International Copyright and Neighbouring Rights

Stephen M. Stewart LL D
of the Inner Temple,
one of Her Majesty's Counsel

London
Butterworths
1983

England	Butterworth & Co (Publishers) Ltd, 88 Kingsway, LONDON WC2B 6AB
Australia	Butterworths Pty Ltd, SYDNEY, MELBOURNE, BRISBANE, ADELAIDE and PERTH
Canada	Butterworth & Co (Canada) Ltd, TORONTO Butterworth & Co (Western Canada) Ltd, VANCOUVER
New Zealand	Butterworths of New Zealand Ltd, WELLINGTON
Singapore	Butterworth & Co (Asia) Pte Ltd, SINGAPORE
South Africa	Butterworth Publishers (Pty) Ltd, DURBAN
U.S.A.	Mason Publishing Co, ST PAUL, Minnesota Butterworth Legal Publishers, SEATTLE, Washington; BOSTON, Massachusetts; and AUSTIN, Texas D and S Publishers, CLEARWATER, Florida

© Butterworth & Co (Publishers) Ltd 1983

All rights reserved. No part of this publication may be reproduced or transmitted in any form or by any means, including photocopying and recording, without the written permission of the copyright holder, application for which should be addressed to the publisher. Such written permission must also be obtained before any part of this publication is stored in a retrieval system of any nature.

This book is sold subject to the Standard Conditions of Sale of Net Books and may not be re-sold in the UK below the net price fixed by Butterworths for the book in our current catalogue.

Stewart, Stephen M.
   International copyright and neighbouring rights.
   1. Copyright, International
   I. Title
   341.7′582 Z552
   ISBN 0 406 66220 7

Printed by Butler & Tanner Ltd, Frome and London

International Copyright and Neighbouring Rights

Preface

Three considerations have prompted me to attempt a book on international copyright and neighbouring rights. The first is that in view of the increasing economic importance of these rights more and more lawyers, both in private practice and in industry and commerce, as well as executives and public servants are confronted with copyright problems in their daily work. They are international problems. This is so because copyrights, being intellectual property, travel more easily and more quickly than most other property. A copy of a book, a recorded tape, a film, can be taken as hand luggage to a dozen countries today and thousands of copies made from it tomorrow. On the air, by radio and television, they travel even faster. To be effective, therefore, copyright control has to be international. Today, those dealing with copyrights must often advise on international situations governed by one or more foreign laws under which the scope, duration and methods of enforcement of the rights they are concerned with may differ widely. They must master the principles of international copyright law and must consider the position under national laws other than their own.

The second consideration is that the development of both national and international copyright law has speeded up considerably in the last three decades. Major copyright laws were passed in France, the United Kingdom and India (Chapters 14, 18 and 23) in the 1950s, in Germany and the Scandinavian countries (Chapters 15 and 17) in the 1960s, in the United States, many Latin American countries and Japan (Chapters 21, 22 and 24) in the 1970s. This seemed the moment to take stock.

The third consideration is that whereas international copyright has made steady, indeed remarkable, progress for a century since the first Berne Convention in 1886, it is said to be going through a crisis at present which may threaten its further progress, and even its survival. Although some of the fears expressed have proved by no means groundless, others, when analysed and considered in their historical context, are shown to be exaggerated. A few examples must suffice here. It is said that copyright is a luxury which developing countries particularly cannot afford. Yet analysis shows that leaders of the developing world like India and many Latin American countries have most sophisticated and modern copyright legislation and that the revisions of the two major copyright conventions in 1971 which made major concessions to the developing countries have yet to be fully explored. It is said that the fundamental differences between the Anglo-Saxon concept of copyright and the Latin concept of droit d'auteur will make assimilation or reconciliation (eg in the European Community) very difficult. Yet history shows that the two systems have common roots and that assimilation began with the Berne Convention in 1886, of which both the major Latin countries and the United Kingdom as the representative of the copyright system were founder members, and that it has been growing apace ever since. It is said that copyright and neighbouring rights are rivals and may militate against each other. Yet analysis shows that in fact they complement each other and that in many national laws the distinction is not even made. Finally it is said that technological progress is so rapid, making the copying of copyright material so easy, that the control of copyrights may become very difficult and may even become impossible. Yet analysis shows that the gradual development of international copyright is the story of the law continually adjusting to new technology for the benefit of creators of copyright material in the constant struggle against piracy. These challenges to the copyright system have to be put in their context and examined. Again, this seemed the right moment to do it.

If these are good reasons for undertaking the task, and world wide coverage had to be attempted in one volume, some fundamental questions of structure and presentation arose. I came to the conclusion that the structure which would best serve the user of the book would be to deal with international law in Part 1 and with the most important jurisdictions in Part 2. Thus Part 1 presents the history, the philosophy and the general principles of international copyright and neighbouring rights (Chapters 1 to 4 and 7), an analysis of the international conventions (Chapters 5, 6 and 8 to 11) and risks a glimpse into the future (Chapter 12); Part 2 presents a synopsis of the world's most important jurisdictions. To achieve a proper balance one had to concede that although very many countries are important, some had to be given more space than others. I concluded that this applied to the major continental European jurisdictions, France, Germany and Italy as the representatives of the droit d'auteur system; to India as one of the leaders of the developing world; and to the United States, both as the largest importer and exporter of copyrights and as the major country with the most recent and up-to-date Copyright Act. Countries in Scandinavia and Latin America whose laws are very close to each other are presented in groups.

To give an authoritative account of the national laws in Part 2 I asked the most eminent experts to present a synopsis of their respective laws following a previously agreed scheme of work. That they all accepted was fortunate indeed as presenting the essentials of a national legislation in twenty or thirty pages is a formidable task. If there turn out to be imperfections in the picture, they will be mine not theirs since I constantly had to cut, adjust or trim to make presentation in one volume possible. To integrate the two parts of the book I have tried to illustrate the principles presented in Part 1 by examples from the national laws dealt with in Part 2 and provided cross-references. There is also a personal link between the two parts. Among the authors of Part 2 are most of the chief architects of the conventions I have dealt with in Part 1: they represented their countries at the meetings of governmental experts and at the diplomatic conferences which made these conventions. They are, (in order of seniority): Valerio de Sanctis of Italy, Eugen Ulmer of Germany, William Wallace of the United Kingdom, Barbara Ringer of the United States, Robert Dittrich of Austria, Agne Henry Olsson of Sweden.

Translations presented a formidable problem. I have tried to render them both faithful and readable and have adopted the same terminology throughout so as to be useful to readers of all nationalities. The conventions quoted in the text and printed in the Appendices are the official English versions of the current Acts, and the sections or articles of national laws cited in the text follow the English version of *Copyright Laws of the World* published by WIPO (the World Intellectual Property Organisation in Geneva) and UNESCO.

I have not attempted a table of cases because there are no cases at the international level: the Court of Justice at the Hague, to which disputes under the conventions are to be referred, has not yet had a copyright case. The most important cases dealing with private international law are dealt with in the national chapters under their respective jurisdictions.

The bibliography consists mainly of recently published books and articles. It does not pretend to be complete but it contains the leading textbooks and the most important articles and monographs which will guide the international lawyer dealing with the conventions or with rights in foreign countries to the relevant sources. The bibliography is presented chapter by chapter and country by country to make it more convenient for the user.

The lists of countries which have ratified the international conventions, the national statutes referred to, and the case law cited are as of 1 January 1983.

Whether all the choices that have had to be made were the right ones and whether they will help practitioners, advisers in industry, academics and students to use the book both as a textbook and as a reference book when dealing with complex and sometimes difficult problems, only the readers will be able to judge. To them 'cher lecteur – mon semblable – mon confrère'* this book is dedicated.

London SS
March 1983

* After Baudelaire: 'Au Lecteur' from 'Les fleurs du mal'.

Acknowledgments

My sincere thanks are due to the eminent authors of Part II for contributing to the work and for their patience and indulgence in putting up with all the difficulties of translation, synchronisation and revision which are an inevitable part of trying to wield their contributions into one work to serve the needs of practitioners and experts.

I am very indebted to the copyright experts in many countries who have read relevant chapters of the book and made most valuable suggestions: Robert Abrahams, Dr David Attard, Marcel Cazé, Professor W. R. Cornish, Gillian Davies, Ivor Davis, Marie Claude Dock, Professor Gerald Dworkin, Professor James Lahore, Claude Masouyé, John Morton, Patricia Robinson, Victor Tarnofski, Ian Thomas, Edward Thompson, Professor Eugen Ulmer, William Wallace, and to Richard Mawhenny for his assistance with research for Part 1 and David Llewelyn for his invaluable help with Part 2.

Last but not least I am grateful to the admirable staff of Butterworth for guiding my faltering steps through all the technical difficulties which are inherent in a work of this kind.

Contents

Preface v
Acknowledgments ix

Part 1   International Law

Chapter 1   The Ideology of Copyright   3
Chapter 2   The History of Copyright   13
Chapter 3   Copyright in International Law   28
Chapter 4   Author's Rights   50
Chapter 5   The Berne Convention (1886–1971)   86
Chapter 6   The Universal Copyright Convention (1952–1971)   133
Chapter 7   Neighbouring Rights   174
Chapter 8   The Rome Convention (1961)   202
Chapter 9   The Phonogram Convention (1971)   238
Chapter 10   The Satellite Convention (1974)   250
Chapter 11   Regional Agreements   266
Chapter 12   The Future of International Copyright Law   277

Part 2   National Laws

Chapter 13   Austria, by Robert Dittrich   311
Chapter 14   France, by Pierre Chesnais   326
Chapter 15   Germany (Federal Republic), by Eugen Ulmer   368
Chapter 16   Italy, by Valerio De Sanctis and Vittorio De Sanctis   399
Chapter 17   Scandinavia, by Agne Henry Olsson   419
Chapter 18   United Kingdom, by William Wallace   435
Chapter 19   The Soviet Union, by Mark Boguslavski   455
Chapter 20   European Economic Community (EEC), by Hans Hugo von Rauscher auf Weeg   466
Chapter 21   United States of America, by Barbara Ringer   480
Chapter 22   Latin-America, by Henry Jessen   533
Chapter 23   India, by Krishnaswami Ponnuswami   568
Chapter 24   Japan, by Yoshio Nomura   599
Chapter 25   Australia, by James Lahore   620

Appendices

Appendix 1   Berne Convention for the Protection of Literary and Artistic Works (Paris Act 1971)   643
Appendix 2   Universal Copyright Convention as revised at Paris 1971   667

Appendix 3   Rome Convention 1961   679
Appendix 4   Convention for the Protection of Producers of Phonograms 1971   687
Appendix 5   Convention Relating to the Distribution of Programme-Carrying Signals Transmitted by Satellite 1974   691
Appendix 6   European Agreement Concerning Programme Exchanges by means of Television Films 1958   694
Appendix 7   European Agreement on the Protection of Television Broadcasts 1960   697

Contributors to Part 2   703
Bibliography   707
Index   719

Part 1
International Law

Summary

A. *Copyright (General)*
   Chapter 1   The Ideology of Copyright   3
   Chapter 2   The History of Copyright   13
   Chapter 3   Copyright in International Law   28

B. *Authors' Rights and Conventions for their Protection*
   Chapter 4   Authors' Rights   50
   Chapter 5   The Berne Convention (1886–1971)   86
   Chapter 6   The Universal Copyright Convention (1952–1971)   133

C. *Neighbouring Rights and Conventions for their Protection*
   Chapter 7   Neighbouring Rights   174
   Chapter 8   The Rome Convention (1961)   202
   Chapter 9   The Phonogram Convention (1971)   238
   Chapter 10 The Satellite Convention (1975)   248
   Chapter 11 Regional Agreements   264

D. *The Future of International Copyright Law*
   Chapter 12 The Future of International Copyright Law   275

Chapter 1
The Ideology of Copyright

Summary

1. The justification of copyright   1.01
2. The nature of copyright   1.06
3. The general principle of copyright   1.11
4. The major systems of copyright   1.12
    (1) The 'droit d'auteur' or 'continental European' systems   1.13
    (2) The 'Anglo-Saxon' or 'copyright' systems   1.15
    (3) The 'socialist' systems   1.17
    (4) The systems of the 'developing countries'   1.18
5. The social and political significance of copyright   1.19

1. The justification of copyright

1.01   As copyright in the modern form is a comparatively recent legal concept[1] and long and fruitful periods of Western civilisation have existed without it, the first question to ask is: What is the justification for a copyright system?

Four major arguments can be advanced in favour of a copyright system.

1   See ch 2 below.

1.02   The principle of natural justice.   The author is the creator or maker of the work which is the expression of his personality. He should be able to decide whether and how his work is to be published and to prevent any injury or mutilation of his intellectual offspring.

The author, like any other worker, is entitled to the fruits of his efforts. The royalties he is paid are the wages for his intellectual work.

1.03   The economic argument.   In the modern world considerable investment is needed to make the creation of some works, such as works of architecture or films, possible. As the purpose of the creation of practically all works is to make them available to the public, that process too, such as publication and distribution of books or records, is expensive. These investments will not be made unless there is a reasonable expectation of recouping them and making a reasonable profit. Furthermore the doctrine of unjustified enrichment may apply if those who make creative contributions on the road of the work from its creator to its user, were not compensated.

1.04   The cultural argument.   The works produced by creators form a considerable national asset. Therefore the encouragement and the rewarding of creativity is in the public interest as a contribution to the development of the national culture.

1.05 The social argument. The dissemination of works to large numbers of people forges links between classes, racial groups and age groups and therefore makes for social cohesion and the creators thus render a social service. If the ideas and experiences of creators can be shared by a wide public within a short space of time they contribute to the advance of society.

Different social and political philosophies and different systems of copyright put the emphasis on different arguments for the justification of copyright.[1]

1 See paras 1.12–1.18 below.

2. The nature of copyright

1.06 Copyright is a *property right* but the subject matter of the property is incorporeal. The property in the work is justified by the fact that the right owner has created or made it. As he is the owner he can dispose of it by outright sale (assignment of his right) or by licensing. The subject of the property is incorporeal, it gives a *dominium* over the work, a right in the work erga omnes. The property is an 'intellectual property' in that it originates in the mind of a person or persons before it is reduced to material form.

1.07 Copyright is a right of *limited duration*. Unlike physical property, which lasts as long as the object in which it is vested (a chair, a camera, a house) copyright is limited in time. After the expiration of the time fixed by statute the work passes into the 'public domain', that is it becomes public property and can be freely used by anyone.

1.08 Copyright is an *exclusive right*. This means that the right owner can prevent all others from copying the work. This is often referred to as a 'monopoly' but that is rather misleading. It is recognised that the produce of a person's skill and labour is his property. If someone makes a movable object such as a chair it belongs to him. He can use it in any way he likes. He can keep it in his home and sit on it or sell it. If it is a very rare and beautiful chair he can exhibit it. If anyone steals the chair he commits an offence and can be prosecuted. But anyone else can also make chairs and compete with him. He has no monopoly in making chairs.

If someone writes an article or a book on that chair he will be the owner of the work; that is, the thoughts that come to his mind when contemplating the chair and its uses, the way he expresses them, the choice of words he uses in describing its appearance and its uses. When he writes it down or types it he will own the manuscript. But anyone can write an article about chairs in general or about this particular chair and compete with him. He has no monopoly in writing articles on chairs or even on this chair. If anyone else writes an article about chairs or about this particular chair which is similar in kind to the original one he will probably acquire himself a copyright in his own article about the chair. The only thing he is prevented from doing is attempting to avoid the intellectual effort of writing the article and instead copying the author's article or substantial parts of it and then publishing it in his own name. That would be the equivalent of stealing the chair.

It is therefore misleading to say that a copyright creates a monopoly or is a monopolistic right. On the other hand, holding all or most of the copyrights in a particular field on behalf of all or most copyright owners as collecting societies do[1] may in practice constitute a monopoly.

1 See para 20.09 below.

1.09 Copyright is a *multiple right*, a 'bundle of rights' in one work. They can be assigned or licensed either together or separately. Both the categories of works protected by copyright and the number of specific rights which form the bundle known as 'the scope' of copyright have been gradually extended over the years as technology has advanced.

1.10 In the 'copyright' countries[1] (as opposed the 'droit d'auteur' countries)[2] copyright now subsists in nearly all works which represent the product of skill and labour if they are fixed on a material support so that they can be reproduced. However the scope of the copyright may vary considerably according to the class of work and so does the term granted to different works. Whereas the term of the old established categories of works: 'literary and artistic' works is well settled as the Berne Convention[3] demands 50 years from the death of the author, the term of the new categories of works: sound recordings, cinematograph films, broadcasts, are less settled and still vary from country to country. As in many cases the term of copyright is the most apparent distinction between classes of works it is also still the most controversial. For instance, should a street directory or a price list be given the same term as a film?.[4] The former are in many copyright countries literary works and get 50 years post mortem auctoris the latter is 'only' a cinematograph film and therefore gets 50 years from publication, a shorter term. In practice the differentiation is not substantial as the street directory will be out of date after a few years and the price list probably after a few months, but the classification of works still leaves a lot of room for readjustment both nationally and internationally.

1 See para 1.15 below.
2 See para 1.13 below.
3 See para 5.54 below.
4 See UK report of the Whitford Committee, para 30.

3. The general principle of copyright

1.11 Each copyright system has to strike a balance between two public interests, the rights accorded to the copyright owner and the reasonable demands of organised society. Both sides of the copyright coin are well set out in article 27 of the Declaration of Human Rights.[1] The rights of organised society in paragraph (1) and the rights of the copyright owner in paragraph (2):

'(1) Everyone has the right freely to participate in the cultural life of the community, to enjoy the arts and to share in scientific advancement and its benefits.
(2) Everyone has the right to the protection of the moral and material interests resulting from any scientific, literary or artistic production of which he is the author.'

The basic limitations which are peculiar to copyright flow directly from this balance between the interests of the copyright owner and the interests of the copyright users and the public as a whole. These limitations which, as copyright is a creature of statute, are statutory limitations, are of three kinds:

1. Copyright is of limited duration. After the stated term the work falls into the 'public domain'.
2. Some uses of protected works are free. These are usually referred to in general terms as 'fair use' or 'fair dealing' in the Anglo-Saxon jurisdictions. Other jurisdictions state the exceptions where the use of copyright works is free, specifically in the statute.
3. In some cases the right owner is not given an absolute right subjecting all uses of the protected work to his prior authorisation, but only the right to

equitable remuneration for each use. This is known as a 'compulsory licence'.[2]

1 Brownlie *Basic Documents on Human Rights* (OUP).
2 See para 4.33 below.

4. The major systems of copyright

1.12 Although copyright is a comparatively young right it has both grown into a system of rights which affect a large variety of matter from books, photographs, films, records, broadcasts to pictures, sculptures, buildings and has gained worldwide general acceptance. This means that it has been accepted in countries whose economic, social and political philosophies differ widely. The four major arguments in favour of copyright[1] have been generally accepted, but different legal systems give priority to one and put greater emphasis on some than on others. Of the three main systems the 'droit d'auteur' system puts the emphasis on the principles of natural justice, the Anglo-Saxon system on the economic argument and the socialist system on the social argument. There are however considerable variations between different countries within the same system.

1 See paras 1.01–1.05 above.

(1) The 'droit d'auteur' or continental European systems

1.13 These are essentially individualistic. The right in the work springs from the act of personal creation, the work is part of the personality of the author and remains linked to him throughout its life. It is a human right with distinctly religious overtones: 'la plus sacrée, la plus personelle de toutes les propriétés'.[1] In the terms of the 'droit d'auteur' at the beginning is the 'work'. It is the creation of the author's mind and is intellectual and incorporeal until it is fixed in writing or any other tangible form. That fixation is the physical embodiment of that work such as a book or a sheet of music which its owner can use, lend or sell as he pleases like any other property.

1 Le Chapelier, le Moniteur Universel, 15 January 1791.

1.14 The property in the work is described as intellectual property ('Propriété Intellectuelle', 'Immaterialgüterrecht'). In the case of literary works the fixation can be a manuscript or a book; in the case of musical works sheet music, a musical score or a record; in the case of artistic works, a picture, a drawing, or a statue. All these physical objects have one thing in common, that they can be reproduced in small or large quantities and by various processes. The technological processes by which reproduction can be achieved vary and new ones are constantly being added, but they are all reproductions of the work. The work which by the process of its creation becomes the property of the author gives him the right to exploit it economically (economic rights) but the work also has an intellectual and moral link with its author as his brainchild which gives him the right to publish it or not as he wishes, when he wishes and in such form as he wishes and to defend it against any distortions or abuses (moral rights).

Several important results flow from this concept:

(a) Copyright is a natural right and thus in theory, absolute and should not be restricted. Although in practice restrictions are imposed, they must be kept to a minimum. As, in theory at least, the right should be perpetual the extension of the right beyond the life of the author is justified. France pioneered the duration of 50 years after the death of the author which is now very widely accepted. The moral rights are in theory also perpetual as they attach to the work which lives on after the economic rights come to an end and continue to bear the expression of the personality of the author and his fame. However, internationally the duration of the 'droit moral' for the whole term of the economic rights was only accepted by the Berne Convention as recently as 1967.[1]

(b) The 'droit moral' occupies a place of major importance. It is inalienable in order to protect the author against commercial pressures which he may find irresistible, particularly at the early stages of his career. To renounce his moral rights would be 'moral suicide'.[2]

(c) Contracts between the author and those he has to deal with such as publishers are put into a special category with safeguards for the author as the financially weaker party.

(d) Drastic restrictions of the rights of the author such as compulsory licences are acceptable only in very exceptional circumstances.

(e) Perhaps the most far reaching consequence in twentieth century terms is that because the 'droit d'auteur' is a natural and therefore individual right, it can only originate in an individual and not in a company or corporation. This means that 'making' a film, or record, or broadcast, which is in almost all cases done by a company cannot give rise to a 'droit d'auteur' as such film producers or record producers cannot be authors. As a result, under the French system film companies have to acquire a large number of rights from individuals who are classed as authors ranging from the stars to cameramen and 'cutters' and producers of phonograms have to seek protection under the law of unfair competition and broadcasting companies under public law provisions, whilst in other continental European systems they are given 'neighbouring rights'.[3] Historically the concept of the 'droit d'auteur' is a child of the French Revolution and has been applied most rigorously in French law[4] but other Latin countries such as Italy[5], the Iberian countries (Spain and Portugal) and the Latin American countries[6] have also adopted the 'droit d'auteur' system in a more or less pure form. The Germanic jurisdictions (Germany, Austria, Switzerland) whilst based on the concept of the 'droit d'auteur' show significant variations. For instance the 'droit moral' is not a perpetual right as in French law but terminates with the copyright term 50 years after the death of the author, based on the experience that at that time there may be no heirs left who are morally entitled or able to safeguard the purity of the work. The Scandinavian jurisdictions[7] also stem from the 'droit d'auteur' concept but are closer to German than to French law and have developed special traits particularly in recent decades under the influence of their own social philosophy.

1 See para 5.37 below
2 Desbois *Le droit d'auteur en France* (3rd edn, 1978) para 382.
3 See ch 7 below.
4 See ch 14 below.
5 See ch 16 below.
6 See ch 22 below.
7 See ch 17 below.

(2) The Anglo-Saxon or 'copyright' systems

1.15 The philosophical foundation of 'copyright' as opposed to the 'droit d'auteur' is more humble. It is simply the right to prevent the copying of physical material and its object is to protect the owner of the copyright against any reproduction of that material which he has not authorised. Copyright, in its essence is a negative concept. It is the right to prevent people from dealing with something that is yours and has been improperly taken by someone else. It focuses on the material support rather than on the creation. Copyright, as the word suggests, was in its origin a right to prevent copying, that is reproduction.

The modern concept of copyright stems directly from the Statute of Queen Anne, 1709 in the United Kingdom. Then the main objective was to protect the investment of the booksellers who fulfilled the function of a modern publisher. As the economic argument has always been in the foreground, this system found no difficulty in extending an eighteenth-century notion to twentieth-century technology. When the film, the phonogram and the broadcasting programmes joined 'writing' as a means of communicating the work the proponents of the 'copyright' concept had no difficulty incorporating the film producer, the phonogram producer and in some cases the broadcasting organisations into the copyright system. On the other hand the proponents of the pure 'droit d'auteur' concept could not bring themselves to give these entities, whom they see more as users than as creators a 'droit d'auteur'. Thus the notion of 'neighbouring rights' which signifies rights neighbouring on authors' rights and is mainly applied to the rights of performers, producers of phonograms and broadcasting organisations[1] had to be invented whereas most copyright systems granted copyrights albeit with lesser scope and of shorter duration. Furthermore, as the economic argument had always been in the foreground, copyright countries were not shocked by the notion that the first copyright owner in the case of films or phonograms or broadcasting programmes is a company or a corporation.

The general philosophy of copyright is that whoever takes the initiative in creating the material and makes the investment to produce it and market it, taking the financial risks that such activities involve, should be allowed to reap the benefit. He can only do that if he is protected by a right because, if he is not protected, the copyist will produce the same product at a lower cost because he does not have to take the initiatives and risks or make the investment. He will therefore undersell the originator of the material in the market place. This will have two consequences. The first is that the copyist will reap an unjust (and sometimes very large) enrichment, the second is that the originator will be deprived of the incentive to create similar materials and the public will be deprived of the widest base for competitive creativity.

The test of the economic value of copyright must therefore be: 'What measure of protection is needed to bring about the creation and production of new works and other material within the copyright sphere?'[2] In answering the question, 'What is a work?' the basic idea of the copyright system is to protect products of intellectual endeavour from the sublime to the most humble demanding sometimes only modest efforts and little originality. To qualify as a protected work, the subject matter has to be the direct result of someone's skill and labour and capable of being reproduced. In the United Kingdom for instance the list of protected works includes a trade catalogue[3] or a football coupon[4] among 'literary works', as well as engineering drawings among 'artistic works'. The standard reply to the defendant's challenge, 'you say that what the plaintiff did is so easy you could do it yourself with very little effort' is: 'Very well then do it and you will have a copyright; but if you copy it from the plaintiff instead you must pay for it.'

When rights like the right of public performance, the recording right and the broadcasting right became as important or more important than the original reproduction right (the right against copying) the term 'copyright' was already too deeply embedded in the legal language to change it to something like 'the right in the work'.

Many copyright systems, unlike continental European 'droit d'auteur' systems, do not specifically recognise moral rights as such, but some of the remedies which the moral right gives to authors are available not under copyright but under other headings, such as defamation if the author's reputation has suffered, breach of an implied term of the contract or breach of trust if the author's 'droit de divulgation' is violated or the tort of 'passing off' if the defendant tries to mislead the public into thinking that he is the author of the plaintiff's work.

The copyright system stemming from the 1709 statute of Queen Anne has spread to all the English speaking countries[5] and to many countries which are or were part of the British Commonwealth.[6]

Several states like Germany[7], Austria,[8] the Scandinavian countries[9] and Japan[10] which ideologically belong to the continental European 'droit d'auteur' system are in some respects closer to the copyright system than to the French system, particularly granting performers, producers of phonograms and broadcasting organisations rights which they term neighbouring rights as they are exclusive rights which are close to and 'neighbouring' on copyrights and do not see the fact that some of these rights may originate in legal entities as opposed to natural persons as an inhibiting factor.[11]

1 See ch 7 below.
2 Cornish *Intellectual Property* (1981) p 309.
3 *Purefoy v. Sykes Boxall* (1955) 72 RPC 89, CA.
4 *Ladbroke v Wm Hill* [1964] 1 WLR 273, HL.
5 Eg USA; see ch 21, Australia; see ch 25.
6 Eg India for the former; see ch 23: eg Republic of Ireland, South Africa, Israel for the latter.
7 See ch 15.
8 See ch 13.
9 See ch 17.
10 See ch 24.
11 See para 7.02.

1.16 Philosophically the difference between the personal, individualistic and idealistic 'droit d'auteur' system and the more commercially orientated copyright system may be fundamental, but in practice the differences should not be overestimated. Historically both systems were created when the system of privileges, which had been in operation both in England and on the European mainland from the fifteenth to the eighteenth century,[1] was abandoned. The continental European countries under the influence of the French Revolution followed the French Act of 1783 whereas the countries of the Anglo-Saxon legal tradition followed the main lines of the 1709 Statute of Queen Anne, but when international copyright became a commercial necessity in the nineteenth century the protagonists of each system, England and France, became founder members of the Berne Union in 1886. That convention achieved a set of compromises between the two systems that have served both the world and the copyright owners well. Most states adhering to the 'droit d'auteur' system have ratified it and most states adhering to the copyright system have also done so, the United States being the most notable exception. The development of the Berne Union has decisively influenced the copyright systems. The acceptance by the United States of the term of 50 years pma in the Copyright Act 1976[2] and the recommendation by the Whitford Committee in the United Kingdom in 1977 to 'make proper provision for moral rights under Copyright law'[3] are the most important recent examples of that influence. The acceptance of 'neighbouring rights' into the copyright statutes of most continental European and Latin American countries of the 'droit d'auteur' tradition and their ratification of the neighbouring rights conventions like the Rome Convention[4] and the Phonograph Convention[5] are examples of the influence of the copyright concept on basically 'droit d'auteur' countries.

With the recognition of the increased importance of 'neighbouring rights' in the 'droit d'auteur' countries and the development of the moral rights in the 'copyright' countries under the influence of the Berne Convention a synthesis of the two philosophies will gradually be achieved which will greatly strengthen the position of copyright as a legal discipline both nationally and internationally.

Both systems presuppose a free market economy and grant a high level of protection. The copyright system seems to adapt more easily to the demands of new technology (see the difficulties the pure 'droit d'auteur' system still has in coping with films or phonograms). On the other hand in coping with the difficulties posed by the fact that more and more works are produced in employment and by team-work, the 'droit d'auteur' doctrine has an important contribution to make.[6]

1 See ch 2.
2 See para 3.02, US copyright Law 1976.
3 Whitford Report, paras 56-57.
4 See ch 8.
5 See ch 9.
6 See 4.25 below.

(3) The socialist systems

1.17 The law of the USSR[1] is based on the socialist doctrine which emphasises the social importance of the author but claims that he can only truly function if he represents and depicts the ideas and the life of a socialist society. Copyright is regarded as 'an instrument for the management of cultural processes'.[2] As the interests of society as a whole are paramount and must therefore prevail in the situations where that interest may conflict with that of the author, the economic rights of the individual authors may become less valuable, but some of the moral rights of authors like the right of paternity and the right of the integrity of the work are safeguarded. The publication and dissemination of the work is in the hands of state publishing houses, film companies, phonogram companies or theatres and the selection of what works are disseminated is made by them under state control. This aspect shows some similarities with the system of privileges in eighteenth-century Europe[3] and shares with it the close affinity between the concept of copyright and state censorship.

In the USSR public performance of copyright works by the mass media, mainly broadcasting and film, is free from the payment of copyright, as is the press. Other performances in public are subject to a compulsory licence granting the author a right to equitable remuneration and the same applies to the author's recording right. On the other hand the term of copyright has been lengthened in order to comply with the Universal Copyright Convention.[4]

Most of the other socialist countries in Eastern Europe are members of the Berne Union and have modern laws which occupy a middle ground between the Soviet Union and Western Europe.[5]

1 See ch 19.
2 Püscher 'Copyright in the German Democratic Republic' Copyright Bulletin of the USA Vol 10 No 3 (1976).
3 See ch 2.
4 Soviet Civil Law 1961 revised in 1973. See ch 19 below and Boguslavski *Urheberrecht in den Internationalen Beziehungen*' (1977, published in East Germany).
5 Czechoslovakia, Law of 1965; Hungary Law of 1969; Yugoslavia, Law of 1978.

(4) The systems of the 'developing countries'

1.18 The developing countries are sometimes put into a separate category in respect of copyright mainly because they are all able to benefit from the compulsory licence system created for them in 1971 both by the Berne Convention and the Universal Copyright Convention.[1] However, the laws of the former British and French colonies in Africa and Asia are shaped by the copyright system and the 'droit d'auteur' system respectively. This is particularly the case in India[2] where the Copyright Law of 1957 follows the United Kingdom Copyright Act very closely. Equally the Latin American Republics although classed as developing countries have sophisticated, 'droit d'auteur' orientated copyright laws.

1 See paras 6.38 et seq.
2 See ch 23.

5. The social and political significance of copyright

1.19 All the conditions for the birth of a copyright system were present in eighteenth-century Europe. A long tradition of individual creation and competition for public recognition had laid the foundation for a positive philosophical and cultural attitude towards intellectual property. The invention of the printing press had created a trade which expected to reap the economic benefits of its investment in the works of authors and had achieved it by the system of privileges. The doctrine of natural law and the political changes brought about by the French Revolution swept away that system as it was connected with repression and censorship. It may be significant that of the four major original copyright laws three were passed in the wake of revolution and the fourth (the Statute of Queen Anne) in a situation of rapid change following the Revolution of 1688.

In England the Stuarts were finally removed by the 'glorious' because bloodless revolution which, in 1688, put William of Orange on the English throne and Parliament into power. In 1702 the House of Commons refused to continue the Licensing Acts because the whole apparatus of licensing had broken down and the censorship which was based on it, with it freedom of speech and freedom of expression in print by the press and in pamphlet and books was being recognised as common law rights.

> 'The Statute of Anne marked the end of autocracy in English Copyright and established a set of democratic principles: recognition of the author as the ultimate beneficiary and fountainhead of protection and a guarantee of legal protection against unauthorised use for limited times, without any elements of prior restraint of censorship by government or its agents.'[1]

The fundamental French copyright statute was passed in 1793 in the wake of revolution, four years after the storming of the Bastille.

In the United States after the Declaration of Independence in 1776, 12 of the 13 original States enacted copyright statutes based on the Statute of Anne and the constitution contains in its first article the establishment of the copyright (and the patent) system. The first Federal copyright statute followed in 1790.

The first copyright Act of the USSR was passed in 1917, merely two years after the Russian Revolution.

Since the nineteenth century, if not before, the question that has most often occupied the centre of the political stage has been the proper balance between the rights of the individual and the rightful demands of an organised society. Because this is also the central question of copyright with the creators of works of all kinds representing the individual and Parliament representing the public interest the copyright system must always have a political dimension. In the highly industrialised and sophisticated societies of today a highly developed copyright system is one of the characteristics of a free society. 'It is harder to determine that the inter-relationship between strong copyright protection and individual freedom of expression is one of cause and effect, but I believe that, on the basis of the historical evidence, a causal relationship can be shown.'[2] The converse is even plainer to see. If authorship of all kinds is remunerated by a proper copyright system new ideas or new expressions of creative personality will reach the public quickly unless they are artificially suppressed. Without copyright, creators have to resort to patronage to survive. That patronage came in European history from the church, from the great aristocratic houses or from the Crown. In modern times it comes largely from the state. If creators were to be dependent on the state a subtle censorship of taste or a crude censorship of reasons of state could be exercised in literature and the arts. The absence of such censorship is an essential ingredient of a free society. An up-to-date and virile copyright law alone cannot create a free society but it can greatly assist its preservation. A bad copyright law may help to destroy it. A free society does not seem possible without an effective copyright law as no other system has so far been devised which ensures creators the necessary freedom of thought and action whilst ensuring the general public as consumers the widest access to their works.

1   Barbara Ringer, Bowker Memorial Lecture, 1974 (Publisher's Weekly, 18 November 1974, p 27).
2   Barbara Ringer 'Two Hundred Years of American Copyright Law' Bicentenary Symposium of the American Bar Association, 1976, p 118.

Chapter 2
The History of Copyright

Summary

1. Antiquity   2.02
2. The Middle Ages   2.03
3. From the invention of the printing press to the first multinational copyright convention   2.04
   (1) Germany   2.05
   (2) France   2.09
   (3) England   2.11
   (4) The United States of America   2.17
   (5) Conclusions   2.19
4. From the Berne Convention to the present   2.20

2.01 The profession of author is one of the oldest in the world but copyright has its origins in Western Europe and the need for it does not emerge until the fifteenth century.

1. Antiquity

2.02 During the first flowering of Western Civilisation in ancient Greece and Rome authors did not regard themselves as a profession. The Greek writers often regarded themselves as teachers like Socrates or Plato or as practical philosophers like Euclid. The Roman writers were often politicians like Caesar or advocates like Cicero, or public servants like Catullus, although they at times regarded themselves as authors. Many of them wrote to achieve fame and recognition rather than to earn a living. They were concerned that their authorship should be recognised and were unanimous in condemning those who sought to appropriate their works. It was generally thought very wrong when Hermodorus, a disciple of Plato, wrote up the master's lectures and speeches and took them to Sicily to sell them. On the other hand, had he and others not done just that, much of the masters' teaching may not have survived.

There were also those who took the opposite view. Cicero in his correspondence with Atticus, who in modern terms would have been called his publisher, praised him for having splendidly 'sold' his speeches for Ligarius and offered him all his future works for publication.[1] The Latin *vendere*[2] had the same double meaning as 'selling' in modern English. It could mean selling them for money or it could mean just publicising them as 'selling an idea' and herein lies the two-sided attitude of Roman writers to authorship. Others, particularly the poets, expressed themselves very strongly in favour of being paid. The poet Martial, in one of his epigrams, addresses himself directly to the reader:

'Whereas you should be well satisfied with so long a work, you are asking me for another few couplets. But Lupus asks for his interests and my young slaves for their wages. Pay! dear reader! You remain silent, pretending not to hear? Good-bye then!'[3]

Martial gives short shrift to plagiarists: 'My books need neither your witness nor your judgment! Your page turns against you and it says to you: You are a thief!'[4] The expression *plagiarium* is taken from the lex Fabia, the law which deals with what we would today call kidnapping, then the stealing of slaves or children. Martial, regarding his works as his children, in an epigram calls one who steal his verses a *plagiarius*, a kidnapper.[5]

Although the moral right of the author was thus strongly asserted, the economic rights were not sufficiently developed to lead to the concept of an author's 'right' in his work and neither the laws of the Republic nor the Codification of Justinian make any reference to such a right.

1   Ad Atticum XIII, 12.2. 'Ligarianam praeclare vendisti. Posthac quidquid scripsero tibi praeconium deferam'.
2   Marie Claude Dock 'Genése et évolution de la notion de propriété littéraire' RIDA (January 1974) pp 127 ff at p 135.
3   Martial, Epigrams XI, 108: cited by Dock, op cit, p 137: 'Quamvis tam longo possis satur esse libello Lector: adjuc a me disticha pauca petis.
    Sed Lupus usuram, puerique diaria poscunt.
    Lector Solve: taces, dissimulasque? Vale.'
4   Martial, Epigrams I, 53: cited by Dock, op cit, p 149:
    'Indice non opus est nostris nec judice libris. Stat contra dicitque tibi tua pagina: "Fures".'
5   Martial, Epigrams I, 52. See also Ulmer *Urheber und Verlagsrecht* (3rd edn) p 50.

2. The Middle Ages

2.03 In the Middle Ages the situation was different but equally unsuitable for the notion of a copyright to emerge. Many works were written in monasteries and were of a religious nature. The monks were both authors and duplicators. The result of their labours was often team-work which would have been difficult to identify with any one person. It was the work of the whole community of the monastery though probably transcribed by one monk. In any event they had taken a vow of poverty and would probably not have been very interested in money. Many works were of a semi-political nature and their authors only desired the widest possible distribution. They wanted to proselytise, not to commercialise their work. However they too were sometimes keenly aware of the moral rights of an author. Saint Columba once paid a visit to the monastery of his old teacher, the Abbot Finnian. During the visit he apparently copied the abbot's psalter. Finnian was very cross and demanded the return of the copy. Columba refused. The suit was referred to King Dermott. Finnian pleaded that the book was largely his work and that Columba had taken it without his permission. Columba pleaded that he was going to give it wide circulation and thus propagate the faith. The King ruled in favour of the author, using somewhat agrarian language: 'to every cow her calf and consequently to every book its copy.'[1]

Eike von Repkow in the introduction to his *Sachsenspiegel* (the laws of the Saxons) seeks to forestall those who would cite him, but slightly alter his text so as to further their case and then attribute the passage wrongly to him.[2]

Thus the paternity claim to the work is strong and so is the desire not to have works wrongly attributed to an author thus damaging his authority or reputation, but the commercial element is still missing.

Beckmesser in Wagner's *Meistersinger* is the classic story of the plagiarist getting it all wrong and coming to grief. He tries to win the prize of the singing competition, the hand of Hans Sachs' beautiful daughter by copying a poem he finds in Sachs' house, but he is merely made the subject of public ridicule, not of a law suit.

Public reading of poetry and the story telling before the birth of the novel was largely practised by troubadours and travelling minstrels and they were mainly representatives of the oral tradition. With only very few manuscripts the case for copyright did not arise.

1 The story is told by George Putnam in *Books and their makers during the Middle Ages, 1476-1600* (New York, 1962) and quoted in Ploman and Hamilton *Copyright* (1980) p 8.
2 Ulmer, op cit, p 51.

3. From the invention of the printing press to the first multinational copyright convention

2.04 With the invention of the printing press the situation changed radically. With the mechanisation of the reproduction method (printing press instead of copying by hand) the speed of multiplication increased a hundredfold and consequently the end product could be produced and sold much more cheaply. Whereas in the Middle Ages only a small section of the population could read, the number of people able to read increased greatly. The combination of these two circumstances was the modest start towards a mass circulation for a mass market.

This also meant that the author could not reach this new public without the intervention of an intermediary who was prepared to make the initial investment. A new trade emerged: printers and booksellers, in England called 'stationers', who were the forerunners of modern publishers. They had to make a considerable investment. Paper was costly and so were the presses. The processes of early printing were slow and therefore labour costs were substantial. The initial capital investment and the current expenditure in wages and material could be recouped only over a long period particularly as prices were not very high. Here was, for the first time, the classic situation of the entrepreneur who made an investment and wanted to recover it and make a profit. He was soon faced with competition which often was unfair. Much care and cost might go into the first edition of a book and soon afterwards a less scrupulous competitor might take it and at much smaller cost and less trouble, produce his own edition. Here was the classic case of a commercial grievance that needed redress. It was easy to understand and the stationers, who formed a political pressure group were in a strong position to put it forward as it had assumed serious proportions. Some printers were ruined and others did not dare to embark on any new publications which demanded a heavy investment. The crisis of the new trade had come and they turned to the authorities to redress their grievance. The authors had sometimes complained but never campaigned for their rights. The publishers did campaign and succeeded in obtaining protection. They thus became the beneficiaries of the privileges or, in modern terminology, the right owners.

The authorities were the King in England and in France and the sovereign princes in the German states. They were prepared to help and began to grant 'privileges'[1] to the booksellers early in the sixteenth century.

It did not take the authorities long to realise that by restricting the rights to privileges, which were granted only to a small number of people they could control all publications quite easily. Many of the publications in the sixteenth and seventeenth centuries were of a religious or political nature advocating the Reformation or the Counter-Reformation and this gave the governments an easy and effective weapon allowing them to exercise a very tight censorship over this new medium.

The privileges had three essential characteristics of modern copyright:

(a) an exclusive right of reproduction and distribution was granted,
(b) the right had a limited term, and
(c) remedies for infringement of the right were fines and seizure and confiscation of the infringing copies and in some cases damages.

It is often said that from the earliest days when the printing press began to revolutionise the publication and dissemination of all 'writings', from news and political and religious pamphlets to literature and the arts, the ideology and development of copyright and the attitude of governments towards copyright problems shows a great divide. That division is between 'copyright' pioneered in England by the Statute of Anne 1709 which was the first copyright law in the world spreading to the whole English speaking world on one side and the 'droit d'auteur', the creation of France, spreading to all Latin countries and most of continental Europe on the other. This, it is submitted, is a fallacy. The development was completely parallel throughout Europe from the fifteenth to the eighteenth century. The two main streams divided at the time of the French Revolution with the French Copyright Acts (the decrees of 1791 and 1793). They started to approach each other again at the time of the Berne Convention, the first multinational copyright convention (1886)[2] less than 100 years later. They have been converging mainly under the influence of that convention ever since and what divides them today are presumptions, albeit very important ones, not principles. To demonstrate this a very brief history of the development of copyright in leading countries in this field is attempted with France and Germany representing the so-called 'droit d'auteur countries' and England and the United States representing the so-called 'Copyright countries'.

1 The term *privilegium* is an abbreviation of the latin *privata lex* a private bill for the redress of grievances which was known to both Roman and Canon law.
2 See ch 5.

(1) Germany

2.05 In Germany, the country where printing with movable types was invented[1], the necessity of protecting printers and booksellers became urgent very early. The first reported *privilegium* was granted to Johann von Speyer by the city of Venice. It was a monopoly to print all books in the city for five years.[2] The early privileges were given by granting a general monopoly, the use of certain types of script, for a limited time for the purpose of furthering trade and as such were the forerunners of patents rather than of copyrights. Only later were privileges given for certain works or a number of works, to printers and publishers as had been done in the other countries for a number of years. They were also granted to authors which included artists. (A privilege was granted in the sixteenth century for etchings of Dürer.)[3] The first privileges recorded (1501) were granted in the name of the Emperor of the Holy Roman Empire, but with the gradual decline of the Empire they were granted more and more by the sovereign German princes. (Mainly in the centres of the book trade: Frankfurt and later Leipzig.) Privileges were given mainly for individual works but there were also general privileges for dictionaries, calendars and particularly schoolbooks.[4] Compulsory deposit was a condition precedent for the grant, a forerunner of the requirement of deposit in England which in turn was taken to the United States. The term was generally one to ten years. The privilege was given to enable the printer and publisher to recoup his investment, but in practice the granting of the privilege was often made dependent on the proof, to be delivered by the publisher, that the author had given his consent.[5]

1 The invention is attributed to Johannes Gutenberg of Mainz where the first book printed on movable type, the Forty-two Line Bible (it had 42 lines to each page) was printed in 1455. A few years later Mainz was partly destroyed and the printers emigrated to other European countries mainly to Flanders where William Caxton learned the art. He printed the first book in English in Bruges in 1476 (a history of the siege of Troy) and set up the first printing press in England at Westminster. There he printed in 1477 the first known book printed in England (a book of the sayings of the philosophers) and a year later in 1478 he produced the first 'best seller', Geoffrey Chaucer's *Canterbury Tales*. There was no significant change in the technique of printing for over 300 years when Lord Stanhope invented the iron press which replaced Gutenberg's wooden one.
2 See Ulmer, op cit, p 51.
3 See Ulmer, op cit, p 51.
4 See Gieseke *Die Geschichliche Entwicklung des Deutschen Urherberrechts*, (Göttingen, 1957) and Fohlmann *Das Neue Geschichtsbild der Deutschen Urheberrechtsentwicklung* (1961).
5 See Ulmer, op cit, p 52.

2.06 As in other countries, authors were more concerned with their moral rights than with the reproduction right. Martin Luther addressed a complaint to the Council of Nuremberg that his works had been published in altered and amended form. The manuscript had been stolen from the printing shop in Wittenberg and sold to a printer in Nuremberg who published it apparently in an expurgated edition. The Council decreed that such a reproduction must show the name of the printer and the place where the reprint was published. There was, however, no penalty imposed. Luther published a pamphlet in 1525 'Warning to the Printers' in which he accused them of 'highway robbery' of his work and theft of his manuscript. The first allegation was staking a claim for his printers who suffered losses through the activities of the pirates. The second was literally true. Dürer, although he could not stop the copying of his pictures, obtained from the same Tribunal protection against the copying of his signature on the copied pictures. A reported lawsuit before the same Tribunal of the City of Nuremberg in 1581-82 shows that when the plaintiff, a publisher, relied on a general privilege granted for all his publications for the printing of a work by Orlando di Lasso and the defendant on a special privilege given to the author with whose knowledge and permission he was printing the work, judgment was given for the defendant.[1]

Towards the end of the seventeenth century the first attempts were made to base the right of the publisher who publishes with the consent of the author on the natural law. Leading philosophers like Kant, Hegel, and Schopenhauer began to develop the idea of intellectual property. Basing themselves both on philosophy and on logic they worked on the problem of how to draw the line between the intellectual property in the work and the physical property in the copy.[2]

1 Ulmer, op cit, p 53.
2 Centuries later the same problems were raised again when it came to defining copyrights in films and phonograms as opposed to books. See para 7.02 below.

2.07 Unlike in France, the change from the protection by privileges to a copyright protection was one of evolution not of revolution. The main difference between the development of privileges in Germany as opposed to France or England is that whereas in France and England a privilege was valid for the whole country, Germany consisted of large numbers of sovereign Principalities and the privilege of the publisher was only valid for the 'land' by which it was granted. As a result piracy of literary works was rampant during the major period of the flowering of German literature in the eighteenth and the first half of the nineteenth centuries. The leading poet and dramatist Wolfgang von Goethe, in many ways Germany's Shakespeare, had to secure 39 privileges for his publisher which he may not have managed had he not been so eminent a writer as well as a minister of the Court and government of Weimar.

2.08 On the other hand, the multiplicity of states in Germany brought about the first attempts towards placing copyright on a supranational level by bilateral agreements between the German states. In 1832, the Alliance of German states ('Deutscher Bund') assured reciprocity between the German states in respect of the protection by privileges. The Alliance decided in 1837 to require each state in the Alliance to grant protection for 10 years after publication and extended this term in 1845 to the Prussian term of 30 years pma.[1] Thus the first foundations for interstate copyright treaties and for a term exceeding the life of the author were laid.

When the German Empire ('Reich') was created in 1871 and Germany thus became one country, copyright was made a matter for the central government and the first German copyright law was promulgated in the same year. By the time the Berne Convention came to be drafted in 1886 German copyright law was fairly well developed and the German input was probably second only to that of France.

1   See Ulmer, op cit, p 59.

(2) France

2.09 In France, as in other European countries, the publishing of books was in the hands of printers and booksellers and authors did not as a result publish their works.

In the fifteenth century the number of presses was not very great and the new trade of booksellers and publishers was thus not subject to much competition, but at the beginning of the sixteenth century the number of publishers increased, competition grew and much of it was unfair competition in the form of counterfeiting.

Towards the second half of the sixteenth century high costs of materials and comparatively low prices for books made publishing a long term investment and growing competition and a good deal of piracy made it a very risky one. The publishers turned towards the authorities for protection. However, 'instead of invoking a general principle ... they asked, in accordance with the concepts of the period, for private guarantees'.[1] All individual rights were considered as flowing from the royal prerogative. Thus the privilege covered one work and for the benefit of the publisher prohibited all others to print or copy it. It was 'an institution of industrial protection meant to indemnify the booksellers for the general cost of publishing and the commercial risks of their enterprise.'[2] Infringers were subject to fines. Printers also formed a Guild to which one had to belong to have the right to print and publish books.[3]

The authorities soon realised the political implications of the system of privileges and used it to maintain a censorship of all books. An ordinance of 1537 established a compulsory deposit. An edict of 1547 forbade the publication of books concerning holy scripture until it was examined by the theological faculty of Paris. An ordinance of 1566 forbade the printing of anything with the seal of approval of the Royal Chancellery. No fines for infringement here! The penalty was death by hanging or strangling.

At the beginning of the eighteenth century a conflict[4] arose between the Paris booksellers and their counterparts in the provinces. The Parisians had obtained most of the privileges from the authorities, whereas the provincial publishers had obtained only very few. When it came to the renewal of a privilege for a Parisian publisher the provincial publishers opposed it. They argued that wider publication of great works and the spreading of learning was in the public interest. They stressed what today we would call the public domain. The Parisians on the other hand, arguing for the renewal and extension of their privileges, discovered the author. Their advocate, Louis d'Hericourt, argued that the work was the creation of the author and belonged to him and he transferred his property in the work to the publisher who took the risks of publication.[5] One of the consequences of this theory was that the publisher acquired the author's right in the work in perpetuity. Thus, they argued, the renewal of the privilege was merely the recognition of this state of affairs. In 1767 the Parisian publisher, le Breton, secured the support of one of the most renowned authors of the day, Diderot, who, whilst supporting the claim for renewal, strongly affirmed the rights of the author.[6]

Almost on the eve of the Revolution, in 1777, Louis XVI issued six decrees dealing with the book trade. One, the '*Arrêt sur les privilèges*', speaks of two privileges. One of the publisher, granted in the public interest as a monopoly of limited duration to recoup his investment, the other of the author granted, because of his creation of the work, an exclusive right in perpetuity.

1   Dock, op cit, p 161.
2   Dock, op cit, p 163.
3   Olivier-Martin '*L'organisation corporative de la France d'Ancien Régime*' (Paris, 1938) cited by Dock, op cit, p 161.
4   Cf the 'battle of the booksellers' in eighteenth-century England, see para 2.14 below.
5   See Dock, op cit, p 187.
6   Lettre sur le Commerce de la librairie, 1767.

2.10   The French Revolution abolished all privileges in 1789 and the privileges of publishers were no exception. They were replaced by two decrees of the Constituent Assembly. The decree of 13–19 January 1791 was concerned with the liberty of the theatre. It established the performance right of the author.

The decree of 19–24 July 1793 established the exclusive reproduction right of the author.

Both decrees, in accordance with the philosophy of the Revolution based themselves firmly on the personal right of the author who becomes the proprietor of his work. The report of Le Chapelier to the Assembly calls it 'la plus sacrée, la plus personelle de toutes les propriétés.'[1]

These two decrees gave the author the two essential property rights in his work, the reproduction right and the public performance right. They also provided for damages for infringement. Apart from an amendment in 1910 which prolonged the term of copyright they stood until the present law of 1957 was enacted.

The decrees contained two entirely new principles:

1. The right was firmly placed in the hands of the author and was a personal right.
2. It was a right in the work, whatever type of work it may be.[2]

These general principles enabled the courts to develop the theory and practice of the 'droit d'auteur' without any further legislation for a century and a half until the present Copyright Act of 1957.[3]

1   Le Moniteur Universel, 15 January 1791.
2   By contrast in England the statutory right was mainly a commercial right which arose with publication and was a right in books so that the rights in all other works (paintings, musical works etc) had to be added by statute one by one in the nineteenth century.
3   See para 14.01 below.

(3) England

2.11 William Caxton had learned the art of printing in Flanders where the refugee printers had emigrated after the destruction of their presses in Mainz.[1] He returned to England and set up the first printing press at Westminster and printed his first book in England in 1477 and his first best seller, Chaucer's *Canterbury Tales*, in 1478. He never seems to have obtained a grant of monopoly,[2] which he could have done under common law and thus the art of printing was freely practised in England. This freedom was encouraged by a statute of Richard III in 1483 which lifted any restraints on foreigners importing manuscripts and books into England and also printing them here. Soon much of the book trade was in the hands of foreigners.[3] Although this freedom lasted only for one generation this was long enough to make England one of the centres of the printing trade in Europe.

1   See para 2.05 above, note 1.
2   The forerunner of a patent.
3   Caxton died in 1491 and was succeeded by his foreman and friend Wynkyn de Worde who had come with him from Flanders. Neither became 'King's Printer', that office went to their main English competitor Richard Pynson.

2.12 The policy was reversed under Henry VIII who, after introducing restrictions in 1523 and 1528, prohibited the importation of books altogether in 1533 on the grounds that there were enough printers and book-binders in England. The main reason however was the King's determination to control the dissemination of religious and political books and this was easier if there were no imports and the trade was in the hands of comparatively few citizens who could be licensed. An Act of Henry VIII of 1529 had set up the system of privileges[1] for the printing of books. The granting of privileges was the prerogative of the Crown. The control was exercised through the privilege system and through the bye-laws of the Stationers' Company. The company originated as a craft guild early in the fifteenth century and was made into a company by Henry VIII in 1557. It consisted of 97 London publishers, who were called 'stationers' or 'booksellers'. Only the Company's registered members had the right to print books. All works which were printed or reprinted had to be entered into the register of the company before being published. The entry had to show the name of the member (publisher), the title of the work, and the date of publication. The works on the register were known as 'copies'. The members claimed the right to publish these copies in perpetuity and the right was later referred to as 'copyright'. Although the right was not limited in time it lapsed if the book was out of print. In such cases the court of the company could award the privilege to 'poor brethren' as an act of 'relief'.[2] In case of infringement of the privilege the company could levy fines, confiscate the infringing copies and award damages to the registered owner of the work.[3] In the early days of the company, book entries were made only when a registration fee was charged, but 'as the grip of authority went on tightening ... until it climaxed in the Star Chamber Decree of 1637, as books also became more and more a power, and therefore dangerous things ... the book entries became a permission, an 'Imprimatur', rather than a cash receipt.'[4]

Although the privileges bear many of the characteristics of a copyright system they were trading licences creating a monopoly for the owner of the right. Whereas a right in the work at common law flowed from the act of the production and publication of it, the right under the privilege flowed from the prerogative of the Crown, the royal grant of the privilege. It involved no recognition of authorship.

The system created by the Acts of Henry VIII and the bye-laws of the Stationers' Company regulated the publishing of all printed matter in England for one and three quarter centuries until the lapse of enclosing systems and the Statute of Anne 1709. It represented the parallel interests of the publishers and of the Government. The stationers could by their regulations limit both the number of master printers and the number of presses and at times even the number of copies printed of each publication. The Government by controlling the stationers could control all publications. Infringement cases were heard by the Stationers' Company's own court, which had power to seize and destroy all illegal copies and the presses on which they had been printed. There was, as a result, very little 'piracy' of books.

The reading public was small and the investment made by the publisher had to be recouped over a long period. The rights in Milton's *Paradise Lost* were sold outright for £5 and it took the publisher almost seven years to sell the first printing.[5]

The Court of Star Chamber sought to tighten its control over printed matter further by restricting the number of presses and listing them. When the Court of Star Chamber was abolished in 1641 all regulations controlling the printing of books were abolished with it but the Stationers' Company was to ensure under an order of the House of Commons in 1642 that nothing was printed without the name and consent of the author. If the order was not complied with, proceedings could be taken against the printer, treating him both as printer and author.

1 The full title was 'Cum privilegio regali ad imprimendum solum'.
2 Greg and Boswell *Records of the Court of the Stationers' Company* (1930) p 5.
3 For a full account of the system see Edward A. Arber, *Transcript of the Registers of the Stationers' Company* Vol 1 (London, 1875).
4 Arber, op cit, Vol I, p XVI.
5 P. Wittenberg *The Protection of Literary Property* (1957) p 14.

2.13 The system of privileges thus survived the Cromwellian revolution and was confirmed after the restoration of Charles I by the Licensing Act of 1662 which prohibited the printing of any book unless licensed and entered in the register. This, and subsequent licensing Acts which had to be renewed periodically by Parliament, were used mainly for controlling the press but towards the end of the century the system began to crumble. The power of members of the Stationers' Company to claim copyright in perpetuity had led to very high prices as the number of copies of a work was controlled by the members of the company and kept low. When the House of Commons refused to renew the licensing Acts there followed a period during which piracy flourished.

'Proprietors of Copyright had so long been protected by summary measures that they regarded an action at common law as an inadequate remedy.'[1] In it a publisher could recover no more costs than he could prove damage and the defendant was always a pauper. The booksellers repeatedly petitioned Parliament asking for forfeiture of offending copies which they regarded as the only effective remedy.

1 *Copinger and Skone James on Copyright* (8th edn) para 29.

22 The History of Copyright

2.14 In 1690 the philosopher John Locke had demanded a copyright for authors which he justified by the time and effort expended in the writing of the work which should be rewarded like any other work.[1]

The result was the Act of Queen Anne in 1709 which was the world's first copyright Act. Barbara Ringer called it 'the mother of us all', referring to all English speaking nations, 'and a very possessive mother at that'.[2] It is a fairly short Act establishing in the main three basic rules:[3]

1. Authors of books not yet printed were to have the sole right of printing for 14 years from the date of publication. After the expiration of the 14 years term, the sole right of printing returns to the author, if then living, for another term of 14 years.
2. Infringers shall forfeit the infringing books found in their custody and pay a fine of a penny for every sheet (a swinging penalty which for a 300 page book could amount to approximately $50 per copy at today's prices). Half went to the Crown and the other half to the plaintiff or any person who sued for it.
3. No suit can be brought unless the title of the book has been entered before publication in the 'Register Book' of the Company of Stationers. The clerk of the company is to give a certificate of such entry (cost six pence) and the register may be inspected without a fee.

Thus was established at a stroke the first clear acknowledgment of the legal right of authorship (only hinted at in the licensing Acts and the Star Chambers Decrees).

A clear distinction was drawn between the right in the work and the *corpus mechanicum*, the tangible object which contained the work. The only object referred to in the statute was the book, but the phrase used in the title 'books and other writings' already foreshadowed extension to other objects.

The term of 14 years plus another 14 if the author was alive after the first 14, and the return of the right to the author after the first 14 years, even if he had sold the right originally found its way into the law of the United States and in that form (the term was later doubled to 28 plus 28) survived there until 1976. The principle of registration has also survived in some countries, including the United States though not in England.

The Act was a compromise between the demands of the publishers and what Parliament considered the public interest. The authors lost their common law right after publication, the publishers lost their claim to buy a perpetual copyright from the author. The compromise is expressed in the title of the Bill: 'A Bill for the Encouragement of Learning and for Securing the Property of Copies of Books to the rightful owners thereof'. The legal monopoly which the printers had in perpetuity was broken but they were still left in a strong position. The character of the Act is that of a Trade Regulation, but the law nevertheless recognised that the source of the copyright is the work created by the author.

It is to be noted that the rights under the Statute of Anne are neither restricted to British subjects nor to books printed in the United Kingdom. This is in stark contrast to the American law, both before and after 1780.

When the appointed day came on 10 April 1731 (21 years after the Act of Anne came into effect) the London booksellers, who were the owners of nearly all the titles published before 1710 as they were entered in the Register of the Stationers' Company, maintained that these entries gave them a copyright in perpetuity in these works. The provincial booksellers who did not own such entries started to publish the old titles claiming that the Act of 1709 had terminated the copyright and the works were now in the public domain. The ensuing struggle was known as 'The Battle of the Booksellers'.[4]

1 John Locke *Two Treaties on Civil Government* (1690).
2 Paper at WIPO Seminar, Montreux, 1971.
3 See Stewart 'Two Hundred Years of English Copyright Law', Bicentenary Symposium of the American Bar Association, 1976.
4 For same development in France see para 2.09 above.

2.15 The publishers won the first round when the court of first instance held in 1769[1] that the 'natural right of the author under Common law' was to print, publish and sell his work and that this right was in perpetuity and could be conveyed to the bookseller. However the opposition won the second round and therewith the battle in the House of Lords in 1774. In *Donaldson v Beckett*[2] it was held that:

1. At common law an author of any literary work had the exclusive right of first printing and publishing that work in perpetuity.
2. Once the work was published, however the common law right was extinguished and he could only bring an action on the terms and conditions of the Statute of 1709.[3]

Thus, the exclusive right of the author or publisher in the work was balanced against the public interest in the free dissemination of all works.

Inherent in the judgment of the House of Lords in *Donaldson v Beckett* are the two rights of the author in his work: the rights that are the author's from the time he creates the work and those that arise from the first publication of the work. The former, the natural rights, include the right to publish or not to publish it, to alter the work before publication and to maintain the integrity of his work by preventing others from altering it without his consent. The latter, the rights arising from publication, are prescribed by statute and are economic in nature. The exact shape and content of the natural right ('droit moral')[4] has never been settled in Anglo-Saxon countries in spite of the fact that many of them have ratified the Berne Convention which contains an obligation to that effect.[5]

1 *Millar v Taylor* 4 Burr 2303.
2 *Donaldson v Beckett* (1774) 4 Burr 2408. The case arose over the copyright in the same book as *Millar v Taylor*: Thomson's poem 'The Seasons'.
3 It is interesting to note that on these two decisive points (of a total of five points of law which were put to the House of Lords) the majority was only six to five. On this one vote the laws of all English speaking countries were based for the next two centuries.
4 See para 4.15 below.
5 Article 6 bis; see para 5.37 below.

2.16 The impact of the Statute of Anne, once its effect had thus been clarified by the courts was such that no changes of fundamental significance were made for over two centuries (1709-1911). The changes that were made were of three kinds:

1. The term of copyright was gradually extended.[1]
2. Where the Statute of Anne only covered 'books and other writings', engravings, prints, lithographs, sculptures, dramatic works, musical compositions were gradually added to the list by piecemeal legislation.[2]
3. Works of foreign authors were being protected which enabled Great Britain to be represented at the Diplomatic Conference in 1885 which framed the Berne Convention and to ratify it within a year, being one of the first countries to do so.

The revision of the Berne Convention in 1908 (Berlin Act) brought major extensions of copyright which needed national legislation to ratify it.[3] This was done in the Copyright Act of 1911 which also consolidated the piecemeal legislation of the nineteenth century (14 different Acts).

1 The landmark in the extension of the term of copyright was the Copyright Act 1842 because it extended the term beyond the death of the author. The passage of the Bill caught the imagination of Parliament and of sections of the public because of the personal clash between two protagonists, Sergeant Talfourd, a barrister with literary interests, and the famous historian Macaulay. The case against copyright was put by Macaulay: 'It is a tax on readers for the purpose of giving bounty to writers. The tax is an exceedingly bad one on the most innocent and most salutary of human pleasures; and never let us forget that a tax on innocent pleasures is a premium on vicious pleasures'. (Hansard Vol 56, 5 February 1841). Talfourd's oratory on the major issue of extending copyright beyond the life of the author is still remembered '... at the moment when his name is invested with the solemn interest of the grave - when the last seal is set upon his earthly course, and his works assume their place among the classics of his country – your law declares that his works shall become your property, and you requite him by seizing the patrimony of his children'. Copyright was eventually extended to seven years pma or a term of 42 years, whichever was the longer.
2 Most of these Acts got on to the Statute Book because of the efforts of men who took a personal interest in the matter and were sufficiently famous and eloquent to achieve their objectives among an only moderately interested Parliament. Bulwer Lytton, the writer, whose Dramatic Copyright Act 1833 became known as 'Bulwer Lytton's Act' and William Hogarth, the painter, to whose efforts the Engraving Copyright Act 1734 was due, are outstanding examples.
3 See para 5.11 below.

(4) The United States of America

2.17 Although the Pilgrim Fathers undertook their voyage to the American colonies to escape from religious oppression, the regulation of the press and printing generally was not very different there. 'The traditional European idea of monopolising the press to cement the social order was successfully transplanted to the American shores.'[1]

However, much of the printed matter produced did not consist of literary works. Government proclamations, printed forms, maps, handbooks were of little interest to the censors and printing in the American colonies remained free from the economic control of the Stationers' Company or any guild and was run on purely commercial lines. 'Exclusivity and protection of markets was secured by agreements among printers in different colonies, guaranteed at least in part by the fundamental difficulties of colonial transportation and communication'.[2] Perhaps the most important difference between colonial America and Europe in the seventeenth and eighteenth centuries was that literature did not rely as much on patronage in America as it did in Europe and therefore American writers looked to the general public rather than wealthy or influential individuals for their financial rewards.

Most of the books sold were being imported, but newspapers and periodicals carried much of the new American literary output in serialised form. Papermaking was based on cheap home grown material and received a big boost when the Townshead Act of 1767 put a tax on imported paper.

Thus, when the Revolution came in 1776, as Barbara Ringer points out, 'all the necessary resources, human and material, for the publication of books were present in the Colonies',[3] and by the time the Constitution came to be drafted 12 of the 13 colonies had passed copyright legislation.[4] Although these laws varied in their contents all followed more or less closely the Statute of Anne. More than half of them had reciprocity clauses in them stipulating that only authors of states which also gave copyright protection would be protected – an early forerunner of the multinational conventions.

1 Boorstin *The Americans; The Colonial Experience* (1958) p 330. For the history of American Copyright before 1790 see Patterson *Copyright in Historical Perspective* (1968) and Boynton *Annals of American Bookselling: 1638-1850* (1932). Also: Kaplan *An Unhurried View of Copyright.*
2 Ringer 'Two hundred Years of American Copyright Law' Bicentenary Symposium of the American Bar Association, 1976, p 124.
3 Ringer, op cit, p 124.
4 The campaign for legislation was lead by Noah Webster, the author of the first American dictionary, who persuaded Congress to assist his campaign for state legislation (see Ringer, op cit, p 125). For a compilation of these state statutes see US Copyright Office, Library of Congress, Bull No 3, Copyright Enactments: 'Laws Passed in the United States since 1783 Relating to Copyright' (1973).

2.18 The American Constitution (1789) contains a copyright and patent clause):[1] 'The Congress shall have the power ... to promote the progress of science and the useful arts, by securing for limited time to authors and inventors the exclusive right to their respective writings and discoveries'.

The Constitution was followed within a year by a federal law: the Copyright Act of 1790. It contains most of the characteristics of the English law of that period. the distinction between common law rights in unpublished works and statutory rights in published works, registration and deposit provisions, the same two-tier term of copyright, the remedies for infringement and the lack of any provisions dealing with the moral right of authors.

The 'Federalist' contains a succinct comment on the clause:

> 'The utility of this power will scarcely be questioned. The Copyright of authors has been solemnly adjudged in Great Britain to be a right of Common Law. The right to useful inventions seems with equal reason to belong to the inventors. The public good fully coincides in both cases with the claims of individuals. The States cannot separately make effectual provision for either of the cases, and most of them have anticipated the decision of this point, by laws passed at the instance of Congress.[2]

The law also contains one major deviation from English law: foreign authors were not protected. Ploman and Clark Hamilton comment: 'Complete with the piracy provision it can be viewed as the action of a developing country to protect its burgeoning culture while exploiting the cultural products of more developed nations'.[3] Barbara Ringer views it as damaging American authors in this respect: 'By protecting only works of American authors, the new law sanctioned the unrestrained reprinting of popular English writers, to the disastrous competitive disadvantage of the very indigenous American literature it was pledged to encourage. It took a century of agitation to remedy this fatal error.'[4] The results were more striking in the United States than in most other post-revolutionary or developing countries because the United States and England speak the same language and English literature, and particularly the novel, flourished in the post-revolutionary period so that 'almost half the best sellers in America between 1800-1860 were pirated'[5] mainly from English novels. As always in cases of large scale piracy prices also had something to do with it. Towards the end of the nineteenth century English novels from Charles Dickens to Walter Scott and from Trollope to Thackeray cost a guinea and a half in England whereas the pirated American version cost 25 to 50 US cents, approximately one-tenth as much. It would appear therefore that had the law protected foreign works, American publishers would have paid royalties and still made a profit.

By the same token, when American literature began to flourish Edgar Alan Poe, Melville and Cooper were pirated in England and the reprints sold at cheap prices so that the legitimate product could not compete and the American authors lost their royalties.

When the Copyright Law of 1891 was passed this situation was remedied and the United States entered 'the family of Copyright countries', although the Act still had a manufacturing clause to the effect that books of foreign authors were protected in the United States only if they were printed in the United States. This clause was finally removed only by the 1976 Copyright Law, long after the United States had ratified the Universal Copyright Convention.

The 1976 Law, to date the most modern major copyright law in the world, tries to grapple with most of the problems twentieth-century technology poses for copyright legislation.[6]

1 Art 1, para 8.
2 The Federalist 43 (New American Library ed 1961) 271-272.
3 Ploman and Hamilton, op cit, p 16. However this seems less than fair to many developing countries like India, see ch 23, or the Latin American countries, see ch 22, who accepted in their national laws general copyright principles from the beginning and even in 1971 only insisted on compulsory licences for strictly defined and limited purposes (see para 6.41 below). The large scale piracy of the whole of English literature which took place legally during the nineteenth century in the US would have been illegal under the laws of the leading developing countries then and now.
4 Ringer, op cit, p 127.
5 Tebbel *A History of Book Publishing in the United States* (1972).
6 See ch 21 below.

(5) Conclusions

2.19 A short synthesis of the history of these four major jurisdictions thus shows the common origins, the parting of the main streams and the gradual coming together.

1. The first germs of copyright are found in the 'privileges' granted to publishers. Privileges were based on a mercantilist concept of monopoly to reward enterprise and encourage investment.
2. The privilege system was used to exercise control of all publications by confining privileges to members of a guild or corporation and requiring the deposit of a copy of every publication.
3. A struggle ensued between those who had obtained these privileges, mainly the publishers in the capital, and those who had not, mainly the publishers in the provinces.
4. Those trying to combat the privileges were advancing the right of the author as the creator of the work, as opposed to the entrepreneur who published and distributed it.
5. The philosophers put forward the case for the author's right based on natural law (Locke, Rousseau, Hegel, Kant).
6. After the first copyright Act, the Statute of Queen Anne in 1709, copyright became largely a creature of statute, granting an exclusive right for a limited time. That term was then gradually lengthened over a long period until it reached 50 years after the death of the author.
7. The English concept of copyright was taken to the United States, where the revolution of 1776 gave it a strong nationalistic flavour, and eventually to the whole English speaking world.
8. The French concept of 'droit d'auteur' was taken to many countries of continental Europe, to the French colonies and Latin America and thus acquired an international flavour.
9. The first attempt to create an international copyright system, the Berne Convention 1886, built a bridge between the two main systems.
10. That bridge was gradually strengthened and extended during the next century.[1]

1 See paras 5.10 et seq.

4. From the Berne Convention to the present

2.20 With the passing of the Berne Convention the initiative in the development of copyright had passed from national legislation to international conventions which became the pacemakers. The standards were set by the countries with the most highly developed laws giving the widest protection. Other countries followed and amended their legislation in order to ratify each new version of the Convention.

The history of the development of international copyright law in the 60 years between 1886 and 1948 is thus largely the history of the Berne Convention.[1] From the 1950s to the 1980s, it is the history of the development of that convention and of the Universal Copyright Convention[2] which brought the two superpowers, the USA and the USSR, into the orbit of international copyright. It is also the history of the conventions dealing with neighbouring rights[3] which enlarged the subject matters of copyright to bring it into line with technological advance.

It is perhaps significant that the tempo of the development of copyright accelerates throughout history. Over 2000 years of Western civilisation without any copyright (fifteenth century BC–eighteenth century AD) are followed by 180 years from the first copyright statute to the first international convention (1709–1886). Over 60 years under the aegis of the Berne Convention (1886–1952) are followed by 30 years under the aegis of the Revised Berne Convention, the Universal Copyright Convention, and the Rome Convention[4] (1952–1982). Increasing pressure from a rapidly developing technology thus increases the pressure on the development of the copyright system. The future will require ever speedier action both on the national and on the international level if the system is to be kept viable.[5]

1 See ch 5.
2 See ch 6.
3 See chs 7–11.
4 See ch 8.
5 See ch 12.

Chapter 3

Copyright in International Law

Summary

1. The two disciplines of international law   3.01
   (a) Public international law
   (b) Private international law
   (c) International copyright law
2. The questions arising in a 'conflict of laws'   3.02
   (a) What is the legal issue?   3.03
   (b) To what category does this issue belong?   3.04
   (c) What 'connecting factor' is relevant to solve the conflict?   3.05
3. The Sources of private international law   3.08
   (a) International custom   3.08
   (b) International conventions   3.09
   (c) National legislation   3.10
   (d) Judicial decisions   3.11
   (e) Writings of academic lawyers   3.12
4. International copyright law   3.13
5. The treatment of foreigners in copyright law   3.14
6. The history of international copyright treaties   3.15
7. The principles of international copyright conventions   3.16
   (a) General   3.16
   (b) National treatment (assimilation)   3.17
   (c) Extensions of the principle of national treatment   3.18
      (1) Minimum rights   3.18
      (2) Formalities   3.19
   (d) Limitations of the principle of national treatment   3.20
      (1) Reciprocity   3.20
      (2) Reservations   3.21
   (e) Challenges to the principle of national treatment   3.22
8. The connecting factor   3.24
   (a) The country to which the author belongs   3.25
   (b) The country of origin   3.26
   (c) The country of first publication   3.27
   (d) The protecting country   3.28
9. The systems of creating rights in international copyright conventions   3.29
10. The systems of applying international copyright conventions to national Law   3.30

1. The two disciplines of international law

3.01 The two disciplines of International law are (a) public international law and (b) private international law.

(a) **Public international law ('Jus Gentium', 'Droit des Gens', 'Völkerrecht')** is a system of law which is general in its source as it is based on customary law with a superstructure of international treaties and general in its scope as it is to be applied everywhere. It comprises those parts of the law which are international by definition, like the law of the sea, air law or space law as well as international humanitarian law ranging from the abolition of slavery as a personal status to international labour law and to the latest form of the law on personal status: human rights law. It also encompasses international economic law which deals with the ownership and use of natural resources and the production and distribution of goods (trade agreements, such as GATT, international financial agreements, such as the World Bank). This is the part of public international law nearest to copyright if you view authorship as a 'national resource,' which it is, and the carriers ('supports matériels') of copyright works such as books, films or phonograms as 'goods', which they are.

It is therefore from this part of public international law that international copyright law has taken its principal tools and adapted them to its purpose. These tools are:

1. The application of minimum standards.
2. Preferential treatment. This can be:
   (i) Most favoured nation treatment;
   (ii) Reciprocal treatment;
   (iii) National treatment, ie the equality of treatment between foreigners and nationals.

'Most favoured nation treatment is characteristic of bilateral treaties, which is how international copyright started both in Europe and in the Americas. This technique was abandoned in international copyright in favour of multinational treaties of which the Berne Convention[1] was the first and most important. Since then, 'national treatment' and 'reciprocity' are the tools used by the conventions on international copyright and neighbouring rights together with the application of minimum standards.

1 See ch 5.

(b) **Private international law is really a misleading term** because it is not international law but part of national law. It is a discipline within each national legal system. There is no such thing as an 'international' private international law. There is only that part of French or English law which deals with international situations (in federal states there may even be a private international law of the State of New York or of New South Wales). On the other hand there is no such thing as the public international law of France or England; that would be a contradiction in terms. There is only one public international law.

Private international law is the body of rules (part of national law) which deals with international situations, that is, legal situations with a foreign element (eg contracts of sale between persons belonging to different countries). The rules of private international law are either rules of customary international law, that is, general principles recognised by all civilised nations, such as pacta sunt servanda, or rules laid down by international treaties which have been ratified by the country concerned and thus have become part of its national law or rules of national law applied to foreigners as well as to nationals.

(c) **International copyright law.** International copyright law is a hybrid. In this area the main source of international copyright law is international conventions which are treaties between sovereign states and as such part of public international law. The principle applied in these conventions like the principle of reciprocity or the principle of national treatment are principles of public international law but the situations to which they are applied are private international law situations that is situations of conflict of law.

Private international law is sometimes called 'conflict of laws', meaning the conflict being between various national laws which may be applicable to one legal issue.

2. The questions arising in a 'conflict of laws'

3.02 There are three questions to be answered in a case of conflict of laws:
(a) What is the legal issue?
(b) To what category does this issue belong?
(c) What 'connecting factor' is relevant to solve the conflict?

(a) What is the 'legal issue' ('la question de droit')?

3.03 The question which private international law has to solve is: From which legal system do we derive the rule which will decide the legal issue before us? There may of course be several legal issues in one case, but each issue has to be decided separately and the answer may well be that the first issue in a case has to be decided acccording to one law and the second issue according to another law.

(b) To what category does the issue belong?

3.04 Is the issue the validity of a will or of a marriage? Or is it the distribution of a person's movable estate? Or a delictual liability?

A simple traffic accident case may present the choice of three legal systems. An English motorist on holiday in France injures a pedestrian who is also a tourist but domiciled in Germany. If the issue is liability, that is whether the motorist or the pedestrian is to blame, it will probably be judged according to French law as the lex loci delicti. If the issue is whether the motorist was covered by his insurance policy which is probably an English contract, that issue will be judged by the lex loci contractus which is English law. If the pedestrian was killed, it would probably be for German law to decide – if he is held to have been negligent – who his heirs are and whether his estate is liable.

To choose a copyright example: if an English author makes a publishing contract to have his work published in France and the published work is then performed in a slightly altered form without permission in Germany, the issue whether that performance constitutes an infringement will probably be judged according to German law as the country where protection is claimed, that is where the infringement was committed (the lex loci delicti, whether the 'delict' is a crime or a civil wrong or a tort) but the validity of the transfer of the right to the French publisher will probably be judged according to French law if the contract is a French contract (the lex loci contractus).

(c) What is the 'connecting factor' ('point de rattachement', 'Anknüpfungspunkt')?

3.05 In other words what is the feature which connects the issue with one particular legal system? In the traffic example the question would be: is it the nationality of the motorist, or the nationality of the victim or the country where the accident took place? In the copyright example the question would be: is it the law of the country of the author or the law of the country of the publishing contract or the law of the country where the alleged infringement has taken place?

3.06 Thus the judge or the administrator dealing with the case or the legal practitioner advising on it will have to decide first what the issue is, then to which class the issue belongs and finally which is the relevant point of attachment.

The dilemma in all cases of conflict is between consistency (similar decisions in similar cases) and international harmony (same decision on the same issue in whatever country the issue may be tried). In an ideal world the decisions would be both consistent and harmonious. In practice this is not possible as legal systems vary widely and the rules of private international law are part of a national legal system which may be different from most other legal systems. Therefore, choices have continuously to be made, usually by judges, which are neither perfect nor completely logical but the best that can be done in the circumstances. If one views consistency and harmony as a parallelogram of forces within which the solution has to be found, the strongest force among the connecting factors which will decide a case is the lex fori. This is so because private international law, being part of the national law which the courts apply every day, the natural tendency of the judges will be to apply their national law, and those rules of private international law which are part of it, rather than a foreign law. In France the 'Rapporteur' in the Cour de Cassation in the *Soulier* case[1] in 1910 put it very succinctly: 'I prefer that French courts, if they are permitted to do so, should judge according to French law which they know, rather than according to a foreign law which they do not know. I prefer French law to foreign law'.

Kahn Freund[2] calls this the 'homeward trend',[3] pointing out that courts do not only prefer to apply their own law, but also do so more efficiently than if they have to apply foreign law. He concludes that 'the homeward trend' should not necessarily be considered as an aberration, or as a sign of intellectual inertia.

It is also an expression of the craftsman's pride in his work and of an unwillingness to jeopardise the quality of the produce through the use of unfamiliar tools. One suspects that many phenomena of private international law are partly the result of the homeward trend: the rule of 'ordre public', 'fraude à la loi', treating as a rule of jurisdiction what might have been treated as a rule of choice of law, 'renvoi', insistence on the need to assert the applicability of foreign law in the pleadings, the need to prove it by calling an expert rather than just producing the written law, are all signs of the conscious or unconscious desire of the courts to avoid the application of foreign law.

1 Cour de Cassation 9.3 1910, DP 1912 1.262.
2 Kahn–Freund *General Principles of International Law* (1980) p 321.
3 Adapting a term used by Arthur Nussbaum *Principles of Private International Law* p 37.

3.07 The solution of applying the lex fori is thus usually satisfactory for deciding cases. On the other hand it may make life difficult for the legal practitioner. If the client is an 18-year-old student resident and domiciled in England, but of Swiss nationality because his parents were Swiss, and he was born in Switzerland, and he has fallen in love with and wants to marry next month a fellow student who is American, at her parents' home in Florida, the legal adviser has to solve a private international law problem. The law of the boy's domicil (English law) says that the question is governed by the law of his domicil, (English law), which says he can contract a valid marriage at 18. The law of his nationality (Swiss law) says that the question is governed by his nationality and under Swiss law you cannot validly marry until you are 20. The lex contractus (the law of Florida) says that the validity of the marriage is governed by the law of the place where the marriage takes place. If the legal advice is that the safest course would be to wait until he is 20 it may be wise counsel but may not be very popular with the client. If the advice is that whether his marriage is valid or not will depend on the context in which the question may arise later (divorce or legitimacy of children or succession to property on death) it would be accurate advice but really not much help to the young client. There is no lex fori here because there is no 'forum' as there is no law suit, just two young people in love who would like to get married.

3. The sources of private international law

(a) International custom

3.08 Since, as we have seen, private international law is a set of rules which forms part of national law, it follows that, as Justice Storey put it[1] 'whatever force and obligation the laws of one country have in another, depend solely upon the laws and municipal regulations of the latter; that is to say, upon its own proper jurisprudence and polity, and upon its own express or tacit consent'. However both foreign laws and customary international law can, applying the terminology of English courts, have 'persuasive authority'[2] meaning that the court adopts the reasoning of a judgment without being bound by it. This is close to the position of customary law in private international law, when it fills a gap in the national law.[3] German jurists call it 'Erkenntnisquelle' (as opposed to 'Rechtsquelle') a source of reasoning as opposed to a source of law. More ambitiously French jurists try to adduce general principles from the 'comity of nations' which constitute generally recognised rules of private international law based on 'natural law'.[4] This doctrine is often referred to as the 'universalist' or 'international' doctrine. Levy-Ullman defines it[5] as 'a doctrine which seeks to see adopted by the whole civilised world, identical rules on the conflict of laws and aspires to this goal by natural sentiment. It is a doctrine which, in the domain of action, seeks to get adopted, by the greatest possible number of nations, that identity of rules which may eventually lead to uniformity'.

Applied to private international law generally this perhaps is no more than the elegant expression of a pious hope.[6] It is cited here because it is precisely the philosophy which in international copyright inspired the Berne Convention and other copyright conventions which followed it. It is most gratifying that in this sphere of international law it has proved highly successful.

1 Joseph Storey, a Justice of the Supreme Court of the USA and Professor of Harvard University: *Commentaries on the Conflict of Laws* (2nd edn, 1841) p 30.
2 The term is applied by the English courts usually referring to decisions of the courts of other common law countries, mainly the USA, Canada, Australia and New Zealand.
3 See Kahn-Freund op cit, p 20.
4 The definition of 'comity' used in The United Kingdom by Diplock LJ in *Garthwaite v Garthwaite* [1964] P 356 at 389.
5 'La doctrine universaliste en matiere de conflict des lois' (1938) cited in the original French by Kahn Freund, op cit, p 21, freely translated here into English.
6 Levy-Ullman's 'Seven International Principles' of private international law are neither universally accepted, nor do they cover the whole ground, but they will serve as an illustration of what may be covered by 'customary international law': 'Territoriality of the law of immovable property'; 'Extraterritoriality of the law of personal status'; The rule locus regit actum (the law

of the country where an act takes place governs that act); 'Respect of vested rights'; The principle of 'ordre public' (in matters touching the public interest national law is paramount); The rule 'mobilia sequuntur personam', (the movable estate of a deceased person is governed by the personal law of the deceased); The rule of 'autonomie de la volonté' (the parties to a contract are free to choose expressly or by implication what law shall apply to it).

(b) International conventions

3.09 The sparsity of customary law and the imprecise nature of what little there was, proved a major incentive in the nineteenth century to regulate international situations by state treaties. Such treaties can be either inter partes – seeking to deal with conflict situations arising between contracting states – or erga omnes – seeking to be generally applicable. The early conventions were of the first variety, either bilateral treaties[1] or multilateral treaties specifying that they only applied between contracting parties. There is a tendency in the twentieth century towards conventions erga omnes, seeking to codify the widest achievable international consensus in one specific field of law.[2] One of the main influences producing both the trend towards conventions erga omnes and towards specialisation of subjects were the Hague Conventions on private international law.[3] Against this trend the international conventions in the field of industrial property[4] and in the field of copyright[5] and neighbouring rights[6] are notable and most successful exceptions.

1. The Franco-Swiss Treaty of 1869 on Civil Jurisdiction and the Enforcement of Civil Judgments is one of the earliest and outstanding examples.
2. Geneva Convention on the Execution of Foreign Arbitral Awards, 1927 and New York Convention on the Recognition and Enforcement of Foreign Arbitral Awards, 1958.
3. All conventions since 1951 when the Hague Conference on Private International Law was set up on a permanent basis are contained in *Recueil des Conventions de la Haye*.
4. The Paris Convention for the Protection of Industrial Property, 1883, several times revised, lastly at Stockholm 1967, and the Madrid Agreement for the Repression of False or Deceptive Indications of Source on Goods 1891, several times revised, lastly at Stockholm, 1967.
5. See chs 5 and 6.
6. See chs 7 to 10.

(c) National legislation

3.10 As private international law is in fact part of national law, one would expect national legislation to be the main source of this part of the law, particularly in those countries which rely on codification rather than development of the law by court decisions. That there has been comparatively little national legislation dealing with private international law is due to two reasons. The first is that many aspects of the subject are controversial and many of the controversies have grown rather than diminished during the nineteenth and twentieth centuries so that national legislators did not find the measure of agreement which would enable a statute to represent a consensus of opinion or at least a predominant majority opinion.[1] The first major codification of private international law which has proved the most influential was contained in the French Civil Code of 1804.[2] Of later national codifications the two in the major European countries, the German Law of 1900[3] and the Italian Law of 1942,[4] were passed by fairly authoritarian regimes. The Anglo-Saxon democracies did not attempt codification. The other reason is that the task of regulating international situations by national legislation is politically highly sensitive as no country wants to give away more than it receives.

The French Civil Code 1804 contains three main rules. The laws dealing with 'ordre public' (such as police and security matters) govern all persons living in France, whether French citizens or not. This is the origin of the 'ordre public' doctrine which has since been much enlarged. Land is governed by

French law, whether owned by Frenchmen or foreigners and the rules dealing with personal status and capacity apply to all Frenchmen whether living at home or abroad. On this comparatively narrow base[5] the French courts have been able to build over a century and a half a fairly elaborate system of private international law.

In the United Kingdom and other common law countries on the other hand there has been no attempt to deal with private international law by general legislation. Only laws dealing with particular subjects (mainly in the twentieth century) contain some private international law provisions.[6]

This explains why, when the first international convention in the copyright field was created,[7] French legal thinking and experience dominated the scene.[8]

1 See Kahn Freund, op cit, p 80.
2 Art 3, Code Civil.
3 Einführungsgesetz arts 7-31.
4 Codice Civile, Disposizioni sulla lege in generale art 16-31, (revising the original law of 1865).
5 There are a few other private international law provisions to be found in other parts of the Civil Code, eg art 170 on marriages and art 999 dealing with wills, both establishing the principle 'locus regit actum'.
6 The Legitimacy Act 1916, Foreign Judgments (Reciprocal Enforcement) Act 1933, the Recognition of Divorces and Judicial Separations Act 1971, the Wills Act 1963 in the United Kingdom.
7 The Berne Convention 1886 see ch 5.
8 The Swiss Law of 25 June 1891 which deals with private law applicable to persons domiciled and resident in Switzerland was also influential in the development of the Berne Convention.

(d) Judicial decisions

3.11 The courts have an important role in the development of private international law not only in the common law countries but also in countries which rely to a larger extent on codification to formulate the rules of conflicts of law such as France.

(e) Writings of academic lawyers ('Rechtswissenschaft') (the science of law), ('la doctrine')

3.12 Savigny's seminal work on private international law[1] in its preface puts it thus:

> 'The state of the subject is chaotic but the lively interest in the subject creates an endeavour to arrive at a rapprochement, a harmonisation and understanding, the like of which cannot be found in any other legal subject'. One can say that this subject has already become the common property of educated nations, not because it has firm general principles, but through the community of scholarly inquiry, which leads towards such principles.

1 Savigny *System des Heutigen Römischen Rechts* (1849).

4. International copyright law

3.13 In the realm of the law of movable (physical) property the law applicable to decide ownership is generally the law of the counttry where the property is acquired. If one bought goods in country A and takes them to country B, the question whether one has become the rightful owner of the goods is to be decided by the law of country A. The position is different with regard to copyright. The law applying to the physical property of the corpus mechanicum such as the book, the film, the record containing the work is governed by the above mentioned rules. The property in the work, however is governed by the law of country B, if that is where the right is claimed.

Thus 'the centre of gravity'[1] of the work is the country where protection is claimed.

Copyright law, like patent law, started as a privilege conferred by a prince and developed into a right conferred by a statute.[2] Such statute law gave protection to the right owner but, like all other statute law, only within the territory of that state. However, once it was conceded that the creators of new works of many kinds should be protected, such protection becomes at best only partially effective and at worst totally ineffective if it is confined to national frontiers. The idea that copyright arises from the act of creation of the work and not from any administrative act leads naturally to the idea that once the right exists, it should be valid anywhere. There is no good reason why a creator should be entitled both to moral recognition and to the pecuniary rewards of his works only in his own country and not abroad. But even more important than the moral imperative is that Gresham's law on international currencies that 'bad money drives out good money' applies to works and copyright protected matter. If a 'work' protected by copyright in country A is not protected in countries B and C so that it can be freely reproduced in these countries it may be imported into country A where it will then compete with copies on which copyright has been paid. As the imported copies will not have paid any copyright, they will be cheaper and will therefore drive the home-made produce, which has paid copyright, out of the market. The effect is the same as if a tax was put on a home produce, whereas the same produce was allowed to come in from abroad tax free. The greater the mobility of persons and goods the more serious will be the results of this phenomenon. To cope with it (as well as protecting its citizens abroad) a state has to give a certain amount of reciprocal protection to foreigners.

1 Ulmer *Urheberrecht und Verlagsrecht* (3rd end, 1980) p 83.
2 See ch 2.

5. The treatment of foreigners in copyright law

3.14 When faced with the question of the rights of foreigners in a country (country X) the following questions have to be answered in the following order:

1. Can the foreigner claim protection under one of the international conventions to which country X is a party? (in countries where such conventions are self applying).[1]
2. If not can he claim protection under a bilateral agreement to which country X is a party?
3. If not, can he claim protection under the national law of country X relating to foreigners?

In this third case national law may provide that he can claim no greater protection than that granted in his country of origin or it may apply the rule of material reciprocity.

As the great majority of countries which are of importance for copyright purposes are parties to one of the international conventions[2] bilateral agreements have lost most of their importance. Thus in most cases one will have to see whether the foreigner claiming protection is covered by one of the conventions and if not whether he is protected by the national law of the country where protection is claimed, in its provisions relating to foreigners.

The treatment of foreigners, apart from conventional protection, varies considerably and within the confines of this book a summary of comparison between the major European countries treated in Part 2 will have to suffice by way of example.

1. In the *Federal Republic of Germany*[3] works are protected if they are first published in Germany or are works by German nationals or assimilated persons (stateless persons and refugees).
2. In *Italy* works are protected if they were first published in Italy or the author resides in Italy.
   In both the Federal Republic and in Italy foreign authors are protected (over and above conventional protection) subject to reciprocity.
3. In the *United Kingdom* works are protected if their maker at the time of publication is a qualified person (qualified persons are British and Irish nationals or persons domiciled or resident in the United Kingdom), or if they are first published in the United Kingdom or an associated territory.[4]
4. In *France*[5] foreign works are protected even if neither the author is a French national nor the work was first published in France. The only condition is that an exclusive right in the work exists in the country of origin.[6] However, it is perhaps significant that a few years after the French Copyright Act 1957 France passed a law[7] to the effect that if a country which is not a member of any of the conventions to which France is a party does not grant adequate and effective protection[8] to works first published in France, works first published in such a country are not protected in France.[9]
5. The *United States* having won independence from Britain and wanting to create their own culture became protectionist.[10] Copyright was granted only to American citizens and residents in the United States. Even a century later when copyright was gradually granted to some foreign authors (country by country) copies of a foreign work had to be printed in the United States (under the so-called 'manufacturing clause').[11]

1 See para 3.30 below.
2 Nearly all important countries are members of the Berne Convention with the notable exceptions of the US and the USSR, but these countries are members of the UCC. See chs 5 and 6.
3 Similar rules apply in Denmark and the Netherlands.
4 In addition, the list of protected persons can be extended by Order in Council on grounds of reciprocal protection of works of British (or Irish) origin.
5 Similar rules apply in Belgium and Luxembourg.
6 See *Rideau de Fer* case, Cour de Cassation, 22 December 1959; Dalloz 1960 I p 93.
7 Law of 8 July 1964.
8 The language of art 1 of the UCC; see para 6.03 below.
9 This is an example of even the most liberal country in the world in copyright matters saying 'enough is enough' and applying the rule of material reciprocity. Yet true to its tradition 'moral rights' are protected even in such cases.
10 See para 2.18 above.
11 With various modifications this clause survived until the 1976 Copyright Act.

6. The history of international copyright treaties

3.15 The first international treaties dealing with copyright were bilateral agreements both in Europe and in America. In both cases they were found unsatisfactory as they produced, particularly in America, a mosaic of differing relationships leading away from harmony instead of towards it. They came to an end in Europe with the creation of the Berne Convention in 1886 and in America – for all practical purposes – with the creation of the Universal Copyright Convention in 1952. The 'Pan-American' experience is illuminating in this respect. The first multinational treaty was the Montevideo Convention in 1889, thus almost contemporary with the Berne Convention 1886. Just as the Berne Convention was initially a mainly European convention but open to all countries,[1] so the Montevideo Convention aimed at establishing a pan-American copyright system but was open to all countries and ratified by many American states as well as European ones.[2] However, there was an essential difference. The Berne Convention was based on the principle of national treatment,[3] treating foreigners like nationals if they belonged to member countries, thus accepting broadly speaking the lex fori. Under the Montevideo Convention on the other hand the rights of an author were governed by the law of the country of first publication or the law of the country of origin of the work which followed the work into all other countries of the union, thus accepting the principle of the lex originis. This meant that a court in country A when adjudicating on works originating from countries B, C and D had to apply three different foreign laws, those of countries B, C and D, whereas under the principle of national treatment the court would have applied only the law of country A: its own. The system not surprisingly did not work and provided a 'demonstratio ad occulos' that with all its shortcomings and complications the principle of national treatment is the better of the two.

There followed five further inter-American copyright conventions not open to non-American states.[4] The most successful one was the Buenos Aires Convention 1910 which was ratified by 17 Latin American republics and the United States. It had changed to the principle of national treatment. After the second world war the members of the Pan-American Union signed a revised convention in Washington DC in 1948 which was fashioned on the principles of the Berne Convention: a number of minimum rights and the principle of national treatment. If copyright was obtained in one state, a statement appearing on the work indicating the reservation of copyright confers copyright in all states without any formalities. A notice like 'Copyright reserved' was sufficient. Fourteen Latin American countries ratified it but the United States could not accept the granting of copyright without any formalities which were required under its own national law and did not ratify. With the largest American market outside the convention it could not become really effective and the Latin American republics were clearly seeking worldwide rather than merely Latin American protection, which had to include both the United States and Europe. They turned towards the Universal Copyright Convention created six years later in 1952 and although the Pan-American conventions are still operative, it is the Universal Copyright Convention that governs relations between the Latin American states and the United States and the Berne Convention as well as the Universal Copyright Convention governs the relations between them and the European states. Thus, all copyright and neighbouring rights conventions are now based on the principle of national treatment.

[1] The three non-European countries of the 10 signatories of the original Berne Convention were Haiti, Liberia and Tunisia.
[2] The European countries included the most important markets, France, Germany and the UK.
[3] Article 5(1); see para 5.34 below.
[4] Mexico City Convention 1902, Rio de Janeiro Convention 1906, Buenos Aires Convention 1910, Havana Convention 1928, Washington Convention 1948.

7. The principles of international copyright conventions

(a) General

3.16 Seeking to apply the general principles of private international law to a multinational copyright treaty, theoretically two of the principles would appear to be suitable: the lex loci and the lex fori. The adaptation of the principle of lex loci (or lex originis) leads to the principle of country of origin of the work. This means treating a work like a person and saying that its nationality is either that of its father (the author) at the time of its birth, which would be the time of its creation if it remains unpublished or the time of its first publication, if published. Alternatively it would be the nationality of its birthplace, that is the country of its first publication. Like a person the work would then, so to speak, have a passport and take its nationality with it wherever it goes. For example, if Nigeria is a convention country the work of a Nigerian author, first published in Nigeria, would have in the United Kingdom or France the same rights as it has in Nigeria.

The adaptation of the principle of lex fori to copyright leads (not necessarily but in practice) to the principle of national treatment, or as it is sometimes called, the principle of assimilation. This means that persons protected by the convention can claim in all contracting states the protection that the law of that state grants to its own nationals. Foreigners, if belonging to a convention country are 'assimilated' to nationals.[1]

The work of the same Nigerian author, published in Nigeria, would have in the United Kingdom the same rights as if it were created by a United Kingdom author and first published in the United Kingdom.

It will be seen that the advantage of adapting the first principle, the lex loci, would be that the same work will receive the same treatment in all member countries. The disadvantage is that lawyers and courts will continuously have to apply a large number of foreign laws, sometimes several laws in the same transaction or court case.[2]

The advantage of the second principle, the lex fori, is that courts will always apply their own law. The disadvantage is that the same work will get varying levels of protection in convention countries according to the national law of the country where the protection is claimed.

1 See para 3.17 below.
2 See para 3.26 below.

(b) National treatment (assimilation)

3.17 In practice, the second principle, that of national treatment, has proved to be the only viable one.[1] This is so mainly for two reasons, one psychological and the other political. The psychological reason is that courts prefer to apply their own law which they know, to having to apply foreign law which they do not know, and the quality of judgments will be better and the law therefore more certain under the principle of national treatment. The political reason is that right owners in countries of low level protection will realise that they get better treatment abroad in high level protection countries than they get at home and will bring pressure to bear on their governments to raise the level of protection at home. Thus, as the high level protection countries give a lead, the level of protection will graduually rise everywhere, thus getting nearer to the ideal of uniform treatment but on a high level.

National treatment is also in accord with the ideal of international law that all men are equal before the law, regardless of whether they are nationals or foreigners, and in a period of history where more and more eminent authors and creators are expatriates or refugees, conventions have also assimilated these to nationals so that they enjoy the same privileges in the country of their choice. The principle of national treatment also means that both the question of whether the right exists and the question of the scope of the right are to be answered in accordance with the law of the country where the protection is claimed.

A beneficial spin-off of the principle of national treatment is that confiscating measures valid under the law of the country where the confiscation takes place have no validity in other countries. These countries have to treat the right owner as they treat their own right owners, regardless of how he is treated in his own country. In recent times the division of Germany into the German Democratic Republic (East Germany) and the Federal Republic of Germany (West Germany) provides an example. Where a publisher had been expropriated in East Germany, the West German courts held that his reproduction and distribution right in the Federal Republic were not affected.[2] In the case of *August 14th* by Solzhenitsyn, the German Supreme Court held[3] that a publishing contract between the Russian author and a German publisher made in Switzerland which would be invalid according to Russian law because VAAP, the state agency, has a publishing monopoly that makes contracts with another publisher invalid, was nonetheless valid in Germany.

For these reasons the principle of national treatment was adopted as the basic principle of the Berne Convention in 1886[4] and of the copyright and neighbouring conventions which followed the Berne Convention.

The general application of the principle of national treatment in international copyright means that the major problem arising in almost all other areas of private international law: 'which law is a court to apply in a situation with foreign elements?' hardly ever arises in copyright law. The choice of law is mostly determined by the conventions which apply the principle of national treatment with the result that any right owner who is a national of a convention member state, or who first publishes in a member state, is entitled in every other member state to the same protection as the nationals of that state. Thus the courts in the state where the infringement occurs nearly always apply their own national law.

1   See the failure of the principle of lex loci in the case of the Montevideo Convention (1889), para 3.26 below.
2   OLG Stuttgart (BBL 1956, 14); see Ulmer, op cit, p 81.
3   BGHZ 64, p 183.
4   It was first proclaimed by the 'Societé des gens de lettres' at their conference in Paris 1878, which was the forerunner of the Berne Convention. See Röthlisberger *The Berne Convention* (1906) p 6.

(c) Extensions of the principle of national treatment

(1) *'Minimum rights'*
3.18 The principle of national treatment is extended in the copyright conventions by providing minimum rights which may be claimed in all convention countries jure conventionis regardless of the national legislation. In a strictly conceptual sense, these minima are not rules relating to conflict of laws as they contain no reference to another legal system. They also do not compel a convention country to grant these conventional rights provided as minimum rights to its own nationals because the convention deals only with international situations and therefore, if nothing else is provided in the convention, only compel a state to grant these rights to foreigners who are nationals of member states. However, the principle of national treatment without minimum rights, jure conventionis might produce a serious imbalance which states would find unacceptable. If countries A and B were members of a convention which provides only for national treatment and has no minimum rights and country A grants performance and broadcasting rights as well as a reproduction right, whereas country B grants only a reproduction right, the effect would be that

the nationals of country B would enjoy performance and broadcasting rights in country A, but nationals of country A would not enjoy these rights in country B because the nationals of country B do not enjoy them either. This could produce a serious disequilibrium which would be unacceptable to country A.

The history of copyright and neighbouring rights conventions bears this out. The Berne Convention[1] which was agreed at a time when the level of protection granted to authors still varied greatly from country to country started with only a minimum term and a translation right jure conventionis. The first task was to get as many countries as possible to accept these 'Minimum Rights' in their legislation which they had to do before they could ratify the convention. Having thus created a common minimum level of protection in these respects the Revision Conferences added further minimum rights.[2] The high level protection countries gave a lead to the lower level protection countries and it was hoped that the right owners of the lower level protection countries enjoying rights abroad which they did not have at home would bring pressure to bear on their governments to introduce them. These hopes proved amply justified.

When the Universal Copyright Convention was negotiated over 60 years later, the difference in the level of protection with regard to the rights covered by the convention had become less marked, and thus less stringent measures to insure against unacceptable differences in the level of protection were required. The term of 25 years 'post mortem auctoris'[3] and the translation right[4] are minimum rights, whereas article 1 requiring contracting states to 'provide for the adequate and effective protection of the rights of copyright owners' and article X requiring contracting states 'to adopt ... such measures as are necessary to ensure the application of the convention' are only general guidelines. However this was considered enough to ensure that differences of levels of protection under the national treatment rule were not too great.

In the Rome Convention, the first neighbouring rights convention, the principle of national treatment is accompanied by minimum rights for each of the three beneficiaries: a right against unauthorised fixation for performers, a reproduction right for phonogram producers and broadcasters, a performance right in phonograms (subject to reservations) for producers and performers.[5] If reservations are made the reciprocity rule can be applied to the states making a reservation. Thus, the principle of national treatment combined with minimum rights to assure a common denominator is moderated by the reciprocity rule to avoid injustices being caused by large divergencies of levels of protection.[6]

Minimum rights also make the gradual growth of a convention possible. The convention can start with a small number of minimum rights and add others as the years go by at revision conferences, thus providing a road towards both uniformity and higher standards of protection. The Berne Convention for instance started with the translation right and added the right of public performance and the broadcasting right, the droit moral, the cinematographic right.[7] The UCC (1952) provided for the translation right only and in its revised version (1971) added the reproduction right, the broadcasting right and the public performance right.[8]

1   See ch 5 below.
2   See paras 5.10 et seq below.
3   UCC, art vi; see pará 6.18 below.
4   UCC, art v; see para 6.23 below.
5   See ch 8.
6   Cf Straschnov 'National Treatment and Neighbouring Rights' Droit d'Auteur (February 1961) p 41.
7   See ch 5.
8   See ch 6.

(2) Formalities

3.19 In a sense freedom from formalities is also an extension of the principle of national treatment as it compels national laws to grant rights to works from convention countries without making such rights subject to formalities which may otherwise be required. This can be done either by requiring the granting of rights without any formalities like the Berne Convention,[1] or by laying down a maximum of formalities which may be required to secure protection like the University Copyright Convention with the symbol © or the Rome Convention and the Phonogram Convention with the symbol ℗ accompanied by the name of the copyright owner and the year of first publication.[2]

1 Berne Convention, art 5 (2) see para 5.35 below.
2 UCC, art III, Rome Convention, art 11, Phonogram Convention, art 5.

(d) Limitations of the principle of national treatment

(1) *Reciprocity*

3.20 The principle of national treatment can be limited, sometimes severely limited, by the rule of reciprocity. The 'raison d'etre' of reciprocity is: 'Manus lavat manum.' State A wants its citizens protected in State B and thus offers to protect the citizens of State B in return. Reciprocity in international law can be either 'material' (or 'substantive') reciprocity or 'formal' (or 'partial') reciprocity.

'*Material Reciprocity*' means that country A will protect the citizens of country B in the same manner as country B protects the citizens of country A.[1] As a general rule the copyright conventions are opposed to material reciprocity although there are exceptions.[2] This is made plain in the 'Declaration Against Material Reciprocity' which is included in the Report of the 1971 Paris Revision Conference.[3] One of the advantages of avoiding material reciprocity in copyright conventions is that the courts of member states do not have to interpret the laws of other member states to see whether protection is given in respect of a particular right. The rule of national treatment enables them instead to apply their own law to foreigners. A disadvantage is that it permits sometimes great disparities between the effective levels of protection[4] so that the citizens of high level protection countries get less rights in some convention countries than they enjoy at home, whereas the citizens of low protection countries get better protection in some convention countries than they get at home. However this is balanced by the advantage that wide ranging copyright relations are facilitated between countries of differing ideologies and differing stages of economic development.

'*Formal Reciprocity*' (or partial reciprocity) in copyright conventions means that each member state will protect the works or citizens of other member states in some manner but from such reciprocity nothing is to be implied with regard to the nature of the protection. That is generally determined by the rule of national treatment.[5]

The 'comparison of terms' under the Berne Convention[6] is an example. The term of protection is dealt with in the conventions by laying down a minimum term: 50 years post mortem auctoris, but countries are free to grant a longer term. Comparison of terms means that a country which grants a longer term than 50 years to their nationals need only grant that longer term to foreigners if that term is also granted by their country of origin. For example the Federal Republic of Germany gives 70 years pma, but Germany need only give 50 years pma to United Kingdom right owners because that is the term of their own national law. It does not have to give the full 70 years it gives to its own nationals.

1 Material reciprocity has been described as 'tit for tat'.
2 The 'droit de suite' in the Berne Convention (art 14 bis; see para 5.53 below) or the 'comparison of terms' in the Berne Convention (art 7/8; see para 5.59 below).
3 Report of the General Rapporteur of the Paris Conference 1971, paras 58 and 59.
4 See Ulmer 'Copyright Problems in Relations between East and West' 1 IIC 32, 44 (1970).
5 See Ulmer; 'Copyright Problems in Relations between East and West,' 1 IIC 32, 44 (1970).
6 Berne Convention, art 7 para 8, see para 5.54 below.

(2) Reservations

3.21 The rights granted by conventions can also be limited by reservations, which give countries the opportunity to ratify the convention but to withhold the giving of some rights wholly or partly. Some conventions, eg the Phonogram Convention, permit no reservations, others, eg the Rome Convention, provide for several. The reservations can relate to the scope of a right or to the connecting factor eg the reservations regarding the points of attachment in the Rome Convention[1] or to a whole right, eg the performance right in phonograms in the same convention.[2] The making of reservations is usually accompanied by the application of the rule of reciprocity so that the nationals of country A which has made the reservation can be deprived of the exercise of those rights in country B because the nationals of country B are not granted these rights in country A.

1 Rome Convention, art 5.1; see para 8.10 below.
2 Rome Convention, art 16.1 (a) (i); see para 8.30 below.

(e) Challenges to the principle of national treatment[1]

3.22 Thus the principle of national treatment subject to extensions and limitations has proved itself as the fundamental principle of copyright and neighbouring rights conventions for nearly a century. It is however at present in danger of being undermined as governments try to cope with the rapid development of technology and communications. When a new right is being granted to copyright owners governments have the option of granting it in the course of copyright revision and as a copyright, or of granting it as a new right in a separate law outside the copyright law. If the government decides to grant the new right as a copyright, the international conventions apply and the principle of national treatment may demand that foreigners who are nationals of convention countries which have not yet granted the new right have to be given the same right and thus become entitled to the remuneration which flows from it. If on the other hand the government decides to create the new right outside the copyright law the conventions will not apply and foreigners will not be entitled to national treatment and therefore will not be entitled to participate in any remuneration for the use of the new right. Two practical examples will illustrate the position.

1 See para 12.07 below.

(1) Public lending right

3.23 This right has been introduced in several countries under which authors of literary works receive a royalty when their books are being borrowed from a library by members of the public. In the Federal Republic of Germany this right is granted in the Copyright Law[1] and therefore, as Germany is a member of the Berne Convention and of the Universal Copyright Convention, foreigners who are nationals of convention countries are entitled to remuneration if their books are borrowed. On the other hand the Scandinavian countries[2] the

United Kingdom[3] which also give a public lending right, have chosen to do so by separate legislation outside the copyright laws and are therefore not bound to grant the right to foreigners, although, like Germany, they are also members of both conventions and the remuneration paid for the lending right is therefore limited to works of national authors.[4]

(2) Reprography
This is the production of copies of printed matter by copying machines.[5] One way of dealing with such copies produced for commercial purposes is to subject the reproduction right in respect of such copies to a compulsory licence and give the author a right to equitable remuneration as in the Federal Republic of Germany.[6]

On the other hand France introduced a tax on the sale and importation of all machines producing reprographic copies in its Finance Act 1976. Part of the revenue of this tax is paid to the copyright owners of the material copied, but it is paid only to French copyright owners although France is a party to both copyright conventions. The principle of national treatment does not apply as the compensation does not arise from a copyright and foreigners are thus not compensated.

The distinction between the two examples is that the reproduction right is generally recognised in all copyright laws and is a fundamental right of both international conventions and unauthorised copying is only permissible as an exception (eg for private use), whereas a public lending right, far from being universally acknowledged, only exists in a few countries and does not form part of the jus conventionis of any of the international conventions. Thus, on grounds of natural justice and applying the principle of national treatment to a generally accepted right, the claim of foreigners who are convention nationals to compensation for reprographic use of their works is strong. In the case of the public lending right it is, so far, still weak whilst only few countries grant it.

Another distinction is that in the case of the reprographic right in the United States the royalty will be paid by the user, which is a characteristic of all copyrights, whereas the compensation (it is not termed a royalty) in the case of the public lending right in Scandinavia and in the United Kingdom is paid out of a public fund. That means that it comes from taxpayers' money as opposed to copyright users' money.

Thus by the simple device of calling the right to compensation something other than a copyright and introducing it by a separate piece of legislation[7] the application of the principle of national treatment can be avoided. Particularly in cases where the compensation is paid out of a government fund which can be called taxpayers' money, the temptation to restrict it to nationals is considerable. If that device is generally used by governments when dealing with the new uses of copyright material arising from new technology and new means of communication, the fundamental principle of national treatment and with it the copyright conventions based on it, could be seriously eroded in the near future.[8]

1 Para 27; Copyright Law 1965 as amended 1972.
2 See eg Law on Public Libraries, 27 May 1969 (amended 26 June 1975) art 19 in Denmark.
3 Public Lending Right Act 1980.
4 One of the strange consequences of this method is that the translator of a book if he is a national has a right to remuneration but the author of the same book, if he is a foreigner, has not.
5 See paras 12.07 and 12.16 below.
6 German Copyright Law, art 54(2), see para 12.18 below.
7 A case where 'a rose by any other name' does *not* 'smell just as sweet'.
8 See Elisabeth Steup, Geringer Lecture 1977, Bulletin of the Copyright Society of the USA (1977), p 279.

8. The connecting factor

3.24 On the national level the question whether copyright protection does exist or not is decided by asking first whether the subject matter attracts copyright protection or not. For instance 'literary and artistic works' are protected in all copyright countries (countries whose legislation grants copyrights). Other works like (cinematograph) films or phonograms enjoy copyright in some countries, eg the United Kingdom or the United States, but not in others, eg France. If there is a copyright the second basic question to ask is whether the protection sought is covered by the scope of the right. For instance all works enjoy a reproduction right in copyright countries but not all works enjoy a performance right; for instance phonograms enjoy a performance right in the United Kingdom but not in the United States. The third basic question to ask is what term the legislation grants to the work or subject matter in question. Literary and artistic works in Berne Convention countries enjoy a minimum of the life of the author and 50 years and in Universal Copyright Convention countries a minimum of the life of the author and 25 years, whereas photographic works or works of applied art enjoy a shorter term (under the Universal Copyright Convention a minimum of 10 years). On the international level a further question has to be answered: If the work is a foreign work or the author or right owner is a foreigner, what is the criterion for deciding whether the work or the right owner are protected? This is known as the connecting factor, ('point de rattachement', 'Anknüpfungspunkt'), the factor which connects the work or the author with a particular country. It is usually defined as the country with which there is 'the closest and most real connection'. When considering the possible connecting factors one has to bear in mind that copyright is an intellectual property right. It is a property right in the sense that it is a right erga omnes, thus resembling corporeal property rights, but the subject of that right is incorporeal. That means that although the work appears in the tangible form (corpus mechanicum) of a book, a film, a phonogram in one place, it can be reproduced or performed in lots of other places whilst still remaining the same work. Different criteria from those applied to corporeal property rights have to be found to serve as the relevant factors connecting the work or subject matter or the author or the right owner of the work with one particular country. These factors are:

(a) *Personal status connection* (nationality, habitual residence etc) – referred to as 'the country to which the author (or the maker) of the work belongs').[1]

(b) *Geographical connection of the work* – referred to as 'the country of origin.'[2]

(c) *Geographical connection with the public* – referred to as 'the country of first publication',[3] the country where the work or subject matter of copyright was first made available to the public.

(d) *The lex fori* – referred to as the 'protecting country', the country where protection is claimed, that is where the use of the work, be it legitimate exploitation or infringement, takes place.

1 Berne Convention, art 3 (2).
2 Berne Convention, art 5 (4); see para 5.36 below.
3 Berne Convention, art 3 (1) (b); see para 5.32 below.

(a) The country to which the author belongs

3.25 In accordance with the philosophy of the 'droit d'auteur' that the quintessence of copyright is the progress of the work from the mind of the author to the general public, the personal status connection of the author and the geographical connection of first publication with the public were the essential points of attachment of the first international copyright convention, the Berne Convention. The nature of the personal status connection was defined as nationality, but those persons who have their 'habitual residence' in a country of the Berne Union are 'assimilated' to nationals[1] and the Universal Copyright Convention adopts the same structure using the Anglo-Saxon concept of 'domicil' instead of the Latin concept of habitual residence.

In essence habitual residence is a question of fact for the court that tries the case to be judged by the length of time during which the author has lived in a country, whereas the concept of domicil differs from country to country and may depend on where the author ultimately intends to settle rather than where he resides, a matter sometimes more difficult to ascertain.[2]

In more recent times where refugee and stateless authors have become more frequent than they were in the nineteenth century, they too have been assimilated to nationals.[3]

When the right owner is not a natural person but a legal entity like a corporation or company such as a film producer or a phonogram producer or a broadcasting organisation, the place of its seat or headquarters decide residence or domicil.[4]

In the case of the personal connecting factor the question to which country the author or maker of the work belongs may have to be answered differently at different times as he may change his nationality and even more easily his habitual residence. The relevant date may be the date of the creation of the work in which case different works of the same author may have different connecting factors. It may be his nationality or residence at the time of publication in the case of a published work, or it may be the time when protection is claimed. The Berne Convention is silent on the point.[5] It is, unless the national law provides a solution, a matter for the courts to decide. It is likely that the courts will choose the nationality or residence at the time when protection is claimed for the purely practical reason that it is probably the easiest to ascertain.

1 Berne Convention, art 3 (2).
2 For a recent analysis of the concept of domicil in the United Kingdom see *Re Fuld's Estate* [1968] P 675 and *Re Flynn* [1968] 1 WLR 103.
3 See Berne Convention, art 3 (2) 'authors ... who have their habitual residence' in a Union country.
4 Art 4 (a) of the Berne Convention makes one of its rare concessions to the notion that a corporate body can have a copyright by recognising the headquarters of a maker of a cinematographic work as his residence for the purposes of the convention.
5 See Masouyé/Wallace *WIPO Guide to the Berne Convention* 3.11.

(b) The country of origin

3.26 At the earliest stages of drafting multinational treaties the concept of the country of origin of the work was at the centre of the scene. The underlying thought was that once a work is created or published it should have the same rights abroad as at home. The principle was tried in the Montevideo Convention 1889.[1] It was not successful as a basic principle of a convention because it leads by definition to situations where different rights attach to similar works, because one originates in a country granting a high level of protection and the other in a country with a low level of protection. The creators of the Berne Convention did not make this mistake and based the convention on the principle of national treatment. However the convention contains a definition of the country of origin[2] to the effect that for a published work the country of origin shall be the country of first publication and for an unpublished work the country 'to which the author belongs'. Although the Paris Act 1971 still contains a more detailed definition,[3] to the same effect, the importance of this point of attachment seems to have declined with the years and neither the Universal Copyright Convention nor the neighbouring rights conventions contain the concept of the country of origin.

It must be remembered that conventions deal only with international situations and therefore protection of nationals in the country of origin itself is regulated by the law of that country. Thus if a national author publishes at home no problem arises. If he publishes abroad the country of first publication takes the place of the country of origin. For unpublished works the country of origin becomes important if a subsequent publication, eg of a translation, takes place abroad.

The main importance of the country of origin today is for measuring the duration of protection. The rule of the comparison of terms[4] provides that although the term of protection is governed by the law of the country where protection is claimed, that term shall not exceed the term fixed in the country of origin of the work, unless the national law provides otherwise. When terms of protection varied widely the comparison of terms was often of crucial importance. It is less so now. However examples are to be found in the relation between countries which give the minimum term of 50 years after the death of the author and countries which give a longer term.

1 See para 3.17, note 1 above.
2 Berne Convention 1886, art 2 (3).
3 Berne Convention 1971, art 5 (4).
4 Berne Convention, art 7 (8). Comparison of terms in the Universal Copyright Convention (art IV 4 (a)) is made for published works by comparing with the country of first publication and for unpublished works by comparing with the country of which the author belongs. See para 6.19 below.

(c) The country of first publication

3.27 First publication is an important connecting factor.[1] If a writer writes a book in China (a state not a member of any international convention), it is unprotected anywhere else while it is unpublished. If he publishes it in China it is still unprotected anywhere else. If however he publishes it first in the United Kingdom it becomes protected by the Berne Convention or if he publishes it first in the United States it becomes protected by the Universal Copyright Convention. If the only publication within a convention country is an English translation published in the United Kingdom, or in the United States, that translation becomes protected as a separate work, but the original in Chinese still remains unprotected. The result is that anyone can make another English translation (or indeed a French or German one) and publish it in any convention country without the author's permission.[2] The concept of simultaneous publication is of vital importance as a connecting factor because it may considerably enlarge the protection of the work if the work is published in a non convention country and would otherwise be unprotected. If it is 'simultaneously' published in a convention country this secures its protection.[3] The Berne Convention allows an interval of 30 days between the first and second publication to qualify the second one as a simultaneous publication. So does the Rome Convention for the publication of phonograms.[4] Simultaneous publication is particularly important in cases of works published in the same language (a translation is a new work) in several countries or in the case of musical works or phonograms.[5]

1 For definitions of 'publication' see Berne Convention, art 3 (3); see para 5.33 below and Universal Copyright Convention, art VI; see para 6.32 below.
2 If the work is valuable it may therefore be wise to publish a limited edition of the original in the UK or US first to establish the connecting factor and secure protection by the conventions. See Cornish Intellectual Property (1981) p 340 note 25.
3 Berne Convention, art 3 (4) see para 5.33 below.
4 Rome Convention, art 3 (d). See para 8.13 below.
5 Under the Rome Convention the criterion of first publication can be excluded as a point of attachment, (art 5/1 see para 8.10 below) the result is that the sole points of attachment are the nationality of the producer or the fixation of the recording. If a country excludes the criterion of publication, as the Scandinavian countries have done, it is for this very reason: to exclude simultaneous publication protecting a phonogram which is made in a non-convention country by a producer who is a national of a non-convention country.

(d) The protecting country

3.28 This is shorthand for the country where protection is claimed. As in practice an action is usually brought in the country where the infringement is committed, this usually means the lex fori. However there are exceptions where the infringement is committed in a country other than the one where protection is claimed. It is another question not settled by the convention whether in cases of infringements abroad legal protection based on foreign copyright can be claimed. In the past it has usually been accepted that the principle of territoriality applies and that legal protection before national courts can only be claimed in cases of infringements committed within the country concerned. However as Ulmer points out[1] according to the general rules of private international law 'it seems consistent to expand the rule which may be derived from the conventions into a complete rule of conflict of laws whereby protection of intellectual property rights, irrespective of the country in which the action is brought, is to be governed by the law of the country in whose territory the act of infringement took place, (the lex loci delicti)'.

The answer depends on the view taken by the national courts. The German courts for instance have taken a broad view in trade mark[2] and patent[3] cases. In the United Kingdom the general rule is that a wrongful act committed abroad is actionable in England if it would be actionable as a tort in England had it been committed in England and is also actionable in the foreign country where it was committed.[4] As in copyright cases the legal position is similar whether they are Berne Convention countries or Universal Copyright Convention countries, it is arguable that an action can be maintained.[5]

In the United States the courts seem to take the view that it is a matter for their discretion and have refused to accept jurisdiction, giving as the reason that it would involve a judgment on the validity of a foreign right which would be more appropriately made by the courts of that foreign country.[6]

However the recent EEC 'Convention on Jurisdiction and the Enforcement of Judgments in Civil and Commercial Matters' (22 September 1968)[7] provides in article 5 (3) that in actions for 'delict and quasi delict' persons may be sued in any contracting state in the court competent for the place where the damage or injury has occurred. It would appear therefore that in these countries an action for infringement of copyright can be brought both in the country where the defendant is domiciled and in the country where the infringement has occurred.

1 Ulmer *Intellectual Property Rights and the Conflict of Laws* (1978) p 10.
2 Supreme Court (Reichsgericht, 8 July 1930 RGZ 129, 385).
3 Court of Düsseldorf, GRUR Int 1958 p 430; Court of Appeal Düsseldorf, GRUR Int 1968 p 100.
4 See Boys v Chaplin [1971] AC 356, HL; also Cheshire & North *Private International Law* (9th edn, 1974) p 263. Dicey & Morris *Conflict of Laws* (9th edn, 1973) ch 31.
5 See Cornish, op cit, p 69.

6 *Orsman v Stanway Corp* 163 USPQ (NDIII) 1969; *Vanity Fair Mills Inc v Eutin & Co* 109 USPQ 446 (2nd Circ) 1956; *Packard Instrument Comp Inc v Beckmann Instruments Inc* (ND III) 1972.
7 Ratified by the six original member states of the EEC.

9. The systems of creating rights in international copyright conventions

3.29 There are three systems of dealing with international situations in a convention:

(1) The situation is dealt with in the convention by granting a right jure conventionis and there are no exceptions. *Example*: the translation right in the Berne Convention (1971).[1]

(2) The situation is dealt with in the convention, but it is open to national legislation to introduce restrictions and fix modes of application. *Example*: The broadcasting right in the Berne Convention (1971).[2] Compulsory licence schemes are permitted although their scope is confined to the country permitting them.

(3) The situation is defined in the convention but it is left to national legislation whether it grants a right or not. *Example*: The 'Droit de Suite' in the Berne Convention (1971).[3] The right is optional in the sense that a member country need not introduce it (the United Kingdom for instance, has not yet introduced it). If a country does introduce it for its nationals it can make the application to nationals of other convention countries dependent on reciprocity (which is exceptional in the Berne Convention).

The choice between these systems permits a gradual approach which allows a political judgment to be exercised at every stage during the life of a convention. A new right can be introduced in group 3 giving member countries the choice whether they wish to grant the new right or wish to wait. If a country wishes to introduce the new right but make it subject to a compulsory licence it can do so in group 2. Once a right is established and generally accepted it can then be moved up to group 1.

1 The only possible exceptions are contained in the Protocol, and apply only to developing countries. See paras 6.45 et seq.
2 Art 11 bis. See para 5.43 below.
3 Art 14 ter. See para 5.53 below.

10. The systems of applying international copyright conventions to national law

3.30 The application of an international convention by a country is the method by which the convention which is international law becomes part of the national law of the country.

At the diplomatic conference which establishes the convention, countries which are represented by an accredited plenipotentiary usually sign the convention. However such signature has no legal consequences, although it may carry with it a moral obligation to ratify at a later stage.

If a country was not represented at the diplomatic conference or if its representative did not sign the convention it can later 'accede' to it. The effect of accession is the same as ratification.

How the international law contained in the convention is translated into the national law of a state depends on the constitutional law of that state.

(a) In some countries international conventions are self applying. No further legal or administrative act is necessary. The provisions of the convention become part of the national law and override previous legislation. The convention is 'self-executing'. This is the case for instance in France, Germany, Italy and the Latin-American countries. It leads to interpretation of the text of the convention itself by the national courts.

(b) Some countries, on the other hand, do not regard agreements between sovereign states as part of the law of the land. Conventions are not binding on their citizens until ratified by the legislature. This is the case for instance in the Scandinavian countries, United Kingdom, United States. In these countries national legislation is needed to make the provisions of a convention binding on its nationals. This may be done by making the whole convention part of the national law thereby falling for interpretation by the national courts. It may also be done by drafting national law so as to comply with the convention. In that case it will be for the national courts to decide whether to take the convention text into account when interpreting the national law.

Chapter 4
Authors' Rights

Summary

1. Subject matter of copyright   4.01
   (1) Creation of the work   4.01
   (2) Fixation of the work   4.04
   (3) Publication of the work   4.05
   (4) Categories of works and subject matters of copyright   4.14
2. Economic rights and moral rights   4.15
3. Ownership of copyright   4.24
   (1) General   4.24
   (2) Works created in employment   4.25
   (3) Commissioned works   4.26
   (4) Assignment and licensing   4.27
4. Limitations of copyright   4.28
   (1) Free use   4.29
   (2) The problems of free use   4.31
   (3) Compulsory licences   4.33
   (4) Special provisions for developing countries   4.38
5. Term of copyright   4.39
6. Remedies for infringement of copyright   4.42
   (1) Civil remedies   4.43
   (2) Criminal remedies   4.48
   (3) Administrative measures   4.49

1. Subject matter of copyright – type and quality of the subject matter of copyright

WHAT IS A WORK OR ANY OTHER SUBJECT MATTER OF COPYRIGHT?

(1) Creation of the work

Quality

4.01 There is general agreement that the quality or merit of a work are matters of taste and do not enter into the question of what is a work. Nor is there a prescribed degree of ability or the amount of skill and knowledge necessary to create the work, or a measure of resources used to produce it. In Anglo-Saxon jurisdictions it will in each case be 'a question of degree whether the labour or skill or ingenuity or expense involved' are sufficient to warrant a claim of copyright.[1]

[1] UK: *Ladbroke (Football) Ltd v William Hill (Football) Ltd* [1964] 1 All ER 465 where simple compilations like a 'football coupon' consisting of a list of forthcoming matches with spaces for the punter to put a sign for win, lose or draw, were held to have a copyright. The argument that anyone can do it was met by the House of Lords saying: 'If you can do it yourself then do it yourself, but if you copy someone else's work you must pay for it'.

For the same reason examination papers have been held to be 'literary works' (*University of London Press Ltd v University Tutorial Press Ltd* [1966] 2 Ch 601) as have trade lists (*Purefoy v Sykes Boxall* (1955) 72 RPC 89, CA); street directories (*Kelly v Morris* (1866) LR I Eq 697); timetables (*Blacklock v Pearson* [1915] 2 Ch 376).

Originality

4.02 Unlike for a patent, where novelty is essential, there is no such requirement for copyright. It is sometimes said that to be copyright protected a work must be original.[1] However this has to be understood in a very wide sense and does not mean complete novelty. It means in many cases no more than that the creator can truthfully say – 'This is all my own work'.[2]

It is possible for two different persons quite independent from one another to make the same invention. In such cases the invention first registered at the patent office will have the prior claim and the other will not be protected. Not so in copyright. Infringement of copyright predicates the use of someone else's work. If the similarity or even identity is accidental there is no infringement. Thus if two people set out independently from one another to make a map or a street directory using identical or very similar information and producing very similar results each will have a copyright in his work. The consequence is that the writer, the composer, the painter, the sculptor or anyone creating copyright material need not fear the existence of pre-existing rights which would threaten his copyright.[3] This is the reason why the requirement of registration or deposit is not necessary to a copyright system although some countries (notably the United States) have such systems, for varying reasons. 'All protected works have this in common; they represent the result of someone's skill and labour and they can be reproduced'.[4]

1 The US Copyright Act 1976 refers to 'original works of authorship' (s 102).
2 UK, Whitford Committee Report, p 10.
3 See Ulmer *Urbeber und Verlagsrecht* (3rd edn) p 14.
4 Whitford Committee Report, para 33.

Derivative works

4.03 So far we have only dealt with primary works in the sense that the author starts from nothing and creates a work, however humble or pedestrian may be the creation. There are however also works where the author starts with a pre-existing work and by an additional intellectual input of his own creates a new work.

The earliest examples were translations of a literary work into another language. The translator needs the permission of the author of the pre-existing work to make the translation, but he has himself a copyright in his translation.

There is copyright in the adaptation of a literary work such as a play adapted from a novel or a film script adapted from a play. In the realm of musical works adaptations are usually called arrangements, eg an orchestral work arranged for piano, or conversely a song written with piano accompaniment orchestrated for voice and orchestra. In popular music there are many arrangements of original songs made to suit a particular performer or a particular language version of the text. Each such adaptation or arrangement is a work provided there is a sufficient element of intellectual creation. The intellectual input of the adapter or arranger may be quite modest to be sufficient. An arrangement of the 'March of the Toreadors' from Bizet's *Carmen* for saxophone, xylophone, and drums may sound a little odd but it will have copyright under most jurisdictions, although there already exist dozens of other arrangements of that march.

In an anthology, eg a collection of poetry or extracts from other literary works by different authors, the originality or the intellectual input lies in the selection and the arrangement of the pre-existing works. The creator of the collection has a copyright.

If the translation or the arrangement of a pre-existing work is recorded or the screen play filmed, the producer of the phonogram or the film will have a copyright in the copyright countries (eg the United States or the United Kingdom) or a neighbouring right in many other countries. There will thus exist, superimposed one upon the other, several copyrights or neighbouring rights: the copyright of the author of the primary work, the copyright of the translator or adaptor or arranger and the copyright of the producer of the phonogram or the film. In a song written by A, orchestrated by B, recorded by C, or a novel written by A, dramatised by B and filmed by C, A, B, and C will have copyrights or neighbouring rights in most countries.

(2) Fixation of the work

4.04 In all Anglo-Saxon jurisdictions fixation is crucial. The work has to be fixed in writing or in any other material form to qualify for a copyright. That is not to say that a work cannot be complete whilst merely in the mind of the author eg a composer may play his composition or a poet recite his poetry without having written anything down beforehand. The work is an intellectual creation not a material thing. However in Anglo-Saxon jurisdictions it does not acquire protection until it is reduced to material form. In other words fixation is a condition precedent to the existence of copyright. The work can exist in a complete state in the mind of the author, but he has to take a further step before completing his title and acquiring a copyright, he has to fix it or cause it to be fixed in material form.[1] This is not so in most continental European jurisdictions particularly in France and Germany. In these jurisdictions a lecture given without a script or a musical performance of a work without a score are protected.[2] In view of this position the Berne Convention (1971) does not take sides and provides[3] that it is 'a matter for legislation in the countries of the Union' to require fixation 'in some material form'. This gives each country the possibility to demand fixation either generally or for one or more categories of works.[4]

'Writing' is not required in international law. The Berne Convention defines a literary work as: 'every production in the literary ... domain, whatever may be the mode or form of its expression, such as books, pamphlets and other writings ... dramatic or musical works etc'![5] It seems to follow that in all Berne Convention countries any form of fixation other than writing will suffice to acquire a copyright. Apart from the obligation to honour the Convention the opposite interpretation would lead to very odd results in the light of modern technology, eg a musical work not written down on paper but played and recorded would not be protected as a work and anyone who copied it from the recording would not be an infringer. As this situation arises regularly in recording studios with jazz and popular music, musical copyright would be seriously undermined.

In countries not members of the Berne Convention writing could be required by the national law. The classic case is the United States, where the word 'writings' occurs in the Constitution.[6] This was perfectly logical in the eighteenth century but when other forms of fixation emerged such as films and records, the courts had to wrestle with the problem and eventually gave the term 'writings' of 'authors' a wide meaning in the light of modern technology declaring a recording a form of writing which Congress could protect pursuant to the patent and copyright clause of the Constitution.[7] Therefore under national laws the answer which the law gives to the question: 'What constitutes fixation?' is of crucial importance to what is and what is not copyright material and who is the copyright owner.

The next stage in the life of the work after creation and fixation is publication.

1 See Laddie Prescott and Vitoria *The Modern Law of Copyright* 2.17.
2 See Ulmer, op cit, p 131.
3 Art 2(2); see *WIPO Guide to Berne* 2.9-2.11.
4 For instance for choreographic works and pantomimes.
5 Berne Convention, art 2(4).
6 Art 1, para 8, cl 8.
7 Under the Copyright Act 1976 notation of a work in visually perceptible form is no longer a requirement of copyright protection.

(3) Publication of the work

4.05 The definition of publication is relevant in international copyright in several respects:

1. In the copyright conventions the country of publication is one of the connecting factors (eg in the Berne Convention[1] and the UCC[2] if the author of the work is not a national of a contracting state. In the Rome Convention[3] it is one of two connecting factors which cannot be eliminated by reservation).
2. If formalities are required (eg Universal Copyright Convention) one of them is the year date of publication.
3. It is relevant for the computation of the term of copyright for those classes of work where the term is x years from the date of first publication.
4. It is relevant for the system of compulsory licences in developing countries under the Berne and Universal Copyright Conventions 1971 as the date when the issuing of a compulsory licence becomes possible is computed from the publication of the work.

Whereas in the law of libel publication as a term of art has a very narrow meaning, ie showing *or* communicating the writing containing the libel to any person other than the person defamed, in copyright the meaning is wider and closer to the general meaning of the word: making public. The definition of publication has varied considerably both from country to country and from time to time.[4] In the history of copyright publication meant originally the publication of copies (ie reproductions) of works or other printed matter. When films and phonograms were invented the old definitions began to present new difficulties, which were dealt with in separate ways in different countries.

There are five basic questions to be answered:

1. Does publication imply publication with the consent of the author?
2. Does publication require a fixation in a tangible form (corpus mechanicum) and the making of copies or duplicates which are tangible objects, or does for instance public performance of a literary or musical work constitute publication?
3. Are phonograms or films copies for the purpose of publication?
4. How many copies have to be made available to the public to amount to publication?
5. Do these copies have to be sold, or does hiring out copies for public performance also amount to publication?

1 See Art 3(1)(b).
2 See Art II/1.
3 See Art 5/1 (c).
4 For a detailed and critical exposition of the problems surrounding the concept of publication see: Sylvane Durrande 'The concept of publication in the international conventions' RIDA Vol 111, (January 1982) p 72.

4.06 1. The first question is nearly always answered in the affirmative: unauthorised publication is not 'publication'. The only exception, albeit an important one, is publication under a compulsory licence system.[1]

1 See para 4.33 below.

4.07 2. The answer to the second question varies from country to country. In some countries broad definitions like 'making a work public by any means' (Netherlands)[1] or 'the first exercise of the right to use the work shall be considered its first publication' (Italy)[2] or 'a work has been published if it has been made accessible to the public with the consent of the copyright owner' (Germany)[3] are obviously wide enough to include publication by public performance or recitation of a literary or musical or dramatic work, or exhibition of a picture or statue, and are intended to include such means of publication.

On the other hand the Anglo-Saxon jurisdictions adopt a narrower definition of publication, which requires copies (reproductions) of the work to be issued to the public.[4] This clearly excludes publication merely by public performance or recitation of literary or musical works or the exhibition of any artistic work or the construction of a work of architecture.

The major disadvantage of recognising publication by public performance is the difficulty of ascertaining the date and place of a first performance of a work, and those two factors govern not only the term of protection but often decide when a work is protected internationally. This is the main reason why the Berne Convention[5] excludes performance etc from constituting publication.

In France, where publication is nowhere defined in the law, the courts have developed the concept of publication, starting from the publishing of printed copies and gradually including phonograms and films, thus assimilating the modern media to the original printed copies so that making copies available to the public by any means[6] seems to constitute publication and so does public performance, recitation and any form of communicating works to the public directly.[7]

1 Art 12, Dutch Copyright Law 1912.
2 Art 12, Italian Copyright Law 1941.
3 Art 6/1, German Copyright Law 1965.
4 Eg United Kingdom Copyright Act 1956, s 49 (2), United States Copyright Law 1976, s 101 (Definitions). Similarly Australia, India.
5 Berne Convention (1971), art 3 para 3 (last sentence).
6 Listed in art 28, French Copyright Law 1957.
7 Listed in art 27, French Copyright Law 1957.

4.08 3. In sheer logic it is difficult to see why making available to the public phonograms containing the recording of a work should not be publication of that work, as particularly in the field of music the work reaches the public more quickly and in much larger numbers than by printed copies[1] and the same consideration applies to films. However, in the United Kingdom[2] and other jurisdictions derived from the United Kingdom[3] publication of a recording of a work does not amount to publication in Law. This attitude is based on the essential difference between a copy of a book and a copy of a phonogram. Whereas a printed copy is a 'neutral' reproduction of the work, a phonogram is a reproduction of the recorded performance of the work. Thus the performance comes between the work and the copy whereas there is no such intervention in the printed copy of a book. Thus recognising this difference the publication of a phonogram in Anglo-Saxon jurisdictions is regarded as publication of the recording which is a derivative work, but not of the work recorded. On the other hand the making of a recording or a film provides the certainty of place and time which mere (unrecorded) performance lacks.

The United States, Copyright Law 1976 provides a solution to this problem which has some of the qualities of the egg of Columbus. It provides[4] that 'publication is the distribution of copies or phono-records of a work to the public' thus preserving the traditional and as we have seen not unwarranted distinction between 'copies' and 'phonograms' but widening the concept of publication by including publication of the recorded version of a work.

The practical consequences of excluding recording from the concept of publication is that many works which were recorded but not published in printed form remain 'unpublished works' and if their authors are not nationals of a convention country, they would be unprotected.

The Berne Convention adopts a wide definition of publication.[5] A work is published if, with the consent of the author, it is made available to the public 'whatever may be the means of manufacture of the copies'. However, performance, recitation, broadcasting of literary, musical, cinematographic works, exhibition of works of art, construction of works of architecture are specifically excluded as not constituting publication.

The Universal Copyright Convention is the only convention which contains a definition of publication. (It is the only definition it contains). Publication requires 'reproduction in a tangible form' and the copies must be 'copies from which it can be read or otherwise visually perceived'.[6] This clearly excludes phonograms but includes films, although in the latter case it poses a problem with regard to the soundtrack of a film.[7]

The Rome Convention defines publication of a phonogram as 'the offering of copies ... to the public in reasonable quantity'.[8]

1 In many cases of popular music no 'sheet music' (printed copies) is published, only the recordings.
2 United Kingdom Copyright Act 1956, s 42(2)(a).
3 Eg Australia, India and until 1976 the USA.
4 US Copyright Law 1976, s 101.
5 Berne Convention (1971), art 3(3); see para 5.33 below.
6 Universal Copyright Convention (1971), art VI, see para 6.31 below.
7 In the US Copyright Act 1976 sounds accompanying a motion picture or other audio-visual work ... 'fixed in a material object' are excepted from the definition of 'phono records'. 17 USC para 101.
8 Art 3(d).

4.09 4. What number of copies made available to the public constitutes publication must in the last resort be a matter for the courts to decide in each case. However, the general rule must be that the copies must be sufficient in number to satisfy the reasonable demands of the public. Three points arise:

4.10 (i) The quantity necessary to constitute publication will vary according to the nature of the work. If a book or a record has been a success in the country where it was first published, putting a few copies in a shop for sale in another country will probably not constitute publication there, as it would not satisfy the reasonable demand of the public. On the other hand it was held in the United Kingdom[1] that putting six copies of the sheet music of a song which was unknown on sale was sufficient to constitute publication.

The place of publication is where the offering of the work to the public takes place, not where the copies are made or where they are received. If a book is printed in country A and then copies are shipped to country B where they are stored and then sent to country C where they are offered for sale, publication takes place in country C because that is where the public is for the first time invited to buy them.

1 *Francis Day v Feldman* [1914] 2 Ch 728, CA.

4.11 (ii) Making available means offering them to the public. There is no need for the offer to be accepted, thus it makes no difference if the copies remain unsold.[1] On the other hand, making available must mean that the copies must be displayed or advertised in some form so that the public is aware of their availability. Keeping copies in a basement without anyone being aware of their existence would probably not be sufficient. Some examples from national legislations will illustrate the point. Publication must be 'more than just minimal'.[2] There must be a 'serious attempt to satisfy public demand.'[3] The distribution must be made 'in a scheduled, deliberate and comprehensive manner' and although it may be 'organised from a foreign country' there must be a 'bona fide distribution centre in a Union country'.[4]

1 This is justified by the nature of the work as an intellectual creation with the result that whether to publish or not must depend on the decision of the right-owner and cannot depend on the taste of the public at any particular time.
2 More than 'merely colourable' (United Kingdom Copyright Act 1956, s49(2)(b)).
3 German Supreme Court (Bundesgerichtshof), Judgment of 19 May 1972.
4 Swiss Supreme Court (Bundesgericht), Judgment of 3 November 1970 (*Goldrush* by Charles Chaplin).

4.12 (iii) What is, in this context, the definition of 'the public'? It is submitted that it must mean availability to the general public and that availability to a 'closed group', however large in numbers, is probably not publication, particularly if, as in the Universal Copyright Convention, the language used is 'general distribution to the public'. The problem is of great practical importance in countries where the state exercises censorship of literary works, so that some of them have to be circulated in a clandestine way. The classic example is the Samizdat in the Soviet Union. The literal meaning of Samizdat is 'individual publication'.[1] The publishing industry in the USSR is in the hands of the state and is entrusted to a specialised agency which operates under governmental control.[2] Conversely companies or individuals are not allowed to engage in publishing activities, thus access to printing presses on a commercial scale is denied them. As the state exercises censorship, works which are not approved by the censor are circulated in the form of typewritten copies from hand to hand. Thus these are 'literary works,' they are reproduced in tangible form and they are 'made available', to a closed circle, although most people who are prepared to take the political risk can probably acquire one. If a work so published is then published abroad the question is whether the publication outside the USSR is the first publication, thus securing protection in all Berne Union countries, if the country is a Berne Convention country or whether the first publication is the Samizdat. If it is the latter, ie publication by a Soviet author in the Soviet Union it becomes a Soviet work. The economic importance of the problem lies in the fact that a Soviet author can only make a publishing contract with VAAP. He cannot, for instance make such a contract with a foreign publisher, only VAAP can. Thus if the work is first published in the USSR the royalties including foreign royalties are negotiated or decided by the Soviet authorities and they include translations into foreign languages. If on the other hand first publication takes place outside the USSR because Samizdat is not publication the author can make his contract with the foreign publisher.[3] The question came before the courts in Germany in the case of Alexander Solshenitsyn's novel *August 14*.[4] The German Supreme Court decided that the novel which had been circulated by Samizdat in the USSR and subsequently published in France was first published in France,[5] a Berne Convention country, and therefore protected in Germany, because distribution by Samizdat would 'by its nature' not qualify as publication, as it was clandestine and made the work available only to those 'in the know' ('initiated persons') and was thus by the very nature of its circulation not accessible to the general public.

1   A concept close to the meaning of publication in the law of defamation.
2   A centralised agency, known as VAAP was created for the publication of all works including literary, musical and dramatic works when the USSR ratified the Universal Copyright Convention in 1973 see para 19.01.
3   In normal circumstances he will therefore receive something like 10% of the retail selling price of each copy.
4   Bundesgerichtshof, Judgment of 16 October 1975.
5   It was also important that the work had been published in France both in Russian and in French. As a translation is a new work, publication of a translation of an 'unpublished' work may leave the original work unprotected although the translation is protected, with the effect that anyone else can make a new translation without the author's permission and acquire a new copyright.

4.13 5. The answer to the fifth question – have the copies available to be for sale or is availability for hire sufficient? – is of particular importance in the case of films, where copies are not offered to the public for sale but are made available to distributors for public performance in the cinemas. The answer must be that availability for hire is sufficient for publication, as the opposite would lead to the absurd position that a film which has been seen by millions is an unpublished work because the film producing company only releases a small number of copies for hire to a small number of distributors in any given country. It has to be admitted that this requires a wide interpretation of the wording of the Universal Copyright Convention 'general distribution to the public of copies of a work' as the public is never in possession of any copies of a film as it is in the case of a book or a record. It means that general distribution has to be understood as a general communication of the work to the public.

(4) Categories of works and subject matters of copyright

4.14 Some national legislations contain a definition of the works protected (eg Germany, United States) others do not (eg United Kingdom). Broadly speaking there are two categories of works. The first is the one which includes the works named in the Berne Convention: 'literary and artistic works' which includes dramatical, musical and dramatico-musical works. The second is a category of more recent types of works: cinematograph films, sound recordings, broadcasts. Both categories rank as works or subject matters of copyright in the Anglo-Saxon jurisdictions (eg United States, United Kingdom, Australia). In other jurisdictions the second category ranks as subject matters which enjoy neighbouring rights (eg Germany, Scandinavia). Even more recent subject matters are videograms and computer software. Videograms come within the definition of cinematograph films in nearly all countries and are therefore works in those countries where films are works. The most significant difference between videograms and films is that the latter are mainly shown in public cinemas whereas the former are shown in private homes. This necessitates different methods of distribution but has no bearing on their legal status. Computer software, meaning programmes devised for the working of computers, is generally regarded as coming within the definition of literary and artistic works.[1]

Thus the historical process of extending the categories of works continues. As the British Copyright Council put it:[2] 'Over the years the type of works protected by copyright have been extended, as has the scope of the protection afforded. Today copyright subsists in almost all works representing the product of labour and/or skill, if fixed so that they can be reproduced'. This seems to reflect the majority view among the developed countries but the minority view which is held most strongly in France excludes the more recent categories.

In the majority countries the scope of the copyright granted to works varies greatly between the old works and the new, and the term of the copyright must be different, as in the case of the new works or subject matter of copyright the original copyright owner is usually not a natural person and the term can therefore not be 50 years after the author's death. It varies between 20 and 50 years from first publication and is thus nearly always shorter than the term of the old categories of works.

The latest major Copyright Act, the United States Copyright Law 1976, lists seven categories[3] –

1. Literary works
2. musical works, including any accompanying words
3. dramatic works, including any accompanying music
4. pantomimes and choreographic works
5. pictorial, graphic and sculptural works
6. motion pictures and other audiovisual works
7. sound recordings.

The definition 'original works of authorship fixed in any tangible medium of expression, *now known or later developed*' makes the point that, like the categories of tort, the categories of copyrightable works are never closed.

1 See Professor Ulmer's study 'Problems arising from the computer storage and retrieval of protected works' Copyright (1972) p 37; also Working Group on Copyright Problems arising from the use of Computers 1979' Copyright (1979) p 186.
2 Quoted in the Whitford Committee Report para 28.
3 17 USC section 102.

2. Economic rights and moral rights

4.15 Whilst wishing to sustain the idealistic element in copyright which is an idealistic concept – starry-eyed idealism should be discouraged. Copyright is 90% about money, but that is not saying that the remaining 10% cannot be as important as the 90%. The importance of the 90% was well put by Beaumarchais:

> 'People say that it is not noble on the part of authors to plead sordid interest while claiming to aspire to glory. They are right, glory is attractive, but they forget that, to enjoy it for just one year, nature condemns us to dine three hundred and sixty-five times'.

The importance of the other 10% is contained in the definition of the *droit moral* in French law:

> 'The author shall enjoy the right to respect for his name, his authorship, and his work. This right shall be attached to his person. It shall be perpetual, inalienable and imprescriptible.'[1]

Its main objective is to safeguard the author's reputation, what Shakespeare called 'that immortal part of myself'.

1 French Copyright Law 1957, art 6 ('imprescriptible' is used in WIPO translation and means 'not subject to prescription'!)

Economic rights

4.16 The economic rights of the author are in a large majority of cases assigned to an entrepreneur such as a publisher of books or music, a film producer or a record producer. The latter uses his judgment, both artistic and commercial, and in the case of the film producer or the record producer adds his own artistic and technical input. It is the entrepreneur who carries the risk of failure and reaps the profit of success. He also pays for the marketing and advertising of the work in its fixed form. It is the rationale of copyright that if he is to recoup his investment and make a profit he has to be protected against unauthorised reproduction.[1] If he were not so protected the 'pirate' could almost invariably produce copies at a much lower price. In book publishing the pirate's price would be lower, but he still has substantial costs. In record production the pirated product is sold at a much lower price because the pirate only bears the cost of manufacture and distribution and saves both copyright royalties and recording costs. In film production the pirate's costs are only a small fraction because of the very high cost of making the original film.

About the absolute necessity of copyright protection there can therefore be no doubt even when contemplating only the economic rights of the author. However, controversy is possible on two questions: a) how long should the protection be? and b) should it be absolute, ie including a right to forbid any use of the work, or should, in certain cases, use be permitted without the authorisation of the author, against the payment of a fair and equitable remuneration, ie by a Compulsory Licence?[2] The argument for the term of protection, ie the duration of the Copyright has, throughout the history of copyright, been carried by the moral right of the author. This point is well illustrated by the first Copyright Act in history: the Statute of Queen Anne (1709) in the UK. The copyright term of 14 years was taken from Patent Law and clearly intended to allow the printer/publisher to recoup his costs. It also gave the author a further term of 14 years, making 28 years in all[3] but only if at the end of the first 14 years the author was still alive. The Act thus clearly distinguished between what it deemed necessary for the publisher to recover his investment and what it deemed necessary for the benefit of the author. However, in later statutes the two terms were amalgamated into one, which was assignable as a whole to the publisher. It was gradually lengthened beyond the life of the author until it reached 50 years pma[4] in the Berne Convention in 1908.[5] The motivation for this gradual lengthening of the term was clearly the moral right of the author which links his personality to the work and thus leads to the concept that copyright is a property right in the work which can and should be passed to the creators' heirs and successors.

1 Milton's *Paradise Lost* was sold outright for £5 and it took the publishers 7 years to sell the first edition of a few hundred copies.
2 See para 4.33 below.
3 The term of 28 years was taken across the Atlantic at the end of the eighteenth century and in the form of 28 years plus 28 years on renewal, formed the term of United States copyright law until 1976 when it was replaced by 50 years pma under the influence of the Berne Convention.
4 Post mortem auctoris after the death of the author.
5 There is still a remnant of the division in the 'Reversion' provisions in some Anglo-Saxon countries (UK Copyright Act 1911 s 5(2) repealed in 1956 however still applied to pre-1957 works (Sch 7, para (3) and Sch 8, para (b) of the Copyright Act 1956; US Copyright Act 1976, 304 (6) for works created before 1978, where the rights in a work, although assigned to a publisher revert to the author or his heirs for the last years of the term of copyright).

Droit moral

4.17 Moral rights 'stem from the fact that the work is a reflection of the personality of the creator, just as much as the economic rights reflect the author's need to keep body and soul together'.[1] The moral right is usually referred to by its French name because it originated in French law, from whence it found its way into all continental European and Latin American Laws and into the Berne Convention.[2] Anglo-Saxon laws often give similar protection to the author but base it on other parts of the law, such as the law of defamation, of unfair competition or of contract. There are three basic moral rights:

1. *Droit de divulgation*, (the right of publication) is the right to decide whether the work is to be made public.
2. *Droit de paternité*, (right of paternity) is the right to claim authorship of published works.
3. *Droit de respect de l'oeuvre* (right of integrity) is the right of the author to safeguard his reputation by preserving the integrity of the work.

1   WIDO Guide to Berne 6 bis1.
2   Art 5 bis see para 5.73 below, the UCC only contains rudiments of moral rights in Art V (e) and (f) and V quater, para 1 (7) and (8).

Droit de divulgation
4.18   Although prominent in French law this is the only one of the three moral rights which is not part of the moral rights in the Berne Convention. It consists of two rights: the right of the author to decide whether and when his work is to be published. If his creditors want to publish a manuscript to satisfy their claims the writer can stop them. If a composer wants to hear the first performance of an orchestral work before publishing the score he can prevent publication of it. The other right is the right to withdraw the work after publication if the author wishes to do so. This is described as 'the most audacious manifestation of the Droit Moral' in French law.[1] In Anglo-Saxon jurisdictions the case for withdrawal will have to be a very strong one to succeed eg a philosopher or a scientist who has changed his theory in the light of further work or new discoveries may succeed in having the rest of an edition withdrawn and corrections made in the next edition.

1   Desbois *Le Droit d'Auteur en France* p 392; French Copyright Act 1957, art 32.

Droit de paternité
4.19   This consists of three rights:

(a)   The right to demand that the author's name appears in an appropriate place on all copies of the work and to claim authorship of it at all times.
(b)   Conversely the right to prevent all others from claiming authorship of the work.
(c)   The right to prevent the use of his name by someone else in connection with that other person's work.

Droit de respect de l'oeuvre
4.20   This contains the right of the author to authorise or prohibit any modification of his work. This part of the right is mostly used positively by licensing the modifications, eg turning a novel into a film or a play into a work for television, but can also be used negatively eg by preventing an unauthorised broadcast version or dramatisation of a novel.

It contains the author's right to prevent 'distortion' of his work. All adaptations (eg novel into play, play into film) demand a great deal of alteration by the adapter who becomes himself the owner of a copyright in the adaptation. Where the borderline between adaptation and distortion lies will be a question for the courts to decide in all the circumstances of the case. Generally the courts in civil law countries will apply a subjective test: does the author honestly believe that the action of the adapter would be prejudicial to the honour or reputation of the author? The courts in the common law countries usually apply an objective test: would a reasonable, right-thinking member of the public think that the alteration is prejudicial to the honour and reputation of the author?

4.21 It is of the essence of moral rights that they are 'independent of the author's economic rights'[1] and that he can exercise them 'even after the transfer of the said rights'.[1] It is a moot point under the Berne Convention whether this means that the moral rights are inalienable ie whatever the author agrees to in a contract in which he transfers his economic rights, he can still exercise his 'droit moral' afterwards. If, for instance, the contract says that the adapter can turn the novel into a play in any form that appears appropriate to him, the author of the novel can still object when he reads the play. The alternative interpretation is that the article means that if the author simply transfers the economic rights he is not held to have transferred his 'droit moral' unless the contract is in writing and says so specifically. It is suggested that the latter interpretation is to be preferred. The courts will be vigilant to interpret the contract of transfer strictly. They will usually be able to apply the rule of interpretation of contracts contra preferentem as these contracts are usually drawn up by or on behalf of an entrepreneur rather than by the author. This view is born out by the Rapporteur Général of the Rome Revision Conference of the Berne Convention in 1928 at which the 'droit moral' was first introduced into the Convention.[2] It also receives support from the fact that when the French government proposed at the Brussels Conference in 1948 to make the 'droit moral' inalienable that proposal was rejected.[3]

If moral rights are alienable under the law of the country where protection is claimed, clauses to the effect that the adapter can modify the work as he wishes, or even that he need not mention the name of the author will be valid, if it is clear that the author at the time of making the contract was aware of the clause and agreed to it for valuable consideration.

1 Berne Convention, art 6 bis(1).
2 See Piola Caselli, Droit d'Auteur (June 1935).
3 For arguments on the point see: Mayer Gabay, Geiringer Lecture 1978. For a contrary view see De Sanctis, Copyright (September 1978) p 259.

4.22 It is also of the essence of the 'droit moral' that it lasts during the life of the author. Whether the right can be exercised by the heirs after the death of the author and for how long depends on the law of the country where protection is claimed. The Paris Act (1971) of the Berne Convention provides that the 'droit moral' shall last 'at least until the expiry of the economic rights'. This is thus a minimum of 50 years after the death of the author. However article 6 bis(2) permits a reservation to the effect that the 'droit moral' only lasts for the life of the author. It remains to be seen how many of the common law countries will use this reservation.[1] In some countries, eg France, the 'droit moral' is perpetual.

Perhaps the most up-to-date European law on this point is the Copyright Law of the Netherlands, 1912 (revised October 1972), article 25 which adopts a middle-of-the-road position between the French law and the laws of the common law countries. It gives the author even after the transfer of his copyright the right to object to any modifications of his work except where such objection would be 'unreasonable'. It also permits a valid waiver of moral rights in appropriate circumstances'.[2] Introducing the notion of what is 'reasonable' or 'appropriate' gives the courts a wide discretion to decide each case on its merits. This seems to avoid both undesirable extremes: on the one hand the moral rights of the author cannot be shrugged off easily, on the other hand unreasonable barriers to publication or extortionate money claims can be resisted.

The right of paternity also extends to the uses of the author's work which are free, eg quotations must mention the source and the name of the author if it appears on the source.[3]

1 The Whitford Committee in the UK and the Government Green Paper 1981 recommend the extension of the moral right to the full period of the economic right. (Paras 51-57 Whitford Committee Report; chapter 18, para 8, Green Paper).
2 A similar solution is recommended by the Whitford Committee for the UK (para 56).
3 Art 10(3), Berne Convention.

4.23 In Anglo-Saxon jurisdictions the national laws do not contain moral rights but most of the moral rights of the author can be exercised using other causes of action.

1. *Droit de divulgation* (right of publication)
The author is protected if his unpublished work is published in breach of trust or of confidence. The plaintiff must prove the confidential nature of the information or that the work was given to the defendant in circumstances implying an obligation of confidence and that the defendant has or is about to publish the work or information.

2. *Droit de paternité* (right of paternity)

(a) If the defendant publishes a work masquerading as the work of the real author a 'passing-off' action will lie. The plaintiff has to prove that he has acquired a reputation which the defendant has used to gain an advantage and that the latter has represented to the public that his work is in fact that of the plaintiff.
(b) In the converse case where the defendant claims to be the author of a work which is the work of the plaintiff author an action for 'malicious falsehood' will lie if the plaintiff can prove that the publication is 'calculated to cause pecuniary damage to the plaintiff'. An action for 'defamation' will also lie if the plaintiff author can prove that his reputation was lessened in the eyes of reasonable and right thinking members of the public. As this gives the courts the task of judging what a reasonable member of the public would think of the author, it gives them a fairly wide discretion.

3. *Droit de respect de l'oeuvre* (right of integrity)
The author has the exclusive right to authorise any derivative work based on his work and from this the right to prevent unauthorised adaptations or adaptations which go beyond what was authorised flows.[1] In cases of alterations of the work which go beyond what the plaintiff author authorised in the contract, the courts will imply a term limiting the right to make alterations to what has been authorised. In the United Kingdom a very small alteration in a play for the purpose of broadcasting was held to be a breach.[2] Objections to 'substantial re-writing' of an article were upheld.[3] The plaintiff's story 'as told to the journalist by the plaintiff' was condemned as 90% of it was inaccurate and not told by her.[4]

1 *Chaplin v Leslie Frewin (Publishers) Ltd* [1966] Ch 71.
2 *Frisby v BBC* [1967] Ch 932.
3 *Joseph v National Magazine* [1959] Ch 14.
4 *Moore v News of the World* [1972] 1 All ER 915.

3. Ownership of copyright

(1) General

4.24 The general rule is that creators of works should be the owners of the copyright in those works subject only to contracts providing otherwise. Article 1 of the Berne Convention which speaks of a Union of Countries 'for the protection of the rights of authors in their ... works' clearly supports this proposition. The Convention does not define the term 'author' which it uses throughout. It provides[1] that in the absence of proof to the contrary, the person under whose name the work is disclosed is to be regarded as the author. This provision too should in most cases favour the author as it constitutes a rebuttable presumption which would have to be rebutted either by a contract or by an implied term. In the absence of convention law it is therefore for national legislation to decide who the owner of the copyright is. However there are two situations which are problematical: commissioned works, and works created in employment. It is in these situations that different legal systems supply different solutions and international law through the conventions applies the rule of national treatment[2] which assimilates all nationals of convention countries to the nationals of the country where protection is claimed. One therefore has in every case to look at the law of the country where copyright is claimed.

The questions arising from works either commissioned or created in employment have assumed much greater importance in the last 30 years than they had before because many creators of works are employed and even those who are working 'freelance' are very often financially dependent on work which is commissioned, usually by radio and television, film and record companies, publishers of newspapers or periodicals. The notion that creators of works are intellectual workers working freelance and self-employed which was no doubt encouraged by the copyright philosophy and by the conventions tends to deprive individual creators of the advantages of the modern welfare state in the field of national insurance such as sickness, unemployment benefits and pensions. This is an aspect of copyright which has only begun to be considered but which will probably play an important part in the development of the next decades.[3]

1 Art 15(1).
2 See para 3.17 above.
3 For an analysis of the problem see Professor Cohen Jehoram 'The Author's Place in Society', Copyright (1978) p 385 and Cuvillier 'Employment and Copyright', Copyright (1979) p 112, also Ulmer *Urheberrecht* (3rd edn) p 23 and W.R. Cornish *Intellectual Property* pp 375 ff; Dietz *Copyright Law in the European Community* (1978); Dittrich *Arbeitnehmer und Urheberrecht* (1978) p 23; Keyes and Brunet *Copyright in Canada* (1977) pp 70 ff.

(2) Works created in employment

4.25 The treatment of this problem varies according to whether the national law is of the Anglo-Saxon or of the Roman law tradition. Generally the Anglo-Saxon law approach is one of freedom of contract. Where, however, there is no contract or the contract has no provision the tendency is to ascertain as far as possible the intention of the parties. The Roman law countries approach the problem from a socio-economic point of view and seek to protect the author as the economically weaker party against the entrepreneur with whom he has to deal for the exploitation of his works.

Thus, countries of the Anglo-Saxon tradition regard the employer as the copyright owner unless a contract provides otherwise.[1] These provisions, however, generally apply to works created by the employee in the course of his employment. With regard to all other works, mainly those created in his spare time and unconnected with his employment, the employee is the first copyright owner. The rule stems from patent law on employees' inventions and what is and what is not to be regarded as being within the course of the employment will largely depend on the nature of the employment and the term of the employment contract (express or implied). The borderline is far more blurred than in patent law where it should, as a rule, be fairly clear whether an invention was made in the course of the employment and often as an integral part of the employment. In copyright the problem is much more complex. A work by an employee can be used in several forms, such as an article in a newspaper or in a learned journal, as a lecture, as a pamphlet or as part of a book. The rule is that the employer will, in the absence of agreement to the contrary, be entitled to the copyright only in cases where this was contemplated by the parties to the employment contract. A teacher is employed to teach his subject but if in the course of teaching his subject a textbook grows out of his work, the copyright would be his as he is not employed to write books.

In the United Kingdom it was suggested already in 1951 that the old test of whether the employer controls the activities of the employee is wearing thin in the copyright sphere and that the true test should rather be whether the employee is performing the task out of which the work sprang 'as an integral part of the business'.[2]

In the countries with a Roman law tradition the author will be regarded as the original copyright owner even if he is employed. The employer must generally acquire such rights as he needs by assignment or licence. Compared with the countries of Anglo-Saxon tradition it can be said that, in general, the presumption works the other way. Even in France where the employment contract creates no exception to the absolute right of the author[3] case law permits transfer of the right to the employer if the contract is in writing.[4] In the Federal Republic of Germany the law[5] also presumes in favour of the employee unless the contrary results from the nature of the employment. Any assignment is limited to the purpose of the contract.[6] However in practice many industries formulate standard or model contracts which the employer asks the employee to sign on taking up employment and which provide for the automatic transfer of copyright thus nullifying any presumption. In such cases only mandatory provisions in the copyright laws will have any effect.[7]

Generally it can be said that the system which gives the employed author the original copyright is gaining ground as it is in accord with the general concept of copyright and with the Berne Convention, but at the expense of exceptions and presumptions which seek to do justice to the realities of the employment situation. Perhaps the closest approximation of the existing trends is provided by the Tunis Model Law 1976 for developing countries.[8] It provides two alternatives. Alternative A is meant for countries of the Roman law tradition. The original copyright vests in the author unless a written contract provides the contrary. Alternative B is meant for countries of the Anglo-Saxon legal tradition. The original copyright is deemed to be transferred to the employer (or to the person commissioning the work) unless a written contract provides the contrary, but only to such extent as may be necessary to his customary activities at the time of the conclusion of the employment contract or the commissioning of the work.[9]

The moral right under the Berne Convention[10] remains with the author even after the transfer of the economic rights. An employee author should therefore retain these rights in Berne Convention countries whether they are safeguarded by the copyright law or, as in the countries of the Anglo-Saxon legal tradition by the common law. However the position must be influenced by the employment situation, eg the employee may, if circumstances demand it, have to be content with publication of the work without his name appearing as the author and the employer will have to have wider powers to make alterations than a publisher would have with a work of a freelance author.

1   United Kingdom, Copyright Act 1956, s 4(4), Ireland, Copyright Act 1963, s 10(5), Netherlands, Copyright Law, as amended 1972, art 7, USA, Copyright Law 1976, para 201(6), Canada, Copyright Act 1921, as amended 1971, s 12(3).
2   Per Denning LJ in *Stephenson Jordan v McDonald & Evans* (1951) 69 RPC 10, CA.
3   Copyright Law 1957, art 1, para 3.
4   'Cour de Cassation', Criminal Chamber, 11 April 1975.
5   Copyright Law 1965 (as amended in 1974) para 43.
6   Copyright Law 1965, para 31.
7   See Ulmer *Urhebervertragsrecht* pp 40 ff and Schulze *Copyright Contracts* pp 137 ff.
8   S 11(2).
9   The Whitford Committee in the UK expressed the view (para 570) that 'if a person is employed to do a job of work and paid for his services, the product of his labour should, subject to any agreement to the contrary, belong to his employer'. They give the example of a firm of architects designing a large amount of copyright material such as specifications, site plans, working drawings etc which are produced by a large number of qualified employees. It would be a major exercise to obtain all the necessary assignments of copyright for each piece of work and this would be too heavy a burden to place on the employer. The Report suggests however that if the work produced by the employee is used by the employer in a way which was not within the contemplation of the parties when it was created, the employee should be given a statutory right to an award from the employer which, in the absence of agreement, should be settled by an arbitration tribunal.
10 Art 6 bis(1): see para 5.37.

(3) Commissioned works

4.26 Where a freelance 'author' creates a work as an independent contractor he does so, commercially speaking, as a speculation. In the case of a commissioned work, on the other hand, there is a contract between the author and the person or body commissioning the work which precedes the creation of the work and secures him a remuneration. These contracts, particularly if in writing, should contain provisions as to copyright ownership but they often do not. In that case different legal systems create different legal presumptions. The United States law equates the author of a commissioned work to an employed author.[1] The United Kingdom law creates a presumption of ownership in favour of the author but provides exceptions in the case of photographs, paintings, portraits, engravings, where the commissioner is presumed to be the copyright owner.[2] In French law there is a presumption in favour of the author.

Generally where the author is the original copyright owner, either by contract or by legal presumption, the interests of the commissioning party will be adequately safeguarded if he is licensed by the author to use the work in those respects contemplated by the parties. If, for instance, a broadcasting organisation commissions a play for sound radio the author will remain free to license it for stage performances or publish it in book form or adapt it as a filmscript unless the contract provides otherwise. The example illustrates the 'many-faceted nature of copyright'[3] and consequently the advisability of a written agreement which covers all possible uses of the work. The agreement should also contain certain safeguards for the commissioner, eg in the case of family portraits.

1   See US Copyright Act 1976, para 201(6).
2   Copyright Act 1956, s 4(1) and (3).
3   Cornish *Intellectual Property* (1981) p 379.

(4) Assignment and licensing

4.27 Once the initial copyright ownership is established the exploitation of the work may take many forms. The transfer of copyright from the owner of the initial copyright usually takes the form of an assignment or of a licence. An assignment can be the transfer of ownership of the whole right or of part of it. A licence is the authorisation of acts which, without such authorisation would be infringements.[1] As copyright consists of a bundle of rights, the bundle is often split into its component parts for the purpose of licensing. An author of a novel may grant separate licences for the book rights (hardback and paperback), the serialisation rights (newspapers and magazines), the film rights, the dramatisation rights (novel into a play or novel into a 'musical'), the broadcasting rights (sound and television) and last but not least the translation rights which can be split language by language. Licences can be exclusive (eg book or film rights) or non-exclusive (eg the recording right where, as a rule, many record companies are being licensed, in turn, to record the same work). The term of copyright can also be split by granting a licence or an assignment for a number of years, in which case the right reverts to the initial owner at the end of the period. There thus exists in the case of many works a very large choice in the method of exploitation of the work. Contracts are often not very explicit and purport simply to 'grant an exclusive right'. It is then for the courts to determine whether taking into account all the circumstances and the implied intention of the parties such a contract is an assignment or a licence.[2] Some copyrights (eg musical performing rights) are transferred to a collecting society which grants bulk licences to users for the whole of its repertoire so that the right owner only knows what licences have been granted or what performances have taken place when he gets his (usually quarterly) account. Assignments must under most legislations be in writing and signed by the assigning right owner. A licence does not, as a rule, have to be in any particular form but an exclusive licensee will be well advised to observe the same formalities as are required in the case of an assignment as otherwise proof of copyright may be difficult if he wants to sue an infringer. There are cases where a licence will be implied although not given either in writing or orally, but the circumstances will have to be very clear to sustain such an implied term (eg if a writer submits an article to a journal this will carry the implication that he agrees to its publication on such terms as are customary).

In some countries of the continental European system, eg Germany and Austria, copyrights are not transferable, only a right of user can be granted which can be exclusive or non-exclusive. The granting of an exclusive licence to use the work for an unlimited time, in these jurisdictions, comes close to the concept of an assignment and avoids the sometimes difficult differentiation between an assignment and an exclusive licence.

In the countries of the continental European system all moral rights are inalienable, so that even if the author purports to transfer them, the transfer is not valid and the right remains with the author.

1 See Cornish, op cit, pp 381 ff.
2 In the UK see *Chaplin v Frewin* [1966] Ch 71 at 94, CA.

4. Limitations of copyright

4.28 The limitations of copyright are necessary to keep the balance between two conflicting public interests, the public interest in rewarding creators of 'works' and the public interest in the widest dissemination of works which is also the interest of the users of such works.

There are, in international law, three groups of restrictions on the exclusive right of the creator in his work:

1. Cases where the use of the work is declared free ('fair dealing' or 'fair use' exceptions).
2. Cases where, subject to certain conditions, one of which is the payment of equitable remuneration, the work can be used without the prior authorisation of the creator (compulsory licences).
3. Cases where restrictions on the absolute right of the creator in his work are permitted by international conventions because the use of the work is to be made in a developing country.[1]

1 The Annex to the Berne Convention (Paris Act) 1971 and the Protocol to the UCC 1971; see para 6.38 below.

(1) Free use

4.29 Free use of copyright material is called 'fair dealing' in the United Kingdom and United Kingdom derived legislations and 'fair use' in United States law. In other legislations they are described as 'restrictions' or 'exceptions'. The Berne Convention solution to the problem of free use has the merit of uniformity as a general rule and the advantage of permitting a great deal of flexibility both for variations from country to country and for the future when new technology may pose new problems. Article 9(2) authorises national legislation to permit the reproduction of protected works 'in certain special cases' provided two conditions are fulfilled: (a) the 'reproduction does not conflict with a normal exploitation of the work'; and (b) such reproduction 'does not unreasonably prejudice the legitimate interests of the author'. The provision is cumulative, thus both conditions have to be fulfilled.[1]

The UCC leaves even greater elbow room to national legislations. Article IV bis, paragraph 2,[2] permits the states to make exceptions to the three basic rights of the creator of a work (the reproduction right, the public performance right and the broadcasting right) provided that: (a) they 'do not conflict with the spirit and the provisions of the Convention'; and (b) provided they 'accord a reasonable degree of effective protection to each of the rights'.

It is to be noted that the UCC deals with all three basic rights whereas article 9(2) of the Berne Convention deals only with exceptions to the reproduction right and deals with the exceptions to the other two rights separately[3] and that the reference to the 'spirit of the Convention' and a 'reasonable degree of effective protection' provides a lower level of protection than the two rather strict provisos of not conflicting with a 'normal exploitation of the work' and not unreasonably prejudicing 'the legitimate interests of the author'. Even under the Berne Convention each country has to decide what the legitimate interests of the author are, whether the prejudice to these interests, which is inevitable, is reasonable or unreasonable and what amounts to a normal exploitation of the work which must be safeguarded. Fair dealing must always be a matter of degree. The Anglo-Saxon approach to fair dealing is well characterised by a judgment in an English case[4] dealing with a case of a literary review:

> 'You must consider first the number and extent of quotations and extracts. Are they altogether too many and too long to be fair? Then you must consider the use made of them. If they are used as a basis for comment, criticism or review, that may be "Fair dealing." If they are used to convey the same information as the

author, for a rival purpose, they may be unfair. Next you must consider the proportions. To take long extracts and attach short comments may be unfair. But short extracts and long comments may be fair and other considerations may come to mind also. But after all is said and done, it must be a matter of impression.'

1 See para 5.39 below.
2 See para 6.20 below.
3 See para 5.39 below.
4 Lord Denning in *Hubbard v Vosper* [1972] 2 QB 84 at 94.

4.30 The special cases of free use are of two kinds: free use for all classes of works for special purposes such as reporting of current events, some religious and educational purposes, personal or private use etc and free use of particular classes of works eg public speeches, newspaper articles, broadcast commentaries, reproductions of pictures in catalogues for public exhibitions, etc. There are five categories of exceptional free use of copyright material:

1. Exceptions for public speeches, lectures, speeches in legal proceedings[1]
2. Exceptions justified by the desirability of freedom of information in press and broadcasting[2]
3. Quotations[3]
4. 'Private study and research'
5. Reproduction for 'personal' or 'private' use.

Category 1: mainly speeches made in public meetings or in the broadcasting studio dealing with problems and news of the day and the speeches of counsel in court. The use must be justified by the information purpose.

Category 2: articles in newspapers and periodicals, photographs, films, and broadcasts reporting current events. The extent of use must be justified by the information purpose.

Category 3: quotations from published works and illustrations for the purpose of teaching, criticism, etc. The use must not be greater than is justified by the purpose and must be in accordance with fair practice.

Category 4: both the research and the study must be 'private'. This excludes research carried out by commercial organisation or for industrial or business purposes. It also excludes general teaching purposes in schools or universities which are public not private study.

Category 5: the reproductions must be duplication for private use as opposed to public use. It need not always be personal in the sense that it is only for the use of one person but the circle of persons must be small and strictly definable, eg a scientist makes copies for his collaborators, a student makes copies of a lecture for the use of a small circle of fellow students, a music lover makes copies of a piece of chamber music to play at his home. The method of duplication is not relevant. It could be manuscript, typewritten or mechanically reproduced. The number of copies made must be very small.[4]

The exceptions were conceived mainly with manuscript or typewritten copies in mind, but modern technology has provided two new tools which produce major challenges to the reproduction right: tape recorders and duplicating machines. Their use is usually referred to as 'reprography'[5] and 'home taping'[6]. Most of the equipment for reprographic reproduction is owned and used by organisations, both commercial ones like companies and non-commercial ones like public libraries or schools whereas the equipment for tape recording is owned and used by individuals. Consequently duplicating machines are used in public places or offices, whereas tape recorders are used in private homes. It is also important that a substantial part of the literary material reproduced by duplicating machines is not material in which copyright is claimed, although it may be subject to copyright like office memoranda. On the other hand most of the material copied by tape recorders is copyright material. It is mainly music in the case of copying of phonograms and mainly cinematograph films in the case of copying of videograms.

1 Berne Convention (1971), art 2 (bis) (1) and (2); see para 5.58 below.
2 Berne Convention (1971), art 10 (bis) (1), (2) and (3); see para 5.60 below.
3 Berne Convention (1971), art 10(1) and (2); see para 5.56 below.
4 The German Supreme Court in a case of quotations from school books duplicated for the purpose of teaching, put the maximum at seven copies. Reported in GRUR 1978, 474, cited by Ulmer, op cit, p 300.
5 See para 12.16 below.
6 See para 12.12 below, also Stewart 'Home Taping – The legal basis for the compensation of Copyright owners' EIPR (July 1980) p 207.

(2) The problems of free use

(a) *Reprography*

4.31 The term commonly used is 'photocopying' because most of the processes used for reproduction can be so described. However processes other than light processes are now increasingly used such as laser techniques, holographic reproduction and the use of computers for reproduction. Thus the generic term reprographic reproduction or 'reprography' is currently used to cover all these processes.

The origin and justification of the fair use or fair dealing exception is well illustrated by the much quoted statement of the Royal Society in the United Kingdom in 1956: 'Science rests upon its published record, and ... access to public scientific and technical information is a fundamental need of scientists everywhere ... making single copies of extracts from books or periodicals is essential to research workers, and the production of such single extract copies ... is necessary for scientific practice'. This is generally accepted but the difficulties begin when the copies taken are not 'single' copies but multiple copies and what is copied is not an 'extract' but the whole work or an essential part of it. The making of multiple copies by libraries and other institutions starts a vicious circle as it leads to smaller circulations which lead to higher publication costs which are reflected in prices and the more expensive the publications are the more they are being copied.

The test of what is fair use and what is not may vary from country to country, but factors to be considered which are set out in the US Copyright Act 1976[1] would probably be accepted in most countries:

(i) The purpose and character of the use
(ii) The nature of the copyrighted work
(iii) The amount and substantiality of the portion used in relation to the copyrighted work as a whole
(iv) The effect of the use upon the potential market for, or value of the copyrighted work.

If multiple copies are taken and whole works or the essential parts of works are copied, this probably constitutes an infringement under most national laws but an infringement which is very difficult to police. Different national laws have devised schemes to deal with this problem which can be based on a compulsory licence, but are mostly based on bulk licensing schemes. However it is generally acknowledged that 'a uniform solution on the international level cannot, for the time being, be found'. Thus each state, whilst respecting the conventions to which it is a party, has to set up a system which is politically acceptable as being in conformity with the educational and socio-economic circumstances of the country concerned. Among the measures recommended by the Intergovernmental Copyright Committee is that states should encourage 'the establishment of collective systems to exercise and administer the right to remuneration'.[2]

1   Para 107.
2   Resolution of Sub-Committee of the Intergovernmental Copyright Committee on Reprographic Reproduction, Washington 1975 (Copyright (1975) pp 159 ff at p 175).

(b) *Home taping*

4.32   As most of the equipment used for home taping is used by individuals in their private homes the question is whether it is covered by the private use exception. The Berne Convention in article 9(2)[1] provides for such an exception from the reproduction right of authors, the Rome Convention in article 15(1)(a)[2] from the right of phonogram producers. When the private use exception was conceived in national legislations the intention was clearly to enable private persons to make extracts from books or written material for their own private use. As late as the Brussels Act of the Berne Convention (1948) the reproduction right was so much regarded as the basic and essential right of the author that it was not separately dealt with in the convention. 'Short quotations' from newspaper articles were dealt with in article 10(1); 'excerpts from literary or artistic works in educational or scientific publications' in article 10(2). When the reproduction right was, for the first time, explicitly and separately dealt with in the Stockholm Act (1967) by article 9(1), a new article 9(2) was added[3] to enable national legislation to permit reproduction of protected works 'in certain special cases' and a proviso was added that 'such reproduction does not conflict with a normal exploitation of the work and does not unreasonably prejudice the legitimate interest of authors'. The Report of the Raporteur Général makes the meaning of this proviso plain and gives a clear guide to judicial interpretation: '... if it is considered that reproduction conflicts with the normal exploitation of a work, reproduction is not permitted at all. If it is considered that reproduction does not conflict with the normal exploitation of the work, the next step would be to consider whether it does not unreasonably prejudice the legitimate interests of the author'.

It is fairly plain that home taping conflicts with the normal exploitation of the work as the loss of a sale deprives the author and possibly the performer of a musical work of their royalties and the phonogram producer of the sale of the phonogram. However the main point seems to be that whereas what was envisaged in the Convention was the free copying of extracts, even 'small extracts', home taping involves the copying of the whole work. In the United Kingdom the Whitford Committee considered the problem in 1977. The report[4] states the legal position:

> ',... we reject the suggestion that fair dealing should be extended generally to permit some free audio and video recording because fair dealing to an extent such as is accepted as reasonable for literary works, for example, would not satisfy the need of most users, while a widening of the term would create a virtual free-for-all with copyright owners getting no benefit.'

However although home taping is clearly an infringement of copyright it is impossible to enforce the infringed rights as such enforcement would constitute an intolerable intrusion in the privacy of the home. Thus other and new solutions will have to be adopted on the national level – possibly in the form of a royalty on the recording equipment, as in the Federal Republic of Germany,[5] or of a royalty on blank tape used for this purpose, as in Austria,[6] or both.

1 See para 5.39 below.
2 See para 8.41 below.
3 See para 5.39 below.
4 United Kingdom Command Paper 6732 para 320.
5 German Copyright law 1965, para 55.
6 Austrian Copyright (Amendment) Law 1980, s 42.

(3) Non-voluntary licences (compulsory or statutory licences)

4.33 The concept of compulsory licensing comes from patent law where it is used to prevent the patentee from being the sole producer, forcing him to face direct competition from others, subject only to the payment of a reasonable royalty.

In copyright law the effect of a non-voluntary licence is that the absolute right of the copyright owner is reduced to a right to equitable remuneration. This right to equitable remuneration distinguishes compulsory licences from free uses of the work dealt with under (1).

There are two forms of non-voluntary licensing systems which are often referred to as compulsory licences in the wider sense.

(a) *Statutory licence*. This is 'a licence under which the protected works can be freely used on condition that the user paid a fee, fixed by the competent authority, to the body designated by that authority and distributed in accordance with the rules established by the latter'.[1]

(b) *Compulsory licence*. This is 'a licence requiring the copyright owner to grant the necessary authorisation without, however, depriving him of his right to negotiate the terms of the authorisation, with the proviso that the administrative or judicial authorities (civil courts or special jurisdictions) would fix the amount of remuneration if no amicable agreement can be reached between the parties.[1]

The essential difference is that in the case of the statutory licence the right of the licensee to use the work derives directly and solely from the statute which also regulates the equitable remuneration, whereas under a compulsory licence system the user is not entitled to use the work against the payment of a standard royalty, he must negotiate with the author or with the Collecting Society representing him but these are bound by law to permit the use of the work against payment of an equitable remuneration.

1 Report of the Sub-Committee of the Intergovernmental Committees, Copyright (1978) p 208, paras 48 and 49.

4.34 There are two main reasons for introducing non-voluntary licences. The first concerns cases where the users of certain works have to have access to these works on terms which are known in advance and it is not practical for them to locate each right owner each time and obtain an individual licence from him. The statutory licence for jukebox operators in the United States[1] or for the public libraries with regard to the public lending right in Germany[2] are examples. The other reason for introducing a compulsory licence is to avoid the creation of a monopoly for a user of certain copyrights at the expense of all other users. The statutory licence for the recording of musical works in the United Kingdom[3] and the United States[4] are examples.

The main criticism of the principle of all non-voluntary licences is twofold:

the first criticism relates to the moral right of the author. If he is deprived of the complete control over his work which his copyright should give him, and thus cannot forbid its use, he cannot properly exercise his moral rights, particularly the right to preserve the integrity of his work, until it is too late, as mass distribution has probably already taken place by the time he becomes aware of any alterations made. The second criticism relates to the economic rights. The level of remuneration is said to be lower because the bargaining power of the author is reduced. Likening the author to an intellectual worker it could be said that compulsory licences are the equivalent of depriving a worker of the right to strike which would seriously affect his bargaining position.

In certain copyright situations it can be argued that the author has already lost control over some uses of his work and can only exercise his rights by assigning them to a collecting society which exercises them on his behalf (eg the public performance right in musical copyrights.) This society then negotiates bulk licensing agreements with users or user organisations. Thus the royalty bargaining takes place between two virtual monopolies. It is argued that there is no great difference as far as the economic effect is concerned, between this form of bulk licensing by a monopoly society and a compulsory licence system. This may be so, provided two conditions are met: 1) the moral rights of the author are safeguarded – this means for instance that no unauthorised alterations are permitted[5] and 2) in case of failure to agree the terms of the licence, there is an independent authority such as a copyright royalty tribunal to decide.

In situations where copyrights can no longer be exercised effectively by individual or corporate copyright owners (eg phonogram producers exercising performing rights[6]) the choice between a compulsory licence system and a system of bulk licensing negotiated by a collecting society may be a fine one and will ultimately be decided by the social and philosophical preferences of the country concerned.

A group of experts appointed by WIPO in 1980 to consider the matter stated the problem succinctly:[7]

> 'Where the clearance of the rights must be effected in a comprehensive way because of the great number of the works involved or the practical difficulties of contacting the owner of the copyright in time, national laws should provide, for these practical reasons, for institutionalized collective administration of the said rights. Only where such administration would not work in practice, should national laws provide – subject to the right to equitable remuneration and the respect of moral rights – for the possibility of non-voluntary licenses. But because of the particular situation in which cinematographic works, dramatic works and dramaticomusical works find themselves, provision for non-voluntary licenses for such works should be avoided. The particular situation of the said works is due to the following: (i) their number is relatively small, (ii) their owners can generally be located with less difficulty, (iii) the calendar of their showing on television must, for important economic reasons, be co-ordinated with the calendar of their theatrical showing.'

Recent experience in the United States seems to illustrate the political and philosophical sensitivity of the choice. The United States Copyright Law 1976 introduced a statutory licence for cable system operators with regard to the broadcasting of copyright material. Barely five years later the United States Department of Commerce (National Telecommunications and Information Administration, Office of Policy Analysis and Development) in a staff report of December 1980 recommended the abolition of that licence and concluded:

> 'that a flexible and efficient private bargaining agreement among industry segments is a workable alternative to the present government-administered cable

copyright system. The basic flaw in the current system is the presence of federal government in what essentially should be a privately negotiated Contractual agreement.... The Act not only requires that government agencies collect, invest and distribute cable royalty fees; it also regulates the price for the creative output of private entrepreneurs.... A free market, or even a system of negotiated fees containing a more limited government role than the present system, would permit marketplace forces to determine how the distant signal's value is apportioned among all principals, from cable subscribers to program rights holders.'

1   S 116, US Copyright Act 1976.
2   Para 27, German Copyright Law 1965.
3   S 12, UK Copyright Act 1956.
4   S 115, US Copyright Act 1976.
5   Under para (8) of article II of the Appendix of the Berne Convention for instance even the 'droit de divulgation' is safeguarded to some extent. If the author has withdrawn all copies of his work from circulation no compulsory licence shall be granted.
6   See para 7.30 below.
7   Copyright (1980) p 154.

4.35 On the international level the Berne Convention contains two compulsory licence provisions: article 11 bis (2) relating to the broadcasting right and article 13 (1) relating to the recording right.[1] In both cases three conditions are laid down: 1) The moral rights of authors must be safeguarded; 2) Equitable remuneration must be provided for and the amount of such remuneration must, in the absence of agreement, be fixed by 'competent authority' which may mean a government agency or a special tribunal; 3) The compulsory licence must only be applicable in the country which has provided for it in its law and nowhere else.

Whereas the compulsory licences of the broadcasting organisations relate to all literary and artistic works the compulsory licences of phonogram producers cover only musical works (including the tests authorised to be recorded with the music). In view of the very broad formulation used[2] both statutory and compulsory licensing system would appear to be permissible. However this is not free of doubt.[3]

The UCC (1971) allows much wider scope for non-voluntary licences. Under article IV bis contracting States need only provide effective protection against reproduction, public performance and broadcasting. Thus both compulsory and statutory licences are compatible with the convention and they may relate to each of the main rights.

The original 1952 Convention was wider still. The USSR legislation for instance permits the use of protected works by the mass media (press, broadcasting and film) not only without authorisation but also without compensation.[4] Thus the USSR could ratify the text of the UCC 1952 and did so.

In the sphere of neighbouring rights the broadcasting right and the public performance right of phonogram producers and performers under the Rome Convention[5] is subject to what is in effect a compulsory licence as these performing rights are not expressed as absolute rights to allow or forbid the performance, but as rights to equitable remuneration. Most countries have followed that pattern. The United Kingdom and some jurisdictions whose laws stem from the British Copyright Acts are exceptions as the performing right of the phonogram producers in these jurisdictions is an absolute right which enables them to restrict the number of hours broadcasting organisations can play phonograms (known as 'needletime').

1   See para 5.43 and para 5.46 below.
2   The phrase used 'conditions under which this right may be exercised' is the convention's euphemism for a compulsory licence. It is as if the draftsmen of the convention could not bring

themselves to use the dreaded word, rather like writers in the Middle Ages referred to the devil as 'the evil one' or members of the House of Commons in the UK refer to the House of Lords as 'another place'.
3   See Report of the Sub-Committee of the Intergovernmental Committee 1978, para 50, Copyright (1978) p 208.
4   See para 19.04 below.
5   Art 12; see para 8.26 below.

4.36 Under the *French Copyright Law 1957* there are no compulsory licence provisions.

The *United Kingdom Copyright Act 1956* contains a provision for a statutory licence of a special kind, under which the author is free to allow or forbid the first recording of his work, but once he has given permission to one recording company all other users can record the work on the same terms by paying the statutory royalty.[1] A composer can thus pick the company he wishes to record his work for the first time but once that first recording has been made all other record companies can record the work by giving the required notice and paying the statutory royalty. This is a form of statutory licence tailored to avoid the creation of a monopoly for one recording company in respect of the work in question.

The *German Copyright Law 1965* contains 3 major non-voluntary licences:

(1) The droit de suite[2] which gives an artist a claim of 5% of the increase in the sales price for sales subsequent to the first sale of a work of art.
(2) The public lending right[3] which gives the author of literary works an equitable remuneration where copies of his work are lent by public libraries.
(3) The private use right[4] for home taping which gives the author, the performer and the record producer, through a common collecting society, the right to a royalty of up to 5% of the price of the recording equipment.

The *United States Copyright Act 1976* contains four non-voluntary licences (compulsory licences in the wider sense):

(1) For the making and distributing of phonograms.[5] The royalty is decided periodically by a Copyright Royalty Tribunal.
(2) Public performance by coin-operated phonorecord players (jukeboxes).[6] The jukebox owner applies to the Register of Copyright who issues a certificate after receipt of the fee. The Copyright Royalty Tribunal is charged with the distribution of the royalties.
(3) Cable television.[7] Royalties are worked out according to a formula laid down in the Act and distributed by the Copyright Royalty Tribunal.
(4) Public (ie non-commercial) broadcasting.[8] This relates only to non-dramatic musical works and pictorial graphic and sculptural works and the Copyright Royalty Tribunal sets the royalty rate.

It thus seems, judging from the most recent copyright law revisions of major legislations, that there is a tendency towards the creation of compulsory licences particularly in those fields of copyright where modern technology has created new uses for works giving new rights which can only be exercised effectively by bulk licensing through a collecting society or under a compulsory licence system.

1   UK Copyright Act 1956, s 12.
2   German Copyright Law, para 26.
3   Ibid, para 27.
4   Ibid, para 53(5).
5   Ibid, para 115.
6   Ibid, para 116.

7 Ibid, para 111.
8 Ibid, para 118.

4.37 Anxiety has been expressed that the proliferation of compulsory licences may undermine the copyright system[1] and that the limitations imposed on copyright owners in the public interest may lead to unjustified enrichment by private commercial users of copyrights because of the reduced bargaining power of the copyright owners.

Copyright Royalty Tribunals should be able to counteract such tendencies when fixing or varying royalty rates. The underlying general principle of such determination should, it is submitted, be the same whether the adjudication takes place under a system of voluntary bulk licensing or under a compulsory licence. It has been suggested that the principle should be to fix the royalty at a figure which represents 'the highest rate a willing buyer would pay and the lowest rate a willing seller would accept'[2] which should result in a rate of royalty closest to the rate under a free bargaining system. However in some circumstances this test may be inappropriate because both copyright owners and copyright users are represented by monopolies eg a monopolistic collecting society and a state broadcasting corporation. In such cases the general common law principle of reasonableness in all the circumstances may be the only right one to be applied by the tribunal. Recent adjudications by tribunals in the common law countries seem to show a tendency to increase the rates payable under statutory licence systems.[3]

It is not without significance that the only two compulsory licences which the Berne Convention permits relate to the recording right and the broadcasting right, two mass media which only assumed importance in copyright law comparatively recently. Most cases in national legislation where non-voluntary licence schemes have been introduced are cases where new technology has posed problems for the enforcement of copyright which the legislator thought could only be solved in a practical way by compulsory licence schemes.

With regard to the choice between a compulsory licence and a statutory licence the modern trend seems well expressed in a recent judgment of the German Supreme Court[4] 'There should be no limitations on copyright which serve merely the financial interests of individual users of works. One must also ensure that a limitation imposed in the public interest does not lead to the unjustified advancement of commercial interests of users. In this dilemma, it seems appropriate to control merely the author's power to forbid but to leave him with the right to claim an equitable remuneration for the use of his work'. A clearly expressed preference for a compulsory as opposed to a statutory licence system.

1 Barbara Ringer 'Copyright and the future of authorship' Copyright (1976) p 155.
2 UK Performing Right Tribunal *Scottish Ballroom Association etc v PRS* - PRT 1/58.
3 Eg the Royalty Rate Tribunal in the United States increased the 'mechanical royalty' payable by phonogram producers from 3¼ cents per tune to 4 cents per tune in 1980 within the first few years of the Tribunal being created under the Copyright Law 1976. The Performing Right Tribunal in the United Kingdom laid down a sliding scale rising to 8% of the net advertising revenue for the use of phonograms by commercial broadcasting organisations.
4 17 BGHZ 766, 278.

(4) Special provisions for developing countries

4.38 The compulsory licences introduced into the Paris Acts (1971) of the Berne Convention and the UCC are a special provision to meet a special case.[1] Non-voluntary licences are: a) confined to the exercise of two rights – the translation right and the reproduction right; b) confined to countries recognised as developing countries; c) only permitted if all the prior conditions stipulated in the Annex and Protocol are fulfilled, and d) temporary in the sense that they are permissible under the conventions only as long as the country concerned ranks as a developing country.

It is significant that the Stockholm Protocol 1967 which would have permitted statutory licences, ie a rate of royalty fixed by a statute, ran into serious difficulties and had to be modified in this respect among others. The result of permitting non-voluntary licences has been that in many cases during the decade since 1971 contractual licences have been negotiated and there has thus been no need to resort to non-voluntary licences. It would thus appear that the existence of the power to resort to compulsory licensing may prove sufficient without that power having to be exercised.

1 Appendix, Berne Convention (1971) and art V ter and quater, UCC (1971); see para 6.38 below.

5. Term of copyright

4.39 Unlike property rights in material goods which, once acquired, last as long as the property exists, copyright, like all other intellectual property rights, has a limited duration. This is not due to any inferiority of intellectual property rights in general or copyright in particular but to the special nature of copyright, as a creature of statute law. When legislating on copyright each country has to find a balanced compromise between two public interests: the public interest in encouraging the creation of new works and the public interest in making all works accessible to the widest possible public. The latter interest gives rise to the notion that eventually the work should enrich the national culture and become public property. This is referred to as 'falling into the public domain'. As the duration of the right obviously influences its value to the right owner the question of the term of copyright has always been at the heart of copyright protection.[1] The internationally most widely accepted terms are now the 50 years after the death of the author, usually referred to as 50 years pma (post mortem auctoris) laid down by the Berne Convention and the 25 years pma of the UCC. The reason for tying the term to the life of the author is that he and his family should both benefit materially from the economic rights and that the latter should be in a position to exercise responsibly and in the way the author would have wished, his moral rights after his death. The term of the Berne Convention is approximately three generations, the term of UCC two. After that the connection between the creator of the work and the work itself ceases and the interest of the public at large takes over. Historically the first term of copyright was 14 years from publication under the Statute of Queen Anne in the United Kingdom in 1709 which equated a copyright with a patent as far as duration is concerned and thus gave it 14 years. It was renewable for another term of 14 years if after the first term the author was still alive.

The first question to answer was whether to tie the term to the author, or to the publisher who made the original investment. If recouping the investment is the major objective, the term should obviously be made to start with publication. If protecting the creator is the major objective, the term must somehow be geared to his natural life. The Statute of Anne was thus a compromise between the two. From that modest beginning, the term was slowly and gradually extended in many countries.

Once the idea had taken root that the term should be connected with the life of the author, mainly as a result of the ideas propagated by the French Revolution, the next major hurdle to overcome was to extend it beyond the natural life of the author. During a very emotional parliamentary debate in the United Kingdom on the Bill to extend copyright beyond the life of the author, Lord Macaulay, himself an author of renown who opposed the bill, coined the phrase that the copyright was 'a tax on readers'. Thelford, an eminent barrister advocating the Bill, put the case for 'copyright pma':

> 'At the moment when the author's name is invested with the solemn interest of the grave – when the last seal is set upon his earthly course, and his works assume their place among the classics of his country – your law declares that his works shall become your property, and you requite him by seizing the patrimony of his children'.

The original version of the Berne Convention in 1886[2] gave an even shorter term than the Statute of Queen Anne 1709; 10 years from the end of the year of first publication, but by the turn of the century the majority of the 20 member states had accepted a term of the life of the author and 50 years after his death and that term was written into the Berne Convention in 1908, albeit subject to reservations from member countries which still had shorter terms in their national laws. It was not until 1948 (Brussels Act) that the term of 50 years pma became a Convention obligation, and since then some member states have gone beyond it. However, when the UCC was created a few years later in 1952 the term of 25 years pma was chosen as the highest common denominator acceptable to the countries outside the Berne Convention, most of which had shorter terms in their national laws. Although 25 years pma was made the general rule[3], for those countries which do not compute the term on the basis of the life of the author an exception was created so that they could continue to compute the term as they did, but in that case the minimum was and still is 25 years from the date of first publication. Thus the world remained divided between those countries which put the emphasis on the life of the author and those which put it on publication. The biggest shift toward the 50 years pma term took place when the United States who had been the protagonist of the latter system changed to the Berne Convention system in their Copyright Law of 1976 and introduced 50 years pma as their general rule,[4] although they have not yet ratified the convention.

1 The Masouyé/Wallace *WIPO Guide to the Berne Convention* calls article 7 dealing with duration 'One of the cornerstones of the Convention'. See also Cornish *Intellectual Property* p 308.
2 Art 15, para 5.08 below.
3 Art IV.
4 Until 1976 the USA had the term of 28 years from first publication taken from the UK and renewable for another 28 years making 56 years.

4.40 Ever since the beginnings of international copyright law the term of copyright has in many cases differed from country to country. Thus both to maintain a degree of reciprocity and to encourage countries to lengthen their term of protection to benefit their national authors the rule of comparison of terms was introduced. Its effect is that the term granted to foreign authors in the country where protection is claimed need not exceed the term granted in the country of origin of the work[1]. This is the only major exception from the general principle of national treatment in the Berne Convention and has been applied from its inception to the present day. It applies between the large majority of countries which have accepted the term of 50 years pma and a small number of countries which are still only bound by the Rome Act 1928[2] and apply a shorter term. It also applies between that majority and a small number of countries which have a longer term.[3]

The comparison of terms is complicated by the extensions of the term of copyright which many countries have enacted to make up for the lost opportunities for the exploitation of works during the two world wars.[4] Even for ordinary literary and artistic works there is a term not based on the life of the author, for obvious reasons: if the work is published anonymously or under a pseudonym and the author maintains his anonymity the work is protected for 50 years after it has been made available to the public.[5]

1   Berne Convention 1971, art 7, para (8); see para 5.54 below.
2   At the last revision in 1971 only three member countries still had shorter terms – Poland, Rumania and Bulgaria.
3   The main countries with longer terms are the Federal Republic of Germany, Austria and Israel 70 years pma; Brazil 60 years pma; Spain 80 years pma.
4   These have to be checked in each case as they vary from country to country and are in some cases governed by bilateral agreement.
5   Berne Convention, art 7(3); see para 5.54 below.

4.41   The now largely accepted term of the life of the author and 50 years after his death is obviously not applicable to copyrights the original owner of which is not a natural person but a legal entity, eg a film producer or phonogram producer. In those cases the term must of necessity be calculated from their making or from their publication. However, shorter terms and terms not related to the life of the author have also been given to some works, the original owner of which is a natural person, such as fifty years after the work has been made available to the public for cinematographic works[1] and 25 years from the making of the work for photographs and works of applied art under the Berne Convention[1] and 10 years for such works under the UCC[2]. The rationale of these provisions is that these works either do not need or do not deserve longer terms of protection. These terms are expressed as a rule in the Convention, although they are really minima and they are generally matched in national legislation. On the other hand the conventional terms of 20 years from fixation, performance or broadcast as the case may be under the Rome Convention[3] are expressed as minima in the Convention and are exceeded by many national legislations, eg 50 years from first publication in the United Kingdom[4] and 75 years from first publication in the United States for phonograms.[5] The rights given to performers date from the date the performance took place and the minimum term is 20 years. This is a case where the original owner of the right is always a natural person, (as in most cases of photographs) so that the shorter term which may be far short of the lifetime of the performer or the photographer is not due to the corporate character of the original owner of the right but to the fact that this was considered a sufficient period for a particular work or a particular class of persons. In the case of performers this is less than just.

1   Berne Convention art 7(2) and (4); see para 5.54 below.
2   UCC, art IV/3; see para 6.18 below.
3   Rome Convention, art 14; see para 8.38 below.
4   United Kingdom Copyright Act 1956 art 12(13).
5   United States Copyright Act 1976, 302(c) and 304(a). They have the same term as other classes of works and as most will be 'works made for hire' the term is 75 years from first publication or 100 years from the year of its creation which ever expires first.

6. Remedies for infringement of copyright

4.42   It is self-evident that the remedies provided for the copyright owner to enable him to enforce his copyright are provided by the national law of the country where he claims protection whether it is his own or a foreign country. There is therefore, with the exception of the rather sparse provisions of the conventions, which are dealt with later in this chapter, no international law on the subject. However as enforcement is a vital part of copyright and as the enforcement of certain rights has been rendered particularly difficult by modern technology a brief outline of those factors which are common to nearly all legislations is being attempted here.

Remedies for infringement are of three kinds: civil, criminal and administrative.

(1) Civil remedies

4.43 Although in most cases the original owner of the copyright disposes of it by contract and therefore cases of infringement may arise as breaches of contract, it is of the essence of copyright as a proprietary right that it is enforcible erga omnes including all those with whom the copyright owner has no contractual relations.

The civil remedies for infringement of copyright are of two kinds: preventive and compensatory.

(1) *Preventive remedies*

4.44 The preventive remedies are: a) the power of search and seizure of infringing material; b) an injunction to stop the defendant from committing breaches or further breaches.

(a) The power of search and seizure serves the purpose of discovering infringing copies of the work and the equipment for making them and preventing infringements or further infringements by seizing them.

(b) Anticipatory injunctions[1]. Such injunctions are known and widely used in many jurisdictions. Injunctions are granted in some cases to prevent an infringement of copyright before it is committed (anticipatory injunctions).[1]

If the plaintiff can show that a performance of his play is being rehearsed by a theatrical company or a broadcast version of it is being prepared he need not wait until the first night or the broadcast, he can get an injunction to prevent them. If the plaintiff can show that a film or a record pirate has made illicit copies of his film or phonogram he need not wait until the film is shown in public or the phonograms sold to the public, he can get an injunction to prevent such showings or sales.

As most infringements of copyright consist of a continuing process of successive infringing acts such as printing copies of a written publication or pressing records, the most important remedy and in many cases the only effective one is the injunction. This is always in the discretion of the court and the court has to weigh the possible damage to the plaintiff if the injunction is not granted against the possible damage to the defendant if it is granted. Thus once the infringement and its continuance is proved the plaintiff will usually be entitled to an injunction, but the injunction would not be granted if the damage caused to the defendant by granting the injunction would be out of all proportion to the seriousness of the infringement or to the possible damage to the plaintiff.[2]

The plaintiff must prove a causal connection between the identity or similarity of the defendant's work and his own. The alternatives to such causal connection are that the defendant arrived at the same or similar result by his own efforts and independently of the plaintiff or possibly that the plaintiff and defendant copied from the same source.[3] As Professor Cornish points out this 'distinguishes Copyright from the "full" protection of the patent system'.[4]

As copyright is a proprietary right in case of direct infringements which amount to taking what is not yours, ignorance is not a defence, or putting it the other way the plaintiff does not have to show that the defendant knew he was infringing. On the other hand in the case of indirect infringements which are committed by sale, importation or other dealings in copies of the work the plaintiff has, as a rule, to show that the defendant knew that the goods he was selling or importing were infringing copies. In most cases of indirect infringement where the plaintiff has to sue a wholesaler or a dealer the burden of proof becomes vital in two respects: (a) proving that the plaintiff is the copyright owner and (b) proving that the defendant knew he was handling infringing material.

On the first question of proving copyright international law provides a presumption in the form of article 15 of the Berne Convention (1971). The author of a literary or artistic work shall be presumed to be author and thus entitled to institute infringement proceedings in a Berne Union country if his name 'appears on the work in the usual manner'. Thus the burden of proof is shifted to the defendant to prove the contrary. In this respect the Convention makes one of its rare concessions to corporate bodies as owners of copyright. If the work is a cinematographic work the 'person or body corporate whose name appears on a cinematographic work in the usual manner' will 'be presumed to be the maker of the said work'[5] and if the work is anonymous or pseudonymous the publisher whose name appears on the work 'shall be deemed to represent the author and ... shall be entitled to ... enforce the authors rights'.[6]

The second point, the defendant's knowledge that he is infringing may also be difficult to prove as knowledge is a state of mind and can therefore in the absence of an admission only be proved by inference. Such inference can be drawn from the surrounding circumstances, eg that he bought the infringing copies from an unusual and suspect source, that he is not displaying them openly but keeping them 'under the counter' or possibly the most telling circumstance: that he bought the infringing copies at a fraction of the usual price. However all these circumstances may be difficult to prove in a court. The position of the person dealing in infringing copies is in fact similar to that of the 'receiver', the person dealing in stolen property. 'Receiving' of stolen property is only an offence if the defendant knew that the property was stolen. However in most jurisdictions once it is proved that the goods found in the defendant's possession were in fact stolen, the burden of proof shifts to the defendant who has then to prove that he did not know that he was in possession of stolen property. In some jurisdictions the burden of proof has been reversed in a similar way in copyright infringement cases so that the defendant has to show that he did not know or had no reasonable grounds for suspecting that the copies in his possession which he was importing, buying or selling were infringing copies.[7]

1   'Einstweilige Verfügung' in Germanic countries eg Federal Republic, para 15.40 below. A 'Référé procedure' in Francophone countries; see para 4.46 below.
2   *Nimer on Copyright* (1981) pp 14-53 and 14-54 suggests that under US law when great public injury would result from an injunction, a court could award damages or a continuing royalty.
3   See in the United States *Fisher v Dillingham* (1924) 298 Fed 145 at 150 or in the United Kingdom *Francis Day v Bron* [1963] Ch 587 at 625 per Diplock LJ.
4   Cornish *Intellectual Property* p 345.
5   Berne Convention (1971), art 15(2).
6   Berne Convention (1971), art 15(3).
7   Eg Singapore, Copyright (Gramaphone and Government Broadcasting) Act 1968, s 3(1).

4.45   The most significant development in *Anglo-Saxon* jurisdictions to make the remedies against copyright infringements more effective took place in the United Kingdom when the Court of Appeal and later the House of Lords[1] approved a procedure by which the court can make an order in camera without prior notice being given to the defendant to allow the plaintiff accompanied by his lawyer to inspect the premises of the Defendant and seize infringing copies or make copies or take photographs which are relevant to his case. The order is named after the first reported case where it was granted and is known as an 'Anton Piller' order.[2] To obtain such an order the plaintiff must show 1) that there is a very strong prima facie case of infringement, 2) that the potential damage to the plaintiff is very serious, 3) that there is clear evidence that the defendant has in his possession materials or documents which prove the infringement, 4) that there is a very real possibility that if the defendant would be warned by an ordinary hearing of the application inter partes he would remove the incriminating evidence. The plaintiff must also give an undertaking to pay damages suffered by the defendant if at the end of the trial it was held that there was no infringement. Subject to the safeguards that the plaintiff must be accompanied by his lawyer (a solicitor in the United Kingdom who is an officer of the court and has to answer to the court for his conduct) and that the defendant must be allowed to consult his lawyer if he wishes before he allows the plaintiff entry to his premises, this is probably as close to a search warrant in a civil case as one can get. The court may also order the defendant to disclose the names of the persons who have supplied the infringing copies or of the persons to whom such copies have been consigned if this is the only means by which the plaintiff can find the persons he can act against for the infringement of his copyright.[3, 4]

1   The Supreme Court of the UK.
2   *Anton Piller v Manufacturing Processes* [1976] Ch 55.
3   In a Patent case in the UK *Norwich Pharmacal v CCE* [1974] AC 133 an order was made against the customs authorities to reveal the identity of importers of drugs which were patented.
4   In the United States discovery of documents can be taken to the extent of preliminary cross-examination of the defendant, see *Cornish* p 61 and footnote 77.

4.46 In *French* civil and commercial procedure remedies are available which have similar effects. They are known as an order in chambers[1] obtained in the presence of both parties or an ordinance upon petition[2] obtained by the plaintiff in the absence of the defendant, both are expedited, swift procedures designed to fulfil a need for urgent action.

An expedited procedure ('procedure de référé') is available in the French courts in all but criminal matters at every level of jurisdiction. The defendant is summonsed to appear before a judge in chambers on the plaintiff's application for an order in chambers. The order, if granted, is an interim order. It grants no rights in the subject matter but is binding at the interlocutory stage as it is not subject to appeal. Its object is to secure or to preserve evidence which may be vital to the outcome of the case. As the order is granted in the presence of the defendant it lacks the element of surprise of an 'Anton Piller order'. That can only be achieved by an ordinance upon petition which is an ex parte procedure that can be used without having to inform the defendant or the third party in whose possession the matters forming the subject of the suit are. It is made to a High Court judge.[3] In copyright cases it is used to seize objects or documents from a party before they have an opportunity to hide them, dispose of them or destroy them. French law provides:

'The police commissioners, and where there are no police commissioners, justices of the peace shall be required, upon the demand of any author of a work protected by this law, or his successors, to seize the copies constituting an unlawful reproduction of the work.

If the seizure will have the effect of retarding or suspending public performances which are in progress or which have already been announced, a special authorisation shall be obtained from the president of the "tribunal civil", by an order issued on demand.

The president of the "tribunal civil" shall also be empowered in the same form, to order:

The suspension of all manufacture in progress serving the unlawful reproduction of a work;

the seizure, even at hours not provided by Article 1037 of the Code of Civil Procedure, of the copies constituting an unlawful reproduction of the work, whether already manufactured or in the process of manufacture, of the receipts obtained and of copies unlawfully utilised;

the seizure provided under Article 426 of the Penal Code, of receipts obtained from any reproduction, performance or dissemination, by any means whatever, of an intellectual work, effected in violation of the author's rights.

The President of the "tribunal civil" shall, in issuing the decrees heretofore provided, order that security be given in advance by the plaintiff.'[4]

The judge has discretionary powers to grant or refuse the order. If he refuses the plaintiff can appeal to the Court of Appeal within 15 days. If he grants the order the defendant cannot appeal against the order which takes effect immediately, but he can at any stage of the case request the same judge to rehear the petition and withdraw the order ('voie de retraction').[5]

The ordinance could be either an order on an affidavit made out by a bailiff, or a writ of execution. In the latter case, there are two alternatives: the attachment of property or the 'descriptive seizure' which consists of an inventory made by the bailiff of infringing copies. The goods as described are then transferred to the possession of a third party who will hold them whilst the case is pending.

In order to prevent abuses, such as vexatious seizures or seizures for the purpose of unfair competition, the judge may order payment into court by the person requesting seizure of a sum of money sufficient to indemnify the person against whom the order is made should it prove to have been ill-founded.

Article 67 of the Copyright Law of 1957 also provides for measures to obtain the withdrawal of a seizure order:

'Within thirty days of the making of a report of the seizure provided in the first paragraph of Article 66, or of the date of the decree provided in the same Article, the distrainee or the garnishee may demand that the president of the "tribunal civil" end the seizure or limit its effects, or authorise the resumption of manufacture or public performance, under the authority of an administrator constituted a receiver, so that whoever is the proprietor may benefit by the manufacture or exploitation.

The president of the "tribunal civil," acting "en référé," may, if he allows the demand of the distrainee or garnishee, order the petitioner to deposit a sum applicable as a guarantee for damages to which the author might be entitled.'

1 'L'ordonnance de référé.'
2 'L'ordonnance rendu sur requête.'
3 'President du Tribunal de Grande Instance.'
4 Copyright Law (11 March) 1957, art 66.
5 The respondent must use the 'référé – procedure' (art 497, Code of Civil Procedure), especially when the ordinance upon petition has provided for a seizure (attachment), a sequestration of property, or any other kind of measure provided for by art 493 to 812 of the Code of Civil Procedure. The procedure then becomes contentious.

(2) *Compensatory remedies*

4.47 The compensatory remedies are: a) the award of damages to the plaintiff and b) orders for the destruction or 'delivery up' of infringing copies and the equipment by which such copies are produced.

(a) Damages. The main remedy in civil infringement actions is damages. These can be damages actually suffered which must be proved or under most jurisdictions 'exemplary damages' in flagrant cases, which are, as a rule, in the court's discretion. Generally damages for infringement of copyright are at large but, as a yardstick, the measure of damages can be said to be 'the depreciation of the value of the copyright caused by the infringement'.[1] The injury to the plaintiff's reputation in cases of infringements vulgarising the original work is a proper head of damages in all countries of the Berne Union.

(b) Delivery up. This is an additional remedy consisting of an order to hand over infringing copies and the machinery[2] made or used for the purpose of making these infringing copies. This remedy is usually discretionary as there may be cases where it would be unfair to the defendant to order delivery up of his equipment, but in the majority of cases it would be unfair to the plaintiff to leave the defendant in possession of it as it might encourage him to repeat the infringement.

1 In the UK, per Lord Wright in *Sutherland Publishing Co Ltd v Caxton Publishing Co Ltd* [1936] Ch 323 at 336. In the US the US Copyright Act 1976 (para 504) provides for 'statutory damages', ie amounts of damages laid down in the statute which the court can award if no actual damages are proved.
2 This includes plates, blocks, moulds, printing presses in cases of printed material, negatives in the case of photographs, matrices and all kinds of reproduction equipment in the case of phonograms or films.

(2) Criminal remedies

4.48 The advantages of criminal remedies are obvious. Infringement is likened to theft of the intellectual property involved and the sanctions, fines in the first place and imprisonment in case of recidivism have, as all criminal sanctions are intended to have, a deterrent effect. This is why criminal sanctions have since the beginning of copyright legislation been a part of the copyright owner's armoury just as they are in the case of any owner of material property. In most jurisdicitions where there are criminal sanctions for copyright infringements, these also include seizure followed by delivery up of the infringing copies or destruction of such copies in some countries, also the destruction of the equipment used for the making of the infringing copies.

However, criminal remedies in copyright have their disadvantages.

1. Both the plaintiff's title and the infringement including in many cases the defendant's knowledge have to be strictly proved and in difficult cases the defendant will often either not be prosecuted because the prosecutor does not think the case is strong enough or he will be acquitted because the court will give him the benefit of the doubt.

2. Technology has made infringement of copyright immensely profitable and even high fines will not have the desired deterrent effect. If the defendant is known to have made a very large profit from his infringement even imposing the maximum fine will be seen to be derisory.[1] Furthermore, fines have to be expressed in the currency of the country and if in spite of inflation and devaluation of currencies fines are to remain an effective deterrent they will have to be revised rather frequently.[2]

3. In most developed countries the courts are reluctant to send a defendant to prison for copyright infringements other than in the most serious cases or if the defendant has already a criminal record.

4. As in drug trafficking or smuggling cases, which large copyright infringement

cases sometimes resemble in character, the main culprits often remain in the background and are not on trial.

5. The fines imposed do not compensate the copyright owner but go to the state.

1 In a tape piracy case in Hong Kong in 1976 the defendant was estimated to have made profits exceeding a million dollars in little over a year. The maximum fine was imposed: HK$25,000 = approx US$5,000.
2 At a rate of inflation of 10%, the value of a fine is halved in $3\frac{1}{2}$ years.

(3) Administrative measures

4.49 Administrative measures are mainly provided so that the importation of infringing copies can be dealt with by the customs authorities. This is provided for in most legislations for all printed material. The copyright owner can notify the authorities and customs officers can, without much difficulty, identify infringing material such as books, periodicals or sheet music by titles alone. However if the copyright material has to be performed (the record played, the film shown) to identify it, it is more difficult for customs officers to deal with it. This is particularly so if both legitimate and infringing items which look very similar are imported. Artistic works present similar difficulties. However the control of piracy of all kinds can be dealt with most effectively at the point of entry into the country and 'becomes progressively more difficult once the imports are dispersed'.[1] The difficulty is similar to that encountered in trade mark infringement cases where some jurisdictions require written notice to the customs authorities that goods bearing a protected trade mark 'are expected to arrive ... at a time and place and by a consignment specified in the notice'.[2] International law provides for seizure in the Berne Convention which includes seizure by customs authorities. Infringing copies are 'liable to seizure in any country of the Union where the work enjoys legal protection'.[3] Such seizure shall also be possible if the infringing reproductions are 'coming from a country where the work is not protected, or has ceased to be protected'.[4] This means that in cases of imported infringing copies it is irrelevant whether they infringe copyright in the country where they were made or in the country from which they are exported. If the plaintiff can show that the work is protected by copyright in the country of import, the imported copies are infringing copies. This is an example of the lex loci delictus rule applied to copyright.

In most jurisdictions civil, criminal and administrative remedies are used and are complementary to each other.

1 Whitford Report in the United Kingdom, para 722.
2 United Kingdom, Trade Mark Description Act 1968, s 17 (inserting a new s 64A into the Trade Mark Act 1938).
3 Art 16(1).
4 Art 16(2).

4.50 The Tunis Model Law on Copyright for Developing Countries (1976)[1] contains most of the essence of the provisions against infringement of copyright.

'(1) Any person infringing any one of the rights protected under this Law:
  (i) shall be obliged by the court to cease such infringement;
  (ii) shall be liable for damages;
  (iii) shall, if the infringement was wilful, be punishable by a fine not exceeding ... or imprisonment not exceeding ... months or both, provided that, in the case of recidivism, the above amount or term or both may be doubled.
(3) Infringing copies, receipts arising from acts constituting an infringement of these rights and any implements used for the infringement shall be subject to seizure.

(4) The material proof of such infringement of any one of the rights may be provided by statements of police officers or by the certified statements of the sworn agents of the organisation of authors.'

This section, which eases very considerably the burden of proof by admitting affidavits from officers of a collecting society, goes further than most developed countries have been prepared to go so far, although in France the practice of swearing in agents of authors' societies to establish infringements seems to be accepted by the courts.[2]

1 Adopted by the Committee of Governmental Experts convened by the Government of Tunis with the assistance of WIPO and UNESCO and published by UNESCO/WIPO, s 15.
2 J.L. Tournier 'Perspectives', RIDA (January 1974) p 478 at p 506.

Chapter 5

The Berne Convention

Summary

1. Introduction   5.01
2. The making of the Convention   5.05
3. The 'Berne Union'   5.06
4. History of the Berne Convention   5.07
5. The Berne Convention 1886   5.08
6. The Berne Convention between 1886-1971   5.10
   A. The Paris Additional Act (1896)   5.10
   B. The Berlin Act (1908)   5.11
   C. The Additional Protocol (1914)   5.12
   D. The Rome Act (1928)   5.13
   E. The Brussels Act (1948)   5.14
   F. The Stockholm Act (1967)   5.27
7. The Paris Act (1971)   5.28
   (1) Who is an 'author'?   5.29
   (2) What is a 'work'?   5.30
   (3) Which works are protected? – article 2   5.32
   (4) What is publication? – article 3(3) and (4)   5.33
   (5) The principle of national treatment – article 5(1)   5.34
   (6) The principle of automatic protection and absence of formalities – article 5(2)   5.35
   (7) The notion of 'country of origin' – article 5(3) and (4)   5.36
   (8) The ten major rights – article 6 bis, articles 8 – 14   5.37
   (9) The term of protection – article 7   5.54
   (10) Exemptions from copyright and restrictions on the rights of authors – article 2 and article 10   5.55
   (11) 'Folklore' – article 15(4)   5.63
   (12) Restrictions by government control – article 17   5.64
   (13) Remedies for breaches of the Convention   5.65
8. List of member states of the Berne Union   5.68

1. Introduction

5.01   It is in the nature of copyright that it would be, at best, greatly reduced in value, and at worst, useless, unless it was internationally recognised. It would be greatly reduced in value because the author would not receive royalties for the use of his work in countries other than his own. It may become useless because, as works would be exploited largely in countries where no royalty is payable and then reimported to the country of the author at a cheaper rate. Gresham's law of economics, that bad money drives out good, does apply to copyright in the sense that pirated copies, not having paid any copyright and probably made in a country with cheap labour costs, and reimported at a far lower price, will drive out the legitimate copies of the work.

As the Berne Convention is the first of the international conventions dealing with copyrights it is appropriate to set out the advantages of an international instrument in the copyright field, the objectives of an international copyright convention and the methods by which these objectives are achieved.

Advantages of the Convention

5.02
(1) Copyright owners get full protection in all member countries without any formality, merely by the fact that they have created a work.

(2) Publishers know that when they first publish a work in a convention country, even if it is not a work of a national of their country, or of any convention country, their investment in the publication is protected in all countries that have ratified the convention.

(3) The Convention guarantees the traditional rights: the reproduction right, the translation right, and the public performance right and, as technology progresses, other rights such as the recording right, the film right, the broadcasting right, and the wire diffusion right are gradually added by way of revision.

(4) In the country where an infringement takes place the courts can apply to an international situation all the remedies provided by the domestic law.

Objectives of the Convention

5.03 To establish international relations in the field of copyright by dealing with international situations, ie situations involving the laws of more than one country as opposed to national situations which are dealt with according to the law of the land.

Furthering greater uniformity of the level of protection, which means bringing the countries with a lower level of protection up to the standard of the countries with a higher level of protection.

Methods applied by the Convention to achieve these objectives

5.04
1. *Minimum rights* jure conventionis granted in the substantive clauses of the Convention.

2. *The principle of national treatment*, which has the effect that a national of a country with a low level of protection who gets better protection abroad than he can get at home, will eventually bring pressure to bear on the authorities of his country for better protection.

3. *The principle of reciprocity*, which means that although according to the principle of national treatment a country has to grant foreigners who are nationals of a convention country the same right as it grants to its own nationals, it can, under the rules of some conventions, reduce the level of protection to the same level which its citizens enjoy in the country of origin of the foreign national in question. It is often essential to apply this principle for political reasons when ratification of the convention is sought in national parliaments.

4. *The principle of automatic protection*, which means that a state cannot require formalities as a condition of protection.

5. *The possibility of reservations*. This means that when a new right is introduced, ratifying countries are given the possibility of making reservations with regard to that right which are necessitated by their national laws: They can later be withdrawn when the protection in their national laws has been increased to the required level.[1]

1 Berne Convention, art 27.

2. The making of the Convention

5.05 The first initiatives came from the 'Société des gens de lettres' and from ALAI ('Association Literaire et Artistique Internationale') whose honorary president was Victor Hugo founded in 1878 and from the 'Boersen-verein der deutschen Budhändler' which at the International Congress of ALAI in Rome in 1882 moved a resolution for the formation of an international union. That congress produced the first draft of the Convention. The guiding thought was that all authors, of whatever nationality, of works published in a contracting state, should be assimilated in the other countries of the Union to the national authors of that country without being subjected to any formalities whatsoever.

The programme was worked out in three diplomatic conferences held in Geneva between 1884 and 1886. It was predominantly a European convention with the leading European powers, France, Germany, Italy and Britain to the fore.[1]

From the beginning the Convention contained significant elements which were of crucial importance for its future development:

(1) The countries which took the lead in creating the Union were Western European countries, similar in outlook and stage of cultural and industrial development. However, they included from the start the protagonists of the two *ideologies of copyright*: France, supported by the other Latin countries as the representatives of the 'droit d'auteur', and Britain as the representative of copyright.[2] Although Britain was in a minority of one until it was joined by the major British Dominions,[3] both ideologies had to be accommodated from the beginning and at every revision conference, as the Union subscribed from the start to the unanimity rule.[4]

(2) *The colonial clause* – The founder members included all the colonial powers of the day apart from the Netherlands and Portugal who joined later, with the result that by extending their membership of the Union to some of their colonies, by a simple Declaration,[5] they took the principles of the Convention to all continents. This clause remained almost unchanged until 1948.[6]

1 Belgium, Spain and the host country, Switzerland, also signed it and so did three non-European countries, Haiti, Liberia and Tunisia.
2 See para 1.13 and para 1.15 above.
3 The ratification of the United Kingdom extended from the start to the self-governing dominions: Canada, Australia, New Zealand, South Africa and to India. Other nations with legislation stemming from the United Kingdom Copyright Acts joined it after they had reached independence, eg Pakistan and the Republic of Ireland joined the Union in 1948, Israel in 1951, Cyprus in 1964.
4 Art 17/3, Berne Convention 1886.
5 Art 19.
6 Brussels Act, art 26 – now art 31 of the 1971 Act.

3. The Berne Union

5.06 The underlying thought of the founder members was that the Convention should have a permanent character. This was achieved by creating a 'Union of States'. The declaration that 'the countries to which this convention applies constitute a Union' has several important implications:

(1) The Union was universal from its inception, ie open to all countries. The Berne Convention is an open convention.
(2) Once formed, the Union of member states has an independent existence in that some countries may leave, some others may join. The Union goes on.
(3) The Convention is capable of periodic revision to take account of technical, political and economic developments.
(4) The Union system enables member countries to define their copyright relations although their membership is at different levels of the Convention, eg a country joining the Convention now can have international copyright relations with those countries which have ratified the Paris Act 1971 (eg France) and at the same time with countries who have only so far ratified the Rome Act 1928 (eg Canada).
(5) There is no separate administration of the different Acts; the Union functions as one entity from a legal, administrative and financial point of view.

4. The history of the Berne Convention

5.07 The Berne Convention is a success story among international conventions. It has endured as an effective convention for nearly a century. During that period it has gradually attracted more and more ratifications, reaching 74 by 1982 without any member leaving the Union.[1] The level of protection has, throughout the history of the Convention, been gradually but consistently increased. Even the last Revision Conference (Stockholm, 1967) and the Paris Act (1971) where substantial concessions were made to the developing countries, were no exception as in all other respects protection was consolidated and increased.

Since 1886 the Berne Convention has has two *Additions* and five *Revisions*:[2]
9 September 1886: Berne Convention (entry into force on 5 December 1887);
4 May 1896: Additional Act of Paris (entry into force on 9 December 1897);
13 November 1908: Berlin Revision (entry into force on 9 September 1910);
20 March 1914: Additional Protocol of Berne (entry into force on 20 April 1915);
2 June 1928: Rome Revision (entry into force on 1 August 1931);
26 June 1948: Brussels Revision (entry into force on 1 August 1951);
14 July 1967: Stockholm Revision (no entry into force of the substantive provisions since these were reviewed in the following revision; entry into force of the administrative provisions in 1970):
24 July 1971: Paris Revision (entry into force on 10 October 1974).

This chapter deals with the original Convention (1886) in some detail for historical reasons and presents an analysis of the current state of the Convention (1971 Act). The intermediate stages are dealt with in brief outline.

---

1 Of the members of the United Nations the USA and the Soviet Union (both now members of the Universal Copyright Convention) are the only major exporters and importers of copyright works which have so far remained outside the Berne Union.
2 It was the tendency to keep the general layout and as far as possible the numbering of the articles unchanged but to add to them. Thus 'bis' indicates the insertion in the convention between 1928 and 1948 and 'ter' indicates insertion in 1967/1971 (with the exception of art 11).

5. The Berne Convention 1886

5.08   The countries which accede to the Convention form a single Union.[1]

The protection of the Convention is given to 'authors' and their 'works'.[2] However neither of these terms is defined.

The predominant influence of publishers is recognised by making the act of publication the cornerstone of the Convention.[3] The *country of first publication* becomes the country of origin of the work.[3] This is known as the 'geographical criterion'. Only for unpublished works the country of origin is that to which the author belongs. This is known as the 'personal criterion'. As in the nature of things the overwhelming majority of works are 'published', the criterion of first publication applies to most works.

Even if the author belongs to a non-Union country 'the stipulation of the present Convention shall apply equally to the *publishers of literary and artistic works* published in one of the countries of the Union'.[4]

The right owners are described as 'authors or their lawful representatives'.[5] This was the first English translation of the French 'ayants droits'. It was later changed to 'right owners', but the first translation shows plainly what the draftsmen had in mind: that in the large majority of cases, the publisher was the right owner because the author had assigned his rights to him in the publishing contract.

With regard to authors, the *principle of assimilation* or, as it is now usually called, *the principle of national treatment*[6], stipulates that authors who are citizens of a Union country shall enjoy in another Union country 'the rights which the respective laws ... grant to natives'. It is matched by the *principle of reciprocity* as far as the term of copyright is concerned.[7]

Although the protected rights may be subject to *conditions and formalities* in the country of origin of the work,[8] they must not be subjected to any other formalities which may be required in the country where protection is claimed. It is 'sufficient that their name be indicated on the work in the accustomed manner'.[9] In order to be satisfied that such formalities as are required by the law of the country of origin have been complied with, the courts in the country where protection is claimed may require a certificate to that effect.[10]

Although the title of the convention speaks of 'an International Union for the protection of literary and artistic works', the non-exhaustive definition in article 4, apart from all 'writings', includes such things as 'plans, sketches and charts as well as three dimensional works[11] relative to architecture and science'. The categories of works were not closed from the beginning so that they could be added to as technology progressed.

It is interesting to observe that the omnibus clause in the 1886 definition[12] is much more up-to-date after nearly a century than what was put in its place later. It reads: 'in fact every production whatsoever in the literary, scientific, or artistic domain which can be published by any mode of impression or reproduction'. The words 'every production whatsoever ... which can be published by any ... impression or reproduction' may have fitted both films and phonograms quite adequately. However it was removed by the Berlin Act in 1908 when both the processes of cinematography and recording had already been invented, but neither films nor phonograms had reached the commercial importance they have assumed since. Had the original text of the definition not been removed just when it began to be needed, the considerable intellectual and practical difficulties which the Convention encountered later, particularly at the revision conference in 1948 with regard to films, television broadcasts and phonograms, might have been avoided and the creation of the so-called neighbouring rights[13] may not have been necessary.

The only rights specifically protected were the translation right[14] and the public performance right.[15] The basic right of the author (and his publisher), the reproduction right, was so much taken for granted that it was not even mentioned and had to wait for almost a century until 1967[16] before it was accorded its rightful place as 'the exclusive right of authorising the reproduction of... works in any manner or form'.

With regard to the term of protection the Convention is cautious. Apart from the translation right which runs for 10 years from the date of first publication, it only provides that the term must not exceed the term in the country of origin.[17] This was done in order to encourage countries with short terms for copyright to join the Union in the first place and then gradually work towards a higher minimum term of protection.

The structure of the Convention rests on two pillars: Convention law and Referral Rules. The Convention law consists of those rights which every country has to apply jure conventionis. The Referral Rules indicate to the courts of the country where protection is claimed that they may have to look apart from their own law to the country of origin of the work which may (in the case of published work) be the country of first publication[18] or (in the case of unpublished works) the country of which the author is a national.[19]

Convention law is obligatory for member states except where a convention makes a provision optional so that it can be excluded by a reservation.

1 Art 1.
2 Art 1.
3 Art 2/3.
4 Art 3.
5 Art 2.
6 Art 2/2 (last sentence).
7 Art 2/2 (last sentence).
8 Art 2/2.
9 Art 11.
10 Art 11/3.
11 The English translation of 'oeuvres plastiques' as 'plastic works' is not very meaningful.
12 Art 4 (last sentence).
13 See ch 7.
14 Art 5.
15 Art 9 'public representation' of dramatic or dramatico-musical works is an early translation of the French 'representation public'. It remained 'public representation' in 1908 (art 11), 'public presentation and public performance' (art 11) in 1948, and became 'public performance' in 1967, although the correct term 'public performance' already appeared in the English translation of art 9/3 in 1886.
16 Stockholm Act 1967, art 9.
17 Art 2/2 (last sentence).
18 Art 2/3.
19 Art 2/4.

Exceptions

5.09 The author or his publisher can forbid the reproduction of one of his articles in a newspaper or periodical, but if he does not do so expressly, it can be reproduced or translated without payment.[1] 'Political discussion' and 'news of the day' are free in any event.[2] In 'publications destined for educational or scientific purposes' portions of protected works can be used 'if the legislation of the member country permits it'.[3]

The two main remedies for breaches of copyright are spelt out:

(a) proceedings against 'the pirates' can be instituted in the courts of the country where protection is claimed, with a reduced burden of proof as to title. If the author's name is 'indicated on the work in the accustomed

manner' he is presumed to be the right owner unless there is proof to the contrary.[4]
(b) seizure of copies can be effected on importation into a country of the Union provided that the work and in the case of translations or adaptations, the original work is protected.[5]

The works which were not universally recognised by the original 10 countries are dealt with in the 'Final Protocol'. They are 'photographs' with the proviso that member countries need not protect them 'further than is permitted in their own legislation'[6] and 'choreographic works' if they are 'implicitly included' in their legislation.[7]

The Convention provided for an 'International office' which was placed under the authority of the Swiss government and in 1893 combined with the Buro of the Paris Union (International Union for the Protection of Industrial Property) to form the 'United International Buro for the Protection of Intellectual Property', known by the acronym BIRPI.

1 Art 7/1.
2 Art 7/2.
3 Art 8.
4 Art 11/1.
5 Art 12.
6 Protocol 1/1.
7 Protocol 1/3.

6. The Berne Convention between 1886 and 1971

A. The Paris Additional Act (1896)[1]

5.10 'Publication'[2] was clarified as a concept by referring to it as 'first publication'.

The translation right now runs during the entire term of the right over the original work.[3] However, it comes to an end after 10 years from the date of first publication if the author has not availed himself of it by publishing, in a Union country 'a translation in the language for which the protection is to be claimed'. Thus the convention devised, when the European countries were at an earlier stage of their development, a system which was revived in an only slightly modified form in 1971 to deal with similar needs of the developing countries of our time.[4]

The Act added photographic works to the list of works[5] and created the phrase 'works produced by an analogous process' which was to assume such crucial importance later with regard to cinematographic works.[6] It would appear that the draftsmen had the cinema, then in an embryonic state in mind.

The Act also created protection for 'authorised photographs of protected works of art'.[7]

The Act also established the principle which became important at later stages of the Convention, that states could accede either to the original Act, or to the amended one.[8]

1 The Final Protocol of Diplomatic Conference had stipulated (para 6) that the next conference was to be held in four to six years from the Convention coming into force, but the conference was not a revision in the sense this term is now understood. It produced an 'Additional Act' and an 'Interpretative Declaration', both consolidating the structure of the Convention.
2 Art 2/1.
3 Art 5.
4 Art 30(2)(b) 1971 Act.
5 Art 2 B relating to art 4 of the Convention.

6 Art 14 and 14 bis, 1971 Act.
7 Art 2IB.
8 Art 3.

B. The Berlin Act (1908)

5.11 The Revision Conference achieved important improvements in the level of protection.

1. The principle of national treatment
The two concepts which form the main pillars of the convention are stated, this time side by side: 'the principle of national treatment of Union authors and the rights granted jure conventionis'.[1]

2. Formalities
All formalities were dispensed with. From now on the enjoyment and the exercise of the rights in protected works becomes independent of the existence of protection in the country of origin.[2]

3. The translation right
The general rule that the author of a protected work had the exclusive right to make or authorise a translation of his work, was established. It lasts during the whole term of the right in the original work.[3] However, as in respect of other rights a reservation was possible[4] by making a declaration to be bound only by a previous Act.

4. The term of protection
The term of protection was increased to 'the life of the author and 50 years after his death'.[5] This has remained to the present day. However, as in other respects, a reservation was possible maintaining the previous regime. The system of 'comparison of terms' is firmly established. If the terms of the two relevant countries (the country where protection is claimed and the country of origin of the work or the country of which the author is a national) differ, the length of protection is governed by the term in the country where protection is claimed, but it must not exceed the term fixed in the country of origin of the work.[6]

5. New categories of protected works
The list of protected works was increased by adding choreographic works and entertainment in dumb show if 'the acting form is fixed in writing or otherwise', works of architecture, and 'Cinematograph productions ... if the author had given the work a personal and original character'.[7] The 'reproduction by cinematography of a literary or artistic work' (ie a film) is 'protected as an original work'.

6. The recording right
The author of a musical work is given the exclusive right to authorise the 'adaptation of those works to instruments which can reproduce them mechanically'. He is also given the right to authorise the public performance of the work by means of such a recording.[8]

7. A compulsory licence
The Act introduced for the first time the possibility for member countries to apply a compulsory licence. Domestic legislation may determine 'reservations and conditions relating to the application of this article'[9] 'in relation to

adaptations of ... works to instruments which can reproduce them mechanically'. However if a country introduces a compulsory licence system the effect of such a system is 'strictly limited to the country which has put them in force'.[10] This limitation is enforceable. Such 'adaptations' ie phonograms imported into a member country 'without the authority of the interested parties', ie the representatives of the right owner, they shall be 'liable to seizure in that country'.[11]

The Berlin Act of 1908 was followed quickly by several national legislations both within the Union and without, on which it had an undoubtedly significant influence. Within the Union the German Copyright Act 1909 and the British Copyright Act 1911, which was extended throughout what was then the British Empire, are important examples. Outside the Union, the United States Copyright Act 1909 is the prime example.

1 Art 4/1.
2 Art 4/2.
3 Art 8.
4 Art 27.
5 Art 7.
6 Art 7/1 and 7/2.
7 Art 14.
8 Art 13/1.
9 Art 13/2.
10 Art 13/2.
11 Art 13/4.

C. The Additional Protocol (Berne 1914)

5.12 This Protocol introduced into the Convention the so-called 'Reprisal Clause':
Where a country outside the Union 'fails to protect in an adequate manner' works of Union country authors, Union countries could retaliate by deciding to 'restrict the protection given to the works of authors' who are citizens of such non-Union countries.

The relevant date for deciding whether an author is an author belonging to such non-union country against which reprisals are taken is the date of first publication of the work for which protection is claimed.

D. The Rome Act (1928)

5.13 This Act brought a consolidation and development of the rights granted by the Convention. The Rome Conference was the first conference attempting to deal with the new mass media. The main changes are set out below:

It added two new rights jure conventionis to the rights of authors:

(a) The so-called '*droit moral*'.[1] This right is defined as:
   (i) 'the right to claim authorship of the work'
   (ii) 'the right to object to any distortion, mutilation, or other modification' of the work 'which would be prejudicial to the honour or reputation' of the author.[2]
   As always when a new convention right is introduced, it was done by stages. The conditions under which the right can be exercised were left to the discretion of the national legislation of the member states and the 'moral' right, as opposed to the 'economic' rights, of the author was confined to his lifetime.

(b) The *broadcasting right*,[3] as distinct from the public performance right. The terminology was tentative, a sign that the new technological phenomenon was in its infancy: Broadcasting is described as 'communication of ... works to the public by radio-diffusion'.

The introduction of this new right was accompanied by another provision for a compulsory licence[4] in the Convention. National legislations 'may regulate the conditions under which the right ... shall be exercised'.[5] This gives each member country the option to decide whether it wants to subject the right to a compulsory licence or not. If it does the national law has to fulfil two conditions: it must not 'prejudice the moral right of the author', and it must provide for 'equitable remuneration' which, if the right owner and the right user could not agree, 'shall be fixed by the competent authority'.

In the case of *works of joint authorship* the Act gives effect to the indivisible nature of such a work, so that the term runs until 50 years after the death of the last surviving author.[6] This can add substantially to the length of protection for such works.[7]

Again a rule of comparison of terms was introduced:[8] if the author claiming protection is a national of a country where the term is shorter than in the country where he claims the protection, he can only claim the shorter term. However, a minimum is also laid down: the protection cannot expire before the death of the last surviving author.[9]

Cinematographic works which had been given a full copyright provided the author has given the work an original character[10] are now given protection even if the author has not exercised such originality, but the protection is only that of a photographic work.[11]

The system of reservations which the Berlin Act (1908) had introduced was removed. It had been introduced to further the extension of the Convention to as many countries as possible and had served that purpose. It was removed in order to further the other aim of the Convention for as much legal uniformity as possible. However, the removal was not complete: any reservations which had been made could be maintained, only no new reservations could be made.[12] However here too an exception was introduced for the translation right.[13] A country adhering to the Union after 1928 could still make a reservation to the translation right provided such reservation applies 'only to translations into the language or languages of that country.'[14]

1 See para 5.37 below.
2 Art 6 bis.
3 Art 11 bis.
4 For the system of compulsory licences, see para 4.33 above.
5 Art 11 bis (2).
6 Art 7 bis (1).
7 An example will illustrate: the libretto of Guiseppe Verdi's last two operas *Othello* and *Falstaff* were both by Arigo Boito, based on the two Shakespeare plays. Verdi died in 1901, Boito in 1918. The term for these two works (unlike the rest of Verdi's operas by other librettists) was to expire in 1968 instead of 1951. (It was in fact prolonged to allow for the time of exploitation lost by the war).
8 Art 7 bis (2).
9 Art 7 bis (3).
10 See para 5.11 above.
11 Art 14(2).
12 Art 27(1) and (2).
13 Art 8.
14 Art 25(3).

E. The Brussels Act (1948)

Structure and character of the Convention

5.14 It had been argued prior to 1948[1] that the words 'exclusive rights of authors' were only a kind of shorthand and all it meant was that states undertook to grant certain rights in their national legislations and the courts could therefore not apply any of the rights given by the convention even in jurisdictions where conventions were self applying[2] if the state concerned had not lived up to its obligation and the national law did not provide the right. It was argued that the wording of the Rome Act 1928[3] 'the countries of the Union shall be bound to make provision for the protection of the above mentioned works' support this contention. The wording of the Brussels Act[4] 'the works ... shall enjoy protection in all countries of the Union' now makes it clear, as does the General Report that it was the intention of the conference 'to assure protection based directly on the convention itself'. The Act also removed what had been considered a very serious shortcoming[5] with regard to the principle of national treatment.[6] The Rome Act 1928[7] provided that 'the provisions of the Convention shall not prevent a claim being made for the application of any wider provisions which may be made by the legislation of a country of the Union *in favour of foreigners in general*'. This had been interpreted to mean that authors could claim the wider protection of the national law only when it can be claimed by *all* foreigners, whereas the principle of national treatment demands that convention nationals are entitled to the same protection as the nationals of the jurisdiction concerned regardless of whether such protection is given to all foreigners by the national law. The offending words 'in favour of foreigners in general' were removed by the Conference.[8]

1 By Fritz Ostertag, the Director of the 'Berne Buro'.
2 See para 3.30 above.
3 Art 2(3).
4 Art 2(4).
5 See Alfred Baum *The Brussels Conference for the Revision of the Berne Convention* translated by the US Copyright Office, Washington, 1950.
6 Art 4.
7 Art 19, Rome Act.
8 Art 19, Brussels Act.

The term of protection
5.15 The 50 years pma had been optional as the term could be made the subject of a reservation. It was now made compulsory for Union countries. Therefore the system of comparison of terms is, from now on to apply only in cases where the laws of one of the countries to be compared exceeds the minimum period of 50 years pma.[1]

1 Art 7(1) and (2).

List of 'works'
5.16 Works of applied art, industrial designs and models which had become of great commercial importance, were added to the list of protected works.[1]

The Brussels Act (1948) is the first act which practically corresponds to the notion that copyright is in fact a bundle of rights concentrated in the hands of the copyright owner each of which can be exercised separately and deals with most of the ten major rights granted in the present (1971) Act.[2]

1 Art 2(1) and (5).
2 See paras 5.37 et seq.

1. *The droit moral* – article 6 bis
5.17 The moral right[1] was divided into the author's right during his lifetime, which is granted jure conventionis, and the right of his successors in title after his death, which was granted only as far as national laws permit.

1 See para 5.37 below.

2. The reproduction right

5.18 This is still only implied and was only spelt out in the Stockholm Act 1967.[1]

1 See para 5.38 below.

3. The translation right – article 8

5.19 This is granted as an absolute and exclusive right in its final form.[1]

1 See para 5.40 below.

4. The public performance right – article 11

5.20 Before 1948, the protection of Union works against public performance was based on article 4 granting Union authors national treatment but there had been no right jure conventionis. Such a right was now granted subject only to the possible reservations of articles 11 bis and article 13 which means that in cases of public performance by using phonograms or broadcasts for such performance, reservations can be made by national legislation.[1]

1 See para 5.41 below.

5. The public recitation right

5.21 This right[1] is still treated as part of the public performance right and not spelt out separately.

1 See para 5.42 below.

6. The broadcasting right – article 11 bis[1]

5.22 The broadcasting right had been established jure conventionis in 1928 subject to the possibility of compulsory licences. The right was extended from sound broadcasting to television by introducing the phrase 'wireless diffusion of signs, sounds or images'. Thus the right to authorise the televising of works was firmly established at a stage when the new medium was still in its infancy. This had to be balanced by concessions to the broadcasting industry. They demanded and obtained the extension of the possibility of a compulsory licence to television and to the use of loudspeakers for the communication to the public of sound or television broadcasts. These two rights were then debated as if they were of equal importance. The television right eventually proved of enormous importance, while the right of communication by loudspeaker is hardly ever of any significance.

The other clash between authors and broadcasters' lobbies was solved by a compromise. The broadcasters wanted, as part of their broadcasting right, the right to record their programmes for whatever purpose they need to do so, eg for the rebroadcasting of the programme or for the sale or exchange of the programme with other broadcasting organisations. The authors argued that two separate rights were involved. The compromise was the concept of 'ephemeral recordings'. The broadcasting organisations were not given the right to record works in their programmes on 'mechanical instruments' (ie sound carriers or picture carriers) jure conventionis. However, national legislations can permit such 'ephemeral recordings' to be made if the broadcasting organisation makes them 'by means of its own emissions'. They have, however, to be destroyed within a short period.

1 See para 5.43 below.

7. The right of adaptation – article 12

5.23 A very involved and confused provision[1] of the Rome Act 1928 was replaced by a simple and clear one. The author now has an exclusive right to authorise adaptations and arrangements, indeed any alteration of his work. That means he can refuse permission if he disapproved and can enforce his refusal. Once he has given his permission, the adapter or arranger acquires a copyright in his arrangement which is contained in article 2(2) where adaptations and arrangements are equated with translations.

1   Art 12.

8. *The recording right* – article 13

5.24   The Rome Act (1928) had treated recordings as an 'adaptation' of the work 'to instruments which can reproduce them mechanically'.[1] In fact a recording is the fixation on to a material support of a performance. It is the performance of the work which is being fixed, not the work itself. That performance, if not fixed, is ephemeral, ie vanishes and lives thereafter only in the memory of those who heard it or saw it. Once the fixation, ie the first recording, has been made, the pressing of discs or making of tapes was a mechanical and is now an electronic process which is similar in kind to making copies of a book, ie a reproduction process.

This posed four problems:

1. Should the legal fiction that recording was an 'adaptation' be maintained?
2. When should the author's right be exhausted? Ie should he, once he had authorised the recording have a distribution right ('droit de mise en circulation')?
3. What, if any right should the maker of the recording have?
4. Should the possibility of compulsory licences on the national level be maintained?

The first question was resolved by abandoning the fiction of the Rome Act and replacing the concept of adaptation by that of recording.[2] This clarified the right of the author but excluded from the Convention the right of the performer or the maker (producer) of the recording.

The second question was resolved by refusing a distribution right. The practical importance of this was that with a distribution right the author could, if a recording of his work was broadcast, claim a double remuneration: one for the performance of his work flowing from his performance right, and a second one (the so-called 'sur-tax') for the playing of the recording. Although a distribution right was thus not established jure conventionis, a sur-tax was in fact established in some countries by case law.[3]

The third question was decided against the maker of the recording. The proposal to give the maker of the first recording an exclusive right 'to permit its reproduction and a right to an equitable remuneration in all cases where the recording was used for public performances or for a public broadcast', was not adopted. It led however to a 'voeu' advising member states 'to examine ways and means of protecting record producers'. This 'voeu' linked the rights of the record producer with the rights of performers and broadcasting organisations.[4]

The fourth question was resolved by maintaining the possibility of compulsory licences in article 13/2, but stipulating that if a system of compulsory licences is introduced in respect of the recording, the author must be given the right to receive an equitable remuneration.

1   Art 13/1.
2   However, the concept of adaptation survives in some national laws, eg the German law treats the performer of a literary or artistic work for the purpose of recording it as an 'adapter' giving him thus a right in his recorded performance.

3 Eg France, Belgium. The fact that a claim for 10 million Belgian Francs on behalf of authors against the Belgian state radio was pending before the courts of the host country of the Diplomatic Conference, may have had some influence on the debates.
4 See para 8.01 below.

9. *The cinematographic right* – article 14

5.25 The treatment of the third major medium (films) presented similar difficulties to those encountered with recordings. The attempts made during the preparatory period, particularly by the Berne Buro, to protect 'the author' of a film, failed because it proved impossible to agree who was the author. To consider the producer as author was unacceptable to the delegations representing 'droit d'auteur' countries, as the producers in most cases are corporations and not physical persons, and to define who of the many individuals participating in the making of a film would qualify for personal authorship proved equally difficult. Thus the question was left to national legislations and the Convention contents itself with protecting the 'cinematographic work'. Some expressed the hope that if a new generation became used to regarding a film as a work to be protected by copyright they would eventually, in order to achieve legal certainty and some uniformity in the Convention, also accept the producer as the right owner.[1]

The distribution right of the author of the pre-existing work was recognised[2] whereas it had been refused in respect of recordings.[3] This may at first sight be surprising, but it is explained by economic factors. The recording rights of authors were concentrated nationally in the hands of Mechanical Rights Societies and internationally in the hands of BIEM ('Buro International de l'Edition Mechanique'). These organisations make bulk licensing agreements both with phonogram producers and broadcasters.

On the other hand the distribution right in films was of comparatively little importance because film producers make their contracts mostly with individual authors of the pre-existing works and are usually in an economically strong enough position to acquire the distribution right from these authors by assignment in the contract. There was therefore no opposition to a distribution right.

The qualification that a film was to be protected as a cinematographic work only if the work had 'an original character'[4] was dropped.

The express exclusion of the possibility of a compulsory licence by the Act[5] was due to the fact that during the preparatory work the opinion had been expressed that a film is a 'mechanical instrument' in the sense of article 13 and a compulsory licence could therefore have been applied to it by national legislation.

It is interesting to compare the solutions the Brussels Act 1948 adopted with regard to the three new media – broadcasts, phonograms and films, in articles 11, 13 and 14. Subject to certain exceptions such as broadcasts of news, current events and sport, recordings of birdsong or pure nature films, these media predicate a pre-existing literary or artistic work. It is debatable whether the process is something akin to adaptation or not, but at the end of it a new 'work' may be created – a broadcast, a phonogram, a film. These works are by definition derivative works. They are so treated in Anglo-Saxon jurisdiction but not in jurisdictions which are based on a 'droit d'auteur' as opposed to a copyright system. Furthermore, compulsory licences are rejected by the 'droit d'auteur' countries whereas they are with certain safeguards, accepted in copyright systems as serving the public interest. The result of many years of debate during the preparatory work for revision and culminating in the debates at the Diplomatic Conference was that, in the realms of recording and broadcasting, contracting states are free to introduce or maintain compulsory licence systems, in the realm of films they are not. The reason for the exclusion of films from the possibility of a compulsory licence is a practical one. Whereas film producers may have to acquire several pre-existing rights, they do not have to deal with thousands of works as broadcasters and phonogram producers do and therefore do not need it and did not press for it. The phonogram producers kept the possibility of a compulsory licence largely because it had been in the Convention since 1908 and the unanimity rule made it impracticable for the 'droit d'auteur' countries to get it out. The broadcasters obtained a compulsory licence provision by a show of considerable strength and political influence, based to a large extent on the fact that in most participating countries broadcasting in the 1940s was a state monopoly and therefore the broadcasters were closer to the governments making the decision than any of the other interests involved.

At the other end of the scale, the result was the converse: the film in the form of a 'cinematographic work' obtained protection 'as an original work',[6] the phonogram and the broadcast did not. This fact, supported by the 'voeu' expressed by the Conference, led to the speeding up of the preparations of a new convention which eventually established these rights, but outside the ambit of the Berne Convention.[7]

From a structural point of view the result is that with regard to the two most important technological advances, recording and broadcasting, the right of the author which at the start in 1886 was absolute, can be subjected to compulsory licences in convention countries. This development was to be taken a step further in 1967 when the reproduction right of the author was also subjected to possible compulsory licensing albeit only in developing countries and under strictly defined conditions.[8]

1 Alfred Baum, op cit.
2 Art 14.
3 Art 13.
4 Art 14/2.
5 Art 14/4.
6 Art 14.
7 Rome Convention (1961); see ch 8.
8 See paras 6.38 et seq.

10. *The 'droit de suite'* – article 14 bis

5.26 This right was introduced for the first time for original works of art (and manuscripts). It gives the author (painter, sculptor etc) the right to 'an interest in any sale of the work subsequent to the first disposal of the work by the author'.[1]

1 See para 5.53 below.

F. The Stockholm Act (1967)

5.27 The Brussels Act 1948 marked the end of a period. The structure of the Convention and the principal rights had been settled, a substantial number of states joined the Union (44 by 1 January 1952 and 55 by 1 January 1967) and the membership extended to most parts of the world. From now on new problems began to dominate the scene:

1. Who should be right owners? (neighbouring right owners)
2. How was the Convention to respond to the new technologies?
3. What was to be the relation between the Convention and the United States on the one hand and the Third World countries on the other?

By the time the next revision conference was convened in Stockholm in 1967 three events had taken place which had a bearing on these problems and on the Berne Convention: 1. The Universal Copyright Convention[1] was created in 1952 bringing the United States into the general framework of world-wide copyright conventions. 2. The 'voeu' of the Brussels conference had led to the creation of the Rome Convention in 1961 dealing with the rights of some new right owners.[2] 3. The Third World countries were pressing for a simpler convention with a lower level of protection.[3]

The Stockholm Conference had therefore to deal with two groups of problems: the general revision of the Berne Convention and the problem of accommodating the wishes of the developing countries which were members of the Union. The first was achieved by the revision of articles 1 to 20, the second by the revision of article 21 and the additional Protocol regarding developing countries.

However, the Protocol did not meet with general approval of either the interested parties or the governments concerned and never came into force as it never reached the required number of ratifications. After nearly four years of arduous work the Protocol was radically revised at the Paris Conference in 1971. On the other hand the revision of articles 1 to 20 was confirmed in 1971 with only minor alterations. Furthermore, a special treatment for the developing countries was incorporated into the Universal Copyright Convention[4] as well as into the Berne Convention, in almost identical terms.

Therefore the revision of articles 1 to 20 of the Berne Convention and the current text and structure of the Convention is treated here in the context of the Berne Convention, whereas the Appendix dealing with the developing countries which replaces the Protocol regarding developing countries and is for practical purposes identical with special provisions of the UCC is treated separately in joint form as applying to both conventions.[5]

1 See ch 6, below.
2 See ch 8, below.
3 See ch 6, below.
4 See para 6.38 et seq.
5 See para 6.38 et seq.

7. The Paris Act (1971)

5.28 In its title the Convention refers to 'the protection of literary and artistic works'. In article 1, the Convention speaks of the 'rights of authors in their literary and artistic works'. This raises two fundamental questions: 1. Who is an 'author' and 2. What is a 'work'?

(1) Who is an author?

5.29 The term 'author' is not defined in the Convention therefore the law of the state where protection is claimed decides who is an 'author'. The reason for this lack of definition is that the national laws of member states differ greatly on this point. French law and many systems derived from French law or influenced by it recognise only physical persons as authors (writers, composers, painters, sculptors etc). Anglo-Saxon legislations and others influenced by them recognise legal entities, eg film producers, record producers, broadcasting organisations as authors or original right owners.

Although the Convention does not define the term 'author', it creates a presumption[1] to the effect that if a person's name 'appears on the work in the usual manner' he is presumed to be the author. This shifts the burden of proof so that the infringer has to prove that person is not the copyright owner.

If the work is anonymous or pseudonymous the presumption is to the effect that the publisher is 'deemed to represent the author' and thus 'entitled to enforce the author's rights'.[2]

1   Art 15(1).
2   Art 15(3).

(2) What is a work?

5.30   The term 'work' is also not defined in the Convention therefore again the law of the state where protection is claimed decides what is a 'work'. The Convention gives a long list of works ranging from books and dramatic and dramatico-musical works to works of applied art and three-dimensional works relative to architecture, but they are only given by way of example. The list is not exhaustive. This follows from the words 'the expression "literary and artistic works" shall include every production ... such as ...'.[1] The contents of a work are not material for the protection afforded by the Convention. As the *WIPO Guide*[2] puts it: 'a medical textbook, a treatise on physics, a documentary on interplanetary space are protected not because they deal with medicine, physics or the surface of the moon, but because they are books and films'. The examples show that most but not all works are fixed on a material support (corpus mechanicum), eg a book, a musical score, a picture, a statue. Exceptions are the so-called 'oral works' like 'lectures, addresses, sermons and other works of the same nature' or 'choreographic works'.[3]

The problem presented by works not fixed on a material support has been greatly lessened by the provision of article 2(2) in the Paris Act which enables countries of the Union to stipulate in their national legislations that only works fixed in some material form shall be protected. The national legislation may require all works to be fixed or only specific categories of works. Such a requirement in a national law does not rank as a 'formality' forbidden under article 5(2).

The character, quality or the merit of the work is also immaterial. Judgments on the merit of a work may differ widely from country to country and from person to person but all the court in the country where protection is claimed has to find is that the subject matter for which protection is claimed is a work.

It is clear from the history and the whole tenor of the Convention that a work must be some kind of 'intellectual creation'. This term is actually used in article 2(5) as a requirement if collections such as encyclopaedias and anthologies are to be protected as works as opposed to each work forming part of the collection. It is generally assumed that this test should be applied if the question whether something not named in the list of works is a work or not, has to be decided.

The exclusion from protection of 'news of the day' in article 2(8) is another pointer in this direction. Whilst news of the day and miscellaneous facts 'having the character of mere items of press information' are excluded, the implication seems to be that if a journalist although reporting or working on the news of the day brought to such reporting 'a sufficient element of intellectual creation'[4] then he creates a work and will get a copyright.

This test of the intellectual effort required which will have to be applied by the court in the country where protection is claimed is possibly more stringent than the test applied in some Anglo-Saxon countries. In the United Kingdom for instance a football coupon which only involves the setting out of all the matches played during a week listing the home team first, was held to enjoy a copyright[5] on the grounds that although it is a simple thing to do, if someone else does it and you copy it you ought to pay for it.

Originality is not required. A literal and totally inartistic translation of a French poem into English is a work although any third year language student should be able to do it with a dictionary. So is a very poor adaptation of the triumphal march from *Aida* for a band although there are dozens of similar adaptations in existence and every third year music student should be able to make one.[6]

Novelty is also not a requirement. A photograph of the Eiffel Tower taken by a tourist or a press photographer is certainly not novel, there are hundreds of them, but because of the angle chosen (from a pavement, from a building) the lighting (at night or in sunshine) the foreground (a girl in front of the Eiffel Tower) the background (cloud formation) etc are different every time and chosen by the photographer it constitutes a work.

That the list of works in the Convention is only there by way of example and is not exhaustive has two good reasons. The first is that because of the constant inventiveness of the human mind and the rapid progress of technology, there may tomorrow be new objects which are considered worthy of copyright protection and thus, applying the analogy of torts in Anglo-Saxon law, the 'categories of works' are never closed. The second reason is that in many countries the list of works includes things like recordings or broadcasts, which are not works in other countries.

1 Art 2(1).
2 The Masouyé/Wallace *WIPO Guide to the Berne Convention* is published by WIPO. It was written by Claude Masouyé (Director of the Copyright and Public Information Department of WIPO) and translated into English by William Wallace (formerly Assistant Comptroller in the Industrial Property and Copyright Department at the Department of Trade in Britain). It is succinct and couched in admirably clear and simple language. Although WIPO rightly stresses that by its constitution it is not its function to interpret conventions, this Guide is bound to acquire great persuasive authority whenever national courts have to interpret the convention.
3 Although these works too are now very often reduced to 'writing' in a special form of notation.
4 *WIPO Guide to Berne* 2.27.
5 *Ladbroke (Football) Ltd v William Hill (Football) Ltd* [1964] 1 WLR 273, HL.
6 Art 2(3).

5.31 Works of applied art and industrial designs and models.[1] There are three possible cases of protection of works of applied art:

(1) Those protected in the country of origin as works. They are protected as works in all Union countries.

(2) Those protected in the country of origin 'solely as designs and models' (usually by special legislation) and protected in the country where protection is claimed. They get in the Union country where protection is claimed only the protection that country gives to designs and models.

(3) Those protected in the country of origin 'solely as designs and models' and claiming protection in a Union country that does not grant such special protection. They get protection jure conventionis. This means a term of protection of a minimum of 25 years from the making of the work under article 7(4) of the Convention without any formalities such as registration.

This is another example of solving the problem whether some subject matter is a 'work' or not, by recognising it as a work but giving it a much shorter term than would be the case if it were a literary or artistic work.

1 Art 2(7).

(3) Which works are protected? – article 2

5.32 The conditions to be fulfilled for a work to be protected under the Convention are known as 'points of attachment'. The expression is a literal translation of the French 'points de rattachement' and means the circumstances relating to the work which attach it to the Convention thereby giving it protection jure conventionis. English jurisprudence currently uses the term 'connecting factor'.[1]

For published works the Convention used up to 1967 only the geographical criterion, ie the country of first publication. This is explained by the history of the Convention which from its origin put the emphasis on publication. This was fully justified as published works are the overwhelming majority of works and once the work was published the right owner (apart from moral rights) was usually the publisher and it is the place of publication which in all but exceptional cases is in practice the connecting factor. Only for unpublished works (a small minority) is the person of the author the connecting factor.

However, in 1967 a fundamental change was made.[2] A personal criterion, ie nationality (or habitual residence) of the author, was added to the geographical criterion of the place of first publication.

The Convention now protects the works, published or unpublished, of an author who is a national of a Union country or has his habitual residence in such a country. In times when more and more authors live in countries other than the country of their birth, either from choice or for political reasons or reasons of taxation this is a very important change.[3]

The following are connecting factors:
1. If the author is a national of a country of the Union or has his habitual residence in a country of the Union, his works are protected regardless of whether the work is published or unpublished. Article 3(1)(a) and article 3(2).
2. If first publication takes place in a country of Union. Article 3(1)(b).
3. If simultaneous publication takes place in a country of Union. Article 3(1)(b).
4. If the work is a film and 'the maker' has his headquarters in a country of Union. Article 4(a).[4]
5. If the work is a work of architecture erected in a country of Union. Article 4(b).
6. If the work is a work incorporated in a building or structure located in a country of Union. Article 4(b).

1 See para 3.24 above.
2 See *WIPO Guide to Berne* 3.1.
3 It is an open question whether for instance a work of a Russian author written and published in Russia after he has emigrated to France or Britain and now has his habitual residence there, becomes a protected work.
4 This point of attachment was added in Stockholm (1967). It is the first time the Convention recognises, albeit only by implication, that a corporation can be a copyright owner since 'the maker' is nearly always a legal and not a physical person. This step, which must have been hard for the protagonists of the 'droit d'auteur' to agree to, was taken as Masouyé/Wallace point out because it was clear that it was in the interest of the 'authors' as well as the 'makers', because this 'subsidiary' criterion provides an additional point of attachment and thereby gives protection to films which would otherwise not be protected.

(4) What is publication? – article 3(3) and (4)

5.33 From its inception publication has been the linchpin of the Convention, as in practice nearly all works which are successful and are therefore the subject of copyright transactions are published works. The definition of publication however has been developed over the years. The original Convention contained none. The Berlin Act 1908 and the Rome Act 1928[1] contained a very loose definition of published works: 'works copies of which have been issued to the public'. This made the point that publication can only take place if the public has access to a corpus mechanicum, a physical object incorporating the work. It explicitly excluded[2] performance or exhibition of a work. The Brussels Act 1948[3] narrowed the definition by adding that the work must not only have been issued to the public, but 'made available in sufficient quantities'. The Paris Act 1971 seeks to define 'sufficient quantities' by adding the proviso 'that the availability of such copies has been such as to satisfy the reasonable requirements of the public, having regard to the nature of the work'.

The new definition contains three ingredients:

1. *Publication must take place with the consent of the author.* This had always been understood but is now specifically stated so that publication of a stolen manuscript or of a typewritten copy given to the publisher with the request not to publish it until a certain event (eg after the author's death or after his escape from his native country) is not publication. Copies of a work made under compulsory licence also do not constitute publication unless the author has consented to it.
2. *Public performance in the widest sense (including broadcasting) does not constitute publication.* This is spelt out in the text.[4]
3. *The nature of the work dictates the answer to the question whether the 'reasonable requirements of the public' are satisfied.* This is new and has consequences particularly for the new media, records and films including television films.[5]

Availability to the public does not necessarily mean available to be bought by the public. Whereas books or records are put on sale, films are not, but copies are hired out to exhibitors. Orchestral parts of musical works are often lent and not sold to concert impresarios or recording companies. Publication can thus take place by lending copies, or even by free distribution.

The quantity of copies made available to satisfy the definition depends on the nature of the work. Masouyé points out:

> 'it is not enough to show, in the window in a single bookshop, a dozen copies of a book which has enjoyed massive success in some other country outside the Union. Again a single copy of a cinematographic work sent to a festival to be shown before a restricted audience does not meet the conditions. In neither case are the reasonable requirements of the public satisfied'.[6]

'Simultaneous publication' (article 3(4)) is publication by two or more countries within 30 days of first publication.

This is of particular importance if the first publication takes place in a country outside the Union followed by simultaneous publication in a country of the Union. In the past the most important examples have been those of first publication in the United States, before ratifications of the UCC and simultaneous publication in Canada or the United Kingdom[7] and before the 1914-18 war first publication in Russia and simultaneous publications in Germany. (This was known as 'the backdoor to Berne'.) Before 1948 it was thought that publication may have to take place on the same day but the Brussels Act (1948) extended the period to 30 days.

1 Art 4(4).
2 Art 4(4) (second sentence).
3 Art 4(4).

4   Art 3(3) last sentence.
5   See Bergström Report of Stockholm Conference, para 50.
6   *WIPO Guide to Berne* p 28.
7   See *Nimmer on Copyright* Vol 3, 17.12.

(5) The principle of national treatment – article 5(1)

5.34   The principle means that the authors of Union works, ie works protected by the Convention, enjoy in all Union countries, other than in the country of origin of the work, the same protection as nationals of that country in addition to the rights they enjoy jure conventionis.[1]

Example: An author who is a national of Sri Lanka (Ceylon) who first published a work in India enjoys in the United Kingdom a complete reproduction right if he is a writer, but not a 'droit de suite' if he is a painter. The work is a Union work and enjoys the same reproduction right as a British work but not a 'droit de suite' as British works do not enjoy such a right.

1   Art 5(1).

(6) The principle of automatic protection and absence of formalities – article 5(2)

5.35   The right is subject to no formalities and is independent, ie not dependent on whether the right exists in the country of origin.

A 'formality' is any condition on which the existence or the exercise of the right depends. Registration, payment of fees on registration, deposit of copies with certain national institutions are all formalities, but only if the existence of the copyright or its exercise depends on the compliance with such conditions does it amount to a 'formality' in the sense of the Convention. Many countries for instance require the deposit of a copy of every book published in the country in the National Library, but non-compliance does not lose the author his copyright although it may render him liable to an action or even a fine. It is therefore not a formality. In the United States for instance, which has a registration system, non-registration does not deprive the author completely of his copyright but he cannot sue for an infringement without registering his copyright first. Thus, if the United States became a member of the Berne Convention the registration system as such would not constitute a violation of the Convention, because the 'existence' of the right does not depend on it. However the necessity to register before bringing an action would probably be regarded as a 'formality' as it negates the 'exercise' of the right without such registration.

The protection of the rights enjoyed jure conventionis is granted free of any formalities whatsoever. This is one of the major differences between the Berne Convention and the UCC where the symbol © and the year date of publication is permitted as a maximum of formalities which can be required by national legislation.[1] This automatic protection is independent of any protection the work may enjoy in its country of origin. The country of origin may subject the work to any formalities it chooses as a matter of domestic law, but outside the country of origin the author if he is a 'Union author' is entitled to protection in any country of the Union without any formalities. In the courts of the Union country where he claims protection he need not prove that he has complied with the formalities which may be required in the country of origin of the work. Although as a rule a Union author will probably sue in the country where the infringement has taken place, there is no need to do so. If for instance the infringer has no visible assets in that country but has assets in another Union country the right owner can sue there and still has no need to prove that any formalities have been complied with.

1   See para 6.08 below.

(7) The 'country of origin' of a work – articles 5(3) and (4)

5.36 The Convention lays down the rules to find the country of origin of a work in article 5(4). These rules are to be applied when deciding whether a work is protected and when deciding the term of protection. There are several rules:

1. If the work is first published in a country of the Union that country is the country of origin.[1]
2. If the work is published simultaneously in several countries of the Union and the term of protection is longer in one country than in another, the country which grants the shorter term is the country of origin of the work.[2]
3. If the work is published simultaneously in a country of the Union and in a country outside the Union, the Union country is the country of origin.[3]
4. If the work is first published outside the Union, the country of the Union of which the author is a national is the country of origin.[4]
5. If the work is unpublished, the country of the Union of which the author is a national is the country of origin.[5]
6. Protection in the country of origin is a matter of domestic law. 'However, when the author is not a national of the country of origin of the work for which he is protected' he gets the same protection in that country as national authors.[6]

Examples will illustrate the position, choosing France and Germany as the countries of the Union and the United States and Soviet Union as the countries outside the Union.

Rule 1
The country of origin of a work first published in France is France.

Rule 2
The country of origin of a work published simultaneously in France and Germany is France because the term in Germany is 70 years pma and in France only 50 years pma.

Rule 3
The country of origin of a work simultaneously published in the Soviet Union and in Germany is Germany.

Rule 4
The country of origin of a work first published in the United States by a German national is Germany.

Rule 5
The country of origin of an unpublished work of a French national is France.

Rule 6
If an American or a Russian author first publishes a work in France, the country of origin of the work is France and he will get the same protection as a French author gets when he first publishes in France.[7]

If an author who is a national of a country of the Union publishes a work at home (in the country of which he is a national) the Convention does not apply. This would be a national situation as no foreign element is involved and the Convention only deals with international situations.

1 Art 5(4)(a) (first sentence).
2 Art 5(4)(a) (second sentence) and art 7(8).
3 Art 5(4)(b).
4 Art 5(4)(c).
5 Art 5(4)(c).
6 Art 5(3).
7 This is a case where the principle of the country of origin and the principle of national treatment produce a result which does not conform with the rules of material reciprocity. In some countries the national author who first publishes a work abroad may not get the same protection as he would get at home.

(8) The ten major rights – articles 6 bis and 8–14

1. The 'droit moral' – article 6 bis   5.37
2. The reproduction right – article 9   5.38
3. The translation right – article 8   5.40
4. The public performance right – article 11   5.41
5. The public recitation right – article 11 ter   5.42
6. The broadcasting right – article 11 bis   5.43
7. The right of adaptation – article 12   5.45
8. The recording right – article 13   5.46
9. The film (cinematographic) right – article 14   5.47
10. The 'droit de suite' – article 14 ter   5.53

1. *The 'droit moral'* – article 6 bis

5.37 The moral rights of the author now extend beyond his lifetime 'at least until the expiry of the economic rights'.[1] However a kind of reservation is possible here. Countries whose legislation at the moment of ratification do 'not provide for the protection after the death of the author of all moral rights may provide that some of these rights may, after his death, cease to be maintained'.[2]

Moral rights are inalienable which means that they can be exercised even if the author has purported to transfer his moral rights. It is a protection of the author so to speak against himself similar to the protection most legislations accord to minors. This provision 'stops entrepreneurs from turning the moral right into an immoral one'.[3] The means of redress are governed by the law of the country where protection is claimed. The three basic moral rights are:

1. The right of publication ('droit de divulgation') which enables the author to decide when and where or whether he wants to publish his work.
2. The right of paternity ('droit de paternité') which is the right to claim authorship once the work is published.
3. The right of integrity ('droit au respect de l'oeuvre') which is the right of the author to safeguard his reputation by preserving the integrity of his work.

For a more detailed exposition of these three rights see paras 4.17 et seq.

1 Art 6 bis, para 2.
2 This is of importance in Anglo-Saxon jurisdictions where certain moral rights have to be enforced by an action for defamation which can only be maintained during the plaintiff's lifetime.
3 *WIPO Guide to Berne* 6 bis. 6.

2. *The reproduction right* – article 9

5.38 This is the original and still the most essential right of most authors. It is therefore astonishing that it was not contained in the original Act or any of the early Acts. It was not expressly stated in the Convention until 1967. The reason is probably that it was always understood that the author must have this right jure conventionis but it proved difficult to find a formula which would cover both present and future processes of reproduction. The nettle was finally grasped in Stockholm (1967) and the new text of article 9(1) is both lapidary and embracing both present and future processes: 'the exclusive right of authorising the reproduction of these works in any manner or form.' This covers all methods of fixing a work on any material or transferring it from one support to another, ranging from engraving and lithography to all modern printing processes and photocopying.

It is interesting that by article 9(3) it is also made to cover all sound and visual recordings although a recording is not a reproduction in the strict sense. A reproduction as the word indicates is to produce a copy of a 'production', that is in this context to copy a work already fixed on a material support or to transfer it from one kind of material support to another, eg from typing to printing or from a photograph of a picture to a colour print in a book. Recording on the other hand is the first fixation of sounds or images and sounds on a material support. If what is to be fixed is a work, it is not the fixation of a work but the fixation of the performance of a work (the singing of a song, the playing of a symphony, the recitation of a poem). That first fixation is known as 'the master' or 'the matrix'. The making of copies from that matrix thereafter in form of discs or tapes etc is a reproduction in the true sense. The Stockholm text covers both the first recording and the subsequent copies made from it by providing in article 9(3) that all recordings 'shall be considered as a reproduction for the purposes of this Convention'. This is the same kind of legal fiction that first expressed a film as 'a process similar to photography'. It is neither technologically nor logically accurate but it will serve its practical purpose.

The right not given in the Convention which exists in many national laws is the 'distribution right', sometimes called 'circulation right'. This right where it exists entitles the copyright owner to follow his work beyond the reproduction stage, eg to designate that copies of his book may be sold in countries A and B, but not in countries C and D.

5.39 Exceptions from the reproduction right – article 9(2). The formulation of the exceptions from the general reproduction right proved particularly difficult at the Stockholm Conference and a special working party was set up for the purpose. The problem was posed by the development of technology since the Brussels Act (1948) which had produced two new phenomena: reprography, the private copying of written material in large numbers, and home taping, the private copying of recordings (mainly of music) both from sound carriers (discs and tapes) and carriers of sounds and images (films, videograms) and off the air from sound and television broadcasts.[1]

The Convention leaves it to national legislation to permit reproduction of protected works 'in certain special circumstances'. This leaves to the national legislation the task of defining these special circumstances. The most common circumstances are 'private use' for 'purposes of teaching or research'. However, any exception must comply with two conditions which are cumulative. This is most clearly set out in the Report of the Stockholm Conference:[2]

> 'If it is considered that reproduction conflicts with the normal exploitation of the work, reproduction is not permitted at all. If it is considered that reproduction does not conflict with the normal exploitation of the work, the next step would be to consider whether it does not unreasonably prejudice the legitimate interests of the author. Only if such is not the case would it be possible in certain special cases to introduce a compulsory licence, or to provide for use without payment. A practical example might be photocopying for various purposes. If it consists of producing a very large number of copies, it may not be permitted, as it conflicts with a normal exploitation of the work. If it implies a rather large number of copies for use in industrial undertakings, it may not conflict with a normal exploitation of the work,

but it may not unreasonably prejudice the legitimate interests of the author, providing that, according to national legislation, an equitable remuneration is paid. If a small number of copies is made, photocopying may be permitted without payment, particularly for individual or scientific use'.

Perhaps the most important point to note[3] is that it is not a question of prejudice to the legitimate interests of the author. All copying is prejudicial to the interests of the copyright owner to some extent. The question is whether the prejudice is reasonable or unreasonable. There is little doubt that making one copy of an article from a learned journal for private use may be reasonable although it does deprive the journal of a sale and the author of a royalty. On the other hand there is also little doubt that a large corporation making fifty copies of the article and sending one to each of its subsidiaries would be unreasonable. The answer to the problem posed by the Convention has to be given in two stages:

In the first place by the national legislation which formulates the exception permitted by the Convention, and in the second place by the national courts interpreting that formula in the national law. Only if the national law chose to disregard one or both of the conditions laid down by article 9(2) would the member country be in breach of the Convention.

The *Guide*[4] concludes that 'in cases where there would be serious loss of profit for the copyright owner, the law should provide him with some compensation (a system of compulsory licensing with equitable remuneration)'.

Two national legislations provide examples on these lines: the German Copyright Law 1965[5] which raises the compensation to the copyright owner for private copying in the form of home taping by a charge on the apparatus used for fixing the sounds (tape recorder) or the sounds and images (video recorder) and the Austrian Copyright Amendment Law 1980[6] which raises the compensation from the material on which the sounds (tape) or the images and sounds (videotape) are fixed. The important point about both legislations is that they remain within the framework of the Convention treating the amounts raised not as an impost or a levy which could be used for any purpose the government considered proper but as a compensation or royalty due to the copyright owner or owners emanating from their reproduction right.[7]

1 See paras 12.16 and 12.12 below.
2 Bergström Report para 85.
3 See *WIPO Guide to Berne* 9.8.
4 *WIPO Guide to Berne* 9.8.
5 S 5(5).
6 Art 42(5).
7 See Report of the Working Group on the use of video cassette and videodiscs, Copyright (1977) p 87. Also Ljungman 'La Fonction du droit d'auteur dans la societé contemporaire' RIDA (April 1976) p 51. The author hopes that governments will steer between 'the Scylla of state control and the Charybdis of a collective system'. Collova 'Reproduction sonore et visuelle pour l'usage personel' INTERGU Vol 57, 1979. Stewart, 'Home Taping' European Intellectual Property Review (EIPR) (July 1980) p 267.

3. *The translation right* – article 8

5.40 This right, applying of course mainly to literary works, is a fundamental right which was both at the centre of the Convention at the start of the Convention in 1886[1] and at the most recent revision in 1971.[2] In the first place it was a right for ten years from publication of the original work with limits imposed on its scope (the so-called 'ten-year' regime).[3] At the 1971 revision the limits were put on its exercise by giving the possibility of granting compulsory licences to developing countries. The right was recognised as fundamental in 1886 as translation gives literary works their international dimension and with the advent of modern communications it has even more increased economic value as well as being essential to all educational activities of developing countries.

Although this does not appear in the 1971 text, the General Report of the Stockholm Conference shows that it was agreed that the so-called 'small exceptions' apply to the translation right.[4] They are:
Speeches in press and broadcasts – article 2 bis (2).
Special cases of reproduction – article 9(2).
Quotations and press summaries – article 10(1).
Use of works by way of illustration for teaching – article 10(2).
Articles in newspapers or broadcasts – article 10 bis (1).
Reports of current events – article 10 bis (2).
In all these cases the rules of fair practice have to be observed and moral rights respected.

It is a moot point whether these exceptions also apply in cases of the compulsory licences under articles 11 bis and 13, in other words, whether the right given by these compulsory licences to use the work without the author's consent also allows the user to translate it.[5]

1   Art 5 of 1886 Act.
2   Art 8 of 1971 Act and art 11 of the Annex. Some reservations made under the earlier Acts have been abandoned only in recent years, eg Japan 31 December 1980.
3   See paras 5.10 above, and 6.49 below.
4   Bergström Report, paras 205, 210.
5   Bergström Report, para 205.

4. *The public performance right* – article 11
5.41   This right applies to dramatic, dramatico-musical and musical works. Public performance of literary works is covered by article 11 ter[1] which is parallel to article 11 in all respects.[2]

The performance must be in public. A performance of the work in private is not covered by the Convention. Where the borderline between public and private performance lies is to be decided by the national courts according to the circumstances but it is generally agreed that a performance before a small invited audience whether in a home or in a hired hall is not a public performance. The general public must have access to the performance to make it a public one. On the other hand if the public has access it is not necessary for an entrance fee to be charged. A concert given in a public park or a hall to which everyone has access is a public performance.

The performance can be given 'by any means or process'. This means that the performance need not be 'live', but can be by means of phonograms or films.[3]

If the public performance is communicated to a wider public than that attending the performance this could be done by broadcasting, in which case article 11 bis applies. It could also be done by loudspeaker to another hall or (of much greater economic importance) by cable to subscribers in other buildings. In such cases it is covered by article 11(1)(ii) as a 'communication to the public of the performance'.

Public performance of a translation of the work is protected whilst the original work is in copyright.[4]

1   Since the Brussels Act (1948); see para 5.20 above.
2   See para 5.42 below.
3   The public performance by means of cinematographic works is also covered by art 14(1)(ii).
4   Art 12(2).

5. *The public recitation right* – article 11 ter
5.42   This right is a complete parallel of the public performance right in

article 11, the only difference being that the subject of the former is 'dramatic and musical works' and the subject of the latter is 'literary works'. Thus the performance of a play in a theatre falls under article 11 whereas a reading of the same play in a lecture theatre or concert hall without costumes and decor would be a recitation under article 11 ter.

The separate treatment of these two rights has historical reasons. Many national laws did not grant a recitation right at all and it was therefore introduced in the Brussels Act 1948. In the Stockholm Act 1967, article 11 ter was redrafted so as to mirror article 11.

6. *The broadcasting right* – article 11 bis

5.43 Authors of literary and artistic works have the absolute right to authorise the broadcasting of their works. Broadcasting includes both sound radio and television.

What gives rise to the right is the emission of sounds or of sounds and images. It is not necessary for such signals to be actually received by anyone. Once the broadcast is made, the author has secondary rights. He has the exclusive right to authorise the communication to the public, whether by wire or not if the communication 'is made by an organisation other than the original one'.[1] This act of wire diffusion is different from the one covered by article 11(1). It deals with the diffusion of someone else's broadcast[2] whereas 11(1) deals with the case where the wire diffusion organisation originates the programme.

The result is that the author has – subject to the existence of a compulsory licence in some countries permitted by article 13 bis (2) – an absolute right to authorise or to forbid:

(1) The sound broadcasting of his work, article 11 bis (1)(i).
(2) The televising of his work, article 11 bis (1)(i).
(3) Communication of such broadcasts to the public over wires, ie wire diffusion (CATV), article 11 bis (1)(ii).
(4) Communication of such broadcasts to the public without wires, eg by another broadcasting station (re-broadcasting), article 11 bis (1)(ii).
(5) Communication of the broadcast by loudspeaker, article 11 bis (1)(iii).

Broadcasting is not defined in the Convention (although it is defined in many national legislations). The meaning of broadcasting is defined in the Radio-Communication Regulations. It has two essential characteristics: It must be effected by the emission of Hertzian waves and the broadcast must be directly received by the general public.

It is doubtful whether transmission of a signal via satellite with the help of an earth station is broadcasting. The argument against it is that the transmission via satellite is not intended for the general public. It is intended for reception by the earth station which then transmits it to the general public. There seems no doubt however that once broadcasts transmitted via satellite become 'direct satellite broadcasts' that is directly receivable by the general public who will only need a specially fitted receiver this will be broadcasting in the accepted sense.

The author also has an exclusive right to authorise the communication of the broadcast by loudspeaker or, in case of television, on a screen in a public place, such as a hotel or restaurant, an aircraft or a store.

This means that CATV systems, hotels or stores using sound radio or television, need a licence (usually issued by the national Authors' Society). This use of the work is not covered by the authorisation to broadcast the work. The justification for these secondary rights is that an additional audience is created. By analogy to the law of contracts it can be said that this additional audience was not within the contemplation of the parties (the author and the broadcasting organisation) when authority to broadcast the work was given. In the case of a compulsory licence system, the authority to broadcast is given by law but the equitable remuneration payable by the broadcaster does not cover the further secondary uses of the broadcast.

However, when dealing with the absolute rights of the author jure conventionis according to article 11 bis (1) it has to be borne in mind that article 11 bis (2) leaves the national legislation a very wide discretion in the treatment of the broadcasting right including the application of a compulsory licence system. As most countries deal with the broadcasting right in their national legislation because of its great social and political importance, the right of authors to authorise the broadcasting of their works relies in reality mainly on the principle of national treatment rather than on these rights jure conventionis.

On the other hand the Convention does lay down minimum rights to which the author is entitled under the Convention jure conventionis whatever the national regime – article 11 bis (2). They are:

1. A right to equitable remuneration.
2. Respect for his moral rights defined in article 6 bis.
3. If a country establishes a compulsory licence system its application is limited territorially to that country.

With regard to the 'equitable remuneration' the number of works used by broadcasting organisations is so large that in most cases blanket licensing is the only possible way of dealing with the matter. The 'fair remuneration' has thus to be agreed between one or more collecting societies and the broadcasting organisation. If there is no agreement, usually because negotiations have failed, the national legislation has to provide that the compensation 'shall be fixed by a competent authority'.[3] This means either the fixing of the level of the compensation by statute or regulation or by an administrative decision of a ministry or a named official, or the setting up of a tribunal to adjudicate or arbitrate between the right owners and the broadcasting organisations. The last possibility, ie a tribunal, is no doubt the solution closest to the wording and the spirit of the Convention as, particularly in the case of state owned or state controlled broadcasting organisations, a remuneration will hardly be seen to be 'equitable' if the government which is a party to the suit becomes the judge in its own case, by fixing the remuneration.

1   Art 11 bis (1)(ii).
2   See *WIPO Guide to Berne* 11 bis. 9.
3   Art 11 bis (2).

5.44 It seems to be clear from the structure of the Convention that the broadcasting right and the recording right are separate rights and that therefore authority to broadcast a work does not include authority to record it. However, in practice, most broadcasts are now made from sound or video recordings. This sometimes has technical reasons (better sound and picture can be obtained), sometimes artistic reasons (editing or combining separate recordings is necessary), sometimes practical reasons (programming is greatly facilitated if artists can be recorded when they are available instead of at the time when the broadcast has to go out), sometimes legal or political reasons (in the case of artistically or politically sensitive material, broadcasting organisations sometimes like to see or hear what is to be broadcast before it is). Prerecording of broadcasts has therefore become a virtual necessity. The Convention restates the position that permission to broadcast a work does not include permission to record it in article 11 bis (3). However, in article 11 bis (3), second sentence, it enables national legislations to regulate so-called 'ephemeral recordings'. If such recordings are to be made without permission they must fulfil three conditions:

1. They must be transitory. The term 'ephemeral' which in its Greek origin and in its biological application means lasting only one day, must not be taken literally, but be applied reasonably to mean: 'to be kept only for a short time'. National laws usually provide for between one and six months.
2. They must be made by the broadcasting organisation's 'own facilities', meaning the technical facilities of the broadcasting organisation. It excludes recordings made by third parties even if commissioned by the broadcasting organisation.
3. They must be made 'for their own broadcasts'. This means that such recordings cannot be sold, they cannot be lent or given to other broadcasting organisations or – the most frequent case – exchanged with other broadcasting organisations, without permission of the right owner and they cannot be sold to the public.

However, on one of the most important points, whether such ephemeral recordings have to be paid for or not, article 11 bis (3), unlike article 11 bis (2), is silent. It is therefore possible for national legislations, whilst limiting the use of ephemeral recordings in accordance with the three conditions, to allow the making and temporary use of such recordings without any remuneration.

The national law can provide – usually for one copy – to be kept in official archives.

Ephemeral recordings are of importance mainly in countries where the broadcasting right is subject to a compulsory licence because in countries where there is no compulsory licence the author (mainly in the case of plays or novels) or the collecting society (in the case of music) can and usually does provide for a remuneration for the recording of the work in the same contract which authorises the broadcasting of it.

7. The right of adaptation – article 12

5.45 The author has the exclusive right to authorise any alteration of his work. What amounts to an alteration is not defined and therefore left to the courts to decide in each case. The Convention speaks of 'adaptations, arrangements and other alterations' of the work, which suggests the ejusdem generis rule of interpretation. This would mean that minor alterations can be disregarded provided they do not affect the moral rights of the author[1] and only alterations that amount to something of the kind of an adaptation or an arrangement need the permission of the author. However every case has to be judged on its merits.

Article 12 has to be read together with article 2(3).[2] Together they mean that there are two rights in any derivative work such as adaptations or arrangements – the right of the author of the original work and the right of the author of the derivative work, the former under article 2(3), the latter under article 12.

Anyone wanting to perform or broadcast an arrangement has to get the authorisation of both the original author and the arranger. Both can sue an infringer independently or jointly. The arranger has an independent right of action under article 2(2) even if he made the arrangement without the permission of the author or if the original work is in the public domain. Whether the alterations of a work are sufficiently substantial or original to constitute an arrangement, ie to merit a copyright, is a question of fact to be decided in each case by the courts of the country where protection is claimed.

With the advent of 'musicals', which are often based on plays or novels, adaptation of novels or plays for radio and television and films, this, now very clear provision has proved of great benefit.

1 Art 6 bis.
2 See *WIPO Guide to Berne* p 76.

8. *The recording right* – article 13

5.46 The right relates to musical and dramatico-musical works. The form of dealing with the authors' recording right is a little odd at first sight because instead of granting the right as other articles do, this article deals with the possibility open to Union countries of introducing compulsory licence systems. The explanation lies in the history of the provision. The Brussels Act, in article 13(1), granted both the recording right and the right of public performance by such recordings. The Stockholm text however assimilated the recording right to the reproduction right and dealt with it in article 9(1). It also dealt with the public performance right in article 11(1) granting it for public performance 'by any means or process', thus making no distinction between a live performance and a performance by means of sound carriers. Thus the simple statement that the author has the right to authorise the recording of his work and the right to authorise the public performance of such a recording was thought to be superfluous. The compulsory licence provision now contained in article 13(1) is based on the compulsory licence concept of Britain and Germany[1] that once the author has given his consent to one recording of his work, other recordings can be made by other competing phonogram producers without prior authorisation against payment of an equitable remuneration. The reason behind such a provision is on the one hand not to deprive the author of his absolute right to allow or forbid the first recording of his work, on the other hand once he has given his authorisation to a recording, to avoid a monopoly and stimulate free competition between phonogram producers. Such competition is apt to benefit the author who wants as many uses of his work as possible and to benefit the public by offering a wide choice of recordings.

The new wording makes it clear that in a musical work that contains both words and music both the author of the words and the composer of the music must consent. Words and music 'are considered for this purpose, one entity'.[2]

The rules to be complied with by national legislations are the same as those prescribed for compulsory licences applying to the broadcasting right under article 11 bis (2), ie the compulsory licences have effect only in the country imposing them, the author must receive equitable remuneration and that remuneration will, if there is no agreement be decided by 'competent authority'.[3]

The only overt difference between the treatment of the compulsory licence systems in this article and in article 11 bis, is that here there is no reference to the compulsory licence having to be not prejudicial to the moral rights of authors. However as article 6 bis, granting the moral right, applies to all works including musical and musico-dramatic works this omission is probably of little significance.

The transitional provisions[4] seek to bring to an end the right of record producers to record without the authors' consent works which had been recorded once before 1908. That facility is now reduced to making new pressings of recordings made before 1908 and that only for two years after the country using a compulsory licence system becomes bound by the Paris Act 1971.

Giving effect to the limitation that compulsory licence systems 'shall apply only in the countries which have imposed them'[5] the Convention provides that if sound carriers are exported from a country imposing a compulsory licence system 'without permission from the parties concerned into a country where they are treated as infringing recordings'[6] they are liable to seizure.

1 See Bergström Report, Stockholm, 1967, para 236.
2 *WIPO Guide to Berne* 13.7.
3 Art 13(1).
4 Art 13(2).
5 Art 13(1).
6 Art 13(3).

9. *The film (cinematographic) right* – article 14 and 14 bis

5.47 There are two rights involved: the right of the author of a pre-existing work (article 14) and the right of the owner of the film work (article 14a)[1] The drafting is not easy to follow and one has to view it in the light of the history of the Convention. For over half a century the two main systems (copyright and 'droit d'auteur') held opposing views on the vital question of who should be regarded as the owner of the copyright in a film. As any revision of the Convention demands unanimity each side had a veto. If progress was to be made it could only be by a series of compromises. They had to be compatible with either of the two philosophies and practices of copyright. The wording of the two articles is the somewhat tortuous result of these compromises, but on analysis the meaning becomes quite clear.

1 The rights of the maker of film are dealt with in art 14 and art 14 bis, but they are also referred to in art 2(1) where cinematographic works are listed as protected works, in art 4(a) dealing with points of attachment of cinematographic works, in art 5(4)(c)(i) dealing with the country of origin of a cinematographic work, in art 7(2) dealing with the term of protection for such works and in art 15(2) dealing with the question of who can bring proceedings for infringement.

5.48 I *The rights of authors of pre-existing works* – article 14. The author has the exclusive right of authorising 'the cinematographic adaptation and reproduction' of his work and 'the distribution of the work thus adapted or reproduced'.[1]

Authors of pre-existing works are granted seven separate rights:

1. The adaptation right, eg turning a play or a novel into a film script.
2. The reproduction right, ie the right to record and multiply the acting or playing of that script (synchronisation).
3. The distribution right in the resulting film. This is important as films are as a rule not sold but hired out for showing in cinemas. It is the right to offer the film for exhibition.
4. The public performance right in the film, ie the showing of it in the cinemas.
5. The communication right, ie the right to communicate the film to the public by wire.
6. The broadcasting right. The right to show the film on television, which is covered not in this article but in article 11 bis.
7. The right to the 'subtitling or dubbing of texts'. This is adaptation of the film showing it in languages other than the original one. It is the equivalent to the translation right in a literary work.

1 Art 14(1)(i).

5.49 *The adaptation right in the film* – article 14(2). This means the adaptation of the film 'into any other artistic form'. If for instance a novel is by adaptation made into a film and that film, having been very successful is made, again by adaptation, into a play or a 'musical', the author who adapted the film into the musical would need not only the authorisation of the 'maker' of the film who had acquired all rights in the pre-existing works but also the separate authorisation of the author of the original novel.[1] In other words, the original author can follow the exploitation of his work through all seven stages and exercise his separate rights and presumably his moral right under article 6 bis at each stage.

The result is that although the whole transaction is normally covered by contract, if there were no contracts the author could forbid the use of his novel for a film script, he could then forbid the making of the film from that script, he could then forbid the exhibiting of the film generally or in certain countries, he could forbid the showing of it on television (except in countries with a compulsory licensing system for broadcasting) and even if he had authorised the televising of the film he could forbid it being shown by wire diffusion (CATV) companies to their subscribers. The fact that the author has all these separate rights is of course reflected in the terms of the contract. The countries of the Union are free to introduce any system they wish for the remuneration of the author for the exploitation of the cinematographic work, eg a participation in the receipts resulting from the exploitation.[2]

[1] For a national solution to the problem on the 'droit d'auteur' basis see: France, *l'affaire Tosca*, Cass Civ 22/6/1959, D 1960, J at p 129.
[2] See Report of Stockholm Conference 1967, para 323.

5.50 II *The rights of artistic contributors to the film* - article 14 bis. Whereas the rights of authors of pre-existing works had been dealt with in the Brussels Act 1948[1] and needed little change, the rights in the cinematographic work (the film) itself, dealt with in article 14 bis were very controversial. There are no less than four different systems applied in national legislation to deal with films.

System 1. The Anglo-Saxon jurisdictions give the copyright in the film to the 'maker' of the film. This is in most cases a corporate body which takes the initiative and the financial responsibility for making the film. The socialist countries where the maker is a state-owned corporation do the same. This system is usually referred to as the 'film-copyright system'. It is unacceptable to the philosophy of the 'droit d'auteur' countries mainly because they cannot concede that 'droit d'auteur' can originate in a company or corporation or in any entity other than an individual.

The other systems regard the film as a work of joint authorship. The right originates in the individuals creating the film which include the script writer, the writer of the scenario, the cameraman, the director, the star actors etc. These multiple copyrights have then to be acquired by the film maker. There are three such systems:

System 2. A group of jurisdictions (Austria, Italy, German Democratic Republic-DDR) operate a 'cessio legis' or 'presumptio juris et de jure'. The copyright originates with the individuals who create the cinematographic work but passes at the moment of creation by operation of law to the film maker.

System 3. A group of countries (France, German Federal Republic, the Scandinavian countries) operate a 'presumptio juris'. Unless the contrary is proved it is presumed that the contributors' copyrights have been transferred to the film maker. This system is also known as the 'system of legitimation'.

System 4. Some countries (eg Switzerland) do not give the film maker any special position but treat him simply as a user who has to acquire all relevant rights by contract before he can exploit the film.

The 'Programme' for the Stockholm Revision Conference contained a definition of the maker of a cinematographic work:[2] 'The person or body corporate who has taken the initiative in and responsibility for the making of the film'. It met with strong resistance and was therefore not adopted and the Stockholm Act contains no definition of the maker although for the first time he is referred to in the Convention in three articles, ie article 5(4), article 7(2) and article 15(2). The fact that he may be a body corporate is plainly stated for the first time.

1   See para 5.25 above.
2   Report of Stockholm Conference, para 281.

5.51   As a result the Convention establishes six rules for film copyright:

Rule 1. The cinematographic work is protected as an original work. Article 14 bis (1).

Rule 2. The question who is the copyright owner of this cinematographic work is governed by the national legislation of the country where protection is claimed. Article 14 bis (2)(a). This leaves every national legislation free to adopt the system it prefers. Whatever may be the system in the country of origin of the film, the owner of the copyright in the film when protection is claimed will be the owner in the country of importation where such protection is claimed. Thus if a film made in the United States is exported to France the question who is the copyright owner of the film will be decided according to French law and the fact that in the country where the film was made the 'maker' is the owner of the copyright becomes irrelevant.

Rule 3. If the country where protection is claimed is a country where the artistic 'contributors' to the film are recognised as joint copyright owners they are presumed to have agreed to the exploitation of the film (by reproduction, distribution, public performance, broadcasting, etc).[1] This is known as the 'presumption of legitimation'. Article 14 bis (2)(b). The persons who rank as contributors are defined in article 14 bis (3).

It must be stressed that this presumption only operates if the contributing authors 'have undertaken to bring such contribution'.[2] This simply means that they have consented to the making of the film. Therefore the presumption is not called a presumption of assignment of the rights but a presumption of legitimation.[3] This presumption of legitimation is mandatory for the countries of the Union. In other words it is not possible for countries which regard authors of contributions as owners of copyright in the cinematographic work to maintain or introduce legislation which fails to include a presumption of legitimation in accordance with article 14 bis (2).[4]

It would appear from a 'clarification' inserted in the Report that countries which apply system 4 have to alter their law before they can ratify the Paris Act 1971.

Rule 4. The question of the form of the agreement is to be decided in accordance with the law of the country where 'the maker of the cinematographic work has his headquarters', or, in the rare case where he is an individual, his 'habitual residence'. The written agreement, if writing is required, can be a 'written agreement or a written act of the same effect'. The latter means for instance a collective agreement for the employment of the contributing authors or any legal instrument defining sufficiently 'the conditions of the engagement of persons bringing contributions to the making of the cinematographic work'.[5] If a country requires writing it has to make a declaration to that effect and send it to the Director General of WIPO who will communicate it to all other countries of the Union.[6]

The freedom given for subtitling or dubbing of films if they are to be shown in a country where the language is different from the language of the film does not exclude the right of the author to object if his moral right is not respected as article 6 bis is paramount.[7]

Rule 5. There is an exception to the general application of the presumption. Two categories of contributors are excluded from the presumptions:

(1) 'the authors of scenarios, dialogues and musical works'. They are as the *Guide*[8] describes them, 'authors whose works (scenarios, scripts, music) can enjoy an existence other than in the film itself'.
(2) the 'principal director'. This is to provide for countries which treat the principal director simply as an employee of the film company.

Rule 6. The person or body corporate (usually the latter) whose name appears on the film 'in the usual manner' is presumed to be the 'maker' of the film. This presumption is rebuttable – article 15(2).

The consequence of these rules is that any country of the Union can introduce any system they wish (with the possible exception of system 4) and if it is a 'droit d'auteur' country with systems 2 or 3 it can introduce or maintain (subject to the five rules) any presumption system it chooses.

1   See *WIPO Guide to Berne* 14 bis. 5 and 6.
2   The stilted English is due to a poor translation of the French text which says: 'apporter des contributions'.
3   Report of the Stockholm Conference 1967, para 321.
4   *WIPO Guide to Berne* 14 bis 7.
5   Report of the Stockholm Conference 1967, para 322.
6   The *WIPO Guide to Berne* 14 bis 11 comments that 'this allows those concerned to know the countries in which the presumption depends on the "written" condition and to make their arrangements accordingly'. This is certainly true provided that they have a lawyer at their elbow and that lawyer has a complete and up-to-date list of all declarations sent to the Director General of WIPO! It may be safer to advise film makers to get the written consent of all persons classed as contributing authors in one form or another just in case any one of them should one day object to the showing of the film in a country where such written consent is required.
7   Report of the Stockholm Conference 1967, para 324.
8   *WIPO Guide to Berne* 14 bis 15.

5.52 To summarise the situation created by the presumptions and the exceptions, an example will illustrate the various points. The 'maker' of a film who has made no contracts with the contributors to the film and whose film is being pirated in a country other than that where he made the film may have to go through the following processes:

1. He has to prove that the contributors have undertaken to make their artistic contribution to the film. If he proves this he establishes the 'presumption of legitimation' (article 14 bis (2)(b)) that he is the copyright owner.
2. The form of proving this would, in accordance with the ordinary rules of private international law be governed by the lex loci, the country where he sues. Not so here. He has to provide written proof if his country's law, ie the country where he (ie the company) has his headquarters demands it (article 14 bis (2)(c).

3. The presumption is displaced if his opponent can prove that one of the authors made a 'restrictive condition' (article 14 bis (2)(d)), eg he stipulated either in writing or orally that he reserved the right of synchronisation into another language.
4. If the country where he sues requires writing for the author's undertaking to make his contribution he may then show that the government has failed to notify the Director General of WIPO of that fact. If they have notified him he loses (article 14 bis (2)(c) second sentence).
5. If he wishes to establish his copyright against, for example, the writer of the scenario, he has to prove the latter's agreement in the prescribed form as the presumption does not apply to him (article 14 bis (3)).
6. If he wishes to establish his copyright against the principal director it is presumed that he is protected unless the Director General of WIPO has been notified to the contrary (article 14 bis (3)).

When contemplating these very complex procedural rules one cannot suppress the question Professor Nordemann asks in his analysis of article 14 and 14 bis: 'Does a film "maker" who has to lay out large sums for the making of a film and is so negligent or so ill-advised that he omits to make contracts or agree conditions with his artistic contributors deserve the infinite care taken to solve his problems?'[1] Whatever the answer to this question, whilst the world remains divided into groups of countries with different copyright philosophies and each has a veto at the revision conferences of the Convention the situation will remain complex. A film maker in any country would therefore be wise to have written agreements which qualify under the Convention because otherwise he lays himself open to claims by individual contributors in countries where, because of lack of writing, the presumption does not operate.

In the 'film copyright' countries (mainly the Anglo-Saxon countries) the situation is clear: the 'maker' is the copyright owner. He can bring any action for infringement of the copyright in the film. The presumptions do not apply.

In the countries which have the principle of authorship of the contributors (mainly continental Europe) the presumption applies. However, several of them, ie France, Germany, the Scandinavian countries, already have in their legislation presumptions in favour of the 'maker' of the film, which in some respects are more extensive than article 14 bis (eg they do not exclude the scenario writer, the dialogue writer, and the composer from the presumption).

Thus the field of application of article 14 bis is not as far reaching as would appear at first sight and its great complexity will probably only govern a minority of cases.

[1] Nordemann, Vink, Hertin *Commentary on International Copyright in German speaking Countries and the EEC* p 113.

10. The 'droit de suite' – article 14 ter

5.53 Following a 'voeu' expressed at the Rome Conference 1928 this right was established at the Brussels Conference 1948 as an inalienable right jure conventionis, for works of art.

The underlying thought is that whereas the author of a book gets a royalty every time a copy is sold or the composer of a piece of music every time it is played in public, the painter or sculptor gets his reward only once when he sells his picture or statue. In many cases he has to sell cheaply to make a living but the work greatly increases in value as time goes on and either the owner or a dealer or both make a profit on every subsequent sale. The 'droit de suite' enables the artist to 'follow' his work. If it remains in the same ownership, eg a gallery or a commissioning patron, he gets nothing, but if it is resold he gets a royalty.

This right is granted in many countries of the Union[1] but not in the Anglo-Saxon countries.

Once a government decides to introduce a 'droit de suite' there are three ways of doing it:

(1) To establish the right outside the copyright system. The payment, which takes the form of a levy or sales tax goes into a government fund. This enables the fund to pay only nationals although the country is a member of the Berne Union (eg Norway). It also enables the government to use the fund for social purposes, ie not pay a royalty to the author whose picture or sculpture is sold, but to give subsidies to needy authors or their families or for education in the arts.
(2) To establish the right within the copyright system which necessitates applying the principle of national treatment. This means in the case of a new right not yet generally accepted that a country may have to pay foreign painters or sculptors when its own artists are not being paid in those foreign countries.
(3) To establish the right within the copyright system but moderate the principle of national treatment by applying material reciprocity. This means that you pay only those artists whose countries in turn pay yours (eg Germany). The Berne Convention has adopted the third system, ie material reciprocity.[2]

The right applies to paintings, statues, drawings, engravings, lithographs, but not to works of applied art. It arises on every sale after the first. It is not assignable, presumably to protect the artist who may otherwise be persuaded or forced by poverty to assign it to the first buyer.

The protection may be claimed by any Union author 'to the extent permitted by the country where protection is claimed' but only if it also exists in the country to which the author belongs; ie the principle of national treatment subject to material reciprocity. Whether such reciprocity exists is a question of law to be decided by the courts of the country where protection is claimed.

Material reciprocity can only be said to exist if in the country of the author the 'droit de suite' is also a copyright. Applying the rule of interpretation laid down in article 31 of the Vienna Convention on the law of treaties the Convention terms have to be given their ordinary meaning 'in the context and in the light of its object and purpose'. It cannot be 'the object and purpose' of a copyright convention that the royalty paid for the use of an author's protected work is not paid to him but paid to others whom the government, through a fund committee, considers to have a deserving case.

'The country to which the author belongs' is not the country where the artist resides but the country of origin of the work, ie the country where the work was first published.

The application of material reciprocity was thought necessary because the degree to which the right is granted in Union countries varies greatly. For example in France, Belgium and Germany, the right is not dependent on whether a profit has been made whereas in Italy it is, and the royalty is only levied on the price difference. In Belgium a royalty is only payable on sales in public auctions, in France only if the sale is made by a dealer, whereas in other countries the royalty is also payable on a private sale. The amount of the royalty also varies. In Belgium there is a sliding scale according to price from a minimum of 2% to a maximum of 6%. In France it is 3% for all sales. In Germany it is 5%[3] but only on a price of DM 100 or over.

It is presumably sufficient for the rule of national treatment to apply that the right is generally recognised in the country to which the artist belongs but it can only be claimed to the extent to which it is exercisable in the country where it is claimed. On a sale in Italy, a British artist cannot claim because the right is not recognised in Britain although it is recognised in Italy. A French artist can claim because France recognises the right but he can only claim a royalty on the difference between the price of the last sale and the previous sale as the law provides in Italy, although in France the royalty is payable regardless of whether the price has risen or not. On the other hand, the fact that he would get less at home than he is entitled to in Italy is not material. An American artist could not claim because the United States is not a member of the Union. A Luxembourg artist could presumably not claim because although Luxembourg recognises the right there are no provisions made for its exercise and an Italian artist would therefore not get anything in Luxembourg. A Norwegian artist could not claim because although the right exists in Norway the fund to which the payment goes does not pay foreigners.

It would not be possible to spell out a 'droit de suite' in a country where conventions are self-executing but where there is no special legislation to create it as the norms of application are not sufficiently spelt out to make it a jus conventionis which can be directly applied.[4]

1   Belgium, Brazil, Czechoslovakia, Chile, France, Germany (Federal Republic), Italy, Philippines, Portugal, Senegal, Tunisia, Uruguay. In three further Union countries – Luxembourg, Morocco, Turkey, the right exists in a statute but there are no provisions to enable it to be exercised.
2   It has done so in other exceptional cases where the laws of the member states differ substantially: In art 7(2) for comparison of terms of copyright and art 2(5) in respect of works of applied art.
3   Since 1972; it was originally fixed at 1% in 1965.
4   See Ulmer 'Le droit de suite et sa réglementation dans la convention de Berne', in *Hommage à Henri Desbois* (1974) p 89.

(9) **The term of protection** – article 7

5.54   The term of protection is the life of the author and 50 years after his death (usually referred to as '50 years pma'; post mortem auctoris).

The term is a compromise between those who argue that copyright should be permanent, ie last as long as the work is used because it is appreciated and enjoyed by the public, and those who argue that it is a personal right and should terminate with the life of the author so that the public can enjoy its unrestricted use after his death. The figure of 50 years was introduced in 1908 (Berlin Act) and seems to represent what was then thought the life span of three generations. This is now the most generally recognised period. The British law changed to 50 years pma in the Copyright Act 1911 as a result of the Berlin Revision and many countries which have United Kingdom-type legislations followed suit. The largest copyright country outside the Berne Union, the United States, introduced 50 years pma in the Copyright Act 1976. The fact that the term of copyright is now the same for nearly all members of the Berne Convention and for the largest outsider gives the Convention a major cohesive force. This method of calculation means that copyright can last for only a little over 50 years from publication if the author dies shortly after publication of the work or for a century if the author publishes the work when he is 35 and lives until 85. This compares favourably with copyright in most corporeal property, few of which last longer than 50–100 years and with rights in other incorporeal property such as patents or trade marks. Even in the realm of real property, only few houses last longer than 50–100 years.

The period is lengthened in some countries by the so-called 'wartime extensions'. These countries passed legislation extending the term of copyright by a number of years to compensate copyright owners for the fact that during a period of war there is virtually no exploitation. Apart from unilateral extensions there are also bilateral agreements. This leads to what the *Guide* calls 'a hotch-potch of legal rules and factual situations.'[1]

Therefore in cases where the 50 years pma have elapsed one has to examine the statute law in national situations to see if extensions have been granted by statute and for how long. International situations are governed by the rule of article 7(8). This rule is known as 'comparison of terms'. It says that the duration of copyright is governed by the term in the country where protection is claimed. If the term in that country is longer than the term in the country of origin of the work, foreign authors can, by legislation, be given the same term as national authors but they need only be given the shorter term of the country of origin of the work. This is an exception from the general principle of national treatment.

However, because of the fairly general acceptance of the 50 years pma term by convention countries the comparison of terms rule will come into play only in the comparatively rare case where one of the two countries has a longer term than 50 years pma (eg Germany with 70 years pma) or if one of the two countries has a shorter term because it is still bound by the Rome Act, 1928, and maintains the shorter term on ratification of the Paris Act, 1971. It has a right to do so under article 7(7) of the Act.

The calculation of the 50 years starts on 1 January of the year following the death of the author.[2] There are however shorter minimum terms prescribed for certain types of works. The reasons for the shorter term are mainly of a practical nature. If the copyright owner is a company a term of 50 years pma is not possible as companies do not 'die'. This is the reason why the copyright in a cinematographic work or a television work (work analogous to cinematography) is 50 years 'after the work has been made available to the public'[3] or if the work has not been made available to the public '50 years after the making' of the work.

For similar reasons the minimum term of protection for photographs is 25 years from the making of the work, as is the term for works of applied art.[4] The number of years chosen as opposed to the starting point, is fairly arbitrary. They represent compromises between opposing interests and opposing philosophies. As Masouyé points out[5] the term of 25 years for photographs was chosen because 'the doubts about whether they really merit being treated as works of art' were stilled by the adoption of this shorter minimum for them. The same minimum applies for works of applied art if they are protected as artistic works.

1 *WIPO Guide to Berne*, 7.2.
2 Art 7(6).
3 Art 7(2).
4 Art 7(4).
5 *WIPO Guide to Berne* 7.11.

(10) Exemptions and restrictions on the rights of authors – article 2 and article 10

A. *Total exemptions jure conventionis*

5.55 News of the day – article 2(8). The borderline between 'news' and 'mere items of press information', which are not protected, and reports and pieces of journalism which are 'works', is to be drawn by the national courts. The guideline for the courts is the general principle underlying the Convention that to constitute a work there must be a certain amount of creativity. It is left to the national courts to decide in each case whether the news item in issue is 'merely relating the facts in a dry and impersonal manner or constitutes a story related with a degree of originality'.[1] The degree of originality required may vary from country to country. Where standards of originality required are high, eg in France, the laws of unfair competition may give a remedy where copyright does not, eg one press agency taking its reports from another one.

1 Desbois Françon Kerever *Les Conventions Internationales du Droit d'Auteur et des Droits Voisins* para 146.

5.56 Quotations – article 10(1). This article has had to be modified with the advent of the information age and the introduction of a general reproduction right in article 9.[1] Quotations are now taken not only from literary works but from all works, films, records, radio and television programmes etc. The reference to press summaries is merely a reminder of the history of the Convention.[2] The Convention lays down three conditions for a quotation to be permissible:

1. The work must have been already published. The wording used 'already been lawfully made available to the public' (as in article 7(3)) as opposed to 'published with the consent of the author' (as in article 7(2)) means that quotations can be made from works of folklore where the author is unknown or from works published under compulsory licence where the author need not have given his consent. On the other hand it excludes quotations from unpublished works.
2. The quotation must be 'compatible with fair practice'.[3] This leaves a great deal of discretion to the courts. However, (a) the length of the quotation itself, (the Brussels Act 1948 still said 'short extracts') (b) whether the size of the quotation is a large or a small part of the work quoted, (c) the size of the quotation in relation to the item in which it is used, are all criteria to be applied by the courts.
3. The extent of the quotation must 'not exceed that justified by the purpose'. Thus a piece of literary criticism may justify long quotations, whereas a newspaper article may only justify much shorter ones.

All quotations are subject to the moral right of the author of the work quoted[4] thus demanding correct attribution of the work quoted.

1 See para 5.38 above.
2 Desbois, Françon, Kerever *Les Conventions Internationales du droit d'auteur et des droits voisins* (1976) para 164 point out that whereas a 'quotation' in literature is made for criticism or illustration or to make a point in an argument in a press review, quotations are often presented without commentary leaving the reader to form his own opinion.
3 This is the English equivalent of the French 'conformer aux bons usages' based on the Latin concept of 'contra bonos mores'.
4 Art 6 bis.

B. *Restrictions left to national legislation*

RESTRICTIONS FOR THE PURPOSE OF INFORMATION

5.57 (i) Official texts – article 2(4). These include legislative, administrative and legal texts in the original or in translation but not other government publications. If, for instance, a government decided to publish its own school books they would not fall into this category.

5.58 (ii) Political speeches and speeches delivered in the course of legal proceedings – article 2 bis (1). Such speeches can be totally excluded from protection by national legislation.[1] It is otherwise for *lectures* and *addresses*,[2] works seen or heard in the course of *reports of current events*[3] where the national legislation can 'determine the conditions' suggesting a compulsory licence with the possibility of equitable remuneration.[4]

However, if the author makes a collection of such speeches he has a copyright in the collection.[5] The reason is that 'the information purpose' is served by the right to publish such speeches without remuneration to the author but a collection, made much later would go beyond what is justified for information purposes and is not exempt.

1   Art 2 bis (1).
2   Art 2 bis (2).
3   Art 10 bis (2).
4   See Desbois, op cit, para 17 footnote (1).
5   Art 2 bis (3).

5.59   (iii) Public lectures, addresses and other works of the same nature – article 2 bis (2). These can be subject to a compulsory licence for use in the press and broadcasting 'when such use is justified by the informatory purpose'.

In these cases too the author retains the exclusive right to make and publish collections of these works. Thus a university professor can publish a collection of his lectures, a preacher of his sermons, a politician of his speeches or a barrister of his speeches in court, whether or not all or some of them have been published before by the media, and he will have a copyright in the collection.

5.60   (iv) Articles in newspapers and broadcasts – article 10 bis (1). Articles and broadcasts can be reproduced freely, ie without the consent of the author and without payment if the following conditions are fulfilled:

(a)   the national legislation permits it. This is wider than the previous text.[1] Under the Brussels Act the use was free jure conventionis unless the national legislation excluded it. It also related only to the press whereas it now covers the other news media. This applies both ways, ie press articles can be broadcast and the press can reproduce broadcast items.
(b)   The article must be on a current topic. What is 'current' is a question for the courts but the notion is well understood.
(c)   The subject of the article must be 'economic political or religious'.
(d)   It must be a 'reproduction', ie it must have been previously printed or broadcast.
(e)   Such use by the media must not have been expressly forbidden by the author. As in the other cases of restrictions the author's 'droit moral' must be respected. Only here the point is specifically emphasised by stipulating that 'the source must always be clearly indicated'. It is argued[2] that because the greater always includes the lesser the states of the Union whilst being able to permit free use of articles under the above mentioned conditions can also require such use to be accompanied by the payment of equitable remuneration to the author.

1   Art 9(2), Brussels Act 1948.
2   Desbois, op cit, para 169.

5.61   (v) Report of current events – article 10 bis (2). Under this article current events can be reported freely even when 'literary or artistic works are seen or heard in the course of the event'.

Whereas article 10 bis (1) enables national laws to 'permit the reproduction', article 10 bis (2) enables the national law to 'determine the conditions under which works may ... be reproduced'. It is thus clear that the national law, apart from permitting the report without the author's permission, can also permit it without compensation.

Examples given in the *Guide*[1] are the showing of a statue which is being unveiled or showing the pictures at the opening of an exhibition or music performed during the report of a sporting event. In each case it is clear that the showing of the work is incidental to the report. The facility referred to applies only to works 'which are seen or heard in the course of the event'. On the other hand it cannot be made the justification for exempting the performance of a whole work. Desbois[2] gives the example of a musical work being played in a concert to honour the memory of a composer and the ceremony being broadcast as a report of the event. The inclusion in the report must be 'justified by the informatory purpose'.[3]

1   *WIPO Guide to Berne* 10 bis 6.
2   Desbois, op cit, para 170.
3   This is the same as for oral works like lectures, addresses, etc-art 2 bis (2).

5.62   (vi) Restrictions required for the needs of education – article 10(2). This article permits 'utilisation of works by way of illustration'. Such illustrations can occur in publications, broadcasts or sound or visual recordings provided the following conditions can be fulfilled:

(1)   the use must be for teaching purposes;
(2)   the extent must be 'justified by the purpose';
(3)   the use must be 'compatible with fair practice'.

(1) 'teaching' is 'to include teaching at all levels – in educational institutions and universities, municipal and state schools and private schools. Education outside these institutions, for instance general teaching available to the public but not included in the above categories, should be excluded.'[1] This means a fortiori that research is excluded.

(2) This article is dealing with extracts. As Desbois points out, 'Education can confine itself to extracts, efficiently and wisely chosen'.[2]

(3) Is always in the discretion of the courts.

Do these provisions also include the right to translate? Whereas the Bergström Report[3] makes it clear that the right to reproduce press articles (under article 10 bis (1)) includes the right to reproduce them in the form of translations, the application of the other restrictions on the author's right of reproduction is less clear. The Bergström Report states[4] that:

'while it was generally agreed that Articles 2 bis (2), 9(2), 10(1) and (2), and 10 bis (1) and (2) virtually imply the possibility of using the work not only in the original form but also in translation, subject to the same conditions, in particular that the use is in conformity with fair practice and that here too, as in the case of all uses of the work, the rights granted to the author under Article 6 bis (moral rights) are preserved, different opinions were expressed regarding the lawful uses provided for in Articles 11 bis and 13. Some delegations considered that those articles also applied to translated works, provided the above conditions were fulfilled. Other delegations, including those of Belgium, France and Italy, considered that the wording of those articles in the Stockholm text did not permit of the interpretation that the possibility of using a work without the consent of the author also included, in those cases, the possibility of translating it.'

The Report, however authoritative, cannot of course amend or extend the provisions of the Convention, but it supports the view that the restrictions, except the compulsory licence provisions under article 11 bis and article 13, include the facility to translate. However the question remains open.[5]

1 Bergström, Report Stockholm Conference 1967, para 97.
2 Desbois, op cit, para 171.
3 Report, para 203.
4 Report, para 205.
5 See Desbois, op cit, para 174.

(11) 'Folklore' – article 15(4)

5.63 Folklore is difficult to define and therefore the term is not used in the convention. The article speaks of 'unpublished works where the identity of the author is unknown, but where there is every ground to presume that he is a national of a country of the Union'. In such cases the country in question can 'designate the competent authority which shall represent the author'[1] and notify the Director General of WIPO by a declaration which he then communicates to all Union countries. When that is done the work is protected in all Union countries.

To be designated as folklore the work must be unpublished within the meaning of article 3(3)[2] and the author unknown. In these circumstances the convention 'creates a sort of presumption'[3] that the unknown author is a national of that Union country. This presumption gets over the difficulty that the author in most cases will have been dead for more than 50 years. At the Stockholm Conferenece (1967) which added this article to the Convention it was agreed that in the Convention a work of folklore is assimilated to an anonymous work under article 7(3).[4] This means that the term of protection for such works is 50 years after publication which in this case will be 50 years from the making of the declaration.

This article was put into the convention mainly to enable developing countries to exploit their folklore and it is likely that the competent authority designated by the national legislation will act as the publisher and thus 'be entitled to protect and enforce the author's rights' in accordance with article 15(3).

1 Art 15(4)(a).
2 See para 5.33 above.
3 *WIPO Guide to Berne* 15.10.
4 *WIPO Guide to Berne* 15.13.

(12) Restrictions of circulation, performance or exhibition of works by government control – article 17

5.64 All conventions safeguard the position of ratifying countries with regard to issues of 'public policy'. The formulation which was first adopted by the 'Convention Relating to Adoption'[1] is now generally accepted: 'The provisions of this convention may be disregarded in contracting states only when their observance would be "manifestly" contrary to public policy' ('manifestement incompatible avec l'ordre public').

The Berne Convention has included such a provision since its inception.[2] The principle is that authors can exercise their convention rights as far as they do not conflict with public policy. The main application of this provision is of course censorship, but the protection of free competition and any regulations against monopolies and market domination are also matters of public policy. The establishment of copyright tribunals to adjudicate in cases of disputes between collecting societies formed by copyright owners which are virtual monopolies and users of copyright, also come under this heading.

1 'Convention relating to adoption' (1965), art 15.
2 Berne Convention, art 7.

(13) Remedies for breaches of the Convention

1. *Remedies under public international law*

5.65 'Any country party to this Convention undertakes to adopt, in accordance with its Constitution, the measures necessary to ensure the application of this Convention'.[1] If a state fails to honour this undertaking or in case of a dispute on the interpretation of the Convention, this will first be the subject of diplomatic negotiations between the countries concerned. If such negotiations fail it may be the subject of arbitration. If arbitration fails, the dispute may be submitted to the International Court.[2] The country bringing the dispute before the Court must inform WIPO which in turn notifies all other member states, thereby giving them an opportunity to intervene in the dispute.[3]

Any country, when ratifying the Convention, can make a declaration to the effect that it does not accept the Court's jurisdiction.[4] The Brussels Act 1948, which introduced this provision, made the reference to the International Court obligatory. The Revision Conference at Stockholm (1967) made it optional in deference to those countries which do not recognise the jurisdiction of the International Court.

The International Court gives an opinion on the interpretation of the Convention, without such an opinion having executory force, thus leaving the countries concerned to settle their dispute by diplomatic means on the basis of the opinion, or by the country which, in the opinion of the Court, is in breach of the Convention, amending its legislation to conform with the Convention. It is significant that in over 30 years since this provision was inserted, no dispute has been referred to the International Court although there have been breaches.[5]

A state within the Union which considers that a state outside the Union has failed to protect the works of authors who are nationals of a Union country 'in an adequate manner',[6] can retaliate against such a country by restricting the protection which it gives to works of authors who are nationals of that country. If the Convention state where the protection is claimed takes such reprisals, other Union countries could do the same, ie they could subject the nationals of the offending state to 'special treatment'[7] of the same kind as that adopted by the member state where protection was claimed. They are, however, not obliged to do so.

An example will illustrate: if an African country, which is not a member of the Berne Union, does not protect British works 'in an adequate manner', the British government could restrict the protection it gives to works of authors who are nationals of that African country. If the British government does that, other countries which are members of the Berne Union could, if they wish, do the same.

The purpose of this clause is to counter the device known as 'back-door protection'. This consists of nationals of countries outside the Union who border on a Union country publishing their works simultaneously in a neighbouring country which is a member of the Union, thereby obtaining full Union protection. In such a case, the country where protection is claimed can reduce its level of protection but it cannot refuse protection altogether.

1 Art 36(1).
2 See also Universal Copyright Convention, art X.
3 Art 33(1).
4 Art 33(2).
5 An example of a clear breach of the Convention was the amendment to the Greek law by the authoritarian Greek government in the 1960s. It abolished the author's broadcasting right in order to enable the broadcasting organisation, which had become part of the propaganda apparatus of that government, to avoid paying any royalties to authors for the broadcasting of

their works, whether they were Greeks or foreigners. The other Convention countries took no action, but when a democratically elected government replaced the authoritarian one it restored the law to its original state, thus complying once more with the country's obligations under the Convention.

6   Art 6(1).
7   Art 6(1).

2. *Remedies under private international law*

5.66 Violations of substantive rights deriving from the Convention fall under the jurisdiction of the national courts of the country where protection is claimed. The obligation to protect Union works stems from article 2(6). The way such protection is assured is dealt with under article 36.

Any member country undertakes 'to adopt, in accordance with its constitution, the measures necessary to ensure the application of the Convention'.[1] What these measures are depends on the constitution of the country concerned.

In countries of the French legal tradition where, in accordance with the legal system, conventions are self-executing, it becomes part of the national law and the courts have to apply it directly in its original terms. This means that international law is accorded priority over national law in the sense that if a convention is ratified and promulgated that makes its provisions part of the law of the land. This is a gracious compliment to international law and makes ratification easier in some cases. On the other hand it can cause difficulties for the courts, for instance if a convention contains alternatives and the national law has no provisions the judge may have to decide which of the alternatives in the convention he wishes to apply.[2]

In countries of the Anglo-Saxon legal tradition, ratification does not by itself confer any rights on individuals. Such rights and obligations must be conferred by the national law as only the national law and not the Convention can be relied upon by an individual bringing suit in the courts. These countries have an obligation to take the 'measures necessary to ensure the application of the Convention'. The word 'measure' indicates that the steps to be taken by such a Union country may be legislative, they may be administrative, or both, as long as when the necessary measures are taken the domestic law of the Union country is in a position to give effect to the provisions of the convention from the date of ratification. The trial judge thus applies his own national law. When interpreting it in relation to Convention rights, he will be guided by the spirit and the tradition of the Convention which his country has ratified although if there were a discrepancy between the Convention and his national law he would have to apply his national law. In such a case the Union country would be held to be in breach of the convention and in accordance with article 36 would be under a duty to amend its national law.

Each country is thus required to see to it that it is 'in a position under its domestic law to give effect to the provisions of the convention.'[3] The necessary legislation must already be in force when ratification takes place.

1   Art 36(1).
2   Art 36 was inserted into the convention by the Stockholm Act (1967) which took it from Art 16 of the Rome Convention (1961). This is simply due to the fact that the majority of Union countries were of the French tradition and it was not until 1967 after the Universal Copyright Convention (1952) and the Rome Convention (1961) that it became clear that it was advisable to ensure that the obligations imposed by convention are complied with in countries of both traditions.
3   Art 36(2).

Points to be considered in action for infringement

5.67 In case of an infringement taking place in country A, (a Union country) in a situation with a foreign element, the following processes have to be gone through:

1. Find the country of origin of the work, article 5(4).
2. If the country of origin of the work is a Union country the work is a 'Union work' and is protected without any formalities and enjoys all the rights granted jure conventionis.
3. If the country of origin of the work is not a Union country find the country of which the author is a national. If he is a Union national the work is protected. If he is not the work is unprotected.[1]
4. As to the scope of protection, the work enjoys national treatment, ie all the rights of a work first published in country A and the use of all rules of procedures in accordance with the law of country A,[2]

Example: An infringement takes place in the United Kingdom, the author is a national of Ghana and the work was first published in the Congo. (Ghana is not a Union country but the Congo is.) The work is a Union work because it is published in a Union country although the author is not a Union national. As the United Kingdom is also a Union country the work gets the protection which the United Kingdom law grants to United Kingdom works.

The question which procedural remedies are available to the copyright owners is always to be answered by the law of the country where protection is claimed. The only procedural remedy specifically dealt with by the Convention is 'seizure of infringing copies'.[3] Copies of a work which is protected in the country where such protection is claimed can be seized as infringing copies even though they are being imported 'from a country where the work is not protected or has ceased to be protected'[4] (fallen into the public domain). Depending on the law of the country where protection is claimed the seizure can be executed by the courts or by government officers (usually customs officials).

1 Art 3(1).
2 Art 5(1).
3 Art 16(1).
4 Art 16(2).

8. List of member states of the Berne Union on 1 January 1983

5.68

Contracting states	Date of entry into force	Latest Act by which state is bound
ARGENTINA	10 June 1967	Brussels (Substance) Paris (Administration)
AUSTRALIA	14 April 1928	Paris (1971)
AUSTRIA	1 October 1920	Paris (1971)
BAHAMAS	10 July 1973	Brussels (Substance) Paris (Administration)
BELGIUM	5 December 1887	Brussels (Substance) Stockholm (Administration)
BENIN	3 January 1961	Paris (1971)
BRAZIL	9 February 1922	Paris (1971)
BULGARIA	5 December 1921	Paris (1971)
CAMEROON	21 September 1964	Paris (1971)
CANADA	10 April 1928	Rome (Substance) Stockholm (Administration)
CENTRAL AFRICAN EMPIRE	3 September 1977	Paris (1971)

List of member states of the Berne Union on 1 January 1983

CHAD	25 November 1971	Brussels (Substance)
		Stockholm (Administration)
CHILE	5 June 1970	Paris (1971)
CONGO	8 May 1962	Paris (1971)
COSTA RICA	10 June 1978	Paris (1971)
CYPRUS	24 February 1964	Rome
CZECHOSLOVAKIA	22 February 1921	Paris (1971)
DENMARK	1 July 1903	Paris (1971)
EGYPT ARAB REPUBLIC OF	7 June 1977	Paris (1971)
FIJI	1 December 1971	Brussels (Substance)
		Stockholm (Administration)
FINLAND	1 April 1928	Brussels (Substance)
		Stockholm (Administration)
FRANCE	5 December 1887	Paris (1971)
GABON	26 March 1962	Paris (1971)
GERMAN DEMOCRATIC REPUBLIC	5 December 1887	Paris (1971)
GERMANY – FEDERAL REPUBLIC OF	5 December 1887	Paris (1971)
GREECE	9 November 1920	Paris (1971)
GUINEA	20 November 1980	Paris (1971)
HOLY SEE	12 September 1935	Paris (1971)
HUNGARY	14 February 1922	Paris (1971)
ICELAND	7 September 1947	Rome
INDIA	1 April 1928	Brussels (Substance)
		Paris (Administration)
IRELAND	5 October 1927	Brussels (Substance)
		Stockholm (Administration)
ISRAEL	24 March 1950	Brussels (Substance)
		Stockholm (Administration)
ITALY	5 December 1887	Paris (1971)
IVORY COAST	1 January 1962	Paris (1971)
JAPAN	15 July 1899	Paris (1971)
LEBANON	30 September 1947	Rome
LIBYAN ARAB REPUBLIC	28 September 1976	Paris (1971)
LIECHTENSTEIN	30 July 1931	Brussels (Substance)
		Stockholm (Administration)
LUXEMBOURG	20 June 1888	Paris (1971)
MADAGASCAR	1 January 1966	Brussels
MALI	19 March 1962	Paris (1971)
MALTA	21 September 1964	Rome (Substance)
		Paris (Administration)
MAURITANIA	6 February 1973	Paris (1971)
MEXICO	11 June 1967	Paris (1971)
MONACO	30 May 1889	Paris (1971)
MOROCCO	16 June 1917	Brussels (Substance)
		Stockholm (Administration)
NETHERLANDS	1 November 1912	Brussels (Substance)
		Paris (Administration)
NEW ZEALAND	24 April 1928	Rome
NIGER	2 May 1962	Paris (1971)
NORWAY	13 April 1896	Brussels (Substance)
		Paris (Administration)

PAKISTAN	5 July 1948	Rome (Substance)
		Stockholm (Administration)
PHILIPPINES	1 August 1951	Brussels (Substance)
		Paris (Administration)
POLAND	28 January 1920	Rome
PORTUGAL	29 March 1911	Paris (1971)
ROUMANIA	1 January 1927	Rome (Substance)
		Stockholm (Administration)
SENEGAL	25 August 1962	Paris (1971)
SOUTH AFRICA	3 October 1928	Brussels (Substance)
		Paris (Administration)
SPAIN	5 December 1887	Paris (1971)
SRI LANKA	20 July 1959	Rome (Substance)
		Paris (Administration)
SURINAM	23 February 1977	Paris (1971)
SWEDEN	1 August 1904	Paris (1971)
SWITZERLAND	5 December 1887	Brussels (Substance)
		Stockholm (Administration)
THAILAND	17 July 1931	Berlin (Substance)
		Paris (Administration)
TOGO	30 April 1975	Paris (1971)
TUNISIA	5 December 1887	Paris (1971)
TURKEY	1 January 1952	Brussels
UNITED KINGDOM	5 December 1887	Brussels (Substance)
		Stockholm (Administration)
UPPER VOLTA	19 August 1963	Paris (1971)
URUGUAY	10 July 1967	Paris (1971)
VENEZUELA	30 December 1982	Paris (1971)
YUGOSLAVIA	17 June 1930	Paris (1971)
ZAIRE	8 October 1963	Paris (1971)
ZIMBABWE	18 April 1980	Rome (Substance)
		Paris (Administration)

TOTAL NUMBER OF STATES: 74

Chapter 6

The Universal Copyright Convention (UCC)

Summary

1. History   6.01
   The Revised Universal Copyright Convention 1971   6.03
2. Protected works – article I   6.03
3. The field of application – article II   6.05
4. Formalities – article III   6.08
   (1) The symbol   6.09
   (2) The name   6.10
   (3) The date   6.11
5. Duration – article IV   6.16
   (1) History   6.16
   (2) The rule of national treatment   6.17
   (3) The minimum term   6.18
   (4) The comparison of terms   6.19
6. The basic rights – article IV bis   6.20
7. The system of compulsory licences (general) – articles V/2, V ter, V quater   6.22
8. The translation right – article V   6.23
   (1) The right   6.24
   (2) The exceptions: compulsory licences   6.25
   (3) Procedures to be followed for the issuing of a compulsory licence   6.26
   (4) Compensation   6.27
   (5) Moral rights   6.28
   (6) Exports   6.29
   (7) System of compulsory licences in developing countries   6.30
9. Publication – Article V   6.31
   (1) History   6.31
   (2) Definition of publication   6.32
   (3) General distribution to the public   6.33
10. Works permanently in the public domain – article VII   6.34
11. Links between the 1952 Convention and the 1971 Convention – article IX   6.35
12. The Intergovernmental Committee – article XI and the Appendix Declaration   6.36
13. The 'Berne Union Safeguard Clause' – article XVII and the Appendix Declaration   6.37
14. The special provisions for developing countries – article V bis UCC and article I Appendix (Paris Act) Berne Convention   6.38
    1. General   6.38
       (1) Definition of a developing country   6.39

133

(2) The main characteristics of the compulsory licences issued in developing countries   6.40
(3) Procedures   6.41
(4) Duration   6.42
(5) The rights which can be subjected to a system of compulsory licences   6.43
2. Compulsory licences applied to the translation right – article V ter UCC and article II Appendix to the Berne Convention   6.45
3. Translations for broadcasting purposes   6.48
4. The 'ten-year regime' for translations – article V Appendix, Berne   6.49
5. Compulsory licences applied to the reproduction right – article V quater and article III Appendix, Berne Convention   6.50
15. State of ratification and accessions   6.53

1. History

6.01 There is no doubt that the Berne Convention had beeen successful as the first and original international copyright convention. From its almost entirely European origin it had spread to the other continents and the Union had at the time of the Brussels Act in 1948 39 member states. It protected both the moral and the main economic rights of authors and the level of protection had been systematically increased and strengthened with each revision conference. Its weakness, as seen after the 1939–45 war, was twofold. First, the Union had always striven for quality of rights rather than quantity of membership and it therefore lacked universality. The two states which had emerged from the war as the 'superpowers', the United States and the Soviet Union, were not members, neither were many Asian, and African states who were members of the United Nations. Secondly, the very fact that its level of protection was high prevented countries from joining the Union. The copyright systems not only of the United States but also of many Latin American countries differed from that of the Berne Union and 'by the late 1940s the Berne and the Pan-American systems[1] were fundamentally incompatible'.[2] The impetus for a universal convention which would embrace the states of all five continents, including states of very different stages of economic and cultural development, came from the newly founded cultural organisation of the United Nations—UNESCO.[3] It aimed at attracting all countries, particularly the United States without forcing the Berne Union members to lower their standard of protection. It also aimed at bridging the gap between the two basic philosophies of copyright, one stemming from the French Revolution and the concepts of the 'droit d'auteur', and the other from the Anglo-Saxon concept of copyright originating in the statute of Queen Anne of 1709, and the American Constitution of 1776. The existence and the development of the Berne Convention had proved that the two were not incompatible and could even be said to be complementary.[4]

The Universal Copyright Convention gets its inspiration from the aims of the United Nations and 'one of their articles of faith that if people know each other they will understand each other, and that there is no better means of knowing than through reading the books of other peoples, listening to their music, viewing their motion pictures and in general becoming acquainted with what their minds have created'.[5]

Before this aim could be realised the promoters of the new convention had to 'open a difficult double lock'.[6] The first part of the lock was to allay the fears of the member states of Berne Union that the new convention would undermine the Berne Convention by offering wider international protection on a lower level and lure the members of the Union, as one of their representatives put it 'by a bargain basement offer' to leave the Berne Union and join the new convention instead. The other lock to be opened was the insistence of some states particularly the United States, the main promoter of the convention, to maintain their own copyright systems based on the requirement of formalities as a condition of copyright protection, which was anathema to the suppporters of Berne Convention, and on a duration based not on the life of the author but on the publication date. The key to unlock the first lock was the so-called 'Berne Safeguard Clause' (article XVII and the Appendix Declaration) and the key to the second lock was the © notice (article III). The 'Berne Safeguard Clause' made sure that no member of the Berne Union could leave the Union and then ratify the new convention instead. Any member of the Union can of course leave it by denouncing the Convention,[7] but that state could not subsequently ratify the UCC and claim the protection of the UCC in countries of the Berne Union.

This was a somewhat radical provision which, not surprisingly, came under heavy attack by the developing countries 15 years later at the Stockholm Conference in 1967.[8]

The solution to the problem of duration is rather subtle because it permits a double standard. A member state is free to maintain its copyright term based on publication by granting a term of 25 years from publication to its nationals (the United States at that time gave a 28-year term with the possibility of renewal for another 28 years). However, in protecting other UCC works it has to grant a minimum term of the life of the author plus 25 years.[9] The solution to the problem of formalities is also a compromise as it cuts down permitted formalities to the © notice but does not abolish them altogether. In the first quarter of a century of the life of the UCC the policy of widening the net and of compromising on duration and formalities won two big prizes, apart from many smaller ones: the ratification of the Soviet Union in 1973 and the adoption of the 50 years pma term by the United States in 1978.

Apart from the 'Berne Safeguard Clause'[10] and the minimum duration[11] the original 1952 Convention was based on four further principal provisions:

(1) It abstained from providing a minimum of specified rights jure conventionis and limits itself to demanding 'adequate and effective' protection (article I).
(2) The principle of national treatment (article II)).
(3) The symbol © together with the year date of publication and the name of the copyright owner as satisfying all formalities that may be required (article III).
(4) The exclusive translation right (the only authors' right dealt with specifically by the Convention in its original form) subject to a compulsory licence after seven years under specific rules (article V).[12] This was the model for the compulsory licence system for developing countries in 1971.

---

1 See para 3.15 above.
2 Barbara Ringer 'The UCC and its future' Nordic Copyright Symposium 1975.
3 United Nations Educational, Scientific and Cultural Organisation.
4 See paras 1.13 and 1.15 above.
5 Arpad Bogsch *The Law of Copyright under the Universal Convention* (3rd revised edn, 1972) p 4.
6 Ringer, op cit, 1975.
7 Berne Convention, art 35(2).
8 See para 5.27 above.

9   Art IV/2.
10 Art XVII.
11 Art IV.
12 See paras 6.23 et seq, below.

6.02 At the Stockholm Conference in 1967 when the Berne Convention was to be revised (about 20 years had become the traditional period for revision), a crisis occurred which nearly swept away the whole edifice of international copyright, built up painstakingly over nearly a century.

The challenge came from the developing countries led by India, followed by Tunisia, who demanded special concessions, especially in the field of education in respect of the translation right and the reproduction right. They made a strong case to the effect that without easy access to the literary and scientific works of the developed countries they could not achieve the economic and social progress they were trying to achieve, an aim to which particularly UNESCO was devoted. They were too diplomatic to point out that both the superpowers of the present day had disregarded the rights of foreign copyright owners and copied or translated what they needed at a stage when their economic development was already far more advanced than most developing countries in Asia, Africa and Latin America are today; the United States in the nineteenth century and the Soviet Union until the present day. They did however make it clear that unless they were given the concessions they were asking for, they may have to renounce the Berne Convention and – because of the 'Berne Safeguard Clause' – the UCC as well. Under this pressure and because of the great fund of good-will towards the developing countries, the leading developed countries were prepared to make far-reaching concessions which were enshrined in the so-called 'Stockholm Protocol'. However, it appeared that the delegates of the Stockholm Conference (1967) had gone too far too quickly because as soon as they got home, a storm of protest broke, particularly in the countries from which most of the works which the developing countries needed had to come – France, the United Kingdom and the United States. The case made against the Protocol was that if the developing countries needed help in this sphere and no-one denied that they did, that help should be given by governments as part of their development programmes and should not be given at the expense of copyright owners in developed countries. It became quite clear that the leading developed countries were not prepared to ratify the 'Stockholm Protocol' and it became a dead letter within a few months of the Stockholm Conference. The developing countries voiced their disappointment in measured but firm language and the crisis reached its peak during the next three years of frantic activity. The pace and the intensity of the negotiations were in marked contrast to the usually somewhat leisurely progress of international copyright. Everybody had understood that the survival of international copyright was at stake. Fortunately the crisis occurred at a time when the leaders of the most important delegations, the United States, the United Kingdom, the Federal Republic of Germany and Italy among the developed countries, India, Tunisia, Brazil among the developing countries, were men and women not only of great experience in the field but also of vision, who rose to the occasion. The breakthrough was largely achieved at a conference in Washington in 1969, which worked out a set of compromises which were seen as workable by all concerned and which were on most points adopted by the Diplomatic Conference in Paris in 1971.

The essential features of these compromises are:

1. The 'Berne Safeguard Clause' was removed for the developing countries

with the result that they could now renounce the Berne Convention but still rely on the UCC for their copyright relations.
2. They can impose compulsory licence systems in strictly defined circumstances in respect of both the translation right and the reproduction right.
3. The 'adequate and effective protection' of the rights of copyright owners must now include the exclusive right of 'reproduction by any means' and the broadcasting and public performance right.

The necessary ratifications of the revised conventions were coming forward with commendable speed and both the revised Berne Convention (Paris Act 1971) and the revised UCC (1971) came into effect in 1974.[1]

It is probably too early to say whether the solutions found are only temporary or whether they will endure but what has been proved is that international copyright had reached a degree of maturity which enabled it to overcome such a crisis and that the necessity of having an international legal system in this field is appreciated by developed and developing countries alike.

However, political and financial compromises which have to be couched in legal language are very rarely simple and straightforward, and the 1971 Revision of the UCC is no exception. The convention emerged much stronger and the new minimum basic rights bring it much closer to the Berne Convention level, but it is also twice its original size.

1 The UCC on 10 July 1974 and the Berne Convention on 10 October 1974.

The Revised Universal Copyright Convention 1971

2. Protected works – article I

6.03 The contracting states undertake to provide *'adequate and effective protection'*. When read together with the principle of national treatment laid down in article II, this means that the level of protection depends largely on the law of the country where protection is claimed. If the level of protection in that country is low but 'adequate', the national of another convention country will get a low level of protection. If the level is high he will get a high level of protection. However, to be adequate the protection must now provide the minimum duration[1] and the basic rights: the translation right[2] which is old, as well as the reproduction right, the public performance right and the broadcasting right[3] – which are new.

Under article X each contracting state undertakes to adopt 'such measures as are necessary to ensure the application of the Convention and such state must be in a position under its domestic law to give effect to the terms of the Convention'.

The responsibility to provide 'adequate protection', which since the 1971 Convention includes these new minimum rights rests therefore firmly with the contracting states.

However the fundamental criticism remains: It is that the convention obliges ratifying states to grant the rights given in the convention, but it does not confer these rights on the right owner jure conventionis.[4] Whereas under the Berne Convention the right owner entitled under the convention can claim the basic rights granted by the Convention[5] regardless of the national legislation of the country where the protection is claimed, under the UCC he cannot do that, he has to rely on the obligation of the contracting state in which protection is claimed to fulfil its obligations. This is why some critics say[6] that the rights granted since 1971 in article IV bis are not minimum rights in the true sense of the Berne Convention.

This and the fact that the obligations of the ratifying states with regard to the basic rights are only to ensure 'the author's economic interests'[7] (excluding the 'droit moral') are two of the fundamental differences between the UCC and the Berne Convention.

1 Art IV.
2 Art V.
3 Art IV bis.
4 Nordeman, Vink, Hertin *Commentary on International Copyright in German speaking Countries and the EEC* Art I, 1 (p 170).
5 See Ch 5.
6 Nordemann, op cit, Art IV bis 1 (p 202). Debois *Conventions Internationales* p 80.
7 Article IV bis.

6.04 In 1952 it was thought that the somewhat vague term 'adequate' would have the advantage of flexibility and as the level of protection generally accepted in 'civilised countries' (a term used by the Conference President and quoted in the Report)[1] rose, so the level of protection under the convention would rise as nothing short of that level would be considered adequate and the convention would thus 'automatically keep itself modern'.[2]

An example of the advantage of flexibility is the ratification of the UCC by the Soviet Union which had never been a member of any copyright convention.[3]

Unlike the Berne Convention the UCC refers to 'authors and *other* Copyright proprietors' for two reasons. The first reason is that it seeks to build a bridge between the 'droit d'auteur' philosophy which recognises only an individual as an author and the Anglo-Saxon philosophy which recognises corporate copyright proprietors. The second reason is that the protection includes the successors in title to the author such as assignees or heirs. Protected 'works' are not defined. The description of works as 'literary, scientific and artistic' must not be taken in a literal sense. These terms are overlapping: an opera could be a literary or an artistic work or both. The word 'scientific' which is added to the term 'literary and artistic' in the Berne Convention was considered necessary 'to cover clearly such things as logarithm tables and works on nuclear physics'[4] although such writings would probably rank as 'literary works' under most legislations.

The word 'writings' is taken from the United States Constitution where it has been given a very wide meaning by the courts (eg a phonogram has been held to be a 'writing').[5] Whether it would be given an equally wide meaning in the Convention has not yet been decided by a court. It may well be that it will undergo the same development as it did in the United States courts which at first decided that phonograms were not 'writings' and could thus not be protected under federal law, and only much later permitted the wider interpretation. Perhaps the best definition is that 'writings' are works expressed by signs which can be read on a physical support. This includes works in a little known language or in a code or on the grooves of a record but excludes oral works such as speech which has not been written down.

'Cinematographic works' are protected regardless of whether they are shown in a cinema or on television or on a screen to a narrower group of spectators. 'Paintings, engravings and sculpture' should probably be interpreted widely so that drawings or etchings are 'paintings' and lithographs are 'engravings' and all forms of three dimensional works are 'sculptures'. Whether three dimensional works of applied art are 'sculptures' is less certain and will probably depend on the law of the country where protection is claimed.

1 Report of Rapporteur Général of 1952 Conference under art 1.
2 See Bogsch, op cit, p 6.
3 The Soviet Union adhered to the UCC in 1973, ie before the revised convention came into effect (1974) and thus had the option to choose either the 1952 text or both the 1952 and 1971 texts. It chose the 1952 text presumably among other reasons because under the revised UCC it would be in breach of the obligation to grant a broadcasting right to authors. (Art IV bis).
4 See Report of Rapporteur Général.
5 See para. 21.57 below.

3. The field of application – article II

6.05 To qualify for protection under the Convention the creation must:

(1) Be a 'work' under article I.
(2) Be 'in copyright' ie not have fallen into the public domain by the effluxion of time under article IV.
(3) Comply with the formalities prescribed in article III; and
(4) Be the work of a 'national' of a contracting state or it must have been first published in a contracting state (article III, para 1).

If these criteria are fulfilled the work is protected. The scope of protection is deecided according to the principle of national treatment. The principle applies both to published and to unpublished works. In each case the work must be given, in the country where protection is claimed, the same protection as is accorded to works of nationals of that state first published in its territory or unpublished works of its own nationals. The law of that state also decides whether persons domiciled in that state are to be treated as nationals of that state. The only exception from this equal treatment is to be found in article IV(4)(a) which permits the application of the principle of reciprocity to the duration of the protection.[1]

Nationals of a contracting state can publish their works anywhere and must be given national treatment. Right owners who are not nationals of a contracting state can only claim national treatment in respect of one of their works if it has been first published in a contracting state. This leads to the result that an author who first publishes his work outside his own country but in a contracting state of the Convention can claim national treatment in each contracting state but not at home. It equally leads to the result that an author who is not a national of a contracting state but first publishes his work in a contracting state can claim national treatment in all contracting states but not in the state where he first publishes the work.

The double point of attachment for published works, ie works of a national of a contracting state or works first published in a contracting state is due to the desire of the Convention here, as in other respects to create a bridge between two legal systems: The systems (eg the United States) where protection depends on the nationality of the author and those (eg France) where protection of published works depends on the place of first publication.

1 See para 6.19 below.

Who is a national?

6.06 It is clear that not only citizens and all persons who owe allegiance to the state are nationals but also corporations which have their seat within the state. It is the author who must be a national. This is so because of his close connection with the work but also because to permit eg a licensee of the author to qualify as a national would lead to absurd results. It would be sufficient for an author who is not a Convention national to transfer or licence the work to a national to get the work protected without having to publish it for the first time in a Convention country.[1]

The problem of nationality becomes more difficult if the author changes his nationality or loses his nationality without acquiring another, thus becoming a stateless person. Which moment is relevant for answering the question of his nationality? The question is not answered in the Convention but the only reasonable solution stems again from the author's connection with the work. If one examines the question against that background the solution must be that for published works the relevant moment is the author's nationality at the time of publication. This follows from the language of the article which speaks of 'works of nationals' and from the fact that other possible solutions would lead to unsatisfactory results. If published works were allowed to change nationality every time the author changes nationality the same work could move in and out of the public domain several times destroying acquired right in the process as well as making acts which were lawful unlawful, and vice versa.[2]

The relevant moment to decide the nationality of unpublished works is controversial. One opinion prefers the moment when the work comes into existence. This seems logical but suffers from the difficulty that probably only the author knows when a work was created and could therefore so place the moment as to get it protected. The other opinion[3] prefers the moment of the infringement against which the plaintiff claims relief. The Bergström Report of the Stockholm Conference[4] although dealing with article 4(2) of the Berne Convention would also seem to point in that direction.

In countries that require formalities national authors could see article II to get round these formalities by publishing in another Convention country. The work would then be protected in all Convention countries apart from his own eg an American author who first publishes his work in the United Kingdom thereby protects it in all Convention countries apart from the United States. If he wanted to bring an infringement action in the United States he would have to register the work first (article III/2).

1   See Bogsch, op cit, p 17.
2   See Bogsch, op cit, p 17: Nordemann, op cit, p 182: Ulmer GRUR (1959) p 21.
3   Nordmann, op cit, p 184 and Ulmer (cited by Nordemann).
4   Paras 29 and 30.

Who is the author of a work under the Convention?

6.07 This question arises in cases where different jurisdictions regard different persons or entities as the author of the same work, eg if a work is created in employment the United Kingdom generally regards the employer as copyright owner, whereas the Federal Republic of Germany generally regards the employee as copyright owner. In the United States or the United Kingdom the film producer is regarded as the copyright owner whereas in France the authors of the pre-existing work or the scenario, the director etc are all regarded as authors. The Convention does not give an answer, but the underlying principles of the Convention lead one to the answer that the country where protection is claimed will apply its own law to the question of who is a 'national' in these circumstances and having done so will have to apply the same interpretation to foreign nationals as it does to its own nationals. The Report of the Rapporteur-General of the 1952 Convention under article II suggests this solution.[1]

The results of such a rule, albeit complex, seem satisfactory. If a work is created by an employee who is a national of a contracting country but in the employment of a company incorporated in a non-contracting country and the country where protection is claimed recognises the employee as copyright owner in the circumstances of the case, the work will be protected. If it recognises the employer as copyright owner in the circumstances of the case, it will be unprotected.

If a film producer is a national of a contracting country but the author of the pre-existing work, the director, the composer of the music, the principal actors etc are nationals of non-contracting countries, the film will be protected if protection is claimed in a country where a corporation (the film producer) is recognised as a copyright owner, eg the United States or the United Kingdom but will not be protected if protection is claimed in a country which regards only the individual creators of the cinematographic work as copyright owners, eg France.

The additional Protocol 1 deals with stateless persons and refugees and Protocol 2 with works first published by the United Nations and its specialised agencies and the Organisation of American States.

[1] Report, Conference Records p 76, see Bogsch op cit p 19.

4. Formalities – article III

6.08 This is one of the key provisions of the Convention. To appreciate its importance one has to remember that in some jurisdictions a copyright is viewed, as a patent is in all jurisdictions, as a right which either only arises or can only be enforced if certain formalities, eg registration and deposit, are complied with. The United States and some Central and South American countries as well as Spain have such systems. As these countries could not be expected to alter their laws – at least not immediately – to ratify the Convention a compromise had to be found, which amounts in fact to a derogation from the principle of national treatment[1] and enables these countries to ratify without altering their law.

Article III in fact exempts foreign works protected by the Convention from all formalities with one exception: that they bear a copyright notice containing three elements: 1. The symbol ©; 2. The name of the copyright proprietor; 3. The year of first publication. On the other hand, any contracting state can require formalities for the 'acquisition and enjoyment of copyright' provided such requirements are confined to the works of its own nationals or works first published in its territory. In practice one finds that at least printed publications even when first published in a Berne country now usually carry the copyright notice required by the UCC.

[1] See Desbois, Françon, Kerever *Les Conventions Internationales du droit d'auteur et des droits voisins* (1976) p 81/para 85.

(1) The symbol

6.09 Although the form is taken from the United States copyright system[1] and the letter C stands for the English word 'Copyright' it has been successfully internationalised and presents no problem.

1 Bogsch, op cit, art III, para 6.

(2) The name

6.10 It is usually the name of the publisher which appears with the ©. This is done because the 'copyright proprietor' under the Convention can be the author or the publisher who acquires the copyright in the publishing contract and it will be the latter whom a prospective user will wish to locate to obtain the permission to use the work. It will also usually be the publisher who will want to bring an infringement action on behalf of the author.

This practice meets the requirements of both copyright systems. There are those legal systems under which copyright is indivisible so that it can only be owned as a whole by the author or his heir or his assignee whereas anyone who acquires part of the right is a licensee. The other group are the copyright systems under which copyright is divisible and the copyright owner can assign part of his copyright, eg reproduction right and the film right, separately. In that case the name of the part owner will be the one to appear on the notice. In either case the assignee or the licensee if he cannot give the permission sought by the user, because he does not own the right in which the user is interested, will be able to inform the user to whom he should address himself. 'It is believed that no contracting country will consider a notice insufficient because ownership is interpreted according to one system rather than the other'.[1]

In case of further editions of a book which are identical with the first edition this will present no problem, but if subsequent editions vary substantially from the first edition because of additions, omissions or alterations it may well be that a subsequent edition has to be regarded as a new work. In some countries it is the practice to cite all subsequent editions. However, as it cannot be seen from such citations whether any of the new editions is or may be a new work this does not seem to alter the question the court of the country where protection is claimed has to decide. That question will usually be whether the matters added or the alterations are sufficiently substantial to make it a new work in which case the date of first publication will be the date of publication of that edition or whether it is still to be regarded as the same work in which case the date of first publication will be decisive.

With regard to the name of an author or other copyright proprietor there are no established rules, but it stands to reason that it should be acceptable if it complies with the national law of the country of publication or the country of which the author is a national. This must be so as in some countries there are no surnames, in others there are several. With corporations it may be wise to spell out the name in full instead of using abbreviations which may not be generally understood. With anonymous works it will be the name of the publisher. A pseudonym will probably do if it is widely known as otherwise it would frustrate the purpose of the notice. In both cases it would probably be wise to give the name of the publisher. If the validity of the notice is challenged it is suggested that the test will always be whether the notice is such as to enable a prospective user to get in touch with the right owner who is in a position to authorise the particular use.

1 Bogsch, op cit, art III, para 6.

(3) The date

6.11 The year must always be the year of first publication. In the United States the rule is that for an antedated notice the term runs from the last day of the year in the notice (*Callaghan v Myers* 128 US 645) whereas a postdated notice invalidates the notice (*American Code Co v Bensinger* 282 F 829).[1]

However, in most countries including now the United States, for works published after 1977 this will be of no consequence as the relevant time is the death of the author not of the publication of the work. However, in cases where the copyright runs from publication, eg photographs or works of applied art, it is crucial.[2] It may well be that national courts would adopt the above-mentioned American practice on the grounds that an antedated notice does not harm the public interest whereas a postdated notice does.

Article III prescribes that the symbol © must be 'accompanied' by the other elements. This seems to suggest that the three required elements should appear together and not in different places. There are no rules laid down in the Convention as to the location of the notice (whereas under United States copyright law there are) or the manner of it[3] as long as they are 'placed in such manner and location as to give reasonable notice of claim of copyright', to the person who reads it or otherwise 'visually perceives' it (article VI). Both elements must be questions of fact for the court in the country where protection is claimed.

With regard to the placing of the notice, particularly on copyright material other than books, an advisory opinion of the Intergovernmental Committee of the UCC given in 1957 gives very adequate guidelines.[4]

> In the case of *books or pamphlets*, on the title page or the page immediately following, or at the end of the book or pamphlet, in the case of a *single sheet*, on either of the sides.
>
> In the case of *printed music*, on the title page or first page of music, or at the end of the printed music, in the case of *newspapers*, *magazines* or other *periodicals*, under the main title or the 'masthead'.
>
> In the case of *maps*, *prints* or *photographs*, on their face side, either on the actual map or picture (but somewhere near the title or the margin) or on the margin.
>
> In the case of *independent parts of a whole* (if a separate copyright is claimed in the independent parts), under the title of the independent part.
>
> In the case of *motion pictures*, on the frames which carry its title (whether appearing at the beginning or the end) or credits.'

1 Both cited by Bogsch, op cit, under art III, para 7; and see Desbois, op cit, p 86.
2 Art IV.
3 As Desbois (op cit, p 87) observes with a tinge of irony: 'it should be such that those concerned do not need a magnifying glass'.
4 Cited by Bogsch, op cit, art III, para 9.

6.12 The remaining points on the notice follow from the text of Article III/1:

1. The notice must appear 'from the time of first publication'. This means that if an adequate notice did not appear on all copies constituting first publication, notices on subsequent copies will not save the copyright in countries requiring formalities.
2. The notice must appear on *all* copies. If some copies with a valid notice are produced and evidence is given to the effect that all copies bear the notice, the courts will probably assume that all copies bear that notice until the contrary is proved.[1] If the other side then produce copies without notice

the result will depend on the facts of the case. A dozen copies without notice in a first edition of ten thousand will probably be disregarded as de minimis; on the other hand against a background of a very limited edition of a book or a photograph or an engraving, a dozen copies may be significant.

3. The work must have been 'published with the authority' of the copyright owner. This is of importance because it disqualifies unauthorised publications. Were it otherwise it would be possible for a clandestine first edition of a work to deprive subsequent legitimate editions of the protection of the Convention.

4. A valid notice will be regarded as satisfying any formalities which 'domestic law requires as a condition of copyright'. Those requirements mentioned in article III/I such as deposit, registration, notice etc are 'listed as examples only and not limitatively'[2] as indicated by the words 'such as'.

This means a contrario that formalities which, if not complied with do not invalidate the copyright are permitted. Such formalities may range from the requirements of customs or censorship to deposit with national libraries or any other purely administrative requirements which are common in many countries. They are all permissible and will have to be observed as long as they do not amount to 'a condition of copyright'.

On the other hand many formalities, eg ministerial or consular certificates or proof of certification of protection in the country of origin, can be disregarded.

As most national laws require some formalities it is essential that a copyright notice under article III of the Convention is placed on every copy of a work wherever published and this has in fact become common form all over the world. Bogsch expresses the view that Belgium, France, Luxembourg and Portugal would be the only countries which would apply the Convention to works, copies of which do not bear the notice.[3]

The notice is of particular importance to works first published in the United Kingdom and other countries of the British Commonwealth to counteract the so-called 'manufacturing clause' of the old United States Copyright Act 1909[4] so that copies of books and periodicals bearing a valid notice do not have to be manufactured in the United States.[5]

1 See Report of Rapporteur General Sir John Blake (1952) on art III.
2 Report of Rapporteur General, Records, p 78.
3 Op cit, art III, para 21.
4 17 USC para 16.
5 Whilst the representative of the UK at the Diplomatic Conference pointed out that this lifting of the manufacturing clause is vital if the UK is to ratify the Convention, the French commentary acidly remarks 'a formality now replaces an operation of an industrial or commercial kind' (Desbois, op cit, para 88).

6.13 Article III/3 was inserted in parts purely to safeguard the United States copyright system. It would not have been strictly necessary to say that the procedural requirements of the courts where protection is claimed must be complied with; that is a principle of international law. On the other hand the permissible condition slipped into the middle of a rather convoluted sentence 'the complainant must deposit with the court or an administrative office or both, a copy of the work involved in the litigation' obscures, but does not hide, the fact that an action brought before the United States courts based on a valid notice will not be maintainable unless a copy of the work is deposited with the United States Copyright Office and is registered with that office.[1] However, the significance of the provision is that the copyright is not lost and the procedural defect may be cured by deposit and registration and by bringing a new action. Equally important, an action against another defendant for infringement of the same right will lie after the defects have been cured.

1   See Bogsch, op cit, art 3, para 23.

6.14   Article III/4 Unpublished works of Convention nationals must be protected without requirements of formalities. The contracting states have to provide 'the legal means' of enforcing copyright in unpublished works. This is important because of the fairly narrow definition of publication.[1] The provision is inspired by United States law where there is common law protection (as opposed to protection by statute, ie the Copyright Act) for unpublished works which is unlimited in time.

It is important to note that sales of a work in recorded form (phonograms) do not amount to publication so that the music and text of a song, although it has been recorded and the records sold in large quantities, can be 'unpublished'.

1   Art VI.

6.15   Article III/5 is another provision which applied solely to the United States. The effect of it was that the copyright notice under the Convention avoided the formalities required in the United States in respect of the first term of 28 years but not of the second term of 28 years. To get the second term of 28 years one had to comply with the renewal formalities. Under the new 1976 Act this does no longer apply as there is only one term computed from the death of the author.

5.   Duration – article IV

(1) History

6.16   The provisions governing duration which were left unchanged by the 1971 revision[1] – like much else in the UCC – are an attempt to bridge the gap between the copyright system of the United States and those of most other countries. At the time of the creation of the Convention the terms in the United States was 28 years from first publication with the possibility of renewal for an equal period giving a total of 56 years from publication. This means that in some cases of works written early in the life of an author who lives into his eighties or in the case of works in respect of which the application for the renewal of copyright has not been made or made too late, the work will fall into the public domain in the lifetime of the author which is impossible by definition in Berne Convention countries.

In the new United States Copyright Act 1976 which took effect on 1 January 1978 the basis of the term of copyright for literary and artistic works was changed, undoubtedly under the influence of the Berne Convention, to 50 years pma. However with regard to United States works published before 1 January 1978 the rather complicated rules in article IV dealing with duration calculated from the date of publication are still of importance.

Article IV contains one basic rule and two major and some minor exceptions. The basic rule is – like for the convention as a whole – the rule of national treatment, ie a work to which the convention applies must be protected for the same term as a domestic work.[2] The *first* major exception is that of the *minimum term*, ie if a country gives a longer term to domestic works than the minimum provided by the Convention it need only give that minimum to Convention works.

The *second* major exception is the application of the reciprocity rule to the term producing *comparison of terms* or 'the rule of the shorter term' thus a country which gives to domestic works a term longer than the terms given by the country of origin of the work.

1   Apart from changing lettering and numbering for easy reference (Report of 1971 Conference, para 39).
2   Art IV1 and Art III.

(2) The rule of national treatment

6.17   Published works of convention nationals are protected for the term given to published works of the home state. Published works first published in a Convention state are protected for the term given to works first published in the home state. Unpublished works of nationals of a convention state are protected for the term given to unpublished works of a home national.

(3) The minimum term

6.18   The minimum term of protection is 25 years pma.[1] This means that if a country calculates the term on the basis of the life of the author, as nearly all countries do, and its term is shorter than 25 years pma it must give 25 years pma to Convention works.[2]

1   Art IV/2(a).
2   The USSR had to lengthen the period of protection from 15 years pma to 25 years pma to ratify the Convention. There are now however very few countries which give less. Haiti (10 years pma if no descendant of the author is alive) and Liberia (20 years pma) are examples given by Bogsch op cit, art IV/4.

Exception 1
There is an exception for states (eg the United States) which on the effective date in that state compute the term of protection from first publication or from registration prior to first publication. For those states the term is 25 years from first publication or registration.[1] This is now only of practical importance for old works in the United States.

1   Art IV2(b).

Exception 2
There is also an exception for states which (again on the effective date in that state) have limited the protection 'for certain classes of works' to a period computed from first publication. For these states and those works the term is 25 years from first publication.[2] This exception is important because many countries treat different 'classes of works' in different ways. The classification may vary according to the work, eg literary, dramatic, artistic or published or unpublished works or works published in the author's lifetime or posthumously. It may be according to whether the author is a physical person or a legal entity (corporation etc). It may be according to the status of the author, ie self-employed or employee. Thus any circumstances which give rise to a different treatment of the work constitute a 'class of work'. Some countries in the case of pseudonymous or anonymous works calculate from the death of the publisher (eg France, Spain); some countries, in the case of posthumous works, from the date of first performance in a specific case (eg United Kingdom); some countries, in the case of employees' works from the death of the employer (eg Netherlands).[3]

Article IV/2(c) seems to have no practical application as only the United

States and the Philippines granted two terms of copyright and in both cases the first term exceeded the minimum of 25 years and both countries have now introduced the 50 years pma term.

2   Art IV/2(a).
3   See Bogsch, op cit, art IV, para 9.

Exception 3
Photographic works and works of applied art, in so far as they are protected as artistic works, need only be given a minimum of 10 years.[4] The Convention does not specify the date of commencement of the term. It could be the date of creation, or the date of publication, but as the former would in many cases be very difficult to ascertain presumably the latter is to be applied.[5]

4   Art IV/3.
5   See Report of the Rapporteur General of the 1952 Conference under article IV.

(4) The comparison of terms or 'rule of the shorter term'

6.19   This is the rule applied by the Berne Convention to the term of copyright. There are however significant differences.

1. The 'cutting back' to the term given in the country of origin[1] is permissive. The Convention says: 'No contracting state shall be obliged to grant protection for a longer period' (article IV/4(a)).

Bogsch points out[2] that according to the wording of the article the Convention leaves the question open whether the state where protection is claimed may have to legislate to bring the mechanism of comparison of terms into play. Under the Berne Convention (article 7/8) the comparison is applied automatically if the national law of the country where protection is claimed is silent. However, Desbois[3] points out that French jurisprudence is inclined to establish a parallelism between article 7 of the Berne Convention and article IV of the UCC.

Ulmer[4] and Nordemann[5] also take the view that if the law of the country where protection is claimed is silent the Convention should be directly applied, ie the comparison takes place. They point out that the provision is not a retaliation measure but that there is no reason why a work should be protected for a longer term than in its country of origin.

2. The comparison of terms may be applied not only to the same work as in other conventions but to the term given to the whole 'class of work' to which the work belongs.

Bogsch sets out the thought process to be followed when applying the rule of the comparison of terms very succinctly:[6]

> '(i)   first one has to determine the duration which the national law of the country where protection is sought would grant to the work if this work were a domestic work.
> (ii)   then one has to determine to what class of works the particular work belongs, according to the laws of the country of origin;
> (iii) finally, one has to determine the duration which the laws of the country of origin of the work grant - not necessarily to the particular work in question - but to the class of works to which the particular work belongs.
> If the duration under (iii) is shorter than that under (i), the duration under (iii) may be applied.'

1   The UCC does not use this expression but spells it out: in the case of unpublished works the country of which the author is a national and in the case of published works, the country in which the work was first published.

2 Bogsch, op cit, art IV, para 22.
3 Desbois op cit, para 99 citing a judgment of the 'Court of Paris' of 24 April 1974.
4 GRUR 1960/p57, and Ulmer *Urheber und Verlagsrecht* (3rd ed, 1980) p 102, 103.
5 Op cit, p 200.
6 Bogsch, op cit, Art IV, para 22.

6. The basic rights – article IV bis

6.20 This article was inserted in 1971 'to give further body and meaning to the general obligation contained in Article 1 that each Contracting State undertakes to provide adequate and effective protection of the rights of authors and other copyright proprietors'.[1] These are 'the basic rights ensuring the author's economic interests': the reproduction right, the broadcasting right and the public performance right. Each is an exclusive right.

The three basic rights granted must be interpreted broadly as they are to include works 'either in their original form or in any form recognisably derived from the original.'[2] Thus the author has the exclusive right to authorise translations or adaptations, or arrangements of his work.

These basic rights are a minimum that every state must grant but the list is 'not to be interpreted as limitative or exhaustive'.[3] This follows from the wording of the article: 'the rights ... shall *include* the basic rights'.

On the other hand, they exclude the moral right of authors. The exclusion was deliberate[4] on the grounds that several countries, now parties to the UCC (particularly the United States) did not recognise it.

It must also be emphasised that the Convention does not, unlike the Berne Convention, give the copyright owner any rights jure conventionis. It merely places a contractual liability on the state ratifying the 1971 Convention to grant such rights to authors and other right owners in their domestic legislation.[5]

The *'reproduction right'* is the making of copies from a tangible corporeal fixation 'by any means'. This is sufficiently wide to include all forms of reproduction. The *'right of public performance'* on the other hand does not need a fixation before the performance is given or indeed of the performance. The *'broadcasting right'* includes sound broadcasting and television. Unlike the Berne Convention (article 11 bis) nothing is said about secondary uses of broadcasting ie rebroadcasting or CATV.

It was also understood that no country party to the UCC (1952) that now respects the fundamental rights of authors and other right owners need change its domestic law to specifically include these basic rights or 'assume new obligations in order to adhere to the 1971 Convention'.[6]

This point is taken further by *article IV bis/2* which enables contracting states to provide for exceptions in their domestic legislation but only if two conditions are fulfilled:

1. These 'do not conflict with the spirit and provisions of the Convention' and
2. The state making the exception does nonetheless 'accord a reasonable degree of effective protection to each of the rights'.

It is clear that these formulations are the result of considerable bargaining resulting in a series of compromises 'capable of accommodating a great variety of legal systems, economic and social situations, and cultural factors'.[7]

1 Kaminstein Report 1971, para 41.
2 Art IV bis, para 1.

3 Kaminstein Report, para 43.
4 See Kaminstein Report, para 42.
5 See Nordemann, op cit, p 202.
6 Kaminstein Report, para 44.
7 Kaminstein Report, para 45.

6.21 The delegations at the Diplomatic Conference were obviously aware of the dangers of very different interpretations being put on the meaning of this fundamental article and the General Rapporteur was asked to include in his report what amounts to a kind of authoritative interpretation of the article:[1]

'The conference agreed that, subject to very minor drafting changes, the IGCC text should be accepted and that various points raised by its wording should be interpreted as follows:

1. *The exceptions must not 'conflict with the spirit' of the 1971 Convention.* It was considered that, in addition to the requirement for "adequate and effective protection" in Article I, the "spirit" of the Convention also comprehended the convictions expressed in paragraphs 1 and 2 of the Universal Declaration of Human Rights: that everyone has a right "freely to participate in the cultural life of the community", and that everyone equally has a right "to the protection of the moral and material interests resulting from any scientific, literary or artistic production of which he is the author".

2. The *"contrario principle"*. Paragraph 83 of the Intergovernmental Copyright Committee Report accompanying the IGCC text (UCC/4, Annex IX, p. 9) stated the view of the Committee that "the inclusion in the Convention of special provisions allowing developing countries to publish certain works and translations under compulsory licences, means *a contrario* that, except as provided in Article V, there could be no question of developed countries instituting a general system of compulsory licensing for the publication of literary, scientific or artistic works". The Conference adopted this principle, it being understood that a "general system" referred either to a system applying to a specific type of work with respect to all forms of uses, or to a system applying to all types of works with respect to a particular form of use.

3. *The exceptions must not "conflict with the provisions" of the 1971 Convention.* As a corollary to the "*a contrario*" principle, the Conference understood the references to "the provisions" of the revised convention as referring to Articles V*ter* and V*quater*. This means that a State not qualifying as a developing country under Article V*bis* would not be entitled to institute licensing systems similar to those provided in Articles V*ter* and V*quater*.

4. *The State must accord "a reasonable degree of effective protection" to each of the rights named.* It was understood that, under the second sentence of paragraph 2 of Article IV*bis*, no State would be entitled to withhold entirely all rights with respect to reproduction, public performance, or broadcasting, that where exceptions are made they must have a logical basis and must not be applied arbitrarily, and that the protection offered must be effectively enforced by the laws of the Contracting State.'

From the records of the Revision Conference and this authoritative interpretation six basic principles can be extracted, which are the achievement of the 1971 Revision:

(1) No country 'developed' or 'developing' can 'withhold entirely', ie fail to grant, any one of the three basic rights.
(2) No 'developed country' can institute 'a general system of compulsory licensing for the publication of literary, scientific or artistic works' apart from the restrictions of the translation right permitted in article V.
(3) Even a 'developing country' cannot introduce compulsory licensing systems other than for the purposes and on the terms specified in articles V bis to V quater.

(4) Any such 'general system of compulsory licensing' must be 'either a system applying to a specific type of work with respect to all forms of uses or to a system applying to all types of works with respect to a particular form of use'.[2]
(5) All countries both 'developed' and 'developing' must ensure that the rights granted under the Convention are 'effectively enforced by the laws of the Contracting State'.
(6) The necessary counterpart of permitting compulsory licences is the provision for equitable renumeration to the right owners and the respect of the moral rights granted in these circumstances by the Convention.[3]

[1] Kaminstein Report, para 46.
[2] However, art 2 bis(2), Berne Convention, permits the restriction of the broadcasting right with respect to particular categories of works.
[3] Art V/2(d), (e) and (f).

7. The system of compulsory licences (general)

6.22 The three articles which follow (*articles V/2, Vter, V quater*) establish the possible exceptions to the basic rights granted in article IV bis, article V ter and V quater for developing countries regarding the translation right and the reproduction right respectively.

The procedures which have to be established by states introducing compulsory licences are similar in all three cases: the person seeking a licence must show either that he has requested a licence and his request has been denied or that after exercising 'due diligence' he has been unable to find the right owner concerned. 'The request for authorisation addressed to the owner of the right must indicate that, if authorisation is denied, the denial might serve as the basis for applying for a compulsory licence'.[1] It is for the courts of each country to decide the validity of the compulsory licences granted by the authorities of that country.

Article V/2 (1952 Act, substantially unchanged) establishes an exclusive translation right but permits all member states to grant compulsory licences after seven years under stated conditions.

Article V ter imposes the same obligation to grant exclusive translation rights on developing countries but permits compulsory licences after periods of three years or one year, under the conditions laid down in that article.

Article V quater enables developing countries to grant compulsory licences in respect of the reproduction right after periods of five years and in respect of specially named works of seven years or three years respectively under the conditions laid down in that article.

[1] General Report of the Berne Revision Conference 1971, para 37.

8 The translation right – article V

6.23 This article which, apart from changes of terminology, was already in the 1952 text of the Convention establishes the only compulsory licence system permissible under the Convention in both developed and developing countries. The other permitted compulsory licence systems (articles V bis, V ter, and V quater) are permissible only in developing countries. Article V thus served as the precedent and example for the preferential system of compulsory licences for the benefit of developing countries to be established in 1971.

(1) The right – article V/1

6.24 The author or other copyright proprietor who is the owner of the translation right has the exclusive right to (a) make a translation (b) publish a translation (c) authorise the making of a translation (d) authorise the publication of a translation. It is (d) that is in practice the important right and it has to be read together with the definition of publication in article VI: 'the reproduction in tangible form and the general distribution to the public of copies of a work from which it can be read or otherwise visually perceived'. Thus neither the recording nor the public performance nor the broadcasting of a work are 'publication' in the sense of article V and therefore recordings and public performances and broadcasts and any other use of a translation which does not amount to a 'publication' of the work is outside article V and no compulsory licences can be issued in respect of it.

Furthermore, it follows a contrario from article V/2: a) that if the work is not a 'writing' no compulsory licence is permissible; b) if the translation is into a language which is not 'a national language' no compulsory licence is permissible; c) if a translation into the language in question has been published within seven years of the first publication of the original and is not out of print, no compulsory licence is permissible.

The translation right must be subject to the same term as other rights in the country where protection is claimed unless it is subject to a compulsory licence under article V/2. Thus even if a compulsory licence system is established in a contracting state the exclusive translation right of the author must be respected for seven years from the first publication of the work. The author or other copyright owner will therefore be entitled to an exclusive right for seven years and to equitable remuneration for the rest of the term. (Usually life plus 50 years.)

(2) The exceptions: compulsory licences – article V/2

6.25 'A compulsory translation licence may be granted under certain conditions to "any national" of a contracting state.' Thus this facility is available to all member countries developed and developing. The exceptions must be made by legislation. No contracting state can issue compulsory licences with regard to one work or with regard to one author or with regard to a category of works other than by passing a law.

The translation must be a translation of 'writings'. The term stems from the United States Constitution[1] where it is very widely interpreted.[2] It includes, apart from books, periodicals etc, dramatic works, dialogues of films, which are mostly in written form, libretti of dramatico-musical works, the texts of songs if they exist in written form and are published.

A compulsory licence can be issued by the competent authority to a national of the contracting state where it is issued. This may be a corporation or other legal entity situate in that state. The licence must be personal and 'non-exclusive'. This means that the competent authority can issue more than one licence in respect of the same work. It also means that the right of the authority and the right of the right owner could exist side by side and none can prevent the other granting a licence.[3]

A translation may be published without the permission of the right owner or even against his wishes in either of the two following cases:

(1) No translation in a language in general use in the contracting state has been published within seven years from the date of first publication, or
(2) A translation into such a language has been published within the first

seven years, but all editions are out of print at any time after the seven years have expired and whilst the work is still in copyright.

The Convention does not define a 'language in general use' but it was understood by the 1952 Conference that a state could designate which were regarded as the national languages 'in general use'.[4] The 'competent authority' is not defined. It was suggested at the 1952 Conference that such competent authority should always be a tribunal but as the constitutional requirements of states differ so widely in this respect an administrative authority, eg a ministry, cannot be excluded.

Thus after expiry of the seven-year period a compulsory licence can be issued for any translation, not only translations for the privileged purposes, and copies of these translations can be exported within the limits stated in V/2 (e).

The difference between such a compulsory licence under V(2) and a compulsory licence issued by a developing country under article V ter[5] is that the latter will remain in force even after the seven-year period has elapsed subject to the terms on which it has been granted. The licensee will be able to request that such licence now be replaced by a new 'Article V – licence' subject only to the more liberal provisions of article V. However this course, if chosen, has the disadvantage that he will have to go through the procedure demanded by article V at that stage.[6]

There is a difference here between the UCC and the Berne Convention. Under the Berne Convention a developing country can, instead of a compulsory licence, avail itself of the ten-year reservation on the conditions provided for under article 30(2).[7]

1 US Constitution, art I/8.
2 See para 21.57 below.
3 See Bogsch, op cit, art V/4.
4 Report of 1952 Conference. 'Thus India could provide for translation into the official regional languages which are used in parts of that country, and which are not the national languages of other countries as well as providing for translation into the national languages used more generally in India.'
5 See para 6.45 below.
6 See Kaminstein Report, para 88.
7 See para 6.49 below.

(3) Procedure to be followed for the issuing of a compulsory licence to publish a translation

6.26 A compulsory licence may be granted if the following steps have been taken:

1. The applicant has requested permission to make and publish a translation and has been refused or, after due diligence he has been unable to find the owner of the right.[1] Refusal must relate to the work to be translated (a general refusal would probably not suffice)[2] and to the person of the applicant. Such refusal could however be implied from the circumstances, ie no reply for a substantial period of time. Inability to find the right owner may mean that he literally cannot be found or that his identity cannot be established after using due diligence.
2. If the right owner cannot be found in either of the two above-mentioned cases the applicant has to send copies of his application to the publisher whose name appears on the work.[3] This is a logical step as the publisher, if he is not the right owner, is the most likely person to know who the right owner is.
3. 'If the nationality of the right owner is known copies of the application

have to be sent to the diplomatic or consular representative of the State of which the owner is a national or the organisation which may have been designated by the government of that state.[3]

It seems to follow that if, as will often be the case, the applicant can, after the exercise of due diligence not find out either who the right owner is or what his nationality is, sending off the application to the publisher will be the only practical step.

4. After sending copies of the application, the applicant has to wait for two months before the compulsory licence can be issued.

If the steps listed above have been taken and either the right owner cannot be found or if he is found but he and the applicant cannot agree on the conditions under which the latter may publish the translation, there is a denial of authorisation and a compulsory licence can be issued.

1 Art V/2 (b).
2 See Bogsch, op cit, V para 5.
3 Art V/2 (c).

(4) Compensation

6.27 The legislation in the contracting state must provide for compensation to the right owner. Such compensation must:

(a) be 'just'
(b) 'conform to international standards'
(c) be transmitted to the right owner.[1]

What is just must be left to the tribunal or other competent authority to decide, but to avoid derisory amounts being awarded the Convention requests that it must conform to international standards. It is suggested that this must mean a percentage of the price which the public pays for the copy of the work.[2] However, the amounts, ie the percentage, may well differ substantially from country to country.[3] This is probably the most important provision. If it is interpreted as meaning, that in countries where currency regulations prohibit the sending of money out of the country a deposit in the country is sufficient, the provision would not be very satisfactory to the right owner. He would have to go to the country and spend the money there or buy goods which he can take home.[4] The better view is that the obligations on a contracting state are only fulfilled if the state assures payment in a convertible currency.[5]

1 Art V/2(d).
2 Nordemann, op cit, p 210.
3 Desbois, op cit, para 109.
4 George Bernard Shaw remarked wryly in similar circumstances that his royalties for the translations and the performances of his plays in the USSR could only be recovered by taking a holiday in the Crimea or buying a fur coat for one of his lady friends. (This was of course at a time when the USSR was not a member of any international Convention.)
5 Nordemann, op cit, p 211.

(5) Moral rights

6.28 The moral rights of the author must also be respected although they are not referred to as such.

(1) A 'correct' translation must be ensured.[1]
(2) The original title and the name of the author must be printed on all copies of the translation.[2]
(3) When the author has withdrawn all copies of the work from circulation, no compulsory licence must be granted.[3]

These requirements must not be taken too literally. Thus if the method of duplication is other than printing 2(e) would have to be applied, eg, copies made by duplicating equipment. It is also difficult to see how a competent authority can 'ensure' a correct translation. It will probably be sufficient if a competent translator has been employed and has done his best.

1   Art V/2(d)
2   Art V/2 (e)
3   Art V/2(f)

(6) Exports

6.29   The compulsory licence is valid only for the purpose of publication in the country which has granted it. It would seem however, from the text[1] that exports and distribution outside the country after 'publication' inside the country is permissible.[2]

However, one case of exportation is specifically referred to as permissible if three conditions are fulfilled: (1) the same language as that into which the work has been translated is in general use in the country of importation, (2) that country provides for such compulsory licences and (3) that the importing country does not prohibit such importation.[3]

An example will illustrate the restrictions.[4] A German novel is translated into the Kurdic language in the USSR in accordance with a compulsory licence. Copies can be exported to Turkey which is a contracting state, but not into Iraq or Iran which are not contracting states, although the Kurdic language is in general use there. However, the penultimate sentence of V(2)(e) seems to dispense with these restrictions and substitute for them the sole conditions that the importing state does not prohibit such importation and sale. The result of these provisions therefore seems to be that export of copies of the translation is permissible provided the importing country does not prohibit the importation.[5]

The licence is not transferable by the licensee.[6] This provision is necessary because otherwise the provision that compulsory licences can be granted only to nationals of the state granting them, could easily be circumvented.

1   Last sentence of art V/2(e).
2   See Bogsch, op cit, art V para 8.
3   Art V/2(e).
4   Given by Nordemann, op cit, art V, 10.
5   See Bogsch, op cit, Art V para 8. See also Desbois op cit, p 109 who points out that two contracting states who share the same language could get together to share the cost of the translation and supply their respective markets from the same source.
6   Art V/2(e) last sentence.

(7) The system of compulsory licences in developing countries (general)

6.30   Since 1971 the system of compulsory licensing available to developing countries is basically the same under the Berne Convention and under the Universal Copyright Convention. It is laid down in articles V bis, V ter and V quater of the UCC 1971 and in the Appendix to the Berne Convention 1971, respectively. To avoid repetition the provisions for the benefit of the developing countries are therefore dealt with separately in paras 6.38–6.52 below with references to the relevant articles of each Convention as they apply to both.

9. Publication – article VI

(1) History

6.31 The definition of 'publication' is the result of the origins and history of copyright and of the American influence on the Convention. Copyright originated in the sixteenth century from the privileges of printers which prohibited the copying of what they had printed.[1] It was thus not so much a right to protect authors as a right to protect publishers who were identical with printers in those days and who made the financial investment without which the work would not reach the public. Seen against this political and economic background it is clear that the vital moment in the history of the work is its publication and that publication happens at the moment when the work is available for sale to the general public. It is at that moment that the work starts its journey from its author to its public. This has remained true. The additional factor which weighed heavily with the 1952 Conference was that the United States Constitution[2] provides for copyright only in 'writings', although this term has been given a wide interpretation by the courts.

It is not surprising that a definition grown from an invention of the printing press of the fifteenth century and rooted in legislation of the eighteenth century (the Statute of Queen Anne in 1709 and the American Constitution in 1776) should pose problems in the twentieth century.

The Convention defines 'publication, as used in this Convention' because both many national laws and the Berne Convention contain different definitions.

Some national legislations only require availability to the public without requiring physical copies (eg Federal Republic of Germany, Switzerland, Austria).[3]

At the time of the 1952 Conference the concept of publication did not have an important role in the United States law because copyright protection was dependent on the nationality of the author rather than on the place of first publication. On the other hand in Europe the reverse was the case as a published work is in most cases only protected if it is first published in the country where protection is sought particularly if it is the work of a foreign author.[4]

The concept of publication in the Berne Convention[5] also requires the existence of copies as well as availability of the copies to the general public, but readability or visual perception is not required. The Berne Convention does not specifically stipulate that publication must have been with the authorisation of the author of the work; however it seems clear from the general philosophy of the Convention that rights which belong to the author or other right owner in the work can only be acquired from him and that thus only authorised publication is publication in the sense of the Convention.

1 See para 2.04 above.
2 Constitution of the USA, I/8.
3 German Copyright Law 1965, para 6; Swiss Copyright Law 1911, para 11; Austrian Copyright Law (as amended) 1972, para 8.
4 See Bogsch, op cit, art VI/1.
5 Art 3(3); see para 5.33 above.

(2) Definition of publication

6.32 The definition in article VI has two essential ingredients:

(1) The reproduction of the work must be 'in tangible form', ie copies, from which the work 'can be read or visually perceived'.
(2) Such copies must have had a 'general distribution to the public'.

156 *The Universal Copyright Convention (UCC)*

The main debate over the definition of publication at the 1952 Conference (the article was not altered in 1971) was largely on what should be excluded, ie what should not constitute 'publication'. This is conveniently set out in the interpretation section of the United Kingdom Copyright Act 1956: 'the performance or the issue of records, of a literary, dramatic or musical work, the exhibition of an artistic work, the construction of a work of architecture, and the issue of photographs or engravings of a work of architecture or of a sculpture, do not constitute publication of the work'.[1] The performance of a work in a theatre or a concert hall is not publication because such performance is ephemeral, it *does not* result in copies which can be read. The same is true of broadcasts. Neither amounts to the 'distribution of copies'. The exhibition of a picture or sculpture in a gallery is not 'publication' because it is the work itself that is being exhibited not 'copies' of it.

Copies of a 'derivative' or 'secondary' work are not copies of the underlying original work. Copies of an English translation of a French novel are copies of that English translation (which is a work) but not copies of the French novel. A copy of an arrangement for piano of a symphony is a copy of that arrangement (which is a work) but not of the symphony.

The question whether the issuing of a phonogram amounts to 'publication' depends (according to the Convention) on whether such a phonogram is a 'copy' of the work recorded. The record of the Brussels Conference (1948) shows that the British delegation took the view that it was not a copy, whereas the French delegation took the view that it was.[2]

The Report of the Rapporteur General of the 1952 Convention records that some countries proposed a reference to works which can be 'visually or orally perceived'. This was opposed by some on the practical grounds that it would 'result primarily in the protection of works of nationals of non-contracting States issued first as phonograms in a contracting State'.

Thus the history of copyright and of the Convention explains the definition of publication but cannot hide the absurdity that when thousands of members of the public hear a work in a theatre or a concert hall or hundreds of thousands buy it in recorded form or millions hear it on radio or see it on television that is not 'publication' whereas in many cases putting a few dozen copies of a new book on sale in a bookshop is.

1 S 49(2) (a).
2 Bogsch, op cit, art VI/10 recalls that the first meeting of the Interim Copyright Committee established by the 1952 Convention expressed a view that the 'sole purpose' of art VI was to exclude phonograph records.

(3) General distribution to the public

6.33 'Distribution' cannot be accurately defined but generally it means handing out copies whether it is giving them away or selling them, ie putting them at the disposal of the public, making them available.

Although the English word 'distribution' may suggest that putting copies on sale is not enough, but they have actually to be sold, ie change hands, to be distributed, the French and Spanish texts 'mise à disposition' and 'poner a disposicion' makes it clear that offering is enough without acceptance. Gratuitous distribution is also 'distribution'. Whether leasing or lending is is another question.

The relevant date is the date of distribution, not of reproduction as this is the act that turns an unpublished work into a published work.

'The 'public' must be the general public as the Convention speaks of 'general distribution to the public'. Distribution to a circle of friends or to a definable group is not publication. Thus distribution to a 'Samiszdat' in the USSR was held not to amount to publication because the distribution was to a defined group of people and not the general public.[1]

The concept of 'publication' is relevant to the interpretation of articles II, III, IV and V of the Convention.

Relevance to protection (article II)
'Publication' is a connecting factor relevant if the author is not a national of a contracting country. In such case his work is protected only if published and published in a contracting country.

Relevance to formalities (article III)
First 'publication' of a work outside the country where protection is claimed and the author of which is not one of its nationals (article III(1)) is a prerequisite of substituting the copyright notice under the Convention for domestic formalities. The notice must contain 'the year of first publication' and must appear on the copies 'from the time of first publication'.

Relevance to the term of protection (article IV)
Some countries where the term of copyright for certain works is computed from first publication apply the minimum of 25 years 'from the date of first publication'. Simultaneous publication is calculated 'within 30 days of first publication'.

Relevance to the right of translation (article V)
A compulsory licence can be issued if a translation has not been 'published' within seven years from the date of first 'publication' of the writing.

1 Case of Solzhenitsyn's *August 14th*, BGH (German Supreme Courts) Judgment of 16 October 1975.

10. Works permanently in the public domain – article VII

6.34 If a work is in the public domain it does not matter why it is in the public domain. It may be because it is not eligible for protection. It may be because the term has expired. It may be because essential formalities had not been complied with.

As the article says 'works or rights in works' it is possible that the work as such is not in the public domain but a particular right in the work is. If a country grants 50 years pma for the reproduction right but only 10 or 20 years from first publication for the translation right, the translation right may be in the public domain well within the lifetime of the author.

11. Links between the 1952 Convention and the 1971 Convention – article IX

6.35 The Revised Universal Copyright Convention came into force on 10 July 1974 which was three months after the deposit of 12 ratifications.[1]

The Convention thereby encountered a problem which other international conventions (eg the Berne Convention or the Paris Convention in the industrial property field) had encountered before: how to regulate the relations between states which are bound by different texts of the same convention. The problem was accentuated by the fact that it was novel for the Universal Copyright Convention as this was the first revision and by the desire to make as many developed countries as possible grant the new preferential treatment for developing countries which are contained in the 1971 Convention.

The solution adopted consists of three rules:

(1) No state can, after 11 July 1974 (coming into force of the Convention), accede solely to the 1952 Convention.[2]
(2) A state acceding to the 1971 Convention becomes automatically party to the 1952 Convention.
(3) Relations between two states, one of which is a member of the 1952 Convention whereas the other is a member of the 1971 Convention, shall be governed by the 1952 Convention.[3]

The links between the two versions of the Convention:

Whereas the Berne Convention is regarded as a unit and the different revisions only result in special 'acts' of the Convention, the 'Revised Universal Copyright Convention' is a new convention. This necessitates the creation of links between the two conventions:

1. Article IX (3)
For a state which is not party to the 1952 Convention accession to the 1971 Convention also constitutes accession to the 1952 Convention. Thus treaty relations are established between all states bound by the 1952 Convention or the 1971 Convention.

2. Article IX (4) (First sentence)
Relations between states of which only one has acceded to the 1971 Convention are governed by the 1952 Convention. This is in line with the principle of international law that no state can have its treaty relations with other states changed other than by an express declaration to that effect made by both sides to the treaty.

3. Article IX (4) (Last sentence)
However, any state party only to the 1952 Convention may make a declaration that it will allow all states which have ratified the 1971 Convention to apply the rules of the 1971 Convention 'to works of its nationals or works first published on its territory'.

The emphasis is on 'all'. It means that such a state cannot discriminate between member countries of the 1971 Convention once it has made the declaration.

The purpose of this provision is to speed up the coming into operation of the provisions in favour of developing countries without waiting for the passage of the necessary legislation which may be a lengthy process. A simple declaration addressed to the Directors General of UNESCO (or the Director General of WIPO for members of the Berne Convention), takes effect immediately when it is deposited.

1 Art IX/1
2 Art IX/3
3 Art IX/4

12. The Intergovernmental Committee – article XI

6.36 Like the Berne Convention the UCC also provides for a permanent committee to assure the life and development of the Convention.

The task of the committee is to study 'problems concerning the application and operation'[1] of the Universal Copyright Convention as well as other problems of international copyright in conjunction with other international bodies.

It was agreed that there will be 'two Conventions (1952 and 1971) sharing the same name and a number of the same provision and with links between them'.[2] Thus although strictly speaking there are two conventions merged into one, the sittings and the work will be done together and the decision will be taken in the name of the Intergovernmental Copyright Committee as a single body.[3]

In fact over the last ten years the Intergovernmental Copyright Committee and the Permanent Committee of the Berne Union have at least once every two years met in the same place and during the same period and sat together in meetings during which the current problems of international copyright have been debated and some common resolutions developed, thus ensuring a close co-operation in these matters.[4]

The Intergovernmental Copyright Committee was enlarged in 1971 from 12 to 18 who can be members of the 1952 Convention or of the 1971 Convention and 'shall be selected' with due consideration to a fair balance of national interests on the basis of geographical location, population, languages and stage of development.'[5]

Thus the Committee forms a link between the two conventions.

1 Art XI, 1(a).
2 Kaminstein Report, para 129.
3 Kaminstein Report, para 131.
4 A proposal of the Italian Delegation (UCC/22 Corr 1) for a 'link' between the two international copyright conventions was not adopted. Several delegations favoured a single secretariat under WIPO auspices 'as an ultimate goal'. This goal has not yet been achieved.
5 Art XI/3.

13. The 'Berne Union Safeguard Clause' - article XVII and the appendix declaration relating to article XVII

6.37 Article XVII and the Appendix Declaration together represent what is generally known as the 'Berne Union Safeguard Clause'.

The effect of this safeguard clause is that works which (according to the Berne Convention) have as their country of origin a country which has withdrawn from the Berne Convention after 1 January 1951 shall, in the countries of the Berne Union, not be protected by the UCC. This clause was inserted in 1952 to prevent members of the Berne Union withdrawing from the Berne Convention and then ratifying the UCC, thus reducing the level of their copyright protection.

As many developing countries were members of the Berne Union, they were thus prevented from switching from the Berne Convention to the UCC. To enable them to do this, at least temporarily whilst they have the status of a developing country[1] a new para (b) was added to the Appendix Declaration in 1971 and para (b) redesignated as para (c). The effect of it is that by a unilateral declaration notified to the Director General of UNESCO that a country regards itself as a developing country it can withdraw from the Berne Union and confine itself to membership of the UCC without incurring the sanctions laid down in the safeguard clause.

The developed countries on the other hand can do no such thing. The safeguard clause remains effective for them which means that they cannot withdraw from the Berne Convention and rely on the UCC for the protection of their copyright interests.[2]

This is of some importance because in spite of the raised level of protection of the UCC considerable differences of the levels of protection between the two conventions remain.

1. The 'droit moral' is not specifically recognised in the UCC (although there are some oblique references to it).[3]
2. No formalities of any kind are permitted under the Berne Convention, whereas there are in the UCC.[4]
3. The term of protection is substantially longer under the Berne Convention (50 years pma) than under the UCC (25 years pma subject to the proviso of article IV).
4. However, the most significant difference seems to be the fact that whereas the Berne Convention guarantees authors a number of minimum rights jure conventionis the UCC does not. It merely refers to 'adequate and effective protection' and to a 'reasonable degree of effective protection'. What is 'adequate' or 'effective' is left to the judgment of each state. Perhaps the most effective safeguard is the principle of national treatment in article II which means that if a country wants to adopt a low level of protection which it considers adequate it has to subject its own right owners to the same regime as it wishes to introduce for foreigners.

However compared to the situation before the revision of 1971 the situation seems much eased. Whereas before many developing countries were firmly locked into the Berne Convention and the difference in levels of protection was very considerable now developing countries can freely choose between the Berne Union and the UCC and the difference in the level of protection between them has been much reduced and the clauses benefiting the developing countries are basically identical.

The combination of these factors leads to the somewhat surprising result that now that change from one convention to the other is possible, no developing country has made the change during the decade following the Paris revision. For the reasons set out above it may well be that none or only very few will do so in future.

1 This is due to the reference to art V bis. If a country loses the status of a developing country later on, the now developed country will have to accede once more to the Berne Convention or face the sanctions provided for in the Appendix Declaration.
2 Appendix Declaration, para (a).
3 Respect of authorship – art 5 para 2, subpara 5; Respect of integrity of the text – art 5, para 2, subpara 4; Right to withdraw a work from circulation – art 5, para 2, subpara 6. See para 6.28 above.
4 Art III.

14. Special provisions for developing countries – Article V bis – Article V quater UCC and Article I – Article VI of Appendix, Berne Convention

1. General

6.38 These articles establish the criteria a state must meet and the procedure to be observed by developing countries before they can introduce a compulsory licensing system with respect to translations and reproductions.

Five essential questions have to be answered:

(1) Which countries can benefit from the provision to issue compulsory licences?
(2) What are the main characteristics of such compulsory licences?

(3) What is the procedure to be adopted if a country wishes to benefit?
(4) During what period can these exceptional concessions be claimed?
(5) To which rights of the author can compulsory licence systems be applied?

(1) Definition of a developing country
6.39 The Appendix to the Paris Act (1971) of the Berne Convention and article V bis of the UCC (1971) seem to lay down a double test. The first test is objective in the sense that it is decided by the General Assembly of the United Nations. The country has to be 'regarded as a developing country in conformity with the established practice of the General Assembly of the United Nations'. The practice is not uniform. The test proposed by the US delegation of an 'annual *per capita* income of less than 300 dollars' which is the test applied triannually by the Committee fixing membership contributions, was not accepted by the Conference and there is thus, as Professor Ulmer points out, 'not inconsiderable scope for interpretation'.[1] The second test is subjective in the sense that the country concerned decides whether 'having regard to its economic situation and its social or cultural needs it does not consider itself immediately in a position to make provision for the protection of all the rights as provided for in this Act'. However this second test was not adopted by the Universal Convention 'because of the general feeling that it added nothing to the basic criterion'.[2] Thus the scope for interpretation remains. There is also scope for flexibility because the economic and social conditions of a country may change and also because the practice of the United Nations Assembly may change. It would appear that the decisive factor is that the country in question deposits a 'notification' at the time of ratification or thereafter declaring that it will avail itself of the faculty with regard to the translation right or with regard to the reproduction right or both, as it is difficult to imagine that such a declaration would be challenged unless it were totally unreasonable in view of the country's economic and cultural situation.

It has to be added however that there are countries which are developed countries in accordance with this definition but have no or only very rudimentary copyright laws,[3] whilst there are other countries which are developing countries in accordance with the definition but which have highly sophisticated copyright laws.[4] There are also countries which although they may qualify have stated that they would not avail themselves of the faculty.[5]

1 Ulmer 'The Revisions of the Copyright Conventions' EBU Rev (1971) p 86, para 19.
2 Kaminstein Report, para 53.
3 Eg some Arab countries.
4 Eg India or most Latin American countries.
5 Eg Israel.

(2) The main characteristics of the compulsory licences which could be issued in developing countries
6.40
(1) They are non-exclusive. That means that when a compulsory licence has been issued and copies of a work produced under the compulsory licence have been put into circulation this fact does not prevent anyone else from competing by applying for another licence provided the applicant is a national of the same developing country.
(2) They are non-transferable.
(3) The compulsory licence can be granted only for educational purposes. They are defined for a reproduction licence as 'systematic instructional activities' and for translation licences as 'for the purpose of teaching, scholarship or research'.

(4) They can be granted only after the prescribed periods have expired and the prescribed procedures have been gone through. This means that provided the right owner can be found, the compulsory licence is issued only after prior consultation with that right owner.

(5) The competent authority can issue a compulsory licence only against payment of an equitable remuneration.

(6) Exporting copies made under a compulsory licence is generally forbidden (subject to certain minor exceptions) and each copy must bear a notice to the effect that distribution is allowed only within the country which has granted the compulsory licence.

(7) According to the Report the rules imply that the competent authority issuing the compulsory licence will notify the right owner of the terms on which the licence has been granted. As these include the compensation and the transmittal of the compensation he will be in a good position to ensure that he gets paid.

The most important difference between this sytem adopted by the two conventions in 1971 and the system of the rejected Stockholm Protocol of 1967[1] is that under the Protocol it would have been permissible to publish reproductions and translations of works in copyright without prior consultation with the right owner and without any waiting period. The waiting period and the consultation with the right owner (usually the publisher) whenever he can be found open the way to negotiations. This means that in these negotiations the applicant for a licence will presumably offer conditions which are not unreasonable under the circumstances because he must fear that if he does not and he meets with a refusal he may not get the compulsory licence from the competent authority. On the other hand the right owner will negotiate in the knowledge that if he refuses a licence when the conditions offered are not unreasonable a compulsory licence will be issued. Thus there will be willingness to contract on both sides.

The compulsory licensing provisions for the benefit of the developing countries have been criticised for being unnecessarily complicated. They certainly are very complicated. The complications are due to the fact that the texts had to enshrine a large number of detailed compromises reached only with great difficulty and after protracted negotiations. The language of democratic compromises is almost invariably as lengthy and as complicated as the processes of democracy itself. Their value can only be appreciated by 'contemplating the alternatives'.[2] The alternative in this case was the breakdown of the structure of international copyright. This alternative was avoided by a remarkable piece of international co-operation and compromise. The texts are a portrait of that co-operation 'warts and all'.[3]

1 Art I(e).
2 Sir Winston Churchill's phrase about democracy itself.
3 Oliver Cromwell's phrase when asking Lilley to paint his now famous portrait.

(3) *Procedures*
6.41 The procedure is a simple notification sent to the Director General of WIPO in the case of the Berne Convention, and to the Director General of UNESCO in the case of the UCC.

Thus anyone concerned can always ascertain the status of the country he is dealing with by a simple enquiry.

(4) *Duration*
6.42 The duration of the effectiveness of the notice is in the first place ten years. It may be renewed in whole or in part for one or more periods of ten

years by further notifications. The notification can be made at the date of ratification or at any time thereafter but the ten-year period runs from the date the 1971 Act entered into force.[1] As a minimum period of 3 months and a maximum of 15 months for notification of renewal is provided, all renewals must be effected between 10 July 1983 and 10 July 1984. This will therefore be the year when the developing countries who have made such declarations will have to decide on their future course of action.[2]

Once a country ceases to be regarded as a developing country it can no longer renew the period, however it can avail itself of the exceptions for the rest of the current ten year period. This reflects the fact that development is a gradual process. Furthermore copies made under the compulsory licence may be distributed 'until their stock is exhausted'.[3]

1 10 July 1974 UCC, 10 October 1974 Berne Convention.
2 See *WIPO Guide to Berne* AI.9.
3 Art V bis/4 and Art 1, para (4) of the Appendix.

(5) *The rights which can be subjected to a system of compulsory licences*
6.43 The words 'any or all of the exceptions' show that a country may for instance claim the exceptions to the translation right but not those to the reproduction right or vice versa.

No reciprocity
6.44 It was essential to the special exceptions permitted for the developing countries that the developed countries should not apply material reciprocity to those countries which availed themselves of the exceptions. In other words any developed country must accord to works originating from a developing country which has availed itself of the exceptions, the same protection as it gives to its own works. Whereas this principle has been enshrined in article 1, para (6) of the Berne Convention Appendix, in the UCC it was relegated to the Report of the General Rapporteur[1] but expressed there in greater detail. The principle applies to both conventions.

> '(1) With regard to material reciprocity, no discrimination should be made between the exceptions in Articles V ter and V quater and those in Article IV bis.
> (2) The fact of a state availing itself of any exceptions should in no case permit other contracting states to reduce the level of protection granted by them to works originating in the state in question.
> (3) The principle of the absence of material reciprocity already exists in the 1952 Convention. It derives from the principle of the assimilation of foreign authors and works to national authors and works.
> The fact that such reciprocity is permitted on only one, precisely specified point, viz the duration of protection, underlines the fact that this constitutes the sole exception to the general principle and that where the text is silent, it can only be interpreted in the light of the principle of non-reciprocity.'

The reason for not putting this into the text of the Convention but into the Report as propositions generally agreed by the conference, was that put into the text it might have been interpreted 'as a reversal of the presumption of absence of material reciprocity which governed the 1952 Convention and that consequently, States remaining party to the 1952 Convention alone, would in future be able to interpret that Convention as being governed by the principle of material reciprocity.'[2]

The former 'colonial powers' defined as countries 'responsible for the external relations of another territory' can make a declaration and follow the same procedure if the situation of a dependent territory 'is analogous to that of a developing country'.[3] However, the sending of copies made under compulsory licence in the dependent territory to the colonial power shall be considered an export within the meaning of articles V ter and V quater.

1 Kaminstein Report, para 59.
2 Kaminstein Report, para 59.
3 Art V bis/5 and art I, para (5) of the Berne Convention Appendix.

(2) Compulsory licences applied to the translation right – article V ter UCC and Article II Appendix to the Berne Convention

6.45 The UCC (1952) already provided for a system of compulsory licences for translations in article V (2).[1] Therefore the new translation licence for the benefit of developing countries is treated as a compulsory licence of a specific kind under specific conditions to which the rules of article V apply. The Berne Convention on the other hand so far contained no provision for a system of compulsory licences with regard to the translation right. Thus a complete set of rules is set out in article II which in all material respects is identical with that of the UCC.

In all cases the exclusive translation right of the right owner is preserved but if he does not exercise his right and does not cause a translation to be made within the stated period after first publication his exclusive translation right is temporarily lost and a compulsory licence can be imposed. However, such compulsory licences are not exclusive and the right owner can always try to recover the situation by publishing his own translation.

His short term remedy is to offer a licence on reasonable terms. If the right owner makes such a reasonable offer for the licensing of the translation and the applicant for a compulsory licence refuses it, such refusal does not entitle him to a compulsory licence.[2]

His long term remedy is actually spelt out in the Convention.[3] If he publishes a translation of the work in the developing country in question 'at a price reasonably related to that normally charged in the same state for comparable works the compulsory licence will terminate. He will however, have to compete with the translation made under the compulsory licence until the stock is exhausted.

The compulsory licences can only be granted 'for the purpose of teaching, scholarship or research'.[4] The term 'scholarship' covers instructional activities at all levels, ie primary and secondary schools, colleges and universities[5] as well as other educational activities intended for all age levels and for the study of any subject. The term 'research' may be widely interpreted in the educational sphere but excludes industrial research institutes or industrial or commercial companies undertaking research for commercial purposes.

A guide for the parameters of both 'scholarship and research' may be the fact that the definition 'translations for the benefit of official or officially recognised establishments of education or research'[6] was rejected by the Conference as too narrow.[7]

The purpose of these licences is clearly to facilitate translations of school books, textbooks of all kinds, encyclopaedias, technical and scientific manuals etc. As the Masouyé/Wallace *Guide to the Berne Convention* puts it: 'not the latest song hit or the new London or Paris stage success.'[8]

1 See para 6.25 above.
2 Kaminstein Report, para 87(4).
3 Art V ter 6, and Berne, art II, para 6.
4 Art V ter 3 of the UCC and Berne, art II, para(5).
5 The French text says: 'usage scolaire, universitaire' etc.
6 Proposal of Argentina (Document UCC/7).
7 Kaminstein Report, para 73.
8 *WIPO Guide to Berne* A.II.3.

6.46 The Convention thus sets up three tiers of compulsory licences for translations:

1. For developed countries; after *seven years* of no publication (into a language in general use): a non-exclusive licence.[1]
2. For developing countries; after *three years* if there has been no publication, for a translation into a language in general use.[2]
3. For developing countries; after *one year* if there has been no publication, for translation into a language *not* in general use in one or more developing countries.[3]

The distinction between case 1 (seven years) and cases 2 (three years) and 3 (one year) is clear. It is between developed and developing countries as defined in article V bis.

The distinction between case 2 and case 3 depends on whether the language into which the work is to be translated is a language 'in general use in one or more developed countries'. The Kaminstein Report summarises the conditions to be fulfilled:[4]

'(1) if the translation is not into one of the three world languages, (English, French and Spanish);
(2) if it is into a language in general use in one or more developed countries party to either the 1952 or 1971 texts of the Universal Copyright Convention;[5]
(3) if these countries unanimously agree among themselves that another period of one year (or more) may be substituted;
(4) if the Director General of UNESCO is notified of the written agreement.'[6]

It is clear that formal action on the executive level is required in each developed country and that it could stipulate conditions, eg that it applied only to certain types of works such as technical and scientific works.[7]

The term 'language in general use' is used instead of the alternative 'national language' because in some developing countries there is a language in general use although not a national language, eg English in India or French in the Maghreb countries.

The translation under compulsory licence can be from a language of a developed country into the language or languages of the developing countries or from the language of one developed country into the language of another developed country, eg French speaking African countries may translate English textbooks into French, or English speaking Asian countries may translate French works into English.

The periods of three years or one year from first publication are minima. The countries concerned could choose longer periods. The minimum period of one year was considered the shortest possible time to set for the copyright owner to find a translator of his own choice.[8]

1 Art V/2 see para 6.25 above.
2 Art V ter, and Berne, art II, para 2(a).
3 Art V ter, and Berne, art II, para 3(a).
4 Kaminstein Report, para 66.
5 Or the Berne Convention.
6 The Director General of WIPO in the case of the Berne Convention.
7 Kaminstein Report, para 66.
8 A proposal of India to reduce this period to six months was rejected on these grounds.

6.47 The procedure to be followed to obtain a compulsory licence[1] is similar to the case of a compulsory licence for reproduction (article V quater) and to the procedure of the Berne Convention (article IV of the Annex). This is so as they both stem from the procedure laid down for compulsory licences in developed countries under articles V of the UCC 1952.

The applicant has to show either that he has requested the authorisation of the right owner and been denied or that after using 'due diligence' has been unable to find him.

It is clear that if the publisher of the work has sent to the countries in question a catalogue of his publications, it could no longer be claimed that he cannot be found if due diligence is used. When making his request the applicant has also to inform either the International Copyright Information Centre of UNESCO or a national or regional information centre designated by the state in which the publisher is believed to have his principal place of business. If the right owner cannot be found the applicant for the compulsory licence has to send copies of his application to the publisher whose name appears on the work.

After the date of the request an additional period of six months in the case of the three-year period or of nine months in the case of the one-year period has to elapse before the compulsory licence can be granted.

Copies made under compulsory licences are not for export and must bear a notice to the effect that they are for distribution only in the country granting the licence. This is to prevent publishers in developing countries or western publishers established in developing countries from putting copies made under compulsory licence on to the markets of developed countries and undercutting authorised copies there.[2]

There is however an exception to the ban on exports: copies can be sent to nationals of that country abroad by a public entity of the licensing state if this is done for a non-commercial purpose[3] and the copies are used only for the purpose of teaching, scholarship or research and the country into which they are sent has agreed to allow the receipt and the Director General of UNESCO or WIPO has been informed of such agreement.[4] If compulsory licences are granted on these terms, 'provision shall be made at the national level' for 'just compensation'.

Such provisions may be made by statute or regulations or by administrative measures (eg in currency regulations).

The Convention states two conditions which must be fulfilled if the compensation is to be considered 'just': (a) it must be 'consistent' with standards of royalties normally operating in the case of similar licences freely negotiated and (b) it must not only be paid but also transmitted to the right owner. (a) means that although the level of royalties need not and, for the time being, cannot compare with the level of royalties paid in the country of the right owner, it should not be lower then what is usually paid in the developed country concerned for freely negotiated licences. (b) means that the royalties must be paid in an internationally convertible currency and not into a frozen national bank account. The competent authority is to 'make all efforts to that effect.'

For art books (described in the Convention as 'works which are composed mainly of illustrations') the conditions of article V quater as well as the above conditions of article V ter must be fulfilled.[5]

This is logical as such publications involve not only the translation right (article V ter) but also the reproduction right (article V quater). Whether a work is 'mainly' composed of illustrations is left to the competent authority to decide. It follows that if the main component is the text and not the illustrations, only the conditions for the translation licence need be met.

1   Art V ter 1 sub-paras (c) and (d) and Berne, art IV, paras (1) and (2).
2   Art V ter 4 (a) and (b) and Berne, art IV, para 4(a).
3   This does not preclude the governmental organisation from making charges simply to cover their costs.

4   Article V ter 4(c) and Berne, art IV, para 4(c).
5   Art V ter 7 and Berne, art II, para (7).

(3) Translations for broadcasting purposes

6.48 In view of the increasing importance of television in the field of education, broadcasting organisations in a developing country are also permitted to apply for a compulsory licence to translate protected works[1] under certain conditions. These are broadly the conditions for publishers set out above adapted to the broadcasting field and very tightly defined. The translation must be lawfully made, must be for use only in broadcasts intended exclusively for teaching or for the dissemination of the results of research, to experts in a particular profession and 'without any commercial purpose'.[2] The broadcasts must be intended for recipients within the country, not outside it. They may be exchanged but only with a broadcasting organisation within the country, ie not exported.

The broadcasts may be live or 'through the medium of sound or visual recordings'. The term 'sound or visual recordings' includes all types of aural and visual fixations, including films, phonograms and audio and video tapes.

It must be emphasised that what is acquired under this compulsory licence is the making of a translation for the purpose of broadcasting, not the broadcasting of the work itself. Thus the translation can be recorded and then used for broadcasting on the same conditions as an original work. The broadcasting of the original work is still subject to the ordinary copyright rules. Thus under the Berne Convention, article 11 bis applies. Under this article, Berne Union countries can introduce a compulsory licence subject to the author's right to equitable remuneration and the respecting of his moral rights.[3] In view of the parallelism of the provisions it must be assumed that the same applies to the member states of the UCC.[4]

If all the above conditions are fulfilled the broadcasting organisation can also get a licence to translate any text 'incorporated in an audio-visual fixation' if its sole purpose is systematic instructional activities and it is used for that purpose.[5]

Article V ter 9 sets the relationship between article V (dealing with compulsory licences for translations in all countries) and article V ter (dealing with the same licences in developing countries). As Masouyé points out,[6] article V constitutes the 'common law' in the matter and article V ter stipulates, by way of 'statute law', certain exceptions from the common law rules of article V for the benefit of the developing countries. The consequences which flow from this concept are set out in the Report.[7]

1. The work translated must be a 'writing'. This term does not include musical, dramatic and cinematographic works, nor paintings, engravings or sculptures.

    'The Conference expressly stipulated that words, lyrics or text of musical compositions were not covered by the translation privileges of Articles V ter.'

    Because of the limited definition given to the expression 'publication' in article VI, no compulsory licence can be granted to distribute the work in the form of sound recording or any other form which cannot be 'read or otherwise visually perceived.'[8]
2. All conditions and safeguards of authors' rights built into article V apply to article V ter including the moral rights (originally title and name of the author must appear on the copies of the translations, correct translations must be assured[9]).

3. Where the work for the translation for which a compulsory licence is sought is itself a translation, permission must be applied for both from the owner in the copyright of the translation and from the author of the original work. The same applies to any form of adaptation or 'derivative work incorporating copyrighted material of diverse ownership'.

1 Art V ter 8, and Berne Appendix, art II, para (9) (a).
2 This means that the broadcasting organisation is not a commercial broadcasting organisation and that the programme incorporating the translation carried no advertisements. It does however not preclude the broadcasting organisation from broadcasting other programmes which include commercial advertising nor from charging the owners of receivers a licensing fee. (Kaminstein Report, para 84/(b)).
3 See para 5.43 above.
4 See Ulmer 'The Revisions of the Copyright Conventions', op cit, para 41.
5 Art V ter 8(b) and Berne Appendix art II(9) (c).
6 Claude Masouyé 'Convention universelle sur le droit d'auteur; La Revision de 1971' para 66.
7 Kaminstein Report, para 87.
8 Art VI; see para 6.32 above.
9 See para 6.28 above.

(4) The 'Ten-Year Regime' for translations under the Berne Convention (Appendix, Article V) and the restrictions on the right of translation under the UCC (Article V)

6.49   There is one significant difference between the Berne Convention and the UCC with regard to the translation right

(a) A developing country which is a member of the Berne Union can choose between the provisions of article II of the Appendix and the 'ten-year regime' which was first provided in 1896 (Additional Act of Paris) for all union countries.[1] This regime is less complicated than the 1971 provisions. If no translation in a language in general use in the country concerned has been published within ten years of the first publication of the work, the copyright owner loses his right to translate into that language in that country. As the *WIPO Guide* puts it: 'the work thereafter falls into the public domain in that country so far as translation in that language is concerned, and can be translated freely'. In fact few countries had made that reservation after 1896 but it would have been difficult to repeal the provision at a time when new reservations with regard to the translation right were made possible. Thus developing countries which are members of Berne Union and had made the reservation previously may retain the benefit of the reservation.[2] Developing countries which are members of the Berne Union but had not previously made that reservation or are non Union countries can choose the ten-year regime of 1896 instead of that of the system of article II of the Appendix.[3] However, the choice, once made, is irrevocable.

A country choosing the ten-year regime cannot subsequently change to the system of compulsory licences and a country choosing the system of compulsory licences cannot change to the ten-year regime.[4]

If a country ceases to be a developing country but wishes to maintain or to adopt for the first time the ten-year regime it may make the declaration under article 32(2)(b). However, whereas whilst it was a developing country other countries could not apply reciprocity to its works, now they can if they wish to do so.

There must however be one exception to this application of reciprocity. If a developing country which has previously made the ten-year reservation retains it on acceding to the Paris Act (1971) and later ceases to be a developing country and makes the reservation afresh no one can apply reciprocity to its works otherwise it would be worse off than a developed country acceding to the Paris Act (1971) and retaining the benefit of the previously made reservation under article 30(2)(a).[5]

(b) Under the UCC the system of compulsory licences for translation under art V applies to all convention countries after seven years from first publication of the original work to be translated.

1 See para 5.10 above.
2 Berne Convention, art 30, para (2)(a).
3 Berne Convention, art 30, para (2)(b).
4 See WIPO Guide to Berne A.V.4
5 See Ulmer 'The Revision of the Copyright Conventions,' op cit, para 49.

(5) Compulsory licences applied to the reproduction right – article V quater and article III (Appendix to the Berne Convention)

6.50 Whereas article V ter deals with the right to translate and to publish the translation, article V quater deals with the right to reproduce a work and publish the reproduction. The two articles are constructed on the same lines, the only variations stemming from the fact that whilst both articles were inserted in 1971 for the benefit of developing countries – article V ter dealing with translations for developing countries had to be fashioned in accordance with the regime of compulsory licensing already provided for all Convention countries in article V of the 1952 Act whereas article V quater dealing with reproductions for developing countries was completely new having no parallel. Thus, the substantive differences are only those that stem from the intrinsic difference between the translation right and the reproduction right. The formal differences stem from the fact that article V ter was shaped on the precedent of article V, whereas article V quater stands alone for developing countries only.[1]

These remarks do not, of course, apply to article III of the Appendix to the Berne Convention as in the Berne Convention there had previously been no exception to the right of reproduction and article III spells out the new provisions for the benefit of the developing countries afresh on parallel lines with the UCC.

The basic rule is that a compulsory licence authorising the reproduction and publication of a particular edition of a work may be issued only if after a stated period from the first publication of that edition in the developing country concerned copies of that edition have not been distributed either to the general public or in connection with systematic educational activities by the owner of the reproduction right. These copies must have been distributed 'at a price reasonably related to that normally charged in the state for comparable works'.[2]

The reference to an edition of a work means that the period for each successive edition has to be calculated separately. Therefore even if the period for an earlier edition had expired a compulsory licence to reproduce the latest edition can only be granted if the period for that latest edition has expired.[3]

That period is normally five years. However for 'works of the natural and physical sciences' 'and of technology' the period is three years and for 'works of fiction, poetry, drama and music and for art books' the period is seven years.[4] In general no edition of the work will have been put on sale in the developing country. However if an edition has been on sale but has not been available for six months a compulsory licence can be granted.[5]

The shorter period of three years is justified by the rapid progress of science and technology and the need of developing countries to keep their education up to date. On the other hand the latest works of literature or music do not play such a vital role in the education which is essential for the development of a country. Hence the longer period of seven years.

It is important to note that whereas for a translation[6] the criterion for a longer or shorter period is the language concerned, for Reproductions the criterion is the subject matter of the publication.

The use of the edition published under the compulsory licence must be 'in connection with systematic instructional activities'.[7] It was agreed that that term is to be interpreted widely so as to include all forms of education. This means not only publications for formal and informal instructions in an 'educational institution' but also 'systematic out-of-school education'.[8] Whilst this is a wide interpretation of education, the connection of the publication with such educational activities must be firm. If such activities were in fact merely incidental to the actual purpose of the reproduction a licence must be refused.[9]

National law must provide for 'just compensation' consistent with the standards applicable to 'licences freely negotiated between persons in the two countries concerned'[10] and such compensation must be transferable.

An 'accurate reproduction' of the edition must be assured. This means a reproduction faithful to the original[11] and is a reference to the author's 'droit moral' although no such right is explicitly provided in the UCC.

Article V ter, sub-para (h), deals with the combination of an article V ter licence and an article V quater licence, ie the reproduction of a translation. A licence to publish a reproduction of a translation can only be granted if the translation was published with the right owner's consent and is in a language in general use in the state with power to grant the licence. If the author withdraws all copies of an edition from circulation no compulsory licence shall be granted.[12] This too is a recognition of the author's 'droit moral'.

Applying for a licence to publish a translation, the applicant has to apply both to the right owner of the translation and to the right owner of the original work.

1 Kaminstein Report, para 90.
2 Art V quater 1(a) and Berne, Appendix, art III (2)(a).
3 See Kaminstein Report, para 93.
4 Art V quater (1)(c) and Berne, Appendix, art III (3).
5 Art V quater 1(b) and Berne, Appendix, art II(2)(b).
6 Art V ter and Berne, Appendix, art 2, para 2.
7 Art V quater 1(a) and Berne, Appendix, art 2, para 5.
8 See Kaminstein Report, para 92.
9 Kaminstein Report, para 93.
10 Art V quater (2)(b)(i) and Berne, Appendix, art 4, para 6(a)(i).
11 Art V quater 1 (g) and Kaminstein Report, para 106.
12 Art V quater (2) (d) and Berne, Appendix, art II(8).

6.51 *Procedure.* The procedure for obtaining a compulsory licence under article V quater is mutatis mutandis the same as under articles V and V ter.

As under the above-named articles the applicant must be in good faith, ie he must have used 'due diligence' to find the right owner and if he finds him must request a licence and be denied before a compulsory licence can be issued.

As with the above-named articles the name of the author and the title of the edition must be printed on all copies.

Unlike under article V, but like under article V ter the applicant must inform the International Copyright Information Centre at UNESCO.[1] If the publisher whose name appears on the copy cannot be found, an additional copy must be sent to the designated national or regional information centre or if there is none, to the UNESCO Centre.

In order to provide a last chance for negotiations with the right owner the convention provides for an additional waiting period after dispatch of the application. If the work is in the five or seven year category the additional waiting period is three months. If the work is in the three-year category (scientific) the additional period is six months.[2]

Any compulsory licence shall terminate if the owner of the reproduction right distributes an edition in the same language and with 'substantially the same contents' as the edition published under the compulsory licence 'and at a price reasonably related to that normally charged in the state for comparable works'. Existing copies can be distributed until their stock is exhausted.[3]

It was agreed by the conference that no requests or applications leading to the granting of a compulsory licence may be made from any developing country until that country has ratified the 1971 Convention and it has come into effect in that state.[4]

The field of application of compulsory licences is confined to literary, scientific and artistic works 'published in printed or analogous form of reproduction'.[5] Sound recordings are not included. However in view of the importance of films and videograms in education this covers the reproduction of the work in audiovisual form as well as the translation of any texts contained therein.

The audiovisual reproduction or translation must have been lawfully made and published 'for the sole purpose of being used in connection with systematic instructional activities'.[6]

It follows that commercial films and videograms produced for entertainment cannot be the subject of a compulsory licence. Nor could the reproduction of a cinematographic work based on a work of fiction, as neither can be said to have been published 'for the sole purpose of use in systematic education'.[7] 'Publication' in this context includes the distribution of fixations of images or sounds and images, which can be bought, leased or rented.[8]

1 Art V quater (1) (d).
2 Art V quater (1)(d) (last sentence) and (1)(e) and Berne, Appendix, art III 4(a) and 4(b).
3 Art V quater 2(c) and Berne, Appendix, art III(6).
4 Report, para 104 (last sentence).
5 Art V quater (3)(a) and Berne Appendix, art III(7)(a).
6 Article V quater (3)(b) and Berne Appendix, art III(7)(b).
7 See Kaminstein Report, para 112.
8 See Kaminstein Report, para 113.

6.52 The Report clarifies the interplay between translations of text incorporated in an audiovisual fixation under article V ter (8)(b) and under article V quater (3)(b).[1]

(1) 'Under article V ter the licence can cover only translations of text for broadcasting purposes. Typically, it would be employed for the translations of the sound track of a teaching film or video tape that had been lawfully acquired on the market and the use of the translation in a new ('dubbed') sound track or for visible sub-titles.

(2) Under article V quater (3)(b), the licensee would reproduce the entire audo-visual fixation, and as part of the process he would translate the sound track and reproduce the translation orally or visually along with his reproduction of the visual images. The periods applicable in that situation would vary depending upon the nature of the work in accordance with article V quater (1)(c).'

A compulsory licence does not extend to copies exported into another country.[2] However an exception was agreed by the Conference for states which do not yet have the technical facilities for printing and for reproduction. In such cases exports are permitted both under article V ter (4)(a) and under article V quater (i)(f) if the following conditions are met:[3]

The country where the work of reproduction is done is a party to one of the two international copyright conventions. All copies are sent to the licensee in bulk shipments for distribution exclusively in his country. The establishment doing the work of reproduction has not been created specially for that purpose. All copies reproduced bear a notice in accordance with article V ter (4)(b) and article V quater (2)(a). *No* country can be forced by these provisions to permit operations which would be an infringement under its national law.

1 Kaminstein Report, para 111.
2 Art V quater (i) (f), and Berne Appendix, art IV(4).
3 Kaminstein Report, para 115.

15. Universal Copyright Convention (UCC)

State of ratification and accessions as on 1 January 1983

6.53

Contracting states	Date of entry into force of Convention	Latest text by which state is bound
ALGERIA	28 August 1973	1971 Text
ANDORRA	16 September 1955	1952 Text
ARGENTINA	13 February 1958	1952 Text
AUSTRALIA	1 May 1969	1971 Text
AUSTRIA	2 July 1957	1971 Text
BAHAMAS	27 December 1976	1971 Text
BANGLADESH	5 August 1975	1971 Text
BELGIUM	31 August 1960	1952 Text
BRAZIL	13 January 1960	1971 Text
BULGARIA	7 June 1975	1971 Text
CAMEROON	1 May 1973	1971 Text
CANADA	10 August 1962	1952 Text
CHILE	16 September 1955	1952 Text
COLOMBIA	18 June 1976	1971 Text
COSTA RICA	16 September 1955	1971 Text
CUBA	18 June 1957	1952 Text
CZECHOSLOVAKIA	6 January 1960	1971 Text
DEMOCRATIC KAMPUCHEA	16 September 1955	1952 Text
DENMARK	9 February 1962	1971 Text
EQUADOR	5 June 1957	1952 Text
EL SALVADOR	29 March 1979	1971 Text
FIJI	10 October 1970	1952 Text
FINLAND	16 April 1963	1952 Text
FRANCE	14 January 1956	1971 Text
GERMAN DEMOCRATIC REPUBLIC	5 October 1973	1971 Text
GERMANY, FEDERAL REPUBLIC OF	16 September 1955	1971 Text
GHANA	22 August 1962	1952 Text
GREECE	24 August 1963	1952 Text
GUINEA	13 November 1981	1971 Text
GUATEMALA	28 October 1964	1952 Text
HAITI	16 September 1955	1952 Text
HOLY SEE	5 October 1955	1971 Text
HUNGARY	23 January 1971	1971 Text

Contracting states	Date of entry into force of Convention	Latest text by which state is bound
ICELAND	18 December 1956	1952 Text
INDIA	21 January 1958	1952 Text
IRELAND	20 January 1959	1952 Text
ISRAEL	16 September 1955	1952 Text
ITALY	24 January 1957	1971 Text
JAPAN	28 April 1956	1971 Text
KENYA	7 September 1966	1971 Text
LAOS	16 September 1955	1952 Text
LEBANON	17 October 1959	1952 Text
LIBERIA	27 July 1956	1952 Text
LIECHTENSTEIN	22 January 1959	1952 Text
LUXEMBOURG	15 October 1955	1952 Text
MALAWI	26 October 1965	1952 Text
MALTA	19 November 1968	1952 Text
MAURITIUS	12 March 1968	1952 Text
MEXICO	12 May 1957	1971 Text
MONACO	16 September 1955	1971 Text
MOROCCO	8 May 1972	1971 Text
NETHERLANDS	22 June 1967	1952 Text
NEW ZEALAND	11 September 1964	1952 Text
NICARAGUA	16 August 1961	1952 Text
NIGERIA	14 February 1962	1952 Text
NORWAY	23 January 1963	1971 Text
PAKISTAN	16 September 1955	1952 Text
PANAMA	17 October 1962	1971 Text
PARAGUAY	11 March 1962	1952 Text
PERU	16 October 1963	1952 Text
PHILIPPINES	19 November 1955	1952 Text
POLAND	9 March 1977	1971 Text
PORTUGAL	25 December 1956	1971 Text
SENEGAL	9 July 1974	1971 Text
SPAIN	16 September 1955	1971 Text
SWEDEN	1 July 1961	1971 Text
SWITZERLAND	30 March 1956	1952 Text
TUNISIA	19 June 1969	1971 Text
UNITED KINGDOM	27 September	1971 Text
UNITED STATES OF AMERICA	16 September 1955	1971 Text
USSR	27 May 1973	1952 Text
VENEZUELA	30 September 1966	1952 Text
YUGOSLAVIA	11 May 1966	1971 Text
ZAMBIA	1 June 1965	1952 Text

TOTAL NUMBER OF STATES: 74

Chapter 7
Neighbouring Rights

Summary

1. Ideology and history   7.01
2. Relations between authors' rights and neighbouring rights   7.06
3. Ownership, scope and term of neighbouring rights   7.08
4. Rights of performers   7.09
5. Rights of producers of phonograms   7.16
6. Remedies for infringements of rights of producers and performers   7.19
7. Performance rights in phonograms   7.27
8. Rights of broadcasting organisations   7.36

1. The ideology and history of neighbouring rights

7.01 The history of copyright reflects the development of technology. Copyright develops as the means by which 'works', ie materials deserving copyright protection reach the public. At the beginning was the invention of the printing press which gave copyright its impetus. The protection of printed material against unauthorised reproduction was the main concern of copyright and the right to protect such reproduction, the reproduction right, was the basic and the main right. The next right which became important for literary works was the translation right. Until the second half of the nineteenth century the printing press was the sole technology involved in taking literary works of all kinds to their public. In the case of dramatic and musical works the route of the work to its public was live performance and in the case of artistic works, exhibition.

In the second half of the nineteenth century technology added photography, sound recording and silent films and in the twentieth century films with sound tracks, radio and television. By these additions the copyright scene was entirely transformed. Two new problems arose. The first was to decide what rights authors were to have in these new uses of their work. The second was to decide whether, in the terminology of 'copyright', these new 'materials' needed and deserved copyright protection or, in the terminology of the 'droit d'auteur' whether they constituted 'works' to be protected.

7.02 It became fairly clear by the first decade of the twentieth century that photographs, cinematograph films and sound recordings deserved and needed copyright protection. The difficulties and debates arose over the question who the initial copyright owner should be and what the scope and term of the right should be.

With the first of these materials, photographs, most legislators seemed to have little difficulty. Photographs were 'works' and the photographer was their 'author'. However some photographs which lack artistic or documentary character were excepted by many legislations. 'Photomatons' machines which take passport photographs are an obvious modern example.[1] At the international level the right was at first granted, like in all other 'works', regardless of the subject (landscapes, portraits, current events), regardless of the purpose (professional photographer or amateur, art or advertisement), and regardless of artistic merit (portrait or snapshot) in the Final Protocol of the original Berne Convention by simply adding photographs to the list of works to be protected[2]. Eventually the Stockholm Revision of 1967 put photographs in the same class of works as 'works of applied art' and left national legislation to decide how long a term of protection they should be given if they are protected as artistic works. However it provides a minimum term of 25 years.

The next step beyond photographs was taken by the Paris Additional Act 1896 adding to 'photographic works', 'works produced by an analogous process'. This meant films – then in their infancy. The cinematograph film presented the first doctrinal problem: who should be the initial owner of the copyright? The Anglo-Saxon legislations answered: the 'producer' meaning the company that produced the film. The French and other European legislations answered: 'the author of the cinematographic work' which in practice means a plurality of individuals as joint authors ranging from the camera man (the person 'analogous' to the photographer) to the actors starring in the film. The problem of how to treat cinematograph films was the first problem to show the great divide between those legislations which followed the doctrine of the 'droit d'Auteur' (all Europe with the exception of the United Kingdom and the Republic of Ireland and all Latin America) and those which followed the doctrine of 'copyright' (mainly countries of the British Commonwealth and the United States of America). The main difficulty is not, as has often been maintained, the lack of originality or of quality of these new works. Right from the beginning copyright recognised derivative works which by definition demand a pre-existing work. Such works are not original in the sense that they create something out of nothing like writing a book or a song. Translations and arrangements were the first examples of such works to be recognised as suitable for copyright protection. Thus its derivative nature is not the reason why the 'droit d'auteur' doctrine found it impossible to recognise the producer of a film or later of a phonogram or a broadcast as an initial right owner. Lack of artistic or intellectual input is not a convincing reason either. There is as much or more artistic input in the making of a film or a record or a broadcast as there is in adapting an orchestral score for piano and as much skill and labour as there is in compiling a street directory. Doctrine has never had any difficulty in recognising such adaptors or compilers as initial owners of copyright. The real difficulty lies elsewhere. It lies in the fact that the adaptor or the compiler are, like the photographer, physical persons whereas film producers, phonogram producers and broadcasting organisations are companies or corporations. The difficulty is emphasised when one contemplates the moral as opposed to the economic rights. Moral rights, it is said, which are based on the expression of the author's personality and his intellectual link with his work, cannot exist in a company or corporation. The 'copyright' legislations of common law countries which, whilst recognising moral rights, do not put so much emphasis on them, do not consider this difficulty insuperable and give a copyright to the producer of a film or a phonogram.[3] In the light of the history of 'copyright' this is not illogical. The first copyright owners were printers, in modern terminology publishers, of books who combined artistic skills and judgment with technical skills and made the initial investment. They were individuals in the seventeenth and eighteenth century but in the nineteenth century many became companies. Thus the copyright resided in the company. When broadcasting was invented 'copyright' legislations had no difficulty in granting a copyright to the broadcasting organisations which were responsible for creating and disseminating the programmes.

1 See *WIPO Guide to Berne* 2.6(h).
2 Berne Convention 1886 Final Protocol, para 1, adding a para to art 4.
3 Eg United Kingdom Copyright 1956, ss 12 and 13; United States Copyright Act 1976, para 102(a); Australia Copyright Act 1968 ss 86 and 185.

7.03 Conceptually an infringement of copyright has similar features to a tort. Both are acts which cause damage to a person who should in the opinion of the law be protected and have a remedy, although there is no contractual relationship between the tortfeasor and the injured party. In tort the damage is usually to material property (eg land or goods) but may be to immaterial property (eg reputation in the law of defamation). In copyright too the damage may be material (loss of royalties) or immaterial (loss of reputation). The development of the law of copyright resembles the development of the law of tort. Just as 'the categories of tort are never closed' so the list of acts which are infringements of copyright should never be closed as new materials are added to the list of protected matter. In most countries copyright is a creature of statute, so that new copyrightable matter has to be protected by new legislation whereas the law of torts was largely, although not entirely, developed by the courts. However, in the history of copyright too there are exceptions to development by statute. In France, for instance, the development of the 'droit d'auteur' was left entirely to the courts for over a century and a half (between the first law of 1783 and the second of 1957) which covered a period of rapidly developing technology. Thus the list of copyright owners has been added to from time to time mostly by legislation but sometimes by the courts, as new technology demanded it.

7.04 The 'droit d'auteur' has roots which are different from the common concept of 'copyright'. It stems from the doctrine of natural law and the ideas of the French Revolution;[1] this results in a highly personalised approach to copyright which links the work with the personality and individuality of the author.

The difficulty of recognising such rights as dwelling in a limited company thus becomes almost insuperable. When faced with the new technology these jurisdictions reacted differently to each new invention. The photograph could still be fitted in by giving the original right to the individual who takes it. Nowadays most photographs that have commercial value are taken by employees of companies (press, news agencies etc) but that can be dealt with by the law under the separate heading of 'employed authors'.[2] Films produced a major problem. It was resolved by a fiction, ie that a film is no more than a series of thousands of photographs stuck together and cinematography was until 1948 (Brussels Act) classed as a 'process analogous to photography'. That makes all the individuals who participated in this process or at least most of them co-authors: camera men, cutters, actors (at least the stars), producers, scriptwriters, scenario writers, composers of accompanying music etc. The film producing company has to acquire these rights from the individual co-authors. This is very cumbersome but still feasible. When sound recording was invented the difficulty became insuperable. To recognise the sound engineer or the 'producer' who is in charge of recordings in the studio or the performing artist as the co-authors of a recording was felt to be stretching the point too far and the experience of treating films in this way had not been too encouraging.

The making of a recording in a studio might still be accepted as a team effort by named individuals, although that approach would have produced great difficulties. When it comes to the making of a broadcast, the analogy becomes too strained. A broadcasting corporation is too large an enterprise to conceive as a team of co-authors. Thus for phonograms and broadcasts a new solution had to be found which would be acceptable to 'droit d'auteur' countries.

The international compromise which led 'droit d'auteur' doctrine and legislation out of this philosophical impasse was to say that the initial right in the new material is not a 'droit d'auteur' but is nonetheless an intellectual property right and as such it is close to, connected with, or neighbouring on the 'droit d'auteur'. Italian law, one of the first to recognise these new rights in 1941, called them 'Diritti Conessi' (connected rights), German Law 'Verwandte Schutzrechte' (related rights), French Law 'Droit Voisins' (neighbouring rights). In English the term 'neighbouring rights' is now most commonly used.

1 See para 1.13 above.
2 See para 4.25 above.

7.05 The term 'neighbouring rights' in the narrow sense covers only the rights of performers, producers of phonograms and broadcasting organisations. In a wider sense it also covers other rights similar to copyright, such as the rights in photographs in certain countries,[1] the rights of film producers in certain countries[2] or the rights in first editions of books. These other rights will be referred to as 'related rights'.

The difference between granting these right owners a copyright or a neighbouring right can, as Professor Françon remarks[3] be both in space and in time. 'A given work may enjoy a copyright in one country, but only a neighbouring right or related right in another. This is the case with photographs, enjoying a copyright in France but only a neighbouring right under several other laws. Other works, formerly granted only a Neighbouring Right, may one day become the beneficiary of a Copyright'. He adds: 'This is, perhaps, the present direction of French jurisprudence with respect to performing artists'.[3] They were prophetic words, which seem to have been heeded by the 'Cour de Cassation' in 1982 in the *SPEDIDAME* case.[4] There is a third solution to the phonogram problem – apart from that of giving a copyright to the phonogram producer and that of giving a neighbouring right to the phonogram producer and to the performer; the solution chosen by the German law as early as 1910. It gave the performing artist a derivative copyright, likening his performance to an arrangement or an adaptation. When one considers how different a musical work may sound when sung by different singers or conducted by different conductors or how differently a role may be played by different actors, this approach seems very close to reality. It has now, nearly three quarters of a century later, been followed by the 'Cour de Cassation' in France.[4]

In international law the first move towards 'neighbouring rights' was made in 1928 by the Rome Revision Conference of the Berne Convention when the Conference, although refusing to grant a copyright to performers, as had been suggested, expressed a 'voeux'[5] at the end of the Conference that members of the Berne Convention should 'Consider the possibility of measures intended to safeguard the rights of performers'. It was envisaged that a convention or later two conventions (one for performers and producers of phonograms and one for broadcasting organisations) should be 'annexed to the revised Berne Convention'. Meanwhile some countries, eg Austria in 1936 and Italy in 1941, granted neighbouring rights to performers and record producers. At the Brussels Revision Conference in 1948 three 'voeux' were again expressed pointing in the same direction. On this occasion most states took the view that the rights of performers, phonogram producers and broadcasters were inter-linked and that a fair and equitable balance between them could only be achieved in one instrument. This view was widely shared and led, more than two decades later, to the signing of the Rome Convention in 1961.[6]

1 Eg Italy.
2 Eg Federal Republic of Germany.
3 André Françon 'International Protection of Neighbouring Rights' RIDA (1974, Anniversary Number) p 406 at p 410.
4 *SPEDIDAME v Radio France*, Cour de Cassation (1er Chambre Civile) 5 November 1980, see para 7.12 below.
5 A wish expressed by the Conference which is not binding on Governments but should encourage them to take action.
6 See paras 8.01–8.03 below.

2. Relations between authors' rights and neighbouring rights

7.06 Neighbouring rights are nearly always rights in derivative works because they presuppose a pre-existing work. Performers are only protected if they perform works[1] (thus excluding variety and circus artists). Phonograms are nearly always recordings of works (birdsong or background noises being the unimportant and rare exceptions). Broadcasts consist largely of performances of works (the broadcasting of sporting events or public functions being the notable exception). Thus the comparison to be made is with copyrights in other derivative works.

Derivative works can be of many kinds. The first historically was the translation of a work of literature into another language[2] and transcriptions of musical works (either upwards, eg orchestrating a vocal or piano score, or downwards, eg by reducing an operatic score to a version for the piano). Later followed the derivative works which are achieved by changing the medium, eg novel into film or play into radio or television play.

There is little merit in the argument that these works as derivative works are inferior because they demand only technical and not 'artistic' skills. It is difficult to argue that there is more artistry in transposing the orchestral score of the triumphal march from *Aida* for piano than in making a recording, or more artistry in arranging the march of the toreadors from *Carmen* for a brass band, than in creating a broadcast programme, yet the copyright in such arrangements has never been questioned. The argument becomes untenable when giving a copyright to the photographer who (sometimes at any rate) only presses a button, and denying it to the maker of a film.

The only distinction which is valid beyond argument is that the initial copyright owner in the case of neighbouring rights is almost invariably a corporate body (with the notable exception in the case of 'performers') whereas the initial owner of other copyrights is almost invariably a natural person (with the notable exception of the case of employed authors). Whereas this – the only valid distinction – does not justify division of all copyrights in 'copyrights' stricto sensu and 'neighbouring rights', it does have several consequences. 1) Moral rights will (with the exception of performers' rights)[3] by definition in most cases be confined to 'authors'. 2) The scope of 'copyrights' is, also by definition, wider than the scope of neighbouring rights, which encompasses only three categories of rights: the reproduction rights, the public performance rights and the broadcasting rights 3). The term of the neighbouring rights is, again by definition almost invariably shorter than that of other copyrights as 50 years from the death of the author is always longer than 20 or 30 or even 50 years, from publication, performance or broadcasting. In most cases it is much longer.

The quality of the reproduction right is often equal. The phonogram producer, for instance, has the same absolute right to prohibit the unauthorised copying of his phonogram as the author of a book has to prohibit the unauthorised copying of his book. On the other hand the performance right of the author is almost invariably stronger than that of the neighbouring right owner. The author usually has an absolute right, with the exception of broadcasting, where article 11 bis (2) of the Berne Convention[4] permits a compulsory licence which, if a country makes use of the provision, may reduce the author's right in effect to a right to equitable remuneration. The phonogram producer or the performer have in most countries only a right to equitable remuneration such as under article 12 of the Rome Convention.[5]

1   Rome Convention, art 3(a).
2   See para 5.08 above.
3   See para 7.15 below.
4   See para 5.43 above.
5   Exceptions are the United Kingdom and some countries whose laws stem from UK law where the performance right of the Phonogram Producer is an absolute right.

7.07 Three fears were expressed by authors' societies with regard to the establishment of neighbouring rights. The first was that some countries may protect neighbouring right owners whilst not protecting authors. This fear was allayed by articles 23 and 24 of the Rome Convention which provide that a country can only ratify the Rome Convention if it has already ratified either the Berne Convention or the Universal Copyright Convention.[1]

The second fear was that where several authorisations were required, one from the author and one from the neighbouring right owner, the former may give his authorisation but the latter may withhold it, thereby frustrating the use of the work and depriving the author of his royalty. An example would be a pianist performing a copyright work in a concert hall but objecting to the recording of the concert thus depriving the composer of his royalties on the sales of the record. Such cases are rare and in practice the pianist will only object if he fears the conditions are not conducive to a good recording, in which case the moral right of the author would suffer together with the reputation of the pianist.

The third fear was the most substantial of the three and concerned the performance right. If a user had to pay two royalties for the same performance, one to the author and one to the neighbouring right owners it was feared that he would only be prepared to pay less to the author. This is known as the 'cake theory'. There is supposed to be only one cake and if the neighbouring right owners get a slice of it, the slice of the author would be smaller. Practice has proved these fears to be unjustified. The intergovernmental committee of the Rome Convention finally laid this fear to rest in 1979. After a very thorough investigation of the problem their report[2] says:

> 'Several States members of the Subcommittee expressed the firm view that the evidence in their countries, and the evidence available to the Subcommittee, indicates conclusively that copyright royalties have not decreased as a result of the remuneration paid to performers and producers of phonograms. It is, therefore, clear that there is no evidence to support the proposition that authors' revenue has decreased as a result of neighbouring rights. It has been argued further that the revenue of authors and composers would have increased even more than it has done if there had been no secondary use rights in phonograms. This proposition has never been proved and is, by its nature, impossible to disprove. The Subcommittee, therefore, concludes that the second argument cannot be sustained either. In addition, the Subcommittee believes that a possible adverse effect on authors' royalties would not in any event constitute a sufficient reason for opposing the rights provided for in the Rome Convention since justice demands that performers and producers of phonograms should be remunerated for secondary use of phonograms.'

180 *Neighbouring Rights*

1   See Article 1 Rome Convention, para 8.05 below.
2   Recommendations of the Intergovernmental Committee of the Rome Convention 1979 (Annex 1 of document ILO/WIPO/UNESCO/ICR/SCi/IMP/5 para 28 – Reprinted in Copyright (April 1979) p 105).

3. Ownership, scope and term of neighbouring rights

7.08   Once it was conceded that these new materials deserve copyright protection three major questions had to be answered:

1. Who is to be the initial owner of the right?
2. What is to be its scope?
3. What is to be its term?

The answer to the first question is almost invariably a company or corporation in the case of phonogram producers and broadcasting organisations. It is an individual or a group of individuals (orchestra, chorus, pop group) in the case of performers.

In the case of authors' rights the scope or content of the right is a large bundle of rights which comprises, apart from the basic reproduction right, inter alia the translation right, the performance right, the broadcasting right and the film rights. The scope of these new rights, whether they are classed as copyrights or as neighbouring rights, is confined to the reproduction right, the performance right and the broadcasting right.

The term of protection for authors' rights under the Berne Convention is the life of the author plus 50 years[1] and under the Universal Copyright Convention the life of the author plus 25 years.[2]

Throughout the history of copyright the duration of the right has always been 'at the heart of the policy argument'.[3] The statutory term represents the compromise between the interest of the right owner and the public interest in the widest possible access to all works.[4] For published works most countries have now accepted the 50 years after the death of the author term of the Berne Convention. For works not published in the author's lifetime the period is usually 50 years from the end of the year in which the work was first 'published'. It is the latter type of term, ie a number of years from publication, that has become the rule for neighbouring rights. In the case of phonograms and broadcasts where the original right owner is not a physical person this is the only logical solution.

The minimum term under both the Rome Convention and the Phonogram Convention is 20 years.[5] Under national laws the term varies from 25 years in Scandinavia and Germany.[6] and 30 years in Italy[7] to 50 years in the United Kingdom and 60 years in Brazil and 75 years in the United States.[8] The lower bracket is the equivalent of rights in photographs in several countries,[9] the 50 years term is the equivalent of the copyright term for unpublished works in some countries.[10] Apart from the different term the calculation of the duration of the right is made more difficult by the fact that the starting point is different under different legislations. That point is either the date of fixation, eg Denmark[11] or the date of publication, eg Federal Republic of Germany.[12] The period is computed from the end of the year in which the event (fixation or publication) took place.[13]

In the case of performers the starting point of the term is in most national laws the time when the performance took place[14] or when the performance was fixed.[15] As performers, unlike producers of phonograms or broadcasting organisations, are physical persons with a natural life span, such a term if it is as short as 20 years leads to abnormal situations. When the performer who has made a recording in his twenties or thirties reaches the forties or fifties his new and protected recordings may have to compete in the market with his own earlier recordings which are already in the public domain.

Thus the rights in the new materials are always of shorter duration by definition and sometimes much shorter. In works created at a young age by an author who lives to old age the copyright term may add up to a hundred years, compared with the minimum of 20 years for neighbouring rights.

1   Art 7; see para 5.54 above.
2   Art IV; see para 6.18 above.
3   Cornish *Intellectual Property Rights* (1981) p 340.
4   See para 1.07 above.
5   Rome Convention, art 14; Phonogram Convention, art 4.
6   Denmark, Copyright Act 1960, arts 45 and 47; Germany, Copyright Act 1965, art 82.
7   Copyright Act 1941, art 85 and Presidential Decree of 14 May 1974.
8   Copyright Law 1976, sections 302-305.
9   Eg UK, Republic of Ireland, Luxembourg.
10 Eg UK, Copyright Act, s 3(4).
11 Art 47, Copyright Law 1960.
12 Art 82, Copyright Law 1965.
13 Rome Convention, art 14.
14 Denmark, art 45, Copyright Law 1960; Italy, art 85, Copyright Law 1941.
15 Eg Italy, art 14(a) Copyright Law 1941.

4. The rights of performers

7.09   The position of performers, viewed internationally, is rather paradoxical. Although of all neighbouring rights owners, they are closest to the author, their rights are in many jurisdictions and in international law the weakest. Unlike the other neighbouring right owners, they are physical persons, like the authors and from a purely philosophical point of view it is difficult to see the essential difference between the work of a derivative author, say a translator, or an arranger and that of a performer. Just as the translator renders the original work as faithfully as possible in another language, so the performer interprets the spirit of the work as truly as he can musically or on the stage. Just as the arranger, although basing himself on the original work adds another dimension to the work, so does the performer and different performances by different artistes vary greatly from one another. Most languages emphasise the creativity of the performer by expression like an actor 'creating' a part or a pianist presenting a most 'personal' or 'original' rendering of a well-known concerto. That is applying the more stringent tests of the 'droit d'auteur'. In 'copyright' there is not much doubt that performers 'spend sufficient skill and labour' to merit copyright protection.

There seem to be two reasons for the weakness of the performers' position in law. The first is social and historical, actors or 'strolling players' were regarded as 'vagrants' by the law during the formative period of copyright. Adam Smith in his work *The Wealth of Nations* gave 'players, buffoons, musicians, opera-singers, opera-dancers' as classical examples of 'unproductive labour'.[1] Modern times have removed this social stigma and from the bottom of the social scale star performers have gone to the top and some have become the idols of modern society. The second reason is historical and technological. Adam Smith goes on to say: 'The work of all of them perishes in the instant of its production'. This was perfectly correct in his day. We have seen that fixation of the work in a tangible form, so that it can be copied, is in many jurisdictions an essential ingredient of a copyright protected work. The ephemeral nature of a performance may therefore have provided a valid reason for denying a copyright to performers. This reason was removed with the invention of records, films, radio and television. From the time when performances could be fixed and the fixations both reproduced in large numbers and performed to large audiences, thus involving the two basic rights in the copyright 'bundle', the reproduction right and the performance right, the second reason too had been removed. The question what, if any, rights performers should have in law has been debated among jurists and legislators ever since.

1 Adam Smith *The Wealth of Nations* Book II, ch III, quoted by Edward Thompson 'Twenty Years of the Rome Convention' Copyright (1981) at p 274.

7.10 When eventually some protection was given it took different forms in different countries. Germany, which was the first, followed the way shown by the Berne Convention. When faced with the new phenomenon of the film the Convention declared it a 'process analogous to photography'. Although this is like saying that modern man is analogous to the Neanderthal man it seemed to serve the purpose of appeasing the traditionalists. Granting a right appeared not as an entirely new departure but as a gradual development. German law followed this example. It said in effect that the performance of a musical work by a performer is analogous to an adaption of the original work.[1] This followed the philosophy of Josef Kohler who had argued that whereas before the invention of recording a performer could only have a personality right, once his performance can be fixed on a corpus mechanicum, his performance which had been ephemeral acquires permanence and the fixed performance is a work which is an arrangement of the original work and the performer is its author.[2]

1 Art 2/2 Copyright Law 1910.
2 See Ulmer *Urheber und Verlagsrecht* (3rd edn) p 514.

7.11 In Italy the Copyright Law 1941, the first of the laws to use the term 'neighbouring rights'[1] did not give performers a right to allow or forbid the fixation of their performance but a right to equitable remuneration if their performance was recorded or broadcast.[2] The term is 20 years. By subjecting the right to a kind of compulsory licence and giving it a much shorter term the law indicated that it was not quite like a 'droit d'auteur' but a neighbouring right.

1 'Diritti connessi' (related rights).
2 Art 80/2, Copyright Law 1941.

7.12 In France statute law completely disregards performers' rights as is the case with other neighbouring rights. The laws of 1791 and 1793 were not revised until 1957 and then proposals for such a right were rejected. However the courts recognised a performer's 'droit Moral' as early as 1937[1] saying that whereas performers had no copyright it was 'equitable to recognise a right in their personal creation, ie the interpretation they give to their roles, which is the sole manifestation of their art perceptible by the senses and thus published'.[2] Later in a prolonged law suit known as *l'affaire Furtwängler* the courts went further. Furtwängler had conducted Beethoven's *Eroica Symphony* with the Berlin Philharmonic Orchestra during the 1939–45 war and consented to the performance being recorded and subsequently broadcast. After the war the recording was found by the occupying forces, issued by two American companies (Thalia and Urania) and the records were sold in France. They were inferior recordings and the famous conductor (and after his death his widow) objected. The 'Tribunal civil de la Seine'[3] found for the plaintiff saying that he had 'a right to forbid any use he had not authorised by contract.'[4] He had contracted for his performance to be recorded for the purpose of broadcasting not for the purpose of pressing and selling records. The Appelate Court 'Cour de Paris' in its judgment speaks of moral and economic rights of the performer but studiously avoids the expression 'droit d'auteur', as a right of the performer in his performance.[5] The 'Cour de Cassation' (Supreme Court) was more specific:[6] 'the Performer is entitled to prohibit any use of his performance other than that authorised by him and this ... is sufficient ground to amount to a violation of the Performer's right in the *work*[7] which is constituted by his performance'. The court, choosing its language carefully, leaves no doubt that they regarded at least the performance of a famous conductor as a work. Other decisions in a similar vein followed. One says: 'on account of its originality the performance therefore constitutes an intellectual work, and particularly an artistic one.'[8] The courts also recognised the moral right of a performer in the case of Jacques Brel, a poet performing his own works. The court says that he has 'the moral rights of the artist including the right to prepare and carefully perfect the intellectual work constituted by his singing of a work.'[9]

In the *SPEDIDAME* case[10] the 'Cour de Cassation' held that 'whereas artists do not benefit from the protection of the Copyright Law 1957 they are nonetheless entitled by virtue of the rules of the common law to demand that their performance is not used for a different purpose from that which they have authorised'. The rule of the common law referred to is article 1382 of the Civil Code which establishes the French equivalent to a general tort. It says: 'If anyone commits an act which causes damage to another person, the person through whose fault the damage has occurred shall be obliged to repair it'.[11] Basing itself on this principle the court concludes that a performer's authorisation to have his performance recorded and to have copies of such recording sold, does not include his authorisation to have those recordings broadcast. The result seems in line with article 12 of the Rome Convention, although it is arrived at by another route. Instead of a right to equitable remuneration based on statute the court says that the unauthorised broadcasting of the recordings which he has made for private use entitles the performer to damages against the broadcasting organisation.[12] The French courts put the emphasis on the 'artiste interprete' which is the equivalent to the Rome Convention concept of persons who 'perform literary and artistic works',[13] with the emphasis on soloists.

The German courts, on the other hand, when called to interpret the performance right in recorded performances, held[14] that the right was given to all artists as performers of works from the star to the last violin in the orchestra and the last member of the chorus in an opera.

1 Tribunal civil de la Seine JCP 1937 II 247.
2 See Desjeux *La Convention de Rome* (1966) pp 13-17.
3 Tribunal civil de la Seine JCP 1937 II 247.
4 4 January 1956 (RTDC 1956 p 275).
5 13 February 1957 (RTDC 1957 p 653).
6 Ch Civ (1ᵉ ch) 4 January 1964, Dalloz 1964, 321, note Pluyette and JCP 1964, 13712.
7 Emphasis added.
8 Cour de Lyon, 11 March 1971, Gaz Pal 1971, Jur p 497.
9 Cour de Paris, 22 March 1968, cited in RIDA (1969) LXII p 121.
10 Tribunal de Grande Instance (3ᵉ ch) 14 December 1972 (RIDA, April 1975 p 180). Court of Appeal of Paris (4ᵉ ch.) 30 November 1974 (RIDA, April 1975 p 196). Cour de Cassation (1ʳᵉ ch,) 15 March 1977 (RIDA, July 1977 p 141).
11 Freely translated by the author.
12 The measure of damages was referred back for decision to the lower court.

13 Art 3(a).
14 BGH (Bundesgerichtshof) 31 May 1960.

7.13 In the United Kingdom performers were not given either a copyright or a neighbouring right but protection by way of criminal sanctions.[1] The offence is to make a phonogram or a film of a 'live' (unfixed) performance without the consent of the performer or to broadcast such a live performance (including diffusion by wire) without his consent. In each case to constitute the offence the user has to act both knowingly and without the written consent of the performer. The advantage of this method of protection is immediacy. A private prosecution for an infringement can be undertaken by the performer and be concluded by a fine very quickly. The disadvantage is the practical difficulty of securing the presence of the artist, particularly foreign artists, in court to give evidence and the fact that the penalties being fines have to be constantly kept under review because of inflation otherwise they cease to be an effective deterrent.

Faced with the problem of the illicit recording of live performances (known as 'bootlegging') the courts in the United Kingdom had to 'reconsider both the scope of the general economic torts and the extent to which injunctive relief may be available against the commission of criminal offences'.[2] It has been held in the United Kingdom that a performer whose performance has been recorded without his permission and phonograms made from this illicit recording and sold, is entitled to an injunction.[3]

Thus it seems that even in those countries like the United Kingdom where performers do not have a copyright or a neighbouring right the courts are beginning to fill the gap in different ways and the position of performers seems to be in a state of development. Professor Cornish's summing up seems to point to the most likely outcome: 'The reality ought to be faced: in principle, performances are an independent activity deserving and needing Copyright; the precise scope of the right is then for discussion'.[4]

Such discussions are being conducted on the national level and have, as shown above, led to different solutions fitting in with the general system of copyright in the country, but the general principle seems no longer in doubt.

1 Dramatic and Musical Performers' Protection Acts, originally 1925, now 1958–1972.
2 Cornish, op cit, p 445.
3 *Ex p Island Records* [1978] Ch 122, [1978] 3 All ER 824.
4 Cornish, op cit, p 449.

7.14 It has to be said that even the granting of a copyright or a neighbouring right does not fully compensate the profession of performers, particularly musicians, for the fundamental changes brought about by the new media (films, records, broadcasts), usually referred to as technological unemployment. Once a performance is recorded it can be repeated in public without the necessity of engaging the performer whose performance has been recorded or indeed without the presence of any performer at all. Performers have thus lost countless employment opportunities.[1] This explains the desire of performers in the early history of these rights to obtain an absolute right to authorise or forbid the public performance of their recorded performances so that they could in certain cases have prevented the use of recorded music (eg dance bands instead of discotheques, live performances on radio instead of records) but this did not succeed. It is also being pointed out[2] that the performance right in their recorded performances benefits the stars far more than the rank and file musicians who rarely get into a recording or film studio and therefore do not benefit from any additional income for the profession as a whole. Some collecting societies seek to alleviate this problem by paying some of their income to members who have lost their employment (particularly monies which are undistributable because the beneficiary cannot be identified)[3]. However if the law can make any contribution to solving the problem of technological unemployment which is doubtful, it seems to lie in social legislation rather than in copyright.

[1] A government report in the Federal Republic of Germany in September 1973 stated that unemployment of singers, actors and dancers averaged 11.6%. Among all workers it was 1% at the time. It also showed a steady drop in the number of persons engaged in the performing arts. (Quoted in Frank Gotzen's study 'Performers' Rights in the European Economic Community' 1977 published by the Commission of the European Communities.)
[2] Edward Thompson 'International, Protection of Performers Rights', International Labour Review (1973) pp 303-314 and 'Twenty Years of the Rome Convention' Copyright (1981) p 270.
[3] See para 7.33 below.

7.15 The exercise of any rights performers have under various national legislations suffers from the additional difficulty that quite frequently many performers are participating in one performance. There may be two or three co-authors of a work and national and international copyright law makes provision for this, but the number of performers participating in one performance may be far larger, eg the cast of actors in a play or musicians in an orchestra, or singers, musicians and chorus in an opera. Provision had therefore to be made for the collective exercise of their rights.

The rights given to performers under various legislations are:

1. The right to control the fixation of a live performance.
2. The right to control the broadcasting or public performance of a live performance.
3. The right to control subsequent reproductions of the first fixation.
4. The right to control the broadcasting or public performance of such a fixation.

The first two rights are usually expressed as the right to authorise or forbid. They are absolute rights. The right to 'control' subsequent reproductions of the first fixation is under the Rome Convention exercisable if the reproduction is made for purposes different from those for which the performers gave their consent.[1] The right to control the broadcasting or public performance of the first fixation, ie a phonogram, is almost invariably granted in the form of an equitable remuneration for the use of phonograms on the air or in public. This is a form of a compulsory licence. It is being justified by the fact that the user would not be able to obtain the authorisation of the performers for each separate use. He will want to make agreements for the payment of an equitable remuneration with a collecting society acting on behalf of all performers.

In view of the fundamental differences of approach between national legislation the first international instrument, the Rome Convention, adopts the solution of the lowest common denominator.

Performers have 'the right to prevent' unauthorised fixations of their live performances. This can be implemented on the national level by an absolute right (eg Germany) or a neighbouring right (eg Japan) or protection by criminal provisions (eg the United Kingdom).

Some countries grant certain moral rights to performers in respect of their performances. Italian law[2] provides that performers who play leading parts in a dramatic, literary or musical work are entitled to have their names indicated when their performances are broadcast or recorded on a phonogram or film. The 'moral right to respect' for the integrity of the performance is also given in some legislations. German law[3] prohibits any distortion or other alteration of a performance which might injure the reputation of an artiste. Italian law[4] gives the performers the right 'to oppose any diffusion, transmission or reproduction of their performance which might be prejudicial to their honour or reputation'. These provisions are echoes of articles 6 bis (1) of the Berne Convention equating the performer to an author in this respect. However in international convention law there is as yet no recognition of such a moral right.

1   Rome Convention, art 7(c)(ii); see para 8.19 below.
2   Art 83, Italian Copyright Law 1941.
3   Art 83, German Copyright Law 1965.
4   Art 81, Italian Copyright Law 1941. In a judgment of 9 December 1971 the Cour de Cassation held that this implied that the artiste cannot be required to perform (live) under conditions which are detrimental to his reputation because he cannot demonstrate his artistic ability to best advantage. See Diritto d'Autore (1972) p 284.

5. The rights of producers of phonograms

7.16 Producers of phonograms enjoy the three basic rights in the 'bundle of rights'[1] granted to neighbouring right owners: the reproduction right; the public performance right; and the broadcasting right.

The reproduction right is a right erga omnes to authorise or prohibit any reproduction of a protected phonogram. The Rome Convention[2] gives the right to prohibit reproduction whether such reproduction is 'direct or indirect'. These words replaced the words 'directly or when broadcast' and it was understood[3] that 'indirectly' covered reproduction from a matrix (in the case of discs) or from a pre-existing phonogram, such as a tape or from a 'recording off the air'. The last mentioned method of reproduction is known as 'home taping', an activity which is simple with the equipment available on the market in most countries. Home taping would be contrary to international law in countries which have ratified the Rome Convention unless it is covered by the private use exception of article 15(1)(a) which is a matter of national law.

If the phonogram which is home taped contains works protected by copyright, usually musical works, it infringes the author's right under the Berne Convention.[4] The Report of the 1967 Revision Conference of the Berne Convention made the meaning of article 9(2) very plain:

> '... If it is considered that reproduction conflicts with the normal exploitation of a work, reproduction is not permitted at all. If it is considered that reproduction does not conflict with the normal exploitation of the work, the next step would be to consider whether it does not unreasonably prejudice the legitimate interests of the author'.

It seems clear that the practice of home taping both 'conflicts with a normal exploitation of the work' and does 'unreasonably prejudice the legitimate interest of the author'. Therefore the practice does not seem to be covered by any fair use exception but is an infringement. The Whitford Committee in the United Kingdom came to the same conclusion.[5]

> '... we reject the suggestion that fair dealing should be extended generally to permit some free audio and video recording because fair dealing to an extent such as is accepted as reasonable for literary works, for example, would not satisfy the need for most users, while a widening of the term would create a virtual free-for-all with copyright owners getting no benefit'.

1   See para 1.09 above.
2   Art 10; see 8.29 below.

3   See Report of the Rapporteur General on article 10.
4   Art 9(2), see para 5.39 above.
5   Whitford Committee Report 1977, para 320.

7.17   However the exercise of the reproduction right both by the author and by the phonogram producer in these circumstances would be an intolerable intrusion in the privacy of the users' home and the right is therefore unenforcable in practice. The practice of 'home taping' is a good example of new technology eroding the most basic right of the copyright owner, the reproduction right to such an extent that only legislation can restore the balance.[1] The only practical legislative approach seems to be the one adopted in Germany and Austria. The law of the Federal Republic of Germany provides for a royalty on the recording equipment[2] and the law of Austria[3] for a royalty on the blank tape used for the recording. Under these provisions a royalty is based on the sale of each piece of recording equipment or on the sale of each blank tape. That royalty is shared by authors, performers and phonogram producers. The German law stipulates a maximum percentage of the price which can be levied as a royalty. The Austrian law provides a temporary overall ceiling for the bulk of the revenue. Both legislations leave the distribution of royalties between the parties entitled to them to negotiations between the collecting societies representing these parties.[4]

In the United States an appelate court decided in the *Betamax* case[5] that off-the-air copying of telecasts of copyrighted audiovisual materials by means of video tape recorders was not 'fair use' but constituted a copyright infringement even if done at home and for private non commercial use. The court also held that the manufacturer of the videotape recorder, as well as the distributor and the retail seller of such equipment are liable for 'contributory infringement' because they knew that tape recorders would be used for the purpose of home taping and therefore 'induced, caused or materially contributed to the infringing conduct'. On the mens rea of the contributory infringer the court held that it is only necessary that he knew of the infringing activity, ie home taping. It is not necessary to prove that he also knew that the activity which he made possible was an infringement of copyright.[6]

1   See paras 12.12 et seq.
2   Copyright Act 1965, s 53(5).
3   Copyright Amendment Act 1980, s 42.
4   For an analysis of the available legislative options see Stewart 'Home Taping – the legal basis for the compensation of Copyright owners' EIPR (July 1980), p 207.
5   US Court of Appeals (Ninth Circuit) *Universal, et al v Sony et al* 19 October 1981.
6   As to the appropriate relief the Appelate Court suggested that 'statutory damages' would be more appropriate than an injunction on the grounds that although a permanent injunction is provided for in the Copyright Act a court could award damages or a continuing royalty 'when great public injury would result from an injunction'. The judgment is under appeal to the Supreme Court.

7.18   The reproduction right in phonograms applies to parts of phonograms since, as the Rome Convention Report states, 'the right of reproduction is not qualified, and is to be understood as including rights against partial reproduction of a phonogram'.[1] This is important as it prevents the copying of one track of an LP (long playing record) and probably even part of a track if the part is substantial.

The right owner is the entity which first fixes the sounds. This excludes both the technicians or operators employed by the recording company and any entity merely pressing records, ie duplicating the fist fixation which is the original recording.

The protection under the Phonogram Convention[2] is on the one hand wider and on the other hand less strictly defined. It is wider because it gives a distribution right and a right against importation of illicit reproductions as well as a reproduction right.[3] It is less strictly defined because the means of implementing the reproduction right is left to national legislation which is free to assure protection by such means as the law of unfair competition (eg France) without granting a reproduction right. However most legislations give the Phonogram Producer a reproduction right.[4]

As the copying of pre-recorded tapes is now a very simple operation which almost anybody can carry out and even the illicit copying of discs which requires a pressing plant can be made extremely profitable, 'piracy' (the illicit copying of phonograms for commercial purposes) is today practised in many more countries and in far larger numbers of copies than piracy of books and printed matter ever had been. Thus the enforcement of the reproduction right and the remedies available to authors and phonogram producers at the national level have become of prime importance.

1 See Rome Convention, General Report on Article 10 and *WIPO Guide to Rome* 10.3.
2 See para 9.05 below.
3 Phonogram Convention, art 3.
4 See Stewart 'The Phonogram Convention' Copyright (June 1973) p 110.

6. Remedies for infringements of rights of phonogram producers and performers

(1) Introduction

7.19 Like other copyrights, the copyrights and 'neighbouring rights' of producers of phonograms and performers are usually governed by contracts and these contracts provide contractual remedies in cases of breaches of contract. These remedies include injunctions and actions for damages for breaches of contract. However the distinguishing feature of copyright is that being a right erga omnes it can be enforced against all manner of persons with whom the owner of the copyright or the neighbouring right has no contractual relation, but who have infringed his rights. The effectiveness of such enforcement is measured by three factors: speed, burden of proof and cost. It is also characteristic of these rights that whereas the rights are invariably statutory, the remedies often rest on judge-made law, eg France and the United Kingdom.

In countries where both civil and criminal remedies are available, right owners, as a rule, prefer the civil remedy. The reasons lie in the first two criteria: speed and burden of proof.

Criminal proceedings may take months and in some countries years, whereas in civil proceedings interim orders are usually immediately available. They include orders to desist from the infringing conduct pending the trial of the action, eg making further unauthorised copies. In some countries, eg the United Kingdom, the courts have developed pre-trial procedures such as discovery of documents and information from defendants which enable the plaintiff to uncover breaches by persons other than the defendant so that he can stop further infringements.

The second reason is the burden of proof. In most countries the plaintiff in a civil case will succeed if he convinces the court on the balance of probabilities that the defendant has infringed his right. In criminal cases, on the other hand, the case against the defendant has to be proved strictly or beyond reasonable doubt, a much heavier burden. This difference is particularly significant if mens rea is a necessary ingredient of the offence, ie the defendant will only be found guilty if it can be proved that he knew he was infringing the plaintiff's right. In cases of piracy of phonograms brought against dealers this can only be proved by inferences to be drawn from such factors as very low price or a suspect source of supply or the outward appearance of the record or the cassette. This type of infringement is thus reminiscent of the offence of receiving stolen goods where the receiver's knowledge that the goods were stolen has to be proved by similar inferences. Some criminal statutes have reversed the burden of proof, in receiving cases[1] so that once it is proved that the goods were in fact stolen the defendant has to show that he did not know they were stolen. Such a shift in the burden of proof in Copyright infringement cases has so far only been enacted in very few countries.[2] In some countries, eg Italy and the United States, retailers displaying and selling unauthorised, ie pirated, copies of phonograms have in fact been treated as receivers of stolen goods.[3]

1 Eg the Theft Act 1968 in the United Kingdom.
2 Egs 3(1), Copyright (Gramophone Records and Government Broadcasting) Act 1968 in Singapore.
3 Court of Appeal of Naples, 11 April 1980; case of *Salvatore Molinaro and Antonia Moccia*. United States Court of Appeals for the District of Columbia *US v David L Whetzel* 589F 2d 707 (DC Cir, 1978); illegal copies of sound recordings were treated as stolen goods constituting the offence of interstate transport of goods knowing them to be stolen.

(2) Civil remedies

Search and seizure

7.20 In the United Kingdom the courts make orders ex parte, after a hearing in camera and in the absence of the defendant, ordering the defendant or the occupier of his premises to permit the plaintiff and his lawyer to inspect the defendant's premises, the order enables the plaintiff's lawyers to take possession of infringing copies and documents and other relevant materials or require the defendant to keep infringing stock, thus securing or preserving the evidence. The order is known as 'Anton Piller Order' after one of the first reported cases in which such an order was made.[1] The order is only granted if there is a very strong prima facie case of an infringement and clear evidence that the defendant has in his possession documents or materials which prove the infringement and which he may destroy or dispose of. The plaintiff must also show that the actual or potential damage caused to him, is very serious. The order which is close to being a 'search warrant' in a civil case requires strict safeguards. The plaintiff's lawyer must be present, the defendant must be given time to consult his lawyer if he wishes to do so and the plaintiff must give an undertaking to the court as to damages which the defendant may suffer. Subject to these safeguards a defendant's refusal to permit the inspection can be used as evidence against him and can amount to 'contempt of court' which means that the defendant can be brought before the court and imprisoned until he 'purges his Contempt' by permitting the inspection. The making of the order is always in the court's discretion.[2]

1 *Anton Piller K.G. v Manufacturing Processes Ltd* [1976] Ch 55; see para 4.45 above.
2 Such orders although originating in copyright cases (proceedings against record pirates) can also be made in trade mark cases or cases of breaches of confidence see *Universal City v Mukhtar* 1976 FSR 252 and although originating in the United Kingdom have been made in other common law jurisdictions (eg Australia, Hong Kong).

'*Injunction*'

7.21 This is an order made by the court directing the defendant to desist or refrain from committing acts which infringe the plaintiff's copyright or 'neighbouring right'. Such injunctions can be granted at the end of the trial ('final injunctions') or at the outset ('interlocutory injunctions'). For wilful breaches of an injunction the courts can impose fines or even imprisonment.

It is the interlocutory injunction which, because of its immediacy in stopping the defendant from infringing the plaintiff's right, is the most important remedy to guarantee the efficacy of a copyright. It has the advantage of both speed and relatively low cost. In practice it often has the effect of settling the case as the defendant, deprived of the opportunity to make a quick profit, desists and allows final judgment to be given against him without trial. This is particularly so in the case of phonograms of popular music or newspaper articles or topical broadcasts where at the end of the trial many months later the infringing copies would no longer be of much value. The courts require an undertaking from the plaintiff to make good the damage which may be caused to the defendant should the defendant succeed at the trial. This remedy is always discretionary at the interlocutory stage and the judge has to weigh the risk of damage to the plaintiff if the remedy is refused, against the risk of damage to the defendant if it is granted. In weighing this the courts have to consider whether damages awarded at the end of the trial will adequately compensate the plaintiff and whether the defendant is and will be in a position to pay them. In the case of relatively small retailers dealing in large numbers of infringing copies the answer to this question will usually be negative and the injunction will thus be granted. This remedy of an interlocutory injunction is widely used in all Anglo-Saxon jurisdictions.[1]

In French jurisprudence the Référé-procedure is available in interlocutory proceedings leading to an interim order to preserve the evidence, if necessary also on an 'ex parte' basis.[2]

1 The approach to granting or refusing injunctions has recently been considered in the UK in *American Cyanamid v Ethicon* [1975] AC 396; in Australia in *Firth v Polyglas* [1977] RPC 213 (HC Australia); in South Africa in *Beecham Group v BM Group* [1977] RPC 220 (PD South Africa).
2 Art 497, Code of Civil Procedure, see para 4.46 above.

(3) The law of unfair competition

7.22 In the countries where neighbouring rights do not form part of the law[1] the remedies under the law of unfair competition have to serve to deal with cases of infringement of neighbouring rights.

In some cases where a trademark violation can be established[2] a criminal remedy may be available but the main remedy is provided by the civil law under the law of unfair competition. It is based on article 1382 of the Civil Code: 'If anyone commits an act which causes damage to another person, the person through whose fault the damage has occurred shall be obliged to repair it.[3] The unauthorised reproduction of a legitimate recording constitutes such a 'fault' (tort) and is thus actionable under article 1382.

Civil liability under article 1382 requires three conditions: 'fault', damage and a causal connection between the two. French jurisprudence has always refused to find in favour of a plaintiff who, despite the proof of an existing 'fault', cannot prove damage and its relation to the fault.

It is thus necessary for the phonogram producer to establish the existence of a 'fault', the damage due to the act of unfair competition and the causal connection between the 'fault' and the damage ('préjudice subi').

The courts take the view that unauthorised duplication is an act of unfair competition.[4] It leads to a distortion of competition and creates an evident prejudice to the legitimate record producer, who suffers financial loss from the unfair competition.

In as much as the system of civil liability based on an action for unfair competition was already part of French law, ratification of the Phonogram Convention did not require alteration of French legislation.

It should be added that authors and phonogram producers have agreed that all phonograms should bear a 'label' notice to the effect that unauthorised duplication is prohibited. This has provided an additional safeguard as non-observance of this notice by anyone acquiring the phonogram may render him liable for a quasi-delict.

Based on civil law principles the French courts have held that performers had both a moral right in their performances and a right to forbid any unauthorised use of these performances including fixed (recorded) performances.[5] After France's ratification of the Phonogram Convention (1971) in April 1973 which obliged France to protect phonogram producers protected by the Convention against the unauthorised copying of their phonograms[6] it was thought that it would no longer be necessary for the plaintiff to prove 'fault' in the defendant, but that proof of unauthorised duplication of the plaintiff's phonograms would suffice. However in two subsequent cases the Court of Appeal of Paris[7] held that as the Convention only deals with 'international situations' and not with 'domestic' ones, in cases of 'pirated' French as opposed to foreign phonograms protected by the Convention 'fault' has still to be proved. However in practice it would appear that the burden of proving the existence of 'fault' in the defendant has been reduced as the judges often exercise their discretion, in the plaintiff's favour, no doubt finding it odd that in mixed cases (foreign and French phonograms) they should be constrained to favour foreign plaintiffs against French plaintiffs.[8] In a case where counterfeited phonograms were made in the United States and imported into France the French Authors' Society (SDRM) acted as plaintiff on behalf of its author members and the defence was that copyright was not involved but 'only a sale of material product'. The court rejected this defence[9] It also held that even if the phonograms were made under the compulsory licence in the United States, the principle of national treatment under article 2 of the Universal Copyright Convention,[10] of which both France and the United States were members, meant that the compulsory licence applied only to the United States, and the royalty would have been paid only for the United States, so that distribution in France was an infringement.

In Belgium, where as in France neighbouring rights are only protected by the law against unfair competition[11] unauthorised copying of phonograms and unauthorised recording of an artist's performance have been held to be acts of unfair ('parasitical') competition.[12] The courts have ordered confiscation of infringing copies and damages; however injunctions or orders for inspection or 'seizure by description' which are remedies available to copyright owners are not available to neighbouring rights owners.[13]

1 Mainly France, Belgium and the Netherlands.
2 Particularly cases of counterfeiting.
3 Translation by the author; see para 7.12 above.
4 RIDA (January 1979) p 182. Tribunal de Grande Instance, 7 April 1977. *Sté. Barclay v Paul Lederman, Productions Lederman, Stés. Pathé, Marconi, EMI, MM. Green et Lejeune*. RIDA (April 1980) p 156. Court of Appeal, 6 October 1978. *Sté. Francaise du Son v J-C Roche, Sté. Pacific Vogue Compagnie Générale du Disque*. RIDA (October 1980) p 132. Tribunal of Grande Instance, 19 March 1980 *Soc. Sonodisc and SNEPA v Rezzoug, Negadi, E1 Madjouli*.
5 *Furtwängler* case (Appeal Court, Paris, 13 February 1957) and 'Cour de Cassation' (Supreme Court) 4 January 1964. Followed in *Orane Demasis* 'Cour de Cassation', 30 January 1974, *Spyket* and others, Cour de Cassation', 29 April 1976.
6 Phonogram Convention, art 3; see para 9.06 below.
7 *Société Francaise du son and Allanne v Société Pacific, Vogue, Compagnie Generale du Disque et Roche*, 6 October 1978; *SA Pickwick France v SA Vogue*, 19 January 1979.

8 The Tribunal de la Grande Instance in *La Société Sonodisc SA and SNEPA v Driss Rezzong*, 19 March 1980 finding unfair competition proved, ordered the destruction of the infringing copies and 25,000 francs damages.
9 Tribunal de Grande Instance de Paris 17eme Chambre *SDRM v Beatrice G* 24 April 1980. The court ordered confiscation of all infringing copies, payment of 10.000 F Francs 'provisional' damages and appointed an expert to assess final damages.
10 See para 6.05 above.
11 The Belgian Copyright Law dates back to 1886.
12 *Inelco NV, SABAM and RCA v Suits and others*, Tribunal Correctionel, Louvain, 5 December 1975; *SIBESA v Labion*, Tribunal de Commerce, Brussels, 30 May 1979 a case of a clandestine recording made at a concert without consent of authors or performer.
13 See Davies *Piracy of Phonograms* (a study prepared for the EEC) (1981) 4.2.11.

(4) Compensatory remedies

Damages

7.23 Generally, the purpose of an award of damages is to restore the plaintiff to his position before the infringement. Such damages are thus 'compensatory'. However the courts can also award 'punitive' damages in copyright cases. Whereas the measure of damages in the case of compensatory damages will generally be what the plaintiff could have charged for a licence or the value of lost sales or royalties, the measure of punitive damages is always in the discretion of the Court. They are awarded in cases where the breach is flagrant and the defendant stood to make substantial profits from his conduct,[1] as 'it is necessary for the law to show that it cannot be broken with impunity'.[2] In most countries the awards of the courts itemise the separate heads of damages.[3]

1 In the case of *US v EC Tape Service Inc* the Court of Appeals of Wisconsin awarded 'punitive damages' of a million dollars on top of compensatory damages (27 October 1981).
2 United Kingdom, per Lord Devlin in *Rookes v Barnard* [1964] AC 1129 at 1220 ff.
3 Sweden, Case of *Haken Verner Libjegnen* 31 January 1980. Damages were awarded against a record pirate (1) to NCB (the Authors Society) (a) 37.000 Sw Krs in respect of loss of royalties which would have been paid on legitimate sales of the phonograms (b) 20,000 Sw Krs as general damages (2) To the three performers 20.057 Sw Krs on the basis of the average royalty which would have been paid to each artist in respect of the sale of the records and (3) 10.000 Sw Krs to each artist whose live performance was recorded without his consent. On appeal the Court of Appeal of Gota upheld the award of damages. (It reduced the prison sentence from four months to one month but held that a fine would have been an insufficient penalty). Sweden, Case of *Sten Oskar Vilhelm Borglin*, District Court of Helsingborg. Import of infringing 'Video Cassettes' of over 50 different films. Apart from one month imprisonment, general damages under s 54, para 2, Copyright Act, 1000 Sw Krs for each infringing copy in the possession of the accused and special damages 150 Sw Krs for each infringing copy sold.

'Delivery up'

7.24 This is a remedy usually coupled with an injunction which orders the defendant to surrender the infringing copies and the machinery or other equipment used in the process of production. If delivery up is not obtained at an interlocutory hearing it is usually ordered as an alternative to destruction at the end of the trial.

(5) Criminal remedies

7.25 In the countries where the producers of phonograms have a copyright or a neighbouring right the law usually provides criminal as well as civil remedies by making infringements an offence. Such offences usually show three characteristics:

1. A public prosecution will only be undertaken on the application of the injured party.[1] In countries where the legal system permits private prosecutions the injured party can itself prosecute.[2]
2. The prosecutor must prove that the infringement was intentional.

3. The primary sentence will be a fine and only in cases of recidivism or exceptionally large scale infringements a prison sentence.

The general trend has been to leave the protection of copyright to civil proceedings with confiscation of infringing copies and damages as the main remedies. This has the advantage that it gives the courts the opportunity to extend copyright protection by judge-made law and thus adapt it gradually to the effects of developing technology, whereas in criminal cases judge-made law is much rarer and gaps can often only be filled by legislation. However in view of the large scale infringements of copyright and neighbouring rights in phonograms and films in the 1970s the trend has been partially reversed and criminal remedies have been widely used in copyright and neighbouring rights cases as was the case in the early years of the twentieth century to deal with piracy of sheet music.[3]

Criminal remedies have three disadvantages: a) the strict proof of copyright is sometimes very difficult;[4] b) fines fixed by law become derisory in countries with high inflation rates and have to be periodically revised to remain effective;[5] c) in many countries the courts are reluctant to impose prison sentences for copyright offences.

In the United Kingdom it is an offence, without the consent of performers in writing and knowingly, to make a phonogram or film of their unfixed ('live') performance or to use a phonogram or film for the purposes of public performance or to broadcast such a performance or diffuse it by wire.[6] The necessity of having the performers' consent in writing ensures that the users get in touch with performers or their representatives before using their performances unless, as in the case of making a film or a phonogram, such consent is obtained in advance as part of a contract. As the prosecution is a private prosecution, the remedy is not dependent on the discretion of a public prosecutor. The United Kingdom legislation is exceptional in this respect in that the criminal sanctions are the only remedy available for infringements of the performers' rights in their performance.

1 See German Copyright Law 1965, art 109.
2 See UK Copyright Act 1956, s 17; German Copyright Law 1965, art 110.
3 Musical Copyright Act 1906 in the UK.
4 In cases of complicated licensing and sublicensing contracts ownership of the original copyright is often difficult to ascertain. The presence in Court of a famous star to give evidence in a foreign court is often difficult to secure.
5 In the United Kingdom the Whitford Committee Report recommended that 'penalties be kept under constant review so as to provide an effective deterrent, in particular to ensure that an offender is not left in a position where he can make a profit from his misconduct' (Report, para 412).
6 Performers Protection Acts 1958-1972.

(6) Publication of judgments in the press

7.26 This is a remedy which can be effective particularly in the case of dealers who deal in infringing copies who fear that adverse publicity may affect their trade. It is successfully applied in countries, eg France, Belgium, where the copyright remedies are not available to enforce neighbouring rights.

7. Performance rights in phonograms

7.27 This right is granted either to the phonogram producer[1] or to the performer[2] or to both[3]. In most cases the right is subject to a compulsory licence being expressed as a right to 'equitable remuneration'.

1 Eg United Kingdom, India.
2 Eg Federal Republic of Germany.
3 Eg Denmark, Sweden.

The public performance right

7.28   Producers of phonograms usually have a right in the public performance of their phonograms. This takes the form of a right to equitable remuneration when protected phonograms are played in public.[1] This right (like most public performance rights in musical works) can in practice only be exercised by a collecting society negotiating bulk licensing contracts with users.

Performers often have a parallel right in the public performance of their recorded performances.[1] This right is also a right to equitable remuneration and therefore also has to be exercised by a collecting society. If both producers and performers have a right to equitable remuneration it has to be exercised jointly as the users are only bound to pay 'one *single* equitable remuneration'.[1]

1 Rome Convention, art 12; see para 8.26 below.

The broadcasting right

7.29   Producers of Phonograms have a right in the broadcasting of their phonograms[1] which also takes the form of a right to equitable remuneration. This right is always exercised by a bulk licensing contract with a broadcasting organisation or with a group of broadcasting organisations.[2]

Performers also have a right in the broadcasting of their recorded performances which also takes the form of a right to equitable remuneration. It also has to be exercised in conjunction with record producers as the user is only bound to pay 'one single equitable remuneration' to both.

1 Rome Convention, art 12; see para 8.26 below.
2 Eg with the nine regional broadcasting organisations in the Federal Republic of Germany or with the Federation of Commercial Broadcasting Organisations in Italy.

Collection

7.30   In some countries[1] the remuneration for the broadcasting right and the remuneration for the public performance right are both collected by a neighbouring rights collecting society. In many countries however a national authors' society[2] is mandated to collect the public performance revenue whereas a neighbouring rights society collects the remuneration for the broadcasting right. The purely practical reason for joint collection of the performance right is that it can be done most effectively and cheaply by the authors' society which has to collect the royalties for the authors' right from the same location (eg hotels, cafés, jukeboxes) in any event, and the commission charged provides an additional income for the authors' society which is a contribution towards their administrative expenses, thus increasing their cost effectiveness.[3] The broadcasting right on the other hand can be administered effectively by authors' societies and neighbouring rights societies separately as the bulk licensing contracts which are negotiated separately are usually long term contracts and the collection is from one source, ie a public broadcasting organisation or a federation of commercial broadcasting organisations.

1 Eg PPL (Phonographic Performance Limited) in the United Kingdom.
2 Eg GEMA in the German Federal Republic, SIAE in Italy, KODA in Denmark.
3 See recommendations of the Intergovernmental Committee of the Rome Convention, op cit, para 32.

Distribution

7.31 In some countries the whole protected repertoire is licensed in bulk for an annual sum (eg in the United Kingdom) and that sum is then divided among right owners according to the amount of time their records have been played (known as 'needle time'). In other countries (eg Denmark) payment is made according to a minute rate for protected music.[1] The broadcasting organisation provides so-called 'logs' which show all programmes broadcast and all phonograms used in them. They are then analysed to ascertain which phonograms are protected and the total of minutes broadcast is ascertained and charged for. The advantage of such a system is that the result reflects the copyright position accurately as only protected phonograms are paid for. The disadvantage is that programme makers may be tempted to broadcast not always the best phonograms available or even the ones the audience would prefer to hear, but those that are free of copyright, because they are in the public domain. With the use of data processing machinery the collection, analysis and distribution has become both more accurate and less expensive.[2]

1   On 1 January 1982 the rate in Denmark was approximately US$7 per minute.
2   Gramex, the senior European collecting society in Denmark, operates at a cost of approximately 15% which compares well with the costs authors paid for the collection and distribution of their royalties for the broadcasting and public performance of their works.

7.32 In the field of public performance of phonograms bulk licensing at an annual rate is the rule. The rates are negotiated between the collecting society and the users, and in cases of failure to agree the courts or special tribunals decide the amounts. As detailed evidence of user is very rarely obtainable for public performance the total revenue due to phonogram producers is often distributed among right owners in proportion to sales of phonograms or in the same proportion as their entitlement to revenue from broadcasting. This is based on the assumption that the phonograms most sold and the phonograms most broadcast are the most popular ones and are therefore also those most played in public performance. It is on the face of it a rough and ready method of distribution but when tested by occasional 'spot checks' has proved fairly accurate.

Distribution among performers is more difficult. Although in most cases the artists' names are shown on the labels it is often difficult, particularly many years after the recording was made, to find the right owners. The larger the membership of the national collecting society the more accurate will be the distribution[1] In the case of foreign performers the distribution is most accurate if effected by their own national collecting society under bilateral agreements between the collecting society in the country of user and the collecting society in the country of which the performer entitled to remuneration is a national.

1   Eg at the end of 1980 the Danish Collecting Society, Gramex, had 7606 Danish performers in their data bank of which 5883 were members of the Society. Orchestras and established groups are registered under one number.

7.33 Even after every effort to find the right owners has been made there usually remains a residue of 'undistributable revenue'.[1] This residue is much larger in the case of performers' royalties than in the case of phonogram producers' royalties as most record companies have either a subsidiary or sister company of at least an agency in each country so that royalties can be paid to a local representative of the right owner. In the case of undistributable revenue due to performers the two international federations IFPI and FIM[2] have agreed to the so-called 'London Principles' (1969) the effect of which is that undistributable revenue remains in the country of collection and is 'devoted to the general benefit of the Performers' professions'. This can be bursaries for students, pensions for widows of musicians, subsidies for unemployed musicians etc. This use of undistributable revenue meets at least partially the case of those who argue that recorded music has in many places replaced live music and thrown musicians out of work ('technological unemployment') and that therefore part of the remuneration should go to those deprived of work places by the use of recorded music.[3]

1   Most collecting societies have in their statutes a provision under which they can declare royalties for which right owners cannot be traced as 'undistributable' if they have not been claimed for a number of years (eg five years in Denmark, three years in Austria).
2   The International Federation of Producers of Phonograms and Videograms and the International Federation of Musicians.
3   See para 7.14 above.

7.34   Even before the Rome Convention confirmed the option[1] some countries gave the performance right in phonograms to the producer, some to the performer and some to both. As giving the right to the producer was the most frequent case, an agreement was made between the two international federations representing producers (IFPI) and performers (FIM) in 1956[2] in accordance with which the producers undertook voluntarily to pay a quarter of the remuneration they received for the broadcasting of their phonograms to the musicians' union of the country concerned. The 'FIM agreement' was confined to Europe[3] and was applied in all countries regardless of whether the remuneration paid to phonogram producers was paid under a statutory provision or under a contract between broadcasting organisations and producers of phonograms. The agreement contained a term under which it automatically ceased to apply if performers were granted a right by statute.[4] The agreement was varied by a protocol in 1976 increasing the performers' share to a third of the net distributable revenue. FIA (International Federation of Actors) became a party to the agreement and the agreement was made reciprocal so that if any country gave the right to remuneration solely to the performers they in turn would share it with the producers by paying them a third of the net distributable revenue.

Legislators were aware of this agreement, hence the tendency of legislations from the 1950s onwards towards giving the right to remuneration to both parties or giving it to one party whilst giving a share to the other party. Both methods are in accordance with the provision of the Rome Convention for 'a single equitable remuneration' to be 'paid by the user to the performers, or to the producers of phonograms, or to both'.[5] The 'Model Law concerning the Protection of Performers, Producers of Phonograms and Broadcasting Organisations' provides that the equitable remuneration should be paid to the producers of phonograms and that 'unless otherwise agreed between Performers and the Producers, half of the amount received by the Producers shall be paid by the Producers to the Performers'.[6] This sharing in equal halves, based on the rule of equity that 'equality is equity', has now become the rule. The payment of the single equitable remuneration to the producers with an obligation to share with the performers was chosen because the former is usually more easily identifiable. In practice both the 50/50 rule and the Model Law's suggestion of the payment to the producer with an obligation to share have led to the establishment of joint collection societies in most countries.

1   Art 12; see para 8.26 below.
2   The agreement became known as the 'FIM Agreement'.
3   Israel was treated for this purpose as a European country.
4   The agreement still applies in the European countries where the law gives no rights in the

public performance of phonograms but phonogram producers have negotiated voluntary agreements with broadcasting organisations under which such revenue is paid, mainly Belgium, the Netherlands and Switzerland.
5   Rome Convention, art 12; see para 8.26 below.
6   Model Law, s 5(2).

7.35 Applying the ordinary rules of private international law, the law of the country where the revenue arises and is collected should determine who is entitled to remuneration. Foreign beneficiaries are entitled to the same treatment as nationals under the principle of national treatment. That means that in a country where only phonogram producers are entitled to revenue under the national law, foreign producers are equally entitled to remuneration, whereas foreign performers are not.[1] In a country where only performers are entitled to revenue under the national law, foreign performers are equally entitled to remuneration, whereas foreign producers would not be so entitled. In a country where both producers and performers are entitled to remuneration both foreign producers and foreign performers are entitled to be paid.[2]

The arrangements to deal with national situations (collection and distribution of remuneration due to national performers and producers) usually present no difficulties. Dealing with international situations (collection and distribution of remuneration due to foreign performers and foreign producers) may present problems. The recommendation of the Intergovernmental Committee says:[3] 'The legal problems at the international level can best be satisfied by setting up collection/distribution societies in all countries where national legislation establishes rights for Performers or Producers or both corresponding to those provided for in Article 12 of the Rome Convention'. This has been done and in most countries there is now one joint collecting society for both performers and producers. It is a prerequisite for the effective functioning of these societies that they have valid mandates or assignments of individual rights from those entitled to remuneration. In accordance with the general rules of private international law the validity of such mandates or assignments is governed by the law of the country where such mandates are given or such assignments are made. Experience of administering these article 12 rights in various countries showed that there is more than one type of contractual arrangement that can be made to implement these rights. The practice closest to the general rules of private international law is a bilateral agreement between the two collecting societies to the following effect:

> 'The collection and distribution to nationals would be governed by the law of the country and the rules of the national society in the country of collection, whereas distribution of any revenue transmitted to a second country would be governed by the rules of the national society of that country, provided both societies have valid mandates or assignments from those entitled to remuneration.'[4]

An alternative arrangement distributes the remuneration

> 'to both nationals and foreigners according to the rules of the collecting society in the country of collection. The collecting society in the country of collection then sends to the society in the country of distribution a list of names of performers and the sums they are entitled to without the evidence of the user. In such cases the society in the country of distribution consequently has no possibility of changing the beneficiary or the amounts of distribution since it has no evidence of the extent of use.
>
> If the principles of distribution of the society in the country of collection are felt to be inappropriate or inequitable by the society in the country of distribution it can change the method of distribution, provided it has valid mandates or assignments from all those entitled to remuneration.[5]'

This type of arrangement seems only appropriate in cases where the general principles of distribution adopted by the two societies in question are at variance.

In all cases only the balance of the total distributable remuneration is transmitted to the collecting society of the other country on the principle of clearing house arrangements between banks.

1. Eg United Kingdom, India.
2. Eg Federal Republic of Germany, Denmark.
3. Recommendations of the Intergovernmental Committee of the Rome Convention, 1978, published in Copyright (April 1979) p 105.
4. See Recommendations of the Intergovernmental Committee, op cit, note 3 above, para 31. This arrangement is also advocated by the international federations representing producers of phonograms (IFPI) and performers (FIM and FIA) and is reflected in the so-called 'London Principles' agreed by these organisations in 1978.
5. Recommendations of the Intergovernmental Committee, op cit note, 3 above, para 31.

8. The rights of broadcasting organisations

History

7.36 In order to understand the relative dearth of private international law relating to broadcasting organisations one must look at the nature of broadcasting organisations and the history of their international relations. Among the beneficiaries of the Rome Convention, performers are private individuals and phonogram producers are private or public companies whereas broadcasting organisations are either departments of state (usually in authoritarian countries) or public law corporation with a charter (mainly in Western Europe) or commercial organisations (mainly in North and South America) which need a licence from the government in order to be able to operate. Thus their dependence on the government or their proximity to the government and also their influence on the government is far greater than that of either authors or publishers among the copyright owners or of the other two neighbouring right owners. They perform a public service and their task is cultural and artistic as well as being a leading agency of news and current affairs. It is thus not surprising that the problems being encountered by broadcasting organisations with regard to their rights tended to be dealt with either at the diplomatic level or by public international law, whereas copyright is in its essence the exercise of a private right. Thus in the early days of broadcasting (sound broadcasting) in the 1930s and 1940s the interest of broadcasting organisations in solutions based on copyright were not of prime importance to them. They were also rapidly becoming one of the largest users of copyright works and at the Brussels Revision Conference of the Berne Convention in 1948 played that role of the largest user achieving a compulsory licence and other user benefits.

Thereafter and in the 1950s broadcasters represented by the EBU[1] (European Broadcasting Union) actively participated in the preparatory work for the Rome Convention. This period did however also see the advent of television which made broadcasting organisations the largest single user of copyrights of all kinds (news, literature, drama, music).

1. The OIR (Organisation International Radio) was founded in 1946. In 1950 the EBU (European Broadcasting Union) was founded by 23 European broadcasting organisations. The OIR moved to Prague and changed its name to OIRT (International Radio and Television Organisation) covering Eastern Europe. As Simone Courtex points out: 'The EBU is currently by far the largest and most influential of the international associations of broadcasting organisations; it is the linchpin of a whole system of such associations and serves as a model each time a new one is set up.' (Télévision sans frontières: un problème de cooperation internationale Recherche Panthéon – Sorbonne: Série sciences juridiques – droit de relations internationales (1981)).

The other regional broadcasting organisations are the Inter-American Broadcasting Association (AIR) founded in 1946 mainly for Latin America; URTNA (Union of National Radio and Television Broadcasters of Africa), in 1962, ABU (Asian Pacific Broadcasting Union) in 1964; ASBU (Arab States Broadcasting Union) in 1969; CBU (Caribbean Broadcasting Union) in 1970; OIT (Ibero-American Television Broadcasting Organisation) in 1971. There is a North-American National Broadcasters Association but the major US networks and the CBC (Canadian Broadcasting Corporation) are associate members of the EBU.

7.37 In the 1950s and 1960s broadcasting organisations felt several anxieties about their rights in their broadcasts:

1. The 'Pirate Radio Stations' operating from the high seas, broadcasting news and popular music exclusively from phonograms and not paying any royalties (or taxes) to anybody and not subject to any licensing or controlling body which broadcasters rightly viewed as unfair and undesirable competition. A European Agreement[1] signed in 1965 and entering into force in 1967 followed by national legislation put an end to nearly all pirate radio operations.

2. There was a widespread fear in the 1950s that hotels, restaurants and other public places would increasingly charge entrance fees to their customers (either openly or through increased charges for food and drink or other services) for watching television programmes and that cinemas would run them as films. Test cases were brought[2] and diplomatic activities resulted in the 'European Agreement on the Protection of Television Broadcasts' which was concluded in 1960[3] and is still in force. However this threat to the rights of broadcasting organisations subsided as soon as most households acquired television sets and there was no further need to see television programmes in public places.

3. Cable networks and community aerials were taking television programmes particularly in the United States where they are known as CATV (Community Antennae Television) and making them available to private homes charging subscription fees but denying the rights of broadcasting organisations in their programmes. Broadcasting organisations pleaded for a right against cable operators at the Diplomatic Conference for the Rome Convention in 1961, but failed because hardly any of the countries represented had any legislation to support such a right. The problem is still largely unsolved.[4]

4. When the first communication satellites were launched the major broadcasting organisations represented by the EBU were concerned that other less scrupulous broadcasting organisations would take their programmes off the satellites instead of entering into agreements with the organisation originating the programme and paying royalties or at least entering into programme exchange agreements. They succeeded in achieving the 'Satellite Convention' 1974[5] but during the preparatory stages due to legal and political difficulties copyright or neighbouring rights protection had to be abandoned and replaced by public law commitments to be entered into by ratifying governments. The subject of protection is not the programme, which should be the subject of either a copyright or a neighbouring right but the 'programme carrying signal' regardless of the programme content of such a signal. Thus, with respect to this problem at any rate, the broadcasting organisations were forced to return to protection by public as opposed to private international law, which is where they had started from, half a century earlier. However this history, like the history of CATV, is not concluded because with the advent of 'direct satellite broadcasting' in the 1980s when broadcasts transmitted via satellite will be receivable in private homes without the help of a receiving earth station, the protection of the programme (as opposed to the signal) will once more return to the sphere of private international law. The transmitting of programmes by

the originating broadcasting organisation which are receivable by the public in their homes via satellite is likely to be regarded as 'broadcasting' within the definition of the Rome Convention and thus protected under it.[6]

1 The 'European Agreement for the Repression of Broadcasts Effected by Stations Outside any National Territory' was signed in Strasbourg 22 June 1965 and entered into force on 19 October 1967.
2 *Nord-und Westdeutscher Rundfunkverband v Aktualitäten-kino Theater* (AKI) Hamburg, Hanseatic Court of Appeal, 7 July 1960.
3 See para 11.03 below.
4 Apart from the regional 'European Agreement on the Protection of Television Broadcasts';
5 Rome Convention, art 3(f); see para 8.32 below.
6 Rome Convention, art 13(a); see para 8.32 below.

7.38 (1) Broadcasting organisations have an absolute right to 'authorise or prohibit the rebroadcasting of their broadcasts'.[1] This can be said to be the basic broadcasting right, the equivalent to the reproduction right of copyright owners.

'Rebroadcasting' in the strict sense[2] means the simultaneous relay of the programme. 'Deferred rebroadcasting' must by definition imply the fixing of the broadcast first so that, if done without the consent of the original broadcasting organisation the infringement already takes place at the time of fixation and before the fixation is rebroadcast.

(2) Broadcasting organisations have an absolute right to authorise or prohibit the fixation of their broadcast.[3] The right is the equivalent of a recording right but usually takes the form of a reproduction right as a copy of the first fixation is made and sent to the other broadcasting organisation under a contract between the two broadcasting organisations (either against payment or by way of a programme exchange agreement).

(3) Broadcasting organisations have an absolute right to 'authorise or prohibit the communication to the public of their television broadcasts';[4] this right is the equivalent of a public performance right and is subject to a Compulsory Licence. The right is however restricted to the public performance of television broadcasts as opposed to sound broadcasts and exercisable only if the communication to the public is made 'in places accessible to the public against payment of an entrance fee'. This right is now rarely exercised because the public places which instal television sets, eg hotels, restaurants, bars, public houses, do not charge an 'entrance fee' and the cinemas (film theatres), do not show television programmes on the screen.

1 Rome Convention, art 13(a); see para 8.32 below.
2 Rome Convention, art 3(g).
3 Rome Convention, art 13(b).
4 Rome Convention, art 13(d).

7.39 The basic right of broadcasting organisations is therefore a kind of reproduction right. The subject of the right is the 'broadcast'. This means the contents of the programme which is being broadcast. Like the phonogram the broadcast is a derivative work. It may, and usually does, include other works such as the script of a talk or a play or a musical work, all of which are separately protected as original works. It may include derivative works such as the performances of actors or singers or phonograms, or it may contain a combination of all of these which is very common. On the other hand it may, if it is a live broadcast of a state occasion – like a coronation or a funeral, or a sporting event – not contain any original protected works, yet it is still the subject matter of a copyright or a neighbouring right. As in the case of a phonogram, if the legislation gives broadcasting organisations a reproduction right it does not matter whether it is called a copyright or a neighbouring right. It entitles broadcasting organisations to allow or forbid the rebroadcasting or the fixation of their programmes without their consent.

Apart from this reproduction right, the right commercially most important to broadcasting organisations is the right to allow or forbid the relay of a broadcast by cable. This right is not covered by the Rome Convention or any international convention, apart from the regional 'European Agreement on the Protection of Television Broadcasts'.[1] Only a few national legislations grant it. Examples are the Copyright Law of the Federal Republic of Germany[2] and the Copyright Act of the United States.[3]

On the other hand the right of the author to authorise or prohibit the relay of his work by cable television has, at least in Europe, been upheld in several countries by the highest courts.

Austria: Decision of the Austrian Supreme Court of 25 July 1974 and again in respect of a foreign broadcast: Decision of the Supreme Court of 12 November 1979.
Belgium: *Coditel v Ciné Vog Films* – Judgment of the Belgian Supreme Court 3 September 1981.
Netherlands: *Columbia Pictures v CAI Amstelveen* – Judgment of the Supreme Court of the Netherlands, case no 11–739 of 1981.
Switzerland: *SUISA v Rediffusion AG* – Supreme Court of Switzerland – 1st Civil Chamber 20 January 1981.

All these decisions base themselves directly or indirectly on article 11 bis (1) of the Berne Convention.[4]

The overall position is thus that whereas the copyright of the author against the cable television operator which is a broadcasting right, has been fairly clearly established, on the other hand the neighbouring right of the broadcasting organisation against the cable television operator which is in essence a reproduction right still lacks confirmation by an international instrument.[5]

1 See para 11.03 below.
2 German Copyright Law 1965, arts 15 2.2 and 20.
3 US Copyright Law 1976 para 111.
4 See para 5.43 above.
5 Apart from the 'European Agreement on the Protection of Television Broadcasts'; see para 11.03 below.

Chapter 8

The Rome Convention (1961)

Summary

1. History of the Convention   8.01
2. Structure of the Convention   8.04
3. Safeguard clause for copyright – article 1   8.05
4. National treatment – article 2   8.07
5. National treatment and points of attachment – articles 4–6   8.08
6. Rights of performers – article 7   8.16
7. Group performances – article 8   8.22
8. Variety artists – article 9   8.23
9. Reproduction right of producers of phonograms – article 10   8.24
10. Formalities for phonograms – article 11   8.25
11. Secondary uses of phonograms – article 12   8.26
12. Reservations – article 16   8.30
13. Protection of broadcasting organisations – article 13   8.31
14. Term of rights (duration) – article 14   8.36
15. Exceptions – article 15   8.40
16. Acquired rights – article 20   8.45
17. Other sources of protection – article 21   8.46
18. Special agreements – article 22   8.47
19. Closed convention – articles 23 and 24   8.48
20. Application of the convention – article 26   8.49
21. Denunciation – article 28   8.50
22. Intergovernmental committee and revision – articles 32 and 29   8.51
23. State of ratifications and accessions   8.52

1. History

8.01   Unlike the Berne Convention which took a few years from conception to the Diplomatic Conference[1] and the Phonogram Convention[2] which took only 18 months, the gestation period for the Rome Convention was over half a century. There were two main reasons for this slow progress. The first reason was that the technology of recording and later of radio and television, was novel and no-one could fully appreciate the influence this would have on the exploitation of literary and musical works. The second reason was the innate fear of those representing the interests of authors that their hard-won rights would suffer, if anyone else in this field of law also became a right owner. Time has proved these fears groundless but the view was strongly held by authors' societies and vigorously defended by some states.

The matter was first raised in 1908, at the Berlin Conference for the Revision of the Berne Convention, by the British government proposing international protection for record producers. The Conference was of the opinion 'that the subject was on the borderline between industrial property and copyright and might conceivably be held to belong more properly to the former category'.[3]

The matter was raised again in 1928, at the Rome Conference for the Revision of the Berne Convention. The Italian government proposed the protection of performing artists against the broadcasting of their performances and against the 'adaptation' of musical works to reproduction on mechanical instruments. It proposed an 'equitable remuneration' when such instruments were used for 'public broadcasts or public performance'. This idea was too novel to be inserted into the Berne Convention. The Conference took the view (expressed as a 'vœu') that governments should study the question. The matter was raised again at the Brussels Conference for the Revision of the Berne Convention in 1948, by the Belgian government and the British government. The Belgian government proposed a new article 11 quater, protecting recorded performances, but leaving the conditions of protection to national legislation. Both proposals referred to recorded performances of works, in copyright and in the public domain. As before these proposals were not adopted. This time it was mainly on the grounds that after a world war, which was largely ideological, in which some of the main members of the Berne Union had been on opposing sides no new problems should be introduced, which would lead to lengthy debates, which could be divisive. Another 'vœu' was adopted, this time in more general terms and using for the first time the expression rights 'near to' or 'neighbours of' authors rights ('droits voisins' in the French original). Three such 'vœux' were expressed, one on behalf of performers, one on behalf of record producers and one on behalf of broadcasters.[4]

By that time several national laws had created rights in this field. Austria,[5] Switzerland,[6] Italy[7] by statute, Germany[8] and the United Kingdom[9] by statute and court decisions. The Danish Copyright Law of 1933 and the Norwegian Copyright Law of 1910 contained similar provisions which were developed by the courts.[10]

1 See para 5.05 above.
2 See para 9.01 below.
3 It is interesting that the same mistake was made 60 years later, when the problem of protection of computer programmes was raised and the initial answer was that they should be patented rather than copyrighted; see para 12.21 below.
4 Benigne Mentha the former Director of the 'Berne Bureau' (the predecessor of WIPO) in a paper in the 'Recueil de Travaux Suisses' (presented at the 4th Congress of international comparative law 1965, pp 165 ff) described the authors societies' attitude towards the so-called neighbouring rights as 'platonic solicitude'.
5 Austrian Copyright Law 1920, s 23, para 3 and s 28, para 2 and Copyright Law 1936, art 76.
6 Swiss Copyright Law 1922, s 4, para 2.
7 Italian Copyright Law 1941, ss 72-85 inclusive.
8 German Copyright Law 1910 and RGZ (German Supreme Court) 11-14-1936 Vol 153, 1.
9 Copyright Act 1911, s 19. Performers Act 1925 and *Gramophone Co v Cawardine* [1934] Ch 450.
10 *Gramophone Co Ltd and Norges Musikhandler Vorbund v Norsk* Case 154/1934, Court of Ostrehandsrat (Dept IV) Rikskoring Kasting 1940.

8.02 In 1939 the Director of the Berne Buro, M. Fritz Ostertrag, had drafted a project for an international convention 'connected with' the Berne Convention which was discussed at Samaden in Switzerland in 1939. He had dropped from the group of rights originally proposed a copyright in private letters and in portraits. He had included a copyright in 'informations de presse' and the so-called 'droit de suite' of the painter or sculptor and the rights of performers, producers of phonograms and broadcasting organisations.

The idea of a copyright in news was dropped but the 'droit de suite' was incorporated, optionally in the Berne Convention in 1948 as article 14 bis. Doctrinally, both the 'droit de suite' and the rights of performers, record producers and broadcasters were 'connected' with the authors' rights but the connection was different. The connection of the 'droit de suite' with the 'droit d'auteur' lies in the fact that the creator of the work, the painter or sculptor is an author. The reason why it was thought not an original 'droit d'auteur' was that the painter, unlike a writer or composer, sold the canvas, ie the material support to which the picture is forever attached, whereas the books or sheets of music which were sold were only copies of the original work. The idea of the painter being able to follow his picture (hence 'droite de suite') from sale to sale and get a percentage of the price every time (whether or not it had gone up) was once removed from the 'droit d' auteur'. On the other hand the other three 'connected rights' were connected to the 'droit d'auteur', because the authorship of the three right owners is derivative. The right-owner takes the original work and by his contribution (performance, recording, broadcast) makes it into another protected work. The closest analogies in the Berne Convention are the rights of the translator of a literary work, or the arranger of a musical work. They too use a pre-existing work and add their own contributions (translation or arrangement) making it into a new work and the user of the translation or the arrangement has to pay two royalties, one to the writer and one to the translator or one to the composer and one to the arranger. The Berne Convention had no difficulty in accommodating the translator or arranger and gave him a full copyright and managed in 1948 to accommodate the 'droit de suite'[1] of the painter/sculptor but they could not accommodate the three neighbouring rights. The only rational and logical explanation seems to be the one that was not given at the time, that the painter or sculptor is, like the writer or composer, a physical person, whereas the record producer and the broadcaster are almost always companies or corporations. This also explains the great difficulties (still partly unresolved), which the Berne Convention has with the film producer who is also a derivative creator using a pre-existing work and also nearly always a company or corporation. It also explains why Anglo-Saxon laws have no difficulties in giving a copyright to a record producer, a film producer or a broadcaster. Whereas the 'droit d'auteur' inspired legislations (particularly French law) do not.[2]

The performer, who is also an individual, seems to have suffered in this respect because of the link with the other two. To draw a doctrinal distinction between the activity of a performer on the one hand and an arranger on the other seems extremely difficult. The reason given in the debates was that there are often large numbers of performers engaged in the performance of a single work like orchestras or choirs in musical works, large casts in dramatic works. However the Berne Convention solved similar problems in dealing with collective works and anthologies where there are many authors, without too much difficulty in its early stages.

The three remaining 'connected' rights, apart from being connected to the author's right, were also interconnected. There are few records without a performance (birdsong or background noises are the rare exceptions) and few broadcasts without either a performance or records or both. It is the interconnection between the three rights to be protected and the necessity to create an equilibrium between the three that lead to the creation of a separate convention dealing with the rights of the three right-owners in one instrument. This is unique in international conventions in the intellectual property field.

1 See para 5.53 above.
2 See para 1.13 above.

8.03 Once it was decided to attempt a new independent convention, the 'Road to Rome' was open but it still took over 12 years and three drafts made by meetings of experts. The preparatory work was carried forward by three intergovernmental organisations: BIRPI (now WIPO), UNESCO and the International Labour Office (ILO) and by three international non-governmental organisations: FIM (the International Federation of Musicians) later joined by FIA (The International Federation of Actors); IFPI (the International Federation of Producers of Phonograms) and EBU (the European Broadcasting Union).

The drafts were: the Rome Draft of 1951, emanating from a meeting of experts under the auspices of the ILO, the Geneva Draft 1956 and the Monaco Draft emanating from meetings called by BIRPI, ILO and UNESCO. These three Drafts, which differed substantially were co-ordinated in 1960 by a meeting of governmental experts called by the three intergovernmental organisations at the Hague. The 'Hague Draft' formed the basis of the Rome Convention (1961).

The nature of this convention is therefore different from other conventions, in that it seeks to create a balance between three different right owners to be protected. It is also different from the Berne Convention and the Universal Copyright Convention, in that these conventions based themselves on an existing common denominator between many national legislations, whereas the Rome Convention was a pioneer convention, although similar rights to those granted by the Convention were granted in the legislations of many countries but usually only to one or two of the beneficiaries.

Its tripartite nature, which was a precondition for its creation, proved to be its main difficulty, because the broadcasting organisations which were, with the other two beneficiaries, instrumental in achieving the Convention, changed their minds and inclined to the view that the equilibrium created was not to their advantage. They complained that the rights they rightly claimed against cable operators which used their broadcasts were not included in the Convention[1] and later that their anxieties to protect their programme-carrying signals broadcast via satellite were not protected.[2] They also felt that the protection against their television programmes being shown in public places, to which they attached great importance during the preparatory stages, had ceased to be of great significance once the large majority of households in the developed countries had television sets so that they would no longer go out to cinemas to watch great sporting or public events. Thus they felt that the obligations undertaken under articles 7 and 12[3] outweighed the advantages.

Because the Convention was a pioneer convention many countries had to legislate to create the minimum rights provided for before they could ratify and the progress of the Convention by ratifications was therefore slower than was the case with other conventions. However 23 states have ratified the Convention, and many legislated to grant rights or additional rights to one or more of the three beneficiaries of the Convention, many for the first time. 'Indeed, the Convention has had a great impact on national legislation. As of July 1978, 84 states had legislated to protect producers of phonograms, 66 to protect broadcasting organisations and 35 to protect performers'.[4]

---

1 See para 12.28.
2 See para 12.33.
3 See paras 8.16 et seq and 8.26 et seq.
4 Report of the Intergovernmental Committee of the Rome Convention 1979, Annex 1 para 15.

2. The structure of the Convention

8.04 Like all conventions in the copyright field, the Rome Convention deals only with international situations, that is situations where foreign right owners are involved.

Like the Berne Convention,[1] the Rome Convention is based on the principle of national treatment.[2] National treatment is defined separately in respect of each of the three beneficiaries (article 2/i) and dealt with in article 4 for performers, article 5 for producers and article 6 for broadcasters.

Also, like the Berne Convention[3] the Rome Convention makes such national treatment subject to certain minima of protection: article 7 for performers, article 10 for producers, article 13 for broadcasters as well as article 12 for performers and producers.

Unlike the Berne Convention, the Rome Convention contains the principle of reciprocity in respect of certain rights expressed by reservations which any member state can make at any time (article 16).

Like the Berne Convention,[4] the Rome Convention permits exceptions for private use etc in article 15.

Like the Berne Convention[5], the Rome Convention lays down a minimum term of protection: 20 years in article 14.

Like the Universal Copyright Convention[6], the Rome Convention lays down a maximum of formalities, which a contracting state may require, in article 11.

1 Art 5(1) see para 5.39 above.
2 See para 3.17.
3 See paras 5.37 et seq above.
4 Art 9(2).
5 Art 7(9).
6 Art III.

3. The safeguard clause for copyright – article 1

8.05 The arguments on this subject put forward by the authors' societies voiced mainly by the French delegation were:

(1) It was said that all the situations envisaged could be regulated by contract and there was therefore no need for a convention. This was shown by the debates to be erroneous. A performer may be able to authorise both the fixation of his performance and the reproduction of such a fixation by contract but once the performance is fixed and records reproduced from the fixation and sold to the public he can no longer control the use made by third parties of these recordings, for example by a discotheque, because although he has a contract with the phonogram producer he has no contractual relationship with the owner of the discotheque. If a record producer sold a recording he made under contract with a performer to a film producer who uses it for the sound track of a film the performer may have an action for breach of contract against the record producer if the contract he had made prohibits any uses of his performance other than for making records, but he has no remedy against the film producer and cannot stop the making or showing of the film because he has no contractual relationship with the film producer.

(2) It was also said that the Convention was 'premature' because, whereas when the Berne Convention was made most countries already granted the rights given to authors so that the Convention had only to find a common denominator, in this case only a few countries gave the rights granted by the Convention in their national laws. Historically this was only partly correct, as many countries had to grant authors additional rights in their national

legislations when they ratified the Berne Convention in order to be able to ratify it. It was correct that fewer countries granted rights to the three beneficiaries of the Rome Convention at the time when it was made than countries granting rights to authors at the time the Berne Convention was made. To conclude from this that the Convention was premature was a kind of political 'chicken and egg' argument. If states want to ensure that their nationals get the rights abroad which their laws grant them at home, should they wait until most other states grant these rights before making a convention, or should they make a convention in the hope that it will encourage other states to grant these rights in order to qualify for ratifying the convention? The years since the making of the Rome Convention seem to have justified the choice made as 51 states have given rights to one or more beneficiaries of the Convention and 24 of them have done so for the first time[1].

(3) It was feared that if performers and possibly phonogram producers were to be given rights to allow or forbid the use of their performances or their phonograms they would use them to forbid the use and thereby deprive the author of his royalty for that use.

(4) With regard to the right of equitable remuneration for the use of phonograms for broadcasting and public performance (article 12) it was feared that the exercise of such a right would adversely affect the economic rights of authors as the same user would be paying both authors and performers and/or producers of phonograms and as there was only one cake to be divided the share of the author would be diminished (so-called 'cake theory'). This fear has proved groundless and in 1979, after many years of experience in the application of the Convention, the Intergovernmental Committee in its report observed that:

> 'there is no evidence to suppport the proposition that authors' revenue has decreased as a result of neighbouring rights. It has been argued further that the revenue of authors and composers would have increased even more than it has done if there had been no secondary use rights in phonograms. This proposition has never been proved and is, by its nature, impossible to disprove. The Subcommittee, therefore, concludes that the second argument cannot be sustained either. In addition, the Subcommittee believes that a possible adverse effect on authors' royalties would not in any event constitute a sufficient reason for opposing the rights provided for in the Rome Convention since justice demands that performers and producers of phonograms should be remunerated for secondary use of phonograms.'

1 See Report of the Intergovernmental Committee, op cit.

8.06 The Conference was anxious to assuage the fears that authors' rights would be adversely affected and tried to avoid this by the safeguard clause in article 1. The Kaminstein Report[1] puts the concept succinctly:

> 'Whenever, by virtue of the Copyright Law, the authorisation of the author is necessary for the reproduction or other use of his work, the need for this authorisation is not affected by the Convention. Conversely, when, by virtue of this Convention, the consent of the performer, recorder, or broadcaster is necessary, the need for his consent does not disappear because authorisation by the author is necessary.'

Whilst safeguarding copyright, as the Masouyé/Wallace *Guide* points out, 'It does not proclaim its superiority by laying down that neighbouring rights may never be stronger in content or scope than those enjoyed by authors. Indeed there are a number of examples showing that neighbouring rights are not necessarily inferior'.[2]

The *Guide* suggests that, apart from being a safeguard clause, article 1 is also 'in a way a guide to contracting states when they legislate to cover national neighbouring rights situations. They are not allowed to do so in ways which affect the protection of Copyright'.

1 Abraham Kaminstein was the Register of Copyright of the USA and the 'Rapporteur General' of the Rome Conference 1961.
2 Masouyé/Wallace *WIPO Guide to the Rome Convention* 1.10.

4. National treatment – article 2

8.07 National treatment is the fundamental principle of the Rome Convention as it is of the other conventions.[1]

The Hague draft attempted to deal with the problem basing itself on the country of origin.[2] It provided that each state must grant protection if the country of origin of the performance, of the phonogram or of the broadcast was another contracting state. It then sought to define country of origin in each of the three cases. The Rome Conference found this ambiguous and preferred to drop the term 'country of origin' and to state explicitly who is to be protected and in what circumstances.

Article 2.2 provides that 'national treatment shall be subject to the protection specifically guaranteed ... in this Convention'. That means that a state must grant the minimum rights provided in the Convention (articles 7, 10, 13) to the nationals of other Convention countries even if it does not grant them to its own nationals.

Article 2.2 also provides that national treatment shall be subject to 'the limitations specifically provided for, in this Convention'. That means, for instance, that (under article 16) a country could deny performers or producers of other Convention countries the right to equitable remuneration for the public use of their phonograms, because its own performers or producers do not enjoy such rights in that other Convention country, whereas it grants such rights to its own nationals.

The result of applying the principle of national treatment in the Rome Convention, ie the assimilation of foreigners to nationals, is the same as in the Berne Convention. The difference however is that whereas in the Berne Convention the subject of the protection is the work, the subjects of the protection of the Rome Convention are the beneficiaries. It is as if the Berne Convention had protected authors and publishers instead of works and then applied the principle of national treatment.

In many countries the combination of the principle of national treatment and the conventional minima is only effective if they honour their obligation under article 26.2 to the effect that on ratification a state 'must be in a position under its domestic law to give effect to the terms of this Convention'. However in countries where conventions are self-applying, even if the minimum protection required is not assured by the existing national law, the minima laid down in the Convention will become part of the national law, and thus become effective.

1 See para 3.17 above.
2 See para 3.26 above.

5. National treatment and points of attachment – articles 4–6

8.08 As all conventions only deal with international situations the interaction between the principle of national treatment, the conventional minima and the points of attachment works as follows between country A and country B which are both convention countries. If a performer in country A, which does not protect performers against the fixation of their live performances without their consent, claims such protection at home he will fail, because national law applies and national law does not protect him in this respect. If on the other hand he claims such protection in country B where performers are protected in this respect he will succeed because, in accordance with the convention, country B has to treat him as if he was a 'national' of country B. The question: 'Who is a national'? is decided according to the 'points of attachment' laid down in articles 4, 5 and 6. They are different for each category of beneficiaries, so that these articles lay down 'who is protected and in what cases'.[1]

1   Kaminstein Report under art 4.

Protection of performers

8.09   Performers are protected if the performance takes place in a Convention country (art 4(a)), or the performance is incorporated in a protected phonogram (art 4(b)) or carried by a protected broadcast (art 4(c)).

Producers of phonograms

8.10   Producers of phonograms are protected if the producer is a national of another contracting state (art 5.1(a)), or the sounds were first fixed in another contracting state (art 5.1(b)) or the phonogram was first published in a contracting state (art 5.1(c)).

Nationality of producer

8.11   The producer of phonograms is nearly always a company, that is, a legal not a physical person. In private international law the nationality of a company is to be defined according to one of two criteria: under continental European legal systems it is the seat of the company's administration, headquarters or head office; under Anglo-Saxon legal systems it is the country under the laws of which the company is organised. In the case of the nationality of a broadcasting organisation the Kaminstein Report says that it was agreed that the Anglo-Saxon definition should be applied.[1] It seems likely therefore that the courts would apply the same rule to the nationality of the record producer: the country under whose law the company is organised. In the case of multinational companies this may be of importance.

1   Rome Convention Report, art 8.

Country of first fixation

8.12   This is the country where the recording of the performance of the work is made. The act of recording, that is fixing the sounds on a material support decides the nationality of the phonogram.

Country of first publication

8.13   Between 'fixation', which is the artistic activity of recording a work, and publication of the records is the process of manufacture, ie the pressing of the records, which is the duplication of the master recording. The place where the records are pressed is irrelevant under the Convention. The relevant stage is publication which is defined in article 3(d) as 'the offering of copies of a phonogram to the public in reasonable quantity'.

Unlike the Berne Convention (article 3.3) the Rome Convention does not mention that such copies must have been produced with the consent of the right owner. However as the term 'publication' is taken from the Berne Convention and the definition is similar to the Berne Convention it must be assumed that legality is implied and that the offer of pirated copies to the public would not constitute publication.

Publication within 30 days is 'simultaneous publication', another concept taken from the Berne Convention,[1] which means that a phonogram first published in a non-Convention country becomes protected if it is published within 30 days in a Convention country.

'Publication' is defined in article 3(d) as 'the offering of copies of a phonogram to the public in reasonable quantity'. What is a 'reasonable' quantity is a matter for the courts to decide on the facts of each case. However, applying the criteria the courts have applied to the simultaneous publication of books they will probably not be too difficult to meet.

The common sense reason of this provision is that the place of fixation or publication can be arbitrary. You can record in any place provided it has the necessary technical facilities and is conveniently located. Within reason you can publish the recording where you choose to publish it but the nationality of the record company is where its seat is and you cannot easily change that and each country wishes, for reasons of employment policy and taxation policy, to protect its own companies.

1   Art 3(4); see para 5.33 above.

'Offering in reasonable quantities'

8.14   The 'offer' can be made either by publishing a catalogue which lists the phonogram or by advertisements in the press.[1]

How many copies have to be available to constitute 'reasonable quantities' must depend on the circumstances of the case. The most important factor is probably the nature of the phonogram concerned. The demand for the latest LP of a well-known pop group is obviously a multiple of that for the recording of a little known eighteenth century opera for which the market consists largely of connoisseurs.

It is suggested[2] that it may be sufficient to prove that, although only a few copies were available in the shops at first, larger quantities could be made available at short notice and that the producer has the facilities to make such larger numbers of copies available on demand.

It seems an open question whether offering of a reasonable quantity for hire in a record library ('phonoteque') would be sufficient but on the wording of the definition both sale and hire would seem to qualify.

The situation is further complicated by the possibility of another possible reservation. If a country has in its national law protected phonograms on the basis of the criterion of fixation only, at the time of the making of the Convention (26 October 1961) it can maintain fixation as the sole criterion (article 17). This reservation is of limited application as the countries with such a law are the five Scandinavian countries and Italy.[3] The underlying reason for the inclusion of article 17 was that the Scandinavian countries were determined not to have to give protection to United States phonograms which are, as a rule, published simultaneously in the United Kingdom, and would thus qualify. They would only give that protection when the United States ratified the Convention, thus protecting Scandinavian phonograms. Diplomatic courtesy demanded that this was never said at the Conference and the Report, written by an American, not unnaturally does not mention it. It well illustrates the point that on certain matters which are considered important in the national interest even a small number of small states can make a successful stand against large ones.

Countries can make a reservation is respect of these three points of attachment. They can exclude the criterion of publication, thus applying nationality and fixation as criteria or they can exclude fixation thus applying nationality and publication as the criteria. The criterion they cannot exclude is that of nationality (article 5.3). The three criteria are like a sandwich with publication and fixation as the bread and nationality as the meat of the sandwich. If you remove the top piece of bread or the bottom piece of bread you still have a kind of sandwich. If you remove the meat you are left with only two pieces of dry bread.

The result of the possible reservations is that there will be four categories of countries:

1. Countries which make no reservations and thus protect phonograms if any one of the points of attachment is met (all Latin American countries).
2. Countries which protect on nationality and publication (having excluded fixation) like the Federal Republic of Germany and the UK.
3. Countries which protect on nationality and fixation (having excluded publication) (none so far).
4. Countries which protect only on fixation (having made the reservation on article 17): the Scandinavian countries and Italy.

1 See Nordemann, Vink, Hertin *Commentary on International Copyright in German speaking Countries and the EEC*, p 298.
2 Nordemann, op cit, p 298.
3 Denmark, Norway, Sweden and Italy have ratified the Convention and made this reservation. No doubt when Finland and Iceland ratify they will make it also, but no other country can do so in future by altering its national law and adopting fixation as the sole criterion.

8.15 *Broadcasting organisations* are protected if either the headquarters or the transmitter are situated in another contracting state (article 6(1)(a) and 6(1)(b)).

Countries can make a reservation to the effect that they will only protect broadcasts if *both* the headquarters of the organisation and the transmitter are situated in a contracting state (article 6.2). The rationale of this provision is to enable ratifying countries to exclude from protection some so-called 'peripheral stations' where the headquarters is in one state and the transmitter in another, being a short distance from the national frontier. For example 'Radio Monte Carlo' has its seat in Monaco (article 6.1a), however, for geographical reasons, the broadcasts destined for the public in Monaco are broadcast from French soil (article 6.1b).

The broadcasting organisation is the entity which has the administrative, organisational and economic responsibility for the broadcasting of programmes. It need not be the owner of the buildings from which the broadcast is made (the Ministry of Post and Telegraph is the owner in most European countries) nor the producers of the broadcast material (which can be an independent producer of programmes or an advertising agency or the sponsor of advertising programmes). If the owner of the building or the independent producer of the programmes are different entities from the entity responsible for the broadcasts, it is the latter not the former which is considered the 'broadcasting organisation'.[1]

The principle of national treatment as applied to broadcasting organisations was well illustrated in the case of Goldoni's *Love affairs in Chioggia* (1968). A studio production of the play had been recorded by 'Piccolo Teatro Milano' in Milan under the direction of Giorgio Strehler. Exclusive permission to broadcast the performance had been given to RAI (the Italian State Broadcasting

Organisation). The Second German Television Network (FDF) proposed to broadcast the production of the play which RAI had recorded in Italy. The performers having given an exclusive licence to RAI were trying to prevent the broadcast by suing in the German courts as they would have been entitled to do under German law (para 76, German Copyright Law). At the time Germany had ratified the Rome Convention but Italy had not. The plaintiffs failed before the Court of Appeal in Koblenz, Germany.[2] Had the Rome Convention applied between Germany and Italy the plaintiffs could have claimed protection under the principle of national treatment.

The variety and combinations of the points of attachment and the possibility of reservations makes for a fairly complex system and as the *WIPO Guide* wrily comments it 'is likely to provide a good deal of work for the courts'. However once the system is explained and understood the courts should not find decision making too difficult.

1 Kaminstein Report, art 3.
2 Reported in GRUR Int (1968) p 164.

6. Rights of performers – article 7

8.16 Unlike the parallel rights of the phonogram producer (article 10) and the broadcaster (article 13) the performer does not have a right to 'authorise or prohibit' the fixation or the reproduction of his performance. Instead the contracting states are bound to provide protection to the performer which will enable him to 'prevent' such acts. In sheer logic it is difficult to see why only the performer of the three protected interests should not be given an absolute right. There were three reasons, all political not legal. First those representing authors saw in an absolute right given to performers a right competing with that of the author. Secondly the broadcasters strongly opposed such a right, because they feared that it might be transferred to the performers' unions and could interfere with the broadcasters' freedom and put too strong a weapon in the hands of the unions.[1] Thirdly, an absolute right was opposed by the countries which had, like the United Kingdom, legislation protecting performers by penal sanctions rather than by giving them absolute rights. The *WIPO Guide* puts the problem very neatly:[2]

> 'by the simple decision to appear or not on the stage or in the studio, the performer carries in himself the exclusive right to authorise his performance. But from the moment modern technology intervenes (phonograms, broadcasting) their performance, once fixed, may be used in ways never envisaged. It is then one asks whether they should not have a right, like that of the author in his work, which allows him to follow its fortune, and retain a control over their performances'.

The result is that the Convention prescribes the aim, ie protecting performers against certain specified acts, but leaves the means by which this is to be achieved to national legislation.

That the states wanted to give the performers 'rights' but could not quite overcome the political difficulties is shown first in the Convention itself, when in article 8, dealing with collective performances, the Convention speaks of representation 'in connection with the exercise of their rights'. It is also shown in the Model Law of 1974[3]. There, after 13 years of reflection, section 2(1) says: 'Without the authorisation of the performers, no person shall do any of the following acts'. The section is worded in the same way as section 4 giving an absolute right to producers of phonograms and section 6 giving an absolute right to broadcasters. This would reduce – on the national level – the balance aimed at in the Convention.

The Nordemann Commentary argues that, as article 26.2 obliges each state to be in a position 'to give effect to the terms of the Convention', if national law does in fact not have the effect of 'preventing' the acts stipulated in article 7, such a country would be in breach of its obligations under the Convention.[4]

1   See *WIPO Guide to Rome* p 7.6.
2   *WIPO Guide to Rome* p 7.7.
3   'Model Law concerning Protection of Performers, Producers of Phonograms and Broadcasting Organisations' pub by ILO, WIPO, UNESCO, 1974.
4   Nordemann, op cit, p 302.

8.17   The rights to be given to performers are, however, absolute in the sense that they cannot be replaced by a compulsory licence.[1] Each state has the choice of implementing the Convention by basing the protection of performers on an exclusive right, or on the law of employment, or of unfair competition, or of unjust enrichment, or any other suitable means. The Convention obligations of the national law are fulfilled by achieving the purpose of the Convention, ie preventing the acts enumerated in article 7.[2] These acts are a) the broadcasting and communication to the public; b) the fixation; c) in some cases the reproduction of those fixations of performances without the performer's consent.

(a) The broadcasting and communication to the public of the performance without consent. Communication to the public in this context envisages the transmission of, for example, a concert to a public other than that present in the concert hall either by loudspeaker or by wire. At the Conference it was argued that such communication to the public could only in very rare cases involve the crossing of frontiers. However, as the Kaminstein Report puts it[3] the Conference did not omit it because they did 'not regard their occurrence as outside the realm of the possible'. They had mainly the loudspeaker situation in mind. Since then television programmes are often carried across frontiers by cable and the decision to leave the reference to public performance in, has proved right although for a reason which was not foreseen in 1961.

There are however four exceptions to this rule in article 7.1(a):

1. If the performance has itself already been broadcast. It then becomes a rebroadcast under article 7.2.
2. If the broadcast is made from a fixation, eg a recording made for the purpose of broadcasting (article 7(2)) or a commercial phonogram (article 12) or a permitted ephemeral recording (article 15(c)).
3. If the public performance is made by way of a broadcast (eg radio in a restaurant, or television in an hotel).
4. If the public performance is made by way of a fixation of the performance (eg by a record in a jukebox).

The effect is as the Model Law[4] puts it: 'in general, the performers' rights with respect to broadcasting and public communication are limited to performances not already fixed or broadcast'.

(b) The fixation of a performance without consent. This is fixation on a soundcarrier (record or tape) or on a picture carrier (film or videogram) of a live performance. It covers fixations by a record company, a film company, a broadcasting organisation or an amateur with a tape-recorder in a concert hall.

(c) The reproduction, without consent, of a fixed performance, but only in special stated circumstances. The performer has no general reproduction right in his fixed performance, that right lies solely with the right owner in that fixation that is, a phonogram producer, a film producer, a broadcasting organisation, as the case may be. This failure to give the performer a reproduction right in the fixation of his performance was mainly due to the resistance of the broadcasters who argued that as most broadcasts are made from a fixation it would be putting too much of a burden on them to have to get the permission of the performer every time if they had made the fixation themselves or the permission of the performer as well as that of the phonogram producer if the fixation broadcast was a commercial phonogram.

The three special circumstances when the performer has the right to allow or forbid the reproduction of the fixation of his performance are:

1   Kaminstein Report on article 7. A proposal by Poland (Document 41) which would have had that effect was rejected by the Conference.
2   See also *WIPO Guide to Rome*, p 7.24.
3   Report, art 7 (para 4).
4   Model Law, Commentary to s 2 of the Model Law.

8.18   *Article 7, para 1(c)(i)*: Consent is required where the first fixation was made without consent, eg someone makes a recording of a concert given by a star performer and sells it to a record company who issue it as a commercial record. This is known as 'bootlegging'.[1]

1   The term goes back to the days of prohibition in the USA when those who were illicitly trafficking in spirits hid the bottles in the legging of their boots. The expression became strangely apposite again as with high boots being fashionable again with the young, this was where the recording equipment was being hidden when attending a 'pop' concert.

8.19   *Article 7, para 1(c)(ii)*: Consent is required where the reproduction is made for purposes different from those for which the performers gave their consent, eg if a phonogram made with the consent of the performer is incorporated into the sound track of a film without the performer's consent. He had consented to the fixation of his performance for making phonograms for sale to the public but not for making a film. This needs separate consent and thus separate payment, unless the phonogram producer has acquired that right by contract when he contracted for the making of the original recording.

8.20   *Article 7, para 1(c)(iii)*: Consent is required when a recording has been made lawfully under national law without the consent of the performer in one of the four cases stated under *article 15* of the Convention and is subsequently used for different purposes:

Case 1: Private use, eg someone records some songs, sung by a famous artist, off the air and uses the recording at home to play to his friends. This is covered by the private use exception in article 15.1(a) if the national law permits it, as it does in most countries. If he then either sells the recording or plays it in the village hall charging an entrance fee that is an infringement.

Case 2: Short excerpts in connection with reports on current events, eg a band plays a piece of music at the opening of a public building or the funeral of a statesman and this is recorded as a news item on television. This is covered by article 15.1(b). If the recording is subsequently used for a commercial film it is an infringement.

Case 3: Ephemeral fixation of a performance by a broadcaster without the performer's consent. This is covered by article 15.1(c) if it is made by the broadcasting organisation 'by means of its own facilities and for its own broadcasts' eg a broadcasting organisation makes a recording of a studio performance of a famous orchestra. They do so because they wish to broadcast the concert a week after the performance was given. This is covered by article 15.1(c). They then decide that the recording is so good they want to give it to another broadcasting organisation in another country, so that it can be broadcast there and they get in exchange a recording made by the foreign broadcasting organisation to fill a slot in one of their progrmmes. That is an infringement.

case 4: The original fixation was made 'solely for the purposes of *teaching or scientific research*'. Eg a famous singer gives a public recital of Schubert songs at a university. The music department records it as a videogram and general lecturers use it when analysing Schubert's music in their lectures. This is covered by article 15.1(d). The recording of one of the songs is so good that one of the lecturers sells it to a commercial company which issues it as a videogram. This is an infringement.

It is to be noted that 'fixation' is not defined in article 7 or elsewhere in the Convention. It clearly includes fixations of sounds, of images or of both sound and images. The Model Law[1] contains a definition: 'the embodiment of sounds, images or both in a material form, sufficiently permanent or stable to permit it to be perceived, reproduced, or otherwise communicated during a period of more than transitory duration'. (The last phrase is inserted to exclude ephemeral recordings.)

1 Model Law, s 1(ii).

8.21 *Article 7 para 2*: In spite of the fact that performers, unlike phonogram producers and broadcasters are not given a property right in their performances, the rights given to them in article 7.1 are substantial and important. However, in their relation to broadcasters they are substantially cut down in article 7.2. The question to be answered was: once a performer has given his consent to the broadcasting of his performance can he still claim protection against: a) rebroadcasting, b) fixation for broadcasting purposes, c) reproduction of such fixation for broadcasting purposes and generally the use the broadcasting organisations can make of such fixations? The answer given by the Convention is that it is a matter for the domestic law of the country where protection is claimed. This means that national legislation may prescribe that once the performer has given consent for his performance to be broadcast and the contract is silent on the use the broadcaster can make of the performance, the broadcasting organisation is free to rebroadcast, fix and reproduce for broadcasting purposes. Equally, national legislation may prescribe that even if the performer consents to the broadcasting of his performance and the contract is silent, the broadcaster needs further consents for fixing the broadcast, reproducing it or any further use he wants to make for broadcasting purposes of the fixation. If the latter is the law the performer would obviously demand further payments for rebroadcasting or selling or exchanging the fixations with other broadcasters.

Whereas performers are given the right to control the reproduction of unauthorised fixations, the Convention is silent as to their right to control other uses of a fixation of a broadcast made without his consent. The reason lies in the practical difficulties facing users who would have to decide not only whether the fixation they are using is lawful but also which national law they have to look at to decide whether the fixation is lawful or not.

Faced with this dilemma the Conference decided to leave this problem to national legislation and thus the vacuum in the protection of performers remains.

There is however one brake on the freedom of national legislation in this matter. Domestic law must not deprive performers of the ability to control their relations with broadcasting organisations, by contract (article 7.2(3)). Thus freedom of contract between the parties is paramount on the above named points. Only if the contract is silent can domestic law intervene. If domestic law does intervene it is free to do so on behalf of one side or the other.

The case made for performers was that the protection given to them should enable them to demand reasonable supplementary fees when the broadcaster extends the audience that can hear and see the performance. The case made for the broadcasters was that deferred relays which demand fixation of performances are the rule in modern broadcasting and exchanges of programmes are essential to good broadcasting. To give performers and their unions the power to stop such relays or exchanges would be against the interest of the public who benefited greatly from them as 'Eurovision' in Western Europe or 'Intervision' in Eastern Europe show.[1]

The solutions chosen by the Convention are compromises between the two competing interests.

It was agreed at the Conference[2] that 'contract' in this context includes collective agreements between performers and broadcasting organisations as well as decisions of arbitration boards or tribunals if 'arbitration was the mode of settlement ordinarily applying between performers and broadcasters'.

As the *WIPO Guide* points out, the Convention is silent on the question of moral rights. Performers 'would have the strongest case for such a right, particularly to be identified by name with their performances and that these should not be mutilated in ways likely to spoil them'.[3] The only provision which could be interpreted as a nod towards a 'droit moral' is to be found in article 11 where in connection with formalities which may be required in contracting states, mention is made of identifying performers or the name of the person who owns the rights of such performers.[4] Desbois comments[5] that 'a right to the name' and a 'right to respect' would have been welcome.

However some national laws, eg French law, protect the 'droit moral' of artists by their jurisprudence.[6] In Anglo-Saxon jurisdictions the law of defamation may provide remedies if the artist's name or reputation is affected, as his or her reputation often depends on performances as a recording artist or as a radio or television star.

1 In fact the public had not been deprived of Eurovision because when the Performers' Unions threatened to strike the European Broadcasting Union made a voluntary agreement with FIM and FIA, the international organisations representing them, under which artists get supplementary fees when national broadcasts are relayed on Eurovision.
2 Kaminstein Report under art 7/2(3).
3 *WIPO Guide to Rome*, p 7.28.
4 See Nordemann, op cit, p 305, Desjeux, *La Convention de Rome* (1966), p 156.
5 Desbois, Françon, Kerever, *Les Conventions Internationales du droit d'auteur et des droits voisins* (1976), p 288.
6 L'affaire Furtwängler, Civ, 4 janvier 1964, D 1964, J p 322.

7. Group performances – article 8

8.22 As most performances involve more than one person the question of representation is important. There are many 'groups' of performers from a singer and an accompanist or a trio or quartet to an orchestra or chorus or the cast of a play. There are also many kinds of representatives of performers from agents and professional groupings[1] to trade unions and orchestras which have turned themselves into limited companies.[2] In view of the great variety of these combinations 'the manner in which performers will be represented in connection with the exercise of their rights'[3] is left to national legislation. However, national laws cannot regulate the exercise of these rights. Generally they have to limit themselves 'to the question of how members of a group were represented when they exercised their rights'.[4] The Report indicates that the expression

'Conditions of exercise of rights' was avoided because it has been used, particularly in the Berne Convention, as a euphemism for compulsory licences.[5]

It is to be noted that, representation apart, the rights of performers are freely transferable and are usually transferred by contract.

1 In Denmark conductors are separately represented. In Italy there is a separate union of singers as opposed to other musicians.
2 So have some stars mainly for tax reasons.
3 Art 8.
4 Kaminstein Report under art 8.
5 See para 5.35, note 2 above.

8. Variety artists – article 9

8.23 Article 3 defines performers as persons who 'perform literary and artistic works'. As all provisions of the Convention are minima and contracting states can give greater protection if they so choose this article is really superfluous, as it only gives the contracting states a faculty which they already have. It is intended, as the Report points out,[1] as a 'reminder' to contracting states that they need not confine the protection they give in their laws to performers of literary and artistic work but can extend it to others. The main group in question is variety and circus artists (clowns, acrobats, jugglers etc), who may find that their act is devalued by unauthorised filming or televising as the public may already have seen it when they come to a particular town to perform it. They should therefore be compensated.

It is to be noted that if their act is reduced to writing, eg a sketch performed by a comedian, the script would constitute a work which would be protected under the copyright conventions. The performance of it would be protected by the Rome Convention. A 'mime' would also be protected, if it is 'fixed in some material form'.

It was indicated at the Conference that some countries may wish to include sportsmen such as footballers, iceskaters or golfers, but so far no country has done so.

1 Kaminstein Report on art 9.

9. Reproduction right of producers of phonograms – article 10

8.24 This is a minimum right which contracting states have to grant to fulfil their obligation under article 26.2.

The right extends to 'direct' and 'indirect' reproduction of phonograms. By direct reproduction is meant the reproduction from a matrix, by indirect reproduction the recording of a phonogram 'off the air', that is from a radio or television programme. The most frequent form of piracy of phonograms, which had developed since the Rome Conference is the unauthorised copying of tapes. This may be 'direct' or 'indirect' according to whether the original recording is in the form of a matrix for producing discs, or in the form of a master tape for producing cassettes.

The Rome Convention does not include provisions to prohibit distribution or importation of unauthorised phonograms. Both rights were proposed[1] but they were rejected, mainly on the ground that they were not recognised in the Berne Convention for works such as books, although the Berne Convention does give a distribution right in respect of films (article 14) and a right to seize infringing copies (article 16).[2] The granting of these rights had to await the

Phonogram Convention (1971), after the need had been demonstrated by the widespread piracy of phonograms.[3]

Taking article 10 together with the definition of a 'producer of phonograms' in article 3(c) as 'the entity which first fixes the sounds of a performance', makes it clear that the right owner is the person or the company making the original recording and that neither any of the technicians involved in making the recording such as the 'Sound Master', nor the company which subsequently manufactures (presses) the records from the original recording is a right owner.

It is also clear that, as the reproduction right in article 10 is not qualified in any way, the unauthorised reproduction of a part of a phonogram also constitutes an infringement. This is important as record pirates often copy only one or two, usually the most successful tracks (songs) and put them together to make a long-playing record or tape, often combining them with other successful songs from other records, thereby making up a new LP (long-playing record) consisting of 10 or 12 tracks. In such cases, each track constitutes an infringement.[4]

On the other hand, the term 'reproduction' cannot be stretched to cover so-called 'sound-alikes'. These are recordings on which a performer imitates the performance of a famous artist, usually a singer, making it sound as near the original as he can. This constitutes a new performance and is not a reproduction. Thus no action for infringement lies. In this respect the reproduction right of the phonogram producer is narrower than that of the author under article 9 of the Berne Convention[5] as imitating a 'work', if the imitation is sufficiently close, would be an infringement of the author's right. If this 'sound-alike' recording is marketed honestly under the name of the performer who does the imitation and with a title like 'John Roe taking off Elvis Presley' no infringement is committed. If, on the other hand, it is marketed under a title like 'the sounds of Elvis Presley', possibly with a picture of Elvis Presley on the cover, an action for deceit, passing off or unfair competition will probably lie under most legislations, although it is not an infringement against the copyright of the original phonogram producer under the Convention.

If a live performance is being fixed with the permission of the performers (as is sometimes the case in concerts which are broadcast as well) and person other than the record company or broadcasting organisation which are authorised to do so, fixes the performance without such permission, then the unauthorised recording is not an infringement of the reproduction right of the legitimate phonogram producer or broadcaster, as it is not his recording that is being reproduced. It is however an infringement of the right of the performers under article 7(1)(b) 'the fixation, without their consent, of their unfixed performance' and each phonogram made from such fixation is an infringement under article 7(1)(c)(i), as it is a reproduction of a fixation which 'itself was made without their consent'.

1 The prohibition of distribution by Austria (Convention Document 76) and the prohibition of importation by the five Scandinavian countries (Convention Document 24).
2 See para 5.67 above.
3 See para 9.05 below.
4 The same rule applies to the partial reproduction of other fixations, such as fixations of a live performance or a broadcast.
5 See para 5.38 above.

10. Formalities for phonograms – article 11

8.25 With regard to formalities the Rome Convention does not follow the example of the Berne Convention, which stipulates that the rights granted by the Convention are not subject to any formalities,[1] but follows the example of the Universal Copyright Convention, which provides a maximum of formalities permitted under the Convention.[2]

As the UCC created the symbol © and the year date of publication as notice of a claim of copyright so the Rome Convention creates the symbol ℗ and the year date of publication as notice of claim of the rights under the Convention.[3]

Most legislations protect phonograms without requiring any formalities, as is the case in respect of other 'works'. The reason for providing for a maximum of formalities that can be required is the same as in the UCC: the system of registration of copyrights in the United States.[4] Once the symbol was established by the Rome Convention (1961) and the provisions repeated in the Phonogram Convention (1971) its usefulness was generally recognised, even in countries requiring no formalities and today the symbol ℗ is found on most phonograms wherever published just as the symbol © is found on most books, whether published in a Convention country or not. The symbol ℗ and the year date of publication on a phonogram does not, therefore, necessarily mean that it is protected under the Convention, although this is very likely.

The Report confirms the principle that in countries where no formalities are required as a condition of protection, protection under the Convention must be given, even if the phonogram does not bear the notice.[5] However, if formalities are required as a condition of protection (as for instance in the United States) then the symbol ℗ and the year date of first publication satisfies any formalities which may be required.

It is interesting to note that the Rome Convention, following the UCC, chooses the year date of publication rather than the year date of fixation, which is the date when the phonographic work comes into existence whether it is published in that year or not. This does not accord very well with the term of protection which runs from the end of the year when the first fixation is made.[6]

Most phonograms are published in jackets, sleeves, boxes or containers of some sort and for reasons of publicity these usually bear the name and trademark of the record company and the names of the principal performers (often with their photographs). Thus the alternatives which this article provides in case the label or the container 'do not identify the producer' are rarely of importance. If the label or the container do not identify the producer, the notice 'must include the name of the owner of the rights of the producer'. If they do not identify the principal performers the notice must contain 'the name of the person who, in the country in which the fixation was effected, owns the performers' rights'.

1 Berne Convention, art 4.2.
2 Universal Copyright Convention, art III.
3 Whereas © is based on the English term 'copyright' as opposed to 'droit d'auteur' ℗ stands for phonogram which, being Greek in origin, applies in all major languages.
4 See para 6.08 above.
5 Kaminstein Report under art 11.
6 Art 14(a).

11. Secondary uses of phonograms – article 12

8.26 The expression 'secondary use' is not used in the Convention, but it is used in the chapter heading of the Report to make the point that the primary use of a phonogram is in the home, that is a private use with an audience of a few people, whereas the use of a phonogram in public places with an audience of hundreds or thousands or on the air with an audience of millions, is not the use for which it was primarily intended. It is a 'secondary use'. Therefore, in accordance with the general principles of copyright, it involves a performance right and therefore, remuneration. The 'secondary uses' regulated in article 12 are the use of phonograms in broadcasting and communication to the public.

The Report describes the question of secondary uses as 'doubtless the most difficult problem before the Conference'. The eventual outcome was the result of three formal votes (one in the Work Group on Phonograms, one in the Main Committee and a third in Plenary Conference).[1]

It had been agreed at an early stage that the performance right in phonograms was to be the subject of a compulsory licence in favour of the users, with an equitable remuneration for the right-owners. The difference of opinion was represented by two of the drafts produced by committees of experts years before the Conference. The Monaco Draft, which did not impose an obligation on contracting states to grant secondary use rights and the Hague Draft, which made the performance right a minimum right which could, however, be avoided by contracting states making a reservation. It was, as the *WIPO Guide* puts it 'a question of emphasis and approach'.[2] Yet the emphasis proved important. Of all ratifying countries so far only three developing countries[3] and Luxembourg[4] excluded the right, so that the granting of the right became the general rule.

1 The two former votes produced majorities of 14 to 12 and 21 to 11 respectively and the last for which a ⅔ majority was necessary under the rules of the Conference 20 to 8.
2 *WIPO Guide to Rome.*
3 Congo, Niger and Fiji.
4 Luxembourg has no performers, no phonogram producers, but the most successful commercial broadcasting organisation in Europe.

8.27 The article contains the following rules:

1. The phonogram used for broadcasting or communication to the public must have been 'published for commercial purposes'. This excludes unpublished phonograms or recordings made by a broadcasting organisation.

2. The use must be 'direct'. That means that in the case of 'rebroadcasting' (article 3(g)) only the original broadcast is paid for, the rebroadcasting by other stations is not.

3. The uses to be paid for are broadcasting and communication to the public. Other uses are not covered by the Convention. Relay of a broadcast by cable, for example, is not covered. It is neither direct broadcasting, nor communication to the public.

4. The payment is 'a single equitable remuneration':

a) The user has to pay once only. If an opera is broadcast from a recording, phonogram producers (the producer of the original recording and/or his licensee in the country where the broadcast takes place) and a large number of performers (soloists, orchestra and chorus) may be entitled to remuneration but the broadcaster has to make only one payment. This means that in practice a collecting society is necessary. It receives the 'single' payment on behalf of all right owners and gives the user an indemnity against all possible claims.

b) In cases where the parties cannot agree, what is an 'equitable' remuneration, this has to be decided by the courts of the country where the remuneration is payable.[1] Some legislations have established a special copyright royalty tribunal which adjudicates on such claims.[2]

5. It is left to national legislation to determine which right owner shall be entitled to equitable remuneration. The national legislator has a choice between five possibilities. He can give the right to remuneration to:

(1) the performers alone, (eg Brazil)
(2) the phonogram producers alone, (eg the United Kingdom)
(3) the performers and the producers (eg Sweden)
(4) the performers, with a provision requiring them to pay a share to the producer (eg Federal Republic of Germany)
(5) the producer, with a provision requiring him to pay a share to the performers (eg Austria)

The fifth alternative is the one chosen by the Model Law.[3] It has proved the most practical system. The producer is the most clearly identified right owner, as his name is on the label of the phonogram and can be found in a catalogue. If it is a foreign company it nearly always has a licensee or distributor in the country where the phonogram has been used and where the remuneration is therefore payable. The burden of distributing the performers' share is placed on the phonogram producer who either discharges it directly or through a collecting society.

1 Eg Sweden.
2 Eg Germany (Federal Republic).
3 It is known as 'the Lenoble Solution' as it had been proposed at an early stage of the preparatory conferences by Mauric Lenoble, then legal adviser of the French National Broadcasting Organisation.

8.28 The article 12 right, like all Convention rights, is a minimum which states must grant unless they make a complete reservation under article 16.1(a)(i). There is, however, nothing to prevent a country which gives a copyright to the phonogram producer (eg the United Kingdom) from giving an absolute performance right to the phonogram producer. If a country gives a property right to the performer, it can give him an absolute performance right or broadcasting right when a phonogram containing his performance is used publicly (eg Mexico).

The decision on the sharing of the 'single equitable remuneration' is, in the first place, left to the parties. In the 'absence of agreement between the parties', national legislation 'may lay down the conditions as to the sharing'. Some legislations have done so,[1] but most have left it to negotiations between the parties. If the parties fail to agree, the decision is left either to a special tribunal or to the ordinary courts.

In Europe the international organisations representing the producers of phonograms and the performers[2] have made an agreement[3] which provides that, if national legislation gives the right only to the producer, or only to the performer, they will share the remuneration.

The trend of national legislations seems to be to give the right to both parties.[4] In most countries there is one collecting society acting on behalf of all right owners. The trend of sharing between the parties is towards 50/50, on the basis that when distributing an equitable remuneration 'equality is equity'.[5] The amounts of the equitable remuneration is in all countries left to negotiations between the parties and 'the accent is on agreement'.[6] In case of failure to agree, national laws usually provide for a tariff to be fixed by a competent authority. This jurisdiction is given either to the ordinary courts, or to a special tribunal.

There is no uniform method of measuring the remuneration. In the case of public service broadcasting organisations it can be a lump sum, or a sum per minute of broadcasting of phonograms, both being adjusted periodically in accordance with a cost of living index (eg Scandinavian countries) or a sum related to the number of holders of radio and television licences.

In the case of commercial broadcasting organisations it can be a percentage of the revenue from advertising (eg United Kingdom) or of the cost of advertising spots (eg Republic of Ireland).

In the case of communication to the public it can be a yearly lump sum (eg juke boxes in the United Kingdom), or a percentage of the remuneration paid by the user to the authors' society (eg hotels, restaurants and other public places in Germany). Because phonograms are defined as exclusively oral fixations in article 3(b) and also in view of the total exemption of films in article 19, videograms do not qualify for equitable remuneration under the Rome Convention, but are protected by the copyright conventions.

Whereas in the field of patent and trademark law each right owner is quite capable of exercising the right granted to him by statute, this is not always the case in copyright, particularly as far as performance rights are concerned and especially in the field of musical copyrights. To exercise the latter rights the authors and, in the case of neighbouring rights, the performers and phonogram producers have to form societies which they either mandate or to which they transfer their rights because there is no other practical possibility to exercise them. These societies are monopolistic in the sense that one society represents the rights of practically all right owners in one country as it is virtually impossible for a performer or phonogram producer to exercise his rights himself without a national society.

1   Austrian Copyright Law 1972, lays down a 50/50 sharing unless the parties agree otherwise; see para 13.08 below.
2   IFPI (International Federation of Producers of Phonograms and Videograms) and FIM (Federation Internationale des Musicians) and FIA (Federation Internationale des Acteurs).
3   It is known as the FIM/IFPI Agreement 1953 (Revised 1976).
4   Eg Austria, Denmark, Federal Republic of Germany, Sweden.
5   The Model Law also provides for 50/50 sharing (s 5(2)).
6   *WIPO Guide to Rome* 12.14.

8.29 The Intergovernmental Committee of the Rome Convention made detailed recommendations on 'Collection and Distribution of Remuneration' by such collecting societies dealing with the principles of national and international law applicable to them.[1]

'Collection and Distribution of Remuneration

(A) *Introduction, alternative arrangements and practical considerations*

29. Experience in 32 countries of administering rights of performers and producers of phonograms granted in accordance with article 12 of the Rome Convention has shown that, by harmonizing the interests of the beneficiaries, arrangements, both efficient and reasonably cheap, may be made for the purpose of collecting, distributing and applying remuneration due in respect of broadcasting and communication to the public of phonograms published for commercial purposes. Indeed such arrangements have been found not only to be economically feasible, but also to present fewer difficulties than appear at first sight. In fact, four such systems exist in countries with no legislation to this effect. The functioning of all of these systems refute the argument that the Convention is difficult to apply in practice. According to the interpretation of the Convention, entitlement to remuneration shall in all cases be determined by the country of collection in accordance with private international law. Foreign beneficiaries are entitled to national treatment.

30. The arrangements required must deal with both national situations (collection, distribution and application of remuneration due to national performers and producers) and international situations (collection, distribution and application of remuneration due to foreign performers and producers). The former normally present few problems. The legal and practical requirements for solution of these

problems at the international level can best be satisfied by setting up 'collection/ distribution societies' in all countries where national legislation establishes rights for performers or producers, or both, corresponding to those provided for in article 12. These societies should represent performers and producers and there are certain advantages in having one society only, representing both. A prerequisite for the functioning of these societies is that they must have valid mandates or assignments of individual rights of those entitled to remuneration. The validity of these mandates or assignments is to be judged (in accordance with the principles of private international law) by the law of the country where the mandates or assignments are given. Practical guidance for the establishment and operation of such societies, and for bilateral agreements between them, are set out below.

31. The experience in various countries of administering article 12 rights illustrates that there are several alternative arrangements that can be established to implement such rights. Different arrangements can include:
(a) Remuneration distributed to both nationals and foreigners according to the rules of the collecting society in the country of collection. The collecting society in the country of collection sends to the society in the country of distribution a list (names of performers and the sums they are entitled to), without evidence of the user. In such cases the society in the country of distribution consequently has no possibility of changing the beneficiary or the amounts for distribution since it has no evidence of the extent of use. Only the balance of the total sum of traceable remuneration due to identifiable performers would be transmitted. If the principles of distribution of the society in the country of collection are felt to be inappropriate or inequitable by the distributing society, this society can change the distribution without having agreed to such a change in a bilateral agreement, provided it has valid mandates or assignments from those entitled to remuneration.
(b) Collection and distribution of remuneration based on a practice whereby the collection and distribution to nationals would be governed by the law of the country and the rules of the national society in the country of collection, whereas distribution of any remuneration transmitted to a second country would be governed by the rules of the national society of that country, provided these societies have valid mandates or assignments from those entitled to remuneration. In contrast to (a) above this arrangement is based on bilateral agreements. This arrangement is advocated by the international federations representing producers of phonograms and videograms (IFPI) and performers (FIM and FIA) and is reflected in the 4th London Principle agreed to by these organizations in 1978.
(c) Remuneration remaining in the country of collection and distributed according to the rules of the society in that country, provided the society has valid mandates or assignments from those entitled to remuneration. This arrangement calls for bilateral agreements with collection/distribution societies in other Contracting States. Reasons for the remuneration remaining in the country of collection may include national economic conditions, problems of currency regulation or incompatible methods for calculating the remuneration and the methods of distribution in two given countries.
(d) Remuneration due to one beneficiary remaining in the country of collection and used for collective purposes.

32. A number of practical considerations should be taken into account regardless of the choice made among any of the above arrangements. For example, the collection and distribution societies have, in some countries, found that the most effective way of collecting public performance revenue, as opposed to broadcasting revenue, is to ask the national authors' society to do it on behalf of the article 12 beneficiaries on a commission basis. This is so because they collect from the same users in any event and the additional cost incurred in the collection of article 12 remuneration is marginal. The commission, which provides an additional income for the authors' societies, is a contribution towards meeting their own administrative expenses, thus increasing their cost effectiveness.

33. The experience of existing collecting societies has shown that practical difficulties in identifying the individual performers and producers, whether nationals or foreigners, entitled to broadcasting revenue are less than those involved in dealing with public performance revenue, in respect of which identification of every participating performer is not likely to prove possible. Similarly, it may not be possible to establish precisely the extent to which any particular phonogram is used. In such cases, however, the principle of benefiting performers can be observed by collective application of an appropriate proportion of the revenue received. When revenue is deemed undistributable, at present, it remains in the country in which it arises. Some bilateral agreements based on the FIM/IFPI "London" Principles, 1969, expressly so provide.

34. Legislation in some countries provides that, in the absence of agreement between performers and producers of phonograms, the sharing of remuneration from performance rights should be 50/50. The Model Law concerning the Protection of Performers, Producers of Phonograms and Broadcasting Organizations in section 5(2) provides that "unless otherwise agreed between the performers and the producer, half of the amount received by the producers under paragraph (1) shall be paid by the producers to the performers." It is recalled that the "amount received by the producers" refers to the total sum due to both producers and performers. The Model Law as a whole has the support of FIM, FIA and IFPI and it is common ground between the three organizations that any country adhering to the Convention on the basis of the Model Law should apply this provision.

35. The Rome Convention leaves open the question whether remuneration due to performers should be distributed to individual performers or used for collective or social purposes, that is, for the benefit of the profession as a whole (see paragraph 688.1 of the Summary Records of the proceedings of the Diplomatic Conference). Subject to the provisions of the national law, performers in a given country may control the use to which the remuneration to which they are entitled under article 12 is put, by giving appropriate mandates or assignments of their rights to their national collection/distribution societies.

(B) *Guidelines for the establishment and operation of collecting societies for article 12 rights*

36. The following guidelines are presented to facilitate the practical application of article 12 rights:

(1) In all countries where national legislation establishes rights for performers or producers of phonograms, or both, corresponding to those specified in article 12 of the Rome Convention, societies should be set up for the purpose of collecting, distributing and applying revenue due in respect of broadcasting and communication to the public of phonograms published for commercial purposes. Such societies must have valid mandates or assignments of individual rights of those entitled to remuneration.

(2) Collecting societies representing performers and producers of phonograms may be established either as a single joint society or as separate societies. Both solutions have been adopted by Contracting States. Joint societies, as mentioned in paragraph 28 above, should be composed of performers and producers of phonograms who would be represented on an equal footing. Performers and producers should choose their own representatives, either directly or through representative organizations.

(3) Where broadcasting and/or public performance revenue is due either to producers or to performers, or to both, as a result of legal provisions, and, in the last case, in the absence of any legal provision relating to the division of the revenue between performers and producers, the rules of the society or societies referred to in paragraphs (1) and (2) above should specify that the revenue shall be divided equally between performers and producers.

(4) The society or societies referred to in paragraphs (1) and (2) above should work on a non-profit basis and wherever possible be established in accordance with the national legislation governing non-profit making institutions or analogous organizations. Whatever the legal form adopted, such societies

should have the legal personality required:
- (i) to enter into binding contracts, both at the national and at the international level;
- (ii) to exercise the mandates received from performers and producers.

(5) Membership of a performers' union or association or a producers' organization should not be made a condition of admittance to the society or societies referred to in paragraphs (1) and (2) above.

(6) Within a joint society, as envisaged in paragraph (2) above, the interests of performers and producers respectively may each be represented in one or more separate sub-units, provided that:
- (i) there should be a joint executive organ, with equal representation of performers and producers;
- (ii) the voting strength of performers and producers should remain equal in the joint executive organ or in any other joint organ, irrespective of the number of sub-units representing either performers or producers;
- (iii) the joint executive organ should be responsible for all negotiations concerning the remuneration payable in respect of broadcasting and public performance of phonograms published for commercial purposes;
- (iv) the distribution and application of the revenue allocated to each group of beneficiaries should be decided by separate sub-units representing performers and producers, respectively.

(7) Should the executive organ of a joint society so decide, it may be presided over by an independent person, appointed by agreement between the representatives of performers and producers.

(8) Wherever possible, decisions of a joint society should be adopted unanimously or by consensus, the rules governing voting being framed to this end. On occasions when this does not prove possible, and where there is an independent chairman, the latter may be given a vote.

(9) The question as to whether a representative or representatives of the public authorities should participate in meetings of or be a member of the executive organ of a joint society should be decided in each case in the light of national practice.

(10) The rules of the society or societies referred to in paragraphs (1) and (2) above should provide, *inter alia*:
- (i) that the administrative costs necessarily incurred in the efficient conduct of the business of the society should be a first charge on the revenue received;
- (ii) that administrative costs and capital expenditure, including the acquisition or rental of real property, should be subject to effective scrutiny of the membership;
- (iii) the conditions under which a proportion of the revenue received may be used, either directly by the society itself or otherwise (for example, through representative organizations of performers and producers) for the defence and promotion of the rights of performers and producers at both the national and international level; such uses should be without prejudice to the right of the sub-units representing performers and producers to make separate allocations for these purposes;
- (iv) the establishment of an adequate reserve fund;
- (v) the general objectives in pursuance of which the two groups of beneficiaries may distribute and apply the revenue allocated to each of them, and the procedures by which decisions regarding such uses shall be made, including the methods by which members of the society shall be informed of such decisions;
- (vi) the manner in which indemnities arising from bilateral agreements should be fulfilled.

(11) A report on the activities of the society or societies referred to in paragraphs (1) and (2) above should be made available to members periodically (nor-

mally annually). This report should include:
  (i) a detailed statement of account, duly certified by an independent auditor;
  (ii) explanatory information concerning expenditure incurred by the society pursuant to paragraph (10) above;
  (iii) explanatory information concerning any other expenditure incurred by the society or its sub-units.
(12) With particular regard to the collection of public performance revenue, every effort should be made to obtain the co-operation of existing collecting agencies such as authors' societies, provided that this can be done at reasonable cost.

(C) *International bilateral agreements*

37. The following guidelines are presented in order to facilitate the establishment of bilateral agreements between collecting societies:
(1) *Bilateral agreements* between collection-distribution societies in different countries should be legally binding contracts.
(2) *Such agreements* should be made for a substantial period (not less than two years) and should be automatically renewed unless denounced by either party.
(3) *Such agreements* should contain provisions for the settlement of any dispute as to their interpretation and application. The suggested mechanism would be an international arbitration tribunal consisting of an equal number of representatives nominated by FIM and FIA on the one hand, and by IFPI on the other, with a chairman appointed by mutual agreement. The agreement should provide that either party may require arbitration and that both parties undertake to accept and apply the decision of the arbitration tribunal. The determination of who is to pay arbitration costs, if any, may be decided by the tribunal.
(4) *Such agreements* should be consistent with the arrangement and practice chosen to implement article 12 rights.
(5) (i) Such agreements should clearly indicate where the responsibility for meeting claims, and costs properly incurred in relation thereto, should lie.
  (ii) The two societies party to such an agreement should grant each other mutual indemnities against successful claims, and costs properly incurred in relation thereto, from performers and producers in their respective countries. Such indemnities should take effect to the extent that such claims cannot be met from revenue received by the defendant society in respect of performers or producers in the country whence the claim originates and retained by the defendant society because deemed not for distribution. For the purposes of this calculation, revenue received in respect of performers should not be brought into account in relation to claims by producers, nor vice versa.'

1 Published in Copyright (April 1979), p 107.

12. Reservations – article 16

8.30 The reservations fall into two groups. Reservations in the first groups (article 16/1(a)(i) and (ii)) are to be used by states which do not want to give a performance right in phonograms at all (a(i)); and by states which do grant these rights but only in respect of broadcasting, or only in respect of communication to the public (a(ii)).

Reservations in the second group (article 16/1(a)(iii) and (iv)) are used by states which grant the right but want to stop an excessive outflow of royalties to countries which are either not Convention countries ((a(iii)), or do not grant the rights to the same extent or for the same term ((a)(iv)). The second group of reservations are applications of the principle of material reciprocity.[1]

Reservation under (a)(i): This is a total reservation. Its effect is ratification of the Convention as if article 12 were not part of it.

Reservation under (a)(ii): This makes it possible to restrict the payment of equitable remuneration to payment for use in broadcasting only, or to payment for use in communication to the public only. It also makes it possible to exempt certain kinds of broadcasts from payment, eg cultural or religious broadcasts, or certain kinds of communications to the public eg uses in development areas, or in places where no entrance fee is charged.

Reservation under (a)(iii): This makes it possible to exempt from payment cases where the phonogram producer is not a national of a contracting state. This enables a country to be liberal in its choice of the points of attachment under article 5. It can protect phonograms which are either fixed or first published in a contracting state, but to pay the equitable remuneration only if the producer is a national of a contracting state. This means that the country wishes to protect virtually all phonograms against illicit reproduction but wishes to pay only for secondary use of phonograms which are the produce of a country which in turn pays equitable remuneration. The most obvious example is the wish to exclude from payment phonograms from the United States, because the United States is not a member of the Convention and does not grant payment for secondary uses in its own law.[2] If such a country has chosen publication and nationality as the points of attachment, which is the most frequently used choice, or has chosen all three points of attachment it would have to pay for secondary use of American phonograms, if they were simultaneously published in another convention country (which is often the case). By making a reservation under (a)(iii) this can be avoided, whilst still protecting United States phonograms and United States artists in other respects.

Reservation (a)(iv): This is the reservation which enables a country to apply the rules of material reciprocity strictly to the secondary use situation, to 'cut back the protection it grants to the extent of the protection it receives'[3] and for the term of protection which it receives. This possibility of reservation is necessary, because without it countries which make no other reservations would be worse off as far as their balance between incoming and outgoing royalties is concerned than countries which make a complete reservation under (a)(i) or a partial reservation under (a)(ii) or (a)(iii).

The two examples given in the *WIPO Guide* illustrate the position:[4]

Example 1:

'State A makes the declaration in (a)(iv); State B applies Article 12 without reservation; State C rules article 12 out altogether by making the declaration under (a)(i). A commercial phonogram made by a national of State B is broadcast in State A: there is material reciprocity and payment may be claimed. The same is not true of a phonogram made by a national of State C, since his own country gives no remuneration and there is no reciprocity.'

Example 2:

'State A limits remuneration to broadcasting; State B makes no reservation; the Performers and/or Producers of a State B recording can only claim, in State A, for broadcasting use: whereas those of State A can claim payment, in State B, for both broadcasting and public communication.'

There is however one limit to the application of the material reciprocity rule. A state which gives the right of equitable remuneration only to performers cannot cut back rights in respect of a state which gives the right only to phonogram producers and vice versa and a state which gives the right to both cannot cut back in respect of a state which gives it only to one.

Any of these reservations can be made at any time, not only at the time of ratification. Equally each reservation can be withdrawn at any time, or reduced in its scope, by notifying the Secretary General of the United Nations.[5] This gives all member states a great deal of flexibility.

1 See para 3.20 above.
2 See para 21.57 below.
3 Kaminstein Report on art 16.
4 *WIPO Guide to Rome* 16.9.
5 Art 18.

13. Protection of broadcasting organisations – article 13

8.31 The broadcasting organisations are granted an absolute right similar to phonogram producers in article 10, but the structure of the article is similar to article 7 dealing with the rights given to performers. They have the right to authorise or prohibit the rebroadcasting and the fixation of their broadcasts and the reproduction of fixations of their broadcasts made without their consent or for different purposes.

Rebroadcasting – article 13(a)

8.32 It is clear from the definition of 'broadcasting' in article 3(f) that as it covers only the transmission by wireless means, cable transmission is excluded.

It is also clear from the definition of 'rebroadcasting' in article 3(g) that this covers only simultaneous broadcasting by another organisation. The case of a deferred relay is covered by 13(b) as the broadcast must be fixed first before a deferred relay can take place.

Fixation of a broadcast – article 13(b)

8.33 It was agreed by the Conference that the prohibition against fixing the broadcast shall extend to fixing parts of the broadcast.[1] On the other hand the Conference refused to decide the much debated question whether a slide picture of a telecast is part of it. This question is therefore to be decided by national legislation, or in its absence, by the courts. The point is not without importance, particularly in the field of 'news of the day', where television competes directly with the press. Even if national legislation is silent on the point, it seems likely that a newspaper taking from a telecast a picture of an important event, eg the police dealing with demonstrators, or the winning goal of a football match and publishes it in the morning edition of the paper, this would be considered an act of unfair competition in most jurisdictions.

From a technical point of view, it would appear that a picture out of a telecast is as much 'part of the film' as a track or even a few characteristic bars are 'part of a phonogram'.[2]

1 Kaminstein Report under art 13.
2 See para 8.24 above.

Reproduction of a fixation of the broadcast – article 13(c)

8.34 This is an infringement if either the fixation itself was made without the broadcaster's consent (article 13(c)(i)), or if the fixation was made under article 15 (private use, etc) and the reproduction is made for purposes different from those named in article 15. This provision is exactly parallel with article 7(c)(i) and (iii).[1]

As soon as the broadcasting organisation has authorised the fixation of the broadcast, the right under article 13(c)(i) is exhausted. If, for instance, national legislation provides an exception for the fixation of television programmes in schools solely for the purposes of teaching, this is covered by article 15(1)(d). If, however, the school makes reproductions of the broadcast in the form of videocassettes and sells them article 13(c)(ii) is infringed.

1 See paras 8.18 and 8.20 above.

Communication to the public of television broadcasts – article 13(d)

8.35 The originating broadcasting organisation has a right to prohibit such communication to the public, if it is made in places accessible to the public against payment of an entrance fee. This provision was thought to be of great importance by the broadcasters, because in the case of sport the public showing of a football match or an athletic meeting would reduce the 'gate' for the promoters and they would therefore insist on a higher fee for the televising of the event. Thus it was argued that it is essential for the broadcasting organisation to be able to control the public showing of the event, at least within a certain radius of the location where the sporting event took place. However, the 1950s, when the drafts for the Rome Convention were made, were only the early days of television. As soon as most households in the country concerned have a television set the problem becomes far less important, though it can be said never to disappear completely.

The fee payable must be an 'entrance charge'. Charges made for food and drink in an hotel or restaurant where the event is shown on the television screen do not qualify under the article.

The most important omission from article 13 is the right to control transmission by wire, which is excluded because article 3(f) defines broadcasting as 'the transmission by wireless means'. This was realised by the Conference but, as at the time of the Conference hardly any country had legislation to protect broadcasters in this respect, it was not included. The phenomenon usually referred to 'cable' or CATV (Community Antennae Television) may have to be dealt with at a possible Revision Conference.

Whether the transmission of a programme by space satellite constitutes 'broadcasting' was the subject of argument during the preparatory stage of the Satellite Convention.[1] It would appear that whilst satellite broadcasting is transmitted via an earth station (known as 'point to point satellite') the definition of broadcasting in article 3(f) excludes it, as the definition prescribes transmission by wireless means 'for public reception' and reception by an earth station from a satellite may not be held to be 'public reception'. If however, in the 1980s broadcasts via satellite become directly receivable in the home by fixing an additional gadget to a television receiver, the broadcasting of programmes via satellite would be 'for public reception' and the Convention would apply. In any event the definition of broadcasting in article 3(f) would have to be re-examined by a possible Revision Conference in the light of the technology then available.

If protection under article 13(d) is claimed, national law may 'determine the conditions under which it may be exercised'. This seems to be a reference to the possibility of countries introducing a compulsory licence.[2]

1 See para 10.01 below.
2 See Nordemann, op cit, p 320.

14. Term of rights (duration) – article 14

8.36 As the Report points out there are two questions to be settled with regard to the duration of protection: when the term should start and how long it should be.[1] There is also a third: whether there should be comparison of terms as in the Berne Convention.[2] The duration is always determined by the law of the country in which protection is claimed. This is the result of the rule of national treatment in article 2. It is only if the country in which protection is claimed grants to its own nationals a shorter term than 20 years that the Convention comes into play and a foreign right owner protected under the Convention can claim the 20-year term.

1 Report on art 14.
2 See para 4.33 above.

8.37 *Starting point.* The Convention provides two starting points:

(a) For live performances and live broadcasts the period starts, logically, when the performance or the broadcast takes place (article 14(b) and (c)) as that is the time from which possible infringements, eg by unauthorised fixation or rebroadcasting, can start.
(b) For fixations, that is phonograms and the performances incorporated therein, and fixed broadcasts, which in law constitute a phonogram, the term starts when the fixation is made.

8.38 *Length of protection.* The Convention provides a minimum term of 20 years. The computation is from the end of the year when the first fixation was made, or the performance or broadcast took place, to the end of the twentieth year. However, this is only a minimum and many legislations exceed it. The most common term seems to be either 50 years (United Kingdom and the legislations stemming from the United Kingdom like Australia or India) or 25 years (Germany and Scandinavia). The longest term is that of the United States: 75 years.[1]

There are good arguments for a duration exceeding the minimum for phonograms and broadcasts. The most successful recordings are often still popular, or experience a revival, after 20 years have passed, famous broadcasts are often 'quoted' and there seems no reason why national legislation should not protect them. The strongest case is that of the performer where – if the duration is only 20 or 25 years – the recordings of the same performer at the peak of his or her career in the 20s or 30s would have to compete with his or her own recordings made in middle age. It had been envisaged that the protection for performers should cover their lifetime. Against this the representatives of users (mainly the broadcasters) pointed out that as famous artists often fade from public life in their latter years it would be very difficult to find out whether and when an artist who had been famous in his 20s or even 50s had died and in the case of group performances such as orchestras, this would be impossible. Fifty years from fixation or performance which would cover all but very exceptional cases, would seem the fairest solution on the national level.

It has to be stressed however that under the Convention the right of the performer is only 'the possibility of preventing' (article 7) and if that is implemented by a protection under criminal law, time for prescription would run from the date of the offence, that is the infringement, regardless of how long after the performance that infringement took place. Equally, if the protection is based on the law of unfair competition there is no time limit.

1 US Copyright Law 1976, para 302(6).

8.39 *Comparison of terms.* The Hague Draft had a provision for comparison of terms[1] on the lines of the Berne Convention.[2] However, it was pointed out that with the different points of attachment in articles 5–7 the comparisons would be very complicated and at times conflicting.[3] The concept was therefore abandoned by the Conference. An exception is the term for secondary rights, where it is open to national legislations to introduce a comparison of terms by making the reservation under article 16/1 a(iv).[4] In respect of the right of reproduction of fixations (as opposed to the secondary rights in article (12)), the Report points out[5] that comparison of terms was not considered essential: 'mainly because in most countries unauthorised reproduction is regarded as an act of unfair competition without any well-defined time limits'. It is submitted that that is based on a fallacy. If in a country where the term is 25 years a fixation, say a phonogram, is reproduced without authorisation and published, the right owner would probably fail in many jurisdictions under the law of unfair competition, as the courts would apply the maxim 'lex specialis derogat legem generalem' and hold that when the special law (copyright law) lays down that after the term of protection has expired the work falls into the public domain, it cannot be revived by applying the law of unfair competition. If it were otherwise most copyrights could be made perpetual and the balance struck in the public interest by granting an exclusive right, but for a limited duration, would be upset.[5]

1 See Report under art 14.
2 See para 5.54 above.
3 See Nordemann, op cit, p 322.
4 Kaminstein Report, under article 14.
5 See Nordemann op cit, p 356; for detailed treatment of the problem: see Ulmer *Der Wettbewerbliche Schutz*, pp 189, 194.

15. Exceptions – article 15

8.40 This article deals with the exceptions permissible under national legislations which appear in the copyright conventions.[1]

These exceptional uses are free uses without the payment of compensation. They must not be confused with compulsory licences, where the use of the right is permitted without the authorisation of the right owner under certain conditions, but against equitable remuneration.

It has to be stressed that these are only facultative. If the national legislation of the country in which protection is claimed does not make them explicitly then they do not apply.

The exceptions apply mainly to the rights of phonogram producers (article 10) and broadcasting organisations (article 13). The performers' 'right to prohibit' (article 7) is not self-executing. Thus the rights of performers stem from the national legislation required by article 7 and any exceptions will be contained in the national legislation.

The exceptions permissible under national law are of two kinds:

(a) All exceptions provided in the national legislation 'in connection with the protection of Copyright in literary and artistic works'.[2] There is however a limit to this faculty to provide exceptions: compulsory licences are not permitted, unless they are provided in the Convention (article 7/2(2), article 12 and article 13(d) and nothing else).

(b) The exceptions provided in the Convention (article 15/1). These are:

1 Arts 9/2, 10/2, 10 bis, 11 bis Appendix art II(5) of the Berne Convention and art IV bis/2 of the UCC.
2 Art 15/2. This includes the (unspecified) 'petites exceptions'.

Private use – article 15/1(a)

8.41 Private use can best be defined as use which is neither public nor for profit. Thus if a private person makes a copy of a phonogram from a broadcast and plays it at home that is private use. If he plays it in a discotheque it is not. Equally, if he makes further copies and sells them to his friends or to a shop it is not private use. As the *WIPO Guide* points out,[1] since the making of the Convention 'the ease with which recordings of high quality can be made these days places the idea of private use in a new dimension'. The language of the private use exception in the Berne Convention[2] goes to the heart of the problem. Exceptions are permitted in special cases 'provided that such reproduction does not conflict with a normal exploitation of the work and does not unreasonably prejudice the legitimate interests of the author'. The private copying of phonograms (or of videograms which are films) would seem both to conflict with a normal exploitation and to prejudice the legitimate interests of the author. This is a problem national legislation will have to deal with.[3]

1 *WIPO Guide to Rome* 15.2.
2 Art 9/2 see para 5.39 above.
3 It has done so in Germany and Austria; see 'Home Taping', para 12.12 below.

Use of short excerpts – article 15/1(b)

8.42 This use is to be made 'in connection with the reporting of current events'. It applies mainly in broadcasting. The term 'excerpt' or 'fragment'[1] signifies that it must only be a part and a 'short' part at that. As most usual news programmes are 15 minutes or less, the 'short excerpt' must be quite brief and it must be of such character and only of such duration as is necessary to 'support, underline or illustrate the news item'.[2]

1 In the French text.
2 See Nordemann, op cit, p 324.

Ephemeral fixation by a broadcasting organisation by means of its own facilities and for its own broadcasts – article 15/1(c)

8.43 This exception follows the Berne Convention.[1] Its purpose is to meet the technical needs of broadcasting organisations to make their own recordings, in order to defer the broadcasting of programmes instead of broadcasting them live. These recordings must be destroyed after a reasonable time and the time stipulated in most national legislations is the same time as applies to the 'ephemeral' recordings of copyright works.

The limits of this provision imposed by the words 'by means of its own facilities' and the words 'for its own broadcast' are the same as in the Berne Convention.

1 Art 11 bis, see para 5.43 above.

Use 'solely for the purpose of teaching or scientific research' – article 15/1(d)

8.44 This provision was inserted at the request of the Indian delegation and is a forerunner of the exceptional uses permitted to developing countries introduced by the Berne Revision Conference in 1971.[1] The concept of 'teaching purposes' will no doubt be interpreted by the courts in the same way as when used in other international copyright conventions. Cases of use of performances, phonograms and broadcasts 'for the purpose of scientific research' are not easy to envisage.

The WIPO commentary suggests that 'The paragraph was intended to act as a hint to the member states that they should in principle consider treating both Copyright and Neighbouring Rights equally in this respect.'[2]

1 See para 6.45 above.
2 *WIPO Guide to Rome* 15.9.

16. Acquired rights – article 20

8.45   This article enshrines in the Convention two well-known principles of law which apply both to national legislation and to international conventions. Rights acquired in any contracting state by any of the three beneficiaries of the Convention shall not be affected. They have become the property of a person or organisation and cannot be taken away (article 20.1). In order to qualify as an 'acquired right' it must have existed in the contracting state before the date of coming into force of the Convention in that state.

The second rule is not mandatory like the first: No state shall be bound to apply the provisions of the Convention to protect rights which arise from events (performances, fixations, broadcasts) which took place before the Convention came into force in that state (article 20/2). Conversely, there is nothing to prevent a state from granting rights retroactively, as long as by so doing it does not violate the first rule, ie prejudice someone else's acquired rights.

17. Other sources of protection – article 21

8.46   The Convention shall not prejudice other sources of protection for the three beneficiaries. Such sources can be contained in national or in international law. On the national level these sources could be the law of unfair competition or of 'passing off' or trademark infringements in the case of phonogram producers; personality rights, moral rights or the law of defamation in the case of performers; public laws and regulations in the case of broadcasters.

On the international level the Phonogram Convention (1971)[1] and the Satellite Convention (1974)[2] are examples.

1 See ch 9 below.
2 See ch 10 below.

18. Special agreements – article 22

8.47   The contracting states reserve the right to enter into special agreements among themselves, if those agreements give more extensive rights to the beneficiaries. The precedent for this article is article 20 of the Berne Convention. That article was inserted, because towards the end of the nineteenth century some of the contracting states had concluded bilateral agreements and those bilateral agreements gave in some cases more extensive rights which the new non-multilateral Convention wished to preserve.[1] There is, however, an important distinction: the Berne Convention has only one beneficiary, the author, whereas the Rome Convention has three. As the article speaks of 'Performers, Producers of Phonograms *or* Broadcasting Organisations' as beneficiaries of more extensive rights, it would appear that special agreements could be made for the benefit of one beneficiary instead of the beneficiaries as a whole, which might upset the balance of interests on which the Convention is based.

No bilateral agreements were in fact made under this article. The Phonogram Convention and the Satellite Convention are multilateral agreements and not limited to countries which are parties to the Rome Convention and thus fall under article 21 not article 22. The European Television Agreement,[2] which is a multinational and regional agreement, preceded the Rome Convention.

1 After the Berne Convention few bilateral agreements were made. They were mainly on the duration of protection. Cf in the field of industrial property on the other hand where art 19 of the Paris Convention for the Protection of Industrial Property (1883) contained a similar provision, a number of special agreements were in fact made.
2 See para 11.03 below.

19. Closed convention – articles 23 and 24

8.48 Articles 23 and 24, together with article 1,[1] govern the relations between copyright and neighbouring rights. Articles 23 and 24 make the Rome Convention a closed convention. In order to ratify it a state must not only have been invited to the Diplomatic Conference, or be a member of the United Nations, but also be either a party to UCC or a member of the Berne Union. This is due to the view, which was strongly held by several countries, that the unity of copyright or the primacy of author's rights, cannot be preserved unless there is this 'link' between copyright and neighbouring rights. Without it, it is said there could be countries where the three beneficiaries of the Rome Convention would be protected whilst the author remained unprotected. As the work is the basis of any performance, phonogram or broadcast, that would be an absurd state of affairs. Whilst there is great force in this argument, those in favour of an 'open convention' argue that there are performers who do not perform literary or artistic works and many performers who perform works in the public domain and that there are a few phonograms which do not contain works and many which contain only works in the public domain and that the same is true of a large number of broadcasts.

With the 1971 Revision of the Berne Convention and the UCC and the large number of countries which have ratified either or both conventions, this controversy has lost much of its importance, as most of the countries wishing to ratify the Rome Convention will be members of one of the two copyright conventions and the few wishing to ratify it which are not would be encouraged to ratify one of the two copyright conventions simultaneously in order to qualify.[2]

1 See para 8.05 above.
2 Columbia in 1976 and El Salvador in 1979 have done this, ratifying the Rome Convention and the UCC at the same time.

20. Application of the convention – article 26

8.49 This article sets out the obligation of contracting states. It is fashioned on article X of the UCC (1952) and was incorporated into the Berne Convention at the 1967 Revision.[1] Each state undertakes to adopt 'the measures necessary to ensure the application of the Convention'. What these measures are depends on the country's constitution.[2] The measures necessary to ensure the application of the Convention will be administrative in countries of Group 1 where conventions are self-applying, whereas they will be legislative or legislative and administrative in Group 2.

The Rome Convention is rather exceptional in this respect, as it contains provisions which will need legislative action even in countries where international conventions are self-applying. The rights to be given to performers under article 7 or the choice of the right owner under article 12 are cases where choices have to be made by national legislation. There are, however, no sanctions to enforce this provision. If country A, which has ratified the Convention, does not take the necessary measures to ensure its application, country B which is another convention country whose nationals are aggrieved could use article 30 and ask for arbitration or refer the dispute to the International Court of Justice. So far no dispute in the field of intellectual property law has been referred to the International Court of Justice. If a dispute were referred to the Court, the Court could only give an 'opinion' on the state of international law on the point and the country whose laws do not conform with that opinion would be expected to revise its law accordingly. However, once more there are no sanctions.

Article 26.2 is a little stricter than article 36.2 of the Berne Convention. The latter requires that the law of the ratifying country complies with the Convention, when the Convention comes into force in that country. Article 26.2 of the Rome Convention requires that the national law must conform 'at the time of deposit', that is three months earlier.[3]

1   Art 36.
2   See para 3.30 above.
3   See para 5.66 above.

21. Denunciation – article 28

8.50 Any contracting state may denounce the Convention after five years from the date on which the Convention came into force in that country. The delay is built in to give states an opportunity to test the effects of the Convention on the country.

There is also an automatic cessation, which takes effect if a contracting state ceases to be a party to either of the two copyright conventions (Berne Convention and UCC). This is part of the link between copyright and neighbouring rights.[1]

1   See para 8.06 above.

22. Intergovernmental committee and revision (article 32 and article 29)

8.51 The Intergovernmental Committee is given two functions by the Convention:
(a) 'To study questions concerning the application and operation of the Convention'. A more far-reaching proposal to supervise the life of the Convention under which the contracting states were to file periodic reports on measures taken, under preparation or contemplated in fulfilment of the Convention was rejected and the Intergovernmental Committee was created instead. Its functions have therefore to be seen in this light. They have been interpreted as advisory functions and have played an important part in the life of the Convention. Prior to the ratification of the Convention by Norway the Committee gave an opinion at the request of the Norwegian Government on the interpretation of article 12. In 1974 the Committee adopted a 'Model Law' with a Commentary on the Convention. In 1979 the Committee adopted an extensive report and recommendations on the practical application of the Convention.[1]

(b) 'To collect proposals and to prepare documentation for possible revision of the Convention'. This function has not yet been exercised, but if the Berne Convention is taken as a precedent, the span between revision conferences would be approximately 20 years and the first Revision Conference may take place in the 1980s.

A revision conference can be requested by any contracting state and must be supported by not less than half of the contracting states. It is convened by the three secretariats 'in co-operation with the Intergovernmental Committee'. A revised text has to have two-thirds of the votes of all contracting states and two-thirds of the votes of the states attending the revision conference.[2]

The purpose of a revision is not spelled out, but by analogy to the Berne Convention, where article 27 does spell it out, it is implied that the aim is improvement of the protection granted by the Convention. As the *WIPO Guide* puts it, 'a Revision Conference will probably be called with the aim of filling gaps which exist in the protection given to its beneficiaries'.[3] This applies particularly with regard to the new technological developments which have taken place since 1961, such as cable television satellites and videograms.[4]

1 Report of the Subcommittee of the Intergovernmental Committee on the Implementation of the Rome Convention – ILO/UNESCO/WIPO/ICR/SCI/IMP5 – Geneva, 9 March 1979.
2 Art 29/2.
3 *WIPO Guide to Rome* 29.1
4 See para 12.28, para 12.31 and 12.35 below.

23. State of ratifications and accessions and reservations on 1 January 1983

8.52

Contracting states		Date it came into force	Reservations
AUSTRIA	R[1]	9 June 1973	Article 16(q)(a)(iii) and (iv) and (1)(b).
BRAZIL	R	29 September 1965	
CHILE	R	5 September 1974	
COLOMBIA	A[1]	17 June 1976	
CONGO	A	18 May 1964	Article 5(3) concerning article 5(1)(c) and 16(1)(a)(i).
COSTA RICA	A	9 September 1971	
CZECHOSLOVAKIA	A	14 August 1964	Article 16(1)(a)(iii) and (iv).
DENMARK	R	23 September 1965	Articles 6(2), 16(1)(a)(ii) and (iv) and 17.
ECUADOR	R	18 May 1964	
EL SALVADOR	A	29 June 1979	
FIJI	A	11 April 1972	Articles 5(3) concerning article 5(1)(b), 6(2) and 16(1)(a)(i).
GERMANY, FEDERAL REPUBLIC OF	R	21 October 1966	Articles 5(3) concerning articles 5(1)(b) and 16(1)(a)(iv).
GUATEMALA	A	14 January 1977	
IRELAND	R	19 September 1979	Article 5(3) concerning 5(1)(b); article 6(2) and article 16(1)(a)(ii).

State of ratifications and accessions and reservations 237

Contracting states		Date it came into force	Reservations
ITALY	R	8 April 1975	Articles 6(2), 16(1)(a)(ii), (iii) and (iv), 16(1)(b) and 17.
LUXEMBOURG	A	25 February 1976	Articles 5(3) concerning article 5(1)(a) and (b); 16(1)(a)(i) and 16(1)(b).
MEXICO	R	18 May 1964	
NIGER	A	18 May 1964	Articles 5(3) concerning article 5(1)(c) and 16(1)(a)(i).
NORWAY	A	10 July 1978	Articles 6(2); 16(1)(a)(ii), (iii) and (iv).
PARAGUAY	R	26 February 1970	
SWEDEN	R	18 May 1964	Articles 6(2), 16(1)(a)(ii) and (iv), 16(1)(b) and 17.
UNITED KINGDOM	R	18 May 1964	Articles 5(3) concerning articles 5(1)(b), 6(2) and 16(1)(a)(ii), (iii) and (iv); the same declarations were made for Gibraltar and Bermuda.
URUGUAY	A	4 July 1977.	

TOTAL: 23

1 R = Ratification. A = Accession.

Chapter 9
The Phonogram Convention (1971)

Summary

1. History 9.01
2. Structure of the Convention 9.03
3. Definitions – article 1 9.04
4. The scope of protection – article 2 9.05
5. The means of protection – article 3 9.06
6. Term of protection – article 4 9.11
7. Formalities – article 5 9.12
8. Limitation of protection – article 6 9.13
9. Miscellaneous provisions – article 7 9.14
10. Administrative clauses – articles 8–14 9.15
11. State of ratifications and accessions 9.16

1. History

9.01 Unlike in the case of the Rome Convention the gestation period of the Phonogram Convention was very short. The problem was first raised during a meeting of an ad hoc committee for the revision of the UCC in May 1970[1] and subsequently at the joint meeting of the Intergovernmental Committee of the UCC and the Permanent Committee of the Berne Union in September 1970 dealing with the revision of the UCC. The urgency of the matter was recognised, but it was considered structurally difficult to deal with the problem within the framework of the UCC or indeed the Berne Convention. A working paper was drawn up by experts from France, Germany, United Kingdom and the United States[2] to form the basis for a meeting of a committee of experts held in Paris in May 1971, which produced a draft of a convention. This in turn was put before a diplomatic conference held in Geneva in October 1971 and adopted with some modifications. The Convention came into force (three months after deposit of the fifth ratification) on 18 April 1973.

The interval of only a year and a half between the first recognition of need and the signing of an international convention and another year and a half for its entry into force is, appropriately for a phonogram convention, a record in creating an international instrument, certainly in the intellectual property field. The Convention had been ratified by 36 states[3] on 1 January 1983. As among them are nearly all the major markets for phonograms 'a kind of *cordon sanitaire* has been created by providing that in case of an unauthorised duplication the importation and distribution in the contracting State can thus be prohibited'.[4] The reasons for achieving this speed was that the 'mischief' to be remedied, ie the unauthorised reproduction of phonograms, was wide-spread and required an urgent remedy and that the structure and form chosen for the Convention are simple and based on legal concepts accepted by most countries.[5]

1 See Copyright (1970) p 160.
2 André Kerever of France, Eugen Ulmer and Elisabeth Steup of Germany, William Wallace of the UK and Barbara Ringer of the USA.
3 See list para 9.11 below.
4 Ulmer 'The Phonogram Convention ICC 3/1972, 317 at p 320, and Stewart 'Geneva Convention' Copyright (1973) p 100.
5 The Report, para 25, says: 'These concepts of simplicity and universality should ... be reflected in a Convention, consisting of a relatively restricted number of articles, which should be limited to determining the obligations of contracting States, while leaving to them, the choice of the legal means to assure the protection'.

9.02 A phonogram is a mixture of the exercise of artistic and technical skills.[1] In its creation there are three stages. The first stage is the recording. This involves the choice of a work to be recorded or of its adaptation, the casting of artists, the rehearsals in the studio, the artistic and technical shaping of the performance to make it suitable for a recording and finally the fixing of that performance – unique, but until then ephemeral – on a material support. This is an artistic activity. The second stage is the reproduction of that first fixation, pressing of discs, making of tapes, cassettes etc. This requires technical skill. The third stage is the marketing of the phonograms, taking the work to the general public. This is a commercial operation. The 'pirate' cuts out the first stage entirely, he carries out the second stage mostly very imperfectly and concentrates on the third stage. The profits are large because he pays neither the authors (composers, text writers, arrangers) nor the performers nor the artistic and technical personnel in the studio. He takes no commercial risk, as he pirates only the works and performances which have already proved best-sellers. He thus deprives the authors and the performers of their royalties and endangers the very existence of the producer.

'Record piracy'[2] had become widespread in some developing countries of Asia where in some cases it was not an infringement under the national law and the countries were not parties to any intellectual property conventions[3] as well as in the United States where phonograms were not protected until 1972 and in some European countries where, although legal protection existed, it was difficult to enforce.

Two forms of 'piracy' which are also widespread are not covered by this Convention:

(1) 'Bootlegging' which is the unauthorised recording of a live performance either in a concert hall or off the air. The right involved is that of the performer. It is covered by article 7 of the Roman Convention.[4]
(2) 'Videograms'[5] as a phonogram is defined in article 1 as an 'exclusively aural fixation of sounds'. These audiovisual productions, ie films and videograms (film produced mainly for use in the home) are excluded from the protection of the Convention. The reason for this limitation, in spite of the fact that it was already known in 1971 that videocasettes would become subject to widespread piracy, lies in the differing treatment of audiovisual fixations in national legislations. When there is an original work of authorship it is protected as a 'cinematographic work' and gets copyright protection under the Berne Convention[6] and the UCC.[7] In the Anglo-Saxon jurisdiction the copyright is vested in the producer and he can proceed against unauthorised duplications as a right-owner. In most of the Latin jurisdictions he has to acquire the copyright from the authors, of whom there are many[8] by contract. Some countries, eg Germany and Austria, give the author of the original work a copyright as well as giving a neighbouring right to the producer of the film. In these countries films that are said to lack original creativity, eg nature scenes or daily events

are not protected by copyright but by the 'neighbouring right' of the producer.[9]

1 See Stewart 'Geneva Convention for the Protection of Phonograms' Copyright (1973) p 100.
2 See Davies *Record Piracy* (1981) p 2.
3 Masouyé/Wallace *WIPO Guide to the Phonogram Convention* VIII.
4 See para 8.18 above.
5 See para 12.15 below.
6 Art 14 bis. See para 5.50 above.
7 Art I. See para 6.04 above.
8 See para 5.50 and 5.51 above.
9 See Ulmer, *Phonogram Convention* ICC 3/1972 p 321.

2. Structure of the Convention

9.03 Unlike the copyright conventions or the Rome Convention, the Phonogram Convention is not based on the principle of national treatment. It also does not provide for minima of protection which the national ratifying countries have to grant either by legislation or by direct application of the Convention. Instead the Convention is based on 'the acceptance of mutual obligations between Contracting States.'[1]

The Convention is further based on the principle of non-retroactivity (article 7(3)).[2] The criterion of the nationality of the producer is the only applicable criterion, (unlike the Rome Convention)[3] with a sole exception provided by article 7(4) which allows countries which already apply fixation as sole criterion to keep it.

The protection of phonograms (unlike that under the Rome Convention)[4] extends not only to the making but also to the importation and distribution of phonograms (article 2).

The choice of the means by which the protection is achieved is left to national legislation (article 3).

No reservations are permitted with the sole exception of article 7(4) (article 10).

No compulsory licences are permitted with exception of duplication of phonograms 'solely for the purpose of teaching or scientific research' (article 6).

1 *WIPO Guide to the Phonogram Convention* 3.7.
2 Report para 26.
3 See para 8.10 above.
4 Art 10, see para 8.29 above.

3. Definitions – article 1

9.04 The definitions of 'phonogram' (article 1(a)) and of 'producer of phonograms' (article 1(b)) are the same as in the Rome Convention.[1]

The definition of phonogram as an 'exclusively aural fixation' excludes videograms.[2]

The question of whether the soundtrack of a film is a phonogram was debated at the Conference.[3] One theory is that a film consists of two parts, one visual and one aural and the two are inextricably linked and form a single entity. The soundtrack being an integral part of that entity, the film does therefore not fall under the Convention. The legal result of this theory is that if the soundtrack is 'pirated' and marketed as a phonogram the film producer can take action in those countries where he has a copyright or in the countries where he has not if he has acquired the copyrights of all original authors.

The second theory and – it is submitted – the better view is that 'when an

Definitions – article 1

exclusively aural fixation of the soundtrack is made, the resulting recording is a phonogram within the meaning of the Convention'[4] The Report adds that the 'Soundtrack is almost invariably edited or otherwise altered in the process of producing the recording, so that a new exclusively aural version is created'. Technically the soundtrack of a cinematographic film can be recorded separately and often is and joined later to the celluloid. On the other hand, television films are normally recorded together so that there never is an exclusively aural fixation. An exclusively oral fixation made by a broadcasting organisation in the course of a broadcast is protected as a phonogram.

An 'ephemeral recording'[5] made by a broadcasting organisation is an exclusively aural fixation and therefore protected under the Convention.[6]

The Conference expressed the view that the person to be protected should be the person who first fixes the phonogram as such.[7] The 'duplicate' must embody 'all or a substantial part' of the sounds fixed on the phonogram. The Report[8] makes it clear that 'substantial' expresses not only a quantitative but also a qualitative evaluation and that therefore 'quite a small part may be substantial'. The decision what is or what is not a substantial part is ultimately a question of fact for the courts in the country where protection is claimed. However the courts are likely to interpret the provision widely in favour of the right owner as the methods used may vary widely from cutting and putting together to superimposing or combining extracts and as the *WIPO Guide* puts it 'it is not felt right that an infringer should escape on the pretext that he has not taken the whole'.[9]

'Producer of phonograms' is defined as the person who first fixes the sounds of a performance. This excludes the mere 'presser' of records as under the Rome Convention.[10]

'Duplicate' is defined as 'an article which contains sounds taken directly or indirectly from a phonogram'.

'Indirect copying' is meant to cover copying from the broadcasting of a phonogram[11] or from a copy of a phonogram (two successive pirates, one copying from the other).[12]

'Distribution to the public' is defined as an act of offering duplicates 'directly or indirectly to the general public or any section thereof'.

'Indirect' offering would, for instance, cover the offering to a wholesaler for sale to a retailer or offering copies by advertisement, as the language of the Convention does not require that the infringing duplicates actually change hands.[13] Offering copies to a section of the public would cover, for instance, offering them to the members of a record club or book club.

The definition is also wide enough to cover the hiring, as opposed to the sale of illegitimate phonograms. The Report points out[14] that the definition 'makes no specific reference to commercial purposes in order not to restrict unnecessarily the field of application of the Convention'. It is sufficient that it is intentionally made available to the general public.

1 Art 3(b) and art 3(c).
2 See para 12.45 below.
3 See Report, paras 35 and 36.
4 Report, para 36.
5 See Rome Convention, art 15.1(c) para 8.20 above.
6 Report, para 39.
7 Report, para 38.
8 Report, para 41.
9 *WIPO Guide to the Phonogram Convention* 1.10.
10 See para 9.24 above.
11 Report, para 40.
12 *WIPO Guide to the Phonogram Convention* 1.9.

13 See *WIPO Guide to the Phonogram Convention* 1.13.
14 Report, para 43.

4. The scope of protection – article 2

9.05 The two articles which are the core of the Convention answer the three essential questions:

(1) Who is protected?
(2) Against what?
(3) By what means?

Article 2 deals with the first two questions: the scope of protection, article 3 deals with the third: the means of protection.

(1) Who is protected?

(a) We have already seen that the person or entity protected is the one who first fixes the sounds of a performance on a material support. This, like under the Rome Convention,[1] excludes the mere presser or manufacturer of phonograms or anyone else further down the chain such as a wholesaler or retailer.

(b) The producer, so defined, must be a national of a contracting state. Thus the sole point of attachment is nationality – unlike the Rome Convention, where a choice of options is given to contracting states.[2]

1 See para 9.24 below.
2 See para 8.10 above.

(2) Against what is he protected?

The protection is against (a) the making of illicit duplicates, (b) the importation of such duplicates, (c) the distribution of such duplicates. The three activities which are thereby identified as the three principal acts of piracy.

A duplicate is illicit when it is 'made without the consent of the producer'. The Report[1] makes the point that it was understood that under the domestic law of the contracting state consent may be given 'by the original producer or by his successor in title or by the exclusive licensee in the Contracting State concerned'.

This is wider than article 10 of the Rome Convention, which does not cover importation or distribution. The only limiting factor is the proviso that the making as well as the importation of such illicit duplicates must be 'for the purpose of distribution to the public'. The effect of this is that a person who brings some pirated phonograms home from a trip abroad is not an importer and a person who makes a copy of a phonogram and gives it to a friend as a present is not a distributor. In both cases the purpose is not distribution to the public which in nearly all cases is a commercial purpose.

Whether in each case of making or of importation the purpose of such manufacture or importation was a commercial one, because it was meant for distribution to the public, is a question for the courts in the country where protection is claimed. It will be a matter for the courts to judge from the circumstances in each particular case. In the case of a shop with a stock of illicit records or cassettes it will not be difficult to infer that they were 'for distribution to the public' and there will be no need for the plaintiff or the prosecutor to prove that the shop keeper has actually sold some of the stock, nor that he knew that the stock consisted of pirated copies. Knowledge which will have a bearing on the damages in civil cases and the fines in criminal cases will no doubt be inferred from the price (usually well below the price of legitimate stock) and the circumstances (under the counter). However the important thing is that even discs and tapes openly displayed and offered for sale at ordinary prices will constitute an infringement.

1   Report, para 48.

5. The means of protection – article 3

9.06 Because the means of protection vary greatly the protection was very uneven and the level of protection varied from country to country. In some countries the producers of phonograms have a copyright which is the most effective form of protection. Examples are the United Kingdom and countries of the British Commonwealth, eg Australia, Canada, Ghana, India, Kenya, New Zealand and countries formerly in the British Commonwealth which have legislations similar to that of the United Kingdom, eg Eire, Israel, and South Africa and since 1972 also the United States.

In other countries the producers of phonograms have a neighbouring right which, for this purpose, has the same effect as a copyright, ie an exclusive reproduction right, eg Austria, Germany, Italy, Japan, the Scandinavian countries.

In some countries where there is no specific right, be it a copyright or a neighbouring right, remedies exist under the law of unfair competition, eg France, Belgium, the Netherlands.

The history of the development in the United States is a good example of the comparative merits of the above mentioned systems. The Copyright Act 1909, not surprisingly, did not deal with phonograms. It was in force until it was revised in 1976. To begin with the courts held that unlawful duplication was an act of unfair competition. However, in 1964, the Supreme Court in its decisions in the *Sears* and *Compco* cases[1] held that to forbid the copying of an article, which was neither patented nor copyrighted, would be contrary to the principles of federal law and the Constitution,[2] which provided for the protection of authors and inventors in their works ('writings') and inventions for a limited period.

The uncertainty of the law (the pirates argued that what they were doing was legal and even in the public interest, as they were selling at much lower prices), as well as the difficulties and delays of unfair competition suits, led to a situation where the estimated annual sales of the pirates amounted to a hundred million dollars or a quarter of the total sales.[3]

As a result the government had to intervene and an amendment to the United States Copyright Act 1909 was passed giving phonogram producers a copyright limited to an exclusive reproduction right (United States Law of 15 October 1971, Law 92-140) and was eventually merged into the Copyright Revision Law in 1976.

In view of the uneven levels of protection and the difficulties of persuading some countries to change their laws, as well as the urgency dictated by a worsening of the international situation, which enabled the pirates to shunt the unauthorised duplicates from country to country with impunity, it was decided to go for the solution which would enable at least all the major countries to ratify the Convention, without changing their laws. The Conference thus decided to follow the draft of the experts which was before them and 'to enumerate in this Article the legal means by which the Convention will be implemented, it being understood that these means are not cumulative and that free choice of one or more is left to each Contracting State'.[4] The choice is not entirely free, because article 3 prescribes that domestic law must 'include' one or more of four options: 1) a copyright; 2) other specific rights; 3) protection by the law of unfair competition; 4) protection by penal sanctions.

1   *Sears, Roebuck & Co v Stiffd Co* 376 US 225 (1961) and *Compco Corpn v Day-Brite Lighting Inc* 376 US 234 (1964).
2   Article I, para 1/8.
3   The figures were given in a Statement of Congressman Celler, Chairman of the House Committee, in the Copyright Law Revision Hearings before the Subcommittee on Patents, Trademarks and Copyrights of the Senate Commission on the Judiciary, 90th Congress, 1st Session, ser 7, at 5(1971) and the figure of 100 million dollars was repeated in the presidential message commending the phonogram amendment of the Copyright Act 1909 to the US Congress.
4   Report, para 39.

(1) Copyright

9.07   This system 'treats the recording as not merely an industrial creation, but the product of skill and labour and hence its maker is entitled to the same, or virtually the same, rights as creators of works'.[1]

1   WIPO Guide to the Phonogram Convention 3.2.

(2) Other specific rights

9.08   This means a right similar to copyright which gives the producer the right to allow or forbid the duplication of his phonograms. These rights are often called neighbouring rights (a rather clumsy translation of the French 'droits voisins') or connected rights ('diritti conessi' in Italy) or related rights. All these expressions signify the connection, relation etc of these rights with copyright.

Whereas, however, the 'neighbouring right' sufficient to satisfy article 10 of the Rome Convention need only provide the right to allow or forbid the reproduction of the phonogram, the neighbouring right sufficient to satisfy this Convention must include a distribution right and the right to prevent importation of illicitly made phonograms.

(3) Protection by the law of unfair competition

9.09   Whereas both 1) and 2) are property rights 3) is not. This option is, as Ulmer puts it,[1] 'a concession to French legal doctrine. There is still reservation in France with regard to the recognition of neighbouring rights. Property rights are granted to authors only.'[2]

'Unfair competition' is defined in the Paris Convention for the Protection of Industrial Property[3] as 'any act of competition contrary to honest practices in industrial or commercial matters'. The 'pirates' certainly engage in acts 'contrary to honest practices' but protection by the law of unfair competition is different from protection by a property right in the following respects:[4]

(a)   It is not always applicable to dealers in illicitly made phonograms. Courts have held that although there is 'competition' between the producer of phonograms and the producer of pirated phonograms, there is no competition between the legitimate producer and a dealer in illicit phonograms.

(b)   It is not applicable if only the illicit manufacture had taken place and the illicitly made phonograms had not reached dealers or the general public, eg if a raid takes place on a warehouse where the pirated phonograms are stored or on the place where they are made, deception of the public will be difficult to prove.

(c)   To succeed in an action of unfair competition it is usually necessary for the plaintiff to prove that the illicit duplicate is liable to mislead the public. If the illicit duplicate bears an inscription on the label which is not misleading the action will fail.[5]

(d) The result of an action based on the law of unfair competition is an award of damages. The remedies of injunction and/or seizure of all offending material are often not available to the plaintiff and after a lengthy law suit damages are usually not recoverable as the defendant has by then either gone out of business or simply disappeared.

(e) It is difficult to secure a minimum of 20 years duration for protection by the law of unfair competition. The Report acknowledges this[6] but adds that the Conference 'assumed that in this case the protection should not in principle end before 20 years ... in order to ensure a balance between the different systems'. It is difficult to see how anyone can 'assume' that the courts will find unfair competition proven if the circumstances of the case do not warrant it. If for example a recording is deleted from the catalogue with the intention to reissue it later on in a different form and it is 'pirated', there is no competing phonogram available on the market at the time the illicit issue is offered for sale. It is difficult to see how a court would find unfair competition proven.

For these reasons 'the law relating to unfair competition cannot be considered a solid basis for the protection which is accorded under the Convention'.[7] Many other writers agree with this judgment.[8]

On the other hand it would appear that in France, where conventions are self-applying, the very act of illicit duplication is regarded as unfair competition, so that all the plaintiff has to prove is that he never authorised the duplications made by the defendant to give rise to a claim for damages under article 1382 of the Civil Code.[9] However this only applies to international situations.[10]

1 Ulmer 'Convention for the Protection of Producers of Phonograms against unauthorised Duplication of their Phonograms' IIC Vol 3/1972 p 317 at p 326.
2 France was in fact the first major country to ratify the Convention. On the other hand, of the 36 countries which have so far ratified it, only two chose the law of unfair competition as a means of protection under the Convention.
3 Art 10 bis.
4 See Stewart 'The Geneva Convention for the Protection of Phonograms' Copyright (1973) p 100.
5 In the US many pirated phonograms used to bear a notice saying: 'No permission to produce this recording has been obtained from anyone and no royalties have been paid to anyone'. The label had a skull and crossbones on it. No-one was deceived.
6 Report, para 51.
7 Ulmer, Phonogram Convention, IIC No 3/1972 p 317 at p 326.
8 See De Sanctis 'Some general considerations on the recent Geneva Convention for the protection of Phonograms' Copyright (1972) p 111; Ulmer, op cit; Pedrazzini *Festschrift für Rudolf Reinhardt* p 113 at p 123; Nordemann Vink, Hertin *Commentary on International Copyright in German speaking Countries and the EEC* p 354.
9 *CBS France v FNAC*, Tribunal de Commerce of Paris, 12 January 1976.
10 See para 14.32

(4) Penal sanctions

9.10 If a state adopts penal sanctions as the sole means of protection it must make it a criminal offence to do any of the acts set out in article 2.[1]

In other countries penal sanctions support the property right of the phonogram producer.

As long ago as 1959 Justice Burger, now Chief Justice of the United States, described record piracy as an activity which 'might better be described by other terms connoting larceny'.[2]

In Italy retailers selling 'pirated' phonograms have been convicted as receivers of stolen property. The court equated intellectual property with ordinary property and therefore, taking Chief Justice Burger's observations to their logical conclusion, regarded unauthorised duplication as theft and the retailer as a receiver of stolen property.[3]

On the other hand the burden of proof on the prosecution is heavier than that on the plaintiff in civil cases and particularly the proof of a negative, ie that there was no consent, may be difficult in cases of importation and so may be proof that the defendant knew that the phonograms were illicitly made.

1 *WIPO Guide to the Phonogram Convention* 3.5.
2 *Shapiro Bernstein & Co v Remington Records Inc* 265F2d 263, 269 (21 Cir 1959).
3 Appelate Court of Naples, 11 April 1980; Salvatore Molinari and Antonia Moccia, see para 7.19 above.

6. Term of protection – article 4

9.11 The duration of the protection must be at least 20 years. The 20 years may run from the fixation of the phonogram or from the first publication of it. As publication must always be later than fixation and may be considerably later the 20 years from fixation will be the longer protection but first publication will always be the easier date to ascertain. The term of protection is uncertain in those countries which choose to protect by the law of unfair competition. The courts will have to decide in each case whether X years after publication unfair competition exists. If, for instance, the recording has been removed from the phonogram producers' catalogue and illicitly made reproductions are put on the market, this may be difficult. However the Report[1] says that the Conference 'assumed that in this case the protection should not in principle end before 20 years from the first fixation or first publication ... in order to ensure a balance between the different systems'. As Ulmer puts it[2] 'it is to be hoped that this assumption does not prove too optimistic'.

1 Report para 51.
2 Ulmer *The Phonogram Convention* ICC Volume 3/1972 p 317 at p 327.

7. Formalities – article 5

9.12 No national law has to require compliance with formalities, but if it does the maximum that can be required is that the phonogram or the container bears the notice in accordance with the Convention. This is 'the Symbol ℗ accompanied by the year date of first publication' eg ℗ 1981. In most cases the phonogram or the container will bear the name or trademark or designation of the producer. If however this is not the case and the duplicate does also not identify his successor in title or the exclusive licensee then the notice must do so. The notice must be 'placed in such a manner as to give reasonable notice of the claim of protection'.

This provision is on all fours with article 11 of the Rome Convention.[1] The Rome Convention requires in addition that the principal performers must be identified on the duplicates or the containers or if not in the notice. As however this is almost invariably done in any case the difference is of no practical significance.

As the sole point of attachment of the Convention is the nationality of the producer, it would have been logical to put this on the notice but the overriding importance of having the same notice for the purpose of both this Convention and the Rome Convention prevailed.

The result is that, as article 2 provides that only phonograms whose producers are nationals of member states are protected the nationality of a phonogram may be difficult to ascertain without inquiry. However as most countries which produce and export phonograms have by now ratified the Convention the point is no longer of great importance.

It was understood by the Conference[2] that the term 'exclusive licensee means the person or legal entity that controls all rights in a phonogram for the entire territory of the contracting state in question'. The Delegation of the USA 'indicated that the exclusive licensee would be considered the owner of the copyright for the purpose of the United States law'.[2]

If no formalities are required in the country of origin the phonogram must be protected in another Convention country without any formalities although the law of the latter may require formalities.

In practice the identity of the notice under the Rome Convention and the Phonogram Convention on the one hand and the fact that the notice is required in the USA have lead to an almost universal practice of putting a notice on all phonograms whether that is required under the law of the country of first publication or not. The symbol ℗ on phonograms is now used as generally as the symbol © on books.

1 See para 8.25 above.
2 Report, para 53.

8. Limitation of protection – article 6

9.13 The Convention makes a clear distinction between 1) acts which are permissible without authorisation of the right owner and without compensation ie free use, and, 2) acts which may be permitted by national legislation under certain conditions of which payment of an equitable remuneration is one ie compulsory licences.

(1) The Convention permits the same kinds of limitations as are permitted under national law 'with respect to the protection of authors of literary and artistic works'. This is the same exception as the one provided for by article 15(2) of the Rome Convention.[1]

In countries which protect phonograms by means of unfair competition the question of exceptions does not arise.[2] In these countries the sole question for the courts is whether the excerpt or the quotation or the use for educational purposes etc constitutes competition and if it does whether such competition is unfair.[3]

As this is an 'open' convention a country may ratify it which is not a member of either of the two copyright conventions and has no national copyright legislation. The Conference expressed the view[4] that in such case the principles contained in the multilateral copyright conventions (article 10 and 10 bis, Berne Convention) would nevertheless be applicable to govern the exceptions.

(2) Compulsory licences. The Convention does not permit the establishment of a general system of compulsory licences[5] with one exception: a compulsory licence is permitted if three conditions are fulfilled; a) the duplication is solely for the purpose of teaching or scientific research b) the licence is valid for duplication only within the territory of the contracting state, ie not for the export of phonograms made under the licence c) an equitable remuneration is paid.

The compulsory licence provision is different from that in the Rome Convention[6] in two respects: duplication must give rise to an equitable remuneration whereas under the Rome Convention use solely for purposes of teaching or scientific research is free. On the other hand the protection under this Convention is against the making of duplicates 'for the purpose of distribution to the public'. In most cases of duplicating a phonogram for teaching purposes the duplicate will not be made for distribution to the public but either for the teacher or for a strictly limited number of students and it will therefore not be caught by the Convention at all.[7]

As exports of phonograms made under this compulsory licence are not permitted, it is not permitted to make phonograms under the compulsory licence even for educational purposes, if they are intended for export.

The provision applies to all ratifying countries whereas the analogous provisions in the Berne Convention and in the UCC (1971) apply only to developing countries.[8] However it is thought that it was intended particularly for the developing countries.

1 See para 8.40 above.
2 Report, para 63
3 See *WIPO Guide* 6.1.
4 Report, para 61.
5 See Report, para 58.
6 Art 15/1(d).
7 See *WIPO Guide* 6.8.
8 See para 6.38 above.

9 Miscellaneous provisions – article 7

9.14 Article 7/1 ensures that the Convention cannot be interpreted to limit or prejudice the protection of authors or of performers, producers of phonograms and broadcasting organisations. The conventions concerned are the two copyright conventions; the Rome Convention and the Paris Convention for the Protection of Industrial Property.[1]

The protection of performers against the piracy of phonograms which fix their performances is relegated to contractual provisions. The Report[2] says that whereas the Conference considered that the obligation to take action 'should normally result from the Contract between the producer and the performer', the Conference was of the opinion that these contracts 'should be so drafted as to permit the performers to take action directly against the infringer'. In fact most contracts give the producer the possibility to act in his own name as well as in the name of the performer in persuing infringers.

If a country is a member of both the Rome Convention and this Convention than it follows that if there is an overlap the convention which gives the greater protection applies, giving effect to article 22 of the Rome Convention.[3] The effect is that the two conventions complement each other.

The most important of the miscellaneous provisions is article 7(3) which states that the Convention has no retroactive effect. It corresponds to article 20(2) of the Rome Convention. This means that there is no obligation on any country which has not protected phonograms or not protected foreign phonograms and then ratifies the Convention, to protect phonograms fixed (or published) before the Convention enters into force. This means that a large existing catalogue of recordings can be freely pirated. However as the most frequently pirated recordings are the current popular hits the initial detremental effect of this provision does not last for very long.

1 Art 10 bis (2).
2 Report, para 65.
3 See para 8.47 above.

10. Administrative clauses – articles 8-14

9.15 The Convention is administered by WIPO (the World Intellectual Property Organisation) which is the specialised agency of the United Nations dealing with all intellectual property rights. In that capacity it has published tables showing the legal protection of phonograms worldwide and – together with UNESCO and the ILO – a Model Law of Neighbouring Rights.

11. State of ratifications and accessions on 1 January 1983

9.16

Contracting states		Date into force
AUSTRIA		21 August 1982
ARGENTINA	A[1]	30 June 1973
AUSTRALIA	A	22 June 1974
BRAZIL	R[1]	28 November 1975
CHILE	A	24 March 1977
DENMARK	R	24 March 1977
ECUADOR	R	14 September 1974
EGYPT	A	23 April 1978
EL SALVADOR	A	9 February 1979
FIJI	A	18 April 1973
FINLAND	R	18 April 1973
FRANCE	R	18 April 1973
GERMANY, FEDERAL REPUBLIC OF	R	18 May 1974
GUATEMALA	A	1 February 1977
HOLY SEE	R	18 July 1977
HUNGARY	A	28 May 1975
INDIA	R	12 February 1975
ISRAEL	R	1 May 1978
ITALY	R	24 March 1977
JAPAN	R	14 October 1978
KENYA	R	21 April 1976
LUXEMBOURG	R	8 March 1976
MEXICO	R	21 December 1973
MONACO	R	2 December 1974
NEW ZEALAND	A	13 August 1976
NORWAY	R	1 August 1978
PANAMA	R	29 June 1974
PARAGUAY	A	13 February 1979
SPAIN	R	24 August 1974
SWEDEN	R	18 April 1973
UNITED KINGDOM[2]	R	16 April 1973
UNITED STATES OF AMERICA	R	10 March 1974
URUGUAY		18 January 1983
VENEZUELA		18 November 1982
ZAIRE	A	29 November 1977

TOTAL NUMBER OF STATES: 36

1 R = Ratification.   A = Accession.
2 The United Kingdom declared by Notification, addressed to the Secretary General of the United Nations, and which took effect on 4 March, 1975, that the Convention is applicable to the following territories: Bermuda, British Virgin Islands, Cayman Islands, Gibraltar, Isle of Man, Hong Kong, Monserrat, St Lucia and the Seychelles.

Chapter 10
The Satellite Convention (1974)

Summary

1. The technology of satellite broadcasting   10.01
2. The conceptual problem   10.02
3. The legal problem   10.04
4. The political aspects   10.05
5. Definitions – article 1   10.06
6. The scope of the Convention – article 2(1)   10.07
7. The term of protection – article 2(2)   10.08
8. Direct broadcasting satellites – article 3   10.10
9. Exceptions – article 4   10.11
10. Non-retroactivity – article 5   10.12
11. Safeguard of interests of contributors to programmes – article 6   10.13
12. Abuses of monopoly – article 7   10.14
13. Reservations – article 8   10.15
14. Relationship to other conventions   10.16
15. Nature of the Convention   10.17
16. The economic importance of the 'signal'   10.18
17. The law applicable   10.19
18. State of ratifications and accessions   10.20

1. The technology of satellite broadcasting

10.01 There are three types of transmission of programmes via satellite: 1. point-to-point satellites; 2. distribution satellites; 3. direct broadcasting satellites. A point-to-point satellite (Intelsat system) covers roughly one-third of the earth's surface. With one satellite each placed over the Atlantic, Indian and Pacific Oceans, practically the whole world can be covered. These satellites are used for point-to-point communications over long distances, normally between two points, but not infrequently also between one transmitting point and several receiving points. At both ends, very powerful earth stations are required. Distribution satellites cover smaller geographical regions (eg Europe or a part of the United States). They are designed to feed a signal to a number of different receiving points (eg cable distribution systems). Reception is possible with the aid of receiving equipment which is considerably smaller in size and less expensive than in the case of point-to-point satellites. The common factor of both these systems is that they need a second earth station as well as the satellite: an originating station which emits the signal that carries the programme, and an earth station which receives the signal and transports it to terrestrial transmitters which transmit it in the customary way. The 'direct broadcasting satellite' needs no such intermediary earth station. The signal carrying the programme goes from the originating station via the satellite directly to the receiving sets. Both point to point satellites and distribution satellites, which are merely different versions of transporting a signal via a satellite link, need very powerful earth stations which are very expensive. Direct satellite broadcasting needs the emission of a very strong signal at the originating end and new equipment or at least modified equipment at the receiving end, ie the private home. The state of technology at the time of the making of the Convention was that broadcasting via point to point satellites and distribution satellites was already taking place, whereas broadcasting directly to the general public via satellite was still a thing of the future.

With the point to point satellite there is some danger, and with the distribution satellite there is a very real danger, that the signal can be received and further distributed by broadcasting organisations for which it was not intended, in other words it can be 'poached' or 'pirated'. This is because far less powerful and costly receiving earth stations are required in the latter case, the emitted signal via distribution satellites being far stronger than is possible via point-to-point satellite.

2. The conceptual problem

10.02 The broadcasting industry was thus faced with the old problem of 'piracy', ie unauthorised use of material on an international scale by organisations who are not paying for such use. The piracy of literary and artistic works led to the Berne Convention[1] protecting authors. The piracy of recordings led to the Phonogram Convention[2] protecting producers of phonograms. There was now a need for the protection of broadcasting organisations. The intellectual leap forward necessary for the creation of the Berne Convention was the concept of protecting intellectual, ie incorporeal property, internationally. For the creation of the Phonogram Convention (and of the Rome Convention before it) it was necessary to recognise that there is an intellectual property in a phonogram which should be protected internationally against piracy. It now became necessary to do the same for broadcasting. The step was made more difficult by the fact that whilst phonograms, like broadcasts, are derivative creations, ie nearly all phonograms (apart from birdsong or background noises or family conversations) predicate a pre-existing work, most satellite transmissions do not. Most such transmissions are of sporting events (eg the Olympic games) or of news items or public events (eg an election, a coronation, a state funeral) which are not based on a pre-existing work. The involvement of copyright was therefore, at least at the initial stage, not considered a necessity for combating this particular form of international piracy: the misappropriation of signals. Furthermore, satellite transmissions are also used for purposes other than carrying 'programmes', eg telegraphic communications, weather reports etc, and with those uses in mind international regulations, the 'Radio Regulations' made by the ITU (the International Telecommunications Union) were already in existence.

1 See para 5.05 above.
2 See para 9.01 above.

The concept of 'broadcasting'

10.03 There are two possible interpretations of 'broadcasting' in international law. In the restricted sense it means the emission of signals which can be directly received by the public. In the emission of signals via distribution satellite the 'up leg' is not regarded by some as broadcasting but as a process in the sphere of telecommunications over which intellectual property rights cannot be exercised.[1] The main argument brought forward in support of the restricted interpretation is that transport of signals via communication satellite is not intended for direct reception by the general public. Whether a programme is received through the mail (in cassette form), by microwave link, cable (including optical fibre) or communication satellite, it is the receiving organisation's decision and the receiving organisation's own act (transmission via terrestrial transmitter system or via cable distribution system) which makes the programme available to the general public in the receiving organisation's country. The receiving organisation may record the programme and transmit it later, transmit only extracts thereof, transmit it in an adapted version (eg with its own commentary in the national language), or not transmit it all. The organisation which sent the programme via satellite has no authority to broadcast or to 'co-broadcast' in the receiving country. For all these reasons it is argued that any wider interpretation is contrary to existing telecommunications law and public law in the broadcasting field.

In the wider sense 'broadcasting' includes the emission of a signal towards a satellite intended for reception by the public but only after intervention of a terrestrial station which decodes, ie 'reads', the signal to the public. The satellite is regarded as merely a technical medium through which the signal passes on its way to the public.[2]

It is submitted that in copyright law the second, wider interpretation is to be preferred. The two technical processes both begin with a programme being put on a carrier (the signal), which is intended to be received by the public (viewers and listeners) and both end up by being so received by the public. As André Kerever says:[3] Both the letter and the spirit of the Convention point to 'using the end result as a criterion. It is the purpose sought and achieved by the originating organisation' that matters.

1 Ungern Sternberg, RIDA LXX pp 9ff and Straschnov 'Broadcasting – Satellite Service in Private Law' EBU Review (May 1977).
2 Masouyé RIDA LXII (1972) p 23; GRUR Int 1973, p 344: Ulmer RIDA (July 1977) pp 4ff.
3 Kerever 'The Ambiguities of the Brussels Convention of 21 May 1974' RIDA (January 1977) pp 56ff at p 60.

3. The legal problem

10.04 As with the creation of any international convention, or indeed any national law in this field, the initial questions to be answered were: 1. What is the mischief to be combated? 2. What method is to be applied to combat it? 3. What is to be protected and what rights are to be created? 4. What circumstances will give rise to the protection granted?

The *first question* has already been answered: The mischief is the 'pirating' of programme-carrying signals, meaning the reception or distribution of such signals without the authority of the originating organisation. The *second question*: the question of method proved much more difficult and it was decided to base the Convention on public not private international law. This was a radical departure, unprecedented in the copyright field. It means that the Convention confers no private rights on anyone. It is merely a diplomatic call upon contracting states to take 'adequate measures' to prevent the distribution on their national territory of signals by organisations for whom these signals were not intended. What these measures are to be is left to the contracting state as long as they are adequate. Thus, at a stroke, any questions regarding the granting of exclusive (or non-exclusive) rights to authorise or forbid the distribution of programmes vested in broadcasting organisations or the exercise of any rights vested in the creators of these programmes, eg authors, performers, producers of phonograms, no longer arose.

This means that the very considerable investment of the broadcasting organisation in making the programme is protected regardless of whether the programme contains, or is based upon any pre-existing works. It also means that the owners of rights in the works whose rights are used in the programmes must look for protection either to their national law or to a contract in the country of the originating broadcasting organisation.[1]

It is argued[2] that this is an advantage to the right owners, because the originating organisation bears the responsibility towards the owners of copyrights or neighbouring rights and if that organisation is a member of one of the copyright conventions and the neighbouring right conventions it will have to discharge this responsibility towards foreign as well as national right owners. Furthermore, the law to be applied will be the national law with which both the originating organisations and the collecting society, which will in most cases represent the right owners, are familiar. This is correct, but this responsibility already existed before the creation of the Satellite Convention so that in this respect the Convention has not changed anything.

If the country of the originating broadcast has a developed copyright system the right owners will be able to protect their rights abroad by contracting with the originating organisation. If on the other hand the organisation pirating the signal is in a country without any or with only inadequate copyright legislation the right owners will have no remedy there. They will have to look to the originating organisation for compensation. The broadcasting organisation whose programme has been pirated has no remedy either, because it too will have no rights. If the country where the act of piracy takes place has ratified the Convention, the government of the country of the originating organisation may complain of the violation through diplomatic channels. If the country where the pirating broadcasting organisation is situated has not ratified the Convention no-one of course has any remedy or any grounds for a complaint.

As the means by which protection is accorded is left to each contracting state, it is to be hoped that states will create private rights in exercising their choice of 'adequate measures' and thus keep the protection of programmes within the private international law sphere. In the case of the Phonogram Convention, which also leaves the means of protection to each contracting state, nearly all the countries have chosen to grant private rights in order to fulfil their Convention obligations and the only two major copyright countries which have so far ratified the Satellite Convention[3] have done the same.

The *third question*: what is to be protected has also been answered in a manner which does not fit into an intellectual property or copyright convention. The object of protection is the signal which carries the programme, not the programme itself. The Convention protects the carrier not the content, which means that no rights in the programme are created.

The *fourth question*: What circumstances give rise to the protection granted has also been answered in a narrow sense: the Convention covers the distribution of programme-carrying signals transmitted by point-to-point or distribution satellites. It does not cover direct broadcasting satellites[4] thus programmes emitted via direct broadcasting satellites are either protected by the Rome Convention as 'broadcasts' or they are not protected internationally at all.

1 See Report of the General Rapporteur of the Satellite Convention (Barbara Ringer), para 35.
2 See Straschnov, op cit, p 99.
3 The Federal Republic of Germany and Italy.
4 See Ringer Report, para 47.

4. The political aspects

10.05 Whereas satellite broadcasting by point to point satellite or by distribution satellite necessitates an earth station in the country of reception, satellite broadcasting via direct broadcasting satellite does not. Therefore, whereas the authorities in the receiving country can 'filter' the signals which come via point to point or distribution satellite by controlling the earth station, no such 'filtering' of a signal receivable directly in the home via direct broadcasting satellite will be possible. As filtering is only a polite word for censorship the political aspect of copyright will once more come into focus as it did in European national copyright systems in the sixteenth and seventeenth centuries.[1]

The delegate of the USSR[2] advocated the inclusion of provisions 'concerning the obligations of each state to exclude from programmes transmitted via satellite any material detrimental to the maintenance of international peace and security, aimed at interfering in the domestic affairs of other states or undermining their national laws, customs and traditions'.[3]

The Diplomatic Conference held that this point was 'outside the mandate and competence of the Conference' because direct broadcasting satellites had been excluded from the programme of the conference and because the issue of programme content which arose in connection with direct broadcasting satellites 'was quite properly being considered in the competent bodies of the United Nations.'[4] The political rocks had thus been avoided by careful seamanship, but they will reappear in the future when direct satellite broadcasting becomes a reality and will have to be dealt with.

1 See para 2.09 above.
2 Participating fully for the first time in an international copyright convention.
3 Ringer Report, para 43.
4 See Ringer Report, para 43.

5. Definitions – article 1

10.06 In a convention which is as technical as the Satellite Convention and as contentious, the definition of the terms used is obviously of crucial importance. No wonder article 1 which contains these definitions amounts in length to almost a third of the substantive part of the convention.

It contains three groups of definitions: the group defining the 'signals' and its stages: paragraphs (i), (iv), (v) and (viii); the group defining 'programme' and 'satellite': paragraphs (ii) and (iii) and the group dealing with the organisations involved in the process of satellite broadcasting the 'originating organisation' and the 'distributor' and the concept of 'distribution', paragraphs (vi), (vii) and (viii).

'*Signal*' – paragraph (i) is defined as an electronically generated carrier 'capable of transmitting programmes'. This indicates that it does not matter what electronic means the carrier uses – laser beams or radio waves of all sorts – as long as the signal has the capacity to carry a programme.

The route of the signal is described first as the 'up-leg' from the emitting station to the satellite and then as the 'down-leg' from the satellite to the earth station. Three different stages of the same signal are considered by the convention: when it is 'emitted', when it is 'derived', and when it is 'distributed'.[1] The first two stages are defined in paragraphs (iv) and (v) and the last in paragraph (viii) in the definition of 'distribution'. The important point is that they are all stages of the same signal.

An '*emitted signal*' (paragraph (iv)) is any signal that 'goes to or passes through' a satellite. A '*derived signal*' is an emitted signal whose technical characteristics have been modified regardless of how many modifications have taken place on the way and whether these modifications have involved amplification, modulation or changes of frequency and whether the signal has been recorded or re-recorded or otherwise changed in its physical characteristics or whether these modifications have taken place once or more than once.[2]

The signal is '*distributed*' when the 'derived signal' is taken by a 'distributor' (defined in paragraph (vii) 'to the general public or any section thereof' (paragraph (viii)).

'Distribution' is the most important concept in the convention. Its essentials are the 'distributor', the 'transmission' and the recipients 'the general public or any section thereof'. The 'distributor' is the natural or legal person with the ultimate responsibility for decision making in the process of distribution.[3] The concept of transmission is wide enough to cover any telecommunications methods for transmitting signals, present or future, and includes traditional forms of broadcasting as well as transmission by cable or fixed communications channels, laser transmission and even transmission by a direct broadcasting satellite.[4] Thus, whilst article 3 of the Convention excludes the retransmission of signals taken from a direct broadcasting satellite, it would cover a signal received from a distribution satellite and retransmitted by an unauthorised distributor using a direct broadcasting satellite.

The phrase 'the general public or any section thereof' is taken from the Phonogram Convention[5] and indicates that any defined section of the public, eg subscribers, constitute a public and transmission to them is therefore 'distribution' of the signal. How widely or narrowly 'section' is interpreted will be a matter for the national courts in which protection may be claimed.

'*Programme*' (paragraph (ii)) is defined as a 'body' of 'material'. These words are perhaps a little unfortunate when dealing with something incorporeal but it is only meant to indicate that the material may be live or recorded and consists of images or sounds or both. Such a programme could include privately made films or tapes not originally intended for publication. It excludes private communications, military intelligence, meteorological information or any technical or scientific data carried by satellite.[6]

'*Satellite*' paragraph (III) is defined as a 'device' that is a man-made object capable of serving a particular purpose, in this case the transmission of signals. It is defined as 'extraterrestrial' which means that at least during part of its orbit the satellite must be outside the atmosphere of the earth. It therefore includes satellites which pass through the atmosphere of the earth at some stage of their journey.

The '*originating organisation*' (paragraph (VI)) is the entity which decides what programme the signal will carry. This definition is intended to exclude broadcasting or telecommunication authorities which have administrative functions but exercise no control over what programmes the signals are to carry. The definition also excludes producers of programmes or any of its creators because although they make or control the making of the programme, they have no control over the signal and its emission.[7] In countries where a public body in the form of a broadcasting authority owns the rights in the programmes but delegates the production of the programmes to different regional contractors,[8] the 'originating organisation' is that authority not the contractors as it has the ultimate responsibility and power of decision.[9]

1 Art 1(iv), art 1(v) and art 1(vii) and 1(viii).
2 See Ringer Report, paras 67 to 70.
3 See Ringer Report, para 79.
4 See Ringer Report, para 76.

5 Phonogram Convention, para 1(d), see para 9.04.
6 Ringer Report, para 64.
7 See Ringer Report, para 72.
8 Eg in Britain.
9 See Ringer Report, para 72.

6. The scope of the Convention – article 2(1)

10.07 Article 2 is the central article, of the Convention. It does not give the broadcasting organisation the exclusive right or indeed any right in its broadcasts or in the signal that carries the broadcast or in distribution of that signal. In this respect it differs from all other copyright or neighbouring rights conventions. Instead the 'Nairobi Compromise'[1] puts an obligation on the contracting states 'to take adequate measures to prevent the distribution' of the signal 'by any distributor for whom the signal ... is not intended'. As the French commentators[2] put it: 'In reality the Convention relies on the good faith of the (ratifying) states'. This is indeed so. Whereas no one would wish to question the good faith of such states, which means the good faith of their governments, the fact remains that not only the contributors to the programmes (eg authors, performers, film producers, record producers etc) have no rights ex jure conventionis and cannot enforce the Convention, but the originating broadcasting organisation cannot enforce it either unless the ratifying state grants a specific right to broadcasters. The most likely explanation of the 'Nairobi Compromise' is that it emanates from those states (a majority in the United Nations) where the broadcasting organisation is a state organisation, an arm of government and not an organisation independent of the government, in which case private rights and particularly foreign private rights probably cannot be enforced against such a broadcasting organisation in any event, so that relying on the good faith of that government is the best that can be achieved.

Article 2 contains four basic notions: 'adequate measures', 'prevent', 'distributor', and 'intended'.[3] They will be dealt with in turn.

'Adequate measures' – the contracting states are free to implement their undertaking to grant adequate protection in any form they choose. The granting of a specific right, be it a copyright or a neighbouring right, the adoption of administrative measures, or of penal sanctions, or of telecommunication regulations are all mentioned as possibilities in the report. They are all measures to 'prevent' piracy of the signal.

'Intention' – the criterion whether distribution of the signal is to be permitted or 'prevented' is whether it was 'intended' for the distributor or not. The notion of intention or intended destination is a difficult one. Broadcasting organisations have a certain amount of control over the destination of their signals transmitted via satellite but such control is by no means complete. Furthermore the contributors to the programme have the possibility to negotiate terms with the originating organisation which will depend on the number of countries to which the programme is to be distributed. Writers are critical of the notion of 'intention' and call it 'vague' and 'obscure'.[4] Against that it is argued that the originating organisation will always be in a position to prove whether a particular distributor was authorised to distribute the programme-carrying signal in question or not. However there seems to be agreement that it will be necessary for ratifying countries to specify under what conditions signals are to be considered as 'intended' for a certain broadcasting organisation. This will be so if there are to be administrative regulations and even more so if the protection is to be by penal sanctions as the offence will have to be strictly defined.[5]

The article refers to the signal 'emitted to or passing through the Satellite'. This makes it clear that piracy can occur on the 'up-leg' as well as on the 'down-leg' or thereafter or at any point from the storage unit of the satellite itself.[6]

The article demands measures to prevent distribution 'on or from the territory' of the contracting state. Thus the contracting state has to prevent piratical transmission from a station on its territory, including transmission on its territory, even if the audience for which it is intended is partly or entirely outside its territory.

It is said that this structure also has the disadvantage that it gives no conventional minimum of rights and that therefore the level of protection may vary considerably from country to country as both a higher level of protection and a lower level of protection may be considered 'adequate' and there is no reciprocity.[7] The opposite view is taken by broadcasting organisations pointing out that whatever measures are chosen, the result should be the same: protection against unauthorised distribution.

1   So called because the decision to shift the Convention from the public to the private international law sphere was taken at the fourth and last preparatory conference in Nairobi, Kenya.
2   Desbois, Kerever, Françon, op cit, para 385. See also: Kerever, op cit, p 64 at p 77.
3   Ringer Report, para 78.
4   Kerever, op cit, p 70.
5   WIPO and UNESCO have jointly drafted a Model Law (in two versions) for implementation of the Satellite Convention which they have recommended to states.
6   Ringer Report, para 83.
7   See Desbois, Françon, Kerever para 313.

7. The term of protection – article 2(2)

10.08 The difficulty encountered by the Conference lay in the fact that the 'Nairobi Compromise' had shifted the object of protection from the programme to the signal. If the programme content is to be protected, it has to be protected for a term of years unless the means of protection is the law of unfair competition, in which case the term is not provided for in the law but is one of the elements a court has to take into consideration when deciding whether the competition is fair or unfair.[1] If however the signal, not the content, ie, the programme, is protected the position is more complicated. It was feared that if the Convention contained a term of protection this could be interpreted as imposing a permanent obligation if the signal was recorded or at the other extreme that states would consider their obligation 'to take adequate measures' fulfilled shortly after the emission.[2] The opinion was also expressed that, as this was not a copyright convention and conferred no private rights, a term of protection would be inappropriate.

A series of compromises was eventually adopted in article 2(2). It says that if in a contracting state the 'adequate measures' contain a time limit, then the duration shall be fixed by domestic law. This seems to be stating the obvious because as the Convention does not provide a term, nor state whether or not a time limit should be provided, the only law that can provide it is the national law.

The result is that there will be two groups of states: those who give protection by granting a specific right will have to limit this right to a number of years, but those who do not grant specific rights may have no duration in their legislation. The Report[3] says that 'it was generally considered that a period of 20 years could constitute a reasonable period'. The result will be that the periods chosen by states will probably vary so that the protection will not be uniform even among those states which chose to grant a right for a number of years. The states which fix a term are obliged to notify the Secretary General of the United Nations of the duration of it either on ratification or upon any alteration of the law so that it will be possible to inquire from WIPO what the term of protection, if any, is in the country where protection is claimed at any given time.

1 Art. 4, Phonogram Convention; see para 9.09 above.
2 See Ringer Report, para 86.
3 See Ringer Report, para 98.

Article 2(3)

10.09 This paragraph deals with a situation where a signal has passed through a satellite and thereafter through a chain of distributors and is picked up somewhere along that chain by a distributor for whom the signal was not intended. The paragraph is based on the proposition that the Convention deals with situations of space communications not with terrestrial situations. The result is that if one distributor along the chain of the terrestrial distribution is a distributor for whom the signal was intended and thereafter a pirate picks up the signal, the Convention will not apply. However the piratical act will amount to 'rebroadcasting' under the Rome Convention[1] and if the country where protection is claimed is a member of that Convention a remedy will be available.

1 Art 3(g), defines 'rebroadcasting as 'simultaneous broadcasting by one broadcasting organisation of the broadcast of another broadcasting organisation'.

8. Direct broadcasting satellites – article 3

10.10 This article excludes direct broadcasting satellites from the scope of the convention. If such a satellite is used it is regarded as an extended 'aerial in space' which means that the originating organisation 'broadcasts' in the sense of the Berne or Rome Convention, distributing the signal which is receivable by members of the public in their homes. The DBS System (Direct Broadcasting Satellite System) means that a broadcaster instead of broadcasting for public reception by an aerial situated on the roof of a house, broadcasts via an aerial on a Satellite situated in space with a transmitter sufficiently powerful to send sounds and images directly to receiving sets on earth. This definition of direct satellite broadcasting closely resembles the ITU Radio Regulations[1] without using the word broadcasting. The Regulation says: 'A radio communication service in which signals transmitted or retransmitted by space stations are intended for direct reception by the general public'. A footnote to the regulation explains the term 'direct reception': 'the term "direct reception" shall encompass both individual reception and community reception'. Thus a direct broadcasting satellite is one which transmits directly to private homes or to community antennae.

The Convention also covers the situation where an 'unintended' distributor picks up a signal from a communication satellite and distributes it by direct broadcasting satellite.

Article 3 refers to a signal being emitted by the originating organisation 'or on behalf of the originating organisation' as it may be not the originating broadcasting organisation itself but the Post Office or other telecommunications administration which operates the DBS. Therefore if a pirate distributes conventional satellite signals but does so using a DBS (Direct Broadcasting Satellite) for his distribution this operation will be covered by the Convention if he operates on the territory of a contracting state.[2]

1 International Telecommunication Union, art 84AP-Spa 2 Radio Regulations.
2 See Ringer Report, para 105.

9. Exceptions – article 4

10.11 The exceptions are formulated in the same way as in the Berne Convention.[1] This means that whereas article 2 makes it clear that what is protected is 'the container, not the content', ie not the programmes but the signals, Article 4 clearly deals not with the signal but with the programmes contained in it: eg 'short excerpts of the programme carried by the emitted signal'. Thus the position is that what article 2 defines as a piratical act, ie a broadcasting organisation picking up a signal which is not intended for it is permitted provided the programme content of the signal is of a certain kind, although the Convention avowedly does not deal with the programme content.[2] The exempted programme contents are 'short excerpts ... consisting of reports of current events' (article 4, paragraph (i)) and 'quotations ... compatible with fair practice' (article 4, paragraph (ii)).
Paragraph (i): The short excerpts from the reports of current events are permitted provided they are 'justified by the informatory purpose'. The Report[3] explains: 'to warrant the use of short excerpts under this provision, the programming must be done as part of a report of general news of the day and would therefore, as a rule, have to be transmitted on the basis of fixation.' The term 'current events' means 'events of public life in the broad sense'.[4]
Paragraph (ii) exempts short excerpts of programmes, carried as 'quotations'. They must be 'compatible with fair practice and justified by the informatory purpose of such quotations'. Again the terminology is that of the Berne Convention.[5]
Paragraph (iii) exempts the whole programme if the contracting state where the distribution is effected is a 'developing country'. However the distribution must be 'solely for the purpose of teaching ... or scientific research.'

As a large number of satellite broadcasts of this kind are sporting events and the 'sole' purpose must be teaching the application would appear to be limited.[6]

The concept of teaching is to include adult education. The interpretation of teaching adopted by the Conference 'includes all conventional forms of teaching at every level of education, and instructional television as distinguished from general programming that is cultural or informational in character.'[7]

The exceptions permitted in article 4 are relevant only to the measures contracting states are obliged to take under *this* convention. Conversely obligations undertaken by other conventions[8] are not affected by article 4.

1 See art 10 and 10 bis Berne Convention, Paris Act, p 171.
2 The Commentators (see Masouyé EBU Review (September 1974) p 55; Kerever RIDA (January 1977) at pp 56, 66) politely refer to this piece of Alice in Wonderland logic as 'an anomaly'. Sometimes 'anomalies' of this kind work out in practice.
3 Ringer Report, para 109.
4 Masouyé EBU Review (September 1974) p 56.
5 Art 10 and 10 bis, Paris Act 1971.
6 See Ringer Report, para 109.
7 See Ringer Report, para 110.

8 Eg the copyright and neighbouring rights conventions and the conventions and regulations administered by the ITU. See para 10.10 above.

10. Non-retroactivity – article 5

10.12 No contracting state is required to apply the Convention to any signals emitted before the Convention came into effect in that state.[1]

1 Cf similar provision in art 7(3), Phonogram Convention.

11. Safeguard of interests of contributors to programmes – article 6

10.13 The 'adequate measures' taken by the contracting states to implement the Convention must not 'impinge in any way upon the present or future rights of authors, performers, phonogram producers or broadcasting organisations, whether the protection of those rights is derived from domestic law, from either of the Copyright Conventions, or from the Rome Convention'.[1]

By the same token the purpose of the Convention is 'to complement and supplement the ITU, not to compete with it or weaken it'. This is also expressed in the preamble.[2] The Report makes it clear that 'the protection secured' means the rights existing at the time when the relevant facts occur, ie when the distribution is made not the rights secured in the past.[3]

The question of the protection of contributors to the programmes contained in the signal is dealt with in the Report:[4]

> 'It was ... undisputed that where a satellite is used for the distribution of programme-carrying signals made directly by the satellite itself, the originating organisation, even without the insertion of such a provision in the Convention, is responsible for the distribution vis-à-vis the authors, performers, producers of phonograms and broadcasting organisations and cannot plead that the distribution was made in space and thus outside the sphere of application of any national law.'

The main Commission also expressed 'unanimous appreciation' of the general principle that 'the Contributor or his representative should be able to know in advance where the signals carrying the programmes are intended to go, at least in cases where the contributor has not previously transferred or waived his rights'.

1 Ringer Report, para 113.
2 Third para 'recognising' etc and fifth para 'conscious' etc.
3 Ringer Report, para 118.
4 A statement by the delegations of Austria and Germany which the Conference agreed to insert in the Report (under para 115).

12. Abuses of monopoly – article 7

10.14 This article, like article 4, also seems to refer to the content of the signal, ie the programme rather than to the signal.

It also has to be recognised that in many countries the broadcasting organisation has a monopoly which is sanctioned by national law.

There is also no doubt that a sovereign country can and must apply its laws to prevent abuses of monopoly and many delegations at the Conference felt that this clause was unnecessary.

Its meaning is political rather than legal and becomes clearer in the Report[1]

'... a distributor not designated by the originating organisation may be authorised by the competent national authorities to distribute programme-carrying signals. However, such a measure may not be applied when the originating organisation does not possess the rights to distribute the signals on the territory of the State in question'. This would appear to mean that an originating organisation which has acquired all the necessary rights to distribute the signal in the country concerned can be expropriated but if it does not have all the rights it can not be.

Perhaps the last sentence of the carefully drafted statement which was inserted in the Report at the request of the Main Commission comes nearest to shedding light on the matter: 'A measure under Article 7 would not be justified by the simple fact that the originating organisation is asking for the signal a price considered too high, if it has not been determined that this price is not justified by the production and transport costs of the signal'. Shorn of all the double negatives this means that if a government 'determines' that the price is too high it can expropriate the signal on anti-trust grounds. The Conference was clearly conscious of this and the next sentence of the statement reads: 'In short, the Conference adopted Article 7 with the clear understanding that Contracting States shall apply it in good faith and only where its application appears to them entirely legitimate'. Most commentators are critical of this article, but as one of them puts it: 'Future practice will show whether this conjecture is reflected by the facts'.[2]

1 Ringer Report, para 122.
2 Masouyé, op cit, p 46 at p 57.

13. Reservations – article 8

10.15 Reservations are not permitted except in two stated cases.

The *first case – article 8(2)* deals with the situation in a few countries where the law is based on the criterion of the place from which the signal is emitted as opposed to the criterion of the nationality of the originating organisation. These countries can make a reservation.[1]

The *second case – article 8(3)* permits a reservation for countries where copyright owners cannot fully control retransmission of broadcasts to subscribers of wire and cable systems. Again only a few countries are in this position.[2]

As under article 8(2) the relevant date is 21 May 1974.

The Conference agreed that 'a cable system should not, relying on a reservation under Article 8(3), pick up and distribute signals from a satellite before those signals have been terrestrially distributed in an area where the cable system can receive the terrestrial broadcast'.[3]

1 This article is similar to art 17 of the Rome Convention and art 7(4) of the Phonogram Convention.
2 Among these countries are the UK, Canada, Australia, the Netherlands. See verbatim records of the Conference, para 1120 77.
3 Ringer Report, para 129.

14. Relationship to other conventions

10.16 Article 11 bis Berne Convention[1] and article IV bis UCC.[2] Article 11 bis gives the author the right to forbid the broadcasting of his work without his authorisation and so does article IV bis. The Satellite Convention, where it is implemented by the grant of a private right under the national law concerned gives the broadcaster the right to forbid the unauthorised transmission of his signal.

There could be two possible situations in which these two rights conflict. The first arises if a signal is transmitted without the permission of the originating broadcasting organisation who wants to act against the 'pirate', but the authors of the rights in the programme want the pirate to transmit it. This must be rare as the authors would probably get no remuneration for the additional use of their works by the pirate, but they would have no remedy against the broadcaster's refusal.

The second situation is the converse of the first where the authors refuse to allow their works to be transmitted by satellite to another broadcasting organisation after the originating organisation' has authorised the transmission of the signal. In this case the authors will probably have a remedy against the originating organisation with whom they will have a contract, for a breach of that contract. They will also have a remedy against the transmitting broadcasting organisation if the latter is situated in a country that has ratified the Berne Convention or the UCC.

A third situation and by far the most common, will be the one where the transmission of the signal takes place without the authorisation of the originating broadcasting organisation and without the permission of the authors whose works are contained in the programme carried by the signal. In this case there is no conflict and both will presumably pursue their case together, the authors basing themselves on the Berne Convention or the UCC and the originating broadcasting organisation on its rights in the signal, if the country where the transmission takes place gives such a right.

The relationship to the Rome Convention is limited by the fact that the Satellite Convention does not apply to direct satellite broadcasting[3] whereas the Rome Convention does.[4]

In the case of communication satellites, the Satellite Convention applies and whether the Rome Convention applies is controversial and depends on whether article 3(f) and (g) of that Convention are given a wide or a narrow interpretation. If it does not apply there is no possible conflict. If it does the originating broadcasting organisation will have a specific right in the programme under the Rome Convention as well as a right in the signal under the Satellite Convention. The definition says: '"broadcasting" means the transmission by wireless means for public reception of sounds or of images and sounds'. The Kaminstein Report makes it clear that this means transmission by hertzian waves or other wireless means but excludes transmission by wire. The question is whether transmission by wireless means via a satellite and received directly by receiving sets is 'for public reception'. It is submitted that it is clearly 'for public reception'. The satellite is merely an 'extended antenna in space' which is used by the originating broadcasting organisation to emit the signal and distribute it to the listening or viewing public.[5] On the other hand on the question whether the programme carried by a signal emitted via a distribution satellite is 'broadcasting' and therefore covered by the Rome Convention opinions are divided.[6]

1 See para 5.43 above.
2 See para 6.20 above.
3 Art 3
4 See definition of broadcasting in art 3(f) and (g) and art 13; see para 8.35 above.
5 See Masouyé 'A new international Convention' EBU Review vol no XXV (September 1978) p 49.
6 See para 8.35 above.

15. The nature of the convention

10.17 The Rome Convention is derived from the Berne Convention; although the beneficiaries are different, the basic structure of the Convention, ie rights ex jure conventionis and the principle of national treatment are the same.

The Phonogram Convention is derived from the Rome Convention. Although the beneficiary of the Phonogram Convention is only one of the three beneficiaries of the Rome Convention, the basic structure is the same ie protection of the record producer ex jure conventionis and the principle of national treatment. The deviation is that the convention leaves the means of protection to the ratifying country, but these means are enumerated in the Convention[1] and are, with the exception of penal sanctions, in the field of private international law and most ratifying countries have granted specific rights to the beneficiary.

The Satellite Convention is derived from the Phonogram Convention in that it takes from that Convention the principle that each ratifying state chooses the means of protecting the beneficiary. The further deviation is that it does not protect intellectual property, ie the programme, but the carrier, ie the signal, which may or may not carry intellectual property, and that it does not specify the means of protection.

Whereas the Satellite Convention is in the realm of public international law, whether the Convention is implemented in the realm of private international law or of public international law depends on the means of implementation employed by the ratifying country.[2] If the law of that country gives the broadcasting organisation a distribution right in the signal analogous to a copyright or a neighbouring right, the Convention will be applied in the realm of private international law. If that law contains only administrative provisions protecting the signal, the Convention will be applied in the realm of public international law. In that case the law of the ratifying country will also have to specify under what circumstances a programme-carrying signal is 'intended' for a transmitting organisation. This will be even more necessary if it makes the act of unauthorised transmission an offence where, presumably, such 'intention' will have to be strictly proved.

1 Art 3, Phonogram Convention, see para 9.06 above.
2 See Kerever, op cit, p 56 ff. Also Desbois, Françon, Kerever, op cit, para 313.

16. The economic importance of the 'signal'

10.18 Owing to the need for extensive personnel, the number of cameras to be employed, the distance between the place where the signal is produced and where it is received, the signal may be more costly than the rights (authors rights and neighbouring rights) to be acquired for the making of the programme. If the programme consists of a sporting event (eg a cup final or the Olympic Games) no copyrights are involved but the programme may be more expensive than if there were.

If television 'signals' are sold, the negotiations for such a sale must, therefore, be separate from those conducted with the owners of the copyrights. The rights in the 'signal' are transferable and their value is based on the economic value of the signal and its protection against unauthorised distribution.

The impact of satellite broadcasting on copyright has so far not been very heavy, mainly because most of the programmes broadcast via satellite have consisted of news or current events and sport which do not, as a rule, involve copyright. On the other hand, programmes which contain literary or musical works can be put on tape and easily transmitted by air, in which case they can reach their destination within a few hours after the broadcast has been made, which in nearly all cases is in good time.[1] However if satellite broadcasting becomes a method of ordinary broadcasting, broadcasters will have to be protected in order to be able to protect the programmes they emit.

17. The law applicable

10.19 The Satellite Convention is a convention of public international law and deals with the act of distribution of the signals so that in cases of unauthorised distribution in another country the law of the country where the distribution takes place will be the applicable law.

Under private international law three possible views have been expressed with regard to the copyright law applicable to satellite broadcasts:

1. That no terrestrial law is applicable because the source of the broadcast is in outer space. 2. That the applicable law is the domestic law of the originating organisation. 3. That it is the law of the country where the transmitting earth station is situated, apart from the case of direct satellite broadcasts where there is, by definition, no transmitting earth station.

One must reject the view that no terrestrial law applies because the satellite is in outer space. The origin and the source of the broadcast is terrestrial and 'equity demands that a terrestrial legal system be recognised as applicable'.[1]

With regard to the two remaining possibilities the better view seems to be to choose the country of the originating organisation.[2] There may be several transmitting organisations and if the law were that of the transmitting station several laws which may be different from one another would apply to the same international situation, which is very undesirable. It is far more desirable that the domestic law of the originating organisation should apply to such a situation which ensures legal certainty. As the broadcasting organisation which originates the broadcast will have to conclude contracts with the right owners in its own country it will be able to cover foreign rights more easily if it can apply the law of the land with which it is familiar than if it has to apply foreign law. In most cases the national right owners are represented by a collecting society which also represents foreign right owners and has reciprocal agreements with the collecting societies of other countries, so that the national collecting society can contract with the national broadcasting organisation for all right owners.

The national contracts between broadcasters and copyright owners cover as a rule only the national audience, so that transmission via satellite to other countries will be an extension of the originally intended audience and will therefore require a supplementary remuneration.[3]

1 See Straschnov 'The broadcasting-satellite Service in private law' EBU Review (May 1977) pp 97 ff at p 98.
2 See Straschnov, op cit, p 99, para 5.
3 See Straschnov, op cit, p 99, para 7.

18. State of ratifications and accessions on 1 January 1983

10.20

Contracting State	Date of deposit of instrument	Entry into force
AUSTRIA	6 May 1982	6 August 1982
GERMANY, FEDERAL REPUBLIC OF	25 May 1979	25 August 1979
ITALY	7 April 1981	7 July 1981
KENYA	6 January 1976	25 August 1979
MEXICO	18 March 1976	25 August 1979
NICARAGUA	1 December 1975	25 August 1979
YUGOSLAVIA	29 December 1976	25 August 1979

TOTAL NUMBER OF STATES: 7

Chapter 11
Regional Agreements

Summary

1. The European Agreement concerning Programme Exchanges by means of Television Films 1958   11.01
2. The European Agreement on the Protection of Television Broadcasts 1960   11.03
   (1) History   11.03
   (2) The philosophy of the agreement   11.04
   (3) Protected broadcasts – Article 1   11.05
   (4) The rights of broadcasting organisations – article 1.1   11.06
   (5) The term of protection – article 2   11.07
   (6) Reservations and exceptions – article 3   11.08
      (1) Reservations – article 3.1   11.08
      (2) Exceptions – article 3.2   11.09
   (7) Copyright tribunal – article 3.3   11.10
   (8) Seizure – article 4   11.11

1. European Agreement concerning Programme Exchanges by means of Television Films 1958

11.01 This agreement is a 'special arrangement' under the terms of the Berne Convention.[1] It was made under the auspices of the Council of Europe and is open to members of the Council of Europe[2] and has been ratified by 15 of them.[3] On coming into force it became also open to countries which are not members of the Council of Europe.[4] However no country outside the Council of Europe has ratified it so far and it thus remains a strictly regional agreement. The purpose of the agreement was 'to alleviate the difficulties with regard to copyright ownership in television films which confronted those countries where copyright can be vested only in individual creators and not in a legal entity'[5]. The exchanges of programmes and particularly the joint transmission of major events by 'Eurovision', a joint enterprise of the European broadcasting organisations, highlighted the inability to the 'droit d'auteur' to adapt to modern technology.

According to the laws of several European states, the foremost of which is France, a broadcasting organisation cannot be an original copyright owner mainly because it is a corporation and not an individual. This produced great difficulties when contracts for the making and the exploitation of such television films had to be made and when measures against piracy became necessary. It was clear that broadcasting organisations had to be protected. They take 'the initiative in and take the responsibility for'[6] and the financial risk of 'making' the broadcast and there is no doubt that according to the philosophy of 'copyright' as opposed to the philosophy of the 'droit d'auteur' there is sufficient originality and intellectual effort in the making of a broadcast to justify a copyright in it.[7]

The solution adopted by the agreement is that a broadcasting organisation which is 'the maker' of a television film has the right to 'authorise ... the exploitation of such a film in another country provided both countries are parties to the agreement'.[8] Thus a broadcasting organisation is the copyright owner in the Anglo-Saxon sense although the expression is not used.

1   Art 20, Berne Convention 1971.
2   Art 6.
3   Belgium, Cyprus, Denmark, France, Greece, Ireland, Israel, Luxembourg, Netherlands, Norway, Spain, Sweden, Tunisia, Turkey, UK.
4   Art 8.
5   Ploman and Hamilton *Copyright* (1980) p 75.
    See also Françon 'International protection of neighbouring rights' RIDA (January 1974) p 442.
6   Art 2/2.
7   That a body like the Council of Europe which is dominated by 'droit d'auteur' countries accepted this 'copyright' concept does not prove any weakening of their convictions. It only proves that broadcasting organisations which are in the countries concerned either part of the machinery of government, or fairly close to their governments have sufficient political influence to overcome such ideological or conceptual difficulties when they see the economic necessity to do so.
8   Art 1.

11.02   'Television films' are defined as 'visual or sound and visual recordings intended for television'. The definition is drafted in the form of a non-rebuttable presumption. Such recordings are 'deemed to be television films' within the meaning of the agreement. The agreement does not say whose intention is the relevant intention for this purpose, but it would seem to be the intention of the broadcasting organisation as the broadcasting organisation is also 'deemed to be the maker of it has taken the initiative in, and responsibility for, the making of a television film'.[1]

Equally, if an independent contractor makes a television film he is 'entitled to transfer to a broadcasting organisation the right to authorise the exploitation of the television film in the other countries party to the agreement'[2] but this is so only if such independent contractor is also 'under the jurisdiction of countries which are party to the ... Agreement'.[3]

'Persons who contribute to the making of the television film' can make 'restrictive conditions'[4] in which case neither article 1 nor article 3 of the agreement operate as both these articles provide that they apply only 'in the absence of any contrary or special stipulations as defined in Article 4'.

1   Art 2/2.
2   Art 3/1.
3   Art 3/2.
4   Art 4.

State of Ratifications on Accessions on 1 January 1983
11.03

Contracting State	*Entry into force*
BELGIUM	8 April 1962
CYPRUS	20 February 1970
DENMARK	25 November 1961
FRANCE	1 July 1961
GREECE	9 February 1962
IRELAND	4 April 1965

Contracting State	Entry into force
ISRAEL	15 February 1978
LUXEMBOURG	31 October 1963
NETHERLANDS	5 March 1967
NORWAY	15 March 1963
SPAIN	4 January 1974
SWEDEN	1 July 1961
TUNISIA	22 February 1969
TURKEY	28 March 1964
UNITED KINGDOM	1 July 1961

TOTAL NUMBER OF STATES: 15

2. European Agreement on the Protection of Television Broadcasts 1960 (1965, 1975, 1981)

(1) History

11.04 Like the previous agreement[1] this is a multinational regional agreement created under the auspices of the Council of Europe. The double reason for the Agreement is spelt out in the preamble[2] which states that the exchange of television programmes between European countries 'are hampered by the fact that the majority of television organisations are at present powerless to restrain the re-broadcasting, fixation or public performance of their broadcasts'. It also states that 'organisers of musical or dramatic performances or the like, and promoters of sports meetings, make their consent to broadcasting to other countries conditional upon an undertaking that the relays will not be used for purposes other than for private viewing'. The need for the protection of television broadcasts was thus said to be extremely urgent, particularly because of 'Eurovision'. Thus the Agreement was made as the preamble[3] states 'pending the conclusion of a potentially universal convention on "neighbouring rights".' The agreement is described in the same paragraph of the preamble as 'a regional agreement restricted in scope to television broadcasts and of limited duration'.

As this agreement precedes the Rome Convention[4] by a year it is the first multinational agreement which was faced with the choice of structuring the rights of broadcasting organisations as a copyright or as a neighbouring right.

It originated from the urgent wish of the European Broadcasting Union (EBU) to protect broadcasting organisation against the public performance of their television broadcasts in cinemas during the impending Olympic games in Rome in 1960. The result was an agreement which is restricted in scope (it is solely for the protection of broadcasting organisations) geographically limited to Europe[5] but gives the broadcasting organisations much greater protection than the Rome Convention. According to the preamble the agreement is also of 'limited duration'. Article 13 provided that it was to cease to be effective when a Convention on Neighbouring Rights had been ratified by a majority of members of the Council of Europe that are themselves parties to the Agreement. It was thus to be a provisional agreement. However, when the Rome Convention was agreed a year later in 1961 and the protection for broadcasters turned out to be less than that under the European Agreement, the broadcasting organisations in Europe, quite naturally tried to preserve what they had achieved and succeeded in doing so. The Agreement was revised in 1965 in order to adjust it to the Rome Convention. Article 13 which limited the duration of the Convention to an uncertain date, ie when a majority of the members of the Council of Europe ratified the Rome Convention, was changed to a fixed date, ie 1975, and the term of the coyright for broadcasting organisations was lengthened from 10 to 20 years. The fixed date was extended again from 1975 to 1985 and in 1981 from 1985 to 1995. As long as the international protection of broadcasting organisations is inferior to that granted by the agreement, particularly in the field of cable television, the broadcasting organisations will use their considerable political influence to perpetuate the agreement and lawyers would therefore be well advised to treat it in the same way as any other international convention for the foreseeable future.

1 See para 11.01 above.
2 Preamble, para 4.
3 Preamble, last para.
4 See para 8.03 above.
5 In accordance with Art 9 non-European countries can ratify it if they have 'political ties' with a member of the Council of Europe. This is aimed at members of the British Commonwealth and the French Community, but no non-European countries have in fact ratified it.

(2) The philosophy of the agreement

11.05 The agreement could have chosen the solution of protecting solely original broadcasts. The justification would have been that the originating broadcasting organisation had a copyright because the ingenuity of its employees, or of independent artists had created the broadcast, because it had taken the initiative and provided the technical means for the creation of the broadcast and because it made the financial investment necessary in its realisation. The agreement did not choose this concept. Instead it chose to protect not the original broadcast but 'all' television broadcasts[1] in a country party to the agreement, regardless of whether they were original or relayed. The agreement thus creates an autonomous protection for each broadcast regardless of whether it is original or not.[2] This is different from the philosophy of the Rome Convention[3] where, for instance, the phonogram producer who originates a recording is protected, but the mere presser who duplicates the phonogram under licence is not. The latter would be the counterpart of the broadcasting organisation relaying or repeating an 'original broadcast'. The protection covers both the container and the content. The reason is that the agreement was drafted with 'Eurovision' broadcasts in mind and if only the original broadcast had been protected the objective could not have been achieved. As it is, each broadcasting organisation controls the rights in all its transmissions and can therefore control each of their uses. Apart from the distinct advantage for the broadcasting organisation, this also has the advantage that all right owners who contributed to the broadcast (authors, performers, record producers, film producers) can make their contractual arangements with the national broadcasting organisation in the knowledge that it has absolute control over 'all its broadcasts'.

It has also advantages for the user, who knows that he has to approach his national broadcasting organisation for a licence as the emittor of the broadcast in concreto. If only the originating broadcast were protected and a broadcast was originated in Paris but relayed to London, Rome and Brussels any potential user in England, Italy or Belgium would have to approach French television for a licence.

Thus, in spite of the fact that ideologically the right of the broadcasting organisation under the agreement is not a copyright in the true sense, it is in most respects treated as such. It is for instance transferable by outright sale or by licence and it could be enforced by an infringement action.

Article 6 which is the equivalent of article 1 of the Rome Convention[4] safeguards the rights in respect of television broadcasts which have accrued to third parties, such as authors, performers, film and record producers or organisers of entertainments.

To qualify under the agreement a broadcasting organisation must be 'constituted in the territory' of a contracting state or be 'transmitting from such a territory'. These alternative points of attachment can be turned into a double qualification by any country using the reservation provided for in article 3.1(f) so that the broadcasting organisation has to both be constituted in a member state and be transmitting from a member state. The main importance of the provision is that it excludes pirate stations which may operate from the High Seas and if the reservation is operated may exclude Monaco which is constituted in one country but transmits from another country.[5,6]

1 Art 1, para 1.
2 See Straschnov 'The European Agreement for the Protection of Televison Broadcasts' Copyright (1960) p 263.
3 See para 8.24 above.
4 See para 8.05 above.
5 It may be significant that the two countries with the most successful commercial radio stations in Europe, Monaco and Luxembourg, have so far not ratified the agreement.
6 The reservation was necessitated by the United Kingdom Copyright Act, s 32.1 (e).

(3) Protected broadcasts – article 1

11.06 Provided a broadcasting organisation qualifies under (2), all its television broadcasts are protected. This provision contains several differences from the Rome Convention and other conventions.

(1) Only television broadcasts are protected, not sound radio transmissions.[1] The sound element of a television broadcast is thus protected where it is transmitted together with the picture but if the sound of television broadcast is transmitted separately it is not protected by the agreement.
(2) The protection is not limited to original broadcasts, any relaid transmission is also protected if the relaying broadcasting organisation qualifies[2] but the same broadcast (or 'programme' as the layman would call it) does not preserve its identity, it is so to speak re-born every time it is emitted again and becomes a new broadcast separately protected.
(3) Granting the rights enumerated in article 1 to all television broadcasts 'in the territories of all parties to this Agreement' means that the agreement – unlike other international conventions – deals with national as well as international situations.

'Television broadcasts' is not defined in the agreement but it can be assumed that definitions in the Radio Regulations of the ITU (International Telecommunications Union)[3] 'television transmissions ... intended for direct reception by the general public' or in the Rome Convention:[4] 'The transmission by wireless means for public reception of ... images and sounds', will be applicable. In the absence of a restrictive definition it is submitted that the protected broadcast can be live or from a recording, be it a recording made for the television broadcast or a videogram or a commercial film.

1 Art 5.
2 See para 11.04 above.
3 Reg No 28.
4 Art 3(f).

(4) The rights of the broadcasting organisations – article 1.1

11.07 These are enumerated in article 1:

1. The right to authorise or prohibit:
    (a) Rebroadcasting. This corresponds to article 13(a) of the Rome Convention.[1]
    (b) Diffusion to the public by wire. This is the most important right *not* granted by the Rome Convention.
    (c) Communication to the public by means of any instrument. This is the same right as the one conferred by Article 13(d) of the Rome Convention.[2] Whereas the latter can only be exercised if the communication 'is made in places accessible to the public against payment of an entrance fee' and can be made subject to compulsory licence, the right under the agreement is absolute (unless it is made the subject of a reservation under article 3/1(b) and thereby limited to communication to a 'paying audience').
    (d) 'The fixation of the broadcast' and 'any reproduction of such fixation'. This is the same as article 13(b) and (c) of the Rome Convention.[3] However, the agreement contains the additional right to prohibit 'still photographs' of the broadcast. This can in some circumstances be a valuable right (the winning goal, the kiss on the balcony of Buckingham Palace).
    (e) The use of such fixations or reproductions for 're-broadcasting, wire diffusion, or public performance'. This is similar to, but more specific than, article 13(a), (b) and (c) of the Rome Convention.

It is subject to an interesting exception which applies where the right-owning broadcasting organisation 'has authorised the sale of the said fixations or reproductions to the public'. This makes such reproductions saleable commodities, eg in the form of videograms.[4] Once copies have been sold to the public, their use for broadcasting, wire diffusion or public performance can no longer be prevented by the right owners.

1 See para 8.32 above.
2 See para 8.35 above.
3 See paras 8.33 and 8.34 above.
4 Straschnov 'European Agreement on the Protection of Television Broadcasts' Copyright (October 1960) p 263 on p 266.

(5) The term of protection – article 2

11.08 The term of protection is 20 years, ie 'the end of the twentieth calendar year following the year in which the first broadcast was made from the territory of a member state'. This is the same as article 14(c) of the Rome Convention. It means that if the original broadcast is made in a country which has not ratified the agreement time does not run until it has been retransmitted in a member state. The 'original' broadcast in the non convention country is not protected and can be fixed and reproduced with impunity. As Dr Straschnov points out[1] if the right of the broadcasting organisation was regarded as a pure copyright or neighbouring right this would pose a problem. The first broadcast would be in the public domain and the repetition in a convention country which is protected by the agreement would constitute the passage of a 'work' from the public domain to the private domain becoming protected by copyright, which would be repugnant to most national laws and to the international conventions. It might also create conflict with acquired rights. However if, according to the 'philosophy of the Agreement' the subject of protection is not the content of the broadcast, ie the programme (which always remains the same) but the transmission (which is always a new one), the problem does not arise. This first transmission in a non-convention country is not protected, the second transmission which takes place in a convention country is protected and all the consequences flow from that proposition.

Article 1.2 provides for a kind of national treatment and a comparison of terms analogous to the relevant provisions of the Berne Convention. If a broadcast is made in the territory of one contracting state where the term of protection is longer and then broadcast in a second contracting state where the term is that provided for by the agreement (ie 20 years) the latter country may extend the same term of protection to its broadcasting organisation as that provided for in the first country. This is however not compulsory. If a broadcast has two countries of origin, that of the seat of the broadcasting organisation and a different country where the transmitters are situated, the Berne Convention[2] chooses the term of the country with the shorter protection period. The agreement leaves this question open, but as this position is rare (Monaco seems the only example) its consequences are not serious.

1 Straschnov op cit, p 266.
2 Art 4.3.

(6) Reservations and exceptions – article 3

(1) Reservations – article 3.1.

11.09 By making a declaration under article 10 a contracting state can make any of the following reservations:

(a) It can withhold or restrict the protection of 'diffusion by wire' meaning cable television.[1] This probably is the most important reservation as only two European countries have such protection and therefore the majority of ratifying countries have made the reservation.

Sub-paragraph 1(a) of Article 3 was amended in 1965 and the provision is now a little difficult to follow. It provides that a contracting state may 'withhold the protection' and 'restrict the protection of cable television . . . to a percentage of the transmissions . . . which shall not be less than 50% of the average weekly duration of the broadcasts of each . . . (protected) . . . organisation'.[2] The first part means total exclusion of the right against diffusion as far as broadcasting organisations on their own territory are concerned. The second part means reducing the protection of foreign broadcasting organisations against cable distribution to a minimum of 50% of the average weekly duration of broadcasts by each of these broadcasting organisations. As the two parts are linked one cannot be applied without also applying the other. The history of the protocol suggests that the idea behind the 50% provision was that a large number of broadcasts, eg public events news etc, does not involve large numbers of contributors to the programmes who may be copyright owners whereas another equally large number of broadcasts involves the rights of contributors (authors, performers, producers of films and phonograms) which may be prejudiced by the transmission by cable of programmes to which they have contributed.

It is suggested[3] that the correct interpretation of this rather vaguely drafted provision is twofold:

1. The first part of the reservation means that the original broadcasting organisation whose broadcasts are used by the cable operator must be protected to the extent of minimum of 50% of its average weekly duration of its broadcasts. National legislation can grant more than 50% protection but not less; which 50% is left open. National legislation could for instance choose to protect only evening programmes, as long as they cover an average 50% of the total.

2. The second part of the reservation means that the 50% protection applies to the foreign broadcasts. A country using the reservation must deny protection against cable transmission to its own broadcasting organisations totally.

If this interpretation is correct, the result would be that large countries with powerful broadcasting organisations would find it difficult to free cable distributors from the necessity to obtain licences from the national broadcasting organisations. On the other hand small countries, eg Belgium, which are customarily dependent on broadcasts originating from neighbouring states, will be enabled to improve the quality of the reception of foreign programmes by special cable operators.

However, in practice cable operators have to obtain licences to distribute the protected 50%, which means that they must negotiate with the foreign broadcasting organisations whose programmes they wish to disseminate. As it is impracticable to grant authorisations broadcast by broadcast except in very rare cases, blanket licences have to be negotiated.[4] This being so 'the 50% reservation' becomes a negotiating point which may influence the price paid, rather than the granting of the authorisation.

(b) Contracting states can withhold protection if the communication is not to a paying audience. This is the equivalent of article 13(d) of the Rome Convention.[5] Whereas the Rome Convention defines 'paying audience' as 'communication made in places accessible to the public against payment of an entrance fee', the agreement leaves the definition of the 'meaning' to domestic law. This may affect the classification of borderline cases such as restaurants, which do not charge for the performance but increase the price of the drinks.

(c) Contracting states can withhold protection, if the fixation or reproduction is either for private use, or 'solely for educational purposes' this is the equivalent of article 15/1(a) and 15/1(d) of the Rome Convention.[6] The private use exemption is the same, allowing private copying of television films. The eductional reservation is narrower as it covers only 'eductional purposes' whereas the Rome Convention covers 'scientific research' as well as teaching.

(d) Contracting states can withhold protection in respect of 'still photographs'.[7] However, states making this reservation run the risk that other states retaliate by using the reciprocity provision of article 4.4 of the Agreement.[8]

(e) Contracting states which provide protection for television broadcasts under their national law can exclude the conventional protection. This enables them to regulate domestic protection freely in accordance with their own laws. If the level of protection they grant their nationals is below the level of the Agreement, foreign broadcasting organisations are entitled to the conventional minimum; if the level is higher, foreign broadcasting organisations are entitled to the higher level of protection.[9]

(f) Contracting states can, as already mentioned, require both points of attachment, ie a broadcasting organisation constituted in the territory and transmitting from the territory concerned, instead of one or the other.[10]

1 The UK has made the reservation under the original art 3(i)(a).
2 Belgium has made the reservation under the revised art 3(i)(a).
3 Nordemann, Vink, Hertin *Internationales Urheberrecht, Kommentar* (1977) p 376.
4 Belgian cable distributors have not, so far, made licensing agreements with foreign broadcasting organisations though negotiations are in progress.
5 See para 8.35 above.
6 See paras 8.41 and 8.44 above.

7   See para 11.07 above.
8   Germany and the United Kingdom have made this reservation.
9   Germany has made this reservation.
10 Denmark, Sweden and the United Kingdom have made this reservation.

(2) *Exceptions – article 3.2*

11.10 The agreement states two exceptions from copyright protection: one for short extracts in reporting current events which is analogous to article 10(bis) of the Berne Convention[1] and article 15 1(b) of the Rome Convention;[2] the other for ephemeral fixation, which is analogous to article 11 (bis), paragraph 3 of the Berne Convention[3] and article 15(1)(c) of the Rome Convention.[4]

(a)   The current events exception is much narrower than that under the Rome Convention. Whereas, under the Rome Convention, to fall within the exception of the short excerpts need only be 'in connection with the reporting of current events', in the agreement the broadcast from which the short extracts are taken must 'itself constitute the whole or part of the event in question'. This means that the usual 'News' broadcasts or 'Télé-Journal' do not fall within the exception and they are totally protected. The exception applies only where the whole broadcast is the event, eg a sovereign's Christmas or a president's New Year broadcast, the television confrontation between two or more presidential candidates before an election, a party-political broadcast. It has to be stressed that, as under the Berne and the Rome Convention, the excerpt has to be 'short'.

The main fear of the broadcasting organisations, which motivated the tightening of the exception, was that the news and sports films made by the broadcasting organisations would be used in cinemas disguised as excerpts of current events.[5]

(b)   The exception for ephemeral fixations is identical to that of the Rome Convention.[6]

All exceptions only take effect if they are contained in the national law. They are not exceptions jure conventionis.

1   See para 5.60 above.
2   See para 8.42 above.
3   See para 5.44 above.
4   See para 8.42 above.
5   See Straschnov op cit, p 266. In Germany, the Hanseatic Court of Appeal in Hamburg and the German Supreme Court have found 'unfair competition' proved on similar facts: *Nord und Westdeutscher Rundfunkverband v AKI (Aktulitaten-kino* 7 July 1960 and BGHZ38, 1.
6   See para 8.42 above.

(7) Copyright tribunal – article 3.3

11.11 The Agreement provides the possibility ('the Parties may ...') for contracting states to create a tribunal, which may be administrative or judical, to deal with cable television and/or with the public performance right of broadcasting organisations. The powers given to the tribunal (not the issues to be dealt with) are inspired by the Performing Right Tribunal in the United Kingdom.[1] The tribunal will have jurisdiction to deal with cases where a licence for wire diffusion or for communication to the public has either 'been unreasonably refused' or 'granted on unreasonable terms' by the right owner (the broadcasting organisation). It is submitted that 'unreasonable refusal' or 'unreasonable terms' suggest cases of discrimination or abuse of power. The tribunal could not for instance overrule the motivated refusal of a broadcasting organisation to grant a licence to a cable operator if that organisation, as a matter of policy, refuses to licence any cable operators or if the broadcasting organisation refuses because contracts either with authors or performers or organisers of sporting events forbid it.[2]

The Rome Convention provides for the possibility of a compulsory licence on the performance right of broadcasting organisations[3] but does not deal with cable television.[4]

1 S 27, Copyright Act 1956.
2 See Nordmann, op cit, p 379 and Straschnov, op cit, p 266.
3 Art 13 (d).
4 Unfortunately the suggestion of such a tribunal contained in this paragraph has not been taken up anywhere in this form during the 20 years of the existence of the agreement.

(8) Seizure - article 4

11.12 Reminiscent of article 16 of the Berne Convention[1] and anticipating article 2 of the Phonogram Convention[2] the agreement seeks to deal with the importation of illicit fixations of television broadcasts or still photographs thereof and provides for their seizure. This is based on the thought that it would not be effective to protect fixations of broadcasts in convention countries if infringing copies can be imported with impunity just as this is true in the case of written materials (Berne Convention) or phonograms (Phonogram Convention). Just as the Phonogram Convention[3] the agreement leaves the measures to be taken to produce this result to national legislation, but it goes further than the Phonogram Convention in providing for seizure jure conventionis. Although, as under the Phonogram Convention, compliance with the Convention can be achieved by civil, criminal or administrative measures or a combination of them, seizure predicates some degree of co-operation from the executive organs of the state in question.

By virtue of article 4.1, whether the fixation is illicit has to be judged by the law of the importing country which must be a member state. It is irrelevant whether it was licit or illicit in an exporting country which must not be a member state. Where the exporting country is a member state the injured broadcasting organisation can exercise its rights by virtue of article 1.1(d) to which no reservations are allowed.

Whereas in the case of fixations of broadcasts or their reproduction the measure is compulsory ('shall be liable to seizure') in the case of still photographs and reproductions of them the measure is optional, because of the reservation which states can make under article 3.1(d) in respect of still photographs. In the case of importation of a still photograph of a television broadcast from a contracting state which has made such a reservation the importing state, by way of reciprocity, need not provide for seizure. An example will illustrate the position. A television broadcast is made in country A, a country which has ratified the agreement and is therefore protected. Still photographs are made of it in country B which has not ratified the Agreement. The stills are therefore lawful. They are then imported into country C, which has ratified the agreement. The stills are illicit and can be seized. If on the other hand country C had made a reservation in respect of stills under article 3.1(d) the stills imported would remain licit and could not be seized. Equally, if country A had made the reservation under article 3.1(d) and country C had ratified without reservation, country C would not be obliged to effect seizure (article 4.4) although it would be free do so if it pleased (article 4.2).

1 See para 5.67.
2 Phonogram Convention, art 2; see para 9.05 above.
3 Art 4/3.

State of ratifications and accessions on 1 January 1983

11.13

Agreement

(Strasbourg, 22 June 1960)

Contracting State	Entry into force
BELGIUM[1]	8 March 1968
CYPRUS	22 February 1970
DENMARK[1]	22 November 1961
FRANCE	1 July 1961
GERMANY, FEDERAL REPUBLIC OF[1]	9 October 1967
NORWAY[1]	10 August 1968
SPAIN	23 October 1971
SWEDEN[2]	1 July 1961
TURKEY	20 January 1976
UNITED KINGDOM[1]	1 July 1961

Protocol

(Strasbourg, 22 January 1965)

Contracting State	Entry into force
BELGIUM	8 March 1968
CYPRUS	22 February 1970
DENMARK	24 March 1965
FRANCE	24 March 1965
GERMANY, FEDERAL REPUBLIC OF	9 October 1967
NORWAY	10 August 1968
SPAIN	23 October 1971
SWEDEN	24 March 1965
TURKEY	20 January 1976
UNITED KINGDOM	24 March 1965

Additional Protocol

(Strasbourg, 14 January 1974)

The Additional Protocol entered into force on 31 December 1974, with respect to all States party to the European Agreement on the Protection of Television Broadcasts and the Protocol to the said Agreement.

1 The instruments of ratification were accompanied by reservations in accordance with art 3, para 1, of the Agreement: as to Belgium, see Copyright, 1968, p 147; as to Denmark, see Le Droit d'Auteur, 1961, p 360; as to Germany (Federal Republic of), see Copyright, 1967, p 217; as to Norway, see ibid., 1968, p 191; as to the United Kingdom, see ibid., 1961, p. 152.
2 Sweden availed itself of the reservations contained in subparagraphs (b), (c) and (f) of para 1 of art 3 of the Agreement.

Chapter 12

The Future of International Copyright Law

Summary

1. Challenges to international law
    (1) Political concepts opposed to copyright   12.02
    (2) Needs of developing countries   12.03
    (3) Economic approach of governments   12.04
2. Challenges to national law
    (1) The role of governments and parliaments   12.05
        (a) 'Consumerism'   12.06
        (b) Copyrights and neighbouring rights taken out of the copyright sphere   12.07
        (c) Difficulties of enforcement   12.08
    (2) The role of the courts   12.09
3. Challenges to the effectiveness of copyright
    (1) Challenges to the reproduction right   12.11
        (a) Home taping   12.12
        (b) Reprography   12.16
        (c) Computers   12.20
        (d) Videograms   12.25
    (2) Challenges to the broadcasting right
        (a) Cable diffusion   12.28
        (b) Satellites   12.33
    (3) Challenges to all copyrights and neighbouring rights   12.36
        (a) The sociology of copyright   12.36
        (b) The devaluation of copyright   12.37
        (c) The unity of copyright   12.38
        (d) The control of copyright   12.39
4. The survival of a viable copyright system in a technological age   12.40

12.01 When considering the future of international copyright law one has to remember three things:

First the concept of copyright is of fairly recent origin. There have been periods of great flowering of Western civilisation like the Greek city states, the Roman Empire, the European Renaissance without it, and there are still many countries where that part of the law either does not exist or does not effectively operate.[1]

Secondly copyright deals with the prevention of theft of immaterial or intellectual property which is a concept much more difficult to grasp than ordinary theft and far less deeprooted in the public consciousness of what is right and what is wrong and it is on that consciousness that all laws, and particularly those with a criminal content, are based. The process of convincing the general public that copyright infringement is theft is a long and arduous one which has merely begun.[1]

Thirdly the enforcement of international law, even when laid down in international conventions has not proved easy even in such vital spheres as health regulations or sea or air law.

After a century of very successful development there are now three major forms of the challenges to the concept of copyright: 1. challenges to international copyright law; 2. challenges to national copyright law; and 3. challenges to the effectiveness of copyright arising from the speed of technological development.

[1] See Stewart 'International Copyright in the 1980s' (Geiringer Memorial Lecture 1980) Bulletin of the Copyright Society of the US (April 1981) p 351.

1. The challenges to international law

(1) Political concepts opposed to copyright

12.02 In the 1940s and 1950s it was feared that a challenge to international copyright would come from countries with a communist or totalitarian philosophy which may negate the whole concept of intellectual property on the grounds that all creative people should find their reward and fulfilment in dedicating their works to the community represented by the state and the state in return should look after their material needs and that therefore individual rights are unnecessary and may even be positively harmful. As countries inclining to those philosophies became more common it was feared that this view might spread to many of the new countries which were still uncommitted on the subject of intellectual property rights, that the whole concept of copyright as a private and individual right might be endangered and that at least the general level of international protection might be reduced. This challenge did not materialise. The COMECON countries of Eastern Europe which had fairly sophisticated and successful copyright systems maintained their allegiance to copyright. The Soviet Union which, like France and the United States before her, had enacted a copyright law immediately after the revolution, developed it within the framework of its social and economic systems, revised it in 1973 and eventually ratified the UCC in 1974[1]. VAAP, the state-owned copyright agency, has built up a network of agreements with foreign collecting societies which are based on copyright principles and which will gradually[2] build up copyright relations with the rest of the world. Recent developments in the People's Republic of China suggest that they are not adverse to recognising the concept of copyright and, as a first step, willing to make bilateral agreements[3] and that they may eventually ratify one of the international copyright conventions.

Communist legal theory was recently restated in terms which should completely 'correspond to the basic principles of international copyright'.[4]

Equally, in any countries with rather totalitarian regimes in other parts of the world are members of at least one of the international copyright conventions and have thus accepted the general concept of international copyright.

[1] See para 19.01 below.
[2] The process can only be gradual as the ratification of the UCC has no retrospective effect and therefore most foreign works created before 1974 are not protected.
[3] The Trade Agreement between the US and the People's Republic of China (July 1979)

contains provisions for recognition of copyright. See Jon Baumgarten 'Copyright Relations between the US and the People's Republic of China'. Geiringer Lecture 1979.

4 Mihály Ficsor 'Technological Progress and Crisis Tendencies in Copyright' Copyright (March 1982) p 104 at p 113. See also Aurel Bernard and Gyorgy Boytha 'Socialist Copyright Law – A theoretical approach' RIDA (July 1976) p 45.

(2) Needs of developing countries

12.03 In the 1960s it was feared that the developing countries would challenge the concept of international copyright. This challenge was not based so much on ideological grounds as on the practical proposition that the developing countries needed and welcomed the intellectual property of the developed world, but that they were too poor and certainly too short of hard currency to pay for it in the same way as developed countries did, nor did they have any copyright material which could readily be offered in exchange. The implied challenge was that if they could not be accommodated they might opt out of the international copyright system, at least for the time being, and still take what they needed without payment, pleading that that was, after all, what the two superpowers had done to some extent in the not too distant past.

An attempt to meet this challenge was made at the Stockholm Conference in 1967 and the Paris Revision Conference in 1971. A system of compulsory licences was erected which was carefully structured to give, mainly to the publishers of the western world, an opportunity to meet the needs of developing countries before these compulsory licences come into effect.[1]

Less than a decade after the provisions came into effect (10 July 1974) and with only a few developing countries taking advantage of the 1971 Protocol it is too early to say with any certainty how they will work. At best they will prove to be a modus vivendi between the developed countries and the developing countries enriching the cultures of both and assuring the survival and further development of international copyright. At worst they will assure a breathing space for both developed and developing countries to cope with the demands of rapidly advancing technology and the possibility to try again if some of the provisions do not work satisfactorily. In any event they have prevented a breakdown of the worldwide application of international copyright which might have been the result of failure to find compromise solutions.

1 See paras 6.38ff above.

(3) The economic approach of governments

12.04 As copyright is largely a creature of statute law on the national level and entirely of conventions on the international level, it is self-evident that the development of international copyright necessitates the involvement of governments. The challenge to copyright comes from governments which regard copyright solely from the economic point of view and as a balance of payment problem. Any government will be inclined to ratify an international copyright or neighbouring rights convention if:

$$Ex + NPg = In^1$$

'Ex' is the total of the country's exports of copyrights and 'In' is the total of its imports. 'NPg' is the national prestige attached to the export of the works of national authors. Such works represent a nation's cultural heritage, as well as its spiritual aspirations. They are, in a sense, the nations very own contribution to the cultural achievements of mankind. In most countries imports of copyrights exceed exports. Such countries will thus only ratify a convention if the government is of the opinion that adding the national prestige to the value of exports will balance the import bill. The significance of this equation is that whereas 'Ex' and 'In' should be ascertainable figures, 'NPg' is always a matter of personal judgment. It can be defined as the gain to the country derived from the appreciation of its cultural and intellectual achievements abroad. Thus, the main variable in the equation is not measurable, but a matter of judgment by the government of the day so that the scope of imaginative advocacy, when putting the case for copyright, is very considerable and success or failure may depend on the quality and persuasiveness of that advocacy.

The traditional interval for revision of the Berne Convention seems to be 20 years[2] and the UCC will, after the 1971 revision, probably only be revised in future in conjunction with the Berne Convention in order to preserve the inter-relation of the two conventions and the two-tier effect of copyright protection. Thus, if tradition is followed, the two copyright conventions would not be due for revision until the 1990s. This may be justified in practice as the opinions of governmental experts seem to agree that most of the problems posed by rapid technological development will have to be treated on the national level first before they can be treated on the international level.

On the other hand, applying the same time span to neighbouring rights conventions, the Rome Convention 1961 would appear to be due for revision in the 1980s. The last meeting of the Intergovernmental Committee of the Rome Convention (1981) considered that the time was not ripe. When the time comes the matters to be considered for revision may include the following points:

1. deletion of the exception to performers' rights with regard to films;[3]
2. extension of the reproduction right of phonogram producers and possibly film producers (if the two copyright conventions are not revised for some time) to include a distribution right to enable the right owners to control the hiring of phonograms and videograms;[4]
3. extension of the reproduction right of phonogram producers to include a right against importation and distribution as in Art 2 of the Phonogram Convention;[5]
4. extension of the rights of performers, producers of phonograms and broadcasting organisations to cover cable distribution;[6]
5. making it clear that direct satellite broadcasts are protected in the same way as traditional broadcasts;[7]
6. extension of the 20 year term for neighbouring rights following the trend of several national legislations. (This would follow the pattern of the history of the Berne Convention).[8]

When the Rome Convention is revised a two-tier pattern may develop in the neighbouring rights field with the Rome Convention as the upper tier and the Phonogram Convention and the Satellite Convention as the lower tier similar to the Berne Convention/UCC relationship which has served copyright well.

The fear has sometimes been expressed that in view of the manifold challenges to copyright which exist it may be wiser not to revise the present conventions and rely for development on the existing options for progressive interpretation. This may be so for a short period but in the long run it is difficult to see how, in view of the increasingly rapid development of technology the last ever revision in the history of copyright can have taken place in 1971.[9] Effective copyright or neighbouring rights protection can only be maintained if reform keeps pace with both technological and social development.

1 See Stewart Geiringer Memorial Lecture 1980, op cit p 372.
2 Berne Convention 1886 revised Berlin 1908, Rome 1928, Brussels 1948 Stockholm/Paris 1967–1971. Nb. The Paris Conference 1896 produced an 'Additional Act and Interpretative Declaration and the Berne Conference 1914 an 'Additional Protocol', but were not complete revisions.

3   Rome Convention, art 19.
4   See para 12.37 below.
5   See para 9.05 above.
6   See para 12.32 below.
7   See para 8.35 above.
8   See para 5.08 above.
9   See Ficsor, op cit, p 113.

2. Challenges to national law

(1) The role of governments and parliaments

12.05   In the last 25 years there has been a positive response by governments and parliaments of most leading countries to the need of copyright law reform to adjust the law to advancing technology. New copyright Acts in the United Kingdom in 1956,[1] France, 1957,[2] India, 1957,[3] Scandinavia, 1959/1960,[4] Germany, 1965,[5] Australia, 1968,[6] Japan, 1971,[7] USSR, 1973,[8] United States, 1976[9] are evidence of this trend.

There are, however, three tendencies which constitute challenges to the development of copyright: (a) 'consumerism', (b) the tendency to replace what should be copyrights or neighbouring rights by levies which are a form of taxation, and (c) difficulties of enforcement.

1   See ch 18 below.
2   See ch 14 below.
3   See ch 23 below.
4   See ch 17 below.
5   See ch 15 below.
6   See ch 25 below.
7   See ch 29 below.
8   See ch 19 below.
9   See ch 22 below.

(a) *'Consumerism'*
12.06   More accurately described as consumer politics applied to copyright or neighbouring rights, 'consumerism' means that the consumer should have the widest possible access to all copyright material at the lowest possible cost and in many cases have free access. Almost everybody in a modern society is a consumer of copyrights in several respects; as a reader of books, newspapers or other printed copyright material, as a listener to music, as a viewer of television or as a parent of a child at school who should have his school books cheap or free, to name only the most common uses. Thus, put in electoral terms, on most copyright issues the overwhelming majority of voters are on one side and a comparatively very small number of voters, who are copyright owners, are on the other side of the argument. No politician in a democracy can totally ignore the fact that there are no votes in copyright when taking a position on a copyright issue. The counter argument that without an effective copyright system creative effort would be undermined and the public interest would suffer, is less obvious and will therefore have to be reiterated often and in many different forms. Far from being tediously repetitive it will have to be regarded as a noble pursuit, humanist in the best sense of the word.

(b) *Copyrights and neighbouring rights taken out of the copyright sphere*
12.07   When a new right is introduced such as a public lending right,[1] or an old right has to be reasserted such as the reproduction right in the case of 'Reprography'[2] or 'Home taping',[3] there is a great temptation for governments to take the new right out of the copyright system. In the case of a

public lending right this may be done because a limited fund is created from taxpayers' money as governments do not want borrowers from public libraries to have to pay a royalty and the government wants only nationals to benefit from this fund, which would otherwise be depleted. If a public lending right is introduced as a copyright the international conventions would apply and give all convention nationals the right to claim against the fund.[4] In the case of 'Home Taping' a levy on recording equipment or on blank tape[5] can be treated as a royalty to be divided among copyright owners as in Germany[6] or Austria.[7] However it can also be treated largely as a tax, as in Sweden[8] where 90% goes to public funds and only 10% to the right owners (authors, performers and phonogram producers). It has been said that such solutions are 'inconsistent with a free market economy'. It amounts to an expropriation of the rights of the copyright owner as his most fundamental right, the reproduction right is seriously eroded and the equitable remuneration which is due to him for the copying of his work is taken away from him by the state.

1 See eg Public Lending Right Act 1980 in the UK.
2 See para 12.16 below.
3 See para 12.12 below.
4 For instance in the Federal Republic of Germany; German Copyright Law 1965, 27.
5 See para 12.15 below.
6 German Copyright Act 1965, s 55.
7 Austrian Copyright Amendment Law, 1980, s 42.
8 Law of 24 June 1982, see para 17.29 below.

(c) *Difficulties of enforcement*

12.08 Many copyrights and neighbouring rights, particularly reproduction rights, are becoming increasingly difficult to enforce. 'Reprography'[1] and 'Home taping'[2] are outstanding examples. It would, however, be wrong to conclude from this that these rights should be abandoned and replaced by what would amount to free use exceptions. If this argument is transferred from the field of intellectual property to the field of material property the fallacy becomes clear. It would be like arguing that because in most large modern cities the great majority of burglaries remain undetected and therefore unpunished, the right to one's valuables in the home should be abandoned and housebreaking should be struck from the list of criminal offences. When public performance rights in music were first introduced at the beginning of the twentieth century, it was argued that because of the multiplicity of rights and a very large number of locations where music is performed in public, the right would be unenforcable. These fears have proved groundless and the performance right has become of very great value to copyright owners without in any way harming the public. As the history of copyright shows, different forms of enforcement by collecting societies, blanket licensing and clearing house systems, and only in the last resort compulsory licences and equitable remuneration, would appear to be the correct answers to the problem.[3]

1 See para 12.16 below.
2 See para 12.12 below.
3 See para 4.33 above.

(2) The role of the courts

12.09 'Social necessities and social opinion are always more or less in advance of law. We may come indefinitely near to the closing of the gap between them, but it has a perpetual tendency to reopen. The greater or lesser happiness of a people depends on the degree of promptitude with which the gap is narrowed'.[1] The gap can often be narrowed by the courts. The classic example is the development of the 'droit d'auteur' in France.[2] Two brief copyright laws (1791 and 1793) passed in the wake of the French Revolution were developed in the course of a century and a half into one of the most highly developed copyright systems of the world solely by the courts, until the law was eventually codified in 1957. In the United Kingdom, when piracy of phonograms threatened to erode both the recording right of authors and the reproduction right of producers of phonograms, the judges intervened and created a procedural remedy (the 'Anton Piller Order')[3] which proved swift and effective and enabled copyright to re-assert itself in good time.

As copyright is in essence an individual property right which benefits a small minority, the creators of copyright material, against a large majority, the users of copyright material, the judges who are irremovable under most constitutions may be in a better position to hold the balance between private and public interest fairly than members of Parliament who, however enlightened, have to keep an eye on the next election.

The role of the courts is also essential in holding the balance between copyright owners and copyright users in the process of finding an equitable remuneration for copyrights and neighbouring rights, whether the right is an absolute right or a right to equitable remuneration under a compulsory licence. Royalties must in the first place be a matter of negotiations between the parties, the copyright owners and the copyright users. However, if the negotiating processes are exhausted and the parties fail to agree, it becomes a justiciable issue for the courts. It should not be a legislative issue. Parliament is not the ideal forum for a royalty rate decision as political considerations and the relative strength of lobbies might influence the issue and the end result may be less than 'fair and equitable'. Once the amount of copyright royalty has become a justiciable issue experience seems to show that a special tribunal is preferable to the ordinary courts. Copyright tribunals have been established successively in many countries.[4]

In many cases it can be said that a fair rate for the use of a copyright is the lowest amount a reasonable copyright owner would accept and also the highest amount a reasonable user would pay. The adjudication therefore requires both the weighing of arguments about the philosophy of copyright and of arguments of a commercial kind. The best tribunal for such issues is a professional judge as chairman to preside over the procedure and decide points of law and a number of laymen to fulfil mutatis mutandis the function of a jury in finding what is equitable. When a tribunal has heard a number of cases on the licensing of a particular right a 'going rate' emerges and thereafter both copyright owners and users know approximately what they can expect and more cases are settled by negotiation and fewer cases are brought before the tribunal, thus easing the workload.

1 Sir Henry Maine *Ancient Law* p 24.
2 See para 14.01 below.
3 See para 4.45 above.
4 Canada: Copyright Act 1952, s 50.
   Germany (Federal Republic): Copyright Law 1965 and Regulations on the Arbitration Commission 1965/1970.
   United Kingdom: Copyright Act 1956, ss 23–30 'Performing Right Tribunal'. The Whitford Committee has recommended extension of its jurisdiction beyond performing rights.
   Australia: Copyright Act 1968 ss 136 ff.
   USA: Copyright Law 1976 ss 801 ff.

3. Challenges to the effectiveness of copyright

12.10 (a) The rapid development of technology has given a considerable impulse to copyright law because of the large number of uses to which a work can be put, thus increasing the potential rewards for its creator. 'Copyright is the Cinderella of the law. Her rich older sister, Franchises and Patents, long crowded her into the chimney corner. Suddenly the Fairy Godmother, Invention, endowed her with mechanical and electrical devices as magical as the pumpkin coach and the mice footmen. Now she whirls through the mad mazes of a glamorous ball.'[1] These 'mechanical and electrical devices' are many: recording and audio and video tape recording, broadcasting and broadcasting by cable and satellites, photo copying, storage and retrieval systems. They are all challenges in the sense that they may greatly increase the use of copyright material and thereby the income of the creators or they may seriously undermine it.

(b) The challenge to the copyright system lies in the ease with which one or many copies can be made, and in the fact that such copies are being made in private homes or in offices and other non-public places where any control over the reproduction of copyright material is either impossible (homes) or very difficult (offices etc).

1 Zachariah Chafee 'Reflections on the Law of Copyright,' 45 Columbia Law Review p 719.

(1) Challenges to the reproduction right

12.11 The underlying thought of all copyright protection is that both the reward of creative work and the widest possible dissemination of works are regarded as in the public interest. Thus a property right of limited duration and of varying scope represents the balance struck by legislators between these two public interests. Historically the initial impulse for the creation of copyrights was the invention of the printing press[1] and the first law granting a statutory right to creators, the Statute of Queen Anne (1709) in the United Kingdom is evidence of this fact. The reproduction right, however, was considered so fundamental that when the first international copyright convention, the Berne Convention, was drafted in 1886, the draftsmen apparently did not consider it necessary to include this right jure conventionis. It was fundamental and well understood. The reproduction right was not spelt out in the convention until the Stockholm Act of 1967.[2] By that time the rapid progress of technology had in practice already started to erode the reproduction right. The most powerful challenges to the copyright owners' reproduction right come from duplicating machines and tape recorders.[3] Both machines are capable of reproducing works in which copyright subsists quickly, cheaply and in such numbers as may be required. In both cases control of the use of the works reproduced by the copyright owners is very difficult or impossible. The first phenomenon (reproduction of works by duplicating machine) is known as 'Reprography', the second (reproduction of phonograms or of broadcast performances or films) is known as 'Home taping'.

The main differences between the two phenomena are:

(a) The category of works most frequently reproduced: in the case of 'Reprography' are mainly literary works, in the case of 'Home taping' mainly musical works.
(b) The status of the infringers: in the case of 'Reprography' mainly organisations; (commercial companies, public libraries, educational establish-

ments) in the case of 'Home taping' mainly private persons and as the name suggests mainly in their private homes.
(c) The material copied: in the case of 'Reprography' a substantial proportion of the material reproduced is material in which copyright is not claimed, eg office memoranda, notices etc; in the case of 'Home taping' most of the material copied is material protected by copyright, such as musical works, phonograms, films.
(d) The extent of material copied: in the case of 'Reprography' it is often part of a work, albeit a substantial part, such as a chapter of a book, a part of an article; in the case of 'Home taping' it is nearly always the whole work, such as a song, a symphony, a whole phonogram or at least one whole track of a phonogram, a whole film.

1 See para 2.04 above.
2 See para 5.38 above.
3 See Stewart 'Home Taping' EIPR 1980 p 207.

(A) 'HOME TAPING'

12.12 The facts: a phonogram or a videogram is either borrowed from a friend or from a library or (more often in the case of videograms) hired for a day from a shop or recorded off the air from a radio or television broadcast.

12.13 The law: prima facie the copying is an infringement of the rights of the author of the work, the producer of the film or the phonogram and in some countries of the performers whose performances are recorded. The question is whether the copying falls under the private use exceptions which exist in most national legislations and in article 9(2) of the Berne Convention[1] and article 15(1)(a) of the Rome Convention.[2] It is submitted that it is clearly not covered by the exception. The draftsmen of the convention and national legislators had in mind when creating the exception that private persons should be able, without payment, to take extracts from books or periodicals or other printed matter for their private use. They did not contemplate the copying of the whole work. The Berne Convention allows national legislation 'to permit the reproduction of such works in certain special cases' without payment if two conditions are fulfilled: a) 'such reproduction does not conflict with a normal exploitation of the work' and b) 'does not unreasonably prejudice the legitimate interests of the author'. It is plain that in the circumstances of 'Home taping' of a work protected by copyright, 'Home taping' does prejudice the legitimate interests of the author. It does conflict with the normal exploitation of the work as it deprives him of such benefit as he derives from a sale and it prejudices his legitimate interests as it drastically reduces the potential market for his work.

Article IV bis/2[3] of the Universal Copyright Convention provides that exceptions made from the three basic rights by domestic legislation must 'not conflict with the spirit and provisions of this convention'. Any state whose legislation provides for such exceptions must 'accord a reasonable degree of effective protection' to the reproduction right. As this provision was inserted into the Universal Copyright Convention in 1971 at the same time as article 9(2) of the Berne Convention was drafted it seems not unreasonable to assume, as did the WIPO/UNESCO working party[4] in 1977 and as do Desbois, Françon, Kerever,[5] that the scope of the exceptions permissible under the Universal Copyright Convention does not differ appreciably from that of article 9(2) of the Berne Convention. The use of the words 'effective protection' also seem to support this proposition, as a protection on a lower level than that provided by the Berne Convention in this respect would hardly give effective protection to right owners.

Article 15/1 (a) of the Rome Convention[6] simply provides for domestic law making exceptions as regards 'private use'. This excludes public use or use for profit but gives no guide as to the scope of the exception. This is understandable as 'Home taping' was not a threat in 1961. It had started to become one by 1971, but the Phonogram Convention 1971[7] deals only with the protection of producers of phonograms 'against the making of duplicates ... provided that such making ... is for the purpose of distribution to the public'. Thus the problem of 'Home taping' does not arise within the confines of the Convention.

1 See para 5.39 above.
2 See para 8.41 above.
3 See para 6.20 above.
4 WIPO/UNESCO Working Party, Geneva, February 1977.
5 Desbois, Françon, Kerever 'Les Conventions Internationales du droit d'auteur et des droits voisins' (1976) pp 240 ff. See also Collova 'Reproduction sonore et visuelle pour l'usage personnel' GRUR vol 57 (1979) p 72.
6 See para 8.41 above.
7 Art 2, Phonogram Convention; see para 9.05 above.

12.14 Enforcement: As by definition this form of reproducing phonograms or films and thereby also the works contained in them takes place in the privacy of the home, any attempt by the right owners to enforce their reproduction right would be regarded as an unacceptable intrusion into the privacy of the home and therefore effective control or enforcement is impracticable.

In *Universal et al v Sony et al*, commonly referred to as the '*Betamax*' case, the United States Court of Appeals (Ninth circuit) held[1] that off-the-air copying of telecasts of copyrighted audio-visual materials by tape-recorders used in private homes for private non-commercial use constitutes an infringement of copyright. The court also held that manufacturers and distributors, retail sellers, as well as advertising agencies promoting such video tape-recorders are liable for contributory infringement since they knew that the tape-recorders would be used for such purposes and thus induced, caused or materially contributed to the infringing conduct. The court further held that it is not necessary that the contributory infringer has actual knowledge that the activity which he renders possible or encourages constitutes an infringement of copyright. It is sufficient that he has knowledge of the infringing activity. The court further held that such activities, although carried out in private homes and for non-commercial purposes, are not covered by the 'fair use' exceptions in the law.

Two national legislations have provided a possible answer to the problem. The German Copyright Law 1965[2] provides for a royalty on the recording equipment and the Austrian Copyright (Amendment) Law 1980[3] provides for a royalty on the blank tapes which are used to make copies of phonograms. Such royalties differ from ordinary royalties paid for the use of copyright works in two respects: 1. The royalty is not paid by the user of the work but by the manufacturer of the equipment which enables the user to copy the work. 2. The use is not single use as with other copyright royalties but multiple use. A copy of a phonogram put on tape can be erased and used again a few times and a tape recorder can make large numbers of copies during the 5 to 10 years it may be in use. It is because of the possibility of multiple use that a royalty on the recording equipment as well as a royalty on the tapes used for such copying seems a feasible legislative solution.

1 Judgment of 19 October 1981. Court of Appeal (9th circ) 1981, *Universal City Studios Inc v Sony Corp of America*; see para 21.25 below. The case under appeal.
2 German Copyright Law 1965, s 55.
3 Austrian Copyright (Amendment) Law 1980, s 42.

12.15 The future: The joint subcommittees of the Intergovernmental Copyright Committee (Universal Copyright Convention) and the Executive Committee (Berne Convention)[1] have called attention to these systems which on the one hand affirm the right of the public to this form of private copying for non-commercial purposes and, on the other hand provide a revenue from such use for all right owners. 'In essence, this would be a statutory licence to record works for use in the home. It would obviously eliminate the staggering difficulties of enforcing private rights in private homes.'[2]

This is obviously a matter for national legislation. At the international level it has to be borne in mind that when the private use exceptions of the international conventions were enacted private copying meant the copying of extracts, copying by hand and making one copy. The present position is radically different: the whole work is copied by machine and taking the general public as a whole it is estimated that of some copyright material such as phonograms in some countries as many 'private copies' are made in the home as are sold in the shops.[3] This is a situation totally different from what the private use exceptions of the international conventions had contemplated.

There is however a possible danger in this type of solution to the problem of private copying. A levy or tax could be introduced with the bulk of the income going to the state to be used for general cultural purposes, thus turning copyright, which is a private and personal right, into a source for generating public funds.[4] Copyright owners would lose out as their reproduction right would be greatly reduced in scope and value and the compensation paid by the user for the use of copyright material would go to the state. This would represent a decisive shift affecting the balance, carefully constructed in copyright between private rights and public interest and it is questionable whether what comes close to an expropriation of the copyright owner is consistent with the philosophy of a free market economy.

1   See para 12.13 note 4 above.
2   David Ladd, Register of Copyrights of the USA, at the National Council of Patent Law Association, Washington, October 1981.
3   According to a statement by Warner Communications Inc (26 March 1982) 639 million phonograms (discs and tapes) were sold in the US in 1980 having a retail value of $3,682 million and during the same period phonograms having a retail value of $2,850 million were copied. It is estimated that by 1982 the number of phonograms copied exceeded in value those sold.
4   Eg Sweden, Law of 24 June 1982; see para 17.29 below.

(b) 'REPROGRAPHY'

12.16 The facts: Until the 1960s the customary methods of obtaining multiple copies were carbon copying (resulting in only three or four copies), duplicating by use of stencil, and photostat copying (involving sensitised material and a dark room). All these methods were slow, awkward and expensive. In the 1950s and 1960s machines came on the market which used xerographic and electrophotographic methods which were fast, clean and cheap. By the 1970s these machines were capable of being operated by a reasonably intelligent and adroit 10-year-old. Laser techniques and holographic reproduction methods were developed and the generic term adopted for all these systems of reproduction is 'reprographic reproduction' or 'reprography'. Furthermore, printed matter can be recorded in the shape of microfilms which are very small so that they can be easily stored, the image being minute cannot be read but can be 'blown up' at any time to normal size and copies can be run off at comparatively low cost. The reduction ratio is up to 150 to 1. Thus whole books can be stored in great numbers and with the use of computers, storage and retrieval systems can be established which can cope, in a confined space, with the material so far contained in very large libraries or archives.

12.17 The law: Both the Berne Convention[1] and the UCC[2] now contain a reproduction right. The Berne Convention permits countries of the Union to establish exceptions 'in certain special cases' provided that the reproduction 'does not conflict with a normal exploitation of the work and does not unreasonably prejudice the legitimate interests of the author'. An interpretation of this provision when applied to 'reprography' is contained in the Report of the Stockholm Conference (1967):

> 'If it is considered that reproduction conflicts with the normal exploitation of a work, reproduction is not permitted at all. If it is considered that reproduction does not conflict with the normal exploitation of the work, the next step would be to consider whether it does not unreasonably prejudice the legitimate interests of the author. Only if such is not the case would it be possible, in certain special cases, to introduce a compulsory licence, or to provide for use without payment. A practical example might be photocopying for various purposes. If it consists of producing a very large number of copies it may not be permitted, as it conflicts with the normal exploitation of the work. If it implies a rather large number of copies for use in industrial undertakings, it may not unreasonably prejudice the legitimate interests of the author provided that, according to national legislation, an equitable remuneration is paid. If a small number of copies is made photocopying may be permitted without payment particularly for individual or scientific use.'[3]

This comment was carefully drafted as it was clear by 1967 that many countries, not all classed as developing countries, would like to introduce compulsory licences to reduce their dependence on foreign publishers for reproducing copyright material (mainly educational books) and to reduce the cost to them (mainly in foreign currency). Two distinctions emerge clearly from the report for the guidance of national legislations when they come to deal with these 'special cases': the distinction between single copies and multiple copies of the work and the distinction between individual users on the one hand and corporate users such as libraries, archives, documentation centres, research institutions, schools, universities, government departments on the other. It seems also clear from the history of this provision and of the 'fair use' provisions in national legislations that what was originally envisaged was a) making single copies by hand in a library or later by typewriter at home, b) copying of parts of works only within strict limits, c) copying for purposes of private study and private or professional research. Each of these points is well illustrated by a well known statement made by the Royal Society in the United Kingdom:

> 'Science rests upon its published record, and ready access to public scientific and technical information is a fundamental need of scientists everywhere. All bars which prevent access to scientific and technical publications hinder the progress of science and should be removed. Making single copies of extracts from books or periodicals is essential to research workers, and the production of such single extract copies, by or on behalf of scientists, is necessary for scientific practice'.[4]

Large scale copying, copying of whole works and copying by commercial enterprises or public institutions were clearly not within the contemplation of these provisions.

The two phases in article 9(2) apply cumulatively:

(a) The reproduction must not conflict with a normal exploitation of the work. Schoolbooks, for instance, are normally exploited by being printed and sold to the general public. Article 9(2) does therefore not permit the introduction of a compulsory licence in respect of schoolbooks even if payments were to be made to copyright owners.[5]

(b) The reproduction must not 'unreasonably' prejudice the legitimate interests of the copyright owner. Clearly all such copies prejudice the interests of the author as he may lose a sale and thereby a royalty. The question is whether such prejudice is reasonable or not.

Desbois[6] referring to the two cumulative conditions of article 9(2) gives the example of an industrial undertaking reproducing an article from a scientific magazine for the use of its research department. The first condition is met as this is not a 'normal exploitation' of the work but the second condition is not met as the undertaking acts for a commercial purpose in the same way as if it had obtained a licence and the author loses his royalties so that his legitimate interests are prejudiced

The question whether, if there is prejudice to the interest of the author, such prejudice is reasonable or not leaves great latitude to national legislation and on the national level to the courts. The UCC permits states to make exceptions which do not conflict with the 'spirit and provisions' of the convention and 'accord a reasonable degree of effective protection'.[7] This leaves an even wider discretion to member states.

1 Berne Convention, Paris Act 1971, art 9.
2 Universal Copyright Convention (1971), art IV bis/2.
3 Report of Main Committee, Stockholm Conference 1967, para 85.
4 Statement by the Royal Society to a government committee (Gregory Committee) in 1952.
5 WIPO Guide to Berne 9.7.
6 Desbois 'Le Droit d'Auteur en France' Dalloz (1978) p 945.
7 Universal Copyright Convention (1971), art IV bis/2.

12.18 Two committees of the Berne Union and the UCC[1] jointly made a thorough study of the problem in 1975 and concluded that 'a uniform solution on the international level cannot, for the time being, be found' but recommended that national solutions should be based on two principles: that each of the states should 'establish whatever is best adapted to their educational, cultural, social and economic development' in order to assure the protection of the economic interests of copyright owners under the convention and that states where Reprography is widespread should 'consider among other measures, encouraging the establishment of collective systems to exercise and administer the right to remuneration'.

Several countries have, in fact, dealt with the problem by legislation. Three examples of different schemes will serve to illustrate the variety of national solutions.

The Swedish Copyright Law[2] gives archives and libraries the right to make copies of literary and artistic works 'for the purpose of their activities'. Copyright owners are paid for such use out of a state fund. Payments are based on the number of copies made, to an organisation named BONUS which distributes the revenue using a sampling system to determine the shares of individual right owners.

The law of the Federal Republic of Germany.[3] Authors have a right to equitable remuneration for the reproduction of their works for commercial purposes (the making of single copies for strictly personal use is free). A blanket licence scheme is in operation under which a collecting society called 'Wissenschaft', which represents authors of scientific works and to which such authors assign their rights, collects from commercial enterprises which regularly subscribe to periodicals a fee of 20% of the annual subscription rate. Half of the revenue goes to publishers in accordance with the level of copying from each periodical, the other half goes to societies of authors for general welfare purposes for the benefit of authors.

The United States Copyright Law *1976* contains a 'fair use' exception[4] for purposes of criticism comment, news reporting, teaching (including multiple copies for classroom use), scholarship and research. The law names four factors to be considered 'in determining whether the use made of a work in any particular case is fair use':

'(1) the purpose and character of the use, including whether such use is of a commercial nature or is for non profit educational purposes;
(2) the nature of the copyrighted work;
(3) the amount and substantiality of the portion used in relation to the copyrighted work as a whole; and
(4) the effect of the use upon the potential market for or value of the copyrighted work.'

Reproduction by libraries and archives is dealt with separately.[5]

1   Report of the Sub-committee of the Executive Committee of the International Union for the Protection of Literary and Artistic Works and the Sub-committee of the Intergovernmental Copyright Committee on Reprographic Reproduction, Washington DC, July 1975, Copyright (1975) p 159.
2   Swedish Copyright Law 1960, art 12.
3   German Copyright Law 1965, art 54(2).
4   US Copyright Law 1976, para 107.
5   US Copyright Law 1976, para 108. See para 21.24 below.

12.19   The future: It seems fairly clear when laws refer to 'fair dealing' or 'fair use' four basic categories of exceptions were envisaged: a 'private study' exception which was the original concept,[1] an 'instruction' exception which was intended for teacher and pupil use in educational establishments, an 'anthology' exception for the inclusion of short passages of literary works in various collections, and a 'library' exception. The first category envisaged single use, the second a handful of copies, the third only short fragments of works and the fourth envisaged copies made by a librarian (bearing in mind that nearly all public libraries are non-profit making) for a single user.

None of the four envisaged the multiple copying of whole works in considerable quantities. None can therefore be interpreted to cover the new phenomenon of 'reprography', and it would be surprising if the courts in these circumstances did not interpret the statutory exceptions fairly narrowly.

The nub of the problem is that the individual use may well be 'fair use' but that a million of such 'fair' uses amount to a situation which does in effect 'unreasonably prejudice the interests of the author'.

Private copying to the extent it is practised today is therefore illegal in most countries, certainly in all Berne Convention countries. The only practical answer seems to be blanket licensing by collecting societies representing all copyright owners or groups of copyright owners.

1   A rule of thumb published by the British Copyright Council on behalf of copyright owners illustrates the point. 'Extracts of up to 4,000 words of one work or two or more extracts of 3,000 words each adding up to a maximum of 8,000 words, provided that the total amount copied is not more than 10% of the entire work. Poems and other short pieces are to be regarded as whole works'.

(c)   COMPUTERS

12.20   The facts: Computers are sophisticated machines which carry out a large variety of lengthy processes in a very small fraction of the time it would take a human being to do so and which are also used for the storage and retrieval of information. The great majority of computer operations do not affect copyright materials such as medical diagnosis, seat bookings for transport, calculations for technical and business projects, weather forecasting, payroll records. If such operations deal with copyright works there are three ways in which the operations of a computer impinge upon copyright:

(a) Computer programs. These are sets of instructions for controlling the sequence of operations to be carried out by the computer to achieve the task. They may be written or typed or punched as holes in paper.
(b) Storage and retrieval of copyright material. The Material may be stored as recordings on discs, magnetic tape or cards.
(c) Works created with the help of a computer, such as literary or musical works.

The fact that computers can be linked in networks, the use of simplified 'mini-computers' by commercial enterprises as well as the growth of 'software houses', specialising in the production of computer programs, has rendered the problem of copyright protection more acute.

12.21 The law:

(a) *Computer programs*
A program is the expression of the mind of its author and as such a work of the intellect. Thus, if compiling the program has involved a sufficient measure of skill and labour (copyright laws test) or of originality and creative effort, ('droit d'auteur' laws test) it will constitute a literary work.[1] In international law the definition of the Berne Convention 'the expression "literary and artistic works" shall include every protection in the literary, scientific and artistic domain, whatever may be the mode or form of its expression'[2] seems wide enough to accommodate computer programs. The subject of the protection is not the mathematical concept but the outward and visible emanation of that concept which clearly is a literary work. The same applies to the UCC 'rights of other copyright proprietors in literary ... works, including writings ...'[3]

If that is accepted the term of copyright in the program should be 50 years pma. Although the short commercial life of such programs may suggest a shorter term the obligations of countries of the Berne Union would not permit a shorter term for 'literary and artistic works'. Under the UCC[4] it would be 25 years pma and in countries which had 'limited this term for certain classes of works to a period computed from the first publication of the work' it could be 25 years from first publication as such countries are 'entitled ... to extend them to other classes of works'.[5]

The computer itself is regarded as a very sophisticated tool, but a tool nonetheless comparable to a typewriter, a printing press or a camera. The computer program, on the other hand, has to be protected because like other copyright material it is lengthy and expensive to produce but quick and cheap to copy.

Detection of infringements will be difficult as they will almost invariably not take place in public. However, this is a difficulty shared with private copying of other works.[6]

1   After initial doubts this is now generally accepted. See Ulmer 'Problems arising from the utilisation of electronic computers and other technological equipment', Report for the Executive Committee of the Berne Union and Intergovernmental Copyright Committee, 1971, citing. Report of Committee of Governmental Experts, December 1980. (Copyright (March 1981) p 73).
2   Berne Convention, art 2(1).
3   UCC, art I.
4   UCC, art IV, 2(a).

5   The WIPO 'Model Provisions on the Protection of Computer Software' (1977) s 7, stipulates a maximum term of 25 years 'from the time the computer software was created'.
6   For literature see: Breyer (1970) Harvard LR 281; Ulmer (1971) 2 IIC 56;Gotzen (1977) 13 Copyright 15; Tapper, Computer Law (1978).

(b) *Storage and retrieval of copyright material*

12.22 (1) ACTS SUBJECT TO PROTECTION. There are three possible phases of the process which may give rise to copyright protection: the 'input' stage, the fixation in the 'memory' of the computer and the 'output' stage. The better opinion[1] is that the input of copyright material constitutes 'reproduction' within the meaning given to that term, by both the international conventions.[2] As in almost all cases the input of copyright material into the computer will involve reproduction of the work in a material form when the work is encoded on punched cards, tapes etc, the copyright owner will be able to exercise his right at that stage which will enable him to regulate the remaining stages of the process by contract. However, there is little doubt that fixation of copyright material in the internal computer 'memory' also amounts to reproduction and thus unauthorised fixation would be an infringement.[3] Finally, if the 'output' of the computer takes the form of printouts this should also amount to a reproduction. Protection of 'output' of protected material by a visual display unit (images on a screen or on a cathode ray tube) is less certain.[4] In any event 'output' is probably subject to the generally recognised copyright exceptions for private use and use for purposes of education and research.

(2) SUBJECT MATTER OF PROTECTION. Three uses of copyright material fall for consideration: (1) Storage in the computer of the usual particulars of a work (author, title, publisher, year of publication) – the index method. This will be regarded as free use. (2) Storage of an abstract. If the abstract is either an adaptation of the work or otherwise the result of a creative effort of its author, it will be protected. If it is merely a listing of facts contained in the original work it will not be protected. (3) Storage of the full text of a work. This requires authorisation of the copyright owner. Compilations of data will be protected only if a sufficient degree of skill and labour have gone into their preparation.

(3) ADMINISTRATION OF THIS FORM OF REPRODUCTION RIGHT. In most cases it will not be practical to exercise these rights on an individual basis and collective administration and clearing house systems would seem the obvious solution. On the other hand, compulsory licence systems should not be resorted to unless a clearing house system with the task of entering into contractual arrangements with computer owners on behalf of authors or the devising of model contracts to be collectively administered has proved ineffective.[5] In any event the provisions of the international copyright conventions would appear to militate against compulsory licence systems. Under article 9(2) of the Berne Convention[6] the reproduction of works by computerised information and documentation systems would be very likely to 'unreasonably prejudice the legitimate interests of the author'. With regard to article IV bis, paragraph 2 of the Universal Copyright Convention the General Report says that the conference agreed that the provision did not permit the introduction of a general system of compulsory licences which provided for compulsory licences for all types of works with respect to a particular form of use. The utilisation for storage and retrieval by a computer would appear to be such a particular form of use.[7]

1   Report of the Committee of Governmental Experts on 'Copyright problems arising from the use of computers for access to or the creation of works', December 1980, Copyright (March 1981) p 73.
2   Art 9(1), Berne Convention and art IV bis 1, UCC.
3   See Report of Committee of Governmental Experts, op cit, p 76.

4 According to the Report of the Committee of Governmental Experts, op cit, p 76, some experts took the view that this amounts to public performance but the wording of arts 11 and 14 of the Berne Convention and art IV bis of the UCC and the fact that much of such projection will not take place in public places make this doubtful.
5 See Committee of Governmental Experts, op cit, p 77.
6 See para 5.39 above.
7 See Ulmer 'Problems arising from the use of electronic computers and related facilities for storage and retrieval of Copyright works' Copyright (July–August 1979) p 200 at p 204.

(c) *Works created with the help of a computer*

12.23 If a work is produced by a computer as a result of instructions given to the computer by the author (eg a composer), he will be the author of the work. If a computer program is capable of producing different results and the author exercises the choice he will be the author of the work produced by the computer. If the output is the result of random choices or choices made by a third party there will probably be no copyright in the result.[1]

1 See Committee of Governmental Experts, op cit, p 77.

12.24 The future: At present much of the material stored in computers is information which is not subject to copyright and most of the copyright material stored is stored in the form of abstracts only. However it is possible that the development of more and more sophisticated computers may totally change the dissemination of information 'even to the extent of replacing printed works completely . . . the day may come when all homes and offices throughout the country are linked to a national computer centre via viewer/printer consoles'.[1] The result of such a development would be that the supply of one copy of a new work to a central point would make it or selections from it, available at all offices and homes which are linked to the central point. Bearing in mind that the whole concept of copyright in modern times arose from the invention of the printing press[2] even its partial replacement by computers would amount to a revolutionary change. The copyright owner would then have to exercise his copyright at the input stage and look to the computer disseminator for his royalties in the same way that he has looked towards his publisher in the past.[3] As the copyright owner can both under international law and under most national laws control the reproduction of his work 'there seems no good reason why he should not be entitled to control copying in computers.'[4]

1 'Report of the Whitford Committee' 1977, in the United Kingdom, para 506.
2 See para 2.04 above.
3 See Stewart, Geiringer Memorial Lecture (1980), op cit, p 354.
4 Cornish *Intellectual Property Rights* (1981) p 438.

(d) VIDEOGRAMS

12.25 The facts: The term 'videogram' is now fairly generally used to indicate audio-visual recordings fixed on any form of material support ('videodiscs' if that support is a disc, 'video cassettes' if the support is a tape).[1] In the past most of the recordings issued as videograms were for educational and instructional use or if for entertainment were existing films reissued as videograms, but this is undoubtedly changing and a new medium is developing.

1 See *WIPO Glossary* (1980) No 256.

12.26 The law: As there are no legally significant differences between a videogram and a film there can be little doubt that videograms will be assimilated to cinematographic works in countries of the Latin 'droit d'auteur' tradition and to films in the countries of the Anglo-Saxon tradition. In the Berne Convention[1] the definition of protected works lists 'cinematographic works to which are assimilated works expressed by a process analogous to cinematography'. As the *WIPO Guide* points out: 'It is not so much the process employed which is analogous as the effects, sound and visual, of that process' which means that the 'legal regime applicable, according to the convention is that applicable to cinematographic works'.[2] Although the Universal Copyright Convention does not contain a definition of cinematographic works[3] 'reasonable interpretation leads to the conclusion that a videogram may be assimilated to a cinematographic work in view of the similarities existing between these two types of works'.[4] It is thus not surprising that the subcommittees of the two international copyright conventions came to the conclusion that the advent of videograms did not require a revision of the conventions nor did it 'necessitate the preparation of a new international instrument'.[5]

Thus, article 14 bis which provides that 'a cinematographic work shall be protected as an original work'[6] is applicable and 'the owner of the copyright in a cinematograph work shall enjoy the same rights as the author of an original work'. As the *WIPO Guide* points out this is a compromise between the various legal systems in force.[7] It is left to the national law of the country where protection is claimed to decide who shall be that owner of the copyright.[8] Thus the owner of the copyright in the videogram will be the 'maker' or 'producer' of the videogram in his own right in the Anglo-Saxon countries where there is a film copyright or in other countries the 'maker' of the videogram by reason of a legal assignment or the various artistic contributors to the videogram.[9] Thus the videogram producer will, by virtue of his copyright or by a legal presumption or cessio legis, be able to authorise or prohibit the reproduction or any other use of his videogram without his consent. He will also have to ensure that all pre-existing rights are assigned to him. The courts in most countries interpret copyright contracts restrictively[10] and contra preferentem that is, when in doubt, against the party that has drafted it, which will generally be the producer. Thus any rights not specifically assigned to the producer may be presumed to remain with the author or contributor to the videogram.

Under the Rome Convention both producers of phonograms and broadcasting organisations have a reproduction right[11] and thus, if a videogram contains a telefilm or a phonogram as a soundtrack, the consent of the broadcasting organisation and of the phonogram producer will be necessary. However the position of performers is different because of the exception of article 19 of the Rome Convention which provides that once a performer 'has consented to the incorporation of his performance in a visual or audio-visual fixation' he ceases to enjoy the protection the convention gives him in all other respects.[12] Thus under the convention films or television programmes made with his consent can be reproduced in a videogram without his consent.[13]

1 Berne Convention 1971, art 2(1).
2 *WIPO Guide to Berne* 2.6(f).
3 UCC, art I.
4 Klaver 'Legal Problems of Videocassettes and Audiovisual Discs' para 23, also 'Report of sub-committee of the Intergovernmental Committee of the Rome Convention on Legal Problems arising from the use of videocassettes' Copyright (December 1978) 413.
5 'Report of the subcommittees of the Executive Committee of the Berne Union and the Intergovernmental Committee of the Universal Copyright Convention on legal problems arising from the use of videocassettes and audiovisual discs' para 13.
6 Berne Convention, art 14 bis, para (1).
7 *WIPO Guide to Berne* 14 bis 1 and 2.
8 Berne Convention, art 14 bis, para (2)(a).
9 See para 5.50 above.
10 Davies 'Legal Problems deriving from the use of Vidoegrams' Copyright (October 1979) p 257.

11 Art 10; see para 8.24 above and art 13(c); see para 8.34 above.
12 That means all performers' rights under art 7 of the Convention; see paras 8.16 et seq above.
13 This provision was inserted into the Rome Convention at the express request of the film industry in 1961 when everyone had phonograms and broadcasts in mind, but videograms had not been thought of.

12.27 The future: The development of videograms will require a combining of the so far incompatible systems of hardware so that videograms of all types can be played on all forms of apparatus, just as a modern record player can play 45 and 33 1/3 rotations-per-minute discs or tapes. It will also require the sale of a large amount of 'hardware', that is videogram playing equipment to private homes.[1] When these two things come about, as happened in the development of other media, videograms may develop a new art form and will certainly contain a wide spectrum of copyrights. Whereas videograms resemble films technologically, their material support, their distribution and use will resemble phonograms. Their material support is a disc or a tape, as in phonograms, and they will be used by the public in their private homes as are phonograms, whereas most films are not sold in large numbers of copies but a few copies are hired out to cinemas to be shown in public. Whether more videograms will be sold or hired out will be decided by public taste and choice as is the case already in respect of books, which the public has for many years either bought or borrowed from a library.[2] Thus videograms are as vulnerable to 'piracy' (unauthorised reproduction for the purpose of retail sale) as phonograms are and as vulnerable to 'home taping' both from borrowed or hired copies and off the air from television screens.

1 Whereas at present only 7.5% of households in Western Europe, 5.2% in the United States and 11% in Japan have such equipment it is estimated by way of projection of past trends that by the mid-eighties it will be over 20% in Europe, over 25% in Japan and around 14% in the United States. 'Predicting the future of VCR's' William den Trinden, News Digest of the ITA (International Tape Association) (July, August 1981) p 4.
2 Whereas books are mainly borrowed without payment from public libraries, videograms are mainly being hired out for payment by privately owned shops.

(2) Challenges to the broadcasting right

(a) *Cable diffusion*

12.28 The facts: Whereas in ordinary broadcast transmissions signals are transmitted by Hertzian waves through the ether, in the transmission of programmes by wire diffusion the signals are transmitted by cable to the individual receiver. In short one is 'wireless' transmission, the other transmission by wire. The latter is referred to as cable antennae television or CATV. The essence of CATV is that not the original broadcasting organisation but a third party transmits signals from a simple aerial to more than one television set located in different places such as rooms in a hotel, flats in a block of flats, houses in a town. The original purpose was to give subscribers to the service better reception than their individual aerials could provide, particularly in areas of poor reception (so-called shadow zones), such as in valleys where the mountains obstructed the signal, or in towns where highrise blocks were the obstruction, or where individual aerials were not allowed on environmental grounds. The transmission by the third party is made to a known public, usually subscribers to the service. As CATV developed five forms of cable television emerged, which have to be distinguished from a copyright point of view:

(a) Simultaneous diffusion of programmes by wire to improve reception;
(b) recording of programmes and relaying them at different times by cable;
(c) diffusion of modified programmes usually by the insertion of advertising material;

(d) programmes originated by the cable company;
(e) programmes imported from other regions of the same country or from other countries.

12.29 The law: Broadcasting is the emission of signals by Hertzian waves. It is covered by article 11 bis para 1(1) of the Berne Convention.[1] It is of the essence of broadcasting that the whole operation is carried out by one organisation.[2]

If other means of transmission are used, such as cable, the operation constitutes 'communication to the public by wire' and as the communication is made by an organisation other than the original one, it falls under article 11 bis, para (1)(ii).

The communication to the public by wire of films is covered separately under article 14(1)(ii).

Thus, both authors and film producers have the right to control the use of their protected works by CATV, both in the case of the transmission of captured broadcasting programmes and of programmes originated or partly originated by the cable operator. A large number of these programmes do not contain copyright material such as diffusion of public events, sporting events, weather reports, miscellaneous information and news. That is however a feature common to both wireless broadcasting and CATV.

In the field of neighbouring rights the Rome Convention defines broadcasting as 'the transmission by wireless means ... of sounds or of images and sound',[3] thus excluding transmission by cable and thus neither performers, nor phonogram producers nor broadcasters are protected against the use of their performances, phonograms or broadcasts by CATV operators under the Convention.

On the other hand the Satellite Convention[4] and the European Agreement on Television Broadcasts[5] contain provisions protecting broadcasters against the unauthorised use of their broadcasts by cable operators. However both the Convention and the European Agreement permit member states to make reservations in respect of CATV, thus excluding the rights of broadcasting organisations against cable operators.

1 See para 5.43 above.
2 *WIPO Guide to Berne* 11 bis 8.
3 Rome Convention, art 3(7).
4 See para 10.06 above.
5 See para 11.06 above.

12.30 Under national legislations there is a great variety of approaches to the problem. The United States Supreme Court had held in two judgments in 1968[1] and 1974[2] that to take programme material subject to copyright transmitted by a broadcasting organisation and retransmit it to paying subscribers was not an infringement of copyright. The United States Copyright Act 1976[3] settled the long ranging dispute between copyright owners and cable operators by a complex compulsory licensing provision.[4] The United States Congress was influenced by two main considerations: a) that cable operators were commercial enterprises whose programmes were using copyright materials and that the creators of these materials were therefore entitled to royalties,[5] b) that it would be too great a burden on every cable operator to negotiate with every copyright owner whose work he transmitted and therefore a compulsory licence was the only reasonable and practical solution. The Act distinguishes between 'secondary transmissions' which retransmit programmes within the local service area of a broadcaster or retransmit network programmes on the one hand and retransmission of far away non-network programmes on the other hand. Whereas the former have no adverse economic effect on copyright owners, the latter do because they distribute the programme to an area with a new audience which was not contemplated by the copyright owner when he licensed the transmission. A 'distant signal equivalent' is given to all such distant signals with different values for independent station networks and educational stations.[6] A formula based on these values is applied to the cable operators gross receipts from subscribers and this produces the total royalty fee.[7] The Copyright Royalty Tribunal is charged with the distribution of these royalties to the authors entitled to them. The 'secondary transmission' must be simultaneous with the 'primary transmission'. If it is not, it is an infringement[8] unless the programme is transmitted only once and without deletions or editing and the owner of the cable system is responsible for preventing the duplication of the videotape whilst in his possession. However after only four years of operation[9] of the Act the Register of Copyright of the United States has already challenged the conclusion that a compulsory licence was the only reasonable and practical solution for the exercise of the right[10] and so has the United States Department of Commerce in a staff report.[11] The Copyright Office recommended to Congress the elimination of the compulsory licence subject to certain total exemptions from copyright liability. The suggestion is that 'contractual arrangements along the lines presently used to license carriage of satellite-distributed cable network programming and, indeed traditional broadcast network programming, could be utilised'. The result would be 'to allow the public, using the market, to choose not only what programmes they shall see, but also how they wish to receive them – by broadcast, cable, satellite, videodisc, or otherwise'.[12]

1 *Fortnightly Corpn v United Artists Television Inc* 382 US 390 (1968).
2 *Teleprompter Corpn v CBS Inc* 415 US 394 (1974).
3 S 111, which is the longest section in the Copyright Law. It is characterised by Meyer 'The Feat of Houdini or How the New Act disentangles the CATV-Copyright Knot' 22 NYLSL Rev 545 (1977).
4 See Sidney Diamond 'Compulsory Licences and the Copyright Royalty Tribunal' 6 American Patent Law Association Quarterly Journal 46 (1978).
5 House Report, p 89.
6 S 111(f).
7 S 111(d)(2)(B).
8 S 111(e).
9 The compulsory licence provisions became effective on 1 January 1978 and for 1979 the Copyright Royalties Tribunal awarded 70% of the total revenue collected (after deduction of costs) to the Motion Picture Association of America and other programme syndicators, 15% to the Joint Sports claimants, 5 1/4% to the Public Broadcasting Services, 4½% to Music Performing Arts Society and 5½% to US and Canadian Television Broadcasters and to National Public Radio (5 1/4 and 1/4 respectively). However the 1978 distribution decision has been appealed to the US Court of Appeals (under s 810 of the US Copyright Law).
10 David Ladd: Accommodating Copyright to the tele-technologies, ALAI Symposium, May 1982.
11 US Department of Commerce, National Telecommunications and Information Administration Office of Policy Analysis, Staff Report, December 1981: 'Cable Copyright: Alternatives to the compulsory licence.'
12 David Ladd, op cit, p 16.

12.31 In Europe on the other hand the situation is different. States concerned are bound by the Berne Convention which, in spite of the somewhat old fashioned language very clearly covers all the various CATV situations giving the author a clear right[1] and offers some latitude to national legislation. Nonetheless both some legislations and court decisions show a state of confusion and diversity of opinions reminiscent of the United States situation in the 1960s and 1970s when cable television was in its early stages as it still is in Europe today.

The first law to deal with the problem was the United Kingdom Copyright Act 1956. The programmes of the British broadcasting organisations may be retransmitted by cable in the United Kingdom by licensed operators without incurring copyright liability.[2] It is very doubtful whether this can be squared with Britain's obligations under the Berne Convention.

The *German* Copyright Law 1965 contains a definition of broadcasting which includes both wireless communication and communication by wire. Thus copyright owners are protected for the whole of the copyright term against the broadcasting of their works by cable operators. Broadcasters, including cable operators, have a neighbouring right protecting them against the rebroadcasting of their broadcasts for 25 years. No difference is made between the various categories of CATV.[3]

The latest law to adapt a solution is the *Austrian* Copyright Law Amendment Act 1980.[4] It provides inter alia that simultaneous, unaltered complete transmissions of ORF (the Austrian public service broadcasting station) can be retransmitted within the country and are considered a component part of the original broadcast. There are also exemptions for CATV installations serving an audience within a small radius. On the other hand cable retransmission of foreign broadcasts is subject to copyright under a statutory licence laying down the criteria of remuneration and providing for reciprocity. The conformity of this piece of legislation with the provisions of the Berne Convention has also, understandably, been doubted.[5]

The courts' peregrinations through this labyrinth follow a similar path to that of the United States. Early judgments found against the copyright owners.[6] However, more recently in the 1970s and 1980s the Supreme Courts of several countries have held that unauthorised transmission of a broadcast containing copyright material is an infringement of copyright.[7]

1 Art 11 bis (1)(ii).
2 Copyright Act 1956, s 40(3).
3 Germany Copyright Law 1965, para 54. See also Ulmer: 'CATV and the legal meaning of "broadcast" in German law' GRUR (1980) p 582.
4 S 59a.
5 Walter 'Die Regelung des Kabelfernsehens in der österreichischen Urheberrechtsnovelle 1980' UFITA 91/1981.
6 Supreme Court of the Netherlands HR 3 April 1930 (Radio-Distribution) also HR 6 May 1938 (Caféradio).
7 1. The '*Feldkirch*' case, Supreme Court of Austria, 25 June 1974; GRUR Int (1975) p 68.
  2. The '*Pluton*' case, Supreme Court of Austria, 12 November 1979, GRUR Int (1980) p 308.
  3. *Suisa v Rediffusion* Supreme Court of Switzerland, 20 January 1981, GRUR Int (1981) p 404.
  4. *Coditel etc v Cine Vog Films etc*, Supreme Court of Belgium, 3 September 1981.
  5. *Columbia Picture Industries Inc v Stichting tot Exploitatie, Centrale Anterne – Inrichting Austelveen*, Supreme Court of the Netherlands, case number 11.739, April 1982.
  6. *Performing Right Society Limited v Marlin Communal Aerials limited* Supreme Court of the Irish Republic, 20 April 1982.

12.32 The future: After a lengthy period of study a group of independent experts summoned by WIPO and UNESCO came to four conclusions which seem incontrovertible and point the way forwards:[1]

1. The distribution of broadcast programmes by cable is effected for a public different from the one which the broadcast can reach or only reach with diminished quality; otherwise there would be no need for distrubition by cable. This rejects the distinction between the 'normal or direct reception zone' and the rest of a country because it has been shown that cable distribution services can operate on a commercial basis for subscribers even within the 'normal reception zone'.

2. Because of this difference public broadcasting and distribution by cable are two different acts and the latter is a 'communication to the public' within the meaning of this term in international law. Therefore the exclusive right of the copyright owner should be clearly recognised in this respect. It also follows that the so-called 'small exceptions' should be applicable. The experts rejected the 'mere reception' theory which argues that in cases where the cable distributor effects all the technical operations, which in the case of direct reception are done by the home set, this deprives the operation of the character of communication to the public. It is irrelevant that the signal transmitted required, or did not require, further treatment. When there is an act of transmission of copyright material it does not make any difference by what technological means that act is effected.

3. Because of the great number of works involved or the practical difficulties of locating right owners, national laws should provide for 'institutionalised collective administration' of the rights. 'Only where such administration would not work in practice, should national laws provide – subject to the right to equitable remuneration and the respect of moral rights – for the possibility of non-voluntary licences.'[2]

The experts add that in the case of three categories of works – dramatic works, dramatico-musical works and films (cinematographic works) – non-voluntary licences should be avoided because the number of these works is relatively small, their owners can usually be located and the calendar of their showing on television must, for economic reasons, be co-ordinated with the calendar of their showing in cinemas.

4. In the realm of neighbouring rights national laws should provide for payment of an equitable remuneration for performers and producers of phonograms whose performances or phonograms are used in cable transmission. The necessity for 'institutionalised collective administration' applies to these rights as well. Broadcasting organisations on the other hand should be given an absolute right to authorise the distribution of their programmes by cable. This is the equivalent to a reproduction right for broadcasting organisations and must therefore include the right to forbid the distribution by cable.[3]

1 Statement of the Group of Experts, 13 March 1980 UNESCO/WIPO/IGE/CTV/H/2; Copyright (April 1980) p 154.
2 This means either compulsory or statutory licences; see para 4.33 above. It is significant that only less than a quarter of all Berne Union countries provide for non-voluntary licences for broadcasting organisations although this is permitted under article 11 of the Convention.
3 For literature see: Walter (1976) 12 Copyright 279; Reimer (1979) 10 iic 542; Dittrich (1979) 15 Copyright 26.

(b) *Satellites*

12.33 The facts: So far the satellites in use are 'distribution satellites'. The first telecommunication satellite 'Telstar' was launched in 1962 by the United States. In 1965 the Soviet Union launched 'Molnyija I' (nicknamed 'Sputnik'). These satellites are means of transmission. The signals transmitted are of high frequency and low intensity and therefore cannot be directly received by ordinary television sets. For their reception by the public a transforming station is necessary which fulfils a function similar to an ordinary ground relay station. The uses of these satellites include international telephone traffic, weather forecasting, cartography, agriculture and geology, apart from the transmission of programmes. The types of programmes most frequently transmitted by satellites so far are news and current events where immediacy is essential and sporting events where the viewers can see the game before the result is known. The impact on copyright works has so far not been very great because most programmes with an artistic content can be taped and sent by air to arrive only a few hours after the broadcast itself, which would, in all but a few cases, be in time. However this may not be the case in future. According to the technical experts 'direct broadcasting satellites' may be in use by the mid-80s. They transmit on much lower frequencies allocated by international conventions; the signals are more high-powered and will be receivable by members of the public in their homes after an adaptation of their receiving sets. Direct broadcasting satellites have been called 'aerials out in space' which illustrates the point that when using these satellites the originating broadcasting organisation emits a signal which is directly receivable by the public in their private homes. The only significant difference from traditional broadcasting will be that instead of an aerial on a roof both a satellite in space and a dish on the roof are used. These 'direct broadcasting satellites', possibly combined with cable transmission (CATV), may radically change the pattern of broadcasting and may significantly influence the use of copyright works and make it very difficult for copyright owners to control this new use of their works.

12.34 The law: As the object of transmission by satellite is to make broadcasts available over long distances it is clear that they will nearly always transcend national borders. International law on the subject is contained in article 11 bis of the Berne Convention and article IV bis of the UCC. Article 11 bis was first included in the convention by the Brussels Act (1948) when satellite broadcasting had not been thought of and was not altered in the Stockholm Act (1967) or the Paris Act (1971).[1]

'Broadcasting' is not defined in the Berne Convention. The only definition, which was of course in the minds of those drafting the convention, is to be found in the Radio-Communications Regulations: they refer to 'transmissions intended to be received directly by the general public'.[2] Having dealt with the right of public performance in article 11, article 11 bis speaks of 'the broadcasting of their works or the *communication thereof to the public by any other means of wireless diffusion* of signs, sounds and images'. Thus, two essentials of broadcasting are a specific broadcasting organisation at the emitting end of the signal and the public element in the operation at the receiving end. The copyright owner has a primary right to authorise the broadcasting of his work and the communication of it to the public. 'What matters is the emission of the signals; it is immaterial whether or not they are in fact received.'[3] 'A secondary right is the subsequent use of the emission; the author has an exclusive right to authorise communication of the broadcast to the public, either by wire or without, if the communication is made by an organisation other than the original one.'[4]

Article IV bis of the UCC also grants a broadcasting right in paragraph 1 but the exceptions in paragraph 2 are much wider as states are only required to 'accord a reasonable degree of effective protection', although the exceptions made by national legislation must 'not conflict with the spirit and provisions' of the convention. This would give member states the possibility to interpret the broadcasting right widely or narrowly in respect of satellite broadcasting.

Different opinions have been expressed as to the nature of present day satellite broadcasting. One view is that because the signal is not directly receivable by the public but needs the intervention not only of a satellite but also of an earth station at the other end, it is not broadcasting. The signal is directed not at the general public but to the satellite (the 'up leg' of the signal) then follows the 'down leg' from the satellite to the earth station and then the relay to the general public. Thus the 'up leg' and even the 'up leg' and the 'down leg' cannot be regarded as a complete broadcast. The broadcasting organisations point out that they may have no control over who picks up the signal they emit and can therefore not be held responsible for the communication of the programme containing copyright works to an operator and an audience over which they have no control. Others take the view that all these phases are integral parts of one operation, 'a process which represents an integral whole'.[5] Professor Ulmer takes a middle view to the effect that emitting a signal is the commencement of broadcasting which is an act covered by article 11 bis paragraph (1) of the Berne Convention. He points out that this is a solution 'which is basically in agreement with the principles of copyright and which bears the stamp of what characterizes authors' rights'.[6] He also points out that the responsibility of a publisher towards an author 'does not start only with the distribution of copies to the public, but earlier, with the preceding printing of the work. Thus the author is protected not only against acts prejudicial to his interests but, before that, 'against the dangers to which his interests may be exposed'. However, giving the copyright owner the right to control 'the injection into the spatial circuit' would result in an accumulation of claims as the copyright owner would be able to claim remuneration for the emission of the signal and again for the conveyance of the signal to the general public at the other end. This cannot be the intention of the broadcasting provisions. The most logical view would appear to be to regard the whole technological process by which the programme reaches the audience as constituting one process for which only one single remuneration is due. If that is so, Professor Ulmer's solution that the originating broadcasting organisation and the distributing broadcasting organisation should be regarded as joint debtors, has a lot to commend it. It suffices if one debtor discharges the joint liability. The question is of great practical importance as it could often happen that a very large number of stations simultaneously broadcast a programme, some of which have neither the permission of the copyright owners nor of the originating broadcasting organisation and have no intention of paying any royalties. The importance of the question is reduced in practice by the fact that television programmes which contain copyright works as a rule, although not invariably, are recorded on film or videotape, so that the fixation precedes the broadcast. In law such a fixation constitutes a reproduction within article 9 of the Berne Convention 1971[7] and article IV bis of the UCC 1971[8] and requires the authorisation of the copyright owner. The fixation is not covered by the exception for ephemeral recordings[9] because that exception is limited to recordings 'used for its own broadcasts' which was certainly not intended to cover broadcasts via satellite.[10]

The Satellite Convention 1974 obliges member states to protect the programme carrying signal but does not create any rights for copyright owners.[11]

The Rome Convention (1961) defines broadcasting as 'the transmission by wireless means for public reception of sounds or of images and sounds.'[12] It is arguable whether a broadcast emitted via satellite but needing an earth station is 'for public reception'. The draftsmen of the convention did not have satellite broadcasting in mind in 1961 and two views are possible. The narrower interpretation is that it is excluded because the transmission is not for public reception but for reception by the earth station. The wider interpretation is that whatever the technical means employed the broadcast is eventually destined 'for public reception'.

1 See para 5.22 above.
2 See *WIPO Guide to Berne* 11 bis 6.
3 *WIPO Guide to Berne* 11 bis 3.
4 *WIPO Guide to Berne* 11 bis 4.

5 Ficsor 'Technological Progress and Crisis Tendencies in Copyright' Copyright (March 1982) p 104 at p 110.
6 Ulmer 'Protection of Authors in relation to the 'transmission via satellite of broadcast programmes' RIDA (July 1977) p 32.
7 See para 5.38 above.
8 See para 6.20 above.
9 Berne Convention, art 11 bis, para 3.
10 Ulmer, op cit, p 30.
11 See para 10.07 above.
12 Rome Convention, art 3(f); see para 8.35 above.

12.35 The future: When direct broadcasting satellites 'come into use and broadcasts transmitted via satellites will be directly receivable in private homes, there will be no doubt that these broadcasts will in law constitute 'broadcasting' within the Berne Convention or the Rome Convention as they will have the same characteristics as traditional broadcasting by ground stations. The only remaining problem will thus be contractual as the size of the territory covered by the broadcast, and with it the size of the audience, must be taken into account when determining the royalty payable by the emitting broadcasting organisation.

(3) Challenges to all copyrights and neighbouring rights

(a) *The 'sociology' of copyright*

12.36 It can be said that viewing the history of mankind as a whole from primitive beginnings to the sophisticated civilisations of today, there have been four stages of communications:

1. Speech: ranging from the basic signals of primitive civilisations to the sophisticated languages of antiquity.
2. Writing: ranging from early civilisations to the fifteenth century as the only form of communication in a permanent form.
3. Printing: from the invention of the printing press as the only form of communication suitable for rapid reproduction for mass communications from the fifteenth to the twentieth century.
4. Electronic communications of the twentieth century.

None of these four stages has been replaced by the subsequent stages and today the four co-exist.

The concept of copyright was conceived at the third stage and has until recently been dominated by the reproduction right totally geared to communication by printing. Although copyright has been adapted to the fourth stage by including rights appropriate to recordings, cinematograph films and radio and television broadcasts, the adaptation to the combination of these media of the electronic age has only recently begun. If one includes reproduction which may now be a preparatory act, in the general concept of 'communication to the public' then the object of copyright protection is achieved by granting rights in respect of such communications and granting them to the creators of copyright material and against the communicators of these materials to the public. However during the latest stage of electronic communications this basic situation is changing. In many cases of communicating copyright material to the public, the public is no longer dependent on reproductions made by the communicators; the members of the public make their own. Whilst the machinery enabling the public to make their own copies is still rather expensive and duplicating equipment such as photocopiers, plants for pressing records, equipment for receiving satellite broadcasts will still be owned by governments, corporations or companies, public libraries and the like. In this situation control of copyrights by individual copyright owners is often impossible, but control by collecting societies on behalf of all copyright owners is still possible. Once such equipment becomes sufficiently cheap to be owned by individual members of the public and used in their homes, effective control at the stage of making the copies becomes impossible and copyright protection can only remain effective if exercised at a much earlier stage. Thus the purpose of copyright, which is to assure to the owners of copyright material an equitable remuneration for each use of the copyright material they have created, can only be achieved by a reinterpretation of the concept of copyright in the light of these new circumstances. That widened concept must include the original and most basic copyright; the reproduction right. It does not matter 'whether the rights are directed against a communicator making the work available to the public or against an enterprise producing the equipment making reproduction by the public possible or even against members of the public themselves'.[1] Nothing short of that will assure the effectiveness of copyright protection in the fourth stage of communications.

Committees of experts, both governmental experts and independent experts, have on different occasions expressed the view that the international conventions are wide enough to accommodate this reinterpretation of the concept of copyright, but that in respect of the use of several of the new forms of electronic communication national legislation is both appropriate and urgently needed.

1 Elisabeth Steup, Geiringer Memorial Lecture 1977, Copyright Review of the US, (1977) p 279 at p 286.

(b) *The devaluation of copyright*

12.37 If large areas of the use of copyright material remain uncontrolled and therefore not remunerated and copyright owners cannot 'stop this mass of small-scale infringement, the whole currency of copyright risks devaluation from indifference and common contempt'.[1] What is needed therefore is what Professor Cornish calls 'techniques for converting paper rights into revenue-generating realities'. These techniques could be of three kinds.

1. Maintaining a complete copyright and exercising it by a blanket licensing system administered through a collecting society making collective agreements with large single users or categories of smaller users.
2. Reducing the absolute right to authorise or forbid the use of the protected material to a right to equitable remuneration which will still in most cases be exercised in the same way as those under 1.

    The precedents for the collective exercise of copyrights, whether they are absolute rights or rights to equitable remuneration, are the collecting societies set up by the owners of performing rights, most of which in the field of musical copyrights have half a century of experience of blanket licensing. These licences are granted in advance of the use to organisations which regularly perform copyright material. The societies obtain wherever possible lists of the works used which enable them to distribute the revenue which is often paid as a lump sum, among their members according to the number of times their works have been used.
3. Putting a royalty on the equipment which is used by the public for the reproduction of copyright material.[2]

Whatever the technique used to control the exercise of copyrights and neighbouring rights there will have to be clearly defined exceptions in respect of use of educational and scientific purposes, but there are two schools of thought when it comes to defining such use. The first argues the necessity of making new material containing new ideas freely available as long as the purpose of such use is not a commercial one. The second argues that owners of material goods and services which are necessary for educational and research establishments such as paper and pencils, musical instruments, heating and lighting, do not supply them free and there is no reason why the immaterial goods necessary for education and science should be supplied free at the expense of their creators. Whether the legislative solutions incline towards one side or the other of this argument will depend largely on the political philosophy of the government of the day, bearing in mind that the state is the payor in the case of most educational and in the case of an increasing number of scientific establishments using copyright material. However, in most countries, at least in Western Europe, the argument in favour of copyright in these circumstances is gaining ground and the 'the debate is rapidly shifting to one about means'.[3]

Whatever the national solutions found to these problems, there will be a need of a certain amount of supervision of the collecting societies which exercise a monopoly or market dominating position almost by definition, probably by requiring recognition as a collecting society by a governmental agency and by a 'Copyright Royalties Tribunal' of one form or another which decides what royalty is reasonable in all the circumstances if the collecting societies and the bodies representing users cannot agree. The devaluation of copyright can probably be avoided if the said techniques are applied, the exceptions for education and research are clearly defined and the user interests safeguarded by a tribunal.

1 Cornish *Intellectual Property* (1981) p 430; also Davies and von Rauscher *Challenges to Copyright and Related Rights in the European Community* paras 506-511.
2 See para 12.15 above.
3 Cornish, op cit, p 431.

(c) *The unity of copyright*

12.38 In this context copyright should be understood in its widest sense including both copyrights stricto sensu and neighbouring rights. This is desirable for both doctrinal and political reasons. The doctrinal reason is two-fold. The same right is called a 'copyright' in some countries and a 'neighbouring right' in others. Rights of film producers, phonogram producers and to a certain extent performers and broadcasting organisations are examples. The same uncontrolled or piratical use usually deprives both copyright owners and neighbouring right owners of their remuneration. If a film is copied off the air from a television programme, the authors of the pre-existing works as well as the film producer lose their royalties. If a phonogram is copied off the air from a radio programme the composers, lyric writers, the phonogram producers and performers lose their royalties.

The political reason is that neighbouring right owners are also among the largest users of copyrights and assignees of copyrights. In some countries they are considerable employers and exporters and make an important contribution to the economy and the balance of payments. The combined economic influence of all right owners on legislators may succeed more rapidly to secure wider and more effective copyright protection for all copyright materials, than attempts by particular groups of right owners to secure special rights.

(d) *The control of copyright*

12.39 There can be little doubt that the number of consumers of copyright will continue to grow in the field of information and education as well as in the field of entertainment. Both scholastic and vocational education is constantly being extended and as people become better educated they become more eager for more widely accessible information in all fields. The age span of each consumer of copyright is growing as people earn earlier and live longer. Working hours continue to get shorter thus increasing leisure hours which tends to increase copyright consumption. Whereas in the western world this is a continuing process, in the developing countries it has only just begun. Copyright owners will thus create works for increasing markets which should benefit both their economic and their moral rights, the problem is whether they will be able to control these new markets.

It has been acknowledged a long time that some copyrights can no longer be controlled by individual copyright owners but must be controlled by collecting societies. Performing rights in music are an outstanding example. Control by individual right owners would be impossible, but by collective exercise these rights have become a major source of income for composers and writers in this field. What is new is that more and more copyrights and neighbouring rights are getting into this category. If the challenges described in this chapter – home taping, reprography, computer use, videograms, cable diffusion, satellite broadcasting, – are to be successfully met, this can only be done by collective exercise of the copyrights involved as hardly any of these new uses of copyright material can be controlled by individual copyright owners. In most of these fields, the choice is between this form of control or no control at all and once control of a right is lost it is very very difficult to regain it and in the long run the right will atrophy. The inherent dangers of this inevitable process of collective exercise have frequently been stressed: dangers to the individuality of copyright as a highly personal right[1] if it is to be largely exercised by collecting societies and dangers to economic rights by the more and more frequent introduction of non-voluntary licences.

With regard to the former it cannot be denied that great moral responsibilities as well as great technical and operational burdens are being put on the collecting societies. Experience seems to show that the best guarantee for the right owners is a democratic structure of these societies so that the members can have an effective influence on how their society operates and the best guarantee for the right users is a copyright royalty tribunal to which disputes between groups of users and largely monopolistic collecting societies can be referred.

With regard to the introduction of non-voluntary licences, several markers have been put down recently for the future development of copyright. There are three choices to be made which follow one on the other if the clearance of the rights has to be made in a comprehensive way because the rights cannot be exercised effectively in any other way.

1. The choice between collective exercise by bulk licensing and a non-voluntary licence prescribed by law. The 'Statement of the Group of Experts'[2] summonsed by WIPO and UNESCO in 1980 states the preference for collective exercise in classic form:

> 'Where the clearance of the rights must be effected in a comprehensive way because of the great number of the works involved or the practical difficulties of contacting the owner of the copyright in time, national laws should provide, for these practical reasons, for institutionalised collective administration of the said rights. Only where such administration would not work in practice, should national laws provide – subject to the right to equitable remuneration and the respect of moral rights – for the possibility of non-voluntary licences. But because of the particular situation in which cinematographic works, dramatic works and dramatico-musical works find themselves, provision for non-voluntary licences for such works should be avoided. The particular situation of the said works is due to the following: (i) their number is relatively small, (ii) their owners can generally be located with less difficulty,

(iii) the calendar of their showing on television must, for important economic reasons, be co-ordinated with the calendar of their theatrical showing.'

2. If such administration 'would not work in practice' the choice is between a 'statutory licence' and a 'compulsory licence'. The former is a licence under which protected works could be freely used on condition that the user paid a fee, fixed by the law or by a competent authority. The latter is a licence requiring the copyright owner to grant the necessary authorisation without however depriving him of the right to negotiate the terms of the authorisation.[3] The Supreme Court of the Federal Republic of Germany has in a recent case put the problem in very succinct form:[4] 'There should be no limitations on copyright which serve merely the financial interests of individual users of works. One must ensure that a limitation imposed in the public interest does not lead to the unjustified advancement of commercial interests of users. In this dilemma, it seems appropriate to control merely the author's power to forbid, but to leave him with the right to claim an equitable reward for the use of this work'. This expresses the basic principle that the remuneration in order to be equitable should be freely negotiated, even if such negotiations will in most cases be collective bargaining between two near monopolies.

3. If in accordance with the principles stated above in 1 and 2, the negotiations for the equitable remuneration are to take place in the form of collective bargaining which in many cases will be between two near monopolies, representing right owners and right users, the law should provide for a special tribunal to adjudicate if agreement cannot be reached between these parties. Such copyright royalty tribunals are already provided in some national legislations.[5]

If these priorities are respected it should be possible to maintain the control of copyright owners over their economic rights to a large extent. Moral rights are inalienable[6] and can and are being asserted both in blanket licensing and in compulsory licensing situations.

There is, however, another danger to the control over copyright works. It is that by a new type of legislation, what is essentially a copyright may be turned into a levy and what should be a royalty may be turned into a tax in which case the copyright owner does not only fail to regain control over his rights but loses the whole or a large part of his remuneration as well. Levies on recording equipment and on blank tapes purporting to compensate copyright and neighbouring right owners for the use of their works by 'home taping'[7] are recent examples. So far such cases are rare but state treasuries and ministries of finance, when in sight of a new source of revenue develop predatory instincts which are often hard to curb.

1 Ringer 'Copyright and the future of Authorship' Copyright (1976) p 155 and Donald Brace Lecture, 1976.
2 Statement of group of Exports (Chairman William Wallace) Copyright (April 1980) p 156.
3 See para 4.33 above.
4 17 BGHZ 766, 278.
5 Eg United Kingdom Copyright Act 1956, s 23; German Copyright Law 1965 and para 14, Wahrnehmungsgesetz; US Copyright Act 1976, s 801.
6 See para 3.37 above.
7 Eg Norway, Sweden; see paras 19.28, 19.29 below.

4. The survival of a viable copyright system in a technological age

(a) The raison d'être for a copyright system

12.40 Legislators or courts can only resolve the conflict between two opposing public interests, the public interest in encouraging creativity of all kinds in the arts and sciences on the one hand, and the public interest in the widest possible dissemination of 'works' to the public at reasonable prices, on the other hand in one way: by granting exclusive rights for a limited period to those creating copyright material. This is so for several reasons:

1. There can be little doubt that the remuneration of creative effort stimulates those efforts. 'Despite what is said in some of the authorities that the author's interest in securing an economic reward for his labours is a "secondary consideration", it is clear that the real purpose of a copyright scheme is to encourage works of the intellect, and that this purpose is to be achieved by reliance on the economic incentives granted to authors and inventors by the copyright scheme. This scheme relies on the author to promote the progress of science by permitting him to control the cost of and access to his novelty.'[1] Thus 'the encouragement of individual effort by personal gain is the best way to advance public welfare through the talents of authors and inventors'.[2]

2. The creation, reproduction and dissemination of all sorts of copyright material necessitates in nearly all cases fairly large investments made by copyright owners (publishers, film and record producers are examples). These investments would in many cases not be made if those making them could not recoup them and – at least taking all their activities together over a period – make a profit by exercising their copyrights.

3. If control over the uses of copyright material were lost the creators of copyright material would have to look for their income to one source only; outright sale to an entrepreneur. If they can control the uses of their material the burden of compensating them is shared by a large number, sometimes millions, of users each paying a small amount by way of a royalty, according to the uses made of the work.

4. Many users of copyright material (publishers, phonogram or film producers, broadcasters) could not pay the creators of copyright materials an adequate compensation if they in turn could not protect their product 'erga omnes', that is, against all those who would otherwise use it without authorisation and without paying royalties for such use.

5. The recent rapid advances of technology have immensely increased the audience for each new work and the new media have become most avaricious consumers of copyright works as they have to provide for wider education, enlarged leisure hours and the demand for entertainment practically round the clock. It would be absurd if this vastly increased need for copyright materials resulted in reduced rewards for those creating these materials. With a properly organised copyright system it should get all creators nearer to the ideal state of affairs where every reasonably successful creator can make a living from his work instead of having to supplement his income from his copyrights by having a second occupation, in order to live.

1 Court of Appeals (9th cir) 1981 USA in the *Betamax* case see para 21.25 below.
2 *Mazer v Stein*, 347 United States 201, 219, 74S Ct 460, 471, (*Universal City Studios Inc v Song Group of America*) 98L Ed 630 (1954).

(b) The alternatives to a copyright system

12.41 The only alternatives to a copyright system would seem to be the system of patronage which historically preceded the copyright system[1] and which makes the creator totally dependent on his patron, or a system of subsidies for creators of copyright material paid by the state from public funds.

As the main categories of patrons of pre-copyright days were royal and princely families, the aristocracy and the church, who in most countries have ceased to be effective as patrons and have largely been replaced by the state, the two alternatives amount largely to the same thing. Such a system has in the long run two inevitable consequences. The representatives of the state will subsidise what they would like to see published and widely read, seen or heard, and once they pay for it or subsidise it they will feel that they have a right to censor it. This is as fundamental today as it was in the eighteenth century. It is even more important today than it was then because of the immensely increased volume and speed of communications. Once the state becomes the provider of remuneration for creative effort there is only one short step to making the state or its functionaries, instead of the general public, the arbiters of what is worthy of remuneration and what is not. That is the road towards both artistic and political censorship which is both the road to serfdom and the negation of the economic and the moral rights of creators. In the last resort, all creative efforts have to be sustained apart from the financial reward and the spur of fame, by a further intangible element of reward; the freedom and independence to create according to one's inspiration and one's conscience, and to communicate such creations to a public that can acclaim them or reject them, but must be free in the first place to receive them in order to judge them.

Copyright laws cannot create freedom of speech and freedom of the press and other means of communications, but such freedoms will be diminished unless those who create copyright material can do so without financial dependence on anyone and put what they have created before the public without interference from anyone. 'A bad copyright law can destroy that independence, a good one can help to preserve it'.[2]

1   See para 2.03 above.
2   Barbara Ringer 'Copyright and the Future of Authorship' Copyright (1976) p 155.

Part 2
National Laws

Chapter 13
Austria

by Robert Dittrich

1. History and development of Austrian copyright

13.01 Following the 1914-18 war, the desire to become a member of the Rome Act of the Berne Convention (1928) and technical developments in the field of copyright (particularly concerning records, films and radio) led to endeavours to produce reforms which resulted in the promulgation of the 'Federal Law on Copyright in Works of Literature and Art and on Neighbouring Rights'.[1] The most significant difference between this Copyright Law of 1936 and its predecessor lies in the fact that the new law draws a sharp dividing line between copyright in its narrow sense and other rights. It represents the birth of the protection of neighbouring rights in Austria.

The Copyright Law of 1936 was amended in 1949, 1953, 1972, 1980 and 1982.

The activities of collecting societies have been regulated since 1936 by the Law on Collecting Societies of 9 April 1936.[2] Supplementary provisions were introduced in the copyright law revision of 1980.[3]

1 Federal Law Gazette No 111/1936.
2 Federal Law Gazette No 112.
3 Federal Law Gazette No 321.

2. The relationship between copyright in a narrow sense and 'neighbouring rights'

13.02 The Law on copyright regulates not only copyright in a narrow sense and neighbouring rights but also contains provisions for related rights whose logical location would be elsewhere, such as the right to one's own picture and the protection of letters and other confidential writings which logically belong to the protection of an individual's personality. Also the protection of news and titles of works would systematically come within the Law against unfair competition.

The Copyright Law is based on the concept of copyright in its wider sense, which covers copyright in its restricted sense (protection of authors) and neighbouring rights. The part of the statute which regulates copyright in the restricted sense only mentions once in its first main section several fundamental concepts, in particular reproduction, distribution, public performance and broadcasting. It then makes the provisions dealing with these concepts applicable to neighbouring rights as well.

The subject-matter of copyright protection in its restricted sense is a *work*, in the area of neighbouring rights a performance, a photograph, a phonogram, or a broadcast.[1] The subject of protection is accordingly of a diverse nature. A work may be reproduced simultaneously or at differing moments in time and every reproduction gives rise to differing protection rights, even if the work is reproduced by the same performer (or performers). The same performance may be simultaneously recorded by various producers of phonograms each on a different phonogram (even though, practically-speaking, this does not occur). Various rights then arise in respect of the different recordings in favour of different individual holders of rights. Every performance may be broadcast on radio – live or by using a phonogram or videogram – simultaneously or at different times by various broadcasting organisations. This then gives rise to separate rights, even if the same performance is broadcast at differing times by the same broadcasting organisation. All these rights are independent of one another. As a result, the consent of the author to the exploitation of his work, which at any rate is necessary under copyright in its restricted sense, is not affected by the neighbouring rights. Conversely, any consent required by virtue of a neighbouring right will not become unnecessary by reason of the fact that the consent of the author may not be required (for instance because it is in the public domain). The same applies to the relationship between neighbouring rights owners.

1   'Broadcast' includes sound and television broadcasts.

3. Protection of performers

13.03   The right in respect of recitals and performances of protected or unprotected literary or musical works (hereinafter called performances) is vested in the person giving the recital or performing the work. Thus, the holders of such a right may not only be soloists and artistic directors (particularly conductors, producers and choreographers) but also, in the case of performances which – as in the case of the performance of a stage play or a choral or orchestral work – are created by the collaboration of a number of people under uniform direction; persons who, for example, merely collaborate in the chorus or orchestra. No precise definition of the concept of the performer is provided by the legislation; technical staff (eg lighting technicians) and variety artists are not covered by it as they do not perform a work.

There is no such thing as a secondary neighbouring right such as protection of an adaptation.

The Copyright Law does *not* grant the performer a comprehensive right in his performance but merely a list of rights which is exhaustive.

(a) Reproduction and distribution right

13.04   The *reproduction right* is the right to fix a performance – also in the case of a broadcast – on a videogram or phonogram and to reproduce it. Reproduction also includes use of the reproduction of a performance created with the aid of a videogram or phonogram for transference to another videogram or phonogram. The expression used in the law, 'picture or sound carrier', covers videograms, phonograms and videograms with sound-tracks, ie means which are intended to permit simultaneous, repeatable reproduction to be perceived by sight and sound. Whether the entire performance or only a part of it is recorded is irrelevant. The reproduction right vests, irrespective of the process used and the number if items duplicated. The production of a single copy is sufficient.

Everyone may, for his own use, record performances broadcast and reproductions of performances made with the aid of a videogram or phonogram and may produce individual copies of them, but the performer is given a claim to equitable remuneration. This claim attaches to the material support. Material support in this context comprises blank tapes which are suitable for private reproductions or are intended for such purpose. This includes particular material support onto which a recording has been made solely for the purpose of avoiding the claim to remuneration. Suitability means not only technical feasability but includes economic considerations. It follows from this that only magnetisable carrier material at present comes within this regulation; that, is, in the case of amateur films with magnetic sound-tracks, only the value of such sound track. Videograms or phonograms which are not suitable for private reproduction, such as tape-cassettes for dictating equipment, or those not used for private use such as those sold directly to bulk consumers, like record producers, sound studios or the Austrian broadcasting organisation are not covered. A prerequisite for the claim to equitable remuneration is that the performance has been broadcast or fixed on a videogram or phonogram produced for commercial purposes which is by its nature to be recorded for personal use. The claim is against the first person who brings the material support into trade in Austria, commercially. Private importation and distribution without charge, as well as any intermediary and retail trade stages, are therefore excluded. Thus, the party liable to pay is the domestic importer or manufacturer and claims may be enforced only by collecting societies. When assessing the remuneration, consideration is to be given in particular to the playing time of the tape. Anyone who has purchased such material support at a price which includes the equitable remuneration but who uses it for reproduction purposes not for his own use, may demand from the collecting society the repayment of the remuneration unless such use other than for his own purposes was a permitted free use of the work. An example of this is where a restaurant proprietor purchases sound tapes through a retail outlet in order to record on them himself and then to use them in public. The collecting society agrees the amount of the remuneration in a collective agreement. No strict proof is required for the facts establishing and invalidating rights. Credibility is sufficient.[1]

1 For details see Dittrich *Copyright* (1981) p 81.

13.05 Due to the *distribution right*, no videograms or phonograms may, without the consent of the right owner, be offered for sale to the public or brought into trade. 'Offer for sale' shall mean the public offering of videograms available for sale. A request to order videograms or phonograms which are not yet available (subscription) does not suffice, but videograms or phonograms which are offered for loan (free of charge) or for hire (at a charge) and which are made available for such purpose are 'offered for sale'.

'To bring into trade' means to grant another the actual or legal power of disposal in respect of a videogram or phonogram, particularly by sale or gift or by lending or hiring it out. The pawning of a videogram or phonogram also represents an act of distribution. The distribution right does not apply to any videograms or phonograms which, by assignment of ownership, are brought into trade domestically or abroad with the consent of the party entitled thereto within Austria. However, if the consent has been granted only for a specific territory, the right to distribute outside that territory videograms or phonograms brought into trade within that territory remains unaffected.

The distribution right has three functions: it blocks the further utilisation of videograms or phonograms which have been produced, without any infringement of the right of reproduction, either in accordance with the rule relating to personal use or in a country in which no protection is granted, to performers. Thirdly, it makes it possible to divide rights geographically.

(b) Broadcasting right

13.06 A broadcasting right is the right to broadcast the performance by hertzian waves 'or in a similar manner'. Broadcasting is every activity by which a production is, with the aid of hertzian waves, rendered receivable within the range of such waves to everyone who has the appropriate receiving equipment. It is of course irrelevant whether the broadcast is in fact received: it is sufficient that there is an opportunity to do so. The copyright concept of broadcasting therefore covers radio and television broadcasting. The mention of 'similar manner' is merely to safeguard holders of the rights against any future technological development (eg broadcasting by means of laser beams). Broadcasting is to be differentiated from *directional-transmission* which does not aim at any broad effect: if a microwave link is used to transmit a broadcast to the public within Austria, then this constitutes a part of the transmission in Austria. A broadcast of a work made perceivable to the Austrian public from a location situated within Austria or abroad, by broadcasting or with the aid of cable ranks in law as a broadcast. As is expressly stated in the explanations attached to the original Law, the mere reception of the broadcast remains lawful.

'Broadcasting' in the legal sense is also the simultaneous or deferred transmission of a broadcast of one broadcasting organisation by another broadcasting organisation. However, by virtue of a legal fiction, the simultaneous, complete and unaltered transmission of broadcasts by the Austrian Broadcasting Organisation with the aid of cable within Austria is deemed to be a part of the original broadcast. This means that the lawfulness of the original broadcast always dictates the lawfulness of the onward transmission via cable. In the event of the unlawfulness of the original broadcast, it will have to be established whether the onward transmission via cable is to be classified as a cable-broadcast, therefore also unlawful, or remains lawful as a mere reception process.

The communication of broadcasts 1. by a broadcasting relay system and 2. by a community antenna system, a) where all the receivers are located on contiguous pieces of ground, where no part of the system uses or crosses a public road and where the antenna is not more than 500 metres away from the nearest receiver, or b) where not more than 500 subscribers are connected to the system, shall not be regarded as a new broadcast. The proper use of this technical equipment is thus relegated to the area of mere reception by virtue of a legal fiction.

The broadcasting right of the performer extends only to live performances and to broadcasts made with the aid of videograms or phonograms when either the reproduction or distribution right of the performer (*or* of the organiser) has been infringed or the fixation has been made for one's own use only. However, foreign broadcasts of performances may be used for simultaneous, complete and unchanged onward transmission with the aid of cable. The performer has a right to an equitable remuneration in respect thereof. Such claims may be enforced only by collecting societies. When assessing the remuneration, particular regard must be had a) to the financial significance which the onward transmission has for the performer, b) to the financial benefit which it produces for the onward transmitter, having regard also to the number of broadcasts which can be received simultaneously by cable in one household, and c) to the amount which performers receive for comparable use in the country in which the original broadcast is transmitted.

If the contrary has not been agreed, the conferring of the right to transmit a performance does not cover the right to record the performance on videograms or phonograms during the transmission or for the purposes of the transmission.

(c) Public performance right

13.07 Performances may be given publicly by loudspeaker or by some other technical device outside the location (theatre, hall, place, garden) where they take place, only with the consent of the performer, unless they are made with the aid of videograms or phonograms or broadcasts which may be used for such purpose by virtue of the protection of the performer (*and* of the organiser). Thus, only with the permission of the performer, may live performances be reproduced publicly outside the location where they are made. Thus, for example, the performance of a piano recital may not be used with the assistance of telephonic or loudspeaker equipment for public performance in another hall if the performer does not permit it. On the other hand, a performance made with the assistance of a videogram or phonogram or by using a broadcast for the purpose of a *further* public performance outside the place where the performance takes place, is not subject to any restriction unless the used reproduction is made with the assistance of videograms or phonograms or of broadcasts which it was not permitted to use for such purpose due to the protection of the performer (*and* of the organiser). A broadcast which is permissible by virtue of the protection of the performer (*and* of the organiser) may be used for public performance by means of loudspeakers or by any other technical device. If the broadcast is not permitted, then the public performance is likewise not permissible.

A performance is always public if basically anyone may attend, ie the performance is not limited to any closed circle of participants. It is also public where, although the performance is not generally accessible, the defined or definable circle of participants is not linked by such connections as give the gathering the appearance of a private assembly. The latter is deemed to be the case where the circle of participants is linked by a real, personal tie and distinguished from the outside world by the relations among themselves or vis-à-vis the organiser. Thus, whether a performance is a public or a private performance may be assessed in each individual case having regard to the number of participants, the nature of the personal relations, as well as to the purpose of the assembly. In case of doubt, heed must also be taken of whether the organiser has any financial objectives (whether of his own or on behalf of others). On the basis of these general principles, the television room in a convalescent home and the playing of a radio broadcast during working hours in a factory with more than 100 female employees has been held to be public.

13.08 *Secondary use of phonograms.* The performer has a claim against the record producer for a proportion of the equitable remuneration which the latter receives for the secondary use of phonograms.[1] In the absence of any agreement on the entitlement, such portion amounts to one half of the net remuneration of the producer after deduction of the costs incurred in collection. Such claims may be enforced only by a collecting society.

1 See para 13.18.

13.09 *Protection of moral interests.* At the request of a soloist or artistic director (but not of persons who participate merely in a chorus or orchestra or in similar fashion), his name (pseudonym) is to be stated on videograms and phonograms. This may not be done without his approval. The approval may be withdrawn if a videogram or phonogram reproduces the performance with changes of such a nature or so defectively that its use could damage the artistic reputation of the performer.

13.10 If several persons have collaborated *jointly* as performers in such a way that the results of their performance constitute an inseparable unit, then the rights are vested jointly in all the participants. The connection of a performance with another performance of a different nature, such as the connection of the performance of a musical work with the delivery of performance of a spoken work or with a film work, does not in itself establish any such joint enterprise of the participants. Every participant is entitled to prosecute infringements of the rights. Any amendment or exploitation will require the consent of all participants. If any such participant should refuse his approval without sufficient cause, each of the other participants may by judicial process force him to grant his approval. In such connection, a performer will be guilty of an unlawful misuse of rights only if he refuses his consent for the exploitation of his work solely with the intention of causing harm.[1]

In the case of performances in which several persons collaborate under a unified direction, the rights of those persons who participate merely in the chorus or orchestra or in a similar manner can be enforced only by a common representative. If the representational arrangements have not already been regulated by the law or an ordinance or by any collective agreement or contract, the common representative will be elected by the participants by simple majority. Failing a common representative, the District Court of the Inner City of Vienna has to appoint an administrator who then fulfils the role of the common representative. Every person who credibly demonstrates an interest in the exploitation of the performance is entitled to file an application.

[1] Supreme Court, 20 May 1965, OeBe (Oesterreiche Blätter für gewerblichen Rechtsschutz und Urheberrecht) 1965, p 153 = Schulze copyright case law/40 (Dittrich) = UFITA Vol 50 (1967) p 318.

13.11 Whoever is identified in the normal way on the copies of a published videogram or phonogram as the performer of the recorded performance, that is, for example, in the case of records by the label which is stuck on to the record or by the lettering on the sleeve of the record, is deemed to be such until the contrary is proved. This is so if the identification consists of a statement of his name or of a pseudonym which he is known to use.

So long as the performer has not been identified in such a manner as to justify a presumption of his participation, the promoter or, if no such person is identified on the videogram or phonogram the producer of the videogram or phonogram is deemed to be the participants' agent for the administration of the rights.

13.12 The rights of the performers may be inherited. In fulfilment of a direction made for the event of his death, they may also be assigned to special successors. If the estate of any one of several jointly-participating performers is not acquired by anyone and is also not taken over by the state as being uninherited property, his rights shall pass to the other participants. The same shall apply in the event of a renunciation by one of several joint participants of his rights, so long as such renunciation is effective. Otherwise the rights of the performer are not assignable. If the rights pass to more than one person, the rules as to joint collaboration shall apply analogously.

13.13 A performer may in two ways *permit another to use his performance* by one or all of the methods available to him to exploit it. He may grant a permission or a right to use. In both cases the beneficiary will acquire the unrestricted authority to use the performance or authority which is restricted in time or geographically or by its scope. The difference between these two forms lies in the fact that the permission to use is merely founded on a contractual claim against the performer, whilst the right to use is an absolute right. If the performer has granted to another the permission to use his performance, then although he is obliged to permit his contracting partner to use the performance, albeit within the limits set out in the agreement, the performer himself retains the exclusive right to exploit the performance without any limitations in time, geographically or in scope. He is also not prevented from granting further permissions or rights to use to third parties, even if they are in competition with any permission granted earlier. If, on the other hand, the performer grants a right to use, the beneficiary thereof will acquire an exclusive right to use the performance within the agreed parameters. Even the performer himself must refrain from exploiting the performance insofar as the beneficiary of the right to use has acquired the exclusive right to do so. The performer is put in the position of any third party as against whom the right to use operates as an exclusive right. There is only one exception to this rule: the performer remains entitled to proceed in the civil and criminal courts against anyone who uses the performance without authority, even against the wishes of the beneficiary of the exclusive right to use.

By granting an exclusive right to use, the performer creates a new absolute right differing from his own right.

Exclusive rights to use can be inherited. They are also alienable inter vivos.

13.14 Dispositions of future rights may also be made. Such an agreement is not subject to any formalities and may also be entered into tacitly. The right to use will come into existence, unless otherwise agreed, on completion of the performance without any special action to establish the right being required.[1]

In cases of doubt, the grant of a right or a permission to use is not deemed to be contained in the *assignment* of ownership of a videogram or phonogram.

1   For the field of copyright in its technical sense, see Supreme Court 10 October 1978, OeBe 1978 p 161, =EvBl 1979 No 24, = UFITA Vol 85 (1979) p 351, =Schulze, Copyright Case Law/71.

13.15 If no use is made of a right to use for the purpose for which it was granted, or if such right to use is exploited to such an insufficient degree that important interests of the performer are prejudiced, then, if no fault attaches to him in respect thereof, he may rescind the contractual relationship prematurely insofar as the right to use is concerned. The contract may be rescinded only after expiration of a reasonable additional period of time given by the performer to the beneficiary of the right to use. No additional period of time need be given if it is impossible for the assignee to exercise the right to use, or if he refuses to do so, or if the grant of an additional period would endanger the paramount interests of the performer.

If the performer has undertaken to grant another party rights to use in respect of all performances (which are either not defined or defined only by reference to a category), in which he will participate during his lifetime or within a period in excess of one year, each party may rescind the contract as soon as one year has elapsed from the time it was entered into. No renunciation of the right of rescission may be given in advance. The period of notice is three months, if no shorter period has been agreed. The contractual relationship will be rescinded only in respect of the performances which have not been completed by the time the period of notice expires. Any other rights to cancel the contract will not thereby be affected.

13.16 The question of whether the performer is bound to collaborate with the organiser of a performance and to permit exploitation is to be assessed under the regulations and agreements governing the legal relationship of the participants with the organiser. These will also govern the question of whether a participant has any claim to special remuneration against the organiser. In any event, the organiser with whose approval a performance is intended to be recorded, has to notify the participants in a suitable manner in advance even if such participants are obliged to collaborate. This will apply analogously to the broadcasting of a performance and to its public performance outside the locality where it takes place.

4. Protection of the organiser of a performance

13.17 Provisions for the protection of the organiser are also included in the provisions of the Copyright Law which provide for protection of the performer.

Performances which are made under the direction of an organiser may, without prejudice to the rights of the protected performer,

(a) be recorded on videograms or phonograms;
(b) be broadcast in the case of a live performance or where the videogram or phonogram used for the broadcast should not have been used;[1] or
(c) be performed publicly by loudspeaker or by any other technical device outside the locality (theatre, room, place, garden) where it takes place only with the consent of the organiser. The organiser's protection against public performance is accordingly more comprehensive than that for the performer.

[1] See para 13.04, above.

5. Protection of producers of phonograms

13.18 The right in a phonogram is vested in whoever fixes the acoustic processes on a phonogram. In the case of commercially-produced phonograms, the owner of the enterprise is deemed to be this person.

The *adaptation* of a phonogram (for example, by the mixing of various channels, by filtering out noises in the case of old recordings and/or by incorporating sound effects) gives rise, just as the adaptation of a work, to an independent neighbouring right. The owner of such a right may utilise the phonogram only insofar as he has been granted by the producer of the original phonogram the exclusive right or the permission to do so (adaptation right). A demarcation between slight alterations not giving rise to any protection and protected adaptations is to be drawn in a similar manner as applies to works. In particular, mere cutting or the unaltered re-recording of individual parts of a phonogram (alone or jointly with parts of other phonograms) do not create any adaptation right.

The Copyright Law does *not* give the producer of phonograms a comprehensive right in respect of his recording but (rather) the rights enumerated in the law: a reproduction and distribution right, a broadcasting right and a public performance right.[1]

If a phonogram produced for commercial purposes is used (directly or indirectly, eg by the onward transmission of a broadcast) for the purposes of a broadcast or public performance, the user has to pay to the producer an equitable remuneration. The performer is entitled to a share in that remuneration.[2] Such claims may be enforced only by a collecting society.

1   As regards the extent of these rights in detail, what has been said in the section relating to the protection of the performer applies analogously, particularly with regard to the statutory licence in respect of cable television and the claim to an equitable remuneration for reproduction for personal use.
2   See para 13.08, above.

13.19 What has been stated in the section relating to the protection of the performer on collaboration in such a way that the results of the efforts constitute an inseparable unit[1] apply mutans mutandis.

Likewise, what has been said in the section relating to the protection of the performer applies with regard to the presumption of the producership.[2]

So long as the producer of a published phonogram has not been identified in such a way as to found the presumption that he is the producer, the manufacturer or, if no such manufacturer is given on the phonograms, the supplier is deemed to be the agent of the producer entrusted with the administration of the rights. The manufacturer or supplier is in such event also entitled to sue for any infringements of the rights of the producer in his own name.

1   See para 13.10, above.
2   See para 13.11, above.

13.20 The rights vested in the producer are inheritable and alienable.

If the producer has identified a phonogram with his name (pseudonym, corporate style), any reproductions produced by others and intended for distribution must also bear a corresponding reference to the producer. If a reproduction identified in this manner reproduces a phonogram with significant alterations, the producer designation is to be supplemented by an appropriate addition. In the case of reproductions bearing a producer designation, the designation of the subject matter may differ only from that given by the producer to such extent as complies with ordinary trade usage.

If the producer's rights are assigned, the assignee may also be granted the right to identify himself as the producer of the phonogram.

What has been said in the section relating to the protection of performers on the subject of the right to use and the permission to use,[1] on rights of use concerning future recordings[2] and on the presumption in favour of the holder of the right in the case of assignments of ownership of a phonogram[3] apply correspondingly (but, on the other hand, not what has been said about premature cancellation of the contractual relationship owing to the failure to exploit the right to use or owing to a long-term commitment in advance with regard to future recordings).[4]

1   See para 13.13, above.
2   See para 13.14, above.
3   See para 13.14, above.
4   Compare para 13.15, above.

6. Protection of broadcasting organisations

13.21 The right in respect of a broadcast is vested in whoever broadcasts the sounds, images or sounds and images.[1] Contrary to the provisions regulating the neighbouring right of the record-producer, it is not expressly stated that the rights are vested in the employer and not in the technician who operates the transmitter. This is assumed as a matter of course since, whereas in the case of high-class recordings there is a personal input, the beaming of a broadcast transmission is exclusively a technical process.

1   For the details on the concept of a broadcast, see para 13.06, above.

13.22   The Copyright Law does *not* grant a broadcasting organisation a comprehensive right in respect of its broadcast transmission, but the specific rights enumerated in the law: a right to transmit the broadcast simultaneously through other transmission equipment, to record the transmission in sound or image, particularly also in the form of a photograph, to reproduce and distribute it. The law also grants the right to use videograms or phonograms which have either been fixed, reproduced or distributed for the purposes of a broadcast transmission or for a public performance without the consent of the broadcasting organisation or have been made for one's own use only.

As regards the details of the content of these rights, what has been stated in the section relating to the protection of the performer applies correspondingly, particularly with regard to the statutory licence in respect of cable television.[1] The broadcasting organisation however does *not* have any right to equitable remuneration in respect of reproduction for personal use.

What is stated in the section on the protection of the producer of phonograms concerning the protection of adaptations[2] applies analogously. An example, of an adaptation of a transmission is filtering out noises from an old broadcast transmission. The question of whether a broadcasting organisation which transmits television broadcasts is *also* always protected as the maker of the photographs and as such has a public performance right in respect of its broadcast transmission, is dealt with in the explanations to the Copyright Law revision of 1972:

In the Spring of 1971, the Austrian Broadcasting Organisation instituted proceedings against the proprietor of a cinema. The case was based in law on the view that the Austrian Broadcasting Organisation had, in respect of its broadcast transmissions, an exclusive right to perform them publicly. The Court found for the plaintiff, the Austrian Broadcasting Organisation.[3] The Austrian Broadcasting Organisation has not yet commenced to put the decision into practice by actually making the public performance of its television broadcasts, for example, in restaurants dependent on its consent. In the light of this situation it is advisable that this question of law, which was hotly disputed during the preparatory work for the present bill, should not be decided definitively and further developments should be awaited. To do so, it will be necessary to use the reservation contained in article 16, paragraph 1(b) of the Rome Convention.[4] Because of the considerations on which this reservation is based, no conclusion by analogy or 'a contrario' can be drawn from the making of this reservation. It is submitted that this question should be resolved in favour of the Austrian Broadcasting Organisation but there has been no decision of a higher court.

What is stated in the section relating to the protection of the performer[5] concerning collaboration in such a way that the results of the effort constitute an inseparable unit, applies mutatis mutandis to broadcasting organisations.

What is stated in the section relating to the protection of the performer concerning the presumption of capacity also applies analogously to broadcasting organisations.[6]

Finally it must be borne in mind that broadcasting organisations have a great number of original and derived rights on the basis of copyright in the strict sense, particularly as makers of films and or the basis of the protection of performers, phonogram producers and makers of photographs.

1 See para 13.06, above.
2 See para 13.18, above.
3 Judgment of the High Court of Vienna of 17 May 1971, 24 Cg 67/71.
4 This excludes art 13(d) of the Convention granting broadcasting organisations the right to authorise or prohibit public performance of their broadcasts in places where an entrance fee is charged. See para 8.35 above.
5 See para 13.10, above.
6 See para 13.11, above.

7. Collection and distribution of revenue from neighbouring rights (collecting societies, tariffs, tribunals)

13.23 Until the Copyright Law revision of 1980 came into force, the Law on Collecting Societies,[1] applied only to the enforcement of 'petits droits' in respect of literary works and musical works. Therefore it did not apply to the enforcement of neighbouring rights. Under the new Copyright Law of 1980 it was declared applicable by way of analogy to collecting societies whose objects are the claims to equitable remuneration for reproduction for personal use and claims for simultaneous, complete and unchanged onward transmission of broadcasts by cable. For the purpose of satisfying these claims, collective agreements may be entered into and tariffs issued. The provisions of the Law on Collecting Societies applying to societies representing organisers of performances apply correspondingly to organisations representing users.

This means essentially that such societies can be operated only with a permission of the Minister for Education and Art, that they enjoy a monopolistic position and are subject to state supervision.

Until the coming into force of the law of 1980, two collecting societies in the broader sense have operated without being subject to the law on collecting societies, namely the 'LSG' (Leistungsschutzgesellschaft mbH) collecting the equitable remuneration of performers and of phonogram producers for the broadcasting and public performance of commercial phonograms, and the 'OESTIG' (Oesterreichische Interpretengesellschaft) for the rights of performers in their live performances. Neither society has issued any tariff but both have entered into collective agreements for lump sums. Since 1980 a third collecting society in the neighbouring rights field has been formed; the 'Verwertungsgesellschaft Rundfunk' which has received an operating licence for original and derived rights of broadcasting organisations.

An arbitral tribunal will decide on any disputes as to the amounts of remuneration claimed. This tribunal may, on the application of a collecting society or of an organisation of users, issue regulations relating to the settlement of such claims. It will be established under the authority of the Ministry of Justice. All members are independent in the exercise of their office and are not bound by any directions or instructions. It consists of nine members (and the required number of substitute members). Having regard to the circumstances prevailing at the moment, its composition and decisions will be influenced by the general economic situation, particularly the balance of payments, and to the development of prices and wages. The decisive factor in arriving at this solution was that such a tribunal in arriving at its decisions will require specialist knowledge which cannot be expected of the ordinary courts. This is particularly necessary because in deciding the equitable remuneration claimed by one collecting society, claims for equitable remuneration of other collecting societies will have to be taken into account. Disputes other than over the amount of equitable remuneration are decided by the ordinary courts.

1 Federal Law Gazette No 112/1936.

8. Term of protection

13.24 The right of the performer and of the organiser of performances lapses 50 years after the expiration of the calendar year in which the performance took place. However, moral rights will last until the death of the performer.

The right of the producer of phonograms lapses 50 years after the recording, and if the phonogram is published prior to expiration of this period which is usually the case, 50 years after publication.

The right of the broadcasting organisation lapses 30 years after the transmission.

In calculating these periods of protection the calendar year during which the relevant event takes place is not to be included.

9. Permitted uses

13.25 Neighbouring rights do not inhibit use for purposes of evidence in proceedings before the courts and other authorities or for purposes of the criminal law and public security.

Phonograms and broadcasts produced exclusively or predominantly for official use do not enjoy any protection.

For the purposes of film or broadcast reporting on daily events, performances which are rendered publicly should be allowed to be recorded on videograms or phonograms, broadcast and publicly performed to a degree which is justifiable having regard to the purpose of information. Such videograms or phonograms should be permitted to be reproduced and distributed accordingly. Whether and to what extent the parties entitled to exploit may, in such case, demand that their names be indicated on the videogram or phonogram, will, it is submitted, have to be assessed by reference to normal custom and usage. A similar regulation is applicable in the area of the protection of producers of phonograms, broadcasting organisations and the makers of photographs.

For the purpose of the reproduction and distribution of commercially produced films and other cinematographic products, the otherwise necessary consent of the performer who collaborated in the performances given for the purpose of the production of the film or of the cinematographic product in the knowledge that they would be used for such purpose, is not required.

The provisions relating to the protection of the performer shall not apply in the case of any speeches made in a meeting dealing with public affairs or in proceedings before the courts or other authorities, or in respect of public political speeches.

Use within commercial enterprises, the objectives of which comprise the production or distribution of videograms or phonograms or the manufacture or distribution of broadcasting equipment, is always permissible insofar as it is necessary in order properly to serve their customers.

Use of single performances, phonograms and broadcasts for purposes of science and education to an extent justified by the purpose, is permissible.

Performances may be recorded by the organiser of that performance on a videogram or phonogram and reproduced with the aid of such videogram or phonogram or some other technical device within the building in which the performance takes place for the purpose of rendering the performance visible or audible in another room (such as in a theatre from the stage to the artists' dressing rooms).

10. Remedies for infringement

13.26 Whoever suspects an infringement of an exclusive right or the continuance or repetition of such an infringement may apply to the court for an *injunction* to restrain the party threatening the infringement, even if no fault attaches to the latter. An injunction may be granted against the proprietor of an enterprise where an infringement is threatened within the operation of his enterprise by one of his servants or agents. Interlocutory injunctions may be granted under less than normally burdensome terms.

The injured owner of an exclusive right may demand that the state of affairs which is contrary to the law be rectified. The injured party may, in particular, demand that the copies manufactured or distributed contrary to the provisions of the Copyright Law, as well as such copies as are intended for illegal distribution, be destroyed and that the means (moulds, blocks, plates, film strips and the like) which are intended exclusively for the production of illegal copies be rendered unusable. If the infringing objects or infringing means contain parts whose unaltered existence and whose use by the defendant do not infringe the plaintiff's exclusive right, the court shall have to identify such parts in the judgment pronouncing on the destruction or rendering unusable of the means. In the enforcement of such judgment, these parts are, as far as possible, to be excluded if the party found to be at fault pays in advance the costs associated herewith. If it becomes apparent that the process to render infringing material unusable would involve disproportionately large costs and if such costs are not paid in advance by the party found to be at fault, the court will, after examining the parties, order that such infringing material shall be destroyed. If the state of affairs which is contrary to the law can be rectified in a manner not involving any or only an insignificant destruction, the party prejudiced may apply only for measures of such kind. Instead of the destruction of infringing objects or the rendering unusable of infringing material, the party prejudiced may demand that the infringing objects or infringing material be transferred into his ownership by the owner thereof against payment of reasonable compensation not exceeding the costs of manufacture. The claim for rectification of the situation is to be directed against the owner of the objects in question. The claim may be enforced during the term of the infringed right so long as such objects exist.

The court shall, on application, grant the party successful in the injunction proceedings, if such party has a justified interest, the authority to publish the judgment within a specified period at the expense of the other party. The extent and nature of the publication shall be defined in the judgment.

Whoever uses without authority the subject-matter of a neighbouring right in a way reserved to the right owner shall, even if he is not at fault, pay to the injured party, whose consent should have been obtained, a reasonable compensation. No claim to such compensation shall exist however if a broadcast or public performance was unlawful merely for the reason that it was made with the assistance of videograms or phonograms or broadcasts which were not allowed to be used for such purposes, and if this was not known to their user.

The injured party may also demand the surrender of the profits which the infringer has made by his infringement.

The claim for damages (where fault exists) always covers, notwithstanding the degree of fault, the lost profit and reasonable compensation for such prejudicial effects, as do not consist of any pecuniary loss, which the injured party has suffered owing to the action. As regards the amount of damages the injured party may elect whether to prove the loss suffered or to demand twice the amount of the compensation. In addition to reasonable compensation or the surrender of profits, damages for pecuniary loss may however only be applied for insofar as they exceed the compensation or the profits to be surrendered.

If the infringement founding a claim for compensation is committed within the operation of an enterprise by a servant or agent of that enterprise, the duty to pay the compensation shall lie with the proprietor of the enterprise. If a servant or agent within the operations of the enterprise has acted ultra vires, the proprietor shall be liable, without prejudice to any possible duty on the part of such persons to make good the loss, if such contravention was known to the proprietor or he is precluded from denying knowledge of it. In such a case he also has a duty to surrender his profits.

If the same claim to compensation, to damages or to the surrender of profits is justified against more than one person, they shall be jointly liable.

Whoever under the Copyright Law is obliged to pay an equitable remuneration or compensation or to pay damages or to surrender profits, will have to account to the claimant and to have the accuracy of such account checked by an expert. If, on such examination, any greater amount is found to be due than that given in the account, the costs of the examination are to be borne by the party committed to make the payment.

All claims to equitable remuneration or compensation and the surrender of profits will lapse by prescription after three years. Similarly the claims of individual claimants or groups of claimants against a collecting society will lapse in three years, irrespective of whether or not the claimant had any knowledge of the facts giving rise to the claim.

Whoever wilfully uses the subject-matter of a neighbouring right in a manner reserved to the owner of the right may be prosecuted.[1]

The proprietor or head of an enterprise will also be subject to the penalty if he wilfully fails to prevent any such infringement by any servant or agent within the operations of the enterprise. Prosecution shall take place only at the request of a party whose right has been infringed. What has been said above[2] concerning publication of the judgment will apply correspondingly.

1 Fine of up to 360 daily units or imprisonment of up to six months.
2 See para 13.26, above.

11. Protection of foreign right-owners (points of attachment)

13.27 *Performances* which take place within Austria are protected, notwithstanding the country of which the performer and the organiser of the performance are citizens. Performances which take place abroad are protected if by Austrian nationals. If several persons collaborate jointly in a performance in such a way that the results constitute an inseparable unit, then protection as a result of the Austrian citizenship of one of the participants, shall, it is submitted, not extend to those participants who are not Austrian citizens.

Foreigners are protected with regard to such performances, regardless of state treaties, if such performances are protected in a similar way in the country of which the performer is a national, and in any event to the same extent as such nationals. Such reciprocity is to be assumed if it has been declared by a proclamation of the Minister of Justice in view of the legal situation in the state concerned.

13.28 *Phonograms* are protected, irrespective of whether and where they are published, if the producer is an Austrian citizen. Owing to the lack of any reference to a joint producer in the provision concerned, it is submitted that only an Austrian joint producer is protected. If the producer is a legal entity, it is submitted that the requirement of Austrian nationality is fulfilled if the legal entity has its domicile within Austria.

Other phonograms are protected if they are published in Austria. For phonograms of foreign producers not published in Austria what is said in para 13.27 applies.

There is one exception to this: a claim to remuneration for the broadcasting and public performance of phonograms produced for commercial purposes is vested in foreigners only in accordance with state treaties.

13.29 *Broadcasts* which are not transmitted in Austria are protected only in accordance with state treaties.[1]

1 Eg the Rome Convention; see chapter 8.

Chapter 14
France

by Pierre Chesnais

1. History of the development of copyright in France

14.01 For many centuries authors were more concerned to earn personal reputations or to convert people to their beliefs than to earn an immediate profit from the reproduction of their works. The advent of printing, however, gave these works a commercial value and encouraged authors to sell them for a lump sum to printers (also called 'publishers' or 'booksellers' before a distinction was drawn between the three functions).[1]

In 1507 and 1508 privileges were granted by the King to printers:

> 'Eagerness to get hold of new printed books prevented competition at the time from causing any harm, and up to the end of the XVth century, the number of printing machines was not sufficiently large for such competition to become dangerous to the new trade. However, with the increase of printing presses, printers clashed over the choice of works, and piracy was born, so to speak, with the art itself.
>
> Competition among editions, by increasing the number of copies, reduced the sale. The leading printers found themselves on the verge of bankruptcy; several were ruined and in the early XVIth century no-one dared start a business which required heavy borrowing. This first setback called for a prompt remedy. In order to prevent the collapse of the bookselling-industry recourse was had to royal prerogatives; the sovereign was asked to print a particular work and to forbid all others from printing it'.[2]

The Crown found the further advantage of censorship in the exclusive right to print and publish, but no interest was shown in the rights of the author.

However, at the beginning of the eighteenth century, provincial publishers considered themselves at a disadvantage vis-à-vis their Paris colleagues and, in this clash of interests, the concept of 'literary property' was born: 'the author creates and his creation is his; he conveys the ownership thereof to the bookseller and he conveys it to him in its entirety with all its attributes, the first of which is its perpetuity.'[3]

Economic concepts in France were permeated (and still are) by the doctrines of the Catholic Church, in particular the prohibition of money-lending upon interest and the curtailment of competition which might provoke social upheavals. These doctrines influenced the amendment to the law in 1777[4] which recognised the different economic roles of the author and the book-seller. For an author the 'privilege' of publishing is the price of his work; for a bookseller it is the security covering his advances. The difference in motive governed the difference in the extent of the privilege.

On 4 August 1789, in the wake of the French Revolution, the Constituent Assembly abolished all privileges, including therefore those of authors and booksellers. But what was to become of intellectual creation? In his report to the Assembly when the Decree of 13–19 January 1791 was to be voted on, Le Chapelier proclaimed: 'The most sacred, the most unassailable, and, if I may say so, the most personal of all properties is the work which is the fruit of a writer's mind; however, it is property of an entirely different nature from other properties'.[5] That Decree settled relations between authors and theatre-impresarios; a Decree of 19-24 July 1793 created an exclusive right of reproduction which was based on the concept of property.

These decrees with amendments (concerning in particular the duration of protection), and additions, (such as the Decree of 28-30 March 1852 concerning the offence of infringement of copyright, that of the import and export of infringing works which extended protection to foreign authors, and the Law on the 'droit de suite' of 20 March 1920), remained the basis of protection for authors until the entry into force of the Law of 11 March 1957.[6]

Thus for a century and a half, both legal writers and the courts relied on a few lines of these decrees to adapt authors' rights to the new techniques of communication and reproduction which entirely transformed social and cultural life. The protection thus extended to authors enabled France to take part in the diplomatic conferences on the Berne Union and on the Universal Convention and to ratify their revisions.[7]

However, there came a time when, following the example of many foreign countries, the drafting of a more detailed law was considered. It was then inevitable that discussion should turn to the nature of 'droit d'auteur'.

As early as 28 August 1944, the provisional government in France set up a study group attached to the 'Direction Generale des Arts et des Lettres.' It was given the title of 'Commission on Intellectual Property', and the Conseiller d'Etat Lerebours-Pigeonniere analysed the concept of 'droit d'auteur' under French law:[8]

> 'During recent times, whilst the controversy is not at an end, it seems to me that legal writers have identified the considerations which enable us to reconcile the term literary property with today's concept of the author's moral right supported by an exclusive right of exploitation, whilst at the same time they clarify the divergences existing between intellectual property and tangible property.
>
> The term literary property has been criticised because of the preconceived idea that the concept of property necessarily implied, on the one hand, a direct relation between the owner of the right and the object of such right without the intermediary of a debtor and, on the other hand, the unrestricted rights over the object laid down in Article 544 of the Civil Code. Such a preconceived idea is today held to be erroneous. Appropriation, that is to say the direct relation between the owner and the object of the right, is a sole characteristic of ownership. Unrestricted power is the attribute of tangible property in the Civil Code; it is in no way a prerequisite of ownership. No one disputes the fact that, in the present state of our common law, the author possesses a direct right in his work without the intermediary of a specific debtor. Accordingly, an author's right is, under the general rules of civil law, firstly a right enforceable erga omnes (an absolute right, enforceable absolutely) and is secondly an exclusive right over a work of the intellect. These are the two sole essential characteristics of ownership.'

1 Marie Claude Dock 'Genèse et évolution de la notion de propriété Littéraire' RIDA (January 1974) and Jacques Boncompain *Auteurs et comédiens au XIIIème siècle* (Paris, 1976).
2 Report of Antoine-Louis Séguier Avocat-général (1777) cited by Dock, op cit.
3 Memorandum of Louis d'Héricourt, advocate for the Paris booksellers, 1764, cited by Dock, op cit.
4 See note 2 above.
5 *Moniteur Universel* of 15 January 1791.
6 Law No 57-298 of 11 March 1957 (*Journal Officiel* of 14 March 1957 and amendment in *Journal Officiel* of 19 April 1957).
7 The Paris Act of the Berne Convention, 1971 came into force in France on 10 October 1974. The Paris Act of the Universal Convention came into force in France on 10 July 1974 and the two annexed protocols on 11 September 1972, the date of ratification by France of these three instruments.

8 Quoted by François Hepp 'Copyright as intangible property' RIDA (April 1958) pp 169-171.

2. Definition of a 'work'

14.02 For all these historical reasons, the Law does not lay down any definition of what works are protected as literary and artistic property. Thus, article 2 provides:

> 'The provisions of this law shall protect the right of authors of all intellectual works, regardless of their kind, form of expression, merit or purpose.'

The only criterion which must be taken into account, the originality of form, is not expressly mentioned by the Law (except in so far as article 5 states that the title of a work of the mind shall be protected, as shall the work itself, 'where it is of an original character'). Thus, if two painters choose the same site in the same lighting and in the same perspective, they both produce an original work.

Therefore for copyright purposes, originality must be viewed in a subjective and not in an objective sense, unlike industrial property where the criterion of novelty is an objective concept.

Even when, prior to the Law of 20 March 1925, deposit of the work was required before the author was entitled to bring legal proceedings against infringers, protection did not depend on previous formalities. Also, the Law of 14 July 1909, (which improved the special, voluntary and complementary system for the protection of new designs and models created in 1806 on condition that a deposit be made) does not exclude the common law protection of artistic and literary property where originality is shown.

As protection results from originality of form, ideas are not in themselves protected: 'Everything has been said, and we have arrived too late after more than seven thousand years during which mankind has been in existence and thinking.'[1] However, it should be noted that in certain circumstances ideas can benefit from some protection on the basis of civil liability and particularly under the law on unfair competition:

> 'there is a right to the secrecy of an idea, whether or not it be merely artistic or also industrial or commercial. The protection appears as such as an extension of the scope of the protection of know-how or as a complement to it.'[2]

It can be argued that the vagueness of the criterion of originality was intended by the legislature. Professor Desbois, taking as the basis of his analysis articles 4 and 12 of the Law, distinguishes between 'absolutely' and 'relatively' original works. In his opinion, the problem does not lie in the nature of the works. Thus he distinguishes:

> works of art where the image excludes the idea: the idea and the composition 'anticipate' the future work. Sketches and rough outlines are protected per se, their creation being necessary and sufficient. A copy constitutes a derived work, which is not the case with literary works; and musical works in which the tune is not in any sense an idea because it appeals to the senses and not to the intelligence. Variations on the tune are therefore derived works and relatively original. The difference between a work of art and a musical work lies in the fact that the work of art must be carried out personally by the author, whereas of a musical work, there can be many different interpretations of the author's abstract creation.

1 La Bruyère *Les Caractères*.
2 Xavier Desjeux 'Le droit d'auteur dans la vie industrielle' RIDA (July 1975) p 125.

(1) Joint authors

14.03 Complications arise on two levels as regards 'composite works', 'works of collaboration' and 'collective works' – that of the standing of the author and that of the exercise of the author's 'droit moral' and right of ownership.

In questions relating to the exercise of the rights examined below,[1] the position of each author in works of joint-authorship must be determined.

A *'composite work'* is a new work into which a pre-existing work is incorporated, without the collaboration of the author of the latter (article 9(2) of the law of 1957). These are, as regards literary works: translations, adaptations, anthologies and collections; as regards musical works: arrangements and variations; and as regards plastic art: copies. However, there can be a change in the kind of work, such as turning a poem into music or a pictorial work being inspired by a poem or a novel.

A *'work of collaboration'* is a 'work to the creation of which several physical persons have contributed' (article 9(1) of the Law of 1957). In this case, the contributions of the authors have united so as to contribute to the creation of one and the same work. It could be that the contributions to the work cannot be distinguished (for example, where two writers collaborate to write one book), but in other cases the individual contributions can be distinguished (the libretto and score of an opera, for example). In these cases, section 10, Law of 1957 provides that 'when the contribution of each of the co-authors is of a different kind, each shall be entitled, in the absence of agreement to the contrary, to exploit separately his personal contribution, without, however, prejudicing the exploitation of the common work'. French law differs on this point from the laws of a number of European countries.

The *Prince Igor*[2] case shows the difference between a composite work and a work of collaboration. Borodine having died without completing his opera, Glazounov and Rimsky-Korsakoff completed it. Glazounov's widow wanted to receive the copyright on the whole work. The Paris Court of Appeal took the view that the whole opera was not a work of collaboration because Glazounov and Rimsky-Korsakoff had not touched up Borodine's completed parts of the opera and because Borodine, who had died, could not have collaborated in the creation of the other parts written by the two other composers. On the other hand, the remainder was the fruit of the collaboration between Glazounov and Rimsky-Korsakoff. However, a problem arises here for cinematographic works. As opposed to the many countries which have solved it by treating the producer as an author, first French case law and then the 1957 Law (both faithful to the concept of literary and artistic property) have classified cinematographic works as works of collaboration, and have, moreover, included in such collaboration the authors of pre-existing works as regards the exercise of rights over the cinematographic work (articles 14 and 15, Law of 1957).

The Law adopted the same system for 'radiophonic' or 'radiovisual' works (article 18 of the 1957 Law). It should be noted that doubts subsist as to the interpretation the courts would adopt should all interested parties claim that the provisions applicable to cinematographic works also apply to audiovisual works (obtained by 'a process analogous to cinematography') whether they be works created for television or works created to be used for distribution by cable or for fixing on videogram.

It is likely that the French legislature will in future extend the application of articles 14 to 17 to all audiovisual works so as to make the situation clear.

'A "*collective work*" is a work created by the initiative of a physical person or legal entity who edits it, publishes it and discloses it under his direction and name, and in which the personal contributions of the various authors who participated in its development are merged in the totality of the work for which it was conceived, so that it is impossible to attribute to each author a separate right in the work as realised'. (article 9(3), Law of 1957) 'What does this mean? it means a sort of anonymous work like dictionaries, or encyclopaedias that an editor publishes under his name and which do not cease to be anonymous although the list of contributors is known (the "Dictionary of the Academy" is well-known to be the work of the forty "immortals" (members of the Academy), because it is impossible to determine the role or the part of each of them in the conception and composition of the work). Therefore it is accepted that such a work belongs, as if it were entirely his creation or an anonymous work, to the editor who has directed the composition and under whose name it is published'.[3]

This is the only exception in French law to the principle that authorship can vest only in a natural person, the sole intellectual creator. Although with literary or musical matters, the cases in which it is not possible to distinguish the part of each co-author are rare[4], the same is not true for designs and models, and case-law has repeatedly laid down[5] that legal persons can be included amongst those benefiting from article 8 of the 1957 Law: in such cases 'authorship shall belong, in the absence of proof to the contrary, to the person or persons under whose name the work is disclosed'.

Nevertheless, legal persons cannot claim a 'droit moral' and, in actions for infringement, it is in their interest to rely on article 8 of the Law, without claiming to have created the work, which would involve showing that their rights arise from a collective work or from agreements of assignment.

1 See para 14.12 below.
2 Court of Appeal of Paris (seventh chamber) 8 June 1971, Dalloz 1972. 283, RIDA October 1971. The 'Cour de Cassation' rejected the appeal on 14 November 1973 (RIDA, April 1974).
3 Lerebours-Pigeonniere, Note in Dalloz 1947, 529.
4 'Cour de Cassation' (first civil chamber) 1 July 1970, Dalloz 1970, 770.
5 Court of Appeal of Paris, 27 May 1975, JCP 1976.II.18297; 10 January 1977, JCP 1978.II.18830; 10 December 1980, Dalloz 1981.517, all with notes by Pierre Greffe.

(2) Protected works

14.04 Section 3 of the Law gives a non-exhaustive list (similar to that in article 2 of the Berne Convention)[1] of works protected. It is possible to classify the works by type:

Written works: literary, artistic and scientific writings are protected where there is originality of expression, whatever their form: catalogues, annual publications, notices, forms. Letters are also protected. The person who has the right to disclose a letter and claim a 'droit moral' is not the addressee, who is the owner of the letter, but the author of its contents. Although articles of substance published in the press and interviews are protected, the same is not true of unoriginal news communicated by agencies or the journalists themselves, such as commentaries.[2] Similarly, official documents (laws, decrees, regulations, reports of judicial proceedings) are not protected.

Oral works, such as conferences, public statements, sermons and speeches in court are protected.

Public speeches made in political, administrative, judicial or academic assemblies and public meetings of a political nature and official ceremonies are protected, but their publication, even in full, by press or broadcasting is allowed without consent of the authors, provided that the dissemination is made as current news reports (article 41(3), Law of 1957).[3]

Theatrical works are intended for public performance. Dramatic works are protected as literary works, and dramatico-musical works are protected as literary and musical works. The organiser of the performance does not have any right in the works performed. Authors other than the authors of the dramatic work or of the dramatico-musical work, such as the designer of the scenery and the costume designer, can contribute to the performance if they have produced creative original work, but they are not considered as co-authors. The same applies to the producer, but he must prove the existence of his work so that the reality and substance of his original creation can be appreciated.[4] The Law lays down this requirement of creation established in writing 'or otherwise' so that choreographic works and pantomimes can be protected. It is the person who has decided upon the order of the paces, movements and expressions who is the author, not the performer.

Musical works with or without words are protected, whether it be as regards the tune, the harmony or the rhythm. However, the harmony and the rhythm cannot be protected in isolation from the tune to which they are applied.

'Figurative' works of art are characterised by being capable of visual manifestation. These are cinematographic works or works obtained by a process analogous to cinematographic, and radiophonic and radiovisual works. The Law gives them the special treatment already mentioned.[5] It should be noted here that a cinematographic work 'is considered completed when the first masterprint has been established by common accord between the director or, as the case may be, the co-authors, and the producer' (article 16(1), Law of 1957).

They also include drawings, paintings, architectural works, sculpture, engravings, lithographs, illustrations, geographical maps, plans, drawings and models appertaining to geography, to topography, to architecture or to the sciences. The architect is therefore doubly protected, both as regards his drawings and models and as regards the buildings and monuments resulting from them. However, it is not the technical processes which are protected but rather the original form if it fulfils the requirements as to originality.

They also include works of applied art (for example, furniture, jewellery, cloth, 'couture', chinaware, advertisements and advertising documents). As regards these, in accordance with the principle of the unity of the art, protection is accorded by both the 1957 Law and the Law of 14 July 1909.[6]

Finally, they include photographic works of an artistic or documentary character and those of the same character obtained by a process analogous to photography. The addition of 'artistic character' by parliamentary amendment has introduced a special criterion for this category of works, and has given rise to difficulties of application and contradictions in case law.

The criterion of artistic character requires an assessment of artistic merit or aesthetic quality of the work, and the criterion of documentary character involves judging the value of information given by the photograph. Both assessments are contrary to the spirit of the law.

1 See para 5.32 above.
2 See para 14.44 below.
3 Case of A Malraux, 'Tribunal de grande instance' of Paris (first chamber) 3 April 1973 (RIDA, July 1973, lXXVII).
4 Court of Appeal of Paris, 5 February 1958, JCP 1958.II.10475 and RIDA July 1958 XX - 'Tribunal Civil de la Seine' 24 January 1962, Dalloz 1962 248, note Lyon-Caen, RIDA, April 1962, XXXV.
5 See para 14.3 above.   6 See para 14.2 above.

14.05 The works described as 'derived' from the foregoing are also protected by virtue of section 4. These are the pre-existing works.

Literary works. One can mention anthologies or collections, translations, revisions, updatings, commentaries and adaptations. As regards these, the difficulty of distinguishing what can and cannot be borrowed in order to have an original work has, both before and after the 1957 Law, given rise to piecemeal case law which now seems to be settled[1] for infringement, it is necessary for there to be similarities in the composition, development and arrangement of the ideas and for there not to exist any differences in the personalities of the characters, the course and the conclusion of the plot and the 'feel' of the two works.

Musical works. It is thought that by the word 'arrangements', the legislature has covered arrangements and variations.[2] The distinction between 'arrangement' or 'variation' with orchestration is sometimes difficult. Nevertheless it is important as regards songs and light music, for on it depends whether or not it is necessary to obtain the agreement of the author of the first work. Although his agreement is not necessary for works which are in the public domain or are part of folklore, the author of the arrangement or variations must demonstrate the originality of his personal contribution.[3]

Works of art. Article 4 mentions transformation. The copying of a work of art by other than a purely mechanical process (tracing or moulding, for example) is considered by text book writers and case law to involve the personality of the author of the copy who must ask for the permission of the author of the work of art if the copy is intended to be used for purposes identical to those for which the original work was created (article 41(2), Law of 1957).

Finally, parody, pastiche and caricature could have been viewed as derived works but, by article 41(4), the legislature has dispensed with the requirement that the authors thereof obtain the permission of the authors of works which inspired them. Therefore, they are original works. However, it has been held that there is parody only where the author obtains a caricatural effect or an effect wholly different from that of the original work.[4]

1 'Tribunal de grande instance' of Paris (first chamber) 16 May 1973, RIDA, October 1974, LXXXII.
2 Art 2.3 of the Berne Convention says 'arrangements of music'.
3 'Cour de Cassation' (first civil chamber) 1 July 1970, RIDA, April 1971, LXVIII and Cour de Cassation (first civil chamber) 23 October 1962, RIDA, January 1963, XXXVIII.
4 'Tribunal de grande instance' of Paris 9 January 1971, JCP 1971 16645, Note A Françon.

14.06 'The title of an intellectual work, insofar as it is original in character, shall enjoy the same protection as the work itself' (article 5(1), Law of 1957). Nobody may, even where the work is in the public domain, use that title to indicate a work of the same sort in circumstances likely to give rise to confusion. As in the case of photographs, the legislature has here retreated from the idea of general protection for titles: again, in order to assess the original character of a title, the courts have a tendency to consider artistic merit, which is contrary to the basic tenets of the law. Moreover, they have shown widely different views as to the risk of confusion, which is a concept relevant in the field of unfair competition and consumer protection.

14.07 The 1957 Law does not deal with the legal protection of computer software.[1] A distinction should be made between the act of introducing a work into the memory of the computer, which is an act of reproduction within the meaning of the law, and the creation of a work by means of memorising elements of a program, the person or persons having conceived those elements and the program counting as authors of an original work, which is therefore protected.

But what is the position as regards protection of a computer program itself? The Law of 2 January 1968 does not permit a computer program to be protected by taking out a patent, any more than it does as regards a method of musical notation or of accountancy. It seems, although opinions remain divided, that a program cannot be protected by way of copyright because it consists only of a series of instructions to the machine with a view to a particular result and can be looked upon as an algorithm, which is a non-protectable idea. However, as an idea, the program can be protected under unfair competition law.

1 See para 12.20 above.

(3) Limits to the protection of works

14.08 The 1957 Law has reaffirmed certain limitations on the protection of works already laid down by statute and case law concerning duration and certain uses. However, by a Law of 17 July 1970, the legislature has also added to the protection of the personality rights of third parties already given on the basis of article 1382 of the Civil Code or by the Law of 29 July 1881 on the press.

The case law has already established the right to one's image and the right to respect for private life. The Law of 17 July 1970 takes technical progress into account by laying down penal sanctions, particularly as regards recording, listening devices and the communication of words spoken or images taken in a private place and also as regards mock-ups where it is not obvious that a mock-up is involved and where no express statement that it is a mock-up is made.

14.09 The Law has not limited the duration of an author's 'droit moral': 'It shall be perpetual, inalienable and imprescriptible. It may be transmitted 'mortis causa' to the heirs of the author. The exercise of this right may be conferred on third parties by testamentary provisions' (article 6 of the 1957 Law). Sections 19 and 20 cover the exercise of the right after the death of the author and the exercise thereof can thus pass to a legal person, and in the case of disinheritance or where there are no known beneficiaries, to the Minister for the Arts or to a company whose objects consist of ensuring the respect for works. They can bring proceedings before the courts.[1] However, by article 21 the 1957 Law confirmed the limitation of the duration of the author's monopoly over his work as regards the exercise of his copyright.

It should be borne in mind that as a cinematographic work consists of a work of collaboration, the year to be taken into account is the year in which the last surviving co-author dies.

Notwithstanding the above, as regards certain works, such as anonymous works or works published under pseudonyms, the period of protection is not calculated from the date of the death of the author, but from the date of publication ('publication' being given a wider meaning in article 22 of the 1957 Law than in article 3(3) of the Berne Convention).[2]

Section 23 of the 1957 Law prolonged the period of protection for posthumous works to 50 years from the date of publication.

The period of protection was also extended by the 1919 and 1951 Laws for all work published respectively before 2 August 1914 (the extension being 6 years and 80 days) and before 3 September 1939 (the extension being 8 years and 119 days) and as regards the works of authors who have died for France (the extension being 30 years).

As a consequence of the prolongation of the right of use over works beyond death, article 24 and 25 of the 1957 Law includes provisions covering the rights of the surviving spouse and devolution for inheritance purposes.

1   It seems that professional bodies representing authors have no basis for acting since para 2 of s 65 of the 1957 Law only gives them that basis in order to defend the interests of the profession ('Cour de Cassation,' first civil chamber, 16 April 1975) see also 'Cour de Cassation,' first Civil Chamber, 6 December 1966, JCP II 14937; RIDA, April 1967.
2   See para 5.33 above.

14.10   Article 41 of the 1957 Law makes provision for four sorts of exceptions to the rights of an author:

'When a work has been disclosed, the author shall not be entitled to prohibit:
1. Free, private performances produced exclusively within the family circle;
2. Copies or reproductions reserved strictly for the private use of the copyist and not intended for collective use, with the exception of copies of works of art intended to be used for purposes identical with those for which the original work was created;
3. On condition that the name of the author and the source are clearly indicated: Analyses and brief quotations justified by the critical, polemical, pedagogical, scientific or informational character of the work in which they are incorporated; Reviews in the press;
The dissemination even in their entirety through the press or by broadcast, as current news reports, of speeches intended for the public made in political, administrative, judicial or academic gatherings, as well as public meetings of a political nature and official ceremonies;
4. Parodies, pastiches and caricatures, with due consideration for the laws regarding this type of work.'

It should be noted first of all that, unlike in many other countries, no limitations on the exercise of copyright are laid down concerning education and religious ceremonies, and that, on the other hand, despite the silence of the law, 'official texts' (laws, decrees, regulations and directives, instructions, circulars, notes and ministerial replies concerning interpretation of laws in force, or a description of administrative procedures and the communication itself of administrative documents) are not covered by any protection. However, apart from official texts, works of a type that can be protected may be created and published as part of the activities of the public services.[1]

The first two exceptions can adversely affect the normal use of works or bring about an unjustified disadvantage to the legitimate interests of authors, notwithstanding the obligation laid down by the new article 9.2 of the Berne Convention.[2]

As regards the first exception, representation within the family circle, the courts have chosen a middle course between the most restrictive route (persons related by blood or marriage) and the most extensive (persons belonging to the same association or going to the same hotel) and adopted the view that the family circle means the meeting in the same place of a number of persons who habitually meet each other.[3]

The second exception has already resulted in serious problems, as in most countries in the world, because it is directed at photocopying and reproduction by means of tape and video recorders, which have been developed through technical progress since 1957. Since photocopies of protected works by the user himself do not adversely affect normal use of the works (except musical scores), the courts need not follow the Paris Regional Court ('Tribunal de Grande Instance')[4] which held that a copier is any person who has chosen the contents of the copy having regard to the use, known only to himself, that he intends to make of it. The decisive criterion is some intellectual intervention.' Most photocopies made in undertakings and in educational establishments would not in those circumstances become cases of infringement. Thus, having regard to the impossibility in practice of acting against such infringers, one would have to organise a collective agreement for authorisation and remuneration.[5]

On the other hand, private copying by means of tape and video recorders does adversely affect the normal use of the works and the Commission on Intellectual Property, consulted by the Ministry of Culture in January 1981, unanimously took the view that this was a new way of utilising works and that authors and their beneficiaries should be given the means of obtaining remuneration for it. A draft law is being prepared which would introduce a levy on blank tapes.

1   See 'Le droit d'auteur français et l'état' (French copyright and the state) by André Kerever, RIDA (10 October 1981).
2   See para 5.37 above.
3   Court of Appeal of Grenoble, 26 February 1968, RIDA (July 1968). 'Cour de Cassation' (first civil chamber) 14 June 1972, Dalloz 1972, 659. Compare 'Cour de Cassation' (first civil chamber) 2 November 1971, RIDA (July 1972) and 'Tribunal de Grande Instance' of Paris, 23 May 1973, RIDA (July 1973).
4   'Tribunal de Grande Instance' of Paris (third chamber) 28 January 1974 JCP 75.II.18165, note Françon, RIDA (April 1974). See also 'Le droit d'auteur français et l'état' by A Kerever, op cit.
5   The purpose of the tax on photocopying equipment established by the Finance Law 1976 is not to introduce a legal licence rendering photocopying permissible, but to provide money for the National Book Fund.

(4) The use of the work

The 'droit moral'

14.11   Article 1(2) of the 1957 Law lays down clearly that 'this right includes attributes of an intellectual and moral nature as well as attributes of an economic nature ...'

Although Title II of the Law is headed 'Exploitation of the economic rights of the author', it can be said that the 'droit moral' is constantly pre-eminent as regards exploitation of the work. Article 6 clearly states that 'The author shall enjoy the right to respect for his name, his authorship, and his work'. This right shall be attached to his person, and the right shall be 'perpetual, inalienable and imprescriptible'. The right to respect in the work is here understood in a very wide sense (articles 47 and 56(2)). It is much wider than article 6 bis of the Berne Convention,[1] which only allows the author to object to any distortion, mutilation or other alteration to the work if it would be prejudicial to his honour or reputation. The 1957 law also covers the right to publish the work and the right to correct or retract it. The latter governs all acts of exploitation.

In fact, the author alone has the right to publish and, subject as regards cinematographic works to the provisions of section 17 he alone determines the manner of publication and sets the conditions (article 19, para 1). A reservation should also be made as regards works published in periodicals (article 36) and collective works (article 9). The right is to be considered in the light of the provisions of article 31(3) according to which:

> 'The transfer of author's rights shall be subject to the condition that each of the rights transferred shall be specifically mentioned in the act of transfer, and that the field of exploitation of the rights transferred shall be delimited as to extent and purpose, as to place, and as to duration'.

This right to publish has meant that the French legislature has not needed to give the author a right to put into circulation. It also means that one cannot argue vis-à-vis the author 'the exhaustion of his right',[2] so as to use the work outside the limits laid down as to scope, purpose, place and duration.

The 1957 Law gives, by article 32, the author a right to correct or retract.

The right to correct or retract means that the author has a right which is entirely in his discretion but lays down what must happen in return if he uses it. In the case of a work for which an order has been placed, this right is tantamount to a right of refusal, but it does not go so far as to permit the author to 'expropriate' in some way the purchaser of a work of art (section 29). Nevertheless, problems of application arise not only where an order has been placed for a work, but also where the author receives a salary or has acted on behalf of the state.

Article 1(3) of the 1957 Law provides that 'the existence or the conclusion of a contract to make a work or an employment contract shall imply no exception to the enjoyment of the right recognised in the first paragraph' (an exclusive incorporeal property right effective against all persons). As regards private employers, case law has stuck to a strict interpretation of the law[3], including matters concerning collective works.[4] However, according to Kerever,[5] 'works created as part of an administrative activity are of the same nature as works protected by that law ... and are, within certain limits, the original literary property of the administrative service' and the rights of administrative services 'prevent a property claim on the part of the official in so far as the work is created and made public as part of the activities of the public service'.

1   See para 5.37 above.
2   See paras 20.05 and 20.06 below.
3   'Cour de Cassation' (criminal chamber) 11 April 1975, RIDA (July 1975) and 'Cour de Cassation' (criminal chamber) 30 January 1978, RIDA (January 1979).
4   See para 14.12 below.
5   Kerever, op cit, above.

(5) Exercise of the rights where there is plurality of authors

14.12   Here we meet again the composite work, the collective work and the work of collaboration.

A 'composite work'[1] is the property of the author who has created it, subject to the rights of the author of the pre-existing work. In fact, 'the author of the original work and the authors of the derived work have concurrent rights in the latter work':[2] Victorien Sardou, in agreeing to his work *La Tosca* being adapted to comic opera, has not agreed that a cinematographic work be made from the comic opera.

A 'collective work'[3] is, unless the contrary is proved, the property of the physical person or the entity under whose name it has been divulged.

A 'work of collaboration' is the common property of the co-authors, who must exercise their rights by common agreement. Where they fail to agree, the matter shall be determined by the civil courts. If the participation of each of the co-authors relates to different media, each of them may, unless otherwise agreed, separately use his personal contribution, without, however, adversely affecting the use of the common work.

However, in article 17 the Law laid down a special rule for 'cinematographic works' 'The "producer" is the physical person or legal entity who takes the initiative and responsibility in the making of the work'. He has the benefit of a presumption that the exclusive right of cinematographic exploitation of the co-authors other than the author or composer of music with or without words are transferred to him.

It should be borne in mind that article 15 provides that each of the authors of a cinematographic work may freely dispose of the part of the work which constitutes his personal contribution.

1 See para 4.03 above.
2 'Cour de Cassation' (first civil chamber) 22 June 1959 Dalloz 1960 129 note Desbois.
3 See para 14.03 above.

(6) The exploitation of the author's economic rights

14.13 Article 26 of the 1957 Law states that the right of exploitation includes the right of performance and the right of reproduction.

However, the two rights cannot be intermingled: the assignment of the performance right shall not involve the assignment of the reproduction right, nor vice versa (article 30).

This independence generally leads to royalties under different rights being payable. Thus the right of performance granted to the promoter of a play does not give him the right to copy the text of the drama or comedy for the actors or the music for the orchestra. Since producers of phonograms have only acquired the right to reproduce works for the private use of the public, any user of the phonograms thus sold must pay royalties under the performance right if he wants to give a public performance of a phonogram, broadcast it or otherwise communicate it to the public, and this is in addition to the royalty payable for the performance right in the music. This second royalty is known as 'Surtax'.

The same goes for the public performance of a cinematographic work, a royalty is payable under the performance right to the authors of the music of the work, the music being excluded from the assignment to the producer of the exclusive right to the use of the cinematographic work under article 17.

The fact that different royalties are payable in this way is consistent with the third paragraph of section 31, which requires that the scope and purpose of the exploitation must be stated.[1]

Article 31 of the Law requires that contracts for performance and publication, and authorisations for gratuitous performances, must be evidenced in writing. In other cases, it is the common law which applies.[2] The Law provides on this point that 'when special circumstances so require, the contract may be validly concluded by an exchange of telegrams on condition that the field of exploitation of the rights transferred is delimited in conformity with the provisions of the third paragraph of this article' (article 31(4)). Article 33 prohibits the general transfer of future works by rendering such transfers void, but the following section allows a preferential right to be granted to a publisher, up to a limit of five new works for each kind of work or a period of five years, and lays down the obligations of the parties.

The Law, while providing that an author may make a total or partial transfer of his rights, requires that the assignment give the author a proportionate share in the receipts arising from the sale or use.[3] However, it lays down certain exceptions to this principle. In order to better protect the interests of the author, it enables him to require that the conditions as to price be revised in the case of assignment and inadequate forecast of the fruits of the work.[4]

Similarly, article 38 provides that: 'A clause transferring the right to exploit a work in a manner which is unforeseen or unforeseeable at the date of the contract shall be express, and shall stipulate a participation in the profits from the exploitation'.

Finally, the principle of equitable remuneration is applied as regards the graphic and plastic arts by the institution of a 'droit de suite', a right of the artist to a proportion of the resale price of his picture or sculpture: the authors whose works have, notwithstanding any assignment of the original work, 'an inalienable right to participate in the proceeds of any sale of their works by public auction or through a dealer' (article 42(1)).

It should be noted that the legislator uses the expressions 'total transfer', 'partial transfer', 'consent' and 'authorisation' without stating the nature and the scope of the contracts for the use of works. Section 39 is not a basis for saying generally that the person claiming through the transferor is subrogated to the latter in the exercise of the rights transferred, nor does it lay down any obligation to use the work. From an analysis of the texts, the nature and scope of the two main categories of contracts for the use of works may be summarised as follows. Exclusivity involves the obligation to use. Thus, the performance contract consists of an authorisation without exclusive rights and without the obligation to use the work (articles 43 to 47). Where an exclusive right is granted to a theatrical producer of plays, the right is limited in time and the producer must exercise the right, failing which he loses his monopoly (article 44).

Similarly, the publishing contract (articles 48 to 63) consists of a transfer coupled with an exclusive right, but the publisher must make use of the work in a permanent and continuous manner (article 54).

On the other hand, a phonogram producer who is going to reproduce an interpretation of the work in large quantities without obtaining an exclusive right to reproduce the work on records or tapes, receives a mere authorisation to use without being required to run off a minimum number of copies, not to guarantee a certain amount of remuneration to the author.

Finally, a producer of a cinematographic work who benefits from a presumption of transfer by co-authors other than the composers of music with or without words (article 17) enjoys a monopoly over the work and, being unable to guarantee an adequate use of the work, must very often agree to and advance a minimum remuneration to the co-authors.

It should be noted that contracts for the use of economic rights are made on a personal basis ('intuitu personae') (articles 44 and 62).

1   In Belgium, where the law does not contain the statement in para 3 of s 31, the matter has been decided by the courts in the same way; 'Cour de Cassation' of Brussels, 19 January 1956 RIDA (April 1956).
2   Arts 1341 to 1348 of the Civil Code.
3   Arts 35 and 36.
4   Art 37.

(7) Procedures and sanctions

14.14   The unauthorised use of a work causes, in most cases, irreparable damage to the author and to persons claiming through him. The same is true of other activities, but the law has always hesitated to organise preventive measures, particularly as regards unfair competition for fear that the plaintiff might himself harm a competitor just as irremediably by an unjustified procedure. However, the French legislature has created a special procedure in article 66 seizure for infringement, to protect literary and artistic property.
It should be noted:

1. That the first article only permits 'commissioners' of police and justices of the peace (now called 'magistrates') to seize copies constituting an unauthorised reproduction.
2. That the President of the 'tribunal civil' (which has become the Regional Court: 'Tribunal de Grande Instance') has the same powers but that he

can also authorise seizure outside the hours laid down by the Code of Civil Procedure, and order the seizure of receipts arising not only from an unauthorised reproduction, but also from performances or disseminations made in violation of the author's rights. On the other hand, although he may suspend any manufacture taking place of unauthorised copies, he cannot suspend a performance or a dissemination. Moreover, he must deliver a special authorisation for the seizure of copies (for example, copies of films) where the seizure may delay or suspend performances taking place or already announced. He may, but does not have to, require the furnishing of security by the applicant.

3. That the commissioners of police, justices and magistrates have to carry out the seizure without assessing the substance of the author's application or of the persons claiming through him upon the mere presentation of the document of title (certificate of deposit or authority or total or partial transfer of the work). The President of the Regional Court may refuse to make an order, but the applicants can then appeal.

A debate has arisen as to whether seizure for infringement can be carried out in the case of infringement of the 'droit moral'. It seems that the reference to article 426 of the Penal Code gives the President of the Regional Court this power to make an order in the case of infringement of any of the 'rights of the author, such as they are defined and governed by the law.'[1]

However, it is provided that the person against whom seizure is made can apply within 30 days to the President of the Regional Court for the lifting of, or the giving of security in respect of, the seizure, he can also be made to deposit a sum as security, which would compensate the defendant if the seizure should prove to be unjustified, for the damages which the author can claim (article 67). Moreover, it is provided that the person applying for the seizure order must bring his case before the competent court, failing which the seizure will be lifted (article 68).

This seizure without prior authorisation of a court is exceptional in French law. However, if he considers it desirable, the plaintiff may also apply to a court to exercise its general powers and take measures of sequestration and seizure which will produce analogous effects.

Authors and persons claiming through them (for example, beneficiaries, collecting societies, publishers, producers of cinematographic works) have a choice of either bringing the case before the regional courts or, where a public administrative body is the defendant, the administrative courts, or to lay a complaint before the State Prosecutor or to summon the infringer directly before a court of summary jurisdiction ('Tribunal Correctionnel'). Such proceedings before the court of summary jurisdiction can only be based on one of the infringements in the Penal Code. Article 425 of the Penal Code provides:

> 'Every edition of writings, of a musical composition, drawing, painting or any other printed or engraved production made in whole or in part, contrary to the laws and regulations relating to the copyright of authors, shall constitute an unlawful reproduction and every unlawful reproduction shall constitute an offence.'

Sanctions are laid down in articles 70 to 76 of the 1957 Law, which in this respect complements or modifies the penal code. It should be noted that the burden of proving good faith is on the alleged infringer. However, the same is not true as regards the distribution, exportation and importation of infringing works, when good faith is presumed and the burden of proving the bad faith of the vendor, exporter or importer is on the complainant copyright owner.[2] This obligation does not assist actions by authors or their collecting societies or by persons claiming through them, against the 'piracy' of phonograms or videograms.

1 Court of Appeal of Paris 4 April 1960, Dalloz 1960, 535, note Desbois and RIDA (July 1960).
2 Tribunal de grande instance of Paris (tenth chamber) 20 October 1970: Gazette du Palais 1971.1.266 and Court of Appeal of Paris (thirteenth chamber) 9 November 1972 Gazette du Palais 1973.1.109.

3. Relationship between 'droit d'auteur' and neighbouring rights

14.15 The draft law submitted to Parliament did not refer in its non-exhaustive list of works of the intellect to 'phonographic works'. An amendment for their introduction was presented to the 'Conseil de la République,' but was rejected following an intervention by Marcel Plaisant (who was also Chairman of the Commission on Intellectual Property)[1] in which he stated: 'What would the creation of an ersatz right for the benefit of a record maker lead to? It is placing on the same footing an intellectual creation and that respectable, yet limited, effort of a perfected technique which provides a material instrument for the reproduction of thought'. However, he added '... a right of that type, a sui generis right without a name ... we can create it; we shall create it one day, provided that it is recognised by all producing states so that we will not be at an economic disadvantage when it attains its full strength ...' Although a convention creating such a right, the Rome Convention 1961 has, since, come into force, France has not yet ratified it, and has taken no legislative measures for recognition of those 'derivative rights', although all important producer countries have, by now, done so.

1 Journal officiel des Débats parlementaires: 'Conseil de la République' 1 November 1956, pp 2150 and 2151; Session of 31 October 1956.

14.16 The case for performers is that they have interpreted a work, and so often the value of that work derives from the quality of that particular interpretation: the public often identifies a 'work' by reference to a particular performance. However, all the judicial decisions except one[1] which preceded the coming into force of the Law of 11 March 1957 had specified that the performer has no 'droit d'auteur'[2] and therefore cannot seek to rely on the general law.

Indeed, judicial decisions since the promulgation of the Law of 11 March 1957 have confirmed this refusal.[3] It has been argued that article 14 does not bar the inclusion of contributories to a cinematographic work among its co-authors, and one isolated Court of Appeal decision held that public servants should not be disbarred from being musicians at the same time as civil servants, since 'bearing in mind its originality, performance constitutes a work of the intellect and in particular an artistic work'.[4]

One person may be both author and performer of the work; this frequently happens in respect of musical works. That person enjoys two separate and distinct statuses each carrying separate and distinct rights[5] similar to the stage producer or director between the artistic conception and its actual performance.[6] Sometimes the activity of author and performer merge to such an extent that it is difficult to know whether there is a dual status for performers. It is, for instance, an open question whether an improvisation has sufficient originality to amount to an artistic work.[7] If it does not, the party concerned has no right other than that of performer.

1 'Tribunal Civil de la Seine' 6 March 1903, Gazette du Palais 1903-1-468.
2 'Tribunal Civil de la Seine' 23 July 1902; Gazette du Palais 1903.1.520. 'Tribunal Civil de la Seine' 9 November 1937. Gazette du Palais 1938.1.230, Jurisclasseur Périodique 1937, II, 247, Sirey 1938.2.57. Paris Court of Appeal, 24 December 1940; Jurisclasseur Périodique 1941.II.1649, note H. Desbois.
3 Paris Court of Appeal, 30 November 1961: Dalloz 1962-163. 'Tribunal de Grande Instance' of Paris, 22 March 1968: Jurisclasseur periodique 1968.IV.165, Dalloz-Sirey 1968, summary 118. Social division of the 'Cour de Cassation,' 29 April 1969: Jurisclasseur periodique 1976-IV.204, Dalloz 1976-IR-165. Civil 'Cour de Cassation', 15 March 1977: Dalloz 1976-IR-165. RIDA (April 1977), note H. Desbois.
4 V.R. Badinter 'Le droit de l'artiste sur son interpretation', Jurisclasseur Périodique 1964.I.1844 and Lyon Court of Appeal, 11 March 1971; Gazette du Palais 1971-2-497.
5 'Tribunal de Grande Instance' of Paris, 4 October 1967 summary proceedings and 3 January 1968 – Judgment – RIDA (April 1968) LVI 125 and 'Les disques et les référés' by Castelain and Rouanet de Vigne Lavit, RIDA (April 1968) LVI.41, but confusion in the 'Tribunal de Grande Instance' of Paris, 24 March 1972, RIDA (October 1972) LXXIV, 152.
6 Art 14, 1957 Law and art L.762 – 1 of 'Code du Travail'.
7 Civil division of the 'Cour de Cassation', 1 July 1970, Manitas de Plata, Dalloz, 1970.735, 'Tribunal Correctionnel de la Seine', 9 February 1957. Jurisclasseur Périodique 1957-II-10.031: a music-hall conjuring act in public may be protected by copyright if it is sufficiently original.

14.17 On 13 March 1957, that is to say after the promulgation of the Law of 11 March 1957, but more than 11 months before it came into force, the 'Tribunal Civil de la Seine' delivered a judgment which became final, bringing to an end proceedings between the *Gramophone Co Ltd v Société Concerteum*. The plaintiff alleged that the defendants had taken a record, *The Volga Boatmen*, performed by Feodor Chaliapine, and re-recorded it on an LP record under the title *Feodor Ivanovich Chaliapine Songs*.

Having, by virtue of contracts entered into between 1907 and 1921 with the famous singer, acquired exclusive rights to record on phonograph records all songs performed by Chaliapine and relying on those exclusive reproduction rights, the plaintiff Gramophone Company sought judgment against Concerteum for infringement of copyright.

The court found for the plaintiff by holding that 'the recording and reproduction of musical works and songs constitutes an original work protected by the Laws of 19-21 July 1793, since the production of a work of this nature necessitates on the part of its creator undoubted technical and professional knowledge, skill and research into the use of the best technical methods with a view to ensuring faithful reproduction of the music and of the voice recorded.'[1]

All the court decisions after the entry into force of the 1957 Law have respected the intention of the legislature. It should nevertheless be noted that since the promulgation of the 1957 Law, technical progress has given the phonogram producer many more ways by which he may choose to make recordings of the same performance, to make separate recordings of each part of the orchestra and the vocal performance and to end up with a 'mixture', all the operations being carried out by an artistic team whose task has increasingly resembled closely that of a cinematographic team.

Refusal to recognise the existence of 'phonographic works' has prevented the phonogram producer from persuading authors to assign their exclusive rights to him, and consequently from obtaining protection in this way. Nor is such refusal without repercussions for the people working for the producer: they are denied copyright and in particular a producer is denied the copyright attaching to a co-author. The phonogram producer is not compelled by law, as is the cinematographic producer (section 16), to obtain the consent of a producer and of co-authors in order to treat the first 'standard copy' or 'editing' as the finished product.

1 Jurisclasseur Périodique 1957-II-10210, note Robert Plaisant, see also the cases cited below.

14.18 The subject-matter of radio and television programmes is not always literary or artistic works. Thus, live or recorded broadcasting of a sporting event does not in principle constitute a protectable work, but it has been held that a radio report may constitute a protectable work.[1]

The 1957 Law recognises radiophonic and television works, and lays down, in the absence of a contrary provision, the scope of agreements. It is only by way of exception that a broadcasting organisation may be granted a 'droit d'auteur' when there is a collective work. Contracts with authors or parties claiming through them, for example, collecting societies, may relate to the right to use an existing work, without alteration, or adaptation or to adaptation of an existing work, or to the commissioning of a new work or the adaptation of an existing work. In the case both of a 'composite work' and of a 'work carried out in collaboration', the producer of a television work of this nature becomes one of the co-authors.

Under article 45 of the Law, a broadcasting organisation is not entitled to use the work for purposes other than wireless transmission, and then only for itself. It must therefore acquire under the contract, if it so wishes, the right to authorise another broadcasting organisation to use the programme and the right to exploit it or to have it exploited by other means, including distribution by cable.

Since the broadcasting of a work is regarded as a communication to the public, the use of commercial phonograms which are only published for private use imposes a duty upon the broadcasting organisation to obtain from the authors the right of reproduction and accordingly to pay them an additional royalty for it (referred to by some as a 'surcharge'), but the Law places the broadcasting organisation under no obligation towards phonogram producers or performers.

In order to broadcast cinematographic or audiovisual works, the broadcasting organisation must obtain the producer's permission if the latter has acquired the rights for television exploitation from the authors. Otherwise, it is to the co-authors of the work that the broadcasting organisation must apply and it will also have to deal with the lawful holder of a copy of a work. Whereas, up to now, the absence of a specific right attributed to the cinematographic or videographic producer has not caused any problem in France on a legal level for that type of exploitation, the position will not be the same with regard to the sale or hire of copies of cinematographic or videographic works when their producer is not or is no longer the assignee of the copyright for television exploitation.[2]

As a national public corporation enjoying a monopoly throughout French territory, the ORTF obtained protection under the Ordinance of 4 February 1959. The bodies which succeeded it on 1 January 1975 enjoy a similar protection by virtue of incorporation of the said Ordinance in the Law of 7 August 1974. This enabled France to ratify the European Agreement of 22 June 1960 (and its subsequent protocols) for the protection of television broadcasts.[3] To date, France has not yet adhered to the 1974 Brussels Satellite Convention.

1 'Tribunal Civil de la Seine', 21 May 1954, RIDA (1954) 115. and Paris Court of Appeal, 7 July 1956, RIDA (1956) 167.
2 See para 14.46 below.
3 See paras 11.03 et seq, above.

4. Protection of performers

14.19 The social condition of performers, and in particular that of actors, still suffers in France from the opprobrium to which they had been subject for centuries. Although the Declaration of the Rights of Man and the Law of 24 December 1789 gave them along with Jews, Protestants and executioners, access to all civil and military occupations and made them eligible to stand for election, it was only in 1849 that the 'Concile de Soissons' relieved them from excommunication.

It is not surprising therefore that since the last century, performers and their professional bodies in France have striven above all to obtain, as a first step, the benefit of employment and social security legislation. Thus, the only laws which refer specifically to them and which are comparatively recent relate merely to the legal nature of their employment contracts and the organisation of their placement.

Thus, no provisions are to be found in existing legal and administrative laws and regulations, concerning protection of performers with regard to neighbouring rights.

Nevertheless, Law No 69-1186 of 26 December 1969[1] is of some interest, firstly because it enumerates, on a non-exhaustive basis, those people who are regarded as 'entertainment artistes' and, further and most importantly, because it established a presumption, which is virtually impossible to rebut, that performers are to be employed under the regime of a 'service contract' or 'employment contract':

Every contract whereby either a natural or a legal person secures, for remuneration, the services of a performer for the purposes of his or its production, is deemed to be a service contract when the said performer does not carry on the activity which is the subject matter of the said contract on terms implying his registration in the Register of Commerce.

This presumption subsists whatever the manner and amount of the remuneration, or whatever the description attributed to the contract by the parties. Nor is it rebutted by proof that the performer retains his freedom of expression in his art, that he is the owner of all or part of the equipment utilised or that he himself employs one or more persons to assist him if he takes part personally in the performance.

The contract of employment must be individual, although it may be common to several performers. In such a case, the contract must name all the performers engaged and must show each one's salary. Such a contract of employment may bear the signature of one performer only, on condition that the signatory acts by virtue of a written authorisation conferred by the others named in the contract. A performer contracting on these terms retains the status of employee.

Having regard to the part played by collective employment agreements in France under the terms of the Labour Code, the status of 'employee' conferred on performers has enabled their professional bodies and those of their employers to organise the exercise of rights obtained by the performers under contracts and has enabled the courts to protect such rights by reference to the general law.

In order to facilitate the application of agreements between the artists' organisations and the employers' organisations, the artists created two societies for the collection, control and distribution of royalties for the new primary or secondary uses of their performances. ADAMI (Agence générale pour l'Administration des Droits des Acteurs et Musiciens Interprètes) in 1955 and

SPEDIDAME (Société de Perception et de Distribution des Droits des Artistes Musiciens Exécutants) in 1959.

[1] Now incorporated in the Labour Code (art L.762.1 and 5) and in the Social Security Code (art L.242.1).

(1) Protection through collective agreements

14.20 The successive laws governing collective agreements are now codified under the Third Title of the Labour Code. They forbid any consideration of union membership, or the lack of it, as a requirement for the engagement of a person and the granting or withholding of the benefit of a collective agreement. The result may be summarised as follows:

Every employer who is a signatory to a collective agreement or a member of an employers' federation at the time of signature by him of a collective agreement is bound to extend the collective agreement to all employees in the class concerned, whether or not they are union members and whether they are French or foreigners. Any provision in an individual contract which is contrary to – or less advantageous for the employee than – the corresponding provision in the collective agreement is void, and the provision in the collective agreement is substituted for it. The collective agreement stipulates the conditions upon which the employer may himself exploit the services of the performer or have them exploited by others.

When negotiating the individual contract of employment, the employer may thus neither obtain from the performer an authorisation to use or reproduce his performance when such use or reproduction is denied him in the collective agreement, nor may he pay him a lower remuneration. On the other hand, the performer, provided it is an express term in his individual contract of employment, may withhold the authorisation granted in the collective agreement or obtain additional remuneration higher than that stipulated in the collective agreement.

On occasion, the collective agreement may provide that, for particular kinds of use of performers' services, special agreements or amending agreements shall be entered into between the performers' union and the employer or his federation, to determine the conditions applicable to such cases.

Accordingly, where it has not been possible to sign the special agreement or the amending agreement, some employers take the precaution of stating in the individual contracts of employment that they reserve for the future the right to exploit the services of the performer in certain ways or by particular means of utilisation or reproduction, subject to the conditions of such collective agreements, special agreements or amending agreements as may be in force at the time.

In effect, the shortcoming of the system lies in the fact that if a collective agreement has not provided for utilisation of the services of the performer, or if the performers' union and the employer have failed to reach agreement, the employer will have to obtain the individual authorisation of each one of the performers concerned, thus running the risk of litigation or of a union conflict and the delays and problems which they entail.

Nevertheless, as in labour law, the part played by 'general and constant practice' is recognised and invoked by the Courts[1] or the parties themselves.

Thus, the 1971 collective agreement of the 'Théatre National de l'Opéra' and of the 'Comédie Française' stipulates: 'the Management is entitled to retransmit all or part of its productions, using recordings made within its auditoria or in any other place. The remuneration of the employees concerned shall be that commonly applicable in the profession. Agreements define and set out in detail the rights and duties of such employees'.[2]

1 See para 14.50 below.
2 Art 27 of the Collective agreement of the 'Théatre National de l'Opéra'.

14.21 The collective agreements or collective contracts concluded between performers' unions and the federations of employers or the employers themselves are numerous. Collective exercise of the rights granted to performers in those agreements is the rule. The performer may not restrict the rights granted by the unions, save in his individual contract.

Individual contracts are not used, as a general rule, for the engagement of orchestra musicians and chorus members. If such performers provide services in response to an invitation to work this is tantamount to acceptance of the conditions of the collective agreement.

14.22 With regard to protection of performers for the broadcasting and communication to the public of their non-fixed performances[1] and fixing on a material support of their non-fixed performance,[2] collective agreements concluded with organisers of 'live' shows authorise direct sound-broadcasting and even recorded broadcasting (ie, by means of previous fixations) of shows in return for additional remuneration. Nevertheless, soloists (actors and singers) are entitled to a provision in their contract of employment to the effect that they will not take part in broadcast shows.

For live or recorded television broadcasts, the position of musicians is the same. On the other hand, for actors and singers, the collective agreements stipulate that broadcasts may not take place without prior agreement between the performer and the organisation or television company concerned, with the exception of collective agreements for the national theatres and of extracts from shows rebroadcast as news of the arts. Total or partial fixing of shows for other purposes (for phonographic, cinematographic and videographic exploitation) remains subject to the prior consent of each one of the performers. The performers' employer may therefore be sued by the performer if he allows a third party, even a spectator, to record the show and exploit the recording ('bootlegging').

1 Cf art 7.1, (a) and (b), Rome Convention 1961, see para 8.17 above.
2 Cf art 7.1 (c), Rome Convention 1961; see para 8.18 above.

14.23 As regards reproduction of a fixation of their performance for purposes other than those for which they have given their consent[1] collective agreements are most numerous.

In 1959, the Musician's Union consented to the reproduction of phonograms, in their entirety or in part, for inclusion in the sound-track of cinematographic films in consideration of payment of a royalty calculated by the minute and by reference to the number of musicians.

In 1960, a similar agreement was concluded with the 'Chambre Syndicale des Producteurs de films'[2] to allow reproduction for phonographic exploitation of film music. These two agreements are still in force.

In 1969 and 1970, collective agreements were reached between the Federation of Phonogram Producers and the unions representing all classes of performers to determine their conditions of employment, work and remuneration. All of the collective agreements provided for the making of 'Special agreements for the use of phonograms other than sale or hiring out to the public for private use'. In 1972 a special agreement was concluded with all the performers' unions to allow phonogram producers to authorise reproduction of commercial phonograms by public address systems. The Federation of Phonogram Producers sets aside for the performers a share of the royalties it collects for such use.[3] In June 1980 the same parties signed a collective agreement concerning the use of commercial phonograms in 'live' shows. The agreement invoked the IFPI-FIM principles[4] and in particular the need to preserve employment opportunities for musicians, and the phonogram producers undertook not to authorise the use of their phonograms in a 'live' show without the consent of the Musicians' Union. However, producers are entitled to authorise the use of their phonograms when the use of recorded music in a show does not exceed in total one tenth of its duration. A royalty is fixed by the minute and per show, being collected by the phonogram producer on behalf of the musicians.[5]

With regard to cinematographic films, the Actors' Union have concluded with the Federation of Film Producers a collective agreement which guarantees the 'crediting' of the performer's name and synchronisation of the sound of a part by another actor. It also provided that other than for publicity purposes the permission of the performer is required for any reproduction of the film for other purposes, of its sound-track or of pictures from it. This provision was held to be applicable to the sound in a commercial phonogram in *Crouzet and Bruno v Ste Mediterraneenne de Films*.[6]

Although 'videograms' (on video-cassettes or video-discs) can be regarded as equivalent to a cinematographic work, since either they are made by a process analogous to cinematography or they are merely a reproduction of a cinematographic work, it is apparent from Article 38 of the collective agreement that a cinematographic work reproduced on a video-disc or video-cassette may be exploited in cinema halls, or broadcast by radio or television, but may not be copied and sold to the public without the permission of the performers, in the absence of a specific clause or of an amending contract. For the use of a cinematographic work for other purposes, it is the performer who must specify in his contract that he wishes to forbid or limit it.

1   Cf art 7.1 (c)(ii), Rome Convention 1961; see para 8.18 above.
2   Collective Agreement for Cinematographic Production of 1 September 1967, art 38.
3   See para 14.33 below.
4   IFPI – International Federation of the Producers of Phonograms and Videograms, FIM – International Federation of Musicians.
5   See para 14.34 below.
6   Court of Appeal of Paris, 8 June 1967, unreported.

14.24 As regards direct use of commercial phonograms or of a broadcast reproduction of such phonograms, following the decision of the Court of Appeal of Paris in *ORTF and SNICOP v SPEDIDAME*[1] and the division of the ORTF into four national programme companies at the end of 1974, the Federation of Phonogram Producers (SNEPA) signed a special agreement with all Performers' Unions on 12 December 1975. SNEPA were authorised by the phonogram producers to conclude general agreements with the public corporations, and national or private companies using commercial phonograms for radio or television broadcasting.

This Agreement has been applied between SNEPA and the national broadcasting companies for the TF1, A2 and FR3 but not to 'Radio France' programmes.[2]

1   See para 14.27, note 2, below.
2   Cases against 'Radio France' and against the so-called 'peripheral' broadcasting organisation like Radio Luxembourg, Europe I and Radio Monaco are pending.

14.25 It was not thought necessary to resort to legislation to settle relations between broadcasting organisations and performers. As early as 1946, collective agreements were established embodying three principles for sound broadcasting. The first was that by virtue of his performance the performer authorises the broadcasting of it and the recording of it by the broadcasting organisation. Secondly, the performer's remuneration covers a broadcast of the programme by all transmitters in a network (or 'chain') within a stated time limit: beyond such limit, any fresh broadcast shall entail payment of appropriate additional remuneration. Thirdly, any broadcast on another network or by a foreign transmitter gives rise to the right to additional remuneration, save where such broadcast is simultaneous with the broadcast on the first network and subject to application of the agreement between the European Broadcasting Union (EBU) and the International Federations of Actors (FIA) and Musicians (FIM) relating to sound broadcasting.

This right to additional remuneration is limited to a period of 30 years from the first day of the year following that during which the programme was broadcast for the first time.

Reproduction and use for purposes other than broadcasting of the soundtrack of programmes and of photographs or recordings of pictures made at the time of their production is limited to presentation and illustration of the activities of Radio France. However, as an experiment, the 1977 collective agreement permits the publishing of phonograms based on programmes against payment of remuneration in proportion to the number of phonograms sold. A performer who wishes to oppose this publication of phonograms (which is essential if he is already bound by an exclusive contract with a phonogram producer) must state this expressly in his contract.

The principles governing sound-broadcasting agreements have also been applied to television. The collective agreement signed between the actors' unions and the producers of television programmes (national companies and private companies) was renewed in July 1980; it reproduces the provisions relating to commercial assignment of programmes and telefilms for television and cinema exploitation, but for the first time provides for additional remuneration[1] for exploitation of such programmes and telefilms by the sale thereof to the public for private use on video-cassettes or on video-discs.

A performer who wishes to prevent the televising or the cinema or videographic exploitation of his programmes in another country must therefore stipulate this in his contract of employment.

The supplementary remuneration is due for a period of 30 years from the first day of the year following that during which the programme was broadcast for the first time.

1 6% of the wholesale price (calculated on 90% of the copies sold during the first year) after a lump-sum deduction of 6.50% if the support is a video disc and of 17% if the support is a video-cassette. (Collective Agreement for Performers engaged for Television Broadcasts, 18 July 1980, art 8.15.1).

(2) Protection extended by the courts on the basis of the principles of general law

14.26 Whilst the courts refuse to protect performers as authors of literary or artistic works, they nonetheless grant them, in the absence of special provisions in contracts of employment and collective agreements, two important rights: a 'moral' right and a right to remuneration.

The courts first recognised a 'moral right' in favour of performers, just as they had done in favour of authors, even before the 1957 Law, since every individual is entitled to respect for his personality, honour and reputation. As early as 1931, the 'Conseil d'Etat' had given leave to appeal to two singers who had regarded the broadcasting of their performance without indication that it was fixed on a record as so prejudicial as to bring an action. Although the 'Conseil d'Etat' dismissed the suit,[1] Professor Mestre stated at the time: 'this negative decision of the "Conseil d'Etat" must nonetheless be acknowledged as important. It implies a major conseqence: recognition of the right of the performer.'[2]

In 1937, the 'Tribunal Civil de la Seine' considered that when dubbing is carried out, the public should be informed. It also observed that wherever a performer is deemed to assign his rights to a phonogram producer, unless there is provision to the contrary, so far as his moral right is concerned the presumption is reversed.[3]

In 1955, the 'Tribunal Civil de la Seine', with regard to a short film made without the knowledge of the actors during their break period whilst making a full-length film, held that an actor is entitled to appear only in films and to be presented only in a manner or in parts which he considers to be in keeping with his artistic taste and with the interests of his career.

By making and publicly showing a film which either does not come within the terms of the performer's contract or to which the performer has not otherwise given his express consent, the producer may cause damage by way of lost remuneration, to the performer and also may cause 'moral damage' to the performer's personality.[4]

In the Furtwängler case, decided in 1957 by the Paris Court of Appeal,[5] tapes recorded under the direction of the conductor during the war by the German broadcasting authorities had subsequently been assigned and used without his agreement for the making of commercial discs. The Court held that in the artistic and literary fields, reputation is essentially personal property. The performer is the sole judge of the means and of the timing of its exploitation, and he should draw a commercial profit from its authorisation since he is at liberty to refuse it. So far as a musical performance is concerned, a performer, in the absence of contrary agreement, cannot be deemed to have given his performance other than for a predetermined use, which will exclude any use which might constitute an abuse.

Since then, and notably since the enactment of Law 70.643 of 17 July 1970 intended to reinforce the guarantee of the individual rights of citizens,[6] decisions of the courts confirming the moral right of performers have proliferated. The following judgments are examples:

Abadie v ORTF concerned a 'montage' during a television programme.[7]
J. P. Belmondo concerned the use of photographs for purposes other than advertising the film from which they were taken.[8]
Cl Pieplu v RFP concerned the imitation of the voice of a performer.[9]

There have also been several cases concerning the right of performers not to have their performance 'disfigured' and 'taken beyond its limits.'[10]

So far as the 'non-use' of a performer's performance is concerned, it has been held that although a performer's performance cannot be the subject of any broadcast other than that which he has authorised, the non-use of songs recorded for publication as a phonogram, only constitutes a possible breach of contractual provisions.[11]

1 'Conseil d'Etat' 20 November 1931; Sirey 1932.2.62.
2 Achille Mestre in Revue Juridique de Radioélectricité (1932) p 53 and note Sirey 1932.2.62.
3 'Tribunal Civil de la Seine' (3rd chamber) 23 April 1937 Jurisclasseur périodique 37.II.247, Sirey, 1938.2.57, Dalloz hebdomadaire 1938–107. Le Droit d'Auteur 1939 p 129. Also Tribunal Civil de la Seine (18th chamber) 19 November 1937, Gazette du Palais 1938,1,230, Droit d'Auteur 1940 p 118.

4 'Tribunal Civil de la Seine', (3rd Chamber) Jurisclasseur Periodique 1955 II 8678, note Plaisant. See also Paris Court of Appeal 2nd June 1947, Gazette du Palais 1947, 2.91.
5 'Tribunal Civil de la Seine', Summary Proceedings, 19 December 1953 RIDA III 117 and 9 March 1954; Jurisclasseur Périodique 1954 II 8114 note Plaisant and Scalelli. Paris Court of Appeal, Court No 1, 13 February 1967; Jurisclasseur Périodique 1957 II 9838, Judgment Lindon; RIDA (1957) XVII 144, Revue Trimestrielle de Droit Commercial 1957, 653 remarks Desbois. 'Court de Cassation, Civil Court No. 1, 4 January 1964: Dalloz 1964.321, note Pluyette, Jurisclasseur Périodique 1964.II. 13712. RIDA XXXXV.194. See also Desbois: 'Droit d'Auteur et droit des artistes exécutants' in Dalloz 1964, report 247–183; Badinter 'Le droit de l'artiste sur son interprétation', Jurisclasseur Périodique 1964–I.1844.
6 Journal Officiel, 19 July 1970.
7 'Cour de Cassation' (1st civil chamber) 18 March 1971 and Amiens Court of Appeal (in 'solemn session') 13 December 1971. Gazette du Palais 1972.1.460.
8 Paris Court of Appeal, 13 February 1971; RIDA LXXII, Jeanne Moreau. 'Tribunal de Grande Instance de Paris' 23 March 1972; Dalloz 1972.S.47.
9 'Tribunal de Grande Instance de Paris', 3 December 1975; RIDA (April 1976).
10 'Tribunal de Grande Instance de Paris' (3rd chamber) 16 February 1973; Dalloz 1973.IR. 212; 'Tribunal de Grande Instance de Paris', (3rd chamber) 27 September 1976; RIDA April 1977, 'Tribunal de Grande Instance de Paris' (1st chamber) 19 January 1977; RIDA (January 1978); 'Tribunal de Grande Instance de Paris' (1st chamber) 20 April 1977; RIDA (April 1978), 'Tribunal de Grande Instance de Nanterre (2nd chamber) 25 October 1977.
11 Spycket and another v Ste Disc' az – 'Cour de Cassation', Chambre Sociale, 29 April 1976; Jurisclasseur Periodique 1976 IV 204, Dalloz 1976 IR, 165.

14.27 In cases of conflict between the moral right of an author and that of the performer, it has been held[1] that article 73 of the Decree of 9 September 1971, as amended by article 178 of the Decree of 17 December 1973, enables a judge in chambers to grant an injunction if it is necessary either to forestall imminent damage or curtail 'patently illicit' infringement. Within the meaning of 'patently illicit' is an erotic scene contrary to decent standards of behaviour (within the meaning of articles 6 and 1172 of the Civil Code), and behaviour which is contrary to the wishes of the principal female performer and is detrimental to the standards of human dignity which she intends to retain, especially where she had expressly reserved the right to forbid the showing of such a scene having viewed it. It is irrelevant that such agreement does not bind the director who was not a party to it (even if the producer seemed to have stood surety for the latter, by signing such a clause). In a conflict between the right of the author (ie the director) to respect for his work and the right of the performer to respect for his or her personality, it is appropriate to give the decision which will cause least injury.

In *ORTF and SNICOP v SPEDIDAME*,[2] the Paris Court of Appeal said that the personality of the performer is protected as anyone else's when injury is caused to one or other of his facets such as his image, his name or his private life. The mere fact of making a secondary use of a performance, unauthorised or unremunerated, cannot alone be regarded as causing injury to the performer's personality but might involve contractual or tortious liability on the part of the user.

1 'Tribunal de Grande Instance de Paris Référés' 14 May 1974, Dalloz-Sirey 1974, 766 2ns case and note Lindon.
2 Paris Court of Appeal (4th chamber) 30 November 1974, Jurisclasseur Périodique (1976) II 18336, note Plaisant, RIDA (April 1975); note Desbois, affirmed by the 'Cour de Cassation', (1st Civil Chamber), 15 March 1977, RIDA (July 1977), note Desbois, Dalloz Sirey, 1977, IR.295.

14.28 Thus, quite apart from the moral right accorded to performers, an important question for the courts was whether they should recognise, in the absence of special statutory provisions, exclusive rights in respect of performances.

Some exclusive rights not laid down by law are recognised by the courts as giving rise to an action in tort, such as the right in respect of a shop sign or trade name and more particularly the phonogram producers' right.

The courts went further when technical processes and the importance assumed by phonograms, films and broadcasts in cultural and social life raised serious problems for professional performers.

The first decision on these matters was given by the 'Cour de Cassation' in the *Furtwängler* case:[1] 'Urania Records' had produced and sold the disputed record without the authority of the performer. The court held that a performer is entitled to forbid the use of his performance for a purpose other than that which he has authorised. It is interesting to note that the court referred to injury to the performer's right over 'the work' which constitutes his performance. The use of the term 'work' in this context had initially been criticised. However, in its later judgments the 'Cour de Cassation' has reaffirmed its decision and in this respect without referring to the 'work' and developed it.

In *Orane Demazis v Société Méditerranéenne de Film*[2] the Paris Court of Appeal, confirmed by the 'Cour de Cassation', held that a performance may not be used for purposes other than those which the performer had authorised and, accordingly, the burden is on the film company to establish that it was authorised by the performer to produce records from the sound-tracks of the film and to exploit them commercially.

In *Spycket and another v Société Disc'az*[3] the 'Cour de Cassation' confirmed these precedents. In *SPEDIDAME v ORTF and SNICOP*[4] the 'Cour de Cassation' approved the Court of Appeal of Paris saying that, 'although the performers have a right to object if their performances are used for purposes other than those which they have authorised, they had nonetheless consented without qualifications to the broadcasting of their recorded performances because they knew that these recordings were constantly used by the ORTF as assignee of the producer. Therefore, in the present state of the law, the sole way open to performers to reserve their right of authorisation and their right to receive a supplementary remuneration would have been to reserve these rights in their individual contracts or in their collective agreements'.

Professor Desbois, in his note on the judgment of the Supreme Court[5] draws the following conclusion:

> 'In accordance with the usual rules for proving contracts, it is for the performer to prove, by producing an appropriate clause, that he restrained the freedom of the producer and of parties contracting with the latter. On the other hand, an author may put his opponent to proof that this or that right of exploitation has been granted because in matters of copyright whatever has not been expressly granted remains withheld.'

Emphasis must be placed on the words 'without qualification'. This means that where the contract is silent, the company may make use of the phonograms and, in particular, may sell or hand them over to a broadcasting organisation for the purpose of its broadcasts. This view seems in flat contradiction to the decision of the 'Cour de Cassation' given previously in the *Orane Demazis* case:[6]

> 'But whereas the Court of Appeal, which held that the reference which the letter of engagement made to general conditions (which were not produced), was insufficient to give substance to the existence of a clause assigning the right to reproduce on records the sound-track of the film, the court below was right in concluding from this that such simple reference did not constitute prima facie written evidence of the alleged clause. The court below was also entitled to find that the Compagnie Méditerranéenne du Film could not rely on "general and constant practice".'

It seems clear that both the Court of Appeal and the Supreme Court in the two cases intended to refer to the notion of 'general and constant practice'.

> 'Thus, there is an exception to the ordinary rules governing proof in favour of the performer: it is for the user of his performance to prove that he, or whoever has engaged the performer, obtained the latter's agreement, either by virtue of a contract of employment or of a collective agreement, or by virtue of "general and constant practice".'

This is what the Court of Appeal of Versailles confirmed in a 'solemn session' on 23 June 1982, in the appeal referred back to them by the 'Cour de Cassation' in *SNEPA v Radio France*.[7]

The effect of these decisions may be summarised as follows:

(1) The performer is free to determine the use which is to be made of his performance.
(2) He determines the scope, the purpose, the place and the duration of such use in the contract which he signs with his employer, and in particular if he wishes to restrict the limits fixed in a collective agreement or consecrated by the 'general and constant practice' at the time of signature of the contract, he must do so by inserting express qualifications.
(3) Any use other than that which has been so determined constitutes, in the absence of any subsequent ad hoc authorisation from the performer, a breach of contract or a tort, as the case may be.

Thus the protection achieved by the performers through judge made law and by individual contracts or collective agreements is substantial. It is in some respect wider than the protection under the Rome Convention because it is not subject to the limitations or the exceptions of Articles 9, 14, 15 and 19 of the Rome Convention. Nonetheless it is not sufficient to permit France to ratify the Rome Convention without further legislation. This means that French performers do not enjoy the benefit of reciprocal protection in countries which have ratified the Convention.

1 See note 5, para 14.26, above.
2 See note 8, para 14.27.
3 See note 11, para 14.26, above.
4 See note 2, para 14.27, above.
5 See note 2, para 14.27, above.
6 'Cour de Cassation' (1st Civil Chamber) 30 January 1974, Jurisclasseur Périodique 1974-IV-92 affirming the decision of the Paris Court of Appeal of 17 November 1971 – Revue trimestrielle de Droit Commercial (1972) p 633. Note Desbois.
7 See para 14.34.

5. Protection of phonogram producers generally

14.29 The French legislature has refused to make special provisions for phonogram producers.[1] The law has however very readily treated them as publishers for whom also no special provisions are made. This can be seen from the fact that it was decided to subject phonograms, like books, newspapers and other printed matter destined for publication, to a duty of statutory deposit.

Whilst the Law of 21 June 1943 amending the rules as to statutory deposit and the Decree implementing it[2] mention 'the phonographic work', in the 1957 Law, Parliament refused to include 'the phonographic work' in the list of works of the intellect.

The Law of 29 July 1881, which at the time was only intended for the press and for graphic publishing, was applied to producers of phonograms and a phonogram producer has been fined for having distributed records on which Nazi songs were reproduced.[3]

The 1957 Law refused to extend to the phonogram producer the status of a person or corporation which takes the initiative and responsibility for direction of a work, and so differentiating him from the producer of a cinematographic work who is given the benefit of the presumption of assignment in his favour of an exclusive right to cinematographic exploitation. It seems that relations between authors of phonographic works and phonographic publishers (ie phonogram producers) are not governed by the provisions of Chapter II 'Du contrat d'edition' (the publishing contract) of Title III of the same law: indeed, authors do not assign to phonogram producers the right to mass produce or to have mass produced copies of the work, the burden being on them to provide for its publication and circulation. A phonogram producer is therefore unable to take steps to protect his phonogram as assignee of the exclusive copyright in works the performance of which he has fixed, in contrast with a producer of a cinematographic work and a graphic publisher.

Relations between authors and phonogram producers are regulated either by individual contracts giving permission to record 'work-by-work', or by standard contracts agreed by BIEM (Bureau International de l'édition méchanique) on behalf of authors and IFPI, (the International Federation acting on behalf of phonogram producers), known as the 'BIEM Contract'.[4]

By their nature these contracts correspond therefore more to a 'performance contract'[5] defined in article 4.3 of the 1957 Law, than to a publishing contract.

Under these standard contracts, the labels of the phonograms which are published bear a notice ending as follows:

> 'All rights of the phonogram producer and of the owner of the recorded work are reserved. Re-recording, hiring, loan, and use of this record for public performance and broadcasting without authorisation are forbidden.'

The notice is valid as against anyone in possession of the phonogram as regards the rights of the authors of the works whose performance is fixed thereon, by reason of the rights attributed to authors by the Law on Literary and Artistic Property. However, the same cannot be said of the rights of the phonogram producers and this point remains open.

As it is, a phonogram producer, whether he himself is the actual producer of the phonogram (within the terms of article 3(c) of the Rome Convention or of article 1(b) of the Phonogram Convention) or the sole distributor of the phonogram reproduced on his behalf by virtue of a pressing licence, or of an imported phonogram, may therefore only take legal action in France under the general law by invoking the Paris Convention on Industrial Property or the Phonogram Convention, to which France is party.

1　See para 14.15 above.
2　Law No 341 of 21 June 1943 (Journal Officiel of 1 July 1943) and Decree No 75.696 of 30 July 1975 (Journal Officiel of 5 August 1975).
3　'Cour de Cassation' (criminal chamber) 14 January 1971, Jurisclasseur periodique 1971 IV 43 and II 16 943, note P. Chambon.
4　Art II provides:
'1. The society grants to the Producer, under the terms and within the limits fixed by the present contract, the non-exclusive right to proceed to the making of sound recordings of the works of the Society's repertoire, to press from such recording discs produced and presented for aural use only, and to put such discs in circulation under his mark or marks with a view to their sale to the public for private use.
2. The object of the present contract is expressly limited to discs listed in the Producer's catalogues, supplements to catalogues and lists of new issues which are made available to the public in accordance with the usual practice of the retail trade.
3. The present contract applies exclusively to double-sided discs such as are known and already

exploited at 1st January 1975. Any other form of mechanical reproduction shall be the subject of a separate contract.

4. In the case of the secondary use of discs, either directly (for radio transmission and public performance) or indirectly (by way of re-recording), the Society shall not raise any obstacle to the absolute freedom of the Producer to exercise his rights in regard to the artistic and/or technical recorded performance, it being understood that the copyright owners preserve intact their rights in the work recorded'.

5 Article IV. 3 provides:
A general performance contract is a contract whereby a professional body of authors grants to an impressario the right to perform, during the period of the contract, the existing or future works in the repertoire of the said body, subject to the conditions laid down by the author or his successors-in-title.

Protection against unauthorised reproduction of phonograms

14.30 The importance of protection of this kind emerged in France, as in other countries, only when the technical methods of copying and the phonogram market made it profitable to produce unauthorised reproductions. This is why there is very little case law before the emergence of piracy of phonograms.

Piracy very often takes the form of an offer to the public of phonograms whose appearance is identical to that of the original phonograms. In such cases, the producer, publisher or distributor of the phonogram may sue for trade-mark infringement if the trade-mark is protected in France but this is a remedy unconnected with copyright or neighbouring rights.

There has been some discussion as to whether the offer for sale of a copy of a recording which has packaging or a label different from that of the original phonogram is tortious. Irrespective of whether the authors of the recorded work have given authority for phonographic exploitation of such a copy, case-law indicates that such an act constitutes unfair competition. The courts have also taken the view that to market a copy the making of which required only reproduction and copying, thus avoiding the costs of recording and payment of technicians and performers, causes a distortion of the market, particularly when these copies are sold to wholesalers, retailers and the general public at a price lower than that of the original phonograms, or by bringing together on the same disc or the same cassette copies of performances recorded on different phonograms which have been chosen because they have become hits, something which the producers of the various copied recordings, because of their contractual obligations towards the performers, cannot do.

14.31 This is why the French representatives insisted during the Diplomatic Conference leading to the signing of the Phonograms Convention that the means whereby the future Convention was to be applied should include 'protection by means of legislation relating to unfair competition'[1] which enabled France to be the second state to ratify it, since it was not necessary for it to modify its legislation. An action for unfair competition is an action based on article 1382 of the Civil Code which provides that 'If a person commits an act which causes damage to another person, the person through whose fault the damage occurred shall have an obligation to make good the damage', and on article 1383 which provides that 'Everyone is liable for damage caused by him, not only by his act but also by his negligence'.

The conditions which must be satisfied to bring a successful action include injury or damage, which must be direct, actual and certain. The injury must not be contingent, but if it is certain that it is going to occur, an action may be brought. The injury may be non-material, provided that a legitimate interest protected by law is adversely affected.

The liability deriving from articles 1382 and 1383 is a matter of public policy and the action in tort is barred after 30 years, but if it is based on a criminal offence, a 'delit penal' or 'contravention', it is barred respectively after 10 years, 3 years or 1 year in the same way as a public prosecution.

Finally, article 10 bis of the Paris Convention on Industrial Property, which has been ratified by France, prohibits as unfair competition, 'an act of competition contrary to honest practices in industrial or commercial matters'. Hence, the Paris Court of Appeal held in 1969[2] that the unauthorised copying of a recording constituted an infringement: in that particular case the authorisation to copy a recording given by the manufacturer of the discs to his agent did not prevent infringement, since such authorisation was given subject to the condition that the master tapes used had been lawfully supplied.

1 Art 3, Phonogram Convention; see para 9.06 above.
2 Paris Court of Appeal (4th chamber) 5 May 1969, Jurisclasseur périodique 1970 II. 16386, note R. Plaisant.

14.32 However, ratification by France of the Phonogram Convention has apparently changed certain of the conditions to which the action for unfair competition is subject. In fact, by ratifying the Phonogram Convention, France undertook to 'protect producers of phonograms who are nationals of other Contracting States against the making of duplicates without the consent of the producer and against the importation of such duplicates, provided that any such making or importation is for the purpose of distribution to the public, and against the distribution of such duplicates to the public'.[1] The producer no longer has to prove the offending act, nor prove the existence of damage (other than to fix the quantum thereof): it is sufficient if he proves that he did not authorise the production of the copies in question.

Article 2 of the Phonogram Convention defines the state's commitments and article 3 specifies the means which each state may employ to apply the Convention, and these include legislation against unfair competition. Although the implementing Decree itself is silent as to the means France intends to adopt the legislation on unfair competition is known and applicable, and no other measures provided for by the Convention such as copyright, neighbouring rights, penal sanctions, have been provided by French law. Moreover, prior to ratification of the Convention, the courts already treated this practice, known as 'repiquage' in the trade, as unfair competition.

These are the conclusions which were drawn by the 'Tribunal de Commerce de Paris' in *Société Française CBS Disques v Top Diffusion and FNAC*,[2] a case of an importer, a distributor and a seller of cassettes which consisted of unauthorised copies of phonograms produced by CBS USA, although the 'pirate' cassettes had been produced, imported and distributed before the entry into force of the Convention.

In this case, CBS stated that it was faced with the sale of cassettes under the name Gold Label, pirating at least 25 titles from its catalogue. The defendants confined themselves to saying, that they were assured that all rights had been paid for, although after twenty months of proceedings they had produced no evidence in support of that statement. CBS produced in evidence numerous cassettes bearing the Gold Label mark with poor sound reproduction, great similarity of rhythm and sounds and, above all, the great similarity of the performers and musicians who were the same, which pointed to the conclusion that pirating had actually taken place.

The Court accordingly found that there was unfair competition by the five defendants, and awarded CBS 250,000 Francs. It did not make any pronouncement as to joint and several liability, since each party's liability was to be 'weighed according to the appropriate criteria'. The court also ordered seizure and destruction of all copies and publication of the judgment in two trade journals.

There are three other cases, in 1977 and 1978, in which no reference is made to the Phonogram Convention, since the plaintiff phonogram producers did not consider it necessary to invoke it having regard to the particular facts of the cases.

In the first case, *Barclays v Lederman and others*,[3] a phonogram producer had made a parody of a phonogram but in so doing had pirated 10 seconds from phonograms produced by the plaintiff company. The court recognised that no steps had been taken by the legislature to apply the Phonogram Convention and that neither the producers' rights nor those of the performers were protected by the provisions of the 1957 Law. The plaintiff company had not produced in evidence the contracts by virtue of which it recorded and marketed the discs, and had not proved that Aznavour, the author of the song, assigned to it his rights in respect of the said work. The plaintiff company, therefore, had no grounds for alleging that the defendant was guilty of infringement. On the other hand, the court held that by slavishly reproducing – whatever the duration of the reproduction – the sounds initially recorded by the plaintiff without his prior consent, the defendant improperly appropriated the results of the plaintiff's work. Accordingly, the plaintiff company was held to have a good claim against the defendants on the basis of unfair competition.

Two performers had actively participated in recording this pirated disc. The court held that they did not simply act as authors or performers of the words linking the various extracts of the songs put together in this 'pot pourri' but that both knew that authority from the plaintiff company had not been obtained before the pirate recording was carried out. Accordingly, these performers were held to be jointly liable with the defendants.

It should be noted that the judgment against the two performers illustrates the fact that, on the basis of articles 1382 and 1383 of the Civil Code, the phonogram producer can proceed not only against the 'pirate' of the phonogram, but also against persons who, knowing that the copy or use made thereof had not been authorised, participated in the exploitation of the copies and also against those who agreed to advertise them, journalists or presenters who incited readers or listeners to purchase such unauthorised copies.

In *Barclay v Discophot*[4] the plaintiff company obtained judgment in the 'Tribunal de Grande Instance' of Paris in which the 'pure and simple reproduction of a recording' of a disc without permission was classified as an infringement.

The defendant company, Discophot, had distributed a cassette containing a recording of Ella Fitzgerald singing *Basin Street Blues* in violation of the exclusive rights of the plaintiffs to do so. The plaintiff company sued for infringement of copyright, for an injunction, with a penalty payment of 100 Francs for each infringing copy of the cassette and for payment of the sum of 100,000 Francs on account of damages. The court listened to the two phonograms and found that the recording in issue was a pure and simple reproduction of the original produced by the plaintiff company and therefore constituted an infringement of it.

In *SDRM and Pathe Marconi v MS, J and MZ and others*[5] criminal proceedings were instituted by SDRM (the authors' society) against the reproducers, pressers and sellers of 'pirate' discs. The Pathe Marconi Company, whose discs had been reproduced without its authority and who had been joined as a civil party, were awarded damages on proof that its discs had been 'pirated'.

In *Ste Française du son v J Claude Roche Sté Pacific Vogue Compagnie Générale du Disque*,[6] the Paris Court of Appeal found against the maker of a pirated recording of bird songs, on the ground that his acts constituted a tort under article 1382 of the Civil Code, and that they had caused damage to the producer of the original recordings.

The court also observed that 'the Phonogram Convention provides protection only for producers who are "nationals" of another Contracting State, that is to say international situations and not disputes between nationals' and that, 'even in this respect, France provides no protection in such situations other than in accordance with its own legal system ...'.

This decision in 1978, had serious consequences for French phonogram producers. It has been pointed out during the Geneva Diplomatic Conference that the future Phonogram Convention would, like all conventions, apply only to international situations and thus benefit only producers who were nationals of other contracting states. It had been contended by the French delegation in reply that it would be difficult to withhold this benefit from French national producers when it was accorded to other nationals. French phonogram producers must therefore continue to prove the actual tort and produce evidence of the existence of damage in order to prevent the unauthorised reproduction of their phonograms, and above all, to prevent the sale of copies.

This explains why, for greater efficacy (excepting the case of *Sonodisc and SNEPA against DR, YM and A Elm*,[7] where the police had, on their own initiative, arrested streetsellers and seized suitcases containing the pirated cassettes) since 1978 more than 20 actions against pirates have been brought either in the criminal courts or by the authors' society, SDRM, suing on behalf of the authors whose works were recorded on the pirated phonograms rather than by the producers of the phonograms.

The phonogram producers involved are being joined as civil parties in these actions where there is also an infringement of trade-marks.

1 Phonogram Convention 1971, art 2. See para 9.05 above.
2 'Tribunal de Commerce' of Paris (supplementary chamber) 12 January 1976.
3 'Tribunal de Grande Instance' of Paris (3rd chamber) 7 April 1977, RIDA LXXXXIX, 182.
4 'Tribunal de Grande Instance' of Paris (3rd chamber) 8 February 1978, RIDA LXXXXVIII, 95.
5 'Tribunal correctionnel' of Lyon, 31 March 1978, Public Prosecutor's Office, *SDRM and Pathé Marconi v MS, J and MZ and others*, RIDA 100 (April 1979) 218.
6 Paris Court of Appeal (4th chamber, section B) 6 October 1978, RIDA (April 1980) 104.
7 'Tribunal de Grande Instance' of Paris, 19 March 1980, RIDA 106 (October 1980).

14.33 Despite the absence of a specific right, enterprise and public bodies take care to seek authority from phonogram producers for a total or partial reproduction of their phonograms where these reproductions are made for purposes other than publishing phonograms. The producers of cinematographic works and public-address system operators remunerate performers for such use through the intermediary of the producers, who are their employers.[1] In the case of public-address systems, the phonogram producers' federation, SNEPA, which has been authorised to enter into a bulk contract with them whereby it grants these public-address system operators authority to reproduce the present and future phonograms appearing in the catalogues of its members on terms identical for all public-address systems. The latter must however make an application to each phonographic producer in respect of each phonogram, since if the producer has published a phonogram under licence from another producer, he may not have acquired the right to authorise its reproduction.

'Home Taping'[2] both off the air and from borrowed phonograms is as common in France as elsewhere. The exception of article 91/2 of the 1957 Law (the exception for copying for private use) does not apply to phonogram producers but to pursue claims against millions of people who copy in their homes is not practical. That is why, together with the authors and the performers of the works copied, they have asked the legislature for the means to make their rights effective in this respect.

1 See para 14.22 above.
2 See para 12.12 above.

Protection against broadcasting and public performance

Broadcasting
14.34 In the early 1930s, phonogram producers signed contracts with the French broadcasting organisations whereby, in consideration of lifting the prohibition on broadcasting appearing on the record labels, the broadcasting organisation paid a royalty per minute of record broadcast and so-called 'needle time' limits (a maximum number of hours per day during which records could be broadcast) were fixed. This arrangement continued until the 1939-45 war. A new contract was signed in 1946 between the phonogram producers with 'Radiodiffusion Française' (which became subsequently RTF and then ORTF) which enjoyed a monopoly of broadcasting in France. Phonogram producers received an annual lump sum for the broadcasting of their records and indemnified the broadcasting organisation against any claims from other right owners. After the start of television in 1954, the parties agreed that the royalty would consist of a percentage (0.221%) of ORTF's receipts from all sources. The contract remained in force by tacit renewal until 1974 when it was terminated by ORTF, as it ceased to exist on 31 December 1974.

14.35 After 1 January 1975, the French national broadcasting service was the responsibility of two public corporations ('télédiffusion de France' and 'l'Institut National de l'Audiovisuel'), four national programme companies (TF1, A2, FR3 and 'Radio France') and a public production company (SFP).

Having regard to the 'recommendation' made to performers by the judgment of the Paris Appeal Court on 30 November 1974 in the *SPEDIDAME* case,[1] the performers' Unions signed with SNEPA, representing phonogram producers, a 'collective agreement relating to the use of commercial phonograms for the purposes of radio and television broadcasting' on 12 December 1975. This was done to put an end to 'general and constant practice', to which the court had referred and, again in the terms of the judgment, to establish 'the conditions to which performers would subject the broadcasting of commercial phonograms'.

SNEPA then signed contracts with the TF1, A2 and FR3 companies which came into force on 1 January 1975. SNEPA indemnified them against any claim from the phonogram producers and performers (except 'cases where the applicant claimed damage arising from the use of a phonogram under conditions of use entailing a fault on the part of the broadcasting company'), and each company pays an annual lump sum royalty for the use of commercial phonograms in its programmes. They can only be broadcast however by transmitters in France or abroad or by cable distribution thereof within the provisions of the broadcasting television monopoly defined in Law No. 72-553 of 3 July 1972.

However, these programmes may not be communicated to the public by other means, in particular by distribution by cable other than as envisaged above or by the publication of phonograms or videograms. The agreements are renewed annually, subject to adjustments of the amount of the royalty.

1 See note 2, para 14.27 above.

14.36 No agreement was reached between SNEPA and 'Radio France', and SNEPA brought an action in the courts. The 'Tribunal de Commerce' and the Paris Appeal Court delivered judgments against SNEPA.[1] It held that the label-clause could have no purpose other than that of drawing attention, on the one hand, to the rights of authors and, on the other, to the rights of producers as derived from the Phonogram Convention and, where applicable, from the Rome Convention but that it cannot have the effect of creating 'supplemental rights' for the benefit of the producer who has no rights over and above those attaching to any other industrialist or trader upon the sale of his products. Even if the prohibition on broadcasting of a disc stems from its domestic purpose, its price is calculated only in respect of private use and although the phonogram is the ultimate product of the producer's many skills and investment (technique, savoir-faire and investment) no 'supplemental rights' are created and thus the broadcasters' use of the phonograms did not constitute a breach of contract, nor were they tortious. However, this judgment of the Court of Appeal of Paris was overruled by the 'Cour de Cassation'.[2] The 'Cour de Cassation' upheld the judgment of the Court of Appeal as to the significance of the 'label-notice', holding that it was to serve as a reminder of the rights legally belonging to authors and, where applicable, to phonogram producers, but that such notice could not confer supplemental rights upon them. However, it allowed the appeal on the second ground that the producers of phonograms acted as assignees of the performers and that although performers had no rights under the 1957 Law 'they are nonetheless entitled by virtue of the rules of common law to require that their performances are not used for any purpose different from that authorised by them'. The Court of Appeal was wrong as they had failed to ascertain whether the performers had authorised the broadcasting of their recorded performances. As the 'Cour de Cassation' deals with questions of law, not of fact, the case was sent back to the Court of Appeal of Versailles.

The Court of Appeal of Versailles found, following the directions of the 'Cour de Cassation' that the performers have a common law right to insist that their performances are used only for the purposes which they have authorised. This applies particularly to the broadcasting of their recorded performances as the use made by the radio is not connected with the normal exploitation of a record. The Court also found that after the ORTF had terminated (on 1 January 1975) the agreement of 1954, they were using the recorded performances without paying the royalties which had formed the consideration of the contract. When therefore SNEPA on behalf of the producers of phonograms acting as the assignees of the rights of performers informed 'Radio France' by their letter of 8 January 1975 of their reservations with regard to the use of phonograms, 'Radio France' had from that time no authorisation for the broadcasting of these phonograms and 'Radio France', by continuing to broadcast them, had committed a tort within the meaning of article 1382 of the French Civil Code. The Court also found that the damage suffered by the performers had nothing to do with any promotional advantages the broadcasting of their records may bring them, 'Radio France' incurred a liability in damages under article 1382 and the Court nominated two experts to assess the damages suffered by SNEPA.[3]

1 'Tribunal de Commerce', Paris, 29 May 1978 and Paris Court of Appeal (4th chamber, section B), *SNEPA v Sté Nationale Radio France* RIDA 101 (July 1979) 131.
2 'Cour de Cassation' (first court chamber) 5 November 1980, RIDA 108, (April 1981).
3 Cour d'Appel de Versailles, 23 June 1982, RIDA (October 1982), note P Masouyé.

14.37 Legal proceedings are also pending between SNEPA and French programme companies which deal with advertising, and broadcasting by the 'peripheral stations'. Although, the transmission masts of these stations (with the exception of Radio/Television Monaco) are situated outside French territory (in Luxembourg, the Federal Republic of Germany and Andorra), nearly all of their programmes are produced in France and edited for the purpose of being heard in France.

Public performance

14.38 A right of phonogram producers or performers in the public performance of their recorded performances is not recognised by the law. However the judgment of the Supreme Court in *SNEPA v ORTF* may be interpreted as rendering jukeboxes, discotheques, cafés, hotels, restaurants and other users of phonograms for performances in public places liable under article 1382 in the same way as the ORTF. Users of public address systems had already before that judgment paid a royalty to performers and phonogram producers for their use of phonograms in stores etc which is collected by SACEM, the society of authors. The royalty is calculated on the basis of copyright fees collected in respect of the use of sound tapes 'given the wish of the producers to make the price of authorisation for copying their phonograms proportional to the use which will be made thereof'.[1]

[1] For the use of public-address systems on the terms laid down in the general contract, the royalty is equivalent to 20% of the copyright fee; for those carried out under the terms of the contract granted to the public-address concerns which are members of the Syndicat Professionnel des Distributeurs de Musique d'Ambiance (SPDM) the royalty is equivalent to 10% of the copyright fee, but these public-address enterprises pay in addition a royalty equivalent to 20% of the reproduction fees paid to SDRM (the authors' society collecting mechanical rights).

14.39 In conclusion, the protection for phonogram producers is at the present time wider than that which they would have enjoyed under the exclusive right in article 10 of the Rome Convention[1] since articles 1382 and 1383 of the Civil Code are concerned with public policy, any natural or legal person who is a national of a foreign state may bring an action without having to enquire whether that State grants reciprocal protection to French nationals and has ratified the Phonogram Convention. Furthermore, no copy of a phonogram not authorised by the original producer although lawful in a foreign country (for example, because it was made after the expiry of the period of protection for phonograms) may be reproduced or imported with a view to distribution to the public in France, or distributed to the public without the authority of the producer. This is the case despite, in particular, the free movement of goods ensured by the EEC Treaty.[2]

In spite of these endeavours of the French courts to fill a gap in the legislation it has to be said that without a specific right French phonogram producers cannot so effectively defend themselves against the unauthorised reproduction and public communication of their phonograms as they do not enjoy the full rights accorded to phonogram producers in countries which have ratified the Rome Convention.

[1] See para 8.29 above.
[2] See para 20.09 below.

6. Protection of broadcasting organisations

14.40 Until 1982 broadcasting was a state monopoly in France. No broadcasting organisations other than the state broadcasting organisation was permitted to broadcast. However in practice this monopoly was broken by the so-called 'peripheral' stations (like Radio Luxembourg and Monaco and Europe No 1) operating outside of French territory but broadcasting in French to the French public. In recent years there were also pirate transmitters which operated in spite of the fact that Law No 78.787 of 28 July 1978 had been passed expressly prohibiting such activities and providing fines and imprisonment to enforce the prohibition.

In 1982[1] audiovisual communication to the public was declared 'free'. It was defined as 'putting at the disposal of the public by hertzian waves or by cable sounds, images, documents, facts or messages of all sorts'. However such communication needs prior authorisation by the government or an authority created by the government. The service of sound radio and television is provided by private enterprise and may be decentralised.

1   Law No 82-652 of 29 July 1982.

Legal protection on the national territory

14.41   The law of 7 August 1974 maintained the protection provided by the ordinance of 4 February 1959:[1] 'cable or wireless retransmission, recording or reproduction, of any kind whatsoever, of all or any part of any broadcast with a view to diffusion to the public, whether or not a charge is levied', is prohibited 'subject to the same limitations as those laid down by Law No 57.298 of 11 May 1957 in respect of literary and artistic property'. This protection did not affect direct reception of signals in places open to the public. The Law thus gave every broadcasting organisation the protection granted by article 13 a) b) c) of the Rome Convention,[2] but did not provide for any penalties. A broadcasting organisation could therefore have taken action to have broadcasting stopped where it has not been authorised by the Director General of 'Télédiffusion de France', but it must prove that it has suffered 'direct, actual and certain' damage in order to have damages awarded. The protection was therefore subject to the same limitations as those applicable to copyright as far as its duration and the exceptions to it are concerned.

The Law of 29 July 1982 deliberately did not maintain this protection because the government indicated that it preferred to create legislation based on neighbouring rights.

However, if the author of a work assigns his exclusive right of radio and television exploitation to a broadcasting organisation, the latter may act in the capacity of assignee of the author. This assignment is carried out systematically by the producers of television programmes who, by virtue of the law of 11 March 1957, are deemed to be authors or co-authors of television works.

1   Ordinance No 59.273 of 4 February 1959, art 4; Journal Officiel of 11 February 1959 and amendment in Journal Officiel of 8 March 1959; RIDA XXIV 167.
2   See para 8.32-8.39 above.

Protection under international conventions

14.42   Having regard to the above-mentioned laws and regulations, France was able to ratify without reservation the European Agreement on the Protection of Television Broadcasts, the protocol and the additional protocol thereto. Although few countries are parties to this agreement and its protocols, and sometimes with reservations, the French television organisations thus enjoy some international protection. To date, France has not acceded to the convention concerning the dissemination of programme-carrying signals transmitted by satellite.

The protection provided for the broadcasting organisations has not yet given rise to any case law. However, the broadcasting organisations are faced with two problems in particular, that of private copying and the distribution to the public, particularly abroad, of pirated phonograms and videograms reproducing the broadcasts of what was the ORTF and the programme companies which succeeded it.

As far as protection of broadcasting organisations is concerned, France is since the passing of the Law of 29 July 1982 not in a position to ratify the Rome Convention until new legislation (presumably based on neighbouring rights protection for broadcasting organisations) is passed.

7. Protection of other 'related rights'

14.43 Certain types of enterprises, such as newspapers, graphic publishers, producers of cinematographic works, have the rights of authors assigned to them for a specified term. Where an organisation owns a collective work that work is further protected as literary or artistic property for a specified term. Both in the case of such an assignment or in the case of a collective work, enterprises which suffer damage because of unlawful acts infringing their copyright may institute proceedings for infringement.[1] This remedy is more effective than proceedings for civil liability or unfair competition.

However, where the contract of assignment has expired or the work is in the public domain, the organisation may still have an interest in protecting its product. This applies to newspaper organisations, graphic publishers and producers of cinematographic works or works obtained by a process analogous to cinematography.

1 See para 14.14 above.

Newspaper organisations

14.44 News published in the press is protected by copyright insofar as it displays a minimum of originality. The important question is whether press news is protected in itself, regardless of the form it takes. In this respect a distinction must be drawn between published news and unpublished news.

If a third party publishes a hitherto unpublished news item he can only have obtained it by misappropriation and therefore commits the tort of unfair competition.[1] Whilst the despatches and news of a press agency cannot be regarded as literary property protected by the law, they nevertheless constitute private property conferring on the agency and its subscribers an exclusive right to priority of publication until such time as they are put into circulation by the agency or its subscribers and fall within the public domain.

Once the news is published, anyone can reproduce it. However, unfair competition may arise where there is systematic unauthorised reproduction of news published in a manner liable to lead to confusion.

1 There is a good deal of case law on this point. See for example: 'Cour de Cassation' 23 May 1900; Dalloz périodique 1902. See also 'Cour de Cassation', Requêtes, 8 August 1861: Annales de la propriété industrielle 1861.32 – Dalloz Périodique 1862, 1, 136 – Tribunal de Commerce de la Seine, 24 November 1892 and 11 April 1893; Annales de la propriétié industrielle 1898, arts 3980 and 3982: 'Tribunal de commerce de la Seine' 3 December 1896/ le Droit 4 December 1896; Tribunal de commerce de Marseille, 5 February 1906/ Dalloz 1906/ 5/ 61; 'Tribunal Civil de la Seine, 4 January 1965, Annales de la propriétié industrielle 1865, 23 Art 22, law 75-1278 of 30/12/75 (Journal Officiel 31 December 1975).

Graphic publishers

14.45 Documents which are published graphically reproducing works which are no longer protected by copyright can only be protected by means of proceedings for unfair competition, proceedings for 'unjust enrichment' and more generally on the basis of articles 1382 and 1383 of the Civil Code (liability in tort).

In the case of graphic reproductions of works which are within the public domain and which are hired out, for example 'orchestral materials', the contracts between the publishers and the users specify the purpose, the extent and the duration of the performance or reproduction of the performance for which the graphic material is used. The contracts also specify that the hirer 'undertakes not to make, even for his own use, any partial or total copy of any material hired to him, nor to make any adaptation thereof whatsoever, without obtaining the prior authorisation of the publisher who owns the work'. Where the authorisation is granted, it is usually provided that the copies become the property of the publisher who then bears the cost of the copies.

The exception contained in article 41-2 of the law of 11 March 1957 which permits copies to be made strictly for the private use of the copyer and not intended for collective use, cannot be invoked against the publisher. However in practice right owners nevertheless suffer from the abuses committed by the use of photocopying machines. These abuses constitute actual infringements where the copies are made for collective use, for example within a company or a teaching establishment. In order to remedy such abuses and despite the reservations expressed by authors and publishers, the Finance Act of 1976 established a parafiscal tax on photocopying machines for the benefit of a 'Caisse Nationale du Livre'.[1] However all the copies which are not reseerved for the private use of the copyist still constitute an infringement of the right of the author and an act of unfair competition against the publisher.[2]

1 This parafiscal tax was the subject of an action brought by the Commission of the EEC against the French Republic pending before the Court of Justice of the EEC. The Commission of the EEC commenced an action on 7 June 1979 before the Court of Justice, seeking a declaration that France, by levying royalties on the import of reprographic apparatus, is in breach of its obligations under art 12 of the EEC Treaty, regulation 950.68 relating to the TDC, last amended by regulation 2800/78, and art 113 of the EEC Treaty. The European Court rejected the complaint made by the Commission (Judgment of 3 February 1981, RIDA 109, 191).
2 'Tribunal de Commerce de Paris' (1st chamber) 20 October 1980, RIDA 107, 182. Confirmed by Cour d'Appel de Paris (4th chamber) 8 October 1982, RIDA 115 (January 1983).

The producers of cinematographic or videographic works

14.46 Article 17 of the law of 11 March 1957 provides that the producer of a cinematographic work, whether an individual or a corporate person, who takes the initiative and responsibility for the creation of a work cannot be the author or a co-author of the work unless he falls within the definition contained in article 14, that is unless he, as an individual, is responsible for the intellectual creation of the work in question. Article 17 further provides that the producer acquires from the authors of the work, other than authors of musical compositions with or without lyrics, by means of a contract and unless otherwise provided, assignment in his favour of the exclusive right of cinematographic exploitation.

The interested parties in France are of the opinion that an audiovisual work produced using a 'video recorder' or produced for purposes other than cinematographic or television exploitation is made by a 'procedure analogous to cinematography', and seek by their production and exploitation contracts[1] to assimilate it to a cinematographic work.[2]

The producer of a cinematographic or videographic work may therefore, by virtue of the assignment granted to him by the authors, bring copyright actions to protect their audio-visual fixations.[3] Where the assignment has expired, or the work has fallen into the public domain,[4] he can only bring an action on the basis of articles 1382 and 1383 of the Civil Code.

The legal protection of the film producer is becoming inadequate because of the recent increase not only in the sale and hire to the public of films reproduced on video-cassettes or video-discs, but also because of the private copying which accompanies the trend. Every legitimate holder of a copy of the film can perform it in public once the producer's exclusive right of cinematographic exploitation has expired, provided that he obtains authorisation from the co-authors of the cinematographic work.

It is for this reason that producers and distributors take care to include provisions protecting their rights in their contracts.

In the case of contracts of agency or assignment between producers and distributors, it is provided that the copies of the film shall remain the property of the producer even if the distributor has borne the expense of making the copies. The distributor in turn imposes the same condition on the user, who undertakes to return the copies and is fully responsible for them until he has returned them.

The standard contracts between societies of authors and the federations of videogram producers,[5] stipulated that each video-cassette must carry certain warnings designed to protect the rights of both producers and authors. The usual wording is: 'All rights of the producer and of the owner of the recorded work reserved, copying, sale or hire, use of this recording for radio and television broadcasting, tele-distribution and cinematographic exploitation prohibited'. The producer must also inform his clientèle that they are prohibited from parting with recordings for the benefit of third parties and provided he does so he incurs no liability for the acts of those third parties.

With recording apparatus available to the general public, publishers and particularly the producers of cinematographic, television and videographic works, have become aware that once the protection under the assignment of copyright has lapsed, they are almost without any protection. Their position is even weaker than that of the producers of phonograms who at least have the benefit, at the international level, of the Phonogram Convention.

1 Contract for the reproduction and execution by means of videograms for specific uses implemented by SACEM and SDRM on the one hand and the 'Syndicat National de la Vidéocommunication' on the other (1978). Standard contract for the exploitation of videograms intended for sale to the public for private use, entered into between GICA and SDRM (9 April 1982).
2 The 'Groupement Intersyndical de la Communication Audiovisuelle' (Press - Graphic publishing - Phonographic publishing - Videocommunication - Producers and distributors of films and telefilms) defined a videogram as follows:
   'The fixing of any sequence of images, or images and sounds, whatever the recording and/or reproduction process, and whatever the support - film or magnetic band magnetic tape or film, disc, etc - and whatever the purpose thereof' (Declaration of 17 March 1980).
3 Tribunal correctionnel de la Seine' 14 December 1943, Gazette du Palais 1944, 1, 60; 'Tribunal de Grande Instance de la Seine' 9 April 1963, RIDA LXXIX 257; 'Cour de Cassation' (criminal chamber) 20 October 1977, Gazette du Palais 1978, I, 106.
4 Paris Court of Appeal (3rd chamber) 24 April 1974, RIDA LXXXIII.
5 See note 1, above.

8. Duration of protection

14.47 The limitation period for an action in tort is 30 years, the period for a criminal prosecution is 10 years for a 'crime', 3 years for a 'penal delict' and 1 year for a 'contravention'.

In all proceedings instituted on the basis of articles 1382 and 1383, which includes an action for unfair competition, the limitation period runs from the time of the tortious or quasi-delictual act (unauthorised use of the work or reproduction) and not from the date of the performance, fixation or broadcast.

These rules do not apply to the term of protection provided for by the collective agreements and contracts designed to give certain rights to remuneration.

Since articles 1382 and 1383 are matters of public policy ('d'ordre public') it is of little importance whether the fixation or the reproduction of phonograms distributed to the public or used in France has been carried out lawfully abroad without the authorisation of the performer or producer. Whether he be French or foreign, the performer or producer can bring an action in the French courts to prevent the unauthorised act, and this, as the law stands at the present time, overrides in France the limitations on the duration of protection laid down by the laws of foreign countries.

9. Limitations of rights (exceptions)

14.48 Article 41 of the Law of 11 March 1957 provides for limitations on authors' right of authorisation. Where the work has been published, the author cannot forbid private performance within a family circle, copies for the private use of the copyist, short quotations, parodies and pastiches.

These limitations cannot be invoked against performers or phonogram producers any more than against the producers of cinematographic or videographic works.

Private performances for which no charge is made and which are carried out exclusively within a family circle, do not, if they are effected by means of commercial videograms or phonograms, constitute an exception to the rights of phonogram or videogram producers, nor to the rights of artists and performers whose performance is reproduced on the phonogram or videogram since the very purpose of commercial videograms or phonograms is 'private use by the public'. It is the right of phonogram producers and performers, in the case of private performances where a charge is made or public performances whether or not a charge is made, which is still contested.

Although the exception to the right of reproduction, where the reproductions are reserved strictly for the private use of the copyist, cannot be invoked at law by producers or performers,[1] it exists de facto as private copying has become widespread.[2]

The exception relating to 'short quotations' was originally applied only to manuscript or written texts or music scores.[3] The fixing of sound or sound and images requires a producer and performers. The insertion of short extracts from one of these recordings in a direct communication to the public[4] for a critical, polemic, pedagogical or scientific purpose, does not appear to require the permission of the producer or performers as such uses do not adversely affect the interests of the right owners. On the other hand the reproduction of short extracts in another sound or audiovisual recording, even though it may be for the same purpose, is not permitted without their authorisation since article 41 cannot be invoked against them. Such quotations are dealt with in collective agreements so that the broadcasting organisations are not required to pay additional remuneration but only on the following conditions:[5] that no continuous extract used shall exceed three minutes; and that the total extracts in one broadcast shall not exceed 10% of the duration of the original broadcast.

The same conditions which apply to quotations apply to 'parodies, pastiches, and caricatures'. Accordingly it was held that the making of a phonogram containing a parody which reproduced 10 seconds in all of another phonogram without the authorisation of its producer constituted an infringement.[6]

1 See para 14.33 above.
2 In 1976, 88% of the blank cassettes sold in France were used to make one or more copies; SOFRES Survey, carried out on behalf of SACEM and SNEPA in 1976 (L édition sonore, January 1977 No 1).
3 This explains why, in the absence of a provision similar to that contained in the 2nd paragraph of art 41, it is already causing problems in its application to works of art.
4 Eg broadcasting, a lecture illustrated by extracts from phonograms or audio-visual works.
5 Eg art 8.5(B) of the Collective Agreement for artists engaged for television broadcasts (18 July 1980).
6 See para 14.32 above.

10. Remedies for the infringement of rights

14.49 Remedies for the infringement of copyrights are dealt with in the Law of 11 March 1957 which sets out the procedure and provides for penalties under Title IV, by amending or supplementing existing articles of the Penal Code.[1]

Performers, phonogram producers and, where they are no longer the assignees of authors' rights, the producers of cinematographic or videographic works, can only bring proceedings under articles 1382 and 1383 of the Civil Code. They can only institute penal proceedings if they have been the victim of theft or some other delict, such as fraud. In order to benefit from the special procedure reserved for copyright owners and thus to secure more effective action against infringers, they intervene as often as possible in penal proceedings brought by the authors.

However, they can initiate criminal proceedings where their trademarks have been infringed on the labels or packaging used for the phonograms or videograms, provided those trademarks are protected in France.[2]

A prosecution may also be brought against any person who uses a trademark without authorisation, who holds products which he knows to bear a counterfeited or fraudulently affixed trademark, or who sells, offers for sale, supplies or offers to supply products or services under any such trademark and against any person who knowingly delivers a product or provides a service other than that which was requested of him under a registered trademark. Upon conviction such an offender is liable to a fine of 500 Francs to 20,000 Francs or to a period of imprisonment from three months to three years or to both.

It is an offence to make a fraudulent imitation of a registered trademark in a way such as to deceive the purchaser, or to make use of a fraudulently imitated trademark. It is also an offence knowingly to make use of a registered trademark bearing indications liable to deceive the purchaser as to the nature, essential qualities, composition or content of active ingredients, or the kind or origin of the article described thereby and to stock without legitimate cause, products which the defendant knows to bear a fraudulently imitated mark. It is also an offence to knowingly sell, offer for sale, supply or offer to supply products or services under any such mark. In these cases the defendant is liable to a fine of 500 to 20,000 Francs or imprisonment of one month to one year or to both.

The court may further order that the products confiscated be delivered to the owner of the infringed or fraudulently affixed or imitated trademark, without prejudice to any claim for damages which he may have.

There are, however, two serious disadvantages which hamper the effectiveness of infringement actions. First, although the law[3] provides for seizure in respect of infringement of copyright in order to proceed with such seizure, an order must be obtained from the President of the 'Tribunal de Grande Instance' upon an application from the plaintiff who must prove either registration of the work or an application for registration. Secondly, the services of a bailiff must be obtained, who will be accompanied by an expert appointed by the plaintiff and will make a detailed description of the products which the plaintiff alleges are marked, delivered or supplied in a manner which is prejudicial to him and thus unlawful.

The bailiff will, according to the Court order, merely make a description or else seize the number of copies necessary for the description or will carry out a full seizure, that is to say of all the copies produced, delivered or supplied. But if the plaintiff secures full seizure, the judge may require security, which must be lodged before the seizure is carried out.

As in the case of infringement of copyright there is no presumption of good faith on the part of the infringer. In the case of holders, sellers and suppliers of products whose trademark is counterfeit, the onus is on the plaintiff to prove bad faith.

However, victims of unauthorised recordings, reproductions and use may exhaust their resources in prosecutions which are burdensome and costly and are often ineffective against lawbreakers who know how to organise themselves well, both in their operations and in their insolvency. It would be helfpul if, as is the case in Belgium, the President of the Court could grant an order directing that acts contrary to honest practice in commerce and industry must cease and failing immediate cessation of such acts, those responsible would incur penalties under criminal law.

It would also be necessary for the customs authorities to be able to intervene so as to protect what should not be regarded as merely a private interest but one which involves the national economy: for this reason, the recent measures adopted by GATT to create a code relating to counterfeiting should be extended to infringements of copyright and of neighbouring rights.

1 Art 64-68; see para 14.14 above.
2 Ss 422, 423.1 and 423.2 of the Penal Code.
3 Law No 64-1360, 31 December 1964 (modified by Law 75536 of 30 June 1975).

11. Protection of foreign right owners

14.50 The protection of performers, phonogram producers and broadcasting organisations extends to all foreign legal persons, whatever their nationality and without any requirement as to reciprocity or duration, when the protection is based on articles 1382 and 1383 of the Civil Code which is based on public policy. However protection can be wider or more effective for certain foreign right owners than the protection available to other foreign right owners or to French nationals.

In the case of performers, employers bound by collective agreements must not discriminate between nationals and foreigners, whether members of a union or not. However, a French or foreign performer whose performance has been fixed by a phonogram producer or a cinematographic producer or a broadcasting organisation, in France or abroad and who has not authorised (in his individual contract or in any collective agreement) the use of his performance for other purposes, may obtain protection from a French court, unless the court take the view that the use in question is one of general and constant practice.[1]

The same rules apply if the term of the protection granted by the state of which the phonogram producer is a national, or in which the first fixation or first publication took place (in the case of a phonogram) or in which the principal establishment or the transmitter is situated (in the case of a broadcast) has expired.

If they are nationals of a state which is party to the Phonogram Convention, phonogram producers will enjoy more effective protection in France than French nationals.[2] Phonogram producers who are nationals of non-member states enjoy the same protection as French producers because of the public policy character of articles 1382 and 1383 of the Civil Code.

Since the passing of the Law of 29 July 1982 a broadcasting organisation is no longer in a position to apply article 1 of the European Agreement for the protection of Television Broadcasts to which France is a party, since it provides that:

> 'Broadcasting organisations constituted in the territory and under the laws of a Party to this Agreement or transmitting from such territory shall enjoy, in respect of all their television broadcasts: 1. in the territory of all Parties to this Agreement the right to authorise or prohibit...'

1 See para 14.20 above.
2 See para 9.05 above.

12. Law revision

14.51 For all the above mentioned reasons the French Government is preparing a draft law which will revise the legal status of the audiovisual work, create a right to remuneration for private copying for the benefit of authors, performers and producers of phonograms and grant specific rights to performers, producers of phonograms, producers of audiovisual works and documents as well as to enterprises for audiovisual communications.[1] Such a law would enable France to ratify the Rome Convention[2] and to conclude bilateral agreements based on reciprocity with states which accord their nationals certain other rights which are not part of the Rome Convention.

1 See para 14.40 above.
2 See chapter 8 above.

Chapter 15
Germany (Federal Republic)
by Eugen Ulmer

1. History and development of copyright

15.01 Viewed historically as antecedents of copyright appeared as privileges which were granted following discovery of the art of book-printing in order to offer protection against copying. They were granted in Germany from the beginning of the sixteenth century by the Kaiser or the 'Reich' Government with effect for the German 'Reich' and by the Heads of the 'Länder' with effect for each of those territories. When the power of the 'Reich' disappeared in the seventeenth century, the privileges granted by the Heads of the 'Länder' gained the upper hand. They were awarded to the printer and, as the concept developed, also to the publisher for the protection of their trades. It has become apparent from more recent research into copyright law that they were also granted in a number of cases to authors. The way in which they were formulated in detail was a matter of discretion. The period for which legal protection was granted varied generally between one and ten years but in individual cases was longer.

Works of important artists were also protected by privileges. Drawings by, inter alia, Dürer and Zeitblom were protected by privilege in the sixteenth century.

Progression towards a true form of copyright protection has been, since the end of the seventeenth century, the result of different impulses based on the concept of intellectual property. The source of law drawn upon is natural law. In a work on the reproduction of books summarising the views held of the law in his time, Johann Stephan Puetter writes (in 1774) that the works were 'indisputably the unqualified property of their authors in the same way that anyone may regard as his property everything which owes its existence to his skilfulness and dedication'. In German philosophy the concept of intellectual property has been advanced particularly by Fichte, Hegel and Schopenhauer.

Acceptance of the idea of intellectual property in practice was achieved only slowly. In legislation, the protection afforded by privileges starts to blend with a direct protection, the emphasis being laid however on the right of publishers. The fragmentation of the country into its various states was a significant barrier to any comprehensive protection. The privileges and the statutory prohibitions on reproduction applied only in the territory in respect of which they were granted. Thus, illicit reproduction was still flourishing in the eighteenth century when German literature achieved great significance.

In the nineteenth century Germany was thus faced with the double task of doing away finally with the remains of the privilege system and creating a system of rules for the whole of Germany. The driving force was the book trade. At the Vienna Congress, a committee of the German book trade obtained a declaration, contained in the instrument constituting the Federation of German States, promising safeguards for the rights of authors and publishers against piracy. The focal point however continued to lie with the legislation of the various 'Länder'. The leading enactment was the Prussian Law of 1837 for the protection of the ownership of works of science and art. This was based directly on the right of the author. Other German 'Länder' have followed the Prussian example. In particular, the Prussian Law proved to be the trend-setter for the period of protection to be the lifetime of the author plus 30 years. Thus, the 30-year protection period became general law in Germany. It was eventually replaced in 1934 by the 50-year period of the Berne Convention[1] and in 1965 by the 70-year period of protection.

After the formation of the North-German Federation and the German 'Reich', the way was set for uniform legislation. As early as 1870, a copyright law was promulgated by the North-German Federation and this became 'Reich' law in 1871. It was superseded in 1901 by the Law on Copyright in Literary and Musical Works, and supplemented by a statute relating to publishing law. Copyright relating to the arts was segregated in 1870, as more preparation was required in order for suitable regulations to be formulated. The result was the Law of 1876, which was replaced in 1907 by the Law on Copyright in Artistic Works and Photography.

1 Art 7; see para 5.54 above.

More recent legal developments

15.02 The Copyright Laws of 1901 and 1907 contributed to significant progress. In particular, protection against translations was extended to the entire duration of the copyright and copyright in respect of musical works was further developed. In the field of copyright relating to the arts, protection was extended to buildings and works of applied art.

The laws did not however mean that legal developments had come to a standstill. The revision conferences of the Berne Convention had an important influence on these developments. The Berlin Act of 1908 took into account phonograms and films for the first time. This was reflected in an amendment to the Copyright Law in 1910. The Rome Conference held in 1928 took broadcasting into account and led to the 'droit moral' being embodied in the text of the convention.

German case law was able to keep pace with the results of the Rome Conference, owing to a liberal interpretation of the texts of the statutes. On the whole, however, a new law appeared desirable. The intention was for the protected works and the rights of their authors to be regulated afresh in an improved systematic form taking into account new types of work creation and work utilisation. It was also intended to reinforce the legal protection of authors of works and to dismantle some existing limitations. Further development of the rules relating to the author's personality right ('droit moral') was also a matter of urgency.

The work required to reform German copyright started after the Revision Conference in Rome in 1928. After a number of private drafts had been submitted, an official draft followed in 1932 which had been worked out jointly by the German and the Austrian justice ministries. In Austria, the Federal Law of 1936 concerning copyright in works of literature and art and neighbouring rights developed out of a revision of the joint draft. The preparatory work was recommenced after a pause during the 1939-45 war in the Federal Republic of Germany after the Brussels Revision of the Berne Convention (1948) and resulted after a fruitful public discussion in the new unified Law on Copyright and Neighbouring rights of 9 Septembeer 1965 replacing the two existing separate laws. The Law takes into account the wishes which had been expressed in favour of a reform. In addition, copyright and neighbouring rights became clearly distinguishable. The period of protection was extended 50 to 70 years from the death of the author.

The Copyright Law was supplemented by a simultaneously-promulgated law relating to the administration of copyright and neighbouring rights which provides for state supervision of collecting societies. The statute relating to publishing law of 1901 remained in force with some minor amendments.

A major source of law which has also proved significant in respect of copyright is the 'Fundamented Law'[1] of the Federal Republic of Germany of 23 May 1949. The essential factor is that the substance of copyright is guaranteed by the Constitution: the protection of economic rights by the rules on the guarantee of property, the moral right by the rules on the protection of personality (human) rights.

The federal Constitutional Court has handed down a number of important decisions on copyright law protection based on the guarantee of property afforded by the 'Fundamental Law'. Although it is true that the legislature has a certain latitude when defining the content of and restrictions on copyright, the basic content of the guarantee of property must be safeguarded. The Constitutional Court held,[2] inter alia, that although it was justifiable on cultural grounds for copyright law to allow within certain bounds the incorporation of protected works or parts of such works in collections intended for use in churches, schools or educational establishments without the consent of the author, the latter must be paid a reasonable remuneration contrary to what was provided in the Copyright Law.

The result of this decision has been taken into account in the Revision of the Copyright Law dated 10 November 1972. The revising law also extended the rule relating to the right of the author of a work of the visual arts to participate in the proceeds of the sale of his original work ('droit de suite'), as well as the rules relating to the remuneration which authors may claim for the hiring or lending of copies of their works ('public lending right'). Proposals for law reform go even further. They contain, among other things, a fresh regulation of the rights in respect of photographs and, in view of its increasing significance, the rules on reprographic reproduction and the rules relating to reproduction for personal use.

1 Grundgesetz.
2 B Verf G 31, 229 (Constitutional Court, Judgment of 7 July 1971) also B Verf G 49, 382 (Constitutional Court, Judgment of 15 October 1978).

2. Copyright – General

(1) The works and their author

15.03 In defining the works which were protected by copyright, the old copyright laws proceeded on the basis of individual types of work, such as written works, musical works and work of the visual arts. This scheme however gives rise to the danger of gaps in the law when new types of works arise. For example, this was the case with film works, which were not taken into account in the old copyright laws. The new Copyright Law therefore provides generally for protection of authors of literary, scientific and artistic works but stipulates in addition that literary works, musical works, pantomimes, artistic works, photographic works, film works and illustrations of scientific or technical nature are included in the list of protected works, but the list is not exhaustive. The types of works mentioned above are however examples which are of significance in interpreting the general notion of 'literary, scientific and artistic works'.

The term 'work' is moreover defined in greater detail by the provision that works in this context are only personal intellectual creations. The decisive criterion is the individuality of the work, which is based on personal intellectual creative activity. On the whole, it is true to say that the case law on the subject does not lay down very strict requirements. Thus, in particular in the case of literary works, there is the so-called 'kleine Münze' ('small change') of copyright, such as printed forms, pre-printed contracts, summaries of facts in catalogues, prospectuses and the like. Protection here may result from the intellectual effort involved in the elaboration or arrangement of the material. On the other hand, more strict requirements are made by case law, in particular for works of applied art. Here, it is relevant that, in addition to copyright in artistic works, there is also the Design Law, which depends on the fulfilment of formalities and provides for a shorter period of protection; it is based on the Law of 1876 the so-called 'Geschmacksmustergesetz'. The difference is recognised as a difference in degree: where mere adaptations to new trends in fashion and taste are involved, only the registered design protection is relevant. The more extensive protection afforded by copyright requires a higher degree of artistic achievement.

The author is the creator of the work. By way of divergence from a number of foreign legal systems, the principle applies without exception that the author is the first owner of copyright. Therefore, an author's right cannot be vested in a legal entity. Even in the case of works which are created in employment the copyright is vested in the creative employee. The only possible, and the usual, solution in this situation is for the employee to grant licences (expressly or by implication) to the employer for purposes of his business. The law has special rules for cinematographic works. Here too the law proceeds on the assumption that copyright originates as a right of the intellectual creators of the work. In order properly to take into account the interests of the film producer in using the work without hindrance, it is presumed that the authors have granted him the rights necessary for the exploitation of the film in the contracts they entered into with him.

If several persons have jointly created a work, without it being possible for their contributions to be separated, they are regarded as joint authors. As such they are only entitled to publish, exploit and alter the work jointly. However, an individual joint author may not in bad faith refuse approval to publish, utilise or alter. The period of protection will be calculated from the death of the last survivor.

Joint authors must be distinguished from the authors of composite works. These are cases where the works may be separated but which are combined by their authors for exploitation in common, as in the case in particular with operas and operettas and literary works with illustrations. In these cases too, each author may demand of the other his consent to the publication, exploitation or alteration of the combined works if it is reasonable and in accordance with the principle of good faith to request the other to give such consent. The term of protection however runs for each work from the death of its author.

(2) The author's rights

15.04 The Copyright Law provides, by way of general formulation, that the author is protected in his intellectual and personal relationship with the work and in the use of the work. The Law divides the rights of the author into the author's personality right, the exploitation rights and other rights.

15.05 The author's personality right safeguards the non-commercial interests connecting the author with his work. In this context, the Law is concerned with personal and intellectual interests: for the author it may be a matter of his reputation and honour and thus his personal interests which may be put at risk by the work's publication or the nature of the communication. More objectively, the author, composer or artist may prevent the misrepresentation of his work, not because he fears for his reputation but because what is important to him is the subsistence and integrity of his work. These two interests are, however, closely interwoven.

The most significant aspects of the author's personality right are his right to determine whether and how the work should be published, the right to his authorship being acknowledged, as well as the right to prohibit distortions or other misrepresentations which might endanger his justified intellectual or personal interests in the work.

15.06 The exploitation rights are split by the Law into an exclusive right to exploit the work in material form and the exclusive right publicly to communicate the work in non-material form.

(a) Exploitation in material form comprises, in particular, the right of reproduction, of distribution and of exhibition.

The right of reproduction is the right to make copies of the work, by whatever process and in whatever number. Printing and photocopying are equated with writing by hand or typing. Reproduction in the legal sense also comprises the copying of works of the visual arts, as well as the manufacture of carriers of sounds and images like phonograms and videograms for repeated communication of the work.

The right of distribution is the right to offer copies of the work to the public or to market the same. It has independent significance alongside the right of reproduction. If, for example, copies of the work are produced without the consent of the author in a foreign country in which the period of protection is shorter than in Germany or no copyright protection exists, then the distribution of the copies in Germany is not permitted. Distribution basically also includes secondary distribution of copies. If, however, copies are marketed by the party entitled so to do by way of sale, the secondary distribution is permissible (so-called 'exhaustion of the right of distribution'). This right will likewise be exhausted by a distribution abroad if the party marketing the copies is also empowered to distribute within Germany. Within the Common Market, the rules of the EEC Treaty relating to the free movement of goods must, in addition, also be observed.[1]

The right of exhibition is the right publicly to display the original or copies of an unpublished work of the visual arts or of an unpublished photographic work. The right lapses on publication. The author, if he has disposed of the original of a work, may likewise not prevent the owner of the original from displaying it unless, when selling the original, he precluded by express agreement the right to exhibit.

(b) The right publicly to communicate the work in non-material form comprises in particular:

1. The right of recitation, performance and presentation of the work. Presentation is defined in the Law as the right to make an artistic work, a photographic work, a cinematographic work, or an illustration of a scientific or technical character perceptible to the public by means of technical devices;
2. The right of broadcasting the work (including rebroadcasting[2]). Broadcasting in the sense of the Law is not only the wireless transmission, but also the transmission by wire;

3. The right to communicate the work by means of sound or picture carriers and the right to communicate broadcasts by means of a screen, a loudspeaker or analogous technical devices.

(c) The extent to which exploitation of the work is reserved to the author is widened by the rule that the consent of the author is also required if the work is being adapted or otherwise reformulated. The terminology used is that of the adaptation right of the author, which includes in particular the translation right and film right. If the adaptation is in itself a personal intellectual creation, as is normally the case with a translation or the making of a film, then the adapter is entitled to a copyright. So long as the original work remains protected however, he may exploit the adaptation only with the consent of the author of the original work. Such consent may be dispensed with only if the new work is an independent work created in free use of the protected work. The case law on the subject has laid down strict requirements as regards the independent nature of the new work: use is deemed to be free only if, having regard to the individuality of the new work, the characteristics of the used work have faded. In the case of musical works the Law itself prescribed a strict standard: use shall in no event be permitted if a melody can be recognised as having been extracted from the protected work (so-called 'extensive protection of melodies').

1 See para 20.04 below.
2 See also para 15.35 below.

15.07 The Copyright Law encompasses under 'other rights' those which have for the first time been recognised by the new Law. These concern the right of the author to have access to copies of his work, the 'droit de suite' and the public lending right.

The author may demand access to copies of the work from the holder of the original or of copies thereof, insofar as it is necessary for the manufacture of copies or adaptations of the work and no justified interests of the holder preclude this from being granted. For example, an architect may demand access to buildings for the purposes of making photographs or sketches. The right is of particular significance if the work exists only in the form of a manuscript or a score which is held by a third party. Although under these circumstances the author cannot demand that the copy is delivered up to him, he can however require that it be made accessible to him so that he has the opportunity of making copies or having copies produced.

The 'droit de suite' is the right of authors of works of the visual arts to participate in the proceeds of a further sale of the original. It has been greatly reinforced by the Revision Law of 1972. In particular, the share in the proceeds on a further sale has been increased from 1% to 5%. The claim presupposes that an art-dealer or auctioneer participates in the further sale as the acquiring party, seller or agent. Rights to information in favour of the author exist against art-dealers and auctioneers for the purposes of implementing the claim. They may, however, only be enforced by a collecting society. In Germany, the collecting society 'Bild-Kunst' is the organisation which administers this right.

An author has a claim to equitable remuneration for the hiring out and lending of copies of a work if the hiring out or lending process forms part of the business of the hirer or lender, or if the copies are hired out or lent by an organisation to which the public has access (eg a bookshop, collection of records or other reproductions). The current version of the provision, which is based on the Revision Law of 1972, has made it possible in particular to enforce the right against public libraries. In this context, the collective agreement entered into in 1974 by the federal and the 'Länder' governments with the relevant collecting societies (GEMA, 'Wort' and 'Bild Kunst'), under which an annual amount of DM 12 million is presently provided for as a lump sum for the settlement of claims, is of practical significance.

(3) Limitation of copyright

15.08 In the interests of effective protection, the limits of copyright are less in the Copyright Law of 1965 than in the earlier laws. Nevertheless, there are still a number of restrictions, the emphasis being on restrictions relating to exploitation rights. The author's personality right basically remains intact. In particular, there are rules relating both to the prohibition against making modifications and to the indication of source, by virtue of which, where exploitation rights are restricted, protection of the personal and intellectual interests of the author is guaranteed.

Apart from the limits which are provided for in the interests of the administration of justice and public security, and other minor limitations, the restrictions are basically those set out below:

The rules relating to freedom of 'quotation' and of 'borrowing' from works concern intellectual and cultural interests. In the case of the freedom to quote a work, the Law differentiates between major quotations, which are permitted in independent scientific works, and minor quotations, which are permitted in independent literary works. Musical quotations are also allowed: individual passages of a musical work already published may be quoted in an independent musical work.

The freedom to borrow from a work is permitted in the case of collections for religious, educational and teaching purposes. Parts of works, literary or musical works of small size, as well as individual works of the visual arts and individual photographic works, may be incorporated without consent of the author in collections in which works of a considerable number of authors are collected. The author must however be paid equitable remuneration.

A further category of limitations serves to make information freely available. In addition to the reproducing of public speeches on daily events in newspapers and other media of information, as well as parliamentary speeches, there is the reproduction of newspaper articles and radio commentaries relating to current political, economic or religious questions by printing them in newspapers or radio programmes. Reproduction is permissible if no rights are reserved in respect of the articles or commentaries. The authors are, however, to be paid equitable remuneration. Only if it is a matter of the reproduction in the form of a summary of brief extracts from several articles and commentaries need no remuneration be paid, as for example in 'press round-ups'.

It is permitted without restriction to reproduce, distribute and publicly communicate information of a factual content and news of the day which has been published by the press or on the radio.

15.09 Particular significance is attributed to the rules as to whether, and to what extent, reproduction of protected works for private use is permitted. Originally, it was assumed that copyright lapsed in the private sphere and that, as for private performances, the manufacture of copies for private use was permitted. What was contemplated were copies made by hand, by typewriter, or hectographic copies which did not essentially impinge on the interests of the author. However, the situation has changed as technical developments have led to novel appliances which are particularly suitable for mechanically producing individual copies for private use. Such machines are tape-recorders, by means of which radio broadcasts can be recorded and phonograms re-recorded and, in recent times, also video-recorders which make the recording of television broadcasts possible and the replaying of films, particularly videograms. Above all, there are the reprographic machines by which photocopies, xerox and microcopies can be made.

The German Law on Copyright, as it stands at present, differentiates between reproductions for personal use and reproductions for other internal use such as internal use by the authorities, schools, technical colleges, research institutions, libraries and companies.

(a) The manufacture of individual copies for personal use is basically unrestricted. This also applies to copies produced photo-mechanically. On the other hand, there is a special rule particularly for copies which are made for personal use by fixation of radio broadcasts onto videograms and phonograms by rerecording from one videogram or phonogram onto another. Although such copies for personal use are permitted, the authors of works which are, by their nature, expected to be reproduced in this way, are entitled to claim against the manufacturers of equipment suitable to make such copies, payment of equitable remuneration for the opportunity provided to make such reproductions. In the case of importation of such equipment, the claim is against the importer. Analogous claims are provided for also in respect of performers and producers of phonograms and films. The remuneration consists of an equitable share of the proceeds resulting from the sale of the equipment, but the total amount of the claims by all parties involved must not exceed 5% of the proceeds of sale.

(b) The manufacture of individual copies for other internal use is permitted only in special cases. The most important special case is the copying, particularly the reprographic copying, of small sections of a work which has been published, as well as of individual articles published in newspapers and magazines. If the copying is done for commercial purposes, for example by a business enterprise for use by employees, the author has to be paid equitable remuneration. On the other hand, in the special cases of manufacture of individual copies without a commercial purpose, for instance in schools or institutes, no remuneration has to be paid.

Overall, the rules represent progress as against the old Law. However, from the authors' and publishers' point of view they are at present proving to be no longer satisfactory. Consequently, plans for reform are being considered: in the case of copying by tape recorders and video recorders it is proposed that blank cassettes will have to bear a levy. As regards reprographic copying, the intention is that an equitable remuneration will, without exception, have to be paid, but may be claimed only by collecting societies.

(c) The limitations on copyright also include the compulsory licence for the production of phonograms envisaged under the Copyright Law. If a producer has been granted a right to use a musical work, entitling him to make sound recordings of the work and to distribute them for commercial purposes, then every other producer domiciled or resident within Germany may demand, after publication of the work, that he should likewise be granted a corresponding right to use the work on reasonable terms.

In practice, such a compulsory licence is not of great significance: the rights of the author in respect of mechanical reproduction are, as a rule, like the rights in respect of public performance, administrated by GEMA. If the mechanical reproduction right is administered by a collecting society, no-one can avail himself of the compulsory licence. Therefore only the obligation to enter

enter into a contract with the user which is provided for in respect of all collecting societies is relevant in practice. Moreover, it must be noted that the licence is not a legal licence as in English law on the basis of which the right may, without entering into any agreement, be claimed against payment of the statutory royalty. The producer can only sue the collecting society to force it to enter into a contract with him. As far as is known, no judicial proceedings of this nature have been instituted in Germany since the compulsory licence was introduced in 1910.

(4) Term of protection

15.10 The usual term of protection for works was extended by the Copyright Law of 1965 from the old limit of 50 years to 70 years from the death of the author. The extension applies also to those works which were still protected in 1965. Works whose term of protection had already expired at the end of 1964 remain in the public domain. A transitional rule applies to copyright agreements which were entered into before the extension of the term of protection: any transaction by which a disposition is made in respect of the copyright will, in cases of doubt, also extend to the period by which the duration of protection was extended. The holder of the right, however, shall have to pay equitable remuneration to the assignor or licensor if it is to be assumed that the latter, on entering into the agreement, would have procured a higher fee if the extended period of protection had been envisaged at the time.

Special rules are provided for the period of protection in respect of anonymous and pseudonymous works with the exception of works of the visual arts. If the name or the known pseudonym of the author is indicated neither on the copies of a work which has been published nor when the work is publicly communicated, then the copyright therein will extinguish seventy years after the publication including public communication of the work.

In certain cases, however, the 70-year period is still calculated from the death of the author:

(a) If the name or known pseudonym of the author is indicated within a period of seventy years from publication on copies of a work which has been published or the author has otherwise become known as the creator of the work;
(b) If, within 70 years of publication, the true name of the author is notified for inscription in the Register of Authors which is kept at the German Patent Office in Munich;
(c) If the work has been published after the death of the author.

As regards the publication or issue of posthumous works, a period of protection of 10 years should in any event be guaranteed. The Copyright Law differentiates here between protection of the heirs of the author and protection of the editor.

(a) If a posthumous work is published more than 60 years but less than 70 years after the death of the author, the copyright therein shall end not less than 10 years after publication. The extension therefore benefits the heirs of the author.
(b) If the copyright has lapsed, the editor who publishes for the first time within the Federal Republic of Germany an unpublished work has a 'related right' which protects him for a period of 10 years against copying and distribution, as well as against the use of copies for public performances.[1]

In respect of photographic works, the Copyright Law provides for a term of protection of 25 years. It runs from the publication of the work or, if the work has not been published within this term, from its production. An extension of the term of protection is planned in the next revision of the law.

As regards international relations, it is of significance that the Federal Republic of Germany claims the comparison of terms of protection[2] both under the Berne Convention and under the Universal Copyright Convention. If the country of origin of the work is a member of the Berne Union, a term of protection longer than that in the country of origin will not be granted. Thus, if, as is normally the case, the term of protection is 50 years from the death of the author, protection is also restricted in the Federal Republic to this period. Exceptions apply for member countries such as, in particular, France, which have extended the 50 year period on account of the World Wars. In relation to countries which, as in the United States and the Soviet Union, belong only to the Universal Copyright Convention, protection will be granted for a period no longer than that fixed for the class of works to which the work in question belongs, in the contracting state in which the work was first published or, if an unpublished work, in the contracting state of which the author is a national.[3]

1 See also below, para 15.38.
2 Art 7(8), Berne Convention.
3 As to the significance of this rule for the protection of American works in the Federal Republic, see Ulmer, in International Review of Industrial Property and Copyright Law (1979) pp 287–295.

(5) Legal succession. Granting of rights to use

15.11 Copyright is inheritable. It passes to the heirs under a will, a testamentary agreement or by virtue of the statutory rules of inheritance. A testator may by his will appoint an executor not only to administer his estate as a whole but also to exercise his copyright in some or all of his works. The executor thereby becomes the guardian of his intellectual estate.

Copyright may also be assigned on death. A testator may, by will or testamentary agreement, bequeath to a legatee the copyright in his works or in any number of them. The copyright in this case also initially passes to the heirs. The heirs, however, are obliged to assign it to the legatee. It is also possible for joint heirs, to which the copyrights have passed, to assign as part of a settlement any or all of such rights to one or more of them.

15.12 In other respects copyright is not assignable.

By way of divergence from the above, the Copyright Laws of 1901 and 1907 provided that copyright could also be assigned by contract subject to restrictions. Under the old Laws, however, a development manifested itself in case law and literature which formed the germ of the new rules. With the development of the author's personality right the legal principle arose that, at least as regards its fundamental nature, it could not be assigned. Indeed, an author may empower others to exercise his personality right by, for example, empowering a theatrical publisher to prohibit theatrical companies, to which he grants the right to perform his work, from making any distortions or prejudicial changes in his work. He may also permit certain changes to the work, but in any event he retains the right to prohibit distortions.

In addition, with regard to exploitation rights, the difference which exists between the transfer of physical assets and the assignment of rights in respect of intellectual works is, however, also to be taken into account. The Copyright Law therefore only permits a grant of rights to use – by its very nature a grant of licences – with the consequence that the copyright as such remains with the author and reverts to a full-blooded right when the derived rights lapse.

In the context of international trade this means that the legal result of agreements relating to the assignment of world copyright, which, for example, are entered into in the United States or in the United Kingdom, as far as the Federal Republic is concerned, is the granting of rights to use.

15.13 The grant of rights to use is made by contract. Such a contract may be entered into informally and even tacitly. The law prescribes the written form only in respect of contracts relating to future works which are not defined at all or are defined only by reference to their nature, particularly option agreements.

The scope of a grant of rights to use depends on the contract and its interpretation. Basically, the Law permits great latitude, under the principle of the freedom of contract: the author may grant another the right to use the work in one or more ways. The right to use can also be limited as to place, time or purpose.

Nevertheless, a number of limitations must still be heeded:

(a) Agreements are ineffective insofar as they relate to means of utilisation which are not yet known. In this respect, the Law relies on the experience gained in cases where rights were assigned at a time when films and radio broadcasts were not yet known. Means of exploitation not conceived by the parties when entering into the contract remain the prerogative of the author.

(b) An important rule of interpretation is the doctrine of purpose-restricted assignment. It is based on the principle that, in cases of doubt, the author is not held to assign more extensive rights than is required by the objective pursued by the grant.

Accordingly, the statutory rule reads: If, when a right to use is granted, the types of use to which the right is intended to extend are not defined in detail, the extent of the right to use is determined according to the objective pursued by its grant. If therefore, for example, it is agreed in a publishing contract that the author grants the publisher all rights to use, the publisher will nevertheless acquire, in accordance with the typical objective of a publishing agreement, only the right of reproduction and distribution of the work. This does not preclude the author from also granting to the publisher other rights, such as the broadcasting, translation and film rights. The individual rights must, however, in such a case be expressly defined in the agreement. In other words, the freedom of contract is not limited but the law ensures that the author is conscious of the extent of the grant he is making.

The rule is, in particular, also of significance for agreements with employees. In cases of doubt, it is to be assumed that an employee who creates works in the performance of his duties within his service relationship grants to the employer the rights to use, to the extent that they are required for the purposes of the business. More extensive grants are permissible but require express agreement in the service contract or collective agreement.

(c) In cases of doubt, contracts concerning the grant of rights to use relate only to the use of the work in its original form. If they are to extend to adaptations, particularly to translations, this must be specially agreed. Accordingly, where a publisher's agreement has been entered into and nothing else is expressly provided, the translation right remains vested in the author.

(d) If the author sells the original of a work, in cases of doubt he does not thereby grant the assignee the right to use. Practically speaking, the rule is of significance mainly in the field of the visual arts: An artist who sells or gives away a painting or a drawing does not, in cases of doubt, grant the purchaser or donee any right of reproduction. In cases of doubt, an architect who constructs a building on the orders of a principal retains, in addition to his personality right, also the exploitation rights including the right to make reproductions, on the basis of which he may prohibit any copying.

15.14 Rights to use may be granted *as exclusive rights*.

An exclusive right is, in particular, the right to publish a work, on the basis of which the publisher can prevent others from reproducing and distributing the work. Accordingly, a film producer will, as a rule, be granted the exclusive right to make the film. Also, in the case of theatrical works, a theatrical company can be granted the exclusive right to perform the works, very often subject to a restriction to a particular city or a particular territory. In such cases, both the author and the person who has acquired the exclusive right may take proceedings against infringement of the rights.

It is normal to give non-exclusive rights for the use of the work where rights are granted by collecting societies, including the musical performance right and the mechanical-reproduction right. Rights to show films are also mainly granted only as non-exclusive rights. The question arises as to the legal position where the right to use is initially granted as a non-exclusive right to A and later as an exclusive to B. The Copyright Law comes down, in cases of doubt, in favour of the continuance of the non-exclusive right: This right retains its effectiveness against the holder of the exclusive right if nothing to the contrary is agreed between the author and the holder of the non-exclusive right.

15.15 The remuneration of the author will be regulated in the agreements which the author enters into with users of the works.

Basically, freedom of contract applies. A participation in the proceeds derived from the use of the works is often agreed. However, it is also possible for compensation to be agreed in the form of a specified sum. An adjustment of the fee agreed is provided for under the Copyright Law if there is gross inequity, as could be the consequence of an agreement on a lump sum in cases where the success of the work significantly exceeds expectations. The term 'Best-seller paragraph' is used. A pre-requisite is that the agreed fee, having regard to the whole of the relationship between the author and the user is manifestly out of proportion to the income derived from the use of the work. The author may, in such event, require the user's consent to an amendment to the agreement which will then give him an equitable share in the income and, if necessary, force him to give his agreement by bringing proceedings against him.

15.16 The legal effects of the exercise and existence of the right to use are also influenced by the author's personality right. The holder of a right to use is basically not empowered to make modifications to the work or its title without the consent of the author; only those modifications which the author cannot, in good faith, refuse are permissible.

In addition, the author's personality right is the source, in particular, of the author's right of revocation because the right has not been exercised or because he has changed his opinion.

(a) The right of revocation on account of non-exercise of a right is relevant in cases where exclusive rights to use have been granted. It is possible that the acquirer of the right is contractually obliged to exercise his right, as is the case particularly in a contract with a publisher. In such event, the author can set the publisher a reasonable time limit for performing his duty with the threat that he will withdraw from the contract with the publisher should the time limit expire without the right being exercised.

The obligation to exercise rights may however be lacking. In practice, this is particularly the case in contracts to film or broadcast a work. In such cases, there is the danger that the author's personal interests in the communication of his work will be infringed. The Copyright Law provides, therefore, regardless whether or not commitments exist on the part of the person who has acquired the right, for the opportunity to revoke the right to use. A pre-requisite is that the exclusive right has not been exercised or has been exercised only insufficiently within a certain period of time and that this has led to the author's justified interests being significantly infringed. The period of time is, as a rule, two years or, in the case of a contribution to a newspaper or a magazine, six months or one year respectively. The declaration of revocation must be preceded by a warning in which the holder of the right to use is set a reasonable period of time within which he has to exercise the right to a sufficient degree. The right to use lapses when the revocation becomes effective and the author will have to pay compensation if, and insofar as, it is equitable for him to do so.

(b) The author's personality right is also the source of a right of revocation because the author has changed his mind on the subject. The author may revoke a right to use by declaration as against the holder of the right, if the work no longer accords with his views and for such reason he can no longer be expected to agree to the use of his work. Examples are: changes in religious or political conviction or, in the case of scientific works, the recognition that the work has been superseded by new research.

As the grounds for the revocation reside in the author, he must pay the holder of the right to use reasonable compensation. He must at least refund him his expenses. The revocation will become effective when the author has refunded the expenditure or has provided security in respect of it.

(6) Copyright agreements

15.17 Copyright agreements are those agreements which are entered into for the grant of rights to use works protected by copyright and contain a statement of the duties of the contracting parties. Depending on the purpose of the grant, differentiation has to be made between a contract for the administration of rights and contracts to use.

Contracts for the administration of rights. The right of collecting societies
15.18 Contracts for the administration of rights may be entered into in respect of individual or collective administration of authors' rights.

(a) *Individual administration* is administration of authors' rights in respect of stage works by theatrical publishers (also known as theatrical agencies). The publishing houses enter into contract with the authors of dramatic, dramatic-musical or choreographic stage works and on the basis of these contracts, they administer the rights to use on behalf of the authors.

The rights administered are primarily performance rights in respect of stage works. The administration of other rights, in particular broadcasting rights and filming rights, may however also be agreed in the contract.

Owing to the lack of a special statutory rule, the general civil law rules apply as well as the special rules of the commercial law on commission agreements. The authors grant to publishers the rights to use on the basis of which the latter are able to enter into contracts with promoters in their own name and to enforce the rights against unauthorised use. The duty imposed on the publishers of stage works is a duty of careful administration. It covers the duty to advertise, to enter into user agreements with the promoter under normal commercial terms, as well as the duty to collect the fee and to pay it to the author (less a commission).

(b) *Collective administration* means the administration of authors' rights by collecting societies. It is effected by joint exploitation of all works.

Collecting societies were set up initially for musical copyrights. They go back to the year 1903 when the 'Genossenschaft deutscher Tonsetzer' was formed by, among others, Richard Strauss. Today, the performing rights in musical works, as well as the mechanical reproduction rights are administered by 'GEMA' ('Gesellschaft für musikalische Aufführungs und mechanische Vervielfältigungsrechte'). The members of GEMA are composers, lyricists and publishers of music.

Collecting societies to administer other rights of authors, as well as neighbouring rights, were set up considerably later. Of particular significance is the society 'Wort', for authors and publishers of literary works, the society 'Bild-Kunst' which administers the rights of visual artists, photographers, filmscriptwriters and authors of illustrations of a scientific or technical nature, as well as 'GVL' (the 'Gesellschaft zur Verwertung von Leistungsschutzrechten') which administers certain neighbouring rights, particularly the rights of performers and of producers of phonograms.

(c) The law on collecting societies is specially regulated by the 1965 Law on the Administration of Copyright and Neighbouring Rights. In the interests of the authors and of the owners of neighbouring rights as well as of the users, the Law lays down the duties of the collecting societies and puts them under state supervision.

(i) The supervisory body is the German Patent Office. It grants permission to carry on the activities of a collecting society, supervises the observance of the obligations put on the societies by the law, is entitled to participate in the meetings of the organs of the societies and has to be kept informed in detail of the activities of the collecting societies, any changes in their statutes, tariffs and resolutions, as well as the annual accounts and directors reports.

(ii) As regards their legal relations with the users of the works, the rules relating to the setting of tariffs and the obligation to contract with users are important.

The collecting societies must issue tariffs showing the fees which they collect under the rights administered by them. The tariffs are published in the Federal Gazette; they are those which the collecting societies issue unilaterally and also those on which they agree in collective agreements with associations of users. If no accord can be reached on the execution of collective agreements or of agreements with broadcasting companies, the (arbitration) tribunal set up under the auspices of the Patent Office may resolve the matter.

The obligation to contract with the users is provided because the collecting societies have in fact a monopoly position within their field of activities. The societies must, on demand, grant anyone rights on reasonable terms. It is also possible for the reasonableness of any conditions to be examined by the courts. Such an examination may, in particular, be relevant if no collective agreements have been entered into with users' associations.

(iii) The rules on the obligation to administer rights and on the apportionment schemes of the collecting societies serve the interests of the authors and the holders of neighbouring rights.

The obligation to administer rights is, like the obligation to enter into contracts, provided for because of the practical monopoly of the collecting societies. The societies are obliged, at the request of interested parties, to administer the rights within their spheres of activities on reasonable terms if no other effective administration of the rights is possible.

The income of the collecting societies has to be distributed on the basis of distribution schemes governed by fixed rules which preclude arbitrary action. In this connection, it is also intended that classes of work of cultural value are to be promoted and that collecting societies should set up welfare funds for the holders of the rights administered by them.

The publishing contract

15.19 Publishing contracts relating to literary and musical works are regulated in detail by the Statute on Publishing Law of 1901. Despite continued developments in the field of publishing, the law has proved adequate for the task. The most important reason for this is that, as a whole, the legal provisions are not mandatory. The only provisions of a mandatory nature are those dealing with the bankruptcy of the publisher.

(a) The author's duty to allow the work to be reproduced and distributed by the publisher stems from the publishing contract.

The transfer of the work to the publisher includes the obligation on the author to refrain from certain activities and to secure title for the publisher. Under the statute, the author has to refrain from any acts of reproduction or distribution which are forbidden to a third party during the period of the copyright. More extensive arrangements are possible, but may not be so wide as to affect the author's creative freedom. The duty to secure rights is basically the duty to secure the publishing right, ie the exclusive right to reproduce and distribute the work, which the publisher may enforce both against third parties and against the author himself. The publishing right arises under the statutory rule, not when the publishing contract is executed but, rather, when the manuscript is delivered. The author is responsible for any failure to secure the right. In practice publishers, particularly publishers of 'belles-lettres', are in most cases also granted other rights, such as the translation right, filming right and broadcasting right, as well as the right to arrange paperback and other special editions. The prerequisite for validity is that these rights are expressly mentioned in the agreement. The publisher is then obliged effectively to exploit the rights, in particular to grant licences, and to pay to the author a share in the income derived therefrom.

(b) The principal duty of the publisher is the duty to reproduce and distribute the work in the appropriate and customary fashion. The duty to pay a fee is not essential for the publishing contract: even where an author pays an amount towards the printing costs the contract is a publishing contract. In most cases, however, a fee will be agreed. The fee can be a lump sum, or a fee according to the number of lines (particularly for newspapers and magazines) or of printed sheets. However, the generally-accepted method of calculation of the fee is by reference to the price of copies sold, for example a fee of 10% of the retail price.

If nothing else has been agreed, the retail price will be fixed by the publisher. It is traditional within the German book trade for the fixed retail price system to be adopted. The maintenance of the system, which at times appeared to be endangered by antitrust law, has been ensured by a special provision in the 'Law against Restrictions on Competition'. It is permissible to lay down a fixed price in written contracts entered into by the publishers with booksellers. In practice, collective undertakings are signed, which are submitted to booksellers by an agent on the instructions of the publishers.

The number in an edition may be agreed contractually. If nothing is agreed, an edition will consist of 1000 copies. Under the statute, a publisher is entitled only to one edition. In most cases, however, publishers are granted in the publishing contract the right to print several or all editions. The publisher is not obliged to make new editions. The author can, however, set the publisher a reasonable period for the exercise of his right and withdraw from the contract on expiration of that period.

(c) The duration of the publishing contract follows from the agreements relating to editions and from the sales. If the relationship with the publisher is restricted to a particular number of editions or copies, it will come to an end when the number of editions or copies have been achieved. If the publisher is granted the publishing right in respect of all editions, the publishing contract will, in cases of doubt, end with the term of copyright protection.

It is possible to end the relationship between publisher and author prematurely. In particular, both the author and the publisher may withdraw from a contract if the contracting partner, despite being warned, fails to comply with essential duties encumbent on him. The publisher will also have a right of cancellation if the objective which the work is intended to achieve disappears after execution of the publishing contract. The author has a right of cancellation if circumstances arise which were not envisaged when the publishing contract was entered into and which would have caused him to refrain from publication had he been aware of the situation. This right exists in addition to the revocation right when the author has changed his convictions.

The possibility of termination for good cause is also of general importance in the case of long-term publishing contracts. Case law relies on the rule that such publishing contracts may be terminated by the author or publisher for good cause if it is no longer reasonable to expect him to continue the publishing relationship owing to a breakdown of mutual trust.

(d) Special provisions exist for the publication of periodicals, particularly for the publication of newspapers and magazines. Where contributions are made to a newspaper, the publisher, in cases of doubt, acquires only a non-exclusive right. If, however, an exclusive right is granted, such right will be extinguished when the contribution appears. In the case of contributions to other periodicals, such as magazines, calendars, almanacs etc, the publisher will, in cases of doubt, acquire an exclusive right to reproduce and distribute the work. The author can, however, reproduce and distribute the work through other sources after expiration of one year from its publication.

Other contracts to use
15.20 (a) There are no special statutory provisions for other user agreements. Important bases for such legal arrangements and their interpretation are found in specimen contracts, standard-form contracts, collections of rules, the customs of the book trade, and theatrical usage. In general, freedom of contract prevails. Regard must, however, be had to the fact that in such agreements the author is usually the weaker and the user the stronger party. It is therefore important to bear in mind that unfair terms may be successfully opposed by authors as being contrary to public policy. Where agreements are based on specimen contracts and printed forms drafted in advance by the users, the provisions of the 'Law regulating Standard forms of contracts' of 9 December 1976 are also applicable. These provide, inter alia, that terms contained in standard form

contracts are ineffective if they unreasonably prejudice the contracting partner of the user in a manner which is inequitable.

(b) If user agreements are administered by collecting societies, in most cases collective agreements which relate to an entire repertoire are entered into. This applies particularly to collective agreements relating to rights in musical works which GEMA enters into with concert agencies and broadcasting organisations. On the other hand, contracts for the performance of stage works are entered into individually. The rights of the authors are mainly administered by theatrical publishers. The rules, which are based on experience, including the rules relating to fees, are comprised in a collection of rules agreed between theatrical publishers and theatres. The theatres are, as a rule, not only entitled but obliged to perform the works concerned. Changes to the works are permissible only to the extent to which the author is unable, in good faith, to deny his consent. Any more extensive changes require special agreement which, under the rules, must be in writing.

(c) Among the other user contracts, broadcasting contracts and contracts in the film industry are of particular significance.

(i) In addition to collecting societies, publishers and employee-authors, the contracting partners of broadcasting organisations are in particular also freelance writers writing for broadcasting. Their contracts are based on the fee scales of the broadcasting organisations which contain provisions on the production of commissioned works, single broadcasts, repeated broadcasts and onward transmissions, as well as on the fee to be paid in respect of them. A broadcasting obligation is normally excluded in such agreements. In the case of television works, the broadcasting organisation will as a rule obtain an exclusive broadcasting right. Statutory regulation of the law relating to broadcasting contracts is at present being considered in view of complaints from authors and their associations on various contractual terms.

(ii) Within the film business there are, on the one hand, contracts to make films which the producers enter into with the authors of the works on which the films are to be based and with filmscript writers. The Copyright Law lays down wide presumptions in favour of the granting of rights. As regards the authors of pre-existing works, it is presumed that they have granted in the contracts which they enter into with the film producer the exclusive rights to produce, reproduce and distribute, adapt and otherwise reshape the film and, in the case of film works which are intended for performance, the exclusive right to perform them, and in the case of film works which are intended to be broadcast, the exclusive right to broadcast them. As regards the film authors, it is also provided that they grant the film producers the exclusive right to use the film work by all known methods of such use.

On the subject of the use of films, the relevant contracts are those which producers enter into with film distributors, as well as the contracts which are entered into with cinemas relating to the showing of films. Film producers customarily grant film distributors exclusive rights for particular areas. Contracts for the showing of films are entered into by a film producer or film distributor with cinema owners. Contracts which are entered into using written order forms contain detailed provisions on showing dates. The theatre owners have to pay the agreed fee. In cases of doubt, they too are not only entitled to present the work but also obliged to do so.

3. Neighbouring rights

(1) The development of neighbouring rights

15.21 The German Copyright Law distinguishes between copyright and neighbouring rights. This arrangement is based on the idea that there exist in the cultural sphere not only the creations of authors but also certain other accomplishments demanding the law's protection. These accomplishments differ according to their nature, but they have one common feature, that to a greater or lesser extent their legal protection is related to copyright protection.

Performers are closely related to authors. Fundamentally, however, their task is not the creation of works but the interpretation of the works of others. It is only in those special cases where performers during their performances adapt a work by way of improvisation or complete an unfinished work, as for example the kind of music known as outline music, that they may become authors themselves.

The protection of performers became necessary for the first time when it became possible to record their performances on phonograms. Protection was envisaged, therefore, in 1910 in an amendment to the Law concerning Copyright in Literary and Musical Works, providing that the transcription of works on to phonograms by way of a personal performance was deemed to be equal to an adaptation of the work. The performer was deemed to be an adaptor, who, like for example a translator, was entitled to copyright. However, the intention of the legislator was that performers would transfer their rights to the producers who on that basis would be able to claim protection against counterfeit pressings of the records.

In the long run, this method of regulation has not proved satisfactory. The recognition of copyright meant that the performer was granted protection which was too far-reaching. Likewise, the transfer of rights to the producer does not happen as a matter of course. Rather, it became evident that the grant of legal protection to both performers and producers of phonograms, to the extent of their respective interests, was required. In this way, the distinction between copyright and neighbouring rights was conceived and this became the basis of the system adapted by the Copyright Law of 1965.

In the course of the preparatory work for the new law, the work done in preparation for the international regulation of neighbouring rights and the ensuing Rome Convention[1] was taken into account, particularly the minimum rights of the three groups of beneficiaries of the Convention. However, the scope of protection, in particular of performers has been extended beyond the minimum envisaged in the Convention. Furthermore, it was logical that besides the protection of the producers of phonograms, a right has been accorded also to film producers in the visual and audiovisual recordings ('Videograms')[2] in which a film is fixed. These records are, in the case of cinematographic works, the physical embodiment of the intellectual creations concerned.

The distinction between copyright and neighbouring rights has turned out to be beneficial. It makes it possible to restrict the notion of copyright to those rights which arise out of work creation while at the same time satisfying the requirements of the justified subjects of protection.

The legislation also provides for rights other than those of performers, of producers of phonograms and films and of broadcasting organisations which are related to copyright. Thus, for example, the right in photographs which are not photographic works as such is a related right. The new Copyright Law also provides rights related to copyright in scientific editions of works and texts not protected by copyright and in editions of posthumous works. Thus, by by virtue of the protection of the editio princeps in particular, a lacuna which had existed in the earlier Law and which had often been pointed out in legal literature was closed.

1   See chapter 8, above.
2   See para 12.25 above.

(2) **The protection of performers**

15.22   A performer within the meaning of the Copyright Law is anyone who recites or performs a work or who participates artistically in the recitation or performance of a work. Artistic participants are, in particular, conductors of music and directors.

The subject-matter of legal protection is therefore the performance of works, as well as artistic participation in such performances. This is so irrespective of whether such performance is of protected or unprotected works. As is the case under the Rome Convention, no protection has been extended to other activities, such as those of variety-artists and athletes. It may be possible however to derive protection under other legal provisions, such as the right to one's own image and in particular the protection of promoters under the rules on unfair competition or by virtue of an unlawful interference with their business.

15.23   The protection of the rights of performers embraces both rights to give consent and claims for royalties.

(a)   The performance of a performer may only be fixed on videograms or phonograms with his consent. Likewise, such videograms or phonograms may only be reproduced with his permission. As a rule, therefore, an artist will give the phonogram producer, at the time of recording the performances on phonograms, permission both to make and to reproduce the phonogram. Reproduction may not, however, be undertaken for purposes other than those for which it has been authorised: for instance, a producer of phonograms may not, in the absence of an agreement to do so, use the phonograms for the production of videograms or film soundtracks. Both performer and producer may bring proceedings against any unauthorised reproduction by third parties, in particular against unauthorised pressings or re-recordings of phonograms.
(b)   Only with his consent may a performer's performance be publicly communicated outside the room in which it is taking place by way of a screen, loudspeaker or similar technical devices.
(c)   A performer's performance may be broadcast only with his permission. Such permission is also required for repeat broadcasts or onward transmissions. However, the Copyright Law provides an important restriction in those cases in which videograms or phonograms are used for broadcasting. Where a performance has been recorded with the consent of the performer on videograms or phonograms and these have been published, the performer has no right to give or to withhold consent but only a right to claim for the payment of an equitable remuneration.
(d)   If a performance is publicly communicated by means of videograms or phonograms or if a broadcast performance is publicly communicated, the performer has a claim to equitable remuneration.

15.24   The claims for remuneration envisaged by the Copyright Law are claims for secondary exploitation. The level of protection in the Copyright

Law exceeds the minimum provided in the Rome Convention. For instance, claims for remuneration may be enforced not only in the case of a broadcast by way of phonograms but also in the case of the public performance of broadcasts (including the public performance of live broadcasts).

The question, which is left unanswered by article 12 of the Rome Convention, as to whether the remuneration is to be paid to performers, to producers of phonograms or to both, has been decided by the German Copyright Law in favour of performers. The producers of phonograms however have a claim to a fair share in the remuneration received by the performers.[1]

[1] See para 15.31 below.

15.25 The right to give or withhold consent and the claim for compensation are, in certain cases, restricted.

(a) Generally speaking, the rules concerning limitations of copyright – with the exception of the rules concerning compulsory licences for the production of phonograms – are to be applied by analogy to the rights of performers. Important from a practical point of view is, in particular, that, as in copyright, the production of individual copies for personal use is in principle permissible without the performer's consent. However, performers have, in the case of the recording of broadcasts and the transferring from one phonogram to another for personal use, a claim for equitable remuneration against the manufacturer or importer of the equipment involved (the equipment levy). This is a compensation by way of substitution for the restriction of their rights.

(b) A far-reaching restriction of the rights of performers is provided by the Copyright Law in the case of the use of performances contained in cinematographic work. Although the consent of performers is necessary for the recording of their performances, on the videograms and soundtrack of the film, if they give such consent, in particular by participating in its production, their right to give or withhold their consent to the reproduction and broadcast thereof, as well as their claims to remuneration in the case of a public performance, are excluded. The relevant rules, in particular that concerning secondary exploitation, are therefore only of significance in the case of films which are not cinematographic works, such as a broadcast of an opera performance which is shown on the basis of a television recording.

15.26 Under his personality right, a performer has the right to prohibit any distortion or other alteration of his performance which is liable to prejudice his prestige or reputation as a performer. Where a performance is being given jointly by several performers, they will have to show a reasonable degree of consideration for one another in the exercise of this right.

15.27 The question of the period of protection of the rights of performers arises in those cases where their performances are recorded. The Copyright Law distinguishes as follows: The property rights of performers expire 25 years after the publication of the recordings or alternatively 25 years after the performance if the phonograms have not been published within that period. The protection against distortion or other alteration lapses on the death of the performer or, 25 years after the performance, whichever is the later.

15.28 The Copyright Law contains special provisions for performers who are serving under a contract of employment, with regard to choral, orchestral and stage performances and to the protection of organisers of performances.

(a) Even in those cases where performances of performers are rendered in fulfilment of their obligations under a contract of employment, it has to be assumed that they are the right owners. As a rule, however, such performers will grant to their employer rights to use their performances. The extent of such grants may be fixed by agreement, in particular in employment contracts or collective agreements. In the absence of express agreement, the extent of the grant must be deduced from the character of the employment or service relationship. In case of doubt, it is assumed that use is permissible to the extent required by the objectives and scope of the employer's activities.

(b) In the case of choral, orchestral and stage performances the Copyright Law contains a special regulation for the enforcement of the rights of performers participating in the ensemble. The rights of soloists, conductor and director remain unaffected. Apart from this, however, a right of a group of performers can be asserted only by a representative on behalf of the group as a whole. Each ensemble may elect one or more representatives, forming the 'committee'. If no such committee is elected, the right will be exercised by the head of the group of performers such as the choir master or conductor.

(c) It is a peculiar feature of German law that the Copyright Law, by analogy with the rights of the performer, also provides for the protection of the enterprise in which the performance is given. In cases where the consent of the performers is required for use of the performance, the consent of the owner of such enterprise is likewise required. Any claims for compensation arising out of secondary exploitation however are the sole property of the performers.

(3) The protection of producers of phonograms

15.29 In the same way as is provided under the Rome Convention, a producer of phonograms within the meaning of the Law is anyone recording the sounds for the first time. The Copyright Law makes this clear by providing that the producer's right does not arise by virtue of the reproduction of a phonogram. The Law also provides expressly that where the producer is an enterprise, the owner of the enterprise, which may be a legal entity, is deemed to be the producer. The rights of the producer are independent of the subject-matter of the recording. Apart from the performance of works by performers, other kinds of sound sequences are possible such as, for example, the recording of ringing bells or natural sounds.

The rules concerning the rights of phonogram producers do not apply to producers of films concerning the sound-tracks. Instead, their place is taken by the rules concerning the producers of films.[1]

1 See paras 15.32 et seq below.

15.30 The right of the producer of phonograms comprises the exclusive right to reproduce and distribute such phonograms.

(a) Reproduction may be by way of re-pressing and these days mostly by way of re-recording of phonograms. It is immaterial whether such reproduction takes place directly or indirectly. In particular, the recording of the broadcast of a phonogram is not only a physical recording of such broadcast but at the same time a reproduction of the phonogram.

(b) The limitations provided by the Copyright Law for the author's reproduction and distribution rights also apply analogously to the reproduction and distribution rights of the producers of phonograms, with the exception of the rule on compulsory licences for the production of phonograms. As is the case with authors' rights and performers' rights, it is permissible to produce individual copies for personal use. The producers of phonograms have, however, by way of substitution, a claim to the so-called equipment levy in the case of the recording of broadcasts or re-recording from one phonogram onto another.

The producers' right, like the authors' right of distribution, is exhausted once the copies have been marketed by way of sale by a person entitled to sell. Such exhaustion also arises in the case of distribution abroad if the person marketing the copies also has the domestic right of distribution. Moreover, within the Common Market the rules of the EEC Treaty on the free movement of goods must be observed.[1]

(c) The right expires 25 years after the publication of the phonogram or, where the phonogram has not been published within this period, 25 years after the production of such a phonogram.

[1] See paras 20.09 et seq below.

15.31 The producer has no right to permit use of phonograms for public performances. As has already been mentioned, in the case of secondary exploitation it is not the producer but the performer who has a claim to compensation. Producers have, however, a claim against performers for a reasonable share in any compensation received by the latter. In practice, a balance is struck between performers and producers by way of the 'Gesellschaft zur Verwertung von Leistungsschutzrechten', 'GVL' (Society for the Exploitation of Neighbouring Rights), to which both performers and producers assign their rights on trust, and which administers the claims for remuneration and provides a 50% share in the net revenue, each to performer and producer in accordance with its distribution scheme.

(4) The protection of film producers

15.32 It is a peculiar feature of German law that the Copyright Law also provides a neighbouring right in favour of film producers. Both silent films and sound films fall under this provision: in the case of silent films, there is a right in respect of the visual and in the case of sound films in the images and soundtrack of the films.

As in the case of the phonographic recording of musical works, a distinction must be made in the case of cinematographic works between the rights of authors in their intellectual creations and the rights of the producers in the picture carrier. It is true, of course, that the practical importance of the neighbouring right of the film producer in the case of cinematographic works intended for presentation as particular feature films shown in cinemas, is not as great as the importance of the rights which the film producer acquires from the authors. In case of doubt, he is granted in the agreements with the authors, the exclusive rights of reproduction and public presentation of the cinematographic work, on the basis of which he will be able to restrain use by any third party. The neighbouring right is of importance, however, in the case of films which are not cinematographic works, such as, for example, the recording of daily events intended for television news broadcasts. In relation to such films, the film producer may prohibit the use of the film by others on the basis of the neighbouring right vested in him. Furthermore, today, consideration must also be given to videograms. Even though, as a rule, these will be cinematographic works, authors will not always grant the producer an exclusive right of public performance. Where, in such cases, videograms are used not only for private but also for public showing or for broadcasting purposes, the consent of both the author and, by virtue of the neighbouring right, of the film producer will be required.

15.33 The film producer's right comprises the following rights:

(a) As with phonograms, the film producer has an exclusive right of reproduction and distribution. In the same way as a producer of phonograms may prohibit their use for the production of films, a film producer is able to prohibit the use of the sound-tracks of films for the production of phonograms. The limitations on the rights of reproduction and distribution are the same as for phonograms. In particular, although the production of individual copies for personal use is permissible, the film producer has, by way of substitution, a claim to royalty (equipment levy) in the case of recordings of television broadcasts and re-recordings of videograms.

(b) In addition to the rights granted to producers of phonograms, the Copyright Law also grants film producers the exclusive right to use the sound carrier for broadcasting or other public performances. As has already been mentioned, where authors have, in consideration of their contributions to a cinematographic work, reserved the right of public performance, the consent of both the author and the film producer is required for the broadcasting and public performance of the cinematographic work.

(c) In addition, the Copyright Law permits the film producer to prohibit distortion and abridged versions of the film. This protection is similar to the author's personality right. Unlike the moral right of the authors, however, it is assignable. In essence therefore, it must be regarded as a proprietary right. Of decisive importance are the economic interests of the film producer and his successors in title in the use of the film, the value and success of which may be adversely affected by distortions and abridgements.

15.34 The right of the film producer expires 25 years after publication of the film or 25 years after its production, if the film has not been published during that period.

(5) The protection of broadcasting organisations

15.35 In conformity with the Rome Convention[1] and the European Agreement on the Protection of Television Broadcasts,[2] the Copyright Law also provides a neighbouring right for broadcasting organisations. Although, by their nature, radio broadcasts are intended for a wide public, broadcasting organisations have a justified interest in being able to prohibit certain kinds of use of their broadcasts.

The rights of broadcasting organisations comprise the following:

(a) The broadcasting organisation has the exclusive right of re-broadcasting its broadcasts. Re-broadcasting means, as it does in the Rome Convention, the simultaneous transmission of the broadcast. In the case of subsequent transmission by another organisation, the interests of the original broadcasting station are protected by the fact that the recording which is a pre-condition of a delayed transmission requires the consent of the originating broadcasting organisation.

Re-broadcast by way of wire or cable is likewise a re-broadcast within the meaning of the Copyright Law, requiring the consent of the author and the originating broadcasting organisation, notwithstanding certain minor exceptions. In particular, the re-broadcast by way of community antennae serving only individual houses or apartment blocks requires neither the consent of the authors of the works broadcast nor the consent of the originating broadcasting station. Further, in its decision of 7 November 1980, the Federal Supreme Court ruled that the simultaneous re-broadcasting of radio programmes by way of central cable installations does not require consent if they are exclusively intended for a group of recipients living within the transmission range of the originating broadcasting station in an area located in a 'blackout zone' created by high-rise buildings. The grounds for and the effect of the decision have however been the subject of considerable criticism in legal literature.

(b) A broadcasting organisation has the exclusive right to fix its broadcasts on visual or sound recordings, to make photographs of its television broadcasts and to reproduce such recordings and photographs. This right is, in essence, a right of re-production. Accordingly, the limitations imposed by law on the right of reproduction must be applied mutatis mutandis. There exists in particular an exception in favour of the making of individual copies for personal use, without any claim to a royalty by way of an equipment levy.

(c) Broadcasting organisations have the exclusive right to prohibit the public performance of their television broadcasts in places provided that the public has access to such places, only against payment of an entrance fee. As is the case under the Rome Convention, the right is accordingly restricted to the performance of television broadcasts. In addition, performance in guest-houses and in other places where no entrance fee is charged is unrestricted, as it is in the private sphere.

The right of broadcasting organisations is assignable. It expires 25 years after the broadcast. Practically speaking, this time limitation is of importance with regard to the reproduction right in the visual and sound recordings as well as the photographs onto which the broadcast was fixed.

1 See chapter 8 above.
2 See chapter 11 above.

(6) The protection of other 'related rights'

15.36 The Copyright Law provides for related rights to protect photographs as well as certain publications.

Related rights in photographs

15.37 As photography was developed at a time when the notion of neighbouring rights was still unknown, the legislator provided for copyright protection for photographs within the framework of artistic copyright. Legal writers and case law, however, did not demand the same requirements of photographs as for the protection of works of the visual arts, and the term of protection was restricted (initially to ten years). This differentiation gave rise to the idea of including rights in photographs among neighbouring rights. It cannot be doubted, however, that in addition to simple or 'mere photographs' (snap shots) there are 'artistic photographs' which are distinguished by special characteristics deriving from the subject matter, or a particular choice of position or the kind of lighting. The Copyright Law took account of this situation by providing copyright protection for photographic works, but a 'related right' for 'mere photographs'. The subject-matter of related rights may be both photographs taken as a matter of routine in the course of professional activity and 'mere photographs' taken by amateurs.

In view of the practical difficulty in differentiation, however, it was provided that the provisions applicable to photographic works are to be applied by analogy to 'mere photographs'.

(a) Thus, the related right also arises in the person of the photographer. The transfer of this right, like the transfer of copyright, is possible only by way of inheritance. Photographers however may grant rights to use. In particular, in the case of employed photographers it is to be assumed, in cases of doubt, even without express provision to that effect, that they will have granted to their employer the rights required for the purposes of the employer's business.

(b) Apart from this there is equality both as regards the substance of protection and the term of protection. The right includes in addition to the exploitation rights, the author's personality right. Protection expires 25 years after publication of the photograph or 25 years after its production, where the photograph has not been published within that period.

Related rights in certain publications

15.38 The Copyright Law also provides for related rights in certain publications:

(a) There is a related right in editions of works or texts not protected by copyright, if they are the result of scientific analysis and differ appreciably from previously-known editions of such works or texts. Eligible are not only editions of old manuscripts, documents and inscriptions, but also editions of more recent works in which copyright has expired and which have been recreated in their original version on the basis of scientific analysis.

The right vests in the author of the edition. In its substance it corresponds to copyright, but expires 10 years after publication of the edition or 10 years after production where the edition has not been published within that period.

(b) Protection is also accorded to editions of posthumous works. Protection is accorded to the person publishing a previously-unpublished work in the Federal Republic of Germany after expiry of the copyright. This provision has replaced the earlier rule that copyright protection did not expire until 10 years after the publication of the work. This rule was justified by the idea that the protection, albeit shortened in time, of the first edition was based on a legitimate interest. In its effect however, this rule went beyond the intended purpose in that it resulted in eternal protection for unpublished works. A new rule was therefore provided in the 1965 Copyright Law. This differentiates between the protection of the heirs of authors and the protection of the editor. Where a posthumous work is published after 60 years, but before 70 years of death of the author, the copyright expires 10 year after publication. The result is a possible extension of copyright protection by a maximum of 10 years, to the benefit of the heirs of the author. Where a work has fallen into the public domain because the term of protection has expired, the protection of the first edition is assured by a related right for the editor of the work. The publisher has the exclusive right to publish and to distribute the work and to use copies of the work for public performance. This right is transferable. It expires 10 years after publication of the work.

4. Infringement of copyrights and neighbouring rights

(1) Civil law claims

15.39 General:

(a) The consequences of the infringement of rights are dealt with in the Copyright Law under the same heading for infringement of copyrights and neighbouring rights. Of primary concern is protection under the civil law. This is a comprehensive protection against unlawful interference with the exclusive rights granted by the Copyright Law. This protection covers actions for injunctive relief, claims for destruction of copies and for rendering equipment unusable, as well as claims for damages and claims for unjust enrichment.

(b) Infringement of exclusive rights in the context of copyright law are infringements of the author's personality right and the exploitation rights of the author and his successor in title, as well as infringements of the exclusive rights to use granted to others. Apart from the owner of an exclusive right to use, the author himself may also, on the basis of the right retained by him, take steps against infringements. Thus, for example, in addition to the publisher who has been granted the exclusive reproduction and distribution right, the author of the work may himself proceed against a pirate printer. The pre-condition for this is that, despite the granting of the exclusive right to use, there still remains a material or intellectual interest of the author which is worthy of protection.

In the case of the grant of non-exclusive (simple) rights to use, the owner has a right to use, without having a right of prohibition. It remains possible, however, for an assignee of a simple right to use, to bring an action for an injunction against third parties using the right without permission, if he has the authorisation of the author or his successor in title to do so.

(c) Accordingly, the holders of neighbouring rights are protected against infringements of the exclusive rights granted to them. Exclusive rights include, in particular, also the rights of a performer to give or withhold his consent.

(d) The exclusive right protected by the Copyright Law will be infringed by those who undertake or participate in any unlawful interference with the right. A participant is, in particular, anyone who causes the infringement of the rights. An infringement of the rights may therefore, be attributed to a number of persons: Behind the printer stands the publisher who has commissioned him to print the work. The author of an infringing work may also be an infringer. If music is played by a band in a public house, the organiser of the performance is, for the purposes of the law, not only the band leader but also the landlord.

The consequences of an act of infringement are more particularly defined by the requirements for the claim. In particular, fault, (intention or negligence) is required in a claim for damages but not in a claim for injunctive relief or a claim on account of unjustified enrichment. If, for example, there is fault on the part of the publisher and author of the infringing work but not on the part of the printer, only the first two will be liable in damages. Where several persons are liable in damages they are liable jointly and severally.

15.40 The actions for injunction may be brought for unlawful infringement of copyright and neighbouring rights. The injured party may bring an action for injunctive relief requiring the wrongdoer to remove the infringement or, if there is a danger of repetition, to prohibit further infringements.

(a) The claim for injunction prohibiting further infringement which is particularly important in practice, is directed against threatened infringements. Where the owner of an exclusive right learns of an act of infringement, such as where the author learns of any reproduction, distribution or public performance of his work without his permission, he may, where there is a danger of repetition, bring an action for an injunction restraining further infringements. Instead of an infringement, however, the mere threat to a copyright or a neighbouring right by conduct suggesting an impending infringement will be sufficient. Where, for example, an unauthorised stage production is publicly announced or prepared by way of rehearsals, the author need not wait for the infringement, but may bring an action for an injunction on the basis of the threatened infringement. This is termed a preventive injunction.

Actions for an injunction are of crucial importance for the protection of copyright and neighbouring rights. Quick action is often necessary in order to prevent material or moral damage. In this connection, it is important that the person entitled, where there is danger that the enforcement of his right will be frustrated or made substantially more difficult, may, by application for an interlocutory injunction, secure a temporary prohibition.

(b) The claim for an injunction to remove an infringement is directed against continuing infringements. Such a claim may for instance be brought in the case of infringements of the author's personality right. Where, for example, a work of art is defaced by painting over it, the removal of the overpainting may be demanded. Such claims have been recognised in leading cases.

By their very nature, acts of public performance are acts of infringement of a temporary nature. In the case of unlawful reproduction and distribution, a claim for injunction may be brought with a view to prohibiting further acts of reproduction and distribution. In addition, however, the distribution of an edition may amount to a continuing infringement. A claim may be brought against a publisher distributing reprints through the book trade to withdraw them, as far as is still possible, from circulation.

(c) In order to avoid unreasonable hardship, the Copyright Law provides for, under certain conditions, a right to indemnify the injured party by a money payment, the exercise of which may avoid a claim for an injunction. It is a requirement of this right that the claim is directed against a person guilty neither of unlawful intent nor of negligence, that unreasonably severe damage would be suffered by such a person as a result of the injunction and that money may reasonably compensate the injured party. This may be the case, for example, where a large cinematographic work or an extensive publication has been produced at great cost but where one of the participating authors, without this being apparent to the film producer or the publisher, committed an infringement of another's rights.

15.41 Claim for destruction and similar measures; the right of 'delivery up'. Claims for destruction and similar measures serve to protect the interests of entitled persons. The injured party, however, may instead claim a right of delivery up.

(a) Liable to be destroyed are all copies unlawfully produced, unlawfully distributed or intended for unlawful distribution, such as books, sheet music, films and phonograms, as well as copies of works of the visual arts, photographic works and photographs. Liable to be rendered unusable are equipment which exclusively serve the unlawful manufacture of reproductions, such as plates, lithographic printing equipment, printing blocks, stencils and negatives. They may be rendered unusable by grinding down the plates, melting down and similar measures, but where this is not possible, destruction may be demanded.

(b) Compared with destruction, rendering unusable is the more lenient measure as some value of the equipment is preserved. In addition, the Law reflects the notion that the complete destruction of valuable articles should, if possible, be avoided. Accordingly, buildings are not subject to destruction. Where copying of a building is threatened, the architect of the original building may prohibit the construction of such a building, but the building, once erected, need not be pulled down. Apart from this, the general rule applies that where the unlawfulness of the copies and equipment may be remedied by means other than destruction or rendering unusable, only the milder remedy may be demanded. Thus, for example, in the case of books the blacking-out of individual passages or in the case of photographs, touching-up may be sufficient to remedy the infringement.

(c) The circle of persons against whom a claim for destruction or similar measures may be brought is restricted: reproductions and equipment are subject to these measures only if they are the property of the persons participating in the unlawful production or distribution of the copies. These may be, inter alia, printers, publishers, book sellers, art dealers and producers of and dealers in films and phonograms. Copies which have already been distributed to the general public are, however, exempt from destruction.

(d) Instead of a claim for destruction or similar measures, the injured party may claim a right of delivery: he may demand that the copies or equipment be completely or partially made over to him on payment of reasonable compensation amounting to no more than the cost of manufacture. However, he may not be forced to take them over. Rather, it is left to him whether he wishes to claim the right to take over the items in question or not.

(e) In cases of hardship, the infringer may avoid claims for destruction or similar measures and the right of delivery by payment of compensation. The prerequisites for this are the same as in those cases where the claims for an injunction may be avoided because unreasonable hardship would be caused.

15.42 Claims for damages and on account of unjust enrichment:

(a) Claims for damages may be raised in the case of unlawful and culpable infringement of the rights of the authors and their successors in title, the owners of exclusive rights to use and the owners of neighbouring rights.
  Liability to pay damages requires that the infringement was intentional or the result of negligence. The courts in general impose a strict standard. They expect, in particular of specialists in the field, such as publishers, phonogram and film producers and broadcasting organisations, that they take care to inform themselves of the factual and legal position.

(b) A claim for monetary compensation may in any event be brought on the basis of economic loss. This may also arise out of an infringement of the author's personality right: distortions of the work or false designations of authorship may lead to a loss of orders or to a reduction in sales.

In addition, the Copyright Law – adopting a legal concept which has gained acceptance in recent case law concerning the infringement of the general personality right – also provides for the possibility of demanding monetary compensation for moral damage: authors, holders or rights in scientific editions, photographers and performers may demand monetary compensation for damage other than economic loss insofar as this accords with the principles of equity. Relevant examples are, first and foremost, infringements of the author's personality right, such as a distortion of protected works or performances, but also an infringement of exploitation rights. For instance, the making of a film version of a work without the consent of the author, may injure his intellectual interests in a way which justifies a claim for monetary damages.

(c) Special principles apply for the calculation of economic damage. In going beyond the limitations normally imposed on claims for damages, the courts have developed the law in a way which accords with the particular interests involved in copyright law. It leaves the plaintiff a choice of several methods for calculating damages:

(i) The injured person may claim damages in accordance with the general rules relating to damages. He may demand to be put into such a position with regard to his property rights as he would have been if his rights had not been infringed. Thus, for example, a publisher may in the case of unauthorised reprinting demand compensation for the reduction in sales which is a consequence of the reprinting.

(ii) The injured party may demand payment of equitable remuneration. In particular, the author may demand fees for the reprinting, royalties for the performance and remuneration for broadcasts. In this way, account is taken of an equitable principle: where, for example, a literary work which had been published and printed is being broadcast without the permission of the author it may well be that the broadcast does not lead to a reduction but on the contrary, like advertising, to an increase in sales. Nonetheless, it would seem appropriate that the author whose rights are being infringed may demand compensation: whoever infringes a copyright or a neighbouring right must expect to be treated as if an agreement on the usual terms had been entered into.

(iii) The plaintiff may demand the surrender of the net profit of the infringement without it being relevant whether he himself has lost any corresponding profit. This extension of the claim for damages has been developed by the courts and has, following the judicature, been recognised in the Copyright Law. The more precise terminology used in the Copyright Law is that the injured person may demand the surrender of the profit which the infringer has achieved as a result of the infringement of the plaintiff's rights 'in lieu of damages'.

(d) Assessment of economic loss is not conclusively dealt with by the provisions on damages. Rather, the plaintiff has, in the case of an infringement of his rights, also a claim for unjust enrichment. This has the advantage that it may be claimed without proving an intention or negligence on the part of the infringer. The successful plaintiff may demand the delivery of the amount of the enrichment which the infringer has obtained at his expense by virtue of the unlawful use. The author or performer may therefore also demand equitable remuneration by virtue of his claim for unjust enrichment because the infringer has, at the expense of the plaintiff, saved an amount which he would have had to pay if he had acted lawfully. The enrichment of the infringer also includes the net profit which he has obtained through the use of the work. It is debatable whether the injured party may demand the net profit in full, as he can in the case of a claim for damages, or only the amount which he himself might have been able to obtain. Prevailing opinion inclines towards the former point of view.

(2) Criminal law sanctions

15.43 The punishment of infringements of copyright and neighbouring rights presumes that certain illegal actions will have been committed. The detailed definitions are contained in the Copyright Law.

(a) A criminal prosecution shall only be initiated on the demand of the injured party. Only intentional infringement is punishable. The penalty is imprisonment up to one year or a fine.
(b) The punishable actions may be prosecuted by injured parties by way of a private prosecution in the criminal courts. Public prosecutions will be brought by the public prosecutor only where they are in the public interest. The remittal of criminal prosecution to private prosecution in those cases where there is no public interest, which was effected by a statute of 1924, has had important consequences: the emphasis of legal protection has shifted to civil proceedings. Criminal penalties have become rare. This state of affairs is appropriate in as much as in the majority of cases the bringing of claims in the civil courts is a more suitable method: the injured party need not prove intent. Additionally, as distinct from criminal proceedings, gaps in the Law can be filled by analogous interpretation.

On the other hand, recent developments have shown that at least in cases of grave infringements, such as in the case of large scale piracy of phonograms, there is a need for prosecution by the public prosecutor. In this context, official proceedings have in recent times again been increasing in importance.

15.44 In the case of criminal prosecutions a distinction must be drawn between infringements of rights to use and infringements of the author's personality right.

(a) Punishable infringements are intentional acts of interference with the rights of authors, their successors in title and the owners of exclusive rights to use. Any person is punishable who, in cases other than those provided for by law, intentionally reproduces, distributes or publicly performs a work without the consent of the right owner.
(b) A protection of the author's personality right in criminal law only exists in two special cases for the protection of designation of authorship in the case of works of the visual arts. Both the attachment of a designation of authorship to the original of a work without the consent of the author, as well as the attachment of a designation of authorship to reproductions so as to pass them off as originals, are punishable.

15.45 In the case of an infringement of neighbouring rights, only acts of interference with exclusive exploitation rights are punishable; punishable acts are the unlawful reproduction, distribution and public performance of scientific editions, of posthumous works and of photographs, as well as use of the performances of performers which take place without the required consent. In the case of films, videograms and phonograms, as well as broadcasts, any use infringing the exclusive right of the producer or the broadcasting organisation is punishable.

15.46 A complaint may be filed with the public prosecutor's office, the police authorities and the district courts. Entitled to file the complaint is the injured party, not only the first owner of the right, but also the holder of an exclusive right granted to him.

15.47 Where the public prosecutor brings a public prosecution, the injured party may at any stage join the proceedings as a subsidiary prosecutor.

The injured party may, within the framework of the criminal proceedings, even where he is not involved as a private claimant or subsidiary prosecutor, by way of joinder proceedings make a proprietary claim arising from the criminal act, provided such claim has not yet become the subject of other legal proceedings. Where the accused is acquitted or where the claim for compensation of the proprietary damage appears to be unfounded, the criminal court will refrain from making a finding, leaving the injured party to assert the claim in civil proceedings.

Chapter 16
Italy

by Valerio de Sanctis and Vittorio de Sanctis

Copyright

(1) Origins of copyright law

16.01 It is said that even in Roman law, the rights of an author were protected by the 'actio iniuriarium aestimatoria' but it is certain that only after the invention of printing did the problem of unauthorised reproduction of works arise, a problem which was resolved in the first instance by giving privileges to publishers. The commonest examples of such privileges occur in the Venetian Republic, which by various enactments dating from 1516, granted a monopoly to printers. The Law of 1603 granted this exclusive right of sale for 20 years.

The first laws recognising authors' copyright arose from the reforms which followed the French Revolution and which were imported into Italy in the wake first of the Republican and then of the Napoleonic army. A Milan law of 30 November 1810 defined copyright as a 'right of property' capable of being inherited by the sons and the widow of an author for a period of 20 years after his death. Similarly, as regards musical and theatrical works, a Decree of the King of the Two Sicilies during the Napoleonic era (7 November 1811) entitled authors to claim damages for 'abusive use of the property of others' in the event of performances of their works taking place without their consent. Even after the Napoleonic era when the reaction to it had passed, the Italian states again took their inspiration from France in protecting copyright.

Upon the Unification of Italy, the problem was considered by the new national Parliament to which numerous Bills were submitted which finally resulted in the Law of 25 June 1865[1] which remained in force with few alterations until 1925.

The Law of 7 November 1925[2] and the decree putting it into effect[3] was without doubt the most advanced piece of legislation on copyright in the international field as it abolished all formalities connected with the acquisition of such right and increased the period for which it remained in force to 50 years after the death of the author.

Even more important was the recognition of the author's moral right, making provision for the protection of authorship, of the integrity of the work and the so-called right to repent.

These innovations made by the Italian Law found an echo during the Rome Conference for the revision of the Berne Convention in 1928.

The Austrian Law of 1936 was the first in Europe to recognise neighbouring rights and the present 1941 Italian Law[4] owes much to it.

The initiative for the 1941 Law came from the contemporaneous reform of the Civil Code, articles 2575 to 2583, which summarise the principles on which the protection of intellectual property rights is based.

[1] Law No 2337.
[2] No 1950 and amendments of 13 January 1927.

3   Royal Decree No 1369 of 15 July 1926.
4   22 April 1941, No 633.

(2) Post-1941 law

16.02   The 1941 Law has subsequently been amended by several decrees.

A decree enacted in the immediate post-war years[1] made alterations in particular to the duration of rights and formalities for the filing of foreign works with respect to the scheme of the 1941 Law, reflecting the principle of comparison of protections. This Decree provided for the protection of the works of foreign authors on conditions of simple reciprocity, subject only to international conventions.

Presidential Decree Law No 490 of 14 May 1974 altered Art. 79 of the Law by extending the rights of wireless broadcasting organisations to television broadcasts. This gave formal recognition to what was already judicial practice.

Law No 103 of 14 April 1975 instituted a system of permits for the installation of cable transmission relay stations for radio and television. This Law in fact provides that the permit holder shall be liable to the owner of the copyright in respect of works broadcast by him on radio and television.

The 1941 Law incorporates protective measures and penalties for the violation of copyright and a recent Law[2] has substantially increased the penalities for unauthorised duplication, reproduction, import, distribution and sales of phonograms.

Presidential Decree Law of 8 January 1979 introduced further changes of particular importance which arose from the ratification and implementation of the Paris Act (1971) of the Berne Convention. Article 2 of the Law was amended to include in the number of protected works, photographic works and the like.[3] Furthermore, with respect to the protection of photographic works, article 32 bis has been added to state that the duration of the right is 50 years from the date of the production. The same term has been granted to cinematographic works.

Article 20 of the Law protecting the author's personality has been amended to include among the author's moral rights, in addition to those of preventing any deformation, mutilation or other alteration to his works, the right to prevent 'any other act capable of damaging the work itself'.

1   Decree law No 82 of 23 August 1946.
2   No 406 of 29 July 1981.
3   Mere photographs, however, remain protected by the rights arising from Title II of the Law.

(3) The works

16.03   Law No 633 on Copyright and articles 2575-2583 of the Civil Code define as the subject matter of protection, 'intellectual works'.

In particular, the first article of the Law states that intellectual works, if they are to enjoy the protection of copyright, must be of a 'creative nature' and belong to 'literature, music, the graphic arts, architecture, theatre and cinematography'. This definition relates to the means of expression used by the author. The provisions of article 2 then define by way of example the literary, artistic and scientific 'genre' in terms almost identical to many other national laws and to the Berne Convention.[1] Article 1 of the Law completes the definition by stating that intellectual works are protected 'regardless of the method or form of expression'.

Copyright does not protect intellectual or material effort alone, however great, but does protect any external manifestation of the creative personality of the author, however modest (summaries, translations, creative digests) without having regard to its 'objective merit' or 'creative level'.

The position of works of art applied to industry is different as they, in accordance with Article 2, para 4 of the Law, are not protected by copyright when their artistic value cannot be separated from the industrial character of the product with which they are associated, but are protected by a special patent for ornamental models and designs governed by Royal Decree No 1411 of 25 August 1940.

1 Berne Convention art 2; see para 5.32 above.

(4) The creators of the works

16.04 The basis on which copyright is acquired is the creation of the work.[1] The problem of the authorship of the work and the copyright ownership becomes complicated where the act of creation is not the act of a single person, either because the work is the result of the intellectual creative effort of several persons, or because it is produced by a legal person. The question has been raised as to whether such a legal person can be regarded as an author. The received view subdivides intellectual works relating to their authors into three categories: simple works, composite works and collective works, the first expression being works created by a sole author, the second to designate works created by several authors, and the last to describe the works of one or more authors who organise and direct the creation of contributions made by other authors.

When several authors contribute to the realisation of a work, one talks of creative collaboration and it is of no importance whether their contributions are distinguishable to a greater or lesser degree provided that they are inseparable from the work which is the result of their united effort. Since copyright protects the personality of the individual only to the extent that he is the creator of a specific work and because therefore the protection of the personality of the author is identified both in fact and in law with the protection of the work, in the event of works produced in collaboration, the right must be exercised jointly by the co-authors. An unreasonable refusal by one co-author to agree to publication or alteration of the work can only be overcome by a Court Order.[2] The fact that the law views the co-authors as connected by a single personality is demonstrated by the term of protection of such works, which is calculated from the date of the death of the last surviving co-author.

Italian law uses the same rules to calculate the term of copyright also for works where distinct contributions are made, such as musical dramas, operettas, choreographic works and pantomimes, but rules for the exercise of the right are different, as these rules allow the individual co-authors to agree between themselves. However, in the absence of such agreement it is the author of the most relevant element who is granted, subject to some constraints, the management of the rights to the entire work.[3]

The Copyright Law[4] sets out separate rules for collective works that is those works where two classes of creative contribution can be distinguished, namely those contributing to the formation of the work as such (which may be one or more) and those involved in the creation of individual contributions (necessarily multifarious), so that the existence of a collective work appears conditional on its independence from the works and parts of works which form its contents. The most common examples of such works are newspapers, dictionaries, encyclopaedias and anthologies.

Legal writers are divided on whether a legal person can be regarded as an author, be it of works created within the ambit of the company, or works created within the ambit of employment by the company, or of a contract between the company and the author.

However, even those who would go along with the idea that commercial bodies can have rights of intellectual property over works created within their ambit do not thereby imply an indiscriminate extension of this doctrine to every work created within a business relationship. If there is no contribution of the legal entity which is expressed in the work, the copyright will vest in the individual creator even if the rights to use the work are acquired by the entity commissioning the work as soon as it is created, under an assignment or exclusive licence, by virtue of the contract of employment which governs the relation between the parties.

1 Art 6.
2 Art 10/3.
3 Arts 33-37.
4 Arts 38-43.

(5) The contents of copyright

16.05 It is often said that copyright constitutes a bundle of rights, as though the various rights of the author are independent from each other.

This distinction is based also on the literal arrangement of the special Law, which deals in two separate sections with the protection of the economic exploitation of the work, and the protection of the author's personality rights. The so-called dualistic concept is then in particular founded on the apparent distinction, in the structure and the rules, between moral and economic protection, with particular reference to the length for which the rights remain in force and their transferability.

The dualistic concept therefore governs the two fundamental aspects of the contents of copyright in different ways; the right to withhold publication as the main protection for the personality of the author, and the right of publication as the basis of all the author's exclusive rights in the utilisation of the work. The Law does not expressly speak of a right of non-publication[1] but gives the author the exclusive right to publish the work[2] which, being a positive aspect of the right of non-publication, must be considered to have the character of a personality right.

It is however to be borne in mind that the Law provides for transferability, albeit limited, of the right of utilisation and non-transferability, albeit subject to exceptions of moral rights. The duration of the first is measured in terms of the specific period which normally begins after the death of the author. The moral right is capable of being enforced after the death of the author without limitation as to time, but only by certain categories of heirs.

Transferability of copyright is a complex issue, with which we will deal in greater length below. Copyright in its totality is most certainly non-transferable, and the fact that the rights of utilisation of the work are transferable does not mean that they have a different legal nature. Rights of personality are by their nature inalienable. This is so to the extent necessary to protect the individual author not only from third parties but even from himself.

Finally, it should not be forgotten that the Law covers (a) the independence of the individual exclusive rights of utilisation,[3] and thereby enables the author to exercise any one of them independently of the others and to place precise limits on his right of non-publication, and (b) the right to withdraw the work from commercial use ('right to repent'),[4] by virtue of which serious moral objections are a basis for the termination of any contract transferring copyrights.

These and other limitative provisions concerning the transferability of rights[5] are further evidence of the non-proprietary nature of copyright considered as a whole, which however protects economic interests if it is in the moral interest of the author.

1   Except with respect to the criminal sanctions set out in the last para of art 171.
2   Art 12.
3   Art 19.
4   Art 142.
5   See for example the rules relating to publishing contracts, arts 118-135 of the special Law.

(6) The use of the work

16.06   In articles 13 and 18, the Copyright Law enumerates in detail the various rights of the author and in particular the exclusive right to reproduce the work by any means, the right to transcribe, the exclusive right to execute, represent or recite the work, the right to broadcast the work by any technical broadcasting method, the right to translate it into other languages and to elaborate, alter or transform the work into another literary and artistic form.

Finally, the author has the right to place a work in circulation for gain which relates to all methods of utilising the work, and includes the duty put on third parties to desist from engaging in acts prejudicial to the exclusive enjoyment of the financial rewards which may be drawn from the work.

The author of a work of plastic art created as a unique specimen must have access to the work even after its assignment to third parties if he wishes to exercise other rights which have not been assigned, for example, the right of reproduction.

The Copyright Law sets out specific rules for the protection of only some of these authors' rights which are on an especially moral nature, but which have immediate proprietary repercussions. For example, - article 20 of the Law protects works of plastic art, as with any other work, from alterations, but not, according to case-law, from destruction, which is an adjunct of the right of ownership.

Article 109 provides that the assignment of one or more copies of a work of plastic art does not involve transfer of the rights of utilisation, unless a mould, an engraved plate or any similar medium is also transferred.

Article 144 gives the author of works of plastic art (painting, sculpture, drawings etc) the right to a percentage, varying between 2% and 10% of the amount by which the price of the first *public* sale of the original copies of such works exceeds the price of first alienation.

It must be emphasised that financial enjoyment of the work is never exclusive to the author and his heirs-at-law in as much as it relates to the ideas, techniques and scientific principles which may be contained therein. After publication of the work these contents are within the public domain unless they are otherwise protected (industrial property). Equally, there is freely available to the public the aesthetic enjoyment of the work once published.

(7) Limits on copyright

(i) *The duration*
16.07   Temporal limits are not usually considered to be limits on copyright as most writers consider the limited duration to be inherent in the nature of copyright. It should, however, be noted that the right to publish the work in any one of its various forms, which is the fulcrum and the motor for all rights of utilisation, has no true temporal limit, being capable of being exercised at any time by the heirs or legatees of the author, and to the extent that such is

not prohibited, or made subject to special conditions, by the author himself, by virtue of a disposition inter vivos or mortis causa.

Italian law provides that the protection period shall run from the first exercise of the right of utilisation throughout the life of the author and for a period of 50 years after his death.

This general rule, however, is subject to numerous exceptions: Anonymous works and works written under a pseudonym are protected for 50 years from the date of publication unless the author reveals his identity before the end of the period either personally or through his heirs or through persons authorised by him in the manner laid down by article 28 of the Law.

Collective works including cinematographic works, are protected for 50 years from the date of first publication.[1]

1 Art 26/2.

(ii) *Personal use and free utilisation*

16.08 Articles 65 to 71 of the Law govern the 'free utilisation of intellectual works', and the textbooks for the most part consider that in this case the author's exclusive right is subject to a genuine legislative limit.

Copyright, however, understood as the law of paternity and the right to publish (or not to do so), is at no time affected by these provisions which are intrinsically connected with the structure of the right.

The limits refer to two separate requirements which justify the free reproduction of an otherwise protected work.

On the one hand, there is the personal consumption by the private user of a work, who to meet his personal needs or at most, the needs of his family circle, may reproduce copies, or perform and execute a protected work or extracts therefrom. Such reproduction includes reproductive means such as mechanical, magnetic or photographic reproduction provided they are not suitable for the sale or distribution of the work to the public.[1]

The concept of free personal use is widened to cover existing works in libraries when the reproduction is for personal use or library use.

On the other hand, there is the requirement of free discussion of ideas and of the contents of intellectual works which are the basis for the right to summarise, to quote, to reproduce extracts or parts of works for critical purposes and for the purposes of discussion or education.

Likewise, public information forms the basis for the right to reproduce items of news of an economic, political or religious nature published in magazines or newspapers, when also published in other magazines or newspapers, and when the author by failing to reserve the right to reproduce, has by implication given the work a public purpose.[2]

A similar justification exists for the reproduction in magazines and newspapers of discourses on political or administrative matters[3] and the free reproduction of works in legal or administrative procedures.[4]

1 Art 68.
2 Art 65.
3 Art 66.
4 Art 67.

(iii) *Compulsory licences*

16.09 Genuine limits, that is to say rules which curtail, though only partially, the exclusive copyright are the provisions of the special law which compel the author to grant a type of compulsory licence in favour of certain uses which are in the public interest. A case in point is the reproduction of extracts from published works for the purposes of anthologies or scholastic use.[1]

Another more important case in point is the right of a public body such as the Radio and Television Authority (RAI) to broadcast by radio and television works already performed by theatres, concert halls and other public places, for a remuneration paid to the author which in the event of disagreement between the parties can be determined by the Courts.[2]

Analogous in its structure is the right of a public commercial concern to relay radio broadcasts by loudspeaker, but again subject to a remuneration payable to the authors.[3]

Similar, on the other hand, to the right to reproduce the work for personal use, is the right of a broadcasting organisation to record the work on disc or tape or by similar means for the purpose of broadcasting it at a future time, for reasons of timetable or technical reasons, provided that after use the said recording is destroyed or rendered unserviceable.[4]

1 Art 70.
2 Arts 52–54.
3 Art 58.
4 Art 55, 'Ephemeral' recordings; see para 16.20 below.

(8) Transfer of rights of utilisation of intellectual works

16.10 Article 107 of the Copyright Law states that the rights of use belonging to authors of intellectual works may be transferred in any way and any form allowed by law.

Subsequent provisions reserve the right of the author to withdraw the work from commerce,[1] to alter it, even if printing or more generally reproduction has begun,[2] although subject to the payment of damages.

These rules, together with those in article 22 on the express inalienability of the moral right of the author, are a reflection of the non-transferability of copyright considered as a whole.

The enjoyment of financial rewards from the use of a work is however transferable either inter vivos or mortis causa, although subject to the above conditions, and subject to such other conditions as the law may impose.

In particular the Law provides as follows. Transfers inter vivos must be evidenced in writing;[3] a contract of assignment which purports to cover all the works, or categories of works, or works of a particular type, which the author may in future create without time limit is null and void.[4]

Transfers of copyright cannot include future rights which may be conferred by later laws;[5] the assignment of one or more copies of a work does not constitute, unless otherwise agreed, a transfer of the rights relating to use.

In more general terms, since in accordance with article 19 the utilisation rights are independent of each other, transfers relating thereto take effect to the extent indicated by the person entitled, there remaining available to him all such rights as have not expressly been transferred.

The work itself as opposed to copies of the work, until published and to the extent that it belongs personally to the author, may not be charged or pledged or taken in distraint or expropriated in the interest of the state.[6]

The author of the work, even after the assignment of particular utilisation rights, retains a legal interest in their safeguard and for such purpose he is given inter alia the right to take part in legal proceedings brought by the assignee to protect the rights.[7]

Within the wide and comprehensive wording of article 107 may be included all types of transfer of the right and of each independent right in the work, including even the disposal of the work as such and the disposal of the various utilisation rights.

The law distinguishes between transfers of rights for the purpose of distribution and transfers which are not for such a purpose. Whilst the first category is covered by the Law which expressly deals with the most important transfers, ie the publishing contract for printed works and those for performance and representation,[8] the second are not, except from the reference to them in article 107. Case law and writers are agreed that in copyright assignments in the case of doubt, the intention to disseminate the work must always be presumed.

1 Arts 142–143.
2 Art 129.
3 Art 110.
4 Art 120 No 1.
5 Art 119 No 3.
6 Arts 111, 112.
7 Art 165.
8 Arts 118–141.

(9) Copyright contracts

16.11 We will now examine in greater detail contracts most commonly made by authors for the management and distribution of their works. The Law specifically deals with two types of contract: publishing, and public performance, and further provides for the collective management of copyright through the 'Societa Italiana degli Autori ed Editori' (SIAE).

Under article 180 the SIAE has the exclusive right in Italy and abroad to act as an intermediary for the safeguarding of the rights of performance, execution, recital, radio-broadcasting, and mechanical and cinematographical reproduction of literary theatrical and musical works, as well as exercising other duties for the protection of intellectual property pursuant to its statutes. The SIAE therefore, having a legal monopoly, acts for the authors as intermediary for the receipt of royalties and for their distribution between the persons entitled to them. For this purpose SIAE enters into contracts with various categories of users of works, those of the greatest importance being those with the radio and television authorities (with RAI-TV and now with private broadcasters) and with phonogram producers.

The publishing contract is a typical contract which all copyright contracts follow because it is the one which the law governs in most detail, also because its numerous rules are applicable to all transactions for the transfer of the copyright.[1]

The publishing contract whereby the author grants a publisher the right to publish the work by printing it at his own cost and for his own account. The contract can be 'per edition', that is to say granting the publisher the right to publish one or more impressions for twenty years or 'on terms' whereby the publisher is bound to print a certain number of copies per impression but is at liberty as regards the number of impressions which he considers necessary to publish within the period, which may not however exceed 20 years.

The publisher must publish the work within the period agreed in the contract, which may not exceed a period of two years from delivery of the completed work to the publisher.

The remuneration paid to the author is either a share of the receipts which is the rule, or a fixed price. The latter type of contract can be used only in respect of certain categories of works.[2]

Contracts for public performance are also governed by the Law (articles 136 to 141). They are contracts by which the author assigns the right to publicly perform a dramatic work, musical drama, choreography, pantomime or any other work destined to be performed, including cinematographical and radio and television works. The rules concerning such contracts are based in part on the publishing contract and in part on the general provisions for the protection of the integrity of the work.

1 See in particular the rules of arts 119, 120, 121.
2 Dictionaries, encyclopaedias, anthologies and other collaborative works, translations, newspaper and magazine articles, discourses or conferences, scientific works, cartographical works, musical works or musical drama, works of figurative art.

(10) Notification of works and of transfers

16.12 The protection of works against unauthorised use by third parties caused the legislator as early as 1925 to institute a general system of public notification for all intellectual rights, the owners of which are obliged upon publication to deposit and register at the Office of Literary, Artistic and Scientific Property which is attached to the Under-Secretariat of the Presidency of the Council. Transfers inter vivos or mortis causa which refer to deposited works may also be notified. This form of public notification is of a merely declaratory nature and the only consequence of failure to comply is the payment of a fine.

Foreign authors are not subject to this filing requirement. The purpose of the public notification is to create a presumption, in the absence of evidence to the contrary, of the existence of the work and its publication and a presumption of priority in respect of an act of transfer of an earlier date.

Neighbouring rights

(1) General concepts, legislative sources and points of contact with 'copyright'

16.13 The 1925 Copyright Law[1] was the forerunner of the Law of 1941[2] which is still in force. The former did not include specific protection for neighbouring rights. However, provisions as to photographs, rights to correspondence and portraits, rights in respect of engineering drawings, the title of the work, articles and news, were included.

The rights of performers, albeit only within the field of broadcasting, were already regulated by the 1925 Law on broadcasting. Protection was also accorded to radio broadcasts but only on the basis of penal provisions.

It is said that the 1941 Law drew its inspiration for the protection of neighbouring rights from the 1936 Austrian Law.[3]

The 1941 Law lays down in Part I, 'Provisions relating to copyright', and in Part II, 'Provisions concerning rights connected with the exercise of copyright', in Part III, 'Common provisions' and in Part VI, 'Field of application of the law'.[4]

Provisions relating to copyright are also to be found in Chapter V of the Civil Code under title IX which deals with 'rights in respect of works of the intellect and industrial inventions'. Amongst these provisions, reference is made to the rights of performers[5] and to drawings for engineering under the title of 'related rights'.[6] A number of general principles of copyright, which formerly appeared under 'Property', are in the present Civil Code in the Chapter entitled 'Labour'.[7]

With regard to copyright, article 2576 of the Civil Code provides that: 'The originating basis for the acquisition of authors rights is the creation of a work as a particular expression of intellectual effort'.

1 Law No 1950 of 7 November 1925.
2 Law No 623 of 22 April 1941.
3 See para 13.01 above.
4 Part IV deals with 'Domain public payant' and Part V with collecting societies.
5 Art 2579 of the Civil Code.
6 Art 2578.
7 In addition to the general principles of copyright and industrial inventions there are provisions on 'business' (arts 2555-2568) and on 'competition' (art 2598) as these subjects are closely connected with copyright and, in particular, 'related rights'.

16.14 The related rights, governed by the Law of 1941 include neighbouring rights, that is the rights of producers of phonograms, performers and broadcasting organisations. Protection under this head is also granted to authors of sketches for theatrical scenes; photographs; written correspondence; portraits; engineering drawings. Titles, headings and the external appearance of a work; newspaper articles and news receive protection by virtue of the prohibition of certain acts of unfair competition.

The principles upon which these related rights are based are diverse, as are the grounds justifying their protection. Some are properly described as copyright (protection of the title, headings, external appearance of the work, articles, news and certain acts of unfair competition). Others have only a de facto connection since an author of a work in the exercise of his right may find himself confronted by competing or parallel rights relating to other types of subject-matter which are also regulated in the Copyright Statute. This arrangement is made in order to avoid conflicts between the various categories of rights such as the rights of producers of phonograms, rights of performers, rights of broadcasting organisations and copyright as there may be competing interests arising out of their co-existence in a single object.

On the other hand, performances could also be regarded as intermediate links between the author's work and the public in the same way as printing is a link between a book and the public. Some rights relate to works which are on the borderline between intellectual creations and industrial productions (photographs, drawings of theatrical scenes, engineering drawings); finally, other rights (those relating to written correspondence and portraits) may be called rights bordering on copyright, ie rights which are not even allied to copyright and are of a personal nature, which may be infringed by the exercise of copyright. Consequently the owners of such rights, are entitled to either grant or refuse permission for their use.

Certain related rights, despite the description given to them by the legislation, may also, in fact, have no connection with protected intellectual work, at least from the economic and structural point of view. Works with no artistic character such as letters and works of a like nature, are certainly alien to copyright, although they may constitute the subject-matter of a related right. Under the Italian legal system the rights of performers, producers of phonograms, broadcasting organisations may be referred to as neighbouring rights, that is, rights related to or neighbouring upon copyright. However, they are specific rights and classified as such in Italian law.

There have been numerous amendments to the Law of 1941. The enactments which have implemented these amendments are nearly all concerned with related rights.

Provisions applicable equally to copyright and to related rights are contained in the Law of 1941, particularly in the chapter relating to 'free use':[1] that is use for which no consent of the right owners is necessary, generally for social or cultural reasons, nor does such use give any right to equitable remuneration. The provisions as to free use, enacted essentially for copyright, are extended, where possible, to many of the related rights, by analogy. Other common provisions are those relating to fulfilment of requirements of an administrative nature, such as those relating to sanctions. A Public Register is kept by the Office of the President of the Council of Ministers, the Intellectual Property Office, whilst the Special Register for cinematographic works is kept by the 'Società Italiana Autori ed Editori' (SIAE). Registration is conclusive evidence of the existence of the work or of the product, and of its publication (article 103).

1 Chapter V, arts 65–71.

16.15 In Italian law, no definitions are given of the notions of use 'in public', use 'in private' and 'personal use'. 'Use in private' as opposed to use in public indicates use within the confines of one's own home or business undertaking and for the purposes of that undertaking. 'Personal use', however, is use in pursuit of enjoyment, use only on an individual basis. Although they are two distinct concepts, use in private and personal use sometimes coincide, in that personal use of a work generally takes place in private.

However, use in private is a concept of fundamental importance in relation to those kinds of use which the Law limits exclusively to 'public' use, that is, the right of performance, presentation or recitation of a work. As regards the right of reproduction, it is only personal use, not private use, which is of legal importance. For this reason, personal use[1] is limited to reproduction not suitable for circulation among the public (as for example copying by hand). However, by express legal provisions,[2] the sale of such copies to the public is prohibited, as is in general any use competing with the author's rights to use.

With the numerous technical advances, such as videograms, the distinction between 'personal' and 'private' use has taken on an importance not envisaged by the framers of the 1941 Law.

The infringement of copyright and of a number of related rights is not only a tort, but in many cases a crime[3] subject, by virtue of the same Law, to specific penal sanctions.

1 Art 68.
2 Art 68, last para.
3 Arts 171–174.

(2) **Rights of performers**

16.16 In the Civil Code, in the chapter entitled 'Labour', the rights of performers are placed alongside copyright proper although a performer's right is only a right to equitable remuneration. Italian law does not give the performer an exclusive right of reproduction, or of diffusion of his interpretation or performance. However, his right is effective erga omnes and therefore can be enforced, analogously with rights in rem, even when there is no contractual relationship. The right to equitable remuneration therefore does not derive from any employment contract but from law. Equitable remuneration, to be paid by a non-contracting third party, does not take the form of compensation for damages for reproduction by the user of the performer's performance without the latter's consent, as would be the case if there was an exclusive right. On the contrary, it must be regarded as a means of paying the performer in relation to the profit which the third party in question has obtained from the performance. Where there is no contractual relationship and, in the absence of effective administrative rules, determination of the equitable remuneration is, in the event of disagreement between the parties, made by the courts. This is also the case when the sound-track of a film is reproduced on a disc without the consent of the conductor of the orchestra.[1]

The performer's moral right, is recognised as a personal right in Article 20 of the 1941 Law, a right to his name and a right to respect of his performance.

The 1941 Law, in the Chapter on 'related rights', provides as follows:

> 'Artists who act or interpret dramatic or literary works, as well as artists who perform musical works or compositions, even if such works or compositions are in the public domain, shall, independently of any remuneration in respect of their acting, interpretation, or performance, have the right to equitable remuneration from any person who diffuses or transmits by broadcasting, telephony or like means, or who engraves, records or reproduces in any manner, upon a phonograph record, cinematographic film or other like contrivance, their acting, interpretation or performance.
>
> A like right shall belong to them in relation to any person who by similar means, subsequently diffuses or reproduces the work already diffused, transmitted, engraved, recorded, or reproduced within the meaning of the preceding paragraph.
>
> This right shall not apply where the citation or performance is given for the purpose of such broadcasting, telephony, cinematography, engraving or recording upon the mechanical contrivances indicated above, and remuneration is paid therefor.
>
> Likewise, no remuneration shall be due in the case of a recording upon records, metal tape or any other similar means, within the provisions of Articles 55 and 59.'[2]

As regards the protection of moral rights, the Law provides that 'Artists who act, interpret or perform shall be entitled to oppose any diffusion, transmission or reproduction of their recitation or performance which might be prejudicial to their honour or reputation'.[3]

Besides these particular provisions the performers may also rely on the general rules of the Civil Code[4] to protect his right to his name, pseudonym and image. Any protection of the so-called 'stage mask', or the 'style' of the performer, must be sought in the provisions of the general law.

1 Court of Rome, 9 July 1977, *Vitali-Ortolani v Soc EMI Italiana*.
2 Art 80.
3 Art 81.
4 Arts 7, 8, 9, 10.

16.17 Presidential Decree No 490 of 1974, promulgated to implement Italy's ratification of the Roman Convention (1961)[1] recognised that performers themselves should have a share in the payment which the producer of phonograms may claim for use of the phonogram on which their performance is recorded.[2] However, even before Decree No 490 of 1974 where there was secondary use of a performance in a broadcast programme, it had been held that the performer was entitled to equitable remuneration, in addition to his moral right to his name.[3]

Performers, vested with the right to equitable remuneration are defined as '1) persons who, in [the performance of] any dramatic, literary or musical work or composition, play an important artistic part, even if subsidiary to the leading performers; 2) the conductors of an orchestra or choir; 3) entire orchestras or choirs, provided that the orchestral or choral part [of the performance] has artistic value in itself and is not a mere accompaniment'.[4]

The performers' have a right 'to have their names indicated in the diffusion or transmission of their recitation or performance and applied in an indelible manner to any phonograph record, cinematographic film or other like contrivance'.[5] The right is restricted to performers who play the leading roles in the dramatic, literary or musical work or composition.

The performer's right is protected for 20 years from the date of the recital, presentation or performance.

By virtue of article 25 of the General Regulations, the determination and appointment of the payment is made by the parties in accordance with collective agreements. Only where such collective agreements do not exist, and failing agreement between the parties, does article 25 of the regulations refer determination of the payment to administrative bodies. However, this administrative procedure has not been invoked so far.

In Italy a performance must always be paid for according to the principles of labour law. This general principle of labour law has various effects on the exercise of the right and its protection. The term of 20 years relates only to the legal right to equitable remuneration, whereas the duration of any right to participate in proceeds in respect of a 'primary' performance is based on the principle of contractual freedom.

There are no specific penal rules protecting the rights in question; there are, however, obviously, the general rules of the criminal law where they are applicable.

1   See chapter 8, above.
2   This is known as 'secondary use' – article 12 of the Rome Convention; see para 8.26 above.
3   Milan Court, *Petrella v Cetra-Loria Records and Others*, 4 October 1952.
4   Art 82.
6   Art 83.

(3) Rights of producers of phonograms

16.18   Having regard to the many modifications made to the Law of 1941, by subsequent legislation connected with the ratification and implementation by Italy of the Rome Convention (1961) and subsequently the Geneva Convention (1971),[1] the law relating to phonogram producers is best explained not by reference to the original text and amendments, but by a summary of the essential outlines of the protection of phonograms by way of neighbouring rights.

It should be remembered that, under the Italian system, the basis for protection of phonograms is not the principle of intellectual creation, but factors of an industrial, technical and artistic nature. However, the phonogram is also subject to the general discipline of the provisions of the Civil Code and other special laws, as a commercial product.

The fundamental principle of protection of the phonogram is laid down in the Law as a neighbouring right: 'Without prejudice to the rights belonging to the author under the provisions of the preceding Part, the producer of a phonograph record or like contrivance for reproducing sounds or voices shall have the exclusive right, for the term and subject to the conditions specified in the following articles, to reproduce by any process of duplication the record or contrivance which he has produced, and to put it into commercial circulation.'[2]

The exclusive right under this article is restricted to a simple right to equitable remuneration 'for the utilisation for profit', of the phonogram in broadcasting, cinematography, television, public dance festivals and public performances.[3] The phonogram producers' right can be transferred inter vivos or mortis causa; in the case of any commercial enterprise the right may therefore be maintained regardless of any change in the form of the enterprise. No remuneration is payable for use 'for instructional or propaganda purposes by the State administration or by institutions authorised by the State for such purposes.'[4]

The level of the equitable remuneration payable by a party who uses a phonogram with a view to profit, in accordance with the article mentioned above, is determined by administrative procedures. However, since the tariff system is only applied in the absence of any agreement between the parties, in effect both the level of the remuneration, and the procedures for collecting it, are established between the parties themselves, by collective agreement.

In accordance with article 74, the producer is entitled to oppose any use of the phonogram which is likely seriously to prejudice his commercial interests. The administrative remedy,[5] which can be invoked by either of the parties, is by proceedings before a panel of experts. The right in question is a kind of moral right but one which rests essentially on commercial interests.

The original wording of article 76, which has remained unchanged, provides that copies of a phonogram may not be put on the market unless the particulars laid down by article 62 are indelibly imposed on the phonogram. They are: the title of the work reproduced, the name of the author, the name of the performer, (orchestral or choral groups to be indicated by their customary name) and the date of production.

The moral right of the author of the work reproduced in the phonogram must be respected, but without prejudice to the lawfulness of modifications to the work rendered necessary by technical recording requirements. The exclusive right to public performance of music or of words and music embodied in a phonogram is vested, originally, in the author of the work. The right can be transferred, wholly or in part.

The original wording of the Law of 1941 made protection of phonograms dependent upon deposit of a copy of the phonogram at the appropriate offices of the Department of the President of the Council of Ministers. The amending Law,[6] following the provisions of the Rome Convention, provided that the deposit formalities are deemed to have been satisfied if, on all the copies of the phonogram the symbol ⓟ appeared in permanent form, together with the year date of first publication.

The term of the right in a phonogram is 30 years from deposit and not more than 40 years from the date of production of the original phonogram. If the deposit is not made, the duration is 30 years from the date of production.

Article 171 sets out offences which may be committed in relation to phonograms. Article 171(e) provides 'Any person who reproduces, by any process of multiplication, records or other like contrivances, or sells same, or introduces reproductions produced abroad in this way into the territory of the State, is liable to a fine and also to imprisonment'. The increase in the penalty by the Decree of 1976, followed by the recent Law No 406 of 29 July 1981 specifically intended to stop the trade in unauthorised reproductions of phonograms, is the result of the struggle, in Italy and elsewhere, against the 'piracy' of phonograms which has, particularly in recent years, increased both in Italy and internationally. Legal remedies against piracy are also part of Italy's obligations under the Phonogram Convention (1971).[7]

1   Decree No 490 of 14 May 1974 and Decree No 404 of 5 May 1976.
2   Art 72.
3   Art 73.
4   Art 73(3).
5   Arts 24 and 28 of the General Regulations.
6   Decree No 404 of 1976.
7   See chapter 9, above.

16.19 There have been a number of recent prosecutions under the penal provisions. These have concerned the unlawful reproduction and forgery of identifying marks on music-cassettes.[1] An attempt to improve the protection of phonograms against unlawful reproduction was made by an agreement entered into between the Italian phonogram producers and the 'Societa Italiana Autori ed Editori' (SIAE) whereby the mark 'SIAE' is placed on the phonogram. The unauthorised copying of this mark constitutes forgery which carries heavier penalties. Unfortunately, this mark too is being forged in the unlawful reproductions.[2]

To date, no legal amendment has been made to the provisions which govern the freedom of personal or private use. Therefore, in the face of the ever-increasing use of modern technology for the reproduction of works, in particular musical compositions, the liberty of the individual to copy is restricted only in so far as sale of such copies to the public is concerned and, in general, any use which conflicts with the author's right is unlawful.

1 Court of Palermo, 27 September 1979, *Impresa Benfanti and others;* Court of Genoa, 24 April 1980, *Impresa Amato Nunzio and others;* Court of Naples, 27 May 1980, *Impresa Colucci e Brancaccio;* 'Pretura' of Florence, 19 May 1980, *Impresa Menicatti.*
2 More than 1000 criminal complaints laid before the courts for piracy of phonograms were cancelled by the 1978 General Amnesty Law.

(4) The rights of broadcasting organisations

16.20 The Law provides that:

'Without prejudice to the rights granted by this Law in favour of authors, producers of phonograph records and like contrivances, and of actors, the organisation carrying on the broadcast service shall have the exclusive right: (1) to re-transmit the broadcast emission, by wire or by radio; (2) to record, with gainful intent, upon phonograph records or like contrivances for the reproduction of sounds or voices the transmitted or re-transmitted broadcast emission – (3) to utilise the records or contrivances referred to in the preceding sub-paragraph for new transmissions, re-transmissions or for new recordings'.[1]

Law No 490 of 1974 then made it clear that these rights extend to television.

It is important first to set out the structure of broadcasting in Italy. Firstly, 'RAI – Radiotelevisione Italiana S.p.a.', a private company with state participation, provides the public service of broadcasting on a monopoly basis, as concessionaire of the state. The state monopoly is sanctioned by the Consolidating Law.[2] However, the Constitutional Court, on a reference from the lower courts, pronounced in two judgments[3] on some matters of a constitutional importance in respect of the activity of broadcasting in Italy. In these decisions, the Court declared that the state monopoly of public service broadcasting does not conflict with the Constitution. These judgments and Decree No 103 of 14 April 1975 made it possible to uphold the principle that the State monopoly operates only at national level, whilst the setting up of private radio and television transmitters at local level is permitted. Having regard however to the limitation (not, in fact, all that much limited) of channels reserved for Italy, it is not easy to implement such a principle strictly.

Originally, it had been held that private transmitters without proper concessions or authorisations were unlawful. However, a recent judgment of the Supreme Court affirmed that where the state administration allocates broadcasting channels to a private transmitter, an administrative authorisation or concession is implied. This new legal, and above all de facto situation of recent years, has also raised other problems, in particular regarding the applicability to such private transmitters of numerous legal provisions, including those contained in articles 52-60 of the 1941 Law, under the title 'Broadcast Works'.

These special provisions are supported by a preamble in article 51 of the same Law under the title relating to 'copyright' and linked to article 16 of the same Law which grants 'the exclusive right of diffusion': 'By reason of the nature and purpose of broadcasting as a service reserved to the State, which carries on such service either directly or by means of concession, the exclusive right of broadcasting, either directly or by any intermediate means, shall be regulated by the following special provisions'. The limitations on the author's exclusive right, contained in these articles, are due essentially to the social and cultural aspects of public service broadcasting.

'Ephemeral recordings'[4] are dealt with 'without prejudice to the rights of the author in connection with the broadcasting of his work, the organisation carrying on the broadcasting service is authorised to record the said work upon a record or metal tape or by some analogous process, for the purpose of its deferred broadcast, when this is necessitated by considerations of time or technology, provided that after its use, the said recording is destroyed or rendered unusable.'[5] Article 5 of the General Regulations deals with the exercise of such a right by the broadcasting organisation. The deferred broadcasting of a recorded work, unless otherwise agreed by the parties, shall be deemed to have been agreed to for a period of 15 days.

The rights of broadcasting organisations are also protected by criminal law. In particular, anyone who retransmits by cable or by wireless or records transmissions or retransmissions of broadcasts on phonograms and sells or markets recorded phonograms unlawfully made is liable to a fine.

There are no domestic provisions dealing with satellite broadcasts.

1 Art 79 of the Law of 1941.
2 Royal Decree No 645 of 27 February 1936.
3 Judgments No 225 and 226 of 1974.
4 See para 5.22 and Cf Rome Convention, Art 15/1(c); see para 8.42 above.
5 Art 55.

(5) Rights in respect of photographs

16.21 In the 1925 Law photographs were protected as copyright works. By the law of 1941, the protection of photographs 'slipped' wholly into title II devoted specifically to related rights. This transposition of the protection of photographs from the chapter on copyright proper to that on related rights was due essentially to the consideration that in photographs the technical factor usually outweighs the creative factor. Moreover, in 1941, no difficulty from the point of view of international commitments prevented such a transfer of protection.

However, photographs which reproduced works of figurative or architectural art of conspicuous artistic value enjoyed longer protection under the original wording of the 1941 Law, on the condition that a reservation was indicated on the photograph. It was therefore, essentially, a question of 'classification'. However, reform of the whole subject of photographs was ripe for implementation and when Italy implemented the Paris Act of the Berne Convention (1971), the 1941 Law was substantially amended. The 'photographic work' was distinguished from the 'mere photograph'. Photographs of writing, documents, business letters, technical drawings and similar products are in no way protected by the Law of 1941.

'Photographic works and those produced by an analogous procedure' whose protection was transferred from the chapter on related rights to the chapter on copyright, thus being added to the various categories of works of the intellect listed in article 2 of the Law, are therefore now also protected as far as the moral right of the photographer is concerned.

The duration of protection of the right to use a photographic work, having been thus brought into line with the general term for copyright, is fixed at 50 years from the year of production of the work. However, the Decree of 1979 left open a number of questions and some of the old case law may therefore still apply. Difficulties may also arise in distinguishing between a 'photographic work' and a 'mere photograph'.

'Pictures of persons or of aspects, elements or events of natural or social life, obtained by photographic or analogous processes, including reproductions of works of graphic art and stills of films, shall be considered to be photographs.'[1] The photographs protected by related rights are thus 'static' productions, even if they are 'in series'. Productions of photographs 'in movement' on the other hand fall within the protection of works in the strict sense as cinematographic or television films or videograms. The photographer has an 'exclusive right of reproduction, diffusion and circulation' of the photograph.[2] A simple presumption of assignment of the rights in the photograph applies in the case of assignment of the negative.[3]

The exclusive right in photographs which are commissioned or made in the course of an employment relationship is not vested in the photographer but in the commissioning party or the employer.[4] In these cases, the photographer is entitled to an equitable remuneration which may consist, in the latter case, of the salary paid to him for that purpose.

Finally, a right to equitable remuneration also arises in respect of reproductions of photographs for anthologies for scholastic use, and in scientific and educational works.

In general, the tariff system referred to by the Law of 1941, for the exercise of the right to remuneration, has either not been implemented or has been superseded by direct agreements between the parties, or through trade associations or by the courts in judgments in private disputes. What is important is that a person entitled to equitable remuneration cannot exercise an exclusive right and thereby forbid reproductions without consent. But even that principle is not always followed in court decisions.

Copies of photographs must bear, even if in abbreviated form, an indication of the name of the photographer or of the employer or person who commissioned it, and the date and year of production of the photograph.[5] Where copies do not bear these particulars, reproduction of the photograph is not considered an infringement. However, the formalities mentioned above are now limited to 'mere photographs' and do not affect 'photographic works', thus resolving a number of problems which arose in the past regarding possible infringement of the principle laid down by the Copyright Conventions; of protection of copyright without formalities. The duration of protection for 'mere photographs' is 20 years from production of the photograph.[6]

1   Art 87.
2   Art 88.
3   Art 89.
4   Arts 88 and 91.
5   Art 90 of the Law and art 9 of the Regulations.
6   Art 92, 1st para.

16.22 Following ratification by Italy (1953) of the Brussels Act of the Berne Convention (1948) which included photographic works in article 2 among 'works', only international situations covered by the convention had the benefit of the rules relating to copyright because the rule had not been carried over into the wording of domestic law, until this was done by a Decree of 1979.[1] However, a number of judgments,[2] both at first instance and in the Supreme Court, had already recognised, on the basis of general principle, an author's moral right in respect of artistic photographs, even in purely national situations. Support for the general principle within the framework of protection of works originating in a country outside the Berne Union had been given by the Constitutional Court.[3]

The Constitutional Court, rejecting the objection of unconstitutionality raised by the Milan Court, affirmed that the legal provisions which do not grant an Italian photographer the moral right referred to by articles 20 ff of the Law and 6 bis of the Berne Convention, do not conflict with the principle of equality in article 3 of the Constitution.

1   Delegated Decree No 19 of 8 January 1979 (published on 30 January 1979).
2   Judgment of the Supreme Court, No 1440 of 16 April 1975, and the judgment of the Court of Milan of 8 January 1979, which immediately preceded the publication of the Decree.
3   Judgment No 48 of 15 March 1972 in respect of an order by the Court of Milan of 19 January 1970.

(6) Rights relating to sketches of theatrical scenes, engineering drawings to written correspondence and portraits, the title, headings, and external aspect of works, newspaper articles and news. Prohibition on some acts of unfair competition

16.23 The rights relating to sketches of theatrical scenes, engineering drawings, written correspondence and portraits, the title, headings and external aspect of works, newspaper articles and news are variously described as 'related rights' in the 1941 Law. They are grouped in this way because they are really all specific examples of the law on related rights.

A number of these rights appear to be obsolete, in particular sketches of theatrical scenes and, although to a lesser extent, drawings for engineering. The former is largely governed by copyright in the strict sense, and the latter by industrial property rights.

The group of rights in written correspondence;[1] rights relating to portraits;[2] protection of the title, headings, external aspect of works as well as newspaper articles and news – prohibition on certain acts of unfair competition,[3] are rights of a diverse nature, and have been the subject of legal literature and numerous decided cases.

1   Arts 93–95.
2   Arts 96–98.
3   Arts 100–102.

16.24 The protection of sketches of theatrical scenes is limited to a right to equitable remuneration which is analogous in certain aspects, to the right of performers. The right to equitable remuneration for the use by other theatres may be exercised for a period of five years starting from the first public use of such a product of a technical and artistic nature. The short duration of the period of protection, and above all the specific denial that they are works of the intellect, explains why authors of productions of this kind have not attempted to avail themselves of such special protection. A further reason is that they can invoke in certain cases the Law on industrial drawings and models.[1]

1   Law No 1411 of 25 August 1940, amended by Decree No 338 of 22 June 1979.

16.25 The producer of drawings for engineering and similar works, which constitute original solutions for technical problems, has not only an exclusive right of reproduction of the plans and drawings for the projects in question, but also a right to equitable remuneration from those who carry the project into effect with a view to profit without the consent of the author. To exercise this right, the author must place on the plan or drawing a declaration of reservation and register it in accordance with the specific rules of article 11 of the General Regulations. The right lasts for 20 years from the time of registration of the project in question. This right has been incorporated in the Civil Code, article 2578.

The judgments in this area show how this legal institution has been misunderstood and misinterpreted by the courts and by the interested parties themselves. In fact, there has sometimes been confusion between protection of copyright in the strict sense, related rights, and protection of industrial patents, thus not attributing to this entitlement to equitable remuneration a precise meaning of its own.

The Supreme Court held,[1] that 'the original solutions of technical problems referred to by Article 2578 of the Civil Code and 99 of the Copyright Law are to be regarded as deriving from the application of new principles or technical rules, or the application of pre-existing principles and rules, marked by ingenuity, and conceived with creative character'.

1   Case No 1678 of 3 July 1968.

16.26 In the Law of 1925 rights in respect of written correspondence and portraits were part of copyright. The Law of 1941[1] lays down detailed rules as to the duties of a person wishing to use in a publication letters, family and personal memoirs of a confidential character or those which refer to the intimacy of private life. Such publications are not allowed without the authorisation of the author and of the addressee or of specified categories of their descendants or ascendants. Similar detailed provisions are laid down regarding portraits, including photographic portraits.[2] In particular, consent is not necessary if the portrait sitter is a famous person, or because of judicial or police requirements, or if reproduction is connected with events of public interest.

1   Art 93.
2   Arts 96–98.

16.27 There is no copyright in the title and the permanent headings of certain publications including journals. The grounds of their protection are to be found, under the 1941 Law in their individualising function, which is analogous to that of distinctive industrial symbols in general, including trade marks. The title and permanent headings are protected only where they individualise the work, and do not therefore extend to a prohibition on works of a kind and character so different as to exclude any possibility of confusion.[1] The title of a newspaper cannot be reproduced unless two years have expired since publication of the paper ceased. In *Agostini v Titanus*[2] an order was made restraining publication of the title of a film which reproduced a similar title of a literary work.

Certain acts are regarded as unfair competition and are therefore prohibited by the Law of 1941: reproduction of articles and news contrary to fair practice in journalism,[3] and 'reproduction of headings, emblems, ornamentations, arrangements of printing signs' and other features of the external aspect of a work.[4]

The Law provides that reproduction of newspaper articles and news is lawful, provided that it is not effected by acts contrary to fair journalistic practice, and provided that the sources are quoted. Systematic reproduction, with a view to profit, of published or broadcast information or news is regarded as an unlawful act. Journalistic copyright in the field of related rights is closely linked to general constitutional principles,[5] in particular to the Press Law of 8 February 1948, No 47. Newspapers are in the same position as radio, television and cinema news programmes for which there are special provisions.

Neither the Copyright Law nor the law on related rights contains any provisions on computers and data storage and retrieval systems.[6]

1 Art 100.
2 Judgment given by the Rome 'Pretore' of 27 July 1979. See also judgment of the Supreme Court, No 2702 of 14 July 1976, *Societa SIEM v fratelli Crespi*.
3 Art 101.
4 Art 102.
5 Art 21.
6 See para 12.21 above.

Chapter 17
Scandinavia

by Agne Henry Olsson

1. History and development of copyright in the Nordic countries

17.01 Copyright is an ancient concept in the Nordic countries. In fact, one of the first copyright laws of the world was enacted in Denmark when the system of privileges was replaced in 1741 by a regulation under which reprinting of books was prohibited without the consent of the publisher. As in many other European countries, the gradual development brought about an acknowledgment of the independent right of the author in his work. When the first law on the protection of works of art was enacted in Denmark in 1837, protection was granted to the artist himself.

The development was more or less the same in the other Nordic countries, where the system of privileges was replaced by legislation granting rights in works to the publishers and later on this protection was gradually extended to the creators – authors, artists, composers – themselves. For example, in Sweden authors' rights were recognised for the first time in the Freedom of the Press Act of 1810, where it was stated that all printed matters were the property of their authors or successors in title. During the nineteenth century and the first decades of the twentieth century, a continuous development took place which resulted in recognition of authors' rights in more and more areas, for example the right in public performance and moral rights.

Another important development was that the five Nordic countries (Denmark, Finland, Iceland, Norway and Sweden) started to co-operate in this field. During the 1930s, formal deliberations took place between representatives of the five countries on the possibilities of harmonising the copyright laws. The result was that, at the end of the 1930s, committees for the revision of the copyright laws were appointed in Denmark, Finland, Norway and Sweden. Iceland participated in this revision process in an observer capacity. During the 1950s the Committees submitted to their governments proposals for nearly identical new copyright laws. After extensive hearings of all interested circles, new copyright laws were enacted in most of the Nordic countries at the beginning of the 1960s. The Swedish legislation was enacted in 1960[1] and during the following year corresponding legislation was enacted in Denmark,[2] Finland,[3] and Norway.[4] In Iceland a new law on copyright entered into force in 1972.[5]

The copyright legislation of the Nordic countries constitutes a remarkable example of successful regional co-operation. It was also a pioneer work in the sense that the Acts contained – before the Rome Convention was established – provisions on the protection of neighbouring rights. The inter-Nordic co-operation has also continued after the enactment of these laws and when a new revision process started at the beginning of the 1970s this was done on a co-operative basis.[6]

All the Nordic countries are party to the Berne Convention and the Universal Copyright Convention. Four of the countries, viz Denmark, Norway, Sweden and, in the beginning of 1983, also Finland have ratified the Rome Convention of 1961. Denmark, Norway and Sweden have also ratified the European Agreement on the Protection of Television Broadcasts and these three countries plus Finland are also party to the Phonograms Convention of 1971.

1 Law No 1960:729.
2 Law No 158/61.
3 Law No 404/61.
4 Law of May 12, No 2.
5 Law No 73.
6 See Para 17.27 below.

2. General principles of the protection of copyright

17.02 As has been mentioned, the Copyright Acts of the Nordic countries are very similar. This is reflected in the structure of the Acts, which all contain eight chapters under the following headings: *Chapter 1* Subject matter and contents of copyright; *Chapter 2* Limitations on copyright; *Chapter 3* Transfer of copyright; *Chapter 4* Term of protection; *Chapter 5* Neighbouring rights; *Chapter 6* Special provisions (protection of titles, etc); *Chapter 7* Liability; and *Chapter 8* Applicability of the Act.

17.03 The Nordic Copyright Acts are based on the concept of the exclusive right of the author to control the use made of his work (Chapter 1). With some slight differences – partly of a linguistic character – in the various Acts the exclusive right of the author comprises the right to produce copies of the work and the right to make the work available to the public in the original form or a changed form in translation or adaptation and in other literary or artistic form or by other technical means. The recording of the work on a material support from which it can be reproduced is considered a production of copies. A work is made available to the public by public performance[1] and by having copies of it placed on sale, leased, loaned or otherwise distributed to the public or publicly exhibited. A performance which takes place within the framework of business activities for a comparatively large, closed group of people is also considered to be a public performance.

The other basic right of the author is the moral right (also Chapter 1). This right comprises the 'droit à la paternité', meaning that when copies of a work are produced, or when it is made available to the public, the name of the author shall be stated to the extent and the manner required by proper usage. The 'droit au respet' is also recognised: a work may not be changed in a manner which is prejudicial to the author's literary or artistic[2] reputation or personality, nor may it be made available to the public in such a form or context as to prejudice the author's reputation in the sense mentioned.

These basic economic and moral rights of the authors are drafted in a comprehensive and relatively brief manner, without a detailed enumeration and description of the various rights and their contents. In this respect the laws of the Nordic countries differ from those of many other countries. The method has the advantage that the provisions can easily be made applicable to new techniques for the utilisation of protected works. On the other hand, there is a disadvantage in the sense that it is not always easy to find a solution to a practical copyright problem directly in the law.

1 Norway: performed outside the private sphere.
2 Norway also 'scentific'.

17.04 Copyright, both the economic rights and the moral right, subsists during the life of the author and for 50 years after his death (Chapter 4). For, inter alia, anonymous works, the term of protection is 50 years from the year in which the work was first disseminated to the public.

17.05 The Copyright Acts also contain certain limitations on copyright (Chapter 2). These limitations vary to some extent between the Nordic countries but the main provisions are basically the same. Among the most important ones is the right to make single copies for private use of works which have been disseminated to the public. Such copies may not be used for other purposes. Quotations may be made from publicly-disseminated works to the extent necessary for the purpose. In educational activities, recordings for occasional use may be made of works without the consent of the author. The provisions in this respect differ, however, to some extent between the Nordic countries. In some of the countries, only sound-recordings are allowed whereas in others video recordings may also be made. In certain situations, public performance may take place without the consent of the author, viz during religious services, in connection with educational activities and in certain other cases, eg for charitable purposes. Once a literary or musical work has been published, the published copies may be further distributed and publicly exhibited. In principle, the same applies to copies of works of art, the ownership of which has been transferred or published. The laws also contain provisions producing a so-called extended collective agreement effect for the benefit of the national broadcasting organisations. If the broadcasting organisation has concluded an agreement with an organisation representing a substantial number of authors in a particular field in the country concerned, the broadcasting organisations may also broadcast published works of the same kind of authors who are not represented by the organisation. This does not, however, apply if the author has prohibited the broadcast or – in Finland, Norway and Sweden – there is reason to assume that the author will oppose the broadcast. The Acts also contain provisions on the right of broadcasting organisations to make so-called ephemeral recordings.

17.06 All the Nordic countries have adopted public lending right schemes. These schemes mean, generally-speaking, that authors of books and certain other contributors receive compensation for the utilisation of their works in public libraries. These schemes are, however, differently organised in the various countries. Thus, eg, the compensation in Denmark is based on the fact that the books are put at the disposal of the public in the libraries. In Sweden the compensation is based, in principle, on the extent of the lending, determined by means of a sampling system. In Finland and Norway compensation takes the form of a system of fellowships granted for purposes of study, which is not related to the actual lending. In no Nordic country, however, does the public lending right take the form of a right under copyright law.

17.07 The Copyright Acts also contain provisions on transfer of copyright (Chapter 3). These are to some extent of a general character but there are also specific provisions on certain aspects of the transfer of copyright, for example, as regards public performance, publishing contracts, film contracts and change of copyright ownership upon the author's death. The general provisions state, inter alia, that in the absence of an agreement to the contrary the person to whom a copyright has been transferred may not make changes in the work or transfer the copyright to others. The specific provisions on transfer apply only in the absence of agreement to the contrary.

17.08 A special feature of the Copyright Acts in the Nordic countries is that the provisions on the protection of neighbouring rights are included in the Copyright Acts as a special chapter.[1]

1 See paras 17.14 et seq below.

17.09 The special provisions contained in Chapter 6 of the Acts are essentially of two kinds. One aims at preventing works from being made available to the public under such a title, pseudonym or signature that the work or its author may easily be confused with a previously-disseminated work or its author. The other provision provides for the possibility of issuing injunctions against utilisation of works in a manner which violates cultural interests.

17.10 The provisions on liability for copyright infringements are basically the same in all the Nordic countries, although they differ in details, inter alia, because of different procedural rules (Chapter 7). Infringement of copyright may entail criminal sanctions, liability for damages and also certain other measures. Anyone who wilfully or with gross negligence[1] infringes a copyright or a neighbouring right can be punished by fines or by imprisonment. The maximum term of imprisonment is two years in Sweden, six months in Finland and three months in the other Nordic countries.

In the case of an exploitation in violation of the Copyright Act, such compensation shall be paid as would constitute a reasonable remuneration for the exploitation. In the case of wilful or negligent infringement, the infringer shall also pay damages for losses other than lost remuneration, for mental suffering and for other injury. Such damages shall also be paid in certain other cases of wilful or negligently committed violations of the provisions of the Copyright Act eg infringements of moral rights.

The courts may order that property involved in the infringement or violation shall, in return for compensation, be surrendered to the owner of the right. The courts may also direct that such property be destroyed or altered in specific ways.

In Finland, Norway and Sweden criminal actions for violation of the Copyright Act may be brought by public prosecutors. A prerequisite is, however, that there is a complaint from the injured party. In Norway such actions may be brought by the public prosecutor if it is considered necessary in the public interest. In Denmark and Iceland criminal actions may only be brought by the injured party. In Sweden as from 1 July 1982, the public prosecutor is entitled to bring action also without a complaint from the injured party if an action is called for in the public interest.

1 According to Norwegian law 'ordinary' negligence suffices.

17.11 The final chapter (Chapter 8) of the Copyright Acts of the Nordic countries contains provisions on the applicability of the Acts to foreign right owners. The provisions on copyright in the strict sense, (the parallel provisions on neighbouring rights are dealt with under secction 12) apply to works of persons who are citizens of or domiciled within the country concerned and to works which have been first published within that country. As mentioned earlier, all the Nordic countries are parties to the Berne Convention and the Universal Copyright Convention. This means that the protection granted to authors and their works under the Nordic Copyright Acts also applies to works having the corresponding points of attachment to countries which are parties to those Conventions.

17.12 Rights in photographic pictures are included in the Icelandic Copyright Act but are in Denmark, Finland, Norway and Sweden dealt with in separate Acts on Rights in Photographic Pictures, enacted in connection with and at the same time as the Copyright Acts. Under these specific Acts, any person who produces a photographic picture has the exclusive right to make copies of it by photography, printing, drawing or other process and to exhibit it publicly. The Acts also contain provisions on moral rights (mention of the photographer's name and prohibition of certain changes) and limitations on the photographer's rights similar to those applicable to works under the Copyright Acts. The greatest variations appear with regard to the period of protection: Denmark provides for 25 years from the production of the picture, Finland for 25 years from the first dissemination of the picture to the public, Norway 15 years from the death of the first owner of the right in the picture and Sweden 25 years from the year of the production of the picture or, in the case of pictures having an artistic or a scientific value, 50 years from the death of the photographer.

The provisions on criminal liability (sanctions, liability for damages, etc) correspond to those applicable to infringement of copyright. However, in Finland the maximum penalty is imprisonment for one year (for copyright infringement six months) and in Norway the only criminal sanction is fines (for copyright infringement imprisonment for three months).

The provisions on the applicability of these Acts to foreign right-owners correspond to those concerning the applicability of the Copyright Acts.[1]

1 See para 17.11 above.

3. The relation between copyright and neighbouring rights

17.13 The provisions on copyright only apply to the result of creative activity. However, it was recognised at an early stage in the Nordic countries that certain categories of persons who were not authors but who utilised protected works and offered important and often independent contributions to the dissemination of those works should be given protection. How this protection should be structured was already discussed during the initial stages of the work on revision of the Nordic Acts in the 1930s. It was, however, not until the end of the 1940s that substantive discussions took place. Various alternatives were considered and the discussions were influenced by not only the suggestions of the interested circles but also by the preparatory work for the future Rome Convention. It was decided not to await the outcome of the international discussions but to submit proposals for national legislation as soon as agreement had been reached on their contents. It also became clear at an early stage that Norway wanted to solve the social and economic problem which the use of recorded music caused for beneficiaries in a way which differed from the solutions envisaged in the other countries. The Norwegian Church and Education Department drafted a proposal which later became the Norwegian fund for the benefit of performers and phonogram producers.[1] This was not, however, meant to constitute a complete solution of the question as to how to protect performers and other categories of persons now enjoying so-called neighbouring rights. The revision committees of the other countries could not accept the Norwegian system but decided that the question should be solved within the framework of private law. In subsequent discussions, Denmark, Finland, Norway and Sweden agreed on all essential points concerning the protection of performers, producers of phonograms and broadcasting organisations. As far as secondary use was concerned, Norway chose the collective fund approach whereas Denmark, Finland and Sweden proposed a system of individual rights to remuneration for use of recordings. Iceland later also adopted the latter approach.

This means that – with the exception of the Norwegian system concerning secondary use – the beneficiaries are granted individual rights, either in the form of a right to authorise or prohibit certain use of their works or in the form of a right to remuneration for such use. In principle, these individual rights are similar to rights granted under copyright law. In the Nordic legislation these rights are brought together under the title 'Neighbouring Rights' in Chapter 5 of the Copyright Acts. This description of the rights, as well as their placing in the Copyright Acts, clearly shows the inter-relation between the two sets of provisions. Another indication of this inter-relation is that the scope and contents of the different neighbouring rights are often determined by reference to copyright provisions, for example, as regards the possibility to make copies for private use. To what extent neighbouring rights should be determined by reference to copyright provisions is one of the questions being discussed in the on-going revision process in the Nordic countries.[2]

As was stressed above, the protection granted to neighbouring rights is very similar in the different Nordic countries. They are therefore treated together in the following survey. Where there are substantial differences between the provisions this is indicated.

1   See para 17.18 below.
2   See para 17.27 below.

4. Protection of performers[1]

17.14 The protection granted to a performer implies that nobody may without his authorisation:

(a)   record his performance on a gramophone record, audiotape, film or similar material support from which the performance can be reproduced,
(b)   broadcast (Danish and Norwegian law use here the word 'immediately' or 'directly') his performance over radio or television or make it available to the public by direct communication; (Danish and Norwegian law add here; 'to a public other than that for which the performer directly performs'),
(c)   make copies of recordings of his performance. This protection, however, only lasts for 25 years from the year in which the first recording took place.

In addition Danish law contains special provisions on right to broadcast from the Royal Theatre gala performance or performances on the occasion of official visits.

Furthermore, performing artists have a right to remuneration when sound recordings of their performances are used.[2]

There is a court case in Sweden on the scope of the rights mentioned in a) and c).[3] It concerned still-pictures of an artist which had been taken during the recording of a motion picture and used, inter alia, as illustrations in a magazine. The Supreme Court stated that the concept of 'recording' should be interpreted as meaning at least a sequence of the play showing the performance by the artist. Consequently, the use of the still-pictures could not be considered an infringement of the artist's rights.

The legislation also contains provisions on so-called moral rights. The artist's name shall be stated when his performance is made available to the public or copies of it are made. Furthermore, the performance may not be changed in a manner which is prejudicial to the performer's artistic reputation or to his individuality, nor may it be made available to the public in such a form or context as to prejudice the performer's reputation.

There are court cases in both Finland and Sweden concerning the interpretation of moral rights. The Swedish case[4] concerned a motion picture in which a well-known actress participated and where the film producer had inserted, without her consent, a sequence containing a scene in bed. This scene had been made with the collaboration of a woman other than the actress. Her body but not her face was visible. The court held that the moral rights of the actress had been infringed by the insertion of this scene. The Finnish case concerned a similar situation.[5]

1   S 45 of the Copyright Acts of Denmark, Finland, Iceland and Sweden; s 42 of the Norwegian Copyright Act.
2   See para 17.18 below.
3   Reported in 'Nytt Juridiskt Arkiv' Supreme Court Reports NJA 1976 p 282.
4   Judgment by the City Court of Stockholm, 1968, DT 3/1968.
5   Reported in Nordiskt Immateriellt Rättsskydd/Scandinavian Journal on Intellectual Property/ NIR 1976 p 303.

5. Protection of producers of phonograms[1]

17.15 The main effect of these provisions is that nobody may without the authorisation of the producer make copies of his recording for 25 years from the year in which the recording was made.[2]

This protection applies only to sound-recordings, including the soundtrack of audiovisual recordings. It covers all kinds of sound-recordings, regardless of their character (music, birds' singing, traffic noise). The 'copies' mentioned in this provision may be made by means of either mechanical or electromagnetic reproductive processes.

1   S 46 of the Copyright Acts of Denmark, Finland, Iceland and Sweden; s 45 of the Norwegian Copyright Act.
2   As regards remuneration for certain uses see para 7.18 below.

6. Protection of broadcasting organisations[1]

17.16 Certain kinds of use of radio or television broadcasts are not permitted without the authorisation of the broadcasting organisation; namely, to

(a)   re-broadcast radio or television programmes
(b)   make broadcasts available to the public[2]
(c)   record the broadcasts on a gramophone record, audiotape, film or similar material support from which the broadcast can be reproduced[3]
(d)   make copies of such recordings; this protection, however, only lasts for 25 years from the year in which the recording was made.

The protection applies to all kinds of broadcasts regardless of content. It should be stressed, however, that the protection applies to the broadcast as such, ie the signal but not to the programme; it is thus quite legal for other broadcasting organisations to transmit a programme which is composed in exactly the same way as the protected programme (provided, of course, that it is with the consent of the authors and other contributors).

1 S 48 in the Copyright Acts of Denmark, Finland, Iceland and Sweden; s 45 in the Norwegian Copyright Act which provision authorises the government to issue regulations in this respect. These provisions, contained in Decrees of 5 April 1968 and 28 July 1978, correspond basically to the provisions embodied in the Copyright Acts of the other countries.
2 Finnish and Swedish law limits this provision to the showing of broadcasts in cinemas or similar places. Danish law applies in this respect to both sound and television broadcasts but limits the exclusive right to acts undertaken with gainful interest.
3 Danish law also stresses in this context that the producing of photographs of television broadcasts presupposes an authorisation.

7. Protection for other related rights (producers of catalogues)[1]

17.17 The Copyright Acts of the Nordic countries contain special provisions aiming at the protection of producers of catalogues, tables and similar productions in which a large number of information items has been collected. Danish, Finnish and Norwegian law (and possibly also Icelandic law because of its rather broad wording) covers not only catalogues and the like but also programmes. The protection means that such productions may not be reproduced without the consent of the producer until 10 years have elapsed from the year in which the production was published. The provisions protect only national productions and consequently have no international application.

The Copyright Acts of Denmark, Finland[2] and Norway[3] also contain provisions on the protection of press news from other countries. Such press news may not, without the consent of the person entitled to receive them, be published or otherwise made available to the public before 12 (in Norwegian law 16) hours have elapsed since their first publication in the receiving country. Norwegian law also provides that the source shall be indicated when press news is reproduced or mentioned in other media.

1 S 49 of the Copyright Acts of Denmark, Finland and Sweden; s 50 of the Iceland Copyright Act; and s 43 of the Norwegian Copyright Act.
2 S 50 of the respective Acts.
3 S 44.

8. Secondary use[1]

17.18 Secondary use of performances takes place when recordings of performances are used in radio or television broadcasts. It has long been recognised that such secondary use should not be free. The Nordic countries do not grant an exclusive right in this context, but instead there is a compulsory licence in the sense that such use may take place without the authorisation of the beneficiary but an equitable remuneration shall be paid to him.

There are certain differences between the provisions on secondary use in the Nordic countries. The Copyright Acts of Finland and Sweden state that, if a sound recording mentioned in section 46[2] is used in a radio or television broadcast, a remuneration shall be paid both to the producer of the recording and to the performer whose performance is recorded. This applies if the use takes place within the period of 25 years mentioned in section 46. If two or more performers have participated in the performance their right may only be claimed by them jointly. As against the radio or television organisation, the performer's right shall be claimed through the producer. The provision applies only to sound-recordings and not to sound-films.

The corresponding provisions in the Copyright Acts of Denmark and Iceland are drafted in mainly the same way but in these countries a remuneration shall also be paid when the recordings are used for commercial purposes in other public performances than those on radio or television, for instance in discotheques or shops. Another difference is that in these countries the right to remuneration may also be claimed by an organisation common for the performers and the producers of phonograms.

The Norwegian Copyright Act contains no provisions on remuneration for secondary use. Provisions with that aim are instead included in the Act[3] concerning Levy on Public Presentation of Artists' Performances etc. Under this Act, a levy shall be paid to a fund by anyone who for commercial purposes publicly; a) presents a recording of the performance of a performer by means of gramophone discs, tapes or similar technical recording devices; or b) transmits from a radio receiver a broadcast in which a performer takes part or which presents a recording of the artist's performance, provided that such transmission constitutes a significant element of the business concerned. Furthermore, such a levy shall also in principle be paid by anybody who for commercial purposes and for use in Norway transfers or arranges for the transfer of recordings of a performance to cinematographic films. The projection of films in cinemas and the Norwegian Broadcasting Corporation's broadcast of recordings made solely for broadcasting purposes are exempt from the obligation to pay such a levy. The Board of the fund shall calculate and collect the levies but the level is determined by the government. The main part of the money going to the fund is used to support Norwegian (not foreign) performers and their surviving dependants. However, a certain amount, each year determined by the government (at present about 20%), shall be paid to the producers of phonograms. The act contains no provisions on the use of this part of the money. It can thus, according to internal agreement, also be used for foreign producers and independently of how old the recordings are.[4]

1 S 47 of the Copyright Acts of Denmark, Finland, Iceland and Sweden; special law in Norway.
2 See para 17.15 above.
3 14 December 1956, No 4.
4 See also paras 17.23 et seq below.

9. Term of protection

17.19 As mentioned above, the general term of protection for the neighbouring rights relating to performers, producers of phonograms and broadcasting organisations is 25 years. Thus, performers and phonogram producers' protection against unauthorised copying of recordings subsists for 25 years from the year in which the first recording (fixation) took place. The same term of protection applies to broadcasting organisations' protection as regards copying of their radio or television broadcasts.

The protection of catalogues and similar compilations subsists for 10 years after publication.

10. Limitations on neighbouring rights

17.20 In most countries copyright law provides for limitations on the rights granted under the law. Such limitations could have a more general scope, such as the provisions on 'fair use' or 'fair dealing' in the Anglo-Saxon legal tradition, or be of a specific nature. In Chapter 2 of the Copyright Acts the legislation in the Nordic countries has adopted the latter approach. Some of these limitations have, by means of references in the provisions on neighbouring rights, also been made applicable to these rights. Consequently, in particular the following limitations apply, mutatis mutandis, to the rights of performers, producers of phonograms and broadcasting organisations:

(a) Single copies may be made for private use; such copies may not be used for other purposes.
(b) Quotations may be made, in accordance with proper usage, to the extent necessary for the purpose.
(c) Sound-recordings may be made for occasional use in educational activities; commercially-produced recordings may, however, not be directly copied. Copies made under this provision may not be used for other purposes. In Denmark, not only sound but also video-recordings of television broadcasts may be used within the framework of educational activities. The right owners can claim remuneration for such recordings if they are made from non-educational broadcasts. In Norway, recordings of television broadcasts are also allowed under certain conditions.
(d) Radio or television broadcasts or films of new events may include brief excerpts of performances which take place in connection with the event.
(e) Radio and television organisations may make so-called ephemeral recordings for use in their own transmissions.
(f) Performances may be broadcast or communicated to the public at religious services or in connection with education or for certain other purposes for the common good.
(g) Recordings may in certain cases be treated as documents drawn up by public authorities; such documents may under certain conditions be copied without the consent of the owner of the rights.
(h) In Sweden certain provisions apply to preservation and use of recordings of performances (broadcast or others) in the Archive for Recorded Sound and Moving Images.

When performances or recordings are used under these provisions the moral rights of the beneficiary in question are safeguarded.

11. Remedies for infringements

17.21 As was noted above, the provisions on neighbouring rights are incorporated in the Copyright Acts. This also means that the provisions on criminal sanctions,[1] liability for damages and seizure apply equally to copyright and neighbouring rights.

[1] Fine or imprisonment for up to two years in Sweden or six or three months respectively in the other Nordic countries.

12. Protection of foreign right owners

17.22 The national Copyright Acts, including their provisions on neighbouring rights, are applicable in the national territory to performances according to criteria which vary in the different Nordic countries. Denmark, Finland and Sweden have adopted the criterion of territoriality as the connecting factor, so that, in principle, performances, sound-recordings and radio or television broadcasts are protected if they take place in the country. In Denmark, the phonogram producers' protection against unauthorised copying applies to all phonograms regardless of origin. Norway and Iceland have adopted the criterion of nationality as the connecting factor which means that the provisions on neighbouring rights apply to beneficiaries who are Norwegian nationals or who have their domicile or habitual residence in Norway or are Norwegian companies having a Norwegian board and its seat in Norway. The protection of performers also applies to performances which take place in Norway. As in Denmark the protection for producers of phonograms applies to all phonograms.

As regards the protection of catalogues and tables, the main principle is that such protection is granted to persons (physical or legal) who are nationals of the country in question or have their domicile or their habitual residence there. Protection generally also applies if the catalogue is produced by a national company or is first published in the country in question.

As mentioned earlier, Denmark, Norway, Sweden and Finland are party to the Rome Convention. For Denmark, Finland and Sweden this means that, in principle, the provisions on the protection of performers, producers of phonograms and broadcasting organisations also apply when the performance, the production of the phonogram or the broadcast takes place in another country which is party to the Rome Convention. However, in Norway the point of attachment is the nationality of the beneficiary.[1]

The Norwegian legislation provides[2] that remuneration for secondary use of recordings shall be paid to performers in the form of a support from a special fund. The beneficiaries of this support are only Norwegian artists and not artists from other countries, even the Rome Convention countries. On the other hand, as regards the remuneration to producers of phonograms, there are no particular limitations as to, for example, nationality, place of fixation or age of the recording. Also, record producers from other countries, inter alia the Rome Convention countries, can be entitled to part of the compensation. The Norwegian system is considered to be compatible with the Rome Convention, inter alia because article 16.1.a (iv) of the Convention states that the fact that a contracting state grants protection to a different category of beneficiaries than another state shall not be considered to be a difference in protection giving a right to restrict the protection.

Denmark, Norway, Finland and Sweden are party to the phonogram Convention of 1971. This means that the protection of phonogram producers against copying without their authorisation also applies to phonograms which have been fixed in a country which is a party to the Convention or, as regards Norway, the producer of which is a national etc of such a country.

Furthermore, Denmark, Norway and Sweden are party to the 1960 European Agreement on the Protection of Television Broadcasts. Consequently, the protection of broadcasting organisations under the national coyright laws of these countries also covers broadcasters from other contracting countries according to the same criteria as have been described above.

In accordance with the generally-accepted principle of national treatment in the system of international copyright conventions, the level of protection under national laws also applies to foreign beneficiaries if the level of protection in the country of origin is lower. Thus, for instance, the protection of broadcasters against cable transmissions also applies to broadcasters from countries party to the Rome Convention, even if those countries do not grant corresponding protection. An exception to this principle of national treatment is that the legislation can provide that protection shall not be granted when the term of protection in the country of origin has expired. The legislation in the Nordic countries contains such provisions on comparison of terms.

The protection for catalogues and tables, as earlier mentioned, applies only to national productions and has no international application.

1   See above.
2   See para 17.18, above.

13. Collection and distribution of revenues

17.23 *General.* With the exception of the Norwegian fund system,[1] each individual performer is under the legislation, granted a right to control the use of his performance. The same principle applies, mutatis mutandis, to phonogram producers and broadcasting organisations. It is, however, impracticable to rely on individual agreements between, for instance, the performer and the person using his performance. Instead, the beneficiaries of neighbouring rights have formed organisations which have concluded collective agreements with the users.

1 See para 17.26 below.

17.24 Distribution of remuneration for the use of recordings in broadcasts in Sweden, Denmark and Finland. (*Sweden* taken as a point of departure.)

The producers of sound-recordings and of videograms are organised in the International Federation of Producers of Phonograms and Videograms (IFPI) which has national groups, inter alia, in the Nordic countries.

Under Swedish law, the phonogram producers represent performers in relation to broadcasters. Consequently, the Swedish Group of IFPI represents performers in relation to the Swedish Broadcasting Organisation and collects, also on their behalf, the remuneration paid for the use of recordings in broadcasts. Half of this sum is then paid to the performers' organisation SAMI.

The performers have, however, another organisation apart from their trade unions, which has the form of a *collecting society*. Its main aim is to collect and to distribute remunerations to artists and musicians for use of their recordings in radio or television broadcasts by the Swedish Broadcasting Organisation.[1] The Swedish name of the organisation is abbreviated to SAMI (in English 'The Professional Organisation of Swedish Artists and Musicians'). It is an incorporated association founded by the two trade unions mentioned above. Membership in the association can be granted to all performers who are members of one of the two trade unions and who appear on a phonogram giving a right to remuneration for use in broadcasts by the Swedish Broadcasting Organisation. Under his membership contract, the member transfers to SAMI the right to enter, on his behalf, into agreements concerning such remuneration. In return, SAMI undertakes, inter alia, to pay remuneration to the member in accordance with the rules on distribution. Artists who are not members of the trade unions can be associated members. These associated members have no right to take part in the decisions of the association and have to pay a service charge of 10% but are, of course, entitled to the remuneration. SAMI has about 1,300 members and about 1,500 associated members. The amount of remuneration for the broadcasting rights was decided in Sweden by the Supreme Court of 1968[2] in the form of a rate per minute of protected phonograms.

That rate multiplied by the number of minutes played gives the annual amount of which one half goes to the performers, the other half to the producers of programmes. The Swedish Broadcasting Organisation supplies a complete record of all programmes played on which a distribution schedule for performers is based (eg seven points to soloists, five points to conductors, one point to orchestral musicians) and the computer works out the amount due to each beneficiary. There are bound to be some royalties the beneficiaries of which cannot be traced. These are held in reserve for a number of years after which, if still undistributable, they are added to the amount for annual distribution to the identified beneficiaries as a bonus payment.

Most of the fees collected from the Swedish Broadcasting Organisation are distributed to Swedish artists and musicians. There are, however, agreements with similar organisations in other countries. SAMI has such agreements with corresponding organisations in Austria, Denmark and the Federal Republic of Germany. The agreements in force between Austria, Denmark and Sweden provide in principle that the organisation in one of these countries also collects those royalties for the use of recordings in radio or television to which artists and musicians in the other country are entitled. The organisations exchange relevant information once a year and the balance of the two sums of individual remunerations is then transferred in the form of a lump sum by the organisation liable for payment to the other organisation. As far as possible, this remuneration is then distributed to the individual beneficiaries.

The agreement between SAMI and its sister organisation in the Federal Republic of Germany is much simpler than the other bilateral agreements mentioned. The reason is that the methods for the calculation of royalties and the methods for the distribution to the beneficiaries are totally different in the two countries. Consequently, the agreement stipulates that remuneration for the use of recordings in radio or television shall remain in the country where they are collected and shall be distributed there. Thus, no transfer of royalties from one country to the other takes place. The bilateral agreements follow the so-called 'London principles' of 1969 which have been adopted by FIA, FIM and IFPI. They essentially provide the following:

(a) Remunerations under article 12 of the Rome Convention, the beneficiaries of which are known, should be sent from the country of collection directly to the recipients in the other country or, preferably, through their organisation in that country.

(b) Remunerations to unknown recipients are kept for a certain time (up to five years) and are then, if the addressee is still unknown paid to the performers in the collecting country to be used for collective purposes for the benefit of that profession.

(c) Remunerations which cannot be distributed due to lack of information as to which phonograms have been used (generally speaking, public performances other than those which take place in radio or television) are kept in the country of collection to be used in the same way as is mentioned under (b).

1   Remuneration under art 12 of the Rome Convention; see para 8.26 above.
2   'Nytt Juridiskt Arkiv' Supreme Court Reports/NJA 1968 p 104 (Judgment of 22 March 1968). The Court awarded 10 Se K for each minute of protected phonograms played and added an annual increase measured by the official cost of living index. The current amount is 37 Se K per minute resulting in an annual payment of 9,799.000 Se K in 1980 (1 Se K = approximately 0.15 $US for a population of approximately 8.5 million.

17.25 The organisational structure is similar in *Denmark*. The most important difference is that the remuneration for the use of recordings in broadcasts is collected by one institution (GRAMEX) common to performers and phonogram producers. The legislation in Denmark also provides for remuneration to performers and phonogram producers when recordings are used in public performances other than broadcasting. This means that, for instance, restaurants, shopping centres and discotheques have to pay a fee to these categories of beneficiaries. Public performance users consequently pay two kinds of remuneration for the music they use,[1] one to authors and one to performers and phonogram producers. For practical and administrative reasons these two claims are combined. KODA (the authors society) collects the authors' remuneration, calculated according to an agreed schedule, plus a 50% additional amount which is then transmitted to GRAMEX (the society of performers and the phonogram producers) and the other half to the performers. The phonogram producers distribute their part of the remuneration to the individual producers in relation to their share of the market as no detailed information on the phonograms used for such public performance is available. Foreign producers are also entitled to a remuneration, provided that the recording has been made in a country which is party to the Rome Convention. The performers' part of the remuneration is distributed to the Danish artists' unions. The largest share goes to the musicians (39%). In principle, performers from the countries of the Rome Convention also get their share as GRAMEX has concluded agreements with its sister organisations in Sweden (1971), the Federal Republic of Germany (1972), Austria (1975) and Czechoslovakia (1979). The amount of royalty payable for the playing of phonograms by the Broadcasting Organisation was fixed by a special tribunal[2] at a minute rate for protected phonograms plus an annual increase measured by the cost of living index.[3]

1 When it is performed by means of phonograms.
2 Award 19 May 1965, D Kr 15 per minute (on 1 October 1982: D Kr 61.70 per minute).
3 At the end of 1981 it stood at D Kr 56.41 per minute for a population of 5.1 million (1 Danish Kroner = 0.11$US). 55% of the phonograms played were protected. The total income for performers and producers of phonograms stood at 14.2 million D Kr (11.8 million from broadcasting and 2.4 million from public performance). The administration costs of the collecting society (GRAMEX) amounted to approximately 15%.

17.26 The *Norwegian* fund system for collection and distribution of remuneration for use of recordings is different as the main reason for the passing of the Fund law in 1956 was that because of the use of phonograms the need for live performances had decreased, with consequent 'technical unemployment' of musicians. This development, which also hurt phonogram producers, could, at least partly, be mitigated by a fund system. All users of phonograms for broadcasting and public performance pay into the fund in accordance with rates fixed annually. The fund distributes the remuneration. Approximately three quarters go to performers but not necessarily to those whose recorded performances have been played, but are distributed according to social considerations. Approximately one quarter goes to producers of phonograms. The fund pays only to Norwegian beneficiaries.

The question whether the Norwegian system, with its strong collective elements, could be compatible with article 12 of the Rome Convention was discussed by the Intergovernmental Committee of the Convention in 1967. The Committee itself did not express any opinion on this matter because it considered that the problem mainly concerned the interpretation of the Convention and of Norwegian law. However, the majority of the members and of the observers expressed the opinion that Norway could accede to the Rome Convention without reservation as regards article 12. It did so in 1978. In the instrument of accession, the Norwegian Government declared, inter alia, that the régime of the 1956 Act, being fully consistent with the requirements of the Convention, will be maintained.

Of particular importance as regards the compatibility between such a fund system and the Rome Convention is the fact that the lump sum allocated to the phonogram producers can, as of right, also be used for beneficiaries who are nationals of Rome Convention countries.

14. Plans for revision and recent amendments to copyright laws

17.27 When they entered into force in the beginning of the 1960s the Nordic Copyright Acts were for their time modern and well-designed to serve their purpose. In their original form they worked remarkably well during the 1960s. The period betweeen 1960 and 1970 was also, however, a decade of events having considerable impact on copyright. Apart from the problems presented by the needs of 'developing countries',[1] the advent of new technology for the dissemination of works and performances, eg reprography, audio and video recording equipment, cable television, and computers had a far-reaching impact on the position of the beneficiaries of copyright legislation, both in the sense that the demand for protected works increased considerably and in the sense that to a large extent the beneficiaries lost control over the use of their works.[2]

In 1974 the Nordic governments, in particular those of Norway and Sweden, began to show a political interest in developments in the copyright field. They expressed concern about what they considered to be a constant increase in the scope of the rights. They were largely concerned with the difficulties encountered by certain projects in the educational and the cultural sectors.

In 1975 the Nordic Council of Ministers adopted common guidelines for the revision of their Copyright Acts. These stress that whereas the exclusive rights under the copyright system give individual authors protection and are a valuable stimulus for cultural life, the system of individual rights has its shortcomings. In more and more areas authors are losing control over the use of their works. On the other hand, the need for specific authorisation by the author could result in less utilisation of the work than would otherwise have been possible.

Even if the individual exclusive right has to be the basis of copyright legislation, one should, within the limits set by the international conventions, increase the possibilities to use protected works without individual consent and for a remuneration negotiated collectively. The solutions should result in a situation in which the economic position of authors and other rightowners, taken as a group, is not diminished. On the basis of these guidelines, terms of reference were established for the national revision committees which were appointed in Denmark, Finland, Norway and Sweden and (since 1981) Iceland.

Some have published reports on some specific items. The *Danish* committee has published a report on the fundamental principles on which the copyright system is based and containing proposals for new provisions on reproduction for private use and photocopying in educational establishments, commercial organisations, etc. In 1982 the Danish Committee also published a report containing proposals for 1) an increase of the penalties for infringement of the rights under copyright legislation and 2) a levy on blank tapes for the benefit of the right owners under this legislation. In addition, in 1983 the Committee published a report on neighbouring rights, mainly dealing with the protection of performing artists. These reports have not so far resulted in legislation. In 1980 the *Finnish* committee published a report on reproduction for private use and on photocopying and recording of television programmes in educational establishments. The *Norwegian* committee has submitted proposals on changes of the provisions on public performance and on a levy on recording equipment for the benefit of authors and other right owners who are affected by the increased reproduction for private use. The *Swedish* committee has submitted a report on photocopying in educational establishments which has resulted in legislation. In June 1981 a report was published containing proposals for stronger measures against infringements of copyright, including an increase in the maximum penalty from six months to two years, the reason being the need to fight the growth of piracy.

As regards neighbouring rights the principal matters under consideration are (i) an extension of the period of protection (possibly to 50 years instead of, as now, 25 years), (ii) remuneration for public performances (other than broadcasting), in Finland and Sweden, (iii) the points of attachment, which at present are fixation only.[3]

1 See para 12.03 above.
2 See para 12.39 above.
3 See paras 8.12 et seq above.

15. Legislation

17.28 In a 'Regulation Concerning a Tax on Blank Cassette tapes for Recording and Reproduction of Sounds or Images'[1] *Norway* introduced a tax part of the yield of which goes to the Norwegian Broadcasting Corporation, the other part to general cultural purposes. The tax is payable on the importations, sale or renting of equipment for the recording or reproduction of sounds or images.

1 Reg No 1108 of 23 June 1982.

17.29 *Sweden*. In accordance with the Law of 24 June 1982 introducing a 'Tax on Certain Cassette Types' law[1] a tax shall be paid to the state for blank audio cassettes and for blank and pre-recorded video cassettes. The tax amounts to 0.02 Se K (Swedish Kroners) per playing minute for audio cassettes and 0.25 Se K per minute for video cassettes. However, with regard to pre-recorded video cassettes a deduction may be made for the amount of the levy according to an agreement concluded between the government and the Swedish video distributors for the support of the Swedish Film Institute. This means in practice that no tax will be paid for pre-recorded video cassettes placed on the market for hire, because the levy paid under the agreement is higher than the tax.

The tax is estimated to produce approximately 135 million Se K[2] a year. Of this amount two thirds goes directly to the general budget and the rest is to be used for various purposes in the cultural field, in particular for the support of music. Of this amount a sum of 8 million Se K will go directly to the organisations for right-owners in the music field as compensation for the extensive use of their rights by home taping. The beneficiaries of this sum of 8 million Se K will be the composers, the phonogram producers and the performers. The sharing of the sum between these categories of right-owners is left to them. The bill introducing the new law to Parliament states that the proposed tax does not prevent the Committee for the Revision of the Copyright Law – which is working, inter alia, on the problem of home taping and reproduction for private use – to propose a levy on blank tapes under private law. The question on how compensation for home taping shall be finally framed will be reconsidered when the Committee puts forward its proposals. Thus the above scheme for taxation could be regarded as a provisional solution.

1 Statute Book 1982 No 691.
2 0.15 Se K (Swedish Kroner = 1 $US).

Chapter 18
United Kingdom

by William Wallace

1. History and development of copyright

18.01 There are two distinct theories justifying the grant of copyright protection. The first is that the grant of exclusive rights stimulates investment in the production and making public of literary and artistic creations. It induces publishers to sink their capital in bringing such works to the public at large, and thus increases the spread of knowledge, stimulates interest in aesthetic creation, and offers the man-in-the-street enjoyment which he would otherwise never have. This is the 'public interest' theory.

The second is the 'natural justice' theory. The creative activity of a man's mind is as much his property as work created by his hands, and no-one must be allowed to take it from him, at least for a limited period. He and only he must be allowed to exploit it for his lifetime, and to pass on this opportunity to exploit to his immediate heirs.

It was the 'public interest' theory which originally prevailed in Britain. It must be remembered that patents for inventions were granted not only to those who actually evolved the invention, but also to those who found the invention abroad and introduced its manufacture into Britain. Patents were granted not so much to stimulate invention as to stimulate investment in new manufacture within the realm. It is only recently that we have ceased to grant patents to those who 'imported' inventions.

In the same way, after the advent of the printing press, it was by the grant of letters patent that monopolies were conferred on approved printers and publishers. Indeed, a monopoly in the King James Bible is still enjoyed by virtue of letters patent. Also, the first copyright statute, that of 1709, was aimed at regulating the book trade. It was with publishers and printers in mind rather than with authors that the limited statutory monopoly was conferred, though the Act was later construed as having provided an author's copyright. In 1774 the House of Lords held[1] that the Act had substituted a statutory copyright for the author's (perpetual) common law copyright so far as published works were concerned (though a perpetual copyright persisted, and still persists, for unpublished works).

Under the 'public interest' theory, protection for published works, like protection for inventions and industrial designs, depended on registration. It was the influence of continental European (and particularly French) thinking and that of the Berne Convention which changed British ideas. Acceptance of the 1908 Berlin Act[2] of that Convention meant that copyright could no longer be subject to any formality, and this principle was accepted in the British Copyright Act of 1911. Copyright thereafter subsisted, whether the work was registered or not, for the life of the author and 50 years after his death. However, notwithstanding any assignment, the rights reverted to the author's heirs during the last 25 years – a principle which went back at least as far as the

Statute of 1709, and which was only abolished, for future works, in the Copyright Act of 1956.

1 *Donaldson v Beckett* (1774) 4 Burr 2408.
2 See para 5.11 above.

18.02 Although the Berne Convention countries (particularly France) have never agreed that neighbouring rights owners merited a true *'droit d'auteur'*, and that Convention does nothing to protect such rights, it was nevertheless the Berlin Revision of that Convention which, indirectly, gave rise to the first of the related rights in the United Kingdom and the countries of the then British Empire. The Berlin Act[1] for the first time, gave authors of musical works the exclusive right of authorising

(i)   the adaptation of those works for instruments which can reproduce them mechanically; and
(ii) the public performance of the said works by means of these instruments.

It was the British government's intention to ratify the Berlin text and hence the Copyright Bill so provided. However, in order to overcome the opposition of the rapidly-growing record industry and the makers of 'pianola' rolls, a provision was inserted in the 1911 Act as follows[2]:

'Copyright shall subsist in records, perforated rolls, and other contrivances by means of which sounds may be mechanically reproduced, in like manner as if such contrivances were musical works, but the term of copyright shall be 50 years from the making of the original plate from which the contrivance was directly or indirectly derived and the person who was the owner of such original plate at the time when such plate was made shall be deemed to be the author of the work ... '

Perhaps because it was a copyright rather than a 'droit d'auteur' which was being conferred, the British Parliament had no qualms about bestowing it on a corporate body. Film companies and broadcasting organisations now also enjoy the protection of copyright legislation for their films and broadcasts.

It is reasonably clear that the intention of the 1909 Committee which recommended this provision was simply to protect record-makers against piracy. However, in 1933, the case of *The Gramophone Co Ltd v Carwardine & Co*[3] decided that the record companies had a right not only to stop copying of their records but also to control their public performance. They have enjoyed both these rights (subject to certain limitations) ever since.

There is however no such thing as a 'neighbouring right' in British law. The only property right known in this field is a copyright, and phonograms and broadcasts enjoy copyright proper.

Protection for performers arose in a different way: in 1925 a Private Member of Parliament succeeded in securing the passage of the Dramatic and Musical Performers Act. This made it a criminal offence for any person 'knowingly' to make a record directly or indirectly from or by means of the performance of any dramatic or musical work without the consent in writing of the performers, and to deal commercially or to use for the purpose of a public performance a record made in contravention of the Act. It was a defence to prove that the record was not made 'for the purposes of trade'. This principle has been extended to cover the clandestine filming or broadcasting of a live performance.

1 See para 5.11 above.
2 S 19(1).
3 [1934] Ch 450.

2. Copyright in 'works' and films

18.03 Copyright in the United Kingdom is purely a creature of statute. All copyrights and two of the three neighbouring rights covered by the Rome Convention are governed by the Copyright Act 1956. The Act is law in the whole of the United Kingdom of Great Britain and Northern Ireland and also in certain countries to which it 'extends'[1]

Part I of the Copyright Act deals with 'Copyright in original works, namely literary, dramatic, musical and artistic works', whereas Part II deals with copyright in other subject-matter – sound recordings, cinematograph films, broadcasts, etc.

1 Copyright Act 1956 and the Copyright (International Conventions) Order 1979, SI 1979/1715, Sch 6: Bermuda, Belize, British Virgin Islands, Cayman Islands, Falkland Islands and its Dependencies, Gibraltar, Hong Kong, Isle of Man, Montserrat, St. Helena and its Dependencies.

3. Acquisition of copyright

18.04 The basic rule is that the author owns the copyright in his work. Protection under United Kingdom law depends either on the author being a 'qualified person' (basically a British or Irish subject) or resident in the United Kingdom when the work was made[1] or on the work being first (or simultaneously) published in the United Kingdom. Either will suffice.

A work is 'made' when it is first reduced into writing or some other material form, eg recorded on disc or tape, either by the author himself or by someone else. Unless a work is 'made' it is unprotected.

'Publication' means the issue of copies to the public with the intention of satisfying their reasonable requirements. It does *not* include public performance or the issue of records or the exhibition of an artistic work. Publication is 'simultaneous' if it occurs within 30 days of any other publication.[2]

'Foreign works'. Section 32 of the 1956 Act permits the government to make Orders in Council to confer copyright on 'foreign' works as if they were 'British'.[3]

International Conventions to which the United Kingdom is a party do *not* form part of British law. The rights of convention nationals are those conferred by the Copyright Statute and Orders made under it. If they fail to meet the United Kingdom's convention obligations, this is a matter between governments. Individuals cannot sue on the Convention.[4]

To the basic rule that the author is the first owner of copyright in the work, there are two exceptions. If the work is made 'in the course of the author's employment by another person under a contract of service' *all* rights belong to the employer. For this to operate, it must be a contract of service, ie of employment, and the work must be made in the course of that employment. The exception does not apply in the case of an independent contractor. In the case of a staff journalist, however, the employer only gets the newspaper and periodical rights; the journalist retains any other rights.[5] The other exception arises in the case of a commissioned photograph or portrait in which case the copyright belongs to the person commissioning the photograph or portrait.[6]

These provisions only apply, of course, in the absence of agreement to the contrary. It is possible to assign the copyright not only in existing works[7] but also in works not yet created.[8] Transmission of copyright[9] may be by assignment, by testamentary disposition or by operation of law. In order for an assignment to have legal effect it must be in writing. A licence to exploit copyright may be oral or in writing or may be implied, for example, a freelance who supplies an article for publication. Any assignment or licence may be of the whole or of part of the copyright.

Thus, an author may wish to assign his public performance and broadcasting rights to a collecting society and either retain his reproduction right himself or assign it to a publisher. Exclusive licensees may bring actions for infringement (on joining the copyright owner) but only if their licence was in writing.[10]

1 S 1(5).
2 S 49(2).
3 The operative Order is the Copyright (International Conventions) Order 1979, SI 1979/1715. The countries in question are listed in the Schedule to that Order.
4 S 4(4).
5 S 4(2).
6 S 4(3).
7 S 36.
8 S 37.
9 S 36.
10 S 19.

4. Subject-matter of protection

18.05 Part I of the 1956 Act is concerned with copyright in original works. 'Original' can be contrasted with 'novel'. It means that the work is a creation of its author, arrived at without copying; even if it closely resembles some earlier work it is itself original if independently arrived at. To be a 'work', the author must have devoted sufficient skill, judgment and/or labour to its creation. In a recent case it was held that the word 'Exxon' by itself did not qualify.[1]

Literary works. These include, in addition to books, articles and similar works, 'any written table or compilation' and in 1964 the House of Lords held a football fixture list to be protectable.[2] Things like broadcasting schedules, directories, and railway guides have been protected as compilations.

Dramatic works. Dramatic works are not defined in the Act, but include a choreographic work or entertainment in dumb show, if reduced to writing in the form in which the work or entertainment is to be presented. The expression does not include a cinematographic film as distinct from a scenario or script for such a film. It will be noted that copyright in choreographic work does not arise until the work is reduced to writing. In the case of all other works, recording on tape or film suffices. But so far as ballets, etc, are concerned, it would appear from the restricted wording in section 48(1), that it is insufficient if only a visual recording is made; the choreographic work must be reduced to writing or some form of notation.

Musical works. The expression is not defined. As with all other works, to be made, they must be fixed in some way, not necessarily by the composer himself. Artistic merit, or the lack of it, appears to be irrelevant. Any new arrangement of a piece of music will attract a copyright, provided sufficient skill and/or labour has gone into it to qualify as a work. The arranger becomes author of his arrangement. In a recent case it was held that there may be two separate copyrights in a song: a literary work in the lyrics and a musical work in the musical score.³

Artistic works. Section 3 of the Act defines 'artistic works' as meaning works of any of the following descriptions;

(a) the following, irrespective of artistic quality, namely paintings, sculptures, drawings, engravings and photographs;
(b) works of architecture, being either buildings or models for buildings;
(c) works of artistic craftsmanship, not falling within either of the preceding paragraphs.

The categories of artistic works are important, as the term of protection, rights and defences may vary from category to category. Whereas it is plain that aesthetic merit is not necessary for the protection of drawings and the like, the position in relation to categories (b) and (c) of artistic works is different. If an article is mass-produced industrially from drawings, there is copyright in the drawings, and hence in the article, without artistic quality. However, if it starts life in three dimensions it can only be an artistic work if it is a 'work of artistic craftsmanship'.

The leading case on this point is *Hensher v Restawhile Upholstery Ltd*⁴ in which the plaintiff claimed that his furniture was a work of artistic craftsmanship and failed, showed the difficulty of establishing that an article which has a functional purpose like furniture is a 'work of artistic craftsmanship'. Only if that can be proved the degree of artistic merit becomes irrelevant. In practice, the existence of drawings is therefore extremely important commercially. An industrial object made up of drawings which qualify as 'works' is protectable without the need for artistic character and without the need for registration. Given sufficient skill or labour, copyright arises automatically on completion of the work, whereas protection of the design under the Registered Designs Act 1949⁵ is only available after official examination for 'novelty', and registration. In either case protection lasts for 15 years⁶. Designs of the following objects have been held to be entitled, on the basis of drawings, to copyright protection: furniture, garments, parts for machinery, taps, light fittings and electric meter fronts.

1 *Exxon Corporation v Exxon Insurance Consultants International Ltd* (1981) 3 All ER 241.
2 *Ladbroke (Football Ltd) v William Hill* (1964) 1 WLR 273.
3 *Chappell v Redwood Music* [1981] RPC 337.
4 [1976] AC 64.
5 See para 18.18 below.
6 This view disregards *Dorling v Honnor Marine* [1964] Ch 560 and [1965] Ch 1 in which case the plaintiff had designed a kit, for amateur builders, of parts to be assembled into a boat. It was held that the parts shown in the plans were not registrable and therefore the artistic copyright in them remained unaffected for the full term of life plus 50 years. In *Amp v Utilex Proprietary Ltd* [1972] RCP 103 the House of Lords held that if the design of an article of a certain shape is functional only and does not appeal to the eye of the customers it is not registrable under the Registered Design Act 1949. This means that many designs may not be registrable and would thus be eligible for full copyright protection, which is a bizarre result.

5. Restricted acts – infringement

18.06 The restricted acts are those acts which only the author, his successors or assignees, have the exclusive right to do or authorise others to do in relation to the work. The restricted acts in respect of literary, dramatic and musical works are found in section 2 of the Act, and, in respect of artistic works in section 3.¹

1 See para 18.18 below.

Acts restricted by the copyright in literary, dramatic or musical works

18.07 These are: a) reproducing the work in any material form; b) publishing the work; c) performing the work in public; d) broadcasting the work; e) causing the work to be transmitted to subscribers to a diffusion service; f) making any adaptation of the work; g) doing, in relation to an adaptation of the work, any of the acts in a) to e). It is also an infringement to do any of these acts in relation to a 'substantial part' of a work (section 49(1)). Quite a small part may be 'substantial' for this purpose.

18.08 Reproduction. To reproduce simply means to copy. Any form of copy which reproduces the original in a recognisable form is sufficient. A handwritten work may be reproduced by photocopying, typing, duplication or printing. A work may be reproduced by being recorded on tape or in a film. Thus, for example, whenever a piece of music is embodied in a sound-recording the permission of the music copyright owner is required.[1] The provisions of section 48(1) are not definitive of 'other material form' but merely examples of reproduction. Thus, it is probably an infringement of a literary work to store it in a computer.

1 Subject to the exception in para 18.17.

18.09 Publishing. The expression 'publish' is mainly of importance in relation to the subsistence of copyright.[1] The House of Lords in *Infabrics Ltd v Jaytex Ltd*[2] held that the provisions of section 49(2) on the meaning of 'publication' relate only to the subsistence and not to infringement of copyright. The use of sections 2(5)(b) and 3(5)(b) is therefore not extensive. In the *Infabrics* case it was pleaded against a seller and distributor who obtained copies made abroad but who could not be proved to have the knowledge required under section 5(2) of the Act. As the House of Lords found that 'selling' of infringing copies does not, per se, constitute publication, the scope of sections 2(5)(b) and 3(5)(b) is reduced as a result of that case.

1 See para 18.04, above.
2 [1981] 1 All ER 1057.

18.10 'Performing' is not defined in the Act but section 48(1) specifies that 'performance' includes delivery, in relation to lectures, addresses, speeches and sermons, and in general includes any mode of visual or acoustic presentation by the use of a radio or television set, the showing of a film or the playing of a record. Thus, to play in public a sound-recording embodying a piece of music for example, is to cause the music to be performed in public. A licence is required from both the maker of the sound-recording[1] and the author of the musical work, both of whom will normally have assigned the public performance right to a collecting society. If the work is performed in public 'by the operation of any apparatus' (eg a jukebox) which is either supplied by, or supplied with the consent of the occupier of the premises where the performance occurs, then that occupier is the person giving the performance.[2] This rule applies irrespective of whether he operates the apparatus. 'In public' is best contrasted with domestic or quasi-domestic. One must look at the nature of the audience. The recent trend in the decided cases is to give a wide rather than narrow meaning to 'in public'. The Act makes an exception[3] in favour of performances in schools, provided the audience is limited to teachers and pupils. The exemption does not extend to universities nor to audiences which include pupils' parents.

1 See para 18.29 below.
2 S 48(b).
3 S 41(3) and (4).

18.11 'Broadcasting' is defined by reference to the Wireless Telegraphy Act 1949.[1] It does not include wire diffusion. Broadcasting may be either sound or television broadcasting and is taken to be made by the body by whom, at the time when, and from the place from which the broadcast emanates.[2]

1 S 48(2).
2 S 14(10).

18.12 'Diffusion Service'. Causing the work to be transmitted to subscribers to a diffusion service (namely, CATV or wire diffusion) is defined as the transmission of a work in the course of distributing broadcast programmes or any other programmes over wires or paths provided by a material substance to the premises of subscribers to the service.[1] The person who 'causes the work to be transmitted' is he who undertakes to provide the service to the subscribers, irrespective of whether he originates the programmes himself. It is not an infringement to transmit by wire a BBC or IBA broadcast, provided the transmission is immediate and is not taped and subsequently broadcast.[2]

1 S 48(3).
2 S 40(3).

18.13 'Adaptation' is defined in section 2(6) of the Act and includes converting a literary work into a dramatic work and vice versa, translating the work, or conveying the story or action in the form of pictures suitable for reproduction in a book, newspaper or magazine or similar periodical. In relation to a musical work, an adaptation is an arrangement or a transcription of a work.

Acts restricted by the copyright in artistic works

18.14 These are:[1] a) reproducing the work in any material form; b) publishing the work; c) including the work in a television broadcast (otherwise than incidentally)[2]; d) causing a television programme which includes the work to be transmitted to subscribers to a diffusion service.

Reproduction includes 'a version produced by converting the work into a three-dimensional form, or, if it is in three dimensions, by converting it into a two-dimensional form', but only if a layman would recognise the one as being a reproduction of the other[3], ie the design of a machine is not protected by virtue of the blueprint on which it is based.

1 S 3(5).
2 S 9(5).
3 S 9(8).

18.15 Primary infringement. The owner of copyright in a work has the exclusive right to do certain restricted acts in relation to that work. He therefore has the right to prevent others from doing any of those restricted acts. A prospective plaintiff must show: firstly that he owns the copyright, secondly that what he is seeking to protect is a work, and thirdly that the defendant has infringed the copyright by committing one of the restricted acts. If two works are identical or substantially similar, then the second is only an infringing copy if it was made by copying the first. A second but independently arrived at identical work is not an infringement.

18.16 Secondary infringement. Acts of primary infringement do not require guilty knowledge, though lack of knowledge may mitigate the damages. There are however a number of other acts, the doing of which may be an infringement of copyright, provided that the defendant knew that such an act would infringe. These are set out in section 5 of the 1956 Act. First, any work is infringed by a person who, without the licence of the owner of the copyright, imports an article (otherwise than for his private and domestic use) into the United Kingdom if to his knowledge the making of that article constituted such an infringement of that copyright or would have constituted such an infringement if the article had been made in the place into which it is so imported.[1] Secondly, there are similar provisions governing any person who sells, lets for hire, or by way of trade offers or exposes for sale or hire any article or by way of trade exhibits any article in public.[2] Thirdly, similar provisions apply to anyone, who either for the purpose of trade or for other purposes, but to such an extent as to affect prejudicially the owner of the copyright in question, distributes any articles.[3] There is also provision for secondary infringement in respect of the public performance of literary, dramatic and musical works. It applies to any person who allows a place of public entertainment to be used for the public performance of a work where the performance itself of the work constitutes an infringement. There are two defences: first, there is no infringement if the person had no reasonable ground for suspecting the performance was an infringement, or secondly he had given permission gratuitously or for only nominal consideration or for a fee which only covered his reasonable expenses.

1   S 5(2).
2   S 5(3).
3   S 5(4).

18.17 Exceptions. 'Fair dealing' for purposes of research or private study, criticism or review or reporting current events is permissible. One test of fairness is whether the copy competes with the original. Again, it is no infringement to reproduce a work in toto for the purpose of a judicial proceeding or a report of such a proceeding. Broadcasting organisations have a (limited) freedom to record for broadcasting and keep for a limited time works which they have been licensed to broadcast solely for the purpose of broadcasting the work ('ephemeral' recordings).[1] Statues and the like permanently situated in public places, and works of architecture may be painted or photographed and the photographs published or broadcast without infringement. These exceptions are found in sections 6 and 9 of the 1956 Act.

1   S 6(7).

18.18 Section 7 allows certain non-profit making libraries to make and supply single copies of articles in periodicals to persons requiring them for research or private study, and allows some latitude to publish 100 year-old unpublished manuscripts.

Once an author (usually a composer of music) has allowed his work to be recorded for retail sale, other record-makers may make and market their own recordings of the work on payment of the statutory royalty.[1]

Finally, section 10 of the Act provides that once a design, which is itself an artistic work[2] is 'applied industrially' with the consent of the copyright owner, and the articles to which it is applied are marketed, the protection of the Copyright Act is lost for those articles. The only protection (if any) is that available under the Registered Designs Act 1949. This loss of copyright protection does not apply if the articles in question are 'primarily literary or artistic in character' and are so listed in rules made under section 4 of the 1949 Act above (eg greetings cards, book jackets, wall plaques).

An amendment of great commercial significance was made to this section by the *Design Copyright Act* 1968 the effect of which was to postpone for 15 years this loss of copyright protection for the industrial articles concerned.[3]

1 S 8. The rate of royalty is fixed by law in 1911 and raised in 1928 to 6¼% of the retail selling price of the phonogram. This rate now in the 1956 Act was the subject of an inquiry provided by s 8(3) of the Act and was confirmed by the Tribunal of Inquiry.
2 See para 18.05 above.
3 See para 18.05, Artistic works, above.

6. Films

18.19 Although protected by the Copyright Conventions, cinematograph films are dealt with in Part II of the British Act, together with sound-recordings and broadcasts, as 'other subject matter' of copyright. Copyright subsists if *either* the 'maker' is a qualified person ie a national or body incorporated, of, or under the law of, a country to which the Act extends or applies *or* if first (or simultaneously) published in such a country.[1] 'Maker' means the person who makes the necessary arrangements for the making of the film and 'film' means any sequence of visual images recorded on material of any description so as to be capable of being shown as a moving picture (and includes the soundtrack). Videotapes and video discs are thus to be regarded as films within this definition. 'Publication' in this case means 'the offer for sale or hire of copies to the public'.[2] The maker of the film owns the copyright in the film (as distinct from any works (script, music) included therein). The acts restricted by the copyright[3] are: a) making a copy of the film; b) causing the film to be seen or heard in public; c) broadcasting the film; d) causing the film to be transmitted to subscribers to a diffusion service. It is not an infringement to make a copy of the film or to show it for the purposes of a judicial proceeding.

1 S 13(1) and (2).
2 S 13(10).
3 S 13(5).

7. Term of protection

18.20 The basic term of protection for all works is, in accordance with the Berne Convention, the life of the author plus 50 years. The exact term is from the date the work was created until the end of the period of 50 years from the end of the calendar year in which the author died. This means the term ends on 31 December of the fiftieth year after death. However, if, before the author's death, a literary, dramatic or musical work has not been published, performed in public, offered to the public for sale in the form of a record, or broadcast, then the term of protection will run from the date when one of these acts is first done and will run for 50 years. The term ends as before at the end of the fiftieth year after the act in question. An unpublished and 'unperformed' manuscript therefore enjoys perpetual copyright.

The general rule for artistic works is the same as for literary, dramatic and musical ones with the important difference that, except for engravings and photographs, no perpetual copyright is possible.[1]

In this case the protection continues to subsist until the end of the period of

50 years from the end of the calendar year in which the photograph is first published and shall then expire.

Films. Protection for cinematographic films lasts for 50 years from the year of registration or, if not registrable, 50 years from publication.

Anonymous works and works of joint authorship. An anonymous or pseudonymous work enjoys protection from the end of the calendar year in which it is first published. If during that period it becomes possible for someone to ascertain the author's identity by reasonable enquiry then the normal rules apply. A work of joint authorship is treated for these purposes as a work of the author who died last.[2]

1   S 3(4).
2   S 11(2), Sch 3, para 2.

8. Remedies

18.21   Remedies for infringement of copyright are the subject of Part III of the 1956 Act. A copyright owner or exclusive licensee[1] whose copyright has been infringed may have one or more of the following objectives: he may want compensation for the loss he has suffered, he may wish to prevent further infringement or distribution of the infringing copies and he may require information containing the names or details of the 'piracy' operations. The remedies available are, damages, 'exemplary' damages, an account of profits, delivery up, and an injunction.

1   S 19.

Damages

18.22   Infringement of copyright is a tort. The overriding principle in tort damages is to put the plaintiff in the position he would have been had the tortious act not occurred. Therefore, if the plaintiff's business has suffered as a result, for example, of the defendants selling infringing copies in competition with the plaintiff, the plaintiff will recover loss of profits he would have made if the defendant had not been in competition.
(a) *Normal damages.* The copyright owner can choose whether to ask for the provable damage suffered by him (such as loss of sales) or he can ask the court to treat the infringer as his agent who must hand over all his profits (regardless of whether the copyright owner would have made the same profits). The first choice is called 'damages', the second 'an account of profits'.

(b) *Conversion damages.* The law 'deems' all infringing copies of the work to be the property of the copyright owner. If such infringing copies are sold the seller is thus deemed to have sold what does not belong to him (that is to have 'converted it to his own use') and the receipts of such sales must be handed over to the copyright owner.[1]

(c) *Additional or exemplary damages.* Section 17(3) of the Act makes special provision for additional damages if the infringement has been flagrant and the defendant has benefitted considerably from the infringement. If a court is satisfied that in those circumstances effective relief would not otherwise be available to the plaintiff, it may award additional damages as it deems appropriate in the circumstances. Although the court has a wide discretion under these provisions, it is in practice unusual for an award to be made.

1 S 18.

Account of profits

18.23 This form of relief is rarely sought in copyright actions as it can be extremely complicated and therefore very expensive. The relief is in the form of an order that the defendant pays to the plaintiff, a sum equal to the net profits made by the defendant. Although in the case of 'innocent infringement' the Act says the defendant shall be entitled to an account of profits it seems that at all times, including 'innocent infringement', the remedy is a discretionary one, as are all equitable remedies.

Delivery Up. An order for delivery up of infringing articles is within the inherent jurisdiction of the court although not specifically mentioned in section 17(1). It seems in any event that this remedy is little used because of the effect of section 18 and an action in conversion.

Injunctions

18.24 The court has power to make an order restraining the defendant from infringing or continuing to infringe the plaintiff's copyright. Normally an injunction will be granted if the plaintiff has established his loss and it is not unlikely that the defendant will continue to infringe. However, the court may grant an injunction even though the plaintiff's loss to date is a nominal one, if there is the possibility of the defendant infringing in the future. In many cases the defendant may be willing to give an undertaking to the court not to infringe. If he does so and it is accepted by the plaintiff and the court, his undertaking has the effect of an order and he may be committed for contempt of court for breach of such an undertaking.

There are three main types of injunction:

(a) *Final injunction*. This is the permanent injunction granted at the end of the full trial as part of the final judgment forbidding the defendant to repeat any infringing acts.

(b) *Interlocutory injunction*. This is a temporary injunction granted at the very start of the action and pending the trial of the action. The main purpose is to preserve the status quo until the end of the trial.

(c) *Ex parte injunction*. This is an injunction granted in the absence of the defendant and without his knowledge in cases of extreme urgency. It must be of short duration.

Interlocutory injunctions

18.25 In a copyright action a plaintiff can expect to have to wait between the time he first issues proceedings and the date of trial. In many cases the plaintiff will want speedy relief to prevent further infringements and further damage to his own business. A trial in two years time may be of no use if the market for the articles is a temporary one and the defendant may 'disappear' with the proceeds of infringement. Such a plaintiff will need interim relief. If the matter is extremely urgent he may apply ex parte, that is without notice to the defendant, for an injunction. However, most injunctions are sought on an interlocutory basis on notice.

In *American Cynamid v Ethicon*[1] the court laid down the process through which it should go before granting an injunction:

1. Is there a serious issue to be tried? If there is not, no injunction will be issued. If there is, then the court moves to the second question.
2. If the plaintiff can be adequately compensated by damages at trial no injunction will be issued. If the defendant can be adequately compensated at trial by the plaintiff's undertaking to pay the defendant his damages, then an injunction should be ordered.
3. If there is no clear answer to either question of damages then the court should attempt to determine whether the defendant would suffer greater inconvenience if the injunction were granted, or the plaintiff if it is not granted. This is known as the 'balance of convenience' test.
4. It is only if the 'balance of convenience' test does not resolve the matter that the court should look at the relative strength of the parties' case as revealed by their affidavit evidence.

1 [1975] AC 396.

'Anton Piller' Orders

18.26 Since the decision of the Court of Appeal in *Anton Piller KG v Manufacturing Processes Ltd*,[1] the courts have been willing in certain circumstances to grant to the plaintiff an order enabling him to seize articles in the defendant's possession which he has grounds for believing are infringement of his copyright. The most important aspect of an application for an Anton Piller Order is that it is made without notice to the defendant. In the normal course of an action, a plaintiff may require early access to articles or papers in possession of the defendant in order to prepare his case properly. In most cases this can be done by application on notice. However, the copyright owner who has not yet instituted proceedings against a suspected infringer may fear that if he puts the prospective defendant on any sort of notice that he is suing or even going to sue, then the prospective defendant will dispose of infringing articles and details of his distributorship chain. This is quite often the case where the prospective defendants are what are known as 'record pirates' whose business is the selling and distribution of phonograms (records and tapes) made and sold in infringement of copyright. In such a case the plaintiff may apply ex parte ie without notice, for an order for inspection, photographing and delivering up of infringing materials in the defendant's possession or control. The Court of Appeal in the *Anton Piller* case said that such an order would only be made if there is 'a grave danger that vital evidence will be destroyed, that papers will be burnt or lost or hidden, or taken beyond the jurisdiction, and so the ends of justice be defeated'. The availability of the orders has been confirmed by section 72 of the Supreme Court Act 1981. In *Rank Film Distributors v Video Information Centre*[2] the House of Lords held that a defendant in civil proceedings was entitled to rely on the privilege against self-incrimination in order to resist an Anton Piller order for disclosure of, for example, the addresses of suppliers. The *Supreme Court Act 1981* now provides that 'In any proceedings to which this sub-section applies, a person shall not be excused, by reason that to do so would tend to expose that person or his or her spouse to proceedings for a related penalty: (a) from answering any questions, or (b) from complying with any order made in those proceedings'. Thus the privilege against self-incrimination does not apply to proceedings 'for infringement of... intellectual property rights'.

When copyright subsists in a work, it is an offence for any person to make for sale or hire, or to sell or let for hire, or by way of trade to offer or expose for sale or hire or to exhibit in public or to import other than for his private use, articles which he knows to be infringing copies of the work.[3] Thus the prosecution has to prove guilty knowledge which in many cases is difficult. Mainly for this reason the provision is rarely used.

1 [1976] 2 WLR 162.
2 [1951] 2 WLR 668.
3 S 21, Copyright Act 1956.

9. Protection of performers

18.27 In spite of some pressure from bodies such as the Musicians' Union, successive committees (in 1935,[1] in 1952,[2] and in 1977[3]) have recommended against giving the performer a property right in the nature of a copyright. The protection at present afforded to performers is in the Performers Protection Acts 1958/72. The 1958 Act is the principal Act. It was amended in 1963 to bring United Kingdom law into line with the Rome Convention of 1961, prior to ratification; and in 1972 the penalties for offences under the earlier Acts were increased in an effort to curb the growing practice of 'bootlegging', which is the making of clandestine recordings from live performances given at concerts and the pressing and sale of commercial discs and tapes therefrom.

It is an offence, without the consent in writing of the performer or performers, knowingly, (i) to make a record or a film of his 'live', that is unfixed performance, 'directly or indirectly', that is either at the place where the performance takes place or off the air, (ii) to sell or hire or offer to sell or hire records or films so made or to use them for the purpose of public performance, (iii) to broadcast (sound or television) a live performance.[4]

Since 'broadcasting' under United Kingdom law is confined to diffusion by Hertzian waves, the 1963 Act added the offence of 'otherwise than by the use of a record or a cinematograph film or by the receipt of a broadcast', knowingly causing a performance to be transmitted (a) to subscribers to a diffusion service; or (b) over wires or other paths provided by a material substance so as to be seen or heard in public.[5]

The persons who enjoy protection are 'actors, singers, musicians, dancers or other persons who act, sing, deliver, declaim, play in or otherwise perform literary, dramatic, musical or artistic works'.[6] It is immaterial whether or not the work is still in copyright. But the fact that protection is confined to performances of 'works' means not only that tennis or football stars and other sportsmen and wrestlers (unless wrestling from a script!) are excluded, but also certain variety artists (like acrobats and jugglers). The reason no doubt is the difficulty of framing a definition which protects the latter but not the former.

It is a defence to prove that consent in writing was given by a person who represented that he had been authorised by the performers to give it (even if not in fact so authorised) *and* that the person making the record, film or broadcast had no reason to believe otherwise,[7] but the person who, without authority, purported to give that consent is himself guilty of an offence.[8]

Finally, it is an offence to make or have in one's possession a 'plate or similar contrivance' for the purpose of making records in contravention of the Act; and the court has power to order the destruction, forfeiture, etc of offending records, films and plates.[9]

1 The Departmental Committee on International Copyright, 1935 (The Peto Committee).
2 The Copyright Committee 1951 (The Gregory Committee) Cmd 8662.
3 The Committee to consider the Law on Copyright and Designs (The Whitford Committee) Cmd 6732.
4 1958 Act, ss 1–3.
5 1963 Act, s 3.

6 1963 Act, s 1(i).
7 1958 Act, s 7.
8 1963 Act, s 4.
9 1958 Act, ss 4 and 5.

Penalties

18.28 The maximum fines were increased in 1972 from £2 to £20 per record and from £50 to £400 per transaction – filming, broadcasting, etc. In addition, a person may, on indictment, suffer imprisonment for up to two years in addition to a fine.[1] Further the 1972 Act inserted a new section into the 1963 Act:[2]

> 'Where an offence under the principal Act or this Act committed by a body corporate is proved to have been committed with the consent or connivance of, or to be attributable to any neglect on the part of, any director, manager, secretary or other similar officer of the body corporate or any person who is purporting to act in such capacity, he, as well as the body corporate, shall be guilty of that offence and shall be liable to be proceeded against and punished accordingly.'

Although the United Kingdom legislation thus protects performers only by means of a criminal rather than a civil sanction, the Whitford Committee (1977) said 'it is not clear whether civil proceedings under which damages, for instance, could be awarded, are available in respect of offences under these Acts.[3]

The need for the performer's consent enables him to make what bargain he can as to remuneration as a condition of giving it. But he has no right, except by agreement, to control or claim remuneration for the broadcasting or public performance of his fixed performance once his consent has been given to the fixation in question.

1 1972 Act, ss 1, 2 and Sch.
2 Performers' Protection Act 1963, s 4a.
3 Whitford Committee Report, para 406.

10. The protection of producers of phonograms

18.29 As has been pointed out above, these have enjoyed a copyright since 1911. The rights are now embodied in the Copyright Act 1956. By section 12 of that Act 'the acts restricted by the copyright in a sound recording are the following ... that is to say (a) making a record embodying the recording; (b) causing the recording to be heard in public; (c) broadcasting the recording.'[1] The owner of the copyright is the maker of the recording (except in the case of recordings commissioned for money or money's worth).[2] 'Maker' is defined as the person who owns the first record on which the recording is made,[3] and protection lasts until the end of a period of 50 years from the end of the calendar year in which the recording is first published.[4] 'Publication' means the isssue to the public of records embodying the recording or any part thereof.[5] 'Sound recording' means the aggregate of the sounds embodied in, and capable of being reproduced by means of, a record of any description, other than the sound-track associated with a cinematograph film.[6] Thus, the broadcasting organisations, like the record companies, enjoy copyright under this section in any recordings they make of their programmes.

In addition to the civil remedies provided by section 12, it is also a criminal offence under section 21 of the 1956 Act to make, import or deal commercially with articles which the defendant knows to be infringing copies not only of works but also of sound recordings.[7] (The same does not apply to public performance or broadcasting of sound recordings.) Penalties include fines and forfeiture of infringing articles, and in some cases, for a second or subsequent offence, imprisonment.

The rights do not include diffusing the recording by wire. But, in addition to the power to control copying of recordings, phonogram producers also enjoy, subject to the jurisdiction of the Performing Right Tribunal,[8] power to control 'needle time', that is the extent to which their records are used in the making of broadcast programmes. Evidence given to the Gregory Committee (in 1952) showed that the power had also been used, at the behest of the Musicians' Union, to forbid the use of records in theatres, music halls and dance halls where live musicians could, having regard to the size and nature of the place, be employed.[9] This was a principal reason for the establishment of the Performing Right Tribunal. The Whitford Committee (1977) did not think that a requirement for the employment of live musicians as a condition for granting a licence was always going to be unfair, having regard to the powers of the Performing Right Tribunal to override unreasonable refusals or conditions. The Report cited, apparently with approval,[10] the Manx Radio case of 1964[11] in which the record makers proposed that not more than one-fifth of Manx Radio (its first commercial station) broadcasting time should be occupied by the playing of commercial records. Manx Radio asked for more needle time. The BBC and the Musicians' Union intervened in the case (as they are entitled under the rules to do with the leave of the Tribunal), the former on the ground that Manx Radio should not enjoy more needle time than was allowed to the BBC, and the latter on the ground that any extension of broadcasting of records was damaging to the livelihood of musicians and ultimately to the existence of a sound musical profession. The Tribunal increased the amount of needle time allowed to Manx Radio to one half of its total broadcasting time, but increased the royalty during the second to fourth year of the licence.[12] It made the observation that, when the licence fell to be renewed, it would be a matter of interest to the Tribunal to enquire into the amount of help that Manx Radio had seen fit to give to live musicians, either by direct employment, or by the promotion of their interests in the Island. When, in 1980, the Tribunal again considered licences to broadcast commercial records, this time for 19 independent commercial radio stations, it largely reaffirmed its findings in the *Manx Radio* case.[13]

1 S 12(5).
2 S 12(4).
3 S 12(8).
4 S 12(3).
5 S 12(9).
6 S 12(9).
7 S 21(1)-(4).
8 Copyright Act 1956, ss 23-30.
9 Gregory Committee Report, para 149.
10 Whitford Report 1977, para 409.
11 Decision of Performing Rights Tribunal 17/64 of 29 March 1965.
12 To 8% of net advertising revenue per year.
13 *The Association of Independent Local Radio Contractors v Phonographic Performance Ltd and the Musicians Union.*

Remedies. See paras 18.21–18.26 above.

11. Protection of broadcasting organisations

18.30 Broadcasting organisations, too, have a copyright in their broadcasts,[1] in addition to any copyright they may own in works, recordings or films which they broadcast. It lasts for 50 years from the end of the year in which the broadcast is first made.[2] The Acts restricted by the copyright are:

(a) in the case of a television broadcast insofar as it consists of visual images, making, otherwise than for private purposes, a cinematograph film of it or a copy of such a film;

(b) in the case of a sound broadcast, or of a television broadcast insofar as it consists of sounds, making, otherwise than for private purposes, a sound recording of it or a record embodying such a recording;

(c) in the case of a television broadcast, causing it, insofar as it consists of visual images, to be seen in public, or, insofar as it consists of sounds, to be heard in public, if it is seen or heard by a paying audience;

(d) in the case either of a television broadcast or of a sound broadcast, rebroadcasting it.[3]

It should be noted that it is *not* an infringement of this copyright to cause the broadcast to be transmitted to subscribers a diffusion service.

If only a part of a television broadcast is taken, it is an infringement if this part is a sequence of images sufficient to be seen as a moving picture. It is not therefore an infringement for a newspaper to take and to publish one still photograph from a broadcast, eg the winning goal in a football match.

1 Copyright Act 1956, s 14.
2 S 14(2) and (3).
3 S 14(4).

12. Collection and distribution of revenue

18.31 Since performers do not enjoy a property right in their performances, they do not directly collect any revenue from the broadcasting or public performance of recordings embodying their performances. Producers of phonograms however do so collect, both from broadcasting and from public performance of phonograms, and that revenue is shared by voluntary agreement with the principal individual artists whose performances are recorded and with the Musicians' Union. Of the net distributable revenue, 20% goes to the performers who recorded, $12\frac{1}{2}$% to the Musicians' Union for the collective benefit of musicians and a further 8% to the music publishers. The society which collects and distributes this revenue on behalf of phonogram producers is Phonographic Performance Ltd, which was incorporated in 1934, the year after the *Carwardine* case[1] decided that such a right existed. It was because the Gregory Committee felt that there should be some appeal from the terms and conditions imposed by the collecting societies – the Performing Right Society (PRS) on behalf of composers and music publishers and Phonographic Performance Ltd (PPL) on behalf of phonogram producers – that the Performing Right Tribunal was created by the 1956 Act.

The Tribunal consists of a lawyer of at least seven years' standing as Chairman, and of not less than two nor more than four other members.[2] In practice these members are or have been accountants, economists, businessmen and retired civil servants. If there is a dispute over a tariff or a licence to perform in public or broadcast a work or to diffuse it by wire, to perform in public or broadcast a record or to cause a broadcast to be seen or heard in public, the person requiring the licence may refer the matter to the Tribunal, which may make such order as it thinks 'reasonable in the circumstances'.[3]

Its jurisdiction, as its name suggests, is only over performing (including broadcasting) rights. It has no jurisdiction over the author's rights of reproduction, however exercised. So far as the author's rights are concerned, the Tribunal only has jurisdiction when performing rights are exercised by a society which issues 'blanket' licences. An author who retains his own performing rights, such as the composer of an opera or the writer of a play, and who prefers to negotiate his own terms for performing his work cannot have those terms challenged by the Tribunal. The same is true of an organisation, for example a theatrical agency, even though it controls the performing rights and the works of a number of different authors, provided always it is prepared to grant individual licences, or to licence each work separately. The Tribunal's jurisdiction over authors' rights therefore is confined to cases of organisations which grant 'general licences each extending to the works of several authors'. The intention in limiting the Tribunal's jurisdiction in this way was to honour the United Kingdom's obligations under the Berne Copyright Convention which requires that the author should enjoy an exclusive right, though allowing power to control abuse of monopoly. However, so far as phonogram producers and broadcasters are concerned, no Convention on obligations exists and the Tribunal's jurisdiction covers the performing rights of these copyright owners even if exercised individually.

The fees payable to the Tribunal are small although the Tribunal does have discretion to award to any party a contribution from the other party towards the costs he has incurred in the case.

The Tribunal has tended to draw a distinction between undertakings for which music is essential, such as dance halls, and those for which it is not, such as Bingo sessions, being disinclined in the latter case to interfere.

1   *The Gramaphone Co Ltd v Carwardine & Co* [1934] ch 450.
2   S 23(2).
3   S 25(5).

13. Term of protection for neighbouring rights

18.32   Protection for phonograms lasts for 50 years from publication, and that for broadcasts for 50 years from the making of the broadcast. No time limit is set out in the Performers' Protection Acts and therefore the normal rules relating to the prosecution of criminal offences apply. Though not bound by any strict time limits, the courts would expect a prosecution to be brought within a reasonable time of the discovery that an offence had been committed, and would be disinclined to punish a person for an offence in respect of which there has been a long delay in bringing proceedings.

14. Limitation of neighbouring rights (exceptions)

(1) Performers

18.33   For an offence to be committed, it must have been done 'knowingly', and it is a defence to prove that the record or film in question was made for the 'private and domestic use only' of the person making it.[1] The question of someone unauthorised purporting to give consent has been dealt with above.[2] Other defences are for the defendant to prove:

(i) that the record, cinematograph film or broadcast to which the proceedings relate was made only for the purpose of reporting current events, or
(ii) that the inclusion of the performance in question in the record, cinematograph film or broadcast to which the proceedings relate was only by way of background or was otherwise only incidental to the principal matters comprised or represented in the record, film or broadcast.[3]

1 1958 Act ss 1 and 2.
2 See para 18.04, above.
3 1958 Act, s 6.

(2) Producers of phonograms

18.34 The principal exceptions here are to the right of performance in public. It is not an infringement of the copyright in a sound recording to cause it to be heard in public.

(i) at any premises where persons reside or sleep, as part of the amenities provided exclusively or mainly for residents therein, or
(ii) as part of the activities of, or for the benefit of, a club, society or other organisation which is not established or conducted for profit and whose main objects are charitable or otherwise concerned with the advancement of religion, education or social welfare,

unless (in case (i)) a special charge is made for admission to the part of the premises where the recording is to be heard, or (in case (ii)) if a charge is made for admission to the place where the recording is to be heard and any of the proceeds of the charge are applied otherwise than for the purposes of the organisation.[1] Nor is it an infringement to cause it to be heard in public by means of the reception of a broadcast.[2]

It should be noted however that the exception of fair dealing for the purposes of research, private study, criticism or review[3] or 'private purposes'[4] does not apply in the case of reproducing sound-recordings. Parliament in 1956 took the view that commercial phonographs were made for sale to the public for playing in their homes, and it would be wrong to approve the practice of making a private record collection off the air or by borrowing records from friends or the local library, even if it was clear that it happened and was virtually impossible to police.[5]

1 1956 Act, s 12(7).
2 S 40(1).
3 S 6(1)-(2).
4 S 14(4).
5 See para 12.12 above.

(1) Broadcasting organisations

18.35 The public performance rights of broadcasting organisations are limited to television broadcasts to *paying* audiences.[1] This is in any case something of a dead letter since there is now a television set in most homes, and cinemas no longer show broadcasts of the principal sporting events. The other exception is 'anything done in relation to a broadcast for the purpose of a judicial proceeding'.[2]

1 See para 18.21 above.
2 S 14(9).

15. Protection of foreign 'neighbouring rights'

Performers

18.36 Criminal offences under United Kingdom law are only actionable if committed within the jurisdiction. In order to ensure that the United Kingdom meets its obligations as regards performers from other Convention countries, the Performers Protection Act 1963 contains the following provisions:

> Section 1(ii) – For the avoidance of doubt it is hereby declared that the principal Act applies as respects anything done in relation to a performance notwithstanding that the performance took place out of the United Kingdom, but this shall not cause anything done out of the United Kingdom to be treated as an offence. Section 2 – For the purposes of Paragraphs (b) and (c) of Section 1 of the principal Act (by which sales of, and other dealings with, records made in contravention of the Act are rendered punishable), a record made in a country outside the United Kingdom directly or indirectly from or by means of a performance to which the principal Act applies, shall, where the civil or criminal law of that country contains a provision for the protection of performers under which the consent of any person to the making of the record was required, be deemed to have been made in contravention of the principal Act if, whether knowingly or not, it was made without the consent so required and without the consent in writing of the performers.

The Whitford Committee found this latter provision difficult to construe[1] on the question of whether or not reciprocity was required. But it seems reasonably clear that if, in the foreign country in which recording of the performance took place, the performers' consent was required (albeit not in writing) and such consent was given, dealings in the United Kingdom with the resulting records are not criminal offences.

1 Report, para 412.

Producers of phonograms

18.37 Sound-recordings enjoy protection against copying in the United Kingdom if the maker is a national of (or body incorporated in) a country of the Berne Union or of the Universal Copyright Convention. (Since Rome Convention countries must belong to one of these, this also includes all Rome Convention countries.) A recording is also protected if it was first (or simultaneously) published in such a country. 'Simultaneously' has the same meaning as in the Rome and the Berne Conventions (that is within 30 days).[1]

On the other hand, the right to control (and receive remuneration for) public performance and broadcasting is only enjoyed on the basis of reciprocity, that is in respect of recordings made by nationals of, or first published in, countries under whose law control over or remuneration for *either* public performance or broadcasting or both is enjoyed by United Kingdom recordings. The list of such countries includes[2] not only all those Rome Convention countries which have accepted, in whole or in part, article 12 of that Convention,[3] but also a number of Commonwealth and other countries whose law provides the necessary reciprocity.

1 Copyright Act 1956, s 49(2)(d).
2 Schedule 3, Copyright (International Conventions) Order 1979. Countries in whose case copyright in sound recordings includes exclusive right to perform in public and to broadcast are: Australia, Austria, Brazil, Chile, Colombia, Costa Rica, Cyprus, Czechoslovakia, Denmark, Ecuador, El Salvador, Federal Republic of Germany (and West Berlin), Fiji, Guatemala, India, Republic of Ireland, Italy, Israel, Mexico, New Zealand, Nigeria, Norway, Pakistan, Paraguay, Spain, Sri Lanka, Sweden, Switzerland, Uruguay.
3 See para 8.27 above.

Broadcasting organisations

18.38 Broadcasting organisations constituted in or under the laws of certain foreign countries enjoy protection in the United Kingdom for their broadcasts *if* made from places in those countries. The foreign countries in question include all members of the Rome Convention, and, as regards television broadcasts only, all members of the Council of Europe Agreement for the Protection of Television Broadcasts.[1]

1 See para 18.37 above.

Chapter 19
The Soviet Union

by Mark Boguslavski

1. History and development of copyright

19.01 After the 1917 Revolution, Soviet copyright law faced two tasks: to abolish the copyright laws of tsarist Russia and liquidate the relations established in that field, and to formulate new principles regulating the copyright law in order to combine the interests of society with those of the author. The former was achieved by declaring a state monopoly in the works of dead authors for a term of not more than five years (the Decree of 29 December 1917), and by recognising as state property any works in science, literature, music and art (the Decree of 26 November 1917). Under the latter decree works by 47 writers and 17 composers were declared to be state property. The authors whose works were not declared state property retained the right to dispose of them. The Decree of 10 October 1919 declared null and void all the agreements which publishers had hitherto concluded with authors under which their works had become the publishers' sole property.

A new system of copyright norms was set up after the formation of the USSR. On 30 January 1925, 'The Fundamental Principles of Copyright Law' were adopted. This national law only provided basic regulation procedures in this field, stipulating that detailed rules would be fixed in the legislation of the Union republics.

On 16 May 1928, new 'Fundamental Principles of Copyright Law' were adopted. In keeping with this national law, all the Union republics adopted copyright laws. After the adoption in 1961 of a general legislative act in the field of civil law: the 'Fundamental Principles of Civil Legislation' of the USSR and of the Union republics, followed by civil codes of the Union republics, the system of special laws on copyright norms is contained in the 'Fundamental Principles of Civil Legislation' of the USSR and of the Union republics. This is the national law adopted by the USSR Supreme Soviet on 8 December 1961 which came into force on 1 May 1962.[1] Detailed rules for copyright are contained in the civil codes of the Union republics.[2] In accordance with the 'Fundamental Principles of Civil Legislation' and the civil codes, a large number of statutes on copyright have been enacted: resolutions of the USSR Council of Ministers and the governments of the Union republics, as well as orders and instructions of ministries and departments.

Until the early 1970s, international regulation of copyright issues had not had any essential impact on the development of Soviet legislation. This can be shown, above all, by the way in which the USSR solved the problem of translation of works from one language into another.

After the formation of the USSR, the first legislative acts by the Soviet state on copyright recognised freedom of translation. It was decreed that within the Soviet Union a work could be translated without the author's consent or compensation. This principle was proclaimed in 1925 in the resolution 'On the Fundamental Principles of Copyright Law' and was reaffirmed in 1928.

According to article 9a of the Copyright Act of 1928 'the translation of another's work into another language' was not considered to be an infringement of copyright. Soviet legal literature supported the introduction of this principle, and its retention in subsequent legislative acts is justified by the need to ensure unrestricted development of the different national cultures in the Soviet Union.

The principle of freedom of translation was retained in the 'Fundamental Principles of Civil Legislation' and in the civil codes of the Union republics, although detailed rules on questions of translation changed (for example, a provision was introduced for notifying the author of the translation of his work). Since 1947, the legislation of the Union republics has made provision for the payment of royalties to authors of works translated and published in another language. However, essential changes in this field were brought about by the USSR's accession to the Universal Copyright Convention in 1973. These changes, however, had been heralded by developments in Soviet legislation, as well as by international agreements concluded by the Soviet Union with Hungary and Bulgaria in 1967 and 1971.

The rules of translation were revised by the Decree of the Presidium of the USSR Supreme Soviet of 21 February 1973. Article 102(1) of the 'Fundamental Principles' was formulated as follows: 'Translation of a work into another language for the purpose of publication shall be subject to the consent of the author or his successors in title'. At the same time, by way of supplementing article 101, it was provided that the use of the author's work (including translation into another language) by other persons is permitted exclusively on the basis of a contract with the author or his successor in title, except in cases provided for by law. Appropriate changes have also been introduced in the civil codes of the Union republics.

International rules and, above all, the provisions of the Universal Copyright Convention have also had their impact on other provisions of Soviet law: for example, extension of the duration of copyright and the increase of the scope of copyright owners.

Also of essential importance for the development of Soviet copyright law was the establishment of the USSR Copyright Agency (VAAP). A public institution, VAAP, being the only organisation of this kind in the USSR, carries out a number of functions, some of which are directly linked with the USSR's participation in the Universal Copyright Convention and in bilateral international agreements on copyright. These functions include ensuring the protection of the legitimate rights and interests of Soviet and foreign authors, participating in the conclusion of agreements on the use of works of Soviet authors abroad and of works of foreign authors in the USSR, the collection and payment of royalties to authors, and the conclusion of various agreements with authors' societies of other states, in particular dealing with public performance of works.[3]

1 [1961] Vedomosti Verkhovnogo Soveta SSSR, No 50, item 525.
2 For the texts of these acts including all the alterations see Boguslavsky *The USSR and international copyright protection* Progress Publishers (Moscow, 1979) pp 289-303.
3 For greater detail on VAAP and its functions, see Rudakov Yu S, Gringolts I A 'The Copyright Agency of the USSR (VAAP) - Background, Functions, Structure' RIDA (1974) No 1, pp 2-33.

2. Copyright – synopsis of Copyright Act[1]

19.02 Under the USSR Constitution of 1977, 'the rights of authors, inventors and innovators are protected by the state'. However, as already stated, there is at present no specific law on copyright in the USSR.

The basic norms of copyright law are contained in the 'Fundamental Principles of Civil Legislation' of the USSR (Part IV of the Law), in the civil codes of the Union republics and in different decisions taken by the government of the USSR and the governments of the Union republics.

Under Soviet law, copyright extends to scientific, literary and artistic works, irrespective of the form, purpose and merits of a work, or the form of its reproduction. Copyright extends to published or unpublished works in some tangible form which permits the reproduction of the result of the author's creative activity (for example, manuscript, drawing, image, public performance or recital, tape, mechanical or magnetic tape-recording). To ensure copyright protection in the USSR no formal registration of a work is required. An exception is made for photographic works and works produced by means similar to those used in photography: each copy of such a work must indicate the name of the author, as well as the place and year of publication.[2]

The aim of legal regulation of copyright in the USSR is to ensure the most favourable material and legal conditions for creating scientific, literary and artistic works and at the same time to promote the broadest possible publication, performance and other dissemination of these works. The principle of harmony between the interests of the author and society is essential to Soviet copyright law. Personal intangible and tangible interests of the author are protected by different norms of Soviet copyright legislation.

Soviet law grants the following rights to the author:

(a) the right of publication, reproduction and distribution of his work by all legal means under his own name, pseudonymously or anonymously;
(b) the right of inviolability of a work;
(c) the right to compensation for the use of a work by other persons, excepting cases provided for by law.

It is forbidden to use a work in any way, translate it into another language, set it to music or to adopt a narrative work into a play, a cinematographic, radio or television scenario, and vice versa without the consent of the author or his successors in title.

Copyright extends to all literary, scientific and artistic works. A non-exhaustive list of such works is given in article 475 of the Civil Code of the Russian Federation and in appropriate articles of the civil codes of the other Union republics.

Civil codes of the Union republics provide the main rules for concluding an author's contract. Such contracts may be of two types: 1) an author's contract for the transfer of a work for use; 2) an author's licence contract. Under the author's contract for the transfer of a work for use, the author or his successor in title transfers, or the author undertakes to create and within the term specified by the contract to transfer, the said work to a given organisation for use in the way stipulated by the contract, and the organisation undertakes to effect or begin its use within the time limit specified by the contract, and to pay to the author or his successor in title a royalty (except in cases provided for by law).

Authors' contracts for the assignment of a work for use include: a contract for the publication or republication of a work in the original (a 'publishing' contract), a contract for the public performance of an unpublished work (a 'production' contract), a contract for the use of an unpublished work in a film or television film (a 'scenario' contract), in a radio or television broadcast, as well as other contracts on the assignment of a literary, scientific or artistic work for use by some other means. An author's contract must be in writing.

From the general provisions in the civil codes of the Union republics on authors' contracts of the first type stem Model Publishing Contracts which take into account the specific details of individual works and the methods of use (publications, performances, productions of films, radio and television broadcasts). These Model Publishing Contracts stipulating the reciprocal rights and obligations of the author and organisation-user of the work are All-Union acts which have been jointly worked out between appropriate ministries and departments, the creative unions concerned and the USSR Copyright Agency. Specific contracts may contain provisions not stipulated by the Model Contract, but conditions reducing the author's rights as compared with those provided for in the Model Contract are considered null and void.[3]

Another type of author's contract provided for by Soviet law is the licence agreement. Under an author's licence agreement, the author or his successor in title grant the organisation the right to use the work, including use by translating it into another language, or altering it within the limits stipulated by the agreement and for a term provided for by the agreement, and the organisation undertakes to pay royalties for the granting of this right or for the use of the work in the form specified by the agreement.

The terms of a licence agreement for the right to use a work by translating it into another language or by altering it into a work of another kind (in particular by transposing a narrative work into a dramatic one and vice versa) are fixed by the parties to a contract. Agreements on the use of works by foreign authors in the USSR are concluded through VAAP.

A distinctive feature of Soviet copyright law is government regulation of the rates and procedure for payment of an author's royalties for the use of his work. This regulation is usually effected by ordinances of the Council of Ministers of the USSR and the Councils of Ministers of the Union republics. It should not be presumed, however, that government regulation of the author's remuneration leaves the parties to a contract for the use of a work, the author in particular, no leeway in determining the amount of a royalty. This contractual freedom, however, is limited by the minimum and maximum rates in force.

The right to use works by a Soviet author abroad can only be granted through VAAP, which is a state monopoly in the field of granting and acquiring rights to use works. This applies both to works published in the USSR and unpublished works (manuscripts).

[1] For greater detail see I. A. Gringolts 'La Législation Soviétique sur le Droit d'Auteur (en relations avec l'adhesion de l'URSS à la Convention Universelle sur le Droit d'Auteur de 1952)' Interauteurs (1774); E. P. Gavrilov 'Letter from the USSR' Copyright (1976) No 4.
[2] Art 1, Civil Code of the Russian Federation.
[3] Art 506, Civil Code of the Russian Federation.

3. The relationship between copyright and neighbouring rights

19.03 In the USSR there is no problem of the relationship between copyright and 'neighbouring rights', as existing copyright legislation does not directly provide for the protection of performers' rights, nor are rights of producers of phonograms provided for.

4. The protection of performers, producers of phonograms and broadcasting organisations

19.04 Under existing Soviet legislation, the activities of performers are not the subject-matter of copyright. However, in view of technical progress legal writers have suggested copyright protection for performers.[1]

Soviet law does not provide special copyright protection for producers of phonograms. These organisations in the USSR belong to the state. In keeping with the rules of Soviet legislation on copyright, a Soviet producer of phonograms has the right to record a published work on a phonogram, film, magnetic tape or other material support without the consent of the copyright owner.[2] The copyright owner is paid royalties according to rates fixed by the government. Phonograms and pre-recorded cassettes are sold to the public by producers of phonograms who are protected by their monopoly position in the market without any special legal protection of their rights.

Soviet broadcasting and television organisations are also in a special position. They are all non-commercial state organisations financed from the state budget and the owners of radio and television sets do not pay for their use.

Copyright in radio and television broadcasts belongs in the USSR to the radio and television broadcasting organisations.[3] Any published work can be freely broadcast by radio and television, including a tape-recording broadcast. In these cases authors are not paid royalties, although copyright belongs to them. If a work is commissioned by a broadcasting or television organisation, the authors are paid a certain royalty.

1 B. S. Antimonov, Ye. A. Fleishits *Copyright Law* (Moscow, 1957) pp 92-93; Ionas V. Ya. *Creative works in Civil Law* (Moscow, 1972) p 80; S. A. Chernysheva *Legal Relations in Creative Work* (Moscow, 1979) pp 100-101 (all in Russian).
2 Art 104(2) of the Fundamental Principles, para 2, art 495 of the Civil Code of the Russian Federation.
3 Art 486 of the Civil Code of the Russian Federation.

5. The protection of other related rights

19.05 Such protection is not provided for in Soviet law.

6. Collection and distribution of revenue from copyright and neighbouring rights

19.06 VAAP carries out a number of tasks with regard to the collection and payment of royalties to authors. It collects and pays royalties accruing to Soviet and foreign authors and their successors in title for the public performance of their works in the territory of the USSR and for the reproduction in industry of works of fine arts, collects and pays royalties to Soviet authors and their successors in title for the public performance, as well as for other kinds of non-contractual use, of the works of Soviet authors abroad. VAAP collects and pays royalties for the use of works of foreign authors in the USSR and of works of Soviet authors abroad on the basis of agreements concluded through VAAP.

VAAP also collects and pays additional remuneration for motion pictures and television films, as well as for reproduction of phonograms.

The royalties due to foreign authors for the use of their works in the USSR can, at the author's wish, be paid in Soviet currency or freely remitted in the currency of the country which is the permanent residence of the author or his heir, or the permanent seat of the legal person if an agreement on the use of the work in the USSR was concluded with the latter. Exchange transactions are carried out by VAAP through 'Vneshtorgbank SSSR' (the Bank for Foreign Trade of the USSR).

VAAP deducts commission from all sums of an author's remuneration received (from publishing houses, editorial boards of journals, and other organisations). The remaining sum, after deducting income tax, is remitted to the foreign recipient. VAAP is charged with the assessment and deduction of taxes from all sums of royalties payable by it, including taxes collected from foreign recipients. The procedure and rates of taxation to be levied on the author's royalties have been fixed by the Decree of the Presidium of the USSR Supreme Soviet of 12 May 1978.[1]

The Decree prescribes in principle the same tax rates that are applied to Soviet citizens. An annual income under 1,200 roubles is taxed at a progressive rate of 1.5 to 12%; an income over 1,2000 roubles is taxed at 13%.

The same Decree, however, provides for the application of the principle of material reciprocity with respect to the tax levied on a foreign beneficiary. In practical terms, this means that a foreign copyright owner may estimate his possible income from the use of a work in the USSR from the tax rates applied in his country to the payment and transmittal of compensation to Soviet beneficiaries.

The income tax levied on sums paid to foreign authors may be abolished on condition of reciprocity. On this basis (as of 1 November 1981) income tax has not been deducted from authors' royalties transmitted to Denmark, Canada, the Netherlands, Portugal, the Federal Republic of Germany, Switzerland, Sweden, Senegal and West Berlin.

Deduction of income tax from the sums payable to foreign authors and their successors in title may be restricted or abolished on condition of reciprocity by the conclusion of appropriate international agreements between the USSR and other states. As of 1 November 1981 the USSR had concluded such agreements with Bulgaria, Hungary, the German Democratic Republic, Norway, Mongolia, Poland, Rumania, Czechoslovakia, Finland and the United States.

[1] Vedomosti Verkhovnogo Soveta SSSR, 1978, No 20, Item 313.

7. Term of protection

19.07 Soviet legislation[1] stipulates that copyright lasts for the author's life and 25 years after his death, the author's heirs enjoying copyright for 25 years after his death, calculated from 1 January of the year following the author's death.

At the same time, Soviet legislation stipulates that the Union republics may provide shorter terms of protection for copyright with regard to certain categories of works, in particular for photographic works and works of applied art. These terms cannot be less than 10 years from the date of publication (reproduction). Legislation of the Russian Federation, as well as of Byelorussia, Latvia, Lithuania, Kirghizia, Tajikistan, Turkmenistan and Estonia have not availed themselves of this opportunity; thus, the above republics apply the general term of copyright protection to these two categories of works.

However, several Union republics (Azerbaijan, Georgia, Kazakhstan, Moldavia and Uzbekistan) have provided shorter terms of copyright protection for certain categories of works. For instance, the Civil Codes of Moldavia and Uzbekistan stipulate that photographic works and works of applied art are protected for 15 years from the date of publication (reproduction); in Kazakhstan a shortened term of protection applies only to photographic works, which are protected for 10 years, and collections of such works for 15 years from the date of publication.

The Decree of the Presidium of the USSR Supreme Soviet of 21 February 1973 which revised the 'Fundamental Principles of the Civil Code' introduced new rules on the term of protection of copyright which do not apply to works for which the term of protection expired before 1 January 1973. This means that if the author of a protected work died, for example, in 1958 or earlier the period of copyright protection for the work shall not be prolonged by the new law. If the author of a protected work died after 1958 the duration of copyright for the work shall be determined on the basis of the new law. If the work had not been protected in the USSR by 1 January 1973, the rules of the new law always apply to it.

At the same time, it should be stressed that an agreement for the use of a work cannot prolong the term of copyright protection: the expiry of the term of protection terminates the commitments of the parties to the agreement in question, in particular the commitment to pay royalties except, of course, commitments undertaken earlier.

1   Art 105 of the Fundamental Principles.

8. Limitation of rights

19.08   Article 103 of the Fundamental Principles and article 492 of the Civil Code of the Russian Federation stipulate that for educational, scientific and enlightenment purposes a work may be used without the author's consent and without payment of royalties. These rules were established in the public interest, but it should be borne in mind that works may be freely used only provided the author's name and the source are indicated. In case of free use of a work, other personal rights, above all the right to inviolability of a work, must be observed.

Let us examine some examples of free use provided for in article 492 of the Civil Code of the Russian Federation (as revised in 1974).

Firstly, reproduction is permitted in newspapers of public speeches, reports, as well as published works of literature, science and art in the original and in translation.[1]

Secondly, in the periodical press (newspapers and journals), motion pictures, radio and television it is permited to use information about published literary, scientific and artistic works,[2] in particular, in the form of annotations, abstracts, reviews and other documentary form.

Thirdly, in scientific and critical works, educational and political-educational works it is permitted to reproduce separately published scientific, literary and artistic works and excerpts therefrom. Reproduction in the form of quotation may be permitted within the limits justified by the purpose of the edition and reproduction in a different form, for example in collections, providing it does not exceed one 'author's sheet' from works of one author.[3] In the USSR an 'author's sheet' should contain 23 pages typed in double spacing, which equals 40,000 characters. Such 'legal reprinting' is permitted only in editions of a specified character, for instance, in scientific and critical works (monographs, surveys, articles, reviews), educational and 'political-enlightenment' editions (textbooks, teaching aids, posters, calendars).

Fourthly, there is a provision for reproduction of 'printed publications for scientific, educational and enlightenment purposes without earning profits'.[4] This provision applies in the first place to reproduction (for example, production of xerox copies, microfilms) in libraries and information centres at the request of other libraries, scientific and educational institutions. The user pays only for the work done, and copies are not sold. Reproduction for personal use is also allowed (for example, copying of articles from scientific journals, separate pages or sections of monographs). Such copies are also not sold and payment is made only for the making of copies themselves.

Of considerable importance are two other exceptions. Firstly, under article 492(1) of the Civil Code of the Russian Federation use may be made, without the author's consent and without payment of compensation, of another author's published work for the purpose of creating a new, artistically-independent work. However, adapting a work of fiction into a dramatic work (for the theatre, variety, circus, cinema, radio or television) and vice versa, as well as adapting works for the stage into works for the cinema, radio or television, or vice versa, requires the author's consent. Secondly, under article 492(4), reproduction may be made of public speeches, reports and published literary, scientific and artistic works, without the author's consent and without payment of compensation, in motion pictures, over the radio and on television. Thus, any published work, including a literary one, can be freely reproduced in the USSR in motion pictures, over the radio and on television; it can also be reproduced in a recording made with the help of a technical device. Article 492(4) of the Civil Code of the Russian Federation stipulates that 'radio and television broadcasts of a public performance of works direct from the place of performance are also considered reproduction' (for example, from a theatre or concert hall).

The right of free reproduction, however, does not apply either to translation or adaptations of a work for a motion picture, or a radio or television broadcast. If a work has not yet been published in a given language, a contract has to be concluded with the copyright owner.

In addition to the provision for use free of charge, Soviet law contains rules permitting the use of a work without the author's consent, ie without concluding a contract, but with the indication of his name and the payment of compensation. A case where remuneration is paid while no consent of the owner of copyright is required is the fixation of a published work on a phonogram, film, magnetic tape or other material support which may then be put on sale.[5] A reservation is made concerning cinematography, radio and television, as, for example, published music on the sound track of a motion picture or recording for a broadcast come under the operation of the above mentioned provisions for free reproduction without compensation.

Practically speaking, the provision for recording applies to the fixation of concerts and other programmes on phonograms, magnetic tape and cassettes sold to the public. In the future, with the development of videograms, it will probably be extended to include them.

Another example is public performance of published works.[6] This refers to 'live' performance of dramatic, musical, dramatico-musical and literary works. The rates of compensation are laid down in the legislation of the Union republics as a percentage of box-office returns. If admission is free the author's compensation is paid as a percentage of the fees paid to the performers.

The above cases are not considered by Soviet juridical doctrine to be 'restrictions of the author's rights', as they refer to measures promoting broader distribution of works of literature, science and art, in the interests, above all, of public education and enlightenment, all personal rights of authors being fully observed.

1 Art 492(5) of the Civil Code of the Russian Federation.
2 Ibid, art 492(3).
3 Ibid, art 492(2).
4 Ibid, art 492(7).
5 Ibid, art 495(2) and art 104(2) of the Fundamental Principles.
6 Art 104(1) of the Fundamental Principles and art 495(1) of the Civil Code of the Russian Federation.

9. Remedies for infringement

19.09 Soviet legislation provides for civil law or criminal responsibility for copyright infringement.

If the author's personal rights are infringed (for example, infringement of the inviolability of a work), in accordance with the provisions of Soviet legislation,[1] re-establishment of the infringed work (the making of appropriate corrections, and announcement in the press or by some other means concerning the infringement), or the prohibition of publication of the work or the termination of its distribution may be demanded.

If losses are inflicted on an author or his successors in title by infringement of copyright, the author or his successors in title have the right to demand compensation for the losses caused, including both the positive damage and lost profit.[2] Unlike copyright in some other countries, Soviet legislation precludes cash indemnities for the 'droit moral'. Actions brought for copyright infringement are considered by general courts. In accordance with article 21 of the Law on the Legal Status of Foreign Nationals in the USSR of 1981,[3] foreign nationals in the USSR have the right to protection in the courts or other state bodies against encroachments on their personal, property and other rights. In court they enjoy the same legal rights as citizens of the USSR. All suits stemming from copyright are exempted in the USSR from duties and from other costs in favour of the state.

Any disputes arising under an agreement concluded between a foreign partner and VAAP, are resolved in accordance with the procedure laid down in the agreement (generally through arbitration at the Foreign Trade Arbitration Commission in Moscow).

Criminal liability is also possible. Thus, if a person issues under his own name another person's scientific, literary, musical or artistic work or appropriates in any way the authorship of such a work, a court may impose on the offender a fine of up to 500 roubles or sentence him to imprisonment for a term of up to one year.

1 Art 499 of the Civil Code of the Russian Federation.
2 Ibid, art 500.
3 Vedomosti Verkhovnogo Soveta SRSR, 1981, No 26, art 336.

10. Protection of foreign rights owners, application of international conventions

19.10 Protection of foreign copyright owners in the USSR is determined, above all, by the participation of the USSR in international conventions. The Soviet Union joined the Universal Copyright Convention of 1952 in 1973. (The Soviet Union's accession to the Convention has been effective since 27 May 1973).

The USSR adhered to the original text of the Convention, ie to the text of 1952. As a signatory to the 1952 Convention only, the Soviet Union declared its decision to apply the Paris text of the 1971 Convention to the works of its nationals or to the works first published in the USSR for all countries participating in the 1971 Convention. This means, above all, that Soviet works may be used in developing countries on more favourable terms than provided under the Paris text of 1971, even though the USSR has not ratified this text.

The USSR does not participate in the Berne Convention, nor in other multilateral agreements on copyright.

The Soviet Union has concluded bilateral agreements for reciprocal copyright protection with Bulgaria, Hungary, the German Democratic Republic and Czechoslovakia.

Copyrights of foreigners are protected in the Soviet Union in accordance with article 97 of the 'Fundamental Principles' of Civil Legislation, which states that 'Copyright in works first published in the territory of the USSR, or not published but located in the territory of the USSR in any tangible form, shall be declared to belong to the author and his heirs regardless of their citizenship, as well as to their successors in title'.

'Copyright in works of citizens of the USSR which are first published or located in any tangible form in the territory of a foreign state shall be declared to belong to such citizens as well as to their successors in title.'

'Other persons shall be granted protection for works first published or present in any tangible form in the territory of a foreign state in conformity with international treaties or international arrangements to which the USSR is a party'.[1]

With regard to foreign copyrights, the above article has three provisions:

1. Soviet legislation takes account in the first place of where a work was first made available to the public, ie where it was first published. If a work was first published in the USSR it is subject to protection. The notion of 'publication' is determined in this case in accordance with the rules of Soviet law. Publication implies any communication of a work to the public by any means or process, the principal ones being listed in article 476 of the Civil Code of the Russian Federation (printing, public performance, public presentation, radio or television broadcast), but this list is not complete.

Protection also extends to unpublished works existing in Soviet territory in tangible form (for example, in the form of a manuscript). In all of the above cases, protection of foreigners' works is granted on the same terms as to works of Soviet citizens, that is foreign authors are granted national treatment.

2. If a work of a foreign author was first published abroad or it is in some tangible form abroad, such a work is not entitled to protection if the international agreement to which the USSR is a party does not extend to it. Thus, legislation proceeds from the well-established principle in international practice according to which copyright is of territorial nature, ie it operates within the territory where the work was first published.

3. If international agreements are concluded such works are protected.

In compliance with article 97 of the Fundamental Principles, the following categories of works of foreign authors belong to the works protected in the USSR:

Firstly, works first published in the contracting states of the Universal Copyright Convention after it came into force in the USSR, ie after 27 May 1973.

Secondly, works first published by nationals of the contracting states of the Universal Copyright Convention in other states after it came into force in the USSR.

In granting protection in the USSR, in compliance with the Universal

Copyright Convention, the fact of publication in the territory of a foreign state is determined in accordance with the provisions of the Convention. Under the Convention 'publication' means the reproduction in tangible form and the general distribution to the public of copies of a work from which it can be read or otherwise visually perceived.

It follows from the bilateral agreements on reciprocal copyright protection concluded by the USSR that in the territory of the USSR protection is granted to works of the citizens of Bulgaria, Hungary, the German Democratic Republic, Poland and Czechoslovakia, as well as to works of all foreign authors first published in the territory of Hungary and Poland.

In all other cases, a work by a foreign author is not entitled to protection in the territory of the USSR. Copyright principles are not applied to unprotected works, although in the Soviet Union there has traditionally been a practice by which Soviet organisations using these works (publishing houses and others) observe the rules concerning the protection of the author's name and the inviolability of his work.

In the case of works by foreign authors protected in the USSR, the rights of owners of appropriate copyrights will be protected in accordance with the principle of national treatment.

In accordance with the principle of national treatment, a foreign author is granted the same personal and property rights as are granted by Soviet law to Soviet authors. It is a matter for Soviet legislation to determine the extent of protection afforded to foreign authors. The extent of protection granted to the author by the law of the country of which he is a national is irrelevant. He will enjoy only the rights provided for in Soviet legislation.

It is against the law to afford foreign authors lesser benefits of protection and, in general, different conditions of protection than those granted to Soviet citizens. Exceptions to the rights of authors made in the USSR in the interests of society as a whole and discussed above apply to foreign authors as well. For example, under Soviet legislation in certain specified cases a work may be used without the author's consent or compensation.[2] The provision also extends to foreign authors.

The use of works of foreign authors (publication, performance) is governed by the same rules that apply to works of Soviet authors.

A foreign author or his assignee may conclude a contract with a competent Soviet organisation for the publication of a work in the USSR.

The rates of compensation paid to the author for the publication in print, public performance and the use of works of foreign authors by other means are determined by Soviet legislation on the principle of national treatment, ie royalties due to foreign authors are paid according to the rates and procedure established in the USSR for Soviet authors.

1   As amended by the Decree of the Presidium of the Supreme Soviet of the USSR of 21 February 1973.
2   Art 103 of the Fundamental Principles, art 492 of the Civil Code of the Russian Federation.

Chapter 20

European Economic Community (EEC)

by Hans Hugo von Rauscher auf Weeg

1. Treaty of Rome

20.01 EEC Law is not international law in the generally accepted sense, like the international copyright conventions,[1] it is supranational law[2] and thus sui generis. The Treaty of Rome ('the Treaty') is considered the source of primary community law. The Council and the Commission have power[3] to create Community law which is neither inter-state law nor public international law but is supranational law originating from those bodies as an 'autonomous source of law'[4] Community law has thus its own legislative authorities, it also has its own means of enforcement and its own Court.

Article 2 of the Treaty reads:

> 'The Community shall have as its task, by establishing a common market and progressively approximating the economic policies of Member States, to promote throughout the Community a harmonious development of economic activities, a continuous and balanced expansion, an increase in stability, an accelerated raising of the standard of living and closer relations between the States belonging to it.'

The aims, as far as they are relevant in this context, are set out in articles 3, 5 and 7 of the Treaty.

Article 3:

> 'a. the elimination as between Member States of customs duties and of quantitative restrictions on the import and export of goods, and of all other measures having equivalent effect;
> c. the abolition, as between Member States, of obstacles to the freedom of movement for persons, services and capital;
> f. the institution of a system ensuring that competition in the common market is not distorted;
> h. the approximation of the laws of Member States to the extent required for the proper functioning of the common market;'

Under Article 5, the member states are to take all appropriate measures for the fulfilment of the obligations resulting from the Treaty or from the actions of the institutions of the Community, namely the Assembly, the Council, the Commission and the Court of Justice.

Article 7 of the Treaty prohibits within the EEC any discrimination on grounds of nationality.

In a decision of 18 October 1967[5] the Constitutional Court of the Federal Republic of Germany declared that the member states have by the EEC Treaty divested themselves of their sovereign rights in favour of the Community to such an extent that a new public law authority has been created which is autonomous and independent of the authority of individual member states. The result of this is that national parliaments of member states of the Community cannot supplement or improve the provisions of Community law as this would 'lead to an obscuring of the limits between national and supranational jurisdiction and to unequal legal protection in the Member States'.

1 See Chapters 5 and 6.
2 German Federal Constitutional Court, Judgment of 18 October 1967, B Verf GE, Vol 22, p 293, 296.
3 Art 189, Treaty of Rome.
4 Sammlung Vol VIII p 97 (110); Vol X p 1251 (1270).
5 B Verf GE Vol 22, No 28, pp 296, 298.

20.02 The power of the Community institutions, to make laws for the purpose of fulfilling their obligations under the Treaty is set out in article 189, paragraph 1, of the Treaty: 'In order to carry out their task the Council and the Commission shall, in accordance with the provisions of this Treaty, make regulations, issue directives, take decisions, make recommendations or deliver opinions'. A regulation has general applicability. It is binding in all its parts and applies directly in every member state. A directive is binding on each member state to which it is addressed as far as the objective to be achieved is concerned, but leaves to the domestic authorities of that state the choice of the means and the form to achieve that objective. Recommendations and opinions, on the other hand, are not binding. Decisions are binding in all their parts for those to whom they are addressed.[1] Harmonisation of the laws of member states can be achieved by means of directives or regulations.

Articles 100 to 102 provide for the approximation of national laws by means of directives, which may be relevant to copyright law.

Regulations may only be issued on the basis of specific powers contained in the Treaty. Copyright and neighbouring rights are not mentioned in the Treaty, and consequently there is no such specific authorisation for regulations to be enacted in this field. However, article 235 of the Treaty provides a basis for action where this should prove necessary to attain one of the objectives of the Community, in the absence of specific powers in the Treaty.

The European Court of Justice in its recommendation on European Union[2] called the attention of the heads of states and governments to article 235: 'If, in conformity with the Treaty, the procedure of Article 235 were to be applied, Community Law would have the prospect of developing by a gradual extension of its area of applicability. If however, such procedure were to be replaced by another one of a purely public international law nature, the law of the community would run the risk of becoming 'sterilised', without any prospect of further development.' Precisely this risk exists in the area of the copyright conventions if individual states would refuse to ratify them. Between 1976 and August 1981 the Council has availed itself of the power given by article 235 of the Treaty in other fields in 228 cases[3] and this may one day induce it to act similarly in the culturally and economically significant field of copyright, including neighbouring rights.

The duties of the European Community are carried out by the Assembly, the Council, the Commission and the Court of Justice,[4] the last three being entrusted with detailed powers of decision-making.[5]

The competent institutions in the field of copyright have so far not dealt with harmonisation, thus recourse must be had to the case law of the European Court of Justice. The fact that the Treaty nowhere expressly mentions copyright, despite the fact that it is of great economic significance, has lead in the past to considerable controversy.

The European Court of Justice is still a relatively new court consisting of 10 judges, one from each member state, and one should perhaps pay as much attention to the direction in which it is heading on a particular issue as to the individual decisions contained in each of the judgments which have been handed down.

Ritter[6] has stated pertinently: 'The Court has *increasingly* emphasised the connection with the general objectives of the European Community ..., has created a *close connection* with the general principle of the elimination of all quantitative restrictions (free movement of goods, Article 30 et seq) and, after *initial tentative attempts*, has developed the latter into an equally important pillar of competition policy (in its broader sense) in order to enable the same procedures to be adopted against all measures which falsify competition'. In the Court of Appeal in the United Kingdom Lord Justice Templeman described the position of the European Court of Justice as 'the supreme arbiter in questions of European law'.[7] Article 177 of the Treaty enables national courts and tribunals to refer questions of EEC law to the Court for a preliminary ruling. On this basis, the Court is in a position to ensure a uniform interpretation of provisions of Community law in each member state.

1 Art 189, paras 2 to 5 of the Treaty.
2 Bulletin of the European Communities Appendix 9/75, pp 17, 19.
3 Off-Line Edition Mistral CII HB V 4-01-03.
4 Art 4 of the Treaty.
5 Arts 145, 155, 164 et seq of the Treaty.
6 Ritter *Aktuelle Grundsatzfragen des EWG-Kartellrechts* (Köln, 1978).
7 *Polydor v Harlequin* (1980) FSR 362, CA, in the UK and case 270/80 (1980) CMLR 247.

2. Intellectual property

20.03 The application of Community law to the field of intellectual property law does however present considerable difficulties. In addition to the fact that laws of the member states have not yet been harmonised, certain substantial provisions of the Treaty, for example articles 30 et seq and articles 85 and 86, impinge on the exercise of national intellectual property rights.

The first copyright case before the European Court was *Deutsche Gramophon Gesellschaft v METRO*[1] which deals with a neighbouring right, the reproduction and distribution right of phonogram producers. The concept of a 'neighbouring right' is somewhat out of place in the law of those countries which equate these rights with copyrights (eg producers of phonograms have a copyright in the United Kingdom and in the Republic of Ireland although the scope of these rights is less wide than the scope of other copyrights, whereas in other countries of the community they only have a neighbouring right). As there is no express mention of either copyright or neighbouring rights in the Treaty, the question whether the Treaty applies to copyright and neighbouring rights was originally regarded as an open question. There are, however, recent decisions[2] which seem to indicate fairly clearly that in some respects at any rate the Treaty applies to copyright and neighbouring rights.

Articles 30-37 of the Treaty provide for the elimination of quantitative restrictions on trade between member states. Article 36 is in effect a derogation from this principle. It provides that prohibitions or restrictions on imports, exports or goods in transit are not prohibited if they are for the purpose of protecting 'industrial and commercial property', provided that they do not constitute a means of arbitrary discrimination or a disguised restriction on trade between member states.

The argument that copyright is not covered by the concept of 'national treasures possessing artistic, historical or archaeological value' or by the concept of 'industrial and commercial property' under article 36, sentence 1, EEC Treaty,[3] is unconvincing. Nevertheless, one should not adopt a 'formalistically rigorous stance and deny Copyright the privilege of Article 36 sentence 1 for the sole reason that it is not mentioned therein.[4] Thus, construction by way of analogy offers itself as the only sensible legal rule.[5]

1 Case 78/70 of 8 June 1971, (1971) CMLR 631.
2 Judgment of 20 January 1981 in associated cases 55/80 and 57/8: *Musikvertrieb Membran GmbH and K-tel International v GEMA* (Gesellschaft fur Musikalische-Aufführungs und Vervielfältigungsrechte) (1981) 2 CMLR 44; and *CODITEL v Cine Vog Films*, Decision of 18 March 1980, Case 62/79.
3 Gotzen *'Artistieke eigendom en mededingsregels van de Europese Economische Gemeensschap'* (1971) pp 6, 7 and 47 et seq; also Dietz *Copyright Law in the European Community* (1978) para 13 et seq.
4 Johannes *Gewerblicher Rechtsschutz und Urheberrecht im Europäischen Gemeinschaftsrecht* (1973) p 56.
5 Johannes, op cit and Dietz, op cit, para 29.

3. Free circulation of goods

20.04 The European Court of Justice in the recent *K-tel and Membran* case[1] dealt unequivocally with questions which have been disputed for a long time, and still were even in the course of these proceedings, by the governments involved. It clearly establishes that article 36 of the EEC Treaty is applicable to copyright – and thereby also to neighbouring rights.[2] Therefore this decision and the 'opinion' of Advocate General Warner in the proceedings are taken as the starting point of an explanation of the somewhat complicated development of the case law in the field of industrial property and copyright law. The facts were as follows:

Musikvertrieb Membran imported into the Federal Republic of Germany records and cassettes from, inter alia, member states of the Community. The fees paid for the recording, reproduction and distribution of the phonograms, containing music which was protected by copyright, were at the lower rate of royalty of $6\frac{1}{4}\%$ fixed by statute in the United Kingdom, whereas in the Federal Republic of Germany the legal basis of such royalties is governed by contract and agreed at 8%. No additional copyright royalty was paid for the sale of records imported into Germany. GEMA (the German authors' society) therefore instituted proceedings before the German courts for payment of the 'difference' (ie $8\% - 6\frac{1}{4}\% = 1\frac{3}{4}\%$).

In 1974 *K-tel International* imported 100,000 records of music protected by copyright into the Federal Republic of Germany from the United Kingdom. Through the Mechanical Copyright Protection Society, MCPS, (the British collecting society for mechanical rights), the British affiliate of the German firm K-tel (K-tel International Limited) was granted the right to record the musical works on to phonograms and to sell them against payment of a royalty of 6.25% of the customary retail price of the record in the United Kingdom. MCPS attempted to procure in respect of the phonograms exported to the Federal Republic of Germany the payment of the difference between the royalties customarily charged in the United Kingdom and in the Federal Republic of Germany. The German collecting society GEMA instituted proceedings against K-tel on the basis of article 97 of the German Copyright Law:

> 'As against any person who infringes a copyright or any other right protected by this Act, the injured party may bring an action for injunctive relief requiring the wrongdoer to cease and desist if there is a danger of repetition of the acts of infringement, as well as an action for damages if the infringement was intentional or the result of negligence.'

Under national German law, as emphasised by the Federal Supreme Court in its reference, the claim to the difference is justified on account of the exclusive distribution right. The Court doubted whether this enforcement of copyright was compatible with the provisions of the EEC Treaty relating to the free movement of goods.

1 *Membran and K-tel v GEMA* (1981) 2 CMLR 44.
2 Dr Reischl, First Advocate General of the Court of Justice of the European Communities in 'Copyright Law and the Free Movement of Goods in the European Market', in Copyright (March 1982) p 116.

20.05 In the opinion of the Court, in a common market distinguished by free movement of goods and freedom to provide services, an author, acting directly or through his publisher, is free to choose the place, in any of the member states, in which to put his work into circulation. He may make that choice according to his best interests, which involve not only the level of remuneration provided in the member state in question but other factors such as, for example, the opportunities for distributing his work and the marketing facilities which are further enhanced by virtue of the free movement of goods within the Community. In those circumstances, the Court held that a copyright collecting society is not permitted to claim, on the importation of sound recordings into another member state, payment of additional fees based on the difference in the rates of remuneration existing in the various member states.

It considered that *the disparities which continue to exist in the absence of any harmonisation of national rules on the commercial exploitation of copyright may not be used to impede the free movement of goods in the Common Market.*

The European Court referred to the concept of 'protection of industrial and commercial property' in article 36 and ruled: 'The ... expression includes the protection conferred by copyright, especially when exploited commercially in the form of licences capable of affecting distribution in the various Member States of goods incorporating the protected literary or artistic work'.[1]

The European Court also emphasised[2] that phonograms, even if they contained copyright-protected music, were products to which the system of free movement of goods envisaged in the Treaty applied. It concluded that the internal legal provisions of a state which could lead to an obstacle to trade in phonograms between member states, 'are to be regarded as measures of equal effect to quantitative restrictions within the meaning of Article 30'. This was also the case where the copyright provisions of one member state permitted a collecting society to oppose the sale of phonograms from another member state on the basis of exclusive national rights, for example, on the basis of the exclusive right of reproduction and distribution.

The European Court also resolved another point of controversy in this case: Although articles 30 et seq prohibit between member states quantitative restrictions on imports, exports and all measures having equivalent effect, these provisions do not preclude import prohibitions or restrictions which are justified on the grounds of the protection of industrial and commercial property. The case law established by the European Court restricts this principle on the basis of the reservation contained in sentence 2 of article 36, which states that such prohibitions or restrictions shall not constitute a means of arbitrary discrimination or a disguised restriction on trade between member states.

The European Court has developed the concept, that the Treaty does not affect the substance of the industrial and commercial property rights granted by the national laws of the member states, but that the exercise of these rights may well be limited by the prohibitory rules of the Treaty, according to the circumstances. Article 36 therefore allows restrictions of the free movement of goods only in so far as they are justified for the protection of those rights which constitute the 'specific subject matter' of industrial commercial and therewith also other intellectual property.[3]

The European Court has also developed the principle that the owner of an industrial or commercial property right is unable to rely on the protection afforded him by his national law in order to oppose the importation of a product which has already been lawfully put into circulation in another member state by him or with his consent.[4] In its judgment in the *Dansk Supermarked* case[5] the European Court remarked:

> 'It may be recalled that the effect of the provisions of the Treaty of the free movement of goods and in particular of Article 30, is to prohibit between Member States quantitative restrictions on imports and all measures having equivalent effect. However, according to Article 36 that provision does not preclude prohibitions or restrictions on imports justified on grounds of the protection of industrial and commercial property. Nevertheless it is clear from that article, in particular the second sentence, as well as from the context, that whilst the Treaty does not affect the existence of rights recognized by the legislation of a Member State in matters of industrial and commercial property, yet the exercise of those rights may none the less, depending on the circumstances, be restricted by the prohibitions of the Treaty. Inasmuch as it provides an exception to one of the fundamental principles of the common market, Article 36 in fact admits exceptions to the free movement of goods only to the extent to which such exceptions are justified for the purpose of safeguarding rights which constitute the specific subject-matter of that property. The exclusive right guaranteed by the legislation on industrial and commercial property is exhausted when a product has been lawfully distributed on the market in another Member State by the actual proprietor of the right or with his consent'.

The European Court thus held that Articles 30 and 36 of the Treaty are to be construed in such a way that the courts of a member state cannot prohibit the *distribution* of goods which are protected within the territory of that state by reason of any copyright or trade mark right if the goods in question have been lawfully placed on the market in the territory of another member state by the owner of such rights or by a third party with his permission.

The European Court of Justice, in the *Deutsche Grammophon* decision[6] has already differentiated between the 'specific subject-matter of the rights' with reference to which restrictions may be placed on the free movement of goods because they form part of the protected matter, *which are permitted*, and the exercise of those rights which may lead to an arbitrary discrimination or to a disguised restriction of trade, *which is prohibited*.

The European Court stated in that case:

> 'If a right related to copyright is relied upon to prevent the marketing in a Member State of products distributed by the holder of the right or with his consent on the territory of another Member State on the sole ground that such distribution did not take place on the national territory, such a prohibition, which would legitimize the isolation of national markets, would be repugnant to the essential purpose of the Treaty, which is to unite national markets into a single market. That purpose could not be attained if, under the various legal systems of the Member States, nationals of those States were able to partition the market and bring about arbitrary discrimination or disguised restrictions on trade between Member States.
>
> Consequently, it would be in conflict with the provisions prescribing the free movement of products within the common market for a manufacturer of sound recordings to exercise the exclusive right to distribute the protected articles, conferred upon him by the legislation of a Member State in such a way as to prohibit the sale in that State of products placed on the market by him or with his consent in another Member State solely because such distribution did not occur within the territory of the first Member State'.

1   Statement of Grounds of Decision Number 9.
2   Statement of Grounds of Decision Number 8.

3 Reischl, op cit, p 117; cf *Deutsche Grammophongesellschaft v Metro* (1971) CMLR 631, also: Cases 15 & 16/74: *Centrafarm BV v Sterling Drug Inc; Centrafarm BV v Winthrop BV* (1974) 2 CMLR 480. Case 102/77: *Hoffman-La Roche v Centrafarm* (1978) 3 CMLR 217. Case 3/78: *Centrafarm v American Home Products Corp* (1979) 1 CMLR 326.
4 Case 119/75: *Terrapin Overseas Limited v Terranova Industry CA Kapferer & Company* (1976) 2 CMLR 482.
5 Case 58/80: Judgment of 20 January 1981 *Dansk Supermarked A/S, Aarhus v A/S Imerco Glostrup/Copenhagen*
6 Case 78/80: *Deutsche Grammophongesellschaft v Metro* (1971) CMLR 631.

20.06 In the fields of patent and trade-mark law, the European Court of Justice has developed extensive case law.[1] This may be summarised as follows: The substance of such rights is guaranteed by the Treaty and therefore everything necessary for the protection of such substance is permissible. However the exercise of such rights is subject both to the principle of the free movement of goods (articles 30-36) and to the competition rules (articles 85, 86). It is clear that this differentiation causes difficulties in practice. Does, for example, the national statutory period of protection relate to the substance of the right or is such a period considered to fall within the sphere of the exercise of the right? From the case law of the German Federal Constitutional Court[2] it could be inferred that it forms part of the substance, an opinion which may well be shared in other countries.

However broadly or narrowly one might wish to draw the line between the substance and exercise of copyright, the case law developed by the European Court lays down, in essence, that the holder of an industrial and commercial property right (and now also of a copyright or neighbouring right) is unable to have recourse to the legal provisions available to him in order to oppose the importation of a product which has been lawfully marketed in the territory of another Member State by him or with his consent. The European Court pointed out in the *K-tel and Membran* case[3] without again reverting to the difference between the substance and exercise of a right, that an author is indeed at liberty, either personally or through his publisher, freely to select the place in any one member state of the Community in which he wishes to market his work. He is permitted to make his choice having regard to his own interests – including his financial interests – so that he may obtain advantages in terms of the level of royalties, marketing opportunities and sales. The European Court states[2]:

> 'It should be observed ... that no provision of national legislation may permit an undertaking which is responsible for the management of copyrights and has a monopoly on the territory of a Member State by virtue of that management to charge a levy on products imported from another Member State where they were put into circulation by or with the consent of the copyright owner and thereby cause the Common Market to be partitioned. Such a practice would amount to allowing a private undertaking to impose a charge on the importation of sound recordings which are already in free circulation in the Common Market on account of their crossing a frontier, it would therefore have the effect of entrenching the isolation of national markets which the Treaty seeks to abolish It follows from these considerations that this argument must be rejected as being incompatible with the operation of the Common Market and with the aims of the Treaty.'[3]

Reischl[4] quite rightly points out that the European Court therewith explains that the claim for payment of a royalty difference could only be justified if the importation of the phonograms constituted an infringement of the exclusive distribution right of the copyright owner; however, according to the established case law of the Court of Justice this right has been exhausted by the fact that the sound recordings have already been brought into circulation in other member states with the consent of the owner of the right.[5] Such a practice would amount to allowing a private undertaking to impose a charge based solely on the fact that the phonograms had crossed a frontier. The European Court felt that the claim for payment of the royalty difference came very close to a levy having equivalent effect to customs duties, which was incompatible with the operation of the Common Market and with the aims of the Treaty.'

1 Cases 56 and 58/74: *Consten SA and Grundig-Verkaufs v Commission* (1966) CMLR 418.
Case 24/67: *Parke Davis & Co v Probel and Centrafarm* (1968) CMLR 47.
Case 40/70: *Sirena SRL v EDA SRL* (1971) CMLR 260.
Case 119/75: *Terrapin (Overseas) Ltd v Terranova Industrie* (1976) 2 CMLR 482.
Case 86/75: *EMI Records Ltd v CBS Grammofon A-S* (1976) 2 CMLR 235.
See also the 'Centrafarm' cases para 20.05, note 3, above.
2 BVerfGE 31, 275.
3 Decision of 20 January 1981, *Musikvertrieb Membran and K-tel International v GEMA* (1981) 2 CMLR 44.
4 Reischl, op cit, p 119.
5 Cf especially the decision in the case *Deutshe Grammophon Ges v Metro-SB-Grossmärkte* (1971) CMLR 631 and *Dansk Supermarked v Imerco*, see para 20.05, note 5.

4. Divided publication and distribution rights

20.07 Another question related to the distinction between the substance and exercise of a right is that of the divided publishing right. If, as in many systems of law, the right of publication is regarded as an exclusive right available without restriction to the holder of the right, there is nothing – if the doctrine of exhaustion is disregarded – precluding it being exclusively granted for certain territories. Does this, because it is only afforded statutory protection in each country separately, come within the sphere of the substance of the right in such a country or merely within the sphere of the exercise of the right? Do film use, television use or cable or satellite use form part of the 'specific subject-matter' of intellectual property or do they fall merely within the exercise of the rights? These are examples of a number of questions which can only at present be raised but not answered.

The detailed application of articles 30 et seq of the Treaty to the substance of copyright and neighbouring rights throws up a number of problems. The most difficult problem area is in the field of the shared publication right or distribution right or both.

In the case *Polydor v Harlequin*[1] the basic issue at stake was whether the case law established by the Court as regards the interpretation of articles 30 to 36 of the Treaty, which provide for the free movement of goods between member states, could be extended in order to apply to goods originating from Portugal, a country with which the EEC has a free trade agreement containing provisions almost identical to those articles.

The European Court held that the free trade agreement did not have the same purpose as the EEC Treaty, as although it made provision for certain restrictions on trade between Portugal and member states to be abolished, there was no intention to create a single market. In this connection, the Court emphasised the lack of means at the disposal of the Community for achieving the approximation of laws in relations between the Community and Portugal. In the Polydor case the Court held that the owner of the copyright in the sound recording in the United Kingdom could prevent the import of records manufactured in Portugal which would infringe his copyright, even when the records had been put on the market in Portugal by a licensee, ie with the consent of the United Kingdom copyright owner.

1   Case 270/80 *Polydor Ltd and RSO Records Inc v Harlequin Record Shops Ltd and Simons Records, Ltd* (1980) FSR 362, CA in the UK and case 270/80, [1980] CMLR 247 in the European Court. See para 20.02, note 7.

20.08   The rules of member states on the protection of distribution rights differ widely.

The *French Copyright Law of 1957* recognises the '*droit de divulgation*', this right has to be distinguished from the distribution right which is contained in the penal regulations.

Article 19 reads:

'The Author alone shall have the right to divulge his work. He shall determine the method of divulgation, and in the case of cinematographic works shall fix the conditions thereof, subject to the provisions of Article 17 ...

This right may be exercised even after the expiration of the exclusive right of exploitation determined by Article 21.'

Article 71 reads:

'Article 426 of the Penal Code shall be modified as follows: "Any reproduction, performance or dissemination of an intellectual work by any means whatever, in violation of the author's rights as defined and regulated by law, shall equally constitute an offence of unlawful reproduction."'

The decision of the 'Tribunal de Grande Instance' of Paris dated 24 April 1980[1] proceeds from the view that the unauthorised importation into France of phonograms properly made in the United States under a compulsory licence or contractual licence, infringe the author's right of distribution and reproduction. The court relied particularly on article 31, para 3 of the Copyright Law which reads:

'The transfer of authors' rights shall be subject to the condition that each of the rights transferred shall be specifically mentioned in the act of transfer, and that the field of exploitation of the rights transferred shall be delimited as to extent and purpose, as to place and as to duration'.

Therefore, when the copyright works in question were imported into France, the importer was obliged to pay the authors of such works the fees demanded by the collecting society (SDRM), even if they were made abroad with the required consent.

The ratio decidendi of this decision largely corresponds to the principle of the distribution right in the *Federal Republic of Germany*. This is also similar to what, in German law, has been developed by case law and jurisprudence as the 'doctrine of the purpose of assignment' ('Zweckübertragungstheorie'), which has found its statutory expression in article 31(5) of the German Copyright Law: 'If the terms of the licence do not specifically enumerate ways in which the work may be used, the scope of the grant of rights shall be determined in accordance with the purpose envisaged in making the grant'.

In *Belgium*[2] the law was laid down by the decision of the 'Cour de Cassation' of 19 January 1956.[3] It recognises the right of the owner of mechanical reproduction rights to forbid the use of phonograms which are licensed merely for private use, for broadcasting purposes by the Belgian Broadcasting Organisation. In the proceeding between *Time Limit SA v SABAM*,[4] the 'Cour d'Appel de Bruxelles' confirmed that the person entitled to the copyright is the only person who may lay down the conditions for the reproduction and distribution of copies of the work. In particular, territorial restrictions are also recognised under Belgian law. This has made it possible to make the importation into Belgium of phonograms, licensed in the United Kingdom for hiring, dependent on payment of a separate fee for such hiring in Belgium.[5]

The *Italian* Copyright Law of 22 April 1941 states in article 17:

> 'The exclusive right of commercial distribution has for its object the putting into circulation, with gainful intent, of a work or copies thereof, and includes also the exclusive right of introducing into the territory of the State, for the purpose of putting into circulation, reproductions which have been made abroad.'

The legal situation in Italy is therefore quite clear as the domestic right of distribution is expressly reserved by statute.

This survey shows that several member states acknowledge a distribution right. However, all their national laws are subject to the supranational Community law which therefore takes precedence over national distribution rights. This situation has met with considerable jurisprudential criticism and also criticism from the section of the economy concerned with copyright and neighbouring rights. The financial consequences arising from EEC law are particularly severe in the book publishing trade between the United States and the United Kingdom, where no language barriers exist. Whilst economically it was a wholly justified and indeed necessary custom for American and British publishers to grant licences restricted to their respective territories, this is now legally and practically precluded by the case law of the European Court. The American publishers are able, for example, to supply their books to Holland or Denmark and then export them from there to the United Kingdom. In this way, the divided publishing rights may be circumvented by a publisher who is not subject to EEC law. In order to avoid this result, which without doubt is unwelcome and perhaps in practice even ruinous for publishers, it has been proposed that the unrestricted onward distribution of works should be permitted only if they are manufactured in an EEC country and not merely distributed there by way of exports.[6] The British Publishers Association has warned that the present situation threatens the existence of British publishers and has demanded that an exception be made to the application of articles 30 and 36 of the Treaty.

1 Tribunal de Grande Instance de Paris (17 ème Chambre Correctionelle) 24 April 1980.
2 See Reimer in GRUR Int 1981, p 72.
3 Droit d'Auteur 1956, p 58; see also Gotzen, *Het Bestimmingsrecht van de Auteur* supplemented by a resume in French entitled: *Le droit de destination de l'auteur*, (Brussels, 1975).
4 *Time Limit SA v SABAM* RIDA (1979) p 198; GRUR Int (1980) pp 145 et seq; [1976] 2 CMLR 684, [1979] 2 CMLR 578.
5 See Reimer, op cit.
6 See Dietz, op cit, para 241.

5. Collecting societies

20.09 In all member states, collecting societies are monopolies or in a position of market dominance, and article 86 of the Treaty therefore applies to their activities. Article 86 prohibits conduct by an undertaking in a dominant position which is an abuse of that position and may affect trade between member states. In the GEMA case[1] the Commission decided that GEMA, the German collecting society, had abused its dominant position in the Federal Republic by inter alia (a) discriminating against nationals of other member states by, for example, denying their full voting rights; (b) binding its members with unnecessary obligations, such as requiring the assignment of rights for a minimum of six years; (c) extending copyright through contractual means to non-copyright works; and (d) charging the full royalty on records imported into Germany by independent importers on which royalties had already been paid to the author's collecting society in the country of origin.[2] The Commission, in applying Article 86, decided however that GEMA was at liberty to demand from dealers the difference between the lower royalty applicable in the country of manufacture and the higher royalty contractually agreed in the Federal Republic of Germany.

In the decision of the Commission in the *'GVL' case*,[3] relating to the German collecting society of that name which administers the rights of phonogram producers and performers, the Commission confirmed that article 86 applies, not only to authors' societies but also to societies of owners of neighbouring rights. GVL was found, by the Commission, to be in abuse of its dominant position, within the meaning of article 86 of the EEC Treaty. The abuse consisted in refusing to represent, in respect of their performing rights, performers who were not German nationals or resident in Germany, but who nonetheless had rights in Germany as a consequence of the Rome Convention[4] and who are nationals or residents of a member state of the EEC.

The European Court decided in *Belgische Radio en Televisie v SABAM* (the Belgian Association of Authors, Composers and Publishers)[5] on a reference under article 177, that in determining whether a collecting society is imposing unfair restraints on its members or third parties, account is to be taken of all the relevant interests in order to ensure a balance between the need to preserve maximum freedom for authors to dispose of their works, on the one hand, and the effective management of these rights by the collecting society to which they have to assign them, on the other hand.[6]

The practices in dispute must therefore be examined to see whether they exceed the limits absolutely necessary for the attainment of that object. With regard to the compulsory assignment by a composer of all his existing and future copyrights to a collecting society in a dominant position, the Court held that this may be an unfair condition under article 86, especially if the assignment is required for an extended time after the member's withdrawal from the society.[7]

1 (1971) CMLR D 35.
2 Such a practice was held by the European Court to be contrary to arts 30–36 in *Musik-Vertrieb Membran GmbH v GEMA*, (1981) 2 CMLR 44.
3 Commission Decision of 29 October 1981 (IV/29.339-GVL) OJ of 28, December 81 No L 370/49.
4 See Chapter 8.
5 (1974) 2 CMLR 283.
6 In *Re GEMA (No 2)* (1972) CMLR D 115, the Commission was of the opinion that the abusive nature under art 86 of the exclusive contract between author and authors' rights society was dependent on two factors: the length of the period the author is bound and the breadth of the rights covered. A longer period should cover a narrower range of rights, and vice versa.
7 See however *Greenwich Films SA v SACEM* decision of the French 'Cour de Cassation' (1982) I CMLR 577, where it was held that the mere fact that a performing rights society requires an author, as a condition of membership, to transfer all existing and future rights for the whole world does not per se affect trade between member states and therefore is not per se an abuse of a dominant position.

6. Performing rights

20.10 In *Re CODITEL v Ciné Vog Films*[1] the European Court stated:

'The provisions of the Treaty relating to the freedom to provide services do not preclude an assignee of the performing right in a cinematographic film in a Member State from relying upon his right to prohibit the exhibition of that film in that State, without his authority, by means of cable diffusion if the film so exhibited is picked up and transmitted after being broadcast in another member State by a third party with the consent of the original owner of the right'.

The owners of the copyright in the film have, following the statement of grounds by the Court, a justified interest in calculating the royalty due to them for the showing of the film on the basis of the actual or probable number of performances and in agreeing to a television transmission of the film only after a certain period of showing it in the cinemas. 'The possibility given to the owner of the copyright to claim a royalty for each showing of the film belongs to the essential content of the copyright in such literary or artistic work.'[2]

With regard to article 59 of the Treaty, concerning freedom to provide services, the European Court stated, that the rule contained in article 36 of the Treaty is also applicable to the freedom to provide services. It held: 'Whilst Article 59 of the Treaty prohibits restrictions upon freedom to provide services, it does not thereby encompass limits upon the exercise of certain economic activities which have their origin in the application of national legislation for the protection of intellectual property, save where such application constitutes a means of arbitrary discrimination or a disguised restriction on trade between Member States.' Such would be the case if the application enabled parties to an assignment of copyright to create artificial barriers to trade between member states.

The effect of this is that, whilst copyright entails the right to demand fees for any showing or performance, the rules of the Treaty cannot in principle constitute an obstacle to the geographical limits which the parties to a contract of assignment have agreed upon in order to protect the author and his assigns in this regard. The mere fact that those geographical limits may coincide with national frontiers does not point to a different solution in a situation where television is organised in the member states largely on the basis of legal broadcasting monopolies, which indicates that a limitation other than the geographical field of application of an assignment is often impracticable.

The exclusive assignee of the performing right in a film for the whole of a member state may therefore rely upon his right against cable television diffusion companies which have transmitted that film on their diffusion network, having received it from a television broadcasting station established in another member state, without thereby infringing Community law.'[3]

The Court also qualified the royalty for each showing of the film as being part of the substance of the performing right in the film.

Reischl concludes from this that the European Court considers the grant and effect of a territorial licence in respect of the performance right limited to *one* member state differently from the exercise of the distribution right in a protected work.[4]

1 *CODITEL v Ciné Vog Films*, Decision of 18 March 1980, Case 62/79.
2 Reischl, op cit, p 120.
3 *CODITEL v CineVog Films*, Case 62/79, paras 15 to 17.
4 Reischl, op cit, p 120.

7. Relationship between European Community law and the copyright and neighbouring rights Conventions

20.11 Unlike the directly applicable law of the EEC the copyright and neighbouring rights conventions[1] contain only an obligation under international law for states to enact national legislation in conformity with these conventions. If a contracting state fails to comply with an obligation under the conventions, the only course open to the other contracting states is an appeal to the International Court of Justice.[2] All international copyright conventions[3] and neighbouring rights conventions are based on the principle of national treatment[4] which means that convention nationals have to be treated, ie given the same rights, as nationals of the state concerned. The system of the international copyright conventions therefore results in convention law becoming an integral part of national law which applies to foreigners. It does not, however, create any supranational law as EEC law does. The national copyright laws are based on the 'principle of territoriality' which means that the extent of the legal protection granted will in each convention state depend on the rules of the law of that state.[5] Even where convention law is directly applicable (self-executing) the conventions do not create supranational law, but provisions of the convention are made part of the domestic legislation of member states which have adhered to the convention.

The aim of the conventions is to achieve, by the principle of national treatment, uniformity of protection in all convention countries. The Treaty of Rome expresses a similar aim in article 3(b): 'the approximation of the laws of Member States to the extent required for the proper functioning of the common market'. The approximation of laws in the EEC is thus, for the first time in European history 'not abandoned to chance and the free play of unfettered agreements in international law'[6] such as lie at the basis of the copyright conventions, but is an obligation associated with the establishment and ordering of the operation of the Community.[7]

However Community law, it is submitted, is not in conflict with the obligations of the member states under the copyright and neighbouring rights conventions.[8] In any event the EEC Treaty which is 'res inter alios acta' cannot relieve member states of their commitments to third countries.

The Berne Convention (all Acts until the Brussels Act 1948) and the Universal Copyright Convention[9] (1952) precede the EEC Treaty but all the neighbouring rights conventions[10] came into effect after the EEC Treaty and so did the Paris Acts (1971) of the Berne Convention and of the Universal Copyright Convention.

The relationship between Community law and international agreements made before the entry into force of the EEC Treaty by one or more member states on the one hand, and one or more third countries on the other hand, is dealt with in article 234 of the Treaty which provides that 'the rights and obligations arising from "such agreements" shall not be affected by the provisions of this Treaty'. The second paragraph of the Article provides:

> 'to the extent that such agreements are not compatible with this Treaty, the Member State or States concerned shall take all appropriate steps to eliminate the incompatibilities established'.

As far as the conventions which came into force after the EEC Treaty are concerned, it is submitted that it must be presumed that all those member states of the Community which signed these conventions considered these international treaties as being compatible with community law.[11] The same applies 'a fortiori' to those countries which have since ratified or adhered to these conventions.[12]

The European Court has so far not been called upon to deal with these questions.

Finally it should be emphasised that Community law dealing with intellectual property rights is in a state of rapid development. Thus, the decisions of the Commission and the European Court in this field should be subjected to constructive legal criticism as they will be of crucial importance to economic and cultural development within the EEC.

1 See chapters 5 and 6 and chapters 7 to 10 above.
2 Art 33(1), Berne Convention; art XV, Universal Copyright Convention; art 30 Rome Convention. See para 5.65 above.
3 With the sole exception of the Montevideo Convention which is now practically obsolete see para 3.15 above.
4 See para 3.17 above.
5 See Ulmer *Urheber und Verlagsrecht* (Copyright and Publishing Law) (3rd edn) pp 80 et seq.
6 Hallstein *Angleichung des Privat - und Prozessrechts in der Europäischen Wirtschaftsgemeinschaft* (Comparison of Private and Procedural Law within the European Community), Rabels Zeitschrift (1964) p 214.
7 Ipsen *Europaisches Gemeinschaftsrecht* (EEC Law) p 686, referring to Hallstein, op cit, p 214.
8 See Davies and von Rauscher auf Weeg *Challenges to Copyright and Related Rights in the European Community* (1982) para 127.
9 See chapters 5 and 6 above.
10 See chapters 8-10 above.
11 See Nordemann, Vinck, Hertin, Internationales Urheberrecht, 1977 Introduction, para 37.
12 See Davies and von Rauscher, op cit, para 129.

Chapter 21
United States of America

by Barbara Ringer

A prefatory note

21.01 According to Chafee's magisterial essay on the American copyright system,[1] there are six ideals to which a copyright law should aspire: (1) subject matter coverage should be complete, so that new forms of creative expression are protected; (2) the scope of protection should be broad and unified so that new forms of infringement can be prevented; (3) protection should be international in scope; (4) protection should not go substantially beyond the purposes it is intended to serve; (5) protection should not be allowed to stifle independent creation by others and (6) the legal rules for securing and maintaining copyright should be convenient to handle.

Writing in 1945, roughly half-way through the 70-year reign of the Act of 1909 and a decade before the Universal Copyright Convention finally brought the United States into a global copyright arrangement, Chafee found that the US copyright law stopped far short of achieving these ideals. It is interesting to consider how he might have judged the copyright system of the United States in 1982, after five years of experience with a new statute which, to the extent possible, was revised with his ideals in mind.

From the viewpoint of traditional copyright principles, the new American copyright law is a substantial improvement over the old, but it still falls far short of the ideal. Subject matter and scope of protection have been broadened but not enough. The individual author's rights as against licensees and infringers are more secure and less subject to meaningless technicalities; but a number of formal requirements, including the infamous manufacturing clause, remain, and in the case of works made for hire the employer is still regarded as the 'author'. Some users are given outright exemptions, and concessions in the form of compulsory licenses are given to other special interest groups: record producers, jukebox operators, cable television systems and non-commercial broadcasters. The duration of statutory protection has been lengthened to meet the international norm, but subsisting copyrights in their first 28-year term under the old law must still be renewed. The moral right of the author is still not given statutory recognition. And, to the intense disappointment of many, including this writer, the United States is still a long way from accepting the whole range of international ideals embodied in the Berne Convention.

From the viewpoint of neighbouring rights, the situation in the United States is even less satisfactory. Looked upon simply as the aggregate of protection offered to performers, producers of phonograms and broadcasting organisations, neighbouring rights can be said to exist in the United States in one form or another. But, lacking a systematic or coherent jurisprudential framework such as the Rome Convention, the American protection for performers, recordings and broadcasts is unpredictable, uncertain, illogical and grievously incomplete. Neighbouring rights in the United States remains a patchwork of copyright, unfair competition, communications and other legal concepts, woven into a variety of common law precedents, statutes and regulations, and stitched together loosely in interrelated federal and state laws. And it is in a constant state of flux, with many conflicting precedents and even more unsettled and untested issues.

This highly unsatisfactory situation is made all the more regrettable by the failure of the United States to make any of the necessary moves toward becoming a party to the Rome Convention. It is well known that United States government representatives played an active role in the development of the Convention and in the Rome Conference itself, and left their stamp upon many of the treaty's provisions. Yet no legislation aimed specifically at implementing the Rome Convention has ever been placed before the United States Congress, and the Convention itself has never been submitted to the Senate for its approval.

Within the last generation the ongoing revolutions in communications technology have begun to break down the supposed distinctions between copyright and neighbouring rights, and have thrown a bright spotlight on the reasons for and consequences of these forms of protection. One copyright crisis follows another as front page news, and issues of intellectual property have become matters of urgent public debate. Continuing developments that are currently having profound copyright consequences include cable television and satellite transmissions, audio and video recording and the inevitable use of computers in nearly every aspect of daily life.

These and other sweeping changes have brought with them new forms of copyrightable subject matter, new kinds of infringing uses, new demands for and against copyright protection and new alliances among the interested groups. Perhaps most important, there appears to be a vague but growing realisation among copyright owners that their rights cannot be compartmentalised – that all copyright owners' interests are linked together – that if uncompensated use of someone's property is allowed to go unpunished, this 'piracy' not only fails to benefit other copyright owners but ultimately works to damage them.

Moreover, there is reason to hope that the long period when the American Congress, and especially the American courts, were consistently hostile to intellectual property rights may be coming to an end. It is becoming more generally realised that decisions actively calculated to deter creativity in the name of 'competition' or 'consumers' rights' could not be more self-defeating, and that hostility to copyrights, as well as other forms of intellectual property, has actually hurt the public and the nation. Instead of straining to invalidate creators' rights, the courts in some recent cases actually seem to be straining to uphold them.

1 Z. Chafee 'Reflections on the Law of Copyright' 45 Col L Rev 719, 734 (1945).

The structure of intellectual property law in the United States

21.02 To understand the evolution and present scope of protection for copyright and neighbouring rights under US law it is necessary to have some grasp of the American legal system, and particularly the inter-relationship between federal and state laws.

The fountainhead of intellectual property protection in the United States is the US Constitution itself, which gives to Congress the authority to enact copyright laws protecting the 'writings of an author'. The Constitution also empowers Congress to regulate interstate and foreign commerce, and the 'commerce clause' is the source of federal laws dealing with trademarks, unfair competition and communications.

In addition to federal laws applicable uniformly throughout the United States, American intellectual property protection derives from the laws of the 50 states, consisting both of statutes and, more often, of judge-made common law. Where a federal statute is found to have pre-empted a particular form of intellectual property protection, the states are excluded from the field. Where there has been no federal pre-emption, the states are free to offer intellectual property protection on a wide variety of legal theories: common law copyright,[1] trademark, unfair competition or misappropriation,[2] right of privacy,[3] right of publicity,[4] interference with contract relations,[5] interference with employer-employee relations,[6] moral right,[7] and various state and local criminal statutes dealing with the 'piracy' and 'counterfeiting'.[8] These laws differ widely from state to state and are often conflicting and irreconcilable.

Throughout the history of intellectual property protection in the United States the question of federal pre-emption has been a major unsettled issue. Before 1978, American copyright law consisted of a dual system of common law state protection for unpublished works and federal protection for published works. The question of how far the states could go in offering protection to published works remained unclear and highly controversial. The Copyright Act of 1976 (effective 1 January 1978) expressly pre-empted the field, offering federal copyright protection for both published and unpublished works and forbidding the states to do so,[9] but this has by no means settled the question. There are still wide areas of intellectual property that the states can protect on one theory or another, and the limits of these areas will undoubtedly be before the courts for generations to come.

And the problem does not end there. The American judicial system provides for a federal judiciary, which exists in addition to the courts of each state. The federal courts deal not only with cases involving federal statutes, but also with controversies in which the parties are citizens of different states. Before 1938 it was assumed that in these 'diversity of citizenship' cases the federal courts could apply the so-called 'federal common law' and were not bound by any state court precedents. Following the 1938 Supreme Court decision in *Erie Railroad Co v Tompkins*,[10] however, the federal courts are required to apply the law of the state where the district court in which the action was brought happened to be located. This has not only cast some of the earlier federal precedents dealing with common law copyright and neighbouring rights into doubt, but has also presented the courts with problems of extreme complexity. For example, in an unfair competition case involving performers' rights, the court may be called upon to determine (1) the state conflict of laws rule, (2) which state laws apply, (3) what the various state laws are, and (4) how to resolve conflicts among the applicable state laws.[11]

All of this means that, with respect to areas of traditional copyright covered expressly by the federal statute, the protection offered is now defined exclusively by that statute. However, in those areas – notably performers' rights, broadcasters' rights and certain designers' rights where the statute is silent or inapplicable, the nature and scope of protection in the United States are unsettled. In these areas some precedents can be described and some trends can be discerned, but definitive rules are extremely rare and generalisations are risky.

1 See eg, *Waring v WDAS Broadcasting Station Inc* 327 Pa 433, 194 A 631 (1937).
2 See eg, *Metropolitan Opera Association Inc v Wagner-Nichols Recording Corp* 199 Misc 786, 101 NYS 2d 483 (1950); affd 279 App Div 632 (1951).
3 See eg, Maxey J's concurring opinion in *Waring v WDAS Broadcasting Station Inc* 327 Pa 433, 456, 194 A 631, 642 (1937).
4 See eg, *Factors Etc Inc v Pro Arts Inc* 579 F 2d 215, 205 USPQ 751 (2d Cir 1978).
5 See eg, *Metropolitan Opera Association Inc*, above.

6 *Darmour Productions Corpn v H.M. Baruch Corpn* 135 Cal App 351 (1933).
7 See eg, Frank J's concurring opinion in *Granz v Harris* 198 F 2d 585, 589 (2d Cir 1952).
8 See eg, McKinney's Cons Laws (of New York), Penal Law paras 275.05, 275.10; West's Ann Cal Penal Code paras 653h; Fla St Ann paras 543.041.
9 17 USC para 301.
10 304 US 64 (1938).
11 *Ettore v Philco Television Broadcasting Corpn* 229 F 2d 481, 108 USPQ 187 (3d Cir), cert denied 351 US 926, 109 USPQ 517 (1956).

The purpose and organisation of this chapter

21.03 This chapter has two aims: to provide an introduction to the copyright law of the United States as embodied in the new Copyright Act of 19 October 1976 (effective 1 January 1978); and to summarise in somewhat more detail the American law on neighbouring rights as it is derived from various federal statutes and regulations and from state statutes and common law precedents. Since the Act of 1976 provides statutory copyright protection for performances and sound recordings under certain circumstances, the subjects of copyright and neighbouring rights under American law can be said to overlap. Thus, to avoid repetition, the statutory copyright protection offered to performers and record producers will be referred to generally in the section on copyright, and will be dealt with in more detail in the section on neighbouring rights.

Organisationally, Part I of this paper on the US copyright statute will follow generally the structure of the Act of 19 October 1976. Part II, the section on neighbouring rights, will be divided into subsections dealing respectively with performers' rights, rights of reproduction and performance in sound recordings and rights of broadcasters.

Part I: Statutory copyright in the United States

A. The Act of 1976

21.04 The Copyright Act of 19 October 1976, which came into force on 1 January 1978, was only the fourth general revision of the copyright law of the United States since its original enactment in 1790.[1] The 1976 statute was the product of over 20 years of active legislative efforts, and it represents a radical change in the philosophy and direction of the American copyright system. It replaces the antiquated Act of 4 March 1909,[2] and it pre-empts the entire field of state common law copyright protection for unpublished works of authorship.

1 1 Stat 124 (1790).
2 Act of 4 March, 1909, ch 320, 35 Stat 1075.

B. Subject matter of protection

1. General subject matter coverage
21.05 Under section 102 of the Act of 1976, copyright protection extends generally to 'original works of authorship' that are 'fixed in any tangible medium of expression, now known or later developed, from which they can be perceived, reproduced, or otherwise communicated either directly or with the aid of a machine or device'. This language embodies the three fundamental criteria of copyrightability under US law: originality, authorship and fixation.

The subject matter coverage of the statute is thus extremely broad; as long as a work can be said to be the product of authorship, to be original, and to be fixed tangibly, it is copyrightable without regard to the nature of the work, the intentions of the author, the commercial applications of the work, its aesthetic value, its novelty or ingenuity, its potential audience, or the number of copies or phonorecords reproduced. As long as the work is fixed, the form, medium and manner of the fixation are irrelevant.

The legislative history of the 1976 Act makes clear that it was intended to cover everything that had previously been subject to statutory protection, to add some new classes of copyrightable material,[1] and to leave the door open for the courts to expand statutory coverage in step with technological advances. At the same time, the drafters were careful to make clear that, broad as it is, the coverage of the 1976 Act is still smaller than the whole field of the 'writings of an author' that the US Constitution empowers Congress to protect. In the future it will be possible for the courts to hold that a type of work is the 'writing of an author', and hence potentially subject to copyright legislation, but that it is not an 'original work of authorship' within the coverage of the 1976 Act.[2]

[1] While some choreographic works and pantomines had been protected under the earlier law, they had not previously been listed as a class.
[2] House Report No 94-1476, 3 September, 1976, p 56.

2. Categories of copyrightable works

21.06 Section 102(a) of the statute states that 'works of authorship shall include the following categories', and then goes on to list seven specific classes: (1) literary works; (2) musical works, including any accompanying words; (3) dramatic works, including any accompanying music; (4) pantomimes and choreographic works; (5) pictorial, graphic and sculptural works; (6) motion pictures and other audiovisual works; and (7) sound recordings. Use of the word 'include'[1] in referring to these categories in relation to 'works of authorship' makes clear that the list is not exhaustive, although the courts will certainly be likely to view it as indicative of what Congress intended the new law to cover in a general way.

[1] 17 USC para 101 provides that, 'The terms "including" and "such as" are illustrative and not limitative'.

21.07 *'Literary works'*. All of the listed categories are broad, and the broadest of all is 'literary works'; these are defined as 'works, other than audiovisual works, expressed in words, numbers, or other verbal or numerical symbols or indicia, regardless of the nature of the material objects, such as books, periodicals, manuscripts, phonorecords, film, tapes, discs, or cards, in which they are embodied'. This is generally the category applicable to computer data bases, and to a 'computer program' which, under a 1980 amendment to the new Act, is defined as 'a set of statements or instructions to be used directly or indirectly in a computer to bring about a certain result'.[1]

[1] Pub L No 96-517, Sec 10(a), 12 December 1980, 94 Stat 3028.

21.08 *'Pantomimes and choreographic works'*. The one entirely new category in the listing of copyrightable works consists of 'pantomimes and choreographic works'. Pantomimes and at least some choreography were undoubtedly subsumed in 'dramatic works' under the earlier law, but their express listing in the copyright statute has removed uncertainties about their status, and has encouraged choreographers to rely more heavily on copyright law for their protection.

21.09 *'Pictorial, graphic, and sculptural works'.* The category of 'pictorial, graphic, and sculptural works' is defined in a way that includes the whole range of two-dimensional and three-dimensional artistic and graphic expression, but that excludes certain industrial designs. The design of a 'useful article'[1] is considered a 'pictorial, graphic, or sculptural work' only if, and only to the extent that, it 'incorporates pictorial, graphic, or sculptural features that can be identified separately from, and are capable of existing independently of, the utilitarian features of the article'.

This dividing line between copyrightable pictorial, graphic and sculptural works on the one hand, and uncopyrightable industrial designs on the other, can be called the doctrine of separability. It has been established by Copyright Office regulations and practice under the previous law,[2] and has been endorsed by the courts.[3] What it means in practice is that virtually any original two-dimensional design – for example, designs for textile fabrics, wallpaper and other sheet-like materials – is fully copyrightable, and the same is true of three-dimensional designs that can be actually or conceptually separated from the utilitarian aspects of the article embodying them. However, where the design of the useful article is inseparable from the utilitarian or functional aspects of the article, protection, if any, must be sought under the design patent law[4] or under common law theories of unfair competition or misappropriation.[5]

1   17 USC para 101 defines 'useful article' as follows: A 'useful article' is an article having an intrinsic utilitarian function that is not merely to portray the appearance of the article or to convey information. An article that is normally a part of a useful article is considered a 'useful article'.
2   CFR para 202.10 (c), revoked 1 January, 1978, 43 Fed Reg 965, 966 (1978).
3   *Kieselstein-Cord v Accessories by Pearl Inc*, 632 F 2d 989, 208 USPQ 1 (2d Cir 1980); *Esquire Inc v Ringer* 591 F 2d 796, 199 USPQ 1 (DC Cir 1978), cert denied, 440 US 908, 201 USPQ 256, reh denied 441 US 917, 99 S Ct 2019 (1979); *Eltra Corpn v Ringer* 579 F 2d 294, 194 USPQ 198, 198 USPQ 321 (4th Cir 1978); *Durham Industries Inc v Tomy Corpn* 630 F 2d 905, 208 USPQ 10 (2d Cir 1980).
4   35 USC para 171.
5   See eg, *Vuitton et Fils SA v J Young Enterprises Inc* 644 F, 2d 769, 210 USPQ 351 (9th Cir 1981).

21.10 *'Motion pictures and other audiovisual works'.* 'Audiovisual works' and 'motion pictures' are defined in such a way that they comprise a single category of copyrightable material, with motion pictures constituting a sub-species of audiovisual works. Motion pictures include all types of audiovisual works that impart an illusion of motion, including traditional cinematographic works, recorded television programming of all sorts, video recordings of every type and computer recordings where motion is simulated. Any soundtrack or audio component of a motion picture is considered an integral part of the motion picture, and is given protection whether used with the motion picture or separately. Thus, a performance recorded on a motion picture soundtrack has performing rights under the copyright law, while, as we shall see, a performance embodied in a sound recording with no visual component is denied any right of performance.[1]

The general category of 'audiovisual work' is defined as comprising 'works that consist of a series of related images which are intrinsically intended to be shown by the use of machines or devices such as projectors, viewers, or electronic equipment, together with accompanying sounds, if any, regardless of the nature of the material objects, such as films or tapes, in which the works are embodied'. This very broad definition was intended to cover not only all types of motion pictures but also photographic works, such as filmstrips and slide sets, and material intended for sequential visual display or performance by means of computers. Interestingly, certain key portions of one of the extraordinarily popular video games has recently been held to constitute an 'audio-visual work'.[2]

1   See Part II, Section B, below.
2   *Stern Electronics Inc v Kaufman* 523 F Supp 635, 213 USPQ 75 (EDNY 1981), affd 669 F 2d 852, 213 USPQ 443 (2d Cir 1982).

21.11 *'Sound recordings'*. The copyrightability of sound recordings was rather tentatively established by an amendment to the 1909 statute adopted as a temporary measure in 1972, and later extended.[1] The 1976 Act finally placed sound recordings on a firm footing as copyrightable works but severely limited their protection. The nature of sound recordings and the scope and conditions of their protection under the 1976 Copyright Act will be discussed in Part II of this chapter, in the context of neighbouring rights.

1   Act of 15 October 1971 (PL 92-140, 85 Stat 391), as amended by the Act of 31 December 1974 (PL 93-573, 88 Stat. 1873).

3. Compilations and derivative works

21.12   Section 103 of the 1976 Act makes clear that copyright protection extends to the two types of works employing pre-existing material or data: 'compilations' (works 'formed by the collection and assembling of pre-existing materials or of data that are selected, co-ordinated, or arranged in such a way that the resulting work as a whole constitutes an original work of authorship'), and 'derivative works' (where the pre-existing works have been 'recast, transformed, or adapted'). The new statute also seeks to clarify a point that has often been misunderstood in the past: that copyright in a compilation or derivative work 'covers only the material added by the later author, and has no effect one way or the other on the copyright or public domain status of the pre-existing material'.[1]

Several recent cases in the United States have dealt with the situation arising when a derivative work – typically a motion picture – has been made from a copyrighted work – typically a play or novel – and the copyright in the underlying work was renewed but the copyright in the derivative work was not renewed and expired. Is the public free to use the derivative work without infringing the rights of the owner of the underlying copyrighted work? The decisions on this question have left the matter in some doubt[2] but, at least where the underlying work is the subject of a valid statutory copyright, the weight of authority appears to hold that, even where a derivative work has fallen into the public domain, it cannot be used without permission from the owner of copyright in the underlying work.[3]

1   House Report No 94-1476, 3 September 1976, p 57.
2   Most cases hold that although a derivative work enters the public domain, matter contained therein that derives from matter still covered by statutory copyright is not dedicated to the public. See eg *Russell v Price* 612 F 2d 1123, 205 USPQ 206 (9th Cir 1979); *Grove Press Inc v Greenleaf Publising Co* 247 F Supp 518, 147 USPQ 99 (EDNY 1965); *Filmvideo Releasing Corpn v Hastings*, 426 F Supp 690, 193 USPQ 305 (SDNY 1976). Conversely, expiration of the copyright of the underlying work has been held not to affect the copyright of so much of the derivative work as is a new work and entitled to be independently copyrighted as such. See eg *G. Ricordi & Co v Paramount Pictures Inc* 189 F 2d 469, 89 USPQ 289) 2d Cir 1951), cert denied, 342 US 849, 91 USPQ 382 (1951). But see *Rohauer v Killiam Shows Inc* 551 F 2d 484, 192 USPQ 545 (2d Cir 1977), cert denied 431 US 949, 194 USPQ 304 (1977) (holding that a new property right' is created in the proprietory of a derivative copyright independent of the continued vitality of the copyright renewal in the underlying work).
3   Id In *Classic Film Museum Inc v Warner Bros Inc* 453 F Supp 852, 199 USPQ 265 (D Me 1978), affd 597 F 2d 13, 202 USPQ 467 (1st Cir 1979), the underlying work was covered by a common-law copyright of perpetual duration, thus not to allow free use of the derivative work would, the court reasoned, violate the limited monopoly character of copyright.

4. Uncopyrightable works

21.13 *'Works in the public domain'.* Section 103 of the Transition and Supplementary Provisions of the Act of 19 October 1976, provides specifically that 'This Act does not provide copyright protection for any work that goes into the public domain before January 1st, 1978'. The Copyright Act thus precludes any retroactive effect in restoring protection in cases where copyright had been lost or had expired. With respect to works subject to protection under the 1976 Act, copyright can be lost by failure to comply with formalities of notice and registration,[1] or by expiration of the relevant copyright term.[2] Once a work has fallen into the public domain in the United States it is no longer eligible for copyright protection under any circumstances, short of a special Act of Congress.[3]

1 See Part I, Section G, below.
2 See Part I, Section F, below.
3 Act of 15 December 1971 (Private Law 92-60).

21.14 *The question of obscenity.* A recurring question in US law is whether works thought to be obscene are subject to statutory copyright protection. In a recent case[1] an appellate court reversed a lower court decision that had denied relief to the copyright owners of a pornographic motion picture on grounds of obscenity. The appeals court effectively ruled out any restrictions on copyrightability based on the content of a work; it concluded that the constitutional purpose of copyright legislation 'is best served by allowing all creative works (in a copyrightable format) to be accorded copyright protection regardless of subject matter or content, trusting to the public taste to reward creators of useful works and to deny creators of useless works any reward'.

1 *Mitchell Brothers Film Group v Cinema Adult Theater* 604 F 2d 852, 203 USPQ 1041 (5th Cir 1979); *Jartech Inc v Clancy* 213 USPQ 1057 (9th Cir 1982).

21.15 *Works lacking original authorship.* The criterion of originality in American copyright law constitutes a very modest requirement. As stated by Judge Frank in *Alfred Bell & Co Ltd v Catalda Fine Arts Inc*[1] one of the classic decisions on the subject:

> '"Original" in reference to a copyright work means that the particular work "owes its origin" to the "author". .... All that is needed to satisfy both the Constitution and the statute is that the "author" contributed something more than a "merely trival" variation, something recognizably "his own". Originality in this context "means little more than a prohibition of actual copying". No matter how poor artistically the "author's" addition, it is enough if it be his own.' (citations omitted)

Even though very little in the way of originality is required to support a copyright, there are a number of American decisions ruling against copyright protection on grounds of lack of originality. Some of these cases seem to turn on the triviality or minimality of the author's contribution;[2] others are based more upon the mechanical or rote-like nature of what the author was called upon to do.[3] As expressed in the Copyright Office's regulations, these areas of 'material not subject to copyright' include:[4]

> Words and short phrases such as names, titles, and slogans; familiar symbols or designs; mere variations of typographic ornamentation, lettering or coloring; mere listing of ingredients or contests; ...

1 *Alfred Bell & Co Ltd v Catalda Fine Arts Inc* 191 F 2d 99, 102-103, 90 USPQ 153, 156-157 (2d Cir 1951).
2 See eg, *L Batlin & Son Inc v Snyder* 536 F 2d 486, 189 USPQ 753 (2d Cir 1976), cert denied 429 US 857.

3 See eg, *Gardenia Flowers Inc v Joseph Markovits Inc* 280 F Supp 776, 157 USPQ 685 (SDNY 1968).
4 37 CFR para 212.1(a).

21.16 *Unfixed works.* Works such as a live performance, a musical improvisation, an unrecorded choreographic work, or an extemporised speech are not subject to statutory copyright, since they are not 'fixed in any tangible medium of expression'.[1] However, it is clear from the case law that unfixed works of authorship are subject to common law or state statutory protection.[2] This form of protection will be dealt with in more detail in Part II, in connection with live performances.

1 House Report No 94-1476, 3 September 1976, pp 52-53.
2 *Metropolitan Opera Association Inc* above; *Zacchini v Scripps-Howard Broadcasting Co* 433 US 562, 205 USPQ 741 (1977).

21.17 *Ideas, systems, blank forms.* Section 102(b) restates the familiar distinction between uncopyrightable ideas and copyrightable expressions of those ideas: 'In no case does copyright protection for an original work of authors extend to any idea, procedure, process, system, method of operation, concept, principle, or discovery, regardless of the form in which it is described, explained, or embodied in such work'. With respect to computer programs, this language was intended to rule out any protection for the 'methodology or processes adopted by the programmer', as distinguished from the programmer's step-by-step written instructions as expressed in the program.[1] The statutory prohibition is also relevant in judging the copyrightability of printed material intended to be used by filling in blank lines or spaces. In its listing of 'material not subject to copyright', the Copyright Office Regulations include:

> Blank forms, such as time cards, graph paper, account books, diaries, bank checks, scorecards, address books, report forms, order forms and the like, which are designed for recording information and which do not in themselves convey information.[2]

1 House Report No 94-1476, 3 September 1976 p 54.
2 37 CFR para 212.1(c).

21.18 *US Government works.* Section 105 of the 1976 Act declares that copyright protection is not available for any 'work of the United States Government', and section 101 defines such a work as one 'prepared by an officer or employee of the United States Government as part of that person's official duties'. This provision, which covers both published and unpublished works, does not apply to works prepared under government contract[1] or with the use of government funds,[2] and its impact is limited to works by officers or employees of the United States federal government; works of state or local governments are not affected.[3]

1 *Schnapper v Foley* 471 F Supp 426, 202 USPQ 699 (DCDC 1979), affd 667 F 2d 102, 212 USPQ 235 (DC Cir 1981).
2 *Children's Television Workshop v Royal Mold Inc* No 77 Civ 3890 (SDNY 1978), reprinted in CCH Copyright Law Reporter, 25,013.
3 *Building Officials & Code Administrators International Inc v Code Technology Inc* 628 F 2d 730, 207 USPQ 81 (1st Cir 1980).

5. *National origin*

21.19 As long as they remain unpublished,[1] all original works of authorship are entitled to US copyright regardless of the nationality or domicile of their author. As for published works, section 104 of the 1976 Act established four conditions, under any one of which a work will be eligible for copyright in the United States:

'(1) The author of the work is a national or domiciliary of the United States, or of a country linked to the United States by a copyright treaty, or is a stateless person;
(2) The work is first published in the United States or in a country party to the Universal Copyright Convention;
(3) The work is first published by the United Nations, a specialized agency of the UN, or the Organization of American States;
(4) The work comes within a special presidential proclamation on copyright.'

1 17 USC para 101 states that: 'Publication' is the distribution of copies or phonorecords of a work to the public by sale or other transfer of ownership, or by rental, lease, or lending. The offering to distribute copies or phonorecords to a group of persons for purposes of further distribution, public performance or public display, constitutes publication. A public performance or display of a work does not itself constitute publication . . .

C. The scope of copyright protection

1. *Exclusive rights generally*
21.20 Unlike the statute that it replaces, the Act of 1976 first states the five basic rights of the copyright owner – the rights of reproduction, adaptation, publication, performance and display – in broad, unqualified terms in section 106. Then, in the following sections 107 through 118, it specifies the limitations on the copyright owner's exclusive rights. Taken together, sections 106 to 118 define the 'bundle of rights' of which American copyright now consists.

21.21 *Rights of reproduction, adaptation, and publications.* The first three exclusive rights specified in section 106, which apply to all types of copyrighted works, are the following:

'(1) To reproduce the copyright work in copies or phonorecords;
(2) To prepare derivative works based upon the copyrighted work;
(3) To distribute copies or phonorecords of the copyrighted work to the public by sale or other transfer or ownership, or by rental, lease or lending; . . .'

As explained in the legislative report on the Act of 1976,[1] the right of reproduction comprehends the right to produce a material object (a copy or a phonorecord) in which the work is duplicated, transcribed, imitated, or simulated in a fixed form from which it can be 'perceived, reproduced, or otherwise communicated, either directly or with the aid of a machine or device'. The right of reproduction and the right to prepare derivative works overlap to some extent, where the activity in question involves both reproductions of the copyrighted work and the preparation of a new work based upon it.

The right of public distribution – the equivalent of the right of publication – extends to the first act of distribution (sale, gift, loan, rental, or lease) of an authorised copy or phonorecord of a work, and to any act of distribution with respect to copies or phonorecords that have been unlawfully made. However, under the so-called 'first sale doctrine' embodied in section 109 of the 1976 Act, the right to control the distribution of an authorised copy or phonorecord ceases as soon as the copyright owner has transferred ownership of it.[2]

1 House Report No 94-1476, 3 September 1976, p 61.
2 *American International Pictures Inc v Foreman* 576 F 2d 661, 198 USPQ 580 (5th Cir 1978); *United States of America v Whetzel* 200 USPQ 193 (DC Cir 1978).

21.22 *Rights of public performance and display.* The remaining two rights in the copyright owner's bundle are stated in section 106 as follows:

'(4) In the case of literary, musical, dramatic, and choreographic works, pantomimes, and motion pictures and other audiovisual works, to perform the copyrighted work publicly; and

(5) In the case of literary, musical, dramatic, and choreographic works, pantomimes, and pictorial, graphic, or sculptural works, including the individual images of a motion picture or other audiovisual work, to display the copyrighted work publicly.'

Unlike the equivalent right under the 1909 law, the general right of public performance in the 1976 Act is not qualified by any 'for profit' limitation. Thus, as a general rule, non-profit performances are covered by the statute; some exemptions are provided under specific circumstances in section 110 and elsewhere, but unless one of these exemptions is applicable an unauthorised public performance will be an infringement even if no commercial motive or profit is involved.

The express statutory recognition of a right of public display represents a major innovation in American copyright law – one that seems sure to assume great importance with the increased use of computers and of video displays of textual and graphic materials. Like the right of publication, the right of public display is qualified by the equivalent of a 'first sale doctrine'; section 109 provides that the owner of a lawfully-made copy, or any person authorised by the owner, is entitled to display the copy publicly, 'either directly or by the projection of no more than one image at a time, to viewers present at the place where the copy is located'.

Under the 1976 Act, the concepts of public performance and public display are extremely broad. As stated in the legislative report,[1] they cover 'not only the initial rendition or showing, but also any further act by which that rendition or showing is transmitted or communicated to the public'. Under section 101:

'To perform or display a work "publicly" means—
(1) To perform or display it at a place open to the public or at any place where a substantial number of persons outside the normal circle of a family and its social acquaintances is gathered; or
(2) To transmit or otherwise communicate a performance or display of the work to a place specified by clause (1) or to the public, by means of any device or process, whether the member of the public capable of receiving the performance or display receive it in the same place or in separate places or at the time or at different times.'

2. *General limitations on exclusive rights*

1   House Report No 94-1476, 3 September 1976, p 63.

21.23   a. Fair use. Although the doctrine of fair use has been an important limitation on the rights of American copyright owners since it was first recognised in 1841,[1] section 107 of the 1976 Act represents its first statutory articulation. Section 107 recognised the principle that 'the fair use of a copyrighted work ... for purposes such as criticism, comment, news reporting, teaching (including multiple copies for classroom use), scholarship, or research, is not an infringement of copyright'. It then sets four 'factors to be considered' in determining whether a particular use is 'fair':

'(1) The purpose and character of the use, including whether such use is of a commercial nature or is for non-profit educational purposes;
(2) The nature of the copyrighted work;
(3) The amount and substantiality of the portion used in relation to the copyrighted work as a whole; and
(4) The effect of the use upon the potential market for or value of the copyrighted work.'

During the development of the 1976 Act the scope of fair use in the context of various educational practices, particularly the practices of photocopying and tape recording for use by pupils, students and teachers in various classroom situations, became a major bone of contention. As it finally emerged, section 107 itself contains little language reflecting this controversy, but the legislative history contains long and, presumably, authoritative comments on the line between fair use and infringement in a number of different classroom situations. In particular, the final report of the House of Representatives on the legislation reproduces two detailed sets of guidelines for classroom copying, one with respect to books and periodicals and the other with respect to music. These guidelines, which had been developed by representatives of the various affected interests at the urging of the House Committee, were expressly endorsed in the Committee report,[2] and must be taken into consideration in judging whether particular educational practices constitute fair use.

1 *Folsom v Marsh* 9 F Cas 342, No 4901 (CCMass 1841).
2 House Report No 94-1476, 3 September 1976, pp 68-72. Under these minimum standards, copying to create or substitute for compilations is prohibited, as is copying of 'consumable' material, such as workbooks. A copy of a work of prose or poetry, with copyright notice, may be distributed to each pupil in a class under certain prescribed tests of brevity (measured according to the number of pages copied), spontaneity ('at the instance and inspiration of the individual teacher'), and cumulative effect. This last test seeks to prevent an unreasonable amount of copying from one compilation, or of the works of one author, and to limit the instances of multiple copying in one term. The guidelines further specify that limited copying of copyrighted music may be made for academic purposes other than performance, and that performance is prohibited except to replace a purchased copy which for some reason is unavailable for an imminent performance.

21.24 b. Reproduction by libraries and archives. The scope of fair use and permissible reproductions by libraries and archives was another burning issue during the evolution of the 1976 Act; the controversy over this question was fuelled by a somewhat inconclusive court decision in the highly-publicised *Williams and Wilkins* case.[1] Unlike the classroom situation, which was resolved by general language in the fair use section and copious interpretations in the legislative history, the so-called 'library photocopying' issue produced its own statutory provision, section 108.

Section 108 is a long and, at least in places, somewhat obscure provision whose basic purpose is to sanction certain practices by libraries and archives and their employees in providing reproductions of copyrighted material to their patrons. In order to come within the section, the library or archive must meet the following conditions:

(1) *No multiple reproductions.* The reproduction and distribution must be limited to 'no more than one copy or phonorecord of a work'. 'Isolated and unrelated reproduction or distribution of a single copy or phonorecord of the same material on separate occasions' is permitted, but the section does not permit cases of 'related or concerted reproduction or distribution of multiple copies or phonorecords of the same material, whether made on one occasion or over a period of time and whether intended for aggregate use by one or more individuals or for separate use by the individual members of a group'.

(2) *No systematic reproduction.* The provision of section 108(g) ruling out 'the systematic reproduction or distribution of single or multiple copies or phonorecords of the same material' kicked up a storm of opposition from librarians, who feared it would interfere with very widespread inter-library 'loan' arrangements under which, instead of lending copies, libraries furnish photocopies which the patron can keep. As a result of this controversy, a

proviso was added to permit participation in 'interlibrary arrangements' as long as the library or archives receiving the copies or phonorecords for distribution does not do so 'in such aggregate quantities as to substitute for a subscription to or purchase' of the work. This language was in turn made the subject of detailed interpretative guidelines which were incorporated in the legislative history and given congressional endorsement.[2]

(3) *No commercial purpose.* The reproduction must be made 'without any purpose of direct or indirect commercial advantage'.

(4) *Public access.* The collections of the library or archives must be open to the public or to specialised researchers not affiliated with the organisation.

(5) *Notice of copyright.* The reproduction or distribution must include a 'notice of copyright'.

(6) *Certain types of works not covered.* The privileges of library reproduction and distribution under section 108 do not apply to musical works, pictorial, graphic and sculptural works, and audiovisual works other than those dealing with news.[3]

(7) *Purposes of reproduction.* Section 108 permits library or archival reproduction and distribution only for certain specified purposes: in general, for preservation or security, to replace lost or damaged copies of out-of-print works, to supply a patron with a copy of all or part of an out-of-print work, and to supply a patron with a copy of a single article from a periodical or collection, or of a small excerpt from a work. The library or archive is freed from any responsibility for the use by others of coin-operated reproducing equipment on their premises, but section 108 makes clear that the persons using the equipment may be copyright infringers if what they do exceeds fair use.

1 *Williams & Wilkins Co v United States* 172 USPQ 670 (Comm'r Ct Cl 1972), revsd on other grounds 487 F 2d 1345 (Ct 1973), affd per curiam by an equally divided court 420 US 376 (1975).
2 House Conference Report No 94-1733, 29 September 1976, p 72.
3 News programmes, but not documentary or magazine-format broadcasts, are exempt from the limitation on reproduction by lending set forth in s 108. Documentaries involving news reporting fall within the exemption. 17 USC para 108(f) (3).

21.25 The single most talked about, and probably the most important, copyright question of the 1980s in the United States involves the use of millions of audio and video tape recorders being manufactured, advertised, sold, and used to reproduce radio and television broadcasts. Under what circumstances does the use of this equipment constitute fair use or infringement of the copyrighted works being recorded by the millions? Can the manufacturer, the advertiser, or the vendor of the equipment be considered a contributory copyright infringer?

The way these questions are ultimately answered seems sure to change the course of copyright law, but it is now too soon to predict the forms that change will take. The most that someone writing in 1982 can do is to make a few preliminary observations.

Where the activity involved is what is commonly called 'piracy' – the unauthorised reproduction of copyrighted material and the distribution for purposes of commercial gain – it will clearly be looked upon as copyright infringement whether the reproduction is made directly from another copy or record or indirectly from a radio or television broadcast or other transmission.[1] When commercial piracy is involved, the source from which the unauthorised duplication was made, and whether or not the 'pirate tape' is an audio or a video recording, is irrelevant.[2]

When the activities in question are not for commercial gain, however, the answers are somewhat less clear, and when we are talking about individuals making off-the-air recordings for personal purposes in their private homes, the situation becomes still more problematical. In a recent decision, a school system was held to have violated the copyrights of various educational motion picture producers when it systematically recorded programs off-the-air and used them for classroom purposes.[3] And, in the famous '*Betamax*' case,[4] a federal appeals court held that home taping of copyrighted motion pictures is an infringing rather than a fair use, and that the manufacture, advertising, and merchandising of equipment for home recording constitutes contributory infringement.[5] The Supreme Court has agreed to review the *Betamax* decision,[6] and there has been a flurry of legislative proposals to deal with the problem.[7]

1 See eg, *United States v Drebin* 557 F 2d 1316, 195 USPQ 619 (9th Cir 1977), cert denied 436 US 904, 197 USPQ 848 (1978); *United States v Atherton* 561 F 2d 747, 195 USPQ 615 (9th Cir 1977). In both cases the court upheld convictions for the interstate transportation of stolen property in the form of unauthorised duplicates of copyrighted motion pictures.
2 See eg, *United States of America v Sam Goody Inc* 210 USPQ 318 (EDNY 1981) (interstate transportation of unauthorised duplicates of sound recordings).
3 *Encyclopedia Britannica Educational Corpn v Crooks* 477 F Supp 243, 197 USPQ (WDNY 1978).
4 *Universal City Studios Inc v Sony Corpn of America* 659 F 2d 963, 211 USPQ 761 (9th Cir 1981).
5 The court first stated that 'the grant of exclusive rights is only limited by the statutory exceptions', of which home video recording is not one. In fact, unlike with sound recordings, Congress had shown a 'special solicitude for [copyright protection of] audiovisual works'. The court then considered the fair use doctrine, as codified in 17 USC para 107, and concluded that home taping is not fair use. With regard to the third factor in s 107 - 'the amount and substantiality of the portions used in relation to the copyrighted work as a whole' -the court added that 'the fact that the infringement will not affect the sale or exploitation of the work or pecuniarily damage [the copyright owner] is immaterial'. Indeed, the harm to a copyright plaintiff is 'inherently speculative'. Nor would liability on the corporate defendants be inappropriate, for videotape recorders, unlike cameras, are not 'suitable for substantial non-infringing use'. Finally, the court said that the innocence of the infringers would not bar a finding of liability, but only reduce the damages under 17 USC para 504(c) (2).
6 Cert granted 14 June, 1982. 584 PTCJ 153.
7 Eg, S 1758, introduced by Senators Dennis DeConcini (D-Ariz) and Alphonse D'Amato (R-NY), and Amendment No 1333 thereto, introduced by Senator Charles Mathias (R-Md); HR 5705, introduced by Representative Don Edwards (D-Calif); HR 4808, introduced by Representative Stan Parris (R-Va); HR 4783, introduced by Representative John Duncan (R-Tenn).

3. *Specific limitations on exclusive rights (other than compulsory licenses)*

21.26   a. Exemption of certain performances and display. Section 110 of the 1976 Act consists of nine subsections exempting certain performances and displays from copyright liability. Some of the exemptions are fully justified, while others are more the result of special interest pressures than of reasoned justice. Nevertheless, although these nine exemptions may seem at first glance to make substantial inroads into the copyright owner's exclusive rights, they actually add up to much less of a limitation than existed under the 1909 statute.

The following is a brief outline of the nine exemptions which, as expressed in the statute, are full of detailed exceptions, conditions and qualifications:

(1) *Face-to-face teaching activities*. This exemption applies to performance or display of all types of works by instructors or pupils in non-profit educational institutions.

(2) *Instructional transmissions*. Performance of non-dramatic literary works, and display of all types of works, are exempted if done in certain types of non-profit educational transmissions.

(3) *Religious services*. Performances of certain types of works, and displays of all types of works, are exempted if done in the course of religious services.

(4) *Non-profit live performances*. This important but rather complicated exemption applies to performances of non-dramatic literary or musical works

otherwise than in a transmission to the public. Such performances are exempt if there is no commercial purpose, no payment to any of the performers or promoters, and no admission charge. Or, if admission is charged, the performance is exempted if the net proceeds are used exclusively for eleemosynary purposes and no objection to the performance has been lodged by the copyright owner. The effect of this provision has been to require payment of royalties in a number of cases that had formerly been exempted – typically, large money-making concerts sponsored by non-profit organisations – and legislation to change it has been introduced in Congress.[1]

(5) *Home receiving apparatus.* This exemption covers the operation of 'single receiving apparatus of a kind commonly used in private homes', and allows entrepreneurs to communicate transmissions to the public by this means, unless they charge admission or unless 'the transmission thus received is further transmitted to the public'. The legislative history of this provision suggests that it is to be narrowly construed,[2] and a recent decision involving radio performances piped throughout a clothing store ruled that, because of the sophistication of the sound system and the large size of the store, there was 'further transmission' and hence an infringement.[3]

(6) *Agricultural fairs.* This exemption covers performances of music at annual agricultural or horticultural fairs; it applies only to the governmental or non-profit sponsors of the fairs and does not excuse concessionaries from liability.

(7) *Promotional Performances.* Performances of music by vending establishments are exempted 'where the sole purpose of the performance is to promote the retail sale of copies or phonorecords of the work'.

(8) *Transmissions of nondramatic literary works to the blind and deaf.* Certain types of transmission aimed at blind and deaf audiences are permitted under this exemption.

(9) *Transmissions of dramatic works to the blind.* This exemption allows a single performance of a dramatic work under very strict conditions.

1 HR 4441 (97th Cong 2d Sess) exempting non-profit veterans' and fraternal organisations from liability for infringement of non-dramatic literary or musical works performed for charitable purposes has now been enacted into law effective 24 November 1982 as PL 97-366.
2 House Conference Report No 94-1733, 29 September 1976, pp 74-75.
3 *Sailor Music v The Gap Stores Inc* 213 USPQ 1089 (SDNY 1982).

21.27 b. Ephemeral and other recordings for broadcasting purposes. Although the title of section 112 of the 1976 Act refers to 'ephemeral recordings', only the first of its subsections embodies the traditional exemption under which a broadcasting organisation licensed to transmit a performance or display of a work is given a temporary privilege of recording the work as a technical convenience. Section 112(b) gives a much broader exemption to non-profit broadcasters, sanctioning the marking of up to 30 reproductions which can be exchanged with other non-profit broadcasters and can be retained up to seven years. Subsection (c) of section 112 provides a rather broad exemption allowing religious organisations to make recordings of religious music or records and to distribute them to non-profit broadcasters without copyright liability under certain circumstances. And, under subsection (d), recordings for use in transmissions to the blind are also permitted, subject to specified conditions.

21.28 c. Reproduction of pictorial, graphic and sculptural works of useful articles. Section 113(a) restates the fundamental principle first enunciated by the Supreme Court in the famous 'lamp base' case[1] and now firmly rooted in US copyright law: that 'the exclusive right to reproduce a copyrighted pictorial, graphic, or sculptural work in copies ... includes the right to reproduce the work in or on any kind of article, whether useful or otherwise'. However, a related question on which the courts have not provided a definitive answer, involves the extent of protection for a pictorial, graphic or sculptural work that portrays or depicts a useful article as such. Does copyright in a painting of an automobile give the owner rights as against someone who makes an automobile of the same design?

This question is one of the most subtle and difficult in copyright law, and Congress deliberately decided not to attempt to answer it. Under section 113(b), the question is left to the courts to decide on a case-by-case basis, using the applicable precedents as they existed before the new law came into effect.

1   *Mazer v Stein* 347 US 201 (1954).

21.29   d. Use of computer programs. During one phase in the development of the Act of 1976 a great deal of concern was expressed that, unless free input of copyrighted material into computer programs were permitted, the growth of computer science would be inhibited and its benefits to the public would be lost. This controversy had two intermediate results: Congress created a consultative body – the National Commission on New Technological Uses of Copyrighted Works (CONTU) – to study the problem; and, in section 117 of the Act of 1976, it temporarily froze the law on the point. As originally enacted, section 117 provided that copyright owners were to be afforded 'no greater or lesser rights with respect to use of the work in conjunction with computers than those afforded to works under the law ... in effect on December 31st, 1977'.

After the new law had come into effect the Commission completed its work, concluding that unauthorised input of copyrighted material into a computer is clearly copyright infringement, and recommending that section 117 be revised. Congress responded in 1980 by adopting an amendment dropping the freeze and substituting a kind of fair use provision for computer programs.[1] As revised, section 117 permits the owner of a copy of a computer program to make and use new copies and adaptations of the program under certain conditions.

1   Pub L No 96-517, 12 December, 1980, 94 Stat 3028.

21.30   e. Sound recordings. Section 114 of the 1976 Act, which sharply limits the scope of copyright protection for sound recordings, is dealt with in Part II of this chapter.

4. *Exclusive rights subject to compulsory licensing*

21.31   a. Compulsory licenses and the Copyright Royalty Tribunal. As a middle ground between exclusive rights and complete exemption, the 1976 Act provided forms of compulsory licensing governing four important uses of copyright material: recordings of musical works, cable television, jukeboxes and non-commercial broadcasting. Each of the compulsory licenses is dealt with differently in the statute, but they all call upon the services of a newly-created government body, the Copyright Royalty Tribunal,[1] for either the establishment of the royalty rate, the distribution of royalties among copyright owners or both.

Some copyright experts have criticised the 1976 Act for its complicated compulsory licensing provisions with their heavy government involvement in the process, and have deplored the trend that this is said to represent. Certainly one could wish for simpler methods of recompensing copyright owners for the use of their works. But it must be recalled that in each of the four cases the compulsory licensing system was preceded by a complex exemption from copyright liability,[2] and that enormous industries had been built upon a foundation of free use of copyrighted material. Given the strength of the special interest pressures generated in these situations, the establishment of any degree of copyright control—even one subject to a compulsory license—must be considered something of an accomplishment.

1   17 USC Chapter 8. The Copyright Royalty Tribunal was created as part of the Copyright Act of 1976, Pub L 94-553, s 102. The Tribunal is to adjust royalty rates based on the economic conditions peculiar to the industries affected by such adjustment, and to review rates on a staggered basis according to the industries affected. Rates for retransmission of copyrighted works by cable television systems were reviewed in 1980 and thenceforth each fifth year; rates established for mechanical reproduction were reviewed in 1980, then in 1987 and thereafter each tenth year; rates for performance by jukebox were reviewed in 1980 and thenceforth each tenth year; and rates and terms in connection with non-commercial broadcasting are reviewable in 1982 and each subsequent fifth year.
2   In *United Artists Television Inc v Fortnightly Corpn* 392, US 390, 158 USPQ 1 (1968) reh denied 393 US 902, the Supreme Court held that cable television operators, 'like viewers and unlike broadcasters, do not perform the programs that they receive and carry', and therefore would not be liable for copyright infringement. See also, *Columbia Broadcasting Systems Inc v Teleprompter Corpn* 415 US 394, 181 US 65 USPQ (1974). In *White-Smith Music Co v Appollo Co* 209 US 1 (1908), the Supreme Court held that grooves in phonorecords, not being 'a written or printed record in intelligible notation', were not copyrightable. Jukebox operators were completely exempted from copyright liability by s 1(e) of the 1909 Act. Non-Commercial broadcasts were formerly exempted from liability due to the requirements that musical 'performances subject to liability be 'for profit', and because there then existed no right of display in the copyright owner.

21.32   b. Phonorecords of musical works (the 'mechanical license'). The familiar 'mechanical royalty' system of section 1(e) of the 1909 Copyright Act—under which, as soon as a copyrighted musical composition had been licensed for recording, anyone else was entitled to record the work upon payment of a royalty of two cents per 'part' manufactured—was for the most part retained in the 1976 Act. The new law increased the amount of the royalty, refined the details of the system, and provided for involvement of the Copyright Royalty Tribunal in setting the royalty rate.

Rather surprisingly, when the question of whether the 'mechanical license' should be retained came to the test, it became apparent that the parties had become comfortable with the system and were loath to dispense with it. Section 115 thus follows the general outlines of the old law, as it had been interpreted in practice and by the courts. The debates that emerged had more to do with the basis for computing the royalty and the amount of the royalty rate than with the loss of exclusivity implicit in a compulsory licensing system.

Under the 1976 Act, the owner of copyright in a non-dramatic musical work has exclusive rights to make and distribute phonorecords of the work up to the time when authorised records are first distributed to the public. At that point, any other person may make and distribute phonorecords of the work without permission, under the conditions of the compulsory licensing provisions of section 115. These conditions can be summarised generally as follows:

(1) The compulsory licensee's primary purpose in making the phonorecords must be 'to distribute them to the public for private use'.

(2) Compulsory licenses are not available to 'record pirates'—that is, persons duplicating another sound recording without authority from the owner of rights in the recording.

(3) Compulsory licensees are given some leeway in arranging or adapting the musical work, but 'the arrangement shall not change the basic melody or fundamental character of the work'.

(4) A compulsory licensee must serve a 'notice of intention' on the copyright

owner within certain time limits; failure to do so will make the unlicensed recording and distribution into acts of infringement. At the same time, the copyright owner must be identified in the registration or other records of the Copyright Office in order to be entitled to royalties.

(5) The compulsory licensee must pay a specified royalty for 'every phonorecord made and distributed'; a record is considered 'distributed' if the 'person exercising the compulsory license has voluntarily and permanently parted with its possession'. Because of the rather loose practices concerning record shipments, returns and reshipments prevalent in the American record industry, this provision raised controversial accounting questions and is the subject of a complex Copyright Office regulation.[1]

(6) The compulsory licensee must make monthly royalty payments and file detailed annual accounts. The royalty fee provided in the 1976 Act was, with respect to each musical work embodied in a phonorecord, either two and three-fourths cents, or one-half cent per minute of playing time (or fraction) whichever is larger. In early 1981, the Copyright Royalty Tribunal, following hearings and comments as authorised in the statute, readjusted this rate to four cents or three-fourths cents per minute.[2] This rather large increase was immediately challenged in the courts, but was upheld in a thoughtful and scholarly opinion by Judge Mikva of the US Court of Appeals for the District of Columbia.[3] Thereafter, the Tribunal determined that there should be annual increases in the rates through 1986, reaching a level of five cents or .95 cent per minute.

1 37 CFR para 201.19.
2 37 CFR para 307.2.
3 *National Association of Broadcasters v Copyright Royalty Tribunal* 214 USPQ 161 (DC Cir 1982).
4 46 Federal Register 10466.

21.33 c. Secondary transmission (the 'cable license'). The longest, most complicated and most controversial in the Copyright Act of 1976 is section 111, dealing generally with secondary transmissions of copyrighted works and, in particular, establishing a compulsory licence for secondary transmissions by cable television systems. The cable question—whether cable operators were liable under the 1909 Act when they picked up broadcasts containing copyrighted material and retransmitted them to subscribers—had reached the Supreme Court twice, in 1968 and 1974.[1] In both cases the court ruled against the copyright owners, thus making the imposition of any sort of copyright liability in the new legislation an extraordinarily difficult and delicate task. As it emerged in the Act of 1976, section 111 is a complex and rather uneasy amalgam of copyright and communications law, incorporating a number of compromises and private understandings.

In approaching this problem the 1976 statute first draws a distinction between 'primary transmissions'—including broadcasts by radio and television stations that are retransmitted by cable systems to their subscribers—and 'secondary transmissions'—the basic service of retransmitting television and radio broadcasts to subscribers. Under section 111, every cable system in the United States is required to obtain a compulsory licence, and to pay at least a minimum of royalties twice each year in order to make secondary transmissions to its subscribers without copyright liability. Primary transmissions by cable systems (such as cablecasting, pay-cable and background music services) are not, of course, subject to compulsory licensing; as under the previous law, any copyrighted material used in them must be licensed. A compulsory license also does not permit cable systems to alter programming, to substitute commercial advertising, to import foreign signals (except those of certain Mexican and

498 *United States*

Canadian stations), or, except under very special circumstances, to record programming for simultaneous retransmission.

To obtain a compulsory license, a cable system must first file with the Copyright Office an initial 'notice of identity and signal carriage complement', and must notify the Office of any change in the information originally given. Then, twice each year within specific deadlines, the system must file a statement of account containing a good deal of detailed information, and must pay a semi-annual royalty, the amount of which varies depending upon the system's gross receipts from subscribers for secondary transmissions during the preceding six months. For smaller systems the royalty is a small flat amount; for medium-sized systems the royalty is computed by using a fairly simple formula based on gross receipts. For larger systems the royalty is based on a complex formula based primarily on a concept known as a 'distant signal equivalent' or 'DSE'—a numerical value given by the Copyright Act to each of various kinds of television stations carried by a cable system. The amounts established in the 1976 Act with respect to gross receipts and DSE values were substantially increased by the Copyright Royalty Tribunal following rate review proceedings in 1980;[2] the Tribunal's action has been appealed.

A key feature of the cable compulsory license is that it applies only to those signals that the cable system is permitted to carry under the regulations of the Federal Communications Commission (FCC); should the cable operator violate the FCC regulations and retransmit unauthorised signals it would automatically become fully liable for copyright infringement. At the time of the 1976 Act was passed the FCC's cable regulations were stringent and sweeping in their effect; in particular, the importation of distant signals into major television markets was strictly limited, and cable operators could be required to 'black out' syndicated programming for which an exclusive broadcasting license had been granted within the cable system's area. It was assumed that these regulations would remain in effect, and would continue to provide a form of protection for copyright owners' exclusive rights.

As part of the epidemic of 'deregulation fever' that struck Washington in the late 1970s and early 1980s, the Federal Communications Commission repealed its cable rules on distant signals and syndicated program exclusivity, thus significantly altering the balance of section 111. The FCC's action was upheld by the courts,[3] and as a result there has been a clamour for revision of the copyright law to improve the rights of copyright owners as against cable operators.[4] Meanwhile, the Copyright Royalty Tribunal has opened proceedings looking toward further readjustment of the cable royalty rates in light of the FCC's actions.[5]

Royalties paid by cable operators under their compulsory licenses are placed in interest-bearing funds until they can be divided among copyright owners as determined by the Copyright Royalty Tribunal after distribution proceedings. The determinations of the Tribunal have been sustained by the courts on appeal.[6]

1   *United Artists Television Inc v Fortnightly Corpn* above; *Columbia Broadcasting Systems Inc v Teleprompter Corpn* above.
2   37 CFR paras 201.11 and 201.17.
3   *Malrite TV of New York v FCC* 652 F 2d 1140 (2d Cir 1981).
4   HR 5949 (97th Cong 2d Sess).
5   47 Fed Reg 8808 (2 March, 1982).
6   *National Association of Broadcasters v Copyright Royalty Tribunal*, above.

21.34   d. Coin-operated phonorecord players ('the jukebox license').

Among the various blots on the face of the 1909 Act, the so-called 'jukebox exemption' was one of the largest and blackest. A multi-million dollar industry, based entirely on the performance of copyrighted music for profit, was enabled to escape the payment of any royalties whatsoever on the basis of an ill-considered exemption for performances on coin-operated machines adopted at the last minute in 1909. The political power of the American jukebox industry was such that it was able to resist all efforts at legislative reform until 1976. By then popular tastes had changed; and a right that once would have been of great financial importance to musical copyright owners had become one of greatly diminished value.

As enacted in 1976, section 116 of the statute is relatively simple as compulsory license provisions go. Jukebox operators are freed of copyright liability for performance of copyrighted music on their machines if, once each year, they file a statement with the Copyright Office, pay a fee of $8 for each of their phonorecord players, and place a certificate on their machines showing that they are licensed. The fees thus collected are paid out to copyright owners by a distribution procedure like that for cable royalties.

Something that is startling to observe about the operation of jukebox compulsory license is the disparity between the estimates of annual royalties that would be generated and the actual amounts brought in: some $4,000,000 had been predicted and some $1,100,000 was actually distributed for 1978. Either the use of jukeboxes has waned tremendously, or some jukebox operators are ignoring the law—or perhaps both factors are at work. Be that as it may, the jukebox royalties for 1978 were divided as agreed upon among the performing rights societies representing copyright owners, without the necessity for Copyright Royalty Tribunal proceedings. At the outset, however, agreement could not be reached among the royalty claimants for the 1979 royalties; following lengthy proceedings the CRT determined that it could not resolve the dispute on the basis of the material presented to it, and requested the parties to 'submit proposals for a joint survey that they would agree to beforehand and whose execution they would supervise jointly.'[1] This prompted the performing rights societies to try again, and this time they reached substantial agreement covering the 1979 and 1980 divisions.[2]

Meanwhile, as part of the 1980 cyclical review of compulsory licensing rates mandated by the 1976 Act, the Copyright Royalty Tribunal determined that, beginning in 1982, the $8 rate per box should be increased to $25, and that in 1984 the amount would be set at $50, leaving the door open to further increases, based upon possible changes in the cost of living as determined by the Consumer Price Index, to be effective in 1987.[3] On the appeal of this determination to the courts, the Tribunal's action was fully sustained.[4]

1 46 Fed Reg 58139 (30 November 1981).
2 47 Fed Reg 18406 (29 April 1982).
3 37 CFR para 306.3.
4 *National Association of Broadcasters v Copyright Royalty Tribunal*, above.

21.35 e. Public broadcasting. Toward the end of the efforts to revise the copyright law in the mid-1970s, the representatives of public broadcasting organisations began a major campaign to obtain compulsory licenses to use dramatic literary and musical works, and pictorial, graphic and sculptural works. Faced with the loss of the 'nonprofit' exemption covering performances of music and non-dramatic prose and poetry, and with the addition of a right of public display covering graphic material, the public broadcasters sought a means to avoid clearance negotiations and to place a cap on the royalties they would have to pay.

A compulsory license provision along the lines sought by the public broadcasters passed the Senate in 1975. The House of Representatives, recognising that 'public broadcasting may encounter problems confronted by commercial broadcasting enterprises' because of 'the special nature of programming, repeated use of programs, and, of course, limited financial resources', agreed that 'the nature of public broadcasting does warrant special treatment in certain areas.'[1] However, instead of the Senate's broad form of compulsory license involving government rate making and royalty distribution, the House adopted a system encouraging voluntary agreements and royalty payments directly between the parties.

The House version, which became section 118 of the 1976 Act, applies only to 'published nondramatic musical works and published pictorial, graphic, and sculptural works'. Literary works were not included in the obligatory scheme, though a way was found to encourage voluntary licenses of literary material.[2] With respect to music and graphics, the Copyright Royalty Tribunal was directed to institute proceedings aimed at establishing the terms and rates for various uses in public broadcasting, and the parties were exhorted to bargain 'in an effort to reach reasonable and expeditious results'. Any voluntary agreements thus reached were to be placed on public record, and were to be given effect regardless of any determinations by the Tribunal. After taking into account the terms and rates established in the voluntary agreements, the Tribunal was directed to publish a schedule of rates and terms to be binding on all parties not covered by voluntary agreements. Royalty payments were to be handled between the parties, and the whole procedure is to be repeated at cyclical intervals.

This system, which resembles a procedure sometimes known as 'agreed licensing', seems to have worked fairly well. While ultimately compelling the licensing of the works in question, and dictating the rates and terms of the licenses, it places a premium on voluntary negotiations, gives primary force and effect to agreements voluntarily achieved, and reduces the government's role to a minimum. People wanting to ameliorate the harsh effects of straight compulsory licensing in other areas would do well to take a close look at section 118.

On 8 June 1978, the Copyright Royalty Tribunal issued its final determination in the first public broadcasting proceedings.[3] Noting that the two other major performing rights societies had already reached voluntary agreements, it ruled in favour of an annual payment of $1,250,000 for performances of ASCAP music by Public Broadcasting System (PBS), National Public Radio (NPR), and their member stations. It also ruled that local and regional programming should be subject to copyright royalties, and set up detailed royalty schedules for these and other purposes. These determinations of the CRT were not appealed.

1   House Report No 94-1476, 3 September 1976, p 117.
2   17 USC para 118(e) exempts public broadcasting entities and owners of copyright in nondramatic literary works from antitrust liability arising from the terms and rates of royalty payments under voluntary agreements among themselves. That section also required the Register of Copyrights, on 3 January 1980 to submit to the Congress a report on the extent of such arrangements and describing any problems that may have arisen.
3   43 Fed Reg 25070 (8 June, 1978).

D. Ownership and transfer of copyright

1. *The philosophy of the 1976 Act*
21.36   A fundamental principle underlying the Act of 1976 was that, as the primary beneficiaries of copyright, individual authors should be accorded greater protection in their dealings with the first line of users of their works—

the publishers, producers, broadcasters and other entrepreneurs responsible for exploiting the authors' works and making them available to the public. For nearly 200 years the legislatures and the courts had treated authors very nearly the same as any other property owner; all too often, through no fault of their own, authors found themselves deprived of the benefits of their creation while businessmen made fortunes from them. There is only so much that a copyright statute can do to safeguard the property rights of authors against unintentional, improvident, unfair and unremunerative transfers; but, given the special pressures and the weight of a long tradition favouring 'freedom of contract', the 1976 Act did what it could. Specifically:

(1) It narrowed the scope of 'works made for hire';
(2) It safeguarded the rights of authors of contributions to collective works;
(3) It made copyright divisible, assuring that authors retain any rights they do not transfer;
(4) It prohibited involuntary transfers of the rights of individual authors;
(5) It reversed the common law presumption that, when an author or artist transfers a prototype copy (a painting or manuscript, for example), the copyright is transferred also;
(6) It established a system for terminating unremunerative transfers after a period of years;
(7) It established various requirements with respect to the execution and recordation of transfers and the registration of copyright claims. Taken together, these provisions rule out oral transfers, require the authors' signature for any rights they transfer and, in one way or another, require that anyone claiming copyright ownership must be able to trace their chain of title back to the author.

2. Initial ownership of copyright; joint works
21.37 Section 201(a) of the 1976 Act makes clear that copyright 'vests initially in the author or authors of the work', and adds that the 'authors of a joint work are co-owners of copyright in the work'. The term 'joint work' is defined as 'a work prepared by two or more authors with the intention that their contributions be merged into inseparable or interdependent parts of a unitary whole'. This important definition is further interpreted in the legislative report on section 201:

> '... a work is "joint" if the authors collaborated with each other, or if each of the authors prepared his or her contribution with the knowledge and intention that it would be merged with the contributions of other authors as "inseparable or interdependent parts of a unitary whole". The touchstone here is the intention, at the time the writing is done, that the parts be absorbed or combined into an integrated unit, although the parts themselves may be either "inseparable" (as in the case of a novel or painting) or "interdependent" (as in the case of a motion of a picture, opera, or the words and music of a song).'

3. Words made for hire
21.38 The legal fiction making the employer the 'author' for copyright purposes is retained in the new copyright law, but with some important changes. Section 201(b) states the principle as follows:

> In the case of a work made for hire, the employer or other person for whom the work was prepared is considered the author for purposes of this title, and, unless the parties have expressly agreed otherwise in a written instrument signed by them, owns all of the rights comprised in the copyright.'

Thus, where a work falls within the rather elaborate definition of a 'work made for hire' in section 101, the rights of the employee are governed by the terms of that person's employment—typically, by an individual employment contract or collective bargaining agreement. However, as section 201(b) makes clear, the employee can bargain with the employer for some of the rights under the copyright, and can become a copyright owner to the extent of those rights.

Initially an employed creator may be compensated better than a free-lance author who is guaranteed no income from the work and must take the risks of finding someone to exploit it. But the employee can never be an 'author', and can never assert claim under the copyright statute. For example, if the employment agreement calls for royalties and the employer stops paying them, the employee, unlike an author, cannot sue to rescind the contract and reclaim the copyright.

Most important, as will be explained later, there is no right of termination under sections 203 and 304 of the copyright statute in the case of works made for hire. Authors and their heirs may, by filing notices within specified time limits, terminate any existing 'exclusive or nonexclusive grant of a transfer or license of copyright or of any right under a copyright, executed by the author'. This right of termination cannot be transferred or bargained away, and it is looked upon very seriously by publishers and motion picture producers, among others. Employees and their heirs are foreclosed from exercising this right, and for this reason the question of whether or not a work is 'made for hire' can assume critical importance.

Under the law in effect before 1978, the term 'author' was defined to include the employer in the case of a 'work made for hire',[1] but the term 'work made for hire' was undefined. Beyond cases where the work was prepared within the scope of the employee's assigned duties,[2] the courts had expanded the meaning of 'work made for hire' to include many works prepared on special order or commission,[3] especially when the commissioning party could be shown to exercise some control over the preparation of the work.[4]

The definition of 'work made for hire' in the new law is divided into two clauses. Under the first, a work is considered 'made for hire' if it is 'prepared by an employee within the scope of his or her employment'. Under the second clause, a work that is 'specially ordered or commissioned' can be considered a work made for hire, but only under certain narrow conditions: (1) the parties must 'expressly agree in a written instrument signed by them that the work shall be considered a work made for hire'; and (2) the work must have been 'specially ordered or commissioned for use as a contribution to a collective work, as a part of a motion picture or other audiovisual work, as a translation, as a supplementary work, as a compilation, as an instructional text, as a test, as answer material for a test, or as an atlas ...'.[5] Thus, only certain very limited types of commissioned works can now be considered 'works made for hire', even if the parties agree otherwise.

1 Act of 4 March 1909, s 26.
2 See eg, *Sawyer v Crowell Publishing Co* 46 F Supp 471, 54 USPQ 225 (SDNY 1942), affd 142 F 2d 497, 61 USPQ 389 (2d Cir), cert denied, 323 US 735, 63 USPQ 359 (1944) (map created by a government employee).
3 See eg, *Brattleboro Publishing Co v Winmill Publishing Corpn* 369 F 2d 565, 151 USPQ 666 (2d Cir 1966); *Lin-Brook Builders Hardware v Gertler* 352 F 2d 298, 147 USPQ 264 (9th Cir 1965).
4 See eg, *Picture Music Inc v Bourne Inc* 457 F 2d 1213, 173 USPQ 449 (2d Cir 1970), cert denied, 409 US 997 (1972).
5 17 USC para 101. This section further provides that: 'For the purpose of the foregoing sentence [relating to the definition of "work made for hire"] a 'supplementary work is a work prepared for publication as a secondary adjunct to a work by another author for the purpose of introducing, concluding, illustrating, explaining, revising, commenting upon, or assisting in the use of the other work, such as forewords, afterwords, pictorial illustrations, maps, charts, tables, editorial notes, musical arrangements, answer material for tests, bibliographies, appendixes, and indexes, and an "instructional text" is a literary pictorial, or graphic work prepared for publication and with the purpose of use in systematic instructional activities.'

4. *Contributions to collective works*
21.39 Section 201(c) represents an effort to bring light to one of the murkiest corners of American copyright law, and to remedy situations in which, over the years, some great injustices have been done to authors. At the outset it makes clear that copyright in an individual contribution to a collective work (such as an issue of a periodical, a symposium or an anthology) is separate and distinct from copyright in the collective work as a whole, and that the author of the contribution is the first owner of copyright in it.

As stated in the legislative report,[1] the rights of the owner of copyright in the collective work 'extend to the elements of compilation and editing that went into the collective work as a whole, as well as the contributions that were written for hire by employees of the owner of the collective work, and those copyright contributions that have been transferred in writing to the owner by their authors'. However, in the absence of such a written transfer, the author remains the owner of copyright in the contribution, even where the contribution does not bear a separate copyright notice in the author's name. The second sentence of section 201(e) establishes a presumption that, in the absence of an express transfer from the author conveying broader rights, the owner of the collective work acquires 'only the privilege of reproducing and distributing the contribution as part of that particular collective work, any revision of that collective work, and any later collective work in the same series'.

[1] House Report No 94-1476, 3 September 1976, p 122.

5. *Transfers and divisibility of copyright*
21.40 Section 201(d) expressly establishes the free alienability of copyright ownership: ownership may be transferred 'in whole or in part'; the transfer may take place 'by any means of conveyance or by operation of law'; and the copyright may be transferred by will or pass as personal property upon the owner's death. Clause (2) of section 201(d), an extremely important innovation in the 1976 Act, provides for divisibility of copyright:

> 'Any of the exclusive rights comprised in a copyright, including any subdivision of any of the rights..., may be transferred... and owned separately. The owner of any particular exclusive right is entitled, to the extent of that right, to all of the protection and remedies accorded to the copyright owner by this title.'

Since authors who are not employees are the initial owners of all rights in their works, the principle of divisibility means that any rights authors do not transfer will remain their property. Transfers of anything less than 100% of the rights they own will now leave the transferors with full copyright ownership in the residuum; and, even when there has been a blanket transfer, it should now be easier to argue that rights in certain uses—especially those resulting from new technology—were not contemplated when the transfer was made and were thus retained by the transferor.[1]

[1] *Ettore v Philco Television Broadcasting Corpn* above.

6. *Prohibition against involuntary transfers*
21.41 Section 201(e) provides that, where an individual author has not voluntarily made a transfer of copyright ownership, any purported seizure, expropriation, transfer or exercise of rights of ownership will be given no effect. The immediate aim of this provision was to prevent suppression of dissident writings under a cloak of copyright, but the statutory language could be interpreted to cover other situations.

7. Ownership of copyright and material object: effect of transfer

21.42 Though supposedly a basic principle of copyright law, the rule stated in section 202—that copyright ownership 'is distinct from ownership of any material object in which the work is embodied'—has often been obscured in practice and confused in some of the court decisions. The typical question is whether, when an author or artist or photographer sells the prototype or sole copy of a work—the manuscript or original painting or negative, for example—the rights of copyright ownership are presumed to be transferred along with material object. Under the so-called 'Pushman doctrine',[1] the author in this situation was presumed to have disposed of all rights of ownership that are not expressly reserved at the time of the sale. This presumption is reversed under the new law: sale 'of any material object, including the copy or phonorecord in which the work is first fixed, does not of itself convey any rights in the copyrighted work embodied in the object', and an express written transfer, signed by the author, would be required to convey rights in the work.

1 *Pushman v NY Graphic Society Inc* 25 NYS 2d 32 (Sup Ct 1941), affd 287 NY 302, 39 NE 2d 249 (1942); *Chamberlain v Feldman* 300 NY 135, 89 NE 2d 863 (1949). Prior to the enactment of s 202, state statutes in New York and California had already reversed the 'Pushman doctrine'.

8. Right of termination

21.43 Under the law in effect before 1978, the duration of copyright was divided into two terms: a first term of 28 years, and, if renewal registration was made, a second term of 28 years. The old law, in an effort to guard authors against unremunerative transfers, provided for ownership of the second (renewal) term automatically to revert to the author or other specified beneficiaries in certain situations. The provisions of the 1976 Act with respect to duration and ownership of copyrights secured before 1 January 1978, are discussed below.

For transfers of United States rights made by an author on or after 1 January 1978, the Act of 1976 drops the renewal feature and substitutes a right of termination. Post-1977 transfers, whether of exclusive or non-exclusive rights, can be generally terminated by the author, or certain heirs of the author, within a five-year period beginning at the end of 35 years from the date of the grant—or, if the grant covers the right of publication, 35 years from the date of publication or 40 years from the date of the grant, whichever is shorter. The right of termination is not automatic; to be effective, a written notice of the termination must be served on the transferee within specified time limits.

As noted above, the right of termination does not apply to works made for hire. With respect to a derivative work prepared under the authority of the transfer being terminated, section 203(b)(1) provides that it 'may continue to be utilised under the terms of the grant after its termination', but this privilege does not extend to the preparation of other derivative works based on the work in question.

The right of termination cannot be waived or transferred in advance; section 203(a)(5) provides for the effectiveness of a termination 'notwithstanding any agreement to the contrary, including an agreement to make a will or to make any future grant'. To prevent trafficking in future interest such as occurred under the renewal provision of the 1909 law, section 203(b)(4) provides that 'a further grant, or agreement to make a further grant, of any right covered by a terminated grant is valid only if it is made after the effective date of the termination'. However, something in the nature of a 'right of first refusal' is given to the original grantee in this situation.

9. *Execution of transfers*

21.44 Under section 204 of the 1976 Act, a copyright transfer (other than one occurring by operation of law) is valid only if a written instrument of conveyance, or a note or memorandum of it, bears the signature of the owner of the rights conveyed, or, of that owner's agent. Notarial certificates of acknowledgment are not required for the validity of a transfer but will constitute prima facie evidence of the execution of the instrument; in the case of documents signed outside the United States, the certificate can be furnished by a US consular officer or by an official whose authority is certified to by such an officer.

10. *Recordation of transfers*

21.45 Section 205 of the 1976 Act sets forth the conditions for recordation of documents in the Copyright Office, the conditions that must be met in order for a recorded document to provide constructive notice of the facts it contains, and the rules as to priority between conflicting transfers, and between a conflicting transfer of ownership and a non-executive license. Section 205(d), entitled 'Recordation as Prerequisite to Infringement Suit', provides a new requirement in the nature of a formality, and will be discussed below.

E. A single copyright system: pre-emption of common law copyright

21.46 The most sweeping, and probably the most important change in the US copyright system brought about by the 1976 Act is found in section 301, headed 'Pre-emption with respect to other laws'. From its beginnings in 1790 to 1978 the US copyright law had consisted of a dual system of state common law (or, in a few cases, statutory) copyright for unpublished works and statutory copyright for published works. Describing the dual system as 'anachronistic, uncertain, impractical, and highly complicated', the legislative report on the 1976 Act[1] declared that a single federal copyright system, by providing national uniformity in interpretation and enforcement would greatly simplify, clarify and strengthen the law.

Under the 1976 Act, federal statutory copyright in any 'original work of authorship' comes into existence at the moment of its 'creation'—that is, the point at which it is fixed for the first time. The concept of 'publication' is still significant for certain purposes under the new law, but it no longer has supreme importance in determining whether a work is protected by state common law or federal statute, or is in the public domain.

For works, other than those in the public domain, created before or after 1 January 1978, whether published or unpublished, section 301(a) provides that from 1 January 1978 on their protection is to be governed exclusively by the 1976 Act:

1. *Rights covered by the pre-emption.* '... all legal or equitable rights that are equivalent to any of the exclusive rights within the general scope of copyright as specified by section 106'.
2. *Works covered by the pre-emption.* 'Works of authorship that are fixed in a tangible medium of expression and come within the subject matter of copyright as specified by sections 102 and 103'.
3. *Laws covered by the pre-emption.* From 1 January 1978, 'No person is entitled to any such right or equivalent right in any such work under the common law or statutes of any State'. However, 'nothing in this title annuls or limits any rights or remedies under any other Federal statute'.

Under this language, federal pre-emption is certainly clear with respect to traditional common law copyright in traditionally copyrightable material. But the situation becomes much more obscure when the rights in question have similarities to copyright but are called something else—trade secrets,[2] right of publicity,[3] misappropriation,[4] resale royalties,[5] etc. And the situation becomes still murkier when the works involved come within a general class of copyrightable matter but do not qualify for copyright under the 1976 Act.[6]

Section 301(b) sought to provide some guidance on these questions by setting forth three areas of 'rights and remedies under the common law or statutes of any State' that are not annulled or limited by the pre-emption:

> 1. 'subject matter that does not come within the subject matter of copyright as specified by sections 102 and 103, including works of authorship not fixed in any tangible medium of expression';
> 2. causes of action that arose before 1 January 1978; and
> 3. 'activities violating legal or equitable rights that are not equivalent to any of the exclusive rights within the general scope of copyright as specified by section 106'.

The third of these clauses was hurriedly amended on the floor of the House of Representatives to delete several examples of activities that the states could regulate, which had the effect of making its scope even fuzzier than before. The American courts are now wrestling with the problem, and some clear-cut lines of demarcation will emerge eventually; but it is still too early to make any tentative, much less firm, predictions as to where they will fall.

Subsection (c) of section 301 deals with the special problem of sound recordings fixed before 15 February 1972, and is discussed below in connection with neighbouring rights.

1 House Report No 94-1476, 3 September 1976, p 129.
2 *Walker v University Books Inc* 193 USPQ 596 (ND Cal 1977), affd 602 F 2d 859 (9th Cir 1979).
3 *Hicks v Casablanca Records* 464 F Supp 426, 204 USPQ 126 (SDNY 1978).
4 *Mitchell v Penton/Industrial Publishing Co Inc* 486 F Supp 22, 205 USPQ 242 (ND Ohio 1979).
5 *Morseburg v Baylon* 621 F 2d 972, 207 USPQ 183 (9th Cir 1980), cert denied, 449 US 983, 208 USPQ 464 (1980).
6 *Leonard Storch Enterprises Inc v Mergenthaler Linotype Co* 202 USPQ 623 (EDNY 1979).

F. Duration of copyright

1. *The life-plus-fifty system*

21.47 Another important and sweeping change brought about by the 1976 Act was the adoption of the international norm governing the duration of most copyrights: the life of the author, and an additional 50 after the author's death. This major breakthrough in American copyright, which has both symbolic and practical significance, was not achieved without a struggle. And, because of the peculiarities of the copyright system being replaced, the duration provisions of sections 302 through 305 are not simple. In effect, they lengthen the potential duration of all copyright, including the millions of statutory copyrights already secured and subsisting when the new law came into effect, but they apply the life-plus-fifty system only to copyrights secured on and after 1 January 1978.

2. *Works already under statutory protection before 1 January 1978*

21.48 For works that had already secured statutory copyright protection before 1 January 1978, section 304 retains the old system of computing the duration of protection, but with some changes.

21.49 a. Duration under the old law. Under the law in effect before 1978, copyright was secured either on the date the work was published, or on the date of registration if the work was registered in unpublished form. In either case, the copyright lasted for a first term of 28 years from the date it was secured. During the last (28th) year of the first term, the copyright was eligible for renewal. If renewed, the copyright was extended for a second term of 28 years (and, for a number of copyrights, the second term was extended beyond 28 years by special legislation). If not renewed, the copyright expired at the end of the first 28-year term.

21.50 b. Effect of new law on length of subsisting copyrights. For statutory copyrights subsisting on 1 January 1978, the pre-1978 law on duration was carried over into the new statute, but with one major change: the length of the second term was increased to 47 years. In other words, the maximum total term for subsisting copyrights was increased from 56 years to 75 years (a first term of 28 years plus a renewal term of 47 years).

The situation for works copyrighted before 1978 depends on whether the copyright had been renewed before the new law came into effect on 1 January 1978, or was still in its first term on 31 December 1977:

1. *Works originally copyrighted before 1950 and renewed before 1978.* These older works have automatically been given a longer copyright term; their copyrights will last for a total term of 75 years from the end of the year in which they were originally secured, without the need for any further renewal or other formality. This extension applies not only to copyrights less than 56 years old on 1 January 1978, but also to even older copyrights that had previously been extended in duration by a series of congressional acts beginning in 1962. As in the case of all other copyrights subsisting in their second term between 31 December 1976, and 31 December 1977, inclusive, these copyrights will (or did) expire at the end of the calendar year in which the 75th anniversary of the original date of copyright occurs.

2. *Works originally copyrighted between 1 January 1950 and 31 December 1977.* Despite the longer terms and other liberalised features of the Act of 1976, one hard fact of US copyright life remains: works originally copyrighted between 1 January 1950 and 31 December 1977 must still be renewed to be protected for the second term. If a valid renewal registration is made at the proper time, the second term will last 47 years (19 years longer than the old term). But if the copyright is not renewed before the statutory deadline, the copyright still expires at the end of its 28th year, and the work enters the public domain permanently.

The renewal provisions of the pre-1978 law have been carried over virtually intact into the 1976 Act. Renewal of copyright is a whole field of US law by itself, and it is too much to burden this chapter with its quirks and convolutions. In summary, then:

a. *Copyrights still subject to renewal.* Copyrights secured between 1 January 1950 and 31 December 1977.

b. *Renewal procedure.* Within the prescribed time limits, submit to the Copyright Office a renewal fee (currently $6) and a renewal application on Form RE, identifying the work and stating the proper renewal claimants and statutory basis of claim.

c. *When to renew.* The renewal time limits have changed because of section 305 of the 1976 Act, which provides that all terms of copyright now run to the end of the year in which they would otherwise expire. Renewal registration must now be made between 31 December of the 27th year of the copyright and 31 December of the copyright's 28th year.

d. *Renewal claimants.* Renewal copyright is considered a 'new estate' which, subject to various exceptions and qualifications, is taken free and clear of rights and interests in the first copyright term. Only certain persons are entitled to claim renewal: the author (or certain of a deceased author's heirs); or the proprietor of the copyright in four specific cases, the most important of which comprises works made for hire.

3. *Works originally copyrighted on and after 1 January, 1978.* For works coming under the federal copyright statute for the first time on or after 1 January 1978, the Act of 1976 does away with all renewal requirements, establishes a single copyright term, and provides different methods for computing the duration of a copyright. Works of this sort fall into two categories:

a. *Works created on or after 1 January 1978.* A work that is created (fixed in tangible form for the first time) after 1 January 1978, is automatically protected from the moment of its creation, and, as a general rule, is given a term lasting for the author's life, plus an additional 50 years after the author's death. For joint works, the term is 50 years after the last surviving author's death. For works made for hire, and for anonymous and pseudonymous works (unless the author's identity is revealed in Copyright Office records), the duration is 75 years from publication or 100 years from creation, whichever is shorter.

b. *Works in existence but not copyrighted on 1 January 1978.* As explained above in connection with pre-emption, works that had already been created before the new law came into effect but that had neither been published nor registered for copyright before that date were automatically brought under the new federal statute. The duration of copyright in these works will generally be computed in the same way as for new works: the life-plus-fifty or 75/100-year terms will apply to them as well. However, some of the works in this category are very old, and it was considered unfair to throw them into the public domain without at least some minimum period of federal statutory copyright. Thus, all works in this category are guaranteed at least 25 years of statutory protection; in no case will copyright in a work of this sort expire before 31 December 2002, and if the work is published before that date the term may be extended by another 25 years, through the end of 2027.

4. *Termination of grants covering extended term.* The 19-year extension that has been or will be added to the second (renewal) term of subsisting copyrights is, in effect, a new grant of copyright and, for reasons of fairness and constitutional validity, Congress felt that authors or their heirs should have a crack at it. Thus, section 304 contains provisions, closely but not precisely paralleling those already discussed in section 203, for the termination of transfers covering the extension. A grant of rights made by the author and covering any part of the 19-year extension can be terminated by the author, or certain specified heirs of the author, by filing a notice within strict time limits. This right to reclaim ownership of all or part of the extended term is optional; it can be exercised only by certain specified persons and in accordance with prescribed conditions.[1]

1 *Burroughs v Metro-Goldwyn-Mayer* 491 F Supp 1320, 210 USPQ 579 (SDNY 1980).

G. Copyright formalities

21.51 Another feature of the American copyright system that many look upon as a bane—its reliance upon various formal requirements as conditions for securing and maintaining copyright protection—is retained in the Act of 1976, but with changes that soften the impact of these formalities in various respects.[1] The range of formal requirements under the new law can be summarised very generally as follows:

1   17 USC paras 401 et seq.

1. *Copyright notice*
21.52   A notice of copyright is supposed to be placed on all visually-perceptible copies of a work whenever it is published in the United States or elsewhere. With some variations and exceptions, the notice is to consist of three elements: (1) the symbol '©' (the letter 'C' in a circle), or the word 'Copyright', or the abbreviation 'Copr.'; (2) the year of first publication; and (3) the name of the copyright owner. The notice is to be affixed to the copies 'in such manner and location as to give reasonable notice of the claim of copyright', and, as directed in the statute, the Register of Copyrights has issued regulations giving examples of how this requirement might be fulfilled in specific cases.[1]

For works other than sound recordings, the only notice requirement applies to visually-perceptible copies. Thus, for example, when a musical composition is reproduced aurally and published on a phonorecord, no notice is required to cover it. A special type of notice is required to appear in connection with the phonorecord, to cover the sound recording as such; this requirement is discussed below in connection with neighbouring rights.

Sections 403 and 404 contain special provisions dealing with the notice requirements for publications incorporating US government works and contributions to collective works. The latter makes clear that an author's ownership of copyright in a contribution is not impaired even if the only notice is that 'applicable to the collective work as a whole', but that persons innocently dealing with the wrong copyright owner in this situation are insulated from liability.

Sections 405 and 406 deal with the consequences of various errors with respect to the copyright notice, ranging from errors in the name, in the date, and in both name and date, to complete omission of the notice. If caught in time, almost any error can be cured, subject to protection of the rights of truly innocent infringers. With respect to complete omission of the notice, section 405 provides that this will not invalidate the copyright if 'the notice has been omitted from no more than a relatively small number of copies or phonorecords distributed to the public', or if 'the notice has been omitted in violation of an express requirement in writing that, as a condition of the copyright owner's authorisation of the public distribution of copies or phonorecords, they bear the prescribed notice'.

But what of the situation—alas, much too common—where the notice has been omitted from every copy in an authorised edition? Even here all is not lost. Section 405(a)(2) provides that copyright is not invalid in this situation if two conditions are met: (1) if 'registration for the work has been made before or is made within five years after the publication without notice', and (2) if 'a reasonable effort is made to add notice to all copies or phonorecords that are distributed to the public in the United States after the omission has been discovered.[2]

1   37 CFR para 202.2.
2   It should be emphasised that this provision does not apply to copies outside the United States.

2. *Deposit for the Library of Congress*
21.53   Under the old law deposit and registration were conjoined in a single, rather weak formal requirement. Under the Act of 1976, the provisions govern-

ing deposit of published copies and phonograms for the Library of Congress are separate from the provisions governing copyright registration. Unfortunately this is not quite as simple as it sounds, since the registration provisions still call for deposit of copies or phonorecords to accompany the application and fee, and deposit and registration can be combined so as to satisfy both provisions at once. Nevertheless, it is true to say that, under the 1976 Act:

> '*Deposit for the Library of Congress* is mandatory in the sense that it can be demanded; and, if the the demand is not fulfilled, the result can be criminal prosecutions and substantial fines. However, even if a demand for deposit is deliberately ignored or denied, it will have no effect whatever on copyright in the work in question.
>
> *Copyright registration* (including deposit for purposes of registration) is optional rather than mandatory in the sense that it cannot be demanded. However, a failure to register before or within five years after publication without notice will forfeit copyright protection. And, as will be shown below, the statute provides other instances in which, without being a condition of copyright, registration has advantages to copyright owners.'

The mandatory deposit provisions of section 407 apply generally to all works 'published with notice of copyright in the United States', and require, within three months following US publication, the deposit of 'two complete copies of the best edition'.[1] 'Best edition' is defined as 'the edition, published in the United States at any time before the date of deposit, that the Library of Congress determines to be most suitable for its purposes'.[2] The Register of Copyrights is given rather broad leeway to issue regulations exempting categories of material from these requirements, requiring only one copy instead of two, or alternative forms of deposit.

1 *National Conference of Bar Examiners v Multistate Legal Studies Inc* 495 F Supp 34, 205 USPQ 720, 211 USPQ 144 (ND Ill 1980).
2 17 USC para 101. See the Library of Congress acquisitions policies reprinted in 37 CFR paras 202.19 and 202.20.

3. *Copyright registration*

21.54 The rather detailed statutory provisions dealing with copyright registration, including the requirements with respect to deposit for purposes of registration, provisions dealing with administrative classification, optional deposit, group registrations under certain conditions, procedures for correcting and amplifying registrations, the contents of the application, and the responsibilities of the Copyright Office in the registration process, and certain inducements to register a claim, are laid out in sections 408 to 412 of the 1976 Act.

The purpose of copyright registration is to place on public record the basic facts of a particular copyright: identification of the copyrighted work and its contents; authorship; ownership; facts concerning its creation and publication; and information distinguishing between material in which copyright is being claimed for the first time and older material that is already under copyright or is in the public domain. Having this information comprehensively available to all users and to the public at large, through widely published Copyright Office catalogues and other official records freely open to public inspection, has been a unique feature of the United States copyright system for over a century.

Yet, since copyright registration is not mandatory, and is not a condition of copyright except in rare cases, one may wonder why the number of annual registrations is steadily increasing and is now approaching half a million. What induces so many copyright owners to go to the trouble and expense of voluntarily registering their claims? Motives doubtless vary, but seven advantages of copyright registration have been singled out:

1. Only one deposit required. For many if not most published works, deposit of one copy for the Library of Congress is a mandatory requirement under section 407. Since copyright owners must make this 'section 407 deposit' anyway, many of them have chosen to apply for registration at the same time, thus gaining the advantages of early registration and avoiding the need to make another 'section 408 deposit' later on.

2. Registration as a prerequisite to certain remedies against infringers. The most direct and deliberate inducement to copyright registration in the statute is found in section 412. This section, which is often misunderstood, *does not provide* that registration is a condition for recovery of ordinary remedies against infringement, or that registration must be made within three months after publication in order to recover the extraordinary remedies of statutory damages and attorney's fees. What section 412 does provide, in general, is that unless a work had been registered before a particular act of infringement occurred, the copyright owner cannot recover statutory damages and attorney's fees for that infringement. However, the section also provides for a three-month grace period beginning on the date of publication. If an infringement occurs during that period, and if registration is made before the end of the three-month time limit, the copyright owner still gains the full range of remedies. For any other infringement, the copyright owner of a work that had not been registered at the time the infringement began can recover ordinary damages and profits, and enjoin the infringement, and can benefit from the other ordinary remedies available under the copyright statute; but, in seeking recovery, that owner cannot claim attorney's fees or rely on the special schedule of minimum damages set out in the statute.

3. Registration as a prerequisite of filing an infringement suit. Under section 411, registration must ordinarily be made before an action for copyright infringement can be instituted; the infringer is still liable for all acts of infringement, including those committed before registration is made, but the courts will not accept the case for trial until registration is properly applied for.

4. Value of certificate of registration. For registrations made before or within five years after publication, section 410(c) obliges the courts to treat the certificate of registration as 'prima facie evidence of the validity of the copyright and of the facts stated in the certificate'. For registrations made later, the court is free to give the certificate any evidentiary weight it chooses.

5. Constructive notice of transfers of ownership and other documents. Almost any signed or authenticated document can be recorded in the Copyright Office, but for recordation to be treated as 'constructive notice' of what it says, registration must have been made for the work to which the document pertains.

6. Curing errors or omissions of copyright notice. As explained above, there is one situation in which copyright registration is an actual condition of copyright protection: where the copyright notice on more than a few copies of a published work is fatally defective or is omitted entirely. In this situation the copyright owner must complete registration within five years after the defective publication if copyright protection is to be preserved.

7. Practical advantages. There are many circumstances involving licensing, royalty collections, transfers or other business dealings where it is convenient, if not essential, to have a copyright certificate. Having a work catalogued and preserved in the Copyright Office or Library of Congress may also have practical advantages.

4. Recordation of transfer to plaintiff

21.55 A 'sleeper' formality that had no counterpart in the law before 1978, but that has been used as a defence in several recent cases,[1] is found in section 205(d). Entitled 'Recordation as Prerequisite to Infringement Suit'. The subsection provides that 'no person claiming by virtue of a transfer to be the owner of copyright or of any exclusive right' can institute an infringement action 'until the instrument of transfer under which such person claims has been recorded in the Copyright Office'. However, a 'suit may be instituted after such recordation on a cause of action that arose before recordation'.

The case law interpreting this section is still evolving; but, on the basis of the decisions so far, it seems clear that section 205(d) cannot be ignored, and that the courts will not permit a case to go on to trial until a document supporting the plaintiff/transferee's ownership is on record.[2] However, when the required document is not on record, the courts seem disposed to allow the matter to be handled through late recording and amended or supplemental pleadings rather than dismissing the complaint out of hand.[3] In a recent case the court also held that recordation of the document by which the plaintiff acquired title from another transferee, was sufficient, and that it would not be necessary to record all of the transfers in a chain of title.[4]

1 *Co-Opportunities Inc v National Broadcasting Corpn* 510 F Supp 43, 211 USPQ 103 (ND Cal 1981); *Ruskin v Sunrise Management Inc* 506 F Supp 1284 (D Colo 1981); *Burns v Rockwood Distributing Co* 481 F Supp 841, 209 USPQ 713 (ND Ill. 1979).
2 See eg *Burns v Rockwood Distributing Co* above.
3 See eg *Frankel v Stein & Day Inc* 470 F Supp 209, 205 USPQ 51 (SDNY 1979); *Co-Opportunities, Inc v National Broadcasting Corpn* above.
4 *Co-Opportunities Inc v National Broadcasting Corpn* above.

5. Manufacturing requirement

21.56 The so-called 'manufacturing clause' of the US copyright law—a provision requiring certain types of works to be manufactured in the United States to be fully protected—has been a running sore on the body of the American copyright system for over 90 years. Successive amendments have watered it down, and the version enacted in 1976 is the least objectionable from the viewpoint of copyright owners; but the fact remains that protectionist legislation discriminating in favour of American printers at the expense of American authors and publishers has no place in a copyright law or anywhere else. In recognition of this principle, the Act of 1976 supposedly provided for the prospective repeal of the manufacturing clause; it was scheduled to expire on 1 July 1982.

In the summer of 1982 a strange little drama was played out in Washington. Claiming that enormous numbers of American jobs would be lost to printers in other countries if section 601 were repealed, representatives of the printing industry and unions persuaded Congress to extend the manufacturing clause for another four years, to 1 July 1986. President Reagan then vetoed the extension bill, whereupon—for the first time in his administration—Congress overrode his veto and enacted the extension into law.[1] One can hope that sooner or later, and preferably in 1986, American copyright can finally rid itself of the manufacturing clause; but, for the present at least, it seems to be a sore that will not heal.

As it now exists in section 601, the scope and effect of the manufacturing clause are not very broad. In general, the requirement applies only to works consisting preponderantly of copyrighted non-dramatic literary material in the English language, written by an American author domiciled in the United States. Where the clause applies, section 601 generally prohibits the importation of more than 2,000 copies manufactured outside the United States; however, there are several exceptions to this limit, including one for the benefit of individual American authors who have to go abroad to find a publisher. The manufacturing processes that must be performed in the United States or Canada include typesetting in certain cases, plate-making, printing and binding, but the clause permits some of the most technically advanced processes of composition to be done outside the United States or Canada. Section 601(c) declares that 'importation or public distribution of copies in violation of this section does not invalidate protection for a work under this title', but provides that, in an action for infringement of the right to reproduce and distribute copies, the infringer will have a complete defence if violation of section 601 can be proved.

1 PL 97-215 ('The Copyright Manufacturing Clause Extension Act'), enacted into law as a result of the Congressional veto on 13 July 1982.

Part II: Neighbouring rights in the United States of America

A. Performers' rights

1. PERFORMERS AS CREATORS

21.57 It now appears settled beyond dispute under American law that the contributions of performing artists to a sound recording constitute an original intellectual creation capable of protection as the 'writing of an author'.[1] In 1937, the Pennsylvania State Court in *Waring v WDAS Broadcasting Station Inc*[2] posed the following question for the first time in any American court: 'Does the performer's interpretation of a musical composition constitute a product of such novel and artistic creation as to invest him with a property right therein?' In a courageous decision that ultimately changed the direction of US intellectual property law, Judge Stern of the Pennsylvania Supreme Court answered this question affirmatively, but with several qualifications. In the view of the Court:

> 'A musical composition in itself is an incomplete work; the written page evidences only one of the creative acts which are necessary for its enjoyment; it is the performer who must consummate the work by transforming it into sound. If, in so doing, he contributes by his interpretation something of novel intellectual or artistic value, he has undoubtedly participated in the creation of a product in which he is entitled to a right of property, which in no way overlaps or duplicates that of the author in the musical composition.'

The court in the *Waring* case drew an analogy between recorded performances and musical arrangements: 'The law has never considered it necessary for the establishment of property rights in intellectual or artistic productions that the entire ultimate product should be the work of a single creator; such rights may be acquired by one who perfects the original work or substantially adds to it in some manner'. Having thus equated performances with traditionally copyrightable musical arrangements, the court was required to consider whether publication of records embodying the performances would destroy common law protection and throw the performances into the public domain. The records involved in the case bore the legend 'Not licensed for radio broadcast'; the court held that this 'equitable servitude on a chattel' was reasonable, and that it sufficiently limited the publication to permit a court of equity to protect the recorded performances. The majority of the Waring Court also felt that the misappropriation doctrine of unfair competition provided an alternative basis for protection.

The *Waring* decision embodied a possible limitation on performers' rights. The majority opinion implied that 'the ordinary musician does nothing more than render articulate the silent composition of the author', and indicated that, in order to claim protection, the performer must 'elevate interpretations to the realm of independent works of art'. The concurring opinion of Judge Maxey took strenuous issue with this aesthetic standard. In his view it was clear that '*any* interpreter of a musical or any other kind of composition has an interest in his interpretation to which the law accords the status and which it will protect'. Judge Maxey felt that the proper legal theory on which this protection should be based was the right of privacy.

Read together, the majority and minority opinions in the *Waring* case provide a fountainhead for neighbouring rights protection in the United States as it now exists, 45 years later. The copyrightability of performances, without any requirements of aesthetic values or restrictive legends, is well established; the right of privacy, now regarded more as a personal 'right of publicity', is also available to protect performers in appropriate cases.

As for unfair competition, the courts had strongly reinforced protection of performances against misappropriation through record piracy before 1972, when the federal copyright statute pre-empted at least some of the field. Unfair competition is still available to protect unfixed performances and performances fixed before 1972; whether it can be relied on to protect post-1972 recordings remains a controversial question.

The decision in the *Waring* case was followed by other courts,[3] and created such consternation among broadcasters that legislatures in three southern states were induced to enact laws nullifying its effect within their borders.[4] Three years later, however, the judicial trend initiated by the *Waring* decision came to a long, if ultimately temporary, halt. In *RCA Mfg Co v Whiteman*,[5] decided in 1940, a federal court sitting in New York held that the sale of records destroyed all common law rights in the performances fixed on them, regardless of any printed legends they might contain. The decision in the *Whiteman* case was written by Judge Learned Hand, one of the greatest jurists in American history and by far the most influential intellectual property judge of his time. Judge Hand did not deny the potential copyrightability of recorded performances, but held that, in the absence of statutory copyright, sale of the records threw the performances into the public domain. For many years, the *Whiteman* case was regarded as representing good law in New York and in other jurisdictions outside Pennsylvania.

In 1950, in a sweeping decision that was to assume great importance a few years later, a New York court restrained the distribution of unauthorised recordings of broadcasts of Metropolitan Opera broadcasts on grounds of unfair competition.[6] The *Metropolitan Opera* decision substantially expanded the misappropriation concept of unfair competition, and in so doing Judge Greenberg's opinion had this to say about the performances themselves:

> 'The law has also ... protected the creative element in intellectual productions—that is, the form or sequence of expression, the new combination of colors, sounds or words presented by the production. The production of an opera by an opera company of great skill, involving as it does, the engaging and development of singers, orchestra, the training of a large chorus and the blending of the whole by

expert direction into a finished interpretative production would appear to involve such a creative element as the law will recognize and protect against appropriation by others.'

Five years later, an even more important and influential case arose involving the right of one record company to restrain another from issuing reproductions of performances recorded by others. The basic question in the *Capitol Records* case[7] was whether the earlier sale of the records had destroyed common law rights in the recorded performances. The court, rejecting the Whiteman rule and basing its decision squarely on the New York precedent in the *Metropolitan Opera* case, held that performances represented creative works entitled to protection, and that this protection survived publication of the records. The majority of the court had this to say about the performances:

'There can be no doubt that, under the Constitution, Congress could give to one who performs a public domain musical composition the exclusive right to make and vend phonograph records of that rendition.'

In the Capitol Records case Judge Learned Hand, clinging steadfastly to his *Whiteman* case opinion that the sale of records throws the recorded performance into the public domain, found himself in the minority. On the question of the creativity and potential copyrightability of performances, however, his dissent agrees fully with the majority opinion; his dissent observes:

'Musical notes are composed of a 'fundamental note' with harmonics and overtones which do not appear on the score. There may indeed be instruments—e.g. percussive—which do not allow any latitude, though I doubt even that; but in the vast number of renditions, the performer has a wide choice, depending upon his gifts, and this makes his rendition pro tanto quite as original a "composition" as an "arrangement" or "adaptation" of the score itself, which §1(b) makes copyrightable. Now that it has become possible to capture these contributions of the individual performer upon a physical object that can be made to reproduce them, there should be no doubt that this is within the Copyright Clause of the Constitution.'

In 1956, the following year, the *Capitol Records* decision was followed in a New York case involving performances of Walter Gieseking, the renowned piano virtuoso.[8] And, in *Ettore v Philco Television Corpn*[9] an interesting case also decided in 1956, a professional prizefighter sought to restrain television broadcasts of an old film of one of his fights. The federal court in which the case was tried found it necessary to apply the laws of Pennsylvania, Delaware, New Jersey, and New York, and to consider the precedents in the *Waring*, *Whiteman*, *Metropolitan Opera* and *Capitol Records* decisions. The court held that, under the laws of all four states, the prizefighter had rights in his 'performance' and that these rights had not been lost by general distribution of the film. With respect to the creative or aesthetic value of a fighter's contribution to a film of a sports event, the majority of the court, while acknowledging that 'Ettore is not such an artist as the Supreme Court of Pennsylvania described Waring to be', concluded that 'we do not think that the quality of the performance can supply the criterion. ... If the artistry of the performance is used as a criterion, every judge perforce must turn himself into a literary, theatrical or sports critic'.

The *Ettore* decision seems to have settled the question of the artistic or creative nature of the performer's contribution for good. Nearly all of the many later cases[10] dealing with piracy of sound recordings have either assumed that the performers' contributions were protectable property, or have stated the principle with little if any discussion. During these intervening years the explosion of tape piracy produced a large number of state statutes protecting recorded performances against unauthorised reproduction,[11] but neither these statutes nor the common law precedents culminating in the *Metropolitan Opera*, *Capitol Records* and *Ettore* decisions, were effective in stopping the pirates. Performers, record producers and music publishers therefore banded together in what proved to be a successful effort to obtain federal copyright legislation to combat piracy.

The argument that recorded performances do not constitute the 'writings of an author', and that copyright legislation purporting to protect them could therefore be unconstitutional, was resurrected as the Congressional hearings on anti-piracy legislation, but without much conviction or impact. Effective 15 February 1972, Congress enacted section 543, amending the copyright law to make sound recordings copyrightable and to protect them against unauthorised duplication.[12]

About a year after the sound recording amendment came into force, the US Supreme Court handed down its decision in *Goldstein v California*,[13] an action challenging the constitutionality of the California anti-piracy statute as it applied to records fixed before 1972. Chief Justice Burger, writing for the majority of the Court, suggested that the term 'writings of an author' in the US Constitution is not to be construed in its 'narrow literal sense but, rather, with the reach necessary to reflect the broad scope of constitutional principles'. Since the term 'author' in its constitutional sense can be construed to mean an 'originator', 'he to whom anything owes its origin', and since the term 'writings' 'may be interpreted to include any physical rendering of the fruits of creative intellectual or aesthetic labor', the Chief Justice declared that 'recordings of artistic performances may be within the reach of [the constitutional clause].'

The *Goldstein* decision goes on to hold that, although recorded performances may be regarded as the 'writings of an author' within the meaning of the Constitution, this does not mean that Congress is obliged to protect them: 'whether any specific category of "writings" is to be brought within the purview of the federal statutory scheme is left to the discretion of Congress'. Since, before 1972, Congress had left the protection of sound recordings unattended, the states were free to occupy the field and the California statute was constitutional. At the end of his opinion Chief Justice Burger adds the following comments:

> 'In earlier times, a performing artist's work was largely restricted to the stage; once performed it remained "recorded" only in the memory of those who had seen or heard it. Today, we can record that performance in precise detail and reproduce it again and again with utmost fidelity. The California statutory scheme evidences a legislative policy to prohibit "tape" and "record piracy", conduct that may adversely affect the continued production of new recordings, a large industry in California.'

Although, in the strictest possible interpretation, the Supreme Court's *Goldstein* decision stops just short of a direct holding that recorded performances are the 'writings of an author' within the meaning of the US Constitution, it nevertheless is a very strong authority for that proposition. The 1977 Supreme Court decision in *Zacchini v Scripps-Howard Broadcasting*[14] can also be cited as supporting the protection of performers' rights; here the 'performer' was a 'human cannonball' whose variety act had been recorded and performed on television against his will. In holding that the performer had the 'right of exclusive control over the publicity' for his act, the court described the act as 'the product of petitioner's own talents and energy, the result of much time, effort, and expense'.

Thus, throughout a wide range of performances, from Fred Waring's to those of the Metropolitan Opera, from Ettore's losing prizefight to the coloratura of Erna Sack,[15] from Walter Gieseking to the human cannonball, the American courts have established beyond cavil that recorded performances are entitled to legal protection. The congressional report on the Bill that became the Copyright Act of 1976, in its discussion of the section incorporating the 1972 anti-piracy legislation in the new copyright code, had this to say on the point:

> 'As a class of subject matter, sound recordings are clearly within the scope of the "writings of an author" capable of protection under the constitution, and the extension of limited statutory protection to them was too long delayed. ... The copyrightable elements in a sound recording will usually, though not always, involve "authorship" both on the part of the performers whose performance is captured and on the part of the record producer. ...'[16]

1   *Capitol Records Inc v Mercury Records Corpn* 221 F 2d 657, 105 USPQ 163 (1st Cir 1955); *Goldstein v California* 412 US 546 (1973).
2   *Waring v WDAS Broadcasting Station Inc* above.
3   *Waring v Dunlea* 26 F Supp 338 (EDNC 1939); *Gieseking v Urania Records Inc* 17 Misc 2d 1034, 155 NYS 2d 171 (Sup Ct 1956); *National Association of Performing Arts v Wm. Penn Broadcasting Co* 38 F Supp 531 (ED Pa 1941); *Noble v One Sixty Commonwealth Avenue* 19 F Supp 671 (D Mass 1937).
4   NC Code Ann (Mitchie, 1939) para 5126(s); SC Acts 1939, No 28, para 2.
5   114 F 2d 86 (2d Cir 1940).
6   221 F 2d 657 (1st Cir 1955).
7   *Capitol Recording Inc v Mercury Records Corpn* above.
8   *Gieseking v Urania Records Inc* above.
9   229 F 2d 481 (3rd Cir), cert denied, 351 US 926 (1956).
10 See eg, *A & M Records Inc v MVC Distributin Corpn* 574 F 2d 312, 197 USPQ 598 (6th Cir 1978o; *United States v 1,934 Stereo Eight-Track Tape Sound Recordings*, more or less (D Mass 1980); *Gaio Audio of New York Inc v Columbia Broadcasting System Inc* 27 Md App 172, 340 A 2d 736, 188 USPQ 75 (1975).
11 See eg, McKinney's Cons Laws (of New York), Penal Law paras 275.05, 275.10; West's Ann Cal Penal Code paras 653h, 653s.
12 Act of 15 October 1971, PL 92-140.
13 412 US 546, 178 USPQ 129 (1973).
14 433 US 562, 205 USPQ 741 (1977).
15 *Capitol Records Inc v Mercury Records Corpn* above.
16 House Report No 94-1476, 3 September, 1976, p 56.

2. OWNERSHIP OF PERFORMANCES

a. *Rights of individual performers who are not employees*
21.58 (1) *Under the law before 1978.* Before the new copyright law came into effect on 1 January 1978, independent performers were usually not treated much better than employees when it came to judicial recognition of their rights. Oral agreements would be honoured if their terms could be proved.[1] Most important, the decisions established a general rule that, unless the performer expressly reserved specific rights in the performance, those rights passed to the owner of the work in which the performance was given.[2] This presumption in favour of the assignee was first enunciated in some of the earliest cases involving performers' rights. In the primal case of *Waring v WDAS Broadcasting Station Inc*[3] the right of public performance had been the subject of negotiations between the performer and the record company, and the rights of the performer with respect to 'public performance for profit' had been expressly reserved. The court in *Noble v One Sixty Commonwealth Avenue Inc*[4] held that in contrast to the Waring situation, an orchestra leader had no standing to sue a restaurant owner for playing his records because he had transferred all of his rights in them:

> 'Looking to the contract between plaintiff and the RCA Manufacturing Company, it is clear that there is no reservation contained in the contract of any rights by the plaintiff. He gave to the RCA Manufacturing Company "the right to sell, lease, or otherwise dispose of" his recordings. ... This is a broad and all inclusive grant.'

The question became critical with the advent of television and the demands of some motion picture actors to a share of the benefits from the use of their old films in the new medium. In the early 1950s, two leading cowboy stars, Gene Autry[5] and Roy Rogers,[6] separately sued Republic Productions Inc in an effort to stop the television licensing of some 137 western films in which they had starred. Both failed; and, while the decisions in both cases were based on interpretation of particular contractual language, apparently that language was sufficiently typical of the era that other stars were deterred from suing under their old contracts. Needless to say, after the lessons of the *Autry* and *Rogers* decisions sank in, the issues involved in contract negotiations between performers and motion picture producers changed drastically, and rights with respect to television and other future uses became a hotly contested bargaining chip.

The contracts in the *Rogers* and *Autry* cases were similar; neither mentioned television and both contained separate clauses dealing with the performers: (1) 'acts, poses, plays and appearances', and (2) their 'name, voice, and likeness'. The first of these contractual clauses granted broad and perpetual rights to the motion picture producer. The second contained limitations: the rights in each actor's 'name, voice, and likeness' expired with the contracts and did not permit use in advertising anything other than the motion pictures themselves. The actors argued that, since commercial television in the United States is an advertising medium, the film producer should be enjoined from licensing films embodying their 'name, voice, and likeness'.

The courts rejected this argument, though not without some difficulty. Acknowledging that '[t]he fact that artist's name, his voice, and his likeness are contained in and throughout the motion pictures in which he appears is superficially confusing', the court emphasised the need to 'read the whole of the contracts, and read each part in relation to the other parts'. Having done this, the court held as follows:

> '[W]e interpret these two sets of words as applying to two different and distinct subject matters. The former refers to the artist's activities or appearances in a motion picture as such; the latter set of words refers to a reproduction of the name, voice or likeness of the artist apart from his activities or appearance in the former, and lacking the motion and dynamic and dramatic qualities contained in motion pictures.'

The *Autry/Rogers* courts held that, with respect to the 'acts, poses, plays and appearances' in the films, the actors had granted all of their rights without limitations and for valuable consideration, and that therefore the ownership rights of the producer were unrestricted.

The *Autry* and *Rogers* decisions may well be correct as a matter of contract interpretation, but it is hard to escape the conclusion that, underlying them, was a conviction favouring the absolute nature of the motion picture producer's property rights, and a strong desire not to hamper the film industry with restrictions on the licensing of its property. The lower court in the *Autry* case made these observations:

> 'It is clear from the foregoing that the parties understood Republic had absolute ownership of the photoplays in controversy and that there was no restriction upon the exhibition. The same films used for televising are used in the exhibition of

photoplays in conventional motion picture theatres, and that being true I must hold Republic's unrestricted ownership rights of the films include the right to license their exhibition on home television receivers. ... If plaintiff is worthy of his hire, certainly Republic is entitled to the full use of the fruits of his labor.'

If the courts in the *Autry* and *Rogers* cases, indeed of assuming the existence of a presumption in favour of the performer/transferor rather than the producer/transferee, had been willing to recognise a presumption running the other way, the results might have been different. A court predisposed toward creators' rights could have held that, since television rights had not been bargained for, the performers had transferred only those rights within the contemplation of the parties, and retained all other rights.

This is precisely what the court in *Ettore v Philco Television Broadcasting Corpn.*[7] was able to do. Here a prizefighter was seeking to restrain television showing of films of a boxing match that had occurred nearly 20 years earlier. The films had been made with the fighter's knowledge and consent, and the majority of the court acknowledged that it was troubled by the fact 'that Ettore did not expressly reserve rights against the televising of the films by any legend on the film or, insofar as it appears, by his contract'. Nevertheless, and over a dissent on this point, the court held as follows:

> 'Commercial television ... was not in existence at the time of the Ettore-Louis contest. Fairness would seem to require that a court treat the absence of the new or unknown media, television in the instant case, as about the equivalent of a reservation against the use of the work product of the artist or performer by a known medium, radio broadcasting in Waring's case.'

It is interesting that Judge Riggs, writing for the majority in the *Ettore* case, thought that the problem had been solved for the future. He described the typical situation as follows:

> 'The performer, as a means of livelihood, contracts for his services with an entrepreneur. The finished product is, for example, a motion picture in which the performer's services are embodied. If the motion picture is employed for some use other than that for which it was intended by the performer and the entrepreneur, the motion picture is employed in such a way as to deprive the performer of his right to compensation for the new use of the product. It is usual today to provide specifically by contract between the performer and the entrepreneur as to what uses the product may be put; so, as to services performed and products made in the future, the issues presented by the cases will become largely academic.'

This prediction is probably overly optimistic. Performers' contracts are still written in broad or ambiguous terms that may or may not cover new uses that are complementing and, in some cases, superseding television as it was known in the 1950s and 1960s: cable television, subscription services, video recordings, computer databases, direct satellite broadcasts and who knows what. In future disputes over ownership of performers' rights in these and other new uses, the results will still depend on whether the court adopts the *Autry/Rogers* anti-performer presumption that a grant carries all rights not expressly reserved, or the *Ettore* pro-performer presumption that, in fairness, performers should not be held to have granted rights to uses that were not in existence or contemplation.

1 *R R Donnelly & Sons Co v Haber* 43 F Supp 456 (EDNY 1942); *Linn-Brook Builders Hardware v Gertler*, above.
2 *Brattleboro Publishing Co v Winmill Publishing Corpn* above; *Electronic Publishing Co v Zalytron Tube Corpn* 151 USPQ 613 (SDNY 1966), affd 376 F 2d 593 (2d Cir 1967); *Yardley v Houghton Mifflin Co* 108 F 2d 28 (2d Cir 1939).
3 327 Pa 433, 194 A 631 (1937).
4 19 F Supp 671 (2 Mass 1937).

5   *Autry v Republic Productions Inc* 213 F 2d 667, 101 USPQ 478 (9th Cir 1954).
6   *Republic Picture Corpn v Rogers* 213 F 2d 662, 101 USPQ 475 (9th Cir 1954).
7   229 F 2d 481, 108 USPQ 187 (3rd Cir) cert denied, 351 US 926 109 USPQ 517 (1956).

21.59 (2) *Under the law after 1 January 1978.* For performers who are not employees the chances of claiming ownership in their performances have improved under the new copyright Act. Although the revised statute left unfixed (ie 'Live') performances subject to the vagaries of common law protection, and effectively deprived independent performers on sound recordings of any claim of rights of public performance remaining under the decisions stemming from the Waring case, these factors were balanced by a general improvement in the status of authors of copyrighted works, including performers in sound recordings and motion pictures. As explained above,[1] one of the principal goals of the 1976 Act was to accord individual authors greater protection in their business dealings with those who exploit their works. Since performers must now be recognised as 'authors', the seven ways in which the new law seeks to safeguard the copyright ownership of individual authors will benefit individual performers as well.

1   See Part I, Section C, above.

b. *Rights of performers who are employees for hire*

21.60 Among American men and women who support themselves by performing, the large majority are employees for hire, though not necessarily on a continuous or year-round basis. Their compensation and rights are governed by collective bargaining agreements negotiated by their unions. To understand neighbouring rights in the United States, one must have some knowledge of the battles waged by and within the unions of organised performers since the early 1930s and the outcome of those battles.

The efforts of the performers' unions, notably the American Federation of Musicians (AFM), to combat technological unemployment among their members and to protect performers' property rights is a complicated, dramatic and thought-provoking story. This history, which combines plot elements from *Oedipus Rex* with characters from *Guys and Dolls*, has been well told by Professor Robert Gorman of the University of Pennsylvania,[1] and can only be briefly summarised here.

1   R. Gorman 'The Recording Musician and Union Power', reprinted in Report on Performance Rights in Sound Recordings, at p 1071, Subcommittee on Courts, Civil Liberties and the Administration of Justice, 95th Cong, 2d Sess (1978).

21.61 1. *Technological displacement of live performers.* The communications revolution of the twentieth century devastated the performing arts as a livelihood. Every new development restructured the means by which performances reached the public and forced more and more live performers into other professions. As each new invention or advancement came into use, the impact on performers was two-fold:

(a) Performers by the thousands lost their jobs. Faced with having to compete with their own or others' recorded performances, performers in vaudeville, movie theatres and radio stations, among others, were forced into unemployment, and into part-time and full-time employment in other fields;

(b) Among those performers who remained, many found work as recording musicians. But they soon discovered that they had lost control over the value of their performances, which could be used over and over again with profit to others but not to them. When a performer's recording could displace that performer's live performance, a time payment was not enough.

Bad as these two effects were separately, the efforts to cure them were bound to come into conflict. Attempts to help live performers proved detrimental to recording performers and their rights, and produced explosive conflicts within the unions that are still felt today.

21.62 2. *Response of performers and their unions to technological displacement.* In reaction to the damage being wrought on their livelihood by the new technology, performers undertook two concurrent programs:

(a) *Legal recognition of performing rights in recorded performances.* The efforts of Fred Waring and his National Association of Performing Artists (NAPA) to obtain judicial decision upholding property rights in recorded performances and enjoining unlicensed radio broadcasting of them were initially successful, as we have seen. The performers' unions obviously supported these efforts, although they were not parties to any of the suits. However, when the Whiteman decision—a strong opinion by a highly-respected judge on an influential court—ruled against performance rights in recorded performances, the unions in effect abandoned the property-rights approach for nearly 30 years. Waring and the NAPA also reacted to the Whiteman decision by changing tactics: instead of pursuing their claims against broadcasters in the courts, they sought legislation under copyright principles. Their legislative efforts continued for many years, but ultimately faded away in frustration and boredom.

(b) *Labour demands and pressure.* Instead of pursuing what they considered the will-o'-the-wisp of property rights, the performers' union decided to attack the problem frontally, using all the weapons of organised labour at their command. Under the uncompromising leadership of the president of the American Federation of Musicians, of James Caesar Petrillo, the union did everything in its power to inhibit the use of recorded music for anything other than personal enjoyment in private homes. Petrillo's contract demands included 'featherbedding' (required employment of stand-by performers when records were used), quotas on the amount of recorded music that could be used, quotas on the employment of live musicians, restrictions on the use of 'canned music' for various purposes, and prohibitions on the licensing of old films (including soundtracks) for performance on television. These demands were backed by vigorous labour action: strikes and boycotts, including an effective ban on virtually all recording by union musicians that lasted for two years, from 1942 to 1944. The union pressure during this period was very strong, and the public outcry was very loud.

The 1942 recording ban was settled by the signing of contracts in 1943 and 1944 that involved the establishment by the union of the Recording and Transcription Fund, and the agreement by the record companies to pay a certain percentage of receipts from their recordings into this fund. The purpose of the fund was in no way to compensate employed performers for the use of their recorded performances. Instead, it was intended to be divided among the union locals to provide employment for their unemployed members by means of free live concerts.

21.63 3. *Legislation restricting union activities.* The public reaction to the union's activities in general, and to Petrillo in particular, was one of outrage. Demands for legislation brought results: the so called Lea Act of 1946,[1] which in effect made it a crime for the musician's union to use most of the weapons of organised labour in their dealings with broadcasters. In very sweeping terms the statute forbade the use of union pressure, including strike threats, picketing and boycotts, to require employment of un-needed musicians and to inhibit the use of recorded music in radio broadcasting.

During the debates on the Lea Bill, Representative Emanuel Celler of New York proposed the establishment of a system of royalties to be paid to performers for playing their recordings on the radio. His prescient statement on this point is worth quoting in part:

> 'Why should we not provide that where a record is replayed unlimitedly and has the result of putting out of business the very man who created the record, ... then in the first instance the royalty should be increased, and every time there is a replaying of that record there should be another royalty, or additional royalties, paid to those who originate the record.'[2]

Yet the anti-Petrillo sentiment was running too high. Congress not only failed to adopt this proposal for performance royalties, but in effect outlawed union pressure aimed at achieving a royalty system through collective bargaining. The Lea Act, which survived a constitutional challenge[3] and remained on the federal statute books until repealed very recently,[4] stalled the efforts to obtain legal recognition of performers' rights for more than a generation.

1   Act of 16 April 1946, 60 Stat 89.
2   92 Cong Rec 1547 (1946).
3   332 US 1 (1947).
4   Act of 8 December 1980, 94 Stat 2747.

21.64 4. *Establishment of the Music Performance Trust Funds.* The AFM's Recording and Transcription fund survived the Lea Act debacle, but the following year it was threatened by enactment of the Taft-Hartley Act of 1947,[1] a comprehensive statute restricting labour practices generally. One provision of that act outlawed the use of trust funds administered solely by a union. In October 1947, Petrillo sailed directly into the whirlwind; he announced a complete and permanent ban on all recording by AFM musicians, stating that upon expiration of the union contracts with the record companies it was the union's 'declared intention, permanently and completely, to abandon that type of employment'. The recording ban went into effect on 1 January 1948, and, after one year of litigation, negotiation and controversy, produced a compromise.

A major element of this compromise was the creation of new five-year trust agreements, under which the record companies were to pay percentages of their receipts from record sales to an independent trustee, nominated by the record companies and appointed by the Secretary of Labour. The trustee was to be completely independent of the record companies and the performers, representing solely the public interest, with the purpose of providing free live music and the employment of musicians whether union members or not. By 1952 there were four Music Performance Trust Funds receiving payments from record producers, transcription companies, motion picture and television producers, and advertising agencies.

1   Act of 23 June 1947, ch 120, 61 Stat 136.

21.65 5. *The 'Local 47 Revolt'.* When the 1948 contracts were renegotiated in early 1954, the 1948 wage scales were not increased, but the record companies agreed to substantial increases in their payments to the trust fund. This was consistent with Petrillo's basic philosophy, which was clearly revealed in his answers during 1958 deposition:[1]

> *Question.* Have you personally favored the establishment of performers' rights, ... either in the Federation or elsewhere?

Answer. Well, performance rights is all right if a performer can get his rights, but my idea as a labor leader is always trying to get some employment for the fellow that is out of work.... The guy that I want to help is the fellow that is going out of business.
Question. You don't have any interest in securing additional benefits for the man who is making the recording, who is doing the work?
Answer. Well, the fact is, I guess, his is the highest wage scale in the country. How can you say we are not doing anything for them? The best conditions, the best wage scale is the recording musician. What are we supposed to do, get them some more money, some more conditions, residual rights? What about the guy that is out of work here? Aren't you thinking about him at all, this fellow that has been put out of work?... You are for the guy that is making the dough, and I am for the guy that is out of work; that is the difference between the two of us.

The members of Local 47 of the American Federation of Musicians were professional musicians working in the Los Angeles area; numerically they were a small percentage of the AFM's total membership, but their proportion of the total income of AFM members was high. They felt that income and wage increases that were rightly their property were being bargained away unfairly by the union leadership, and that the trust funds severely impaired their economic position. Their appeals within the union fell upon deaf ears, and ultimately some of their members arose in open revolt.

In the late 1950s a stark melodrama was played out within the AFM. To summarise a long and complex story very briefly: the Local 47 dissidents tried to take over the local and were rebuffed and punished by the union; some of them broke off and formed a new union, the Musicians Guild of America, under the leadership of the foremost dissident, Cecil Read; the MGA instituted four massive lawsuits in California against the trust funds and the AFM; the MGA won several union representation elections, including one major one, ousting the AFM from representing musicians in their contracts with motion picture procedures; the MGA negotiated several new agreements, de-emphasising trust fund payments, though they were unable to achieve some of their major goals and were coming under increasing criticism; Petrillo resigned as President of the AFM, citing his health and the pressures of the job; the new leadership of the AFM, under President Herman Kenin, immediately and openly shifted the union's philosophy toward direct support of recording musicians and away from the trust funds; ultimately peace was restored and the dissidents were brought back into the AFM fold.

The demands of the dissidents fell roughly into three categories: 1) higher wages; 2) reduction or elimination of payments to trust funds and substitution of royalty or residual payments to recording musicians for re-use of their performances; and 3) 'the explicit adoption by the Federation of the principle of performance rights, and the making of a concerted effort (with actors, singers, writers, directors and other performing artists) to change the copyright law to recognise such performance rights'.[2] All of these goals were ultimately achieved within the AFM, but some were reached much sooner than others.

1 Quoted in Gorman, above, at p 1099.
2 Quoted in Gorman, above, at p 1102.

21.66 6. *The trust fund lawsuits.* Between 1955 and 1965 the trust funds came under massive legal attack on three fronts: (1) an action by a movie studio claiming illegality of the motion picture trust fund under the anti-trust laws; (2) derivative actions by shareholders of major record companies attacking the legality of the trust funds under the Taft-Hartley Act; and (3) four lawsuits by recording musicians attacking the legality of the trust funds on the ground of breach of their fiduciary obligations by the union and the trustee. All three of these groups of suits were of serious concern to the union, but it was the third that posed the greatest threat to Petrillo's trust fund philosophy and the zealous union policies it spawned.

The tangle of litigation during this period ultimately resulted in judgments upholding the legality of the trust funds under the anti-trust statutes,[1] and under the Taft-Hartley Act.[2] It also resulted in a decision *Anderson v American Federation of Musicians* holding that the union had indeed breached its fiduciary responsibilities to its recording-musician members.[3] In the Anderson case the court concluded that the recording musicians had a property right in the wage increases which, the court held, had been improperly diverted to the trust fund. It directed that these amounts be paid over to the musicians.

Shortly after the court's decision in the *Anderson* case, negotiations were undertaken in an effort to settle all of the recording musicians' pending suits. These negotiations were successful, and under the settlement agreement a total of $3,500,000 was paid out to the musicians. Even more important, the negotiations marked the beginning of a process of reconciliation among the warring factions.

[1] *Republic Productions Inc v American Federation of Musicians* 245 F Supp 475 (SDNY 1965).
[2] *Shapiro v Rosenbaum* 171 F Supp 875 (SDNY 1959).
[3] *Anderson v American Federation of Musicians*, Case No 669, 990, Cal Super Ct, LA County (1959).

21.67 7. *Compromise and reconciliation.* Following James Caesar Petrillo's resignation as president of the American Federation of Musicians, and even before negotiations to settle the lawsuits had started, the new leadership of the union had begun to negotiate collective bargaining agreements on a changed basis. Far less stress was placed on trust fund payments, and major emphasis was placed on wages and pensions. Under the presidency of Herman Kenin the union also began to embrace more and more enthusiastically the concept of re-use payments or 'residuals' along the lines already negotiated on behalf of motion picture and television actors. As time went on the Musicians Guild of America lost strength while the AFM gained support from its recording-musician members and successfully negotiated contracts in which wages and benefits were increased, trust fund payments were reduced or eliminated, and residual payments were introduced.

In 1961 peace talks between the Guild and the Federation resulted in complete reconciliation. The AFM agreed to reinstate all of the dissidents to refund their fines, and to set up a committee of recording musicians to advise the AFM on the terms of collective bargaining negotiations. Most important, the Federation agreed that, in negotiations with the phonograph record industry, it would seek payments of which half would go to the trust fund and half would go to the musicians in the form of residuals. The AFM also committed itself 'to seek residual or re-use payments for the recording musicians in all other recording fields'. On their side the Musicians Guild of America agreed to dissolve their union and to permit their current agreements to lapse in favour of the Federation.

21.68 8. *Trust fund and residuals: the situation today.* The turmoil of the 1940s, and 1950s, and the harmonising efforts of the 1960s, led to a much more stable situation with respect to the rights of employed performers in the 1970s and 1980s. Having regained their right to represent all instrumental performers in the United States, the AFM lived up to its commitments to its recording-musician members, and successfully negotiated contracts with the record industry calling for residuals on record and tape sales. The trust fund still exists, though its function has changed substantially. To summarise the situation as it exists in the early 1980s:

21.69 (a) *Residuals*. Today nearly all collective bargaining agreements between organised performers and producers of records, films and video recordings call for 'residuals' – re-use payments based on a percentage of the employer's income from sales, license fees, etc. The performer's residual has been judicially recognised as a property right of the employee – one which the employee's union could not 'unfairly or discriminately ignore'.[1] The principle behind residuals – that employee-performers are entitled to share in the commercial success of the productions to which they contribute – is now firmly established. The issues in collective bargaining are no longer whether employees are entitled to residuals, but rather at what point in the re-use cycle the residuals are to start, the formula for computing them, and the amounts or percentages to be established.

The contract now in effect between the record manufacturers and the AFM follows a pattern established in 1964. In effect, the amounts previously contributed by the manufacturers to the trust fund were divided into two equal parts, with one half going to the trust fund and the other half going into the newly-created Phonograph Record Manufacturers' Special Payments Fund. This Special Payments Fund is administered by the United States Trust Company and is independent of the union. After the appropriate deductions from this fund, the administrator distributes the proceeds to each person who performed on a record during the preceding year, the amount of the distribution being based on a weighted formula. Under the contract now in effect the record companies pay a specified percentage of the manufacturer's suggested retail price for each record and tape sold; the percentages are .6% for records and .5% for tapes.

1   *Anderson v American Federation of Musicians*, above.

21.70 (b) *Trust fund*. As things stand now, the only remaining music performance trust fund is that deriving from the sale of phonograph records and audio tapes. Some 4,400 recording companies are signatories to the trust fund agreement, and in fiscal year 1977 the fund distributed a total of over $10,000,000 to 350,000 individual musicians for performing in over 50,000 live performances. However, as Professor Gorman observes:

> Although President Petrillo originated the trust fund concept as a way of moderating the impact of unemployment resulting from the exploitation of recorded music, the Trust Fund today, and for most of its existence, cannot properly be regarded as a welfare or unemployment fund. For one thing, the average Trust Fund allocation for each musician performing in fiscal year 1977 was some $30.50. Moreover, the Trustee has for some time announced that the principal objective of the Trust Fund is not relief from unemployment but the development of a public appreciation for live music. In any event, most of the payments from the Fund are not received by workers who are unemployed. The great majority of the recipients are employed full-time outside the field of music ... and play on occasion for their enjoyment and as a small supplement to their income.[1]

Given the precipitous decline in record sales in the United States in recent years and the current economic slump, it will be interesting to see how the trust fund is dealt with in the next round of collective bargaining between the AFM and the record manufacturers. Unquestionably the free concerts made possible by the trust fund have been the source of public enjoyment and enlightenment, and have been of some benefit to a great many trained musicians who cannot make a living at their art. But every dollar that they receive is a dollar that would otherwise go to a recording musician. One may wonder whether, under these circumstances, the Music Performance Trust Fund can continue to survive indefinitely.

1 Gorman, above, at pp 1133-34.

21.71 (c) *Ownership of performances by groups*

A difficult question, on which US law offers no definitive answer, arises where several performers participate in the same performance. Assuming that the issue is not settled by the terms of an individual or collective contract, does a second-chair violinist in a symphony orchestra have the same rights as those of the orchestra conductor? Is one of a group of anonymous accompanists entitled to the same share as a virtuoso soloist? Are the star of a motion picture and a bit player with one line of dialogue equal as far as property rights are concerned? And, assuming that everyone contributing to a performance has some share in the property rights in that performance, how are the rights in an individual share to be exercised?

It is interesting that one of the very few American cases dealing with this question was *Waring v WDAS Broadcasting Station Inc*[1] the first US case on performers' rights. In the *Waring* case the action was brought in the orchestra leader's personal name, rather than that of the incorporated orchestra. The court held that the performance was collective enterprise in which no-one, including the orchestra leader, could claim individual rights and that properly the action should have been brought in the name of the corporation; however, since the orchestra leader owned all but two shares in the corporation, the court recognised him as the true party in interest.

Oddly enough, in the early performers' rights cases[2] following the *Waring* decision, this point was not mentioned; the courts seemed to assume that the plaintiff orchestra leaders could have 'distinct and separate'[3] rights based on their own creative contributions, and were not concerned about the rights of other contributors to the collective performance.[4]

In *Metropolitan Opera Association Inc v Wagner-Nichols Recorder Corpn*[5] the rights of the corporate opera company were upheld on grounds of unfair competition, without any consideration of the rights of the individual opera stars, conductors and members of the opera company who contributed to the performances in question. With respect to theatrical motion pictures, the decisions in the *Autry*[6] and *Rogers*[7] cases – that star performers must expressly reserve their rights contractually in order to preserve them – would seem to apply equally to any performer in the cast of a motion picture. However, in view of the evident disposition of the courts in these cases to rule against anything that threatens to hamper the free exercise of the motion picture producer's rights in a completed film, the chances of a featured actor or bit player in a motion picture successfully asserting anything other than contractual rights seem remote. In contrast, the reasoning of the court in the *Ettore* case,[8] upholding the 'right of privacy' of one participant in a boxing match, would appear equally applicable to the other contestant.

In *Capitol Records Inc v Mercury Records Corpn*[9] the majority of the court upheld rights in recorded performances by 'singers, instrumentalists, orchestras, bands, conductors and elocutionists, and other artists of established reputation',[10] but did not explore into the rights of these artists among themselves since, it rather brusquely ruled, all of the rights of all of the artists had been transferred to the original record company. In his famous dissent Judge Learned Hand agreed that, in principle, performers were entitled to property rights in their performances, and suggested that this principle applies to all instrumental performers:

> 'There may indeed be instruments – e.g. percussive – which do not allow any latitude, though I doubt even that; but in the vast number of renditions, the performer has a wide choice, depending upon his gifts, and this makes his rendition pro tanto quite as original a "composition" as an "arrangement" or "adaptation" of the score itself, which § 1(b) makes copyrightable.'

Two years after the *Capitol Records* decision a singer who had been employed briefly as vocalist with Glenn Miller's popular orchestra complained of the issuance of recordings of broadcasts of several of his performances with the orchestra, arguing that cases such as *Waring v Dunlea*[11] and *Radio Corporation of America v Whiteman*[12] established that he had a common law copyright in his performances.[13] The court disagreed, observing:

> '[E]xamination of these cases shows that in each instance such right as was declared to exist inhered in the leader as proprietor of the orchestra, rather than in the various employees of the orchestra.'

To summarise, then, the American law on rights in group performances is sketchy and inconclusive. When the action is predicated on unfair competition principles, the courts seem reluctant to recognise any rights of individual performers; property in the collective performance is generally accorded to the entrepreneur responsible for organising it. Where copyright principles are involved, rights of individual performers such as virtuoso soloists and leading actors have been recognised, and artists such as orchestra conductors and band leaders have been assimilated to this group. However, all too often these leading performers will be held to have transferred all rights contractually, and there are no cases recognising separate property rights in instrumentalists in an orchestra or other similar contributors to a collective performance.

Statutory legislation with respect to copyright in sound recordings has so far been silent as to the respective rights of record producers and performers, and as to the division of rights among the various performers contributing to a collective performance. However, proposed legislation aimed at establishing a performing right in sound recordings has some interesting provisions on this point. The most recent Bills in effect give copyright ownership to the record producer but require a 50–50 division of compulsory licensing royalties between the producers and the performers, whether the performers are employees or not. For this purpose all performers who contribute to the performance – from the conductor and soloist down to the most obscure instrumentalist – are to receive equal shares.

1 327 Pa 433, 194A. 631 (1937).
2 See eg, *Waring v Dunlea* 26 F Supp 388 (EDNC 1939); *RCA Mfg Co v Whiteman* 114 F 2d 86 (2d Cir) cert denied, 311 US 712 (1940); *Noble v One Sixty Commonwealth Avenue* 19 F Supp 671 (D Mass 1937).
3 *Waring v Dunlea*, above, at 26 F Supp 339.
4 See eg, *Noble v One Sixty Commonwealth Avenue*, above; *RCA Mfg Co v Whiteman*, above.
5 *Metropolitan Opera Association Inc v Wagner-Nichols Recording Corpn* above.
6 *Autry v Republic Productions Inc* above.
7 *Republic Pictures Corpn v Rogers*, above.
8 *Ettore v Philco Television Broadcasting Corpn* above.
9 221 F 2d 657 (1st Cir 1955).
10 221 F 2d at
11 26 F Supp 338 (EDNC 1939).
12 114 F 2d 86 (2d Cir 1940).
13 *Nelson v RCA*, 148 F Supp 1 (S D Fla 1957).

3. PERFORMANCES AS PROPERTY: THE SCOPE OF PERFORMERS' RIGHTS

21.72 The line of cases, beginning with the *Waring* decision,[1] dealing with the rights of performers against unauthorised use of sound recordings for which they had given their consent, will be dealt with below, in connection with rights of record producers. Aside from those decisions, the American cases on performers' property rights are relatively few in number; but their thrust in favour of upholding the right of the performer against unauthorised fixation of an unfixed performance, or against reproduction for purposes not contemplated by the performer, is quite strong.

Section 301(b) of the Copyright Act of 1976 specifically preserves state common law rights in 'works of authorship not fixed in any tangible medium of expression', and the legislative report on the 1976 Act cites unfixed performances as an example of works still eligible for state protection. The fountainhead case in this area, *Metropolitan Opera Association Inc v Wagner-Nichols Recorder Corpn*[2] established that property rights exist in unrecorded performances – in that case live opera broadcasts – and that these rights are not lost by widespread dissemination. Other cases adopting this principle include a decision enjoining unauthorised records made from a broadcast of President Kennedy's funeral,[3] and another involving an unauthorised recording of an interview with the Beatles.[4] The strongest recent decision on the point is that of the US Supreme Court in the 'human cannonball' case, discussed above.[5]

Where the performer has consented to recording of a performance for one purpose and seeks to enjoin exploitation for an entirely different purpose, the decisions upholding the performer's right are somewhat less conclusive, since they will ordinarily turn on what the court finds the parties intended in the contract.[6] In the *Ettore* case, discussed above,[7] the court found that a prize-fighter's consent to filming of a fight did not convey television rights in the film. Other decisions suggest that, where a contract covered the issuance of phonorecords playing at a particular speed, the issuance of records at a slower speed (with some attendant editing) would give rise to additional rights.[8] However, where a famous ballerina's performance was used in an advertising commercial on television without her consent, the court refused to enjoin use of the commercial since, it thought her appearance was too fleeting to be recognisable.[9]

In *Baez v Fantasy Records Inc*[10] the well-known folk-singer, Joan Baez, sought to enjoin the commercial issuance of some demonstration or audition tapes made some years before she became famous. The court held for the plaintiff, ruling that she had not transferred or abandoned her common law property rights in the recorded performances.

1 *Waring v WDAS Broadcasting Station Inc* above.
2 199 Misc 786, 101 NYS 2d 483 (1950), affd 279 App Div 632 (1951).
3 *Time Inc v Bernard Geis Associates* 293 F Supp 130 (SDNY 1968).
4 *Lennon v Pulsebeat News Inc* 143 USPQ 309 (NY Sup Ct 1964).
5 *Zacchini v Scripps-Howard Broadcasting Co* above.
6 *Autry v Republic Productions Inc* 213 F 2d 667, 101 USPQ 478 (9th Cir 1954); *Republic Pictures Corp v Rogers* 213 F 2d 662, 101 USPQ 475 (9th Cir 1954).
7 *Ettore v Philco Television Broadcasting Corpn* above.
8 *Nelson v RCA* 148 F Supp 1 (SD Fla 1957).
9 *Hayden v Briston-Myers Co* (Sup Ct, Special Term, New York County, Part 1—24 January 1968).
10 *Baez v Fantasy Records* 144 USPQ 537 (Calif Super Ct 1964).

4. PERFORMERS' RIGHTS: OTHER THEORIES FOR PROTECTION

21.73 In addition to the cases according protection to performers' property rights, there is a substantial body of American law recognising personal rights of performers on theories of defamation,[1] right of privacy[2] and especially the fast-evolving right of publicity.[3] The area of personal rights of performers is outside the scope of this chapter, but it should be noted that some of the decisions come close to recognising property rights in performers' personal attributes as expressed in their performances. At present an important unsettled issue is whether the right of publicity, like a property right, can descend to a performer's heirs.[4]

1   *Lahr v Adell Chemical Co Inc Inc* 300 F 2d 256 (1st Cir 1962).
2   *Waring v WDAS Broadcasting Station Inc*, above.
3   *Factors Etc Inc v Pro Arts Inc* above.
4   Various cases dealing with the commercial exploitation of the name and likeness of the late Elvis Presley have held that there exists a right of publicity which is descendible at death. See *Factors Etc Inc v Creative Card Co* 444 F Supp 279 (SDNY 1977); *Factors Etc Inc v Pro Arts Inc* 444 F Supp 288 (SDNY 1977) (granting plaintiffs a preliminary injunction), affd 579 F 2d 215, 205 USPQ 751 (2d Cir 1978) cert denied, 440 US 908 (1979); *Estate of Elvis Presley v Russen* 513 F Supp 1339, 211 USPQ 415 (DCNJ 1981); *Factors Etc Inc v Pro Arts Inc* 496 F Supp 1090, 208 USPQ 529 (SDNY 1980) (granting plaintiffs summary judgment in action seeking a permanent injunction). This last action was reversed on appeal, at 652 F 2d 278, 211 USPQ 1 (2d Cir 1981), on the grounds that the question of whether plaintiff's licensor had a right of publicity in Presley's name and likeness would be decided by the law of Tennessee, Presley's domicile. Tennessee is in the Sixth Circuit, which decided in *Memphis Development Foundation v Factors Etc Inc* 616 F 2d 956, 205 USPQ 784 (6th Cir), cert denied, 449 US 953 (1980), that after death, the opportunity for gain from the use of a celebrity's name and personality shifts to the public domain. The Second Circuit's decision reversing the grant of a permanent injunction was granted certiorari on 1 February 1982, and is now pending before the US Supreme Court (*Factors Etc Inc v Pro Arts Inc* No 81-1535). Interestingly, the Sixth Circuit in *Memphis Development*, while bound to rule according to Tennessee law under the law of *Erie RR Co v Tompkins* 304 US 64, could only surmise what Tennessee law would be, as no relevant case law then existed. However, since the Sixth Circuit ruled, a Tennessee court, in *Commerce Union Bank v Coors of the Cumberland Inc* No 81-1252-III (Chancery Ct Tenn 1981), ruled in favour of the descendible right of publicity.

B. Rights in sound recordings

1. *Copyright protection for sound recordings under the 1976 Act*
21.74   a. *Recognition of sound recordings as copyrightable works.* Section 104 of the Copyright Act of 1976 lists 'sound recordings' as one of the seven categories of copyrightable 'works of authorship'. Section 101 defines 'sound recordings' as 'works that result from the fixation of a series of musical, spoken, or other sounds, . . . regardless of the nature of the material objects, such as discs, tapes, or other phonorecords, in which they are embodied'. The definition excludes 'the sounds accompanying a motion picture or other audiovisual work' from the meaning of 'sound recordings'.

As with other works, including motion pictures, the statute does not identify the authors of a sound recording. However, the legislative report on the 1976 Act[1] makes clear that the authors of a sound recording include anyone who made a creative contribution to the recorded sound and that, in the case of a typical sound recording, this would include not only the performers but also the 'record producer responsible for setting up the recording session, capturing and electronically processing the sounds, and compiling and editing them to make the final sound recording'.

1   House Report No 94-1476, 3 September 1976, p 56.

21.75   b. *Scope of protection for sound recordings.* The victory represented by the statutory recognition of sound recordings as copyrightable works is a qualified one. Section 106 excludes sound recordings from the categories of works accorded exclusive rights of public performance, and section 114 states explicitly that the exclusive rights of the owner of copyright in a sound recording 'do not include any right of performance under section 106(4)'. The 1976 Act left the legislative door open for further consideration of performing rights in records. However, despite a favourable report from the Register of Copyrights[1] and additional hearings on Bills aimed at establishing a compulsory license with modest royalties for commercial performances of records, the chances for legislation in the near future appear slim. The opposition from the American broadcasting industry is too strong.

Section 114(b) also makes clear that copyright protection for a sound recording does not include the right to prevent imitations or simulations of the performance or of the manner or style of the performers. Copyright covers only the aggregate of the particular sounds fixed in the recording, and is infringed only when some or all of those specific sounds are reproduced by some technical method, including repressing, electronic transcription, or recapture from a broadcast. The owner of copyright in the sound recording can prevent 'counterfeiting' (exact reproduction) and various forms of 'piracy' (including cases where 'the actual sounds fixed in the sound recording are rearranged, remixed, or otherwise altered in sequence or quality'). However, as the legislative report on section 114 states: 'Mere imitation of a recorded performance would not constitute a copyright infringement even where one performer deliberately sets out to simulate another's performance as exactly as possible'.

Decades after home use of audio tape recorders began eroding the market for commercial recordings, record producers and performers have finally become aware of what this pervasive activity is costing them. Whether ordinary home taping for personal use is a copyright infringement or fair use under the present law is an unsettled question; but, in any case, audio taping in the home would be extraordinarily difficult to restrain. Legislation aimed at establishing surcharges on recorders and unrecorded tape for the benefit of copyright owners is still in a formative stage. However, two developments are making the problem an urgent one for record producers:

(1) Record distributors have started renting, rather than selling, records, with the obvious expectation that the record will be taped before it is returned. Under the 'first sale' doctrine expressed in section 109, once the copyright owner has parted with ownership of a particular phonorecord, all rights to control the later use of that phonorecord are lost. The ability of the record producers to control the rental of their records is thus extremely limited, and this has led to proposals for legislation to amend section 109.

(2) There have also been proposals for systems combining satellite and computer technology that would allow members of the public to call up a performance of a particular sound recording at will, destroying all incentive to purchase phonorecords. Should these proposed systems ever become operational, the lack of an exclusive right to control performances of sound recording would become even more serious for performers and record producers.

[1] Performance Rights in Sound Recordings, House Judiciary Committee, Committee Print 15, 95th Cong, 2d Sess, 1978.

21.76 c. *Effect of federal pre-emption on sound recordings.* During consideration of section 301 of the Act of 1976, a tricky question arose as to the status of sound recordings fixed before 15 February 1972 – the effective date of the amendment bringing recordings fixed after that date under federal copyright protection. Rather than pre-empt the many state anti-piracy statutes already in effect, section 301 makes an exception for sound recordings fixed before 15 February 1972. They are exempted from immediate pre-emption, but they are also not to be accorded perpetual state common law or statutory rights. Section 301(c) establishes a future date – 15 February 2047 – when the pre-emption of rights in these earlier recordings is to take place.

21.77 d. *Copyright formalities for sound recordings.* For the most part the same formal requirements applicable to other copyrightable works[1] extend to sound recordings. There is one exception however: section 402 provides special requirements for the form and position of the copyright notice to appear on phonorecords of sound recordings. In general, whenever a copyright sound recording is 'published in the United States or elsewhere by authority of the copyright owner', a special notice 'shall be placed on all publicly distributed phonorecords of the sound recording'. The notice is to consist of three elements: (1) the symbol 'P' (the letter 'P' in a circle); and (2) the year of first publication of the sound recording; and (3) the name of the owner of copyright in the sound recording. A recognisable or generally known abbreviation or alternative form of the owner's name is acceptable, and the statute provides that, 'if the producer of the sound recording is named on the phonorecord labels or containers, and if no other name appears in conjunction with the notice, the producer's name shall be considered a part of the notice'. With respect to the position of the notice, the statute allows for fixation on the surface of the record, or on the label or container, as long as reasonable notice of the copyright claim is given.

1 See Part I, Section G, above.

2. Protection for sound recordings fixed before 15 February 1972
21.78 With respect to sound recordings fixed before 15 February 1972, it seems clear that, under the US Supreme Court decision in *Goldstein v California*[1] and under section 301 of the 1976 Act, there will be no federal pre-emption of state laws protecting sound recordings until the year 2047. Each state is free to offer whatever protection it chooses, and most, though not all, have enacted statutes making record piracy a crime.[2] Many states undoubtedly would also uphold private property rights of performers and record producers against record pirates; either on theories of common law copyright, unfair competition or both.

An interesting question involves the possibility of asserting rights of public performance in pre-1972 sound recordings. On the authority of the *Waring* decision and other precedents, a strong theoretical case can be made out that, in at least some states, broadcasters are violating common law rights when they perform pre-1972 recordings. It would take a brave plaintiff to face the storm of controversy that such a suit would stir up, but the effort might not be in vain.

1 412 US 546, 178, USPQ 129 (1973).
2 See eg McKinney's Cons Laws (of New York), Penal Law paras 275.05, 275.10; West's Ann Cal Penal Code paras 653h, 653s; Fla St Ann para 543.041.

C. Rights of broadcasters

21.79 Broadcasters in the United States are, of course, owners of substantial numbers of copyright that they have acquired by employment, transfers or exclusive licenses. They are also the direct and indirect beneficiaries of some of the copyright restrictions placed on cable television systems under section 111. However, when it comes to their broadcast signals – electromagnetic emissions as distinguished from the programming carried – the American copyright law is powerless to offer protection. The constitutional concept of the 'writing of an author' has been construed very broadly, but it cannot be stretched to cover physical impulses wholly lacking in human authorship or creativity.

Emissions of broadcasters licensed by the Federal Communications Commission are protected against rebroadcasting under the Federal Communications Act of 1934; rebroadcasting is prohibited, and broadcasters can bring suit to restrain unauthorised rebroadcast of their signals. There are also situations in which broadcasters can protect their emissions on theories of unfair competition or misappropriation.[1] However, in the face of a cascade of new communications technology – including cable services, microwave and retransmissions, subscription television, direct broadcast satellites, and other competing methods of signal delivery – American broadcasters are increasingly losing control over what once were exclusive markets.

1 *WGN Continental Broadcasting Co v United Video Inc* 685 F 2d 218 (7th Cir, 1982).

Chapter 22
Latin-America
by Henry Jessen

Authors' rights

22.01 Concern for the protection of intellectual works has been a constant political theme in the Latin-American states. In the years following the achievement of their independence, protective laws were passed one by one in all the various countries. By way of example, Mexico may be mentioned where, according to Ramón Obón,[1] the Decree of December 1826, 'a document of great sensibility and legislative vision', represented the first systematic treatment of the subject. In Argentina, Mouchet and Radaelli[2] tell us that the National Constitution of 1853, in article 17, confirmed the legal status of 'the author as exclusive owner of his work', and mention that as far back as 1823 there had been a provincial decree referring to intellectual property. In Brazil, an Imperial Decree of 1827 attributed a 10-year right to teachers in respect of educational works, and the Penal Code of 1830 punished illegal reproduction during the author's life and for 10 years after his death. According to Costa Netto,[3] Law No 496, of 1898, represented the first comprehensive and developed view of the matter, including the recognition of moral rights. Furthermore, a Pan-American protective network was established by means of various, international conventions, the first of which – the Montevideo Convention[4] – was also open to other nations, and was signed by seven European states.

However, it would be a mistake to imagine that there exists a perfect homogeneity among the various laws as regards intellectual property rights. They undoubtedly follow the general principles derived from Roman law and, initially, took their inspiration from the French legislation of 1793.[5] Nevertheless, as a result of the amendments to which they were submitted from time to time, the influence of national idiosyncrasies and differing doctrinal tendencies, the positive law has evolved differently in these countries. Thus, we have today the modern Ecuadorean law of 1978, side by side with the obsolete law of Panama, which dates from 1916. These two laws have little in common, other than basic principles. Further, there coexist in Latin America the system of registration as a condition of protection, as in the case of Honduras, and the system of registration as evidence of copyright ownership which applies in Colombia, for example.

Consequently, any generalisation as regards interpretation is rash, and it is essential to analyse each case in the light of the national legislation and case law in order to avoid being led into error.

1 J. Ramón Obón L. 'Los Derechos de Autor en Mexico' CISAC (1974) p 30.
2 C. Mouchet and S. Radaelli 'Derechos Intelectuales' Ed. Kraft (1948) TI, p 32.
3 J.C. Costa Netto 'O Direito Autoral no Brasil' CNDA (1980) p 8.
4 See para 3.15 above.
5 See para 2.10 above.

22.02 The first legislative measures relating to author's protection were based on the theory of property, in accordance with the French system. With the emergence of new ideas, in particular those of Kant, Koehler and Picard, there was a definite tendency towards the recognition of a moral right, establishing an indissoluble link, of a personal nature, between the author and his work. At the present time, with the exception of very few countries, the Latin-American legislation provides for the two types of rights, those of a moral and those of an economic nature, recognising both.

As regards moral rights, specific recognition is, as a general rule, accorded to the right of the author to claim the paternity of his work, that is the right to assert that he is its creator, the so-called 'right of respect', that is the right to object to any distortion or other modification of the work and the 'right of divulgation',[1] that is, the right to decide whether the work shall be made public. These rights are unrenounceable, non-transferable and perpetual. Certain countries, such as Brazil, also recognise the 'right to withdraw the work' ('droit de repentir'), whereby the author may take his work out of circulation.

1 See para 5.37 above.

22.03 The author's economic prerogatives cover all forms of exploitation of his work, and constitute an exclusive right, exercisable erga omnes. The public performance, broadcasting and reproduction of a work are provided for in detail, and the author is granted the right to authorise or prohibit the use thereof and to stipulate the price for such use. Publication, considered a contract sui generis, is subject to detailed rules.

Broadcasting is considered, for legal purposes, as a form of public performance in the majority of countries. For example, article 50 of Argentinian Law No 11.723 accords identical treatment to both situations, and article 115 of Brazilian Law No 5.988 makes reference to 'the public performance, including broadcasting and cinematographic presentation' of musical works.

The exceptions to protection are those generally recognised as such, namely: short citations of the work, private use, news reports, political speeches, copying for personal use and such like. An interesting innovation introduced in the Brazilian, Chilean and Peruvian laws is the exception in favour of retailers of sound equipment and phonograms limited exclusively to demonstrations to their customers.

In principle, therefore, all the economic rights referred to in the Universal Copyright Convention and the Berne Convention are granted by the national laws, with the exception of the 'droit de suite' (provided for by the Berne Convention) which is only contained in the laws of Uruguay, Peru, Chile, Brazil and Ecuador (citing the countries in the order in which the laws were promulgated).

22.04 There exists a wide disparity, however, in the duration of the terms of protection granted by the various countries, and this led to the adoption of a recommendation by the II Continental Conference of the Inter-American Copyright Institute, held in Buenos Aires, in April 1981, to adopt a uniform term of 80 years 'post mortem auctoris' (the terms in force in Colombia and Panama). The existing periods of protection are:

Argentina	50 years pma
Bolivia	30 ,, ,,
Brazil	60 ,, ,,
Chile[1]	30 ,, ,,
Colombia	80 ,, ,,
Costa Rica	50 ,, ,,
Cuba	25 ,, ,,

Dominican Republic	30 ,, ,,
El Salvador	50 ,, ,,
Ecuador	50 ,, ,,
Guatemala	50 ,, ,,
Haiti	10 ,, ,,
Honduras	10–15 or 20 years from registration
Mexico	50 years pma
Nicaragua	variable
Panama	80 years pma
Paraguay	50 ,, ,,
Peru	50 ,, ,,
Uruguay[1]	40 ,, ,,
Venezuela	50 ,, ,,

It should be noted that the terms of protection listed above represent the general rule, and that there may be variations in special cases. Thus, El Salvador reduces the term of protection to 25 years from publication when the right belongs to a legal entity, Colombia to 30 years from fixation or publication in the same circumstances, and the Dominican Republic protects cinematographic works for only 25 years. Brazil gives protection for the life of the parents, children or spouse, when they are the heirs of the author. Chile, in a similar provision, limits the protection to the lifetime of the spouse and unmarried or widowed daughters, or to a married daughter if her husband is incapacitated and unable to work. Haiti extends the protection post mortem auctoris to the lifetime of the widow, or to 20 years when the child is the author's heir. Accordingly, it is necessary, as already explained, to study the applicable law carefully in each specific case in order to avoid error.

1   50 years for works protected under the Berne Convention.

22.05 Many national laws took their list of protected works, with minor alterations, from article 2 of the Berne Convention, and all original literary and artistic works enjoy legal protection, even those not included in the official list, which is merely illustrative and not exclusive. In addition, it should be noted that translations and other adaptations are also protected.

22.06 Payment for the use of works in the public domain ('domaine public payant') has been instituted in several countries (Argentina, Brazil, Chile, Mexico and Uruguay), and there is a movement to introduce it elsewhere. Two schools of thought justify the adoption of the system: the first, on social grounds, holds that it is unjust for the user to take advantage of a free work in order to increase his earnings, and that the proceeds of its use should be applied for the benefit of needy authors and their families; the other, arguing on economic grounds, takes the view that competition between works in the public domain, which can be used free of charge, and protected works, for which the user has to pay, is unfair, since it results in an obvious preference for the former, whenever the user has an option, to the detriment of authors who are living or recently deceased.

22.07 In some Latin American countries, the system of registration as a condition of protection persists, with the result that failure to register implies loss of protection. This legal requirement in no way affects the protection of creators of intellectual works who are nationals of states which are parties to international conventions, provided that their works and other protected material bear the conventional symbols of protection and the required references, assuming always that the legal requirements, if any, in the country of origin have been complied with.

The prevailing opinion at the present time is in favour of the abolition of registration as a condition of protection in the field of copyright. The present writer supports this opinion unreservedly on the grounds that the protection should arise from the act of creation and not from registration in public records and that the formality of registration should be optional, merely constituting evidence of copyright ownership, thus providing a service for authors who wish to publicise and guarantee their rights.

A strange result has been produced in the Ecuadorean law of 1976. It provides that the author is not obliged to register his work[1] but in the case of musical works, transfers this obligation to the producer of phonograms, who, as well as being obliged to register his phonogram, must also register the original work in the name of the author, unless the latter has already effected registration of his own accord.[2] This is an abnormal situation, a left-over from former attitudes which, understandably, many people are reluctant to change.

The fact that certain states are attached to the system of registration as a condition of protection derives from the theory of property, which required possession of a document of title as evidence of the right. The gradual disappearance of this theory as a basis for protection, and its replacement by concepts more in keeping with the subject matter, will in time eradicate registration as a pre-condition for copyright protection as a result of the passing of new laws.

At present, however, copyright is still governed by registration in a few countries. For example, in the Dominican Republic, failure to register within one year from publication causes the work to fall into the public domain for the next five years. Moreover, it will remain there permanently unless the interested party effects registration within two years following that period. As this country is not a signatory to the Berne Convention or the Universal Copyright Convention, the above rules apply to all foreign works, except those having their origin in Spain, with which the Dominican Republic has entered into bilateral agreements, and in those States which are parties to Pan-American Conventions to which the Dominican Republic is party.

1 Art 2.
2 Art 60.

22.08 An author's economic rights may be assigned, wholly or in part, by act inter vivos, and by way of example[1] the Mexican Law of 1956, revised in 1963 may be cited, which provide for the transfer of such rights by any legal means. These rights may be assigned for any period up to the expiration of the term of protection. There are, however, countries which impose restrictions on the freedom to contract. For example, Colombia requires a public instrument, duly registered, and, when the author leaves legal heirs, the rights assigned will revert to the latter 25 years after the author's death[2] unless otherwise agreed with the author.

Another general rule is the retention by a practitioner of the plastic arts of the right of reproduction, unless agreement is reached to the contrary in the contract of sale. In Brazil, however, this rule is inverted, and the author must reserve the right expressly on selling the work of art.

1 Arts 4 and 5.
2 Arts 21 and 23 of Law 23 of 1982.

22.09 The most serious problem affecting literary works at the present time is reprographic reproduction, a world-wide abuse which has spread to Latin

America, where thousands of copies of protected works are reproduced daily, in countless places, resulting in substantial losses to the authors and their publishers.[1] For the time being, no legislative solution has been adopted. Opinions are divided into two opposing camps. The first, which has a numerous following, supports a compulsory licence system, by means of payment to the authors of the works used or, if their identity is unknown, for the sake of simplicity, a flat fee payment to a writers' fund. The other point of view, to which this author subscribes, is that the state should uphold the exclusive right of the author to authorise the use of his creation as this right is the corner-stone of copyright protection, and that the best solution lies in the collective administration of this right, as already occurs in the musical and theatrical areas.[2] As Villalba and Lipszyc[3] point out, 'copyright should be conceived as an individual right exercised collectively', and it is not clear why legislators should permit indiscriminate reproductions by any user, when it would evidently be preferable for them to establish a legal mandate in favour of a national society of holders of such rights, with the power to fix tariffs, grant licences and establish conditions depending on the nature of the user and the ultimate destination of the copies.

Another source of anxiety to the Latin-American nations is the defence of their folklore. Several countries are considering the introduction of legislation on this subject, and there are a number of projects under consideration to ensure the genuineness of folk music, in order to preserve the national culture and identity from foreign influences, which become more and more widespread and intense with the constant improvement of the communications media. Up to now only Bolivia has effectively produced a law[4] with these objectives, protecting traditional Bolivian music and music produced by folk groups. Since authorship is anonymous, the Decree attributes authorship to the community itself, acting as a legal entity. It may be questioned if this is in fact the most appropriate way to achieve the desired result, since strictly the problem is more one of preserving the country's cultural heritage rather than one of transferring it to the field of copyright.

1   See para 12.16 above.
2   See Koumantos 'Le Droit de Réproduction et L'Evolution de la 'Technique' RIDA LXXXXVIII p 3.
3   Villalba e Lipszyc, Il Diritto d'Autore, No 2-3, p 681.
4   Supreme Decree No 08396.

22.10 In this very brief review of the protection of authors' rights, we may conclude that, in successive stages, albeit without any co-ordination between the individual states, national legislation in Latin America has reached a point of maturity at which it may be considered satisfactory in the majority of these countries. Obviously such an observation does not reflect a static position, since intellectual rights are in a constant state of evolution and the rules governing such rights require regular revision.

Neighbouring rights

22.11 Neighbouring rights are known in Latin America as 'Derechos Conexos' (in Spanish) or 'Direitos Conexos' (in Portuguese) (equivalent in English to the expression 'related rights'), but only acquired this name after the signature of the Rome Convention[1] in 1961, which constitutes a landmark in the treatment of the rights of performers, producers of phonograms and broadcasting organisations. Those countries which had legislation concerning these rights prior to the adoption of the Rome Convention, classified them as authors' rights in spite of criticism of this criterion on the part of some specialists. It is necessary here to recall the profound conceptual difference between 'copyright' and 'droit d'auteur'.[2] The latter term contains an entirely subjective and personal element, absent from the meaning of copyright. Thus, while an Anglo-Saxon jurist has no difficulty in saying that a broadcasting organisation is the owner of the 'copyright' in its programmes, a practitioner of the 'droit d'auteur', in the Latin tradition, will deny that a broadcasting organisation can have an 'author's right' in its broadcasts, since such a right necessarily includes rights of a personal nature, which are considered inconceivable in the context of a corporation.

Another interesting peculiarity of the pre-Rome legislation is the use of the word 'interprète' (performer) to mean artists in general. Argentina, for example, in 1970, in order to adapt this generic term to the situation of accompanying musicians, adopted the formula of sub-dividing performers into two types: 'principal performers' and 'secondary performers' (who accompany the former).

To the writer's knowledge, the first legislative provision in favour of performers was article 119 of the Mexican Civil Code of 1928, which secured to them special rights, akin to an author's right, in respect of their performances. Subsequently, Argentina, Colombia, El Salvador, Paraguay and Uruguay introduced provisions protecting performers, producers of phonograms and broadcasting organisations, into their legislation regarding intellectual rights, recognising them as authors of their respective productions and performances.

1 See chapter 8 above.
2 See paras 1.12 et seq above.

22.12 To a large extent, the Rome Convention of 1961, met the requirements of the three categories of beneficiary concerned, both at the national and international level and, furthermore, introduced a logical treatment of their rights and a terminology more consistent with the existing circumstances. In addition, the Convention drew the attention of Latin American legislators to the necessity of providing legislation for the protection of its beneficiaries. Brazil, for instance, following the example of France, had previously completely ignored the three classes of beneficiaries under the Convention, considering them merely as users of the works of others.

In 1966, however, Brazil passed Law No 4.944, modelled on the Rome Convention, which introduced neighbouring rights and was the first comprehensive legislation on the matter in the Americas. Chile followed in 1970, as did Ecuador in 1976 and Colombia in 1982, which leads one to suppose that the influence of the Rome Convention will spread through the whole of Latin America during the present decade.

It must be remembered that, according to the laws of Latin American countries, the ratification and consequent promulgation of an international treaty incorporates its provisions into the internal positive law.[1] Consequently, the rules adopted by the Rome Convention are valid in all the countries which have adhered to it, even though they may not be expressly reproduced in the national legislation of such countries.

1 See para 3.30 above.

22.13 In order to examine in detail the protection granted to performers, producers of phonograms and broadcasting organisations, the Latin American states can be divided into groups, in accordance with the degree and extent of the protection granted, thereafter giving a short analysis of the legislation applicable in each country.

The first group of countries consists of those which are parties to the Rome Convention and those whose national laws recognise all or a substantial part of the rights contained therein. These are: Argentina, Brazil, Chile, Colombia, Costa Rica, Ecuador, El Salvador, Guatemala, Mexico, Paraguay and Uruguay.

The second group consists of those countries which grant protection to one or other of the beneficiaries of neighbouring rights, either by virtue of their national law, or by reason of having adhered to another international treaty which has a supplementary internal effect. To this group belong: Cuba, the Dominican Republic, Nicaragua, Panama and Venezuela.

The third group comprises those states which have no rules regarding neighbouring rights. These are: Bolivia, Haiti, Honduras and Peru.

Group 1

1. ARGENTINA

Legislation: Law No 11.723, of 1933, revised in 1957; Decrees No 746, of 1973, and Nos 1670 and 1671, of 1974

International agreements: Phonograms Convention

Legislative synopsis

(1) *Performers*

22.14 The Laws of 1933–1957 refer to performers under the general title of 'Intérpretes', without defining the term or giving examples of the activities of the individuals covered by the expression. However, Decree No 746, in its article 1, evidently inspired by the Rome Convention, filled that gap by defining as 'Intérpretes' the classes of persons set out in article 3(a) of the Convention. Decree No 1670, relating to phonograms, establishes two categories of performer: (a) principal performer and (b) secondary performer, there being a consensus of opinion to the effect that the latter means accompanying musicians.

Article 4 of Decree No 1670 guarantees to the principal performer the moral right to require his name or pseudonym to be mentioned in the reproduction of the fixation and in its publicity.[1] Article 56 of the Law also recognises the moral right of the performer to oppose the communication of the performance to the public when this may cause 'serious and unjust prejudice to his artistic interests'. This right is exercisable by the director, in the case of choirs or orchestras.

The fixation of a performance requires the prior consent of the principal performer[2] and its reproduction or publication will entitle the performers to receive a remuneration, to be determined by a judicial authority in the absence of agreement between the parties.[3]

1 Henceforth, since this right derives from authorship, it will be referred to as 'the right to paternity'.
2 Art 3, Decree No 1670.
3 Art 56, Law 1933–1957.

(2) *Producers of phonograms*

22.15 The producer of phonograms is an author, in accordance with article 1 of the Law, as a result of which he has the exclusive right of reproduction and publication,[1] as well as communication thereof to the public, without prejudice to the rights of the authors of the works included therein.[2]

[1] Art 2.
[2] Art 1, Decree No 1670.

(3) Broadcasting organisations

22.16 Article 1 of the Law guarantees protection to 'every scientific, literary, artistic or educational production, whatever its process of reproduction'.

(4) Term of protection

22.17 Article 5 of the Law establishes the term of protection as life of the author plus 50 years in favour of his heirs and successors.

(5) Registration

22.18 The registration of the work is obligatory and is a condition of copyright protection.[1] 'Failure to register shall result in the suspension of the rights of the author until such registration is accomplished'. However as Argentina is a member of the Berne Convention, the UCC and the Phonogram Convention, only Argentine citizens and nationals of States not parties to the Berne Convention, the UCC and the Phonogram Convention are subject to the formality of registration.

[1] Art 63.

(6) Protection of foreign works and other subject matter of copyright

22.19 Article 13 of the Law extends the provisions of that law to foreign works and other copyright material, the authors of which are nationals of states which grant protection to intellectual property. Such works are exempt from the requirement of registration in Argentina, provided they comply with the formalities of the country of origin. The term of protection shall not exceed the term in force in the country of origin.

(7) Communication of phonograms to the public

22.20 Decree No 1671 grants to the 'Asociación Argentina de Intérpretes (AADI)' the monopoly of representation of national and foreign performers for the purpose of collecting their public performance and broadcasting fees on phonograms.[1] It grants a similar monopoly to the 'Camara Argentina de Productores e Industriales de Fonogramas (CAPIF)' as regards both national and foreign producers.[2] The Decree requires the constitution of an organisation by AADI and CAPIF, for the purpose of collecting their fees jointly.[3] Accordingly a society was set up under the style of 'AADI-CAPIF Sociedad Civil Recaudadora'.

The distribution of the fees is governed by article 5, which provides that 45% shall go to the principal performer, 22% to the secondary performers and 33% to the producer of the phonogram.

[1] Art 1.
[2] Art 2.
[3] Art 7.

(8) Sanctions

22.21 Criminal sanctions applicable in the case of infringement include fines and imprisonment.[1] Other remedies include seizure of the illegal copies, suspension of the unauthorised performance,[2] and civil damages.[3]

1 Arts 71-74.
2 Art 79.
3 Art 77.

Comments

22.22 (a) The Argentinian legislation on intellectual rights is based on the theory of property. Further, it extends the status of author to legal entities. There were doctrinal arguments as to the validity of such extension to the producer of phonograms, referred to in the law as 'phonographic discs'. However, various judicial decisions and Decree No 1670 have dispelled any remaining doubts, since article 1 of the Decree says: '... phonograms may not be communicated to the public ... without the express authorisation of their authors...'

(b) The remuneration for the communication to the public of phonograms by way of broadcasting and public performance is freely negotiable with the users, who may have recourse to arbitration. In practice, however, the collecting society, AADI-CAPIF, applies a tariff approved by the authorities.[1]

1 Resolution 894/0200.

BRAZIL

Legislation: Laws Nos 4.994, of 1966, 5.988, of 1973 and 6.533, of 1978; Regulations No 1.023, of 1962, and No 61.123, of 1967

International Agreements: Rome and Phonograms Conventions

Legislative synopsis

(1) Performers

22.23 The definition of 'performer' corresponds to that contained in article 3 (a) of the Rome Convention, although it also specifically includes 'announcers, narrators and declaimers'.[1]

Article 1 of the Law of 1966 makes it obligatory to obtain the prior express authorisation of the performers to fix, reproduce, broadcast or rebroadcast their performances. Article 95 of 1973 reiterates this provision, adding the 'use in any form of communication to the public'.

The performer has the moral right to claim the paternity of his performance[2] and the Law of 1973 provides[3] for the extension to neighbouring rights of the applicable rules relating to author's rights, which undoubtedly includes the moral right to respect and the right to divulge.

The person entitled to exercise the right is the performer, his heir or successors.[4] In the case of orchestras, instrumental and vocal groups, the person so entitled is the director.[5]

The Law of 1978 deals with performers and technicians in shows, presented live or by means of fixations. It protects a wide range of performers, which includes performers of literary or artistic works as well as animal tamers, magicians, jugglers, etc, and others in non-musical shows. This Law, clearly inspired by the trade unions, lays down rules for the exercise of the performer's profession and basic contractual conditions.

1 Art 2(a) of the Law of 1966 and art 4, XII of the Law of 1973.
2 Art 9 of the Law of 1966.
3 Art 94.
4 Art 1 of the Law of 1966.
5 Art 95, of the Law of 1973.

(2) *Producers of phonograms*
22.24 The definition of producer of phonograms differs in form from that contained in the Rome Convention, although it has the same meaning: 'the natural person who or legal entity which produces the phonogram for the first time'.[1]

The producer has the right, exercisable erga omnes, to authorise or prohibit the reproduction, whether direct or indirect, broadcasting, rebroadcasting and public performance in any form of his phonogram.[2]

1 Art 4x(a), of the Law of 1973.
2 Art 4, of the Law of 1966 and art 98, Law of 1973.

(3) *Broadcasting organisations*
22.25 Article (c) of the Law of 1966 defines these as: 'radio-broadcasting and television organisations which transmit programmes for public reception'. Article 4, XI of the Law of 1973 provides a wider definition: 'organisations for radio or television, or for any other process, which transmits programmes to the public, whether by wire or wireless'. Thus cable television is included in the protection.

Article 5 of the Law of 1966 grants to broadcasting organisations 'the right to authorise or prohibit the rebroadcasting, fixation and reproduction of their broadcasts'. Article 99 of the Law of 1973 added the communication to the public of television broadcasts in places accessible to the public against payment of an entrance fee.

The ephemeral fixation of performances is permitted, to be used for the number of times agreed with the performer.

(4) *Term of protection*
22.26 Article 7 of the Law of 1966 provides for a term of protection of 60 years. This is confirmed by article 102 of the Law of 1973, which provides that the term shall commence on 1 January of the year following the date of the fixation, transmission or performance.

(5) *Registration*
22.27 Registration is optional[1] except if there is an assignment of the right, in which case registration of the instrument will be essential in order for the transfer of the right to be effective against third parties.

1 Art 17, Law of 1973.

(6) *Protection of foreign works and other subject matter of copyright*
22.28 The Law of 1973[1] extends to foreigners domiciled abroad the protection provided for in international agreements to which Brazil is a party. Furthermore, article 48, III, provides that works protected by states not linked to Brazil by treaties only fall into the public domain when such states do not grant protection to Brazilian works; thus the principle of reciprocity applies, irrespective of conventional obligations. Article 105 of the same law obliges foreign collecting societies to be represented by Brazilian societies.

1 Art 1, para 1.

(7) *Communication of phonograms to the public*
22.29 The Law of 1966, which governs the matter, grants to performers and phonogram producers the right to receive remuneration for communication to the public. Article 6, para 1, empowers the producer to collect the money from

the users, and obliges him to share it with the performers in the proportions provided for by contract or, if the contract is silent on the matter, in accordance with the following formula: 50% for the producer, 33% for the performer and 17% for the accompanying musicians.

Article 115 of the Law of 1973 delegates to a Central Office the monopoly to collect authors' and neighbouring rights fees from public performance (including broadcasting). This office, known by the initials ECAD, is constituted and administered by the various societies representing the beneficiaries. It is a private entity under state supervision.

(8) Sanctions

22.30 Failure to name the principal performer when 'using an intellectual work by any means or process', obliges the party in default to issue a public correction, as well as to pay an indemnity by way of moral damages.[1]

Copyright infringement is punished by imprisonment of 3 months to one year or a fine of CRS 2,000 to 10,000. However, when the infringement consists in the unlawful reproduction of an intellectual work, a phonogram or a videogram for commercial purposes or the selling of same, the penalty is imprisonment for one to four years and a fine of CRS 10,000 to 50,000.[2] The seizure of infringing copies is provided for by article 122 of the Law of 1973 which also provides for damages to the injured party. The penalty for unauthorised communication to the public of performances, broadcasts and phonograms consists of suspension of the use and damages.[3] Articles 127 and 130 provide for police intervention to suppress violations of copyright and neighbouring rights.

1 Art 126, Law of 1973.
2 Art 184, Penal Code.
3 Art 123, Law of 1973.

Comments

22.31 The Law of 1966, introduced neighbouring rights into Brazilian legislation. It was modelled on the Rome Convention, although it excluded the exception embodied in article 19 of the Rome Convention. Moreover, the text of article 1 of the Law effectively grants performers the right to authorise and prohibit the utilisation of their performances, instead of the mere possibility of preventing such use.

(b) The general rule under Brazilian law is that patrimonial rights may be assigned.[1] This rule was partly modified by the Law of 1978[2] which prohibits the performers referred to therein from assigning rights resulting from the rendering of their services.

(c) As a consequence of the ratification of the Phonograms Convention by Law No 6.895, of 17 December 1980, two provisions of the Penal Code[3] were amended to include protection for phonograms against fraudulent reproduction, establishing cumulative penalties of fines and imprisonment and making such reproduction a public offence.

1 Art 52, Law of 1973.
2 Art 13.
3 Arts 184 and 186.

CHILE

Legislation: Law No 17.336, of 1970, amended in 1971; Regulation No 1.122, of 1971

International agreements: Rome and Phonograms Conventions

Legislative synopsis

(1) *Performers*

22.32 The definition contained in item (j) of article 5 of the Law is practically identical to that in the Rome Convention.[1]

The Law expressly recognises the moral right to the paternity of a performance in a cinematographic work[2] and in a phonogram,[3] by making it an obligation for the producer to mention the name(s) of the principal performer(s), such mention to appear in the film or on the record label or sleeve. The right of divulgation stems naturally from the performer's right to authorise or prohibit the communication of his performance to the public.[4]

In accordance with article 66, the authorisation of the performer is required to fix, reproduce, broadcast and rebroadcast or in any other way use performances for profit.

1 Art 3(a), Rome Convention.
2 Art 30.
3 Art 65.
4 Art 65.

(2) *Producers of phonograms*

22.33 The producer of phonograms is defined in paragraph (k) of article 5 as being 'the natural person or legal entity responsible for the publication of phonograms'. Although it is not the act of publication that gives rise to the right of the producer, the fact that he is responsible for it presupposes earlier legal acts, such as the obtaining of the author's licence, the intervention of the performers and, above all, the fixation of the sounds which is the act that gives rise to the right of the producer. Thus the producer is clearly the same person as that described in article 3(c) of the Rome Convention.

The producer of phonograms is obliged to state the title of the work and its author, the performer, his trade mark and the year of the publication.[1]

The same article grants to the producer the right to authorise or prohibit the reproduction of his phonograms.

1 Art 68.

(3) *Broadcasting organisations*

22.34 Radio and television organisations have the right to authorise or prohibit the fixation and the reproduction of their broadcasts.[1] However, as regards rebroadcasting, the same article only gives them the right to remuneration.[2] With the later ratification of the Rome Convention in 1974, it would appear, however, that the right to prohibit laid down in article 13 of the Convention will prevail for rebroadcasts.

The same legal provision,[3] without requiring the condition of the payment of an admission fee by the audience, deals with the situation referred to in paragraph (d) of article 13 of the Rome Convention,[4] and provides that the user shall compensate the broadcasting organisation.

Ephemeral fixation by broadcasting organisations is permitted for use for as many times as is agreed with the performer, provided it is destroyed immediately thereafter.[5]

1 Art 69.
2 Art 9, reg no 1.122 fixed this at the symbolic sum of one Escudo.
3 Art 69.
4 See para 8.35 above.
5 Art 69.

(4) *Term of protection*
22.35 The term of protection for neighbouring rights is 30 years as from the end of the year in which the event took place.[1] The determining events are 'the fixation' of the phonogram, the 'transmission' of the broadcast and 'the giving' of the performance.

1 Art 70.

(5) *Registration*
22.36 Although it is not a pre-condition for copyright protection,[1] registration is obligatory both for works[2] and for contracts for the assignment of rights.[3]

1 Art 1.
2 Art 72.
3 Art 73.

(6) *Protection of foreign works and other subject matter of copyright*
22.37 Foreigners domiciled abroad enjoy the protection granted by the conventions adhered to by Chile.[1]

1 Art 2.

(7) *Communication of phonograms to the public*
22.38 Article 67 of the Law obliges the user of phonograms for profit to pay to the performers a remuneration stipulated by the Regulation which provides for an amount equal to that paid for author's remuneration, by article 8. Of the amount collected for national performers, 20% must be paid to the Chilean Cultural Corporation,[1] a state organisation with cultural aims; in the case of foreign performers, 50% has to be paid to that organisation.

1 Art 104 of the Law.

(8) *Sanctions*
22.39 Anyone infringing neighbouring rights is subject to a fine 'equivalent to two to ten times the annual minimum wage, scale A of the department of Santiago'.[1] The injured party may request the court to order the seizure of the illegal copies, together with the material used in the reproduction, or the proceeds of the performance. The Court may, if asked to do so, order the immediate suspension of the sale or performance.[2]

On the application of the injured party, the judge may order the sentence to be published in the press, at the expense of the party at fault.[3]

The publication of a work, with a declaration of reservation of ownership, without prior registration, is punishable by a fine equivalent to the annual minimum wage, scale A.[4]

1 Art 79.
2 Art 82.
3 Art 83.
4 Art 80.

COLOMBIA

Legislation: Law No 23, of 1982

International agreements: Rome Convention

Legislative synopsis

(1) *Performers*

22.40 Item 'K' of article 8 of the Law defined performers in practically the same words as article 3(a) of the Rome Convention.

Article 171 extends to performers all the moral rights granted by article 30 to authors, ie the inalienable, unrenounceable and untransferable rights of paternity, respect, divulgation and withdrawal, the latter subject to the prior payment of an indemnity to any party thereby prejudiced.[1]

In the case of a performance by a number of performers, the group shall be represented by its legal representative or, in his absence, by its director.[2]

Performers have the right to authorise or prohibit the fixation, reproduction, communication to the public, broadcasting and any other form of utilisation of their performances.[3] Furthermore, the Law expressly provides that the authorisation for one form of use does not extend to any other form.[4]

Article 168, however, introduces the exception contained in article 19 of the Rome Convention regarding visual and audio-visual fixations, denying therefore to the performer the right to oppose the use of such of these fixations for purposes other than those agreed upon.

Creditors of an impresario cannot seize the amounts due by him to the performers.[5]

1 Art 30, para 4.
2 Art 170.
3 Art 166.
4 Art 167.
5 Art 250.

(2) *Producers of phonograms*

22.41 The producer, defined as in the Rome Convention,[1] has the right to authorise or prohibit the total or partial reproduction of his phonogram.

All copies of a phonogram must mention on the label or packaging the title of the work, the name of its author, the principal performers, the year of fixation, the producer's trademark or style, the reservation of his[2] and the author's[3] rights as well as the symbol of protection ℗, the year of first publication and other information referred to in article 11 of the Rome Convention.[4]

The contract between the author of a work and the producer of phonograms is non-transferable, it does not extend to public performance,[5] or other uses[6] and, if based on a royalty on sales, it gives the author the right to examine the books and warehouses[7] of the producer.

1 Art 3(c) Rome Convention.
2 Art 175.
3 Art 151.
4 Art 180. For Rome Convention see para 8.25 above.
5 Art 151.
6 Art 154.
7 Art 152.

(3) *Broadcasting organisations*

22.42 Broadcasters have the power to authorise or prohibit the rebroadcast, fixation and reproduction of their programmes[1] which is to say they enjoy all the rights provided for in paragraphs (a) to (c) of article 13 of the Rome Convention.

Broadcasting organisations may make ephemeral fixations of performances for use for the number of times agreed by authors and performers, provided they are destroyed thereafter.

1   Art 177.

(4) *Term of protection*

22.43   As regards individuals, the protection endures for life plus 80 years after death in favour of their heirs and assigns; for legal entities it is limited to 30 years from the date of the performance, fixation or broadcast.

(5) *Registration*

22.44   Although the law states that protection is granted by virtue of the intellectual creation,[1] the formality of registration is compulsory[2] for works and aural and audio-visual fixations, as well as for contracts regarding copyright.

Registration of foreign works which are protected in their country of origin is optional.[3]

1   Art 9.
2   Arts 192 et seq.
3   Art 208.

(6) *Protection of Foreign works and other subject matter of copyright*

22.45   The law protects foreigners to the extent provided for in the international conventions to which Colombia has adhered or when their own national law applies the principle of reciprocity to Colombian nationals.[1]

1   Art 11.

(7) *Communication of phonograms to the public*

22.46   Article 12 of the Rome Convention is incorporated into the law[1] which also specifies[2] the classes of users who are obliged to pay remuneration to performers and producers.

The power to collect the remuneration is vested in the producer, who shares the revenue with the performers in agreed proportions, which must be no less than 50% of that revenue.

Performers and producers have recently set up an organisation, known as 'ACINPRO', the object of which is to collect and distribute revenue resulting from broadcasting and public performance rights.

1   Art 173.
2   Art 176.

(8) *Sanctions*

22.47   The law provides for an imprisonment of three to six months and a fine of 50,000 to 100,000 pesos, for unauthorised reproduction, duplication or divulgation of performances,[1] and the fraudulent reproduction, importation or distribution of phonograms.[2]

A fine of 20,000 to 50,000 pesos is imposed for the public performance of phonograms without authorisation or payment of the remuneration due.[3]

All illicit reproductions shall be seized and handed over to the plaintiff.[4]

All copyright violations are public offences[5] but damages can be awarded in the criminal proceedings.[6]

1   Art 232, paras (1) and (2).
2   Art 232, para 7.
3   Art 233.

4 Art 236.
5 Art 239.
6 Art 238.

Comment

22.48 The new Law of 1982 is a modern, comprehensive piece of legislation. A certain lack of precision, will most probably be clarified by the regulations to be issued by the government.

COSTA RICA

Legislation: Law no 6683, of 3 August 1982

International Agreements: Rome and Phonograms Conventions

Legislative synopsis

(1) *Performers*

22.49 The definition of 'performer' corresponds to that contained in article 3(a) of the Rome Convention.[1]

The Law invests the performers with the right to authorise or prohibit the fixation, the reproduction, the communication to the public, the broadcasting and rebroadcasting by radio or television, or any other form of utilisation of their performances.[2]

The principal performer has the moral right to oppose the broadcasting of his performance if it causes a serious and unjust injury to his artistic or economic interests; also he may demand the mention of his name when his performance is communicated to the public by broadcasting or public performance.[3]

The donation of a contract dealing with future performances cannot exceed five years.[4]

The person entitled to exercise the right is the performer, his heirs, successors or assignees.[5] In the case of orchestras, instrumental and vocal groups, the person so entitled is the conductor,[6] who is also considered the principal performer, for the purpose of the remuneration referred to in article 84(a) of the Law (see 7 below), of instrumental recordings.

1 Art 77(a) of the Law.
2 Art 78 of the Law.
3 Art 79 of the Law.
4 Art 93 of the Law.
5 Art 78 of the Law.
6 Art 80 of the Law.

(2) *Producers of phonograms*

22.50 The definition of producer of phonograms corresponds to that contained in the Rome Convention.[1]

The producer of phonograms has the exclusive right to authorise or prohibit the direct or indirect reproduction, the broadcasting or rebroadcasting by radio and television, the public performance and any other form of utilisation of his phonograms.[2]

1 Art 81(a) of the Law.
2 Art 82 of the Law.

(3) *Broadcasting organisations*

22.51 Broadcasting organisations are defined as: 'radio or television organisations which transmit programmes to the public'[1] but the definition of 'transmission'[2] leaves no doubt that it is by way of 'radio-electric waves'.

The Law grants to broadcasting organisations the right to authorise or prohibit the rebroadcasting, the fixation and the reproduction of their broadcasts, as well as the communication to the public of their programmes in places accessible to the public.[3]

1 Art 85(a) of the Law.
2 Art 85(b) of the Law.
3 Art 86 of the Law.

(4) *Term of protection*
22.52 The Law provides for a term of protection of 50 years, commencing at the end of the year during which the broadcast, the performance or the publication took place.[1]

1 Art 87 of the Law.

(5) *Registration*
22.53 Registration is optional, including registration of documents assigning rights.[1]

1 Arts 101 and 102 of the Law.

(6) *Protection of foreign works and other subject matter of copyright*
22.54 The Law extends to foreigners domiciled abroad the protection provided for in international agreements to which Costa Rica is a party.[1]

1 Art 3 of the Law.

(7) *Communication of phonograms to the public*
22.55 The Law empowers the producer to authorise the broadcast and the public performance of phonograms published for commercial purposes and to collect from the user a remuneration which he shall share with the performers in accordance with their contract.[1] If there are no contractual stipulations among them, the producer shall pay to the performers half of the net amount received (less collecting and administration expenses), which shall be distributed to them in the following proportions: 50% to the principal performer and 50% in equal parts to musicians and members of accompanying choirs.[2] Amounts not collected by musicians shall be transferred by the producer to their union, after 12 months.

1 Art 83 of the Law.
2 Art 84 of the Law.

(8) *Sanctions*
22.56 The fixation and reproduction or broadcasting of a performance without authorisation of the performer is punished by imprisonment of eight to twelve months.[1] The same penalty applies to the unauthorised reproduction of a phonogram,[2] or fixation, reproduction or rebroadcasting of a broadcast.[3]

The public performance or broadcasting of a phonogram without authorisation of the producer[4] is punished by imprisonment from one to three months.

Whoever sells, distributes, keeps in wharehouses, imports or exports unlawful reproductions of performances, phonograms and broadcasts, or in any way conspires to defraud the right owner, is liable to imprisonment of eight to twelve months.[5]

Recidivism shall increase the above penalties by one third.[6]

Copyright infringements are public offences.[7]

Proceeding for civil damages can be requested by the injured party in a criminal case.[8]

The author, the performer and the producer may request in the civil courts the seizing of all printed copies and of the equipment utilised for the reproduction, as well as the amounts received by the selling of such copies.[9]

1   Art 119(ch) of the Law.
2   Art 119(c) of the Law.
3   Art 119(d) of the Law.
4   Art 117(b) of the Law.
5   Art 119(h) of the Law.
6   Art 122 of the Law.
7   Art 126 of the Law.
8   Art 128 of the Law.
9   Art 130 of the Law.

Comments

22.57 There is no doubt that this most recent of the Latin American laws is a comprehensive and effective instrument, which is based on the most modern principles in this field.

ECUADOR

Legislation: Decree No 610, of 1976, and Regulation of 30 November 1977; Decree No 2821, of 1978; Decree No 3303 of 1979

International agreements: Rome and Phonograms Conventions

Legislative synopsis

(1) *Performers*

22.58 The Decree No 610 of 1976[1] defines performers in similar terms to those contained in the Rome Convention.[2]

Under this Decree performers are expressly granted moral rights, specifically in relation to the right of respect for their performances,[3] and the right to claim the paternity of their performances in published phonograms[4] or in other uses.[5]

Moreover, article 147 of the Decree extends to performers those provisions relating to authors which are of a non-conflicting nature. This permits the application to performances of the provisions of article 17, including the moral right of divulgation and withdrawal and the right to anonymity.

The Decree grants to the performer the right to oppose the public dissemination of his work, the fixation of broadcasts and the reproduction of fixations, when these have not been authorised by him.[6] The law refers to the 'fixation', which obviously includes both visual and sound recordings. Furthermore, it requires the prior authorisation of the performers for the publication of a cinematographic work in videograms or any other form of use.[7] The performer is entitled to remuneration for any use, ie when the performances are 'fixed on a material support' for broadcasting or rebroadcasting, transmission by cable television or videocassette or recorded on a disc or tape or 'any other similar medium'.[8] Such remuneration is freely negotiable.[9]

The Decree of 1979, entitled 'the Performer's Protection Law', governs the labour relations between the performer and his employer and institutes certain unrenounceable rights in favour of the former.[10] In addition to artists who perform literary or artistic works, protection includes circus and variety artists.[11] Clearly inspired by the trade unions, it specifies in detail the contractual conditions for artistic performances, including the permitted proportion between national and foreign performers.[12] It introduces highly praiseworthy concepts, such as tax exemption for programmes featuring national performers[13] and the granting of social security benefits to performers.[14] It also contains certain discrepancies, such as the reference[15] to 'conductors of symphony orchestras', when these should be included under the title of musicians' in article 4(a).

The nullity of a contract made by a performer may be pleaded only by the performer and not by the other party to the contract.[16]

1 Art 139.
2 Art 3(a) Rome Convention.
3 Art 142(d).
4 Art 60(2)(c).
5 Art 142(d).
6 Art 142.
7 Art 80.
8 Art 140.
9 Art 141.
10 Art 3.
11 Art 4(6).
12 Arts 29–30.
13 Art 32.
14 Art 20.
15 Art 4(c).
16 Art 7.

(2) *Producers of phonograms*
22.59 The law dedicates an entire chapter to the 'contract of phonomechanical fixation'. Although the definition of 'producer'[1] makes his right conditional upon authorisation by the author of the recorded work, there is no doubt that the producer is the same person as that referred to in articles 3(c) and 1(b) of the Rome and Phonograms Conventions respectively.

The producer's obligations include registration of the phonogram and of the work and the inclusion of a notice giving the year of the recording (year of cutting the original matrix) with the name or trade mark of the producer as essential requirements for protection. Omission would deprive the producer of his exclusive right of reproduction.[2]

The producer has an exclusive right of reproduction, whether direct or indirect.[3]

1 Art 59.
2 Art 60.
3 Art 62.

(3) *Broadcasting organisations*
22.60 The chapter on 'broadcasting contracts' lists the duties of the radio and television organisations, without granting any protection to their broadcasts.[1] However, since Ecuador is a party to the Rome Convention, it is submitted that the minimum rights contained in article 13 of the Convention are applicable.

Broadcasting organisations may effect ephemeral fixations of works,[2] which presupposes the fixation of such performances, for a single broadcast. Further broadcasts will give rise to an additional remuneration for the performers.[3]

1 Arts 65 and 69.
2 Art 67.
3 Art 140.

(4) *Term of protection*
22.61 Protection of performers is for 25 years from the date of the fixation or performance.[1] The decree is silent, however, on the term

for phonograms, which it expressly protects.[2] One may therefore conclude that the provision applicable to this case is the general principle contained in article 88, which stipulates a term of 50 years 'post mortem'. With regard to broadcasts, which, as we have seen above (item 3), are not afforded specific protection in the law, it would appear that the applicable term is that provided for in article 14 of the Rome Convention.

1 Decree of 1976, art 146.
2 Art 62.

(5) *Registration*
22.62 Registration merely provides evidence of ownership of copyright,[1] but is nevertheless obligatory in the case of phonograms,[2] within 30 days of publication.

1 Art 17 of the Regulation.
2 Art 60(2).

(6) *Protection of foreign works and other subject matter of copyright*
22.63 The decree accords to foreigners the protection granted under international conventions and adopts the principle of reciprocity.[1] This provision relates to authors, but by virtue of articles 145 and 147, is also applicable to performers. It probably extends to phonograms and broadcasts originating in countries which are not parties to the conventions but grant protection to producers and broadcasters who are nationals of Ecuador.

1 Art 5.

(7) *Communication of phonograms to the public*
22.64 Performers are entitled to receive the remuneration agreed upon for the use of the fixation of their performances, sharing the amount thereof between them.[1] In the absence of any agreement, the remuneration is distributed in equal shares, except in the case of the director of a group or orchestra who receives 25% of the total.[2]

There is no legal provision prohibiting the participation of the producer in the performer's remuneration resulting from a broadcast or public performance of a phonogram, provided this is the subject of a written agreement duly registered at the National Registry.

1 Art 140.
2 Art 141.

(8) *Sanctions*
22.65 The performer may apply to the court for an injunction to prevent the infringement of his rights, and to obtain seizure of illegal copies and damages.[1] The offender is also liable to a fine of 5,000 to 20,000 sucres and imprisonment of six months to two years.[2]

The producer of phonograms may institute legal proceedings to curb illegal reproduction or use.[3] The reproduction, stocking, distribution for commercial purposes or sale of illegal copies is punishable by imprisonment of two to five years, and a fine of 5,000 to 20,000 sucres, as well as forfeiture of the infringing copies and material, and also gives rise to a claim for damages.[4]

1 Art 120.
2 Art 129.
3 Arts 62 and 120.
4 Art 1 of Decree of 1978.

Comments

22.66 The whole tenor of the Decree of 1976 favours the author very strongly, affording him the widest possible protection, while offering fairly scanty protection to the beneficiaries of other rights, which are subordinated to the principal right of the author, in accordance with the theoretical viewpoint (which is not shared by this writer) that neighbouring rights should be dependent on the author's right. For example, article 138 provides that, in the event of conflict, author's rights shall prevail over performer's rights, and article 62 states that protection for phonograms is derived from the authorisation of the author.

(b) The Decree of 1978, which was promulgated as a direct consequence of the Phonograms Convention, constitutes the first piece of legislation in Latin America which seeks to curb the piracy of phonograms. The defendant in an action must prove that he had the express and written consent of the producer to copy his phonogram.[1] Thus the burden of proof is reversed.

1 Art 3.

22.67 Registration or deposit is not a condition of copyright protection[1] but is compulsory for works, contracts, statutes of authors and performers' societies and '... the distinguishing marks of publishing houses and the names ... and addresses of natural persons and legal entities regarded as impresarios or users in terms of this law'.[2]

Producers of phonograms must register their phonograms within 30 days of publication and must also register the reproduced work in the name of the author or his successors in the title.[3] The omission of certain formalities such as the mention of the year of cutting the original matrix on each copy of the phonograms will deprive the producer of his exclusive right of reproduction.

1 Art 2, Decree of 1976 and art 17, Regulations.
2 Art 111.
3 Art 60.

EL SALVADOR

Legislation: Decree No 376, of 1963

International agreements: Rome and Phonograms Conventions

Legislative synopsis

(1) *Performers*

22.68 The Decree of 1963 defines 'performers' as 'musicians, singers, actors and other persons who, in the course of their activities, make use of their own works or the works of others',[1] which clearly shows that the legislation refers to the same beneficiaries as are granted protection under the Rome Convention.

The Decree provides for the performer's moral rights, obliging broadcasting organisations to respect them, and in particular the right to claim the paternity of their performances.[2]

It also provides that 'interpretative creations' of intellectual works likewise enjoy the applicable legal protection.[3] Thus, the provisions of article 2, which grant the author an exclusive property right exercisable erga omnes, are applicable to performers, as are the provisions of article 8 which lists the uses entitling the author to remuneration, and of article 9 which empowers him to authorise or prohibit use.

The use of the performance by third parties shall be determined by contract, which presupposes prior authorisation.[4]

1 Art 56.
2 Art 59.
3 Art 17.
4 Art 53.

(2) *Producers of phonograms*
22.69 Article 18 extends protection to 'all artistic productions', which clearly includes phonograms. Furthermore paragraph 6 of article 79, which deals with the registration of works, makes express reference to 'phonographic discs'.

Since the producer is the author of the production, article 2 grants him the exclusive ownership of the phonogram, including the right to permit or prohibit its reproduction.[1]

1 Arts 8 and 9.

(3) *Broadcasting organisations*
22.70 Article 18 lists broadcasting and television works among the 'protected creations', but article 20 refers specifically to radio and television broadcasts, which it assimilates to 'derivative works', thereby securing to the broadcasting organisation full author's rights, with all the legal consequences.

Organisations that fix broadcasts must remunerate the performers when they re-use the programmes containing the performances.[1]

1 Art 57.

(4) *Term of protection*
22.71 The standard term is 50 years from the author's death, which is applicable to all individuals, including performers.[1]

With regard to legal entities, the term of protection is reduced to 25 years from first publication.[2]

1 Art 61, para 1.
2 Art 61, para 4.

(5) *Registration*
22.72 Registration is not a pre-condition for protection,[1] but is essential for litigation purposes,[2] and documents assigning rights will only be valid against third parties after registration.[3]

1 Art 49.
2 Art 77.
3 Art 65.

(6) *Protection for foreign works and other subject matter of copyright*
22.73 Protection is extended to nationals of countries which adopt the principle of reciprocity and who have complied with the necessary formalities required in the country of publication.[1]

Furthermore, the law attributes to an official office ('Oficina de Marcas de Fabrica, Patentes de Invención y Propriedad Literaria') the task of taking all necessary steps to ensure the observance of the international conventions on copyright.[2]

1 Art 16.
2 Art 74.

(7) *Communication of phonograms to the public*

22.74 The right owner can authorise or prohibit the use of a work for commercial purposes and its public performance[1] and receive remuneration on the public performance, broadcast and dissemination of the work by any means.[2]

1 Art 9.
2 Art 8.

(8) *Sanctions*

22.75 The penalty for infringement of the performer's right of paternity is forfeiture of the copies, unless the infringement can be remedied by the subsequent inclusion of his name.[1]

The unauthorised reproduction of a performance or a phonogram constitutes an infringement,[2] and subjects the offender to forfeiture of the copies and payment of an indemnity of not less than the retail value of all the copies illegally reproduced.[3]

The unauthorised broadcast or communication to the public by any means of a performance or a phonogram, for profit entitles the injured party to sue for an injunction and damages.[4]

The injured party may petition the court for an injunction ordering the preventive seizure of the proceeds.[5]

1 Art 70.
2 Art 68.
3 Art 69.
4 Art 69.
5 Art 72.

Comments

22.76 (a) An interesting provision of the law[1] requires the immediate payment to the copyright owners of the remuneration due to them following the use of their works unless otherwise agreed between the parties.

(b) Models who pose for paintings or artistic photographs are entitled to remuneration.[2]

(c) The law of El Salvador regarding authors' rights is one of the best in Latin America, and deserves attention on account of its correct doctrinal approach to the subject. It undoubtedly contains some omissions, for example, the absence of the 'droit de suite' or criminal remedies for infringement of the law. However, this in no way detracts from the merits of the law.

1 Art 52.
2 Art 60.

GUATEMALA

22.77 Law No 1037, of 1954, governs authors' rights satisfactorily, but makes no provision whatsoever for neighbouring rights. These are protected by the provisions of the Rome Convention, as from January 1977 and the Phonograms Convention, with effect from February 1977, which are to a great extent self applying.

MEXICO

National legislation: Federal Law of November 4, 1963 and Decree of 30 December 1981.

International agreements: Rome, Phonogram and Satellites Conventions

Legislative synopsis

(1) Performers

22.78 The Mexican legislation granting protection to performers is very detailed. It contains a definition of performers in Article 82 which is similar to that of article 3(a) of the Rome Convention. The first part of article 82 introduces a certain element of confusion by requiring that the performance must have 'artistic value in itself' and not constitute a 'mere accompaniment'. This would appear to exclude musicians who merely accompany a principal performer, but, in practice, it seems that the requirement does not deprive them of protection, which in any case, they can always claim under article 3(a) of the Rome Convention. Apart from the right of divulgation, contained implicitly in the prohibition against communication to the public,[1] the 1963 Law does not provide for any specific moral right in favour of the performer. Nevertheless the Official Agreement with broadcasting organisations on tariffs stipulates that 'the moral interests of the author and/or the performer' must be respected,[2] from which one may presume that such interests are contractually defined by agreement between the parties.

Economic rights are covered in great detail in the Law, and the lengths to which the Mexican legislation has gone to protect the performer in this respect are praiseworthy. All the situations in which protection is envisaged in the Rome Convention are contained in several articles fixation of broadcasts:[3] fixation of phonograms, secondary use of phonograms,[4] rebroadcasting, fixation and reproduction of broadcasts,[5] fixation communication to the public and use other than the authorised use).[6] In short, a performer may object to any form of abusive utilisation of his performances, whether such performances are given solely to be heard or to be heard and seen.

There is an interesting provision in article 25 which permits the protection for renewable terms of 5 years by means of registration, of 'human persons playing character roles in artistic performances'.

1 Art 75.
2 Agreement establishing the tariff regulating the payment of Copyright Royalties (August 1966); art 2.
3 Art 75—Rome Convention, art 13(b); see para 8.33 above.
4 Arts 77 and 78—Rome Convention, art 12; see para 8.26 above.
5 Art 86—Rome Convention, art 13(c); see para 8.34 above.
6 Art 87—Rome Convention, art 7; see para 8.16 above.

(2) Producers of phonograms

22.79 The national law does not accord specific protection to phonograms, although it does make reference to the 'case of phonograms'[1] and to 'phonograms of protected performances'[2] making it obligatory to place the conventional symbol P on them. As this symbol is the characteristic mark of a protected production this would appear to indicate the intention of the legislature to protect phonograms, even though in fact such protection was not embodied in the law. It is submitted that producers will have to rely on the protection provided by the Rome and Phonograms Conventions, both of which Mexico has adhered to, for details of their protection in Mexico.

1 Art 27.
2 Art 92.

(3) *Broadcasting organisations*
22.80 Identical considerations apply in the case of radiophonic and television broadcasts, protection of which is governed by the provisions of the Rome and Satellites Conventions.

Broadcasting organisations have the right to make ephemeral fixations, for a single deferred broadcast, without additional payment, whenever there is no simultaneous broadcast.[1]

1 Art 74.

(4) *Term of protection*
22.81 Article 90 of the Law, which has been recently amended by the Decree of 30 December 1981, protects performances for a term of 30 years from the date of the event. Prior to this decree, which came into force on 12 January 1982, performances were protected for a term of 20 years which is the minimum term under the Rome Convention.

As the domestic law is silent on the matter, the term applicable to phonograms and broadcasts is that stipulated in the Rome Convention.

(5) *Registration*
22.82 The registration merely provides evidence of ownership of copyright in Article 122.

(6) *Protection of foreign works and other subject matter of copyright.*
22.83 A foreigner domiciled abroad may avail himself of the rights contained in the treaties and conventions to which Mexico is a party.

(7) *Communication of phonograms to the public*
22.84 The broadcasting of phonograms is remunerated in accordance with the Official Agreement published in the Official Gazette of 25 August 1966.

Public performance on jukeboxes is remunerated by means of a surcharge on the sale of all singles records put on the market in favour of the performers.[1] The Official Agreement published in the Official Gazette of 19 July 1962 fixes the tariff for jukeboxes and also the tariffs payable by other users (bars, restaurants, etc).

Performances in jingles and other commercial announcements entitle the performer to receive a further remuneration if they are used for a period exceeding six months.[2]

Cinematographic exhibitions give rise to a right to remuneration, fixed in an Official Tariff, in favour of the performers,[3] including accompanying musicians.[4]

Article 84 which grants performers the right to receive a remuneration for the exploitations of their performances has recently been amended by the Decree of 30 December 1981. Under the new article the remuneration granted to performers for the use of their performances for 'direct or indirect financial gain' shall be inalienable.

These provisions weaken substantially article 85 which expressly permits the performer to dispose freely of his 'patrimonial rights'.

The law permits performers to create societies similar to those set up by authors.[5] Various categories of performers have done so, for example, principal performers have founded the 'Asociación Nacional de Intérpretes' (ANDI), and the musicians have the 'Sociedad Mexicana de Ejecutantes de Musica' (SOMEM).

558 Latin-America

1 Art 80.
2 Art 74.
3 Law of 26 October 1965, Official Gazette, 9 November 1965.
4 Official Gazette, 13 July 1976.
5 Art 117.

(8) Sanctions
22.85 The law provides for imprisonment from 30 days to one year and/or a fine from 50 to 5,000 pesos for unauthorised use of a performance.[1]

The law also provides for imprisonment from two months to one year, and a heavier fine (50 to 10,000 pesos) for persons exploiting phonograms which are produced for private use only.[2]

Illegally produced copies, as well as the equipment utilised in such illegal reproduction, are subject to confiscation.[3]

1 Art 137.
2 Art 142.
3 Art 150.

Comments

22.86
(a) The author's right prevails over that of the performer, when there is a conflict between the two.[1]

(b) Undoubtedly, the revision of the Mexican law of 1963 was influenced by the Rome Convention of 1961, which was reflected in the protection granted to performers, in spite of the exclusion of the other two beneficiaries. The 1981 Amendments strengthen the protection granted to performers. The duration of protection is extended to 30 years and some of their patrimonial rights are made inalienable.

1 Art 6.

PARAGUAY

Legislation: Law No 94, of 1951; Regulation No 6.609, of 1951

International agreements: Rome and Phonogram Conventions

Legislative synopsis

(1) Performers
22.87 Performers have the same right as authors, they are defined as 'singers, declaimers, performers, etc'[1] which automatically includes all the beneficiaries referred to in article 3(a) of the Rome Convention.

As well as the right of respect[2] and to claim the paternity of their performances,[3] performers have the moral right to oppose the use of their work, when such use may harm their artistic interests. In the case of choirs and orchestras this right is exercisable by the director.

Article 39 confirms the performer's economic right to remuneration for the various types of use of their performance. This provision is in fact redundant, since articles 2 and 3 grant the same right to the author, and as we have already observed, the rights of the authors are extended to performers by virtue of article 37.

1 Art 37, Law of 1951.
2 Art 9.
3 Art 45.

(2) *Producers of phonograms*

22.88 Although phonograms are not expressly mentioned in the list of works or intellectual property for which protection is granted, article 4 states: 'the works protected by this Law are all ..., artistic productions which may be published or reproduced...' Furthermore, the Decree of 1951 which lays down the requirements for registration of works, provides:[1] 'For photographs, plans, maps and phonographic discs, a copy thereof shall be deposited', which it is submitted, taken together with the ratification of the Phonogram Convention and the Rome Convention seems to indicate that phonograms are covered by legal protection.

Consequently, the provisions of articles 2 and 3, which grant to the author the exclusive right to authorise the publication, reproduction, public performance or broadcasting of his work are applicable to phonograms.

1 Art 16.

(3) *Broadcasting organisations*

22.89 Although radio and television organisations are referred to in the Law and in the Regulation merely as users,[1] Article 4[2] could be construed as covering broadcasts. In any case, they are protected by the Rome Convention.

1 Arts 3(d) and 38.
2 See para 22.88 above.

(4) *Term of protection*

22.90 The term of legal protection is life plus 50 years under article 19.

(5) *Registration*

22.91 Registration of the performance and of the phonogram which is regarded as a work, is a condition of protection under article 58.

(6) *Protection of foreign works and other subject matter of copyright*

22.92 The Law automatically extends protection to any foreign works, provided the necessary formalities in the country of origin are complied with.[1]

The term of protection for foreign works may not exceed that of the country of origin.[2]

1 Art 47.
2 Art 48.

(7) *Communication of phonograms to the public*

22.93 As already mentioned in items 1 and 2 above, performers and producers of phonograms have the exclusive right to authorise broadcasts and public performances and are entitled to remuneration in respect thereof.

(8) *Sanctions*

22.94 The unlawful reproduction or sale of a work, the omission of the performer's name, are considered to be fraudulent acts and are punishable under article 416 of the Penal Code.[1] Unauthorised public performances are punishable by imprisonment from one month to one year or by a fine the amount of which is fixed by the Regulations and paid into an 'Encouragement Fund'.[2]

1 Art 62.
2 Art 63.

Comment

22.95 There is a bill currently before the National Congress, based on the Phonograms Convention, for the curbing of phonographic piracy and bootlegging.

URUGUAY

Legislation: Law No 9.739, of 1937, amended in 1938; Regulations of 21 April 1938; Law No 15.289 of 1982
International Agreements: Rome Convention, Phonogram Convention

Legislative synopsis

(1) *Performers*

22.96 The law of 1937 lists the various beneficiaries of rights and makes express reference[1] to 'the performer of a literary or musical work in respect of his performance'.

The performer is entitled to oppose the reproduction of his performance when this may cause grave and unfair injury to his artistic interests.[2] This right is exercisable by the conductor when the performance is given by a choir or orchestra.[3]

The law of 1982 increases the protection granted to performers in providing that the recording and subsequent use of a live performance must be authorised in writing by the performer[4] and the non-observance of this provision carries criminal penalties.[5]

Article 36 assures to the performer a remuneration for the use of his performance in radiotelephony, television, or when recorded on disc, tape, film, wire or any other material form suitable for sound or visual reproduction. In the absence of agreement, such remuneration shall be determined by the court.

1 In para (d) of article 7.
2 Art 37.
3 Art 38.
4 Art 1, para 2.
5 See para 22.95 below.

(2) *Producers of phonograms*

22.97 The rights of producers of phonograms are now specifically referred to by the law of 1982 which aims at tackling the problems of piracy of phonograms and videograms. It also adopts the terminology of the Rome and Phonograms Conventions for the definitions of 'phonogram' and 'producer'.[1] The law prohibits the unauthorised reproduction and distribution of phonograms.[2] It is particularly strict on the form of authorisation of the producer which must be given in writing. The Law of 1982 makes a general reference to the Law of 1937 by providing that 'the provisions of the Law of 1937 will be applicable when relevant'.[3] It thus assimilates the rights of the producer to those of the author and grants him a 'right of ownership'[4] and the right to reproduce, publish, perform, and disseminate[5] his production. It is submitted that even before the adoption of the Law of 1982 phonograms were protected by the Law of 1937 by virtue of article 5 which lists the intellectual works subject to protection and terminates the list with the generic formula 'all intellectual production'.

1 Art 3(b) and Art 3(c) Rome Convention.
2 Art 1.
3 Art 5, last para.
4 Art 1, Law of 1937.
5 Art 2, Law of 1937.

(3) *Broadcasting organisations*
22.98 The Law includes television among the productions entitled to protection, but does not refer expressly to sound broadcasts.[1] It is submitted that sound broadcasts in so far as they contain originality, are included in the generic formula which protects all intellectual productions. Accordingly, sound and television broadcasts, enjoy protection against reproduction and dissemination by telephone, broadcasting and analogous processes.[2]

The free use of protected productions is conceded to state cultural broadcasting organisations for non-commercial purposes.

1   Art 5.
2   Art 2, second and last para.

(4) *Term of protection*
22.99 The protection granted to the work of an individual lasts for 40 years after his death, in favour of his successors[1]. However, the work will fall into the public domain if it is not used within the 10 years following the death. These provisions apply equally to performances.

The term of protection in favour of corporate entities is fixed at 40 years as from first publication.[2] This applies to phonograms and broadcasts.

1   Art 14.
2   Art 17.

(5) *Registration*
22.100 Registration is obligatory,[1] and constitutes an essential formality for protection.

An assignment of rights will only be valid against third parties after registration of the appropriate agreement.

Registration of a performance must be applied for by the performer.[2]

Registration of a phonogram must be applied for by the producer, who is obliged to deposit two copies.[3]

Application for registration must be made within two years from first publication, if this occurred in Uruguay, or three years if the work was first published abroad.[4]

1   Art 6.
2   Art 15, Regulations.
3   Art 19, Regulations.
4   Art 53, Law, paras 4 and 5.

(6) *Protection of foreign works and other subject matter of copyright*
22.101 The law accords equal protection to the works of nationals and works of foreigners domiciled abroad[1], provided that the latter have complied with the legal formalities required in the country of origin.[2] This obviates the necessity for registration in Uruguay.

1   Art 4.
2   Art 6.

(7) *Communication of phonograms to the public*
22.102 Performers and producers of phonograms enjoy the right to receive remuneration and to authorise the broadcast and public performance of their performances and their phonograms.[1]

1   Arts 2 (penultimate and final paras) and 36.

(8) *Sanctions*
22.103 The law of 1982 provides that the unauthorised reproduction and distribution of phonograms as well as the unauthorised recording of a live

performance shall be punished in accordance with article 46 of the Law of 1937[1] which provides for a fine or a corresponding prison sentence. The amount of the fine ranges from 5,000 to 50,000 pesos and will be revised annually.[2] The infringing copies will be confiscated[3] If the offence is repeated within five years, the penalty will be imprisonment.[4]

The court will suspend a public performance or broadcast if these have not been authorised by the right owner.

In addition the injured party can bring a civil action since any violation of rights gives rise to a claim for damages.[5]

1 Art 1.
2 Art 3.
3 Art 2.
4 Art 4.
5 Art 51.

Comments

22.104 The Law of 1937 was a fine piece of legislation, which was a leader in the field.[1] It has been further enhanced by the passage of the new Law of 1982. Even though nearly 50 years have passed since its promulgation, it is still up-to-date in its application, in spite of the rapid evolution of technology. It was for instance the first law in Latin America to include the 'droit de suite'.[2] It also reflected perfectly the highly personal characteristics of the moral right. It was, however, based on the theory of property, which was still in vogue at the time but is no longer accepted by Latin American copyright jurists.[3] The new amending law of 1982 modernises the copyright legislation of Uruguay, and brings it into line with the Rome Convention. It also grants specific remedies to performers, producers of phonograms and videograms[4] thus reinforcing their rights.

1 See Austrian Law of 1936 and Italian Law of 1941.
2 See Sciarra Quadri 'The "droit de suite" in Latin America' RIDA No 102, p 73.
3 See Romeo Grompone *El Derecho de Autor en Uruguay* (Publicaciones AGADU, 1977) p 16.
4 For the problems relating to the definition of a videogram see Davies 'Legal Problems deriving from the Use of Videograms' Copyright (1979) p 257.

Group 2

CUBA

22.105 The only reference in the Copyright Law of 1977[1] to a right recognised by the Rome Convention is to be found in article 24, which grants to broadcasting organisations an author's right with regard to radio and television broadcasts. Such protection is granted ad aeternum, by virtue of article 46 which provides that 'the term of validity of author's rights belonging to legal entities is of unlimited duration'.

NICARAGUA

22.106 The Nicaraguan Civil Code dedicates to literary and artistic property approximately 140 articles, none of which however, relate to neighbouring rights.[1] This is so in spite of a reference to 'musicians'[2] which is incorrect since it applies to 'musical composers'. Nevertheless, Nicaragua has adhered to the Satellite Convention,[3] a strange situation for a country which does not even protect its own nationals in respect of the broadcasting of programmes for direct reception by the public.

1 Law No 14 of 1977.
2 Art 789, para 5.
3 See chapter 10 above.

PANAMA

22.107 The Administrative Code of Panama of 1916 contains the entire legislation regarding to the protection of literary and artistic property in articles 1889 to 1966. Broadly speaking, the main features of this legislation are in conformity with accepted principles although the obsolescence of certain provisions, as well as the terminology employed, call for urgent revision which is now being undertaken by the Ministry of Education and Culture. It is submitted that phonograms and broadcasts come within the scope of the old law.[1] They are thus protected until 80 years after death,[2] if registration is effected[3] within one year from the date of publication.[4] Foreign productions are protected by the principle of reciprocity.[5] Panama has adhered to the Phonograms Convention, thereby specifically protecting phonographic productions against illegal reproduction.

1 Art 1894.
2 Art 1903.
3 Art 1911.
4 Art 1915.
5 Art 1910.

DOMINICAN REPUBLIC

22.108 The Law of 1947,[1] expressly protects phonograms[2] and it would appear that Article 3(h) covers broadcasting. Unfortunately this Law contains no provision at all regarding performers. Protection derives from registration[3] which must be effected in the year of publication. The term of protection is 30 years after death.[4] Foreign productions are protected in accordance with the relevant treaties[5] for a term not exceeding that in the country of origin.[6]

1 Law No 1381 of 1947.
2 Art 3(e).
3 Art 16.
4 Art 30.
5 Art 42.
6 Art 31.

VENEZUELA

22.109 The copyright law of 29 November 1962 does not contain provisions on neighbouring rights. However, Venezuela has recently made a step toward the recognition of those rights by acceding to the Phonogram Convention, with effect from 18 November 1982. A draft aiming to bring the law of 1962 up to date to add neighbouring rights is under consideration by the congress.

Group 3

22.110 The author has been unable to find any reference to neighbouring rights in the legislation of the following countries: Bolivia, Haiti, Honduras.

The law of Peru also does not deal with neighbouring rights with the exception of Law No 13.714 of 1961, which deals[1] with the obligations of the producer of phonograms which include the obligation to respect the performer's moral right to claim the paternity of his performance.[2]

1   Arts 52 to 55.
2   Art 54.

General considerations

22.111   As regards the interpretation of legislation relating to the protection of intellectual property, the rules adopted by the Latin American countries generally include the following principles: (a) the later law repeals any conflicting provisions in the earlier law; (b) on the ratification of or accession to an international convention, the provisions thereof are automatically incorporated into the domestic legislation of the country concerned, thereby producing the effect mentioned in (a) above: (c) the protection afforded by a state to its own nationals cannot be less than that which it grants to foreigners domiciled abroad.

Accordingly, a country that limits the term of protection to 40 years after death and subsequently adheres to the Berne Convention, which establishes a minimum period of 50 years, thereby extends the protection for this minimum period not only in favour of foreign authors protected by the Berne Convention, but also to its own nationals, in respect of those works specifically referred to in the text of the Convention. On the other hand, as regards works which, because they do not appear in the Berne Convention are protected only under domestic law, the term of 40 years 'post mortem auctoris' will remain in force. This is the case, for example, of Uruguay which protects television broadcasts as 'works',[1] whereas broadcasts as such are not protected by the Berne Convention. This situation remained unaltered by Uruguay's subsequent adhesion to the Rome Convention, which expressly protects television broadcasts, because the Rome Convention imposes a minimum term of only 20 years after publication. In this case, the lex loci, which provides for a longer term, prevails so that television broadcasts are protected for 40 years pma.

The adoption of the above principles has allowed the majority of Latin American states to keep up-to-date in the field of copyright by merely ratifying international agreements. These sometimes bring about innovations by introducing rights hitherto not recognised in the area of domestic legislation. The problem of application only arises when the Convention offers alternatives, or requires definition at the national level. In the event of litigation, the courts will establish the relevant rules by means of case law, pending legislative action. For this reason, it is convenient that the texts of conventions should be applicable automatically as has been the case in fact with the majority of the treaties relating to copyright.

1   Art 5, Law of 1937.

22.112   The Rome Convention contains no provisions regarding moral rights, except, by inference, the right of divulgation. This is not surprising in view of the fact that it was the first international agreement to deal with neighbouring rights. It was necessary therefore to conform, as far as possible, to the various national laws in force and to avoid problems which would have been aroused by a doctrinal debate on moral rights.

On the national level, however, such difficulties do not exist, and various

Latin American states have introduced into their legislation provisions granting to performers rights of a personal nature. As may be seen from an examination of the legislation of the individual states, Argentina (the pioneer in this respect), followed by Uruguay, Colombia and Paraguay, granted performers the right to prevent the communications of their performances whenever this might unjustly harm their artistic interests. A videotape which, by reason of faulty camera-work, portrays the performer in a grotesque fashion, a faulty record which, played at too fast a speed, makes the performance ridiculously high-pitched, a film in which a romantic singer has his voice synchronised in an improper scene, are examples of injuries to the moral right of the performer for which an appropriate legal remedy should be available. Obviously, performers, like authors, must exercise their personal rights in a responsible manner. If it is shown in the proceedings that the plaintiff's action was prompted by a temperamental outburst, the desire to emulate the defendant or mere caprice, then the court will reject the complaint as an abuse of legal process, as it does in the case of any other person who invokes the protection of the law in an irresponsible manner. It is essential, however, to provide the performer with the necessary means to protect his reputation in appropriate circumstances.

Another moral right long recognised in Latin America is that of the right to claim paternity of works. The legislation of various countries expressly accords to the performer the right to attach his name to the performance. As this right is the logical and natural result of a right to claim paternity, the writer has chosen to adopt this expression, which is sometimes translated as 'the right to claim authorship'.[1] It is the right to assert that he is the author of the work, in this case the performer of the performance. A performance being the very expression of the performer's artistic personality, is in itself an act of creation which, like a separate branch of the same tree, is analogous to the author's right, and to which are applied the same general principles which protect artistic and literary works. Accordingly, by providing that the performer's name is to be cited in connection with his performance, the legislation is effectively assuring him the right to claim paternity, expressed in its most natural form.

1 See Masouyé/Wallace, *WIPO Guide to the Berne Convention* 6 bis 3.

22.113 The writer has always supported the view that the word 'phonogram' refers to the 'fixed sound', understood as a res immaterialis, independent of the form in which it is embodied. Others take the view that the disc or tape constitutes the phonogram, whereas strictly a disc or tape is merely a reproduction of the phonogram, or a repitition of the 'fixed sound' in a new material form. In other words, the disc or tape contains the phonogram, but does not itself constitute a phonogram.

This apparently subtle distinction is in fact of fundamental importance in the identification of the producer of phonograms. It has been argued, for example, that the 'producer' of a phonogram taken from the sound track of a motion picture is the manufacturer of the disc, since it is he who, for the first time, effects the exclusively aural fixation of these sounds, which were previously, in the film associated with images. On reflection, it is impossible to agree with this view. A phonogram consists of the capturing of sounds in some material form permitting them to be repeated and consequently reproduced. The producer is the person who fixes the sounds for the first time. The fact that the immediate and principal object of such fixation is the synchronisation of a motion picture, a complex work consisting of a combination of sounds and images, does not mean that the film-maker was not the first to fix the sounds, thereby becoming the producer of the phonogram when those sounds, isolated from the images, are published separately. In these circumstances, the disc manufacturer is a mere reproducer, as is the licensee of a phonogram producer who publishes under contract a phonogram belonging to another.

Following another line of thought, it is the writer's opinion that the protection due to the producer of phonograms, apart from the other factors inherent in his activity, which it is unnecessary to repeat in this work, derives essentially from the fact that he produces something which previously did not exist, an incorporeal thing, a res nova – the object of the right – consisting of the fixation of the performance of an authorised work by performers chosen and brought together at the initiative of the producer, and under his technical and artistic supervision. The recognition of a right exercisable erga omnes, analogous to an author's right, for the protection of phonograms, not only against their reproduction but also against all other uses appears to the writer to be necessary. Moreover, such protection must be in harmony with the principles adopted for the defence of other intellectual property rights, not only to avoid conflicts of interest, but also to make the protection effective; this is particularly relevant as regards the term of protection, which should never be less than that relating to the performance embodied in the phonogram.

22.104 *In Brazil* the application of the provisions of article 12 of the Rome Convention regarding the collection of remuneration payable for the communication to the public and the broadcasting of phonograms is effected by 'SOCINPRO' (Sociedade Brasileira de Intérpretes e Produtores Fonográficos). This organisation, established in January 1962, was among the first in the world to unite performers and producers for the common purpose of administering their rights.[1] By virtue of Law No 5.988, SOCINPRO joined the authors' societies in a Central Office (ECAD) which has the monopoly in Brazil over the collection of revenue arising from broadcasting and public performance. ECAD is also entrusted with the distribution of the income. The unification of tariffs, collection, systems and rules of distribution through ECAD represents an enormous advance in the methods of effecting such operations, and has resulted in a substantial reduction in costs. ECAD is administered by a Board, elected by the collecting societes. It is a private non-profit-making organisation, under the supervision of the National Copyright Council (Conselho Nacional de Direito Autoral).

In Argentina the secondary use of phonograms in broadcasts and public performances, has been remunerated since the 1930s, although, oddly enough, producers, who were legally entitled to an author's right, did not exercise the right, preferring to share with the performers the latter's right. Moreover, accompanying musicians were excluded from this benefit. This anomaly was resolved with the passing of Decrees No 1670 and 1671, as a result of which the artists' association (AADI) and the producers' association (CAPIF) formed a collecting society which receives revenue on behalf of all interested parties, to the satisfaction of all concerned. This has resulted in the collection of some five million US dollars in 1980, a very high sum for such rights in a Latin American country.

In view of the general acceptance of the Rome Convention in the area, 10 states have already ratified the convention, it is to be expected that the initiatives referred to above will be repeated in all the Latin American countries.

Logically, the next stage will be the establishment of bilateral relations between all the collecting societies thereby giving to the economic aspects of article 12 of the Rome Convention the international dimension intended by its creators. The need for such a development and its feasibility was confirmed by the recommendations adopted in 1979, by the Sub-Committee of the Intergovernmental Committee of the Rome Convention concerning the collection and distribution of revenue deriving from article 12 rights which resulted from the enquiry into the implementation of the Rome Convention.[2]

1 In Columbia, ACINPRO has already begun its activities and, in Uruguay, SUDEI, the performers' society has joined with the producers' association and the authors' society AGADU for the collection of neighbouring rights resulting from broadcasting and public performance.
2 See para 8.29 above.

Chapter 23
India

by Krishnaswami Ponnuswami

1. History and development of copyright*

23.01 The roots of the Copyright Act 1957 lie firmly embedded in the past, when the copyright law of British India was closely intertwined with that of Britain. It replaces the Indian Copyright Act 1914, which made applicable to British India, with additions and modifications, the Imperial Copyright Act 1911.[1]

Developments which occurred in this field in the international arena forced the pace of development of national copyright laws. The Imperial Copyright Act 1911 is a clear example of such interaction. The extensive modifications of the Berne Convention at Berlin in 1908, to which Britain was a party, made it imperative for her to consolidate and amend her copyright laws, which lay scattered in over a dozen statutes enacted during the course of two centuries.[2]

The Imperial Copyright Act 1911 was the culmination of this enormous exercise of consolidation. The important changes made by the Act were (i) the abolition of the formal requirement of registration of copyright; (ii) the extension of the term of copyright from 42 years to one of life of the author plus 50 years (subject to certain conditions); (iii) the extension of the scope of copyright; and (iv) the substitution of one Act for the numerous Acts on the subject. By proclamation, the Government of India brought the Imperial Act 1911 into force in British India with effect from 31 October 1912, and the Indian Copyright Act 1914 was passed by the British Indian legislature, embodying necessary modifications in, and additions to, the Imperial Act. In effect, therefore, the copyright law of India had been substantially identical with that of Britain and conformed to the Berne Convention as modified at Berlin in 1908.

The further revision of the Berne Convention at Rome in 1928 and at Brussels in 1948 and the adoption of the Universal Copyright Convention in 1952 made it necessary for Britain to enact the present Copyright Act in 1956. Similar compulsions made it inevitable for India to attempt a complete revision of her copyright law, but the simple technique of adopting the British statute with peripheral modifications was no longer appropriate to Free India's sovereign status. After much deliberation and consultation with concerned interests, the present Copyright Act was on the statute book by mid-1957 and was brought into effect from 21 January 1958. Thus began a new chapter in the development of copyright law in India.

The Copyright Act 1957 does not break away from the past, but renovates and builds a modern superstructure on the old foundation. For the first time, it established a Copyright Office[3] under the immediate control of the Registrar of Copyrights, a civil servant in charge of administrative matters pertaining to the Act, and provided for the maintenance of a Register of Copyrights.[4] The

* The author is indebted to Mr M. L. Chopra, Deputy Registrar of Copyrights, Government of India, for his invaluable help with this chapter.

Act also introduced a quasi-judicial Copyright Board under the chairmanship of a sitting or retired judge of the Supreme Court of India or of a High Court or of a person who is qualified to be appointed as a judge of a High Court[5] and vested the Copyright Board with important powers.[6] The Act gave recognition for the first time to cinematograph films as a distinct class of work eligible for copyright protection[7] and to a special right, called 'broadcast reproduction right', in programmes broadcast by radio and television.[8] It also recognised for the first time the 'moral rights' of the author[9] (described in the Act as 'special rights').

1 The subject of copyright law has yet to arouse much scholarly attention in India and the literature on it is not extensive; see bibliography.
2 *Copinger and Skone James on Copyright* (11th edn, 1971) ch 2.
3 Copyright Act 1957, s 9 (hereinafter referred to as the Act).
4 Ibid, Ch X (ss 44-50).
5 The Act, ss 11, 12.
6 Eg to grant compulsory licences under ss 31, 32; decide objections to fees, charges or royalties levied by performing rights societies: see ss 33-35; rectify the Register of Copyrights: see s 50.
7 See the Act, ss 2(y)(ii), 13(1)(b), 14(1)(c).
8 The Act, Ch VII (ss 37-39). Audio and visual broadcasting of programmes to the public by wireless diffusion is termed 'radio-diffusion' in the Act: see s 2(v).
9 The Act, s 57; see para 5.37 above.

2. Copyright – general

23.02 Section 13 of the Copyright Act 1957 confers copyright throughout India in the following classes of 'works', namely:

(a) Original literary, dramatic, musical and artistic works;
(b) Cinematograph films; and
(c) Records.[1]

1 S 2(y).

A. Original literary, dramatic, musical and artistic works

(1) *Original literary works*
23.03 The Act does not define the term 'literary work' except to state that it 'includes tables and compilations'.[1] Literary merit is not a prerequisite for a work to be a literary work. A literary work is just the good old 'book' of the earlier two centuries of copyright law, that is, anything written, printed, or expressed in any other form of notation, however elementary, pedestrian or even absurd its contents may be.[2] To be original, it need not be inventive, innovative, intellectual, or new. All that is required is that it must originate from the author, not be copied by him from elsewhere, and be the result of his labour. A full ten years prior to the English case of *Walter v Lane*[3] the same approach was adopted by Sir Arthur Wilson in the Calcutta High Court in *Macmillan v Suresh Chunder Deb*[4] (the *Golden Treasury* case). The book by Professor Palgrave entitled *The Golden Treasury of Songs and Lyrics*, published by Macmillan and registered as the law then required, contained a selection of poems from many English authors of various periods. One section of the book was prescribed by the Calcutta and Bombay Universities for their BA examinations. An enterprising Indian publisher brought out 'a sort of variorum edition' of the poems. The court held that the defendant's book was a piracy of Professor Palgrave's, as it had borrowed his selection of poems, though the arrangement of the poems was altered and other changes introduced in the defendant's

book. According to the court, Professor Palgrave's selection of poems was not a mere mechanical exercise in scissoring and pasting, but called for 'extensive reading, careful study and comparison, and the exercise of taste and judgment'. The defendant is free to produce his own selections by similar skill and struggle, but not by the short-cut of appropriating to himself the fruits of Professor Palgrave's labour.

The true principle underlying the law of copyright protection is well-settled: the law will not permit one man to make profit out of, and to appropriate to himself, the labour, skill, and capital of another.[5] But copyright law does not confer any monopoly in the ideas or knowledge embodied in the subject of copyright which others are free to make use of and utilise as the raw material for their own creative endeavours.[6]

1 S. 2(o).
2 *University of London Press Ltd v University Tutorial Press Ltd* [1916] 2 Ch 601.
3 [1900] AC 539.
4 ILR 17 Calcutta 951 (1890) (Wilson J).
5 *Walter v Lane* [1900] AC 539 (see the opening sentence in the judgment of the Lord Chancellor, Lord Halsbury).
6 *RG Anand v Delux Films* AIR 1978 SC 1613.

(2) *Original dramatic and musical works*
23.04 'Dramatic work' includes 'any piece for recitation, choreographic work or entertainment in dumb show, the scenic arrangement or acting form of which is fixed in writing or otherwise.'[1] It does not include cinematograph films which have now become an independent subject of copyright in their own right.

'Musical work' is defined as 'any combination of melody and harmony or either of them, printed, reduced to writing or otherwise graphically produced or reproduced'.[2]

1 S 2(h).
2 S 2(p). The definition is taken from the (now repealed) British Musical (Summary Proceedings) Copyright Act 1902, s 3. The words 'or otherwise *graphically* produced or reproduced' are, in the modern context, too narrow and instead the words 'or some other material form' would be preferable.

(3) *Original artistic works*
23.05 'Artistic work' is defined as follows:[1]

(i) a painting; a sculpture; a drawing (including a diagram, map, chart or plan); an engraving (including etchings, lithographs, woodcuts, prints and other similar works, not being photographs); or a photograph (which term includes photo-lithograph and any work produced by any process analogous to photography but does not include any part of a cinematograph film); whether or not any such work possesses artistic quality;
(ii) an architectural work of art;[2]
(iii) any other work of artistic craftsmanship.

1 S 2(c).
2 S 2(b) speaks of these as being either buildings or models for buildings.

(4) *Industrial designs*
23.06 Section 15 denies copyright under the Act to any design which is registered under the Designs Act 1911.[1] Also, by virtue of the same section, copyright ceases in any design which is capable of being registered under that Act[2] but has not been so registered, as soon as any article to which the design

has been applied has been reproduced more than 50 times by an industrial process by the owner of the copyright or, with his licence, by any other person. It follows that a purely industrial design capable of being registered under the Designs Act 1911, but not so registered, is still entitled to artistic copyright under the Act of 1957, as long as any article with that design applied has not been reproduced more than 50 times by an industrial process.[3]

1   Until 1970 the Act dealt with patents as well as designs. After the enactment of the Patents Act 1970, that Act deals with designs and bears the short-title 'The Designs Act 1911'.
2   The Designs Act 1911 provides for the registration of 'any new or original design not previously published in India': s 43(1). Upon such registration the registered proprietor of the design becomes entitled to copyright in the design, ie the exclusive right to apply the design to any article in any class in which the design is registered during the period of five years from the date of registration, renewable for two further terms of five years each: ss 47, 2(4).
3   'Design' '*does not include any trade mark as defined in clause (v) of sub-section (1) of section 2 of the Trade and Merchandise Marks Act, 1958, or property mark as defined in section 479 of the Indian Penal Code.*' s 2(5) (italics supplied). The exclusion of trade marks from the definition of 'design' in s 2(5) of the Designs Act 1911 (above, the italicised words) would mean that trade marks are not capable of being registered as designs under the Designs Act 1911 and can therefore claim artistic copyright under the Copyright Act 1957. For a decision upholding such claim in an interlocutory injunction application see *Anglo-Dutch Paint, Colour and Varnish Works, P Ltd v M/s India Trading House* AIR 1977 Delhi 41. It appears that the Copyright Registry is flooded with applications for the registration of artistic copyright in labels under s 44 of the Copyright Act 1957. In fact this was also done by the proprietor of the trade mark in the case just referred to.

(5) *Published editions of existing works*

23.07   A publisher who publishes a new edition of a non-copyright work has no remedy, if another publisher multiplies copies of his edition by photographic or similar process as the Act confers no protection in typographical arrangements only.

(6) *Tainted works*

23.08   There is nothing in the Act itself denying copyright protection to obscene, immoral, defamatory or other tainted works,[1] although the courts in India will presumably be guided by British precedents and will not extend protection to them on the ground of public policy. It must however be borne in mind that the Constitution of India guarantees to all citizens of India the fundamental right to freedom of speech and expression. Reasonable restrictions can be imposed by the state on the exercise of the right 'in the interests of the sovereignty and integrity of India, the security of the State, friendly relations with foreign States, public order, decency or morality, or in relation to contempt of court, defamation or incitement to an offence'.[2] The courts will strike down any legislation imposing unreasonable restrictions. Works falling within the ambit of prohibition of such laws are obviously illegal and cannot claim copyright protection. But in other cases, it is submitted the court cannot, in the absence of valid legislation restricting the fundamental right to freedom of speech and expression, deny copyright protection to a work on any common law doctrine of public policy.

1   Cf The Trade and Merchandise Marks Act 1958 (Act 43 of 1958), s 11, which provides that a mark which comprises or contains scandalous or obscene matter, or any matter likely to hurt the religious susceptibilities of any class or section of the citizens of India, or a mark the use of which would be likely to deceive or cause confusion or would be contrary to any law for the time being in force, or a mark which would otherwise be disentitled to protection in a court shall not be registered as a trade mark.
2   Constitution of India, Preamble, art 19 (1) (a), (2). It may be noted that the right cannot be restricted 'in the interests of the general public as, for example, in the cae of the fundamental rights to property or business': see art 19 (5), (6).

B. Cinematograph films

23.09 The Act for the first time treats cinematograph films as an independent subject of copyright. Section 2(f) makes it clear that the expression 'cinematograph film' includes any sound track. Under this section 'cinematograph' should also be construed as including any work produced by any process analogous to cinematography. Care has been taken to exclude cinematograph films from the definition of dramatic work[1] and from that of 'photograph'[2] and also to exclude the sound track associated with a cinematograph film from the definition of 'record'.

The Act makes it clear that no copyright will subsist in a cinematograph film if a substantial part of the film is an infringement of the copyright in any other work:[3] the same applies to records (see below).

The copyright in a cinematograph film does not affect the separate copyright in any work in respect of which, or a substantial part of which, the film is made[4] (also with records below). When the copyright in the cinematograph film expires, a person who causes the film to be seen, or to be seen and heard, in public does not, however, thereby infringe the separate copyright in the work in respect of which, or a substantial part of which, the film is made.[5] What is protected is the physical material containing the visual images rather than any dramatic or artistic matter embodied therein.

1 S 2(h).
2 S 2(s).
3 S 13(3)(a); for records, s 13(3)(b).
4 S 13(4).
5 S 52(1)(y).

C. Records

23.10 The Act defines the term 'record' to mean 'any disc, tape, perforated roll or other device in which sounds are embodied so as to be capable of being reproduced therefrom other than a sound track associated with a cinematograph film'.[1] It also defines the term 'recording' to mean 'the aggregate of the sounds embodied in and capable of being reproduced by means of a record.'[2]

1 S 2(w).
2 S 2(x).

Subjects of copyright

23.11 Under the Act copyright may subsist in unpublished works as well as published works.[1] Copyright subsists under the Act:[2]

(i) in all works first published in India (irrespective of the citizenship, nationality, domicile or residence of the author of the work);
(ii) in works first published outside India, if the author of the work is a citizen of India at the date of such publication;
(iii) in works first published outside India posthumously, if the author of the work was a citizen of India at the time of his death;
(iv) in unpublished works (other than an architectural work of art), if the author is at the date of the making of the work[3] a citizen of India or domiciled[4] in India; and
(v) in an architectural work of art,[5] if the work is located in India.

In the case of a work of joint authorship,[6] the conditions conferring copyright specified above should be satisfied by all the authors of the work.[7]

1   This is clear from the language of the Act in various sections: eg ss 13(2)(i) and (ii); 16.
2   S 13(2).
3   When the making of the work is extended over a considerable period, the author of the work is deemed to be a citizen of, or domiciled in, that country of which he was a citizen or wherein he was domiciled during any substantial part of that period: s 7.
4   S 8 of the Act lays down that a body corporate shall be deemed to be domiciled in India, if it is incorporated under any law in force in India.
5   Section 2(b).
6   Section 2(z).
7   *Explanation* to s 13(2).

Publication

23.12 Copyright subsists in a work throughout India, if the work is 'first published' in India. Copyright can subsist in a work 'first published' *outside* India only if its author was a citizen of India at the date of such publication, or in the case of a posthumous publication he was a citizen of India at the time of his death. However, copyright can subsist in an 'unpublished' work (other than an architectural work of art) only if the author is at the date of the making of the work a citizen of India or domiciled in India.[1]

Again, copyright subsists for an unlimited term in 'unpublished' literary, dramatic and musical works, unpublished engravings and photographs, unpublished cinematograph films and unpublished records, whereas if these works are published, the copyright is for the limited term as prescribed in the Act. In several cases the term of copyright runs from the date of 'publication' or 'first publication.'[2]

The factum of publication, the place of publication and the time of publication are of practical importance for determining whether copyright subsists in a work under the Act.

In the case of a literary, dramatic, or musical work 'publication' means the 'issue' of copies of the work to the public in sufficient quantities.[3] The 'issue' of any records recording a literary, dramatic or musical work is, however, not publication.[4] But 'the sale, or offer for sale' of any records made in respect of a literary, dramatic or musical work, or of any adaptation thereof, or the public performance of such work or adaptation, is deemed to be publication for the purpose of determining whether the work was published posthumously or during the lifetime of its author. This is a crucial question for reckoning the term of copyright in the work.[5]

In the case of an artistic work, 'publication' means the issue of copies of the work to the public in sufficient quantities,[6] but does not include in the case of a work of sculpture or an architectural work of art the issue of photographs and engravings of such work.[7]

'Publication' of a record means the issue of records to the public in sufficient quantities.[8] 'Issue' of copies to the 'public' will include not only an issue for purpose of sale but also free distribution.

An unauthorised publication by public performance of a work without the licence of the owner of the copyright does not amount to 'publication' of the work, except, of course, in relation to infringement of copyright in the work.[9]

The Act empowers the Copyright Board to decide any question as to whether copies have been issued to the public in sufficient quantities so as to amount to 'publication' of the work. The decision of the Board on the question is final.[10]

A work published in India is deemed to be first published in India despite its simultaneous publication in some other country, unless that other country provides a shorter term of copyright for such work. A work is deemed to be published simultaneously in India and another country, if the time between the publication in India and in that other country does not exceed 30 days or such other period as may be fixed by the central government in relation to any specified country.[11] The Copyright Board is empowered to determine any question as to whether the term of copyright for any work is shorter in another country than that in India for the same work. The decision of the Board thereon is final.[12]

1   S 13(2).
2   SS 22–29.
3   S 3(a).
4   S 3.
5   S 24(2).
6   S 3(a).
7   S 3(a).
8   S 3(c).
9   S 4.
10 S 6(a).
11 S 5.
12 S 6(b).

The first owner of the copyright

23.13   (1) *'Author'*. The general rule is that the 'author' of a work is the first owner of the copyright in the work.[1] The term 'author' is defined[2] to mean in the case of:

(i)   a literary or dramatic work, the author of the work;
(ii) a musical work, the composer;
(iii) an artistic work (other than a photograph), the artist;
(iv) a photograph, the person taking the photograph;
(v)   a cinematograph film, the owner of the film at the time of its completion;
(vi) a record, the owner of the original plate from which the record is made, at the time of the making of the plate.

To the general rule that the copyright in a work belongs to the author, there are exceptions, namely:

As regards a literary, dramatic or artistic work (but not a musical work) made by the author in the course of his employment by the proprietor of a newspaper, magazine or similar periodical under a contract of service or apprenticeship, the said proprietor is, in the absence of any agreement to the contrary, the first owner of the copyright in the work in so far as the copyright relates to the publication of the work in any newspaper, magazine or similar periodical, or to the reproduction of the work for the purpose of its being so published, but in all other respects the author is the first owner of the copyright in the work.[3]

(2) *Commissioned works*.[4] In the case of a photograph taken, or a painting or portrait drawn, or an engraving or cinematograph film made, for valuable consideration at the instance of any person, the person who commissioned the work to be done is, in the absence of any agreement to the contrary, the first owner of the copyright therein. This is subject to the above exception.

(3) *Author's employment under a contract of service*[5]. For work done by an author in the course of his employment under a contract of service or apprenticeship, the employer is, in the absence of any agreement to the contrary, the first owner of the copyright therein. This exception applies to all works, including musical works.

(4) *Government work*.[6] In the case of a government work the government is, in the absence of any agreement to the contrary, the first owner of the copyright therein.

(5) *Works of international organisations.* In the case of works of international organisations to which copyright protection has been extended by the order of the central government as provided by the Act, the international organisation concerned is the first owner of the copyright therein.

1 S 17.
2 S 2(d).
3 S 17.
4 S 17, proviso (b).
5 S 17, proviso (c).
6 S 2(k).

Transfer of copyright: assignment and licensing

23.14 The Act contains specific provisions relating to assignment of copyright[1] and the granting of any interest in the copyright by licence.[2] The transfer by the owner of the material object in which copyright subsists does not by itself necessarily operate as a transfer of the copyright therein. Copyright can be transferred by the owner inter vivos by assignment or he can grant an interest therein by licence in accordance with the provisions of the Act. It can be transferred by testamentary disposition or can pass to the heirs upon the owner dying intestate. It can also pass by operation of law in the case of the insolvency of the owner. As regards the testamentary disposition of the manuscript of an unpublished literary, dramatic or musical work or of an unpublished artistic work, the copyright of which is owned by the testator immediately before his death, a rule of construction is enacted by the Act that the bequest includes the copyright in the work, unless the contrary intention is indicated in the testator's will or any codicil thereto.[3]

1 Ss 18, 19.
2 S 30. Ss 31 and 32 deal with 'compulsory' licences, which are treated separately.
3 S 20.

1. *Assignment of copyright*

23.15 A valid assignment of the copyright in any work can be made only in writing signed by the assignor or his duly authorised agent, though it need not be in any special form and no particular words are required to constitute an assignment. Such assignment may be made 'either wholly or partially and either generally or subject to limitations and either for the whole term of the copyright or any part thereof'.[1]

For the first time, the Act makes it possible for the 'prospective owner' of the copyright in a 'future work' to assign the future copyright.[2] In such a case, the assignment takes effect only when the work comes into existence.[3] If the assignee dies before the work comes into existence his legal representatives will be entitled to the rights of the assignee.[4] (Similar rules apply to licences.)

1 S 18(1).
2 S 18(1).
3 S 18(1), proviso.
4 S 18(3).

2. *Licences*

23.16 The Act provides that the owner of the copyright in an existing work, or the prospective owner of the copyright in a future work, 'may grant any interest in the right by licence in writing signed by him or by his duly authorised agent'.[1]

An exclusive licensee[2] is treated as an 'owner of copyright'[3] for the purposes of the civil remedies[4] available under the Act for infringement of copyright and therefore can institute in his own name every suit or other proceeding regarding infringement of copyright. In all such actions the owner of the copyright must be joined as a defendant, unless the court directs otherwise.[5] When the owner is thus made a defendant, he has the right to dispute the claim of the exclusive licensee. If the exclusive licensee succeeds in the proceedings, no fresh suit or other proceeding will lie at the instance of the owner of the copyright.[6]

1 S 20.
2 S 2(j) defines 'exclusive licence' as a licence which confers on the licensee, or on the licensee and persons authorised by him, to the exclusion of all other persons (including the owner of the copyright), any right comprised in the copyright in a work...'
3 S 54(a).
4 Ch XII (ss 54–62).
5 S 61(1).
6 S 61(2).

3. Abandonment of copyright

23.17 The Act also enables the author of a work to 'relinquish' all or any of the rights comprised in the copyright in the work by giving notice in the prescribed form to the Registrar of Copyrights.[1] Thereupon such rights cease to exist from the date of the notice. This is without prejudice to any rights subsisting in favour of any person on the date of the notice.[2]

1 S 21(1). On receipt of such notice the Registrar should get it published in the Official Gazette: s 21(2).
2 S 21(3).

4. Compulsory licences

23.18 The compulsory licensing provision[1] applies to any 'Indian work'[2] as defined in the Act; that is,

(i) any literary, dramatic, musical or artistic work the author of which is a citizen of India;
(ii) any cinematograph film made or manufactured in India; and
(iii) any record made or manufactured in India.

The Copyright Board is empowered to direct the Registrar of Copyrights to grant a compulsory licence in respect of the work in the circumstances specified in the Act. Upon complaint to the Board that the owner of the copyright in the work which has been published or performed in public (a) has refused to republish or allow the republication of the work, or has refused to allow the performance of the work in public, and by reason of such refusal the work is withheld from the public, or (b) has refused to allow the communication of such work to the public by radio-diffusion, or in the case of a record the work recorded in such work, on terms which the complainant considers reasonable. If the Board is satisfied, after giving to the owner of the copyright in the work a reasonable opportunity to be heard and after necessary inquiry that the grounds for such refusal are not reasonable, the Board may direct the Registrar to grant to the complainant, a licence to republish the work, perform the work in public, or communicate the work to the public by radio-diffusion, as the case may be, on such terms and conditions, including the payment of compensation to the owner of the copyright as the Board may determine. If there are two or more complainants, the Board is to prefer the one who in its opinion would best serve the interests of the general public.

In addition to the built-in procedural safeguards in the section, there are constitutional remedies for the judicial control of the exercise of administrative discretion and for the prevention of any abuse. It must be noted that such a compulsory licence may now be granted even during the lifetime of the author.

The Act also contains a provision authorising the making of records in respect of any literary, dramatic or musical work, if records recording that work have previously been made with the owner's licence or consent, on the terms of paying a statutory royalty.[3]

The Act includes a provision empowering the Board to grant a compulsory licence to produce and publish a translation in the circumstances mentioned in the Act[4] to any person who applies to the Board for the purpose. A compulsory licence can be granted by the Board to the applicant only if the following conditions are satisfied, namely:

(i) no translation in that language has been published of that work within seven years of its first publication, or, if published, it has been out of print;
(ii) the owner has denied the applicant authorisation to produce and publish such translation, though he had requested him therefor; or the owner of the copyright could not be found and the applicant had sent a copy of his request for such authorisation to the publisher named in the book not less than two months before his application to the Board;
(iii) the Board is satisfied that the applicant is competent to produce and publish a correct translation of the work and possesses the means to pay to the owner the royalties at rates determined by the Board;
(iv) the author has not withdrawn copies of his work from circulation; and
(v) the owner of the copyright is given, wherever practicable, an opportunity to be heard.

After holding such inquiry as may be prescribed, the Board is empowered to grant, if the above conditions are satisfied, a non-exclusive licence to produce and publish a translation of the work in the language mentioned in the application, on condition that the applicant shall pay reasonable royalties to the owner of the copyright in the work.

1 S 31.
2 S 2(1), read with the *Explanation* to s 31(1). Note that the compulsory licensing provisions do not apply to unpublished works, a work first published in India whose author is not a citizen of India, and works published outside India, and cinematograph films and records made or manufactured outside India.
3 S 52(1)(j).
4 S 32.

Registration

23.19 Registration is not a pre-condition for the subsistence of copyright in any work and India continues to adhere to the principle of 'automatic' protection without compliance with any formality. The present Act, however, provides for the maintenance of a Register of Copyrights and indexes of the register at the Copyright Office.[1] The register, open to public inspection, is prima facie evidence of the particulars entered therein.[2]

1 Ss 44, 46. One court has fallen into the error of viewing registration as a mandatory prerequisite for the subsistence of copyright and the acquisition of ownership thereof under the Act of 1957: see the obiter dictum in *Mishra Bandhu Karyalaya v Shivratanlal Koshal* AIR 1970 Madhya Pradesh 261; but not others: see *Satsang v Kiron Chandra* AIR 1972 Calcutta 533; *Kumari Kanaka v Sundararajan* [1972] Kerala LJ 536; *Manojah Cine Productions v A Sundaresan* AIR 1976 Madras 22. While *Iyengar's Copyright Act* (3rd edn, 1977) correctly states that registration is not compulsory under the Act (at p 158), it persists in stating erroneously that '[T]he effect of the new Act is to afford maximum protection to authors, *if they adopt the simple procedure laid down in the Act as to registration of* their rights' (at p 2: emphasis supplied).
2 S 48.

3. Copyright and 'neighbouring rights'

23.20 The expression 'neighbouring rights' is not commonly used in India. The Rome Convention, to which India has not yet acceded, seeks to provide protection at the international level for three categories of 'auxiliaries' of literary and artistic creation, namely, (i) performers; (ii) producers of phonograms; and (iii) broadcasting organisations. The protection afforded to these auxiliaries at the national level by the Indian copyright statute forms the subject-matter of this section.

4. The protection of 'performers'

23.21 No provisions exist, or have ever existed, in India recognising or protecting the rights of 'performers' of musical or dramatic works – that is, 'actors, singers, musicians, dancers and other persons who act, sing, deliver, declaim, play in, or otherwise perform such works'.[1]

1   In a recent popular work on the subject *Know Your Copyright* (Orient Longman, 1977) by G. D. Khosla, a former Chief Justice of the Punjab High Court and an eminent writer of many literary works of fiction, history, travel and law, it is stated (at p 69) that 'If a gramophone record or tape is prepared of a song sung by a popular singer, or if a musical piece is performed by a musician, the *performer* as well as the composer acquires copyright in the record or the tape' (emphasis added). This statement, which is inaccurate as a whole, is particularly erroneous so far as the performer is concerned. Copyright in a record (which term includes a tape: s 2(w)) lawfully made: see s 13(3)(b) belongs to its author viz, the original owner of the plate from which the record is made at the time of the making of the plate: s 2(d)(vi). The 'performer' is in no case regarded as the author of a copyright work and is therefore not entitled to copyright under the Act at all. Copyright in a musical work belongs to the composer; the singer (musician?) has no part of it.

   Recently, a divisional bench of the Bombay High Court has negatived the claim of a matinee idol, actor Dev Anand, to copyright in his performance in a cinematograph film: *Fortune Films International v Dev Anand*, AIR 1979 Bombay 17. The court had held that the Indian Act does not recognise the performance of an actor as a 'work', as defined in s 2(y), in which copyright can subsist under the Act.

   Krishna Iyer J, of the Supreme Court of India, has pleaded for the legislative recognition of the singer's rights, apart from the copyright conferred on the composer alone in musical works under the present law: see the 'footnote' appended by the judge to the judgment of the Court delivered by Jaswant Singh J, in *Indian Performing Rights Society Ltd v Eastern Indian Motion Picture Assoc* AIR 1977 SC 1433, affg AIR 1974 Cal 257, followed in *Eastern India Motion Pictures v Performing Rights Society Ltd* AIR 1978 Cal 477.

5. The protection of producers of phonograms

23.22 As already stated, 'records' are treated as an independent subject of copyright under the present Act.[1] The definition of 'record' comprehends gramophone records as well as other devices in which sounds are embodied so as to be capable of being reproduced therefrom, other than a sound track associated with a cinematograph film.[2] The Act bestows upon the owner of the copyright in a record the exclusive right to do or authorise the doing of any of the following acts by utilising the record, namely:

(i)   to make any record embodying the same recording;
(ii) to cause the recording embodied in the record to be heard in public; and
(iii) to communicate the recording embodied in the record by radio-diffusion.[3]

Copyright in the record is infringed by any person who, not being the owner or licensee, does any of these acts, or permits for profit any place to be used for causing the recording embodied in the record to be heard in public where such public performance constitutes an infringement of the copyright in the record, unless he was not aware and had no reasonable grounds for believing that such performance would be an infringement of the copyright, or deals in infringing copies of the record.[4]

The protection afforded to the producers of phonograms under the Act is even more extensive than that envisaged by the Rome Convention[5] to which India has not acceded and the Phonograms Convention[6] which India has ratified.

1 See above.
2 S 2(3). The Model Law of Neighbouring Rights, defines a 'phonogram' as any exclusively aural fixation of sounds of a performance or other sounds, images, or both in a material form sufficiently permanent or stable to permit them to be perceived, reproduced, or otherwise communicated during a period of more than transitory duration (art 2). Thus, it appears that the 'phonograms' of the Rome Convention and the Model Law and the 'records' of the Indian Act are co-extensive.
3 S 14(1)(d).
4 S 51.
5 Art 10 and art 12, Rome Convention; see para 8.24 and paras 8.26 et seq above.
6 Art 2, Phonogram Convention; see para 9.05 above.

6. Protection of broadcasting organisations

23.23 The Act, for the first time, confers a special right, called 'broadcast reproduction right'[1] in programmes broadcast by radio-diffusion[2] upon the government or other broadcasting authority lasting for a period of 25 years from the beginning of the calendar year following the year in which the programme is first broadcast.

A broadcasting authority can communicate copyright works to the public by radio-diffusion only if a licence is granted to it by the owner of the copyright. The Act, however, permits 'fair-dealing' with a literary, dramatic, musical or artistic work for the purpose of reporting current events by radio-diffusion.[3] The Act does not permit the broadcasting authority to use a copyright work in its programmes for any other purpose.

Broadcast reproduction right in a programme broadcast by radio-diffusion means the exclusive[4] right conferred upon the broadcasting authority to do, or authorise the doing of any of the following acts, namely:

(i) to rebroadcast the programme in question or any substantial part thereof;
(ii) to cause the programme, or any substantial part thereof, to be heard[5] in public;
(iii) to utilise the broadcast for the purpose of making a record recording the programme or any substantial part thereof.

While acts (i) and (ii) above can be done by any person who is authorised to do so by the broadcasting authority by licence, in the case of (iii) in addition a licence is required from the owner of the copyright in the work embodied in such programme.[6]

The broadcast reproduction right conferred upon a broadcasting authority does not affect the copyright in the literary, dramatic or musical work which is broadcast by that authority, or in any record recording any such work.[7]

The provisions of the Act relating to assignment of copyright,[8] licence,[9] banning of the importation of infringing copies,[10] civil remedies for infringement of copyright,[11] and the penal provisions relating to infringing copies,[12] are made applicable mutatis mutandis to broadcast reproduction rights.[13]

Broadcast reproduction right is infringed by any person who, without a licence of the broadcasting authority, re-broadcasts the programme, or a substantial part of it, or causes it to be heard in public, or utilises the broadcast to make a record recording it.

There is no general limitation recognised by the Act to the infringement of a broadcast reproduction right.

1 S 37.
2 S 2(v).
3 S 52(1)(b)(ii).
4 This language, used in the case of copyright under s 14, is not used in the case of the broadcast reproduction right in s 37 which instead lists these acts as infringements of the broadcast reproduction right, if done without a licence from the broadcasting authority.
5 It is not clear why no mention is made here about causing the programme to be 'seen' in public.
6 S 38, proviso.
7 S 39.
8 Ss 18, 19.
9 S 30.
10 S 53.
11 S 55.
12 Ss 64, 65 and 66.
13 S 38.

7. Collection and distribution of revenue from 'neighbouring rights'

23.24 The newly created Copyright Board is vested with power to inquire into objections to any fees, charges or royalties proposed to be charged by a performing rights society for the grant of licences for performance in public of works in respect of which it has authority to grant such licences and to make such alteration in respect of the fees, charges or royalties as the Board may think fit.[1] A performing rights society is defined as 'a society, association or other body, whether incorporated or not, which carries on the business in India of issuing or granting licences for the performance in India of any works in which copyright subsists'.[2] These societies either act as agents of the owner of the copyright for licensing the performing right, or acquire the copyright themselves.

Every performing rights society is required to prepare, publish and file with the Registrar of Copyrights statements of all fees, charges and royalties which it proposes to collect for the grant of licences for performance in public of works in respect of which it has authority to grant such licences. Failure to do so prevents the society from instituting any action, civil or criminal,[3] for infringement of the performing rights in the work except with the consent of the Registrar of Copyrights.[4]

Any person may lodge objections in writing at the Copyright Office to any fees, charges or royalties, or other particulars contained in the statement filed by the society.[5] Such objections are to be referred by the Copyright Office to the Copyright Board for decision. The Copyright Board is empowered to make such alterations in the statement as it may think fit, after affording an opportunity to the objector and the society of being heard and making such inquiry as may be prescribed. The Board is to transmit the alterations so made by it to the Copyright Office which is required to publish them in the Official Gazette and furnish the objector and the society with a copy thereof. The society can sue for, or collect for, licences granted by it for the performance of the works concerned, only those fees, charges or royalties thus authorised by the Copyright Board.

Any person can perform in public a work the performing rights of which a society has authority to grant licences for, provided he has tendered or paid to the society the fees, charges or royalties specified in the statement published by the society in respect of that work, *if any*, as altered by the Copyright Board. In such a case the society will have no right of action against such person for infringement of the performing rights in the work or to enforce any civil or other remedy for such infringement.[6] A person can perform a work in public, despite lodging an objection to the society's statement at the Copyright Office, after depositing the fees, charges or royalties at the Copyright Office, pending disposal of his objections and he will not be thereby infringing the copyright in the work. After the objections are finally disposed of and the amount deposited, that amount will be paid over to the party or parties who become entitled thereto consequent upon such final decision.[7]

1 Ss 33–36. These sections do not have retrospective operations: s 36.
2 S 2(r).
3 See paras 23.43 et seq, below.
4 S 33(2).
5 S 34.
6 S 35(5).
7 S 35(6), (7).

8. The term of protection

(1) The term of protection in literary, dramatic and musical works and in artistic works other than photographs

23.25 (i) *Published*[1] *within the lifetime of the author.*[2] The general rule is that the term of copyright in such works is 50 years from the beginning of the calendar year following the year in which the author dies.[3] In the case of a work of joint authorship, that is, a work produced by the collaboration of two or more authors in which the contribution of one author is not distinct from the contribution of the other author or authors,[4] the term must be reckoned with reference to the author who dies last.[5]

A shorter term is, however, provided where the identity of the author or authors is not disclosed either because the work is published anonymously or pseudonymously.[6] In such cases the copyright subsists only for 50 years from the beginning of the calendar year following the year in which the work is first published.[7] But even in such cases, if within such period of 50 years the identity of the anonymous author, or of one or more of the anonymous joint authors, is disclosed, then the general rule stated in the last paragraph is applied and the term of the copyright would be until the expiry of 50 years beginning from the calendar year following the death of the disclosed author or the death of the last of the disclosed authors.[8] The identity of an author shall be deemed to be disclosed, if such disclosure is made publicly by both the author and the publisher, or the author otherwise establishes it to the satisfaction of the Copyright Board.[9]

(ii) *Published after the lifetime of the author: posthumous works.* Where a literary, dramatic, or musical work, or an adaptation[10] thereof, has not been published in the lifetime of its author (or joint-authors), and copyright subsists in such work at the time of the death of the author (or of the last surviving joint-author), copyright subsists in such work until 50 years from the beginning of the calendar year following the year in which the work, or an adaptation thereof, is first published posthumously.[11]

This rule also applies to engravings.[12] In the case of artistic works other than engravings, and photographs which are dealt with separately,[13] it would appear that the copyright in them terminates upon the expiry of 50 years from the beginning of the calendar year following the year in which the author died, irrespective of whether such artistic works are published or unpublished.

(iii) *Unpublished works.* Where a literary, dramatic or musical work is not published copyright would subsist for an unlimited term.[14] The unlimited term applies to unpublished engravings (and photographs, which are separately dealt with), but not other unpublished artistic works.[15]

1 S 3(a). 'Publication' is dealt with in para 23.12 above.
2 S 2(d).
3 S 22. In this formulation the date of publication becomes immaterial, the only question being whether the work is a published work. Again the precise date of the death of the author is immaterial as the term will always be reckoned from 1 January next following. This version is based on the Brussels revision (1948). It will be noted that when the term of copyright expires, all the works of the same author fall into the public domain at the same time.
4 S 2(z).
5 S 22, *Explanation.*
6 S 23.
7 S 23(1).
8 S 23(2).
9 See *Explanation* to s 23. On Copyright Board see below.
10 'Adaptation' is defined by s 2(a) to mean:

   (i)   the conversion of a dramatic work into a non-dramatic work;
   (ii) the conversion of a literary or artistic work into a dramatic work by public performance or otherwise;
   (iii) any abridgement or pictorial version of a literary or dramatic work; and
   (iv) any arrangement or transcription of a musical work.

11 S 24(1).
12 S 24(1).
13 S 25, see below.
14 See para 23.12 above.
15 S 3.

Term of copyright in photographs

23.26 In the case of a photograph, copyright subsists until 50 years from the beginning of the calendar year following the year in which the photograph is published.[1] Until publication, the photograph enjoys a perpetual copyright as an unpublished work and after publication the copyright subsists for another 50 years.

1 S 25.

(2) Term of copyright in cinematograph films

23.27 In the case of cinematograph films, copyright subsists until 50 years from the beginning of the calendar year following the year in which the film is published.[1]

1 S 26.

(3) Term of copyright in records

23.28 In the case of a record, copyright subsists until 50 years from the beginning of the calendar year following the year in which the record is published.[1]

1 S 27.

(4) Term of copyright in government works

23.29 A work made or published by or under the direction or control of (i) the government or any department of the government, (ii) any Legislature in India, or (iii) any court, tribunal or judicial authority in India, is called a 'Government work'.[1] In the case of a government work the government is, in the absence of any agreement to the contrary, the first owner of the copyright in the work.[2] The term of the copyright is 50 years from the beginning of the calendar year following the year in which the work is first published.[3]

1 S 2(k).
2 S 17, proviso (d).
3 S 29.

(5) Term of copyright in works of certain international organisations

23.30 The Act contains provisions for extending copyright to works made, or first published by, or under the direction or control of organisations of which one or more sovereign powers, or the government or governments thereof, are members by Order of the central government published in the Official Gazette, if the government deems it expedient to do so.[1] In such cases the term of copyright is 50 years from the beginning of the calendar year following the year in which the work is first published.[2]

1 S 41. Copyright International Organisation Order 1958, SRO 272, dated 21 July 1958.
2 S 29.

9. Infringement and limitation of rights

23.31 Section 14 of the Act spells out the exclusive rights which constitute the copyright in different kinds of works.

Copyright in any work is said to be infringed,[1] when any person, not being the owner or the licensee[2] of the copyright, or in contravention of the conditions of such licence or of any condition imposed by a competent authority under the Act:

(i) does anything the exclusive right to do or authorise the doing of which is by the Act conferred upon the owner of the copyright;
(ii) permits for profit any[3] place to be used for the performance of the work in public where such performance constitutes an infringement of the copyright in the work, unless he was not aware and had no reasonable grounds for believing that such performance would be an infringement;[4]
(iii) 'deals' in 'infringing copies' of the work, ie copies made or imparted in contravention of the provisions of the Act.

In the following pages, the exclusive rights of the copyright owner in different classes of works, the statutory limitations on those exclusive rights, and their infringement are dealt with.

1 S 14(1)(a).
2 Granted either by the owner as provided by s 30 or by the Registrar of Copyrights as provided by ss 31 and 32. S 30 provides for the granting of an interest by the owner by a licence in writing signed by the owner or his duly authorised agent. But there is no provision invalidating a licence which is not thus in writing and signed: Cf s 19 which makes an assignment invalid unless it is in writing and signed by the assignor or his duly authorised agent. Quaere, can there be a valid oral licence or can a licence be implied from conduct?
3 S 51(a)(ii).
4 S 14(1)(a).

(1) Literary, dramatic or musical copyright

23.32 The owner of the copyright in a literary, dramatic or musical work has the exclusive right to do or authorise the doing of the following acts:

(i) to reproduce the work in any material form;[1]
(ii) to publish the work;[2]
(iii) to perform the work in public;[3]
(iv) to reproduce, perform or publish any translation of the work;[4]
(v) to make any cinematograph film or to make any record in respect of the work;[5]
(vi) to communicate the work by radio-diffusion; or to communicate to the public by a loudspeaker or any other similar instrument the radio-diffusion of the work;[6]
(vii) to make any adaptation[7] of the work;
(viii) to do any of the acts specified in clauses (i) to (vi) above in relation to a translation or adaptation of the work.[8]

1 S 14(1)(a)(i).
2 S 14(1)(a)(ii).
3 S 14(1)(a)(iii).
4 S 14(1)(a)(iv).
5 S 14(1)(a)(v).
6 S 14(1)(a)(vi).
7 S 14(1)(a)(vii).
8 S 14(1)(a)(viii).

a. *Infringement of literary, dramatic or musical copyright: infringement by copying*

23.33 As the owner has the exclusive right to reproduce the work in any material form, any person who makes copies of the work without his licence commits infringement of copyright in the absence of any statutory provision authorising him to do so. As long as the defendant's work is an independent product of his own exertions, it cannot be held to infringe the copyright in the plaintiff's work, however great the similarity between them and even if the defendant has derived his ideas or inspiration from the plaintiff's work. There is no infringement unless it is established that the defendant's work both closely resembles the plaintiff's work and has been produced by a substantial use, direct or indirect, of those features of the plaintiff's work in which copyright subsists. The tests for determining whether one work infringes the copyright in another by copying were recently elucidated by the Supreme Court of India in *RG Anand v M/s Delux Films*[1] in which the Court held that the defendant's cinematograph film was not a reproduction of the plaintiff's dramatic work. The case also highlights the difficulties in applying the tests to the concrete facts of a case.

1 AIR 1978 SC 1613. One of the judges (R S Pathak J) confessed to uneasiness in arriving at that decision. For an exposition of the principles applicable where the defence of common source is pleaded, see *Gangavishnu Shri Kisondas v Moreshvar Bapji Hegishte* ILR 13 Bombay 359 (1888), especially the judgment of Scott J in the trial court which was affirmed on appeal by a divisional bench. The plaintiff brought out a new and annotated edition of a certain well-known Sanskrit work on religious observances. The defendant brought out a verbatim copy. The court held that a new arrangement of old matter would give a right to the protection afforded by the law and that the defendant was not at liberty to save himself the labour of going to the sources by simply copying the plaintiff's work. But the onus lies on the plaintiff to clearly prove plagiarism: *Pandit Girdhari Lal v Pandit Devi Dayal* 95 Punjab LR 1910, 8 Ind Cas 497, 1 Hyd's Reps 9 (Punjab Chief Ct, 1910). The plaintiff complained that the defendant had infringed his copyright in a Hindi almanac by publishing an Urdu almanac the tables in which tallied except for minutes and seconds. Admittedly the calculations in both had been worked out in accordance with *Makrand*, an old book of logarithms. The court held that the defendant's failure to prove how he got his calculations done would not make up for want of proof of allegations of plagiarism by the plaintiff. The court observed (at 498): 'In such works similarities must perforce be found, and it is for the plaintiff in such a case clearly to prove plagiarism'.

b. *General limitations*

23.34 The statute also sets limits to the rights granted by expressly recognising specific defences (in the following cases, the identity of the work and its author must be acknowledged):[1]

(a) Fair dealing:[2] fair dealing with the work

  (i) for the purposes of research or private study;
  (ii) for the purposes of criticism or review,[3]
  (iii) for the purpose of reporting current events. Whether the 'dealing' with the work for these purposes is 'fair' or a pretended, excessive, or unfair one will depend on the facts of the particular case.

(b) The reproduction of the work for the purpose of a judicial proceeding or of a report of a judicial proceeding.[4]

(c) The reproduction or publication of the work in any work prepared by the Secretariat of a Legislature exclusively for the use of the members of that Legislature.[5]

(d) The reproduction of the work in a certified copy made or supplied in accordance with any law for the time being in force.[6]

(e) The reading or recitation in public of any reasonable extract from a *published* literary or dramatic (but not musical) work.[7]

(f) The publication in a collection, mainly composed of non-copyright matter, bona fide intended for the use of educational institutions, and so described in the title and in any advertisement issued by or on behalf of the publisher, of short passages from *published* literary or dramatised (but not musical) works, not themselves being works published for the use of educational institutions in which copyright subsists, provided that not more than two such passages from works by the same author are published by the same publisher during any period of five years.[8]

(g) The reproduction of the work (i) by a teacher or a pupil in the course of instruction; (ii) as part of the questions set for an examination or in answers to such questions.[9]

(h) The performance, in the course of the activities of an educational institution, of the work by the staff and students of the institution.[10]

(i) The making of records in respect of the work, if:

  (i) records recording that work have previously been made by, or with the licence or consent of, the owner of the copyright in the work; and
  (ii) the person making the records has given the prescribed notice of his intention to make the records, and has paid in the prescribed manner to the owner of the copyright in the work royalties in respect of all such records to be made by him, at the rate fixed by the Copyright Board. The person so making records ought not, however, to make any alteration in, or omissions from, the work, unless records recording the work subject to similar alterations and omissions have been previously made by, or with the licence or consent of, the owner of the copyright in the work or unless such alterations and omissions are reasonably necessary for the adaptation of the work to the records in question.[11]

(j) The performance of the work by an amateur club or society, if the performance is given to a non-paying audience or for the benefit of a religious institution.[12]

(k) The reproduction in a newspaper, magazine or other periodical of an article on current, economic, political, social or religious topics, unless

(l) The publication in a newspaper, magazine or other periodical of a report of a lecture, address, speech or sermon delivered in public.[14] As copyright subsists only in a literary 'work', ie a work printed or written, there can be no copyright in a mere extempore speech.

(m) The making of not more than three copies of a book (including a pamphlet, sheet of music, map,[15] chart[16] or plan)[17] by or under the direction of a person in charge of a public library for the use of the library, if the book is not available in India.[18]

(n) The reproduction, for the purpose of research or private study or with a view to publication, of an unpublished work kept in a library, museum or other institution to which the public has access, provided that, if the identity of the author of such work is known to the library, museum or other institution, as the case may be, such reproduction can be made only at a time more than 50 years from the date of the death of the author.[19] In such a case the identity of the work and its author should be duly acknowledged.

(o) The reproduction or publication of official matters.[20]

(p) The reproduction or publication of an unauthorised translation in any Indian language of an Act of a Legislature and of any rules or orders made thereunder.[21]

(q) The exhibition of a cinematograph film made in respect of the work after the expiration of the copyright in the film.[22]

1 S 52(1).
2 S 52(1)(a) and (b).
3 S 52(1).
4 S 52(1)(d). This is new.
5 S 52(1)(d), read with the proviso. This is new.
6 S 52(1)(e).
7 S 52(1)(f), read with the proviso; Cf the British Act of 1956, s 6(5), which adds: 'provided that this subsection shall not apply to anything done for the purposes of broadcasting'.
8 S 52(1)(g), read with the proviso to the subsection. See the *Explanation* to the clause relating to works of joint authorship.
9 S 52(1)(h). This is new.
10 S 52(1)(i). This is new. Copinger and Skone James, op cit, p 220 (para 518).
11 S 52(1)(j).
12 S 52(1)(l).
13 S 52(1)(m), read with the proviso to the subsection.
14 S 52(1)(n).
15 These now fall within 'artistic work' as defined in s 2(c)(i).
16 S 52(1)(o).
17 S 52(1)(o).
18 S 52(1)(o).
19 S 52(1)(p). In the case of a work of joint authorship this is 50 years from the date of the death of the joint author whose identity was known, or if the identity of more than one of them was known, from the death of such of these authors who died last.
20 S 52(1)(q). This is new.
21 S 52(1)(q). This is new.
22 S 52(1)(y).

(2) Artistic copyright

23.35 The owner of the artistic copyright has the exclusive right to do or authorise the doing of any of the following acts:[1]

(i) to reproduce the work in any material form;[2]
(ii) to publish the work;[3]

(iii) to include the work in any cinematograph film;[4]
(iv) to make any adaptation of the work;[5]
(v) to reproduce, publish, or include in any cinematograph film, such adaptation.[6]

Artistic copyright is infringed when any person, not being its owner and without a licence, does any of those acts, the exclusive right to do which belongs to the owner, or deals in infringing copies of the work.[7]

1   S 14(1)(b).
2   S 14(1)(b)(i). S 48 of the British Act states that 'reproduction' in the case of an artistic work includes a version produced by converting the work into a three dimensional form, or, if it is in three dimensions, by converting it into a two dimensional form. There is no corresponding provision in the Indian Act. But s 52(1)(w) of the Act provides that the copyright in an artistic work is not infringed by the making of an object of any description in three dimensions, 'if the object would not appear to persons who are not experts in relation to objects of that description to be a reproduction of the artistic work'.
3   S 14(1)(b)(ii), read with s 3(a), according to which 'publication' means in the case of an artistic work the issue of copies of the work to the public in sufficient quantities, but does not include in the case of a work of sculpture or an architectural work of art the issue of photographs and engravings of such work.
4   S 14(1)(b)(iii).
5   S 14(1)(b)(iv). S 2(a) provides that 'adaptation' in relation to an artistic work means the conversion of the work into a dramatic work by way of performance in public or otherwise. It is not clear how an artistic work can thus be converted into a dramatic work.
6   S 14(1)(b)(v).
7   S 51; s 2(m), read with the *Explanation* to s 51; the British Act of 1956, ss 1(2),5. See on infringement of artistic copyright, Copinger and Skone James op cit pp 210-215 (paras 496-505).

a. *General Limitations*

23.36   The following acts do not constitute infringement of the copyright in an artistic work:

(a)   a fair dealing;[1]
(b)   a fair dealing with an artistic work for the purpose of reporting current events;
(c)   reproduction for the purpose of a judicial proceeding or for the purpose of a report of a judicial proceeding;[2]
(d)   the reproduction or publication of an artistic work in any work prepared by the Secretariat of a Legislature (or either house of a bicameral legislature) for the exclusive use of the members of that Legislature;[3]
(e)   the reproduction of an artistic work (i) by a teacher or pupil in the course of instruction; or (ii) as part of the questions to be answered in an examination; or (iii) in answers to such questions;[4]
(f)   the making of not more than three copies of a map, chart or plan by or under the direction of the person in charge of a public library for the use of the library, if the map, chart or plan is not available for sale in India;[5]
(g)   the making or publishing of a painting, drawing, engraving or photograph of an architectural work of art;[6]
(h)   the making or publishing of a painting, drawing, engraving, or photograph of a sculpture or work of artistic craftsmanship (falling within section 2(c)(iii)), if such work is permanently situate in a public place or in any premises to which the public has access.[7]
(i)   the inclusion in a cinematograph film of an artistic work:

   (i)   permanently situate in a public place or premises to which the public has access; or
   (ii)   by way of background or as otherwise incidental to the principal matters represented in the film;[8]

588 *India*

(j) the use by the author of an artistic work, of any mould, cast, sketch, plan, model or study made by him for the purpose of the work, provided that he does not thereby repeat or imitate the main design of the work;[9]
(k) the making of an object of any description in three dimensions of an artistic work in two dimensions, if the object would not appear to persons who are not experts in relation to objects of that description to be a reproduction of the artistic work;[10]
(l) the reconstruction of a building or structure in accordance with the architectural drawings or plans by reference to which the building or structure was originally constructed, provided that the original construction was made with the consent or licence of the owner of the copyright in such drawings and plans.[11]

1 S 52(1)(a).
2 S 52(1)(c).
3 S 52(1)(d).
4 S 52(1)(h).
5 S 52(1)(o).
6 S 52(1)(s).
7 S 52(1)(t).
8 S 52(1)(u).
9 S 52(1)(v).
10 S 52(1)(w).
11 S 52(1)(x).

(3) Copyright in cinematograph films

23.37 The owner of the copyright in a cinematograph film has the exclusive right to do or authorise the doing of the following acts:[1]

(i) to make a copy of the film;[2]
(ii) to cause the film, in so far as it consists of visual images, to be seen in public and, in so far as it consists of sounds, to be heard in public;[3]
(iii) to make any record embodying the recording in any part of the sound track associated with the film by utilising such sound track;[4]
(iv) to communicate the film by radio-diffusion.[5]

The owner of a literary, dramatic or musical copyright has the exclusive right to make any cinematograph film in respect of the work besides the other exclusive rights. He may retain all his other exclusive rights and transfer the exclusive right to make a cinematograph film in respect of the work. In such a case the transferee will own the copyright in the cinematograph film including the sound track, and will have the exclusive rights as owner of the copyright in the film. Thus he will be entitled 'to cause the film, in so far as it consists of visual images, to be seen in public and, in so far as it consists of sounds, to be heard in public' and to communicate the film by radio-diffusion. The transferor would, however, as the owner of the copyright in the literary, dramatic or musical work, be entitled to all his other exclusive rights, and can, for example, communicate the work, as distinguished from the film, by radio-diffusion.[6] While the transferor continues to have the exclusive right to make a record in respect of the work, the transferee, as the owner of the copyright in the film, has the exclusive right to make any record embodying the recording in any part of the sound track associated with the film by utilising such sound track.[7] Applying these principles, the Supreme Court of India has, in *Indian Performing Rights Society Ltd v East India Motion Picture Association*,[8] rejected the claim of the Performing Rights Society that copyright in a literary or musical work incorporated in the sound track of a cinematograph film vests in the author of the literary work or the composer of the musical work, as the case may be, and that when the cinematograph film is exhibited in public, the Society, as the assignee of the copyright, is entitled to collect the fee or royalty due to the author or composer. It must be noted that where a film producer employs a lyricist to write lyrics for his movie, or a composer to compose the music, and the work is made in the course of the author's employment under such contract of service, the copyright in the work belongs to the producer (employer) and not to the employee.[9] When the work has been produced otherwise than under any such contract of service, the first copyright of a literary work vests in the author and of a musical work in the composer. Any cinematograph film or record in respect of the work can be made, only if he confers the right upon anyone by licence or assignment. If he assigns his copyright wholly, nothing else remains with him and the transferee acquires full ownership of the copyright. Where he grants a licence, or makes a partial assignment, entitling the licensee or assignee to make a film or record, the situation of dual ownership of the respective exclusive rights will arise. The Performing Rights Society can get only such rights which belong to the owner or composer, subject to the term of the licence or assignment as the case may be. The decision of the Supreme Court makes it clear that the Society cannot lay any claim to rights which, under the Act, belong exclusively to the owner of the cinematograph copyright.

1   S 14(1)(c). See s 2(f) which provides that 'cinematograph film' includes the sound track, if any.
2   S 14(1)(c)(i).
3   S 14(1)(c)(ii).
4   S 14(1)(c)(iii).
5   S 14(1)(c)(iv).
6   S 13(1)(a)(vi) and s 13(1)(c)(iv).
7   S 13(1)(a)(v) and s 13(1)(c)(iii). No such right is given to the owner of the copyright in a cinematograph film under the British Act; see s 13.
8   AIR 1977 SC 1443 (Jaswant Singh J for the court with a footnote by Krishna Iyer J), affg AIR 1974 Cal 257.
9   S 17, proviso (c).

a. *Infringement*

23.38   Copyright in a cinematograph film is infringed[1] by any person who, not being the owner or licensee of the copyright:

(i)   does anything the exclusive right to do which is conferred upon the owner of the copyright in the film by the Act;
(ii) permits for profit any place to be used for the performance[2] of the film in public, ie for the public showing of its visual images or for the public hearing of its sounds, where such performance constitutes an infringement of the copyright in the film, unless he was not aware, and had no reasonable ground for believing, that such performance would be an infringement of copyright;
(iii) 'deals' in infringing copies[3] of the film, ie a copy of the film or a record embodying the recording in any part of the sound track associated with the film made or imported in contravention of the provisions of the Act.

1   S 51.
2   S 2(d)(v).
3   S 2(m)(ii).

b. *General limitations*

23.39   The only exception stated in the Act is that the 'performance' of a cinematograph film in the course of the activities of an educational institution does not constitute an infringement of the copyright in the film, if the audience is limited to the staff and students of the institution, the parents and guardians of the students and persons directly connected with the activities of the institution.[1]

Again, the inclusion in a cinematograph film of any artistic work permanently situate in a public place or any premises to which the public has access or of any other artistic work, if such inclusion is only by way of background or is otherwise incidental to the principal matters represented in the film does not constitute an infringement of the copyright in such artistic work.[2]

1 S 52(1)(i); Cf the British Act of 1956, s 41(4). Under the British Act, s 13(6), the copyright in a cinematograph film is not infringed by making a copy of it for the purposes of a judicial proceeding, or by causing it to be seen or heard in public for the purposes of such a proceeding. The corresponding exception in s 52(1)(c) of the Indian Act applies only to the reproduction of a literary, dramatic, musical or artistic work.
2 S 52(1)(u).

(4) Copyright in records

23.40 The owner of the copyright in a record has the exclusive right to do, or authorise the doing of, any of the following acts by utilising the record, namely:[1]

(i) to make any other record embodying the same recording;[2]
(ii) to cause the recording embodied in the record to be heard in public;[3]
(iii) to communicate the recording embodied in the record by radio-diffusion.[4]

1 S 14(1)(d).
2 S 14(1)(d)(i).
3 S 14(1)(d)(ii).
4 S 14(1)(d)(iii).

a. *Infringement*

23.41 Copyright in a record is infringed[1] by any person who, not being the owner or a licensee of the copyright:

(i) does anything the exclusive right to do which is conferred upon the owner of the copyright in the record by that Act;
(ii) permits for profit any place to be used to cause the recording embodied in the record to be heard in public, where such public performance constitutes an infringement of the copyright in the record, unless he was not aware and had no reasonable grounds for believing that such performance would be an infringement of copyright;
(iii) 'deals' in 'infringing copies' of the record, ie a record embodying the same recording made or imported in contravention of the provisions of the Act.[2]

1 S 51.
2 S 2(m)(iii).

b. *General limitation*

23.42 (i) The causing of a recording embodied in a record to be heard in public by utilising the record:

(a) at any premises where persons reside as part of the amenities provided exclusively or mainly for residents therein;[1]
(b) as part of the activities of a club, society or other organisation which is not established or conducted for profit.[2]

(ii) The performance, in the course of the activities of an educational institution, of a record, if the audience is limited to the staff and students of the institution, the parents and guardians of the students and persons directly connected with the activities of the institution.[3]

(iii) The making of records in respect of any literary, dramatic or musical work, if:

    (a) records recording that work have previously been made by or with the licence or consent of the owner of the copyright in the work; and

    (b) the person making the records has given the prescribed notice of his intention to make the records, and has paid in the prescribed manner to the owner of the copyright in the work royalties in respect of all such records to be made by him, at the rate fixed by the Copyright Board.

1 S 52(1)(k)(i).
2 S 52(1)(k)(ii).
3 S 52(1)(i).

10. Remedies for infringement

23.43 The Act[1] makes it an offence for any person knowingly to infringe, or abet the infringement of, (a) the copyright in a work, or (b) any other right conferred by the Act. The offence is punishable with imprisonment for up to one year, or with a fine, or with both.[2] We have already seen what is meant by infringement of copyright.[3]

Similarly, it is an offence knowingly to make, or be in possession of, any plate[4] for the purpose of making infringing copies[5] of any work in which copyright subsists and is punishable in the same manner.[6]

Where a magistrate has taken cognisance of any offence of infringement of copyright or other rights conferred by the Act, or abetment thereof, the Act authorises any police officer, not below the rank of sub-inspector, to seize, even without a warrant from the magistrate, all copies of the work, wherever found, which appear to him to be infringing copies[7] of the work and produce them before the magistrate as soon as practicable.[8] The magistrate is empowered to adjudicate upon the rights in such seized copies of anyone claiming an interest in them.[9]

The court trying any offence under the Act can order that all copies of the work or all plates[10] in the possession of the alleged offender which appear to it to be infringing copies[11] be delivered up to the owner of the copyright.[12] Such an order can be passed whether the alleged offender is convicted or not.

Remedies by way of injunction, damages, accounts and otherwise are available to the owner of the copyright in the event of its infringement just as in the case of infringement of 'any other right'.[13] The remedies are available to the 'owner of the copyright', ie the first owner,[14] and anyone deriving title from him by assignment[15] or otherwise.

1 Chapter XIII (ss 63-70); the Indian Act of 1914, Chapter III (ss 7-12). The law provides for civil, as well as criminal, action of infringement of copyright. The court would not stay the criminal proceedings until the disposal of the civil action. See newspaper report of a decision of the Delhi High Court in *The Sunday Statesman*, 24 August 1980, p 2.
2 S 63.
3 S 51. See paras 23.31 et seq above.
4 'Plate' includes any stereotype or other plate, stone, block, mould, matrix, transfer, negative or other device used or intended to be used for printing or reproducing copies of any work, and any matrix or other appliance by which records for the acoustic presentation of the work are, or are intended to be, made: s 2(t).
5 S 2(m).

6 S 65.
7 S 2(m).
8 S 6(1).
9 S 64(2).
10 S 2(t).
11 S 2(m).
12 S 66.
13 Chapter XII of the Act (ss 54 to 62); Cf the British Act of 1956, Pt III (ss 17-22).
14 S 17.
15 On assignment see s 18. The section makes provision for an assignment by a prospective owner of copyright in any future work. The assignment in such a case becomes effective when the work comes into existence: Proviso to s 18.

(1) **Injunction**

23.44 The remedy of injunction is invariably sought in actions for infringement of copyright as it affords preventive relief. Such preventive relief is granted at the discretion of the court by injunction, temporary (interlocutory) or perpetual. Temporary injunction, pendente lite, is sought in copyright actions since damages are rarely an adequate remedy. The principles governing the granting of ad interim injunctions are fairly well settled.[1] In the case of 'innocent infringement', ie if the defendant proves that at the date of the infringement he was not aware and had no reasonable grounds for believing that copyright subsisted in the work, the plaintiff-owner can only claim an injunction in respect of the infringement and a decree for the whole or part of the profits made by the defendant by the sale of the infringing copies, as the court may consider reasonable in the circumstances of the case, but is not entitled to damages in respect of the infringement.[2]

1 See Copinger and Skone James, op cit, pp 235-238 (paras 555-557).
2 S 55(1) proviso. For a similar defence to an action for damages in respect of detention or conversion see s 58, proviso.

(2) **Damages for detention or conversion**

23.45 Infringing copies[1] of any work in which copyright subsists, and all plates[2] used or intended to be used for the production of such infringing copies,[3] are deemed to be the property of the owner of the copyright who accordingly may take proceedings for the recovery of possession of such infringing copies and plates or for the conversion thereof.[4] The remedy of conversion is, however, not available in respect of infringing copies against an innocent infringer.[5]

The remedies of damages for infringement of copyright and for detention or conversion are cumulative and not alternative. But as damages are compensation for the injury or damage caused to the plaintiff by the defendant's wrongful act, in so far as money can do it, it follows that what the plaintiff can recover is reparation and nothing beyond.[6]

1 S 2(m).
2 S 2(t).
3 See s 2(m), read with s 51, *Explanation*. 'Infringing copy' in the case of a literary, dramatic, musical or artistic work means a reproduction thereof, including a reproduction in the form of a cinematograph film, made or imported in contravention of the Act; see above.
4 Proviso to s 58.
5 The British decision in *Sutherland Publishing Co v Caxton Publishing Co* [1936] Ch 323, CA (affd by the House of Lords on this point) has been followed in India: *W B Yeats v Eric Dickinson* AIR 1938 Lahore 173; *Dharam Dutt Dhawan v Ram Lal* AIR 1957 Punjab 161; *Mishra Bandhu Karyalaya v S Koshal* AIR 1970 Madhya Pradesh 261.
6 S 55(1).

(3) Remedy by way of accounts

23.46 The plaintiff is also entitled to require the defendant to account for the profits made by him by his piracy instead of claiming damages for infringement or conversion.[1]

1 S 2(d).

(4) Author's moral rights

23.47 The Act recognises the author's right to claim authorship (the 'right of paternity') of his work independently of his copyright and even after the assignment, wholly or in part, of such copyright by him.[1] It also confers upon him, as well as his legal representatives, the right to restrain or claim damages in respect of any distortion, mutilation or other modification of his work, or any other action in relation to his work which would be prejudicial to his honour or reputation (the 'right of integrity').

1 S 57.

(5) Protection of third parties

23.48 If anyone claiming to be the owner of copyright in any work threatens any other person with any legal proceedings or liability in respect of an alleged infringement of the copyright, but does not with due diligence commence or prosecute an action for the infringement of the copyright claimed by him, any person aggrieved by such threat may institute a declaratory suit that the threat was unfounded or groundless as the alleged infringement was not in fact an infringement of any legal rights of the person making such threats. In such a suit he may also obtain an injunction against the continuance of such threats and recover such damages, if any, as he has sustained by reason of such threats.[1] If, however, the person making such threats commences and prosecutes with due diligence an action for the infringement of the copyright claimed by him, such a declaratory suit will not lie.[2]

1 S 60.
2 S 60, proviso.

11. Protection of foreign right owners

23.49 We have seen that a work first published in India is entitled automatically to the copyright protection conferred by the Act, even if the author is not a citizen of India.[1] The Act, however, empowers the central government to withdraw, by Order published in the Official Gazette, the protection afforded by it to works of foreign authors first published in India in the case of those authors who are subjects or citizens of any foreign country and are not domiciled in India, if it appears to the government that that foreign country does not give or has not undertaken to give adequate protection to the works of Indian authors.[2] If the author is a citizen of India, his work first published even outside India is entitled to such protection.[3] An unpublished work (other than an architectural work of art) qualifies for protection, if the author is a citizen of India or domiciled in India at the time of the making of the work. An architectural work of art is protected if it is located in India.

The Act empowers the Government of India to extend by order published in the Official Gazette all or any of the provisions of the Act.

(i) to works first published in any territory outside India, as if they were first published in India;[4]

(ii) to any work the author of which was at the date of its first publication (or at the time of his death, if first published posthumously) a subject or citizen of a foreign country to which the Order relates, as if the author was a citizen of India at that date or time;[5]

(iii) to unpublished works, or any class thereof, the authors of which are subjects or citizens of a foreign country to which the Order relates, in like manner as if the authors were citizens of India;[6]

(iv) in respect of domicile in any territory outside India to which the Order relates as if such domicile were in India.[7]

It may be noted that no provision is made to extend by an executive order the provisions of the Act relating to 'broadcast reproduction right' in programmes broadcast by radio-diffusion, to television and sound broadcasts made from places outside India by one or more organisations constituted in, or under the laws, of other countries. India has not ratified the 1961 Rome Convention and has not therefore assumed responsibility for the international protection of broadcasting organisations envisaged by it. Similarly, no protection is afforded to 'performances', at the international level (as well as at the national level) as envisaged by that convention.[8] Before thus extending the application of the provisions of the Act by making an Order relating to any foreign country (other than a country which is a party or a country with which India has entered into a treaty), the government should be satisfied that the foreign country has made, or has undertaken to make, reciprocal protection in that country for works entitled to copyright under the Indian Act.[9]

Every executive Order made by the central government must be placed before both Houses of Parliament as soon as may be after it is made and is subject to such modifications as Parliament may make during the session in which it is so laid or the session immediately following.

In pursuance of these provisions the Government of India has issued the International Copyright Order 1958.[10] The Order makes applicable all the provisions of the Act, except those relating to the rights of broadcasting authorities[11] and those which apply exclusively to Indian works, that is, a literary, dramatic or musical work, the author of which is a citizen of India,[12] to the following works:

(i) any work first published[13] in a Berne Convention country or a Universal Copyright Convention (UCC) country listed in the Schedule to the Order in like manner as if it was first published in India;

(ii) any work first published in any other country the author of which was a national of a UCC country at the date of such publication (or at the time of his death, if the work was published posthumously), in like manner as if the author was a citizen of India at that date or time;

(iii) to an unpublished work the author of which was at the time of the making of the work, a national of or domiciled in a Berne or UCC country listed in the Schedule in like manner as if the author was a citizen of, or domiciled in, India.

It also makes those provisions applicable to a body incorporated under any law of a country listed in the Schedule to the order in like manner as if it was incorporated under a law in force in India. Thus the Order implements the principle of 'national treatment' or 'assimilation'[14] to works originating in any member state (that is, works the author of which is a national of such state or works which were first published in such state).

The protection extended to such works is 'automatic' and is not conditional upon the compliance with any formality.

The provision[15] of the Act for the grant of compulsory licence in works withheld from the public applies only to Indian works, that is, a literary, dramatic or musical work the author of which is a citizen of India,[16] and has therefore no application to the works protected by the Order. The provision[17] of the Act for the grant of compulsory licence to produce and publish a translation of a literary or dramatic work in any language (i) does not apply to a work first published in a Berne Convention country and (ii) applies in the case of a work published in a non-Berne or UCC country and a work by a national of a UCC country first published in a non-Berne country only in respect of a translation of the work into any language specified in the Eighth Schedule to the Constitution of India.[18]

The Order makes the Act totally inapplicable to works published before its commencement in a non-Berne or UCC country except those published in the United States of America immediately before such commencement by virtue of an Order in Council made under the British Act of 1911. All Orders in Council then in force in India were revoked by the International Copyright Order 1958, but without prejudice to the copyright subsisting in a work by virtue of such Order in Council and in which copyright does not subsist under the Order of 1958.

1   See para 23.12 above.
2   S 42.
3   S 13(1); see above. In the case of posthumous publications, the author must be a citizen of India at the time of his death.
4   S 40(a).
5   S 40(d).
6   S 40(b).
7   S 40(c).
8   For the position at the national level see para 23.21 above.
9   S 40, proviso (i).
10 SRO 271 (effective 21 January 1958).
11 Act, Chapter VIII (ss 37–39).
12 S 2(t).
13 S 5.
14 See para 3.17 above.
15 S 31.
16 S 2(t).
17 S 32.
18 These languages are all Indian languages.

Works of certain international organisations

23.50 The Act makes provision for conferring copyright in any work made or first published by or under the direction or control of an international organisation of which one or more sovereign powers, or their governments, are members but in which no copyright would otherwise subsist under the Act. The central government is empowered to declare, by Order published in the Official Gazette, any such organisation to be one to which it is expedient to extend the provision. Upon such declaration by the Order copyright will subsist in the work throughout India as provided in the Act.[1] The Copyright (International Organisations) Order 1958,[2] made by the Government of India has declared that it is expedient to apply the provision to the following organisations, namely, United Nations Organisation and its Specialised Agencies and the Organisation of American States.

1   S 41.
2   SRO 272 (effective 21 January 1958), published in the *Gazette of India*, Extraordinary, Pt II, Sec 3, No 34, dated 21 January 1958.

12. Plans for law revision

(1) Need to overhaul the present provisions

23.51 First, it is necessary to undertake a complete review of the provisions of the Act in the light of its working during the past 23 years. No such attempt has been made so far. Some of the provisions of the Act are obscure and some others are inadequate. For example, the owner of the copyright in a literary, dramatic or musical work has the exclusive right to make a cinematograph film or a record in respect of the work. If he assigns the exclusive right to make a cinematograph film to a film producer and the exclusive right to make a record to a record producer, the film producer will have a copyright in the cinematograph film made by him and the record producer will have a copyright in the record made by him. The film producer, as the owner of the cinematograph copyright, has the exclusive right to make any record embodying the recording in any part of the sound track associated with the film by utilising the sound track. The record producer, as owner of the copyright in the record made by him, has the exclusive right to make any other record embodying the same recording. Thus, there are contemplated two kinds of record making, viz records made by utilising the sound track associated with the cinematograph film and records made otherwise than by utilising the sound track associated with the cinematograph films, and the right to make them belongs to different copyright owners. When the cinematograph copyright owner makes any record by utilising the sound track, he is not given the right, quite understandably, to multiply copies of such record, or to cause it to be heard in public, or to communicate it by radio and television broadcast, all of which exclusively fall within the scope of the rights of the record copyright owner. One doubts whether it was at all necessary to clothe the film producer with the exclusive right to make a sound-record by utilising the sound track of his film when he is given no further exclusive reproduction, performing or broadcasting rights in respect of it. If the only purpose of this provision is to make it an infringement of the film producer's copyright in his film for any person to make a sound-recording by utilising the sound track of his film without his consent, it is quite unnecessary, as he has already the exclusive right to make a copy of the film which includes a copy of the sound track as well as the visual images constituting the film as a whole.

Again, when the owner of a literary, dramatic or musical work assigns his exclusive right to make a cinematograph film in respect of it, all his other exclusive rights remain intact with him including the right to make a record in respect of the work which he can assign to a record producer. It may happen that the author of a literary, dramatic or musical right who has assigned the cinematograph rights to a film producer and recording right to a record producer may still have the exclusive right to 'perform' the work in public. While the record producer has the exclusive right to cause the recording embodied in the record to be heard in public, and the film producer has the exclusive right to cause the film in so far as it consists of visual images to be seen in public and in so far as it consists of sounds to be heard in public, it is not clear whether an acoustic presentation of the cinematograph film can be made without a visual presentation. There are conflicting interests involved in such cases which may call for delicate balancing. The rumblings of such conflict could be heard in *Indian Performing Rights Society Ltd v East India Motion Picture Association*,[1] but it turned out that the musical work incorporated in a cinematograph film was made by its author in the course of his employment by the film producer under a contract of service and therefore the copyright therein belonged to the employer film producer and not to its author.[2] The position would be very different where there is no such contract of service and the copyright in the literary, dramatic or musical work had belonged to the author himself and he had authorised the inclusion of the work in a cinematograph film.

Suffice it to say that a careful overhauling clearly identifying the exclusive rights, and reconciling the legitimate interests of the different parties, will have to be undertaken.

1 AIR 1977 SC 1443; affg AIR 1974 Calcutta 257 (reversing the decision of the Copyright Board).
2 S 17(c). The court also invoked s 17(b), though its relevance to the case is far from clear. Nor is any light shed upon the contract *of* service (which is very different from a contract *for* service).

(2) Need to protect the performer

23.52 The total neglect of the rights of the performer by the Indian copyright law is indefensible and the protection of the rights of actors, singers, musicians, dancers and other performers is overdue. This must be done both at the national and international levels, by enacting suitable provisions in the Act and by acceding to the Rome Convention.[1]

1 Art 7, Rome Convention; see para 8.16 above.

(3) Copyright in sound broadcasts and television broadcasts

23.53 The present provisions of the Act which confer a 'broadcast reproduction right' in the programmes broadcast by the state-owned All India Radio and Door Darshan are perfunctory and inadequate and it will be necessary to confer fully-fledged copyright in such broadcasts.[1] A comprehensive revision of these provisions must be undertaken not only to confer this protection on the national broadcasting authority, but to accept the international regime envisaged by the Rome Convention.

1 See Art 13, Rome Convention; see paras 8.31 et seq above.

(4) Paris revisions for the benefit of developing countries

23.54 It is indeed puzzling that India has not yet availed itself of the special concessions extended to developing countries by the Paris (1971) revision of the Berne and Universal Copyright Conventions enabling the grant of compulsory licences for the translation and for the reproduction of foreign works. The existing Indian provisions are inadequate. The present provision for the grant of compulsory licences to reproduce a literary, dramatic, musical or artistic work withheld from the public is applicable only if the author of such work is a citizen of India.[1] It also applies to a cinematograph film or a record made or manufactured in India. It does not apply to foreign works. The 1971 Paris revision[2] makes it possible to extend compulsory licensing for the reproduction of foreign works, if the owner of the copyright in a foreign work has not put in circulation copies of editions of his work at a price reasonably related to what is normally charged in the country for comparable works for a period of three to seven years (depending upon the subject-matter). Obviously such a provision will be to India's advantage as it will enable the production of low-priced editions of expensive foreign works to the benefit of its large student population.

Similarly, the present provision[3] for compulsory licensing of translations, based upon article V of the 1952 text of the UCC, (i) does not apply to works first published in a Berne Convention country; (ii) applies to works first published in a non-Berne or UCC country and to the works of a national of a UCC country first published in a non-Berne or UCC country and to the works of a national of a UCC country first published in a non-Berne country, but only in respect of the translation of the work into an Indian language;[4] and (iii) applies to a work first published in India, or a work of an Indian citizen first published in any other country. A compulsory licence can, however, be granted only after seven years of its first publication without a translation thereof having been published during that time by the owner of the copyright or any person authorised by him, or if a translation so published has gone out of print.[5] The 1971 Paris revision of the Berne and UCC Conventions has further liberalised this enabling provision by reducing the seven-year period to three years in respect of translation into a language in general use in the developing country concerned (which in India includes English), and to one year in respect of translation into any language which is not in use in the developed countries (which would mean all the Indian languages). There again, it will be to India's national interest to avail itself of this provision without further delay.

It will also be necessary to make special provision to authorise the use of copyright works by the broadcasting media in their educational programmes. Radio and television are powerful instruments for mass education and a special exception in their favour will serve the larger public interest.[6]

1 S 31(1).
2 See para 6.50 above.
3 S 32. And see para 6.55 above.
4 Specified in the Eighth Schedule to the Constitution of India.
5 S 32(4).
6 S 52(h), (i).

Chapter 24
Japan

by Yoshio Nomura

1. History and development of copyright

24.01 What might be termed the first comprehensive copyright law of Japan was enacted in 1899. The new Law repealed the former piecemeal legislation and consolidated it into a single statute. The old Laws were the Copyright Law 1869, prohibiting unauthorised reproduction of books, the Copyright Law of 1893, the Dramatic and Musical Copyright Law of 1887 and the Photographic Copyright Law of 1899. The new Copyright Law of 1899 could claim to have attained an international outlook. With its promulgation, Japan acceded to the Berne Convention of 1886.

Since then the 1899 Law had been amended on various occasions, principally in order to bring it into line with the Berlin Act (1908) and the Rome Act (1928) text of the Berne Convention, other amendments being of minor importance. After the 1939–45 war the Berne Convention was twice revised, in Brussels in 1948 and again in Stockholm in 1967, and, in 1961, the Rome Convention was signed. It was against the background of rapid technological change and of these international developments, that pressure was brought to bear in the 1960s in favour of a comprehensive revision of the then dated Copyright Law 1899.[1] The Japanese government asked the Copyright Council to prepare proposals for the revision of the law. The Council, after four years of lengthy discussion, made its recommendation for a comprehensive revision of the whole copyright system. The government submitted the General Revision Bill of the Copyright Law to the Diet in its session of 1969/70 which, after many days debate, agreed it without amendment. The new Copyright Law was promulgated in the Official Gazette on 6 May 1970 as Law No 48 and came into force on 1 January 1971, together with the associated Cabinet Decrees and Ministerial Ordinances.

The new Copyright Law of 1970 rests on certain fundamental principles, namely the improved protection of authors, the consolidation of neighbouring rights, and the encouragement of a wide dissemination of copyright works thereby making a contribution to the development of culture. The following amendments are perhaps worth noting as regards the special characteristics of the new Law: (i) specific remedies to enforce the authors' moral rights and copyright, (ii) recognition of performing rights in musical works fixed on phonograms, (iii) prolongation of the terms of protection, (iv) limitations on copyright, defined and circumscribed, such as private use (v) introduction of neighbouring rights, (vi) use of works by compulsory licence, (vii) settlement of disputes, (viii) civil and penal sanctions.

The new Law (Copyright Law of 1970) comprises 124 articles, as against the 66 of the former Law. In addition, the new Law contains 31 supplementary articles. The following arrangement of the Chapters of the new Law gives a general structure of the law:

Chapter I   General Provisions
  Section 1   General rules (articles 1 to 5)
  Section 2   Scope of Application (articles 6 to 9)
Chapter II   Rights of Authors
  Section 1   Works (articles 10 to 13)
  Section 2   Authors (articles 14 to 16)
  Section 3   Extent of the rights
    Subsection 1   General rules (article 17)
    Subsection 2   Moral Rights (articles 18 to 20)
    Subsection 3   Rights comprised in copyright (articles 21 to 28)
    Subsection 4   Ownership of copyright in cinematographic works (article 29)
    Subsection 5   Limitation on copyright (articles 30 to 50)
  Section 4   Term of protection (articles 51 to 58)
  Section 5   Inalienability of moral rights etc (articles 59 and 60)
  Section 6   Transfer and expiry of copyright (articles 61 and 62)
  Section 7   Exercise of rights (articles 63 to 66)
  Section 8   Exploitation of works under compulsory licences (articles 67 to 70)
  Section 9   Compensation (articles 71 to 74)
  Section 10 Registration (articles 75 to 78)
Chapter III   Right of Publication
Chapter IV   Neighbouring Rights
  Section 1   General rules (articles 89 and 90)
  Section 2   Rights of performers (articles 91 to 95)
  Section 3   Rights of producers of phonograms (articles 96 and 97)
  Section 4   Rights of broadcasting organisations (articles 98 to 100)
  Section 5   Term of protection (article 101)
  Section 6   Limitation, transfer, exercise and registration of the rights (articles 102 to 118)
Chapter V   Settlements of Disputes (articles 105 to 111)
Chapter VI   Infringements (articles 112 to 118)
Chapter VII   Penal sanctions (articles 119 to 124)
Supplementary provision.

---

1   It had been repeatedly pointed out that, owing to developments in means of reproduction and recording, as well as in publishing and broadcasting, the legislation made inadequate provision for the protection of authors' interests. The various restrictions imposed on copyright were also out of tune with the changed conditions.

2. Copyright

(a) Purposes of the copyright law

24.02   The purposes of the copyright law are to provide for 'the rights of authors and rights neighbouring thereto with respect to works of authorship as well as performances, phonograms and broadcasts, to secure protection of these rights, paying due regard to fair exploitation of these cultural products, and thereby to contribute to the development of culture'.[1]

1   Art 1.

(b) Definitions

24.03   While there were no definitions in the old Law, the new Law gives a number of definitions of the terms used.[1]

A *work* is defined as 'a production in which thoughts or sentiments are expressed in a creative way and which falls within the literary, scientific, artistic or musical domain'. This definition has the backing of Japanese legal thinking and case law although few other legislations have defined the contents of a work in terms of expressing thoughts and sentiments.

Joint works are defined as works created by two or more persons in which the contribution of each person cannot be separately exploited. The old Act made no distinction in respect of the possibility of separating the contributions to joint works. *Makers* of cinematographic works are defined as being those who take the initiative and responsibility for the making of the cinematographic works. *A cinematographic work* itself is not specifically defined but includes 'works expressed by a process producing visual or audiovisual effects analogous to those of cinematography and fixed in some material form' and therefore also includes telefilms, videotapes and the like made for television purposes because live television is not considered to be a cinematographic work.

The *recording* of the performance of a dramatic work and the recording of a broadcast of a dramatic work are within the definition of the '*reproduction*' of such a dramatic work. In practice the definition includes the recordings of stage performances of dramatic works or the broadcasting of such works.

Publication is the making available to the public a copy of the work or a translation of the work.

1   Art 2.

(c) Works of authorship protected by copyright

24.04   Works eligible for protection are as follows:

1. Works of Japanese nationals, including legal persons established under Japanese law;
2. Works first published in Japan, including simultaneous publications within 30 days; and
3. Works for which Japan has the obligation to grant protection in accordance with an international treaty.

The Copyright Law[1] lays down eight kinds of work eligible for protection; they are:

(i)   Novels, dramas, theses, lectures and other literary works;
(ii) Musical works;
(iii) Choreographic works and pantomimes;
(iv) Paintings, woodcut prints, engravings, sculptures and other works of art;
(v)   Architectural works;
(vi) Maps as well as plans, charts, models and other figurative works of scientific nature;
(vii) Cinematographic works; and
(viii) Photographic works.

News reports are expressly excluded from being a work of authorship[2]. However, some of the works in the list are defined in article 2. 'Works of art' include 'works of artistic craftsmanship', 'cinematographic works' are defined to include 'works expressed by a process producing visual or audiovisual effects analogous to those of cinematography and fixed in a tangible form' and 'photographic works' include 'works expressed by a process analogous to photography'.

Although not expressed in terms, material support for these works is not deemed necessary, in principle, in accordance with the general philosophy underlying the Copyright Law. There is an exception to this rule where the nature of the works naturally presupposes the existence of a material support, as in the case of cinematographic works and photographic works. For this reason live television broadcasts are not regarded as cinematographic works. As for choreographic works, fixations are not a prerequisite for protection.

Secondary or derivative works are protected. A derivative work is defined by article 2(1)(xi) as 'a work created by translating, arranging musically, transforming, dramatizing, cinematizing or otherwise adapting a pre-existing work'. A derivative work is protected independently of the original work, but protection of a derivative work shall not prejudice the right of the author of the original work.[3] A compilation is protected provided there is some originality in the selection or arrangement of the materials.[4] The rights of authors of component parts of the compilation are not affected.

The following works do not come under the purview of the Copyright Act: laws and regulations, notifications, instructions and the like of the organs of the state or local public entities; judgments or decisions and the like by judicial or administrative courts; translations of these works made by the organs of the state or local public entities.[5]

1   Art 10.
2   Art 10(2).
3   Art 11.
4   Art 12(1).
5   Art 13.

(d) Authors

24.05 An *author* is defined as 'a person who creates a work' and may be a natural person or a legal person. A legal person for the purposes of copyright laws includes unincorporated associations and foundations having representatives or administrators. When a work is created by an employee in the course of his duties and is published under the name of the employer then, unless it is stipulated to the contrary in a contract, work regulation or the like in force at the time of making the work, the employer owns the copyright in the work.[1]

While the old Law provided that 'copyright in a work published or publicly performed under the name of a governmental or public agency, school, shrine or temple, association, company, or any other organisation as its author, shall endure for 30 years from the time of publication or public performance',[2] its purport was not so clear as to the authorship of these works. The Copyright Law provides that the authorship of these works shall rest 'ab origine' with the legal person who is the employer, unless otherwise stipulated. It remains to be seen how far the new conception in respect of the employer/employee relationship will be resorted to by the various interests concerned when they realise the full implication of the new provisions.

As to the authorship of a cinematographic work, the new Law provides for the problem in the following way:

Copyright 603

'the authorship of a cinematographic work shall be attributed to those who, by taking charge of producing, directing, filming, art direction, etc., have contributed to the creation of that work as a whole, excluding authors of novels, scenarios, music or other works adapted or reproduced in that work; provided, however, that the provisions of the preceding Article are not applicable'.[3]

This article means that authors of pre-existing works, including novels, scenarios and music, are precluded from the authorship of a cinematographic work; the authors of creative contributions to the cinematographic work as such or so-called contributory authors are the authors of the cinematographic work. However, as will be seen below, copyright, ie an economic right in a cinematographic work, belongs to the maker of a cinematographic work, leaving only the moral rights in the hands of the contributory authors. News films and similar works which usually do not have contributory authors would come within the scope of the preceding article concerning a work made under the name of a legal person as laid down in the proviso clause in the clauses quoted above. Television fixations are assimilated to cinematographic works as already mentioned. Players and actors are not included among contributory authors. As contributory authors, such as directors, enjoy moral rights, the contents of cinematographic works may not be altered or curtailed without their authorisation. The editing of cinematographic works for showing on television requires the consent of the director and other persons concerned. Videocassettes are generally treated as cinematographic works.

1 Art 15.
2 Art 6.
3 Art 16.

Extent of the author's rights
24.06 (1) *General.* The author enjoys moral rights and copyright without formality.[1] The copyright system (both under the new and old Acts) is based on the dual theory of the rights of authors.

1 Art 17.

24.07 (2) *The moral rights.* Three kinds of moral rights are specified:[1]

1. The right to make the work public;
2. The right to claim authorship;
3. The right of preserving the integrity of the work.

In other words, the first refers to the right of publication, the second to the right of paternity and the third to the right to prevent alterations. In the case mentioned below where copyright in a cinematographic work belongs to the maker, it is presumed that contributory authors have consented to making the work available to the public.[2] Indication of the names of authors may be omitted in cases where there is no risk of causing prejudice and in so far as doing so is compatible with fair practice.[3] Changes may be made without the author's consent in the case of unavoidable modification determined by the nature of a work and the manner of use.

As to the nature of moral rights, the new Copyright Law clearly sanctions them as private rights, while the 1899 Law was not so clear in that respect.[4] Moral rights are personal, exclusive and inalienable[5] and, therefore, expire on the death of the author, but later protection of the interests involved in moral rights may be claimed by certain of his relatives by virtue of the provisions of the relevant Article in the Act.[6] Furthermore, users of works making them available to the public are prohibited, with civil and penal sanctions, from doing any act prejudicial to the moral rights of authors even after their death.[7] The right 'to have second thoughts' or of withdrawal[8] is recognised only in respect of the right of publication.

So far as the right to publish is concerned there are a number of presumptions, rebuttable by evidence of the author's contrary intention, concerning the author's consent in certain circumstances. The effect of these provisions is:[9]

(i) Where the author has assigned copyright in his work which has not been made public, offering to and making available to the public of such work in the exercise of copyright;

(ii) Where the author has assigned the original of his artistic or photographic work which has not been made public, making its original available to the public by exhibition; and

(iii) Where the ownership of copyright in his cinematographic work belongs to its maker, offering to and making available to the public of the work in the exercise of copyright.

The right to claim authorship provides that 'The author shall have the right to determine whether his true name or pseudonym should be indicated or not as the name of the author on the original of his work or when his work is offered to or made available to the public'.[10]

The author's right to 'protect the integrity of his work and its title against any distortion, mutilation or other modification against his will'[11] is subject to certain exceptions, namely:

(i) Change of letters or words or other modification which is necessary for school education when a published work is used in a school textbook under article 33(1) or in a radio or television programme for school education and its textbook is based on the curriculum under the relevant school education laws and regulations under article 34(1).

(ii) Modification of an architectural work by means of extension, rebuilding, repairing or remodelling.

(iii) Other modifications not falling under (i) or (ii) above which are necessary in view of the nature of the work and the purpose and manner of its use.

1   Arts 18–20.
2   Art 18(2) (iii).
3   Art 19(2), (3).
4   Art 18, 1899 Law.
5   Art 59.
6   Art 116.
7   Art 60.
8   'Droit de divulgation' see para 4.17 above.
9   Art 18(2).
10 Art 19.
11 Art 20.

24.08 (3) *The economic rights.* The author's economic rights, are a collection of rights to authorise the use of works of authorship in various different ways. These rights are set out in articles 21–28 and are as follows:

Right to reproduce a work (art 21);
Right to perform a work (art 22);
Right to broadcast or diffuse by cable a work (art 23);
Right to recite a work (art 24);
Right to exhibit a work (art 25);

Right to present publicly and distribute a cinematographic work (art 26); and Right to translate or adapt a work (art 27).

The Act provides that the author of an original work shall have the same rights as the author of a work derived from it in the exploitation of the derivative work.[1] The right of exhibition concerns the exhibition of the originals of artistic works and unpublished photographic works.[2] Television broadcasting of these works is not subject to this right of exhibition. As to the right of broadcasting, it is provided that:

(1) The author shall have the exclusive right to broadcast or diffuse his work by wire;
(2) the author shall have the exclusive right to communicate publicly, by means of a receiving apparatus, his work thus broadcast or diffused by wire.[3]

The most important right is the reproduction right, which is 'to reproduce in a tangible form by means of printing, photography, copying, sound recording, visual recording or other methods' and to include: (a) in the case of a play or a similar work to be used for a drama, acts 'to make sound or visual recording of the performance or broadcasting of such work'; and (b) in the case of an architectural work, acts 'to construct a structure in accordance with the architectural plan'. The cases cited by Professor Doi[4] illustrate the point:

In *Yamada and Max Blondel La Rougery v Nihon Case KK*[5] the defendant reproduced a part of the bird's-eye view map of Paris made by a French artist, Max Blondel La Rougery, and used it as a design for dress boxes and wrapping papers which it manufactured and sold. The map was entitled 'Plan de Paris a vol d'oiseau' and published in France in 1959 for use by tourists. The court held that this was an infringement and granted remedies to the plaintiff.

In *Machiko Hasegawa v Tachikawa Bus KK*[6] the defendant bus company copied the plaintiff's comic characters on both sides of the bodies of sightseeing coaches which it operated. The plaintiff was a leading female comic artist in Japan. Although the plaintiff asserted that her reproduction right was infringed, the court simply held that the defendant infringed the plaintiff's copyright in her comic strips and granted damages.

In *Tsuburaya Productions and KK Bullmark v Omori*[7] it was held that unauthorised use of fictional characters in three-dimensional toys is an infringement of copyright. However there has been no court decision holding that such an unauthorised use infringes the plaintiff's reproduction right.

The Copyright Council of the Cultural Affairs Agency considered the problem of reprography and without coming to a final conclusion indicated that a system of compulsory licensing against the payment of fees according to a tariff or a system of blanket licensing by an organisation of copyright owners may be the best solution. The Law[8] provides that the author shall have 'the exclusive right to perform his work for the purpose of making it seen or heard directly by the public'.

The copyright owner of a musical work has such an exclusive right both in the live performance of his work and in its public performance by phonograms (for instance by a jukebox).

The right of public communication of works broadcast or diffused by wire is a newly sanctioned right subject to certain limitations.

1 Art 28.
2 Art 25.
3 Art 23.
4 Professor Doi *The Intellectual Property Law of Japan* (1980) para 4.3.1.
5 Chosakuken Hanreishu 47, Chosakuken Kenkyu (No 8) 142 (1976) (Osaka Dist Ct, 27 April 1976).

6 Chosakuken Hanreishu 721, Hanrei Jiho (No 815) 28, Chosakuken Kenkyu (No 8) 163 (Tokyo Dist Ct, 26 May 1976).
7 Merchandising Rights Report, March 1973, p 12. (Urawa Dist Ct, Koshigaya Branch, 25 January 1973.
8 Art 22.

24.09 (4) *Cinematographic works.* Cinematographic works include televisual fixations, as stated above. The new Copyright Law solves this controversial problem in two different ways for the categories of (a) cinematographic works in general and (b) those made by broadcasting organisations themselves exclusively as technical means for broadcasting. The relevant article provides that:

'(1) copyright in a cinematographic work to which the provisions of Article 15 are applicable, shall belong to the maker of that work, provided that the authors of the work have undertaken to participate in the making thereof;
(2) in the case of a work of which a broadcasting organisation is the maker and which is made exclusively for broadcasting purposes and to which Article 15 is not applicable, the following rights comprised in the copyright therein shall belong to that organisation as the maker of the cinematographic work:
(a) The right to broadcast that work, and to diffuse by wire and communicate publicly on a receiving apparatus the work thus broadcast;
(b) The right to reproduce the work and to distribute its copies thus reproduced to other broadcasting organisations.'[1]

Thus, copyright in cinematographic works, as already referred to above in connection with article 16, in both categories (a) and (b) above, belongs to the maker 'ab origine'. However, in the case of category (a) the proviso covers the case of an undertaking to participate by contributory authors as stated before, while no such proviso exists as regards televisual fixations. The connotations of the term 'technical means' are wider than those usually accepted with regard to the ephemeral recording.[2]

1 Art 29.
2 The broadcasting organisations seem concerned at present about the fact that their rights thus acquired do not carry over the right of reproduction and distribution of video cassettes to non-broadcasting interests.

24.10 (5) *Limitations on copyright – fair use*
The limitations on copyright are a part of the policy of the Copyright Act to balance the two conflicting interests of authors on the one hand and the general public as 'users' on the other. The policy of balancing these interests is expressed in article 1: 'to secure protection of these rights, paying due regard to fair exploitation of these cultural products, and thereby to contribute to the development of culture'.

The Copyright Law provides for the following limitations in 18 separate articles:[1] reproduction for private use, reproduction in libraries, quotations, reproduction in school textbooks and the like, broadcasting in schools and other educational institutions, reproduction in examination questions, reproduction and similar use in Braille, performances which are not for profit, reproduction of articles on current topics, exploitation of public speeches and the like, reporting of current events, reproduction for judicial purposes, exploitation by means of translation and adaptation and so on, ephemeral recordings by broadcasting organisations, exhibition of an artistic work by the owner of the original thereof, exploitation of an artistic work located in open places, reproduction required for an exhibition of artistic and similar works. It is specifically provided that these limitations may not be interpreted as affecting the protection of an author's moral rights.[2] A number of these limitations are worthy of further explanation.

In the 1899 Law, reproduction for private use was permitted virtually in handwritten form only, thereby excluding the use of mechanical or electronic devices. Naturally, these provisions had not been strictly observed. The 1970 Copyright Law permits reproduction for personal or domestic use by means of modern reproduction equipment on condition that the user himself should make the reproduction. This restriction to private use does not extend beyond the personal and domestic spheres to such areas as reproduction in commercial firms, there being no provisions in the Copyright Law for reproduction for other internal uses, such as stipulated in the German Copyright Law.[3]

The Copyright Law introduced a remarkable innovation in respect of school broadcasting. A compulsory licence system permits the broadcaster to broadcast a work already published, in a school programme and also to reproduce it in teaching materials for such programmes.[4] Such use is authorised subject to the payment of an equitable remuneration.

Reproduction in the course of teaching is freely permitted, including even the video recording of school broadcasts.[5]

A work broadcast or diffused by wire may be communicated to the public freely by means of a receiver for non-profit-making purposes and if no admission fee is charged.[6]

In certain cases specified by the relevant articles,[7] the permitted use of works included the use of translations, adaptations, arrangements and other modifications.

Ephemeral recordings may be made by means of a broadcaster's own facilities or the facilities of other broadcasting organisations that are in a position to broadcast the same work. The latter refers to network broadcasting. Ephemeral recordings may be kept for six months after they have been made or broadcast.[8]

The owners of artistic works may publicly exhibit the works; however, they cannot permanently locate the works in open places;[9] permanently located original artistic works and works of architecture may be exploited by any means, with certain exceptions.[10]

Libraries may reproduce in the course of non-profit-making operations works of authorship contained in their materials in these circumstances:

(i) Where, at the request of the user and for his own research or study, he is furnished with a single reproduction copy of a part of a published work (or the whole of an individual work in a periodical upon expiration of a considerable length of time after its publication);
(ii) Where it is necessary for the preservation of library materials; and
(iii) Where, at the request of another library, it is furnished with reproduction copies of library materials which are not generally available because they are out of print or for similar reasons.[11]

1 Arts 30–47.
2 Art 50.
3 Art 54 of the German Law 1965.
4 Art 34.
5 Art 35.
6 Art 38(2).
7 Art 43.
8 Art 44.
9 Art 45.
10 Art 46.
11 Art 31.

(e) Term of protection

24.11 Copyright in a work comes into being at the moment of the work's creation[1] and now endures under the new Law for the term of 50 years 'post mortem auctoris' or 'post publicationem operis' according to the nature of the works,[2] instead of 38 years as under the 1899 Law. This standard term of protection applies equally to the right of translation. The reservations made by Japan under the Berne Convention in respect of translation will eventually be withdrawn.

The term of protection for an anonymous or pseudonymous work is fifty years after publication and in respect of a work created by a legal person or other entity is fifty years after its publication or fifty years after its creation, if it is not published. A cinematographic work is protected for 50 years from its publication or 50 years after its creation if it remains unpublished until that time.[3]

1 Art 510.
2 Arts 51–58.
3 Art 54(1).

(f) Transfer and expiry of copyright

24.12 The economic rights may be assigned in whole or in part[1], as opposed to moral rights which are inalienable. The right of translation and the right of adaptation in derived works not specifically transferred in a contract remain with the transferor.[2] The general position with regard to partial assignment or licence is not always clear under the Copyright Law. The position is illustrated by Professor Doi:[3]

> 'A good example is found in *K.K. International Music Publishers v Domei Suzuki et al.* In this case, the plaintiff "International Music Publishers", a Japanese music publisher, obtained an exclusive licence to publish in Japan a number of musical works of American composers from the copyright owner Music Publishers Holdings Corp. (MPHC) of the United States under a so-called "catalogue contract". The catalogue included Harry Warren's song "The Boulevard of Broken Dreams". The licence was granted for a period of two years subject to renewal. The agreement used the term "licence" throughout and granted to the plaintiff "sole and exclusive publication, mechanical, radio and small performing rights"; all other rights were reserved by MPHC. Under the agreement, copyright on the sheet music published by the plaintiff and the Japanese translation of the song was to be secured in the name of MPHC. The agreement provided that it should be interpreted in accordance with the law of the State of New York. The plaintiff brought an action for damages in the Tokyo District Court alleging that it was the copyright owner by assignment of Harry Warren's "The Boulevard of Broken Dreams" and that the defendant Domei Suzuki's "One Rainy Night in Tokyo" infringed upon the plaintiff's copyright. The court found that the copyright in question was assigned to the plaintiff by MPHC but dismissed the action on the ground that the defendant's music was not infringing.'

1 Art 61(1).
2 Art 61(2).
3 Doi *The Intellectual Property Law of Japan* para 5.1.

(g) Compulsory licences

24.13 A work already made available to the public may be broadcast by a broadcasting organisation – in cases where negotiations between the parties for broadcasting the work have been unsuccessful or could not take place – by virtue of a compulsory licence issued by the director of the Cultural Agency.

Payment by way of compensation must be made to the owner of the copyright in the work, the amount to be fixed by the director in consultation with the Copyright Council.[1] This is a more elaborate continuation of the similar system adopted under the 1899 Act.[2] However, no actual case of such compulsory licensing has occurred in the last 20 years.

The Copyright Law has also introduced the compulsory licence system for the recording of musical works on commercial phonograms. When three years have elapsed since a commercial recording was first put on sale in Japan, any person intending to manufacture a commercial phonogram by recording a musical work already recorded on such a phonogram may make the recording on the strength of a compulsory licence issued by the director of the Cultural Agency, if negotiations between the parties to record the musical work have been unsuccessful or could not take place. Payment to the copyright owner of the musical work must be made on the basis of the amount fixed by the director in consultation with the Copyright Council. The new system has been introduced to facilitate the free movement of musical works, avoiding a monopoly in such works by record companies.

1 Arts 67 and 71.
2 Art 25.

3. Relation between 'copyrights' and 'neighbouring rights'

24.14 As referred to above the consolidation of the neighbouring right system into the present Copyright Law of 1970 is one of the main features of the revised Law.

The rights granted under the Law are more extensive than those envisaged in the Rome Convention. Without the Rome Convention such a complete system would not have been adopted in Japan. The 1899 Act provided for 'singing and playing music' and 'instruments for the mechanical reproduction of sound' enjoying copyright protection, but the exact scope and extent was far from clear as the broad interpretation suggested by the wording was untenable in the light of the relevant legislative history. Since protection under the 1899 Law was weak and Japan wanted to join the Rome Convention, the new Copyright Law introduced a complete neighbouring rights system (Chapter 4) modelled on the Rome Convention.

The neighbouring rights system envisaged by the 1970 Law is introduced in article 1 which states the purpose of the new statute:

> 'The purpose of this law is, by providing for the rights of authors with respect to their works as well as for the rights of performers, producers of phonograms and the broadcasting organisations with respect to their performances, phonograms and broadcasts, to secure the protection of the rights of authors etc, having regard to a just and fair exploitation of these cultural products and thereby to contribute to the development of culture.'

The secondary use of phonograms is dealt with in article 95 as far as performers are concerned and in article 97 as far as producers of phonograms are concerned. The rights given to them are rights of equitable remuneration, not absolute rights. Japanese law makes a distinction between the absolute right of the producer of phonograms against the reproduction of his phonograms or the absolute right of the performer to allow or forbid the recording of his performance on the one hand, and a right to compensation by way of equitable remuneration for secondary use on the other hand. The right to equitable remuneration is a right akin to the right of an author to equitable remuneration where there is a compulsory licence in existence.[1]

1 See Art 89/5.

4. Protection of performers

24.15 Performers include not only those performing literary and artistic works but also similar performers of entertainments such as acrobats and jugglers. Conductors are included in the class of performers. *'Performance'* is defined in the Copyright Law[1] as meaning the acting on the stage, dancing, musical playing, singing, delivering, declaiming or the performing in other ways of a work, and includes similar acts not involving the performance of a work which have the nature of public entertainment.[2] *'Performers'* are defined as meaning actors, dancers, musicians, singers and other persons who give a performance as well as those who conduct or direct a performance.[3] It is not necessary for a performance to be a performance of a work of authorship.

The following performances are granted protection under the Copyright Law, namely:

(i) Performances which take place in Japan;
(ii) Performances fixed on phonograms mentioned in each item of article 8; and
(iii) Performances transmitted by broadcasts mentioned in each item of article 9, excluding those which are incorporated in sound or visual recordings before broadcasting with the authorisation of the performers.[4]

Performers are protected in respect of the recording (including the reproduction), the broadcasting and the wire diffusion of their performances.[5]

The secondary uses of phonograms giving rise to payment are limited to the use by the broadcasting organisations as well as wire diffusion services principally offering music.[6] There is no protection of phonograms against public performance, other than by broadcasting.

The Performer's right provided in article 92(1) is restricted in Article 92(2) to the following cases: (1) the direct broadcasting of live performances, (2) direct wire diffusion of live performances, (3) rebroadcasting of broadcasts of live performances, (4) broadcasting of wire diffusion of live performances, (5) broadcasting of unauthorised recording of performances, (6) wire diffusion of unauthorised recording of performances. In the cases referred in (1) and (5), where the initial broadcast is authorised by the performer in accordance with the provisions of article 94, broadcasting organisations connected with a relevant network have to pay remuneration to the performers. It is advisable for performers to make the appropriate stipulation in their initial contract with the broadcasting organisation or the wire diffusers, if they wish to control the subsequent use of their authorised performance for broadcasting or wire diffusion.

Under the provision of article 92(2) the exclusive right of the performer does not extend to the diffusion by wire of a performance already broadcast or to performances which have been incorporated in a cinematographic work (film sound tracks).

The Broadcasting Organisation may, unless stipulated otherwise, record performances which the performers have authorised them to broadcast, and may place the recording at the disposal of other broadcasting organisations for the broadcasting purposes. Broadcasting of these recordings gives rise to remuneration payable to the performers by the originating broadcasting organisation. Fixations thus made by the broadcasting organisation may be used not only for the initial broadcast but also for repeat broadcasts by the broadcasters to whom the fixations have been offered. Other broadcasting organisations may also retransmit programmes containing performances duly authorised by the performers and offered by the originating organisation. In practice, this permits the use of these fixations to produce a system of network broadcasting. In such cases of the use of fixations for retransmission, a reasonable remuneration must be paid to the performers concerned.

Payment for the use of commercial phonograms for broadcasting and wire diffusion (except for rebroadcasting or diffusion by wire) must be made to an association which must comprise a substantial number of performers and must be designated as a collecting society by the Commissioner of the Agency for Cultural Affairs.[7] The fees payable to the performers are quite distinct from those payable to the producers of phonograms. This means that the system in Japan in this respect does not adopt the so-called 'single remuneration principle' as envisaged in the Rome Convention.

The performer's right in the recording extends to the reproduction of the recording, giving the performer greater protection than that envisaged in the Rome Convention. The performer's right does not extend to other kinds of reproduction, eg photographs, whereas the right of the broadcasting organisation in article 98 does.

No provision is made for the protection of a performer's moral right. The only non contractual remedy a performer would have for distortion or unauthorised alteration would be an action for defamation.

1 Art 2(1) (iii).
2 Art 2(1) (iii).
3 Art 2(1) (iv).
4 Art 7.
5 Arts 91, 92.
6 Art 95(1).
7 Art 95.

5. The protection of producers of phonograms

24.16 Phonograms are defined as meaning fixations of sounds on discs, tapes and other material forms, excluding those intended for use exclusively with images.[1] Sound tracks of films and videograms are therefore excluded from the definition.

Producers of phonograms are defined as meaning those who first fix the sounds on phonograms[2] and commercial phonograms are defined as meaning copies of phonograms made for sale to the public.[3] A phonogram producer is protected even if the recording is not of a work of authorship.

The Copyright Law recognises the creative element in the initial fixation of sounds by excluding from the definition the pressing process. Thus the owner of a record pressing plant as opposed to the producer of the phonogram does not have a copyright. Broadcasting organisations or producers of cinematographic works are considered as the producers of phonograms when the former make recordings for the purpose of broadcasting and the latter when soundtracks of film are used in making phonograms.

Producers of phonograms are protected on the basis of the exclusive right to reproduce their phonograms,[4] that is the same protection as under article 10 of the Rome Convention. This provision is not applicable to phonograms listed in paragraph 3 of article 8 except in the case where relevant reproduction is made for the purpose of distribution.[5] This exception also relates to phonograms whose protection is mandatory for Japan under the provisions of the relevant international treaty: the Phonograms Convention. The exception was added when ratifying the Phonograms Convention for the purpose of retaining intact the ephemeral recording right of the broadcasting organisations.

The broadcasting right and the public performance right are operative where the broadcast or the performance is made from mechanical reproductions, that is phonograms. Under the 1899 Law, public performance and broadcasting of a musical work recorded on mechanical devices intended for reproduction had been free, subject to indication of sources.[6] Thanks to this limitation of rights, broadcasting organisations and organisers of public performances had long been exempted from paying regular royalties for the use of commercial phonograms to authors, performers and producers of phonograms in respect of their contributions. In the 1899 Law singing and the playing of music as well as recordings of sounds were regarded as the subject matter of copyright. As from 1 January 1971, broadcasters have to pay royalties for the use of recorded music, which is a significant event in the history of broadcasting in Japan. The Government Copyright Council recommended in this connection that the custom of free use of recorded music so long entrenched in Japan must be abandoned in a way that would not involve too sudden a burden on the interested parties. Pursuant to this recommendation, confirmed by the government and the debates in the Diet, the tariff for the use of recorded music, which was to be kept to a moderate level, has to be authorised by the Director of the Cultural Agency in accordance with the provisions of the Copyright Law and the Copyright Intermediary Law, and is subject to the approval of the Copyright Council.

Producers of phonograms have the right only to receive payment for the secondary use of phonograms and only from those broadcasting organisations and wire diffusion organisations which are principally broadcasting music.[7] The payment must be made to an association designated by the Commissioner of the Cultural Agency as stated below.

Producers of phonograms also have a right to equitable remuneration for the public performance of their phonograms in coffee shops or other establishments serving food and drinks to customers if they advertise the fact that their business includes entertainment by music, equally dance halls or night clubs with a dance floor for customers or establishments which show drama, dances etc to the accompaniment of music. However, ordinary coffee shops, hotels, pinball parlours and like establishments are exempted.[8]

1 Art 2(1) (v).
2 Art 2(1) (vi).
3 Art 2, para 7.
4 Art 96.
5 Art 96, para 2.
6 Art 30(8), 1899 Law.
7 Art 89(2).
8 Art 14 of the Supplemental Provisions to the Law of 1970.

24.17 *Connecting factors.* Phonograms protected under the Copyright Act are limited to the following cases: (1) phonograms composed of sounds first fixed in Japan; (2) phonograms the producers of which are Japanese nationals; (3) phonograms not falling under the preceding two items, to which Japan has the obligation to grant protection under an international treaty.[1] Item (3) was added by way of amendment in 1978 to cover the situation produced by the ratification of the Phonogram Convention which adopts the principle of nationality of the producer of phonograms as the criterion of protection.[2]

Foreign producers of phonograms are thus protected in Japan if the sounds are first fixed in Japan. Moreover, these phonograms are protected in Japan by criminal sanction.[3] This article makes it an offence to make in Japan an unauthorised reproduction of a commercial phonogram from a matrix the producer of which is not a Japanese national or which was not first fixed in Japan. The offence is also committed if someone distributes it in Japan without the authorisation of the foreign owner of the copyright in that phonogram.

1 Art 8.
2 Phonogram Convention, art 2; see para 9.05 above.
3 Art 121 (ii).

6. The protection of broadcasting organisations

(a) General

24.18 Broadcasting organisations have, with regard to their broadcasts, the exclusive right of reproduction, of rebroadcasting, of diffusion of their broadcasts by wire and of communication to the public, by means of a 'special instrument for enlarging images', their television broadcasts or those diffused by wire from those broadcasts.

Broadcasting is defined as meaning the transmission by radio communication intended for direct reception by the public.[1] 'Broadcasting organisation' is defined as meaning 'those who engage in the broadcasting business',[1] which covers both commercial and public service broadcasting.

Under article 9 broadcasts are protected under copyright law if they fall into either of the following categories:

(i) broadcasts transmitted by broadcasting organisations of Japanese nationality;
(ii) broadcasts transmitted from transmitters located in Japan.

1 Art 2(1) (ix).

(b) Right of reproduction

24.19 'Broadcasting organisations shall have the exclusive right to make sound or visual recordings of their broadcasts, and to reproduce by means of photography or other similar processes the sounds or images incorporated in their broadcasts or those diffused by wire from such broadcasts'.[1]

The reproduction right of the broadcasting organisation extends to both sound and visual recordings. A right in those recordings[2] covers the fixation of the sound and the sequence of images and their reproduction. This means that the protection of the broadcasting organisation against the reproduction of unlawful recordings of their broadcasts, covers not only the sounds but extends also to reproduction by means of photography including reproduction of such photographs.

1 Art 98.
2 Art 2(1) (xiii), (xiv).

(c) The right of rebroadcasting and diffusion by wire

24.20 The Copyright Law provides as regards this right that: '(1) Broadcasting organisations shall have the exclusive right to rebroadcast and to diffuse their broadcasts by wire; (2) the provision of the preceding paragraph shall not apply to the diffusion by wire which is made by a person who is required to do so under the provisions of laws and regulations.'[1]

The exception in paragraph (2) refers to the provision in article 13 of the Cable Television Law of 1972, which provides for several cases where reception by the general public is difficult and the Minister of Posts and Telecommunications may designate those places where the cable television organisations have to retransmit the relevant broadcasts made by the broadcasting organisations.

1 Art 99.

(d) The right to communicate television broadcasts to the public

24.21 The Law of 1970 provides as follows:[1] 'Broadcasting Organisations shall have the exclusive right to communicate to the public their television broadcasts.' This provision also applies to transmission by cable but only in the case of using enlarging apparatus of television broadcasts, such as Eidephore. The provision is a modified version of the article 13(d) of the Rome Convention.[2]

1 Art 100.
2 See para 8.35 above.

(e) The right of retransmission

24.22 The retransmission occurs either simultaneously or by means of a fixation of an original broadcast. The broadcasting law of Japan forbids the unauthorised retransmission by stipulating: 'Broadcasting Organisations shall not receive and retransmit the broadcast of any other broadcasting organisation unless their consent is obtained'. As a result of this law and the practice prevailing in Japanese broadcasting such simultaneous retransmission rarely occurs.

In Japan there exist several network services linking many stations and providing broadcast programmes through micro-waves, but these services do not correspond to the utilisation of a broadcast of the original broadcasting organisation in the neighbouring rights sense.

7. The protection of other related rights

24.23 There are two items which could be classed as related rights, because they are dealing with copyright matters, but which come under the heading of public law. In one case the public law is that governing broadcasting and wire diffusion (the broadcasting law and the cable television law), and in the other case criminal provisions directed at, what in Japanese law is an act of unfair competition, the illicit copying of foreign phonograms.

Under the broadcasting law a broadcaster has the exclusive right to authorise or forbid the rebroadcasting of his broadcasts. Similarly under the cable sound broadcasting law and the cable television law sound broadcasting and television organisations both have the exclusive right to authorise or forbid the retransmission of their broadcasts by cable diffusion. These provisions serve to protect the interests of these broadcasting organisations in a similar manner to the protection by neighbouring rights provided in the Copyright Law.

The second related right is a protection against record piracy. Article 121 of the Copyright Law does not confer a legal right in the strict sense but makes it an offence to reproduce a commercial phonogram made in Japan from a foreign produced matrix by anybody other than the Japanese licensee of the foreign producer. A prosecution for such an offence may only be brought upon the complaint of either the Japanese licensee or the foreign producer.[1] The provision does not confer a right but is designed to protect the Japanese producers, and is based on the law of unfair competition.

1 Art 123(1).

8. Collection and distribution of revenue from neighbouring rights (Collecting Societies, Tariffs Tribunal, etc)

(a) The collecting society for performers

24.24 As described above, broadcasting and wire diffusion organisations are required to pay a fee to performers in respect of performances embodied in the commercial phonograms broadcast. Payments of this secondary fee are governed by article 95(2) of the Copyright Law 1970, which provides that 'Where there is a Society or a federation of Societies which is composed of a considerable number of performers in Japan and which is designated by the Commissioner of the Agency for Cultural Affairs, the right to receive the fee shall be exercised exclusively through that Society'. The Commissioner may designate only such organisations as satisfy the following conditions (i) that it is a non-profit-making organisation; (ii) that its members are free to join it or not, or are free to withdraw from it; (iii) that its members are given equal voting rights and are eligible for election as officers of the organisation; (iv) that it has a sufficiently large membership to enable it to exercise its functions on behalf of the right owners. Such a society may not refuse the request of the right owners to exercise the right on their behalf. Upon receipt of such a request the society has authority to deal on behalf of the right owners in their own name with all matters concerning their rights. The Commissioner may ask such a society to report on their affairs or to submit its accounts. He can make recommendations to improve the administration of the society.

The amount of these fees is fixed each year by agreement between the society and the broadcasting organisations or their federation. If no agreement is reached the parties concerned may request the Commissioner of Cultural Affairs to issue a ruling fixing the amount of the secondary fee. The law provides that such an agreement between the society, which is a monopoly, and the Federation of Broadcasting Organisations or the broadcasting organisations, which may be monopolies, are exempt from the anti-trust laws.[1] This exemption is subject to the proviso that the trading methods are considered fair and reasonable and do not prejudice the legitimate interests of the enterprises concerned.[2]

1 Law relating to the prohibition of private monopoly and methods of preserving fair trade No 541 of 1947.
2 Art 95(3)-(11).

(b) The collecting society for producers of phonograms

24.25 There is a separate collecting society for the collection and distribution of the fees for producers of phonograms provided for under article 97 of the Law. This society is constructed on exactly the same lines as a collecting society for performers and the rules under (a) above apply to it mutatis mutandis.[1]

Cabinet Order No 35, 1970 makes detailed provisions applying to both types of collecting societies.[2] It provides for:

1. Notification of the recognition of a collecting society in the Official Gazette.
2. Administrative regulations of the societies.

3. The setting up of separate accounts of the fees collected for performers.
4. Yearly plans, budgets and reports to the Commissioner of the Agency for Cultural Affairs. The Commissioner may request the societies to render such reports as he deems necessary. He may decree the suspension or abrogation of services or the cancellation of the designation of the society as such a society. There is also a procedure for inviting a ruling by the Commissioner on the amount of the fee for secondary use.

1 Art 95(3)-(11).
2 Art 5 of Cabinet Order No 35.

9. Term of protection of neighbouring rights

24.26 Under article 101 of the Copyright Law the term of protection for the rights of performers, broadcasting organisations and producers of phonograms is twenty years computed from the end of the year following the date when the performance was given, when the first fixation of sounds of the phonogram was made, when the broadcast took place.

This term is in accordance with article 14 of the Rome Convention.[1]

If phonograms are made from the sound track of films, the starting point of the term is the date when the sounds are fixed on the sound track and not the date when the relevant sound track, which is part of the film, is made into a phonogram.

1 See para 8.36 above.

10. Limitation of neighbouring rights

24.27 The limitations applicable to copyrights are applicable to the neighbouring rights mutatis mutandis.[1]

In applying these provisions to particular cases one has to consider whether it is only a neighbouring right which has been infringed, or whether a copyright is being infringed at the same time. For example, in the case of a quotation, the relevant limitation does not allow the quotation from neighbouring right matters for the purpose of quoting copyright protected matters. A quotation could be made only if it is necessary to quote the performance, recording or broadcast, as, for example, in the case of a review (for broadcasting purposes). The source of the quotation has to be clearly indicated.

The limitations of copyright, such as the reproduction of articles on current affairs[2] or of political speeches,[3] are equally applicable to the broadcasting and the diffusion by wire of such works and to the communication of such broadcasts to the public.

1 Art 102. The relevant provisions are these: art 30 (reproduction for private use), art 31 (reproduction in library etc), art 32 (quotations), art 35 (reproduction in examination question), art 37, para 2 (recording for the purpose of lending such record for the purpose of the blind), art 38, para 1 (wire diffusion for non-profit making), art 41 (reporting current events), art 42 (reproduction for judicial proceedings), and art 44 (ephemeral recording by broadcasting organisations).
2 Art 39(1).
3 Art 40(1), (3).

11. Remedies for infringement

(a) Civil remedies

24.28 Chapter VI of the Copyright Law is concerned with infringement of rights, including neighbouring rights. The remedies provided for in this Chapter are purely civil remedies, being the right to demand the ceasing of the infringement, or the prevention of further infringements, and the right to recover damages.

Neighbouring rights owners may require the ceasing of any infringing act or any act likely to infringe their rights. In enforcing these rights they may demand that measures necessary to effect such ceasing or prevention of further infringement be taken. This includes the seizure of any infringing copy, of any object by which the infringing copies are made or any implements and tools used solely in connection with such infringement.[1]

The following acts are considered infringements of the neighbouring rights:[2] (i) importation into Japan, for distribution, of copies which would have been infringing copies if they had been made in Japan at the time of importation into Japan; (ii) the distribution of infringing copies (including those referred to in (i) above) by a person who is aware of such infringement.

Article 114 provides three rules. Firstly, when the infringer has profited from his infringement, the amount of such profits is presumed to be the amount of damages suffered by the plaintiff.[3] Secondly, the plaintiff may claim from the infringer damages equal to the sum that the plaintiff is normally entitled to receive for the exercise of his copyright or neighbouring rights.[4] Thirdly, the plaintiff may claim damages additional to the amount he is normally entitled to receive for the exercise of his copyright or neighbouring right and, in the absence of intent or gross negligence on the part of the infringer, the court may take this into consideration in the assessment of damages.[5]

These provisions of Chapter VI of the Copyright Law concerning infringement are part of the general civil remedies. Any other remedies not specifically mentioned in this Chapter may be available in accordance with the general principles of the Civil Code.

1 Art 112(2).
2 As well as of the copyright, moral rights and right of publication, art 113(1).
3 Art 114(1).
4 Art 114(2).
5 Art 114(3).

(b) Criminal provisions

24.29 Quite apart from any civil liability for infringement of neighbouring rights such infringements may, under Chapter VII of the Copyright Law, be punished by a sentence of imprisonment for a term not exceeding three years or a fine not exceeding 300,000 yen.

Criminal sanctions may extend to infringements committed outside Japan. Civil remedies, however, are only available in respect of those infringements of the civil law occurring in Japan. There is no specific provision for confiscation of infringing copies in the Copyright Law. This is covered in the general criminal law.

Where a quotation is used without indicating the source, an offence is committed punishable by a fine not exceeding 10,000 yen. Similar fines are provided for failing to quote the source in other cases of limitations of copyright and neighbouring rights. These offences are prosecuted on the basis that the act of infringement is contrary to public policy, consequently a complaint by the party whose rights have been infringed is not a necessary condition for a prosecution. However, offences against moral rights may only be prosecuted on the complaint of the injured party.

The Copyright Law provides measures of so-called 'double punishment' for offences committed by a representative, agent, employee or any other servant of a legal entity. In such a case fines can be imposed on both the legal entity and its representative, agent, employee or servant.

12. Protection of foreign right owners

24.30 Japan has adhered to the Phonograms Convention 1971 with effect from 18 September 1978. It has not yet adhered to the Rome Convention 1961 or to the Satellite Convention 1971.

Japanese law protects foreign performers if:

(i) the performance takes place in Japan; or
(ii) the performance is fixed on a phonogram protected in Japan; or
(iii) the performance is transmitted in a protected broadcast but, excluding those incorporated in a sound or visual recording prior to the broadcast with the authorisation of the performer.[1]

Japanese law protects foreign phonograms if:

(i) the producer is a Japanese national; or
(ii) the phonogram was first fixed in Japan; or
(iii) the phonogram does not fall within those two catagories but Japan has an obligation to grant protection under an international treaty, (ie the Phonogram Convention 1971).[2]

Foreign broadcasts are protected if:

(i) the broadcast is transmitted by a Japanese broadcasting organisation; or
(ii) the broadcast is transmitted from transmitters situated in Japan.[3]

1 Art 7.
2 Art 8.
3 Art 9.

13. Transitory provisions

24.31 The provisions of the 1970 Law relating to neighbouring rights do not apply to:

(i) performances which took place before the date on which the Law came into force;
(ii) phonograms composed of the sounds which were first fixed before the date on which the Law came into force;
(iii) broadcasts which took place before the date on which the Law came into force.

Thus with regard to such performances, phonograms and broadcasts the provisions of the old Law still apply.

The provisions relating to the neighbouring rights of the 1970 Law shall not, for the time being, apply to foreign performers who do not have permanent residence in Japan, provided that their performances do not fall within those referred to in (i) to (iii) above.

14. Plans for law revision

24.32 For the time being, there is no plan for revision of the law regarding neighbouring rights. However, when Japan accedes to the Rome Convention, some changes in the present copyright law may be considered although the present provisions of the copyright law are considered quite adequate for the implementation of the Rome Convention.

Chapter 25
Australia

by James Lahore

1. History and development of copyright

25.01 Australian copyright law has always followed very closely the copyright law of the United Kingdom. The first copyright law passed by the Australian Parliament after federation of the states as the Commonwealth of Australia in 1900 was the Copyright Act 1905. This Australian Act was passed pursuant to the concurrent power given to the Parliament, by s 51 of the Constitution, to make laws for the peace, order and good government of Australia with respect, inter alia, to copyrights, patents of inventions and designs, and trade marks: s 51 (xviii). This Act came into operation on 1 January 1907, and provided the first uniform copyright law for Australia. The Act retained the distinction made in the British Acts of 1833, 1842 and 1862 between 'copyright' in books and artistic works, the 'performing right' in dramatic and musical works, and the 'lecturing right' in lectures.

25.02 Colonial copyright law, and Australian law after federation, had supplemented Imperial Acts, and this concurrent system continued until 1912. After 1912 the Imperial British Act of 1911 applied in Australia pursuant to s 8 of the Copyright Act 1912. The imperial system was abandoned in the United Kingdom when the Copyright Act 1956 was passed. Thereafter, in 1958, the Attorney-General of the Commonwealth of Australia appointed a committee 'to examine the copyright law of Australia, and to advise which of the amendments recently made in the law of copyright in the United Kingdom should be incorporated into Australian copyright law and what other alterations or additions, if any, should be made to the copyright law of Australia'. The Chairman of the committee was Sir John Spicer and the committee is generally referred to as the Spicer Committee. The Report was completed in 1959 and it formed the basis of the Copyright Act 1968. Although the 1968 Act is similar in most respects to the United Kingdom Act of 1956 there are many differences which can cause confusion when reading English commentaries and cases. The 1956 Act was itself based upon the Report of The Copyright Committee, 1952 (Cmd 8662), commonly known as the Gregory Committee. This Report was also relied upon by the Spicer Committee in its consideration of the 1956 Act. The adoption of a new copyright law in the United Kingdom was a result of the revision at Brussels in 1948 of the Berne Convention, and the signing in 1952, of the Universal Copyright Convention. A principal term of reference of the Gregory Committee was a consideration of those changes in the law which should be made as a result of these Conventions. Similarly, in Australia, the Spicer Committee was concerned with the accession by Australia to the Brussels Revision of the Berne Convention and the Universal Copyright Convention.[1]

[1] Australia has now acceded to the Paris Act of the Berne Convention and the Paris Revision of the Universal Copyright Convention.

25.03 Another important reason for reform of copyright law in the United Kingdom was the need to provide a law which would take account of scientific and technical developments since 1911. In particular, the growth of broadcasting and television, the development of the film industry and of new methods of reproduction raised problems which were not foreseen in 1911. The Gregory Committee completed its Report in 1952 and the Report of the Spicer Committee was completed in 1959. To the extent that the 1968 Act reflects the thinking of the previous decade it was already somewhat out-dated at the time it was passed. The increased rate of technological change in the field of communications since the 1968 Act was passed has caused increasing dissatisfaction with many of the provisions of that Act. In Australia a committee was appointed in 1974 to examine the question of reprographic reproduction of works protected by copyright in Australia. The terms of reference of the committee were limited to the question of facsimile reproduction by processes such as photocopying ('reprography'), and there was no general review of copyright law. The Chairman of the committee was Mr Justice Franki. The Report of the committee was tabled in Parliament on 9 December 1976. As a result of this Report substantial amendments were made to the Copyright Act 1968 by the Copyright Amendment Act 1980, which introduced a statutory licence scheme for multiple copying in educational establishments.

25.04 The Copyright Act 1968 came into operation on 1 May 1969 and repealed, in s 6, all copyright legislation then in force in Australia, other than that relating to industrial designs. The subject-matter of copyright recognised by the 1968 Act comprises original literary, dramatic, musical and artistic works, and sound recordings, cinematograph films, radio and television broadcasts and published editions of works (typographical arrangements). Copyright in such material, whenever created, and whether published or unpublished, is now the subject of the 1968 Act. There is no longer a common law 'copyright' in unpublished works, and there is no state copyright legislation.

The effect of the close adherence of Australian copyright law to United Kingdom law has been the failure to develop a concept of the 'author's right' and a concentration on 'copyright' as a right of property.

2. Copyright – general principles

25.05 Copyright under the Copyright Act 1968 is the exclusive right to do, and authorise to do, in Australia, specified acts in relation to works and other subject matter for a limited term. The Act deals separately, in Part III, with 'works', and deals in Part IV with 'Subject-Matter other than Works'. A 'work' is defined in s 10 as a literary, dramatic, musical or artistic work, and copyright subsists in such a work if it is original and the requirements of s 32 in relation to the necessary connecting factor exist.[1] Subject matter other than works comprises sound recordings, cinematograph films, television and radio broadcasts and published editions of works. The copyright in this subject matter is in addition to, and independent of, any copyright subsisting in a work embodied in the recording, film, broadcast or edition: s 113(1). The Act does not specifically require that this subject matter should be original before copyright can subsist in it.

---

1   Section 32 provides as follows:
   (1)   Subject to this Act, copyright subsists in an original literary, dramatic, musical or artistic work that is unpublished and of which the author –
   (a)   was a qualified person at the time when the work was made; or

(b) if the making of the work extended over a period – was a qualified person for a substantial part of that period.
(2) Subject to this Act, where an original literary, dramatic, musical or artistic work has been published –
(a) copyright subsists in the work; or
(b) if copyright in the work subsisted immediately before its first publication – copyright continues to subsist in the work, if, but only if –
(c) the first publication of the work took place in Australia;
(d) the author of the work was a qualified person at the time when the work was first published; or
(e) the author died before that time but was a qualified person immediately before his death.
(3) Notwithstanding the last preceding sub-section but subject to the remaining provisions of this Act, copyright subsists in –
(a) an original artistic work that is a building situated in Australia; or
(b) an original artistic work that is attached to, or forms part of, such a building.
(4) In this section, 'qualified person' means an Australian citizen, an Australian protected person or a person resident in Australia.

25.06 The exclusive rights in relation to works are set out in s 31 of the Act. Copyright confers on the owner the exclusive right: (1) to reproduce the work in a material form; (2) to publish the work; (3) to perform the work, other than an artistic work, in public; (4) to broadcast the work, or, in the case of an artistic work, to include it in a television broadcast; (5) to cause the work to be transmitted to subscribers to a diffusion service,[1] or, in the case of an artistic work, to cause a television programme that includes the work to be transmitted to subscribers to a diffusion service; (6) to make an adaptation of a work (other than an artistic work); and (7) to do, in relation to a work that is an adaptation of another work, any of the acts previously specified. An adaptation of a work means a dramatisation or a fictionalisation of a literary work in a non-dramatic or a dramatic form, as the case may be, a picturisation (picture version) of a literary work, a translation of a literary work, and an arrangement or transcription of a musical work: s 10.

1 A diffusion service means essentially a cable transmission to subscribers to the service (see s 26).

25.07 In the case of sound recordings, cinematograph films, television and sound broadcasts, and published editions, copyright confers on the owner the exclusive right to reproduce or copy the copyright subject matter, and in addition, (1) to cause a sound recording to be heard in public, and to broadcast it; (2) to cause a cinematograph film to be seen or heard in public, to broadcast it, and to cause it to be transmitted to subscribers to a diffusion service; and (3) to rebroadcast a television or sound broadcast.

25.08 The copyright in a work or other subject matter is infringed by a person who does, or authorises the doing, of any act that the owner of the copyright has the exclusive right to do under the Act, without the licence or permission of the copyright owner: ss 36(1), 101(1). In addition, it is an infringement of copyright to import articles for commercial or trade purposes, or to sell or otherwise deal in articles, with knowledge that the articles would have infringed copyright if they had been made in Australia by the importer: ss 37 and 38; 102 and 103. It is also an infringement of copyright in a literary, dramatic or musical work to permit a place of public entertainment to be used for an infringing performance of the work in certain circumstances: s 39.

25.09 In a number of cases the Act provides that an act that would otherwise be an infringement of copyright is not an infringement. These exceptions are either absolute or are the subject of a compulsory or statutory licence.[1]

1 See para 25.43 below.

25.10 In order that copyright might subsist in a work or other subject matter within the protection of the 1968 Act it is not necessary for any copyright registration to be effected. In fact there is no provision for registration at all under the 1968 Act and there is no system whereby searching will disclose whether copyright subsists under it. Copyright now subsists in a work or other subject matter to which the 1968 Act relates, provided that there is the necessary connecting factor. This factor will depend on the particular work, the status of the author, the place of first publication or the place of making.[1]

1 See para 25.05 above.

25.11 The general scheme, in s 33(2) of the 1968 Act, is that copyright subsists in a work from the time it is made, and continues to subsist until the expiration of 50 years after the expiration of the calendar year in which the author died. There are certain exceptions to this general rule. Copyright in literary, dramatic and musical works, not published, publicly performed or broadcast during the life of the author, subsists until the expiration of 50 years after the expiration of the calendar year in which the first of these events happens: s 33(3) and (5). Copyright in photographs also subsists until the expiration of 50 years from the end of the calendar year in which first publication took place: s. 33(6). The same term of 50 years from the end of the calendar year in which first publication took place is applied in s 34, in relation to pseudonymous and anonymous works, and is also applied, in ss 93 and 94, in relation to sound recordings and cinematograph films. Copyright in a sound or television broadcast subsists until the expiration of 50 years after the expiration of the calendar year in which the broadcast was made: s 95(1). The only exception in the 1968 Act to the general period of 50 years is the period adopted for published edition of works. Copyright subsists in a published edition until the expiration of 25 years after the expiration of the calendar year in which the edition was first published: s 96.

25.12 The basic distinction made in the 1968 Act between copyright in original literary, dramatic, musical and artistic 'works', dealt with in Part III of the Act, and copyright in subject matter other than works, dealt with in Part IV of the Act, has particular significance in relation to the ownership of the copyright. In the case of works the general principle, in s 35(2) of the 1968 Act, is that the author of an original work is the owner of copyright in it. The principle is subject to certain exceptions with regard to: (1) the work of journalists, (2) photographs, portraits and engravings made on commission, (3) employment contracts, and (4) contrary agreement. However it is an essential feature of copyright under the Act that copyright in a work gives protection to the literary, dramatic, musical or artistic form which originates from an author. This concept of authorship does not apply to subject matter other than works. The 1968 Act does not recognise an 'author' of a sound recording, cinematograph film, television or sound broadcast, or published edition. The owner of the copyright in a sound recording is the person or company which owns the material (disc, tape, paper or other device) in which the sounds are embodied, unless there is an agreement to the contrary or the recording is made under commission: ss 97(2) and 22(3). This person is usually the recording company. In the case of a cinematograph film the producer is usually the copyright owner: ss 98(2) and 22(4). Copyright in a broadcast is owned by the broadcaster: s 99. Copyright in a published edition is owned by the publisher: s 100. There is no copyright protection for the performer, actor or director as such. In no case under Part IV of the 1968 Act is originality a specific requirement for subsistence of copyright. Copyright in subject matter other than works is not an author's copyright; it may be described more appropriately as a manufacturer's copyright.

25.13 Although the 1968 Act now governs all matters relating to copyright in original works and the other subject-matter of copyright, it is essential to understand the law of copyright as it existed under earlier legislation. The transitional provisions in the 1968 Act deal with two groups of copyright subject matter: that created before 1 May 1969, the date on which the 1968 Act came into operation, and that created before 1 July 1912, the date on which the British Copyright Act 1911 came into operation in Australia pursuant to s 8 of the Commonwealth Copyright Act of 1912. In the former case the transitional provisions of the 1968 Act to a substantial extent re-enact those provisions of the 1911 Act which still apply to material created between 1 July 1912 and 1 May 1969. In the latter case the treatment is different. Rights in works created before 1 July 1912 will in general only subsist under the 1968 Act if rights existed under the 1911 Act as a result of substitution, under s 24 of that Act, for rights existing under earlier legislation.

25.14 An action for infringement of copyright may be brought by the owner of a copyright or by an exclusive licensee (except against the owner of the copyright). The relief, apart from costs, available to a successful party in an action are: injunction, damages for infringement and also for conversion, additional damages, account of profits, and delivery up of infringing copies or plates used for making such copies.

25.15 The injunction is the remedy most often sought in infringement proceedings. It may be an interlocutory or a final injunction. It may be granted in respect only of the infringing part or parts of a work, and may be directed to a threatened future publication. The interlocutory injunction is an injunction granted before the trial of the action to ensure that the specified acts do not take place pending the trial and the final determination of the rights of the parties. The principles on which a court acts in granting interlocutory relief have been stated by the High Court in *Beecham Group Ltd v Bristol Laboratories Pty Ltd* (1967-8) 118 CLR 618. The court held that the test is one of probability of success at the trial. The court considers two questions. The first is whether the plaintiff has made out a prima facie case, in the sense that if the evidence remains as it is there is a probability that at the trial of the action the plaintiff will succeed. The court does not undertake a preliminary trial and grant relief upon a forecast as to the ultimate result of the case. The plaintiff, if he establishes a probability of success, will normally be entitled to have the status quo preserved. The second question is whether other considerations make it unjust to grant an injunction; whether the inconvenience or injury which the plaintiff would be likely to suffer if an injunction were refused outweighs or is outweighed by the injury which the defendant would suffer if an injunction were granted.

25.16 In addition to the injunction, a plaintiff may also claim damages for the infringement. The damages are in respect of a wrong done to an incorporeal right – the copyright – and the measure of damages in the depreciation caused by the infringement to the value of the copyright as a chose in action. However, damages are not recoverable from an infringer who is innocent – that is, who is not aware and had no reasonable grounds for suspecting that the act of infringement was in fact an infringement of copyright: s 115(3). This is an important limitation on the rights of a copyright owner or exclusive licensee.

25.17 The court may award additional damages for the infringement under s 115(4) if it is satisfied that it is proper to do so having regard to the flagrancy of the infringement, any benefit that has accrued to the infringer and all other relevant matters. The court may award such additional damages as it considers appropriate in the circumstances.

25.18 The Copyright Act 1968 also provides in section 116 that the copyright owner can bring an action for conversion or detention in respect of any infringing copies, or of any plates used to make such copies, as though he were the owner of the copies or plates. Section 10 provides that 'infringing copy' means a reproduction or copy the making of which constituted an infringement of copyright or, in the case of an imported article, would have been an infringement if it had been made in Australia by the importer.

25.19 The tort of conversion is essentially a denial, either expressly or by implication, of the plaintiff's right to possession of goods by doing an act inconsistent with that right, and in an action for conversion the plaintiff is asking the court to compensate him for his loss. The Copyright Act treats the copyright owner as having the right to possess infringing copies and plates for the purposes of the action and the measure of damages is the value of the copies and plates at the date of the conversion, not the depreciation caused by the infringement to the value of the copyright. The defendant has a defence to any claim for damages if he can prove that he was not aware, and had no reasonable grounds for suspecting, that copyright subsisted in the work or other copyright subject matter or that he reasonably believed that any infringing copies were not infringing copies: s 116(2).

25.20 Sections 132 and 133 of the Copyright Act 1968 provide for offences and penalties in relation to certain dealings with infringing copies of works if the articles are known to be infringing copies. These offences are concerned with the import, sale and distribution of articles that are known to be infringing copies of a work, making or having a plate knowing that it is to be used for making infringing copies of the work, and causing a literary, dramatic or musical work to be performed in public knowing that the performance constitutes an infringement of the copyright.

25.21 Where the offence is import, sale or distribution of an article which is an infringing copy, the penalty is a fine not exceeding $150 for each article to which the offence relates (or $1500 for each copy of a cinematograph film). If it is not a first conviction there is an additional penalty of possible imprisonment for a maximum period of six months. The maximum fine in any one transaction is $10,000 before the Federal Court or $1500 before any other court. The court may also order the destruction or delivery up of any plate or recording equipment used for making infringing copies.

25.22 The concept of the 'droit moral' as recognised in article 6 bis of the Paris Act of the Berne Convention is not fully accepted in Australian copyright law.

There was considerable debate in Australia before the passing of the Copyright Act 1968 as to whether these rights were strictly within the concept of copyright, and whether it would be within the constitutional power of the federal government to pass a law including such rights under its power to make laws with regard to 'copyrights'. The Copyright Law Review Committee 1959 (the Spicer Committee) was nevertheless prepared to recommend the inclusion of appropriate provisions in the new Copyright Act on the ground that the provisions would not be inappropriate in a Copyright Act, and that the federal government could possibly rely on other powers in order to implement the provisions of article 6 bis if they were otherwise considered to be not with the copyright power. It was also considered that existing common law remedies might not be adequate to deal with the matter. After the report of the Spicer Committee had been completed the Stockholm Act (1967) of the Berne Convention extended the rights secured by article 6 bis of the Convention to the term of the copyright in a work instead of the lifetime of the author. This change was taken into account in drafting the provisions of the 1968 Act. The result of the recommendations of the Committee is that the 1968 Act, while not giving the author a general 'moral right', does provide in ss 189-195 that certain duties are owed to an author of a literary, dramatic, musical or artistic work in which copyright subsists.

25.23 The sections of the Copyright Act referred to give rights to authors that continue while copyright in the relevant work subsists, whether the author is also the copyright owner or not, to prevent or obtain damages for the following:

1. falsely attributing authorship to a work or a reproduction, including performing in public or broadcasting a work as the work of another, knowing that this is not so;
2. falsely and with knowledge representing a work as an adaptation of the work of another;
3. publishing or dealing in a reproduction of an artistic work as being a reproduction made by the author when it is not and this is known;
4. publishing or dealing in a work or reproduction of such work of the author when the work has been altered by someone other than the author and this is known.

These provisions only recognise the right of integrity to the extent that certain alterations of the work in the nature of 'passing off' can be prevented, but there is no general recognition of the right of integrity, nor is there such a recognition of the paternity right, for example a right to recognition of authorship such as by credits, as distinct from a false attribution of authorship.

3. Relation between 'copyright' and 'neighbouring rights'

25.24 The concept of a 'neighbouring right' does not exist in Australian law. In this respect Australian law is similar to British law.

Sound recordings (phonograms), cinematograph films and television and radio broadcasts are protected under the Copyright Act 1968 as subject matter of copyright, although, as previously indicated, no copyright protection is given to performers. The Copyright Act does, however, clearly distinguish between copyright in original literary, dramatic, musical and artistic works in Part III of the Act, and copyright in subject matter other than works in Part IV of the Act. This subject matter is a reference to sound recordings, cinematograph films, broadcasts and published editions of works (typographical arrangements).

It should be pointed out that in Australia the Australian government does not have unlimited powers. Under s 51 (xviii) of the Australian Constitution the Parliament has power to make laws with respect to 'copyrights, patents of inventions and designs, and trade marks'. A question, therefore, has been whether the protection given by the Copyright Act to sound recordings and, in particular, to broadcasts, can be said to come within the concept of 'copyright'. It is possible that other powers of the federal government may justify the protection given, but legislative difficulties are caused in Australia to the extent that rights in such material are regarded not as copyrights but as related rights. Constitutional restrictions on Australian government power have also proved a stumbling block in getting some protection for performers by appropriate legislation.

4. The protection of performers

25.25 In one sense the question of the nature of the rights of performers in their performances is an easy one to answer in Australia for the reason that so far as copyright law is concerned there are no rights and the only legal protection a performer has in his performance, apart from contract, is that which may be given to prevent passing off (unfair competition) or breach of confidence in appropriate circumstances, or that which is provided by the law of libel. But these actions relate to the protection of a business goodwill, a particular relationship, or reputation and are not directed to copying or misappropriation as such, or to dissemination for profit.

The Spicer Committee considered protection for performers involved in the making of recordings and broadcasts and considered that these performers should receive a greater share in the proceeds from these undertakings than they had previously received.[1] The Committee was certainly sympathetic to the claims of such performers and was in favour of the enactment of provisions similar to those contained in the British legislation at that time, namely the Dramatic and Musical Performers' Protection Act 1958. This Act was amended, after the Spicer Committee report in 1959, in 1963 and 1972. However, the Committee, although considering that such provisions were desirable, felt unable to make specific recommendations because of what it considered to be constitutional restrictions on Commonwealth power. For the same reason the Committee felt that it could not recommend the grant to performers of a right in the nature of copyright. In addition the Committee noted that the Gregory Committee in England had rejected claims by performers for new rights on the ground that the concept of copyright in British law had always involved something in a recognisable material form.

Although the report of the Spicer Committee was completed in 1959 it was not until 1968 that the present Copyright Act was passed. As a result the question of whether Australia should implement the provisions of the Rome Convention 1961 in the new copyright legislation arose for consideration. The interesting result was that whereas the provisions relating to the protection of phonograms (or sound recordings) and of broadcasts have been implemented in the Copyright Act 1968, the protection for performers was expressly omitted when the Bill was before the House of Representatives for the second reading. Nigel Bowen, the then Attorney-General, gave the following reasons for this omission:

> 'The present Bill will give effect to that Convention (Neighbouring Rights Convention) in so far as it relates to records and to broadcasts, it being appropriate to deal with these matters in a Copyright Bill. The matter of performers is dealt with separately in the United Kingdom by legislation of a different character. It has not yet proved possible to devote attention to the task of examining what legislation should be enacted in Australia to give effect to those provisions of the Neighbouring Rights Convention relating to performers. I understand, however, that there is as yet no substantial problem caused by the broadcasting or recording of performances

of musical and dramatic works in Australia without the prior approval of the performers themselves.'

Since that time proposals for legislation to give protection to performers have been under review and a Bill was prepared for submission to Parliament some years ago but it was not proceeded with.

1 See Report, paras 472-477.

5. The protection of producers of phonograms

25.26 In Section 10 of the Copyright Act 1968 'sound recording' is defined as meaning the aggregate of the sounds embodied in a record, and a 'record' as meaning a disc, tape, paper or other device in which sounds are embodied. The term 'record' therefore denotes the material substance in which the sounds are embodied, the two together constituting the recording. The definition, by its terms, includes not only gramophone records but also magnetic tapes, cassettes and cartridges. The definition also includes the 'phonogram' as defined in the Rome Convention of 1961 and the Geneva Convention of 1971. By section 24, sounds are regarded as 'embodied' in a record for the purposes of the Act if the sounds are capable of being reproduced from the record with or without the aid of some other device. A sound track of a film is deemed not to be a sound recording, this being the subject matter of an independent copyright in relation to a cinematograph film, as provided in s 23(1).

The owner of any copyright subsisting in a sound recording is the maker of the sound recording unless a person makes a contract with another for that other person to make a sound recording. In that case the person giving the commission is the owner of the copyright, provided that there is valuable consideration and that there is no agreement to the contrary: s 90.

A sound recording is deemed, by s 22(3), to have been made at the time when the first record (ie the disc, tape, paper or other device) embodying the recording (ie the aggregate of the sounds) was produced, and the maker is the person who owned that record at the time, not the artists or the technicians or anyone else responsible for the recording. Thus a recording will be 'made' when the matrix is made, and the maker will usually be the producer or recording company that owns the particular disc, tape, paper or other recording material.

Understandably the term 'author' is not used in the Copyright Act 1968 in relation to recordings or broadcasts since the copyright is not an author's copyright in the sense in which author is used in relation to original literary, dramatic, musical or artistic works. The correlative of authorship, namely originality, is also not a requirement for subsistence of copyright, except presumably to the extent that copyright would be denied to a disc dubbed from another disc in infringement of copyright.

Copyright in relation to a sound recording (phonogram), under s 85 of the 1968 Act, is the exclusive right to do all or any of the acts of: (1) making a copy of the recording, (2) causing the recording to be heard in public and (3) broadcasting the recording.

The reproduction right in sound recordings is limited to the actual copying or dubbing of a recording by making another device such as a tape embodying the sounds recorded on that recording. The act may be done by directly or indirectly making use of a record embodying the recording: s 101(3).

A sound recording can be caused to be heard in public by directly or indirectly making use of a record embodying the recording: s 101(3). In addition to the obvious case of playing a record in public by the use of playback equipment, a recording may be caused to be heard in public by the operation of a receiving apparatus to which the sounds are conveyed by the transmission of signals by wire or wireless telegraphy. In such a case the operation of any apparatus by which the signals are transmitted, directly or indirectly, to the receiving apparatus does not constitute causing sounds to be heard: s 27(3). Where a recording is caused to be heard by the operation of a receiving apparatus or any apparatus for reproducing sounds by the use of a record, the occupier of the premises where the apparatus is situated is considered to be the person causing the recording to be heard if the apparatus is provided by or with his consent, whether he is the person operating the apparatus or not: s 27(4). However, in further limitation of the public 'performance' right in sound recordings, s 199(2) of the 1968 Act provides that it is not an infringement of copyright in a sound recording to cause it to be heard in public by the reception of a television or sound broadcast.

The public performance right and the broadcasting right are separate and distinct rights, and broadcasting does not constitute performance or causing sounds to be heard, even though the sound recording is caused to be heard by the operation of a radio or television receiver: s 27(2) and (3). A sound recording may be broadcast by way of a secondary broadcast. If this secondary broadcast is made by receiving and simultaneously making a further transmission of the primary broadcast transmission, or of a transmission made otherwise than by way of broadcasting (ie by wireless telegraphy), but simultaneously with the primary broadcast transmission, the use of the recording for the secondary broadcast is ignored for purposes of the 1968 Act: s 25(3).

There is no diffusion (cable transmission) right in sound recordings.

The second and third of the exclusive rights – 'performing' right and the broadcasting right – have been the subject of considerable controversy in Australia not only with regard to giving to the copyright owner in a sound recording such rights at all, but also, since the passing of the 1968 Act, with regard to royalty payments by the commercial broadcasters for the playing of discs on radio. These rights would oblige a person playing the record in public or broadcasting it to obtain the licence of the owner of copyright in the record in addition to that of the owner of copyright in the work recorded. These rights are, however, subject to very important limitations which are discussed below.[1]

It is also important to note that copyright in sound recordings, cinematograph films, and television and sound broadcasts is a copyright that subsists independently of, and in no way affects or detracts from, copyright in original literary, dramatic, musical and artistic works. Thus infringement of the copyright in a sound recording or in a television broadcast may also constitute infringement of, for example, the copyright in the music embodied in the record or the dramatic work being broadcast by television. But this will not necessarily be the case. Each copyright is independent, and questions of copyright subsistence and infringement will in each case depend upon the provisions of the Act relating to each separate subject matter of copyright.

1 See paras 25.36 et seq below.

6. The protection of broadcasting organisations

25.27 A 'television broadcast' is defined in section 10 as meaning visual images broadcast by way of television, together with any sounds broadcast for reception along with those images, and a 'sound broadcast' means sound broadcast otherwise than as part of a television broadcast. The references to 'broadcast' and 'broadcasting' mean broadcast and broadcasting by wireless telegraphy, and 'wireless telegraphy' means the emitting or receiving, otherwise than over a path provided by a material substance, of electromagnetic energy. A reference in the 1968 Act to broadcasting includes broadcasting both by radio and television, unless the contrary is stated.

Thus broadcasting refers to the usual form of radio and television broadcasting where the emission and reception of the signals is not over a material path and is to be contrasted with the transmission of material to subscribers to a diffusion service. This form of transmission takes place by way of distribution of broadcast or other matter over wires or other paths provided by a material substance, to the premises of subscribers to the service. Broadcasting does not therefore include cable transmissions.

The Australian Broadcasting Commission or the Special Broadcasting Service is the owner of any copyright subsisting in a television or sound broadcast made by it. In the case of other broadcasts the copyright owner is the person who made the broadcast and who is or has been the holder of a licence for a television or broadcasting station, or who is a prescribed person being the holder of a wireless telegraphy licence when the broadcast was made: s 90. A television or sound broadcast is deemed to be made by the person who transmits at a particular time and place the visual images or sounds constituting the broadcast.

Copyright in relation to a television or sound broadcast, under s 87 of the 1968 Act, is the exclusive right, (1) to make a cinematograph film of a television broadcast in so far as it consists of visual images, or a copy of such a film, (2) to make a sound recording of a sound or television broadcast, in so far as the latter consists of sounds, or a copy of such a recording, (3) to rebroadcast a television or sound broadcast. These acts comprised in the copyright refer to acts done by the reception of the broadcast, or by making use of any article or thing in which the visual images and sounds comprised in the broadcast have been embodied, such as a videotape: s 101(4). There is no public performance right and no diffusion right in broadcasts.

The making of a film of a television broadcast includes a film or photograph of any of the visual images comprised in the broadcast, and any reference to a copy of the film includes a reference to a copy of the film or a reproduction of a photograph of any of those images: s 25(4). The effect of these provisions is that a film or photograph of any part of a television broadcast is an exclusive right of the copyright owner even though there is no 'sequence of images'. The taking of a single picture would therefore be an act comprised in the copyright.

Broadcasting refers to television and sound broadcasting by wireless telegraphy. The exclusive right includes rebroadcasting, not only by the reception of a broadcast, but also by making use of a disc, tape or any other article or thing in which the sounds and images of the broadcast have been embodied: ss 101(4) and 24.

There is no 'performing right' in broadcasts – that is, a right to cause the broadcast to be seen or heard in public by a paying audience – despite the recommendation of the Spicer Committee that such right should be included in the copyright law.[1]

There is also an exception in section 111 of the 1968 Act in respect of films or records of broadcasts made for the private and domestic use of the maker. The making is not for private and domestic use if it is for the purpose of the sale or letting for hire of a copy of the film or record; broadcasting the film or recording; or causing the film or recording to be seen or heard in public. To this extent the broadcast cannot be 'performed' in public.

---

[1] Report, paras 297, 298.

7. The protection of other related interests

25.28 Copyright is given by the Copyright Act 1968 not only to sound recordings and broadcasts but also the published editions of works or typographical arrangements.

Copyright in relation to a published edition of a literary, dramatic, musical or artistic work or works, under s 88 of the 1968 Act, is the exclusive right to make, by a means that includes a photographic process, a reproduction of the edition. No other exclusive rights are given by the 1968 Act. The first owner of the copyright is the publisher.

An edition of a work is published if reproductions of it are supplied to the public whether by sale or otherwise: s 29(1). The definition of reproduction in s 21 of the 1968 Act only applies to works, and the exclusive right to make a reproduction of an edition appears to mean the right to make an exact copy of an edition, such as a photographic reprint of a published work.

The duration of the copyright is only 25 years from the end of the calendar year in which the edition was first published: s 96.

8. Collection and distribution of revenue from related rights

25.29 An important innovation in the Copyright Act 1968 has been the establishment of a copyright tribunal with a wide jurisdiction to determine matters in relation to the grant of copyright licences and the determination of royalties and remuneration. A similar tribunal called the Performing Right Tribunal was established by s 23 of the Copyright Act 1956 (UK). The tribunal established by the Australian Act has a wider jurisdiction but in general the provisions are based upon those in the 1956 Act in England. There are three important licensing organisations in Australia, the Australasian Performing Right Association Ltd (APRA), the Phonographic Performance Company of Australia Ltd (PPCA), and the Australasian Mechanical Copyright Owners Society (AMCOS).

The Australasian Performing Right Association Ltd was founded in 1926 and is an association of authors, composers, and music publishers. Members of APRA assign to the Association the right to perform their works in public, the right to broadcast their works and the right to cause their works to be transmitted to subscribers to a diffusion service. As a prospective owner of copyright can assign the future copyright under s 197 of the Copyright Act 1968 members of APRA cannot effectively assign to another person the above rights in works composed after the assignment to APRA. Similarly, they cannot enter into employment contracts or undertake commissions whereby performing, broadcasting or diffusion rights which have been assigned to APRA are to vest in employers or persons giving the commission who are not members of APRA. Licences granted by APRA do not extend to (1) performances in their entirety of dramatico-musical works, such as operas, operettas, musical plays and musical comedies; oratorios; or choral works exceeding 20 minutes of performance; and to (2) the performance of any excerpts from any such dramatico-musical works or of the whole or any part of a choreographic work, if accompanied by stage costume or scenic accessories or dramatic action.

APRA is affiliated with similar associations in other countries such as the Performing Right Society Ltd (PRS) in the United Kingdom, the American Society of Composers, Authors and Publishers (ASCAP) in the United States, and Société des Auteurs, Compositeurs et Editeurs de Musique (SACEM) in France. These associations grant reciprocal rights to each other and a licence granted by APRA authorises the use of its entire repertoire which comprises almost all copyright music performed in Australia. APRA publishes a Repertoire Guide but a complete list of works controlled by APRA is not available. Standard licensing schemes and tariffs are available for cinemas, dance studios, dance halls, jukeboxes, skating rinks, theatres, background and music systems, radio and television sets, hotels, clubs, restaurants, sports meetings, processions, concerts, recitals, revues, etc. APRA has concluded licence agreements not only with individual users of music but also with the Australian Broadcasting Commission, commercial broadcasting and television stations and cinemas. Fees are assessed on the basis of 'box office' or amounts received, or a flat fee is charged if this is appropriate. Fees are distributed amongst members, after deduction of administrative expenses, on the bases of returns prepared by APRA's principal licensees.

The Phonographic Performance Company of Australia Ltd was established in 1969 to control the rights in sound recordings to cause the recording to be heard in public and to broadcast the recording. The members are producers and manufacturers of sound recordings. PPCA is closely associated with The Australian Record Industry Association established to promote the interests of manufacturers, importers and distributors of sound recordings. The operations of PPCA are limited by the compulsory licensing provisions in ss 108 and 109 of the Copyright Act 1968 which apply to the public performance and broadcasting rights in sound recordings.

The Copyright Owners Reproduction Society Ltd was established in 1956 to protect the interests of Australian music publishers who constituted its membership. On 29 November 1973 its name was changed to Australian Music Publishers Association Limited (AMPAL). Subsequently, the Australasian Mechanical Copyright Owners Society (AMCOS) was formed to take over from AMPAL as the collection society.

AMCOS operates as a centralised licensing office for 'mechanical rights' comprised in musical copyright, ie rights to reproduce musical works (and accompanying words) in various forms, including discs, tapes, video recordings, and cinematograph films. Its licensing activities are mainly restricted to miscellaneous usages, such as recording by radio and television broadcasters, smaller commercial record manufacturers, importers of records, documentary and non-feature films etc. In the case of some works, wider rights are held.

An ancillary activity is the licensing of mood-music sound recording libraries owned by some music publishing houses, so as to permit re-recording by commercial users.

Recording usages outside the authority of AMCOS are licensed direct by the copyright owners, usually a local music publisher.

AMCOS holds its rights by agreements with music publishers, composers and lyric writers, and other copyright owners. It also has direct agreements with similar organisations overseas, and its repertoire of music extends worldwide. Its licensing territory covers Australia and New Zealand, Fiji and Papua New Guinea (when applicable).

The provisions relating to the tribunal are contained in sections 136–175 and 232 of the Copyright Act 1968, and in the Copyright Tribunal (Procedure) Regulations 1969. The tribunal consists of five members. A member of the tribunal must be a justice or judge of a federal court, of the Supreme Court of a state, or a barrister or solicitor of not less than five years' standing. The jurisdiction of the tribunal is exercised in three principal areas: firstly, in cases where a royalty or equitable remuneration must be determined for the exercise of a particular right; secondly, in cases relating to licence schemes; and thirdly, in cases where an individual requires a licence and there is no licence scheme in operation.

The various heads of jurisdiction may be summarised as follows:

(1) Royalties and remuneration

25.30 (a) An inquiry in relation to the royalty payable for the compulsory licence to manufacture records of musical works: s 148.

(b) Applications to determine equitable remuneration for the making of a record or film of a work for certain broadcasting purposes: s 149. It is not generally an infringement of copyright in a work to make a recording or film of it for the purposes of a subsequent 'ephemeral' broadcast if it were not an infringement of copyright to broadcast the work in the first place. But equitable remuneration must be paid to the copyright owner if the recording or film is subsequently broadcast by someone other than the maker of it.

(c) Applications to determine equitable remuneration for the making of a copy of a sound recording, again for certain broadcasting purposes of the same nature as those referred to in (b) above: s 150.

(d) Applications to determine equitable remuneration in respect of the public playing of a recording where the compulsory licence for public performance is exercised: s 151.

(e) Applications to determine the amount payable by a broadcaster of a sound recording where the compulsory licence for broadcasting is exercised: s 152. However, the tribunal cannot make an order requiring a commercial broadcaster to pay an amount exceeding 1% of the amount determined by the tribunal to be the gross earnings of the broadcaster during the relevant period in which the order applies: s 152(8). Provisions also limit the amount the Australian Broadcasting Commission can be required to pay assessed on a population basis: s 152(11).

(f) Applications to apportion equitably the royalty payable in respect of a recording of a musical work which includes a literary or dramatic work under different copyright ownership and which is made pursuant to the compulsory licence provisions relating to the recording of musical works: s 153.

(g) Applications under s 149A for determination of an equitable remuneration to be paid to the owner of copyright in a work for making multiple copies under the statutory licence by educational institutions: s 53B, or for handicapped readers: s 53D.

(2) Licence schemes

25.31 A licence scheme, for the purposes of the Copyright Act 1968, is essentially a scheme such as that operated by APRA whereby it stipulates the charges and conditions upon which licences will be granted on behalf of its members. A scheme may be formulated by a licensor or by licensors on their own behalf or on behalf of other persons on whose behalf the licensor or licensors are acting.

The jurisdiction of the tribunal in relation to licence schemes comprises:

(a) reference of a proposed licence scheme to the tribunal by the licensor: s 154.

(b) reference of an existing licence scheme in the event of a dispute with respect to the terms of the scheme between the licensor operating the scheme and an organisation claiming to be representative of persons requiring licences in cases included in a class of cases to which the scheme applies, or between such licensor and any person who claims that he requires a licence in cases included in the class referred to. The licensor, organisation or person concerned may refer the scheme to the tribunal: s 155.

(c) further references of a licence scheme to the tribunal where an order has previously been made under (a) or (b) above: s 156.

(d) applications to the tribunal where a licence scheme applies and a licence has been refused or the charges or conditions are unreasonable: s 157(1), (2).

(3) Cases where there is no licence scheme

25.32 It is now possible under the 1968 Act for an individual or organisation requiring a licence, when there is no licence scheme in operation, to apply to the tribunal if he has not been able to obtain a licence, and it is unreasonable in the circumstances that the licence should not be granted, or if the licence will only be granted subject to charges or conditions that are unreasonable: s 157(3), (4). The tribunal can make an order, after hearing all parties, specifying the charges and conditions that the tribunal considers to be reasonable.

A licence for the purposes of the jurisdiction of the tribunal is defined in s 136(1) of the 1968 Act. Essentially the jurisdiction is limited to licences for performing and broadcasting rights in works and licences for 'performing' sound recordings in public or copying sound recordings for broadcasting purposes.

25.33 Matters now before the tribunal include a number of applications by sound recording companies and PPCA requesting the tribunal to determine the amounts payable by seven commercial FM broadcasters in respect of the broadcasting of published sound recordings: s 152, and the reference of a proposed licence scheme by APRA in relation to the Australian Broadcasting Commission and the Special Broadcasting Service: s 154.

9. Term of protection

25.34 Sound Recordings. The 1968 Act makes a distinction between sound recordings made before the commencement of the Act on 1 May 1969 and those made after that date. If copyright subsists under the 1968 Act in a sound recording made before the commencement of that Act it continues to subsist, under s 220(3) of the Act, until the expiration of 50 years after the expiration of the calendar year in which the recording was made. If the recording is made after the commencement of the Act, and copyright subsists in it, the copyright continues to subsist, under s 93 of the Act, until the expiration of 50 years after the expiration of the calendar year in which the recording is first published.

25.35 Broadcasts. If copyright subsists in a television or sound broadcast under the 1968 Act it continues to subsist, under s 95(1) of the Act, until the expiration of 50 years after the expiration of the calendar year in which the broadcast was made. Copyright does not subsist in broadcasts made before the commencement of the Act on 1 May 1969, nor in a broadcast made after that date which is merely a repetition of a broadcast made before that date: s 223. There is also no additional copyright term in a repetition by use of a tape, disc, or any other device, of an earlier broadcast in which copyright does subsist: s 95(2).

10. Limitation of rights

Producers of phonograms

25.36 Educational use. One of the exclusive rights of the owner of copyright in a sound recording, under s 85(b) of the 1968 Act, is to cause it to be heard in public. It is not, however, an infringement of that copyright for a teacher or student, in the course of educational instruction, to play a sound recording in class or otherwise in the presence of an audience restricted to those taking part in that educational instruction or directly connected with the place where the instruction is given: s 28(4).

25.37 Public performance: guest houses, hotels, etc. It is not an infringement of copyright in a sound recording to cause it to be heard in public at premises where persons reside or sleep, as part of the amenities provided exclusively for residents or inmates of the premises and their guests: s 106(1)(a). This exemption does not apply if a specific charge is made for admission to the part of the premises where the recording is to be heard, even if the charge is partly for admission and partly for other purposes: s 106(2)(a), (3).

This provision should be read with similar exemptions with regard to the performance of literary, dramatic or musical works in s 46, and the operation of diffusion services in s 26(3). If a sound recording is played in public in the above circumstances there is no copyright infringement in the recording or in the work recorded.

Similar provisions are contained in s 12(7)(a) of the Copyright Act 1956 (UK), but there is an important difference. In the United Kingdom Act the amenities must be provided exclusively or mainly for the residents or inmates therein, whereas it is specifically provided in the Australian Act that these amenities may also be provided for guests of the residents or inmates.

25.38 Public performance: non-profit clubs, etc. It is not an infringement of copyright in a sound recording to cause it to be heard in public as part of the activities or for the benefit of a club, society or other organisation not established or conducted for profit, and the principal objects of which are charitable or are otherwise concerned with the advancement of religion, education or social welfare: s 106(1)(b). This exemption does not apply if a charge is made for admission to the place where the recording is to be heard and any of the proceeds of the charge are applied otherwise than for the purposes of the organisation: s 106(2)(b).

These provisions are similar to those in s 12(7)(b) of the Copyright Act 1956 (UK).

25.39 Copying for broadcasting purposes. Section 107 of the 1968 Act gives to broadcasters who have the authority to broadcast a sound recording, whether by licence, assignment or the operation of the Act, the right to make a copy of that recording in association with other matter for the purpose of broadcasting, without infringing copyright in that recording. The conditions which must be met before this exemption operates are the same as those which apply when reproductions of literary, dramatic, musical or artistic works are made in similar circumstances for broadcasting purposes: ss 47, 70.

25.40 Reception of broadcasts. One of the exclusive rights of the owner of copyright in a sound recording, under s 85(b) of the 1968 Act, is to cause the recording to be heard in public. However, the 1968 Act provides in s 199(2) that a person who causes a sound recording to be heard in public by the reception of a television or sound broadcast does not infringe the copyright which may subsist in that recording. It would be necessary to obtain a licence for the public performance in these circumstances of a copyright work included in the broadcast unless one of the exemptions in s 46 (performance in guest houses, hostels, etc), or in s 199(1) (readings or recitations) was applicable.

A performance of a work can take place for the purposes of the 1968 Act by the display or emission of visual images or sounds by a receiving apparatus to which they are conveyed by the transmission of electromagnetic signals (by cable or otherwise); similarly the operation of the receiver can be regarded as causing a recording to be heard: s 27(3). The reception of a television or sound broadcast includes reception from the original broadcast transmission or from a simultaneous cable transmission either directly or by means of a retransmission made by any person from any place: s 25(2). A retransmission may be made by wireless telegraphy or cable and with the use of tapes, discs or any other article or thing in which the images or sounds of the broadcast are embodied: s 25(5).

It is not one of the exclusive rights of the owner of copyright in a sound recording to cause it to be transmitted to subscribers to a diffusion service.

25.41 Secondary broadcasts. If a record embodying a sound recording is used to make a broadcast, a person who makes a further broadcast (the secondary broadcast) by receiving and simultaneously making a further transmission either of the transmission of the original broadcast or of a simultaneous cable transmission, is deemed, under s 25(3) of the 1968 Act, not to have used the record for the purpose of making the secondary broadcast. Such a person is not, therefore, liable for infringing the exclusive broadcasting right of the owner of copyright in the recording.

The act of broadcasting must be distinguished from the transmission of material to subscribers to a diffusion service. Under s 25(1) of the 1968 Act broadcasting includes sound and television broadcasting, and in s 10 broadcasting is defined as broadcasting by wireless telegraphy, that is, the emitting or receiving of electromagnetic energy otherwise than over a path provided by a material substance. On the other hand, the transmission of material to subscribers to a diffusion service is the act of distribution of material over cable, wire or other paths provided by a material substance: s 26(1). Section 25(3) is concerned only with the act of broadcasting.

25.42 Performing and broadcasting rights in certain foreign recordings. There is no performing or broadcasting rights in certain foreign recordings where there is no international reciprocity.[1]

1 See para 25.43.

25.43 Performing and broadcasting rights and the compulsory licences. The 1968 Act includes provisions in ss 108 and 109 permitting recordings to be played in public, or broadcast, without infringing copyright, upon compliance with certain formalities and upon payment of royalties specified by the Copyright Tribunal.

The general effect of these provisions is that after a record has been released in Australia, subject to complying with the requirements of the Act, it may be publicly performed or broadcast subject to payment of appropriate royalties. If the recording has not been published in Australia, a prescribed period of seven weeks must elapse after the date of first publication before the licence can be exercised.

Not all recordings in Australia are entitled to this protection; and in the case of some imported recordings there is no public performance right and no broadcasting right at all. In the context of international copyright protection Australia has adopted the principle of reciprocity. As Australia is a member of the Berne Convention and its revisions and the Universal Copyright Convention of 1952, the Copyright Act must provide protection for works of foreign origin as required by the conventions. The conventions do not, of course, have the force of law in Australia unless specifically enacted as part of our domestic law. This has been achieved by regulations under ss 184 and 185 of the Act namely, the Copyright (International Protection) Regulations, by applying specific provisions of the Act, so far as relevant, to works or recordings made or first published in a foreign country; to citizens, nationals or residents of a foreign country; to bodies incorporated under the law of a foreign country in the same way as the provisions of the Act apply where Australia, and not the foreign country, is the relevant forum. Under ss 184 and 185 the provisions of the Act may be applied to a foreign country subject to such exceptions or modifications as are specified in the regulations and either generally or in relation to specific classes of works as specified in the regulations.

The Regulations apply the provisions of the Act generally in relation to countries that are members of the Berne Convention or are parties to the Universal Copyright Convention. But there are special provisions relating to matters, including the performing and broadcasting rights in overseas sound recordings, which are subject to complex limitations based essentially on the principle of reciprocity. The general effect of the relevant Regulations is that the performing or broadcasting rights in sound recordings cease after publication in Australia or after seven weeks from the date of first publication elsewhere unless the country of which the maker was a citizen, national or resident, or in which the maker was incorporated at the time the recording was made, or in which the recording was made, was a country where copyright in the recording includes the performing or broadcasting rights. These countries are specified in the Third Schedule to the Regulations. First publication of a recording in one of those countries is not a sufficient qualifying factor. In addition, copyright must not subsist in the recording by virtue of the operation of the Regulations and s 89(3) of the Act which provides that copyright subsists in a published sound recording if the first publication of the recording took place in Australia. If the copyright subsists in the recording by virtue only of first publication in Australia or in a convention country to which the Act extends, the copyright does not include the performance and broadcasting rights: ss 105, 184 and 185, and Regulations 1, 4, 6 and 7. The most important effect of the Regulations is in relation to recordings from the USA where, until 1971, there was no copyright at all in sound recordings. As a result, there were no performance or broadcasting rights in Australia in respect of those records. This could not be overcome by arranging a first publication of the recording in Australia or in a country to which the Act extends. If therefore a sound recording was made in the USA by a corporation incorporated there but was first published in say France, copyright would subsist in a recording in Australia. But if first publication in France was the *only* reason for the application of the Act, then the copyright would be limited only to the right to prevent copying under s 85(a), subject to the limited period for recordings not published in Australia.

25.44 Judicial proceedings. A copyright in a sound recording is not infringed by anything done for the purposes of a judicial proceeding or a report of a judicial proceeding: s 104.

Broadcasting organisations

25.45 Educational use. Under the 1968 Act, the owner of copyright in a television or sound broadcast does not have the exclusive right to cause it to be seen or heard in public; there is no 'performing right' in broadcasts. This is not so in the Copyright Act 1956 (UK), where the act of causing a television broadcast to be seen or heard in public by a paying audience is a restricted act under s 14(4)(c). There is, therefore, no exemption in s 28 of the Australian Act for performance in class of broadcasts as there is for works, recordings and films.

It is not an infringement of copyright in a television or sound broadcast intended to be used for educational purposes to make a record of the broadcast under s 200(2) of the 1968 Act. There is also no infringement of copyright in a work or sound recording included in the broadcast. The following conditions must be met:

1. The record must be made by or on behalf of the person or authority in charge of a place of education that is not conducted for profit: s 200(2)(a).
2. The record must not be used except in the course of instruction at that place: s 200(2)(b).
3. There must be no commercial dealings with the record and no rights are given with regard to importation of articles which would otherwise constitute a copyright infringement: s 200(3), (4).

The exemption refers only to the making of a record of a broadcast. A record is defined in s 10 of the 1968 Act as a disc, tape, paper or other device in which sounds are embodied. It would, therefore, appear that the exemption does not include a videotape of a television broadcast but only a sound recording of that broadcast or of a sound broadcast.

25.46 Private and domestic use. Section 111 of the 1968 Act provides that it is not an infringement of copyright in a television or sound broadcast to make a film or recording of it for the private and domestic use of the maker. The making is not deemed to be for the private and domestic use of the maker, pursuant to s 111(3), if it is for any of the following purposes:

1. The sale or letting for hire of a copy of the film or a record embodying the recording;
2. Broadcasting the film or recording;
3. Causing the film or recording to be seen or heard in public.

25.47 Repeat broadcasts. There is no copyright in a repeat broadcast which extends beyond the copyright in the original broadcast: s 95(2). A repeat broadcast is a repetition of a previous television or sound broadcast made by broadcasting visual images or sounds embodied in any article or thing such as a disc, tape or videotape; it is not a live repeat. The copyright in the repeat broadcast expires at the same time as the copyright in the original, and if the repeat broadcast is made after the expiration of copyright in the original broadcast no copyright subsists in the repeat at all: s 95(2).

There is no copyright under the 1968 Act in a television or sound broadcast made after the commencement of the Act that is a repetition of a television or sound broadcast made before the commencement of the Act on 1 May 1969: s 223(b). It seems that the repetition may be a live repetition.

25.48 Broadcasts made before 1 May 1969. There is no copyright under the 1968 Act in a television or sound broadcast made before the commencement of the Act on 1 May 1969: s 223(a).

25.49 Judicial Proceedings. A copyright in a television or sound broadcast is not infringed by anything done for the purposes of a judicial proceeding or a report of a judicial proceeding: s 104.

11. Remedies for infringement

25.50 Civil remedies and criminal offences have been referred to in section 2 above.

The penalties for conviction of an offence under the Copyright Act were increased substantially by the Copyright Amendment Act 1980 to combat the increasing problem of record piracy. The courts have also made use of ex parte orders similar to the 'Anton Piller' orders developed in England[1] requiring a defendant to allow the plaintiff's representatives to inspect and seize infringing copies and documents relating to importation, sale or supply. There has not, however, been the development of the order to include discovery and interrogatories directed to information and disclosure of a self-incriminating nature as has occurred in England (see *Rank Film Distributors Ltd v Video Information Centre* [1981] 2 WLR 668).

1 See para 18.25 above.

12. Protection of foreign right owners

25.51 Since Australia has acceded to the Paris revisions of the Berne Convention and the Universal Copyright Convention, the Copyright Act 1968 must make provision for the protection of works of foreign origin in the manner required by the conventions. It is only by their enactment in the domestic Australian legislation that the convention provisions have the force of law in this country. This is achieved by regulations made under sections 184 and 185 of the Copyright Act which apply specified provisions of the act to works, recordings, films or editions made or first published in a foreign country; artistic works that are buildings situated in a foreign country; citizens, nationals or residents of a foreign country; bodies incorporated under the law of a foreign country; and authorised TV and radio broadcasts made from a place in a foreign country; in the same way as the provisions of the Act apply in the above cases where Australia and not the foreign country is the relevant forum. The provisions of the Act may be applied to a foreign country subject to such exceptions or modifications as are specified in the regulations and either generally or in relation to specific classes of works or other subject matter. However, if the regulations apply provisions of the Act in relation to a country not a party to one of the international conventions to which Australia is a party, a principle of reciprocity is applied.

The regulations that have been made pursuant to the Copyright Act 1968 are the Copyright (International Protection) Regulations 1969, as amended. Generally these regulations apply the provisions of the Act in relation to countries that are members of the Berne Union or parties to the Universal Copyright Convention.

The 'performing' and broadcasting rights in foreign sound recordings are subject to a number of limitations based essentially on the principle of reciprocity. These are discussed in para 25.43 above.

13. Plans for law revision

Manufacture of records of musical works

25.52 In 1979 the Copyright Tribunal completed an enquiry under s 148 of the Copyright Act into the royalty payable for the manufacture of records of musical works under the statutory licence in s 55 of the Act. The Tribunal reported that the amount of royalty payable in respect of a record should be increased from 5% to 6.75% of the retail selling price of the record. The Tribunal also recommended that the basis of the calculation of royalty should be the net retail price (exclusive of sales tax) so that tax changes did not alter the effective royalty rate.

The Report of the Tribunal has caused considerable controversy and strong lobbying from the Australian Record Industry Association (ARIA) and the Australian Music Publishers Association (AMPA). The Attorney-General has recently stated that the government had decided that, in principle, the Copyright Act should be amended to remove the statutory licence for the manufacture of records of musical works, subject to discussions with interested parties.

Audio and video reproduction

25.53 The Committee on Audio and Video Reproduction and Copyright, established by the Copyright Council of Australia, published its Report in 1981. The Committee recommends that royalties for home taping should be charged on software and/or hardware and that taping for educational purposes should be subject to a system of voluntary or statutory licensing. The government is holding an enquiry into audio-visual reproduction. In July 1982 the Attorney-General's Department published the Review of the Audio-Visual Copyright Law: Issues Paper, setting out issues raised in submissions to the current inquiry.

The paper brings together all issues raised in submissions and summarises the main arguments submitted for and against proposals for changes in the law. It also includes background information on copyright law with reference to audio-visual copying. The purpose of the inquiry is the preparation of recommendations to the government for amendments to the Copyright Act.

Cable inquiry

25.54 The Australian Broadcasting Tribunal has recently conducted an enquiry into cable and subscription television services. A term of reference includes the copyright and related issues to which the introduction of cable television services and subscription television services would give rise.

The Interim Report on Cable and Subscription Television Services for Australia was published in August 1982. The Tribunal recommended a system of compulsory and voluntary licences for copyright in relation to cable and television services.

Appendices

Appendix 1

Berne Convention for the Protection of Literary and Artistic Works (Paris Act, 24 July 1971)

The countries of the Union, being equally animated by the desire to protect, in as effective and uniform a manner as possible, the rights of authors in their literary and artistic works,

Recognising the importance of the work of the Revision Conference held at Stockholm in 1967,

Have resolved to revise the Act adopted by the Stockholm Conference, while maintaining without change Articles 1 to 20 and 22 to 26 of that Act.

Consequently, the undersigned Plenipotentiaries, having presented their full powers, recognised as in good and due form, have agreed as follows:

Article 1

[*Establishment of a Union*][1]

The countries to which this Convention applies constitute a Union for the protection of the rights of authors in their literary and artistic works.

1 Each Article and the Appendix have been given titles to facilitate their identification. There are no titles in the signed (English) text.

Article 2

[*Protected Works:* 1. 'Literary and artistic works'; 2. Possible requirement of fixation; 3. Derivative works; 4. Official texts; 5. Collections; 6. Obligation to protect; beneficiaries of protection; 7. Works of applied art and industrial designs; 8. News]

(1) The expression 'literary and artistic works' shall include every production in the literary, scientific and artistic domain, whatever may be the mode or form of its expression, such as books, pamphlets and other writings; lectures, addresses, sermons and other works of the same nature; dramatic or dramatico-musical works; choreographic works and entertainments in dumb show; musical compositions with or without words; cinematographic works to which are assimilated works expressed by a process analogous to cinematography; works of drawing, painting, architecture, sculpture, engraving and lithography; photographic works to which are assimilated works expressed by a process analogous to photography; works of applied art; illustrations, maps, plans, sketches and three-dimensional works relative to geography, topography, architecture or science.

(2) It shall, however, be a matter for legislation in the countries of the Union to prescribe that works in general or any specified categories of works shall not be protected unless they have been fixed in some material form.

(3) Translations, adaptations, arrangements of music and other alterations of a literary or artistic work shall be protected as original works without prejudice to the copyright in the original work.

(4) It shall be a matter for legislation in the countries of the Union to determine the protection to be granted to official texts of a legislative, administrative and legal nature, and to official translations of such texts.

(5) Collections of literary or artistic works such as encyclopaedias and anthologies which, by reason of the selection and arrangement of their contents, constitute intellec-

tual creations shall be protected as such, without prejudice to the copyright in each of the works forming part of such collections.
(6) The works mentioned in this Article shall enjoy protection in all countries of the Union. This protection shall operate for the benefit of the author and his successors in title.
(7) Subject to the provisions of Article 7(4) of this Convention, it shall be a matter for legislation in the countries of the Union to determine the extent of the application of their laws to works of applied art and industrial designs and models, as well as the conditions under which such works, designs and models shall be protected. Works protected in the country of origin solely as designs and models shall be entitled in another country of the Union only to such special protection as is granted in that country to designs and models; however, if no such special protection is granted in that country, such works shall be protected as artistic works.
(8) The protection of this Convention shall not apply to news of the day or to miscellaneous facts having the character of mere items of press information.

Article 2bis

[*Possible Limitation of Protection of Certain Works:* 1. Certain speeches; 2. Certain uses of lectures and addresses; 3. Right to make collections of such works]

(1) It shall be a matter for legislation in the countries of the Union to exclude, wholly or in part, from the protection provided by the preceding Article political speeches and speeches delivered in the course of legal proceedings.
(2) It shall also be a matter for legislation in the countries of the Union to determine the conditions under which lectures, addresses and other works of the same nature which are delivered in public may be reproduced by the press, broadcast, communicated to the public by wire and made the subject of public communication as envisaged in Article 11bis(1) of this Convention, when such use is justified by the informatory purpose.
(3) Nevertheless, the author shall enjoy the exclusive right of making a collection of his works mentioned in the preceding paragraphs.

Article 3

[*Criteria of Eligibility for Protection:* 1. Nationality of author; place of publication of work; 2. Residence of author; 3. 'Published' works; 4. 'Simultaneously published' works]

(1) The protection of this Convention shall apply to:

(a) authors who are nationals of one of the countries of the Union, for their works, whether published or not;
(b) authors who are not nationals of one of the countries of the Union, for their works first published in one of those countries, or simultaneously in a country outside the Union and in a country of the Union.

(2) Authors who are not nationals of one of the countries of the Union but who have their habitual residence in one of them shall, for the purposes of this Convention, be assimilated to nationals of that country.
(3) The expression 'published works' means works published with the consent of their authors, whatever may be the means of manufacture of the copies, provided that the availability of such copies has been such as to satisfy the reasonable requirements of the public, having regard to the nature of the work. The performance of a dramatic, dramatico-musical, cinematographic or musical work, the public recitation of a literary work, the communication by wire or the broadcasting of literary or artistic works, the exhibition of a work of art and the construction of a work of architecture shall not constitute publication.
(4) A work shall be considered as having been published simultaneously in several countries if it has been published in two or more countries within thirty days of its first publication.

Article 4

[*Criteria of Eligibility for Protection of Cinematographic Works, Works of Architecture and Certain Artistic Works*]

The protection of this Convention shall apply, even if the conditions of Article 3 are not fulfilled, to:

(a) authors of cinematographic works the maker of which has his headquarters or habitual residence in one of the countries of the Union;
(b) authors of works of architecture erected in a country of the Union or of other artistic works incorporated in a building or other structure located in a country of the Union.

Article 5

[*Rights Guaranteed:* 1. and 2. Outside the country of origin; 3. In the country of origin; 4. 'Country of origin']

(1) Authors shall enjoy, in respect of works for which they are protected under this Convention, in countries of the Union other than the country of origin, the rights which their respective laws do now or may hereafter grant to their nationals, as well as the rights specially granted by this Convention.

(2) The enjoyment and the exercise of these rights shall not be subject to any formality; such enjoyment and such exercise shall be independent of the existence of protection in the country of origin of the work. Consequently, apart from the provisions of this Convention, the extent of protection, as well as the means of redress afforded to the author to protect his rights, shall be governed exclusively by the laws of the country where protection is claimed.

(3) Protection in the country of origin is governed by domestic law. However, when the author is not a national of the country of origin of the work for which he is protected under this Convention, he shall enjoy in that country the same rights as national authors.

(4) The country of origin shall be considered to be:

(a) in the case of works first published in a country of the Union, that country; in the case of works published simultaneously in several countries of the Union which grant different terms of protection, the country whose legislation grants the shortest term of protection;
(b) in the case of works published simultaneously in a country outside the Union and in a country of the Union, the latter country;
(c) in the case of unpublished works or of works first published in a country outside the Union, without simultaneous publication in a country of the Union, the country of the Union of which the author is a national, provided that:

(i) when these are cinematographic works the maker of which has his headquarters or his habitual residence in a country of the Union, the country of origin shall be that country, and
(ii) when these are works of architecture erected in a country of the Union or other artistic works incorporated in a building or other structure located in a country of the Union, the country of origin shall be that country.

Article 6

[*Possible Restriction of Protection In Respect of Certain Works of Nationals of Certain Countries Outside the Union:* 1. In the country of the first publication and in other countries; 2. No retroactivity; 3. Notice]

(1) Where any country outside the Union fails to protect in an adequate manner the works of authors who are nationals of one of the countries of the Union, the latter country may restrict the protection given to the works of authors who are, at the date of the first publication thereof, nationals of the other country and are not habitually resident in one of the countries of the Union. If the country of first publication avails itself of this right, the other countries of the Union shall not be required to grant to

works thus subjected to special treatment a wider protection than that granted to them in the country of first publication.

(2) No restrictions introduced by virtue of the preceding paragraph shall affect the rights which an author may have acquired in respect of a work published in a country of the Union before such restrictions were put into force.

(3) The countries of the Union which restrict the grant of copyright in accordance with this Article shall give notice thereof to the Director General of the World Intellectual Property Organisation (hereinafter designated as 'the Director General') by a written declaration specifying the countries in regard to which protection is restricted, and the restrictions to which rights of authors who are nationals of those countries are subjected. The Director General shall immediately communicate this declaration to all the countries of the Union.

Article 6bis

[*Moral Rights:* 1. To claim authorship; to object to certain modifications and other derogatory actions; 2. After the author's death; 3. Means of redress]

(1) Independently of the author's economic rights, and even after the transfer of the said rights, the author shall have the right to claim authorship of the work and to object to any distortion, mutilation or other modification of, or other derogatory action in relation to, the said work, which would be prejudicial to his honour or reputation.

(2) The rights granted to the author in accordance with the preceding paragraph shall, after his death, be maintained, at least until the expiry of the economic rights, and shall be exercisable by the persons or institutions authorised by the legislation of the country where protection is claimed. However, those countries whose legislation, at the moment of their ratification of or accession to this Act, does not provide for the protection after the death of the author of all the rights set out in the preceding paragraph may provide that some of these rights may, after his death, cease to be maintained.

(3) The means of redress for safeguarding the rights granted by this Article shall be governed by the legislation of the country where protection is claimed.

Article 7

[*Term of Protection:* 1. Generally; 2. For cinematographic works; 3. For anonymous and pseudonymous works; 4. For photographic works and works of applied art; 5. Starting date of computation; 6. Longer terms; 7. Shorter terms; 8. Applicable law; 'comparison' of terms]

(1) The term of protection granted by this Convention shall be the life of the author and fifty years after his death.

(2) However, in the case of cinematographic works, the countries of the Union may provide that the term of protection shall expire fifty years after the work has been made available to the public with the consent of the author, or, failing such an event within fifty years from the making of such a work, fifty years after the making.

(3) In the case of anonymous or pseudonymous works, the term of protection granted by this Convention shall expire fifty years after the work has been lawfully made available to the public. However, when the pseudonym adopted by the author leaves no doubt as to his identity, the term of protection shall be that provided in paragraph (1). If the author of an anonymous or pseudonymous work discloses his identity during the above-mentioned period, the term of protection applicable shall be that provided in paragraph (1). The countries of the Union shall not be required to protect anonymous or pseudonymous works in respect of which it is reasonable to presume that their author has been dead for fifty years.

(4) It shall be a matter for legislation in the countries of the Union to determine the term of protection of photographic works and that of works of applied art in so far as they are protected as artistic works; however, this term shall last at least until the end of a period of twenty-five years from the making of such a work.

(5) The term of protection subsequent to the death of the author and the terms provided by paragraphs (2), (3) and (4) shall run from the date of death or of the event referred to in those paragraphs, but such terms shall always be deemed to begin on the first of January of the year following the death or such event.

(6) The countries of the Union may grant a term of protection in excess of those provided by the preceding paragraphs.

(7) Those countries of the Union bound by the Rome Act of this Convention which grant, in their national legislation in force at the time of signature of the present Act, shorter terms of protection

than those provided for in the preceding paragraphs shall have the right to maintain such terms when ratifying or acceding to the present Act.

(8) In any case, the term shall be governed by the legislation of the country where protection is claimed; however, unless the legislation of that country otherwise provides, the term shall not exceed the term fixed in the country of origin of the work.

Article 7bis

[*Term of Protection for Works of Joint Authorship*]

The provisions of the preceding Article shall also apply in the case of a work of joint authorship, provided that the terms measured from the death of the author shall be calculated from the death of the last surviving author.

Article 8

[*Right of Translation*]

Authors of literary and artistic works protected by this Convention shall enjoy the exclusive right of making and of authorising the translation of their works throughout the term of protection of their rights in the original works.

Article 9

[*Right of Reproduction:* 1. Generally; 2. Possible exceptions; 3. Sound and visual recordings]

(1) Authors of literary and artistic works protected by this Convention shall have the exclusive right of authorising the reproduction of these works, in any manner or form.
(2) It shall be a matter for legislation in the countries of the Union to permit the reproduction of such works in certain special cases, provided that such reproduction does not conflict with a normal exploitation of the work and does not unreasonably prejudice the legitimate interests of the author.
(3) Any sound or visual recording shall be considered as a reproduction for the purposes of this Convention.

Article 10

[*Certain Free Uses of Works:* 1. Quotations; 2. Illustrations for teaching; 3. Indication of source and author]

(1) It shall be permissible to make quotations from a work which has already been lawfully made available to the public, provided that their making is compatible with fair practice, and their extent does not exceed that justified by the purpose, including quotations from newspaper articles and periodicals in the form of press summaries.
(2) It shall be a matter for legislation in the countries of the Union, and for special agreements existing or to be concluded between them, to permit the utilisation, to the extent justified by the purpose, of literary or artistic works by way of illustration in publications, broadcasts or sound or visual recordings for teaching, provided such utilisation is compatible with fair practice.
(3) Where use is made of works in accordance with the preceding paragraphs of this Article, mention shall be made of the source, and of the name of the author if it appears thereon.

Article 10bis

[*Further Possible Free Uses of Works:* 1. Of certain articles and broadcast works; 2. Of works seen or heard in connection with current events]

(1) It shall be a matter for legislation in the countries of the Union to permit the reproduction by the press, the broadcasting or the communication to the public by wire of articles published in newspapers or periodicals on current economic, political or religious topics, and of broadcast works of the same character, in cases in which the reproduction, broadcasting or such communication thereof is not expressly reserved. Nevertheless, the source must always be clearly indicated; the legal consequences of a breach of this obligation shall be determined by the legislation of the country where protection is claimed.

(2) It shall also be a matter for legislation in the countries of the Union to determine the conditions under which, for the purpose of reporting current events by means of photography, cinematography, broadcasting or communication to the public by wire, literary or artistic works seen or heard in the course of the event may, to the extent justified by the informatory purpose, be reproduced and made available to the public.

Article 11

[*Certain Rights in Dramatic and Musical Works:* 1. Right of public performance and of communication to the public of a performance; 2. In respect of translations]

(1) Authors of dramatic, dramatico-musical and musical works shall enjoy the exclusive right of authorising:

(i) the public performance of their works, including such public performance by any means or process;
(ii) any communication to the public of the performance of their works.

(2) Authors of dramatic or dramatico-musical works shall enjoy, during the full term of their rights in the original works, the same rights with respect to translations thereof.

Article 11bis

[*Broadcasting and Related Rights:* 1. Broadcasting and other wireless communications, public communication of broadcast by wire or rebroadcast, public communication of broadcast by loudspeaker or analogous instruments; 2. Compulsory licences; 3. Recording; ephemeral recordings]

(1) Authors of literary and artistic works shall enjoy the exclusive right of authorising:

(i) the broadcasting of their works or the communication thereof to the public by any other means of wireless diffusion of signs, sounds or images;
(ii) any communication to the public by wire or by rebroadcasting of the broadcast of the work, when this communication is made by an organisation other than the original one;
(iii) the public communication by loudspeaker or any other analogous instrument transmitting, by signs, sounds or images, the broadcast of the work.

(2) It shall be a matter for legislation in the countries of the Union to determine the conditions under which the rights mentioned in the preceding paragraph may be exercised, but these conditions shall apply only in the countries where they have been prescribed. They shall not in any circumstances be prejudicial to the moral rights of the author, nor to his right to obtain equitable remuneration which, in the absence of agreement, shall be fixed by competent authority.

(3) In the absence of any contrary stipulation, permission granted in accordance with paragraph (1) of this Article shall not imply permission to record, by means of instruments recording sounds or images, the work broadcast. It shall, however, be a matter for legislation in the countries of the Union to determine the regulations for ephemeral recordings made by a broadcasting organisation by means of its own facilities and used for its own broadcasts. The preservation of these recordings in official archives may, on the ground of their exceptional documentary character, be authorised by such legislation.

Article 11ter

[*Certain Rights in Literary Works:* 1. Right of public recitation and of communication to the public of a recitation; 2. In respect of translations]

(1) Authors of literary works shall enjoy the exclusive right of authorising:

(i) the public recitation of their works, including such public recitation by any means or process;
(ii) any communication to the public of the recitation of their works.

(2) Authors of literary works shall enjoy, during the full term of their rights in the original works, the same rights with respect to translations thereof.

Article 12

[*Right of Adaptation, Arrangement and Other Alteration*]

Authors of literary or artistic works shall enjoy the exclusive right of authorising adaptations, arrangements and other alterations of their works.

Article 13

[*Possible Limitation of the Right of Recording of Musical Works and Any Words Pertaining Thereto:* 1. Compulsory licenses; 2. Transitory measures; 3. Seizure on importation of copies made without the author's permission]

(1) Each country of the Union may impose for itself reservations and conditions on the exclusive right granted to the author of a musical work and to the author of any words, the recording of which together with the musical work has already been authorised by the latter, to authorise the sound recording of that musical work, together with such words, if any; but all such reservations and conditions shall apply only in the countries which have imposed them and shall not, in any circumstances, be prejudicial to the rights of these authors to obtain equitable remuneration which, in the absence of agreement, shall be fixed by competent authority.

(2) Recordings of musical works made in a country of the Union in accordance with Article 13(3) of the Conventions signed at Rome on June 2, 1928, and at Brussels on June 26, 1948, may be reproduced in that country without the permission of the author of the musical work until a date two years after that country becomes bound by this Act.

(3) Recordings made in accordance with paragraphs (1) and (2) of this Article and imported without permission from the parties concerned into a country where they are treated as infringing recordings shall be liable to seizure.

Article 14

[*Cinematographic and Related Rights:* 1. Cinematographic adaptation and reproduction; distribution; public performance and public communication by wire of works thus adapted or reproduced; 2. Adaptation of cinematographic productions; 3. No compulsory licenses]

(1) Authors of literary or artistic works shall have the exclusive right of authorising:

(i) the cinematographic adaptation and reproduction of these works, and the distribution of the works thus adapted or reproduced;
(ii) the public performance and communication to the public by wire of the works thus adapted or reproduced.

(2) The adaptation into any other artistic form of a cinematographic production derived from literary or artistic works shall, without prejudice to the authorisation of the author of the cinematographic production, remain subject to the authorisation of the authors of the original works.

(3) The provisions of Article 13(1) shall not apply.

Article 14bis

[*Special Provisions Concerning Cinematographic Works:* 1. Assimilation to 'original' works; 2. Ownership; limitation of certain rights of certain contributors; 3. Certain other contributors]

(1) Without prejudice to the copyright in any work which may have been adapted or reproduced, a cinematographic work shall be protected as an original work. The owner of copyright in a cinematographic work shall enjoy the same rights as the author of an original work, including the rights referred to in the preceding Article.

(2)(a) Ownership of copyright in a cinematographic work shall be a matter for legislation in the country where protection is claimed.

(b) However, in the countries of the Union which, by legislation, include among the owners of copyright in a cinematographic work authors who have brought contributions to the making of the work, such authors, if they have undertaken to bring such contributions, may not, in the absence of any contrary or special stipulation, object to

the reproduction, distribution, public performance, communication to the public by wire, broadcasting or any other communication to the public, or to the subtitling or dubbing of texts, of the work.
(c) The question whether or not the form of the undertaking referred to above should, for the application of the preceding subparagraph (b), be in a written agreement or a written act of the same effect shall be a matter for the legislation of the country where the maker of the cinematographic work has his headquarters or habitual residence. However, it shall be a matter for the legislation of the country of the Union where protection is claimed to provide that the said undertaking shall be in a written agreement or a written act of the same effect. The countries whose legislation so provides shall notify the Director General by means of a written declaration, which will be immediately communicated by him to all the other countries of the Union.
(d) By 'contrary or special stipulation' is meant any restrictive condition which is relevant to the aforesaid undertaking.
(3) Unless the national legislation provides to the contrary, the provisions of paragraph (2)(b) above shall not be applicable to authors of scenarios, dialogues and musical works created for the making of the cinematographic work, or to the principal director thereof. However, those countries of the Union whose legislation does not contain rules providing for the application of the said paragraph (2)(b) to such director shall notify the Director General by means of a written declaration, which will be immediately communicated by him to all the oher countries of the Union.

Article 14ter

[*'Droit de suite' in Works of Art and Manuscripts:* 1. Right to an interest in resales; 2. Applicable law; 3. Procedure]

(1) The author, or after his death the persons or institutions authorised by national legislation, shall, with respect to original works of art and original manuscripts of writers and composers, enjoy the inalienable right to an interest in any sale of the work subsequent to the first transfer by the author of the work.
(2) The protection provided by the preceding paragraph may be claimed in a country of the Union only if legislation in the country to which the author belongs so permits, and to the extent permitted by the country where this protection is claimed.
(3) The procedure for collection and the amounts shall be matters for determination by national legislation.

Article 15

[*Right to Enforce Protected Rights:* 1. Where author's name is indicated or where pseudonym leaves no doubt as to author's identity; 2. In the case of cinematographic works; 3. In the case of anonymous and pseudonymous works; 4. In the case of certain unpublished works of unknown authorship]

(1) In order that the author of a literary or artistic work protected by this Convention shall, in the absence of proof to the contrary, be regarded as such, and consequently be entitled to institute infringement proceedings in the countries of the Union, it shall be sufficient for his name to appear on the work in the usual manner. This paragraph shall be applicable even if this name is a pseudonym, where the pseudonym adopted by the author leaves no doubt as to his identity.
(2) The person or body corporate whose name appears on a cinematographic work in the usual manner shall, in the absence of proof to the contrary, be presumed to be the maker of the said work.
(3) In the case of anonymous and pseudonymous works, other than those referred to in paragraph (1) above, the publisher whose name appears on the work shall, in the absence of proof to the contrary, be deemed to represent the author, and in this capacity he shall be entitled to protect and enforce the author's rights. The provisions of this paragraph shall cease to apply when the author reveals his identity and establishes his claim to authorship of the work.
(4)(a) In the case of unpublished works where the identity of the author is unknown, but where there is every ground to presume that he is a national of a country of the Union, it shall be a matter for legislation in that country to designate the competent

authority which shall represent the author and shall be entitled to protect and enforce his rights in the countries of the Union.
(b) Countries of the Union which make such designation under the terms of this provision shall notify the Director General by means of a written declaration giving full information concerning the authority thus designated. The Director General shall at once communicate this declaration to all other countries of the Union.

Article 16

[Infringing Copies: 1. Seizure; 2. Seizure on importation; 3. Applicable law]

(1) Infringing copies of a work shall be liable to seizure in any country of the Union where the work enjoys legal protection.
(2) The provisions of the preceding paragraph shall also apply to reproductions coming from a country where the work is not protected, or has ceased to be protected.
(3) The seizure shall take place in accordance with the legislation of each country.

Article 17

[Possibility of Control of Circulation, Presentation and Exhibition of Works]

The provisions of this Convention cannot in any way affect the right of the Government of each country of the Union to permit, to control, or to prohibit, by legislation or regulation, the circulation, presentation, or exhibition of any work or production in regard to which the competent authority may find it necessary to exercise that right.

Article 18

[Works Existing on Convention's Entry Into Force: 1. Protectable where protection not yet expired in country of origin; 2. Non-protectable where protection already expired in country where it is claimed; 3. Application of these principles; 4. Special cases]

(1) This Convention shall apply to all works which, at the moment of its coming into force, have not yet fallen into the public domain in the country of origin through the expiry of the term of protection.
(2) If, however, through the expiry of the term of protection which was previously granted, a work has fallen into the public domain of the country where protection is claimed, that work shall not be protected anew.
(3) The application of this principle shall be subject to any provisions contained in special conventions to that effect existing or to be concluded between countries of the Union. In the absence of such provisions, the respective countries shall determine, each in so far as it is concerned, the conditions of application of this principle.
(4) The preceding provisions shall also apply in the case of new accessions to the Union and to cases in which protection is extended by the application of Article 7 or by the abandonment of reservations.

Article 19

[Protection Greater than Resulting from Convention]

The provisions of this Convention shall not preclude the making of a claim to the benefit of any greater protection which may be granted by legislation in a country of the Union.

Article 20

[Special Agreements Among Countries of the Union]

The Governments of the countries of the Union reserve the right to enter into special agreements among themselves, in so far as such agreements grant to authors more extensive rights than those granted by the Convention, or contain other provisions not contrary to this Convention. The provisions of existing agreements which satisfy these conditions shall remain applicable.

Article 21

[*Special Provisions Regarding Developing Countries:* 1. Reference to Appendix; 2. Appendix part of Act]

(1) Special provisions regarding developing countries are included in the Appendix.
(2) Subject to the provisions of Article 28(1)(b), the Appendix forms an integral part of this Act.

Article 22

[*Assembly:* 1. Constitution and composition; 2. Tasks; 3. Quorum, voting, observers; 4. Convocation; 5. Rules of procedure]

(1)(a) The Union shall have an Assembly consisting of those countries of the Union which are bound by Articles 22 to 26.
(b) The Government of each country shall be represented by one delegate, who may be assisted by alternate delegates, advisors, and experts.
(c) The expenses of each delegation shall be borne by the Government which has appointed it.
(2)(a) The Assembly shall:

(i) deal with all matters concerning the maintenance and development of the Union and the implementation of this Convention;
(ii) give directions concerning the preparation for conferences of revision to the International Bureau of Intellectual Property (hereinafter designated as 'the International Bureau') referred to in the Convention Establishing the World Intellectual Property Organisation (hereinafter designated as 'the Organisation'), due account being taken of any comments made by those countries of the Union which are not bound by Articles 22 to 26;
(iii) review and approve the reports and activities of the Director General of the Organisation concerning the Union, and give him all necessary instructions concerning matters within the competence of the Union;
(iv) elect the members of the Executive Committee of the Assembly;
(v) review and approve the reports and activities of its Executive Committee, and give instructions to such Committee;
(vi) determine the programme and adopt the triennial budget of the Union, and approve its final accounts;
(vii) adopt the financial regulations of the Union;
(viii) establish such committees of experts and working groups as may be necessary for the work of the Union;
(ix) determine which countries not members of the Union and which intergovernmental and international non-governmental organisations shall be admitted to its meetings as observers;
(x) adopt amendments to Articles 22 to 26;
(xi) take any other appropriate action designed to further the objectives of the Union;
(xii) exercise such other functions as are appropriate under this Convention;
(xiii) subject to its acceptance, exercise such rights as are given to it in the Convention establishing the Organisation.

(b) With respect to matters which are of interest also to other Unions administered by the Organisation, the Assembly shall make its decisions after having heard the advice of the Coordination Committee of the Organisation.
(3)(a) Each country member of the Assembly shall have one vote.
(b) One-half of the countries members of the Assembly shall constitute a quorum.
(c) Notwithstanding the provisions of subparagraph (b), if, in any session, the number of countries represented is less than one-half but equal to or more than one-third of the countries members of the Assembly, the Assembly may make decisions but, with the exception of decisions concerning its own procedure, all such decisions shall take effect only if the following conditions are fulfilled. The International Bureau shall communicate the said decisions to the countries members of the Assembly which were not represented and shall invite them to express in writing their vote or abstention within a period of three months from the date of the communication. If, at the expiration of

this period, the number of countries having thus expressed their vote or abstention attains the number of countries which was lacking for attaining the quorum in the session itself, such decisions shall take effect provided that at the same time the required majority still obtains.
(d) Subject to the provisions of Article 26(2), the decisions of the Assembly shall require two-thirds of the votes cast.
(e) Abstentions shall not be considered as votes.
(f) A delegate may represent, and vote in the name of, one country only.
(g) Countries of the Union not members of the Assembly shall be admitted to its meetings as observers.
(4)(a) The Assembly shall meet once in every third calendar year in ordinary session upon convocation by the Director General and, in the absence of exceptional circumstances, during the same period and at the same place as the General Assembly of the Organisation.
(b) The Assembly shall meet in extraordinary session upon convocation by the Director General, at the request of the Executive Committee or at the request of one-fourth of the countries members of the Assembly.
(5) The Assembly shall adopt its own rules of procedure.

Article 23

[*Executive Committee:* 1. Constitution; 2. Composition; 3. Number of members; 4. Geographical distribution; special agreements; 5. Term, limits of re-eligibility, rules of election; 6. Tasks; 7. Convocation; 8. Quorum, voting; 9. Observers; 10. Rules of Procedure]

(1) The Assembly shall have an Executive Committee.
2(a) The Executive Committee shall consist of countries elected by the Assembly from among countries members of the Assembly. Furthermore, the country on whose territory the Organisation has its headquarters shall, subject to the provisions of Article 25(7)(b), have an *ex officio* seat on the Committee.
(b) The Government of each country member of the Executive Committee shall be represented by one delegate, who may be assisted by alternate delegates, advisors, and experts.
(c) The expenses of each delegation shall be borne by the Government which has appointed it.
(3) The number of countries members of the Executive Committee shall correspond to one-fourth of the number of countries members of the Assembly. In establishing the number of seats to be filled, remainders after division by four shall be disregarded.
(4) In electing the members of the Executive Committee, the Assembly shall have due regard to an equitable geographical distribution and to the need for countries party to the Special Agreements which might be established in relation with the Union to be among the countries constituting the Executive Committee.
(5)(a) Each member of the Executive Committee shall serve from the close of the session of the Assembly which elected it to the close of the next ordinary session of the Assembly.
(b) Members of the Executive Committee may be re-elected, but not more than two-thirds of them.
(c) The Assembly shall establish the details of the rules governing the election and possible re-election of the members of the Executive Committee.
(6)(a) The Executive Committee shall:
 (i) prepare the draft agenda of the Assembly;
 (ii) submit proposals to the Assembly respecting the draft programme and triennial budget of the Union prepared by the Director General;
 (iii) approve, within the limits of the programme and the triennial budget, the specific yearly budgets and programmes prepared by the Director General;
 (iv) submit, with appropriate comments, to the Assembly the periodical reports of the Director General and the yearly audit reports on the accounts;
 (v) in accordance with the decisions of the Assembly and having regard to circumstances arising between two ordinary sessions of the Assembly, take all necessary

measures to ensure the execution of the program of the Union by the Director General;

(vi) perform such other functions as are allocated to it under this Convention.

(b) With respect to matters which are of interest also to other Unions administered by the Organisation, the Executive Committee shall make its decisions after having heard the advice of the Coordination Committee of the Organisation.

(7)(a) The Executive Committee shall meet once a year in ordinary session upon convocation by the Director General, preferably during the same period and at the same place as the Coordination Committee of the Organisation.

(b) The Executive Committee shall meet in extraordinary session upon convocation by the Director General, either on his own initiative, or at the request of its Chairman or one-fourth of its members.

(8)(a) Each country member of the Executive Committee shall have one vote.

(b) One-half of the members of the Executive Committee shall constitute a quorum.

(c) Decisions shall be made by a simple majority of the votes cast.

(d) Abstentions shall not be considered as votes.

(e) A delegate may represent, and vote in the name of, one country only.

(9) Countries of the Union not members of the Executive Committee shall be admitted to its meetings as observers.

(10) The Executive Committee shall adopt its own rules of procedure.

Article 24

[*International Bureau:* 1. Tasks in general, Director General; 2. General information; 3. Periodical; 4. Information to countries; 5. Studies and services; 6. Participation in meetings; 7. Conferences of revision; 8. Other tasks]

(1)(a) The administrative tasks with respect to the Union shall be performed by the International Bureau, which is a continuation of the Bureau of the Union united with the Bureau of the Union established by the International Convention for the Protection of Industrial Property.

(b) In particular, the International Bureau shall provide the secretariat of the various organs of the Union.

(c) The Director General of the Organisation shall be the chief executive of the Union and shall represent the Union.

(2) The International Bureau shall assemble and publish information concerning the protection of copyright. Each country of the Union shall promptly communicate to the International Bureau all new laws and official texts concerning the protection of copyright.

(3) The International Bureau shall publish a monthly periodical.

(4) The International Bureau shall, on request, furnish information to any country of the Union on matters concerning the protection of copyright.

(5) The International Bureau shall conduct studies, and shall provide services, designed to facilitate the protection of copyright.

(6) The Director General and any staff member designated by him shall participate, without the right to vote, in all meetings of the Assembly, the Executive Committee and any other committee of experts or working group. The Director General, or a staff member designated by him, shall be *ex officio* secretary of these bodies.

(7)(a) The International Bureau shall, in accordance with the directions of the Assembly and in cooperation with the Executive Committee, make the preparations for the conferences of revision of the provisions of the Convention other than Articles 22 to 26.

(b) The International Bureau may consult with intergovernmental and international non-governmental organisations concerning preparations for conferences of revision.

(c) The Director General and persons designated by him shall take part, without the right to vote, in the discussions at these conferences.

(8) The International Bureau shall carry out any other tasks assigned to it.

Article 25

Finances: 1. Budget; 2. Coordination with other Unions; 3. Resources; 4. Contributions; possible extension of previous budget; 5. Fees and charges; 6. Working capital fund; 7. Advances by host Government; 8. Auditing of accounts]

(1)(a) The Union shall have a budget.
(b) The budget of the Union shall include the income and expenses proper to the Union, its contribution to the budget of expenses common to the Unions, and, where applicable, the sum made available to the budget of the Conference of the Organisation.
(c) Expenses not attributable exclusively to the Union but also to one or more other Unions administered by the Organisation shall be considered as expenses common to the Unions. The share of the Union in such common expenses shall be in proportion to the interest the Union has in them.
(2) The budget of the Union shall be established with due regard to the requirements of coordination with the budgets of the other Unions administered by the Organisation.
(3) The budget of the Union shall be financed from the following sources:

(i) contributions of the countries of the Union;
(ii) fees and charges due for services performed by the International Bureau in relation to the Union;
(iii) sale of, or royalties on, the publications of the International Bureau concerning the Union;
(iv) gifts, bequests, and subventions;
(v) rents, interests, and other miscellaneous income.

(4)(a) For the purpose of establishing its contribution towards the budget, each country of the Union shall belong to a class, and shall pay its annual contributions on the basis of a number of units fixed as follows:

Class I.	25
Class II	20
Class III	15
Class IV	10
Class V	5
Class VI	3
Class VIII	1

(b) Unless it has already done so, each country shall indicate, concurrently with depositing its instrument of ratification or accession, the class to which it wishes to belong. Any country may change class. If it chooses a lower class, the country must announce it to the Assembly at one of its ordinary sessions. Any such change shall take effect at the beginning of the calendar year following the session.
(c) The annual contribution of each country shall be an amount in the same proportion to the total sum to be contributed to the annual budget of the Union by all countries as the number of its units is to the total of the units of all contributing countries.
(d) Contributions shall become due on the first of January of each year.
(e) A country which is in arrears in the payment of its contributions shall have no vote in any of the organs of the Union of which it is a member if the amount of its arrears equals or exceeds the amount of the contributions due from it for the preceding two full years. However, any organ of the Union may allow such a country to continue to exercise its vote in that organ if, and as long as, it is satisfied that the delay in payment is due to exceptional and unavoidable circumstances.
(f) If the budget is not adopted before the beginning of a new financial period, it shall be at the same level as the budget of the previous year, in accordance with the financial regulations.
(5) The amount of the fees and charges due for services rendered by the International Bureau in relation to the Union shall be established, and shall be reported to the Assembly and the Executive Committee, by the Director General.
(6)(a) The Union shall have a working capital fund which shall be constituted by a single payment made by each country of the Union. If the fund becomes insufficient, an increase shall be decided by the Assembly.
(b) The amount of the initial payment of each country to the said fund or of its participation in the increase thereof shall be a proportion of the contribution of that country for the year in which the fund is established or the increase decided.
(c) The proportion and the terms of payment shall be fixed by the Assembly on the proposal of the Director General and after it has heard the advice of the Coordination Committee of the Organisation.

(7)(a) In the headquarters agreement concluded with the country on the territory of which the Organisation has its headquarters, it shall be provided that, whenever the working capital fund is insufficient, such country shall grant advances. The amount of these advances and the conditions on which they are granted shall be the subject of separate agreements, in each case, between such country and the Organisation. As long as it remains under the obligation to grant advances, such country shall have an *ex officio* seat on the Executive Committee.
(b) The country referred to in subparagraph (a) and the Organisation shall each have the right to denounce the obligation to grant advances, by written notification. Denunciation shall take effect three years after the end of the year in which it has been notified.
(8) The auditing of the accounts shall be effected by one or more of the countries of the Union or by external auditors, as provided in the financial regulations. They shall be designated with their agreement, by the Assembly.

Article 26

[*Amendments:* 1. Provisions susceptible of amendment by the Assembly; proposals; 2. Adoption; 3. Entry into force]

(1) Proposals for the amendment of Articles 22, 23, 24, 25, and the present Article, may be initiated by any country member of the Assembly, by the Executive Committee, or by the Director General. Such proposals shall be communicated by the Director General to the member countries of the Assembly at least six months in advance of their consideration by the Assembly.
(2) Amendments to the Articles referred to in paragraph (1) shall be adopted by the Assembly. Adoption shall require three-fourths of the votes cast, provided that any amendment of Article 22, and of the present paragraph, shall require four-fifths of the votes cast.
(3) Any amendment to the Articles referred to in paragraph (1) shall enter into force one month after written notifications of acceptance, effected in accordance with their respective constitutional processes, have been received by the Director General from three-fourths of the countries members of the Assembly at the time it adopted the amendment. Any amendment to the said Articles thus accepted shall bind all the countries which are members of the Assembly at the time the amendment enters into force, or which become members thereof at a subsequent date, provided that any amendment increasing the financial obligations of countries of the Union shall bind only those countries which have notified their acceptance of such amendment.

Article 27

[*Revision:* 1. Objective; 2. Conferences; 3. Adoption]

(1) This Convention shall be submitted to revision with a view to the introduction of amendments designed to improve the system of the Union.
(2) For this purpose, conferences shall be held successively in one of the countries of the Union among the delegates of the said countries.
(3) Subject to the provisions of Article 26 which apply to the amendment of Articles 22 to 26, any revision of this Act, including the Appendix, shall require the unanimity of the votes cast.

Article 28

[*Acceptance and Entry Into Force of Act for Countries of the Union:* 1. Ratification, accession; possibility of excluding certain provisions; withdrawal of exclusion; 2. Entry into force of Articles 1 to 21 and Appendix; 3. Entry into force of Articles 22 to 38]

(1)(a) Any country of the Union which has signed this Act may ratify it, and, if it has not signed it, may accede to it. Instruments of ratification or accession shall be deposited with the Director General.
(b) Any country of the Union may declare in its instrument of ratification or accession that its ratification or accession shall not apply to Articles 1 to 21 and the Appendix, provided that, if such country has previously made a declaration under Article VI(1)

of the Appendix, then it may declare in the said instrument only that its ratification or accession shall not apply to Articles 1 to 20.
(c) Any country of the Union which, in accordance with subparagraph (b), has excluded provisions therein referred to from the effects of its ratification or accession may at any later time declare that it extends the effects of its ratification or accession to those provisions. Such declaration shall be deposited with the Director General.
(2)(a) Articles 1 to 21 and the Appendix shall enter into force three months after both of the following two conditions are fulfilled:

(i) at least five countries of the Union have ratified or acceded to this Act without making a declaration under paragraph (1)(b),
(ii) France, Spain, the United Kingdom of Great Britain and Northern Ireland, and the United States of America, have become bound by the Universal Copyright Convention as revised at Paris on July 24, 1971.

(b) The entry into force referred to in subparagraph (a) shall apply to those countries of the Union which, at least three months before the said entry into force, have deposited instruments of ratification or accession not containing a declaration under paragraph (1)(b).
(c) With respect to any country of the Union not covered by subparagraph (b) and which ratifies or accedes to this Act without making a declaration under paragraph (1)(b), Articles 1 to 21 and the Appendix shall enter into force three months after the date on which the Director General has notified the deposit of the relevant instrument of ratification or accession, unless a subsequent date has been indicated in the instrument deposited. In the latter case, Articles 1 to 21 and the Appendix shall enter into force with respect to that country on the date thus indicated.
(d) The provisions of subparagraphs (a) to (c) do not affect the application of Article VI of the Appendix.
(3) With respect to any country of the Union which ratifies or accedes to this Act with or without a declaration made under paragraph (1)(b), Articles 22 to 38 shall enter into force three months after the date on which the Director General has notified the deposit of the relevant instrument of ratification or accession, unless a subsequent date has been indicated in the instrument deposited. In the latter case, Articles 22 to 38 shall enter into force with respect to that country on the date thus indicated.

Article 29

[Acceptance and Entry Into Force for Countries Outside the Union: 1. Accession; 2. Entry into force]

(1) Any country outside the Union may accede to this Act and thereby become party to this Convention and a member of the Union. Instruments of accession shall be deposited with the Director General.
(2)(a) Subject to subparagraph (b), this Convention shall enter into force with respect to any country outside the Union three months after the date on which the Director General has notified the deposit of its instrument of accession, unless a subsequent date has been indicated in the instrument deposited. In the latter case, this Convention shall enter into force with respect to that country on the date thus indicated.
(b) If the entry into force according to subparagraph (a) precedes the entry into force of Articles 1 to 21 and the Appendix according to Article 28(2)(a), the said country shall, in the meantime, be bound, instead of by Articles 1 to 21 and the Appendix, by Articles 1 to 20 of the Brussels Act of this Convention.

Article 29 bis

[Effect of Acceptance of Act for the Purposes of Article 14(2) of the WIPO Convention]

Ratification of or accession to this Act by any country not bound by Articles 22 to 38 of the Stockholm Act of this Convention shall, for the sole purposes of Article 14(2) of the Convention establishing the Organisation, amount to ratification of or accession to the said Stockholm Act with the limitation set forth in Article 28(1)(b)(i) thereof.

Article 30

[*Reservations:* 1. Limits of possibility of making reservations; 2. Earlier reservations; reservation as to the right of translation; withdrawal of reservation]

(1) Subject to the exceptions permitted by paragraph (2) of this Article, by Article 28(1)(b), by Article 33(2), and by the Appendix, ratification or accession shall automatically entail acceptance of all the provisions and admission to all the advantages of this Convention.
(2)(a) Any country of the Union ratifying or acceding to this Act may, subject to Article V(2) of the Appendix, retain the benefit of the reservations it has previously formulated on condition that it makes a declaration to that effect at the time of the deposit of its instrument of ratification or accession.
(b) Any country outside the Union may declare, in acceding to this Convention and subject to Article V(2) of the Appendix, that it intends to substitute, temporarily at least, for Article 8 of this Act concerning the right of translation, the provisions of Article 5 of the Union Convention of 1886, as completed at Paris in 1896, on the clear understanding that the said provisions are applicable only to translations into a language in general use in the said country. Subject to Article I(6)(b) of the Appendix, any country has the right to apply, in relation to the right of translation of works whose country of origin is a country availing itself of such a reservation, a protection which is equivalent to the protection granted by the latter country.
(c) Any country may withdraw such reservations at any time by notification addressed to the Director General.

Article 31

[*Applicability to Certain Territories:* 1. Declaration; 2. Withdrawal of declaration; 3. Effective date; 4. Acceptance of factual situations not implied]

(1) Any country may declare in its instrument of ratification or accession, or may inform the Director General by written notification at any time thereafter, that this Convention shall be applicable to all or part of those territories, designated in the declaration or notification, for the external relations of which it is responsible.
(2) Any country which has made such a declaration or given such a notification may, at any time, notify the Director General that this Convention shall cease to be applicable to all or part of such territories.
(3)(a) Any declaration made under paragraph (1) shall take effect on the same date as the ratification or accession in which it was included, and any notification given under that paragraph shall take effect three months after its notification by the Director General.
(b) Any notification given under paragraph (2) shall take effect twelve months after its receipt by the Director General.
(4) This Article shall in no way be understood as implying the recognition or tacit acceptance by a country of the Union of the factual situation concerning a territory to which this Convention is made applicable by another country of the Union by virtue of a declaration under paragraph (1).

Article 32

[*Applicability of this Act and of Earlier Acts:* 1. As between countries already members of the Union; 2. As between a country becoming a member of the Union and other countries members of the Union; 3. Applicability of the Appendix in Certain Relations]

(1) This Act shall, as regards relations between the countries of the Union, and to the extent that it applies, replace the Berne Convention of September 9, 1886, and the subsequent Acts of revision. The Acts previously in force shall continue to be applicable, in their entirety or to the extent that this Act does not replace them by virtue of the preceding sentence, in relations with countries of the Union which do not ratify or accede to this Act.
(2) Countries outside the Union which become party to this Act shall, subject to paragraph (3), apply it with respect to any country of the Union not bound by this Act or which, although bound by this Act, has made a declaration pursuant to Article

28(1)(b). Such countries recognize that the said country of the Union, in its relations with them:

(i) may apply the provisions of the most recent Act by which it is bound, and
(ii) subject to Article I(6) of the Appendix, has the right to adapt the protection to the level provided for by this Act.

(3) Any country which has availed itself of any of the faculties provided for in the Appendix may apply the provisions of the Appendix relating to the faculty or faculties of which it has availed itself in its relations with any other country of the Union which is not bound by this Act, provided that the latter country has accepted the application of the said provisions.

Article 33

[*Disputes:* 1. Jurisdiction of the International Court of Justice; 2. Reservation as to such jurisdiction; 3. Withdrawal of reservation]

(1) Any dispute between two or more countries of the Union concerning the interpretation or application of this Convention, not settled by negotiation, may, by any one of the countries concerned, be brought before the International Court of Justice by application in conformity with the Statute of the Court, unless the countries concerned agree on some other method of settlement. The country bringing the dispute before the Court shall inform the International Bureau; the International Bureau shall bring the matter to the attention of the other countries of the Union.
(2) Each country may, at the time it signs this Act or deposits its instrument of ratification or accession, declare that it does not consider itself bound by the provisions of paragraph (1). With regard to any dispute between such country and any other country of the Union, the provisions of paragraph (1) shall not apply.
(3) Any country having made a declaration in accordance with the provisions of paragraph (2) may, at any time, withdraw its declaration by notification addressed to the Director General.

Article 34

[*Closing of Certain Earlier Provisions:* 1. Of Earlier Acts; 2. Of the Protocol to the Stockholm Act]

(1) Subject to Article 29bis, no country may ratify or accede to earlier Acts of this Convention once Articles 1 to 21 and the Appendix have entered into force.
(2) Once Articles 1 to 21 and the Appendix have entered into force, no country may make a declaration under Article 5 of the Protocol Regarding Developing Countries attached to the Stockholm Act.

Article 35

[*Duration of the Convention; Denunciation:* 1. Unlimited duration; 2. Possibility of denunciation; 3. Effective date of denunciation; 4. Moratorium on denunciation]

(1) This Convention shall remain in force without limitation as to time.
(2) Any country may denounce this Act by notification addressed to the Director General. Such denunciation shall constitute also denunciation of all earlier Acts and shall affect only the country making it, the Convention remaining in full force and effect as regards the other countries of the Union.
(3) Denunciation shall take effect one year after the day on which the Director General has received the notification.
(4) The right of denunciation provided by this Article shall not be exercised by any country before the expiration of five years from the date upon which it becomes a member of the Union.

Article 36

[*Application of the Convention:* 1. Obligation to adopt the necessary measures; 2. Time from which obligation exists]

(1) Any country party to this Convention undertakes to adopt, in accordance with its constitution, the measures necessary to ensure the application of this Convention.
(2) It is understood that, at the time a country becomes bound by this Convention, it will be in a position under its domestic law to give effect to the provisions of this Convention.

Article 37

[*Final Clauses:* 1. Languages of the Act; 2. Signature; 3. Certified copies; 4. Registration; 5. Notifications]

(1)(a) This Act shall be signed in a single copy in the French and English languages and, subject to paragraph (2), shall be deposited with the Director General.
(b) Official texts shall be established by the Director General, after consultation with the interested Governments, in the Arabic, German, Italian, Portuguese and Spanish languages, and such other languages as the Assembly may designate.
(c) In case of differences of opinion on the interpretation of the various texts, the French text shall prevail.
(2) This Act shall remain open for signature until January 31, 1972. Until that date, the copy referred to in paragraph (1)(a) shall be deposited with the Government of the French Republic.
(3) The Director General shall certify and transmit two copies of the signed text of this Act to the Governments of all countries of the Union and, on request, to the Government of any other country.
(4) The Director General shall register this Act with the Secretariat of the United Nations.
(5) The Director General shall notify the Governments of all countries of the Union of signatures, deposits of instruments of ratification or accession and any declarations included in such instruments or made pursuant to Articles 28(1)(c), 30(2)(a) and (b), and 33(2), entry into force of any provisions of this Act, notifications of denunciation, and notifications pursuant to Articles 30(2)(c), 31(1) and (2), 33(3), and 38(1), as well as the Apendix.

Article 38

[*Transitory Provisions:* 1. Exercise of the 'five-year privilege'; 2. Bureau of the Union, Director of the Bureau; 3. Succession of Bureau of the Union]

(1) Countries of the Union which have not ratified or acceded to this Act and which are not bound by Articles 22 to 26 of the Stockholm Act of this Convention may, until April 26, 1975, exercise, if they so desire, the rights provided under the said Articles as if they were bound by them. Any country desiring to exercise such rights shall give written notification to this effect to the Director General; this notification shall be effective on the date of its receipt. Such countries shall be deemed to be members of the Assembly until the said date.
(2) As long as all the countries of the Union have not become Members of the Organisation, the International Bureau of the Organisation shall also function as the Bureau of the Union, and the Director General as the Director of the said Bureau.
(3) Once all the countries of the Union have become Members of the Organisation, the rights, obligations, and property, of the Bureau of the Union shall devolve on the International Bureau of the Organisation.

APPENDIX

[SPECIAL PROVISIONS REGARDING DEVELOPING COUNTRIES]

Article I

[*Faculties Open to Developing Countries:* 1. Availability of certain faculties; declaration; 2. Duration of effect of declaration; 3. Cessation of developing country status; 4. Existing stocks of copies; 5. Declarations concerning certain territories; 6. Limits of reciprocity]

(1) Any country regarded as a developing country in conformity with the established practice of the General Assembly of the United Nations which ratifies or accedes to this Act, of which this Appendix forms an integral part, and which, having regard to its economic situation and its social or cultural needs, does not consider itself immediately in a position to make provision for the protection of all the rights as provided for in this Act, may, by a notification deposited with the Director General at the time of depositing its instrument of ratification or accession or, subject to Article V(1)(c), at any time thereafter, declare that it will avail itself of the faculty provided for in Article II, or of the faculty provided for in Article III, or of both of those faculties. It may, instead of availing itself of the faculty provided for in Article II, make a declaration according to Article V(1)(a).

(2)(a) Any declaration under paragraph (1) notified before the expiration of the period of ten years from the entry into force of Articles 1 to 21 and this Appendix according to Article 28(2) shall be effective until the expiration of the said period. Any such declaration may be renewed in whole or in part for periods of ten years each by a notification deposited with the Director General not more than fifteen months and not less than three months before the expiration of the ten-year period then running.

(b) Any declaration under paragraph (1) notified after the expiration of the period of ten years from the entry into force of Articles 1 to 21 and this Appendix according to Article 28(2) shall be effective until the expiration of the ten-year period then running. Any such declaration may be renewed as provided for in the second sentence of subparagraph (a).

(3) Any country of the Union which has ceased to be regarded as a developing country as referred to in paragraph (1) shall no longer be entitled to renew its declaration as provided in paragraph (2), and, whether or not it formally withdraws its declaration, such country shall be precluded from availing itself of the faculties referred to in paragraph (1) from the expiration of the ten-year period then running or from the expiration of a period of three years after it has ceased to be regarded as a developing country, whichever period expires later.

(4) Where, at the time when the declaration made under paragraph (1) or (2) ceases to be effective, there are copies in stock which were made under a licence granted by virtue of this Appendix, such copies may continue to be distributed until their stock is exhausted.

(5) Any country which is bound by the provisions of this Act and which has deposited a declaration or a notification in accordance with Article 31(1) with respect to the application of this Act to a particular territory, the situation of which can be regarded as analogous to that of the countries referred to in paragraph (1), may, in respect of such territory, make the declaration referred to in paragrah (1) and the notification of renewal referred to in paragraph (2). As long as such declaration or notification remains in effect, the provisions of this Appendix shall be applicable to the territory in respect of which it was made.

(6)(a) The fact that a country avails itself of any of the faculties referred to in paragraph (1) does not permit another country to give less protection to works of which the country of origin is the former country than it is obliged to grant under Articles 1 to 20.

(b) The right to apply reciprocal treatment provided for in Article 30(2)(b), second sentence, shall not, until the date on which the period applicable under Article I(3) expires, be exercised in respect of works the country of origin of which is a country which has made a declaration according to Article V(1)(a).

Article II

[*Limitations on the Right of Translation:* 1. Licenses grantable by competent authority; 2. to 4. Conditions allowing the grant of such licences; 5. Purposes for which licences may be granted; 6. Termination of licences; 7. Works composed mainly of illustrations; 8. Works withdrawn from circulation; 9. Licenses for broadcasting organisations]

(1) Any country which has declared that it will avail itself of the faculty provided for in this Article shall be entitled, so far as works published in printed or analogous forms of reproduction are concerned, to substitute for the exclusive right of translation provided for in Article 8 a system of non-exclusive and non-transferable licences, granted by the competent authority under the following conditions and subject to Article IV.

(2)(a) Subject to paragraph (3), if, after the expiration of a period of three years, or of any longer period determined by the national legislation of the said country, commencing on the date of the first publication of the work, a translation of such work has not been published in a language in general use in that country by the owner of the right of translation, or with his authorisation, any national of such country may obtain a licence to make a translation of the work in the said language and publish the translation in printed or analogous forms of reproduction.

(b) A licence under the conditions provided for in this Article may also be granted if all the editions of the translation published in the language concerned are out of print.

(3)(a) In the case of translations into a language which is not in general use in one or more developed countries which are members of the Union, a period of one year shall be substituted for the period of three years referred to in paragraph (2)(a).

(b) Any country referred to in paragraph (1) may, with the unanimous agreement of the developed countries which are members of the Union and in which the same language is in general use, substitute, in the case of translations into that language, for the period of three years referred to in paragraph (2)(a) a shorter period as determined by such agreement but not less than one year. However, the provisions of the foregoing sentence shall not apply where the language in question is English, French or Spanish. The Director General shall be notified of any such agreement by the Governments which have concluded it.

(4)(a) No licence obtainable after three years shall be granted under this Article until a further period of six months has elapsed, and no licence obtainable after one year shall be granted under this Article until a further period of nine months has elapsed

(i) from the date on which the applicant complies with the requirements mentioned in Article IV(1), or
(ii) where the identity or the address of the owner of the right of translation is unknown, from the date on which the applicant sends, as provided for in Article IV(2), copies of his application submitted to the authority competent to grant the licence.

(b) If, during the said period of six or nine months, a translation in the language in respect of which the application was made is published by the owner of the right of translation or with his authorisation, no licence under this Article shall be granted.

(5) Any licence under this Article shall be granted only for the purpose of teaching, scholarship or research.

(6) If a translation of a work is published by the owner of the right of translation or with his authorisation at a price reasonably related to that normally charged in the country for comparable works, any licence granted under this Article shall terminate if such translation is in the same language and with substantially the same content as the translation published under the licence. Any copies already made before the licence terminates may continue to be distributed until their stock is exhausted.

(7) For works which are composed mainly of illustrations, a licence to make and publish a translation of the text and to reproduce and publish the illustrations may be granted only if the conditions of Article III are also fulfilled.

(8) No licence shall be granted under this Article when the author has withdrawn from circulation all copies of his work.

(9)(a) A license to make a translation of a work which has been published in printed or analogous forms of reproduction may also be granted to any broadcasting organisation having its headquarters in a country referred to in paragraph (1), upon an application made to the competent authority of that country by the said organisation, provided that all of the following conditions are met:

(i) the translation is made from a copy made and acquired in accordance with the laws of the said country;
(ii) the translation is only for use in broadcasts intended exclusively for teaching or for the dissemination of the results of specialised technical or scientific research to experts in a particular profession;
(iii) the translation is used exclusively for the purposes referred to in condition (ii) through broadcasts made lawfully and intended for recipients on the territory of the said country, including broadcasts made through the medium of sound or visual recordings lawfully and exclusively made for the purpose of such broadcasts;
(iv) all uses made of the translation are without any commercial purpose.

(b) Sound or visual recordings of a translation which was made by a broadcasting organisation under a licence granted by virtue of this paragraph may, for the purposes and subject to the conditions referred to in subparagraph (a) and with the agreement of that organisation, also be used by any other broadcasting organisation having its headquarters in the country whose competent authority granted the licence in question.
(c) Provided that all of the criteria and conditions set out in subparagraph (a) are met, a licence may also be granted to a broadcasting organisation to translate any text incorporated in an audio-visual fixation where such fixation was itself prepared and published for the sole purpose of being used in connection with systematic instructional activities.
(d) Subject to subparagraphs (a) to (c), the provisions of the preceding paragraphs shall apply to the grant and exercise of any licence granted under this paragraph.

Article III

[*Limitation on the Right of Reproduction:* 1. Licences grantable by competent authority; 2. to 5. Conditions allowing the grant of such licences; 6. Termination of licences. 7. Works to which this Article applies]

(1) Any country which has declared that it will avail itself of the faculty provided for in this Article shall be entitled to substitute for the exclusive right of reproduction provided for in Article 9 a system of non-exclusive and non-transferable licences, granted by the competent authority under the following conditions and subject to Article IV.
(2)(a) If, in relation to a work to which this Article applies by virtue of paragraph (7), after the expiration of

(i) the relevant period specified in paragraph (3), commencing on the date of first publication of a particular edition of the work, or
(ii) any longer period determined by national legislation of the country referred to in paragraph (1), commencing on the same date,

copies of such edition have not been distributed in that country to the general public or in connection with systematic instructional activities, by the owner of the right of reproduction or with his authorisation, at a price reasonably related to that normally charged in the country for comparable works, any national of such country may obtain a licence to reproduce and publish such edition at that or a lower price for use in connection with systematic instructional activities.
(b) A licence to reproduce and publish an edition which has been distributed as described in subparagraph (a) may also be granted under the conditions provided for in this Article if, after the expiration of the applicable period, no authorised copies of that edition have been on sale for a period of six months in the country concerned to the general public or in connection with systematic instructional activities at a price reasonably related to that normally charged in the country for comparable works.
(3) The period referred to in paragraph (2)(a)(i) shall be five years, except that

(i) for works of the natural and physical sciences, including mathematics, and of technology, the period shall be three years;
(ii) for works of fiction, poetry, drama and music, and for art books, the period shall be seven years.

(4)(a) No licence obtainable after three years shall be granted under this Article until a period of six months has elapsed

(i) from the date on which the applicant complies with the requirements mentioned in Article IV(1), or
(ii) where the identity or the address of the owner of the right of reproduction is unknown, from the date on which the applicant sends, as provided for in Article IV(2), copies of his application submitted to the authority competent to grant the licence.

(b) Where licences are obtainable after other periods and Article IV(2) is applicable, no licence shall be granted until a period of three months has elapsed from the date of the dispatch of the copies of the application.
(c) If, during the period of six or three months referred to in subparagraphs (a) and (b), a distribution as described in paragraph 2(a) has taken place, no licence shall be granted under this Article.
(d) No licence shall be granted if the author has withdrawn from circulation all copies of the edition for the reproduction and publication of which the licence has been applied for.
(5) A licence to reproduce and publish a translation of a work shall not be granted under this Article in the following cases:

(i) where the translation was not published by the owner of the right of translation or with his authorisation, or
(ii) where the translation is not in a language in general use in the country in which the licence is applied for.

(6) If copies of an edition of a work are distributed in the country referred to in paragraph (1) to the general public or in connection with systematic instructional activities, by the owner of the right of reproduction or with his authorisation, at a price reasonably related to that normally charged in the country for comparable works, any licence granted under this Article shall terminate if such edition is in the same language and with substantially the same content as the edition which was published under the said licence. Any copies already made before the license terminates may continue to be distributed until their stock is exhausted.
(7)(a) Subject to subparagraph (b), the works to which this Article applies shall be limited to works published in printed or analogous forms of reproduction.
(b) This Article shall also apply to the reproduction in audio-visual form of lawfully made audio-visual fixations including any protected works incorporated therein and to the translation of any incorporated text into a language in general use in the country in which the licence is applied for, always provided that the audio-visual fixations in question were prepared and published for the sole purpose of being used in connection with systematic instructional activities.

Article IV

[*Provisions Common to Licenses Under Articles II and III:* 1 and 2. Procedure. 3. Indication of author and title of work; 4. Exportation of copies; 5. Notice; 6. Compensation]

(1) A licence under Article II or Article III may be granted only if the applicant, in accordance with the procedure of the country concerned, establishes either that he has requested, and has been denied, authorisation by the owner of the right to make and publish the translation or to reproduce and publish the edition, as the case may be, or that, after due diligence on his part, he was unable to find the owner of the right. At the same time as making the request, the applicant shall inform any national or international information center referred to in paragraph (2).
(2) If the owner of the right cannot be found, the applicant for a licence shall send, by registered airmail, copies of his application, submitted to the authority competent to grant the licence, to the publisher whose name appears on the work and to any national or international information centre which may have been designated, in a notification to that effect deposited with the Director General, by the Government of the country in which the publisher is believed to have his principal place of business.
(3) The name of the author shall be indicated on all copies of the translation or

reproduction published under a licence granted under Article II or Article III. The title of the work shall appear on all such copies. In the case of a translation, the original title of the work shall appear in any case on all the said copies.

(4)(a) No licence granted under Article II or Article III shall extend to the export of copies, and any such licence shall be valid only for publication of the translation or of the reproduction, as the case may be, in the territory of the country in which it has been applied for.

(b) For the purposes of subparagraph (a), the notion of export shall include the sending of copies from any territory to the country which, in respect of that territory, has made a declaration under Article I(5).

(c) Where a governmental or other public entity of a country which has granted a licence to make a translation under Article II into a language other than English, French or Spanish sends copies of a translation published under such licence to another country, such sending of copies shall not, for the purposes of subparagrah (a), be considered to constitute export if all of the following conditions are met:

(i) the recipients are individuals who are nationals of the country whose competent authority has granted the licence, or organisations grouping such individuals;
(ii) the copies are to be used only for the purpose of teaching, scholarship or research;
(iii) the sending of the copies and their subsequent distribution to recipients is without any commercial purpose; and
(iv) the country to which the copies have been sent has agreed with the country whose competent authority has granted the licence to allow the receipt, or distribution, or both, and the Director General has been notified of the agreement by the Government of the country in which the licence has been granted.

(5) All copies published under a licence granted by virtue of Article II or Article III shall bear a notice in the appropriate language stating that the copies are available for distribution only in the country or territory to which the said licence applies.

(6)(a) Due provision shall be made at the national level to ensure

(i) that the licence provides, in favour of the owner of the right of translation or of reproduction, as the case may be, for just compensation that is consistent with standards of royalties normally operating on licences freely negotiated between persons in the two countries concerned, and
(ii) payment and transmittal of the compensation: should national currency regulations intervene, the competent authority shall make all efforts, by the use of international machinery, to ensure transmittal in internationally convertible currency or its equivalent.

(b) Due provision shall be made by national legislation to ensure a correct translation of the work, or an accurate reproduction of the particular edition, as the case may be.

Article V

[*Alternative Possibility for Limitation of the Right of Translation:* 1. Regime provided for under the 1886 and 1896 Acts; 2. No possibility of change to regime under Article II; 3. Time limit for choosing the alternative possibility]

(1)(a) Any country entitled to make a declaration that it will avail itself of the faculty provided for in Article II may, instead, at the time of ratifying or acceding to this Act:

(i) if it is a country to which Article 30(2)(a) applies, make a declaration under that provision as far as the right of translation is concerned;
(ii) if it is a country to which Article 30(2)(a) does not apply, and even if it is not a country outside the Union, make a declaration as provided for in Article 30(2)(b), first sentence.

(b) In the case of a country which ceases to be regarded as a developing country as referred to in Article I(1), a declaration made according to this paragraph shall be effective until the date on which the period applicable under Article I(3) expires.

(c) Any country which has made a declaration according to this paragraph may not subsequently avail itself of the faculty provided for in Article II even if it withdraws the said declaration.

(2) Subject to paragraph (3), any country which has availed itself of the faculty provided for in Article II may not subsequently make a declaration according to paragraph (1).

(3) Any country which has ceased to be regarded as a developing country as referred to in Article I(1) may, not later than two years prior to the expiration of the period applicable under Article I(3), make a declaration to the effect provided for in Article 30(2)(b), first sentence, notwithstanding the fact that it is not a country outside the Union. Such declaration shall take effect at the date on which the period applicable under Article I(3) expires.

Article VI

[*Possibilities of applying, or admitting the application of, certain provisions of the Appendix before becoming bound by it:* 1. Declaration; 2. Depository and effective date of declaration]

(1) Any country of the Union may declare, as from the date of this Act, and at any time before becoming bound by Articles 1 to 21 and this Appendix:

- (i) if it is a country which, were it bound by Articles 1 to 21 and this Appendix, would be entitled to avail itself of the faculties referred to in Article I(1), that it will apply the provisions of Article II or of Article III or of both to works whose country of origin is a country which, pursuant to (ii) below, admits the application of those Articles to such works, or which is bound by Articles 1 to 21 and this Appendix; such declaration may, instead of referring to Article II, refer to Article V;
- (ii) that it admits the application of this Appendix to works of which it is the country of origin by countries which have made a declaration under (i) above or a notification under Article I.

(2) Any declaration made under paragraph (1) shall be in writing and shall be deposited with the Director General. The declaration shall become effective from the date of its deposit.

Appendix 2
Universal Copyright Convention as revised at Paris on 24 July 1971

The Contracting States.

Moved by the desire to ensure in all countries copyright protection of literary, scientific and artistic works,

Convinced that a system of copyright protection appropriate to all nations of the world and expressed in a universal convention, additional to, and without impairing international systems already in force, will ensure respect for the rights of the individual and encourage the development of literature, the sciences and the arts,

Persuaded that such a universal copyright system will facilitate a wider dissemination of works of the human mind and increase international understanding,

Have resolved to revise the Universal Copyright Convention as signed at Geneva on 6 September 1952 (hereinafter called 'the 1952 Convention'), and consequently,

Have agreed as follows:

Article I

Each Contracting State undertakes to provide for the adequate and effective protection of the rights of authors and other copyright proprietors in literary, scientific and artistic works, including writings, musical, dramatic and cinematographic works, and paintings, engravings and sculpture.

Article II

1. Published works of nationals of any Contracting State and works first published in that State shall enjoy in each other Contracting State the same protection as that other State accords to works of its nationals first published in its own territory, as well as the protection specially granted by this Convention.
2. Unpublished works of nationals of each Contracting State shall enjoy in each other Contracting State the same protection as that other State accords to unpublished works of its own nationals, as well as the protection specially granted by this Convention.
3. For the purpose of this Convention any Contracting State may, by domestic legislation, assimilate to its own nationals any person domiciled in that State.

Article III

1. Any Contracting State which, under its domestic law, requires as a condition of copyright, compliance with formalities such as deposit, registration, notice, notarial certificates, payment of fees or manufacture or publication in that Contracting State, shall regard these requirements as satisfied with respect to all works protected in accordance with this Convention and first published outside its territory and the author of which is not one of its nationals, if from the time of the first publication all the copies of the work published with the authority of the author or other copyright proprietor bear the symbol © accompanied by the name of the copyright proprietor and the year of first publication placed in such manner and location as to give reasonable notice of claim of copyright.
2. The provisions of paragraph 1 shall not preclude any Contracting State from requiring formalities or other conditions for the acquisition and enjoyment of copyright in respect of works first published in its territory or works of its nationals wherever published.

3. The provisions of paragraph 1 shall not preclude any Contracting State from providing that a person seeking judicial relief must, in bringing the action, comply with procedural requirements, such as that the complainant must appear through domestic counsel or that the complainant must deposit with the court or an administrative office, or both, a copy of the work involved in the ligitation; provided that failure to comply with such requirements shall not affect the validity of the copyright, nor shall any such requirement be imposed upon a national of another Contracting State if such requirement is not imposed on nationals of the State in which protection is claimed.
4. In each Contracting State there shall be legal means of protecting without formalities the unpublished works of nationals of other Contracting States.
5. If a Contracting State grants protection for more than one term of copyright and the first term is for a period longer than one of the minimum periods prescribed in Article IV, such State shall not be required to comply with the provisions of paragraph 1 of this Article in respect of the second or any subsequent term of copyright.

Article IV

1. The duration of protection of a work shall be governed, in accordance with the provisions of Article II and this Article, by the law of the Contracting State in which protection is claimed.
2. (a) The term of protection for works protected under this Convention shall not be less than the life of the author and twenty-five years after his death. However, any Contracting State which, on the effective date of this Convention in that State, has limited this term for certain classes of works to a period computed from the first publication of the work, shall be entitled to maintain these exceptions and to extend them to other classes of works. For all these classes the term of protection shall not be less than twenty-five years from the date of first publication.
(b) Any Contracting State which, upon the effective date of this Convention in that State, does not compute the term of protection upon the basis of the life of the author, shall be entitled to compute the term of protection from the date of the first publication of the work or from its registration prior to publication, as the case may be, provided the term of protection shall not be less than twenty-five years from the date of first publication or from its registration prior to publication, as the case may be.
(c) If the legislation of a Contracting State grants two or more successive terms of protection, the duration of the first term shall not be less than one of the minimum periods specified in sub-paragraphs (a) and (b).
3. The provisions of paragraph 2 shall not apply to photographic works or to works of applied art; provided, however, that the term of protection in those Contracting States which protects photographic works, or works of applied art in so far as they are protected as artistic works, shall not be less than ten years for each of said classes of work.
4. (a) No Contracting State shall be obliged to grant protection to a work for a period longer than that fixed for the class of works to which the work in question belongs, in the case of unpublished works by the law of the Contracting State of which the author is a national, and in the case of published works by the law of the Contracting State in which the work has been first published.
(b) For the purposes of the application of sub-paragraph (a), if the law of any Contracting State grants two or more successive terms of protection the period of protection of that State shall be considered to be the aggregate of those terms. However, if a specified work is not protected by such State during the second or any subsequent term for any reason, the other Contracting States shall not be obliged to protect it during the second or any subsequent term.
5. For the purposes of the application of paragraph 4, the work of a national of a Contracting State, first published in a non-Contracting State, shall be treated as though first published in the Contracting State of which the author is a national.
6. For the purposes of the application of paragraph 4, in case of simultaneous publication in two or more Contracting States, the work shall be treated as though first published in the State which affords the shortest term; any work published in two or more Contracting States within thirty days of its first publication shall be considered as having been published simultaneously in said Contracting States.

Article IVbis

1. The rights referred to in Article I shall include the basic rights ensuring the author's economic interests, including the exclusive rights to authorise reproduction by any means, public performance and broadcasting. The provisions of this Article shall extend to works protected under this Convention either in their original form or in any form recognisably derived from the original.

2. However, any Contracting State may, by its domestic legislation, make exceptions that do not conflict with the spirit and provisions of this Convention, to the rights mentioned in paragraph 1 of this Article. Any State whose legislation so provides, shall nevertheless accord a reasonable degree of effective protection to each of the rights to which exception has been made.

Article V

1. The rights referred to in Article I shall include the exclusive right of the author to make, publish and authorise the making and publication of translations of works protected under this Convention.

2. However, any Contracting State may, by its domestic legislation, restrict the right of translation of writings, but only subject to the following provisions:

(a) If, after the expiration of a period of seven years from the date of the first publication of a writing, a translation of such writing has not been published in a language in general use in the Contracting State, by the owner of the right of translation or with his authorisation, any national of such Contracting State may obtain a non-exclusive licence from the competent authority thereof to translate the work into that language and publish the work so translated.

(b) Such national shall in accordance with the procedure of the State concerned, establish either that he has requested, and been denied, authorisation by the proprietor of the right to make and publish the translation, or that, after due diligence on his part, he was unable to find the owner of the right. A licence may also be granted on the same conditions if all previous editions of a translation in a language in general use in the Contracting State are out of print.

(c) If the owner of the right of translation cannot be found, then the applicant for a licence shall send copies of his application to the publisher whose name appears on the work and, if the nationality of the owner of the right of translation is known, to the diplomatic or consular representative of the State of which such owner is a national, or to the organisation which may have been designated by the government of that State. The licence shall not be granted before the expiration of a period of two months from the date of dispatch of the copies of the application.

(d) Due provision shall be made by domestic legislation to ensure to the owner of the right of translation a compensation which is just and conforms to international standards, to ensure payment and transmittal of such compensation and to ensure a correct translation of the work.

(e) The original title and the name of the author of the work shall be printed on all copies of the published translation. The licence shall be valid only for publication of the translation in the territory of the Contracting State where it has been applied for. Copies so published may be imported and sold in another Contracting State if a language in general use in such other State is the same language as that into which the work has been so translated, and if the domestic law in such other State makes provision for such licences and does not prohibit such importation and sale. Where the foregoing conditions do not exist, the importation and sale of such copies in a Contracting State shall be governed by its domestic law and its agreements. The licence shall not be transferred by the licensee.

(f) The licence shall not be granted when the author has withdrawn from circulation all copies of the work.

Article V^{bis}

1. Any Contracting State regarded as a developing country in conformity with the established practice of the General Assembly of the United Nations may, by a notification deposited with the Director-General of the United Nations Educational, Scien-

tific and Cultural Organisation (hereinafter called 'the Director-General') at the time of its ratification, acceptance or accession or thereafter, avail itself of any or all of the exceptions provided for in Articles V *ter* and V *quater*.

2. Any such notification shall be effective for ten years from the date of coming into force of this Convention, or for such part of that ten-year period as remains at the date of deposit of the notification, and may be renewed in whole or in part for further periods of ten years each, if not more than fifteen or less than three months before the expiration of the relevant ten-year period, the Contracting State deposits a further notification with the Director-General. Initial notifications may also be made during these further periods of ten years in accordance with the provisions of this Article.

3. Notwithstanding the provisions of paragraph 2, a Contracting State that has ceased to be regarded as a developing country as referred to in paragraph 1 shall no longer be entitled to renew its notification made under the provisions of paragraph 1 or 2, and whether or not it formally withdraws the notification such State shall be precluded from availing itself of the exceptions provided for in Articles V *ter* and V*quater* at the end of the current ten-year period, or at the end of three years after it has ceased to be regarded as a developing country, whichever period expires later.

4. Any copies of a work already made under the exceptions provided for in Articles V*ter* and V*quater* may continue to be distributed after the expiration of the period for which notifications under this Article were effective until their stock is exhausted.

5. Any Contracting State that has deposited a notification in accordance with Article XIII with respect to the application of this Convention to a particular country or territory, the situation of which can be regarded as analogous to that of the States referred to in paragraph 1 of this Article, may also deposit notifications and renew them in accordance with the provisions of this Article with respect to any such country or territory. During the effective period of such notifications, the provisions of Articles V*ter* and V*quater* may be applied with respect to such country or territory. The sending of copies from the country or territory to the Contracting States shall be considered as export within the meaning of Articles V*ter* and V*quater*.

Article V ter

1. (a) Any Contracting State to which Article V*bis* (1) applies may substitute for the period of seven years provided for in Article V(2) a period of three years or any longer period prescribed by its legislation. However, in the case of a translation into a language not in general use in one or more of the developed countries that are party to this Convention or only the 1952 Convention, the period shall be one year instead of three.

(b) A Contracting State to which Article V*bis* (1) applies may, with the unanimous agreement of the developed countries party to this Convention or only the 1952 Convention and in which the same language is in general use, substitute, in the case of translation into that language, for the period of three years provided for in sub-paragraph (a) another period as determined by such agreement but not shorter than one year. However, this sub-paragraph shall not apply where the language in question is English, French or Spanish. Notification of any such agreement shall be made to the Director-General.

(c) The licence may only be granted if the applicant, in accordance with the procedure of the State concerned, establishes either that he has requested, and been denied, authorisation by the owner of the right of translation, or that, after due diligence on his part, he was unable to find the owner of the right. At the same time as he makes his request he shall inform either the International Copyright Information Centre established by the United Nations Educational, Scientific and Cultural Organisation or any national or regional information centre which may have been designated in a notification to that effect deposited with the Director-General by the government of the State in which the publisher is believed to have his principal place of business.

(d) If the owner of the right of translation cannot be found, the applicant for a licence shall send, by registered airmail, copies of his application to the publisher whose name appears on the work and to any national or regional information centre as mentioned in sub-paragraph (c). If no such centre is notified he shall also send a copy to the international copyright information centre established by the United Nations Educational, Scientific and Cultural Organisation.

2. (a) Licences obtainable after three years shall not be granted under this Article until a further period of six months has elapsed and licences obtainable after one year until a further period of nine months has elapsed. The further period shall begin either from the date of the request for permission to translate mentioned in paragraph 1 (c) or, if the identity or address of the owner of the right of translation is not known, from the date of dispatch of the copies of the application for a licence mentioned in paragraph 1 (d).
(b) Licences shall not be granted if a translation has been published by the owner of the right of translation or with his authorisation during the said period of six months or nine months.
3. Any licence under this Article shall be granted only for the purpose of teaching, scholarship or research.
4. (a) Any licence granted under this Article shall not extend to the export of copies and shall be valid only for publication in the territory of the Contracting State where it has been applied for.
(b) Any copy published in accordance with a licence granted under this Article shall bear a notice in the appropriate language stating that the copy is available for distribution only in the Contracting State granting the licence. If the writing bears the notice specified in Article III (1) the copies shall bear the same notice.
(c) The prohibition of export provided for in sub-paragraph (a) shall not apply where a governmental or other public entity of a State which has granted a licence under this Article to translate a work into a language other than English, French or Spanish sends copies of a translation prepared under such licence to another country if:
  (i) the recipients are individuals who are nationals of the Contracting State granting the licence, or organisations grouping such individuals;
  (ii) the copies are to be used only for the purpose of teaching, scholarship or research;
  (iii) the sending of the copies and their subsequent distribution to recipients is without the object of commercial purpose; and
  (iv) the country to which the copies have been sent has agreed with the Contracting State to allow the receipt, distribution or both and the Director-General has been notified of such governments which have concluded it.
5. Due provision shall be made at the national level to ensure:
(a) that the licence provides for just compensation that is consistent with standards of royalties normally operating in the case of licences freely negotiated between persons in the two countries concerned; and
(b) payment and transmittal of the compensation; however, should national currency regulations intervene, the competent authority shall make all efforts, by the use of international machinery, to ensure transmittal in internationally convertible currency or its equivalent.
6. Any licence granted by a Contracting State under this Article shall terminate if a translation of the work in the same language with substantially the same content as the edition in respect of which the licence was granted is published in the said State by the owner of the right of translation or with his authorisation, at a price reasonably related to that normally charged in the same State for comparable works. Any copies already made before the licence is terminated may continue to be distributed until their stock is exhausted.
7. For works which are composed mainly of illustrations a licence to translate the text and to reproduce the illustrations may be granted only if the condition of Article V*quater* are also fulfilled.
8. (a) A licence to translate a work protected under this Convention, published in printed or analogous forms of reproduction, may also be granted to a broadcasting organisation having its headquarters in a Contracting State to which Article V*bis* (1) applies, upon an application made in that State by the said organisation under the following conditions:
  (i) the translation is made from a copy made and acquired in accordance with the laws of the Contracting State;
  (ii) the translation is for use only in broadcasts intended exclusively for teaching or for the dissemination of the results of specialised technical or scientific research to experts in a particular profession;

(iii) the translation is used exclusively for the purposes set out in condition (ii), through broadcasts lawfully made which are intended for recipients on the territory of the Contracting State, including broadcasts made through the medium of sound or visual recording lawfully and exclusively made for the purpose of such broadcasts;
(iv) sound or visual recordings of the translation may be exchanged only between broadcasting organisations having their headquarters in the Contracting State granting the licence; and
(v) all uses made of the translation are without any commercial purpose.

(b) Provided all of the criteria and conditions set out in sub-paragraph (a) are met, a licence may also be granted to a broadcasting organisation to translate any text incorporated in an audio-visual fixation which was itself prepared and published for the sole purpose of being used in connexion with systematic instructional activities.

(c) Subject to sub-paragraphs (a) and (b), the other provisions of this Article shall apply to the grant and exercise of the licence.

9. Subject to the provisions of this Article, any licence granted under this Article shall be governed by the provisions of Article V, and shall continue to be governed by the provisions of Article V and of this Article, even after the seven-year period provided for in Article V (2) has expired. However, after the said period has expired, the licensee shall be free to request that the said licence be replaced by a new licence governed exclusively by the provisions of Article V.

Article V quater

1. Any Contracting State to which Article V*bis* (1) applies may adopt the following provisions:

(a) If, after the expiration of (i) the relevant period specified in sub-paragraph (c) commencing from the date of first publication of a particular edition of a literary, scientific or artistic work referred to in paragraph 3, or (ii) any longer period determined by national legislation of the State, copies of such edition have not been distributed in that State to the general public or in connexion with systematic instructional activities at a price reasonably related to that normally charged in the State for comparable works, by the owner of the right of reproduction or with his authorisation, any national of such State may obtain a non-exclusive licence from the competent authority to publish such edition at that or a lower price for use in connexion with systematic instructional activities. The licence may only be granted if such national, in accordance with the procedure of the State concerned, establishes either that he has requested, and has been denied, authorisation by the proprietor of the right to publish such work, or that, after due diligence on his part, he was unable to find the owner of the right. At the same time as he makes his request he shall inform either the international copyright information centre established by the United Nations Educational, Scientific and Cultural Organisation or any national or regional information centre referred to in sub-paragraph (d).

(b) A licence may also be granted on the same conditions if, for a period of six months, no authorised copies of the edition in question have been on sale in the State concerned to the general public or in connexion with systematic instructional activities at a price reasonably related to that normally charged in the State for comparable works.

(c) The period referred to in sub-paragraph (a) shall be five years except that:

(i) for works of the natural and physical sciences, including mathematics, and of technology, the period shall be three years;
(ii) for works of fiction, poetry, drama, and music, and for art books, the period shall be seven years.

(d) If the owner of the right of reproduction cannot be found, the applicant for a licence shall send, by registered air mail, copies of his application to the publisher whose name appears on the work and to any national or regional information centre identified as such in a notification deposited with the Director-General by the State in which the publisher is believed to have his principal place of business. In the absence of any such notification, he shall also send a copy to the international copyright information centre established by the United Nations Educational, Scientific and Cultural Organisation. The licence shall not be granted before the expiration of a period of three months from the date of dispatch of the copies of the application.

(e) Licences obtainable after three years shall not be granted under this Article:

(i) until a period of six months has elapsed from the date of the request for permission referred to in sub-paragraph (a) or, if the identity or address of the owner of the right of reproduction is unknown, from the date of the dispatch of the copies of the application for a licence referred to in sub-paragraph (d);
(ii) if any such distribution of copies of the edition as is mentioned in sub-paragraph (a) has taken place during that period.

(f) The name of the author and the title of the particular edition of the work shall be printed on all copies of the published reproduction. The licence shall not extend to the export of copies and shall be valid only for publication in the territory of the Contracting State where it has been applied for. The licence shall not be transferable by the licensee.
(g) Due provision shall be made by domestic legislation to ensure an accurate reproduction of the particular edition in question.
(h) A licence to reproduce and publish a translation of a work shall not be granted under this Article in the following cases:

(i) where the translation was not published by the owner of the right of translation or with his authorisation;
(ii) where the translation is not in a language in general use in the State with power to grant the licence.

2. The exceptions provided for in paragraph 1 are subject to the following additional provisions:

(a) Any copy published in accordance with a licence granted under this Article shall bear a notice in the appropriate language stating that the copy is available for distribution only in the Contracting State to which the said licence applies. If the edition bears the notice specified in Article III (1), the copies shall bear the same notice.
(b) Due provision shall be made at the national level to ensure:

(i) that the licence provides for just compensation that is consistent with standards of royalties normally operating in the case of licences freely negotiated betweeen persons in the two countries concerned; and
(ii) payment and transmittal of the compensation; however, should national currency regulations intervene, the competent authority shall make all efforts, by the use of international machinery, to ensure transmittal in the internationally convertible currency or its equivalent.

(c) Whenever copies of an edition of a work are distributed in the Contracting State to the general public or in connexion with systematic instructional activities, by the owner of the right of reproduction or with his authorisation, at a price reasonably related to that normally charged in the State for comparable works, any licence granted under this Article shall terminate if such edition is in the same language and is substantially the same in content as the edition published under licence. Any copies already made before the licence is terminated may continue to be distributed until their stock is exhausted.
(d) No licence shall be granted when the author has withdrawn from circulation all copies of the edition in question.

3. (a) Subject to sub-paragraph (b), the literary, scientific or artistic works to which this Article applies shall be limited to works published in printed or analogous forms of reproduction.
(b) The provisions of this Article shall also apply to reproduction in audio-visual form of lawfully made audio-visual fixations including any protected works incorporated therein and to the translation of any incorporated text into a language in general use in the State with power to grant the licence; always provided that the audio-visual fixations in question were prepared and published for the sole purpose of being used in connexion with systematic instructional activities.

Article VI

'Publication', as used in this Convention, means the reproduction in tangible form and the general distribution to the public of copies of a work from which it can be read or otherwise visually perceived.

Article VII

This Convention shall not apply to works or rights in works which, at the effective date of this Convention in a Contracting State where protection is claimed, are permanently in the public domain in the said Contracting State.

Article VIII

1. This Convention, which shall bear the date of 24 July 1971, shall be deposited with the Director-General and shall remain open for signature by all States party to the 1952 Convention for a period of 120 days after the date of this Convention. It shall be subject to ratification or acceptance by the signatory States.
2. Any State which has not signed this Convention may accede thereto.
3. Ratification, acceptance or accession shall be effected by the deposit of an instrument to that effect with the Director-General.

Article IX

1. This Convention shall come into force three months after the deposit of twelve instruments of ratification, acceptance or accession.
2. Subsequently, this Convention shall come into force in respect of each State three months after that State has deposited its instrument of ratification, acceptance or accession.
3. Accession to this Convention by a State not party to the 1952 Convention shall also constitute accession to that Convention; however, if its instrument of accession is deposited before this Convention comes into force, such State may make its accession to the 1952 Convention conditional upon the coming into force of this Convention. After the coming into force of this Convention, no State may accede solely to the 1952 Convention.
4. Relations between States party to this Convention and States that are party only to the 1952 Convention, shall be governed by the 1952 Convention. However, any State party only to the 1952 Convention may, by a notification deposited with the Director-General, declare that it will admit the application of the 1971 Convention to works of its nationals or works first published in its territory by all States party to this Convention.

Article X

1. Each Contracting State undertakes to adopt, in accordance with its Constitution, such measures as are necessary to ensure the application of this Convention.
2. It is understood that at the date this Convention comes into force in respect of any State, that State must be in a position under its domestic law to give effect to the terms of this Convention.

Article XI

1. An Intergovernmental Committee is hereby established with the following duties:

(a) to study the problems concerning the application and operation of the Universal Copyright Convention;
(b) to make preparation for periodic revisions of this Convention;
(c) to study any other problems concerning the international protection of copyright, in co-operation with the various interested international organisations, such as the United Nations Educational, Scientific and Cultural Organisation, the International Union for the Protection of Literary and Artistic Works and the Organisation of American States;
(d) to inform States party to the Universal Copyright Convention as to its activities.

2. The Committee shall consist of the representatives of eighteen States party to this Convention or only to the 1952 Convention.

3. The Committee shall be selected with due consideration to a fair balance of national interests on the basis of geographical location, population, languages and stage of development.

4. The Director-General of the United Nations Educational, Scientific and Cultural Organisation, the Director-General of the World Intellectual Property Organisation and the Secretary-General of the Organisation of American States, or their representatives, may attend meetings of the Committee in an advisory capacity.

Article XII

The Intergovernmental Committee shall convene a conference for revision whenever it deems necessary, or at the request of at least ten States party to this Convention.

Article XIII

1. Any Contracting State may, at the time of deposit of its instrument of ratification, acceptance or accession, or at any time thereafter, declare by notification addressed to the Director-General that this Convention shall apply to all or any of the countries or territories for the international relations of which it is responsible and this Convention shall thereupon apply to the countries or territories named in such notification after the expiration of the term of three months provided for in Article IX. In the absence of such notification, this Convention shall not apply to any such country or territory.

2. However, nothing in this Article shall be understood as implying the recognition or tacit acceptance by a Contracting State of the factual situation concerning a country or territory to which this Convention is made applicable by another Contracting State in accordance with the provisions of this Article.

Article XIV

1. Any Contracting State may denounce this Convention in its own name or on behalf of all or any of the countries or territories with respect to which a notification has been given under Article XIII. The denunciation shall be made by notification addressed to the Director-General. Such denunciation shall also constitute denunciation of the 1952 Convention.

2. Such denunciation shall operate only in respect of the State or of the country or territory on whose behalf it was made and shall not take effect until twelve months after the date of receipt of the notification.

Article XV

A dispute between two or more Contracting States concerning the interpretation or application of this Convention, not settled by negotiation, shall, unless the States concerned agree on some other method of settlement, be brought before the International Court of Justice for determination by it.

Article XVI

1. This Convention shall be established in English, French and Spanish. The three texts shall be signed and shall be equally authoritative.

2. Official texts of this Convention shall be established by the Director-General, after consultation with the governments concerned, in Arabic, German, Italian and Portuguese.

3. Any Contracting State or group of Contracting States shall be entitled to have established by the Director-General other texts in the language of its choice by arrangement with the Director-General.

4. All such texts shall be annexed to the signed texts of this Convention.

Article XVII

1. This Convention shall not in any way affect the provisions of the Berne Convention for the Protection of Literary and Artistic Works or membership in the Union created by that Convention.

2. In application of the foregoing paragraph, a declaration has been annexed to the present Article. This declaration is an integral part of this Convention for the States bound by the Berne Convention on 1 January 1951, or which have or may become bound to it at a later date. The signature of this Convention by such States shall also constitute signature of the said declaration, and ratification, acceptance or accession by such States shall include the declaration, as well as this Convention.

Article XVIII

This Convention shall not abrogate multilateral or bilateral copyright conventions or arrangements that are or may be in effect exclusively between two or more American Republics. In the event of any difference either between the provisions of such existing conventions or arrangements and the provisions of this Convention, or between the provisions of this Convention and those of any new convention or arrangement which may be formulated between two or more American Republics after this Convention comes into force, the convention or arrangement most recently formulated shall prevail between the parties thereto. Rights in works acquired in any Contracting State under existing conventions or arrangements before the date this Convention comes into force in such State shall not be affected.

Article XIX

This Convention shall not abrogate multilateral or bilateral conventions or arrangements in effect between two or more Contracting States. In the event of any difference between the provisions of such existing conventions or arrangements and the provisions of this Convention, the provisions of this Convention shall prevail. Rights in works acquired in any Contracting State under existing conventions or arrangements before the date on which this Convention comes into force in such State shall not be affected. Nothing in this Article shall affect the provisions of Articles XVII and XVIII.

Article XX

Reservations to this Convention shall not be permitted.

Article XXI

1. The Director-General shall send duly certified copies of this Convention to the States interested and to the Secretary-General of the United Nations for registration by him.
2. He shall also inform all interested States of the ratifications, acceptances and accessions which have been deposited, the date on which this Convention comes into force, the notifications under this Convention, and denunciations under Article XIV.

Appendix declaration relating to article XVII

The States which are members of the International Union for the Protection of Literary and Artistic Works (hereinafter called 'the Berne Union') and which are signatories to this Convention,

Desiring to reinforce their mutual relations on the basis of the said Union and to avoid any conflict which might result from the co-existence of the Berne Convention and the Universal Copyright Convention,

Recognising the temporary need of some States to adjust their level of copyright protection in accordance with their stage of cultural, social and economic development,

Have, by common agreement, accepted the terms of the following declaration:

(a) Except as provided by paragraph (b), works which, according to the Berne Convention, have as their country of origin a country which has withdrawn from the Berne Union after 1 January 1951, shall not be protected by the Universal Copyright Convention in the countries of the Berne Union;
(b) Where a Contracting State is regarded as a developing country in conformity with the established practice of the General Assembly of the United Nations, and has deposited with the Director-General of the United Nations Educational, Scientific and Cultural Organisation, at the time of its withdrawal from the Berne Union, a notifica-

tion to the effect that it regards itself as a developing country, the provisions of paragraph (a) shall not be applicable as long as such State may avail itself of the exceptions provided for by this Convention in accordance with Article V*bis*;
(c) The Universal Copyright Convention shall not be applicable to the relationships among countries of the Berne Union in so far as it relates to the protection of works having as their country of origin, within the meaning of the Berne Convention, a country of the Berne Union.

Resolution concerning article XI

The Conference for Revision of the Universal Copyright Convention,
Having considered the problems relating to the Intergovernmental Committee provided for in Article XI of this Convention, to which this resolution is annexed,
Resolves that:

1. At its inception, the Committee shall include representatives of the twelve States members of the Intergovernmental Committee established under Article XI of the 1952 Convention and the resolution annexed to it, and, in addition, representatives of the following States: Algeria, Australia, Japan, Mexico, Senegal and Yugoslavia.
2. Any States that are not party to the 1952 Convention and have not acceded to this Convention before the first ordinary session of the Committee following the entry into force of this Convention shall be replaced by other States to be selected by the Committee at its first ordinary session in conformity with the provisions of Article XI (2) and (3).
3. As soon as this Convention comes into force the Committee as provided for in paragraph 1 shall be deemed to be constituted in accordance with Article XI of this Convention.
4. A session of the Committee shall take place within one year after the coming into force of this Convention; thereafter the Committee shall meet in ordinary session at intervals of not more than two years.
5. The Committee shall elect its Chairman and two Vice-Chairmen. It shall establish its Rules of Procedure having regard to the following principles:

(a) the normal duration of the term of office of the members represented on the Committee shall be six years with one-third retiring every two years, it being however understood that, of the original terms of office, one-third shall expire at the end of the Committee's second ordinary session which we will follow the entry into force of this Convention, a further third at the end of its third ordinary session, and the remaining third at the end of its fourth ordinary session.
(b) The rules governing the procedure whereby the Committee shall fill vacancies, the order in which terms of membership expire, eligibility for re-election, and election procedures, shall be based upon a balancing of the needs for continuity of membership and rotation of representation, as well as the considerations set out in Article XI (3). Expresses the wish that the United Nations Educational, Scientific and Cultural Organisation provide its Secretariat.
In faith whereof the undersigned, having deposited their respective full powers, have signed this Convention.
Done at Paris, this twenty-fourth day of July 1971, in a single copy.

Protocol 1

Annexed to the Universal Copyright Convention as revised at Paris on 24 July 1971 concerning the application of that Convention to works of Stateless persons and refugees

The States party hereto, being also party to the Universal Copyright Convention as revised at Paris on 24 July 1971 (hereinafter called 'the 1971 Convention'),
Have accepted the following provisions:
1. Stateless persons and refugees who have their habitual residence in a State party to this Protocol shall, for the purposes of the 1971 Convention, be assimilated to the nationals of that State.
2. (a) This Protocol shall be signed and shall be subject to ratification or acceptance,

or may be acceded to, as if the provisions of Article VIII of the 1971 Convention applied hereto.
(b) This Protocol shall enter into force in respect of each State, on the date of deposit of the instrument of ratification, acceptance or accession of the State concerned or on the date of entry into force of the 1971 Convention with respect to such State, whichever is the later.
(c) On the entry into force of this Protocol in respect of a State not party to Protocol 1 annexed to the 1952 Convention, the latter Protocol shall be deemed to enter into force in respect of such State.

In faith whereof the undersigned, being duly authorised thereto, have signed this Protocol.

Done at Paris this twenty-fourth day of July 1971, in the English, French and Spanish languages, the three texts being equally authoritative, in a single copy which shall be deposited with the Director-General of the United Nations Educational, Scientific and Cultural Organisation. The Director-General shall send certified copies to the signatory States, and to the Secretary-General of the United Nations for registration.

Protocol 2

Annexed to the Universal Copyright Convention as revised at Paris on 24 July 1971 concerning the application of that Convention to the works of certain international organisations

The States party hereto, being also party to the Universal Copyright Convention as revised at Paris on 24 July 1971 (hereinafter called 'the 1971 Convention'),

Have accepted the following provisions:

1. (a) The protection provided for in Article II (1) of the 1971 Convention shall apply to works published for the first time by the United Nations, by the Specialised Agencies in relationship therewith, or by the Organisation of American States.
(b) Similarly, Article II (2) of the 1971 Convention shall apply to the said organisation or agencies.

2. (a) This Protocol shall be signed and shall be subject to ratification or acceptance, or may be acceded to, as if the provisions of Article VIII of the 1971 Convention applied hereto.
(b) This Protocol shall enter into force for each State on the date of deposit of the instrument of ratification, acceptance or accession of the State concerned or on the date of entry into force of the 1971 Convention with respect to such State, whichever is the later.

In faith whereof the undersigned, being duly authorised thereto, have signed this Protocol.

Done at Paris, this twenty-fourth day of July 1971, in the English, French and Spanish languages, the three texts being equally authoritative, in a single copy which shall be deposited with the Director-General of the United Nations Educational, Scientific and Cultural Organisation. The Director-General shall send certified copies to the signatory States, and to the Secretary-General of the United Nations for registration.

Appendix 3

Rome Convention 1961
International Convention for the Protection of Performers, Producers of Phonograms and Broadcasting Organisations

The Contracting States, moved by the desire to protect the rights of performers, producers of phonograms, and broadcasting organisations,
 Have agreed as follows:

Article 1

Protection granted under this Convention shall leave intact and shall in no way affect the protection in literary and artistic works. Consequently no provision of this Convention may be interpreted as prejudicing such protection.

Article 2

1. For the purposes of this Convention, national treatment shall mean the treatment accorded by the domestic law of the Contracting State in which protection is claimed:

(a) to performers who are its nationals, as regards performances taking place, broadcast, or first fixed, on its territory;
(b) to producers of phonograms who are its nationals, as regards phonograms first fixed or first published on its territory;
(c) to broadcasting organisations which have their headquarters on its territory, as regards broadcasts transmitted from transmitters situated on its territory.

2. National treatment shall be subject to the protection specifically guaranteed, and the limitations specifically provided for, in this Convention.

Article 3

For the purpose of this Convention:

(a) 'performers' means actors, singers, musicians, dancers, and other persons who act, sing, deliver, declaim, play in, or otherwise perform literary or artistic works;
(b) 'phonogram' means any exclusively aural fixation of sounds of a performance or of other sounds;
(c) 'producer of phonograms' means the person who, or the legal entity which, first fixes the sounds of a performance or other sounds;
(d) 'publication' means the offering of copies of a phonogram to the public in reasonable quantity;
(e) 'reproduction' means the making of a copy or copies of a fixation;
(f) 'broadcasting' means the transmission by wireless means for public reception of sounds or of images and sounds;
(g) 'rebroadcasting' means the simultaneous broadcasting by one broadcasting organisation of the broadcast of another broadcasting organisation.

Article 4

Each Contracting State shall grant national treatment to performers if any of the following conditions is met:

(a) the performance takes place in another Contracting State;
(b) the performance is incorporated in a phonogram which is protected under Article 5 of this Convention;
(c) the performance, not being fixed on a phonogram, is carried by a broadcast which is protected by Article 6 of this Convention.

Article 5

1. Each Contracting State shall grant national treatment to producers of phonograms if any of the following conditions is met:
(a) the producer of the phonogram is a national of another Contracting State (criterion of nationality);
(b) the first fixation of the sound was made in another Contracting State (criterion of fixation);
(c) the phonogram was first published in another Contracting State (criterion of publication).
2. If a phonogram was first published in a non-contracting State but if it was also published, within thirty days of its first publication, in a Contracting State (simultaneous publication), it shall be considered as first published in the Contracting State.
3. By means of a notification deposited with the Secretary-General of the United Nations, any Contracting State may declare that it will not apply the criterion of publication or, alternatively, the criterion of fixation. Such notification may be deposited at the time of ratification, acceptance or accession, or at any time thereafter; in the last case, it shall become effective six months after it has been deposited.

Article 6

1. Each Contracting State shall grant national treatment to broadcasting organisations if either of the following conditions is met:
(a) the headquarters of the broadcasting organisation is situated in another Contracting State;
(b) the broadcast was transmitted from a transmitter situated in another Contracting State.
2. By means of a notification deposited with the Secretary-General of the United Nations, any Contracting State may declare that it will protect broadcasts only if the headquarters of the broadcasting organisation is situated in another Contracting State and the broadcast was transmitted from a transmitter situated in the same Contracting State. Such notification may be deposited at the time of ratification, acceptance or accession, or at any time thereafter; in the last case, it shall become effective six months after it has been deposited.

Article 7

1. The protection provided for performers by this Convention shall include the possibility of preventing:
(a) the broadcasting and the communication to the public, without their consent, of their performance, except where the performance used in the broadcasting or the public communication is itself already a broadcast performance or is made from a fixation;
(b) the fixation, without their consent, of their unfixed performance;
(c) the reproduction, without their consent, of a fixation of their performance:
   (i) if the original fixation itself was made without their consent;
   (ii) if the reproduction is made for purposes different from those for which the performers gave their consent;
   (iii) if the original fixation was made in accordance with the provisions of Article 15 and the reproduction is made for purposes different from those referred to in those provisions.
2. (1) If broadcasting was consented to by the performers, it shall be a matter for the domestic law of the Contracting State where protection is claimed to regulate the protection against rebroadcasting fixation for broadcasting purposes and the reproduction of such fixation for broadcasting purposes.

(2) The terms and conditions governing the use by broadcasting organisations of fixations made for broadcasting purposes shall be determined in accordance with the domestic law of the Contracting State where protection is claimed.

(3) However, the domestic law referred to in sub-paragraphs (1) and (2) of this paragraph shall not operate to deprive performers of the ability to control, by contract, their relations with broadcasting organisations.

Article 8

Any Contracting State may, by its domestic laws and regulations, specify the manner in which performers will be represented in connexion with the exercise of their rights if several of them participate in the same performance.

Article 9

Any Contracting State may, by its domestic laws and regulations, extend the protection provided for in this Convention to artists who do not perform literary or artistic works.

Article 10

Producers of phonograms shall enjoy the right to authorise or prohibit the direct or indirect reproduction of their phonograms.

Article 11

If, as a condition of protecting the rights of producers of phonograms, or of performers, or both, in relation to phonograms, a Contracting State, under its domestic law, requires compliance with formalities, these shall be considered as fulfilled if all the copies in commerce of the published phonogram of their containers bear a notice consisting of the symbol Ⓟ, accompanied by the year date of first publication, placed in such a manner as to give reasonable notice of claim of protection; and if the copies or their containers do not identify the producer or the licensee of the producer (by carrying his name, trade mark or other appropriate designation), the notice shall also include the name of the owner of the rights of the producer; and, furthermore, if the copies or their containers do not identify the principal performers, the notice shall also include the name of the person who, in the country in which the fixation was effected, owns the right of such performers.

Article 12

If a phonogram published for commercial purposes, or a reproduction of such phonogram, is used directly for broadcasting or for any communication to the public, a single equitable remuneration shall be paid by the user to the performers, or to the producers of the phonograms, or to both. Domestic law may, in the absence of agreement between the two parties, lay down the conditions as to the sharing of this remuneration.

Article 13

Broadcasting organisations shall enjoy the right to authorise or prohibit:

(a) the rebroadcasting of their broadcasts;
(b) the fixation of their broadcasts;
(c) the reproduction:

   (i) of fixations, made without their consent, of their broadcasts;
   (ii) of fixations, made in accordance with the provisions of Article 15, of their broadcasts, if the reproduction is made for purposes different from those referred to in those provisions;

(d) the communication to the public of their television broadcasts if such communication is made in places accessible to the public against payment of an entrance fee, it shall be a matter for the domestic law of the State where protection of this right is claimed to determine the conditions under which it may be exercised.

Article 14

The term of protection to be granted under this Convention shall last at least until the end of a period of twenty years computed from the end of the year in which:

(a) the fixation was made—for phonograms and for performances incorporated therein;
(b) the performance took place—for performers not incorporated in phonograms;
(c) the broadcast took place—for broadcasts.

Article 15

1. Any Contracting State may, in its domestic laws and regulations, provide for exceptions to the protection guaranteed by this Convention as regards:

(a) private use;
(b) use of short excerpts in connexion with the reporting of current events;
(c) ephemeral fixation by a broadcasting organisation by means of its own facilities and for its own broadcasts;
(d) use solely for the purposes of teaching or scientific research.

2. Irrespective of paragraph 1 of this Article, any Contracting State may, in its domestic laws and regulations, provide for the same kinds of limitations with regard to the protection of performers, producers of phonograms and broadcasting organisations, as it provides for, in its domestic laws and regulations, in connexion with the protection of copyright in literary and artistic works. However, compulsory licences may be provided for only to the extent to which they are compatible with this Convention.

Article 16

1. Any State, upon becoming party to this Convention, shall be bound by all the obligations and shall enjoy all the benefits thereof. However, a State may at any time, in a notification deposited with the Secretary-General of the United Nations, declare that:

(a) as regards Article 12:

   (i) it will not apply the provisions of that Article;
   (ii) it will not apply the provisions of that Article in respect of certain uses;
   (iii) as regards phonograms the producer of which is not a national of another Contracting State, it will not apply that Article;
   (iv) as regards phonograms the producer of which is a national of another Contracting State, it will limit the protection provided for by that Article to the extent to which, and to the term for which, the latter State grants protection to phonograms first fixed by a national of the State making the declaration; however, the fact that the Contracting State of which the producer is a national does not grant the protection to the same beneficiary or beneficiaries as the State making the declaration shall not be considered as a difference in the extent of the protection;

(b) as regards Article 13, it will not apply item (d) of that Article; if a Contracting State makes such a declaration, the other Contracting States shall not be obliged to grant the right referred to in Article 13, item (d), to broadcast organisations whose headquarters are in that State.

2. If the notification referred to in paragraph 1 of this Article is made after the date of the deposit of the instrument of ratification, acceptance or accession, the declaration will become effective six months after it has been deposited.

Article 17

Any State which, on October 26, 1961, grants protection to producers of phonograms solely on the basis of the criterion of fixation may, by a notification deposited with the Secretary-General of the United Nations at the time of ratification, acceptance or accession, declare that it will apply, for the purposes of Article 5, the criterion of fixation alone and, for the purposes of paragraph 1 (a) (iii) and (iv) of Article 16, the criterion of fixation instead of the criterion of nationality.

Article 18

Any State which has deposited a notification under paragraph 3 of Article 5, paragraph 2 of Article 6, paragraph 1 of Article 16 or Article 17, may, by a further notification deposited with the Secretary-General of the United Nations, reduce its scope or withdraw it.

Article 19

Notwithstanding anything in this Convention, once a performer has consented to the incorporation of his performance in a visual or audio-visual fixation, Article 7 shall have no further application.

Article 20

1. This Convention shall not prejudice rights acquired in any Contracting State before the date of coming into force of this Convention for that State.
2. No Contracting State shall be bound to apply the provisions of this Convention to performances or broadcasts which took place, or to phonograms which were fixed, before the date of coming into force of this Convention for that State.

Article 21

The protection provided for in this Convention shall not prejudice any protection otherwise secured to performers, producers of phonograms and broadcasting organisations.

Article 22

Contracting States reserve the right to enter into special agreements among themselves in so far as such agreements grant to performers, producers of phonograms or broadcasting organisations more extensive rights than those granted by this Convention or contain other provisions not contrary to this Convention.

Article 23

This Convention shall be deposited with the Secretary-General of the United Nations. It shall be open until June 30, 1962, for signature by any State invited to the Diplomatic Conference on the International Protection of Performers, Producers of Phonograms and Broadcasting Organisations which is a party to the Universal Copyright Convention or a member of the International Union for the Protection of Literary and Artistic Works.

Article 24

1. This Convention shall be subject to ratification or acceptance by the signatory States.
2. This Convention shall be open for accession by any State invited to the Conference referred to in Article 23, and by any State Member of the United Nations, provided that in either case such State is a party to the Universal Copyright Convention or a member of the International Union for the Protection of Literary and Artistic Works.
3. Ratification, acceptance or accession shall be effected by the deposit of an instrument to that effect with the Secretary-General of the United Nations.

Article 25

1. This Convention shall come into force three months after the date of deposit of the sixth instrument of ratification, acceptance or accession.
2. Subsequently, this Convention shall come into force in respect of each State three months after the date of deposit of its instrument of ratification, acceptance or accession.

Article 26

1. Each Contracting State undertakes to adopt, in accordance with its Constitution, the measures necessary to ensure the application of this Convention.
2. At the time of deposit of its instrument of ratification, acceptance, or accession, each State must be in a position under its domestic law to give effect to the terms of this Convention.

Article 27

1. Any State may, at the time of ratification, acceptance or accession, or at any time thereafter, declare by notification addressed to the Secretary-General of the United Nations that this Convention shall extend to all or any of the territories for whose international relations it is responsible, provided that the Universal Copyright Convention or the International Convention for the Protection of Literary and Artistic Works applies to the territory or territories concerned. This notification shall take effect three months after the date of its receipt.
2. The notifications referred to in paragraph 3 of Article 5, paragraph 2 of Article 6, paragraph 1 of Article 16 and Articles 17 and 18, may be extended to cover all or any of the territories referred to in paragraph 1 of this Article.

Article 28

1. Any Contracting State may denounce this Convention, on its own behalf or on behalf of all or any of the territories referred to in Article 27.
2. The denunciation shall be effected by a notification addressed to the Secretary-General of the United Nations and shall take effect twelve months after the date of receipt of the notification.
3. The right of denunciation shall not be exercised by a Contracting State before the expiry of a period of five years from the date on which the Convention came into force with respect to that State.
4. A Contracting State shall cease to be a party to this Convention from that time when it is neither a party to the Universal Copyright Convention nor a member of the International Union for the Protection of Literary and Artistic Works.
5. This Convention shall cease to apply to any territory referred to in Article 27 from that time when neither the Universal Copyright Convention nor the International Convention for the Protection of Literary and Artistic Works applies to that territory.

Article 29

1. After this Convention has been in force for five years, any Contracting State may, by notification addressed to the Secretary-General of the United Nations, request that a conference be convened for the purpose of revising the Convention. The Secretary-General shall notify all Contracting States of this request. If, within a period of six months following the date of notification by the Secretary-General of the United Nations, not less than one half of the Contracting States notify him of their concurrence with the request, the Secretary-General shall inform the Director-General of the International Labour Office, the Director-General of the United Nations Educational, Scientific and Cultural Organisation and the Director of the Bureau of the International Union for the Protection of Literary and Artistic Works, who shall convene a revision conference in co-operation with the Intergovernmental Committee provided for in Article 32.
2. The adoption of any revision of this Convention shall require an affirmative vote by two-thirds of the States attending the revision conference, provided that this majority includes two-thirds of the States which, at the time of the revision conference, are parties to the Convention.
3. In the event of adoption of a Convention revising this Convention in whole or in part, and unless the revising Convention provides otherwise:

(a) this Convention shall cease to be open to ratification, acceptance or accession as from the date of entry into force of the revising Convention;
(b) this Convention shall remain in force as regards relations between or with Contracting States which have not become parties to the revising Convention.

Article 30

Any dispute which may arise between two or more Contracting States concerning the interpretation or application of this Convention and which is not settled by negotiation shall, at the request of any one of the parties to the dispute, be referred to the International Court of Justice for decision, unless they agree to another mode of settlement.

Article 31

Without prejudice to the provisions of paragraph 3 of Article 5, paragraph 2 of Article 6, paragraph 1 of Article 16 and Article 17, no reservation may be made to this Convention.

Article 32

1. An Intergovernmental Committee is hereby established with the following duties:

(a) to study questions concerning the application and operation of this Convention; and
(b) to collect proposals and to prepare documentation for possible revision of this Convention.

2. The Committee shall consist of representatives of the Contracting States, chosen with due regard to equitable geographical distribution. The number of members shall be six if there are twelve Contracting States or less, nine if there are thirteen to eighteen Contracting States and twelve if there are more than eighteen Contracting States.
3. The Committee shall be constituted twelve months after the Convention comes into force by an election organised among the Contracting States, each of which shall have one vote, by the Director-General of the International Labour Office, the Director-General of the United Nations Educational, Scientific and Cultural Organisation and the Director of the Bureau of the International Union for the Protection of Literary and Artistic Works, in accordance with rules previously approved by a majority of all Contracting States.
4. The Committee shall elect its Chairman and officers. It shall establish its own rules of procedure. These rules shall in particular provide for the future operation of the Committee and for a method of selecting its members for the future in such a way as to ensure rotation among the various Contracting States.
5. Officials of the International Labour Office, the United Nations Educational, Scientific and Cultural Organisation and the Bureau of the International Union for the Protection of Literary and Artistic Works, designated by the Directors-General and the Director thereof, shall constitute the Secretariat of the Committee.
6. Meetings of the Committee, which shall be convened whenever a majority of its members deems it necessary, shall be held successively at the headquarters of the International Labour Office, the United Nations Educational, Scientific and Cultural Organisation and the Bureau of the International Union for the Protection of Literary and Artistic Works.
7. Expenses of members of the Committee shall be borne by their respective Governments.

Article 33

1. The present Convention is drawn up in English, French and Spanish, the three texts being equally authentic.
2. In addition, official texts of the present Convention shall be drawn up in German, Italian and Portuguese.

Article 34

1. The Secretary-General of the United Nations shall notify the States invited to the Conference referred to in Article 23 and every State Member of the United Nations, as well as the Director-General of the International Labour Office, the Director-General of the United Nations Educational, Scientific and Cultural Organisation and the Director of the Bureau of the International Union for the Protection of Literary and Artistic Works:

(a) of the deposit of each instrument of ratification, acceptance or accession;
(b) of the date of entry into force of the Convention;
(c) of all notifications, declarations or communications provided for in this Convention;
(d) if any of the situations referred to in paragraphs 4 and 5 of Article 28 arise.

2. The Secretary-General of the United Nations shall also notify the Director-General of the International Labour Office, the Director-General of the United Nations Educationals, Scientific and Cultural Organisation and the Director of the Bureau of the International Union for the Protection of Literary and Artistic Works of the requests communicated to him in accordance with Article 29, as well as of any communication received from the Contracting States concerning the revision of the Convention.

IN FAITH WHEREOF, the undersigned, being duly authorised thereto, have signed this Convention.

DONE at Rome, this twenty-six day of October 1961, in a single copy in the English, French and Spanish languages. Certified true copies shall be delivered by the Secretary-General of the United Nations to all the States invited to the Conference referred to in Article 23 and to every State Member of the United Nations, as well as to the Director-General of the International Labour Office, the Director-General of the United Nations Educational, Scientific and Cultural Organisation and the Director of the Bureau of the International Union for the Protection of Literary and Artistic Works.

Appendix 4

Convention for the Protection of Producers of Phonograms Against Unauthorised Duplication of Their Phonograms of 29 October 1971

The Contracting States,

concerned at the widespread and increasing unauthorised duplication of phonograms and the damage this is occasioning to the interests of authors, performers and producers of phonograms;

convinced that the protection of producers of phonograms against such acts will also benefit the performers whose performances, and the authors whose works, are recorded on the said phonograms;

recognising the value of the work undertaken in this field by the United Nations Educational, Scientific and Cultural Organisation and the World Intellectual Property Organisation;

anxious not to impair in any way international agreements already in force and in particular in no way to prejudice wider acceptance of the Rome Convention of October 26, 1961, which affords protection to performers and to broadcasting organisations as well as to producers of phonograms;

have agreed as follows:

Article 1

For the purposes of this Convention:

(a) 'phonogram' means any exclusively aural fixation of sounds of a performance or of other sounds;
(b) 'producer of phonograms' means the person who, or the legal entity which, first fixes the sounds of a performance or other sounds;
(c) 'duplicate' means an article which contains sounds taken directly or indirectly from a phonogram and which embodies all or a substantial part of the sounds fixed in that phonogram;
(d) 'distribution to the public' means any act by which duplicates of a phonogram are offered, directly or indirectly, to the general public or any section thereof.

Article 2

Each Contracting State shall protect producers of phonograms who are nationals of other Contracting States against the making of duplicates without the consent of the producer and against the importation of such duplicates, provided that any such making or importation is for the purpose of distribution to the public, and against the distribution of such duplicates to the public.

Article 3

The means by which this Convention is implemented shall be a matter for the domestic law of each Contracting State and shall include one or more of the following: protection by means of the grant of a copyright or other specific right; protection by means of the law relating to unfair competition; protection by means of penal sanctions.

Article 4

The duration of the protection given shall be a matter for the domestic law of each Contracting State. However, if the domestic law prescribes a specific duration for the protection, that duration shall not be less than twenty years from the end either of the year in which the sounds embodied in the phonogram were first fixed or of the year in which the phonogram was first published.

Article 5

If, as a condition of protecting the producers of phonograms, a Contracting State, under its domestic law, requires compliance with formalities, these shall be considered as fulfilled if all the authorised duplicates of the phonogram distributed to the public or their containers bear a notice consisting of the symbol ℗, accompanied by the year date of the first publication, placed in such manner as to give reasonable notice of claim of protection; and, if the duplicates or their containers do not identify the producer, his successor in title or the exclusive licensee (by carrying his name, trade-mark or other appropriate designation), the notice shall also include the name of the producer, his successor in title or the exclusive licensee.

Article 6

Any Contracting State which affords protection by means of copyright or other specific right, or protection by means of penal sanctions, may in its domestic law provide, with regard to the protection of producers of phonograms, the same kinds of limitations as are permitted with respect to the protection of authors of literary and artistic works. However, no compulsory licenses may be permitted unless all of the following conditions are met:

(a) the duplication is for use solely for the purpose of teaching or scientific research;
(b) the licence shall be valid for duplication only within the territory of the Contracting State whose competent authority has granted the licence and shall not extend to the export of duplicates;
(c) the duplication made under the licence gives rise to an equitable remuneration fixed by the said authority taking into account, inter alia, the number of duplicates which will be made.

Article 7

(1) This Convention shall in no way be interpreted to limit or prejudice the protection otherwise secured to authors, to performers, to producers of phonograms or to broadcasting organisations under any domestic law or international agreement.
(2) It shall be a matter for the domestic law of each Contracting State to determine the extent, if any, to which performers whose performances are fixed in a phonogram are entitled to enjoy protection and the conditions for enjoying any such protection.
(3) No Contracting State shall be required to apply the provisions of this Convention to any phonogram fixed before this Convention entered into force with respect to that State.
(4) Any Contracting State which, on October 29, 1971, affords protection to producers of phonograms solely on the basis of the place of first fixation may, by a notification deposited with the Director-General of the World Intellectual Property Organisation, declare that it will apply this criterion instead of the criterion of the nationality of the producer.

Article 8

(1) The International Bureau of the World Intellectual Property Organization shall assemble and publish information concerning the protection of phonograms. Each Contracting State shall promptly communicate to the International Bureau all new laws and official texts on this subject.
(2) The International Bureau shall, on request, furnish information to any Contracting State on matters concerning this Convention, and shall conduct studies and provide services designed to facilitate the protection provided for therein.

(3) The International Bureau shall exercise the functions enumerated in paragraphs (1) and (2) above in cooperation, for matters within their respective competence, with the United Nations Educational, Scientific and Cultural Organisation and the International Labour Organisation.

Article 9

(1) This Convention shall be deposited with the Secretary-General of the United Nations. It shall be open until April 30, 1972, for signature by any State that is a member of the United Nations, any of the Specialised Agencies brought into relationship with the United Nations, or the International Atomic Energy Agency, or is a party to the Statute of the International Court of Justice.
(2) This Convention shall be subject to ratification or acceptance by the signatory States. It shall be open for accession by any State referred to in paragraph (1) of this Article.
(3) Instruments of ratification, acceptance or accession shall be deposited with the Secretary-General of the United Nations.
(4) It is understood that, at the time a State becomes bound by this Convention, it will be in a position in accordance with its domestic law to give effect to the provisions of the Convention.

Article 10

No reservations to this Convention are permitted.

Article 11

(1) This Convention shall enter into force three months after deposit of the fifth instrument of ratification, acceptance or accession.
(2) For each State ratifying, accepting or acceding to this Convention after the deposit of the fifth instrument of ratification, acceptance or accession, the Convention shall enter into force three months after the date on which the Director-General of the World Intellectual Property Organisation informs the States, in accordance with Article 13, paragraph (4), of the deposit of its instrument.
(3) Any State may, at the time of ratification, acceptance or accession or at any later date, declare by notification addressed to the Secretary-General of the United Nations that this Convention shall apply to all or any one of the territories for whose international affairs it is responsible. This notification will take effect three months after the date on which it is received.
(4) However, the preceding paragraph may in no way be understood as implying the recognition or tacit acceptance by a Contracting State of the factual situation concerning a territory to which this Convention is made applicable by another Contracting State by virtue of the said paragraph.

Article 12

(1) Any Contracting State may denounce this Convention, on its own behalf or on behalf of any of the territories referred to in Article 11, paragraph (3), by written notification addressed to the Secretary-General of the United Nations.
(2) Denunciation shall take effect twelve months after the date on which the Secretary-General of the United Nations has received the notification.

Article 13

(1) This Convention shall be signed in a single copy in English, French, Russian and Spanish, the four texts being equally authentic.
(2) Official texts shall be established by the Director-General of the World Intellectual Property Organisation, after consultation with the interested Governments, in the Arabic, Dutch, German, Italian and Portuguese languages.
(3) The Secretary-General of the United Nations shall notify the Director-General of the World Intellectual Property Organisation, the Director-General of the United Nations Educational, Scientific and Cultural Organisation and the Director-General of the International Labour Office of:

(a) signatures to this Convention;
(b) the deposit of instruments of ratification, acceptance or accession;
(c) the date of entry into force of this Convention;
(d) any declaration notified pursuant to Article 11, paragraph (3);
(e) the receipt of notifications of denunciation.

(4) The Director-General of the World Intellectual Property Organisation shall inform the States referred to in Article 9, paragraph (1), of the notifications received pursuant to the preceding paragraph and of any declarations made under Article 7, paragraph (4). He shall also notify the Director-General of the United Nations Educational, Scientific and Cultural Organisation and the Director-General of the International Labour Office of such declarations.

(5) The Secretary-General of the United Nations shall transmit two certified copies of this Convention to the States referred to in Article 9, paragraph (1).

Appendix 5

Convention Relating to the Distribution of Programme-Carrying Signals Transmitted by Satellite (Brussels, 21 May 1974)

The Contracting States,

Aware that the use of satellites for the distribution of programme-carrying signals is rapidly growing both in volume and geographical coverage;

Concerned that there is no world-wide system to prevent distributors from distributing programme-carrying signals transmitted by satellite which were not intended for those distributors, and that this lack is likely to hamper the use of satellite communications;

Recognising, in this respect, the importance of the interests of authors, performers, producers of phonograms and broadcasting organisations;

Convinced that an international system should be established under which measures would be provided to prevent distributors from distributing programme-carrying signals transmitted by satellite which were not intended for those distributors;

Conscious of the need not to impair in any way international agreements already in force, including the International Telecommunication Convention and the Radio Regulations annexed to that Convention, and in particular in no way to prejudice wider acceptance of the Rome Convention of October 26, 1961, which affords protection to performers, producers of phonograms and broadcasting organisations,

Have agreed as follows:

Article 1

For the purposes of this Convention:

(i) 'signal' is an electronically-generated carrier capable of transmitting programmes;
(ii) 'programme' is a body of live or recorded material consisting of images, sounds or both, embodied in signals emitted for the purpose of ultimate distribution;
(iii) 'satellite' is any device in extraterrestrial space capable of transmitting signals;
(iv) 'emitted signal' or 'signal emitted' is any programme-carrying signal that goes to or passes through a satellite;
(v) 'derived signal' is a signal obtained by modifying the technical characteristics of the emitted signal, whether or not there have been one or more intervening fixations;
(vi) 'originating organisation' is the person or legal entity that decides what programme the emitted signals will carry;
(vii) 'distributor' is the person or legal entity that decides that the transmission of the derived signals to the general public or any section thereof should take place;
(viii) 'distribution' is the operation by which a distributor transmits derived signals to the general public or any section thereof.

Article 2

(1) Each Contracting State undertakes to take adequate measures to prevent the distribution on or from its territory of any programme-carrying signal by any distributor for whom the signal emitted to or passing through the satellite is not intended. This

obligation shall apply where the originating organisation is a national of another Contracting State and where the signal distributed is a derived signal.

(2) In any Contracting State in which the application of the measures referred to in paragraph (1) is limited in time, the duration thereof shall be fixed by its domestic law. The Secretary-General of the United Nations shall be notified in writing of such duration at the time of ratification, acceptance or accession, or if the domestic law comes into force or is changed thereafter, within six months of the coming into force of that law or of its modification.

(3) The obligation provided for in paragraph (1) shall not apply to the distribution of derived signals taken from signals which have already been distributed by a distributor for whom the emitted signals were intended.

Article 3

This Convention shall not apply where the signals emitted by or on behalf of the originating organisation are intended for direct reception from the satellite by the general public.

Article 4

No Contracting State shall be required to apply the measures referred to in Article 2(1) where the signal distributed on its territory by a distributor for whom the emitted signal is not intended

(i) carries short excerpts of the programme carried by the emitted signal, consisting of reports of current events, but only to the extent justified by the informatory purpose of such excerpts, or

(ii) carries, as quotations, short excerpts of the programme carried by the emitted signal, provided that such quotations are compatible with fair practice and are justified by the informatory purpose of such quotations, or

(iii) carries, where the said territory is that of a Contracting State regarded as a developing country in conformity with the established practice of the General Assembly of the United Nations, a programme carried by the emitted signal, provided that the distribution is solely for the purpose of teaching, including teaching in the framework of adult education, or scientific research.

Article 5

No Contracting State shall be required to apply this Convention with respect to any signal emitted before this Convention entered into force for that State.

Article 6

This Convention shall in no way be interpreted to limit or prejudice the protection secured to authors, performers, producers of phonograms, or broadcasting organisations, under any domestic law or international agreement.

Article 7

This Convention shall in no way be interpreted as limiting the right of any Contracting State to apply its domestic law in order to prevent abuses of monopoly.

Article 8

(1) Subject to paragraphs (2) and (3), no reservation to this Convention shall be permitted.

(2) Any Contracting State whose domestic law, on May 21, 1974, so provides may, by a written notification deposited with the Secretary-General of the United Nations, declare that, for its purposes, the words 'where the originating organisation is a national of another Contracting State' appearing in Article 2(1) shall be considered as if they were replaced by the words 'where the signal is emitted from the territory of another Contracting State.'

(3) (a) Any Contracting State which, on May 21, 1974, limits or denies protection

with respect to the distribution of programme-carrying signals by means of wires, cable or other similar communications channels to subscribing members of the public may, by a written notification deposited with the Secretary-General of the United Nations, declare that, to the extent that and as long as its domestic law limits or denies protection, it will not apply this Convention to such distributions.
(b) Any State that has deposited a notification in accordance with subparagraph (a) shall notify the Secretary-General of the United Nations in writing, within six months of their coming into force, of any changes in its domestic law whereby the reservation under that subparagraph becomes inapplicable or more limited in scope.

Article 9

(1) This Convention shall be deposited with the Secretary-General of the United Nations. It shall be open until March 31, 1975, for signature by any State that is a member of the United Nations, any of the Specialised Agencies brought into relationship with the United Nations, or the International Atomic Energy Agency, or is a party to the Statute of the International Court of Justice.
(2) This Convention shall be subject to ratification or acceptance by the signatory States. It shall be open for accession by any State referred to in paragraph (1).
(3) Instruments of ratification, acceptance or accession shall be deposited with the Secretary-General of the United Nations.
(4) It is understood that, at the time a State becomes bound by this Convention, it will be in a position in accordance with its domestic law to give effect to the provisions of the Convention.

Article 10

(1) This Convention shall enter into force three months after the deposit of the fifth instrument of ratification, acceptance or accession.
(2) For each State ratifying, accepting or acceding to this Convention after the deposit of the fifth instrument of ratification, acceptance or accession, this Convention shall enter into force three months after the deposit of its instrument.

Article 11

(1) Any Contracting State may denounce this Convention by written notification deposited with the Secretary-General of the United Nations.
(2) Denunciation shall take effect twelve months after the date on which the notification referred to in paragraph (1) is received.

Article 12

(1) This Convention shall be signed in a single copy in English, French, Russian and Spanish, the four texts being equally authentic.
(2) Official texts shall be established by the Director-General of the United Nations Educational, Scientific and Cultural Organisation and the Director-General of the World Intellectual Property Organisation, after consultation with the interested Governments, in the Arabic, Dutch, German, Italian and Portuguese languages.
(3) The Secretary-General of the United Nations shall notify the States referred to in Article 9(1), as well as the Director-General of the United Nations Educational, Scientific and Cultural Organisation, the Director-General of the World Intellectual Property Organisation, the Director-General of the International Labour Office and the Secretary-General of the International Telecommunication Union, of

  (i)   signatures to this Convention;
  (ii) the deposit of instruments of ratification, acceptance or accession;
  (iii) the date of entry into force of this Convention under Article 10(1);
  (iv) the deposit of any notification relating to Article 2(2) or Article 8(2) or (3), together with its text;
  (v)   the receipt of notifications of denunciation.

(4) The Secretary-General of the United Nations shall transmit two certified copies of this Convention to all States referred to in Article 9(1).

Appendix 6

European Agreement Concerning Programme Exchange by Means of Television Films
(15 December 1958)

The Governments signatory hereto, being Members of the Council of Europe,
 Considering that the aim of the Council of Europe is to achieve a greater unity between its Members;
 Considering that it is important in the interests of European cultural and economic unity that programmes may be exchanged by means of television films between the member countries of the Council of Europe as freely as possible;
 Considering that national legislations allow different conclusions as regards the legal nature of television films and as regards the rights which they grant in respect of such films;
 Considering that it is necessary to resolve the difficulties arising from this situation;
 Having regard to Article 20 of the Berne Convention for the Protection of Literary and Artistic Works, by the terms of which the Governments of the countries of the Union reserve to themselves the right to enter into special arrangements which do not embody stipulations contrary to that Convention,
 Have agreed as follows:

Article 1

In the absence of any contrary or special stipulation within the meaning of Article 4 of the present Agreement, a broadcasting organisation under the jurisdiction of a country which is a Party to this Agreement has the right to authorise in the other countries which are Parties thereto the exploitation for television of television films of which it is the maker.

Article 2

1. All visual or sound and visual recordings intended for television shall be deemed to be television films within the meaning of the present Agreement.
2. A broadcasting organisation shall be deemed to be the maker if it has taken the initiative in, and responsibility for, the making of a television film.

Article 3

1. If the television film has been made by a maker other than the one defined in Article 2, paragraph 2, the latter is entitled, in the absence of contrary or special stipulations within the meaning of Article 4, to transfer to a broadcasting organisation the right provided in Article 1.
2. The provision contained in the preceding paragraph applies only if the maker and the broadcasting organisation are under the jurisdiction of countries which are Parties to the present Agreement.

Article 4

By 'contrary or special stipulation' is meant any restrictive condition agreed between the maker and persons who contribute to the making of the television film.

Article 5

This Agreement shall not affect the following rights, which shall be entirely reserved:

(a) any moral right recognised in relation to films;
(b) the copyright in literary, dramatic or artistic works from which the television film is derived;
(c) the copyright in a musical work, with or without words, accompanying a television film;
(d) the copyright in films other than television films;
(e) the copyright in the exploitation of television films otherwise than on television.

Article 6

1. This Agreement shall be open to signature by the Members of the Council of Europe, who may accede to it either by:

(a) signature without reservation in respect of ratification; or
(b) signature with reservation in respect of ratification, followed by the deposit of an instrument of ratification.

2. Instruments of ratification shall be deposited with the Secretary-General of the Council of Europe.

Article 7

1. This Agreement shall enter into force thirty days after the date on which three Members of the Council shall, in accordance with Article 6 thereof, have signed it without reservation in respect of ratification or shall have ratified it.

2. In the case of any Member of the Council who shall subsequently sign the Agreement without reservation in respect of ratification or who shall ratify it, the Agreement shall enter into force thirty days after the date of such signature or deposit of the instrument of ratification.

Article 8

1. After this Agreement has come into force, any country which is not a Member of the Council of Europe may accede to it, subject to the prior approval of the Committee of Ministers of the Council of Europe.

2. Such accession shall be effected by the deposit of an instrument of accession with the Secretary-General of the Council of Europe, and shall take effect thirty days after the date of deposit.

Article 9

Signature without reservation in respect of ratification or accession shall imply full acceptance of all the provisions of this Agreement.

Article 10

The Secretary-General of the Council of Europe shall notify Members of the Council, the Governments of any countries which may have acceded to this Agreement and the Director of the Bureau of the International Union for the protection of literary and artistic works:

(a) of the date of entry into force of this Agreement and the names of any Members of the Council which have become Parties thereto;
(b) of the deposit of any instruments of accession in accordance with Article 8 of the present Agreement;
(c) of any declaration or notification received in accordance with Articles 11 and 12 thereof.

Article 11

1. This Agreement shall apply to the metropolitan territories of the Contracting Parties.
2. Any Contracting Party may, at the time of signature, ratification or accession, or at

any later date, declare by notice addressed to the Secretary-General of the Council of Europe that this Agreement shall apply to any territory or territories mentioned in the said declaration and for whose international relations it is responsible.

3. Any declaration made in accordance with the preceding paragraph may, in respect of any territory mentioned in such a declaration, be withdrawn under the conditions laid down in Article 12 of this Agreement.

Article 12

1. This Agreement shall remain in force for an unlimited period.

2. Any Contracting Party may denounce this Agreement at one year's notice by notification to this effect to the Secretary-General of the Council of Europe.

Appendix 7

European Agreement on the Protection of Television Broadcasts (Strasbourg, 22 June 1960)

The Governments signatory hereto, being Members of the Council of Europe,
  Considering that the object of the Council is to achieve a greater unity between its Members;
  Considering that exchanges of television programmes between the countries of Europe are calculated to further the achievement of that object;
  Considering that these exchanges are hampered by the fact that the majority of television organisations are at present powerless to restrain the rebroadcasting, fixation or public performance of their broadcasts, whereas the organisers of musical or dramatic performances or the like, and the promoters of sports meetings, make their consent to broadcasting to other countries conditional upon an undertaking that the relays will not be used for purposes other than private viewing;
  Considering that the international protection of television broadcasts will in no way affect any rights of third parties in these broadcasts;
  Considering that the problem is one of some urgency, in view of the installations and links now being brought into service throughout Europe, which are such as to make it easy from the technical point of view for European television organisations to exchange their programmes;
  Considering that, pending the conclusion of a potentially universal Convention on 'neighbouring rights' at present in contemplation, it is fitting to conclude a regional Agreement restricted in scope to television broadcasts and of limited duration,
  Have agreed as follows:

Article 1

Broadcasting organisations constituted in the territory and under the laws of a Party to this Agreement or transmitting from such territory shall enjoy, in respect of all their television broadcasts:
1. in the territory of all Parties to this Agreement, the right to authorise or prohibit:

(a) the re-broadcasting of such broadcasts;
(b) the diffusion of such broadcasts to the public by wire;
(c) the communication of such broadcasts to the public by means of any instrument for the transmission of signs, sounds or images;
(d) any fixation of such broadcasts or still photographs thereof, and any reproduction of such a fixation; and

(e) rebroadcasting, wire diffusion or public performance with the aid of the fixations or reproductions referred to in subparagraph (d) of this paragraph, except where the organisation in which the right vests has authorised the sale of the said fixations or reproductions to the public;

2. in the territory of any other Party to this Agreement, the same protection as that other Party may extend to organisations constituted in its territory and under its laws or transmitting from its territory, where such protection is greater than that provided for in paragraph 1 above.

Article 2

1. Subject to paragraph 2 of Article 1, and Articles 13 and 14, the protection provided for in paragraph 1 of Article 1 shall continue until the end of the tenth calendar year following the year in which the first broadcast was made from the territory of a Party to this Agreement.
2. No Party to this Agreement shall be required, in pursuance of paragraph 2 of Article 1, to accord to the broadcasts of any broadcasting organisations constituted in the territory and under the laws of another Party to this Agreement or transmitting from the territory of another Party longer protection than that granted by the said other Party.

Article 3

1. Parties to this Agreement, by making a declaration as provided in Article 10, and in respect of their own territory, may:

(a) withhold the protection provided for in sub-paragraph 1(b) of Article 1;
(b) withhold the protection provided for in sub-paragraph 1(c) of Article 1, where the communication is not to a paying audience within the meaning of their domestic law;
(c) withhold the protection provided for in sub-paragraph 1(d) of Article 1, where the fixation or reproduction of the fixation is made for private use, or solely for educational purposes;
(d) withhold the protection provided for in sub-paragraphs 1(d) and (e) of Article 1, in respect of still photographs or reproductions of such photographs;
(e) withhold all protection provided for in this Agreement from television broadcasts by broadcasting organisations constituted in their territory and under their laws or transmitting from such territory, where such broadcasts enjoy protection under their domestic law;
(f) restrict the operation of this Agreement to broadcasting organisations constituted in the territory and under the laws of a Party of this Agreement and also transmitting from the territory of such Party;

2. It shall be open to the aforesaid Parties, in respect of their own territory, to provide exceptions to the protection of television broadcasts:
(a) for the purpose of reporting current events, in respect of the rebroadcasting, fixation or reproduction of the fixation, wire diffusion or public performance of short extracts from a broadcast which itself constitutes the whole or part of the event in question;
(b) in respect of the making of ephemeral fixations of television broadcasts by a broadcasting organisation by means of its own facilities and for its own broadcasts.
3. The aforesaid Parties may, in respect of their own territory, provide for a body with jurisdiction over cases where the right of communication to the public referred to in sub-paragraph 1(c) of Article 1 has been unreasonably refused, or granted on unreasonable terms, by the broadcasting organisation in which the said right vests.

Article 4

1. Fixations of a broadcast in which protection under this Agreement subsists, or still photographs thereof, as well as reproductions of such photographs, made in a territory to which this Agreement does not apply and imported into the territory of a Party to this Agreement where they would be unlawful without the consent of the broadcasting organisation in which the right vests, shall be liable to seizure in the latter territory.
2. The provisions of the last preceding paragraph shall apply to the importation into the territory of a Party to this Agreement of still photographs of a broadcast in which protection under this Agreement subsists and of reproductions of such photographs, where such photographs or reproductions are made in the territory of another Party to this Agreement by virtue of sub-paragraph 1(d) of Article 3.
3. Seizure shall be effected in accordance with the domestic law of each Party to this Agreement.
4. No Party to this Agreement shall be required to provide protection in respect of still photographs or the reproduction of such photographs, of broadcasts made by a broad-

casting organisation constituted in the territory and under the laws of another Party to this Agreement or transmitting from such territory, if the said other Party has availed itself of the reservation provided for in sub-paragraph 1(d) of Article 3.

Article 5

The protection afforded by this Agreement shall apply both in relation to the visual element and in relation to the sound element of a television broadcast. It shall not affect the sound element when broadcast separately.

Article 6

1. The protection provided for in Article 1 shall not affect any rights in respect of a television broadcast that may accrue to third parties, such as authors, performers, film makers, manufacturers of phonographic records or organisers of entertainments.
2. It shall likewise be without prejudice to any protection of television broadcasts that may be accorded apart from this Agreement.

Article 7

1. This Agreement shall be open to signature by the Members of the Council of Europe, who may become Parties to it either by

(a) signature without reservation in respect of ratification; or
(b) signature with reservation in respect of ratification, followed by the deposit of an instrument of ratification.

2. Instruments of ratification shall be deposited with the Secretary-General of the Council of Europe.

Article 8

1. This Agreement shall enter into force one month after the date on which three Members of the Council of Europe shall, in accordance with Article 7 thereof, have signed it without reservation in respect of ratification or shall have ratified it.
2. In the case of any Member of the Council of Europe who shall subsequently sign the Agreement without reservation in respect of ratification or who shall ratify it, the Agreement shall enter into force one month after the date of such signature or deposit of the instrument of ratification.

Article 9

1. After this Agreement has come into force, any European Government which is not a Member of the Council of Europe or any non-European Government having political ties with a Member of the Council of Europe may accede to it, subject to the prior approval of the Committee of Ministers of the Council of Europe.
2. Such accession shall be effected by the deposit of an instrument of accession with the Secretary-General of the Council of Europe and shall take effect one month after the date of deposit.

Article 10

Signature, ratification or accession shall imply full acceptance of all the provisions of this Agreement; provided always that any country may declare, at the time of signature or of deposit of its instrument of ratification or accession, that it intends to avail itself of one or more of the options in paragraph 1 of Article 3 above.

Article 11

The Secretary-General of the Council of Europe shall notify Members of the Council, the Governments of any countries which may have acceded to this Agreement and the Director of the Bureau of the International Union for the Protection of Literary and Artistic Works:

(a) of any signatures, together with any reservations as to ratification, of the deposit of instruments of ratification and of the date of entry into force of this Agreement;

(b) of the deposit of any instruments of accession in accordance with Article 9;
(c) of any declaration or notification received in accordance with Articles 12, 13 or 14;
(d) of any decision of the Committee of Ministers taken in pursuance of paragraph 2 of Article 12.

Article 12

1. This Agreement shall apply to the metropolitan territories of the Parties.
2. Any Party may, at the time of signature, of the deposit of its instrument of ratification or accession, or at any later date, declare by notice addressed to the Secretary-General of the Council of Europe that this Agreement shall extend to any or all of the territories for whose international relations it is responsible.
3. Any Government which has made a declaration under paragraph 2 of this Article extending this Agreement to any territory for whose international relations it is responsible may denounce the Agreement separately in respect of that territory in accordance with Article 14 thereof.

Article 13

1. This Agreement shall cease to be effective, except in regard to fixations already made, at such time as a Convention on 'neighbouring rights', including the protection of television broadcasts and open to European countries, amongst others, shall have entered into force for at least a majority of the Members of the Council of Europe that are themselves Parties to the Agreement.
2. The Committee of Ministers of the Council of Europe shall at the appropriate time declare that the conditions laid down in the preceding paragraph have been fulfilled, thereby entailing the termination of this Agreement.

Article 14

Any Contracting Party may denounce this Agreement by giving one year's notice to that effect to the Secretary-General of the Council of Europe.

Amendment 22 January 1965

The member States of the Council of Europe, signatory hereto,
  Considering the desirability of amending the European Agreement on the Protection of Television Broadcasts, signed at Strasbourg on 22nd June 1960, hereinafter referred to as 'the Agreement';
  Considering that the International Convention for the Protection of Performers, Producers of Phonograms and Broadcasting Organisations, signed in Rome on 26th October 1961, entered into force on 18th May 1964,
  Have agreed as follows:

Article 1

1. Paragraph 1 of Article 2 of the Agreement shall be amended as follows:
  'Subject to paragraph 2 of Article 1, and Articles 13 and 14, the protection provided for in paragraph 1 of Article 1 shall last not less than a period of twenty years from the end of the year in which the broadcast took place.'
2. Paragraph 2 of Article 2 of the Agreement shall be deleted.

Article 2

1. Sub-paragraph 1(a) of Article 3 of the Agreement shall be amended as follows:
'(a) withhold the protection provided for in sub-paragraph 1(b) of Article 1 as regards broadcasting organisations constituted in their territory or transmitting from such territory, and restrict the exercise of such protection as regards broadcasts by broadcasting organisations constituted in the territory of another Party to this Agreement or transmitting from such territory, to a percentage of the transmissions by such organi-

sations, which shall not be less than 50% of the average weekly duration of the broadcasts of each of these organisations.

2. Sub-paragraph 1(e) of Article 3 of the Agreement shall be amended as follows:
'(e) without prejudice to sub-paragraph 1(a) of this Article, withhold all protection provided for in this Agreement from television broadcasts by broadcasting organisations constituted in their territory and under their laws or transmitting from such territory, where such broadcasts enjoy protection under their domestic law.'

3. Paragraph 3 of Article 3 of the Agreement shall be amended as follows:
'3. The aforesaid Parties may, in respect of their own territory, provide for a body with jurisdiction over cases where the right of diffusion to the public by wire referred to in sub-paragraph 1(b) of Article 1, or the right of communication to the public referred to in sub-paragraph 1(c) of Article 1, has been unreasonably refused or granted on unreasonable terms by the broadcasting organisation in which the said right vests.'

4. Any State which in accordance with Article 10 of the Agreement has, before the entry into force of this Protocol, availed itself of the option in sub-paragraph 1(a) of Article 3 of the Agreement may, notwithstanding anything in paragraph 1 of the present Article, maintain the application of such option.

Article 3

Article 13 of the Agreement shall be deleted and replaced by the following:
'1. This Agreement shall remain in force indefinitely.

2. Nevertheless, as from 1st January 1985, no State may remain or become a Party to this Agreement unless it is also a Party to the International Convention for the Protection of Performers, Producers of Phonograms and Broadcasting Organisations signed in Rome on 26th October 1961.'*

Article 4

1. The Governments signatory to the Agreement and the Governments having acceded thereto may become Parties to this Protocol by the procedure laid down in Article 7 or Article 9 of the Agreement, according to whether they are member States of the Council of Europe or not.

2. This Protocol shall enter into force one month after the date on which all the Parties to the Agreement have signed this Protocol without reservation in respect of ratification, or deposited their instrument of ratification or accession in accordance with the provisions of the preceding paragraph.

3. As from the date on which this Protocol enters into force, no State may become a Party to the Agreement without becoming also a Party to this Protocol.

Article 5

The Secretary-General of the Council of Europe shall notify member States of the Council, other States Parties to the Agreement, and the Director of the Bureau of the International Union for the Protection of Literary and Artistic Works of any signature of this Protocol, together with any reservations as to ratification, and of the deposit of any instrument of ratification of the Protocol or of accession to it, and of the date referred to in paragraph 2 of Article 4 of this Protocol.

* Text amended according to the provisions of the Additional Protocol of the said Protocol, which entered into force on 31 December 1974.

Contributors to Part 2

Chapter 13 Austria

Robert Dittrich is a director in the Ministry of Justice and a Professor of Law at the Universities of Vienna and Salzburg. He is a Doctor of Law and a Doctor of Political Science. He was a member of the Austrian Delegation at the Rome Convention (1961) and head of that Austrian Delegation at the Paris Revision Conference of the Berne Convention and the Universal Copyright Convention 1971, at the Phonogram Convention 1971 and the Satellite Convention 1974. He was chairman of the Intergovernmental Committee of the Rome Convention 1975-1977. He is the author of *Austrian and International Copyright Law* (1974) and other books and of numerous monographs in 'Droit d'Auteur' and other learned journals.

Chapter 14 France

Pierre Chesnais holds the degrees of Bachelor of Literature, Master of Law and a Diploma of Financial and Economic Sciences of the University of Paris. He was Secretary of the French actors' union from 1948-1968 and Secretary General of the International Actors Federation (FIA) from 1952-1968, and since 1968 has been Director General of the 'Syndicat National de l'edition phonographique et audio-visuelle' and Secretary General of the 'Federation nationale de la musique'. He is author of the book, *The Actor* (1957) and, since 1960, editor of the French law reports (section arts and entertainment). He is a knight of the national order of merit.

Chapter 15 Germany

Eugen Ulmer is a Doctor of Law of the University of Tubingen and a Doctor of Law 'honoris causa' of the University of Stockholm. He was Professor of Law at the Universities of Rostock, Heidelberg and, since 1955, of Munich. He is a member of the Academies of Science of Heidelberg and of Bavaria. He is a founder of the 'Max-Planck-Institut' whose Director he was until 1973. He represented the Federal Republic at the Diplomatic Conferences for the Universal Copyright Convention 1952 and 1971, the Rome Convention 1961, the Stockholm Revision Conference 1967 (where he was Chairman of the main Commission) the Revision Conference of the Berne Convention 1971 and the Phonogram Convention 1971. He is author of the standard work *German Copyright* (3rd edn, 1980) and co-editor of the journal 'Gewerblicher Rechtsschutz und Urheberrecht' (International Part).

Chapter 16 Italy

Valerio De Sanctis is a Doctor of Law, Doctor of Philosophy and Barrister, and was Professor of Intellectual Property at the International University of Social

Studies, Rome, from 1948 to 1975. He has been legal adviser of SIAE (the Society of Authors), member of the Italian Government's Standing Committee on Copyright, and is still editor of the Italian Copyright Journal, 'Il diritto d'Autore', which he has been from its start in 1930.

He was a member of the Italian delegation at every diplomatic conference between 1948-1974. He is the author of a very large number of works on copyright and industrial property rights, in particular: *The Berne Convention* (1949), *The Universal Copyright Convention* (1953), *The Rome Convention* (1963), *Lectures on Copyright* (1960) and *Publishing Contracts* (1965).

Vittorio De Sanctis is a Doctor of Law of the University of Rome and an alumnus of New York University Law School. He is Professor of Commercial Law at the Gabriele D'Annunzio University and a senior partner in a law firm in Rome. He is the author of several works on intellectual property and competition law, and of two books: *The Creative Character of Works of Art* (1971) and *Italian Competition Law* (1980).

Chapter 17 Scandinavia

Agne Henry Olsson is Legal Adviser to the Ministry of Justice in Sweden. He is a Bachelor of Law of the University of Lund and a Justice of the Court of Appeal. He has represented Sweden at all Intergovernmental Committees and Diplomatic Conferences in the copyright field since 1971. He is the author of the manual *Copyright* and of many articles on copyright in learned journals in Sweden and abroad. He is currently Chairman of the Intergovernmental Copyright Committee (The Executive Committee of the UCC).

Chapter 18 United Kingdom

William Wallace is a Master of Arts of the University of Oxford and a Barrister of the Inner Temple. He was Assistant Comptroller of the Patent Office, Industrial Property and Copyright Department, 1954-1973. He is a Companion of the Order of St Michael and St George. He represented the United Kingdom at Intergovernmental Committees and the Diplomatic Conference of the Rome Convention 1961, the Paris Revision Conference of the Berne and Universal Convention 1971. He was Chairman of the Intergovernmental Committee of the Rome Convention 1967-1969 and Chairman of Intergovernmental Committee of the Universal Copyright Convention and the Executive Committee of the Berne Union 1970. He was Vice-Chairman of the 'Whitford Committee' on Copyright and Designs (Report 1974) in the United Kingdom.

Chapter 19 The Soviet Union

Mark Boguslavski is a Professor of Law of the Institute of State and Law and an eminent Soviet lawyer. He is a member of the Programme Committee of the International Association for the Protection of Industrial Property and Vice-President of its Soviet National Group. He was a member of the Soviet delegation at the Stockholm Conference 1967. He is the author of a large number of works on private international law and intellectual property law, in particular: *Problems of Patent Law in International Relations* (1962), *Protection of Industrial Property in the USSR* (1966) (published also in English, 1967), *The Legal Status of Foreigners in the USSR* (1963) (published also in English), *Private International Law* (1974), *The USSR and International Copyright Protection* (1979) (published also in English). He is Editor-in-chief and co-author of two compendia *Problems of Soviet Copyright* (1979) and *Problems of Modern Soviet Copyright* (1980).

Chapter 20 European Economic Community (EEC)

Hans Hugo von Rauscher auf Weeg is a Doctor of Law of the University of Heidelberg and an alumnus of the University of Washington, Seattle, USA and of the Academy of International Law at The Hague. He is a Barrister practising in Munich. He is the author of several works on intellectual property law, in particular: *Musical Copyright and the Protection of Parts of Musical Works* (1954), *Trade Marks in the US and the Plan for German Law Reform* (1958), *Performing Rights of Performers and Record Producers under German Law* (1960), *Rights under the Rome Convention 1973*, and *Challenges to Copyright and Related Rights in the European Community* (with Gillian Davies) (1982).

Chapter 21 United States

Barbara Ringer is a Master of Arts of George Washington University and a 'Doctor Juris' of Columbia University. In a career in the Copyright Office of the United States she rose from Examiner (1949) to Assistant Register of Copyrights (1965-1972). She was Director of the Copyright Division of UNESCO 1972-1973 and Register of Copyrights of the US 1973-1980. She was Adjunct Professor of Law at the Georgetown University Law Center 1964-1972. She represented the USA at Diplomatic Conferences in the Copyright field from 1971 to 1980 and was Rapporteur-General of the Satellite Convention 1974, and President of the Intergovernmental Copyright Committee (UCC) 1973. She has been a Vice-President of the Interamerican Copyright Society since 1977. She is the author of a large number of articles on copyright and the section 'Copyright' of the Encyclopaedia Britannica. She received the 'President's Award for Distinguished Federal Civilian Service' in 1977.

Chapter 22 Latin America

Henry Jessen is a Doctor of Law of the University of Rio de Janeiro. He is Vice-President of the Interamerican Copyright Institute and President of its Neighbouring Rights Committee, President of the second chamber of the National Copyright Council of Brazil and legal adviser to SOCINPRO (the collecting society for Neighbouring Rights in Brazil). He was the delegate of Brazil at the Rome Convention 1961 and a member of the Brazilian delegation at the Phonogram Convention 1971. He is the author of the Latin American textbook *Intellectual Property Rights* (published in Portuguese and Spanish). Translation of Chapter 22 from Portuguese by P D Coate, MA (Cantab) Solicitor.

Chapter 23 India

Krishnaswami Ponnuswami is a Master of Laws and a Bachelor of Science of the University of Madras, a Master of Laws of Yale University (USA) and Doctor of Civil Law of McGill University (Canada). He is Professor of Industrial Property Law at the University of Delhi and (visiting) Professor of the University of Dar-es-Salaam (Tanzania). He is the author of *Cases and Materials on Contracts* (1974) and numerous articles on commercial and industrial law.

Chapter 24 Japan

Yoshio Nomura is a member of the Government Copyright Council of Japan and Vice-President of the Copyright Society. He was Director of the legal and economic department of the Broadcasting Regulatory Agency of Japan from 1949 to 1952. He represented Japan at Intergovernmental meetings and diplomatic conferences for over half a century, inter alia: the International Telegraph Conference, Paris, 1925; the International Radio Communication Conference, Paris, 1927; International Radio Communication Conference, Cairo, 1938; International High Frequency Broadcasting Conference, Florence and Rapallo, 1950; Diplomatic Conference, Rome Convention, 1961; Berne and Universal Copyright Convention Revision Conference, 1967; International Study Group, Copyright Conventions, Washington, 1969; Diplomatic Conference for Satellite Convention, Brussels, 1974. He was Chairman of the East Asian Copyright Seminar, Tokyo, 1973, and lecturer at the Pacific Copyright Seminar, Sidney, 1976.

Chapter 25 Australia

James Lahore is a Doctor of Laws of the University of Melbourne, a Master of Laws of the University of Pennsylvania, USA, and a Master of Arts and Bachelor of Civil Law of Oxford University. He is a solicitor and was Reader in Law at Monash University, Australia, until 1980; Counsellor to the World Intellectual Property Organisation (WIPO) Geneva, 1973-74 and since 1981 is the first holder of the Herschel Smith Chair of Intellectual Property at the University of London. He is an editor of the European Intellectual Property Review and the Australian Business Law Journal, a member of the Council of the Common Law Institute of Intellectual Property and Vice-President of the British Literary and Artistic Copyright Association. He is the author of the standard work: *Intellectual Property in Australia* (Copyright, 1977, and Patents, Designs, Trade Marks and Unfair Competition, 1981) also: *Photocopying, A Guide to the 1980 Amendments to the Copyright Act, 1980.*

Bibliography

Chapter 1 Ideology

Books

CORNISH: *Intellectual Property* (1981)
COPINGER: *Copinger on Copyright* (12th edn, 1981)
DESBOIS: *Le Droit d' Auteur en France* (3rd edn, 1978)
FIKENSCHER: *Methoden des Rechts* (1975)
FOX: *The Canadian Law of Copyright* (2nd edn, 1967)
PLOMAN AND HAMILTON: *Copyright* (1980)
ULMER: *Urheberrecht* (3rd edn, 1980)

Articles

CHAFEE: 'Reflections on the Law of Copyright' (1945) 45 Columbia Law Review 503
RINGER: 'The Demonology of Copyright' (Bowker Memorial Lecture) (18 November 1974) US Publishers Weekly

Chapter 2 History

Books

COPINGER: *Copinger on Copyright* (12th edn, 1981)
DESBOIS: *Le Droit d' Auteur en France* (3rd edn, 1978)
FOX: *The Canadian Law of Copyright* (2nd edn, 1967)
FRANÇON: *La propriété littéraire et artistique en Grande Bretagne et aux Etats Unis* (1955)
GIESEKE: *Die geschichtliche Eutwicklung des deutschen Urheberrechts* (1957)
KOHLER: *Urheberrecht an Schriftwerken und Verlagsrecht* (1907)
LADAS: *The International Protection of Literary and Artistic Property* (1938)
PUTNAM: *Books and their Makers during the Middle Ages* (New York, 1962)
ULMER: *Urheberrecht* (3rd edn, 1980)

Articles

DE SANCTIS: 'Le dévelopement et la consécration internationale du droit d' auteur' RIDA (1974) 207
DESBOIS: L' évolution du droit d' auteur dans les relations internationales depuis la Conference de Bruxelles (1948)' (1974) RIDA 293
DOCK: 'Genèse et evolution de la notion de la propriete literaire' RIDA (June 1974)
RINGER: 'Two Hundred Years of American Copyright Law' (Bicentennial Symposium American Bar Association, 1976)
STEWART: 'Two Hundred years of English Copyright Law' (Bicentennial Symposium American Bar Association, 1976) Copyright (July 1977) 225

Chapter 3 Copyright in International Law

Books

BARTIFFOL AND LAGARDE: *Droit International Privé* (6th edn, 1974)
BROWNLIE: *Principles of Public International Law* (1979)

CHESHIRE AND NORTH: *Private International Law* (10th edn, 1979)
DICEY AND MORRIS: *Conflict of Laws* (9th edn, 1973)
EHRENZWEIG: *Private International Law* (Vol 1, 1967) (Vol 2, with Jayme, 1973)
GRAVESON: *The Conflict of Laws* (6th edn, 1969)
KAHN-FREUND: *General Problems of International Law* (1976)
LIPSTEIN: *General Principles of Private International Law* (Recueil des Cours de L' Academie de Droit International 135 (1972 I) 104)
SCHWARZENBERGER: *International Law* (5th edn)
ULMER: *Intellectual Property Rights and the Conflict of Laws* (Commission of the European Communities, 1978)
WOLFF: *Private International Law* (2nd edn, 1950)

Articles

BAUM: 'International Law, Berne Convention and National Law' Droit d' Auteur (1946) 85
NIMMER: 'Who is the Copyright Owner when Laws Conflict?' GRUR Int (1973) 202
OSTERTAG: 'La Convention de Berne et le droit national' Droit d' Auteur (1941) 29, 37
STEWART: 'Unlicensed broadcasting from ships on the high seas: a challenge to international copyright' 15 Bull Cop Soc USA (1968) 108
WALTER: 'Contractual freedom in the field of copyright and conflict of laws' RIDA (January 1976) 72

Chapter 4 Authors' Rights

General

DOCK: *Etude sur le droit d' auteur* (1963)
DOCK: 'Radioscopie du droit d' auteur contemporain' (1974) Il Diritto di Autore Vol 45 No 4, 415

Special subjects

Droit moral

CORNISH: *Intellectual Property Rights* (1981) 392
DESBOIS: *Le droit d' auteur en France* (3rd edn) (1978) paras 380 ff
STROMHOLM: *Le droit moral de l' auteur en droit Allemand, Français et Scandinave* (1966)
ULMER: *Urheberrecht* (3rd edn, 1980) 208
GABAY: Geiringer Lecture 1978 (1979) Bull Cop Soc USA 203
MENTHA: 'Einige Gedanken zum Urheberpersönlichkeitsrecht' GRUR Int (1973) 295
VAN ISACKER: 'The moral right in the Berne Convention RIDA (1967/8) 241

Droit de suite

DUCHEMIN: 'Le Droit de Suite' RIDA (April 1974) 77
KATZENBERGER: 'The "Droit de Suite" in copyright law' (1973) 4 IIC 361
NORDEMANN: 'Droit de suite' RIDA (January 1977) 77, RIDA (1967/8) 369
ULMER: 'Droit de suite in international copyright' (January 1975) IIC 12

Publication

DURANDE: 'The concept of publication in the international conventions' RIDA (January 1982) 72
NIMMER: 'Simultaneous publication as a route to Berne protection for non Berne nationals' (Homage to Valerio de Sanctis) 1979

Public performance

REIMER: 'Right of public performance in view of technological advancement' (1976) 5 IIC 541

Copyright contracts

COHEN JEHORAM (ED): *Copyright Contracts, Monographs on Industrial Property and Copyright Law*, Vol 2 (1977)
ULMER: 'Some thoughts on the law of copyright contracts' (1976) 5 IIC 202
WALTER: 'Contractual freedom in the field of copyright and conflict of laws' RIDA (January 1976) 72

Cinematographic works

FERRARA-SANTAMARIA: 'Le régime juridique des oeuvres cinematographiques après la révision de Stockholm' RIDA 56, 83
FERNAY: 'Cinematographic and televisual works' RIDA (1967/8) 319

Employee authors

DITTRICH: *Arbeitnehmer und Urheberrecht* (Vienna, 1978)
CUVILLIER: 'Employment and Copyright' Copyright (1979) 112
PLAISANT: 'The employee author and literary and artistic property' Copyright (1977) 274

Chapter 5 The Berne Convention

Documents

Berne Convention (1971) text, see Appendix
Preparatory Documents, Stockholm Conference 1967 pp 80-136
Records of the Diplomatic Conference, Stockholm 1967 (E)
Report of the Raporteur Général (Svante Bergström) 1967
Records of the Diplomatic Conference, Paris 1971 (E)

Books

BAUM: The Brussels Conference for the Revision of the Berne Convention (translation by the Copyright Office of the USA, 1960) (German original, GRUR 1949)
DESBOIS, FRANÇON, KEREVER: *Les conventions internationales du droit d' auteur et des droits voisins* (1976)
MASOUYÉ, WALLACE: *WIPO Guide to the Berne Convention*
NORDEMANN, FINK, HERTIN: *Internationales Urheberrecht und Leistungsschutzrecht* (Kommentar, 1977)

Articles

BERGSTRÖM: 'Schutzprinzipien der Berner Übereinkunft nach der Stockholm - Paris Fassung' GRUR Int (1973) 238
BOGSCH: 'Four Conventions on Copyright and Related Subjects' [1976] NIR 7
DE SANCTIS: 'The future of international copyright in the light of the Revision Conference 1971' (1972) Interauteurs 205
'The Paris Revision of the Universal Copyright Convention and the Berne Convention' Copyright (1972) 241
'The International Copyright Conventions' Copyright (1978) 254
DESBOIS: 'The Diplomatic Conference for the revision of the Berne and Geneva Conventions' RIDA (1971) 6
'The evolution of copyright in international relations since the Brussels Conference 1948' RIDA (1974) 293
DESJEUX: 'The scope of application of the Berne Convention as revised at Stockholm 1967' Copyright (September 1968) 203
MENTHA: 'A glance at the substantive principle clauses of the Berne Convention adopted at Stockholm 1967' (1967) Copyright 321
MASOUYÉ: 'Stockholm, a landmark' (1967/8) RIDA 9
'The Berne Convention after its Stockholm Revision' (January 1968) EBU Legal Rev, 41

'The Berne Convention: its principles, development and administration' (November 1968) BIRPI Symposium
NIMMER: 'The US Copyright Law and the Berne Convention' Copyright (1966) 94
ULMER: 'The Revision of the Copyright Conventions' (1971) EBU Rev 86, GRUR Int (1971) 423
'International Copyright after the Paris Revisions' Bull Cop Soc USA (1972) 263

Chapter 6 Universal Copyright Convention

Documents

The Universal Copyright Convention, text, see Appendix
Records of the Diplomatic Conference, Geneva (1952)
Report of the Rapporteur General (Sir John Blake) Geneva, 1952
Record of the Diplomatic Conference, Paris (1971)
Report of the Rapporteur General (Abraham Karninstein) Paris, 1971

Books

BOGSCH: *The Law of Copyright under the Universal Copyright Convention* (1964)
DESBOIS, FRANÇON, KEREVER: *Les conventions internationales du droit d' auteur et des droits voisins* (1976)
NORDEMANN, VINK, HERTIN: *Internationales Urheberrecht und Leistungsschutzrecht* (1971)

Articles

(ANONYMOUS): 'The protocal regarding developing countries' RIDA (1967/8) 393
DE SANCTIS: 'The Paris Revision of the UCC and the Berne Convention' Copyright (1972) 241
DOCK: 'The UCC' RIDA (1974) 127-206
MOTT: 'The Relationship between the Berne Convention and the UCC' (1967) 11 IDEA 306
RINGER: 'Relationship between the two texts of the UCC' (January 1968) EBU Legal Rev 42
'The UCC and its future' (Nordisk, 1975) (Copyright Symposium, Helsinki, June 1975)
'Origin and evolution of the UCC' (1977) 4 Copyright Bull UNESCO 47
STEUP: 'The rule of national treatment for foreigners' (Geiringer Memorial Lecture 1977) Bull Cop Soc USA (1977) 279
ULMER: 'The Revision of the Copyright Conventions (November 1971) EBU Legal Rev 86
ZIEGLER: 'Les conférences de révision de la Convention Universelle et de la Convention de Berne, 1971' (1971) Interauteurs 26

Chapter 7 Copyrights and Neighbouring Rights

Books

ADDA: *Theorie Generale des Droits Voisins* (thesis) (1979)
MORAES: *Artistas Interpretes e Executantes* (1976)
STRASCHNOV, BERGSTRÖM, GRECO: *Protection Internationale des Droits Voisins* (1958)
ULMER: *Protection of Performing Artists, Producers of Phonograms and Broadcasting Organisations: a Study in International and Comparative Law* (1957)

Articles

BODENHAUSEN: 'Protection of Neighbouring Rights' (1954) Duke University School of Law, USA 156
BUNGEROTH: 'Schutz der ausübenden Künstler GRUR (1976) 454

DA COSTA: 'Developing countries and neighbouring rights' (1976) Cop Bull UNESCO Vol 10 No 2 69
DE SANCTIS: 'Diritti Connessi all' essercizio del diritto d'autore' (1961, Perugia Academia juridica)
DESBOIS: 'Le droit des auteurs et des artistes sur leur interpretations' (1964) Dalloz chronique xxxv 247
FISHER AND BOGSCH: 'Droit d' auteur et Droits Voisins' Droit d' Auteur (1955) 134
FRANÇON: 'International protection of neighbouring rights' RIDA (January 1974) 407
LJUNGMAN: 'Some current problems as regards neighbouring rights in nordic countries' (1979) Diritto di autore Vol 50 No 2/3 664
MAIWALD: 'Zum Verhältnis von Urheberrecht und Leistungsschutzrecht' Film und Recht 1977 Vol 21 No 6
MENTHA: 'Mouvement en faveur de la protection internationale de certains droits voisins au droit d' auteur' (1954)
MEYERS: 'Copyright for sound recordings, another milestone in the protection of Intellectual Property' Bull Cop Soc USA (February 1972) 184
SCHULZE: 'The protection of neighbouring rights in the Federal Republic of Germany' Copyright (1978) 160

Chapter 8 The Rome Convention

Documents

Rome Convention (International Convention for the Protection of Performers, Producers of Phonograms and Broadcasting Organisations (1961)) text, see Appendix
Records of the Diplomatic Conference, Rome 1961
Report of the Rapporteur General (Abraham Kaminstein)
Model Law concerning the protection of performers, producers of phonograms and broadcasting organisations with a commentary on it - ILO, UNESCO, WIPO, 1974
Report of the sub-committee of the Intergovernmental Committee (1979) Copyright 109
Report of the Intergovernmental Committee (on the functioning of the Convention) (1979) Copyright 311
Report of the Copyright Office of the USA: 'Performance rights in sound recordings' by Ohler, Bostick and Katz, Vol II - International Report, 3 January 1978

Books

DESBOIS, FRANÇON, KEREVER: *Les Conventions du droit d' auteur et des droits voisins* (1976) pp 264 ff
DESJEUX: *La Convention du Rome* (1966)
MASOUYÉ, WALLACE: *WIPO Guide to the Rome Convention* (1981)
NORDEMANN, FINK, HERTIN: *Internationales Urheberrecht und Leistungsschutzrecht* (1977)

Articles

DA COSTA: 'Some reflections on the Rome Convention' Copyright (1976) 80
  'Rome and the developing countries' Cop Bull UNESCO 1976/2 69
DAVIES: 'The Rome Convention 1961 - A Brief summary of its development and prospect (1979) EIPR 154
DE SANCTIS: 'The Rome Convention' Interauteurs 1963 (No 150, 13; No 151, ii; No 152, 115; No 153, 24) 1964 (No 154, ii)
DESJEUX: 'The narrow gate, article 16/i/i(a) Rome Convention' Droit d' auteur (1965) 155
ILOSVAY: 'Article 22 of the Rome Convention on Neighbouring Rights (special agreements)' Droit d'Auteur (1962) 211
LABRA: 'The three subjects protected by the Rome Convention' Copyright (1978) 25
LEDUC: 'National Applications of the Rome Convention on neighbouring rights' Copyright (1972) 228

MASOUYÉ: 'Les droits des artistes interprètes ou executants dans la Convention de Rome' RIDA (May 1965) 161
THOMPSON: 'Twenty Years of the Rome Convention' Copyright (1981) 270
VON RAUSCHER: 'The Rome Convention Rights: a Comparative Review of Legislation and International Legal Development over 12 years' Bull Cop Soc USA (1974) 237

Chapter 9 The Phonogram Convention

Documents

The Phonogram Convention, text, see Appendix
Records of the Diplomatic Conference, Geneva 1971
Report of the Rapporteur General (Samnik)
Model Law, IFPI, June 1978

Books

DESBOIS, FRANCON, KEREVER: *Les Conventions Internationales du droit d'auteur et des droits voisins* (1976) paras 314 ff
MASOUYÉ, WALLACE: *WIPO Guide to the Phonogram Convention*
NORDEMANN, FINK, HERTIN: *Internationales Urheberrecht und Leistungsschutzrecht* (1977) 343 ff

Articles

DE SANCTIS: 'Some general considerations on the recent Geneva Convention for the Protection of Phonograms' Copyright (May 1972) 111
KAMINSTEIN: 'The Phonogram Convention' Bull Cop Soc USA (1972) 175
KAUDINYA: 'Recording and Tape Piracy' (1978) Interauteurs 68
MASOUYÉ: 'A new international convention on the protection of phonograms' (January 1972) EBU Legal Rev 59
STEWART: 'The Geneva Convention for the Protection of Phonograms' Copyright (1973) 100
ULMER: 'The Convention for the Protection of Producers of Phonograms' (1972) IIC 3 317

Chapter 10 The Satellite Convention

Documents

Satellite Convention, text, see Appendix
Records of the Diplomatic Conference, Brussels 1974
Report of the Rapporteur General (Barbara Ringer)
Model Law, EBU Legal Rev, November 1979

Books

DESBOIS, FRANÇON, KEREVER: *Les Conventions Internationales du droit d'auteur et des droits voisins* (1976)

Articles

DITTRICH: 'The Brussels Satellite Convention' (May 1974) EBU Legal Rev 60
KEREVER: 'The Ambiguities of the Brussels Satellite Convention 21/5/74' RIDA (January 1977) 56
MASOUYÉ: 'A new international convention' (September 1974) EBU Legal Rev 46
'The distribution of programme – carrying signals transmitted by satellite: the legal problems' (July 1978) EBU Legal Rev 43
STRASCHNOV: 'The broadcast – satellite service in private law' (May 1977) EBU Legal Rev 97

ULMER: 'Protection of authors in relation to the transmission via satellite of broadcast programmes' (July 1977) RIDA 4

Chapter 11 Regional Agreements

Documents

European Agreement Concerning Programme Exchanges by means of Television Films 1958, text; see Appendix
European Agreement on the Protection of Television Broadcasts, 1960, text, see Appendix
Additional Protocol to the European Agreement on the Protection of Television Broadcasts 1974, text, see Appendix

Articles

STRACHNOV: 'Arrangement européen sur l'échange des programmes au moyen des films de télévision' Droit d'Auteur (March 1959) 41
'Arrangement européen pour la protection des émissions de télévision' (October 1960) Droit d'Auteur 263, (1961) EBU Legal Rev 37

Chapter 12 The Future of International Copyright Law
General

DESJEUX: 'Copyright in industrial life' (July 1975) RIDA 124
FERNAY: 'Greatness, misery and contradictions of copyright RIDA (July 1980) 138
FICSOR: 'Disquieting Report from the Maginot Line of Authors' Copyright (March 1982) 104
HUNNINGS: 'Copyright as a hindrance to free movement of thoughts' (July 1980) EIPR
LJUNGMAN: 'The function of copyright in the present day society' RIDA (April 1976) 51
MASOUYÉ: 'Horizon 2000 ou la grandeur et les servitudes du droit d'auteur' (April/September 1979) Il Diritto di Autore
NORDEMANN: 'Towards a logical copyright system' (1980) ICC Vol II 49
RINGER: 'Copyright in the 1980s' Bull Cop Soc USA (1976) 299
STEWART: 'International Copyright in the 1980s' (Geiringer Memorial Lecture 1980) Bull Cop Soc USA (April 1981) 351
WALLACE: 'The impact of new technology on international copyright and neighbouring rights' 18 Bull Cop Soc USA (1971) 293

Special subjects

COLLOVA: 'Audio and visual reproduction for personal use' (INTERGU series No 57, 1979)
DAVIES: 'Legal problems deriving from use of videograms' Copyright (October 1979) 257
KEREVER: 'Home taping' (July 1980) EIPR 207
KINDERMANN: 'Computer software and copyright conventions' (1981) EIPR 6
MALHOTRA: 'Copyright Aspects of Publishing in Developing Countries' Copyright (October 1980) 310
MASOUYÉ: 'Cable television: Copyright problems and others' (November 1978) EBU Legal Rev 40
'Computers and copyright' (September 1980) EBU Legal Rev 40
SCHULZE: 'Förderung des Welturheberrechts durch Eutwicklungshilfe' (Support for International Copyright by assistance to developing countries) (1970) INTERGU 44
SHER: 'Reflections on copyright in developing countries' (Geiringer Memorial Lecture 1969) Bull Cop Soc USA (1969) 201
STEWART: 'The clearing house system of licences' 13 Bull Cop Soc USA (1967) I
Home taping' (July 1980) EIPR 207

ULMER: 'Problems arising from computer storage and retrieval of protected works' Copyright (1972) 37
WALTER: 'Telediffusion and wired distribution systems, Berne Convention and Copyright legislation in Europe Copyright (1975) 302

Chapter 13 Austria

DITTRICH: *Österreichisches und internationales Urheberrecht* (Austrian and International Copyright Law)
DITTRICH: *Urherberrechtsgesetz* (*The Copyright Act*) *1982*
DITTRICH: '1972 Act amending the Austrian Copyright Law' (1973) 21 Bull Cop Soc USA, 89
'Letter from Austria' Copyright (1981) 81
POCH: 'Amendments to Austrian Copyright, unfair competition and local supply law' (1981) EIPR 147

Chapter 14 France

COLOMBET: *Propriété littéraire et artistique* (Paris, 1976, Precis Dalloz)
DESBOIS: *La propriété littéraire et aristique* (Paris, 3rd edn, 1978)

BOMCOMPAIN: 'Auteurs et Comédiens au XVIII me siècle', Paris 1976 Librarie Académique Perrin
CHESNAIS: 'L'acteur', Paris, 1957, Libraries Techniques
DESBOIS: 'La protection des artistes, interpretes et d'oeuvres musicales et dramatiques en France' (1973) 63 UFITA 109
DIETZ: 'Das "Droit Moral" des Urhebers im französischen und deutschen Urheberrecht' 1968
DOCK: 'Génèse et évolution de la notion de propriété litéraire' RIDA (January 1979)
GAUTREAU: 'La musique et les musiciens en droit privé français' Paris, 1970, Presses Universitaires de France
Juris-classeur 'Propriété littéraire et artistique', par Robert Plaisant, Paris Editions Techniques
Juris-classeur 'civil' – Annexes 'Spectacles et Communication audiovisuelle' par Pierre Chesnais. Paris Editions Techniques
PLAISANT: 'Performers' Rights in France' (1974) 25 EBU Review 43

Chapter 15 Federal Republic of Germany

FROMM/NORDEMANN: *Urheberrecht* (4th edn, 1979)
HUBMAN: *Urheber-und Verlagsrecht* (4th edn, 1978)
MESTMÄCKER-SCHULZE: *Urheberrechts Kommentar*
MÖHRING-NICOLINI: *Urheberrechtsgesetz* (1970)
SCHULZE: *Urheberrecht in der Musik* (4th edn, 1972)
ULMER: *Urheber und Verlagsrecht* (3rd edn, 1980)
VON GAMM: *Urheberrechtsgesetz* (1968)

ULMER: 'Urhebervertragsrecht' published by the Federal Ministry of Justice, 1977

Chapter 16 Italy

DE SANCTIS, VALERIO: 'Il diritto di autore' *Enciclopedia del Diritto* (1951)
'Artisti esecutori' *Enciclopedia del Diritto* (1959)
Il Contrato di Edizione (1965)
Proprietà intellectuale (1967)

DE SANCTIS, VITTORIO: *Il carattere creativo delle opere dell' ingegno* (1972)
ARE: *L' oggetto del diritto di autore* (1963)
CANDIAN: *Il diritto di autore nel sistema giuridico* (1953)
CASELLI: *Codice del diritto di autore* (1943)
CORRADO: *Opere dell' ingegno, privative industriali* (1961)
FABIANI:*Esecuzione forzata e sequestro delle opere dell' ingegno* (1958)
    Il diritto di autore nella Giurisprudenza (1972)
GRECO: *I diritti sui beni immateriali* (1948)
GRECO E VERCELLONE: *I diritti sulle opere dell' ingegno* (1974)
JARACH: *Manuale del diritto d' autore* (1968)
SORDELLI: *L'opera dell' ingegno* (1954)
VOLTAGGIO LUCCHESI: *I beni immateriali* (1962)

DE SANCTIS, VALERIO: 'Le developement et la consécration internationale du droit d' auteur' RIDA (January 1974) 207
DE SANCTIS, VITTORIO: 'Opere dell' ingegno e diritti connessi nei programmi televisivi' Il Diritto di Autore (1968)

Chapter 17 Scandinavia

BERGSTRÖM: *Lärobok i upphovsrätt (Manual on Copyright)* (Sweden, 1980)
OLSSON: *Copyright. Svensk och internationell uphovsrätt* (Swedish and International Copyright) (2nd edn, 1978)
WEINCKE: *Ophovsret (Copyright)* (Denmark, 1976)
KARNELL: *Rätten till programinnehallet i TV (Rights in the Contents of TV Programs)* (1970)
LÖGDBERG: *Upphovsrätten och fotografirätten (Copyright and Rights in Photographs)* (5th edn, 1978)

KOKTVEDGAARD: 'Letter from Denmark' Copyright (1982) 314
LIEDES: 'Letter from Finland' Copyright (1982) 156
OLSSON: 'Letter from Sweden', Copyright (1983)

Chapter 18 United Kingdom

CORNISH: *Intellectual Property: Patents, Copyright, Trade Marks and Allied Rights* (1981)
FLINT: *A User's Guide to Copyright* (1979)
LADDIE, PRESCOTT AND VITORIA: *The Modern Law of Copyright* (1980)
MCFARLAINE: *A Practical Introduction to Copyright* (1982)
SKONE JAMES, MUMMERY AND JAMES: *Copinger and Skone James on Copyright* (12th edn, 1981)
WHITFORD: Copyright and Designs Law, Committee Report, 1977

Chapter 19 USSR

LEVITSKY: *Introduction to Soviet Copyright Law* (1964)
    Copyright, Defamation, and Privacy in Soviet Civil Law (1972)
NEWCITY: *Copyright Law in the Soviet Union* (1978)

BERNARD AND BOTHA: 'Socialist Copyright Law: A Theoretical Approach' RIDA (July 1976) 3
DIETZ: 'Protection of Soviet Authors in International Copyright Law' GRUR Int (1975) 341
IONASCO: 'Protection of Copyright in Socialist Countries', RIDA (January 1973) 84
LOEBER: 'VAAP, The Soviet Copyright Agency' (1979) Univ of Illinois Law Forum 401
VORONKOVA: 'Country Report: Soviet Union (1978)' Regional Seminar on Copyright and Neighbouring Rights for Asian and Pacific States. UNESCO/WIPO Doc ND 1978

Chapter 20 EEC

BELLAMY & CHILD: *Common Market Law of Competition* (1978)
CAMPBELL: *Common Market Law* (1973)
CUNNINGHAM: *The Competition Law of the EEC 1973 (and 1975)*
DAVIES & VON RAUSCHER: *Challenges to Copyright and related rights in the European Community* (1982)
DIETZ: *Copyright in the European Community* (English edition, 1978)
GUY & LEIGH: *The EEC and Intellectual Property* (1981)
JOHANNES: *Gewerblicher Rechtsschutz und Urheberrecht im Europäischen Gemeinschaftsrecht* (1973)
KORAH: *Competition Law in Britain and the Common Market* (2nd edn, 1982)
LIPSTEIN: *The Law of the European Economic Community* (1974)

DIETZ: 'The possible Harmonisation of Copyright Law within the EEC' (1979) 10 IIC 195
HOFFMANN: 'Copyright and the Treaty of Rome – Recent Developments: Another view' (1981) EIPR 254
KOPPENSTEINER: 'Zum Erschöpfungsgrundsatz im Patent und Urheberrecht' GRUR Int (1972) 413
FRANÇON: 'Copyright and the Treaty of Rome instituting the European Economic Community' RIDA (1981) 128
REIMER: 'Der Erschöpfungsgrundsatz im Urberberrecht und gewerblichen Rechtsschutz' GRUR Int (1972) 221
REISCHL: 'Copyright Law and the Free Movement of Goods in the Common Market' Copyright (March 1982) 116

Chapter 21 United States of America

Report of the Register of Copyrights on the General Revision of the U.S. Copyright Law, Report to the House Committee on the Judiciary, 87th Cong, 1st Sess (1961)
Report of the House of Representatives Committee on the Judiciary, H.R. Rep No 94-1476, 94th Cong, 2D Sess (1976)
Performance Rights in Sound Recordings, 95th Cong, 2D Sess (1978) House Judiciary Committee (Print No 15)
Report of the National Commission on New Technological Uses of Copyrighted Works

LATMAN: *The Copyright Law* (5th edn) (Howell's Copyright Law Revised and the 1976 Act)
NIMMER: *Copyright*
Studies on Copyright (Fisher Memorial Edition 1960)
BREYER: 'The Uneasy Case for Copyright: A Study of Copyright in Books, Photocopies, and Computer Programs' 84 Harvard Law Review 281 (1970)
BRYLAWSKI: 'The Copyright Royalty Tribunal' 24 UCLA Law Review 1265 (1977)
CHAFEE: 'Reflections on the Law of Copyright' 45 Columbia Law Review 503 (1945)
GOLDSTEIN: 'Federal System Ordering of the Copyright Interest' 69 Columbia Law Review 49 (1969)
'Preempted State Doctrines, Involuntary Transfers and Compulsory Licenses: Testing the Limits of Copyright' 24 UCLA Law Review 1070 (1977)
GORMAN: 'Copyright Protection for the Collection and Representation of Facts' 76 Harvard Law Review 1569 (1963)
'An Overview of the Copyright Act of 1976' 126 Univ of Pennsylvania Law Review 856 (1978)
'Fact or Fancy? The Implications for Copyright' 29 Bull Cop Soc USA (1982) 560
KAPLAN: 'An Unhurried View of Copyright' Carpentier Lectures (1966)
'Performer's Right and Copyright: The Capitol Records Case' 69 Harvard Law Review 409 (1956)
KORMAN: 'Performance Rights in Music Under Sections 110 and 118 of the 1976 Copyright Act' 22 New York Law School Review 521 (1977)

NIMMER: 'Does Copyright Abridge the First Amendment Guarantees of Free Speech and Press?' 17 UCLA Law Review 1180 (1970)
'Preface – the Old Copyright Act as Part of the New Act' 22 New York Law School Review 471 (1977)
SELTZER: 'Exemptions and Fair Use in Copyright' 24 Bull Cop Soc USA 215, 307 (1977)
WHICHER: 'The Ghost of Donaldson v Becket' 9 Bull Cop Soc USA 102 (1961)

Chapter 22 South America

General

EMERY, M. A.: 'Current Legislative Trends in the Field of Copyright and Neighbouring Rights in Latin America' Copyright (1977) 131

Argentina

DELLA COSTA, HECTOR: *El Derecho de Autor y su Novedad* (1971)
MOUCHET, CARLOS Y RADAELLI, SIGFRIDO: *Derechos Intelectuales* (1948)
STANOWSKY, ISIDRO: *Derecho Intelectual* (1954)
VILLALBA, C. A., Y LIPSZYC, D.: *Derechos de los Artistas* (1976)

Brazil

AMARAL, CLAUDIO DE SOUZA: 'Proteçao Internacional do Direito de Autor e dos Direitos Conexos' (1972) RIDA No 3
AZEVEDO, PHILADELPHO: *Direito Moral dos Escritores* (1930)
BITTAR, C. A.: *Direito de Autor na obra Feita sob Encomenda* (1977)
BOBBIO, PEDRO VINCENTE: *O Direito de Autor na Creaçao Musical* (1951)
CHAVES, ANTONIO: *Proteçao Internacional do Direito Autoral de Radiodifusao*
COSTA NETO, J. C.: *O Direito Autoral no Brasil* (1980)
DUVAL, HERMANO: *Direitos Autorais nas Invençoes Modernas*
EBOLI, J. C. DE CAMARGO: 'Direitos Conexos' (1978, RIDA, 1)
GANDELMAN, HENRIQUE: *Guia Basico de Direitos Autorais* (1982)
JESSEN, H.: *Direitos Intelectuais* (1967)
MASCERENHAS DA SILVA, ILDEFONSO: *Direito de Autor* (1954)
MATTIA, FABIO M. DE: *O Autor e o Editor na Obra Grafica* (1975)
MORAES, WALTER: *Posiçao Sistematica do Direito dos Artistas Interpretes e Executantes* (1973)
OLIVEIRA E SILVA, DIRCEU: *O Direito de Autor* (1956)
ROCHA, DANIEL: *Gestion des Droits d'Execution Publique au Bresil* (1978)
VIEIRA MANSO, EDUARDO: *Contratos de Direitos Autorais*

Colombia

PLAZAS, ARCADIO: *Derechos Intelectuales* (1942)

Ecuador

PROANO MAYA, M. A.: *El Derecho de Autor* (1972)

Mexico

BLANCO LABRA, VICTOR: *La Pirateria de las Imagenes en Movimiento* (1981, 11 DA)
OBON, J., RAMON. L.: *Los Derechos de Autor en Mexico* (1974)

Uruguay

GROMPONE, ROMEO: *El Derecho de Autor en Uruguay* (1977)

Peru

PIZZARO D, EDMUNDO: *Los Bienes y Derechos Intelectuales* (1974)

Venezuala

ANTEQUERA PARILLI, RICARDO: *Derecho de Autor* (1977)

Chapter 23 India

CHOPRA: *Copyright and International Conventions* (1978)
DADACHANJI: *Law of Literature and Dramatic Copyright in a Nutshell* (1960)
    Law of Copyright and Movie-Rights in a Nutshell
KHOSLA: *Know your copyright* (1977)
MITTAL, JAIN: *The Law of Copyright in India* (1957) (3rd edn, 1977, by SINGHAL)

Chapter 24 Japan

DOI: *The Intellectual Property Law of Japan* (1980)
NOMURA: 'The New Copyright Act in Japan' (March 1971) EBU Rev No 126B
    'Letter from Japan' Copyright (September 1977) 260
    'Letter from Japan' Copyright (November 1982) 345

Chapter 25 Australia

LAHORE: *Intellectual Property Law in Australia: Copyright* (1977)
STERLING & HART: *Copyright in Australia* (1981)

Index

Academic lawyers
  writings of, as source of private international law, 3.12
Accounts
  remedy for infringement by way of, 23.46
Adaptation
  film, right in, 5.49
  restrictions, 18.13
  right of—
    Brussels Act, 5.23
    Paris Act, 5.45
    United States, 21.21
Additional Protocol. *See* BERNE CONVENTION
Administrative remedies. *See* INFRINGEMENT OF COPYRIGHT
Agricultural fair
  exemptions, 21.26
Anglo-Saxon system
  droit d'auteur distinguished from, 1.15–1.16
  economic argument, emphasis on, 1.12, 1.15
  history of, 1.16
  philosophical foundation, 1.15
Anonymous work
  term of protection, 18.20
Antiquity
  author's rights, 2.02
Anton Piller order
  remedy for infringement, as, 18.26
Applied art
  protection of works of, 5.31
Archives
  reproduction by, 21.24
Argentina
  comments, 22.22
  criminal sanctions, 22.21
  foreign works, protection of, 22.19
  legislative synopsis, 22.14–22.21
  performers, 22.14
  phonograms—
    communication to public, 22.20
    producers of, 22.15
    secondary use of, 22.104
  registration, 22.18
  term of protection, 22.17
Artist
  droit de suite, 5.53
Artistic contributor
  film, right to, 5.50
Artistic copyright
  infringement of copyright, 23.35
  limitation of rights, 23.36
  rights of owner, 23.35

Artistic work
  acts restricted by true copyright in, 18.14
  meaning, 23.05
  original, India, 23.05
  protection by copyright, 4.14
  subject matter of protection, 18.05
  term of protection, India, 23.25
Assignment
  India, 23.14, 23.15
  transfer of copyright from owner by, 4.27
Audiovisual work
  meaning, 21.10
  United States, 21.10
Australia
  broadcasting organisations—
    limitation of rights, 25.45–25.49
    protection of, 25.27
  copyright—
    general principles, 25.05 *et seq.*
    relation with neighbouring rights, 25.24
  foreign right owners, protection of, 25.51
  history and development of copyright, 25.01–25.04
  law revision, 25.52–25.54
  limitation of rights, 25.36 *et seq.*
  neighbouring rights, relation between copyright and, 25.24
  performers, protection of, 25.25
  phonograms, protection of producers of, 25.26
  related interests, protection of, 25.28
  remedies for infringement, 25.50
  revenue, collection and distribution, 25.29–25.33
  term of protection, 25.34–25.35
Austria
  broadcasting organisation, protection of, 13.21–13.22
  cable diffusion, 12.31
  copyright—
    history and development of, 13.01
    relationship between neighbouring rights and, 13.02
  foreign right-owners, protection of, 13.27–13.29
  neighbouring rights
    collection and distribution of revenue, 13.23
    relationship between copyright and, 13.02
  organiser of performance, protection of, 13.17
  permitted use, 13.25
  points of attachment, 13.27–13.29

Austria—*continued*
    producers of phonograms, protection of, 13.18–13.20
    protection of performers—
        broadcasting right, 13.06
        distribution right, 13.05
        generally, 13.03
        public performance right, 13.09–13.16
        reproduction right, 13.04
    remedies for infringement, 13.26
    royalty on blank tape used for recording, 7.17
    term of protection, 13.24

Author
    Antiquity, in, 2.02
    change of nationality, 6.06
    consent of, publication requires, 5.33
    contract of service, work done under, 23.13
    country to which he belongs, 3.24, 3.25
    creator of work, copyright acquired by, 16.04
    droit d'auteur system, 1.13–1.14
    first owner of copyright, as, 23.13
    foreign, treatment in copyright law, 3.14
    joint—
        composite work, 14.03
        work of collaboration, 14.03
    loss of nationality, 6.06
    meaning, 5.29, 24.05
    Middle Ages, 2.03
    moral rights of, 23.47
    performers as creators, 21.57
    plurality of, exercise of rights where, 14.12
    rights—
        adaptation, of, 5.45
        addresses, 5.59
        broadcasts, 5.60
        contract for administration of rights, 15.18
        current events, report of, 5.61
        decree establishing, 2.10
        derivative works, 4.03, 4.23
        droit de suite, 5.53
        economic, 4.15, 4.16, 4.21
        education, restrictions for needs of, 5.62
        equitable remuneration, 5.43
        exhaustion of, 5.24
        existence of pre-existing rights, 4.02
        extent of, Japan, 24.06–24.08
        folklore, 5.63
        France, 2.10
        Germany, 2.06, 15.04–15.07
        Latin America, 22.01–22.10
        limitations of copyright. *See* LIMITATION OF RIGHTS
        minimum, 5.43
        moral—
            economic rights independent of, 4.21
            expiry of, 4.22
            generally, 4.17
            integrity, right of, 4.17, 4.20, 4.23
            other causes of action used to exercise, 4.23
            paternity, right of, 4.17, 4.19, 4.23
            publication, right of, 4.17, 4.18, 4.23
            neighbouring rights, relations between, 7.06–7.07
        newspaper articles, 5.60

Author—*continued*
    rights—*continued*
        Nordic Copyright Acts, 17.03
        official texts, 5.57
        origins of, 7.04
        ownership—
            assignment, 4.27
            commissioned works, 4.26
            employment, work created in, 4.25
            generally, 4.24
            licencing, 4.27
        pre-existing works, 5.48
        public lectures, 5.59
        public policy, restrictions in interests of, 5.64
        relationship between neighbouring rights and, 14.15–14.18
        remedies for infringement of copyright. *See* INFRINGEMENT OF COPYRIGHT
        restrictions left to national legislation, 5.57 *et seq.*
        Rome Convention, 8.02
        Soviet Union, 19.02
        subject matter of copyright. *See* SUBJECT MATTER
        term of copyright, 4.39–4.41
        total exemptions—
            news of the day, 5.55
            quotations, 5.56
        use of work, 16.06
    term of copyright connected with life of, 4.39
    who is, 6.07

Automatic protection
    principle of, 5.35

Berlin Act. *See* BERNE CONVENTION

Berne Convention
    adaptation, right of, 5.23
    Additional Protocol, 5.12
    advantages, 5.02
    Berlin Act, 5.11
    Berne Union, list of member states, 5.68
    between 1886 and 1971, 5.10 *et seq.*
    broadcasting right, 5.13, 5.22
    Brussels Act, 5.14–5.26
    cinematographic right, 5.25
    colonial clause, 5.05
    compulsory licence, 4.35, 5.11
    development of copyright since, 2.20
    1886, 5.08–5.09
    elements of importance to future development, 5.05
    exceptions, 5.09
    formalities, 5.11
    free use, 4.29
    generally, 5.01
    history, 5.07
    improvements in level of protection, 5.11
    joint authorship, works of, 5.13
    list of protected works, 5.16
    literary work, meaning, 4.04
    making of, 5.05
    minimum rights, 3.18
    moral right, 5.13, 5.17
    national treatment, principle of, 5.11

Berne Convention—*continued*
objectives—
    generally, 5.03
    methods applied to achieve, 5.04
Paris Act. *See* PARIS ACT
Paris Additional Act, 5.10
protected works, new categories, 5.11
public performance right, 5.20
public recitation right, 5.21
publication, meaning, 4.08
recording right, 5.11, 5.24
remedies for breach—
    action for infringement, 5.67
    private international law, 5.66
    public international law, 5.65
reprisal clause, 5.12
reproduction right, 5.18
revision, 12.04
Rome Act, 5.13
Stockholm Act, 5.27
structure and character of, 5.14
success of, 6.01
term of protection, 4.39, 5.11, 5.15
translation—
    right, 5.10, 5.11, 5.19
    ten year regime, 6.49
Berne Union
Berne Safeguard Clause, 6.01, 6.37
list of member states, 5.68
Book
copy of, distinguished from copy of phonogram, 4.08
Bookseller
Battle of, 2.14-2.15
emergence of trade, 2.04
privileges granted to, 2.04
protection, Germany, 2.05
Bootlegging
meaning, 8.18
Phonogram Convention, 9.02
Brazil
broadcasting organisations, 22.25
collection of remuneration, 22.104
comments, 22.31
criminal sanctions, 22.30
foreign work, protection of, 22.28
legislative synopsis, 22.23-22.30
performers' rights, 22.23
phonograms—
    communication to public, 22.29
    producers of, 22.24
registration, 22.27
term of protection, 22.26
Breach of copyright. *See* INFRINGEMENT OF COPYRIGHT
Broadcast
points of attachment, Austria, 13.29
protection by copyright, 4.14
restrictions on author's rights, 5.60
term of protection, Australia, 25.34
translations for, 6.48
Broadcaster
rights of, United States, 21.79
Broadcasting
concept of, 10.03
ephemeral recordings, 5.44, 21.27

Broadcasting—*continued*
essential characteristics, 5.43
minimum rights, 5.43
phonogram producers, protection of, 14.34-14.37
public, compulsory licensing, 21.35
right—
    Brussels Act, 5.22
    compulsory licence provisions, 4.35
    introduction of, 5.13
    Paris Act, 5.43
    recording right separated from, 5.44
satellite. *See* SATELLITE BROADCASTING
secondary use, Scandinavia, 17.18
television. *See* TELEVISION
Broadcasting organisation
absolute rights, 7.38
copyright owner, as, 11.01
ephemeral recordings, Italy, 16.20
foreign, protection of, UK, 18.38
limitation of rights, 18.35
limitation of rights, Australia, 25.45-25.49
national territory, legal protection on, 14.41
national treatment, 8.15
protection—
    Argentina, 22.16
    Australia, 25.27
    Austria, 13.21-13.22
    Brazil, 22.25
    Chile, 22.34
    Colombia, 22.42
    communication of television broadcasts to public, 8.35
    Costa Rica, 22.51
    Cuba, 22.105
    Ecuador, 22.60
    El Salvador, 22.70
    fixation of broadcast, 8.33
    France, 14.40-14.42
    Germany, 15.35
    India, 23.23
    Italy, 16.20
    Japan, 24.18-24.22
    Mexico, 22.80
    Paraguay, 22.89
    rebroadcasting, 8.32
    reproduction of fixation, 8.34
    Rome Convention, 8.31-8.35
    Scandinavia, 17.16
    Soviet Union, 19.04
    United Kingdom, 18.30
rebroadcasting—
    meaning, 7.38
    right of, 24.20
retransmission, right of, 24.22
rights of, 7.36-7.39, 11.07
Uruguay, 22.98
Broadcasting right
Austria, 13.06
challenges to—
    cable diffusion, 12.28-12.32
    satellites, 12.33-12.35
Universal Copyright Convention, 6.20
Brussels Act. *See* BERNE CONVENTION
Bundle of rights
copyright as, 1.09

Cable diffusion
  Australia, 25.54
  facts of, 12.28
  future, 12.32
  law, 12.29–12.31
Cassettes
  tax on, 17.28–17.29
Catalogues
  protection of producer, 17.17
Censorship
  France, 2.09
Chile
  broadcasting organisations, 22.34
  criminal sanctions, 22.39
  foreign works, protection of, 22.37
  legislative synopsis, 22.32–22.39
  performers, 22.32
  phonograms—
    communication to public, 22.38
    producers of, 22.33
  registration, 22.36
  term of protection, 22.35
Choreographic works
  United States, 21.08
Cinematographic work. *See* FILM
Collecting societies
  European Economic Community, 20.09
  guidelines for establishment and operation, 8.29
  international bilateral agreements, 8.29
  performers, for, 24.24
  producers of phonograms, for, 24.25
  right of, Germany, 15.18
Collective agreement
  protection of performer through, 14.20–14.25
Collective work
  contributions to, ownership of, 21.39
Colombia
  broadcasting organisations, 22.42
  comment, 22.48
  criminal sanctions, 22.47
  foreign works, protection of, 22.45
  legislative synopsis, 22.40–22.47
  performers, 22.40
  phonograms—
    communication to public, 22.46
    producers of, 22.41
  registration, 22.44
  term of protection, 22.43
Commissioned work
  ownership of copyright, 4.26
Common law
  pre-emption of copyright, 21.46
Compensation
  translation right, 6.27
Compensatory remedies. *See* INFRINGEMENT OF COPYRIGHT
Compilation
  United States, 21.12
Compulsory licence
  Berlin Act, 5.11
  coin-operated phonorecord players, USA, 21.34
  compulsory licence, meaning, 4.33
  concept of, 4.33

Compulsory licence—*continued*
  Copyright Royalty Tribunal, 21.31
  developing countries—
    duration, 6.42
    generally, 4.38, 6.30
    main characteristics, 6.40
    procedures, 6.41
    rights subjected to, 6.43
  exclusive rights subject to, USA, 21.31–21.35
  forms of system, 4.33
  future development, 12.39
  India, 23.18
  Japan, 24.13
  main criticism of principle, 4.34
  main reasons for introducing, 4.34
  phonorecords of musical works, USA, 21.32
  proliferation of, 4.37
  public broadcasting, USA, 21.35
  recordings, 5.24
  reproduction right, applied to, 6.50–6.52
  secondary transmission, 21.33
  statutory licence, meaning, 4.33
  system of, 6.22
  translation, procedure for issue of, 6.26
  translation right subject to, 6.25
Computers
  challenge to reproduction right, as, 12.20–12.24
  facts of, 12.20
  future of, 12.24
  ideas, systems, blank forms, 21.17
  law, 12.21–12.23
  programs, USA, 12.21, 21.29
  software—
    meaning, 4.14
    protection of, 4.14, 14.07
  storage and retrieval of copyright material, 12.22
  works created with help of, 12.23
Conflict of laws
  legal issue—
    category of, 3.04
    connecting factor, 3.05
    what is, 3.03
  meaning, 3.01
  questions arising in, 3.02–3.05
Connecting factor. *See* CONVENTIONS
Consent
  performer's right to give, Germany, 15.23, 15.25
  without, performers' rights, 8.17
Consumerism
  challenge to development of copyright, 12.06
Continental European system
  generally, 1.13–1.14
Contract
  administration of rights, Germany, 15.18
  assignment, 4.27
  assignment of work for use, Soviet Union, 19.02
  copyright, Italy, 16.11
  employment, of, performer serving under, 15.28
  grant of rights to use made by, 15.13
  licence, 4.27
  publishing, 15.19

Contract—*continued*
  service, of, author's employment under, 23.13
  works created in employment, 4.25

Contracting states
  Berne Convention, 5.68
  European Agreement on Protection of Television Broadcasts, 11.13
  Phonogram Convention, 9.11
  Rome Convention, 8.52
  Satellite Convention, 10.20
  Universal Copyright Convention, 6.53

Contribution
  collective work, to, ownership of, USA, 21.39

Contributor
  programme, to, safeguard of interests, 10.13

Control
  copyright, of, 12.39

Conventions
  application to national law, 3.30
  Berne. *See* BERNE CONVENTION
  connecting factor—
    country of first publication, 3.24, 3.27
    country of origin, 3.24, 3.26
    country to which author of work belongs, 3.24, 3.25
    examples, 5.32
    generally, 3.24
    Paris Act, 5.32
    protecting country, 3.28
  history of international copyright treaties, 3.15
  international, as source of private international law, 3.09
  Phonogram. *See* PHONOGRAM CONVENTION
  principles of—
    generally, 3.16
    lex fori, 3.16
    lex loci, 3.16
    national treatment—
      extensions of principle of, 3.18–3.19
      formalities, 3.19
      generally, 3.17
      limitations of principle of, 3.20–3.21
      minimum rights, 3.18
      reciprocity, limitation by rule of, 3.20
      reservations, limitation by, 3.21
      public lending right, 3.22
      reprography, 3.23
  relationship between EEC law and, 20.11
  Rome. *See* ROME CONVENTION
  Satellite. *See* SATELLITE CONVENTION
  systems of creating rights, 3.29
  Universal Copyright. *See* UNIVERSAL COPYRIGHT CONVENTION

Copying machines
  reproduction of works by. *See* REPROGRAPHY

Copyright
  case law developed by European Court, 20.06
  categories of works protected, 4.14
  challenges to effectiveness of, 12.10
  control of, 12.39
  copyright sphere, taken out of, 12.07
  devaluation, 12.37

Copyright—*continued*
  difference between granting neighbouring rights and, 7.05
  divisibility, USA, 21.40
  dualistic concept, Italy, 16.05
  existence of pre-existing right, 4.02
  foreign, protection of owners of, 19.10
  general principle of, 1.11
  history. *See* HISTORY
  ideology. *See* IDEOLOGY OF COPYRIGHT
  infringement of. *See* INFRINGEMENT OF COPYRIGHT
  international law, in. *See* INTERNATIONAL LAW
  justification of. *See* JUSTIFICATION OF COPYRIGHT
  law. *See* LAW
  limitations of. *See* LIMITATION OF RIGHTS
  material, storage and retrieval of, 12.22
  nature of. *See* NATURE OF COPYRIGHT
  ownership. *See* OWNERSHIP
  political significance, 1.19
  relationship between neighbouring rights and, 13.02
  safeguard clause for, 8.05–8.06
  social significance, 1.19
  sociology of, 12.36
  statutory limitations, 1.11
  subject matter of. *See* SUBJECT MATTER
  system. *See* SYSTEMS OF COPYRIGHT
  term of. *See* TERM OF PROTECTION
  transfer of. *See* TRANSFER OF COPYRIGHT
  unity of, 12.38
  user, 1.11

Copyright agreement
  contract—
    administration of rights, Germany, 15.18
    publishing, 15.19
    user, 15.20
  meaning, 15.17

Copyright countries
  variation of scope of copyright, 1.10

Copyright Royalty Tribunal
  distribution of royalties, 4.36
  royalty rate set by, 4.36, 4.37

Costa Rica
  broadcasting organisations, 22.51
  criminal sanctions, 22.56
  foreign works, protection of, 22.54
  legislative synopsis, 22.49–22.57
  performers, 22.49
  phonograms—
    communication to public, 22.55
    producers of, 22.50
  registration, 22.53
  term of protection, 22.52

Country
  first publication, of, 3.24, 3.27
  origin, of, 3.24, 3.26, 5.36
  personal status connection, 3.24, 3.25
  protecting, 3.24, 3.28

Creator. *See* AUTHOR

Criminal sanctions
  Argentina, 22.21
  Brazil, 22.30
  Chile, 22.39

Criminal sanctions—*continued*
  Colombia, 22.47
  Costa Rica, 22.56
  Ecuador, 22.65
  El Salvador, 22.75
  Germany, 15.43–15.47
  Mexico, 22.85
  Paraguay, 22.94
  performers' protection by way of, 7.13
  Uruguay, 22.103
Current events
  report of, restrictions on author's rights, 5.61
  short excerpts, use of, 8.20, 8.42
Custom
  international, as source of private international law, 3.08

Damages
  additional, UK, 18.22
  conversion, 18.22
  detention or conversion, for, 23.45
  exemplary, 18.22
  infringement of rights of phonogram producers and performers, 7.23
  normal, 18.22
  remedy for infringement of copyright, 4.47
Date
  formalities, 6.11
Declaration of Human Rights
  interests of copyright owner compared with interests of copyright user, 1.11
Delivery up
  remedy for infringement of copyright, 4.47
Denmark. *See* SCANDINAVIA
Derivative works
  creation of, 4.03
  kinds, 7.06
  literary works, 14.05
  musical works, 14.05
  neighbouring rights. *See* NEIGHBOURING RIGHTS
  parody, pastiche and caricature, 14.05
  work of art, 14.05
Developing countries
  challenge to concept of international copyright, 12.03
  compulsory licences—
    duration, 6.42
    generally, 6.30
    main characteristics, 6.40
    procedures, 6.41
    provisions, 4.38
    reproduction right, applied to, 6.50–6.52
    rights subjected to, 6.43
    translation right, applied to, 6.45–6.47
  infringement of copyright, 4.50
  meaning, 6.39
  Paris revisions for benefit of, 23.54
  reciprocity, 6.44
  removal of Berne Safeguard Clause, 6.02
  systems of, 1.18
  translation—
    broadcasting purposes, 6.48
    restrictions on right of, 6.49
    right. *See* TRANSLATION RIGHT
    ten-year regime, 6.49

Developing countries—*continued*
  Universal Copyright Commission, special provisions, 6.38 *et seq.*
Distribution
  general, to public, 6.33
  meaning, 6.33
  performance rights in phonograms, revenue from, 7.31–7.35
  right, Austria, 13.05
Dramatic work
  infringement of copyright, India, 23.32
  limitation of rights, 23.34
  meaning, 23.04
  original, India, 23.04
  owner's rights, 23.32
  restricted acts, UK, 18.07–18.13
  subject matter of protection, 18.05
  term of protection, India, 23.25
Droit d'auteur system
  Anglo-Saxon system distinguished from, 1.15–1.16
  generally, 1.13–1.14
  natural justice, emphasis on principles of, 1.12, 1.14
Droit de suite
  establishment of, 5.53
Droit moral. *See* MORAL RIGHTS
Duration. *See* TERM OF PROTECTION

Economic argument
  Anglo-Saxon system puts emphasis on, 1.12, 1.15
  justification of copyright, 1.03
Economic rights
  author, of, 4.15, 4.16, 14.13
  extent of, Japan, 24.08
  importance of, 4.15
  Latin America, 22.03
  moral rights independent of, 4.21
  non-voluntary licence, criticism of, 4.34
  term of protection, 4.16
Ecuador
  broadcasting organisations, 22.60
  comments, 22.66
  criminal sanctions, 22.65
  foreign works, protection of, 22.63
  legislative synopsis, 22.58–22.65
  performers, 22.58
  phonograms—
    communication to public, 22.64
    producers of, 22.59
  registration, 22.62, 22.67
  term of protection, 22.61
Education
  restrictions on author's rights for needs of, 5.62
El Salvador
  broadcasting organisations, 22.70
  comments, 22.76
  criminal sanctions, 22.75
  foreign works, protection of, 22.73
  legislative synopsis, 22.68–22.75
  performers, 22.68
  phonograms—
    communication to public, 22.74

Index 725

El Salvador—*continued*
phonograms—*continued*
producers of, 22.69
registration, 22.72
term of protection, 22.71
Employment
work created in, ownership of copyright, 4.25
Engineering works
producer of drawings for, right of, Italy, 16.23, 16.25
England. *See* UNITED KINGDOM
Engravings
Universal Copyright Convention, 6.04
Entrepreneur
economic rights of author assigned to, 4.16
European Agreement concerning Programme Exchanges by means of Television Films
broadcasting organisation, position of, 11.01
contracting state, 11.03
purpose, 11.01
television films, meaning, 11.02
European Agreement on Protection of Television Broadcasts
broadcasting organisation, rights of, 11.07
contracting state, 11.13
copyright tribunal, 11.11
exceptions, 11.10
history, 11.04
philosophy, 11.05
protected broadcasts, 11.06
reservations, 11.09
seizure, 11.12
term of protection, 11.08
European Court of Justice
functions, 20.02
European Economic Community
collecting societies, 20.09
distribution rights, 20.08
divided publishing right, 20.07
duties, 20.02
free circulation of goods, 20.04-20.06
intellectual property, application of Community law to, 20.03
law, relationship between copyright and neighbouring rights conventions and, 20.11
performing rights, 20.10
Treaty of Rome, 20.01-20.02

Fair dealing. *See* FREE USE
Fair use
doctrine of, United States, 21.23
Japan, 24.10
Federal Republic of Germany. *See* GERMANY
Film
adaptation right, 5.49
artistic contributor, right of, 5.50
Berlin Act, 5.11
copyright, rules for, 5.51
India, 23.09
Japan, 24.09
maker, action in infringement of copyright cases, 5.52
Paris Act, 5.47
producer, protection of, 14.46

Federal Republic of Germany—*continued*
protection—
cinematographic work, as, 5.25
copyright, by, 4.14
United Kingdom, 18.19
right—
Brussels Act, 5.25
Paris Act, 5.47
Rome Act, 5.13
soundtrack as phonogram, 9.04
television. *See* TELEVISION
term of protection, 18.20, 23.27
United Kingdom copyright, 18.03
Universal Copyright Convention, 6.04
Finland. *See* SCANDINAVIA
Fixation
broadcast—
generally, 8.33
reproduction of, 8.34
condition precedent to existence of copyright, as, 4.04
ephemeral, 8.20, 8.43
first, country of, 8.12
meaning, 8.20
original, made for purposes of teaching or scientific research, 8.20
unfixed works, USA, 21.16
without consent, performers' rights, 8.17
Folklore
restrictions on author's rights, 5.63
Foreign neighbouring rights
broadcasting organisations, 18.38
performers, 18.36
producers of phonograms, 18.37
protection, United Kingdom, 18.36-18.38
Foreign right owners
protection of—
Australia, 25.51
Austria, 13.27-13.29
France, 14.50
India, 23.49-23.50
Japan, 24.30
Scandinavia, 17.11, 17.22

Argentina, 22.19
Brazil, 22.28
Chile, 22.37
Colombia, 22.45
Costa Rica, 22.54
Ecuador, 22.63
El Salvador, 22.73
Mexico, 22.83
Paraguay, 22.92
Uruguay, 22.101
Foreigner
reciprocal protection, 3.13, 3.14
rights of, 3.14
Formalities
absence of, 5.35
Berlin Act, 5.11
date, 6.11
exemptions, 6.08
freedom from, 3.19
meaning, 5.35
name, 6.10

Formalities—*continued*
  Notice—
    appearance from time of first publication, 6.12
    appearance on all copies, 6.12
    valid, 6.12
    United States, 21.52
    phonograms, 8.25
  provisions solely applicable to United States, 6.13–6.14
  publication of work with authority, 6.12
  symbol, 6.09
  United States, 21.51–21.56
  Universal Copyright Convention, 6.08–6.15
  unpublished works, 6.15

France
  author's economic rights, exploitation of, 14.13
  author's rights, 2.10
  broadcasting organisation, protection of, 14.40–14.42
  censorship, 2.09
  cinematographic or videographic works, producers of, 14.46
  Civil Code, 3.10
  compulsory licence provisions, 4.36
  decrees dealing with book trade, 2.09, 2.10
  development of copyright, 2.09–2.10
  droit d'auteur and neighbouring rights, relationship between, 14.15–14.18
  duration of protection, 14.47
  foreign authors, treatment of, 3.14
  foreign right owners, protection of, 14.50
  graphic publishers, 14.45
  history and development of copyright, 14.01
  law revision, 14.51
  moral rights, 4.15, 14.11
  newspaper organisations, 14.44
  performers' rights, 7.12
  private guarantees, 2.09
  privileges, 2.09, 2.10
  producers of phonograms—
    protection—
      broadcasting, against, 14.34–14.37
      generally, 14.29
      public performance, against, 14.38–14.39
      unauthorised reproduction, against, 14.30–14.33
    collective agreement, through, 14.20–14.25
    courts, by, on principles of general law, 14.26–14.28
    generally, 14.19
  related rights, protection of, 14.43–14.46
  remedies for infringement of copyright, 4.46
  rights—
    limitations of, 14.48
    remedies for infringement, 14.49
  work—
    joint authors, 14.03
    limits to protection of, 14.08–14.10
    meaning, 14.02
    plurality of authors, exercise of rights where, 14.12
    protected, 14.04–14.07

France—*continued*
    unauthorised use, procedures and sanctions, 14.14
  use of, 14.11

Free use
  exceptional, categories of, 4.30
  generally, 4.29
  home taping, 4.32
  problems of, 4.31–4.32
  reprography, 4.31
  special cases, 4.30

Germany
  author's rights, 2.06, 15.04–15.07
  broadcasting organisations, protection of, 15.35
  cable diffusion, 12.31
  certain publications, related rights in, 15.38
  collecting societies, right of, 15.18
  compulsory licence provisions, 4.36
  copyright agreements, 15.17–15.20
  development of copyright, 2.05–2.08
  foreign authors, treatment of, 3.14
  granting of rights to use, 15.12–15.16
  history and development of copyright, 15.01–15.02
  infringement of copyright and neighbouring rights—
    civil law claims, 15.39–15.42
    criminal law sanctions, 15.43–15.47
  legal developments, 15.02
  legal succession of copyright, 15.11
  limitation of copyright, 15.08–15.09
  multiplicity of states, effect of, 2.08
  neighbouring rights, development of, 15.21
  performers' rights, 7.10
  photographs, related rights in, 15.37
  producers of phonograms, protection, 15.29–15.31
  protection of performers, 15.22–15.28
  protection of printers, 2.05
  related rights, protection of, 15.36–15.38
  reprography, 12.18
  royalty on recording equipment, 7.17
  term of protection, 15.10
  work, meaning, 15.03

Goods
  free circulation of, European Economic Community, 20.04–20.06

Government
  approach to copyright law reform, 12.05
  attitudes to copyright distinguished from ideology, 2.04
  economic approach to copyright, 12.04

Government work
  first owner of copyright, India, 23.13
  term of copyright, India, 23.29
  United States, 21.18

Graphic publishers
  protection of, 14.45

Graphic works
  United States, 21.09, 21.28

Group
  ownership of performances by, 21.71

Group performances
  Rome Convention, 8.22

Guatemala
authors' rights, 22.77
neighbouring rights, no provision for, 22.77

Hire
availability of copies for, amounts to publication, 4.05, 4.13
employees for, rights of performers, USA, 21.60-21.71
ownership of work made for, 21.38

History
Anglo-Saxon system, 1.16
Antiquity, 2.02
Australia, 25.01-25.04
Austria, 13.01
Berne Convention, 5.07
Berne Convention, since, 2.20
broadcasting organisation, 7.36-7.37
duration, 6.16
England, 2.11-2.16
European Agreement on Protection of Television Broadcasts, 11.04
France, 2.09-2.10, 14.01
Germany, 2.05-2.08, 15.01-15.02
India, 23.01
international copyright treaties, 3.15
Italy, 16.01
Japan, 24.01
Middle Ages, 2.03
neighbouring rights, 7.01-7.05
Nordic countries, copyright in, 17.01
Phonogram Convention, 9.01-9.02
printing press, from invention of, 2.04 *et seq.*
publication, 6.31
Rome Convention, 8.01-8.03
Soviet Union, 19.01
Statute of Anne, 2.14-2.16
synthesis of, 2.19
United Kingdom, 18.01-18.02
United States of America, 2.17-2.18, 21.01
Universal Copyright Convention, 6.01-6.02
Western European origins of copyright, 2.01

Home taping
challenge to reproduction right, as, 12.12-12.15
enforcement of reproduction right, 12.14
facts of, 12.12
future of, 12.15
law, 12.13
phonograms, 7.16, 7.17
problems of free use, 4.32
reprography distinguished from, 12.11
United States, 21.25

Ideology of copyright
general principle of copyright, 1.11
government attitudes distinguished from, 2.04
justification, 1.01-1.05
major systems of copyright, 1.12-1.18
nature of copyright, 1.06-1.10
social and political significance, 1.19

India
artistic copyright, 23.35-23.36
artistic works, original, 23.04

India—*continued*
broadcasting organisations, protection of, 23.23
cinematograph films, 23.09, 23.37-23.39
classes covered by copyright, 23.02
compulsory licence, 23.18
dramatic works, original, 23.04
first owner of copyright—
  author, 23.13
  commissioned works, 23.13
  contract of service, author employed under, 23.13
  government work, 23.13
  international organisation, work of, 23.13
foreign right owners, protection of, 23.49-23.50
history and development of copyright, 23.01
industrial designs, 23.06
infringement of copyright—
  artistic copyright, 23.35
  cinematograph films, 23.38
  generally, 23.31
  literary, dramatic or musical works, 23.33
  records, 23.41
  remedies—
    accounts, by way of, 23.46
    author's moral rights, 23.47
    damages for detention or conversion, 23.45
    generally, 23.43
    injunction, 23.44
    third parties, protection of, 23.48
law revision, 23.51-23.54
limitation of rights—
  artistic copyright, 23.36
  cinematograph films, 23.39
  generally, 23.31
  literary, dramatic or musical works, 23.34
  records, 23.42
literary, dramatic or musical copyright, 23.32-23.34
musical works, original, 23.04
neighbouring rights—
  collection and distribution of revenue from, 23.24
  copyright and, 23.20
original literary works, 23.03
Paris revisions for benefit of developing countries, approach to, 23.54
producers of phonograms, protection of, 23.22
protection of performers, 23.21, 23.52
publication, 23.12
published editions of existing works, 23.07
records, 23.10, 23.40-23.42
registration, 23.19
sound broadcasts, copyright in, 23.53
subjects of copyright, 23.11
tainted works, 23.08
television broadcasts, copyright in, 23.53
term of protection, 23.25-23.30
transfer of copyright—
  abandonment, 23.17
  assignment of copyright, 23.14, 23.15
  licence, by, 23.14, 23.16

Industrial design
India, 23.06
protection of works of, 5.31
Information
restrictions on author's rights for information purposes, 5.57 et seq.
Infringement of copyright
Berne Convention, remedies for breach of, 5.65-5.67
civil law claims, Germany, 15.39-15.42
criminal sanctions. See CRIMINAL SANCTIONS
exceptions, 18.17-18.18
film maker, action by, 5.52
importance of enforcement, 4.42
India, 23.31 et seq.
primary, 18.15
remedies—
  account of profits, 18.23
  administrative, 4.49-4.50
  Anton Piller order, 18.26
  Australia, 25.50
  Austria, 13.26
  civil—
    anticipatory injunctions, 4.44
    compensatory remedies, 4.47
    damages, 4.47
    delivery up, 4.47
    generally, 4.43
    Japan, 24.28
    preventive remedies, 4.44-4.46
    search and seizure, power of, 4.44
  criminal—
    generally, 4.48
    Japan, 24.29
  damages, UK, 18.22
  delivery up of infringing articles, 18.23
  France, 14.49
  generally, 18.21
  India, 23.43-23.48
  injunctions, 18.24-18.26
  Scandinavia, 17.10, 17.21
  secondary, 18.16
  similar features to tort, 7.03
  Soviet Union, 19.09
Injunction
anticipatory, as remedy for infringement, 4.44
ex parte, 18.24
final, 18.24
interlocutory, 18.24, 18.25
remedy for infringement, as, 18.24-18.26, 23.44
Integrity
right of, as moral right, 4.17, 4.20
International copyright conventions. See CONVENTIONS
International copyright law. See INTERNATIONAL LAW
International law
centre of gravity of work, 3.13
challenges to—
  broadcasting right, 12.28-12.35
  copyrights and neighbouring rights, 12.26-12.41
  developing countries, needs of, 12.03
  economic approach of governments, 12.04

International law—*continued*
challenges to—*continued*
  effectiveness of copyright, 12.10 et seq.
  political concepts, 12.02
  reproduction right, 12.11-12.27
conflict of laws. See CONFLICT OF LAWS
disciplines of, 3.01
European Economic Community. See EUROPEAN ECONOMIC COMMUNITY
future of, 12.01 et seq.
hybrid nature of, 3.01
neighbouring rights, first moves towards, 7.05
principal tools, 3.01
private. See PRIVATE INTERNATIONAL LAW
public. See PUBLIC INTERNATIONAL LAW
reciprocal protection given to foreigners, 3.13, 3.14
remedies for breaches of Berne Convention, 5.65-5.67
Italy
contents of copyright, 16.05
copyright contract, 16.11
copyright law—
  origins, 16.01
  post-1941, 16.02
creators of works, 16.04
foreign authors, treatment of, 3.14
intellectual works, 16.03
limits on copyright—
  duration, 16.07
  free utilisation, 16.08
  legal licence, 16.09
  personal use, 16.08
moral rights of performer, 16.16
neighbouring rights—
  broadcasting organisations, rights of, 16.20
  general concepts, 16.13
  performers' rights, 16.16-16.17
  photographs, rights in respect of, 16.21-16.22
  points of contact with copyright, 16.14-16.15
  producers of phonograms, rights of, 16.18
  related rights, 16.23-16.27
  sources of law, 16.13
performers' rights, 7.11, 16.16-16.17
personal use, 16.15
transferability of right of use of intellectual work, 16.05, 16.10
use in private, 16.15
use of work, 16.06

Japan
author—
  extent of rights, 24.06-24.08
  meaning, 24.05
broadcasting organisations, protection of, 24.18-24.22
cinematographic works, 24.09
collecting societies, 24.24-24.25
compulsory licence, 24.13
copyright—
  definitions, 24.03

Japan—*continued*
 copyright—*continued*
  law, purposes of, 24.02
  relation between neighbouring rights and, 24.14
  works of authorship protected by, 24.04
 fair use, 24.10
 foreign right owners, protection of, 24.30
 history and development of copyright, 24.01
 law revision, 24.32
 limitations on copyright, 24.10
 neighbouring rights—
  limitation of, 24.27
  relation between copyright and, 24.14
  term of protection, 24.26
 performers, protection of, 24.15
 phonograms, protection of producers, 24.16-24.17
 related rights, protection of, 24.23
 remedies for infringement—
  civil, 24.28
  criminal, 24.29
 term of protection, 24.11
 transfer and expiry of copyright, 24.12
 transitory provisions, 24.31
Judgments
 publication in press, 7.26
Judicial decisions
 source of private international law, as, 3.11
Justification of copyright
 arguments in favour of system, 1.01-1.05
 cultural argument, 1.04
 economic argument, 1.03
 natural justice, principle of, 1.02
 social argument, 1.05

Latin-America
 Argentina. *See* ARGENTINA
 author's rights, 22.01-22.10
 Brazil. *See* BRAZIL
 Chile. *See* CHILE
 Colombia. *See* COLOMBIA
 Costa Rica. *See* COSTA RICA
 countries without neighbouring rights legislation, 22.110
 Cuba, 22.105
 Dominican Republic, 22.108
 economic rights, 22.03
 Ecuador. *See* ECUADOR
 El Salvador. *See* EL SALVADOR
 Guatemala, copyright and neighbouring rights, 22.77
 Mexico. *See* MEXICO
 moral rights, 22.02, 22.112
 neighbouring rights, 22.11-22.13
 Nicaragua, 22.106
 Panama, 22.107
 Paraguay. *See* PARAGUAY
 phonograms, identification of producer, 22.113
 principles of protection, 22.111
 public domain, payment for use of works in, 22.06
 registration, 22.07
 reprographic reproduction, problems of, 22.09

Latin-America—*continued*
 term of protection, 22.04, 22.111
 Uruguay. *See* URUGUAY
 Venezuela, 22.109
Law
 international copyright. *See* INTERNATIONAL COPYRIGHT LAW
 national—
  application of international copyright conventions, 3.30
  challenges to—
   consumerism, 12.06
   copyright or neighbouring rights taken out of copyright sphere, 12.07
   difficulty of enforcement, 12.08
   role of courts, 12.09
   role of governments and parliaments, 12.05
  source of private international law, as, 3.10
 private international. *See* PRIVATE INTERNATIONAL LAW
 sources of. *See* SOURCES OF LAW
 treatment of foreigners, 3.14
Lecture
 public, restrictions on author's rights, 5.59
Legal proceedings
 speech delivered in course of, 5.58
Libraries
 reproduction by, 21.24
Library of Congress
 deposit for, 21.53
Licence
 legal, Italy, 16.09
 non-voluntary. *See* COMPULSORY LICENCE
 schemes, Australia, 25.31
 transfer of copyright by, 4.27, 23.14, 23.16
Limitation of rights
 Australia, 25.36 *et seq.*
 free use—
  exceptional, categories of, 4.30
  generally, 4.29
  home taping, 4.32
  problems of, 4.31-4.32
  reprography, 4.31
  special cases, 4.30
 Germany, 15.08-15.09
 India, 23.31 *et seq.*
 Japan, 24.10
 literary work, 23.34
 necessity for, 4.28
 neighbouring rights, Japan, 24.27
 non-voluntary licence. *See* COMPULSORY LICENCE
 Scandinavia, 17.05
 Soviet Union, 19.08
Literary work
 infringement of copyright, India, 23.33
 limitation of rights, 23.34
 meaning, 4.04, 23.03
 original, India, 23.03
 owner's rights, 23.32
 protection by copyright, 4.14
 restricted acts, 18.07-18.13
 subject matter of protection, 18.05
 term of protection, India, 23.25
 United States, 21.07

Manufacturing clause
  United States, 21.56
Mexico
  broadcasting organisations, 22.80
  comments, 22.86
  criminal sanctions, 22.85
  foreign works, protection of, 22.83
  legislative synopsis, 22.78–22.85
  performers, 22.78
  phonograms—
    communication to public, 22.84
    producers of, 22.79
  registration, 22.82
  term of protection, 22.81
Middle Ages
  notion of copyright, 2.03
Minimum rights
  equitable remuneration, 5.43
  principle of, 3.18
Models
  protection of works of, 5.31
Monopoly
  abuses of, satellite broadcasting, 10.14
  copyright as, 1.08
Moral rights
  author, of, 23.47
  basic, 4.17 et seq.
  Brussels Act, 5.17
  droit d'auteur system, 1.14
  economic rights independent of, 4.21
  expiry of, 4.22
  extent of, Japan, 24.07
  France, 14.11
  integrity, right of, 4.17, 4.20, 4.23
  introduction of, 5.13
  Latin-America, 22.02, 22.112
  meaning, 4.15, 5.13
  non-voluntary licence, criticism of, 4.34
  origin in French law, 4.17
  other causes of action used to exercise, 4.23
  Paris Act, 5.37
  paternity, right of, 4.17, 4.19, 4.23
  performer, of, Italy, 16.16
  protection of, Austria, 13.09
  publication, right of, 4.17, 4.18, 4.23
  translation right, 6.28
Motion pictures
  United States, 21.10
Music Performance Trust Funds
  establishment of, 21.64
Musical work
  infringement of copyright, India, 23.32
  limitation of rights, 23.34
  manufacture of records, Australia, 25.52
  meaning, 23.04
  original, India, 23.04
  owner's rights, 23.32
  phonorecords, 21.32
  restricted acts, 18.07–18.13
  subject matter of protection, 18.05

Name
  formalities, 6.10
National
  meaning, 6.06
National culture
  justification of copyright, 1.04

National legislation
  restrictions on author's rights left to, 5.57 et seq.
National treatment
  broadcasting organisations, 8.15
  extensions of principle of, 3.18–3.19
  formalities, 3.19
  limitations of principle of, 3.20–3.21
  minimum rights, 3.18
  points of attachment and—
    country—
      first fixation, of, 8.12
      first publication, of, 8.13
    generally, 8.08
    nationality of producer, 8.11
    offering in reasonable quantities, 8.14
    producers of phonograms, 8.10
    protection of performers, 8.09
  principle of, 5.11, 5.34
  principle of international copyright convention, 3.17
  reciprocity—
    formal, 3.20
    limitation by, 3.20
    material, 3.20
  reservations, limitation by, 3.21
  Rome Convention, 8.07 et seq.
  Universal Copyright Convention, 6.05, 6.17
Nationality
  author, of, change or loss of, 6.06
  unpublished work, relevant moment to decide, 6.06
  works entitled to US copyright, 21.19
Natural justice
  droit d'auteur system puts emphasis on, 1.12, 1.14
  justification of copyright through principle of, 1.02
Nature of copyright
  exclusive right, 1.08
  limited duration, 1.07
  multiple right, 1.09
  property right, 1.06
  variation of scope, 1.10
Neighbouring rights
  Australia, 25.24
  author's rights, relations between, 7.06–7.07
  broadcasting organisation. See BROADCASTING ORGANISATION
  challenges to, 12.36–12.41
  collection and distribution of revenue, 13.23
  convention, relationship between EEC law and, 20.11
  copyright sphere, taken out of, 12.07
  difference between granting copyright and, 7.05
  fears of authors' societies, 7.07
  first moves towards, international law, 7.05
  foreign. See FOREIGN NEIGHBOURING RIGHTS
  Germany, 15.21
  ideology and history, 7.01–7.05
  India—
    collection and distribution of revenue from, 23.24
    copyright and, 23.20
  Italy, 16.13–16.27

Neighbouring rights—*continued*
Japan—
   collection and distribution of revenue, 24.24-24.25
   limitation of, 24.27
   term of protection, 24.26
Latin-America, 22.11-22.13
limitation, United Kingdom, 18.33-18.35
meaning, 7.05
ownership, 7.08
performers not compensated by grant of, 7.14
performers' rights. *See* PERFORMERS' RIGHTS
phonogram. *See* PHONOGRAM
relationship between author's rights and, 14.15-14.18
relationship between copyright and, Soviet Union, 19.03
relationship between copyright in narrower sense and, 13.02
Scandinavia, limitations, 17.20
scope, 7.08
sources of law, 16.13
term, 7.06, 7.08
term of protection, United Kingdom, 18.32
United States, 21.57 *et seq.*

News of the day
author's rights, 5.55
degree of originality, 5.55
exclusion from protection, 5.30

Newspaper articles
restrictions on author's rights, 5.60
unfair competition, 16.27

Newspaper organisation
protection of, 14.44

Nicaragua
neighbouring rights, 22.106

Non-voluntary licence. *See* COMPULSORY LICENCE

Obscenity
tainted works, India, 23.08
works subject to US copyright protection, 21.14

Official text
restrictions on author's rights, 5.57

Organiser of performance
collaboration of performer with, 13.16
protection of, 13.17

Originality
news of the day, 5.55
subject matter of copyright, of, 4.02

Ownership
assignment, 4.27
commissioned works, 4.26
employment, work created in, 4.25
first owner of copyright, India, 23.13
foreign rights, protection of, 19.10
initial, 21.37
joint works, 21.37
licencing, 4.27
neighbouring rights, 7.08
performances, of, 21.58-21.71
rights of, compared with rights of copyright user, 1.11
United States, 21.36-21.39
work made for hire, 21.38

Painter
droit de suite, 5.53

Paintings
Universal Copyright Convention, 6.04

Panama
literary and artistic property, protection of, 22.107

Pantomime
United States, 21.08

Paraguay
broadcasting organisations, 22.89
comment, 22.95
criminal sanctions, 22.94
foreign works, protection of, 22.92
legislative synopsis, 22.83-22.94
performers, 22.87
phonograms—
   communication to public, 22.93
   producers of, 22.88
registration, 22.91
term of protection, 22.90

Paris Act, Berne Convention
adaptation, right of, 5.45
applied art, protection of works of, 5.31
author, meaning, 5.29
automatic protection, principle of, 5.35
broadcasting right, 5.43-5.44
connecting factors, 5.32
country of origin, 5.36
droit de suite, 5.53
film right, 5.47
generally, 5.28
major rights, 5.37 *et seq.*
moral rights, 5.37
national treatment, principle of, 5.34
pre-existing works, rights of authors, 5.48
public performance right, 5.41
public recitation right, 5.42
publication, meaning, 5.33
recording right, 5.46
reproduction right—
   exceptions from, 5.39
   generally, 5.38
simultaneous publication, 5.33
term of protection, 5.54
translation right, 5.40
work, meaning, 5.30

Paris Additional Act. *See* BERNE CONVENTION

Paternity
right of, as moral right, 4.17, 4.19

Performance
non-profit live, exemption, USA, 21.26
ownership by groups, 21.71
point of attachment, 13.27
promotional, exemptions, 21.26
property, as, 21.72
right of, EEC, 20.10

Performer
collecting society for, 24.24
creator, as, USA, 21.57
meaning, 8.23, 15.22
protection of, national treatment, 8.09
technological displacement, 21.61-21.62
union activities, 21.62 *et seq.*

Performers' rights
Argentina, 22.14

Performers' rights—*continued*
Australia, 25.25
Brazil, 22.23
broadcasting and communication to public without consent, 8.17
broadcasting right, 13.06
Chile, 22.32
collaboration with organiser of performance, 13.16
collective agreements, protection through, France, 14.20-14.25
Colombia, 22.40
consent, right to give, Germany, 15.23, 15.25
contract of employment, when serving under, 15.28
Costa Rica, 22.49
courts, protection by, 14.26-14.28
dispositions of future rights, 13.14
distortion or alteration of performance, 15.26-15.27
distribution right, Austria, 13.05
Ecuador, 22.58
El Salvador, 22.68
employees for hire, 21.60-21.71
ephemeral fixation of performance, 8.20
first fixation made without consent, 8.18
fixation of performance without consent, 8.17
foreign neighbouring rights, protection of, 18.36
France, 7.12, 14.19-14.28
Germany, 7.10, 15.22-15.28
group performances, 8.22
identification of performer, 13.11
India, 23.21, 23.52
individual performer not employee, 21.58-21.59
inheritance of, 13.12
Italy, 7.11, 16.16-16.17
Japan, 24.15
joint collaboration of several persons, 13.10
law revision, 23.52
limitation, United Kingdom, 18.33
many people participating in one performance, 7.15
Mexico, 22.78
original fixation made for teaching or scientific research, 8.20
ownership of performances, 21.58-21.71
Paraguay, 22.87
performers as creators, USA, 21.57
permission for another to use performance, 13.13
position of performers, 7.09
private use, recording used for, 8.20
protection—
  Austria, 13.03-13.16
  penalties, 18.28
  Soviet Union, 19.04
  United Kingdom, 18.27-18.28
public performance right, 13.09-13.16
reproduction made for different purposes, 8.19
reproduction right, 13.04
reproduction without consent, 8.17

Performers' rights—*continued*
right to use, rescission of contractual relationship, 13.15
Rome Convention, 8.16-8.21
Scandinavia, 17.14
short excerpts, 8.20
United Kingdom, 7.13
United States, 21.57-21.73
Uruguay, 22.96
variety artists, 8.23
various legislations, under, 7.15

Phonogram
adaptation, 13.18
collecting society for producers of, Japan, 24.25
communication to public—
  Argentina, 22.20, 22.84
  Brazil, 22.29
  Chile, 22.38
  Colombia, 22.46
  Costa Rica, 22.55
  Ecuador, 22.64
  El Salvador, 22.74
  Paraguay, 22.93
  Uruguay, 22.102
Convention. *See* PHONOGRAM CONVENTION
copy of, distinguished from copy of book, 4.08
distribution to public, 9.04
duplicate, 9.04
formalities, 8.25
home taping, 7.16, 7.17
identification of producer, 22.113
indirect copying, 9.04
meaning, 9.04, 22.113
performance rights—
  broadcasting right, 7.29
  collection of remuneration, 7.30
  distribution of revenue, 7.31-7.35
  generally, 7.27-7.35
  public performance right, 7.28
performer's share in producer's remuneration, Italy, 16.17
producer—
  meaning, 9.04
  national treatment, 8.10
publication, 4.05, 4.08
remedies for infringement of rights, 7.19-7.26
rights of producers—
  Argentina, 22.15
  Australia, 25.26
  Austria, 13.18-13.20
  Brazil, 22.24
  broadcasting right, 7.16
  Chile, 22.33
  Colombia, 22.41
  Costa Rica, 22.50
  Ecuador, 22.59
  El Salvador, 22.69
  foreign neighbouring rights, protection of, 18.37
  France, 14.29-14.39
  generally, 7.16-7.18
  India, 23.22
  Italy, 16.18-16.19

Phonogram—*continued*
  Japan, 24.16-24.17
  limitation—
    Australia, 25.36-25.44
    United Kingdom, 18.34
    Mexico, 22.79
    national treatment, 8.10
    Paraguay, 22.88
  protection—
    broadcasting, against, 14.34-14.37
    generally, 14.29
    Germany, 15.32-15.34
    public performance, against, 14.38-14.39
    Soviet Union, 19.04
    unauthorised reproduction, against, France, 14.30-14.33
    United Kingdom, 18.29
  public performance right, 7.16
  remedies for infringement—
    civil remedies—
      injunction, 7.21
      search and seizure, 7.20
    compensatory remedies—
      damages, 7.23
      delivery up, 7.24
    criminal remedies, 7.25
    generally, 7.19
    publication of judgments in press, 7.26
    unfair competition, law of, 7.22
  reproduction right, 7.16, 7.18, 8.24
  Scandinavia, 17.15
  Uruguay, 22.97
  secondary uses, 8.26-8.29, 13.08, 22.104
  soundtrack of film, 9.04
Phonogram Convention
  bootlegging, 9.02
  contracting states, 9.11
  definitions, 9.04
  history, 9.01-9.02
  protection—
    means of—
      copyright, 9.07
      generally, 9.06
      other specific rights, 9.08
      penal sanctions, 9.10
      unfair competition, law of, 9.09
    scope, 9.05
  structure, 9.03
  videograms, 9.02
Phonorecord
  coin-operated players, USA, 21.34
  musical works, 21.32
Photocopying
  problems of free use, 4.31
Photographs
  related rights in, Germany, 15.37
  rights in—
    Italy, 16.21-16.22
    Scandinavia, 17.12
  term of copyright, India, 23.26
Pictorial works
  United States, 21.09, 21.28
Piracy
  lack of, 2.12
  United States, 21.25

Points of attachment
  Austria, 13.27-13.29
  broadcasting organisations, 8.15
  broadcasts, 13.29
  country—
    first fixation, of, 8.12
    first publication, of, 8.13
    national treatment and, 8.08 *et seq.*
    nationality of producer, 8.11
    offering in reasonable quantities, 8.14
    performances, 13.27
    phonograms, 13.28
    producers of phonograms, 8.10
    protection of performers, 8.09
Political significance
  copyright, of, 1.19
Pre-existing works
  rights of authors, 5.48
Preventive remedies. *See* INFRINGEMENT OF COPYRIGHT
Printer
  emergence of trade, 2.04
  freedom to practise, 2.11
  protection—
    England, in, 2.11
    Germany, in, 2.05
  registered member of Stationers' Company, 2.12
Printing press
  development of copyright from time of invention, 2.04 *et seq.*
Private international law
  conventions. *See* CONVENTIONS
  general principles applied to multinational treaty, 3.16
  national law, as part of, 3.01
  remedies for breaches of Berne Convention, 5.65-5.67
  rules of, 3.01
  sources—
    international conventions, 3.09
    international custom, 3.08
    judicial decisions, 3.11
    national legislation, 3.10
    writings of academic lawyers, 3.12
  See also CONFLICT OF LAWS
Privileges
  characteristics of, Italy, 16.09
  England, 2.12-2.13
  France, 2.09, 2.10
  Germany, 2.05, 2.07
  granted to booksellers, 2.04
  trading licence, as, 2.12
Producer
  cinematographic work, protection of, France, 14.46
  nationality of, 8.11
  phonogram. *See* PHONOGRAM
  videographic work, protection of, 14.46
Property
  right, copyright as, 1.06
Proprietor of Copyright
  Universal Copyright Convention, 6.04
Protected works
  additions to list of, 5.16
  Brussels Act, 5.16

Protected works—*continued*
   new categories, 5.11
   Universal Copyright Convention, 6.03
Pseudonymous work
   term of protection, 18.20
Public
   availability of work to, 5.33
   broadcasting and communication to, performers' rights, 8.17
   domain, works permanently in, 6.34
   general distribution to, 6.33
   making available copies to, 4.11
Public display
   concept of, USA, 21.22
   exemption, 21.26
   right of, 21.22
Public interest
   theory originating in United Kingdom, 18.01
Public international law
   most favoured nation treatment, 3.01
   national treatment, 3.01
   principal tools, 3.01
   reciprocal treatment, 3.01
   remedies for breaches of Berne Convention, 5.65
   Satellite Convention, 10.19
   scope, 3.01
   source, 3.01
Public lending right
   international copyright conventions, 3.22
   reproduction right distinguished from, 3.23
   Scandinavia, 17.06
Public performance
   concept of, USA, 21.22
   exemption, 21.26
   hiring out copies for, sufficient for publication, 4.05, 4.13
   phonogram producers, protection of, 14.38-14.39
   publication by, 4.05, 4.07
Public performance right
   Austria, 13.09-13.16
   Brussels Act, 5.20
   compulsory licence provisions, 4.35
   Paris Act, 5.41
   producers of phonograms, 7.16, 7.28
   United States, 21.22
   Universal Copyright Convention, 6.20
Public policy
   restrictions on author's rights in interests of, 5.64
Public recitation right
   Brussels Act, 5.21
   Paris Act, 5.42
Publication
   availability for hire sufficient for, 4.05, 4.13
   basic questions to be answered, 4.05
   consent of author, requiring, 5.33
   first, country of, 8.13
   general distribution to public, 6.33
   history, 6.31
   India, 23.12
   meaning, 4.05, 4.08, 5.33, 6.32, 8.13, 24.03
   number of copies to be made available to constitute, 4.05, 4.09-4.12

Publication—*continued*
   offering in reasonable quantities, 8.14
   phonogram, 4.05, 4.08
   place of, 4.10
   public performance, by, 4.05, 4.07
   recording excluded from concept of, 4.08
   relevance of definition, 4.05
   right of—
      moral right, 4.17, 4.18
      United States, 21.21
   Samizdat, 4.12
   simultaneous, 5.33, 8.13
   unauthorised publication is not, 4.06
   Universal Copyright Convention, 6.31-6.33
Publisher
   printers and booksellers, 2.02, 2.09
   stationer as forerunner of, 2.04
Publishing
   distribution rights, EEC, 20.08
   divided publishing right, EEC, 20.07
   restrictions, 18.09

Quality
   subject matter of copyright, of, 4.01
Quotation
   author's rights, 5.56
   when permissible, 5.56

Reciprocity
   developing countries, 6.44
   droit de suite, 5.53
   formal, 3.20
   material, 3.20
   principle of national treatment limited by rule of, 3.20
Recording
   adaptation of work, treated as, 5.24
   compulsory licence, 5.24
   ephemeral, 5.44
   equipment, royalty on, 7.17
   exhaustion of author's right, 5.24
   maker's rights, 5.24
   meaning, 24.03
   performers' rights. *See* PERFORMERS' RIGHTS
   private use, 8.20, 8.41
   right—
      Berlin Act, 5.11
      broadcasting right separated from, 5.44
      Brussels Act, 5.24
      compulsory licence provisions, 4.35
      Paris Act, 5.46
   short excerpts, 8.20, 8.42
Regional agreements
   European Agreement concerning Programme Exchanges by means of Television Films, 11.01-11.03
   European Agreement on Protection of Television Broadcasts, 11.04-11.13
Registration
   Argentina, 22.18
   Brazil, 22.27
   Chile, 22.36
   Colombia, 22.44
   Costa Rica, 22.53
   Ecuador, 22.62, 22.67
   El Salvador, 22.72

Registration—*continued*
India, 23.19
Latin-America, 22.07
Mexico, 22.82
Paraguay, 22.91
United States, 21.54
Uruguay, 22.100
Remedies
Berne Convention, for breaches of, 5.65-5.67
civil—
  injunction, 7.21
  search and seizure, 7.20
compensatory—
  damages, 7.23
  delivery up, 7.23
criminal, 7.25
infringement of copyright. *See* INFRINGEMENT OF COPYRIGHT
infringement of rights of phonogram producers and performers, 7.19-7.26
penal sanctions, protection of phonograms, 9.10
performers, protection of, UK, 18.28
publication of judgments in press, 7.26
unauthorised use of work, France, 14.14
unfair competition, law of, 7.22
Remuneration
blank tape used for recording, on, 7.17
Brazil, 22.104
claims for, Germany, 15.23-15.25
collecting societies, guidelines for establishment and operation of, 8.29
collection and distribution—
  Australia, 25.29-25.33
  Scandinavia, 17.23-17.26
  Soviet Union, 19.06
  United Kingdom, 18.31
equitable—
  right to, 5.43
European Economic Community, 20.04
Intergovernmental Committee on collection and distribution, 8.29
neighbouring rights, collection and distribution of revenue, Austria, 13.23, Japan, 24.24-24.25
performance rights—
  collection of, 7.30
  distribution, 7.31-7.35
public domain, works in, 22.06
recording equipment, 7.17
secondary uses of phonograms, 8.26-8.29
Reprisal clause
introduction of, 5.12
Reproduction
artistic work, 18.14
audio, Australia, 25.53
broadcasting organisations, 24.19
commercial purpose, USA, 21.24
libraries and archives, by, 21.24
notice of copyright, 21.24
pictorial, graphic and sculptural works, 21.28
problems of, in Latin America, 22.09
public access, 21.24
purposes of, 21.24
restrictions, 18.08

Reproduction—*continued*
right—
  Austria, 13.04
  basic right of broadcasting organisation as, 7.39
  Brussels Act, 5.18
  challenges to—
    computers, 12.20-12.24
    generally, 12.11
    home taping, 12.12-12.15
    reprography, 12.16-12.19
    videograms, 12.25-12.27
  compulsory licence applied to, 6.50-6.52
  enforcement, 12.14
  Paris Act, 5.38-5.39
  performers' rights, 8.17
  personal use, Italy, 16.08
  producers of phonograms, 7.16, 7.18, 8.24
  United States, 21.21
  Universal Copyright Convention, 6.20
  video, Australia, 25.53
Reprography
challenge to reproduction right, as, 12.16-12.19
facts of, 12.16
future, 12.19
home taping distinguished from, 12.11
international copyright conventions, 3.23
law, 12.17-12.18
problems of free use, 4.31
Reservations
convention rights limited by, 3.21
Restricted acts
artistic works, UK, 18.14
generally, 18.06
literary, dramatic or musical works, 18.07-18.13
Revenue. *See* REMUNERATION
Right to use
contract, grant made by, Germany, 15.13
exclusive right, granted as, 15.14
granting of, 15.12-15.16
transferability, 16.05, 16.10
Rome Act. *See* BERNE CONVENTION
Rome Convention
acquired rights, 8.45
application, 8.49
author's rights, 8.02
broadcasting organisations—
  communication of television broadcasts to public, 8.35
  fixation of broadcast, 8.33
  national treatment, 8.15
  protection, 8.31-8.35
  rebroadcasting, 8.32
  reproduction of fixation, 8.34
closed convention, 8.48
compulsory licence provisions, 4.35
contracting states, 8.52
denunciation, 8.50
drafts, 8.03
duration, 8.36-8.39
exceptions—
  ephemeral fixation, 8.43
  generally, 8.40

736 Index

Rome Convention—*continued*
exceptions—*continued*
private use, 8.41
short excerpts, use of, 8.42
use solely for teaching or scientific research, 8.44
group performances, 8.22
history, 8.01–8.03
intergovernmental committee, 8.51
minimum rights, 3.18
national treatment—
fundamental principle, as, 8.07
points of attachment and, 8.08 *et seq.*
other sources of protection, 8.46
performers' rights, 8.16–8.21
phonograms—
formalities, 8.25
reproduction right of producers, 8.24
secondary uses, 8.26–8.29
publication of phonogram, 4.08
reservations, 8.30
revision, 8.51, 12.04
safeguard clause for copyright, 8.05–8.06
special agreements, 8.47
structure, 8.04
term of rights, 8.36–8.39
variety artists, 8.23

Samizdat
meaning, 4.12

Satellite
challenge to broadcasting right, as, 12.33–12.35
facts of, 12.33
future, 12.35
law, 12.34
transmission of broadcast programmes by, Italy, 16.20

Satellite broadcasting
conceptual problem, 10.02–10.03
Convention. *See* SATELLITE CONVENTION
distribution, 10.06
legal problem, 10.04
originating organisation, 10.06
political aspects, 10.05
programme, 10.06
satellite, meaning, 10.06
signal—
derived, 10.06
distributed, 10.06
economic importance of, 10.18
emitted, 10.06
meaning, 10.06
technology, 10.01

Satellite Convention
abuses of monopoly, 10.14
contracting state, 10.20
contributor to programmes, safeguard of interests, 10.13
definitions, 10.06
direct broadcasting satellites, 10.10
exceptions, 10.11
law applicable, 10.19
nature of, 10.17
non-retroactivity, 10.12
rebroadcasting, 10.09

Satellite Convention—*continued*
relationship to other conventions, 10.16
reservations, 10.15
scope, 10.07
term of protection, 10.08–10.09

Scandinavia
broadcasting organisations, protection of, 17.16
cassettes, tax on, 17.28–17.29
catalogues, protection of producers, 17.17
collection and distribution of revenues—
Denmark, 17.25
generally, 17.23
Norway, 17.26
Sweden, 17.24
copyright, relationship with neighbouring rights, 17.13
Copyright Acts—
basis of, 17.03
plans for revision, 17.27
recent amendments, 17.27
similarity of, 17.02
foreign right owners, protection of, 17.11, 17.22
history and development of copyright, 17.01
infringement of copyright, 17.10, 17.21
limitations on copyright, 17.05
neighbouring rights—
copyright, relationship with, 17.13
limitations, 17.20
performers, protection of, 17.14
phonograms, protection of producers, 17.15
photographic pictures, rights in, 17.12
protection of copyright, general principles, 17.02–17.12
public lending right, 17.06
related rights, protection for, 17.17
reprography, 12.18
secondary use, 17.18
term of copyright, 17.04, 17.19
transfer of copyright, 17.07

Scientific research
fixation made for purposes of, 8.20, 8.44

Scope
copyright protection, United States, 21.20–21.35
variation in copyright countries, 1.10

Sculptor
droit de suite, 5.53

Sculpture
United States, 21.09, 21.28
Universal Copyright Convention, 6.04

Seizure
European Agreement for the Protection of television broadcasts, 11.12

Social argument
justification of copyright, 1.05
socialist system puts emphasis on, 1.12, 1.17

Social significance
copyright, of, 1.19

Socialist system
generally, 1.17
social argument, emphasis on, 1.12, 1.17

Sociology
copyright, of, 12.36

Index   737

Sound recordings
limitations, USA, 21.30
protection by copyright, 4.14
rights in, United States, 21.74-21.78
term of protection, Australia, 25.34
United States, 21.11
Sources of law
international conventions, 3.09
international custom, 3.08
judicial decisions, 3.11
national legislation, 3.10
neighbouring rights, Italy, 16.13
Treaty of Rome, 20.01-20.02
writings of academic lawyers, 3.12
Soviet Union
broadcasting organisations, protection of, 19.04
collection and distribution of revenue, 19.06
copyright, relationship with neighbouring rights, 19.03
foreign rights owners, protection of, 19.10
history and development of copyright, 19.01
limitation of rights, 19.08
performers, protection of, 19.04
phonograms, protection of producers, 19.04
related rights, protection of, 19.05
remedies for infringement, 19.09
Samizdat, publication by, 4.12
synopsis of Copyright Act, 19.02
term of protection, 19.07
Speech
legal proceedings, delivered in course of, 5.58
political, restrictions on author's rights, 5.58
Star Chamber
Court of, control over printed matter, 2.12
Decree of 1637, 2.12
Stationer
forerunner of publisher, as, 2.04
Stationers' Company
byelaws, 2.12
control exercised through bye-laws of, 2.12
copyright in perpetuity claimed by members, 2.13
infringement cases, 2.12
origins of, 2.12
Statute of Anne
basic rules established in, 2.14
impact of, 2.16
term of copyright, 4.39
Statutory licence. *See* LICENCE
Statutory limitations
types of, 1.11
Stockholm Act. *See also* BERNE CONVENTION
Bergström Report, 6.06
reprography, on, 12.17
Stockholm Protocol, 6.02
Stockholm Protocol
concessions to developing countries enshrined in, 6.02
Subject matter
artistic works, of, 18.05
categories of works protected, 4.14
creation of work, 4.01-4.03
derivative works, 4.03
dramatic works, UK, 18.05
fixation, 4.04

Subject matter *continued*
literary works, 18.05
musical works, of, 18.05
originality, 4.02
protection, of, 18.05
publication. *See* PUBLICATION
quality, 4.01
United States, 21.05 *et seq.*
Sweden *See* SCANDINAVIA
Symbol
formalities, 6.09
Systems of copyright
alternatives to, 12.41
Anglo-Saxon, 1.15-1.16
arguments in favour of, 1.01-1.05
continental European, 1.13-1.14
developing countries, 1.18
droit d'auteur, 1.13-1.14
generally, 1.12
raison d'être for, 12.40
socialist system, 1.17
viable, survival of, 12.40-12.41

Tainted works
India, 23.08
Teaching
face-to-face activities, exemption, USA, 21.26
original fixation made for purposes of, 8.20, 8.44
Television
broadcasts—
communication to public, 8.35
right to communicate to public, Japan, 24.21
cable system, secondary transmission, 21.33
European Agreement on Protection of Television Broadcasts. *See* EUROPEAN AGREEMENT ON PROTECTION OF TELEVISION BROADCASTS
film—
European Agreement concerning Programme Exchanges by means of Television Films, 11.01-11.03
meaning, 11.02
programme exchanges by means of, 11.01-11.03
protected broadcasts, 11.06
Term of protection
Argentina, 22.17
Australia, 25.34-25.35
Austria, 13.24
Berlin Act, 5.11
Brazil, 22.26
Brussels Act, 5.15
Chile, 22.35
Colombia, 22.43
comparison of terms, 4.40, 8.39
Costa Rica, 22.52
developing countries, 6.42
Ecuador, 22.61
El Salvador, 22.71
European Agreement on Protection of Television Broadcasts, 11.08
films, 18.20
France, 14.47

Term of protection—*continued*
generally, 4.39 *et seq.*
Germany, 15.10
India, 23.25–23.30
Italy, 16.07
Japan, 24.11
joint authorship, works of, 5.13
Latin America, 22.04, 22.111
life of author, connected with, 4.39
limited duration, copyright as right of, 1.07
Mexico, 22.81
neighbouring rights, Japan, 24.26
original owner not natural person, where, 4.41
Paraguay, 22.90
Paris Act, 5.54
Rome Convention, 8.36–8.39
Satellite Convention, 10.08
Scandinavia, 17.04, 17.19
Soviet Union, 19.07
starting point, 8.37
United Kingdom, 18.20
United States, 21.47–21.50
Universal Copyright Convention—
  comparison of terms, 6.19
  double standard, 6.01
  exceptions to minimum term, 6.18
  history, 6.16
  minimum term, 6.18
  national treatment, rule of, 6.17
  rule of shorter term, 6.19
Uruguay, 22.99
wartime extensions, 5.54

Theatrical scenes
protection of sketches, 16.23, 16.24

Title
publications including journals, Italy, 16.27

Tort
similar features of infringement of copyright, 7.03

Transfer of copyright
assignment, India, 23.14, 23.15
divisibility of copyright, USA, 21.40
effect of, 21.42
execution of transfers, 21.44
involuntary transfer, prohibition against, 21.41
Italy, 16.05, 16.10
Japan, 24.12
licence, by, 23.14, 23.16
recordation of transfers, 21.45, 21.55
right of termination, 21.43
Scandinavia, 17.07

Translation right
article, 6.23
Berlin Act, 5.11
broadcasting purposes, 6.48
  Brussels Act, 5.19
compensation, 6.27
compulsory licence—
  applied to, 6.45–6.47
  procedure for issue of, 6.26
  subject to, 6.25
exports, 6.29
generally, 6.24
moral rights, 6.28

Translation right—*continued*
Paris Act, 5.40
Paris Additional Act, 5.10

Transmission
dramatic works to blind, exemptions, USA, 21.26
instructional, exemption, 21.26
non-dramatic literary works to blind and deaf, exemptions, 21.26

Treaties
international copyright, history of, 3.15
interstate, foundations of, 2.08
See also CONVENTIONS

Treaty of Rome (EEC)
source of primary community law, as, 20.01–20.02

Tribunal
copyright, 11.11

Trust fund
lawsuits, USA, 21.66
Music Performance, 21.64
residuals, 21.69
situation today, 21.68–21.71

Tunis Model Law
infringement of copyright, 4.50

Unfair competition
acts regarded as, Italy, 16.27
law of, 7.22
meaning, 9.09
phonograms, protection by law of, 9.09

United Kingdom
acquisition of copyright, 18.04
American and English law distinguished, 2.18
'Anton Pillar' Order, 4.45
broadcasting organisations, protection of, 18.30
cable diffusion, 12.31
collection and distribution of revenue, 18.31
compulsory licence provisions, 4.36
criminal sanctions, 7.13
development of copyright, 2.11–2.16
films—
  copyright in, 18.03
  protection of, 18.19, 18.20
foreign authors, treatment of, 3.14
foreign neighbouring rights, protection of, 18.36–18.38
history and development of copyright, 18.01–18.02
infringement of copyright—
  exceptions, 18.17–18.18
  primary, 18.15
  secondary, 18.16
neighbouring rights—
  limitation, 18.33–18.35
  term of protection, 18.32
performers, protection of, 7.13, 18.27–18.28
privileges, 2.12–2.13
producers of phonograms, protection of, 18.29
public interest theory, 18.01
remedies for infringement—
  account of profits, 18.23
  Anton Piller order, 18.26
  damages, 18.22

United Kingdom—*continued*
remedies for infringement—*continued*
delivery up of infringing articles, 18.23
generally, 18.21
injunctions, 18.24–18.26
restricted acts, 18.06–18.14
subject-matter of protection, 18.05
term of protection, 18.20
works, copyright in, 18.03
United States of America
broadcasters, rights of, 21.79
cable diffusion, 12.30
compulsory licence provisions, 4.36
Constitution, copyright and patent clause, 2.18
copyright, generally, 21.01, 21.03
development of copyright, 2.17–2.18
deviation from English Law, 2.18
exclusive rights—
compulsory licence, subject to, 21.31–21.35
general limitations, 21.23–21.25
generally, 21.20–21.22
specific limitations, 21.26–21.30
fair use, doctrine of, 21.23
foreign authors, treatment of, 3.14
formalities, special provisions, 6.13–6.14
government works, 21.18
home taping, 7.16
ideals to which copyright law should aspire, 21.01
ideas, systems, blank forms, 21.17
intellectual property law, structure of, 21.02
libraries and archives, reproduction by, 21.24
neighbouring rights, 21.57 *et seq.*
obscenity, question of, 21.14
performers' rights—
ownership of performances, 21.58–21.71
performers as creators, 21.57
scope, 21.72
theories for protection, 21.73
reprography, 12.18
sound recordings, rights in, 21.74–21.78
statutory copyright—
Act of 1976, 21.04
duration, 21.47–21.50
formalities—
copyright notice, 21.52
copyright registration, 21.54
deposit, Library of Congress, 21.53
generally, 21.51
manufacturing requirement, 21.56
recordation of transfer to plaintiff, 21.55
national origin, 21.19
ownership and transfer of copyright, 21.36–21.45
pre-emption of common law copyright, 21.46
scope of copyright protection, 21.20–21.35
single copyright system, 21.46
subject matter of protection—
categories of copyrightable works, 21.06–21.11
compilations, 21.12
derivative works, 21.12

United States of America—*continued*
statutory copyright—*continued*
subject matter of protection—*continued*
general coverage, 21.05
uncopyrightable works, 21.13–21.18
works lacking original authorship, 21.15
Universal Copyright Convention
adequate and effective protection, 6.03
advantages of flexibility, 6.04
author, who is, 6.07
basic rights, 6.20–6.21
Berne Safeguard Clause, 6.01, 6.02, 6.37
broadcasting right, 6.20
cinematographic works, 6.04
compulsory licence—
developing countries, 6.30
provisions, 4.35
reproduction right, applied to, 6.50–6.52
system of, 6.22
translation right—
compensation, 6.27
exports, 6.29
moral rights, 6.28
procedure for issue of, 6.26
subject to, 6.25
contracting states, 6.53
copyright proprietor, 6.04
developing countries, special provisions for, 6.38 *et seq.*
duration—
comparison of terms, 6.19
exceptions to minimum term, 6.18
history, 6.16
minimum term, 6.18
national treatment, rule of, 6.17
rule of shorter term, 6.19
field of application, 6.05–6.07
formalities—
date, 6.11
exemptions, 6.08
generally, 6.08
name, 6.10
notice—
appearance from time of first publication, 6.12
appearance on all copies, 6.12
valid, 6.12
provisions solely applied to United States, 6.13–6.14
symbol, 6.09
unpublished works, 6.15
work published with authority, 6.12
free use, fair dealing, 4.29
history, 6.01–6.02
inspiration, 6.01
intergovernmental committee, 6.36
links between 1952 and 1971 Conventions, 6.35
minimum rights, 3.18, 6.03
national, meaning, 6.06
national treatment, principle of, 6.05, 6.17
paintings, engravings and sculpture, 6.04
principal provisions, 6.01
public domain, works permanently in, 6.34
public performance, right of, 6.20

Universal Copyright Convention
—*continued*
publication—
general distribution to public, 6.33
history, 6.31
meaning, 4.08, 6.32
reciprocity, 6.44
reliance on contracting state to fulfil obligations, 6.03
reproduction right, 6.20, 6.50–6.52
revised, 6.03 *et seq.*
revision, 12.04
Stockholm Protocol, 6.02
term of copyright, 4.39
translation—
broadcasting purposes, 6.48
restrictions on right of, 6.49
writings, meaning, 6.04

Uruguay
broadcasting organisations, 22.98
comments, 22.104
criminal sanctions, 22.103
foreign works, protection of, 22.101
legislative synopsis, 22.96–22.103
performers, 22.96
phonograms—
communication to public, 22.102
producers of, 22.97
registration, 22.100
term of protection, 22.99

User
rights of, compared with rights of copyright owner, 1.11

Variety artists
Rome Convention, 8.23

Venezuela
neighbouring rights, 22.109

Videograms
challenge to reproduction right, as, 12.25–12.27
facts of, 12.25
future of, 12.27
law, 12.26
Phonogram Convention, 9.02
protection by copyright, 4.14

Videographic work
producer, protection of, France, 14.46

Western Europe
origins of copyright, 2.01

Work
collaboration, of, France, 14.03, 14.12
collective, 14.03, 14.12
composite, 14.03, 14.12
existing, published editions of, India, 23.07
intellectual, protection of, 16.03
joint authors, 14.03
limits to protection of, 14.08–14.10
meaning, 5.30, 14.02, 15.03, 24.03
protected, 14.04–14.05
title, protection of, 14.06
unauthorised use, procedures and sanctions, 14.14
uncopyrightable, USA, 21.13–21.18
unfixed, 21.16

Writings
meaning, 6.04

Written correspondence
rights in respect of, Italy, 16.23, 16.26

REF Z 552 .S76